THE GREEK PARTICLES

THE GREEK PARTICLES

BY

J. D. DENNISTON

FELLOW OF HERTFORD COLLEGE, OXFORD
UNIVERSITY LECTURER IN GREEK AND
LATIN LITERATURE

SECOND EDITION

OXFORD
AT THE CLARENDON PRESS

Oxford University Press, Ely House, London W. 1

GLASGOW NEW YORK TORONTO MELBOURNE WELLINGTON
CAPE TOWN IBADAN NAIROBI DAR ES SALAAM LUSAKA ADDIS ABABA
DELHI BOMBAY CALCUTTA MADRAS KARACHI LAHORE DACCA
KUALA LUMPUR SINGAPORE HONG KONG TOKYO

ISBN 0 19 814307 9

First published 1934
Reprinted 1954, 1959, 1966, 1970 and 1975

Printed in Great Britain
at the University Press, Oxford
by Vivian Ridler
Printer to the University

PREFACE TO THE SECOND EDITION

DURING the fifteen years between the first edition of this book and his death in 1949 Denniston made notes of a large number of additional examples and on many points changed his mind in the light of this fresh material. My principal task in the preparation of this second edition has been to incorporate all these additions and corrections. For the sake of speed and economy photographic reproduction from the first edition has been employed. This has meant that no insertion could be made in the text without an omission of corresponding size on the same or the next page. Accordingly, I have reduced many quotations to bare references; the choice of what to omit or condense has not always been easy, but in all cases I have weighed the new matter against the old and omitted whatever contributed least to the argument. Above all, I have taken the opportunity to redistribute matter between the text and the *addenda* in such a way that, as far as possible, the *addenda* do not accumulate additional examples but are confined to discussion of difficulties of text and interpretation.

The notes which Denniston made in his interleaved copy nearly always made it quite clear what he wanted to insert and where; some other notes, in the margins of review offprints and correspondence, did not make it clear, and I have accordingly been very cautious in using them. In general, I have tried to admit nothing into the text without being certain that it represented Denniston's considered view. But in a few cases the fresh examples which he had added seemed to me to necessitate a slight modification of his original views, and I have rewritten a sentence or two accordingly (p. 188, on postponed *δέ* in Middle and New Comedy; pp. 290–1, on *καί* linking qualitative attributes; p. 462, on *δ' οὖν* in the sense of *δὲ δή*; p. 501, on *τε* linking qualitative attributes).

As thoroughgoing a correction as possible has been made of the few printers' errors and fewer wrong references which appeared in the first edition.

Inevitably, in carrying out a revision of this kind one is faced with two temptations; to add material of one's own, and to modify interpretations of the author's with which one disagrees. The second temptation was naturally not very strong in the case of this book, and where it arose I resisted it, except that I have rewritten the discussion of *καὶ . . . τε* on pp. 535–6 and changed its tone from doubt to disbelief. The first temptation has not been entirely resisted. There was clearly no point in multiplying examples indiscriminately; but here and there I have made additions in order either to make a fresh point or to show the wider distribution of a usage (p. 193, Th.vi 20.2; p. 246, Ant.iiiδ9; p. 282, Ar.*Th.* 63; p. 288, *addendum*, Pi.*Fr.*192; p. 296, Th.vi 68.2; p. 305, Th.vi 38.4; p. 379, Th.iii 82.1, vi 69.1; p. 428, Th.iii 95.1, vi 64.1, vii 6.1). I should have liked to include more material from the language of inscriptions; but Denniston conceived this book as a contribution to the study of Greek *literature,* and I have added only the epigraphical *addendum* to p. 536. I should have liked also to add fuller discussions of the position of particles; but to be worth while, such discussions should be systematic and exhaustive, and this was not possible in the time available.

Denniston believed that this book did not need indexes. Those who have used the first edition for some years were divided on this point; but as those of us who wanted them wanted them strongly they have now been provided. The index of combinations will, I hope, give the reader quicker access than the table of contents to discussion of such phenomena as *καὶ δὴ καὶ . . . γέ που.* The daunting task of compiling the index of references was enthusiastically taken up by Mrs. Denniston and carried out by her with tireless care. I believe that all classical scholars will be greatly in her debt.

K. J. D.

BALLIOL COLLEGE, OXFORD
September 1950

PREFACE TO THE FIRST EDITION

It is seventy-three years since Bäumlein's *Untersuchungen über griechische Partikeln* appeared. Bäumlein and his predecessors are out of print, and the only generally accessible treatment of the particles as a whole is that contained in the Kühner-Gerth *Ausführliche Grammatik der griechischen Sprache*, where much valuable information is compressed into a remarkably small compass. Hartung, Klotz, and Bäumlein are the standard works to which scholars have gone for information on these matters. Hartung's is the most philosophical of the treatises on the subject. He is not easy reading, but his analysis is often penetrating, and his terminology contributes to precision of thought. Klotz, though by no means without value, is rather long-winded, and tends to repeat his main theses over and over again like magical incantations. Bäumlein's is a concise and unpretentious little book. These general works have been supplemented during the last hundred years by a stream of dissertations, 'Programme', and articles on individual particles and the usage of individual authors; a stream which, unhappily, shows signs of drying up, though des Places's monumental study of certain Platonic particles is the best thing of its kind that has been written. Again, the indexes to various authors are of great assistance to a writer on the subject. Few important Greek authors now lack an index, and it is much to be desired that the deficiencies should be made good. The compiler of an index may feel that his laborious task is not worth the labour spent on it. He is apt to forget that what are to him isolated facts devoid of any significance may have a vital bearing on some wide and important issue.

Enough has been said to show that a comprehensive work on this subject is needed, and that the circumstances are more favourable for writing one than they were in 1861. I hope that the present book will do something to fill the gap. In writing it, I have set myself aims rather different from the aims of my predecessors. In the first place, I have cut down etymological discussion to the minimum, partly because I have no competence in this field, partly because I do not believe that etymology can help us much here. Even with regard to the origins of particles there is often little agreement between the experts: and, were the origins certain, I doubt whether we should be much the wiser about the particles as elements of living speech. If we could discover the long-lost parent of Epic τε and connective-preparatory τε, it would, I believe, tell us little about the two extant usages. In my own language, I know that 'albeit' is a poetical and archaic word, called into service nowadays to lend a *fucatus nitor* to undistinguished prose. Knowledge of the prefix 'al-' tells me no more of the place of 'albeit' in English literature: and the primary aim of this book is literary, not grammatical or etymological.

In the second place, I have cited more examples than previous writers have done. The reader should be enabled to *bathe* in examples. If I have selected and arranged mine reasonably well, the mere process of semi-quiescent immersion may help him as much as hours of anxious thought. The more I study the Greek particles, and the Greek language as a whole, the more I feel that the ultimate decision in each case rests with the instinctive judgement: an English prejudice, perhaps, but one I cannot rid myself of.

I regard explanation, then, as less important than illustration, though I have done my best to provide explanations. Translation I put third, and a bad third at that. Translation is always a dangerous business, because it assumes equivalence between expressions which (if we go beyond such simple equations as ποταμός = 'river') are hardly ever equivalent. It is especially dangerous in the case of such intangible and elusive words as particles. Nevertheless, the Delegates of the University Press urged me to 'translate more'. I obeyed them, and I am now convinced that I had carried my antipathy to translation too far. I must warn the reader that the renderings I give are designed solely to bring out the force of the particle. Inessential words are constantly left out, and my English is often a paraphrase or summary rather than a translation. Sometimes, indeed, the particle itself is left untranslated, and its force has to be gathered from the sentence as a whole. I have made free use of italics and exclamation marks, clumsy, but convenient, devices. I have not hesitated in places to employ a style inappropriate to the character of the quotation, if brevity could be secured thereby, or the force of a particle brought out more clearly.

I have taken about 320 B.C. as my *terminus ad quem*. Perhaps I should have gone further, and included at any rate the Alexandrians. But the line I have drawn is a not unreasonable one, and the so-called classical writers provided me with adequate employment. In regard to the literature down to 320 I have relied mainly on my own reading. But dissertations and indexes have enabled me to check my results in many places, and in the case of Aristotle I have relied almost entirely on Bonitz. I have drawn freely on Hippocrates, who has been surprisingly neglected by previous writers.

My obligations are many and various. Hartung, Klotz, Bäumlein, and Kühner have been constantly in my hands. My debts to many of the specialized works enumerated in the bibliography will manifest themselves in the course of the text. I have learned much from Jebb's Sophocles. His exceptionally fine feeling for Greek shows itself here, as in other matters. Professor Pearson's notes in his editions of Euripides have also been valuable.

I have to thank the Secretary to the Delegates of the University Press, Dr. R. W. Chapman, for reading the Introduction in its infancy and in its maturity, for giving me a great deal of useful advice on method of presentation and arrangement, and for generously placing at my disposal an essay on the particles in Isocrates, and a great mass of notes and tables, dealing mainly with Platonic usages. The pages on γε, γοῦν, and καίτοι, and many other parts of my book, show how much I owe to his *Sammelfleiss* and acumen. Mr. J. G. Barrington-Ward readily undertook the laborious task of reading the whole of the slip-proofs, and made a number of valuable suggestions, by which I have profited greatly. Mr. M. Platnauer helped me with advice on several points in the page-proofs. I owe it to Mr. R. McKenzie, who has repeatedly placed his expert knowledge at my disposal, that the etymological observations in this book are not more numerous and more erroneous. But they do not bear his *imprimatur*, and he strongly dissents from my conclusions regarding the use of μάν and μέν in Homer. Other Oxford scholars have helped me in details: Professor Gilbert Murray, the Provost of Oriel (Mr. W. D. Ross), Mr. C. M.

Bowra (who, besides elucidating the obscurities of Pindar, read an early draft of γάρ), Mr. E. C. Marchant, and Dr. E. T. Withington. Mr. E. Harrison, of Trinity College, Cambridge, gave me advice on several passages in Theognis. Through the courtesy of the then librarian of Vienna University, the late Dr. G. A. Crüwell, I was able in 1927 to consult various works otherwise inaccessible to me. Professor Misener kindly obtained for me, through the good offices of Professor Shorey, a copy of her valuable dissertation on γάρ.

I began my thanks with the Clarendon Press, and I will end them with the Clarendon Press. This book bears on almost every page the marks of my Reader's accurate mind and of the meticulous care with which he must have pondered every sentence. I have not always accepted his suggestions, and there are, I know, things he disapproves of in this book. But again and again I have accepted his suggestions, and often, where I have rejected them, they have led me to reconsider a point and to improve what I had written. The book is less unscholarly as a result of the trouble he has taken with it. I am grateful to the officials of the Press for their pains and consideration, and I must not forget the compositors, who have performed a complicated task with really astonishing accuracy.

I know, as I bid farewell to this volume, that it must contain many faults of omission and commission. I hope that those who make use of it will inform me of any errors or deficiencies they may notice, so that I may perhaps one day find it possible to publish further Addenda and Corrigenda in some form or other.

J. D. D.

OXFORD,
9th May 1934

FROM AID TO THE READER (FIRST EDITION)

REFERENCES are usually to the Oxford Classical Text, where one exists; otherwise to Teubner. Where I have referred to other editions, I have said so. Where the particle in question is not concerned, I have been content to follow my editor, whether I approve of his text or not. But where my editor emends a particle, I have often quoted the MS. reading without comment. In a few places I have repunctuated.

Quotations are normally arranged in the following order: verse-writers, non-oratorical prose-writers, orators, each group in chronological order of authors. (The orators form a more or less homogeneous group, and they seemed to me best put in a block.) I have not troubled about the chronological order of an author's works, nor have I attempted, except in glaring cases, to distinguish the genuine from the spurious. The order of quotations is sometimes dislocated on special grounds, where several examples naturally group themselves together. The reason in each case will be obvious to the reader.

References are to the line, section, etc., in which the particle occurs: not to the opening of the quotation.

Brackets round a citation, or citations, denote that a particle is used in the same context as in the previous citation.

A Greek capital letter denotes the opening of a speech. A dash denotes a division between speeches. A double dash denotes the breaking of a speech by an interruption. Where, as often in Plato, a speaker resumes after an interpellation by another speaker whose words are not quoted by me, I begin the resumed speech with a capital, but with no preceding dash. In my translations or paraphrases I open with a capital or small letter according as the words may, or may not, naturally be regarded as following a full stop in a continuous translation.

Where a word followed by dots, representing words omitted, is oxytone, I have always printed a grave accent.

I have adopted the abbreviations of names and titles used in the new Liddell and Scott, except that I print 'Ant.' for Antiphon.

I use italics in translation to mark the word stressed in my English: this is not necessarily the word rendering the word stressed in the Greek.

On the whole, I have avoided the indication 'etc.', which in a work of this kind is often dangerously ambiguous. '*Id. saep.*' denotes that the particle or usage occurs often in the author last cited, '*ib. saep.*' that it occurs often in the work last cited, '*et saep.*' that it occurs often in Greek as a whole.

Where a particle is given in brackets as an emendation, it is to be taken as a substitute for the particle under discussion. E.g. on p. 170 (*s.v.* δέ) '(γάρ Reiske)' means that Reiske conjectures γάρ for δέ. But I have been more explicit in cases where ambiguity was to be feared.

AID TO THE READER (SECOND EDITION)

References to Bacchylides are to the edition of Snell (1949). Fragments of lyric and elegiac poets are numbered as in Diehl's *Anthologia lyrica Graeca* (second edition); tragic fragments as in Nauck; comic fragments as in Kock; but Arn., Diehl, Mette, and Mette (*Nachtrag*) after a tragic fragment refer respectively to the *Supplementum Euripideum* of von Arnim, the *Supplementum Sophocleum* of Diehl, the *Supplementum Aeschyleum* of Mette, and *Nachtrag zu dem Supplementum Aeschyleum*; Dem. after a comic fragment refers to the *Supplementum Comicum* of Demiańczuk. Fragments of Pindar are numbered as in Bowra, with Schroeder's number in brackets; of the Presocratics, as in Diels (fifth edition); of the historians, as in Jacoby; of Epicharmus and Sophron, as in Kaibel's *Comoediae Graecae Fragmenta*.

An asterisk indicates that the *Additional Notes* at the end of the book should be referred to.

CONTENTS[1]

---

[1] In the summary of the text square brackets denote an unimportant, illusory, or highly doubtful usage.

INTRODUCTION

I. THE ORIGINS AND FUNCTIONS OF PARTICLES.

(1) Difficult as it is to arrive at a satisfactory definition of *particle*, an attempt must be made at the outset. I will define it as a word expressing a mode of thought, considered either in isolation or in relation to another thought,[1] or a mood of emotion. It is a probable assumption that the evolution of particles represents a relatively late stage in the development of expression. Their existence betokens a certain self-consciousness. A few Greek particles can be clearly seen to have been, at an earlier stage, other parts of speech. Thus ἀλλά was originally ἄλλα, 'other things', and τοι (pretty certainly) the dative of the second person singular pronoun. που was probably 'somewhere', and the τοι in τοιγάρ a case (perhaps the instrumental) of demonstrative τό. So in English 'well', 'come', 'now', 'why', have come to be used as particles. A loss of definiteness has been accompanied by increased subtlety of nuance. There is less body, more bouquet.

(2) The particles which, in origin, express a mode of thought in isolation are γε, δή, ἦ, θην, μήν, περ, τοι, που. Of these, τοι presses an idea upon the attention of the person addressed; 'I would have you know (or remember)': που conveys doubt, 'I

[1] This distinction cannot, however, be rigidly maintained everywhere. While in the case of adjectives and adverbs, and verbs derived from adjectives, emphasis may be added without any external reference (Καλόν γε, 'Fine!' Εὖ γε, 'Excellent!': Εὐτυχῶ γε, 'I *am* lucky'), emphasis on substantives and most verbs necessarily implies a contrast with some other thing or action, however dimly the contrasted idea may be envisaged. 'It's a *cloud*!' (*sc.* 'not a mountain top', or 'not anything else'). And this external reference, which underlies what I shall call 'determinative' emphasis, becomes patent in limitative emphasis: οἶμαί γε, 'I *think* so' (*sc.* 'but I may be mistaken'). Hence limitative γε comes near to μέν in sense. Conversely, μέν *solitarium* often approximates to γε, and καί, from meaning 'even', 'also', sometimes comes to be little more than a particle of emphasis, when the external reference which 'even' and 'also' imply is only vaguely conceived.

suppose'. The remainder primarily carry emphasis. Further, emphasis may take different forms: (i) Affirmative, denoting that something really and truly is so: (ii) Intensive, denoting that something is very much so: (iii) Determinative, concentrating the attention on one idea to the exclusion of all else: (iv) Limitative, implying that beyond the prescribed limits the reverse may be true. Naturally, fixed lines cannot be drawn between these forms. Thus (i) 'I am really sorry' implies, almost of necessity, (ii) 'I am very sorry'. (i) 'It's really James' suggests (iii) 'It's James and no other'. In certain contexts (iii) suggests (iv). We should not therefore expect to find, and we do not in fact find, precise delimitation of the usages of emphatic particles. Affirmation is expressed *par excellence* by ἦ, which (as its regular position, first word in the sentence, indicates) affects the thought as a whole: while δή and γε tend to cohere with the preceding word. ἦ πολλοὶ τοῦτο ποιοῦσι, 'in truth many do this': in πολλοὶ δὴ τοῦτο ποιοῦσι, δή is almost an adverb, going closely with πολλοί: but not quite an adverb, and πολλοὶ δή, 'really many', is not quite the same as μάλα πολλοί, 'very many'. Of the other emphatic particles, μήν perhaps comes nearest in force to ἦ, though less subjective in tone: and in Homer οὐ μήν in negation appears to be the counterpart of ἦ in affirmation. The intensive and determinative functions are shared by γε, δή, and περ: limitation is expressed by γε and περ. Taking Greek as a whole, γε is the particle most commonly used for expressing determination and limitation.

Interrogation is expressed by ἦ (from which, combined with ἄρα, interrogative ἆρα is probably derived): though, strictly speaking, the interrogation is not expressed by the particle, but understood: *Ποιεῖς τοῦτο;* 'Do you do this?' *Ἦ ποιεῖς τοῦτο;* 'Do you really do this?'

(3) Besides expressing modes of thought, these particles, with some now to be mentioned for the first time, also indicate moods of emotion, nuances.[1] Thus pathos is often suggested by δή, irony or sarcasm by δή and δῆθεν (sometimes by γε), interest and

[1] It may be objected that the particle merely emphasizes, while the emotional nuance lies in the context. But the particle, from constant use in a particular kind of context, acquires a specific emotional tone.

surprise by ἄρα and γε, sympathy, encouragement, threatening hostility, and other attitudes by τοι, sudden perception or apprehension by καὶ μήν and καὶ δή.

(4) These particles of emphasis and nuance I will style 'adverbial'[1] since they are in most cases naturally translated by adverbs, 'really', *profecto*, *certe*, etc.: I shall apply this term to all uses other than connective and preparatory (apodotic uses are difficult to classify: see 5.*d* below). The contribution which these particles make to the force and vividness of Greek has been universally recognized. Often they cannot be appropriately translated into a modern language,[2] and their effect must be suggested by inflexions of the voice in speaking, or by italics, exclamation marks, or inverted commas in writing. It would be too much to claim that the whole expression that a sensitive and intelligent reader can put into a page of English is present already in the corresponding Greek, owing to the presence of particles. Rather, the particles may be compared to the marks of expression in a musical score, which suggest interpretation rather than dictate it. To carry the analogy further, a page of Thucydides bears somewhat the same relation to a page of Plato as a page of Bach to a page of Beethoven.

(5) Hitherto we have considered the function of particles as expressing a mode of thought or mood of feeling in isolation. We have now to discuss their function as establishing a relationship between separate ideas. Relationships may be established in different ways.

(*a*) The second idea is linked to the first by a connecting particle,[3] which may do no more than connect, but may also give

[1] This is not a very happy term, but it is a convenient and customary one. Dr. R. W. Chapman, in some of his notes on the Greek particles, styles this group 'self-contained', 'independent'. We must include among the 'independent' particles the Epic τε of habitual action, which, from its purely objective nature, stands apart from the other members of the group.

[2] German is richer than English in particles, and offers more equivalents. German writers on the subject start at some advantage in this respect.

[3] Naturally, the units connected are normally *eiusdem generis*. But this is by no means a hard and fast rule. E.g. in A.*Supp.* 369 δέ links an adverb to a participial clause. Cases in which a finite verb is linked by a connective

a logical turn (adversative, causal, or inferential) to the connexion.

(*b*) As expression develops, subordination largely replaces co-ordination, the *λέξις κατεστραμμένη* the *λέξις εἰρομένη*, and to that extent hypotactic conjunctions replace connectives. These conjunctions, *ἐπεί*, *εἰ*, and so forth, must themselves be regarded as particles.[1] The only reason that I do not discuss them, as some other writers on the particles have done, is that their importance is grammatical rather than stylistic.

(*c*) The capacity of particles to establish a relationship between ideas is not limited to the sphere of connectives and hypotactic conjunctions. *καί* and *οὐδέ*,[2] in the adverbial senses 'also', 'also... not', or, with a sense of climax, 'even', 'not even', point a reference to a second idea either expressed in the context or supplied by the imagination. Since this use of particles denotes that one term answers another, I term it 'responsive'.[3] (In this class we must perhaps include *οὖν* in its Homeric use, 'in accordance with what I have said', and *δέ* in *καὶ . . . δέ*, if (or when) *καί* is the connective in this combination (p. 199, n. 1).) In certain cases this responsive use has a structural importance: as when, for instance, *καί* in relative and final clauses marks the addition of the content of the subordinate to that of the main clause.

(*d*) *Apodotic uses.* Even in hypotactic constructions paratactic particles (*ἀλλά* (*ἀλλ' οὖν*), *αὐτάρ*, *δέ* (*δ' οὖν*), *καί* (*καὶ μήν*), *οὖν*, *τοίνυν*) are not infrequently found at the opening of an apodosis. This apodotic use is probably a legacy from the earlier, paratactic, stage of expression, retained, perhaps, from a Greek love of clearness and logic: it is significant in this connexion that apodotic *δέ* and *καί* are common in Homer (the former also in early prose, Herodotus). But it is no doubt alternatively possible to regard the apodotic use of at any rate some particles as a relic of an earlier, adverbial, use. For it is by no means certain

to a qualifying word, phrase, or participial clause are due to a form of ellipse common in all languages. Λέγεις, καὶ ὀρθῶς γε (λέγεις). Cf. δέ (p. 164, (3)), μέντοι (p. 406, Th.iv.51 : cf. Pl.*Ap.*29c), τε (p. 502(*g*)). See further p. 497, n.2.

[1] The line between parataxis and hypotaxis is a very thin one where e.g. ἐπεί or ὡς introduces an independent sentence, and thus virtually = γάρ. See Kühner, II ii 461, Anm.1.

[2] That τε can ever mean 'also' is highly doubtful. See pp. 535–6.

[3] I borrow this term from Hartung, but give it a narrower denotation.

that the connective sense of any Greek particle is the original sense.

Further, I class as apodotic the use of an emphatic particle at the opening of an apodosis: *γε* (*γοῦν*, with its negative form *οὔκουν . . . γε*), *ἦ* (*ἦ που*, *ἦ τε*), *μέντοι* (p. 402). Apodotic *δή* clearly belongs to this category, for it makes its appearance long before *δή* has begun to acquire connective force.

Thus I include as apodotic both connectives transferred from parataxis to hypotaxis and purely emphatic particles like *γε* and *δή* which do no more than underline the opening of the main clause. There is some illogicality, but great practical convenience, in embracing both types in a single term. Sometimes, indeed, it is difficult to distinguish one type from the other. Thus apodotic *καὶ δή* may be either connective or adverbial in origin (the latter, I think):[1] apodotic *οὖν* and *αὐτάρ*, and apodotic *τε* (if we are to recognize it at all) similarly admit of either explanation.[2] In both its varieties, the apodotic use possesses a structural function in the architecture of the sentence, serving to stress or clarify the relation between clauses. For this reason I do not, for example, regard *οὐδέ* in S.*OC* 590 (see p. 195) as apodotic. Here *οὐδέ* is not, I think, 'the negative counterpart of *δέ* in apodosis' (Jebb). Rather, *οὐδὲ σοί* seems to be the negative of *καὶ σοί* ('you also', 'you, on your side') and the particle goes closely with the word that immediately follows it. The same consideration leads me to deny the title 'apodotic' to *καί* cohering with a single word at the opening of an apodosis (see p. 309). But the distinction is delicate, perhaps precarious.

Closely allied to the apodotic use is the resumptive, in which *δέ*, *δή*, and *οὖν* pick up the thread of a thought which is beginning to wander.

(*e*) *The corresponsive use of particles.* Coherence of thought is adequately secured by the presence of a backward-pointing particle. The reader or listener, when he has reached a certain

[1] An apodotic use of *καὶ δὴ καί*, based on the connective use of that combination, appears occasionally to present itself, but crumbles to nothingness at the touch (p. 257).

[2] For example, Kühner (II ii 327) regards apodotic *οὖν* as adverbial, and the Homeric use of the particle gives him some support. An adverbial force is also clearly present in *αὐτάρ*, if *αὐτάρ* = *αὖτε* + *ἄρ*.

point, meets a particle which looks back to the road he has traversed, and beckons him on in a certain direction. But greater coherence is attained if in addition a forward-pointing particle warns him in advance what path he will soon have to travel, the connexion being expressed reciprocally, from rear to van and from van to rear. It is characteristic of the Greek love of orderliness and lucidity that this double method of connexion is already present in Homer. The forward-pointing particles, which we may describe as 'preparatory',[1] are *μέν*, *τε*, and *καί*. *μέν* is most frequently answered by *δέ*, but often, too, by other particles: *τε* by *τε* or *καί*, *καί* by *καί*. The mutual relationship between the earlier and the later particle may be expressed by the term 'corresponsive'. In particular, the commonness of *μὲν . . . δέ* in all periods of classical Greek has often been noticed. The tendency to view one idea in the light of another idea more or less sharply contrasted with it was indeed innate in the Greek mentality (and occasionally led to the employment of merely formal antithesis for its own sake).[2] The result is a great gain in clearness and precision. Often, when a writer embarks upon a disquisition which appears to invalidate his own point of view, *μέν* indicates that the aberration is only temporary, and that he will return after a time to the straight path.[3]

The responsive use of *καί* and *οὐδέ* noticed above leads also to a corresponsive use in hypotactic constructions when the particle is present in both the subordinate and the main clause. Thus, *ὥσπερ καὶ ἐκεῖνον φιλῶ, οὕτω καὶ σὲ φιλῶ*: 'as I love him as well as you, so I love you as well as him.' The reciprocal relation between *καί* and *καί* is as clearly marked here as in paratactic construction, *φιλῶ καὶ ἐκεῖνον καὶ σέ*.

[1] A forward-pointing particle demands a backward-pointing one to answer it. Anticipatory *γάρ* is not strictly preparatory: it arises, as the word 'anticipatory' suggests, from a dislocation of the natural order. Nor, consequently, can we class anticipatory *γάρ* picked up by *οὖν*, *δή*, etc., as corresponsive.

[2] Demetrius, *De Elocutione* 24, in discussing this matter, quotes Epicharmus' parody: *τόκα μὲν ἐν τήνοις ἐγὼν ἦν, τόκα δὲ παρὰ τήνοις ἐγών*. Pearson, *Fragments of Sophocles*, vol. ii, p. 298, observes: 'The Greeks saw a contrast everywhere, and sometimes overdid it'.

[3] Writers of Greek prose versions sometimes fall short of the Greek standard of lucidity in this respect.

II. CONNECTING PARTICLES.

(1) *The origin of connectives.* I have remarked above (1) that certain particles (ἀλλά, που, τοι, and τῷ in τοιγάρ) can be traced back to other parts of speech. In other cases, where the derivation of the particle itself is unknown, we can trace the evolution of a connective from an adverbial sense in extant Greek literature. Thus μήν and δή, in Homer affirmative particles, later acquire respectively (among other uses) an adversative and an inferential force.[1] An adversative force of μέν, hardly to be found in Homer, is later present in μέντοι, μὲν οὖν, μὲν δή. An inferential force of ἄρα and οὖν, no more than nascent in Homer, grows to maturity. On the other hand ἀτάρ, γάρ, δέ, καί, τε cannot be traced back to an adverbial stage. But it is on general grounds probable (since the connexion of ideas, even in the simplest form, is not a primitive process) that here also an adverbial sense lies behind. And the plausible derivation of γάρ from γε ἄρ (however little it may help us to understand γάρ) points, if correct, in the same direction.

(2) *Connexion and asyndeton.* As a general rule, Greek sentences, clauses, phrases, and single words are linked by a connecting particle[2] to what precedes. Connexion is, on the whole, not often omitted in verse, still less often in prose. There are, however, certain well-marked exceptions to this principle, and Greek frequently dispenses with connexion in the following cases. (I will call this 'formal', as distinct from 'stylistic', asyndeton.)

(i) The preceding context makes the connexion obvious, and no particle is required to point it. This is the case where a writer or speaker directly or indirectly announces his theme in advance, and where a forward-pointing pronoun or demonstrative adverb, or some other word or phrase (especially such an expression

[1] For tendencies which may have led to the evolution of connective δή, see δή, IV.1, *ad init.*

[2] The line between connectives and non-connectives cannot be rigidly drawn. Thus οὖν in Homer, although it has not yet developed a connective function, shows in μὲν οὖν a tendency to develop one. γε, and in a more marked degree μέν γε, mitigate to some extent the harshness of an asyndeton: while γοῦν in the 'part-proof' usage is almost a full connective. μέν, again, occasionally appears to have a quasi-connective force (p. 360).

as *τεκμήριον δέ, σημεῖον δέ*), supplies the link. E.g.Th.vi 90.2 ... *μάθετε ἤδη. ἐπλεύσαμεν* ...: D.vi 17 *λογίζεσθε γάρ. ἄρχειν βούλεται*: xv 9 ... *τῶν γεγενημένων ὑμᾶς τι* ... *ὑπομνήσω. ὑμεῖς ἐξεπέμψατε* ...: Th.iii 20.3 *ἐνέμειναν τῇ ἐξόδῳ ἐθελονταὶ τρόπῳ τοιῷδε. κλίμακας ἐποιήσαντο.* But in such cases connexion by explanatory *γάρ* is probably commoner than asyndeton.

(ii) To a less degree, a backward-pointing pronoun or demonstrative adverb, usually at or near the opening of the sentence, similarly diminishes the necessity for a connecting particle (*δή, οὖν*, or *τοίνυν*). E.g. in X.*An*.i 2 over twenty sentences begin with *ἐνταῦθα, ἐντεῦθεν, ταύτην*, etc., without a connecting particle. Occasionally the pronoun is placed comparatively late: Th.iii 28.2 *ἡ μὲν ξύμβασις αὕτη ἐγένετο*: Ant.vi 14 *καθειστήκει μὲν ἡ χορηγία οὕτω*: X.*An*.i 8.9: And.i 14: D.xviii 235: xx 55.

(iii) In a long series of co-ordinated nouns, adjectives, or verbs connectives are, on the whole, more often omitted than inserted. Th.ii 9.2 *Μεγαρῆς, Βοιωτοί, Λοκροί, Φωκῆς, Ἀμπρακιῶται, Λευκάδιοι, Ἀνακτόριοι*: Pl.*Phdr*.253E (adjectives). But sometimes, and in Epic normally, connectives are inserted: the ancient critics styled this *polysyndeton*. Thus, Hes.*Th*.205–6 and 320 (series of *τε*): *ib*.243–62 (*τε* and *καί* alternating): Th.iii 101.2 *Ἰπνέας καὶ Μεσσαπίους καὶ Τριταιέας καὶ Χαλαίους καὶ Τολοφωνίους καὶ Ἡσσίους καὶ Οἰανθέας*: Hdt.iv 102: Pl.*R*.618D: *Lg*.758E, 842D, 942B. (Our convention of linking the last two units only, leaving the rest unconnected, is on the whole alien to Greek usage: see *δέ* (p. 164), *καὶ* ... *δέ* (p. 202), *καί* (pp. 289–90), *τε* (p. 501).) Pl.*Lg*.897A is a good example of varied asyndeton and connexion.

In a negatived series, while the employment of asyndeton without repetition of the negative is not excluded, repeated negatives, with or without connectives (*οὔτε* ... *οὔτε* ... *οὔτε*: *οὐ* ... *οὐδὲ* ... *οὐδέ*: *οὐ* ... *οὐ* ... *οὐ*) give an effect of greater force, by eliminating each item individually ('not A, nor B, nor C': 'not A, not B, not C'), instead of eliminating the entire series *en bloc* ('not A, B, C'). E.g. Pl.*Lg*.832C (5 *οὔτε*'s): 898B (8 *μηδέ*'s): 902D, 935B. In Pl.*Smp*.211A the great series of *οὔτε*'s and *οὐδέ*'s, enumerating one thing after another that true beauty is *not*, and leading up to the revelation of what true beauty *is*, *ἀλλ' αὐτὸ καθ' αὐτὸ μεθ' αὑτοῦ μονοειδὲς ἀεὶ ὄν*, lends an astonishing power and passion to the period. Cf. Hom.*I* 369–92, where the *οὐδέ*'s (connective and adverbial) are like hammer strokes: 'No, no, no!' In English, compare St. Paul, *Romans* viii 38–9: 'For I am persuaded, that neither death, nor life, nor angels, nor principalities, nor powers, nor things present, nor things to come, nor height, nor depth, nor any other creature, shall be able to separate us from the love of God, which is in Christ Jesus our Lord.'

The truth of the matter is that a great chain or series is of its essence impressive, whether connectives are inserted or omitted. Whether asyndeton or polysyndeton is the more impressive in a particular place, depends on the nature of the context. The Greek critics rightly regarded both as rhetorical 'figures'.

Stylistic, as distinct from formal, asyndeton is used, sparingly by some writers, freely by others, for emotional effect: the impression given is that the speaker's or writer's feelings are too deeply engaged to allow him to trouble about logical coherence. Longinus has some admirable chapters (19–21) on this subject. He quotes Hom. κ 251–2 as an example of asyndeton in rapid narrative, and acutely analyses the telling use of this device in D. xxi 72. In verse there is no finer example of the effect of asyndeton, combined here, as often, with repetition, than the lines of Aeschylus quoted by Plato, *R.* 383B. Of prose writers, Thucydides and (of course) Isocrates rarely employ asyndeton, while Demosthenes exploits its possibilities to the full. As Aristotle remarks (*Rh.* 1413b17–31), asyndeton is essentially a dramatic device, and is for this reason appropriate to oratory: one must 'act the passage, not merely speak it'. A good instance of accumulated asyndeta is to be found in D. xxiv 11–14, where, to say nothing of clauses, ten consecutive sentences, covering twenty-seven lines, open without a connecting particle. Out of many fine Demosthenic examples I will cite xviii 67, 299 (the latter perhaps the finest of all), and xix 76 (where asyndeton expresses the stunning rapidity of disaster). In Lycurg. 33 asyndeton gives pithiness: *τί γὰρ ἔδει προφάσεων ἢ λόγων ἢ σκήψεως; ἁπλοῦν τὸ δίκαιον, ῥᾴδιον τὸ ἀληθές, βραχὺς ὁ ἔλεγχος.*

In contrast with this stylistic employment of asyndeton Andocides and Xenophon often omit connectives in narrative with a certain naive awkwardness, and without any apparent rhetorical justification. E.g. And. i 41, 42, 82, 120, 123: X. *An.* iii 2.33: iv 5.33: v 6.25: vi 4.18: *Cyr.* ii 1.18: iii 3.40.

(3) The mode of connexion omitted when stylistic asyndeton is used is in most cases 'and'. Less frequently γάρ or γοῦν has to be supplied, as in E.*Or.*234: D.xviii 299. Sometimes 'then' or 'therefore' has to be supplied: Pl.*Prt.*339E σὸς μέντοι Σιμωνίδης πολίτης· δίκαιος εἶ βοηθεῖν τῷ ἀνδρί: Pi.*O.*3.45.

(4) In deciding whether asyndeton is tolerable in a particular place, the usage of the author and the character of the passage must be taken into account. These considerations are sometimes of importance for determining the text. Thus in X.*Hier.*6.6 (p. 551) ὅ γέ τοι φόβος κτλ. (τε *ACM*) a connective seems needed to mark the introduction of a new point: the γοῦν sense of γέ τοι will not suit, and the analogy of *An.*vi 5.24, where γάρ has to be supplied in thought, does not support the asyndeton here. δέ τοι (Bach) should perhaps be read. Again, in Pl.*Grg.*459A (p. 578) Ἔλεγές τοι νυνδή κτλ. a connective is badly needed: nowhere else in this passage of formal dialogue (458E–459C) are the successive stages in Socrates' argument introduced without a connective (γε in 459B carries on the thread from his previous speech). I believe τοίνυν νυνδή (τοίνυν νῦν δή *F*) to be the right reading (*C.R.*xlvii (1933) 216). In E.*IT* 50 Porson's emendation produces a most improbable asyndeton: *ib.*1175 the asyndeton is difficult, and Paley's defence of it hardly convincing: in *HF* 722 I believe Nauck's ⟨δ'⟩ to be necessary.

The question of the permissibility of asyndeton is of vital importance for the true explanation of anticipatory γάρ. The asyndeta resulting from the view that γάρ is adverbial here are often intolerable: see γάρ, IV, and ἀλλὰ γάρ (p. 100).

(5) *Apparently superfluous connectives.* In certain cases connectives are inserted where they are, strictly speaking, unnecessary.

(i) In answers to questions. μὲν οὖν (with preparatory μέν and connective οὖν: 'Well'): Pl.*Phlb.*51B: *Sph.*229D: X.*HG* vi 3.13 (answering a rhetorical question). δέ: Pl.*Chrm.*172C ἆρα . . .;—Τάχα δ' ἄν, ἔφη, οὕτως ἔχοι ('And perhaps it may be so'): often in answering a second question (pp. 171–2).

In answers to commands. Pl.*Euthphr.*15E εἰπὲ . . . .—Εἰς αὖθις τοίνυν, ὦ Σώκρατες ('Well, another time, then'): *R.*337D ἀπότεισον ἀργύριον.—Οὐκοῦν ἐπειδάν μοι γένηται ('When I get some, then '.) For a curious τοίνυν in a rejoinder to a statement, cf. Ar. *V.*1141 (p. 573).

(ii) At the opening of a speech or oracle, or of a whole work. The explanation of this inceptive use of connectives is perhaps not everywhere the same. Often the speaker wishes to put his thoughts into relation to the view of the persons he is addressing, or what he takes to be the generally prevailing view. But often, again, this use of connectives appears to be a mere mannerism of style. It has always a touch of *naïveté* such as is characteristic of Xenophon. See ἀλλά (II.8), δέ (I.C.2.iii), τοίνυν (I.6). μέν is similarly employed in openings: though not a connective, it seems to mitigate the abruptness of the initial plunge (p. 382). In a political or forensic speech, after the recitation of documents, the practice varies, connexion being usually inserted, but sometimes omitted.

(iii) In reported speech an opening connective is naturally omitted. 'He said, "Then I'll come"' becomes 'He said he'd go'. But there are cases where the connective is retained: καί, X.*HG* v 3.10: 3.15: νυν, E.*Tr.*1138: οὖν, Pl.*Prt.*322C (p. 426): τοιγαρῶν, Hdt.iv 149.1 (p. 567, n.1): τοίνυν, X.*Cyr.*vi 3.17 (p. 571).

For possibly superfluous δέ in exclamations, see p. 172.

(6) *The different methods of connexion.* These are, broadly speaking, four: (*a*) Additional, (*b*) Adversative, (*c*) Confirmatory, (*d*) Inferential. But the divisions are everywhere fluid. (*a*) is represented at its purest by καί and τε (though δέ is often hardly tinged with adversative colour): one idea is simply added to another without any indication of a logical relation between the two.[1] A variant of (*a*) is what I shall term the 'progressive'[2] use of particles, or combinations of particles, conveying not merely the static piling-up of ideas, but movement of thought: 'now', 'again', 'further', 'to proceed': e.g. μήν, ἀλλὰ μήν, γε

[1] The logical relation may be inherent in the context, though not expressed by the particle. καί, like 'and', sometimes stands where 'and yet' is implied (pp. 292–3). So, occasionally, τε (p. 514 *ad fin.*). Again, δέ, meaning 'and', is sometimes used where the logical relation would properly be expressed by γάρ, οὖν, or ἤ (pp. 169–71).

[2] I prefer this term to 'continuative', which some writers have employed. A man going round in circles in the desert 'continues', but does not 'progress'.

μήν, καὶ μήν, μέντοι.[1] The same significance may be reached from the direction of (*d*), when *οὖν* and *οὐκοῦν* degenerate from *propter hoc* into *post hoc.*[2] In this progressive sense particles mark something of a new departure in the march of thought. They convey an effect approximating to that produced by paragraphing, though not usually denoting quite so strong a break. An example *ex contrario* will illustrate this. In Pl.*R.*338A *Εἰπόντος δέ μου ταῦτα* starts a new paragraph in the Oxford Text, and is printed, as here, with an initial capital. At such an important joint in the structure *οὖν* or *τοίνυν* would have been more normal. (Cf. the not infrequent use of *δέ* in resuming after *μαρτυρίαι*: e.g. D.xlvii 52.) It goes without saying that particles, when used in the progressive sense, must follow strong stops. But certain particles and combinations regularly so used occasionally follow weak stops: e.g. *δή* (p. 239), *ἀλλὰ δή* (p. 242), *καὶ μήν* (p. 352), *τοίνυν* (p. 577 (5)). *καὶ δή, καὶ . . . δή,* and *καὶ δὴ καί* occupy a position between the purely additional and the progressive particles. Broadly speaking, they are to be classed with the former. But *καὶ δή* sometimes introduces a new point, like *καὶ μήν* (p. 249), and so, rather more often, does *καὶ δὴ καί*, which tends to follow a heavier stop than *καὶ δή* and *καὶ . . . δή. καὶ . . . δέ*, on the other hand, is rare after strong stops (p. 201). Even among the particles which I have described as denoting addition pure and simple some difference of structural function can be detected. There is a certain tendency, I think, to use *δέ*, rather than *καί*, for connecting sentences (in the same way as many English writers avoid 'and' at the opening of a sentence), while it is hardly used at all for connecting single words (p. 162). The case of *τε* is complicated, some writers preferring to use it for joining sentences, others for joining clauses, phrases, or single words.

The line between additional-progressive and adversative is

[1] Even within the limits of this class a certain distinction may be drawn, in the uses of such combinations as *καὶ μήν* and *τοίνυν*, between the mere transition to a new item in an enumerative series, or to a fresh argument, and the arrival at a new stage in the logical process. The former may usually best be rendered 'again', 'further', the latter, 'now', 'well'.

[2] The *post hoc* sense is clearly the later in *οὖν*, and also, I think, in *οὐκοῦν*. In *τοίνυν*, on the other hand, if Wackernagel's etymology is right (p. 568), the *propter hoc* sense is the later.

more sharply drawn in English than in Greek and in Latin. ἀλλά, ἀτάρ, αὐτάρ, δέ, μήν, ἀλλὰ μήν, γε μήν, καὶ μήν, καίτοι, μέντοι, etc., like *at* and *autem*, are used both to add and to contrast.[1] On the one hand, the adversative force of a particle like ἀλλά is at times weakened: on the other, custom attaches an adversative force to a pure connective like καίτοι,[2] or to an originally emphatic particle like μήν, or, in certain combinations (μὲν δή, μὲν οὖν, μέντοι), to μέν. By these new developments the range and variety of adversative expression is considerably increased in post-Homeric Greek.

(*b*) Adversatives are of two kinds: eliminative [3] adversatives, used often where one of two contrasted members is negative, the true being substituted for the false (*par excellence* μὲν οὖν and normally ἀλλά), and balancing [3] adversatives, where two truths of divergent tendency are presented (δέ, μήν, μέντοι, etc.). Intermediate between the two we have adversatives like ἀτάρ and καίτοι (and sometimes ἀλλά) which simply raise an objection, leaving it uncertain whether the objection is a fatal one or not. These distinctions are important in principle, though the dividing lines are everywhere fluid. For example, the readiness of ἀλλά and δέ to exchange functions is illustrated by the abnormal, but not uncommon, use of ἀλλά to answer μέν, and of δέ to contrast a positive with a negative clause. μήν, καὶ μήν, and μέντοι occasionally approach the eliminative force of μὲν οὖν (pp. 335, 358, 405).

Class (*c*) is represented throughout Greek literature by γάρ alone (though γοῦν often approaches γάρ in force, giving partial confirmation). (*d*) is less prominent in Homeric Greek, since

[1] When ἀλλὰ μήν, καὶ μήν, καίτοι, δέ γε, etc., introduce the second (major or minor) premise in a syllogism, it is often difficult to say whether they are adversative or progressive. See καίτοι, p. 563, and *Addenda* to p. 353.

[2] Adversative καίτοι is so common that one may legitimately reckon an adversative sense as one of the senses of the particle. On the other hand, where καί appears to be adversative, the opposition is inherent in the context rather than expressed by the particle (p. xlvii, n. 1). Decision between these two explanations is often a delicate matter. We should not, I think, resort to the second in the case of well-established usages. Thus I cannot agree with des Places when he says (p. 107) that in corrective μὲν οὖν 'l'opposition réside uniquement dans la pensée, non dans la particule'.

[3] I think that these terms express the essence of the distinction better than 'strong' and 'weak'.

supplying an explanation is a more primitive and natural process than drawing an inference. In Homer (*d*) is represented by τῶ and τοιγάρ, the inferential force of οὖν being still in embryo. Subsequently τῶ almost entirely disappears, while τοιγάρ remains (in prose almost only in the strengthened forms τοιγάρτοι and τοιγαροῦν), and additional inferential particles are found in οὖν, δή, δῆτα, ἄρα.

(7) *Abnormalities of reference in connexion.* The connexion established is normally, of course, between consecutive units of speech: words, phrases, clauses, or sentences. There are, however, certain exceptions. In dialogue, owing to the quickness of thrust and parry, or the self-absorption of one of the participants, a speaker sometimes links the opening of his speech to his own preceding words, not to the intervening words of the other person.[1] Thus S.*OT* 1357 (οὔκουν . . . γε): *Ph.*1257 (καίτοι): E.*Hel.*1259 (γε μὲν δή): *Or.*793 (οὖν): *Ph.*608 (γε): δέ γε (p. 154): perhaps εἰ γάρ in A.*Pr.*152[2], *Ch.*345 (p. 92). This is often the case with γάρ (III.5). In S.*El.*1035 (p. 443) ἀλλ' οὖν looks back to 1017–26: or perhaps it would be truer to say that its *point d'appui* is the general situation, the whole attitude of Chrysothemis, rather than any particular set of words, an explanation which applies also to E.*Alc.*713 (καὶ μήν, p. 354), and *IT* 637 (μέντοι, p. 405).[3] γάρ (III) presents, in general, many abnormalities of connexion. Thus it sometimes refers to the motive of the preceding words (not to their content), to a far-back remark in a continuous discourse, to an individual word or phrase, or to an idea suggested rather than expressed. Sometimes, again, two successive γάρ's share a common reference.

[1] The ignoring of this possibility has sometimes led to misunderstandings. A certain flexibility of mind is required in such cases. Jebb on S.*El.*1035, Paley on E.*Alc.*713, have, I think, interpreted the sequence of thought too rigidly.

[2] But see *Addenda* to p. 92.

[3] In some of these examples the opening of the second speech is marked by a particle which is not, strictly speaking, a connective. But the line between connectives and non-connectives is a shadowy one (see p. xliii, n. 2), and the principle illustrated is the same in both cases.

III. COMBINATIONS AND COLLOCATIONS OF PARTICLES.

(1) *The distinction between combinations and collocations.* There has often been occasion in the preceding pages to cite combinations of particles. It is now time to consider how far particles may be said to cohere so as to form a real unity of expression, as opposed to a merely fortuitous collocation.[1]

(i) The combinations which have the most indisputable claim to the title are those in which one or other of the two particles (either the more or the less important of the two) could not have been used without the other, and also bears in the combination a sense which it cannot bear in isolation: for example, adverbial οὖν reinforcing ἀλλά, γάρ, γε, δέ, or preparatory μέν: adversative μέν preceding δή, οὖν, or τοι. In corrective μὲν οὖν neither particle could have been used without the other, and each bears in the combination a sense quite different from its independent sense.

(ii) In other cases, while neither of the two particles bears an unwonted force in the combination, still, the presence of the one depends, at any rate to some extent, on the presence of the other. E.g. Pl.*Lg.*666A μετὰ δὲ τοῦτο (νομοθετήσομεν) οἴνου μὲν δὴ γεύεσθαι τοῦ μετρίου . . . μέθης δὲ . . . ἀπέχεσθαι. Here it might at first sight appear that δή does not adhere to μέν, but emphasizes οἴνου, or the phrase οἴνου . . . γεύεσθαι. But, as we find that in prose δή rarely emphasizes substantives or phrases, while it very frequently follows preparatory μέν, there seems no doubt that the function of δή here is to stress the antithetical form of the sentence, not to underline a single element in the content of it. Similarly, γὰρ δή usually[2] denotes that what is presented as a cause is in truth a fact: 'for actually'. The case of γε μήν is instructive. From the point of view of

[1] I have not seen this question discussed in any treatment of the particles. My thanks are due to Dr. Chapman for urging me to clear up my ideas on the subject. I have not, however, attempted in this book to use the distinction between 'combination' and 'collocation' as a basis of classification. To have done so would have complicated matters needlessly.

[2] For exceptions, see IV below.

abstract analysis, γε emphasizes the word it follows, and μήν is the connective, both particles exercising their forces independently. But γε μήν is used in positive adversative clauses by writers who use simple adversative μήν in negative clauses only. The association of γε with μήν is therefore stylistically important, and the two particles may justly be regarded as forming a real combination. So, too, may ἦ γάρ and ἦ καί, which are used by Plato and Xenophon far more freely than ἦ *simplex*. On the same principle, in Attic, where connective καὶ δή without a following καί is rare, καὶ δὴ καί must be regarded as a combination, whereas in καὶ μὴν καί, where the addition of a second καί is not prescribed by custom, there is less coherence between the first two particles and the third.

(iii) Sometimes, again, while either particle could stand without the support of the other, the two nevertheless tend to cohere. Thus, with καὶ γάρ, though καί often goes closely with a word following γάρ,[1] there are cases where καί seems to bear upon the sentence as a whole, and to cling to γάρ: 'for there is a further fact'. Again, the very frequent occurrence of καὶ δὴ καί in Herodotus seems to suggest that, although he, unlike Attic writers, freely uses connective καὶ δή without a second καί, still even in him the second καί, where it does appear, is an integral part of the combination.

(iv) In other cases the collocation of two particles is purely fortuitous. For example, I see nothing significant in the frequent juxtaposition of preparatory μέν with γάρ and τοίνυν:[2] and if I mention in my text those uses of μὲν δή, μὲν οὖν in which the first particle is preparatory and the second connective, I only do so because of their bearing on the evolution of connective δή and οὖν, and in order to call attention to the importance of distinguishing between two entirely separate usages. This is perhaps the place to mention the tendency of certain particles to gravitate towards certain other words which are not particles, especially towards pronouns. Thus γε, especially in Homer, but also to some extent in later Greek, tends to attach itself to pronouns (pp. 121–2):

[1] See IV below.

[2] Des Places (p. 308) attributes stylistic importance to μὲν τοίνυν, and Shorey (*C.Phil.*xxviii 2) calls attention to the frequency of μὲν γάρ in Pl.*Prt.* 337A–C.

so does emphatic μέν in Homer (p. 360). μέντοι in its affirmative and syllogistic senses is frequently associated with σύ, οὗτος, τοιοῦτος, τοιόσδε, etc. (pp. 400, 408–9). γε tends to follow (often with a word or words intervening) ὡς, εἰ, ὅταν,[1] etc. (p. 151, n. 1). δή tends to adhere to certain words and types of word: e.g. to adjectives expressing indefinite quantity or number, to νῦν, to δῆλος, to superlatives, to ὁρᾶν (pp. 204–18). μήν is predominantly used after negatives (pp. 330, 334–40).

(2) *Avoided collocations.*[2] Certain collocations of particles, which are in themselves natural enough, are for some reason or other wholly or generally avoided. τοῦτό γε γὰρ οὐκ ἐρεῖς seems as unobjectionable as τοῦτό γε μὴν οὐκ ἐρεῖς. But while γε μήν is not merely a tolerated collocation but an established combination, γε γάρ never, I think, occurs (the analogy of γε μήν tells strongly against the explanation I have offered on p. 151). The derivation of γάρ from γε ἄρ might perhaps be the cause of this avoidance (just as δὴ δῆτα is eschewed). For though γὰρ ἄρα is found, a language may tolerate a harshness in one case while avoiding it in another. But I doubt if the Greeks apprehended, whether consciously or unconsciously, this derivation of γάρ (if, indeed, it is the true one). The similar avoidance of γάρ γε[3] is more easily understood, as it violates the normal order of precedence (see V.2.i below). While γάρ που is common (in Plato), δέ που and καί που not rare, and ἀλλὰ μήν που, καὶ μήν που occur several times, που never seems to follow an inferential particle such as connective δή, οὖν, τοίνυν. τε οὖν (τε prospective and οὖν ancillary), in marked contrast with εἴτε οὖν, οὔτε οὖν, is only found once (p. 420), while the collocation of prospective τε with connective οὖν is almost entirely avoided, except by Plato (p. 441). μέν τοι (*separatim*, with preparatory μέν), τέ τοι,[4] and οὖν τοι seem to be avoided, in contrast with γέ τοι, δέ τοι, γάρ τοι: so, on the whole, is τέ γε (p. 161,

[1] I do not include these conjunctions among particles. See I.5.*b*. Nor do I include the negatives, οὐ and μή.

[2] See further IV below.

[3] In E.*Ion* 847 γάρ γε, which Grégoire (in the Budé edition) surprisingly retains, is generally held to be corrupt.

[4] Conjectured by Buttmann in S.*Ph.*823.

and see IV below). τε μέν (τε = 'both'), which might have been expected to occur sporadically,[1] seems not to be found.

Other avoided juxtapositions are οὐ (μή) and γε (p. 148), εἰ and τε *simplex*, οὐ and preparatory μέν (in that order).[2] See also (3) below, *ad fin.*

In some cases it is the toleration of an apparently harsh or awkward collocation that calls for remark. Thus non-connective καὶ δή and corrective μὲν οὖν are juxtaposed with each other, and with other particles (pp. 250–3, 479).

(3) *Split combinations.* Particles may form a combination even when not juxtaposed.[3] There is no distinction in meaning between δέ γε and δὲ . . . γε, ἀλλὰ γάρ and ἀλλὰ . . . γάρ, καὶ μέντοι and καὶ . . . μέντοι. In certain passages μέν and γε separate but in close proximity have almost the same effect as μένγε. μὲν . . . τοίνυν is occasionally used for μὲν τοίνυν. In poetry metrical considerations often tilt the balance towards juxtaposition or separation. In other cases custom changes, or individual preference plays a part. Thus Homer writes καὶ . . . περ, οὐδὲ . . . περ, later authors καίπερ, οὐδέ περ : ἀλλὰ γάρ replaces ἀλλὰ . . . γάρ during the fourth century : Plato prefers καὶ μέντοι, Xenophon καὶ . . . μέντοι. Sometimes the juxtaposition of logically cohering particles is actually avoided : notably in the case of γε following an earlier particle or combination (p. 152).

[1] Plato writes (*Lg.*655A: see p. 373) ἀλλ' ἐν γὰρ μουσικῇ καὶ σχήματα μὲν καὶ μέλη ἔνεστιν . . . . If he had used τε . . . καί instead of καὶ . . . καί, the passage would have run ἀλλ' ἐν γὰρ μουσικῇ σχήματά τε μὲν καὶ μέλη ἔνεστιν . . . . That nothing of the kind turns up in the whole of Greek literature is perhaps not accidental. τε μέν, though logical enough, would have been felt to clash. Even as it stands, the sentence is exceptional. The intrusion of μέν between the corresponsive καί's is awkward, and the natural order would have been ἔνεστι μὲν σχήματά τε καὶ μέλη. In A.*Ag.*396 λιτᾶν δ' ἀκούει μὲν οὔτις θεῶν avoids λιτᾶν δὲ μὲν ἀκούει. τε μέν (τε = 'and') is found in Hp.*Morb.*ii53 (p. 373). But it looks highly suspicious.

[2] Conjectured by Wilamowitz in S.*Ph.*811 (p. 331). This taboo is evidence against taking μέν in οὐ μὲν δή in Pl.*Phlb.*46B (pp. 292–3) as preparatory. My Oxford colleagues tell me that their pupils frequently write οὐ μέν.

[3] But this does not apply to *all* combinations. Thus ἀλλ' οὖν is never split, and Jebb is certainly wrong in associating the particles in S.*Ant.*925 (see p. 473). καὶ μήν is hardly ever split (p. 358).

I have referred above ((1) *ad fin.*) to the association of γε with conjunctions, ὡς, εἰ, ὅταν, etc. Here, again, the association is not dissolved by spatial separation, and it appears to make no difference to the sense whether γε follows at once or after an interval (pp. 142–3). The juxtaposition of εἰ and γε seems to be mainly,[1] that of ὡς and γε (with ὡς = 'for': p. 143) wholly avoided.

(4) *Exceptional combinations.* Generally speaking, a combination cannot rightly be described as such unless it is more or less established in the language. Occasionally, however, we meet with an *ad hoc* combination, in which, though it may be found only once in Greek, there is a close and essential cohesion between the separate parts: thus, οὐ μὴν ἀλλὰ . . . γάρ (p. 30), ἀλλὰ μὴν . . . γάρ (p. 347).

(5) *Double connexions.* In a combination of particles it is normally the case either that one particle (whether the first or the second) is connective or preparatory, the other adverbial (e.g. τε δή, γε μήν, γὰρ οὖν), or that both are adverbial (e.g. γε δή, (γὰρ) οὖν δή, ἦ τοι μέν). For the order of precedence, see V.2 below. In a few cases, however, each particle appears to be connective, the connexions being of different kinds. See ἀλλὰ γάρ, (9) and (10) (pp. 107–8): γὰρ . . . δῆτα, καὶ . . . δῆτα (pp. 272–3): ἀλλὰ . . . τοίνυν, δὲ . . . τοίνυν (p. 579). Adversative καὶ μήν, καὶ μέντοι, should not, I think, be so explained, though the analogy of 'and yet' is tempting (pp. 357, 415).

[1] Perhaps this is putting it too strongly. Certainly Sophocles always separates εἰ from γε. But there are many examples in other authors of εἴ γε, ἐάν γε, ἤν γε: e.g. E.*HF*719: *Or.*1106,1593: Ar.*Fr.*105: Antiph.*Fr.*191.2: Hdt.iii73: Pl.*La.*192C: *Phdr.*242D: 253C (conjectured): X.*Mem.*ii1.17: for Demosthenes, see Preuss's Index. (In B.13.228 Blass conjectured εἴ γ' for εἴκ'.) Wilamowitz is therefore wrong in saying (on E.*Ion*847) 'ὡς εἴγε ist unzulässig, da man in alter Zeit εἰ und γε durch ein Wort trennt'.

On the juxtaposition of γε and ἄν, see Neil, Appendix to *Knights*, p. 197: Pearson on E.*Ph.*1215.

IV. DIVERSITY IN THE USAGES AND MEANINGS OF PARTICLES.

We have seen (and the pages of this book will prove it abundantly) that few Greek particles possess one meaning and one alone. New uses develop out of old, and the old, though they sometimes wither and die, more frequently prolong their existence, often in altered forms, by the side of the new. The meanings of particles, more than those of any other part of speech, are fluid. *πάντα ῥεῖ.* Some, indeed, like *ἀλλά* (and, with all its detailed subtleties, *καί*) remain more or less true to type throughout their course. Others behave more eccentrically, and of these the most unaccountable is *τε*, whose two main currents no philologist has traced convincingly to a common source.

Even in usages which appear rigid and stereotyped, the possibility of unexpected deviations from the normal has to be borne in mind.[1] Thus, while *εἰ καί* usually means 'even if', there are places where 'even if' makes nonsense, and *καί*, detaching itself from *εἰ*, adheres closely to a following expression (p. 304). *καί* following interrogatives is of three distinct types (p. 312). *τοῦτον καὶ λέγω* can mean either 'He is just the man I mean', or 'I *do* mean him' (p. 322). *εἴ γε* is usually 'if, but not otherwise', but sometimes 'even if' (p. 126). *μήν* has perhaps different meanings in the apparently similar idioms *τί μήν*; and *ἀλλὰ τί μήν*; (p. 333). *οὐδέ* in Herodotean *οὐ μὲν οὐδέ* has not always the same force (p. 363).

In combinations of particles the possibilities of ambiguity are naturally increased: all the more so since, as we have seen, spatially separated particles may logically go together, and, as we shall shortly see, juxtaposed particles need not necessarily go together. In *καὶ γάρ, οὐδὲ γάρ, καὶ γάρ τοι* there is nothing but the context to show whether (as usually) *γάρ* is connective and *καί* or *οὐδέ* adverbial, or vice versa (pp. 109–11). Similarly, in progressive *ἀλλὰ γάρ* (p. 105), *γάρ* seems to be adverbial, which in this combination it normally is not. While in *γὰρ δή* the coherence of the two particles is usually beyond doubt (Hdt.i 34 *ἦν γὰρ δὴ κωφός*,

[1] Some scholars have gone astray in discussing S.*OT* 219–21 through assuming that *οὐ γὰρ ἄν*, which *often* means 'for else', *must* mean that. See Jebb.

'For in point of fact he was deaf'), in D.xxi 44 they clearly do not cohere: for τί γὰρ δή ποτ' . . . ; is followed by καὶ πάλιν τί δή ποτ' . . . ; and in both cases δή must go with the interrogative, and strengthen it. Similarly, in καὶ γάρ, καί sometimes refers to a following word or phrase, while contrariwise in καὶ . . . γάρ the particles sometimes, though separated, cohere.

Where καί, at the opening of a sentence or clause, is followed at a short interval by a second particle possessing both adverbial and connective functions, there are two possibilities. Either (as usually) καί gives the connexion, and the second particle is adverbial: or καί is adverbial, and the second particle is connective. Thus in X.*Mem.*iv 7.4 καί means 'also' and μέντοι 'but'. καί is also occasionally adverbial in καὶ . . . δή (p. 255), καὶ . . . τοίνυν (p. 578), and, probably, καὶ . . . δέ (p. 199, n. 1).

That two particles form an established combination does not mean that in no circumstances whatever can they part company and exercise their functions independently. (It is easy to go astray over this matter in reading. The eye catches the juxtaposition, and the brain assumes a logical coherence. In some cases, if the passage were spoken, the ear might detect the distinction by a slight change in inflexion.) In γοῦν, for example, while οὖν usually stresses γε, there are cases where οὖν is connective, detached from γε, which goes closely with the preceding word.[1] In γέ τοι the stereotyping of the 'part-proof' sense (as in γοῦν) does not preclude the juxtaposition of the two particles in independent capacities (p. 551). In οὐ γὰρ ἀλλά we sometimes find ἀλλά separated in sense from οὐ γάρ: 'No, but . . .' (p. 31). Here, obviously, pronunciation would indicate the grouping of the words, and a comma after γάρ would make all clear to the eye. In one passage a similar division of οὐ μέντοι ἀλλά is possible (p. 405).

When we find a Greek author using a collocation of particles which the language in general avoids, we shall often find on closer examination that there is no real coherence between the two particles. Thus, the only instances of δή γε which appear to be sound are those in which δή and γε do not coalesce (p. 247).

[1] Perhaps in such cases γ' οὖν should be written, *separatim*, to mark the distinction. See p. 448, n. 1.

The same is probably true of τέ γε (p. 161). In Pl.*Grg.*454E the γε goes with ἀλλὰ μήν, in *Phd.*59C it is epexegetic of ναί: τέ γε is far less objectionable in these two passages, and in X.*Mem.*i 2.54, than in E.*Alc.*647 and Pl.*Phd.*106D, in both of which the γε can only be taken in close conjunction with the τε. Similar considerations justify the rare juxtaposition μέντοι γε in two Aristophanic passages (pp. 404, 410).

Passages in which two particles normally forming a well-established combination exercise their forces independently are discussed on pp. 132 (οὐδέ γε), 153 (δέ γε), 159 (καὶ . . . γε), 160 (μέν γε), 245 (γε δή), 402 (γε μέντἄν), 412 (γε μέντοι, perhaps), 413 (γε μέντοι).

Different meanings of the same particle or combination are even found in close proximity. Thus it seems likely that in Hes. *Op.*772 γε μέν is adversative, while in 774 the μέν looks forward to a δέ (pp. 387–8). In Hdt.i 214 τε δή is apparently 'and' in one place, 'both' in another. In Pl.*Grg.*503B–C the first *Τί δέ;* is, I think, 'Well' ('And what of this?'), going on to a new question: the second is a surprised question, with no connective force, '*What?*' In *Euthd.*298D the first *Καὶ* . . . γε is 'Yes, also', the second is 'Yes, and . . .' In S.*OC*539 and 546 *Τί γάρ;* bears different meanings (pp. 82–3), in Ar.*Nu.*254,255 τοίνυν ('then' and 'now': p. 574), in Hom.*M* 344,357 μέν (p. 368). In the last example we have different meanings not only in close proximity, but in identical phrases: cf. the different meanings of μέν in *Ω*92, *β*318[1] (p. 368), and of περ in *Α*131, *Τ*155[1] (p. 485, n. 1). Cf. also καὶ μήν in Ant.v 44 (p. 358).

V. THE POSITION OF PARTICLES.

(1) *The position of particles in sentence and clause.* Adverbial particles, especially when they apply to the sentence as a whole, tend to gravitate to its opening,[2] where the emphasis in Greek usually lies. ἦ is in fact almost tied down to the position of

[1] In these two cases the variation of meaning may be ascribed to the repetition of a stereotyped phrase in different contexts.

[2] Neil (*Knights*, p. 186) has called attention to this in the case of γε.

first word in the sentence.[1] The position of certain enclitic particles is further affected, as Wackernagel (*Indog. Forsch.* I (1891) 333–436) has shown, by the general tendency of enclitics to come second in the sentence: a tendency strongly marked in Homer, but considerably modified in later Greek. Thus in Hom.*ΝΠΡ* που occurs fourteen times, always as the second word. Epic τε and ῥα also occupy the second place, and so does τοι, which even in post-Homeric Greek presses to the fore so insistently that it sometimes cuts a compound verb in two: E. *Or.*1047 Ἔκ τοί με τήξεις.[2] θην in Homer, and usually in Theocritus, comes second word, except where two particles precede it (e.g. καὶ γάρ θην). But where the emphasis or tone of nuance is postponed, the particle is postponed with it, and γε and δή sometimes come near the end, or actually at the very end, of a sentence. Even particles like τοι and που, which bear on the general thought, are sometimes postponed. Thus in D.xviii 117 δήπου ends a sentence: for postponement of τοι and affirmative μέντοι, see pp. 547–8, 400–1.

Particles which affect the thought as a whole are comparatively rare in post-positive subordinate clauses. (Where the sentence opens with a subordinate clause, a particle contained in that clause is often to be regarded as belonging to the following main clause: εἴ τοι ταῦτα λέγεις, ψεύδει = ψεύδει τοι, εἰ ταῦτα λέγεις.) But we find γοῦν, for example, in a post-positive relative clause in Pl.*Grg.*509A: and τοι (*q.v.*, III) is quite common in post-positive subordinate clauses.

Where γε (as usually) or δή (as often) emphasizes an individual word, it normally follows it immediately, while καί ('also',

[1] Interrogative ἦ and ἆρα naturally open a sentence, or at least a clause: but there are exceptions. Wackernagel (*Indog. Forsch.* i. 377) suggests that the non-enclitic 'post-positive' particles ἄρα, γάρ, δέ, δῆτα, μέν, μήν, οὖν perhaps gradually became post-positive, like *enim*, and *namque* on the analogy of *enim*, *itaque* on the analogy of *igitur*. δή in Homer can open a sentence, but is beginning to be post-positive. (τοίνυν Wackernagel rightly regards as formed by two enclitics, τοι and νυν: see p. 568.) In τοιγαροῦν, I will add, we can watch a particle becoming post-positive (see VI. 3 below). The converse process is to be seen in ἆρα (in the sense of ἄρα), which writers of the New Comedy sometimes put at the opening of a sentence (p. 48, n. 2).

[2] On particles in tmesis, see Kühner, II i 530–7, and cf. pp. 429–30, 478 ((iv): Archipp.*Fr.*35.2).

'even', 'actually') immediately precedes the emphasized word. But there are many exceptions in verse, and some in prose. Thus the most emphatic word sometimes does not immediately follow καί, and sometimes follows, instead of preceding, γε or δή.

The position of connectives is, naturally, far more definitely fixed. καί, τοιγάρ, τοιγάρτοι always, τοιγαροῦν almost always,[1] occupy first place in clause or sentence. Other connectives normally occupy the second place. The main exceptions to this rule are:

(i) Postponement after closely cohering word-groups, particularly where article, preposition, or negative (or more than one of these in combination) cling tenaciously to a following word.

(ii) Postponement after an apostrophe, oath, or exclamation.

(iii) In verse, postponement due apparently to metrical convenience. Here the practice of different authors varies considerably. Thus Aeschylus postpones δέ more freely than Sophocles (though Sophocles often postpones οὖν) and Euripides, and they more freely than the comic poets: while *per contra* the postponement of γάρ goes to surprising lengths in Middle and New Comedy.

(2) *Order of precedence in combinations.* (i) An adverbial particle attached to a connective usually follows it, either immediately or at a short interval: γὰρ δή, ἀλλ' οὖν, καὶ δή, καὶ ... δή. (In Epic δὴ γάρ, δή has greater independence.)

Except in δέ γε, γε seldom immediately follows a connective. ἀλλά γε, καί γε, καίτοι γε, μέντοι γε are all either rare or unknown in classical Greek. Normally γε either precedes the connective (γε μήν, γε μέντοι, γε μὲν δή) or follows at an interval (καὶ μὴν ... γε, ἀλλὰ μέντοι ... γε). The truth seems to be that γε, even in combinations, demands a firmer *point d'appui* than a mere particle can give.

(ii) Preparatory μέν and τε take precedence of a connective: clearness is gained by placing these particles immediately after the word (or the first word of the group) to which they refer. Σωκράτης μὲν γὰρ ...: οἵ τε γὰρ ἐν τῇ πόλει ὄντες ....

(iii) Preparatory μέν and τε also take precedence of ad-

[1] For the position of τοιγαροῦν second in sentence in Hippocrates and in post-classical Greek, see VI.3 below, and p. 567.

verbial particles. Thus μὲν δή, μέν γε, τε δή. (But γε μέν seems occasionally to be used for μέν γε in Epic and Elegiac. See p. 388.)

(iv) Precedence between two combined adverbial particles.

γε takes precedence of other adverbial particles, as in γοῦν, γέ τοι, γε δή. (The rare reverse order in δή γε is due to special considerations. See IV above.) οὖν almost always takes precedence of δή where neither particle is connective: thus γὰρ οὖν δή, ἀλλ' οὖν δή, μὲν οὖν δή. (μὲν δὴ οὖν is very rare.) Affirmative μέν takes precedence of τοι and becomes μέντοι. (But τοι ousts μέν in Homeric ἦ τοι μέν.) δή τοι is almost always preferred to τοι δή, except in οὔτοι δή. που, a modest particle, readily yields place: γέ που, δήπου.

VI. THE STYLISTIC IMPORTANCE OF PARTICLES.

In the preceding pages I have been concerned with particles mainly from the point of view of grammar and logic, with their origins, natures, and functions. In what follows I shall consider their stylistic features and their distribution over the field of Greek literature, taking into account the distinctions which spring from differences of period, differences of genre, and the individual preferences of various writers. This is a study of great interest and importance. It helps us to appreciate the colour of various styles, to which the use of particles contributes in no slight degree. It may also be of occasional value in establishing the text of a passage, and perhaps even in determining, within broad limits, the date and authorship of a work.[1] For the most part, this aspect of the particles has been neglected. Writers on the subject have

[1] On the whole it must be confessed that the harvest is disappointingly meagre. Particles do not help us to date Sophocles' plays, or to determine whether Euripides wrote the *Rhesus*. On the other hand, as I hope to have shown below, they point to certain conclusions regarding the *Prometheus*, and in the dating of Plato's dialogues they have played a not unimportant part. Here the circumstances are exceptionally favourable. We have in our hands almost the whole of the very considerable output, extending over a long life, of an author whose use of particles varies markedly in different works.

largely ignored these distinctions,[1] except where they are very striking, though Kühner is superior to his predecessors in this respect, and the specialized studies provide more information than the general works.

(1) *Repetition of particles.* Before discussing differences of period and so forth, it will be well to consider the general Greek practice with regard to the repetition of particles at a short interval. The Greeks seem to have felt about the repetition of words in general that, while artistic repetition is stylistically effective, accidental repetition is not a thing to be sedulously and artificially avoided. (Their attitude to assonance was precisely the same.) The exactness of the significance of Greek pronouns, it is true, often makes repetition of nouns unnecessary. But where repetition is the most convenient course, the Greeks do not boggle at it, and their writings are mostly free from the pitiful periphrases by which some of our own authors have sought to avoid calling a spade a spade more than once. (τὸ προειρημένον is, happily, a good deal rarer in Greek than its English counterparts.) The Greeks felt the same about the repetition of particles. When it is convenient to use the same particle two or three times at short intervals, the same particle is used two or three times (though, when undergraduates write Greek prose, they will cut themselves with knives rather than do this). Thus we find accumulations of γάρ (Hdt.i 160.2,199.4: Ant.v 86–7: Pl.*Ap.*30C,40A: *Tht.* 155D: Hyp.*Epit.*18–19: Arist.*Pol.*1261a24–6): γε (Hom.*E*258: *Π*30: and see p. 144): δέ (E.*El.*73–5: *IT*45–52: Pherecyd.*Fr.*18a,105 (δέ and καί): Hdt.i 216.3–4): E.*Ba.*965–6 has δέ thrice in two lines (but see Murray's *app. crit.* and Dodds's note): οὐδέ, connective and adverbial (Pl.*Clit.*408A): adverbial καί Pl.*R*445C: X.*Cyr.*v 4.42: D.xxxv 50): οὖν (Hdt.v 82.1–2): γοῦν (Pl.*R*554B): που (Pl. *Cra.*409B): τε . . . καί (Hdt.ix 31.3–5: Pl.*Phd.*82B–C,108A,110E: *Ti.*40E). In Hom.*ξ* 151, S.*Tr.*1151, ἀλλά comes twice in a line: twice in successive lines, S.*Aj.*852–3, *El.*881–2. In Ar.*Th.*274–5, *Pl.*648–9, two consecutive lines are introduced by τοίνυν (cf. *Nu.* 254–5). In *Pax*820–1 ἔμοιγέ τοι immediately follows ἔγωγέ τοι.

[1] As will often appear in the course of this book, scholars have not infrequently introduced by emendation usages of particles which conflict with the practice of their author, as far as we can know it.

That I draw largely on Herodotus for examples suggests that there is often a certain naïveté in the repetition: but other of my examples are from more formal and self-conscious prose.

Through forgetfulness of this Greek tolerance of repetition, the text has sometimes been needlessly suspected. See S.*Ph.*757–62 (δῆτα four times in six lines), with Jebb's excellent note[1] on this passage and on the threefold ἀλλά in 645–51.[2] It is equally mistaken to see design in repetitions which are really fortuitous. Thus, van Leeuwen, on Ar.*Lys.*848, 'Ipsam dein particulam illudens repetit Lysistrata'. I do not think the repetition is intentional here, or in Ar.*Th.*274–5. But I do not mean to deny that there are places where a character in a play throws another character's particle back at him. Thus in S.*OT* 1005 the Messenger, with a touch of the pawkiness which characterizes Sophoclean messengers, retorts rather impudently with καὶ μήν, as Xanthias does, most effectively, in Ar.*Ra.*526 with οὔ τί που ('*Surely* you can't mean . . . ?'). Cf. δὲ δή E.*El.*236–7. In Ar.*Lys.* 902 τοιγάρ, ἤν δοκῇ echoes the same words in the preceding line (that τοιγάρ belongs to the grand style adds to the joke), just as in *Pl.*929 οὐκοῦν ἐκεῖνός εἰμ' ἐγώ echoes 918. In all these cases the repetition has a mocking tone. Cf. also (with more serious intention) A.*Eu.*727–9 (pp. 540–1): S.*OT*549–51. In S.*Ph.*854–5 the repeated τοι gives urgency to the appeal.

The natural frequency with which common particles recur is not, then, artificially limited by the Greek writers, but is regarded as unobjectionable. In certain cases repetition, while natural or even unavoidable in the context, gives positive gain. I have discussed above (II.2) the effect produced by καί and οὐδέ in polysyndeton.

Further, in addition to the natural tendency of common words to recur, it is probably true that a word will run in a writer's head at a particular time. Like other words,[3] particles have, as

[1] I doubt, however, whether the iteration, if a shade careless, demands much 'palliation'.

[2] See also Pearson's Index to Jebb's Sophocles, and Radermacher in *Wien. Stud.* xlvi (1929), pp. 130–2.

[3] For example, Mr. D. L. Page points out to me that ἄφαρ occurs four times in the *Trachiniae*, nowhere else in Sophocles. εὔτυκος in tragedy is confined to A.*Supp.* (959(?),974,994). The frequency of πλῆθος in the *Persae* and πορθμεύω in *IT* is largely explained by the subject-matter.

Dr. Chapman remarks, 'a certain gregarious tendency'. He points out that in Isoc.xii *τοίνυν* occurs nine times in §§ 42–102, not at all in §§ 103–272: in xv, twelve times in §§ 30–121, not at all in §§ 122–204. I note that out of sixteen examples of *τοίνυν* in Herodotus, three are in vii 50.2–4. Comparative *ὥστε* is commoner in *Trachiniae* and *Bacchae* than in other plays. Most of the Sophoclean examples of *ἦ που* are in the *Ajax*. *ἐφ' ᾧ τε* is particularly common in [D.] lvi.[1] All the examples of *τοιγάρ* in comedy are in the *Lysistrata*. *καί τε* is especially common in the *Hymn to Aphrodite*.[1] *ἦ μήν* occurs fifteen times in the *Parmenides*, as often as in all the remaining Platonic dialogues put together.

(2) *Variations in the employment of particles in different periods, dialects, and styles, and by different authors.* Here, owing to the loss of so much Greek literature, we are on slippery ground. For instance, fourth-century tragedy and comedy have vanished, with the exception of meagre fragments. When we find a fourth-century prose usage to be absent from fifth-century tragedy or comedy, or from both, can we assume that it was known to the fifth century, but deliberately avoided by the tragedians as alien to the tragic style, or avoided both in tragedy and in comedy as inappropriate to verse? Is it not equally possible that the usage is a late comer, that Aeschylus and Sophocles would have employed it had they known it, and that Moschion, say, actually did employ it? Contrariwise, we have very little Attic prose earlier than 400 B.C. (It is true that Aristophanes does something to make good the paucity of prose in the last quarter of the fifth century. Where, as often, we find his practice agreeing with that of Plato and Xenophon, we may usually safely regard it as colloquial practice.) Again, when we are tempted to talk of individual preferences, may we not be mistaking the characteristics of a type for personal characteristics? With the ten orators and, to a smaller degree, with the three tragedians, the risk of confusion is less serious. But other types of composition are not so well represented. The extant historians and philosophers, for

[1] In cases like these, where the authorship of a work is unknown, the recurrence of a particle may be due either to 'gregariousness' or to individual preference.

example, form far less homogeneous groups. Certainly our path is beset with dangers here, and many of the distinctions which I shall draw are highly speculative. Still, it seemed worth while to include all the material which might appear to point to various conclusions, even at the risk of having a certain amount of chaff mixed up with the grain.

(3) *Chronological differences.* In Homeric Greek particles of emphasis (γε, δή, ἦ, μήν), and certain other particles, such as ἄρα and 'Epic' τε, are heaped on in almost reckless profusion, and with but little definiteness of application. As the language develops, it tends, in the first place, towards an exacter delimitation of the functions of particles (especially in prose). Thus emphatic δή comes to be mainly used in association with certain types of word, and ἄρα, from denoting interest in general, becomes specifically an expression of enlightenment or disillusionment. μέν no longer simply expresses emphasis, but emphasis as an element in contrast. περ loses its independence, and survives only in an ancillary capacity. The use of apodotic ἀλλά is confined within narrower limits.

This is not, of course, to say that delimitation is everywhere exact. There is frequent overlapping, the same idea [1] being often expressed by several different particles or combinations. Expression thus loses in clarity, but gains correspondingly in variety, since it is thereby possible, for example, to ring the changes on ἀλλὰ μήν, καὶ μήν, τοίνυν, in an enumerative series.

The crystallizing process is especially discernible in the case of combinations. Particles are, for the most part, no longer simply piled on one another without regard for redundance. ἦ δή and ἦ δὴ μάν hardly survive in post-Homeric Greek: ἦ τοι gradually goes out of use. Contrariwise, certain combinations become stereotyped, and in some cases (e.g. μὲν οὖν, μέντοι) bear meanings irreconcilable with the current usage of their component parts. καί develops an adversative sense in καίτοι (not yet found in Homer) and καὶ μήν.

I spoke above of the exacter delimitation of the functions of

[1] Sematologically speaking, I suppose it is inaccurate to say that two words or word-combinations can mean the same thing. But it is hard to believe that the Greeks felt any essential difference between, say, ἀλλὰ μήν and καὶ μήν in many contexts, or between μὲν δή and μέντοι in answers.

some particles in post-Homeric Greek. The functions of others become more diversified. Thus οὖν, which in Homer is strictly confined to certain associations, with ἐπεί, ὡς, etc., subsequently widens the range of its activities, as τοιγάρ also does. In particular, certain emphatic particles develop a connective sense. (See II.1 above.)

The authors who lie between the Epic and Attic periods are unfortunately represented for the most part by scanty fragments. With the dawn of Attic literature in the early fifth century the thread of development can be picked up again, and we can often trace the adolescence or obsolescence of a usage in the course of the fifth and fourth centuries. We can trace, for example, the gradual growth of connective δή right up to the end of the fourth century, when this use predominates over all others. The case of οὖν is instructive. Transitional μὲν οὖν occurs but once in the *Iliad*, five times in the *Odyssey*. In these passages οὖν has the backward reference ('as I have described, or implied') which normally accompanies it in the two epics. But a connective force is already beginning to appear. In the *Hymns* μὲν οὖν is proportionately commoner (four examples), and the backward reference begins to disappear. We are on the threshold of a new stage, where οὖν is a full connective. In Aeschylus, οὖν is fully established as a connecting particle, but is almost confined to questions, a restriction later removed. A similar restriction applies to οὔκουν, first found as a connective in statements in E.*Med*.890. οὐκοῦν in statements is another late development, and Demosthenes and Aeschines are the first writers to use it with any freedom. μήν is, on the whole, relatively a late-comer in the field of Attic literature. In general, its frequency increases in the later works of Plato, Lysias, Isocrates, and Xenophon. The common use of καὶ μήν in introducing a new character on the stage is hardly yet to be found in Aeschylus. Adversative καὶ μήν is not found in Pindar, and in Aeschylus it only appears in *Agamemnon* and *Prometheus Vinctus*. While ἀλλὰ μήν and καὶ μήν can be seen coming into use, ἀλλὰ μὲν δή and καὶ μὲν δή can be seen passing out of use. The latter are almost confined to Plato, Xenophon, and the earlier orators[1] (Antiphon, Andocides, Lysias,

[1] The appearance of καὶ μὲν δή in [D.]lxi 13 is perhaps of some significance for determining the date of this composition.

and Isocrates). The assentient force of μὲν οὖν, as distinct from the corrective, is absent from fifth-century literature. The formulae of assent, πάνυ μὲν οὖν, κομιδῇ μὲν οὖν, etc., of which Plato was so fond, are common in the *Plutus* (388 B.C.): see especially 833–8 of that play, where κομιδῇ μὲν οὖν is clearly made fun of.[1] Similarly, assentient γάρ is rarely found before the fourth century. Its use with an echoed word, common in Plato and in Xenophon's Socratic works, is clearly parodied, as a new fashion, in Ar.*Ec.* 773–6. Single τε and corresponsive τε . . . τε[2] (excluding εἴτε . . . εἴτε and οὔτε . . . οὔτε) grow rarer, on the whole, during the fourth century.

As further instances of chronological development, we may notice the replacement of τοιγάρτοι by τοιγαροῦν and of ἀλλὰ γάρ by ἀλλὰ . . . γάρ, the increased tendency in the fourth century to add γε to apodotic ἀλλά, and the appearance in the Homeric *Hymns* of corresponsive καὶ . . . καί, hardly found in *Iliad* and *Odyssey*.

In certain cases we can detect a difference in an author's use of particles between his earlier and his later works. Thus juxtaposed τε καί gets progressively rarer in Andocides. Perhaps, as Fuhr suggests, Andocides gradually adapted himself to oratorical usage in this respect (p. 512). δὴ ὦν and ὦν δή are rarer in the later books of Herodotus, which are held by some to have been composed first, than in the earlier. These are but isolated phenomena: but Aeschylus and Plato afford evidence of a more general and more significant character.

Aeschylus has left us only seven plays: but, with one exception, they can be dated exactly, or almost exactly, while the dates of Sophocles' and Euripides' plays are usually quite uncertain. The *Supplices* is beyond doubt very early. The *Persae* was produced in 472 B.C., the *Septem* in 467, and the Trilogy in 458. There remains only the *Prometheus Vinctus*, which has been assigned by some scholars to about 470, by others to the last

[1] The appearance of πάνυ μὲν οὖν in Epich.*Fr.*171.1 is perhaps an argument against the genuineness of this fragment, which Diels assigns on other grounds to the fourth century.

[2] It is difficult to say how far the varying frequency of τε . . τε is to be attributed to difference of period, how far to difference of style. (See (5) *ad fin.* below.)

two years of the poet's life, 458–6. On the whole, a greater variety of particles is to be found in the later plays than in the earlier ones. There is hardly a single instance of a particle or usage being employed in the earlier plays and dropped in the later, though ἠδέ is specially common in the lyrics of the *Persae*,[1] and δῆτα with an echoed word or thought is found only in *Supplices* (3), *Persae* (2), and *Septem* (4). On the other hand, we find a number of usages confined to *Prometheus* and the Trilogy (sometimes with *Septem* thrown in). Thus:—

οὐ δῆτα, μὴ δῆτα: *Pr.* only (3).

ἦ μήν: *Th.* (1): *Pr.* (3): *Ag.* (? 1).

καὶ μήν (adversative): *Pr.* (2): *Ag.* (2). (This use is absent from Pindar.)

μέντοι (excluding γε μέντοι, already found in *Supplices*): *Th.* (1): *Pr.* (5), including the only (possibly) adversative example: *Ag.* (3).

οὖν following relatives: Trilogy only.

εἴτ' οὖν, οὔτ' οὖν: Trilogy and fragments only.

ἀλλ' οὖν: *Th.* (1): *Pr.* (2).

γὰρ οὖν: *Ag.* (2): *Eu.* (1).

γοῦν: *Ag.* (2): *Eu.* (1).

δ' οὖν: *Th.* (1): *Pr.* (2): Trilogy (9).

οὔκουν . . . γε, negative of γοῦν: *Pr.* (2): but see p. 425 on *Supp.* 392.

καίτοι: *Pr.* (3): (*Eu.* 849 is corrupt).

ἔστε:[2] *Pr.* (5): *Ag.* (1), conjectured in line 308: *Eu.* (1).

We must be cautious in drawing conclusions here. In the first place, we have only seven plays to work on. In the second place, we have no contemporary Attic literature with which to compare the Aeschylean practice. But, when we find particles and combinations which were commonly used in the second half of the fifth century occurring in Aeschylus in the later plays only, we can hardly be wrong in concluding that they were coming into use towards the end of his lifetime, rather than that they had been in use all along, but were only adopted by him in his later works. Further, when we find that the *Prometheus* agrees strikingly

[1] For a possible explanation of this, see p. 287.

[2] I include ἔστε here, though it lies outside the purview of this book (p. 528).

with the later plays, as against the earlier ones,[1] we may legitimately adduce this as evidence in support of the view that the *Prometheus* was one of Aeschylus' latest plays (or, if we can bring ourselves to accept the possibility—I find it hard to do so—, was written by an unknown later author).

Plato's employment of particles in his later works diverges in many respects from his earlier practice. The following uses are all either much commoner in the late dialogues, or wholly confined to them:—

οὐ μὴν ἀλλά: καὶ . . . δέ: καὶ δὴ καί, transitional, = καὶ μήν: ὁ μέν, etc., omitted before ὁ δέ, etc.: progressive μήν (once only in dialogues earlier than the *Republic*): καὶ . . . μήν, with intervening word: οὐκοῦν χρή; elliptical, in answers: εἴτ' οὖν, οὔτ' οὖν: γὰρ οὖν, for οὖν: γοῦν, progressive, with οὖν as the dominant partner: οὖν δή (commoner in the late works, both absolutely, and relatively to δὴ οὖν): εἴπερ, elliptical, 'if at all': τε coupling single words: the series καὶ . . . τε . . . καί: ἐάντε . . . καὶ ἂν μή: δὴ τοίνυν: καὶ τοίνυν, καὶ . . . τοίνυν.

In discussing the cause of the divergencies between the earlier and the later Aeschylus we lacked the evidence of contemporary literature, which could have afforded a standard of comparison. In the case of Plato, there is contemporary literature in abundance: but the evidence it affords does not suggest that the variations are due to Plato's adoption of new usages which were coming into existence during his lifetime. Rather, they seem due to a personal, stylistic preference on his part. His employment of particles in his late works is at times (as far as we can tell) purely individual, as in the case of καὶ . . . μήν, δὴ τοίνυν: at other times, it manifests a growing predilection for poetical or Ionic idioms (ὁ δέ, without preceding μέν: εἴτ' οὖν, οὔτ' οὖν: τε coupling words: οὖν δή).

Other usages, again, such as juxtaposed ἀλλά γε and καί γε, seem to be mainly, or wholly, confined to post-classical Greek. Here an interesting point arises in connexion with the Hippocratic corpus. The experts tell us that these works, though few of them are from the hand of Hippocrates, almost all date from the fifth

[1] Certain metrical peculiarities of the play, which have been little noticed hitherto, point in the same direction. I hope to discuss them on another occasion.

and fourth centuries. It is remarkable, then, to find in them ἤγουν (meaning 'that is to say', *videlicet*), a word found in the pseudo-Aristotelian *de Plantis* and in grammarians' glosses, but not elsewhere in classical Greek, and to find τοιγαροῦν placed second, not first, in the sentence, which again can only be paralleled in post-classical writers. Further, γοῦν often appears as a synonym for οὖν, as it does, very occasionally, in Plato's later works (see above), and in the *de Plantis*. It seems possible that these medical treatises, remaining, as they did, practical manuals for doctors throughout many centuries, were edited with more freedom and less reverence than works of a more purely literary value, and that in them the use of particles was brought into conformity with the practice of the day.

(4) *Differences in Dialect.* Differences in dialect play a certain part, but, except for purely formal variations such as μέν—μήν—μάν, ὦν—οὖν, perhaps a rather smaller part than we should have expected. There is not, for instance, a great deal in common between the Herodotean and Hippocratic uses. Probably more divergencies would appear if we possessed a greater bulk of non-Attic Greek, particularly Doric. But, even as it is, certain dialectal distinctions can be detected. μήν (μάν) seems to be Doric in origin, and its employment with imperatives is confined to Doric and Epic. θην is hardly found outside Homer and Sicilian literature. δῆτα and τοίνυν[1] are characteristically Attic, δῆθεν Ionic. οὖν (ὦν) in tmesis, between preposition and verb, is Ionic and Doric.

But the line of cleavage between dialects is for the most part less clear cut. What we usually find is, on the one side, Aristophanes and the orators, representing the purest Attic usage: on the other, the tragedians, Herodotus, Plato, and Xenophon (and sometimes Thucydides). This grouping is, on the whole, not unexpected. The tragedians wrote in an Attic which had not completely dissociated itself from Ionic. Thucydides, though later in date, continues to use the ἀρχαία Ἀτθίς. Xenophon spent much of his life in Asia Minor. The Ionic proclivities of Plato in his use of particles may be explained partly as con-

[1] It is significant that Thucydides uses τοίνυν in *Athenian* speeches only.

sistent with the poetical colour of his style, partly by the fact that Ionic was the language of learning.

The use of ancillary *οὖν* with other particles is instructive in this respect. Except for *ἀλλ' οὖν*, *γοῦν*, *δ' οὖν*, and *μὲν οὖν* in the sense *immo*, these combinations are far more frequent in what I will call the semi-Ionic group than in the purest Attic.[1] Thus *εἴτ' οὖν*, *οὔτ' οὖν* are found in tragedy, Herodotus, and Plato, but never in comedy or the orators. *γὰρ οὖν* (tragedy, Herodotus, and Plato) is absent from oratory, and rare in comedy. *δὴ οὖν* and *οὖν δή* are almost confined to Herodotus and Plato. *καὶ οὖν* and *καὶ . . . οὖν* are found only in Hippocrates and Plato. *περ οὖν* after relatives is found only in the tragedians (especially Aeschylus), Herodotus, and Plato.

The use of ancillary *τοι* illustrates a somewhat similar grouping of writers. *δή τοι* and *τοι δή* are almost confined to Epic and Plato[2] (*ὡς δή τοι* being peculiar to Plato). *ἤτοι* ('either') is rare in oratory, and unknown to comedy (I ignore Ar.*Fr.*905).

I subjoin further examples of usages which are rarely, or never, found in strict Attic prose composition:

ἄρα in its more general sense, expressing lively interest (mainly Epic, Herodotus, and Xenophon).

δέ, following a pronoun, 'marking an antithesis, not of persons, but of clauses' (Jebb on S.*El.*448): Homer, tragedy, Herodotus, Xenophon.

οὐδέ, connective, without preceding negative: Homer, tragedy, Herodotus: rare in Aristophanes: hardly ever in Attic prose (p. 190).

δή τις: tragedy, Herodotus, Plato: once in Thucydides: never in oratory: hardly ever in Aristophanes.

ὅστις (etc.) *δή*, in the sense of *nescioquis*, not of *quicumque*: common in Herodotus: also found in Xenophon and in Aeneas Tacticus (whose diction approximates to the *κοινή*), but not in strict Attic, verse or prose (in Ar.*Ach.*753 a Megarian is speaking).

καὶ δή, connective, without a second *καί* following: Homer, Herodotus, Hippocrates, Plato: very rare in drama, almost all

[1] *Per contra*, ἀλλ' ὦν, γῶν, and corrective μὲν ὦν are hardly found in Herodotus.

[2] This tells against the conjecture δή τοι in A.*Pers.*706.

apparent instances being better taken as non-connective: hardly ever found in the orators (once in Andocides, and conjectured in Lysias xiii 4).

δῆθεν: mainly Ionic: sometimes found in tragedians and Thucydides: once apiece in Plato and Xenophon: never in comedy or oratory.

μέντοι, progressive: Hippocrates, Xenophon: occasionally in tragedy, Herodotus, and Thucydides.

ὥστε (relative): tragedy, Herodotus, Thucydides (rarely).

Sophocles' employment of particles is sometimes more Ionic than that of the other tragedians.[1] He is the only tragedian to use *οὖν δή* (for which, see above), or *οὖν* strengthening a prospective *μέν* (found in philosophical Epic, and in Hippocrates, Thucydides, Plato, Xenophon, and Aristotle: never in comedy or in oratory, except for Hyperides, in whom traces of the *κοινή* are beginning to appear).[2] Apodotic *δέ*, frequent in Homer and Herodotus, is rather commoner in Sophocles than in the other tragedians. *μή τοι . . . γε*, with infinitive or participle, is confined to Sophocles, Plato, and Aristotle.

(5) *Differences in genre.* Here the main line of cleavage is not so much between poetry and prose as between dialogue and continuous speech or formal exposition. Particles, apart from the necessary connectives,[3] are like ignition sparks: they flash at the kindling of a new thought, which, once kindled, burns with a steadier and less vivid flame. Hence the tendency of *γε*, for example, to occur near the opening of an answer. *δῆτα*, in all its uses, affirmative *μέντοι*, *που*, and *τοι* are mainly found in dialogue. *οὔκουν . . . γε* is much commoner in answers than in continuous speech. It cannot be doubted that Greek conversation was full of particles: at moments of excitement and emotional tension the dialogue of tragedy and comedy fairly

[1] His language shows Ionic tendencies in other respects. See Christ, *Gesch. d. griech. Lit.* i. 323.

[2] See Blass, *Att. Ber.* III. ii². 34.

[3] But here, too, we find some divergence between dialogue and continuous speech. Thus *καίτοι*, normally used in continuous speech, is but rarely used in answers (p. 558). Plato for the most part uses *μὲν τοίνυν* in answers, *μὲν οὖν* in continuous speech (des Places, p. 308, n. 1), and *τοίνυν* is, in general, much commoner in answers.

bristles with them. Perhaps women, on the principle that τὸ θῆλυ μᾶλλον οἰκτρὸν ἄρσενος, were peculiarly addicted to the use of particles, just as women to-day are fond of underlining words in their letters. (Tucker's suggestion that γε denotes 'feminine underlining' in the Plathane scene in the *Frogs* is attractive.) Of modern languages, German is much richer in particles than the Romance languages, while English, perhaps because of its hybrid nature,[1] occupies an intermediate position.

An emphatic or expressive particle occurring at the opening of a speech is usually omitted when the speech is reported in *oratio obliqua*. Occasionally, however, it is retained.[2] Thus, μέντοι in a question is retained in Pl.*Phdr.*266D λεκτέον δὲ τί μέντοι καὶ ἔστι τὸ λειπόμενον τῆς ῥητορικῆς: so is γε in an answer in Pl.*Smp.*199D (p. 133). For further examples, see p. 211 (δή), pp. 313, 316 (καί), p. 402 (μέντοι).

I have observed that many usages belong, *par excellence*, to answers in dialogue. But a speaker or writer sometimes employs one of these usages in the middle of a long continuous passage, thereby giving the impression of a man answering his own question, or reaffirming or rejecting his own statement. In some cases this impression of imaginary dialogue is strongly marked. Thus in Pl.*Prt.*310C Hippocrates says Νὴ τοὺς θεούς, ἑσπέρας γε (ἥκει Πρωταγόρας), and then, sitting down on Socrates' bed, continues Ἑσπέρας δῆτα ('Yes, in the evening'), δῆτα accompanying an echo of the speaker's own words, just as it very frequently accompanies an echo of another person's. Similarly δέ γε ('Yes, but', 'Yes, and'), καί preceding an interrogative, καὶ γάρ meaning 'Yes, and', exclamatory γε, and corrective μὲν οὖν ('No'), are in essence proper to dialogue, and, when transferred to continuous speech, convey the impression of imaginary question and answer: epexegetic γε is a development of γε in answers. If in such cases we do not catch the nuance of dialogue (a nuance more pronounced in some cases than in others) we miss something of the colour of the style.

In Homer and the historians certain particles and combinations

[1] I owe this suggestion to Prof. G. E. K. Braunholtz.

[2] For the occasional retention of an opening connective in *oratio obliqua*, see II.5.iii.

are absent from the narrative portions of their works, and are only found in the speeches. Thus in Homer ἦ,[1] ἦ μέν, τοι, μέν τοι, are almost confined to speeches. In Thucydides and Xenophon τοι is hardly used except in speeches. In Thucydides τοίνυν is confined to Athenian speeches.

Particles are commonest, then, at the opening of a speech in verse or prose dialogue: less common during the progress of such a speech: and rarest in formal treatises like the works of Aristotle or the history of Thucydides. (The more conversational style of Herodotus and Xenophon employs particles more lavishly.) The orators occupy an intermediate position. They write works to be spoken to an audience, but there is no close personal touch between the speaker and the persons addressed.[2] Hence one is not surprised to find that intimate particles like τοι [3] or hortative ἀλλά are rare in oratory. The vividness of Demosthenes' style leads him to employ a number of lively, conversational idioms which are not to be found in the other orators. For example: exclamatory γε (ix 66 δουλεύουσί γε, 'They are *slaves*!': *ib.* 65): καὶ δή, non-connective, introducing an imaginary supposition, or at the opening of an apodosis, or elsewhere: μέντἄν (i 26 τῶν ἀτοπωτάτων μέντἂν εἴη, 'It *would* be ridiculous!': cf. Is. x 13): καί following demonstratives: corrective μὲν οὖν (five times in the speeches attributed to Demosthenes, never in the remaining orators).[4]

It is sometimes, perhaps, possible to detect a difference between the usage of the Assembly and that of the lawcourts. Thus τε . . . τε, which is never found (apart from εἴτε . . . εἴτε, οὔτε . . . οὔτε) in the political speeches of Demosthenes or in inscriptions of the classical period, occurs 36 times in the forensic speeches attributed to him.[5] τοίνυν, again, is commoner in his forensic speeches, and the sole example of ἅτε [6] in oratory is in

[1] In prose ἦ is mainly found in dialogue.

[2] These differences will not appear surprising if we compare the narrow range of vocal inflexions used by an average speaker in the House of Commons with the numerous and subtle nuances employed on the Shakespearean stage and in everyday conversation.

[3] Curiously enough, however, καὶ γάρ τοι is almost confined to oratory.

[4] See further, p. lxxxi (6).

[5] But see p. lxvii, n. 2.

[6] The distribution of causal ἅτε (pp. 525–6) is extremely puzzling. As it is absent from tragedy, but fairly frequent in comedy, one might suppose

one of these (xlii 24). In the use of particles, as in other respects, the diction of the lawcourts perhaps comes nearer to the usage of everyday life.

(6) *Colloquial and poetical uses.* I have observed that Greek drama reproduces, as far as one can tell, the free use of particles in everyday speech. Particles are on the whole, I think, rather more often employed in comedy than in tragedy. As regards individual particles and individual usages there is, broadly speaking, not much difference between tragic and comic practice. But there are cases where a particle or combination seems to have been felt to be beneath the dignity of tragedy, or (more rarely) too dignified for comedy. Thus μέν γε is found in comedy and often in prose, but is probably unknown to tragedy.[1] ὥσπερ γε is almost confined to Aristophanes, Plato, and Xenophon. Certain uses of δέ γε (*q.v.* (2) and 4. ii) are almost confined to Aristophanes and Plato. δήπου is frequent in comedy and prose, rare in tragedy. ἀλλ' ἤ, ὁτιή (metrically intractable, it is true), καὶ δῆτα in statements, exclamatory μέντἄν, assentient μέντοι (with or without an echoed word), and μέντοι in questions, are all found in comedy and, except ὁτιή, in prose (mainly Plato and Xenophon), but not in tragedy. γέ τοι and καὶ . . . μέντοι are a good deal more frequent in comedy than in tragedy. Other uses which have the appearance of being colloquial are: ἀλλὰ τί (πῶς, etc.); after a rejected suggestion, 'Well, what?': ἀλλ' οὐδέ, 'why, not even': καλῶς γε ποιῶν, etc., in answers: οὐ γὰρ . . .; presenting an answer as obvious (Aristophanes and Xenophon).

In some cases a particle or usage already found in Homer is more frequent in comedy than in tragedy. Though Homer's dialect is an artificial one and his vocabulary is packed with sonorous compounds, the basis of his style is simple, and I suspect that the particles he employs were, in the main, those of everyday speech, and that some of them were only banished from

that it is colloquial. But von Essen cites eight examples (one is doubtful) from Thucydides. Ast cites 26 from Plato, and three times adds '*al.*': Sturz some 30 from Xenophon.

[1] This tells against the genuineness of E.*Fr.* 909, a very lame piece of work.

serious poetry when the Greek language became self-conscious. I believe, then, that such a word as *τιή*, found only in Homer, Hesiod, and Attic comedy, was colloquial from first to last, though it seems to have gone out of use before the days of Plato and Xenophon. *ἀτάρ*, and *δή* after imperatives, are commoner in Homer and comedy than in tragedy. The same is true of *δαί*, though textual uncertainties complicate matters here.

Euripides, as we should expect, is more colloquial in his use of particles than Aeschylus and Sophocles. Thus he uses *ἀτάρ* and *δαί*, and purely affirmative *γε* in answers (pp. 130–1, 133), more freely than they do, and, unlike them, adopts elliptical *ὡς τί δή* . . . ; (paralleled by analogous idioms in Aristophanes and Plato), and *κᾆτα, κἄπειτα* in indignant questions (also used by Aristophanes). *μέν* in questions (e.g. *Ὑγιαίνεις μέν*;) is confined to Euripides, Aristophanes, and Plato, and certainly looks colloquial. So does *ὡς* . . . *γε* (Euripides and Aristophanes: rare in Aeschylus and Sophocles), though it is rare in prose also. *οὐ γὰρ ἀλλά* is confined to the Iambographers, comedy, Euripides, and Plato: *γοῦν* in exclamations, to Euripides and Aristophanes. I have observed that *δή* following imperatives is rare in tragedy: but *ἄκουε δή νυν* (never in Aeschylus, once in Sophocles) is a common Euripidean formula. Assentient *γάρ τοι* following a demonstrative, otherwise confined to Aristophanes and Xenophon, is found once in Euripides. *τοι* in soliloquies and asides (obviously a homely use, if *τοι* means 'you know') occurs once or twice in Euripides, otherwise in Aristophanes only. *οὔ τί που* questions are characteristic of Euripides and Aristophanes.

But Aeschylus does not shrink from an occasional colloquialism in this respect, any more than in others. *τί δ' ἄλλο γ' ἤ*, *οὐδὲν ἄλλο γ' ἤ*, certainly look colloquial: yet the first is found in a chorus (*Th.*852), the second, on the lips of a queen (*Pers.*209): and Aeschylus is the only tragedian to use the Aristophanic *μἀλλά*.

Contrariwise, certain particles and usages which we find in Homer, and which in him were not, perhaps, associated with any special elevation of style, are in later Greek mainly or wholly confined to serious poetry. Here it is natural that Aeschylus, whose tragedies were 'slices from the great banquet of Homer', should stand nearer than the other tragedians to

Epic usage. He, alone of the three, uses concessive περ without a participle, and separates καί from περ in καίπερ: he uses ἠδέ more freely than the others: he uses fairly often, even in dialogue, ὅς τε (Epic τε), which is rarely found, in lyrics only, in Sophocles and Euripides. All these usages are virtually speaking absent from comedy and from prose. The following uses also are, in the main, peculiar to serious poetry:

εἰ γάρ wishes: δέ postponed after apostrophe: ἦ, affirmative and interrogative (except in combination with other particles):[1] omission of μέν before δέ in the first limb of an anaphora (very rare in comedy: sometimes in Herodotus and Plato): γε μὲν δή: τε in anaphora: οὐ . . . οὔτε: οὔτε . . . οὐ (twice in Herodotus): εἶτε for εἴτε . . . εἴτε: οὔτε for οὔτε . . . οὔτε: τοιγάρ.

A few Epic particles or combinations pass entirely, or almost entirely, out of usage, even poetical usage. Witness the extinction, complete or virtually complete, of αὐτάρ, ἠμέν, ἰδέ, ἦ τοι μέν, and (except in one or two specialized usages) Epic τε. There are a few curious Epicisms in the Hippocratic corpus: ἠδέ (on Galen's authority), and in the *de Victu* δέ τε, καί τε. For Epicisms in Herodotus, see pp. 524–5.

In other cases, again, the dividing line comes, not between the high and the low style, but between prose and verse (including comedy). Thus the following are either wholly avoided in verse or far rarer in verse than in prose:[2]

[1] ἦ που in the *a fortiori* sense is common in prose as well as in verse. So, too, is ἦ μήν introducing an oath. It is not surprising that an archaic and poetical word should be used in a solemn legal formula ('So help me God'): and I think that ἦ μήν always suggested an oath to a Greek: Ar.*Ra.*104 Ἦ μὴν κόβαλά γ' ἐστίν, 'I swear it's rubbish'. Curiously enough, interrogative ἦ γάρ, ἦ καί are used by the tragedians, Plato, and Xenophon, but not by Aristophanes. It is difficult to believe that any poetical colour attaches to them in Plato and Xenophon. Were they, perhaps, regarded as poetical in the fifth century, but introduced into everyday speech in the fourth? Similarly the virtual restriction of οὔτοι in Aristophanes to oaths is curious, in view of the commonness of τοι in his plays, and of the unrestricted use of οὔτοι in fourth-century prose. Perhaps οὔτοι had a solemnity in the fifth century which it subsequently lost.

[2] The reason for this grouping, by which comedy is ranged with tragedy in contradistinction to prose, is not easy to find. In no case does metrical convenience appear to have much to do with the matter. οὐ μὴν ἀλλά is not intractable metrically, and if τοιγάρτοι can be fitted into an iambic line, why

οὐ μὴν ἀλλά: εἰ ἄρα: ὡς ἄρα: τὶ δέ; (transitional): καὶ . . . δέ: γε δή: δή following final conjunctions: καὶ δὴ καί: καί in causal and final clauses: corresponsive καὶ . . . καί in subordinate and in main clause respectively: duplicated μέν: ἀλλὰ μήν: οὖν with indefinite relatives: apodotic ἀλλ' οὖν: δ' οὖν at the end of a series of details, and resumptive.

Contrariwise, one or two uses are commoner in tragedy and comedy than in prose: ἀλλά meaning 'at least': δ' ἀλλά: ἦ μήν in its general use, as distinct from its special use in oaths: permissive δ' οὖν (which one would expect to find in Plato and Xenophon).

(7) *Individual preferences.* The element of personal choice has played some part in the differences of period, dialect, and genre which I have discussed above. We have seen that authors do not always remain true to type in their use of particles: that an Attic writer, for example, may draw on Ionic or Doric usage, an orator on colloquial usage, a dramatist with his head full of Homer on Epic usage. There remain a number of cases where a writer employs particles in a way which is not merely alien to the period, dialect, or genre in which he writes, but peculiar, as far as our knowledge goes, to himself. Caution is necessary here. Only a fraction of ancient Greek literature survives, and if we had the whole of it in our hands many uses which are at present only found in a single author would no doubt be found in others too. But the evidence of the facts, and considerations of general probability, warrant us in hazarding the guess that, even if we possessed the whole literature, instances of personal preference would remain, and that, just as authors had their favourite nouns, adjectives, and verbs, e.g. Aesch. γοεδνός, τιμαλφεῖν (cf. Schol. *Eu.* 626), Eur. ὄρφνη, πίτυλος, ἐξώπιος (cf. Sandys on *Ba.* 638), so, too, they had their favourite particles. That a particle is too colourless a thing to be the object of a personal predilection no one who has read Greek literature with understanding will affirm. Nor are such

not καί δή καί? In the case of οὐ μὴν ἀλλά and ἀλλὰ μήν, the late appearance of most μήν compounds in Attic literature may be the cause of the cleavage between verse and prose: and it is probable that other of these differences are differences of period rather than of genre.

predilections lacking in modern languages. Anatole France parodied Ferdinand Brunetière's fondness for *car*.[1] One of the best lecturers I ever listened to (an artillery captain, not a don) had a curious love of 'consequently therefore'. His audience used to count the number of times it came in an hour's lecture, and the record total was a very high one.

Some of the subjoined examples of individual preference are very striking: others less so. But here, again, I have preferred to include what is of possible, though doubtful, value.[2]

Aeschylus. γε μὲν δή (commoner than in the other tragedians): τοι in choruses (rare in the other tragedians).[3]

Sophocles. ἀλλὰ . . . μὲν δή (not in Aeschylus, Euripides, or Aristophanes): δέ used as a strong adversative, for ἀλλά or μὲν οὖν: οὐ δή introducing an incredulous question, 'surely not': οὐ γὰρ δή clearing the ground by eliminating at least one possibility (especially common in Sophocles and Thucydides): postponement of ἦ που: postponement of οὖν (whereas Aeschylus freely postpones δέ).

Euripides. ἀλλά in hypophora (characteristic of the typically Euripidean ἀγών): ἀλλ' εἶα: μὲν . . . ἀλλ' ὅμως: ὥστε . . . γε, adding something to an affirmative answer: γε with the *figura etymologiae* in answers: δὲ δή preceding the interrogative in emphatic or crucial questions (also Aristophanes): καὶ δή introducing surprised questions (where other authors use simple καί): γοῦν giving a *pro tanto* reason for following a suggested course.

Aristophanes. γε following interrogatives: εἰ μὴ . . . γε: apodotic κᾆτα, κἄπειτα: καὶ μήν responding to an invitation to speak, 'Very well, then' (also Plato): οὖν . . . δῆτα, οὔκουν . . . δῆτα in questions.

Herodotus. Anticipatory γάρ (Homer and Herodotus: but νῦν δὲ . . . γὰρ . . . οὖν (δή) is found in Plato: fusion of clauses is characteristic of Herodotus, though sometimes found in Thucydides also): οὐδέ as an emphatic negative, 'not at all': οὗτος

[1] See P. Shorey in *C.Phil.*xxviii.2.132.

[2] I include some examples of preferences common to two writers: also some cases where the absence or rarity of an idiom in a particular writer, who might be expected to employ it freely, calls for remark.

[3] This tells against the conjecture τοι in S.*Ph.*686.

δή referring to a person previously mentioned: *οὕτω (ὧδε) δή τι*: *καὶ δὴ καί* (conversely, rare in Xenophon): *τε δή*: *εἰ καί* = *siquidem*.

Hippocrates. Progressive *ἀλλά*.

Thucydides. *δή* with superlatives: *οὐ μέντοι* (while Isocrates prefers *οὐ μήν*, and Demosthenes uses both indifferently).

Plato. *ἀλλά* substantiating an hypothesis: *οὐ μέντοι ἀλλά* (once in Thucydides): *οὐδέ* negativing an idea *in toto* (also Aristotle): *ἀλλὰ δή*: *ἵνα δή* (also Herodotus): postponement of interrogative *ἦ*: *καί* in anaphora: positive adversative *μήν*: *καὶ μήν* substantiating a condition (also Sophocles): *ἀλλὰ . . . μέν* (p. 378): *μὲν δή*, affirmative and adversative (also Xenophon: pp. 392–3): interrogative *οὐκοῦν* (also Xenophon, in Socratic works): *ἐπεί τοι καί* (also Euripides).

Xenophon. Inceptive *ἀλλὰ* and *τοίνυν*: *καὶ γὰρ οὖν* = *τοιγαροῦν*: *τί δέ, εἰ μὴ . . . γε . . .;* *καὶ . . . δέ* (especially with a repeated word): *καὶ τίς* (*πῶς*, etc.) *δὴ . . .;* *γε μήν* (the most remarkable of all instances of individual preference): *μὲν δή* in anaphora (p. 258): *οὐ μὲν δή* in answers, following an oath (p. 392): *ἀλλὰ . . . μέν* (distinct from the Platonic use: pp. 365–6): progressive *ἀλλὰ μέντοι*: *γε μέντοι*: *καὶ . . . μέντοι*: transitional *τί γάρ*; ('Well, and what of this?': the absence of this idiom from Plato is remarkable): *δέ τοι*. *μέντἄν* is surprisingly absent from Xenophon.

Aristotle. Appositional *γάρ*.

Antiphon. *τοι* (a puzzling preference: that this most unbending and austere of orators should adopt towards the jury the kind of attitude that *τοι* implies, seems somehow not to fit).

Lysias. *καὶ μὲν δή* (common also in Pl.*Phdr.*230E–34C, a passage either written by Lysias or composed in his manner).

Demosthenes. *οὐ μὴν ἀλλά* (also Isocrates): *ἀλλὰ μήν* in calling for evidence (also Isaeus): *ἀλλὰ μήν* in enthymemes.

With regard to Demosthenes I must warn the reader that throughout this book I have usually spoken as though Demosthenes were the author of all the speeches that bear his name, except for one or two that are very obviously not his work. I do not, in fact, wish to suggest anything so unorthodox. But I shrank, both here and in most other cases, from the task of attempting to separate the genuine from the spurious. I give below a list of the speeches attributed to Demosthenes in which usages are to be found which appear to be characteristic of his style, as contrasted with that of the other orators (though, as I have observed, (1) and (3) are shared by him with Isocrates and Isaeus respectively). I give arabic figures, as a string of roman numerals is confusing to the eye: and I bracket the speeches usually held to be spurious.[1]

(1) *οὐ μὴν ἀλλά*: 1, 2, 4, 5, 8, [10], [12], 14, 15, 16, 19, 22, 23, [26], [34], 37, 38, 41, 45, 54, 57, [60].

(2) *καὶ δή*: 2, 4, 5, 18, 20, 23, 29, 39, 55.

(3) *ἀλλὰ μήν* in a transition to the calling of evidence: 19, 20, 21, 27, 29, 30, 36, 37, 38, 45, [46].

(4) *ἀλλὰ μήν* introducing the major premise of an enthymeme: 1, 3, 18, 21, 24, [25], [34], 37, 41, [46], 55, 57, [60].

(5) *μέντἄν*: 1, 8, 18, 19, 21, [34], [40].

(6) *μὲν οὖν* (corrective): 18, [25], [42]. Here it may be observed that, of five instances, three are in 18: and that 25 is regarded by Blass as genuine (see footnote below).

The speeches which the Oxford editors regard as genuine cover 767 pages of their text: the speeches they regard as spurious, 411 pages. In view of this proportion, my statistics show that most of the uses that I have styled Demosthenic are markedly commoner in the genuine speeches than in the spurious. Their occasional appearance in the spurious speeches may be attributed to the influence which Demosthenes exercised on his contemporaries, an influence very clearly seen in Deinarchus's work.

The group of speeches, 46, 47, 49, 50, 52, 53, 59, which Blass and Thalheim hold to be the work of one writer (perhaps Apollodorus), present two peculiarities in the use of particles. In four places (xlvi 15: 17: lix 17, 79) *μὲν . . . τοίνυν*, with a word intervening, is used in resuming the speech after the recitation of evidence, instead of the common *μὲν τοίνυν*. This split form is occasionally found in Plato (p. 580), but I know of no other instance in oratory. For the frequency of *τε . . . καί* in these speeches, see p. 513.

[1] Except in the case of the *Zenothemis* (32), which does not occur in my lists, the Oxford Text agrees with Thalheim in Pauly-Wissowa, s.v. *Demosthenes*. Blass regards 25 (the first speech against Aristogeiton) as Demosthenic (an 'Uebungsrede').

These examples show that the Greek writers are often highly individual in their employment of particles. This is a consideration which may well be borne in mind when discussing whether, for example, Thucydides can have used *καὶ . . . τε* in the sense 'and also', or Aristotle *τε γάρ* in the sense *etenim* (pp. 535–6). Such abnormalities, which recur reasonably often in particular authors (interrogative *γε* in Aristophanes (pp. 124–5) is perhaps another instance), have a certain right to be taken seriously. But the frequency of the examples, and their homogeneity, must be appreciable. On these tests, we can, I think, reject the possibility of Sophocles' having used *τε* in the sense of 'also', (p. 536). Decision in such cases is precarious. And it is, in general, extremely difficult to decide, when discussing particles or any other element of language, how far the abnormal is to be accepted. I feel that in the course of writing this book I have developed a certain avidity for the recondite, and perhaps admitted out-of-the-way usages too readily here and there. They are often like a rare flower that a botanist thinks he espies in the distance, only to find, on coming nearer, that it is a buttercup with two petals missing. But the quest is not always in vain, and a genuine rarity sometimes rewards the seeker.

Ἀλλά

Ἀλλά presents singularly few difficulties. Its clear and unchallenged etymology (from the neuter plural of *ἄλλος*, with change of accent [1]) is in complete accordance with its usage. The primary sense of 'otherness', diversity, contrast, runs through all the shades of meaning, from the strongest to the weakest: from 'but', or even 'no', to 'further', 'again'.

I. General use, as an adversative connecting particle. The adversative force of *ἀλλά* is usually strong (eliminative or objecting): less frequently, the particle is employed as a weaker (balancing) adversative. The distinction in force between *ἀλλά* and *δέ* is well illustrated in Pl.*R.*335A *τὸν δὲ δοκοῦντα μέν, ὄντα δὲ μή, δοκεῖν ἀλλὰ μὴ εἶναι φίλον*: that between *ἀλλά* and *μέντοι* in Pl.*Cra.*432A.

(1) Eliminative, substituting the true for the false. (i) Here usually, in the nature of things, either (*a*) the *ἀλλά* clause (or sentence), or (*b*) the clause to which it is opposed, is negative. (*a*) Pl.*Phdr.*229D *ἐκεῖθεν, ἀλλ' οὐκ ἐνθένδε, ἡρπάσθη*: 260A *ἐκ τούτων εἶναι τὸ πείθειν, ἀλλ' οὐκ ἐκ τῆς ἀληθείας*: Isoc.iv137 *ταῦτα πάντα γέγονε διὰ τὴν ἡμετέραν ἄνοιαν, ἀλλ' οὐ διὰ τὴν ἐκείνου δύναμιν.* (*b*) S.*Ant.*523 *οὔτοι συνέχθειν, ἀλλὰ συμφιλεῖν ἔφυν*: Th.i2.1 *φαίνεται γὰρ ἡ νῦν Ἑλλὰς καλουμένη οὐ πάλαι βεβαίως οἰκουμένη, ἀλλὰ μεταναστάσεις τε οὖσαι τὰ πρότερα*: D.i5 *οὐ περὶ δόξης . . . πολεμοῦσιν, ἀλλ' ἀναστάσεως . . . τῆς πατρίδος*: Hdt.i88: Pl.*Ly.*223A. (*a*) and (*b*) combined. Pl.*Plt.*283E *Διττὰς ἄρα ταύτας οὐσίας καὶ κρίσεις τοῦ μεγάλου καὶ τοῦ σμικροῦ θετέον, ἀλλ' οὐχ ὡς ἔφαμεν ἄρτι πρὸς ἄλληλα μόνον δεῖν, ἀλλ' ὥσπερ νῦν εἴρηται μᾶλλον τὴν μὲν πρὸς ἄλληλα λεκτέον, τὴν δ' αὖ πρὸς τὸ μέτριον*: *R.*443C: *Smp.*211E.

(ii) *ἀλλ' οὐ* and *καὶ οὐ.*[2] The distinction between the two

[1] Or rather loss of accent. For the presence of a grave accent denotes nothing more than the absence of an acute or circumflex accent: see Wackernagel, *Beiträge zur Lehre vom griechischen Akzent*, p. 15.

[2] I owe much here to Dr. R. W. Chapman's analysis of Platonic usage.

theoretically resides herein, that, strictly speaking, *ἀλλ' οὐ* expresses the incompatibility of two ideas, *καὶ οὐ* merely adds a negative idea to a positive. Hence the frequent use of *ἀλλ' οὐ* in contrasting what Chapman calls 'permanent opposites': *ὕπαρ ἀλλ' οὐκ ὄναρ*: *δωριστὶ ἀλλ' οὐκ ἰαστί*: *ἐμπειρίαν ἀλλ' οὐ τέχνην*: *ἀγαθὰ ἀλλὰ μὴ κακά*. Hence also, as Chapman observes, the 'slackening of interest' in the *ἀλλ' οὐ* clause, which merely restates negatively something already stated positively: whereas *καὶ οὐ* adds something really new and important. E.*Heracl.*270 *Κλαίων ἄρ' ἅψῃ τῶνδε κοὐκ ἐς ἀμβολάς* ('and soon, too'): Pl.*R.*372A *καὶ σκεπτέον γε καὶ οὐκ ἀποκνητέον* (you can carry out an examination in a half-hearted way): 397E *ἐν μόνῃ τῇ τοιαύτῃ πόλει τόν τε σκυτοτόμον σκυτοτόμον εὑρήσομεν καὶ οὐ κυβερνήτην πρὸς τῇ σκυτοτομίᾳ* ('a cobbler, and nothing more than a cobbler'): *Lg.*809A *τὸν ἐντυγχάνοντα οἷς λέγομεν καὶ μὴ κολάζοντα*. In rhetorical questions the order of relative importance is reversed, and the *ἀλλ' οὐ* clause bears the stress. Pl.*La.*185A *ἦ περὶ σμικροῦ οἴεσθε νυνὶ κινδυνεύειν . . . ἀλλ' οὐ περὶ τούτου τοῦ κτήματος ὃ τῶν ὑμετέρων μέγιστον ὂν τυγχάνει*; *R.*366C. In English, *καὶ οὐ* is usually best rendered 'and not', *ἀλλ' οὐ* 'not'. 'I want some blotting paper; red, and not too thick.' 'I want some blotting paper: red, not white.' Greek, like English, often dispenses with a connecting particle altogether: E.*IT*369 *Αἴδης Ἀχιλλεὺς ἦν ἄρ', οὐχ ὁ Πηλέως*.

The above distinction between *ἀλλ' οὐ* and *καὶ οὐ* is not, however, by any means always observed, even in the case of 'permanent opposites'. Deviations should be attributed, perhaps, to mere indifference rather than to any subtler motive. S.*Ph.*91 *πρὸς βίαν . . . καὶ μὴ δόλοισιν*: *OT*58 *γνωτὰ κοὐκ ἄγνωτα*: 1275 *πολλάκις τε κοὐχ ἅπαξ*: E *Cyc.*211 *ἄνω καὶ μὴ κάτω*: Hdt.iii 25 *ἐμμανής τε ἐὼν καὶ οὐ φρενήρης*: 115 *Ἑλληνικὸν καὶ οὐ βάρβαρον*: Pl.*Prt.*337B *μάλιστ' ἂν οὕτως . . . εὐδοκιμοῖτε καὶ οὐκ ἐπαινοῖσθε—εὐδοκιμεῖν μὲν γὰρ . . . ἐπαινεῖσθαι δὲ . . .* (but there is no sense of substitution here, *οὐκ ἐπαινοῖσθε* being merely a parenthetical afterthought: hence neither *ἀλλ' οὐ* nor *καὶ οὐ* is really appropriate, and no connecting particle at all is needed. So, below, *μάλιστ' ἂν οὕτως εὐφραινοίμεθα, οὐχ ἡδοίμεσθα—εὐφραίνεσθαι μὲν γὰρ ἔστιν . . .*): *R.*366C *πολλήν που συγγνώμην ἔχει καὶ οὐκ ὀργίζεται τοις ἀδίκοις*: 454C *ἀνερωτᾶν* ἡμᾶς αὐτοὺς εἰ ἡ αὐτὴ φύσις φαλακρῶν καὶ κομητῶν καὶ οὐχ ἡ ἐναντία: 602B ἀλλ' εἶναι παιδιάν τινα καὶ οὐ σπουδὴν τὴν μίμησιν: X.*An.*ii 1.10 τί δεῖ αὐτὸν αἰτεῖν καὶ οὐ λαβεῖν ἐλθόντα; Sometimes ἀλλ' οὐ and καὶ οὐ are used indifferently in closely parallel and nearly situated passages. Pl.*Chrm.*174E Ἢ κἂν ὑγιαίνειν ποιοῖ . . . αὕτη, ἀλλ' οὐχ ἡ ἰατρική; καὶ τἆλλα τὰ τῶν τεχνῶν αὕτη ἂν ποιοῖ, καὶ οὐχ αἱ ἄλλαι τὸ αὑτῆς ἔργον ἑκάστη; *R.*493E αὐτὸ τὸ καλὸν ἀλλὰ μὴ τὰ πολλὰ καλά, ἤ αὐτό τι ἕκαστον καὶ μὴ τὰ πολλὰ ἕκαστα, ἔσθ' ὅπως πλῆθος ἀνέξεται ἢ ἡγήσεται εἶναι; S.*OT*1230: *Ph.*1349: *OC*397: E.*Hipp.*1043: *Heracl.* 531, 944: *Supp.*684: *Hel.*1185,1529: *Or.*575: *Rh.*967: Ar.*V.* 786: *Av.*378,1650: Hdt.i 91,173,188: viii 16.2: 134.1. See Jebb on S.*OT*58: Pearson in *C.Q.*1930, p. 162. For τε καί coupling opposites see τε I.5.

(iii) Certain varieties of the use of ἀλλά following a negative clause deserve especial notice.

(*a*) οὐ μόνον (οὐχ ὅπως) . . . ἀλλὰ καί is too familiar to need illustration. For this we occasionally find οὐ μόνον . . . ἀλλά, without καί. S.*Ph.*556 κοὐ μόνον βουλεύματα, ἀλλ' ἔργα δρώμεν': 52: X.*Mem.*i 6.2 ἱμάτιον ἠμφίεσαι οὐ μόνον φαῦλον, ἀλλὰ τὸ αὐτὸ θέρους τε καὶ χειμῶνος: Pl.*Phdr.*233E οὐδὲ τοῖς προσαιτοῦσι μόνον, ἀλλὰ τοῖς τοῦ πράγματος ἀξίοις: D.xix 276: xxxvi 29: Aeschin.ii 62: Is.vi 21 οὐχ ὅπως . . . ἀλλά: Pl.*Ap.*40D μὴ ὅτι . . . ἀλλά: D.xix 265 οὐχ ὅτι . . . ἀλλά. In our less logical English the omission of 'also' is the rule rather than the exception. But in cases where the first idea is included in the second, as the less in the greater, the omission of καί is logically correct. Isoc.v 146 οὐ μόνον ἐπὶ τούτων . . . ἀλλ' ἐπὶ πάντων ὁμοίως: xii 87: D.xviii 26. (See Kühner, II ii 257, and authorities there cited.) Conversely, in S.*Aj.*1313 καί is retained and μόνον omitted: ὅρα μὴ τοὐμόν, ἀλλὰ καὶ τὸ σόν: Pl.*Phdr.*233B: in Lys.vi 13 καί, if sound, perhaps means 'actually'.

(*b*) In some passages ἀλλά following a negative clause appears to mean 'except' (like ἀλλ' ἤ): as we say in English 'no one but you'. The Aristotelian passages quoted in Bonitz's Index vary considerably in character. *EN*1176a22 ἡδέα δ' οὐκ ἔστιν ἀλλὰ τούτοις. Here (as Dr. W. D. Ross points out to me) the meaning is οὐχ ἡδέα ἀλλὰ τούτοις (ἡδέα): 'except' would be an inaccurate and misleading rendering. In 1152b30 ἀλλά is obviously normal in sense. *Pol.*1316b15 πολλῶν τε οὐσῶν αἰτιῶν . . . οὐ λέγει ἀλλὰ μίαν. Here, it is true, we can supply in thought πολλάς after λέγει: but the ellipse is an artificial one. *Rh.*1402a27 ἐν οὐδεμιᾷ τέχνῃ ἀλλ' ἐν ῥητορικῇ καὶ ἐριστικῇ. Here the rendering 'except' seems to be absolutely necessary, rhetoric being, *ex hypothesi*, an art. Outside Aristotle, I can find no parallel except S.*OT*1332 ἔπαισε δ' αὐτόχειρ νιν οὔτις ἀλλ' ἐγὼ τλάμων. Passages in which some form of ἄλλος precedes have been cited as parallel, but are really not so: ἄλλος makes the ἀλλά normal, 'no one else, but': e.g. Hom.θ312 οὔ τί μοι αἴτιος ἄλλος, ἀλλὰ τοκῆε δύω: Φ276. Nor, again, is E.*Hipp.* 638 parallel: as Hadley suggests, τό before μηδέν makes a vital difference: and the text is not entirely above suspicion. We may perhaps assume an ellipse of some form of ἄλλος in the negative clause. The elliptical origin is forgotten, and ἀλλά is used as a mere synonym of πλήν. The redundant form πλὴν ἀλλά is found several times in Hippocrates: *Vict.*41 ἐπὶ δὲ γάλακτι τρόφιμοι μὲν πάντες, πλὴν ἀλλὰ τὸ μὲν ὅϊον ἵστησι (ἀτάρ, for πλὴν ἀλλά, some MSS.): 85 μεθυσθῆναι δὲ ἅπαξ ἢ δίς, πλὴν ἀλλὰ μὴ ἐς ὑπερβολήν (text uncertain): *Epid.*v89 (πλὴν ἀλλ' *om.C*). Kühner (II ii 285, Anm. 5) quotes examples from Lucian. For πλὴν ἀλλ' ἤ, see ἀλλ' ἤ (ii).

(*c*) Thucydides sometimes inserts a comparative adverb in the negative clause, and it has been said (e.g. L. & S. *s.v.* ἀλλά, I. 3) that in such cases ἀλλά has the force of ἤ. It seems more natural to regard οὐκ . . . ἀλλά as the primary construction, and the comparative as secondary and redundant. (So Klotz i 17.) Th.i 83.2 καὶ ἔστιν ὁ πόλεμος οὐχ ὅπλων τὸ πλέον ἀλλὰ δαπάνης: ii 43.2 τὸν τάφον ἐπισημότατον, οὐκ ἐν ᾧ κεῖνται μᾶλλον, ἀλλ' ἐν ᾧ ἡ δόξα αὐτῶν . . . καταλείπεται: v 99.

(*d*) The colloquial (see Tucker on A.*Ch.*918) μἀλλά (μὴ ἀλλά[1]), 'No, don't say that, but', 'No, rather' (Aristophanes only, except for μὴ ἀλλά in A.*Ch.*918, retained by most modern

[1] Kühner (I i 219), following Ahrens (*De Crasi et Aphaeresi*), regards μἀλλά as representing, not μὴ ἀλλά, but μὰ ἀλλά (the successive stages being οὐ μὰ Δί' ἀλλά, μὰ Δί' ἀλλά, μὰ ἀλλά), and would write μὴ ἀλλά (synizesis) where an imperative follows (cf. also Ar.*Th.*288). In Ar.*Ach.* 292 Meineke's μἀλλ' ἀκούσατε seems, in itself, quite possible, though it does not open the speech.

editors, and Pl.*Alc.I* 114E (both with imperative)), has usually very much the force of μὲν οὖν, contradicting, or substituting a stronger form of expression. Ar.*Av.*109 Μῶν ἡλιαστά;—Μάλλὰ θατέρου τρόπου, ἀπηλιαστά: *Ra.*745 Χαίρεις, ἱκετεύω;—Μάλλ' ἐποπτεύειν δοκῶ: 103, 611, 751: *Ach.*458 (with imperative): *Th.* 646. In almost all cases a question precedes.

(*e*) A rhetorical question often takes the place of a negative clause. E.*Med.* 310 σὺ γὰρ τί μ' ἠδίκηκας; . . . ἀλλ' ἐμὸν πόσιν μισῶ ('No, it is my husband I hate'): *Heracl.*467 τί γὰρ γέροντος ἀνδρὸς Εὐρυσθεῖ πλέον θανόντος; ἀλλὰ τούσδε βούλεται κτανεῖν: X.*Mem.*i 2.2 πῶς οὖν αὐτὸς ὢν τοιοῦτος ἄλλους ἂν ἢ ἀσεβεῖς ἢ . . . ἐποίησεν; ἀλλ' ἔπαυσε μὲν τούτων πολλούς: *An.*iv 6.19 καὶ τί δεῖ σὲ ἰέναι . . .; ἀλλὰ ἄλλους πέμψον: S.*El.*807.

(2) Balancing, sometimes answering a μέν in the preceding clause: in the main, a poetical use. The strong adversative particle disturbs the equipoise between the clauses, and the second clause states a consideration which goes some way towards invalidating the first: 'Aye, but'.

(i) Without preceding μέν. Hom.*Γ*150 γήραϊ δὴ πολέμοιο πεπαυμένοι, ἀλλ' ἀγορηταὶ ἐσθλοί ('but, for all that, good counsellors'): ι 27 τρηχεῖ', ἀλλ' ἀγαθὴ κουροτρόφος: Archil.*Fr.*103 πόλλ' οἶδ' ἀλώπηξ, ἀλλ' ἐχῖνος ἓν μέγα: S.*Aj.*1355 ὅδ' ἐχθρὸς ἀνήρ, ἀλλὰ γενναῖός ποτ' ἦν: *Ant.*1059 σοφὸς σὺ μάντις, ἀλλὰ τἀδικεῖν φιλῶν: *OC*208 Ὦ ξένοι, ἀπόπτολις· ἀλλὰ μὴ . . . μ' ἀνέρῃ τίς εἰμι: E.*El.*293 λόγους ἀτερπεῖς, ἀλλ' ἀναγκαίους κλύειν: *Ph.*918 Σοί γ' (κακά), ἀλλὰ πατρίδι μεγάλα καὶ σωτήρια: Ar.*Ec.*201 Ἀργεῖος ἀμαθής, ἀλλ' Ἱερώνυμος σοφός: Pl.*Euthphr.* 3A Βουλοίμην ἄν . . . ἀλλ' ὀρρωδῶ μὴ τοὐναντίον γένηται: *R.*348A Ἤκουσα, ἔφη, ἀλλ' οὐ πείθομαι: *Chrm.*154A Οἶσθά που σύ γε, ἔφη, ἀλλ' οὔπω ἐν ἡλικίᾳ ἦν πρίν σε ἀπιέναι: *Tht.*169B: *Smp.*179C.

(ii) μὲν . . . ἀλλά. Hom. *Γ*214 παῦρα μέν, ἀλλὰ μάλα λιγέως: E801 μικρὸς μὲν ἔην δέμας, ἀλλὰ μαχητής: S.*Tr.*328 κακὴ μὲν αὕτη γ', ἀλλὰ συγγνώμην ἔχει: E.*Alc.*749 πολλοὺς μὲν ἤδη . . . ἀλλὰ τοῦδ' . . .: Ar.*V.*482 ἀλλὰ νῦν μὲν οὐδὲν ἀλγεῖς, ἀλλ' ὅταν . . . : Callias*Fr.*19: Pi.*O.*9.51: *P.*1.23: A.*Pers.*179: *Ch.* 747: E.*Hec.*382,799: *Hel.*281,510: *Rh.*65: Ar.*Av.*1118: Hp.

*Fract.*42 ἐλαχιστάκις μὲν τοῦτο γίνεται, ἀλλὰ τί ἂν ἐξαπιναίη ἐκπάλησις οὐκ ἐκβάλλοι; Hdt.viii 46.1 ἦσαν μέν σφι καὶ ἄλλαι πεπληρωμέναι νέες, ἀλλὰ τῇσι μὲν τὴν ἑωυτῶν ἐφύλασσον: Pl. *Cra.*431C γράμματα μὲν καὶ εἰκόνας ἐργάζεται καὶ οὗτος, ἀλλὰ πονηράς; *Prm.*154A ἔστι μὲν δὴ οὕτως ἔχον τε καὶ γεγονός. ἀλλὰ τί αὖ περὶ τοῦ γίγνεσθαι αὐτὸ ...; *Tht.*146B ἥκιστα μὲν ... τὸ τοιοῦτον ἂν εἴη ἄγροικον, ἀλλὰ τῶν μειρακίων τι κέλευέ σοι ἀποκρίνεσθαι: X.*Cyr.*vii 1.16 ἀλλὰ τὰ μὲν καθ' ἡμᾶς ἔμοιγε δοκεῖ καλῶς ἔχειν· ἀλλὰ τὰ πλάγια λυπεῖ με: Arist.*Rh.*1372a8 μὴ δοῦναι δίκην, ἢ δοῦναι μὲν ἀλλ' ἐλάττω τὴν ζημίαν εἶναι τοῦ κέρδους: D.viii 52 τὰ μὲν ἄλλ' ἐάσω· ἀλλ' ἐπειδὰν . . . (viii 63: ix 26: xviii 139: xix 145,331: lvii 63 are very similar): Pl.*R.*348E: *Phdr.*240A: *Lg.*655C: *Prt.*344A–B: *Grg.*511B: *Phd.*91D: *La.*191E: *Thg.*125E–126A: Arist.*Pol.*1260a14,1278a6: Ant.i 18: Isoc.iv 145: D.xlv 11 (In Pl.*R.*400C,463A,497C a second speaker's expression of assent intervenes between the two clauses).

Hp.*Gland.*8 contains a curious example of μὲν . . . ἀλλά without any adversative sense: μασχάλῃσι δὲ ξυρρέει μὲν καὶ ἐνταῦθα, ἀλλ' ὅταν πλῆθος ᾖ, δριμεῖς ἰχῶρες, καὶ ὧδε γίνονται φύματα. (Cf. II.9, Progressive.)

μὲν . . . ἀλλ' ὅμως (μέν, ἀλλ' ὅμως) is particularly common in Euripides, and occurs also in Sophocles and Aristophanes. It is not found in Aeschylus, nor, I think, in prose. E.*Hipp.*47 εὐκλεὴς μέν, ἀλλ' ὅμως ἀπόλλυται: *Hel.*1232 χρόνια μὲν ἦλθεν, ἀλλ' ὅμως αἰνῶ τάδε: *Ba.*1027 ὥς σε στενάζω, δοῦλος ὢν μέν, ἀλλ' ὅμως: Ar.*Nu.*1363 μόλις μέν, ἀλλ' ὅμως ἠνεσχόμην: *Ra.*602 ὅτι μὲν οὖν . . . εὖ οἶδ' ὅτι. ἀλλ' ὅμως ἐγὼ παρέξω: *Ec.*413 ὁρᾶτε μέν με . . . ἀλλ' ὅμως ἐρῶ: S.*El.*450: *OT*998: *Ph.*1373: E.*Alc.*353: *Heracl.*928: *Hipp.*795: *Hec.*825: *Ph.*438,1069: *Or.*1023: *Ba.*776: *IA*688,904: *Tr.*366: *El.*753: *HF*1365: Ar.*Ach.*956.

Passages in which ἀλλά answers a negative μέν clause are somewhere on the border-line between (1) and (2). Ar.*V.*765 ἐκεῖσε μὲν μηκέτι βάδιζ', ἀλλ' ἐνθάδε αὐτοῦ μένων δίκαζε τοῖσιν οἰκέταις (where μέν subtly represents the suggested concession as a bargain, not as a surrender: 'enjoy your trial all the same, although not going to the courts'): Anaxilas, *Fr.*22.23 αἳ λαλοῦσ' ἁπλῶς μὲν οὐδέν, ἀλλ' ἐν αἰνιγμοῖς τισιν (where μέν certainly seems pretty otiose): Hp.*Fract.*29 πεπιέχθω μὲν μή, ἀλλὰ ὅσον ἐρμασμοῦ ἕνεκεν τοῦ ἕλκεος προσκείσθω (where μέν is otiose unless προσκείσθω can imply something like pressure, 'fit closely': 'though there should be no compression, they (the compresses) should be applied firmly', Withington): Hdt.ii 49 ἀτρεκέως μὲν οὐ πάντα συλλαβὼν τὸν λόγον ἔφηνε, ἀλλ' οἱ ἐπιγενόμενοι τούτῳ σοφισταὶ μεζόνως ἐξέφηναν: Pl.*La*.182E εἰ δ' ἔστιν μὲν μὴ μάθημα, ἀλλ' ἐξαπατῶσιν οἱ ὑπισχνούμενοι (where μὲν . . . μὴ μέντοι follows in the second alternative).

(3) In a great number of passages, intermediate between (1) and (2), ἀλλά simply expresses opposition, and it is left undetermined whether the opposite ideas are, or are not, incompatible. These examples occur most frequently in answers, less frequently in continuous speech, where the milder καίτοι is more regular. Some of the instances I shall give incline to (1), others to (2): a pedantically rigid delimitation is not possible or desirable.

(i) In answers, objecting to the previous speaker's words or behaviour. S.*El*.731 Ἀλλ', ὦ φίλη, τούτων μὲν ὧν ἔχεις χεροῖν τύμβῳ προσάψῃς μηδέν ('Nay, dear one'): *Ant*.1253 Οὐκ οἶδ' . . .—Ἀλλ' εἰσόμεσθα ('But we *will* know'): E.*Cyc*.688 κερτομεῖτέ μ' ἐν κακοῖς.—Ἀλλ' οὐκέτ': *Alc*.44 Καὶ νοσφιεῖς με τοῦδε δευτέρου νεκροῦ; —Ἀλλ' οὐδ' ἐκεῖνον πρὸς βίαν σ' ἀφειλόμην: Ar.*Nu*.33 Ἄπαγε τὸν ἵππον ἐξαλίσας οἴκαδε.—Ἀλλ' ὦ μέλ' ἐξήλικας ἐμέ γ' ἐκ τῶν ἐμῶν: *Ach*.407–8 ὑπάκουσον . . . —Ἀλλ' οὐ σχολή.—Ἀλλ' ἐκκυκλήθητ'.—Ἀλλ' ἀδύνατον.—Ἀλλ' ὅμως: S.*Tr*.67,981: *Ph*.839: E.*El*.577: *IT* 754: Ar.*Nu*.660: Pl.*Grg*.473B βούλει καὶ τοῦτο ἐλέγχειν; —Ἀλλ' ἔτι τοῦτ' ἐκείνου χαλεπώτερόν ἐστιν . . . ἐξελέγξαι: *R*.396B: X.*An*.v 8.7 τὰ δὲ τῶν ἐμῶν συσκήνων σκεύη διέρριψας.—Ἀλλ' ἡ μὲν διάρριψις . . . τοιαύτη τις ἐγένετο ('Yes, but').

(ii) In continuous speech. Common in Plato and the orators, rare in *unspoken* Greek (but cf. Th.i 11.2: 132.5: v 64.4: vi 31.3). Usually, but not always, the objection is to the speaker's own words. S.*Ph*. 497 πολλὰ γὰρ τοῖς ἱγμένοις ἔστελλον αὐτὸν . . . πέμψαντά μ' ἐκσῶσαι δόμους. ἀλλ' ἢ τέθνηκεν, ἢ . . . : E.*Tr*.669 'I loathe a faithless wife. ἀλλ' οὐδὲ πῶλος ἥτις ἂν διαζυγῇ τῆς συντραφείσης, ῥᾳδίως ἕλξει ζυγόν' ('Why, even a colt'): *El*.948 ὕβριζες, ὡς δὴ . . . κάλλει τ' ἀραρώς. ἀλλ' ἔμοιγ' εἴη πόσις μὴ παρθενωπός ('Nay, give me no girl-faced husband'): *Alc.*832 ἀλλὰ σοῦ τὸ μὴ φράσαι...: *Med.*550 εἶτα σοὶ μέγας φίλος καὶ παισὶ τοῖς ἐμοῖσιν—ἀλλ' ἔχ' ἥσυχος (checking Medea's angry gesture): 1051 τολμητέον τάδ'. ἀλλὰ τῆς ἐμῆς κακῆς ('Nay, but fie on my craven spirit'): *Hipp.*846 οἷον εἶδον ἄλγος δόμων, οὐ τλητὸν οὐδὲ ῥητόν. ἀλλ' ἀπωλόμην (a protest against the inevitable: 'Oh, I am undone'): Ar.*Ach.*428 οὐ Βελλεροφόντης· ἀλλὰ κἀκεῖνος μὲν ἦν χωλὸς προσαιτῶν ('Yet he too'): Pl.*Euthphr.*3C φθονοῦσιν ἡμῖν πᾶσι τοῖς τοιούτοις. ἀλλ' οὐδὲν αὐτῶν χρὴ φροντίζειν, ἀλλ' ὁμόσε ἰέναι. Sometimes, like ἀτάρ or ἀλλὰ γάρ, marking a break-off in the thought. E.*Alc.*1034 ἀλλ', ὥσπερ εἶπον, σοὶ μέλειν γυναῖκα χρή: *El.*1123 παῦσαι λόγων τῶνδ'· ἀλλὰ τί μ' ἐκάλεις, τέκνον; Ar.*Ach.*186 Οἱ δ' οὖν βοώντων. ἀλλὰ τὰς σπονδὰς φέρεις; 1056 ἀλλ' αὑτηὶ τίς ἐστιν; *Pax*1061 Μεμνήμεθα. ἀλλ' οἶσθ' ὃ δρᾶσον; E.*Med.*731.

A particular variety of this use is with the future indicative. The speaker breaks off his reflections, and announces his plan of action. Especially with verbs of motion. ἀλλ' εἶμι: A.*Ag.*1313: E.*Heracl.*678: *Ph.*753,1009: *IT*636. ἀλλ'... ἄπειμι: E.*Hec.* 1054: Ar.*Th.*457. Also E.*Ion*76 ἀλλ'... βήσομαι: *Supp.*1014 ἀλλὰ... ὁρμάσω: Ar.*Av.*1162 ἀλλ' ἐγὼ μὲν ἀποτρέχων ἀπονίψομαι: *Pax*49. Of the same type are: Ar.*Nu.*78 ἀλλ' ἐξεγεῖραι πρῶτον αὐτὸν βούλομαι: *Th.*924 ἀλλ' ὑπαποκινητέον.

Sometimes the objection is couched in the form of a shocked, indignant, or surprised question. S.*Ant.*568 Ἀλλὰ κτενεῖς νυμφεῖα τοῦ σαυτοῦ τέκνου; E.*Med.*326 Ἀλλ' ἐξελᾷς με κοὐδὲν αἰδέσῃ λιτάς; *Hel.*1630 Ἀλλὰ δεσποτῶν κρατήσεις δοῦλος ὤν; 'What!' So, more commonly, ἀλλ' ἦ;

(iii) The speaker anticipates an objection which another is likely to make, 'But, you will say'. Usually he makes it clear that he is not speaking *propria persona* by adding to ἀλλά either νὴ Δία or an explicit statement that he is quoting: sometimes both. X.*An.*vii6.16 ἀλλ' εἴποιτ' ἂν ὅτι...: vii6.23 ἀλλά, φαίητε ἄν,...: D.vi13 ἀλλὰ νὴ Δί', εἴποι τις ἂν ὡς πάντα ταῦτ' εἰδὼς...: 14 ἀλλ' ἐβιάσθη νὴ Δία: xix158 ἀλλὰ νὴ Δί' ἐν τούτῳ τῷ χρόνῳ τοὺς ὅρκους ἔλαβον. But in other passages only the context shows that the objection is attributed to another person. E.*IA*500 ἀλλ' ἐς μεταβολὰς ἦλθον ἀπὸ δεινῶν λόγων; X.*An.*ii

5.22 ἀλλὰ τί δὴ ὑμᾶς ἐξὸν ἀπολέσαι οὐκ ἐπὶ τοῦτο ἤλθομεν; Aeschin.i 113 Ἀλλὰ περὶ μὲν τὰς κληρωτὰς ἀρχάς ἐστι τοιοῦτος, περὶ δὲ τὰς χειροτονητὰς βελτίων. Again, the addition of νὴ Δία does not of necessity imply that the objection is an imaginary one. D.xviii 129 ἀλλὰ νὴ τὸν Δία καὶ θεοὺς ὀκνῶ μὴ . . . οὐ προσήκοντας ἐμαυτῷ δόξω προῃρῆσθαι λόγους.

II. Special uses. (1) Following a rejected suggestion or supposition. That which remains *sub judice*, and may still therefore be true, is contrasted with that which is already out of court. We may usually render 'well' or 'well then'.

(i) Ἀλλά introduces, not a fresh suggestion, but a question. The speaker throws the burden of selection on the rejecter, and leaves the alternative as an indeterminate, an 'x'. This use appears to be absent from tragedy: perhaps it is colloquial. (In S.*OC*524 Ἀλλ' ἐς τί; does not, of course, mean 'Well, in what respect?', but 'Why, in what respect?')

Ar.*Nu*.827 Οὐκ ἔστιν, ὦ Φειδιππίδη, Ζεύς.—Ἀλλὰ τίς; ('Well, who does exist?'): *Pax*198 Ποῖ γῆς;—Ἰδοὺ γῆς.—Ἀλλὰ ποῖ; *Eq*.955 Οὐ τὸ θρῖον.—Ἀλλὰ τί; *Pax*1080: *Av*.98,1015: *Ra*. 488: *Ec*.928: Pl.*Phd*.89B Οὐκ, ἄν γε ἐμοὶ πείθῃ.—Ἀλλὰ τί; ἦν δ' ἐγώ: X.*Cyr*.i 3.11: *Mem*.ii 6.4. (Or a rhetorical question repudiates the possibility of any alternative: Pl.*R*.349D Ἀλλὰ τί μέλλει; 'Of course': 332C Ἀλλὰ τί οἴει; For ἀλλὰ τί μήν, see μήν, I.4.ii.)

(ii) The speaker himself offers an alternative suggestion, either affirmative, interrogative, or imperative in form. E.*Ph*.615–18 πατέρα δέ μοι δὸς εἰσιδεῖν.—Οὐκ ἂν τύχοις.—Ἀλλὰ παρθένους ἀδελφάς.—Οὐδὲ τάσδ' ὄψῃ ποτέ. . .—Μῆτερ, ἀλλά μοι σὺ χαῖρε (in 618 ἀλλά is not so much connective as adverbial in force, as in δ' ἀλλά and in (3) below): Ar.*Ach*.194 Dicaeopolis has refused the five-year and ten-year truces. Αμ. Ἀλλ' αὑταιὶ σπονδαὶ τριακοντούτιδες: *V*.1154 Οὐκ ἀναβαλεῖ;—Μὰ Δί' οὐκ ἔγωγ' . . . —Φέρ' ἀλλ' ἐγώ σε περιβαλῶ ('Well, *I'll* put it on for you'): *Pl*.1155–7 Στροφαῖον; ἀλλ' οὐκ ἔργον ἔστ' οὐδὲν στροφῶν. —Ἀλλ' ἐμπολαῖον.—Ἀλλὰ πλουτοῦμεν. . . .—Ἀλλὰ δόλιον τοίνυν: S.*Tr*.1211: E.*Or*.777: *Ba*.818: *Tr*.716: Ar.*Eq*.1104: *Pax*927: *Lys*.823: *Ra*.56–7,123: *Ec*.251–2: Pl.*R*.335C,382D–E,402E: *Chrm*.173E: *Euthphr*.2B: X.*Mem*.iii 8.3: 11.4: *Smp*.3.8: 6.10.

Normally ἀλλά stands first in the speech: but Pl.*Hp.Ma.*283B *Πῶς φῄς; ἀλλ' ἐλάχιστον;*

(iii) The use of δ' ἀλλά in drama, and occasionally in prose dialogue, is similar, though here ἀλλά is adverbial rather than connective. (Cf. E.*Ph.*1667–9, Ar.*Ach.*191–4, where successive suggestions are introduced by σὺ δ' ἀλλά and ἀλλά). E.*Ion* 978 *Τὰ δυνατά νυν τόλμησον, ἄνδρα σὸν κτανεῖν.—Αἰδούμεθ' εὐνὰς τὰς τόθ' ἡνίκ' ἐσθλὸς ἦν.—Νῦν δ' ἀλλὰ παῖδα τὸν ἐπὶ σοὶ πεφηνότα*: Ar.*Nu.*1369 Pheidippides refuses to recite Aeschylus. Strepsiades: *Σὺ δ' ἀλλὰ τούτων λέξον τι τῶν νεωτέρων* ('Well, give us a bit of the modern school, then'): E.*Med.*942 (Medea takes Jason's hesitation for a refusal): *Heracl.*565: *Hec.*391: *Rh.*167: Ar.*Ach.* 1033: *Pax* 660: *Lys.*904: Antiph.*Fr.*163.1: Pl.*Sph.*235D *φαίνομαι δύο καθορᾶν εἴδη τῆς μιμητικῆς· τὴν δὲ ζητουμένην ἰδέαν . . . καταμαθεῖν οὐδέπω μοι δοκῶ νῦν δυνατὸς εἶναι.—Σὺ δ' ἀλλ' εἰπὲ πρῶτον καὶ δίελε ἡμῖν τίνε τὼ δύο λέγεις* ('Well, anyhow, describe the two'): X.*HG* iii 4.26.

The use of δ' ἀλλά is strictly circumscribed. It is always followed by an imperative, expressed or understood: and it is nearly always preceded by σύ. (I find one instance each of νῦν δ' ἀλλά, ἡ δ' ἀλλά, ὑμεῖς δ' ἀλλά.) In *Hec.*391 a word intervenes between the particles: *ὑμεῖς δέ μ' ἀλλὰ θυγατρὶ συμφονεύσατε.* The primary sense of ἀλλά, in δ' ἀλλά, is substitution pure and simple. The idea of inadequate substitution, or *pis aller*, is secondary, and, if present at all, is derived from the context. In *Hec.*391 it clearly *is* present, for Hecuba is only partially consoled by the hope of accompanying her daughter to execution, instead of saving her from it. And it is probably to be felt in most of the other passages: clearly not, however, in *Rh.*167: *Δο. Οὐ σῆς ἐρῶμεν πολιόχου τυραννίδος.—Εκ. Σὺ δ' ἀλλὰ γήμας Πριαμιδῶν γαμβρὸς γενοῦ* ('Well, then'): where Hector's whole purpose is to offer an alternative reward adequate in Dolon's eyes. The habit of rendering ἀλλά as '*certe*', 'at least', has its dangers. (In E.*Ph.* 1749–51 it is possible that δ' and ἀλλά go together: and in Achaeus *Fr.*7 *κεκερματίσθω δ' ἄλλα μοι παροψίδων . . . παραφλογίσματα* perhaps δ' ἀλλά should be read.

(iv) Hypophora. Again, the proffering and rejecting of successive suggestions may be done by a single speaker, who conducts, as it were, a dialogue with himself. This stylistic device, known as hypophora, is freely used, for liveliness and variety, by the Greek orators. Gorgias, in the *Palamedes*, rides it to death (*Fr.*11a,(7)–(12)). Ant.v 58 *τίνος γε δὴ ἕνεκα τὸν ἄνδρα ἀπέκτεινα; οὐδὲ γὰρ ἔχθρα οὐδεμία ἦν ἐμοὶ κἀκείνῳ. λέγειν δὲ τολμῶσιν ὡς ἐγὼ χάριτι τὸν ἄνδρα ἀπέκτεινα. καὶ τίς πώποτε χαριζόμενος ἑτέρῳ τοῦτο εἰργάσατο; . . . εἶεν, ἀλλὰ δείσας περὶ ἐμαυτοῦ . . .; . . . ἀλλ' οὐδέν μοι τοιοῦτον ὑπῆρκτο εἰς αὐτόν. ἀλλὰ χρήματα ἔμελλον λήψεσθαι ἀποκτείνας αὐτόν; ἀλλ' οὐκ ἦν αὐτῷ*: And.i 148 *τίνα γὰρ καὶ ἀναβιβάσομαι δεησόμενον ὑπὲρ ἐμαυτοῦ; τὸν πατέρα; ἀλλὰ τέθνηκεν. ἀλλὰ τοὺς ἀδελφούς; ἀλλ' οὐκ εἰσίν. ἀλλὰ τοὺς παῖδας; ἀλλ' οὔπω γεγένηνται*: Lys.xxx 26–7: Isoc.xii 23: xv 223,225: xvii 47: Is.xi 25: D.viii 17: xxi 148: Hyp.*Phil.*10: *Epit.*30–1. So, too, in speeches in the historians. Th.i 80.4: vi 38.5 *ἀλλὰ δή* (the only examples, I think, in Thucydides): X.*HG*ii 4.41: *Cyr.*vii 5.83: *An.*v 8.4. (The last passage has the peculiarity that the successive suggestions are not explicitly rejected, but dismissed by contemptuous silence: *πότερον ᾔτουν τί σε καὶ ἐπεί μοι οὐκ ἐδίδους ἔπαιον; ἀλλ' ἀπῄτουν; ἀλλὰ περὶ παιδικῶν μαχόμενος; ἀλλὰ μεθύων ἐπαρῴνησα;* In *An.*ii 5.18 the rejection takes the form of a rhetorical question.) Euripides, the *ποιητὴς ῥηματίων δικανικῶν*, uses hypophora freely in his set speeches: *Hipp.*1013: *Ph.*1618–19: *Heracl.*515: *El.*377: *HF*298,1285–6,1382: *IA*1188: cf. Anaxandr. *Fr.*52.9–11: S.*El.*537: *OT*1375 (*ἀλλὰ . . . δῆτα*): *Aj.*466 (*ἀλλὰ δῆτα*). In Plato, *Ap.*37c is perhaps the only example (see p. 242). Naturally, where you have a live person to talk to, there is less need for a dummy.

(2) In the apodosis of a conditional (sometimes of a causal) sentence. *ἀλλά* contrasts the ideas expressed in protasis and apodosis: 'if . . . on the other hand': 'even though . . . still'.[1] Hom.*A*281 *εἰ δὲ σὺ καρτερός ἐσσι . . . ἀλλ' ὅ γε φέρτερός ἐστιν* ('yet he, on the other hand'): *Θ*154 *εἴ περ γάρ σ' Ἕκτωρ γε κακὸν καὶ ἀνάλκιδα φήσει, ἀλλ' οὐ πείσονται Τρῶες*: *A*82: *K*226: *M*349: *T*165: *Φ*577: *X*192: *Ω*771: *ξ*151 (*ἐπεὶ . . . ἀλλ'*): *τ*86. In post-Homeric Greek, there is a tendency to limit the use of apodotic *ἀλλά* to cases in which a negative protasis precedes, and

[1] In Arist.*Pol.*1278a 9 *ἀλλά* is not, strictly speaking, apodotic: it marks a contrast, not with the protasis, but with the preceding sentence.

the apodosis gives a more or less inadequate substitute for what is left unrealized in the protasis: 'at all events', with a notion of *pis aller*. Some instances, it is true, are of the more general, Homeric, type. Sapph.*Fr*.1.22 *αἰ δὲ δῶρα μὴ δέκετ', ἀλλὰ δώσει* ('ultro tamen dabit'): Hdt.ix 48.3 *νῦν ὦν ἐπειδὴ οὐκ ὑμεῖς ἤρξατε τούτου τοῦ λόγου, ἀλλ' ἡμεῖς ἄρξομεν* ('we shall begin it instead'): Pl.*Prt*.357C *εἰ μὴ ἔστι τοῦτο τὸ πάθημα ἡδονῆς ἡττᾶσθαι, ἀλλὰ τί ποτ' ἐστὶν . . .;* (*ἀλλὰ T* Stobaeus: *ἄλλο B*: 'well, what *is* it?'): X.*Cyr*.vi 1.14 *στέγαι δέ, εἰ καὶ ἡμῖν αὐτοῖς εἰσιν, ἀλλὰ μὰ Δί' οὐχ ἵπποις*. Pl.*R*.383A is noteworthy in that the protasis is expressed participially: *πολλὰ ἄρα Ὁμήρου ἐπαινοῦντες, ἀλλὰ τοῦτο οὐκ ἐπαινεσόμεθα*. But the more limited, *pis aller*, sense is much commoner in the fifth and fourth centuries. S.*OC*241 *ἐπεὶ γεραὸν πατέρα τόνδ' ἐμὸν οὐκ ἀνέτλατ' . . . ἀλλ' ἐμὲ . . . οἰκτίραθ'*: *Tr*.801 *μάλιστα μὲν . . . εἰ δ' οἶκτον ἴσχεις, ἀλλά μ' ἔκ γε τῆσδε γῆς πόρθμευσον*: E.*Hec*.843 *παράσχες χεῖρα τῇ πρεσβύτιδι τιμωρόν, εἰ καὶ μηδέν ἐστιν, ἀλλ' ὅμως*: *Hel*.990 *εἰ μὴ πρὸς οἴκους δυνάμεθ', ἀλλὰ πρὸς νεκρούς*: *Ph*.946 *κεὶ μὴ γὰρ εὐνῆς ἥψατ', ἀλλ' ἔχει λέχος*: *IA*1239 *ἵν' ἀλλὰ τοῦτο κατθανοῦσ' ἔχω σέθεν μνημεῖον, ἢν μὴ τοῖς ἐμοῖς πεισθῇς λόγοις* (the apodosis coming first): Ar.*Th*.288 *πολλὰ πολλάκις μέ σοι θύειν ἔχουσαν, εἰ δὲ μάλλὰ νῦν λαθεῖν*: S.*Fr*.22.2: Pl.*R*.502A *ἵνα, εἰ μή τι, ἀλλὰ αἰσχυνθέντες ὁμολογήσωσιν* (cf. 509C): *Lg*.646B (*ἀκουσόμεθα*) *κἂν εἰ μηδενὸς ἄλλου χάριν, ἀλλὰ τοῦ θαυμαστοῦ*: *Lg*.814A, 860C: X.*HG*.vi 3.15 *ὅτι ἡμεῖς, ἂν μὴ νῦν, ἀλλ' αὖθίς ποτε εἰρήνης ἐπιθυμήσομεν*: *An*.vii 1.31: 7.43: *Ages*.5.4.

Often the emphatic word or phrase in the *ἀλλά*-clause (which word or phrase follows immediately, or almost immediately, after the particle) is limitatively qualified by *γε*, which accentuates the notion of *pis aller*. The tendency to add *γε* in this case increased during the fourth century. Homer never has *ἀλλὰ . . . γε*. The dramatists also prefer plain *ἀλλά*. Herodotus has plain *ἀλλά* ten times (ii 172: iii 72: iv 120: v 39.2: vii 10ζ: 11.2: 104.5: ix 27.5: 42.2: 48.3): *ἀλλὰ . . . γε* only once (iii 140 *ἔδωκας, εἰ καὶ σμικρά, ἀλλ' ὦν ἴση γε ἡ χάρις*: *ὦν* MSS., but see *ἀλλ' οὖν*). For plain *ἀλλά* in Plato and Xenophon, see above. *ἀλλὰ . . . γε*: Pl.*Grg*.470D *εἰ δὲ μή, ἀλλ' ἀκούω γε*: *La*.183A *εἰ δ' ἐκείνους λέληθεν, ἀλλ' οὐ τούτους γε τοὺς διδασκάλους αὐτοῦ λέληθεν*: *Men*.86E *εἰ μή τι οὖν ἀλλὰ σμικρόν γέ μοι τῆς ἀρχῆς* χάλασον (with ellipse in protasis: cf. *R.*502A above): X.*Mem.*iii 3.7 εἰ δὲ μή, ἀλλὰ νῦν γε πειράσομαι: *HG.*iv 6.13: *An.*ii 5.19: iii 2.3: *Cyr.*i 3.6: viii 6.18 (γε *om. CE*): 7.22: *Hier.*2.10: Arist.*Pol.* 1269b7. Demosthenes has plain ἀλλά in xviii 191: xli 16: ἀλλὰ . . . γε in xv 27: xxii 57: lvi 12.

For the reinforcement of ἀλλά by οὖν, see ἀλλ' οὖν.

(3) A development of this use of ἀλλά *in apodosi* is to omit the protasis, the sense of which can easily be supplied from the context. 'At least.' 'At any rate.' 'Well.' (Here, again, the *pis aller* note is usually, but not invariably, present.) This is common in tragedy and comedy, but very rare in prose. Lys.x 15 ἄν πως ἀλλὰ νῦν ἐπὶ τοῦ βήματος παιδευθῇ: D.iii 33 ἐὰν οὖν ἀλλὰ νῦν γ' ἔτι . . . ἐθελήσητε. In verse the commonest forms are ἀλλὰ νῦν (S.*El.*411: *Ant.*552: Ar.*Av.*1598) and ἀλλὰ τῷ (or σὺν) χρόνῳ (S.*El.*1013: *Tr.*201: *Ph.*1041: E.*Med* 912). Also, S.*El.*415 λέγ' ἀλλὰ τοῦτο: E.*HF* 331 ὡς ἀλλὰ ταῦτά γ' ἀπολάχωσ': *IA* 1239 ἵν' ἀλλὰ τοῦτο κατθανοῦσ' ἔχω σέθεν μνημεῖον: S.*Ant.*779 ἢ γνώσεται γοῦν ἀλλὰ τηνικαῦθ': *Tr.*320 εἴπ', ὦ τάλαιν', ἀλλ' ἡμὶν ἐκ σαυτῆς ('Well, tell me yourself, since Lichas cannot.' Not 'at least', Jebb.): *OC* 1276 πειράσατ' ἀλλ' ὑμεῖς γε ('since I have failed'): 1405 ὦ τοῦδ' ὅμαιμοι παῖδες, ἀλλ' ὑμεῖς, ἐπεὶ τὰ σκληρὰ πατρὸς κλύετε τοῦδ' ἀρωμένου, μή τοί με πρὸς θεῶν σφώ γ' . . . μή μ' ἀτιμάσητέ γε (Jebb, perhaps rightly, prefers to take ἀλλά as 'beginning the appeal'. The position of the particle after the apostrophe does not tell against this view: see III below): E.*Ion* 1304 Ἡμῖν δέ γ' ἀλλὰ πατρικῆς οὐκ ἦν μέρος; *Med.*1073 εὐδαιμονοῖτον ἀλλ' ἐκεῖ[1]: *Or.*1562 ὡς ἂν ἀλλὰ παῖδ' ἐμὴν ῥυσώμεθ': Ar.*Nu.*1364 ἐκέλευσ' αὐτὸν ἀλλὰ μυρρίνην λαβόντα τῶν Αἰσχύλου λέξαι τί μοι (" I said "Well, give us a bit of Aeschylus" '): *Th.*424 πρὸ τοῦ μὲν οὖν ἦν ἀλλ' ὑποῖξαι τὴν θύραν: 449 τέως μὲν οὖν ἀλλ' ἡμικάκως ἐβοσκόμην ('I did manage to get along in a sort of fashion'): Hp.*Vict.*1. In E.*Ion* 426, Λοξίας δ' ἐὰν θέλῃ νῦν ἀλλὰ τὰς πρὶν ἀναλαβεῖν ἁμαρτίας, the position of ἀλλά *after* νῦν is remarkable.

(4) In commands and exhortations. Bäumlein (p. 17) explains ἀλλά here as combating the indecision or reluctance of another

[1] But Prof. Murray's punctuation εὐδαιμονοῖτον, ἀλλ' ἐκεῖ makes the expression far more poignant.

person. But it rather expresses, as Hartung says (ii 35), a break-off in the thought: or, as Klotz (i 5) more specifically and more accurately puts it, a transition from arguments for action to a statement of the action required. Hence ἀλλά, in this sense, usually occurs near the end of a speech, as a clinching and final appeal (whereas at the opening of a speech it introduces an objection in the form of a command: S.*El*.431 'Nay'): as we say, 'Oh, but do'. 'Come' or 'come now' will often get the meaning. This usage is very rare in oratory, being probably too intimate in tone. D.lv 9 ἀλλὰ προσέχετε . . . τον νοῦν: Lys.xix 54: xx 35.

With imperative, usually second person. Hom.*A*565 Zeus, after giving some good advice to Hera: ἀλλ' ἀκέουσα κάθησο: *Δ*100 Athena has impressed upon Pandarus what he will gain by shooting Menelaus: ἀλλ' ἄγ' ὀΐστευσον Μενελάου κυδαλίμοιο: 264 'Idomeneus, I honour you most of all the Danaans. ἀλλ' ὄρσευ πόλεμόνδ'': Tyrt.*Fr*.6–7.15 ὦ νέοι, ἀλλὰ μάχεσθε: S.*Aj*.565 Ajax, after addressing his son: ἀλλ', ἄνδρες ἀσπιστῆρες . . . ὑμῖν τε κοινὴν τήνδ' ἐπισκήπτω χάριν, κείνῳ τ' ἐμὴν ἀγγείλατ' ἐντολήν: Hom.*A*393: *B*331,360: *Δ*268: *E*605: A.*Pers*.619: *Pr*.317: *Ag*.524: S.*El*.1009: *Ant*.718: E.*Hipp*.887: Ar.*V*.428,1009. *Pl*.598: Pl.*Euthphr*.12A τρυφᾷς ὑπὸ πλούτου τῆς σοφίας. ἀλλ', ὦ μακάριε, σύντεινε σαυτόν ('Come, my good man, pull yourself together'): *Phd*.117E 'I sent the women away because I wanted no noisy demonstrations. ἀλλ' ἡσυχίαν τε ἄγετε καὶ καρτερεῖτε': *R*.328A 'It will all be most enjoyable. ἀλλὰ μένετε καὶ μὴ ἄλλως ποιεῖτε' ('Do stop': clinching and reiterating the previous appeal in 327C, μένετ' αὐτοῦ): 358D ἀλλ' ὅρα εἴ σοι βουλομένῳ ἃ λέγω (last sentence of speech: getting to business, after stating his method of procedure in advance): Hdt.vi 11.3: viii 79.4: 140β4: Pl.*Smp*.192E,213A: *R*.327B: *Cri*.44B,45A. Ἀλλ' ἄγε, ἀλλ' ἄγετε, ἀλλ' ἴθι are common in Homer. In Pl.*Phd*. 116D ἀλλ' ἄγε δὴ . . . πειθώμεθα αὐτῷ is clearly a Homeric reminiscence. ἀλλ' εἶα, with second person imperative, is common in Euripides, and perhaps confined to him: A.*Fr*.78 (εἶ' *add*. Nauck): E.*Med*.401,820: *HF*622,704,833: *Tr*.880: *Ph*.970,990, 1708: *Or*.1618: *IA*435: with ὅπως and fut. ind., E.*Or*.1060. In certain phrases the imperative is understood: ἀλλ' ἄνα, often in Homer: *Z*331 ἀλλ' ἄνα, μὴ τάχα ἄστυ πυρὸς δηΐοιο θέρηται:

I 247: S.*Aj.*192 ἀλλ' ἄνα ἐξ ἑδράνων. Ar.*Ach.*239 ἀλλὰ δεῦρο πᾶς ἐκποδών: *Eq.*751 ἀλλ' ἐς τὸ πρόσθε. With 3rd pers. imperative, or with subjunctive: Callin. *Fr.*1.9 ἀλλά τις ἰθὺς ἴτω: Tyrt.*Fr.*6–7.31 ἀλλά τις εὖ διαβὰς μενέτω: S.*Ph.*486 ἀλλὰ μή μ' ἀφῇς: Pl.*Cri.*54C ἀλλὰ μή σε πείσῃ Κρίτων ποιεῖν ἃ λέγει μᾶλλον ἢ ἡμεῖς (last sentence of the Laws' appeal to Socrates): S.*Tr.*492: *OC*1475: Ar.*Ach.*627: *V.*860,1008: Th.v 10.5: Pl. *Lg.*625C. With verbal adjective: Pl.*Phd.*91C Ἀλλ' ἰτέον, ἔφη. With χρή, δεῖ, &c.: Ar.*Ach.*234 ἀλλὰ δεῖ ζητεῖν τὸν ἄνδρα: Pl.*Phd.* 115E ἀλλὰ θαρρεῖν τε χρή: E.*Med.*950: Ar.*Av.*1718. With ὅπως and fut. ind.: E.*Cyc.*595 ἀλλ' ὅπως ἀνὴρ ἔσῃ: *HF*503.

Ἀλλά in commands and exhortations is sometimes repeated at a short interval. S.*Ph.*950 ⟨ἀλλ'⟩ ἀπόδος, ἀλλὰ νῦν ἔτ' ἐν σαυτῷ γενοῦ (I do not think Jebb is right in taking the second ἀλλά as 'limiting': the first ἀλλά is due to Turnebus): Ar.*Eq.* 244–6 ἀλλ' ἀμύνου κἀπαναστρέφου πάλιν . . . ἀλλ' ἀμύνου: *V.*240–5 ἀλλ' ἐγκονῶμεν ὦνδρες . . . ἀλλὰ σπεύδωμεν ὦνδρες ἥλικες ('Come, hurry, lads . . . come hasten'): E *HF.*622–4 ἀλλ' εἶ' ὁμαρτεῖτ', ὦ τέκν' . . . ἀλλὰ θάρσος ἴσχετε: *Or.*1337–40: Pl.*Cri.*46A.

(5) In wishes and prayers. This use is usually classed with (4), but (as regards (i)) it is essentially distinct.

(i) An answer takes the form of a wish or prayer. There is no strong break-off, as in (4): ἀλλά merely marks a gentle transition from the known present to the unknown and desired future, corresponding very closely with the English 'well'. A.*Ch.*306 Orestes has determined on vengeance. *Xo.* Ἀλλ' ὦ μεγάλαι Μοῖραι, Διόθεν τῇδε τελευτᾶν: 1063 ἐλαύνομαι δὲ κοὐκέτ' ἂν μείναιμ' ἐγώ.—Ἀλλ' εὐτυχοίης (a stronger contrasting force would be in place here: but Ἀλλ' εὐτυχοίης is a stereotyped phrase, perhaps 'a familiar form of parting blessing' (Tucker): cf. S.*OT*1478: E.*Alc.*1153: *Med.*688: *IA*716 Ἀλλ' εὐτυχοίτην): *Supp.*966 The king has promised help. *Xo.* Ἀλλ' ἀντ' ἀγαθῶν ἀγαθοῖσι βρύοις: S.*OC*44 'These are the Eumenides'.—Ἀλλ' ἵλεῳ μὲν τὸν ἱκέτην δεξαίατο ('Well, may they receive the suppliant kindly'): *OT*929 γυνὴ δὲ μήτηρ ἥδε τῶν κείνου τέκνων.—Ἀλλ' ὀλβία . . . γένοιτ': E.*Supp.*1182 Χαῖρ' . . .—Ἔσται τάδ'· ἀλλὰ καὶ σὺ τῶν αὐτῶν τύχοις: *Rh.*216 Dolon has explained his plan.

—Ἀλλ' εὖ σ' . . . πέμψειεν Ἑρμῆς: S.*OC*308 : *El.*387 : *Ant.*327 : Pl.*Cri.*43D ἀνάγκη δὴ εἰς αὔριον ἔσται . . . τὸν βίον σε τελευτᾶν.—Ἀλλ', ὦ Κρίτων, τύχῃ ἀγαθῇ . . . ταύτῃ ἔστω. The wish may be a curse: E.*Ph.*151 'This is Parthenopaeus.'—Ἀλλά νιν . . . Ἄρτεμις . . . ὀλέσειεν : S.*OC*421 : Ar.*Pl.*592.

(ii) A wish or prayer is expressed, not at the opening of a speech, but during its course. There is a stronger sense of break-off, and the idiom is more closely in line with (4). A.*Pers.*628 (the Chorus turns from Atossa to Heaven) : S.*OT*904 (a formal prayer at the end of a chorus) : *Ph.*1040, at the end of a speech : ἀλλ', ὦ πατρῴα γῆ θεοί τ' ἐπόψιοι, τείσασθε τείσασθ' : *OC*1552 (a wish closing a long speech) : E.*Ion* 1456 Θεῖον τόδ'· ἀλλὰ τἀπίλοιπα τῆς τύχης εὐδαιμονοῖμεν.

(6) Assentient. This use is at first sight diametrically opposed to the adversative. But in fact assent may include the idea of opposition in two contrary ways. (*a*) Agreement is presented as self-evident and inevitable. The speaker not only agrees, but repudiates the very idea that dissent is possible. In modern languages 'mais oui', 'aber ja', 'but of course', are similarly used. This force of ἀλλά is most clearly present where a question precedes: the particle protests, in effect, against the asking of a superfluous question. (*b*) Agreement is presented, not as self-evident, but as wrung from the speaker *malgré lui.* ἀλλά then points the contrast between the assent given and the considerations which have militated against the giving of it. In (*a*) 'Why', in (*b*) 'Well' is usually the best translation. The assentient force of ἀλλά thus appears to be derived from two contrary elements. While in certain passages (e.g. S.*Tr.*490, 600 : Pl.*Grg.*481B) the first of these, in others (e.g. S.*Ant.*98 : *Tr.*472 : *El.*1055 : *Ph.*645,1278) the second is clearly in evidence, and the note of eagerness or of reluctance is unmistakable, other passages remain in which decision is difficult or impossible. This is no mere matter of theory, it concerns the manner in which certain lines are to be read, or spoken on the stage. E.g. in S.*El.*944,1472 does ἀλλά convey a ready or a reluctant acquiescence? Perhaps to the Greeks there was never any ambiguity, and never any temptation to confuse (*a*) and (*b*): though it is also possible that (*a*) and (*b*) merge in a specifically

assentient force, in which all that is present to the mind is the removal of an obstacle, whether an actual or a supposed obstacle.

(i) Practical consent, expression of willingness to act in a required way. The first speaker usually speaks in the imperative, the second usually in the future indicative, but sometimes in the present (or even the perfect), as though he had forestalled the command: in which latter case the adversative force has a more obvious reference.

S.*Ph.*48 τὸν οὖν παρόντα πέμψον ἐς κατασκοπήν . . .—Ἀλλ' ἔρχεταί τε καὶ φυλάξεται στίβος (see Jebb): *Tr.*389 πεύθου μολοῦσα . . —Ἀλλ' εἶμι: *OC*1284 Λέγ' . . .—Ἀλλ' ἐξερῶ: *Ph.*645 Philoctetes has been urging Neoptolemus to set sail. *Νε.* Ἀλλ' εἰ δοκεῖ, χωρῶμεν (cf. A.*Ag.*944): *Tr.*490 στέργε τὴν γυναῖκα . . . —Ἀλλ' ὧδε καὶ φρονοῦμεν ὥστε ταῦτα δρᾶν: 600 σήμαινε . . . —Ἀλλ' αὐτὰ δή σοι ταῦτα καὶ πράσσω: Ar.*Nu.*431 δέομαι τοίνυν ὑμῶν τουτὶ . . .—Ἀλλ' ἔσται σοι τοῦτο παρ' ἡμῶν: S.*Aj.*1400: *El.*944,1472: *Tr.*472,620: E.*Hel.*702: *El.*420: *IA*1540: Ar. *Ach.*409 (after four adversative ἀλλά's): *Nu.*11 ('All right, if you like'): *V.*457: *Pax*1103: *Av.*665: *Lys.*1030: Pl.*Grg.*462B ἐρώτα ἢ ἀποκρίνου.—Ἀλλὰ ποιήσω ταῦτα: 481B οὐδὲν μέντοι οἷον τὸ αὐτὸν ἐρωτᾶν.—Νὴ τοὺς θεοὺς ἀλλ' ἐπιθυμῶ: *Smp.*185D δίκαιος εἶ ἢ παῦσαί με τῆς λυγγὸς ἢ λέγειν ὑπὲρ ἐμοῦ. . . .—Ἀλλὰ ποιήσω ἀμφότερα ταῦτα: *Euthphr.*6E: *La.*181D: *Men.*82A.

Very frequently in Plato, not seldom in Xenophon, and occasionally in other writers, a word used in command is echoed in consent. S.*Tr.*86 οὐκ εἶ ξυνέρξων . . . ;—Ἀλλ' εἶμι: *Ph.*1278 παῦε . . .—Ἀλλ' ἤθελον μὲν ἂν . . . εἰ δὲ μὴ . . . πέπαυμαι: Ar. *Ach.*1232 ἕπεσθε . . .—Ἀλλ ἑψόμεσθα: Pl.*Grg.*449C καί μοι ἐπίδειξιν αὐτοῦ τούτου ποίησαι . . .—Ἀλλὰ ποιήσω: *Smp.*199C πάρες . . .—Ἀλλὰ παρίημι: *R.*327B ἀλλὰ περιμένετε.—Ἀλλὰ περιμενοῦμεν: X.*Mem.*iii 3.15 πειρῶ . . .—Ἀλλὰ νὴ Δία πειράσομαι: 11.18 βούλομαι . . . σὲ . . . πορεύεσθαι.—Ἀλλὰ πορεύσομαι, ἔφη: *An.*vii 1.6 κελεύει Ξενοφῶντα συμπροθυμεῖσθαι ὅπως διαβῇ τὸ στράτευμα . . . ὁ δ' εἶπεν· Ἀλλὰ τὸ μὲν στράτευμα διαβήσεται: Pl.*Tht.*165D,190D,195E: *R.*431B: *Prt.*320C: *Cri.*49A.

Consent may be implied without being directly expressed:

(*a*) The enjoined task is described as easy or unobjectionable. S.*Tr.*1257 Ἀλλ' οὐδὲν εἴργει σοὶ τελειοῦσθαι τάδε: Ar.*Av.*643

καὶ τοὔνομ' ἡμῖν φράσατον.—Ἀλλὰ ῥᾴδιον: 966 'There is an oracle about Cloudcuckooborough'.—Ἀλλ' οὐδὲν οἷόν ἐστ' ἀκοῦσαι τῶν ἐπῶν ('Well, there's nothing like hearing the exact text'): *Lys.*1112 Ἀλλ' οὐχὶ χαλεπὸν τοὔργον: Pl.*Ly.*206C Ἀλλ' οὐδέν, ἔφη, χαλεπόν: *Euthd.*272D Ἀλλ' οὐδὲν κωλύει: *Men.*71E: *Tht.* 162B: *R.*580B: *Mi.*315B: X.*Mem.*i 2.42: *An.*iv 8.5.

(*b*) A person asked to speak conveys his readiness to speak by speaking: particularly when the answer is to be a long and elaborate one, the speaker winds himself up, as it were, with ἀλλά, 'well'.

S.*OT*14 ἀλλ', ὦ γεραιέ, φράζ' ...—Ἀλλ', ὦ ..., ὁρᾷς μὲν ... (Jebb wrongly renders 'nay'): *Ph.*232 ἀλλ' ἀνταμείψασθ' ...—Ἀλλ', ὦ ξέν', ἴσθι τοῦτο πρῶτον: Pl.*Euthphr.*9E Euthyphro, asked to define τὸ ὅσιον: Ἀλλ' ἔγωγε φαίην ἂν τοῦτο εἶναι τὸ ὅσιον: *Hp.Ma.*288E ἀποκρίνου.—Ἀλλ' οὕτως ... ἔχει: *Grg.*460A: X.*Mem.*ii 6.21: *Oec.*7.3. In opening an answer given by a writer to his own question: Hdt.ii 20 ταῦτα ... βουλόμενος εἰδέναι ἱστόρεον ... ἀλλὰ Ἑλλήνων μέν τινες ... ἔλεξαν ('well').

(ii) Assent, expressing agreement with a statement just made. This may be conveyed:

(*a*) By a favourable judgement of the preceding words. S.*OT* 78 Ἀλλ' ἐς καλὸν σύ τ' εἶπας: *Tr.*588 Ἀλλ' εἴ τις ἐστὶ πίστις ἐν τοῖς δρωμένοις, δοκεῖς παρ' ἡμῖν οὐ βεβουλεῦσθαι κακῶς: Ar.*Eq.* 492 Ἀλλ' εὖ λέγεις: Pl.*Chrm.*155A Ἀλλὰ καλῶς, ἔφη, λέγεις: *Phdr.*235D Ἀλλ', ὦ γενναιότατε, κάλλιστα εἴρηκας: *Phlb.*24B Ἀλλ' εὖ γε ... ὑπέλαβες: *R.*430C: X.*Mem.*ii 7.11. (In E.*IA*990, in the middle of a speech, ἀλλά rather marks a break-off in thought.)

(*b*) By a form of words implying that what has been said is correct. S.*El.*1102 'Does Aegisthus live here?'—Ἀλλ' εὖ θ' ἱκάνεις (Jebb compares *Tr.*229, which is rather different. See iii.*b* below): Ar.*Pl.*962 'Is this the right house?'—Ἀλλ' ἴσθ' ἐπ' αὐτὰς τὰς θύρας ἀφιγμένη ('Why, to be sure'): *V.*912 Philocleon, interrupting the prosecutor's speech: Νὴ τὸν Δί', ἀλλὰ δῆλός ἐστ' ('Why, good Lord, it's as plain as a pike-staff'. But perhaps ἀλλά is more definitely adversative, and means that Philocleon does not want to hear any more): E.*Alc.*826 Ἀπωλόμεσθα ...—Ἀλλ' ᾐσθόμην μὲν ὄμμ' ἰδὼν δακρυρροοῦν ('Why,

I was sure of it'): Pl.*Prt.*340E ἰώμενος μεῖζον τὸ νόσημα ποιῶ.—Ἀλλ' οὕτως ἔχει, ἔφη: 357B ἆρα πρῶτον μὲν οὐ μετρητικὴ φαίνεται . . .;—Ἀλλ' ἀνάγκη: *Phd.*62C Ἀλλ' εἰκὸς . . . τοῦτό γε φαίνεται: *Tht.*184D Ἀλλά μοι δοκεῖ οὕτω μᾶλλον ἢ ἐκείνως. Here again Plato is fond of the echoed word. *Euthphr.*7D ἆρα οὐ ταῦτά ἐστιν περὶ ὧν διενεχθέντες . . .;—Ἀλλ' ἔστιν αὕτη ἡ διαφορά: *Grg.*489A νομίζουσιν οἱ πολλοὶ . . .;—Ἀλλ' οἵ γε πολλοὶ νομίζουσιν οὕτως: 496C ὁμολογοῦμεν ταῦτα; . . .—Ἀλλ' ὑπερφυῶς ὡς ὁμολογῶ: *R.*437B: *Men.*75E: *Cri.*48B: *Phd.*105C: *Tht.*153D,157D: *Prt.*341D: *Lg.*898C (Ὦ ξένε, ἀλλά). In Alexis *Fr.*133 ἀλλά, by itself, apparently carries the force of 'yes'. Ἐπίστασαι τὸν σαῦρον ὡς δεῖ σκευάσαι;—Ἀλλ' ἂν διδάσκῃς.—Ἐξελὼν τὰ βραγχία . . . παράσχισον χρηστῶς ('Why, yes, if you teach me'). I know no parallel.

(iii) Again, ἀλλά may express, neither willingness to act as required, nor agreement with something stated or suggested, but:

(*a*) Acquiescence, ready or reluctant, in the attitude or declared intentions of the previous speaker: 'Well': 'Very good.' S.*El.*1055 Ἀλλ' εἰ σεαυτῇ τυγχάνεις δοκοῦσά τι φρονεῖν, φρόνει τοιαῦθ': *Tr.*1216 Ἀλλ' ἀρκέσει καὶ ταῦτα: S.*Ant.*98: *OC* 1768: *Ph.*1407: Pl.*Cra.*430A Ἀλλ' ἀγαπητὸν καὶ τοῦτο: *Smp.*214D: *Phd.*108E.

(*b*) A sympathetic reaction to the previous speaker's words or actions: 'Well'. S.*Aj.*263 'Ajax is better now'.—Ἀλλ' εἰ πέπαυται, κάρτ' ἂν εὐτυχεῖν δοκῶ: *Tr.*229 χαίρειν δὲ τὸν κήρυκα προυννέπω. . . .—Ἀλλ' εὖ μὲν ἵγμεθ', εὖ δὲ προσφωνούμεθα: *Ph.* 336 ἐκ Φοίβου δαμείς.—Ἀλλ' εὐγενὴς μὲν ὁ κτανών: 557 Ἀλλ' ἡ χάρις μὲν τῆς προμηθίας, ξένε . . . προσφιλὴς μενεῖ: 882 'I feel better now.'—Ἀλλ' ἥδομαι μέν σ' εἰσιδὼν παρ' ἐλπίδα ἀνώδυνον βλέποντα: E.*Heracl.*597 Makaria has offered to die. Io. Ἀλλ', ὦ μέγιστον ἐκπρέπουσ' εὐψυχίᾳ πασῶν γυναικῶν, ἴσθι, τιμιωτάτη . . . ἔσῃ: *El.*550 Οἴδ' ἐκ δόμων βαίνουσι . . .—Ἀλλ' εὐγενεῖς μέν: Ar.*Ach.*752 Διαπεινᾶμες ἀεὶ ποττὸ πῦρ.—Ἀλλ' ἡδύ τοι νὴ τὸν Δί' ('Well, that's very nice'): *Th.*257–60 Ἡδὶ μὲν οὖν κεφαλὴ περίθετος . . .—Νὴ τὸν Δί' ἀλλὰ κἀπιτηδεία πάνυ ('Why, it's the very thing').—Ἆρ' ἁρμόσει μοι;—Νὴ Δί' ἀλλ' ἄριστ' ἔχει: E.*IA* 638 Iphigeneia rushes to embrace her father. Κλ. Ἀλλ', ὦ τέκνον, χρή ('That's right, my child'): Pl.*Phlb.*38A Ἀλλὰ προθύμως ἀμύνεις τῷ τῆς ἡδονῆς . . . λόγῳ τὰ νῦν ('Why, you *are* an enthusiastic champion of the cause of pleasure!'. Ironical admiration).

(7) We may perhaps class as assentient those passages in which ἀλλά introduces the substantiation by the second speaker of an hypothesis or wish expressed by the first, confirming as actual what has hitherto been presented as imaginary.

S.*OT*848 εἰ δ' ἄνδρ' ἕν' οἰόζωνον αὐδήσει . . .—Ἀλλ' ὡς φανέν γε τοὔπος ὧδ' ἐπίστασο, κοὐκ ἔστιν αὐτῷ τοῦτό γ' ἐκβαλεῖν πάλιν ('Well, rest assured that that *was* the report'): 769 δι' ἅ νιν εἰσιδεῖν θέλω.—Ἀλλ' ἵξεται μέν: 1158 ὀλέσθαι δ' ὤφελον τῇδ' ἡμέρᾳ.—Ἀλλ' ἐς τόδ' ἥξεις ('Well, that is what you'll come to'): S.*Ph.*647 (ὅτου virtually = εἴ του): *Aj.*529: Ar.*Nu.*420. Sometimes a word from the hypothetical clause is echoed (by exact repetition or by the substitution of a synonym) in the ἀλλά clause. This is a favourite idiom of Plato's. I have counted quite twenty[1] instances in him, several in Xenophon, and a few in other authors. S.*El.*1204 εἰ τὸ τῶνδ' εὔνουν πάρα. —Ἀλλ' ἐστὶν εὔνουν: *OT*370 Εἴπερ τί γ' ἐστὶ τῆς ἀληθείας σθένος.—Ἀλλ' ἔστι, πλὴν σοί: E.*IA*1360 Ὄναιο τῶν φρενῶν.—Ἀλλ' ὀνησόμεσθα: Ar.*V.*181 τί στένεις, εἰ μὴ φέρεις Ὀδυσσέα τιν';—Ἀλλὰ ναὶ μὰ Δία φέρει κάτω γε τουτονί τιν' ὑποδεδυκότα: *Nu.*797 εἴ σοί τις υἱός ἐστιν . . .—Ἀλλ' ἔστ' ἔμοιγ' υἱός: Pl.*Euthd.* 275B εἰ μή τι διαφέρει . . .—Ἀλλ' οὐδὲν διαφέρει: *Phlb.*41B εἴπερ γε εἰσίν.—Ἀλλ' . . . εἰσίν: *Cri.*49E εἰ δ' ἐμμένεις . . . ἄκουε.—Ἀλλ' ἐμμένω: *Cra.*433A εἰ μέμνησαι. . . .—Ἀλλὰ μέμνημαι: *Chrm.*155B μόνον ἐλθέτω.—Ἀλλ' ἥξει, ἔφη: *R.*394C εἴ μοι μανθάνεις.—Ἀλλὰ συνίημι: *Grg.*469C (where a slightly different turn is given to the idiom): *Euthphr.*9C: *Chrm.*162E: *Tht.*207D: *Hp.Mi.*363C: X.*Cyr.*v I.I: *HG*iii 4.5: iv 3.2: *Mem.*iii 10.10: *An.*vii 3.9. Indirect questions with εἰ may be included here: Pl.*Cri.*48B: *Grg.* 476D.

(8) Inceptive. (Cf. δέ, I.C.2.iii.) Speeches in Xenophon often open with ἀλλά. Logically speaking, this cannot be regarded as a distinct usage, since the examples fall under one or other of the heads, adversative or assentient, enumerated above. (E.g.

[1] Dr. Chapman has collected more than thirty.

Pl.*La.*182D *Λάχητος δ', εἴ τι παρὰ ταῦτα λέγει, κἂν αὐτὸς ἡδέως ἀκούσαιμι.—Ἀλλ' ἔστι μὲν . . . χαλεπὸν λέγειν περὶ ὁτουοῦν μαθήματος ὡς οὐ χρὴ μανθάνειν.*) But Xenophon's fondness for this form of opening has some stylistic importance. Where the particle marks assent or complaisance, it corresponds roughly to the English 'Well', and has the same vague and colloquial tone: hence its absence in the more formal speeches of Thucydides.

(i) Adversative. *HG* ii 3 35 (opening a speech for the defence: cf. vii 3.7: *An.*vii 6.11: 7.4): *HG.*iv 1.34: *Cyr.*ii 2.18 (introducing a change of topic). (ii) Responding to an invitation to speak. (Cf. 6. i. *b* above.) *An.*iii 1.35: *Cyr.*ii 3.5: v 1.24. (iii) Response or approval in general (cf. 6. iii above). *An.*iii 1.45: 2.4: 2.33: vii 6.9: *Cyr.*v 2.8: 4.32: iv 3.15.

The occurrence of *ἀλλά* at the beginning of the Xenophontine *Symposium* and *Respublica Lacedaemoniensium* is somewhat similar, and may perhaps be due to naïveté, real or assumed: though Bäumlein (p. 13) may conceivably be right in attributing this usage to a desire to make these small works look like fragments of a larger whole. (The *Oeconomicus* and the Xenophontine *Apology* open with *δέ*: so does the pseudo-Xenophontine *Resp. Ath.*). Oracles, too, have a way of beginning with *ἀλλ' ὅταν*: Ar.*Av.*967: Hdt.i 55: iii 57: vi 77.2.

(9) Progressive. We have observed above that *ἀλλά*, though normally a strong adversative, is sometimes used where we should expect the weaker *δέ*. And we shall see later that in *δέ*, except where preceded by *μέν*, the sense of contrast is normally so slight that the particle denotes little more than mere addition, like *καί* and *τε*. The same is occasionally true of *ἀλλά*, which is then used as an almost purely connective or progressive particle ('further', 'again'), being sometimes reinforced by *καί* or *οὐδέ*. This progressive use is commoner in Hippocrates than in other writers.

VC 14 *ἀφίκει ἐς πρίσιν ἡ τοιαύτη ξυμφορή. ἀλλὰ χρὴ πρίσαντα τὰ λοιπὰ ἰητρεύειν τὸ ἕλκος*: *Prog.*7. In particular, we often find *ἀλλὰ χρή* after a detailing of symptoms, introducing a description of the regimen recommended: 'Well'. *VC* 14: *Int.*19, 20: *Vict.*73, 74: *Mul.*241 (*ἀλλὰ δεῖ*). *Ἀλλὰ καί*. *Mul.*

188 πρόσωπον ἀγλαΐζει ἧπαρ ταύρου . . . ἀλλὰ καὶ ὁ χυλὸς τῆς πτισάνης ὁμοίως λαμπρύνει: *Vict.*93: *Gland.*16. Ἀλλ' οὐδέ. *Vict.*90 Κατακλυζομένην γῆν . . . ὁρῆν νοῦσον σημαίνει . . . ἀλλ' οὐδὲ μέλαιναν ὁρῆν τὴν γῆν οὐδὲ κατακεκαυμένην δοκεῖ ἀγαθόν (ἀλλ' *om.* (*H restit. al. manu*) θ).

In other prose-writers progressive ἀλλά is rarer, though ἀλλὰ μήν is regularly so used. (In such a passage as Lys.xiii 79 ἀλλά rather denotes a break-off: ἀλλ' ἕτερον, 'But there is another point'.)

Plato and Xenophon, proceeding to a new item in a series. Pl.*R.*470E Οὐκοῦν καὶ ἀγαθοὶ . . . ἔσονται;—Σφόδρα γε.—Ἀλλ' οὐ φιλέλληνες; *Tht.*178C (fresh example): *Smp.*197A πρῶτον μὲν . . . καὶ μὲν δὴ . . . ἀλλὰ . . . γε μήν: *Mi.*316A Οὐκοῦν καὶ ἐν Πέρσαις;—Καὶ ἐν Πέρσαις.—Ἀλλ' ἀεὶ δήπου; *R.*487A: X. *Mem.*i 2.27 (a fresh parallel). Marking transition from major to minor premise (cf. ἀλλὰ μήν): Pl.*R.*335C: cf. *Phd.*93D. ἀλλὰ καί. D.xix 54 ἦσαν ἀπιστοῦντές τινες . . . ἦσαν ἄλλοι τινὲς οἳ . . . ἀλλὰ καὶ μεταμέλειν ὑμῖν ᾤοντό τινες: 257,258: xliii 82: liv 36: X.*Cyr.*viii 8.19 (in a series with καὶ μήν, ἀλλὰ μήν, γε μήν): *Oec.*20.10 (preceded by adversative ἀλλὰ καί): *Smp.*4.32. ἀλλ' οὐδέ. Lys.x 10.

There are few verse examples. Alcm.*Fr.*1.71 οὔτε . . . οὔτε . . . οὐδὲ . . . οὐδὲ καὶ . . . ἀλλ' οὐδ': Pi.*N.*10.45 'They came with cups from Sicyon and cloaks from Pellene. ἀλλὰ χαλκὸν μυρίον οὐ δυνατὸν ἐξελέγχειν': E.*Alc.*79 Τί σεσίγηται δόμος Ἀδμήτου;—Ἀλλ' οὐδὲ φίλων πέλας οὐδείς, ὅστις ἂν εἴποι πότερον φθιμένην βασίλειαν πενθεῖν χρή μ' ('Nor yet is there any friend at hand'): Ar.*Eq.*985 ἀλλὰ καὶ τόδ' ἔγωγε θαυμάζω τῆς ὑομουσίας αὐτοῦ: Eub.*Fr.*120.4 'The Achaeans in Homer never got fish to eat. ἀλλ' οὐδὲ μίαν ἄλλην ἑταίραν εἶδέ τις αὐτῶν'. (Add, perhaps, E.*Ion* 26: 'She put golden snakes in the basket with the child. ἀλλ' ἣν εἶχε παρθένος χλιδὴν τέκνῳ προσάψασ' ἔλιπεν': 'Besides'. But ἀλλά may be adversative here. See Paley and Wilamowitz and A. S. Owen. Hartung (ii 40) explains ἀλλά as resuming after the parenthesis, perhaps rightly.)

III. Position. As a strong adversative, ἀλλά naturally takes the first place in clause or sentence, while δέ, μέντοι and μήν take the second. The only exception to this rule is that an apostrophe, or oath, sometimes precedes the particle. This postponement after apostrophe is also found after other connectives (e.g. δέ and γάρ), and is to be attributed, perhaps, to the liveliness of the Greek temperament, the emotional here outrunning the logical. Ar.*Ach.*579 *Ὦ Λάμαχ' ἥρως, ἀλλὰ συγγνώμην ἔχε* (cf. the postponement of γάρ in 576): S.*OT*1503: *OC*238: *Ph.*799: Hdt.v72.3 *Ὦ γύναι, ἀλλ' οὐ Δωριεύς εἰμι*: Pl.*Euthphr.*3C: *Lg.*898C. S.*El.*881 *Μὰ τὴν πατρῴαν ἑστίαν, ἀλλ' οὐχ ὕβρει λέγω τάδ'* (whereas in the passages cited by Jebb ἀλλά contrasts with the negative oath, not with the preceding speech: Ar.*Ra.*174 *Δύο δραχμὰς μισθὸν τελεῖς;—Μὰ Δί' ἀλλ' ἔλαττον*: 'No, less'). For a similar displacement of ἀλλά by an exclamation, cf. Pl.*Hp.Ma.*283B (II.1.ii). In E.*Supp.*951 the text has been suspected: a full stop after παύσασθ' would, I think, remove all difficulty. For postponement after ἀλλ' ἦ, *v. s. v.*

IV. Ἀλλά combined with other particles.

(1) Ἀλλά γε. The juxtaposition is very rare in classical Greek. Neil (*Knights*, p. 193) and Klotz (i.15) are perhaps justified in doubting its occurrence in classical Greek. Kühner (II ii 177) cites Pl.*Hp.Ma.*287B (ἀλλ' ἄγ' *scr. recc.*: ἀλλά γ' *TWF*): *R.*331B (ἀλλ' ἕν γε Stobaeus): *Phdr.*262A (ἀλλά γε δή *B*: ἀλλὰ δή *T*: ἀλλὰ μήν Galenus): as well as instances from Arrian and Polybius (to whom Neil adds Pausanias and *N.T.*). In Pl.*Hp Ma.*287B ἀλλ' ἄγ' should certainly be read: cf. *Phd.* 86E (where all MSS. read ἀλλά γε): *R.*543C (ἀλλ' ἄγε *D* Thomas Magister: ἀλλά γ' *AFM*). In Hom.*A*82 τε is no doubt right. Add Gorg.*Fr.*11a.10 *ἀλλά γε τὸ φῶς πολεμεῖ τοῖς τοιούτοις* (objecting, in hypophora: cf. *id. ib.* 14): Archestratus, *ap.* Ath.319D *ἀλλά γε χρή* (τί Wil.): Aristot.*EE*1216b20 *οὐ μὴν ἀλλά γε*: Pseud.-Aristot. *Oec.*1343b25. For ἀλλά . . . γε see II.2 above.

(2) Ἀλλ' οὐδέ, 'Why, not even . . .' (For ἀλλ' οὐδέ meaning 'Nor, again' see II.9 above.) Ar.*Nu.*1396 *εἰ γὰρ . . . ἀναπείσει, τὸ δέρμα τῶν γεραιτέρων λάβοιμεν ἂν ἀλλ' οὐδ' ἐρεβίνθου*: Com. Adesp.*Fr.*178: Men.*Sam.*144: D.xix37 *ὑπὲρ δὲ Φωκέων . . . ἀλλ'*

οὐδὲ μικρόν (ἔνεστιν): xxi 14: xxv 5 ὁ δὲ κρινόμενος τῶν μὲν εἰς σωτηρίαν φερόντων ἀλλ' οὐδ' ὁτιοῦν πάρεστιν ἔχων: *Prooem.* 48. In all these closely similar passages the speaker makes as though he would mention something of trifling value or importance, but corrects his unspoken thought by saying that even that trifle is too much. A dash in the text before ἀλλά would bring out the meaning. Pickard-Cambridge renders D.xix 37 well: 'But as to the Phocians . . .—why, there is not the slightest mention of them!' Diph.*Fr.*61.8 seems similar: εὐθέως νοῶ ὅτι τοῦτό μοι τὸ δεῖπνον ἀλλ' οὐδ' αἷμ' ἔχει. X.*Cyr.*iv 3.14 is different: ὅ γε μὴν μάλιστ' ἄν τις φοβηθείη, μὴ . . ., ἀλλ' οὐδὲ τοῦτο ἀμήχανον. Here there is a definite anacoluthon, as though a main verb had preceded: cf. *An.*i 8.13: D.xix 264.

(3) Ἀλλ' ἤ (absent from serious poetry) is used only after negatives and questions expecting a negative answer. The explanation of the combination has been much discussed, and it is not even agreed whether ἀλλ' represents ἀλλά or ἄλλο (with loss of accent caused by fusion with the following word). It will be convenient, before examining the rival views, to set out the evidence, in grouping which I follow Cook Wilson, 'On the use of ἀλλ' ἤ in Aristotle', *C.Q.*iii 121–4, while distinguishing (as he and other writers do not) between (*a*) cases where ἀλλ' ἤ introduces the second of two co-ordinated clauses ('except that', 'but merely'), and (*b*) cases where the ἀλλ' ἤ clause, which often consists of a single word or phrase, has no such independence, but is subordinated to the structure of the immediately preceding words ('except').

(i) A negation (or question expecting a negative answer), containing a word of comparison (some part of ἄλλος), is followed by an exception. (*a*) X.*Oec.*2.13 οὔτε ἄλλος πώποτέ μοι παρέσχε τὰ ἑαυτοῦ διοικεῖν ἀλλ' ἢ σὺ νυνὶ ἐθέλεις παρέχειν ('It is only you now that are willing . . .'). (*b*) Pl.*Phd.*81B ὥστε μηδὲν ἄλλο δοκεῖν εἶναι ἀληθὲς ἀλλ' ἢ τὸ σωματοειδές: *Ap.*34B τίνα ἄλλον ἔχουσι λόγον βοηθοῦντες ἐμοὶ ἀλλ' ἢ τὸν ὀρθόν τε καὶ δίκαιον; *Phd.*68B μηδαμοῦ ἄλλοθι . . . ἀλλ' ἢ ἐκεῖ: 101C οὐκ ἔχεις ἄλλην τινὰ αἰτίαν . . . ἀλλ' ἢ τὴν τῆς δυάδος μετάσχεσιν: Isoc.iv 7 εἰ μὲν μηδαμῶς ἄλλως οἷόν τ' ἦν δηλοῦν τὰς αὐτὰς πράξεις ἀλλ' ἢ διὰ μιᾶς ἰδέας: D.xxxvii 53 μήτ' ἄλλου μηδενός εἰσιν ἀλλ' ἢ τοῦ πλείονος: Arist.*Cat.*3b19 οὐδὲν γὰρ ἄλλο σημαίνει τὸ λευκὸν ἀλλ' ἢ ποιόν: Pl.*Phd.*97D: *R.*427C,429B,553D: *Prt.*356A: *Thg.* 123D: *Mx.*244D: *Mi.*313B: Arist.*Top.*103a21: *EN*1125a1. (Juxtaposition of ἀλλ' ἤ with the word of comparison is very rare. Hp.*Vict.*72 προσφέρειν μηδὲν ἄλλο ἀλλ' ἢ ὕδωρ (text uncertain): *Flat.*3 μετέχοιεν δὲ πῶς ἂν ἄλλως ἀλλ' ἢ διὰ τοῦ ὕδατος . . .;)

(ii) A negation, not containing a word of comparison, is followed by an exception. Cook Wilson points out that, while the use of ἤ in such cases is, strictly speaking, irregular, the notion of comparison may be involved in a negative expression: cf. X.*Cyr.*vii 5.41 μηδένα παριέναι ἢ τοὺς φίλους. (*a*) Th.v 60.1 καὶ οὐ μετὰ τῶν πλεόνων οὐδὲ αὐτὸς ('on his side') βουλευσάμενος ἀλλ' ἢ ἑνὶ ἀνδρὶ κοινώσας ('except that he consulted with one individual'): Is.x 12 κατὰ τὸν νόμον ὃς οὐκ ἐᾷ τῶν τῆς ἐπικλήρου κύριον εἶναι, ἀλλ' ἢ τοὺς παῖδας ἐπὶ διέτες ἡβήσαντας κρατεῖν τῶν χρημάτων (but the last three words have often, and with reason, been suspected: *v.* Wyse *ad loc.* If they are omitted, this example must be transferred to (*b*) below): X.*Cyr.* iv 4.10 οὐδ' ὁτιοῦν καινὸν ἔσται ὑμῖν ἀλλ' ἢ οὐχ ὁ αὐτὸς ἄρξει ὑμῶν ὅσπερ καὶ πρότερον: Hp.*Epid.*i 9 οὐδ' ἡμορράγησεν ἐκ ῥινῶν οὐδενὶ . . . ἀλλ' ἢ σμικρὰ ἔσταξεν (ἀλλ' ἤ W. H. S. Jones in Loeb: ἀλλά Littré, with no mention of variants). (*b*) Ar.*Eq.* 779 οὐχὶ φιλεῖ σ' . . . ἀλλ' ἢ διὰ τοῦτ' αὔθ' ὁτιή σου τῆς ἀνθρακιᾶς ἀπολαύει: *V.*984 οὐδέν ποτ' ἀλλ' ἢ τῆς φακῆς ἐμπλήμενος: *Ra.* 227 οὐδὲν γάρ ἐστ' ἀλλ' ἢ κοάξ: *Lys.*427: *Ra.*443,1073,1130: *Pl.*1172: Th.iii 71.1 μηδετέρους δέχεσθαι ἀλλ' ἢ μιᾷ νηὶ ἡσυχάζοντας: vii 50.3 ὡς αὐτοῖς οὐδὲ ὁ Νικίας ἔτι ὁμοίως ἐνηντιοῦτο, ἀλλ' ἢ μὴ φανερῶς γε ἀξιῶν ψηφίζεσθαι (ἀλλ' ἤ Stephanus: ἄλλο εἰ *codd.* The demand for a secret ballot is a part of τὸ ὁμοίως ἐναντιοῦσθαι: cf. 48.1): Pl.*La.*187D αὐτῷ δ' οὐ συγγεγονέναι ἀλλ' ἢ παιδὶ ὄντι: *Prt.*334C μὴ χρῆσθαι ἐλαίῳ ἀλλ' ἢ ὅτι σμικροτάτῳ: *Phdr.*258E τίνος μὲν οὖν ἕνεκα κἄν τις ὡς εἰπεῖν ζῴη, ἀλλ' ἢ τῶν τοιούτων ἡδονῶν ἕνεκα; Arist.*Po.*1455a5 ὅμοιος δὲ οὐθεὶς ἀλλ' ἢ 'Ορέστης: Lys.xix 28 γῆ μὲν οὐκ ἦν ἀλλ' ἢ χωρίδιον μικρόν: D.l 7 οὐκ ἦλθον οἱ ναῦται . . . ἀλλ' ἢ ὀλίγοι: Pl.*R.*601A: *Cra.*438B: X.*HG* i 7.15: vi 4.4: *An.*iv 6.11. πλὴν ἀλλ' ἤ is similarly used in Arist. *Metaph.*981a18 οὐ γὰρ ἄνθρωπον ὑγιάζει ὁ ἰατρεύων, πλὴν ἀλλ' ἢ κατὰ συμβεβηκός.

(iii) Instead of a general negation, which has to be supplied in thought, a particular instance of it is given. Cook Wilson cites from Aristotle:—(*a*) *HA* 563b19 ἔστι δὲ ὁ μὲν ἱέραξ γαμψώνυχος, ὁ δὲ κόκκυξ οὐ γαμψώνυχος· ἔτι δὲ οὐδὲ τὰ περὶ τὴν κεφαλὴν ἔοικεν ἱέρακι . . . ἀλλ' ἢ κατὰ τὸ χρῶμα μόνον προσέοικεν ἱέρακι ('Nor is the cuckoo like the falcon in the head either: (indeed there is no likeness) except that it is like the falcon in colour only'): (*b*) *HA* 580a20 εἰ δ' ἐστὶν ὁ χρόνος οὗτος τῆς κυήσεως ἢ μή ἐστιν, οὐδέν πω συνῶπται μέχρι γε τοῦ νῦν, ἀλλ' ἢ ὅτι λέγεται μόνον ('We have not the evidence of searching observation: (nor indeed any evidence) but hearsay'): *Metaph.* 1038a14: *Pol.* 1257b21. Instances of this use outside Aristotle are few. Cook Wilson, rightly classing Th.v 60.1 under (2), cites doubtfully D.iv 19 (where, however, ἀλλ' ἢ . . . ἔσται must surely be right) and xxxvi 43 (where Reiske's ἀλλ' ἤ gains some support from *A*'s αλλη (*sic*). Add: (*a*) Ar.*Pax* 476 οὐδ' οἴδε γ' εἶλκον οὐδὲν ἀργεῖοι πάλαι ἀλλ' ἢ κατεγέλων τῶν ταλαιπωρουμένων ('they did nothing but laugh'): *Eq.* 1397 τὸν δὲ Παφλαγόνα . . . εἴφ' ὅ τι ποιήσεις κακόν.—Οὐδὲν μέγ' ἀλλ' ἢ τὴν ἐμὴν ἕξει τέχνην ('I won't punish him severely (or indeed at all), except that he'll just have to ply my trade'): Hp.*Loc.Hom.* 13 μὴ ἔγχριε μηδὲν ἀλλ' ἢ κλύσαι κάτω ('Do not rub anything on (or do anything else at all), except give an aperient'). In all such instances I should print a comma before the particles. (*b*) Hp.*deArte* 6 τὸ αὐτόματον οὐ φαίνεται οὐσίην ἔχον οὐδεμίην ἀλλ' ἢ οὔνομα μοῦνον ('but merely': οὐσίην clearly excludes οὔνομα).

Explanation of the combination ἀλλ' ἤ. There are two main views:—(*a*) That ἀλλ', whether it represents ἄλλο (Klotz), or ἀλλά (Hartung), is adverbial, meaning 'except', not conjunctional: and that ἀλλ' ἤ is analogous to *praeterquam*. Neil (on Ar.*Eq.* 780) is inclined to favour this view. Cf. Brugmann, p. 634. (*b*) That ἀλλ' ἤ represents a fusion of constructions, 'but' and 'than'. So Stallbaum, Kühner, and Cook Wilson, who compares μᾶλλον ἢ οὐ. (G.T.A. Krueger's explanation combines (*a*) and (*b*).) The 'fusion' theory is at its most successful in accounting for the passages grouped under (i), ἀλλά being taken as referring to the negative and ἤ to the word of comparison. And Cook Wilson regards (i) as the 'natural origin of the idiom'. On this view, the word of comparison is an integral part of the original construction. But an examination of the instances shows a marked chronological priority in (ii): which suggests that the word of comparison is not integral, but redundant (Brugmann, *loc. cit.*, compares *πρὶν . . . πρὶν ἤ*), and that the frequency with which it is added by Plato is due to the leisurely fullness of his style. Moreover, Bäumlein quotes a number of instances of *οὐδὲν ἄλλο ἤ* and *οὐδὲν ἀλλ' ἤ* between which it is impossible to draw any essential distinction. E.g.: A.*Pers.*209 *ὁ δ' οὐδὲν ἄλλο γ' ἢ πτήξας δέμας παρεῖχε*: Th.iv14.3 *οἱ Λακεδαιμόνιοι . . . ἄλλο οὐδὲν ἢ ἐκ γῆς ἐναυμάχουν*: Pl.*Euthd.*277E *οὐδὲν ἄλλο ἢ χορεύετον περὶ σέ*: *Ap.*20D *δι' οὐδὲν ἀλλ' ἢ διὰ σοφίαν τινά*: *Men.*76B: *Sph.*226A: X.*An.*iii 2.18: D.xiv 12. I therefore believe that Klotz is right in maintaining that *ἀλλ' ἤ* originates in *ἄλλο ἤ*.* There appear to be four stages:—(i) *οὐδὲν ἀλλ' ἤ*, substantival, where we could, and sometimes do, have *ἄλλο ἤ*. (ii) *ἀλλ' ἤ* = 'except', where *ἄλλο*, substantival, would be ungrammatical. (iii) *ἀλλ' ἤ* = 'except that', *ἀλλ' ἤ* having its own clause. (iv) *ἀλλ' ἤ* = 'merely' (an exception to an implied generalization). Cf. *πλήν* S.*OC*1643.

(4) *Ἀλλ' ἦ.* In *ἀλλ' ἦ*, *ἀλλά* puts an objection in interrogative form, giving lively expression to a feeling of surprise or incredulity. 'Why?' See also Neil on Ar.*Eq.*953: Starkie on Ar.*V.*8.

Most commonly, at the opening of an answer-question. A.*Ch.*220 *Ἀλλ' ἦ δόλον τιν', ὦ ξέν', ἀμφί μοι πλέκεις;* S.*El.*879 *Ἀλλ' ἦ μέμηνας . . .;* E.*Heracl.*425 *Ἀλλ' ἦ . . . οὐκ ἐᾷ θεὸς . . .;* Ar.*V.*8 *Ἀλλ' ἦ παραφρονεῖς ἐτεὸν . . .;* A.*Ag.*276 ('Have you dreamed it?' —'No.'—'Well, have you lent an over-credulous ear to rumour?'): E.*Hipp.*932: *Rh.*560 (divided chorus): Ar.*Fr.*125: Pl.*Prt.*309C *Ἀλλ' ἦ σοφῷ τινι . . . ἐντυχὼν πάρει;* *Grg.*447A: *Phdr.*261B: X.*An.*vii 6.4 *Ἀλλ' ἦ δημαγωγεῖ ὁ ἀνὴρ τοὺς ἄνδρας;* *Cyr.*i 4.28 *Ἀλλ' ἦ, φάναι, ἐπελάθου τι ὧν ἐβούλου εἰπεῖν;*

After an exclamation or apostrophe. E.*Alc.* 58 *Πῶς εἶπας; ἀλλ' ἦ καὶ σοφὸς λέληθας ὤν;* *Ph.*1704 *Ὁ ποῖος; ἀλλ' ἦ . . .;* X.*Cyr.*ii 2.28 *Ὦ Σαμβαύλα, ἔφη, ἀλλ' ἦ καὶ σὺ . . .;* S.*Ph.*414: Ar.*Fr.*607 *τί τὸ κακόν; ἀλλ' ἦ . . .;* Less often, later in a speech. E.*Hel.*490 *Διὸς δ' ἔλεξε παῖδά νιν πεφυκέναι. ἀλλ' ἦ τις ἔστι Ζηνὸς ὄνομ' ἔχων ἀνὴρ Νείλου παρ' ὄχθας;* (essentially, though not formally, an opening: 'Why, is there a man called Zeus . . .?'): A.*Supp.*913: E.*Hipp.*858: *Ba.*922: *Rh.*36.

In Ar.*Ach.*424–6 ἀλλ' ἦ follows a rejected suggestion: 'Well'. *Ποίας ποθ ἀνὴρ λακίδας αἰτεῖται πέπλων; ἀλλ' ἦ Φιλοκτήτου τὰ τοῦ πτωχοῦ λέγεις;—Οὐκ . . .—Ἀλλ' ἦ τὰ δυσπινῆ 'θέλεις πεπλώματα . . .;*

It is usually, and rightly, maintained that ἀλλ' ἦ is used only in questions. Kühner (II ii 145) thinks that the particles can also mean '*At profecto*', in a statement: but cites only E.*Alc.*816, which is clearly a question: *Ἀλλ' ἦ πέπονθα δείν' ὑπὸ ξένων ἐμῶν*; Herakles can hardly credit the truth which dawns upon him. Diehl prints *Fragm.Iamb.Adesp.*14 without a question-mark: *ἀλλ' ἦ λύκος τὰς αἶγας ἐκκαλεῖ μολών*: which, in the absence of context, tells us nothing.

Ἀλλ' . . . ἦ, *separatim*, is hardly to be regarded as a distinctive usage. In S.*OC*26 *Ἀλλ' ὅστις ὁ τόπος ἦ μάθω . . .*; ('Well, shall I find out . . . ?'), as Jebb remarks (on *Ph.*414), 'the peculiar force of ἀλλ' ἦ is not present.'

In several passages where the MSS. give ἀλλ' ἦ . . ., ἀλλ' ἦ . . .; appears to be the right reading. See Neil on Ar.*Eq.*953. Ar.*Ach.* 1111–12 (ἀλλ' ἦ Starkie): *Th.*97 (see μέν, I.B.2): *Eq.*953 (third line of speech), 1162: *Lys.*928. In X.*Smp.*1.15 *Τί τοῦτ', ἔφη, ὦ Φίλιππε; ἀλλ' ἢ ὀδύνη σε εἴληφε*; read certainly ἀλλ' ἦ.

(5) *Οὐ μὴν ἀλλά.* The authorities explain οὐ μὴν ἀλλά, οὐ μέντοι ἀλλά and οὐ γὰρ ἀλλά as elliptical idioms, in which a verb from the preceding clause or sentence has to be supplied before the ἀλλά: citing in support of this view X.*Cyr.*i 4.8 *ὁ ἵππος πίπτει εἰς γόνατα, καὶ μικροῦ κἀκεῖνον ἐξετραχήλισεν· οὐ μὴν* (sc. *ἐξετραχήλισεν*) *ἀλλ' ἐπέμεινεν ὁ Κῦρος μόλις πως.* (Hartung ii 48: Bäumlein, p. 156.) But this artificial explanation does not fit other cases. Ellipse of some kind there certainly seems to be, but not, I think, ellipse of any specific idea contained in the preceding words. Rather 'but nothing happens, or happened, or will or shall happen other than . . .'. In any case, the meaning of οὐ μὴν ἀλλά is clear enough. It normally denotes that what is being said cannot be gainsaid, however strong the arguments to the contrary: marking, in fact, the deliberate surmounting of an obstacle recognized as considerable.

The combination first occurs, in the split form οὐ μὴν . . . ἀλλά, in E.*IT*630: 'Your sister cannot bury you. *οὐ μήν, ἐπειδὴ τυγ-*

χάνεις Ἀργεῖος ὤν, ἀλλ' ὧν γε δυνατὸν οὐδ' ἐγὼ λείψω χάριν'. I know no other example of the split form, though Hartung says it occurs 'bisweilen'. The authorities note that οὐ μὴν ἀλλά is confined to Attic Greek. (But see Hp.*Art.*7, below.) They do not go on to observe that its distribution over Attic Greek is extremely uneven. It is never found (except for the solitary instance of οὐ μὴν . . . ἀλλά) in verse. I know of but one example in Xenophon: of but one in any orator other than Isocrates and Demosthenes (Lyc.124): and of none in Thucydides. There are some ten in Plato (according to R. W. Chapman's statistics: eight are in late works, *Politicus* and *Laws*), more in Aristotle, over twenty in Demosthenes, and about thirty-six in Isocrates. The last two writers, particularly Demosthenes, use οὐ μὴν ἀλλά with great variety and flexibility. οὐ μὴν ἀλλὰ . . . γε is relatively common in Plato and Isocrates: in Demosthenes, only [xxvi]20, and inferior MSS. in [x]28 (not counting ἔγωγε).

(i) General adversative use. Pl.*Lg.*722A ταὐτὸν τοῦτ' ἂν αἱροίμην. οὐ μὴν ἀλλά που καὶ Κλεινίᾳ τῷδ' ἀρέσκειν δεῖ τὰ νῦν νομοθετούμενα: Isoc.xii 75 διὸ δέδοικα μὴ . . . οὐ μὴν ἀλλ' αἱροῦμαι βοηθῆσαι: D.i 4 'Philip's power is formidable. οὐ μὴν ἀλλ' ἐπιεικῶς . . . τοῦθ' ὃ δυσμαχώτατόν ἐστι τῶν Φιλίππου πραγμάτων καὶ βέλτιστον ὑμῖν': v 3 συμβαίνει . . . τὰ δὲ πράγματα . . . ἐκφεύγειν ὑμᾶς. οὐ μὴν ἀλλὰ καίπερ τούτων οὕτως ἐχόντων . . .: Pl.*Plt.*263B, 302B: *Lg.*739A,770B,867A,876D: *Amat.*133A: Isoc. xii 113: D.ii 22: iv 38: xxiii 101.

Answering μέν. Pl.*Grg.*453B σαφῶς μὲν . . . οὐκ οἶδα, οὐ μὴν ἀλλ' ὑποπτεύω γε: *Lg.*636E λέγεται μὲν ταῦτα . . . καλῶς πως· οὐ μὴν ἀλλ' ἀφασία γ' ἡμᾶς λαμβάνει: D.xiv 33 ἔστι μὲν χαλεπὸς πρὸς ὑμᾶς ὁ περὶ τούτων λόγος . . . οὐ μὴν ἀλλὰ δεῖ . . .: xix 201 ἔστι μὲν ἐγγυτάτω μανίας, οὐ μὴν ἀλλ' ἴσως τῷ μηδὲν ἔχοντι δίκαιον ἄλλ' εἰπεῖν ἀνάγκη πάντα μηχανᾶσθαι: Pl.*Grg.*449B: Isoc.iii 10: xii 201: xv 198.

(ii) In Demosthenes and Aristotle οὐ μὴν ἀλλά sometimes introduces a supplementary argument which takes such marked precedence over the previous argument that it is represented as contrasted with it, rather than as reinforcing it.

D.viii 8 ὅτι μὲν δήπουθεν οὔθ' ὅσι' οὔτ' ἀνεκτὰ λέγουσιν . . . δῆλόν ἐστιν ἅπασιν, οὐ μὴν ἀλλ' ἐναντία συμβαίνει ταῖς κατηγορίαις ἃς Διοπείθους κατηγοροῦσι: xxxiv 4 οἱ μὲν οὖν νόμοι . . .

οὐχ οὕτως λέγουσιν . . . οὐ μὴν ἀλλ' ἔγωγε ἐλπίζω καὶ ἐξ αὐτοῦ τοῦ πράγματος δείξειν ('But I think that I shall prove, on the evidence of the bare facts'): xxxvii 23 μεμαρτύρηται μὲν δὴ . . . ὡς ἀπεδήμουν . . . οὐ μὴν ἀλλὰ καὶ ἐκ τοῦ ἐγκλήματος τούτου δῆλόν ἐστιν: xxxviii 11: lvii 46: Arist.*Pol.*1262a14, 1264a11 (where Newman is puzzled), 1276b36. Cf. Isoc.ix 33.

(iii) Sometimes the argument thus stressed represents the speaker's second line of defence, or reserve position. It is then followed by a conditional protasis, in which the speaker affirms (or denies), for the sake of argument, something which he has just denied (or affirmed), the apodosis showing that the position is still impregnable.

D.xv.28 δίκαιον μὲν εἶναι νομίζω κατάγειν τὸν 'Ροδίων δῆμον· οὐ μὴν ἀλλὰ καὶ εἰ μὴ δίκαιον ἦν . . προσήκειν οἶμαι παραινεῖν κατάγειν: xxii 37 ὡς δ' οὐδ' ἔστιν ἁπάσης τὸ πρᾶγμα τῆς βουλῆς, ἀλλὰ τινῶν, . . . ἔχω λέγειν . . . οὐ μὴν ἀλλ' εἰ καὶ τὰ μάλιστα πάσης ἔσθ' ἀγὼν τῆς βουλῆς, ὅσῳ συμφέρει μᾶλλον ὑμῖν καταγνοῦσιν ἢ μὴ θεάσασθε: xxii 6: xli 15, 26. Cf. Isoc.viii 137 (where ὁπότερον ἂν ποιήσωσιν means 'if they do either of these things'): xiv 12: Arist.*Pol.*1270a37.

Conversely, in the following, οὐ μὴν ἀλλά marks the first line of defence. D.xix 135 'They say that to condemn the ambassadors will be an ἀρχὴ πρὸς Φίλιππον ἔχθρας. This, if true, is the strongest possible condemnation of Aeschines. οὐ μὴν ἀλλ' ὅτι καὶ φιλίας ἀρχὴ . . . γενήσεται, καὶ τοῦτ' οἴομαι δείξειν.' The reality of the supposed state of affairs being disproved, its moral implications, if it *were* real, do not come into question. ἀλλὰ γάρ would perhaps have been more regular here.

οὐ μὴν ἀλλά is curiously combined with ἀλλὰ . . . γάρ in Hp. *Art.*7, if the text is sound: οὐ μὴν ἀλλ' ἐμβάλλειν γάρ μοι δοκέει καὶ οὕτω πεπαλαιωμένον ἔκπτωμα τοῦ βραχίονος.

(6) *Οὐ μέντοι ἀλλά.* This combination, much rarer than οὐ μὴν ἀλλά, is identical with it in sense. Th.v 43.2 ᾧ ἐδόκει μὲν καὶ ἄμεινον εἶναι πρὸς τοὺς Ἀργείους μᾶλλον χωρεῖν, οὐ μέντοι ἀλλὰ καὶ φρονήματι φιλονικῶν ἠναντιοῦτο ('but nevertheless his opposition was also due to personal pride and ambition'): Pl.*Cra.*436D μέγιστον δέ σοι ἔστω τεκμήριον ὅτι οὐκ ἔσφαλται τῆς ἀληθείας ὁ τιθέμενος

(τὰ ὀνόματα)· οὐ γὰρ ἄν ποτε οὕτω σύμφωνα ἦν αὐτῷ ἅπαντα ... —'That is an unsound argument. *συμφωνία* proves nothing. οὐ μέντοι ἀλλὰ θαυμάζοιμ' ἂν εἰ καὶ τὰ ὀνόματα συμφωνεῖ αὐτὰ αὑτοῖς' ('But there *is* no *συμφωνία*: therefore conclusions drawn from it do not come into question'. Cf. οὐ μὴν ἀλλά, D.xix 135, above): *Phd.*62B,*bis*: *Smp.*173B,199A.

οὐ μέντοι ... ἀλλά. Pl.*Men.*86C Βούλει ... ἐπιχειρήσωμεν κοινῇ ζητεῖν τί ποτ' ἐστὶν ἀρετή;—Πάνυ μὲν οὖν. οὐ μέντοι, ὦ Σώκρατες, ἀλλ' ἔγωγε ἐκεῖνο ἂν ἥδιστα ... καὶ σκεψαίμην καὶ ἀκούσαιμι, πότερον ὡς διδακτῷ ὄντι αὐτῷ δεῖ ἐπιχειρεῖν. (See, however, *μέντοι*, II.2.iii.)

(7) *Οὐ γὰρ ἀλλά.* This combination is confined to the Iambographers, Old Comedy, Euripides and Plato (οὐ γάρ τοι ἀλλά). (See Neil on Ar.*Eq.*1205. His explanation, that οὐ γάρ means 'Oh, no, no', does not meet the facts.) 'For really'. Hippon. *Fr.*1.1 ἀκούσατ' Ἱππώνακτος· οὐ γὰρ ἀλλ' ἥκω: Phoenix*Fr.*3.15 οὐ γὰρ ἀλλὰ κηρύσσω (ἄλια Wil.): Ar.*Nu.*232 οὐ γὰρ ἀλλ' ἡ γῆ βίᾳ ἕλκει πρὸς αὑτὴν τὴν ἰκμάδα τῆς φροντίδος: *Ra.*58 Μὴ σκῶπτέ μ', ὦδέλφ'· οὐ γὰρ ἀλλ' ἔχω κακῶς ('I really *am* in a bad way'): 498 οὐ γὰρ ἀλλὰ πειστέον ('It's no good, I *must* give in'): Ar.*Eq.*1205: *Ec.*386: Eup.*Fr.*73 (ἀλλά Bentley: ἄλλο *codd.*): E.*Ba.*785 οὐ γὰρ ἀλλ' ὑπερβάλλει τάδε ('this really is beyond everything'): *IT*1005: *Supp.*570. οὐ γὰρ ... ἀλλά. Ar.*Ra.*1180 οὐ γάρ μοὔστιν ἀλλ' ἀκουστέα. Pl.*Euthd.*286B οὐ γάρ τοι ἀλλά (305E).

In Ar.*Ra.*192 it is perhaps best to take οὐ γάρ by itself (cf. *γάρ*, VIII.2), and punctuate before ἀλλά: Δοῦλον οὐκ ἄγω, εἰ μὴ νεναυμάχηκε τὴν περὶ τῶν κρεῶν.—Μὰ τὸν Δί' οὐ γάρ, ἀλλ' ἔτυχον ὀφθαλμιῶν ('No, not I: I happened to have ophthalmia'). I should take Pl.*R.*492E similarly: Οἶμαι μὲν οὐδένα, ἦ δ' ὅς.—Οὐ γάρ, ἦν δ' ἐγώ, ἀλλὰ καὶ τὸ ἐπιχειρεῖν πολλὴ ἄνοια. So, clearly, *R.*495A, *Phd.*84A, both rightly punctuated by Burnet. Cf. also Ar.*Lys.*55 (*γάρ*, VIII.2). Arist.*MM* 1209a15 should probably also be similarly punctuated: ἀλλ' οὐκ ἔσται γε κατὰ τὸ φιλητὸν ἡ τοιαύτη φιλία. φιλητὸν γὰρ ἦν τἀγαθόν, ὁ δὲ φαῦλος οὐ φιλητός. οὐ γάρ, ἀλλὰ κατὰ τὸ φιλητέον. The passage is virtually a dialogue, as the use of μὲν οὖν indicates. The proposition ὁ σπουδαῖος τῷ φαύλῳ οὐκ ἔσται φίλος is met by the objection ἔσται μὲν οὖν κ.τ.λ. The counter-objection, ἀλλ' οὐκ ἔσται κ.τ.λ., is met by the rejoinder οὐ γάρ, ἀλλὰ κ.τ.λ.: 'No, but it *will* exist on the basis of τὸ φιλητέον'

Ἄρα

The form ἄρ is often used in Epic before consonants: the enclitic ῥά, usually following a monosyllable (ἦ, ὅς, γάρ, etc.), sometimes also after a disyllable ending in a vowel or diphthong (e.g. ἐπεί), is found in Epic and also in lyric poets and the lyrics of tragedy. The particle is perhaps connected with Lithuanian *ir̃*, 'and'.

According to the most widely-held view, ἄρα denotes connexion (consequence or mere succession). Thus Kühner: 'Es dient zunächst zur Anreihung, und zwar zur Anreihung von Begriffen, die miteinander in einem gewissen natürlichen Zusammenhange stehen.' Hartung arrives at the quite different conclusion that the root-meaning is 'quickness', and hence 'surprise' (deriving the particle from the same root as ἁρπάζω, an impossible etymology). Neither side has much difficulty in collecting evidence to confound the other. It is, for example, as natural for a cook to cut up meat, or for a host to shake hands with his guest, as it is unnatural for waters to part asunder in the midst, or for a man to enter into conversation with a fish. But Hartung's definition seems to widen as he expounds it. After giving examples of Homeric usage, he sums up (i 430) by saying that ἄρα is used 'bei allen Handlungen und Vorgängen, welche stärker oder schwächer das Gemuth aufregen', and that it marks the impression made by anything 'neu und interessant'. It stands, in fact, for something like 'Siehe!', though it is a word to be felt rather than translated. Whatever one may think of Hartung's etymology, his interpretation, in its wider form, seems to me the only one which will account for the wealth and variety of the Homeric use. The examples given below will show that the idea of 'connexion' is often inappropriate, except in so far as some kind of connexion must be present in all speech or action. Moreover, *ἄρα* is one of the commonest of all Homeric particles (*β*413–17 and *τ*435–66 are instances of the almost reckless profusion with which it is used). And it is surely improbable that in Homer, where logical relationships are, broadly speaking, seldom emphasized or very precisely defined, the idea of connexion should thus be obtruded at every turn. On the other hand, if *ἄρα* betokens 'interest', its frequency, even in the most apparently commonplace scenes, is not surprising. For Homer, as for a child, the most ordinary things in daily life are profoundly interesting.

Here, as always, it is safer to guide our steps by the clearer light of usage than by the will-o'-the-wisp of etymology, and to accept Hartung's explanation, while admitting that the freshness of *ἄρα*, in Epic, may be to some extent staled by constant repetition, so that it sinks almost to the level of a mere Epic formula, like the 'all' of our own ballads.

I. Primary use, expressing a lively feeling of interest: in subordinate as well as in main clauses. This is extremely common in Epic, and occurs also in Lyric, *δ' ἄρα* being particularly frequent in narrative. It continues to be found fairly often in Herodotus, and in the not wholly Attic Xenophon. In purely Attic writers, prose and verse, it is but occasionally met with, having a precarious footing in tragedy (mainly in lyrics), comedy, and Plato. Its character is quite foreign to the more formal style of Thucydides and the orators.[1]

Epic. Hom.*A*46 *ἔκλαγξαν δ' ἄρ' ὀϊστοί*: *B*59 *θεῖός μοι ἐνύπνιον ἦλθεν Ὄνειρος . . . στῆ δ' ἄρ' ὑπὲρ κεφαλῆς*: 103 *αὐτὰρ ἄρα Ζεὺς δῶκε διακτόρῳ ἀργεϊφόντῃ*: 309–10 *δράκων . . . τόν ῥ' αὐτὸς Ὀλύμπιος ἧκε φόωσδε, βωμοῦ ὑπαΐξας πρός ῥα πλατάνιστον ὄρουσεν*: 620 *τῶν μὲν ἄρ' Ἀμφίμαχος καὶ Θάλπιος ἡγησάσθην*: *E*582 *βάλε . . . χερμαδίῳ . . . ἐκ δ' ἄρα χειρῶν ἡνία λεύκ' ἐλέφαντι χαμαὶ πέσον*: 587 *τύχε γάρ ῥ' ἀμάθοιο βαθείης*: *Z*418 *οὐδέ μιν ἐξενάριξε . . . ἀλλ' ἄρα μιν κατέκηε*: *H*472 *ἔνθεν ἄρ' οἰνίζοντο κάρη κομόωντες Ἀχαιοί*: *Θ*386 *πέπλον . . . ὅν ῥ' αὐτὴ*

[1] Hartung (i 432–3) is surely wrong in drawing the line between Epic and Lyric on the one hand, and Herodotus and Attic (including Xenophon) on the other.

ποιήσατο: Μ406 στυφέλιξε δέ μιν μεμαῶτα. χώρησεν δ' ἄρα τυτθὸν ἐπάλξιος: Ν672 ὦκα δὲ θυμὸς ᾤχετ' ἀπὸ μελέων, στυγερὸς δ' ἄρα μιν σκότος εἷλεν: Φ382 ἄψορρον δ' ἄρα κῦμα κατέσσυτο: 495 φύγεν ὥς τε πέλεια, ἥ ῥα ... εἰσέπτατο πέτρην: Ω96 βῆ δ' ἰέναι ... ἀμφὶ δ' ἄρα σφι λιάζετο κῦμα θαλάσσης: η301 'My daughter should have escorted you. σὺ δ' ἄρα πρώτην ἱκέτευσας': θ326 ἄσβεστος δ' ἄρ' ἐνῶρτο γέλως μακάρεσσι θεοῖσι: τ184 ὁπλότερος γενεῇ· ὁ δ' ἄρα πρότερος καὶ ἀρείων: ω234 τὸν δ' ὡς οὖν ἐνόησε ... στὰς ἄρ' ὑπὸ βλωθρὴν ὄγχνην κατὰ δάκρυον εἶβε: Hes.*Th.*867 ἐτήκετο, κασσίτερος ὡς ... ὣς ἄρα τήκετο γαῖα: *Sc.*46 παννύχιος δ' ἄρ' ἔλεκτο: Hom.Β16,522,572,642: Δ520: Η267: Λ464: Μ28: η100: μ413: ν33: Hes.*Th.*689, 848. Lyric. Sapph.*Fr.*136 κῆνοι δ' ἄρα πάντες καρχήσιά τ' ἦχον κἄλειβον: Pi.*O.*10.52 ταύτᾳ δ' ... παρέσταν μὲν ἄρα Μοῖραι σχεδόν: *P.*4.121 ἐκ δ' ἄρ' αὐτοῦ πομφόλυξαν δάκρυα: *N.*10. 69 ἐφορμαθεὶς δ' ἄρ' ἄκοντι θοῷ ἤλασε: *I.*6.49 ταῦτ' ἄρα οἱ φαμένῳ πέμψεν θεὸς ... μέγαν αἰετόν: Mimn.*Fr.*13.5: Stesich.*Fr.*5.2: 15.2: Ibyc.*Fr.*3.41: Phoc.*Fr.*17.3: Thgn.599: Simon.*Fr.*67.1: Pi.*O.*6.52: 10.43: *P.*3.27,57: 4.156: *N.*1.48. Prose. Hdt.i 111 τῷ δ' ἄρα καὶ αὐτῷ ἡ γυνὴ ἐπίτεξ ἐοῦσα ... τίκτει: 141 ἰδόντα δὲ παλλομένους εἰπεῖν ἄρα αὐτὸν πρὸς τοὺς ἰχθῦς: ii 58 πανηγύριας δὲ ἄρα ... πρῶτοι ἀνθρώπων Αἰγύπτιοί εἰσι οἱ ποιησάμενοι: 141 ὀλοφυρόμενον δ' ἄρα μιν ἐπελθεῖν ὕπνον: iii 34 πρότερον γὰρ δὴ ἄρα ... εἴρετο ὁ Καμβύσης: iv 45 πρότερον δὲ ἦν ἄρα ἀνώνυμος: 134 πυθόμενος δὲ ... εἶπε ἄρα: 189 τὴν δὲ ἄρα ἐσθῆτα ... ἐκ τῶν Λιβυσσέων ἐποιήσαντο οἱ Ἕλληνες: v 87.2 ἀπολέσθαι τρόπῳ τοιῷδε· κομισθεὶς ἄρα ἐς τὰς Ἀθήνας ...: ix 9.2 ἀκούσας δὲ ὁ Χίλεος ἔλεγε ἄρα σφι τάδε (ὡς δ' ἄρα is common in Herodotus: i 24,27,86: ii 140: iii 134: *id.saep.*: i 112 ὡς δὲ οὐκ ἔπειθε ἄρα τὸν ἄνδρα): Hp.*Fract.*6 ᾗπερ καὶ ἡ ἐπίδεσις ἐχάλα ἄρα μᾶλλον ἢ ἐπίεζεν (ἐχαλάρα *codd.*): X.*HG*iv 2.22 λέγεται ἄρα τις ἀναβοῆσαι: *An.*iv 6.15 ὅπως δὲ ὡς κράτιστα κλέπτητε ... νόμιμον ἄρα ὑμῖν ἐστιν ... μαστιγοῦσθαι (ἄρα *det.*: μὲν γάρ *CBE*: γάρ *A*): *Cyr.*i 3.2 ἀπεκρίνατο ἄρα ὁ Κῦρος: 3.8 ὁ δὲ Σάκας ἄρα καλός τε ὢν ἐτύγχανε: 3.9 οἱ δ' ἄρα τῶν βασιλέων οἰνοχόοι, ἐπειδὰν διδῶσι τὴν φιάλην ... καταρροφοῦσι: 4.10 ὁ δ' Ἀστυάγης ἄρα εἶπεν: iv 6.4 καὶ τότε μὲν δὴ ἀνιαθεὶς ἄρ' οὗτος κατέσχεν ὑπὸ σκότου τὸν φθόνον: vii 3.6 ταῦτα ἀκούσας ὁ Κῦρος ἐπαίσατο ἄρα τὸν μηρόν: viii 3.25 Σακῶν δὲ ... ἀπέλιπεν ἄρα τῷ ἵππῳ τοὺς ἄλλους ἵππους:

4.7 ἐπεὶ ἐδεδειπνήκεσαν . . . εἶπεν ἄρα ὁ Γωβρύας: *Oec.*12.20 ὅτε βασιλεὺς ἄρα ἵππου ἐπιτυχὼν ἀγαθοῦ . . . ἤρετο: 18.9 καὶ πάλαι ἐννοῶ ἄρα εἰ λέληθα (εἰ ἄρα Cobet): *Ap.*27 ὡς δὲ ᾔσθετο ἄρα . . .: 28 παρὼν δέ τις Ἀπολλόδωρος . . . εἶπεν ἄρα: *Ages.*7.5 οὐκ ἐφησθεὶς φανερὸς ἐγένετο, ἀλλ' εἶπεν ἄρα.

Attic (excluding Xenophon). A.*Pers.*568 τοὶ δ' ἄρα πρωτόμοιροι, φεῦ, ληφθέντες πρὸς ἀνάγκας, ἠέ, ἀκτὰς ἀμφὶ Κυχρείας, ὀᾶ, ἔρρουσι: E.*IT*1222 Τούσδ' ἄρ' ἐκβαίνοντας ἤδη δωμάτων ὁρῶ ξένους (very odd, and suspected by Kirchhoff and Paley): *Ba.*166 ἡδομένα δ' ἄρα . . . κῶλον ἄγει ταχύπουν σκιρτήμασι βάκχα: *IA*1103 μνήμην δ' ἄρ' εἶχον πλησίον βεβηκότος Ἀγαμέμνονος τοῦδ': *Rh.* 823 μετὰ σέ, ναί, μετὰ σὲ . . . τότ' ἄρ' ἔμολον: Ar.*Nu.*410 κᾆτ' οὐκ ἔσχων ἀμελήσας (the haggis)· ἡ δ' ἄρ' ἐφυσᾶτ': *Av.*495 κἄρτι καθηῦδον, καὶ πρὶν δειπνεῖν τοὺς ἄλλους οὗτος ἄρ' ᾖσεν: Pl.*Grg.*524B ἐπειδὰν δὲ διαλυθῆτον ἄρα ἀπ' ἀλλήλοιν: *Cra.*412C ἐπειδὴ γὰρ πορεύεται τὰ ὄντα, ἔνι μὲν ἄρ' αὐτοῖς τάχος, ἔνι δὲ βραδύτης: *Tht.*156E ἐπειδὰν . . . , ὁ μὲν ὀφθαλμὸς ἄρα ὄψεως ἔμπλεως ἐγένετο: 200E Ὁ τὸν ποταμὸν καθηγούμενος . . . ἔφη ἄρα δείξειν αὐτό: *R.*598E ἀνάγκη γὰρ τὸν ἀγαθὸν ποιητήν, εἰ μέλλει περὶ ὧν ἂν ποιῇ καλῶς ποιήσειν, εἰδότα ἄρα ποιεῖν: *Lg.* 894E ἀλλ' ὅταν ἄρα αὐτὸ αὐτὸ κινῆσαν ἕτερον ἀλλοιώσῃ . . .: 943E μὴ διαμαρτών τις ἄρα τῶν ἀναγκαίων ἀποβολῶν . . . ἀναξίῳ ἀναξίας ἐπάγῃ δίκας: Ant.vi 35 καὶ αὐτοῖς ἐκ μὲν τῶν πεπραγμένων οὐδεμία ἦν ἐλπὶς ἀποφεύξεσθαι—τοιαῦτα ἄρ' ἦν τὰ ἠδικημένα—: Pl.*Tht.* 199B: Lys.iii 30.

This is not a long list of Attic examples, and it might be further reduced by assigning some of the passages quoted to the more limited uses which we must now discuss. In this, the predominant Attic usage (but already present, in most of its varieties, in Homer), ἄρα denotes, not interest in general, but in particular the interest or surprise occasioned by enlightenment or disillusionment.

II. ἄρα expressing the surprise attendant upon disillusionment.

(1) Verb in the present. The reality of an event is presented as apprehended at some moment during its occurrence. S.*Tr.*61 κἀξ ἀγεννήτων ἄρα μῦθοι καλῶς πίπτουσιν: *OC*534 Σαί τ' εἴσ' ἄρ' ἀπόγονοί τε καὶ . . .: E.*Hel.*793 Πάντ' οἶσθ' ἄρ', ὡς ἔοικας: Ar.*V.*10 Τὸν αὐτὸν ἄρ' ἐμοὶ βουκολεῖς Σαβάζιον: S.*El.*1454:

*Ph.*1101: E.*El.*965: Pl.*Prt.*325C ταῦτα δ' ἄρα οὐ διδάσκονται . . . ; *Clit.*408B εἰ δὲ . . . , δούλῳ ἄμεινον ἢ ἐλευθέρῳ διάγειν τῷ τοιούτῳ τὸν βίον ἐστὶν ἄρα: *R.*438A πάντες γὰρ ἄρα τῶν ἀγαθῶν ἐπιθυμοῦσιν: *Ap.*26C καὶ αὐτὸς ἄρα νομίζω εἶναι θεούς: *Grg.*493B τὸ δὲ κόσκινον ἄρα λέγει . . . τὴν ψυχὴν εἶναι: Hdt.iv 205: vii 35.2: Lys.xii 36.

(2) Verb in the past. The reality of a past event is presented as apprehended either during its occurrence (as in (1) above): or at the moment of speaking or writing: or at some intermediate moment ('as it subsequently transpired'). Hom.*Λ*604 κακοῦ δ' ἄρα οἱ πέλεν ἀρχή: ψ29 Τηλέμαχος δ' ἄρα μιν πάλαι ᾔδεεν ἔνδον ἐόντα: S.*Aj.*1026 κνώδοντος . . . ὑφ' οὗ φονέως ἄρ' ἐξέπνευσας: *Tr.*962 ἀγχοῦ δ' ἄρα κοὐ μακρὰν προύκλαιον: E.*Andr.*274 Ἦ μεγάλων ἀχέων ἄρ' ὑπῆρξεν, ὅτ' . . . : *HF*339 μάτην ἄρ' ὁμόγαμόν σ' ἐκτησάμην: Ar.*Av.*513 ὁ δ' ἄρ' εἱστήκει τὸν Λυσικράτη τηρῶν: Hom. Ξ85: Φ604: Pi.*N.*8.32: A.*Pers.*472,934: S.*El.*935: *Ant.*1178, 1273: Hdt.vi 62.1 τὸν δὲ Ἀρίστωνα ἔκνιζε ἄρα τῆς γυναικὸς ταύτης ἔρως: viii 8.1 ἐν νόῳ μὲν εἶχε ἄρα καὶ πρότερον αὐτομολήσειν: Pl.*Tht.*161C ἡμεῖς μὲν αὐτὸν ὥσπερ θεὸν ἐθαυμάζομεν ἐπὶ σοφίᾳ, ὁ δ' ἄρα ἐτύγχανεν ὢν εἰς φρόνησιν οὐδὲν βελτίων βατράχου γυρίνου: *Prt.*315C ἐπεδήμει γὰρ ἄρα καὶ Πρόδικος: D.xxxv 8 πλεῖστον δ' ἄρα ἦν ἐψευσμένος: Hdt.iii 64,70: vii 130.2(*bis*): Th.vi 76.4: Pl.*Men.*91E: Lys.viii 12.

Two idiomatic usages deserve special notice:—

(i) With μέλλειν and similar expressions, denoting that the predestination of an event is realised *ex post facto*. Hom.*M*113 οὐδ' ἄρ' ἔμελλε . . . ἂψ ἀπονοστήσειν: δ107 τῷ δ' ἄρ' ἔμελλεν . . . ἔσεσθαι: E674 οὐδ' ἄρ' Ὀδυσσῆϊ . . . μόρσιμον ἦεν: O274 οὐδ' ἄρα . . . κιχήμεναι αἴσιμον ἦεν: S.*Aj.*926 ἔμελλες, τάλας, ἔμελλες χρόνῳ στερεόφρων ἄρ' ἐξανύσσειν: *Ph.*1083 ὥς σ' οὐκ ἔμελλον ἄρ', ὦ τάλας, λείψειν οὐδέποτ': Ar.*Ach.*347 Ἐμέλλετ' ἄρα πάντως ἀνήσειν τῆς βοῆς: *Ra.*269 ἔμελλον ἄρα παύσειν ποθ' ὑμᾶς: *Eq.*138 Τὸν προβατοπώλην ἦν ἄρ' ἀπολέσθαι χρεὼν. . . ;

(ii) With the imperfect, especially of εἰμί, denoting that something which has been, and still is, has only just been realized. In such cases Greek tends to stress the past, English the present, existence of the fact. Hom.*I*316 ἐπεὶ οὐκ ἄρα τις χάρις ἦεν μάρνασθαι δηΐοισιν ἐπ' ἀνδράσι νωλεμὲς αἰεί: Π60 οὐδ' ἄρα πως ἦν ἀσπερχὲς κεχολῶσθαι: Ρ142 Ἕκτορ, εἶδος ἄριστε, μάχης ἄρα πολλὸν ἐδεύεο: Thgn. 788 οὕτως οὐδὲν ἄρ' ἦν φίλτερον ἄλλο πάτρης: A.*Ag*.542 Τερπνῆς ἄρ' ἦτε τῆσδ' ἐπήβολοι νόσου: S.*OC* 1697 Πόθος τοι καὶ κακῶν ἄρ' ἦν τις: E.*IT*369 Ἅιδης Ἀχιλλεὺς ἦν ἄρ', οὐχ ὁ Πηλέως: *Hipp*.359 Κύπρις οὐκ ἄρ' ἦν θεός: *IA*1330 ἦ πολύμοχθον ἄρ' ἦν γένος . . . ἀμερίων: Ar.*Eq*.1170 Ὡς μέγαν ἄρ' εἶχες ὦ πότνια τὸν δάκτυλον: *Nu*.1271 Κακῶς ἄρ' ὄντως εἶχες, ὥς γ' ἐμοὶ δοκεῖς: *Av*.19 τὼ δ' οὐκ ἄρ' ἤστην οὐδὲν ἄλλο πλὴν δάκνειν: E.*Andr*.418: *Hel*.616: *Or*.1667: *Tr*.412,1161,1240: Ar.*Eq*. 384,386: *V*.314,451,821: *Pax*676: Hdt.iv64 'They use human skin for making cloaks and quiver-cases. δέρμα δὲ ἀνθρώπου καὶ παχὺ καὶ λαμπρὸν ἦν ἄρα': Pl.*Smp*.198D τὸ δ' ἄρα, ὡς ἔοικεν, οὐ τοῦτο ἦν τὸ καλῶς ἐπαινεῖν ὁτιοῦν: *Phd*.68B ἱκανόν σοι τεκμήριον . . . ὅτι οὐκ ἄρ' ἦν φιλόσοφος: *Ti*.51C τὸ δ' οὐδὲν ἄρ' ἦν πλὴν λόγος: D.lv1 οὐκ ἦν ἄρα . . . χαλεπώτερον οὐδὲν ἢ γείτονος πονηροῦ καὶ πλεονέκτου τυχεῖν (a characteristically naïve opening to a naïve little speech): Hdt.iii65: Th.i69.5. With variation of tense. Hes.*Op*.11 οὐκ ἄρα μοῦνον ἔην Ἐρίδων γένος, ἀλλ' ἐπὶ γαῖαν εἰσὶ δύω: Timocr.*Fr*.3.1 οὐκ ἄρα Τιμοκρέων μοῦνος Μήδοισιν ὁρκιατόμει· ἀλλ' ἐντὶ κἄλλοι δὴ πονηροί.

(3) Verb in the future (mostly in questions). S.*OT*1444 Οὕτως ἄρ' ἀνδρὸς ἀθλίου πεύσεσθ' ὕπερ; Ar.*Nu*.465 Ἆρά γε τοῦτ' ἄρ' ἐγώ ποτ' ὄψομαι; E.*Ph*.1658: *Or*.794,1525: *IA*676, 1360: Pl.*Grg*.515B ἢ ἄλλου του ἄρα ἐπιμελήσῃ . . .; *Ap*.34C ἐγὼ δὲ οὐδὲν ἄρα τούτων ποιήσω: 37D ἄλλοι δὲ ἄρα αὐτὰς οἴσουσι ῥᾳδίως; *Phd*.68A φρονήσεως δὲ ἄρα τις τῷ ὄντι ἐρῶν . . . ἀγανακτήσει . . .; Th.i121.5: Lys.x22. ἄρα repeated, with variation of tense. Pl.*Cri*.50E ἢ πρὸς μὲν ἄρα σοι τὸν πατέρα οὐκ ἐξ ἴσου ἦν . . . πρὸς δὲ τὴν πατρίδα ἄρα . . . ἐξέσται σοι . . .;

ταῦτ' ἄρα is common in Aristophanes. 'I see: that's why . . .'. *Ach*.90 Ταῦτ' ἄρ' ἐφενάκιζες σὺ δύο δραχμὰς φέρων: *Eq*.125: *Nu*.319,335,353,394: *Pax* 414,617: Hdt.vii130.2.

III. The following varieties of the secondary use are prominent:

(1) εἰ ἄρα, ἐὰν ἄρα. ἄρα in a conditional protasis denotes that the hypothesis is one of which the possibility has only just been realized: 'If, after all'. This usage occurs sometimes in

comedy, but is almost confined to prose, where it is common in all styles. (In Thucydides it predominates strongly over other uses.) Ar.*Av.*601 πλὴν εἴ τις ἄρ' ὄρνις: *Th.*532 πλὴν ἄρ' εἰ γυναῖκες: *Ra.*74 εἰ καὶ τοῦτ' ἄρα: Hdt.ii 28 εἰ ἄρα ταῦτα γινόμενα ἔλεγε: iii 45 ἢν ἄρα προδιδῶσι οὗτοι: Th.i 27 2 εἰ ἄρα κωλύοιντο ὑπὸ Κερκυραίων πλεῖν: 93.7 ἢν ἄρα ποτὲ κατὰ γῆν βιασθῶσι: Pl.*La.*187E ἐὰν ἄρα καὶ περὶ ἄλλου του πρότερον ἄρξηται διαλέγεσθαι: Isoc.vi 72 ἂν δ' ἄρα ψευσθῶμεν: D.iii 26 τὴν Ἀριστείδου . . . οἰκίαν, εἴ τις ἄρ' οἶδεν ὑμῶν ὁποία ποτ' ἐστίν: xiv 5 εἰ ἄρ' ἐγχειρεῖν ἔγνωκε τοῖς Ἕλλησι: Hdt.iv 32: ix 90.2: Th.i 70.7: 84.2: Pl.*Ap.*17B: *Phdr.*233C,238D,243A,255A: *Lg.* 626B: Ant.vi 1: And.iii 15: Lys.iii 40. (Obviously different are passages in which εἰ and ἄρα are not connected in thought. Hom.*Γ*374 εἰ μὴ ἄρ' ὀξὺ νόησε (*id. saep.*): Simon. *Fr.*62.) Aristotle occasionally uses εἰ ἄρα elliptically, 'if anything', 'if at all' (cf. εἰ δ' οὖν, εἴπερ). *Cat.*5b10 τῶν δὲ ἄλλων οὐδὲν καθ' αὑτό, ἀλλ', εἰ ἄρα, κατὰ συμβεβηκός: *Top.*106b7 ἐν φωνῇ δ' οὐδέν, ἤ, εἰ ἄρα, τὸ σομφόν: D.xxi 138 εἰ δ' ἄρα.

(2) In reported speech, and after verbs of thinking and seeming, ἄρα denotes the apprehension of an idea not before envisaged. Usually ἄρα conveys either, at the most, actual scepticism, or, at the least, the disclaiming of responsibility for the accuracy of the statement. But sometimes the context implies acceptance of the idea, and ἄρα merely denotes that its truth has not before been realized.

Hdt.viii 135.1 θῶμά μοι μέγιστον γενέσθαι λέγεται ὑπὸ Θηβαίων, ἐλθεῖν ἄρα . . .: Pl.*Grg.*524D ταὐτὸν δή μοι δοκεῖ τοῦτ' ἄρα και περὶ τὴν ψυχὴν εἶναι: *Smp.*198C καὶ ἐνενόησα τότε ἄρα καταγέλαστος ὤν: X.*Cyr.*i 6.31 λέγεται . . . γενέσθαι ποτὲ ἀνὴρ διδάσκαλος τῶν παίδων, ὃς ἐδίδασκεν ἄρα . . .: D.xix 160 οὐδὲ τοῦτο δειχθῆναι πᾶσιν, ὅτι οὐκ ἄρ' ἡ πόλις ἡ τῶν Ἀθηναίων ἥττητο τῷ πολέμῳ. With variation of tense and repetition of the particle. Pl.*R.*600C–D.

Especially ὡς ἄρα (rarely ὅτι ἄρα). Like εἰ ἄρα, this is almost confined to prose. It is peculiarly common in Demosthenes, with whom the sceptical sense preponderates strongly. In Plato the preponderance is less marked.

Sceptical. E.*HF*759 ἄφρονα λόγον . . . ὡς ἄρ' οὐ σθένουσιν

θεοί. Pl.*R.* 364B λόγοι . . . θαυμασιώτατοι λέγονται, ὡς ἄρα καὶ θεοὶ πολλοῖς μὲν ἀγαθοῖς δυστυχίας . . . ἔνειμαν: *Smp.*192C οὐδενὶ γὰρ ἂν δόξειεν τοῦτ' εἶναι ἡ τῶν ἀφροδισίων συνουσία, ὡς ἄρα τούτου ἕνεκα . . . : *Men.*80E ἐριστικὸν λόγον κατάγεις, ὡς οὐκ ἄρα . . . : X.*An.*v 7.5 ἀκούω τινὰ διαβάλλειν ἐμέ, ὡς ἐγὼ ἄρα . . . μέλλω: Isoc.viii 66 καὶ μὴ καταγνῶναί μου τοιαύτην μανίαν, ὡς ἄρ' ἐγὼ προειλόμην ἂν . . . : And.i 54,137 : D.viii 73. Without scepticism. Ant.Soph.*Fr.*54 ἔστι δέ τις λόγος, ὡς ἄρα ἰδὼν ἀνὴρ ἄνδρα ἕτερον ἀργύριον ἀναιρούμενον πολὺ ἐδεῖτό οἱ δανεῖσαι ἐπὶ τόκῳ: Pl.*Phdr.*249E ἔστι δὴ οὖν δεῦρο ὁ πᾶς ἥκων λόγος . . . ὡς ἄρα . . . : *Ap.*40E καὶ ἀληθῆ ἐστιν τὰ λεγόμενα, ὡς ἄρα . . . : *R.*495A οὐ κακῶς ἐλέγομεν ὡς ἄρα . . . : D.xix 256 ἀληθῆ λόγον . . . ὡς ἄρ' οἱ θεοὶ σῴζουσιν ἡμῶν τὴν πόλιν : lviii 24 ἀκούω δὲ καὶ παρὰ τῶν πρεσβυτέρων . . . ὡς ἄρα . . . : Pl.*R.*375D, 392A,572B : *Ly.*215C,E : *Smp.*174B : *Ti.*90A : *Lg.* 657A. Sometimes the particle is postponed to a later point in the oratio obliqua. Pl.*Grg.*493A ἤδη γάρ του ἔγωγε καὶ ἤκουσα τῶν σοφῶν ὡς . . . , καὶ τοῦτο ἄρα . . . : *Lg.*698D καί τινα λόγον . . . ἀφῆκεν φοβερόν, ὡς οὐδεὶς Ἐρετριῶν αὐτὸν ἀποπεφευγὼς εἴη· συνάψαντες γὰρ ἄρα τὰς χεῖρας σαγηνεύσαιεν πᾶσαν τὴν Ἐρετρικήν. Sometimes the particle is repeated. Pl.*Phd.*97A θαυμάζω γὰρ εἰ, ὅτε μὲν . . . ἦν, ἓν ἄρα ἑκάτερον ἦν . . . , ἐπεὶ δ' ἐπλησίασαν ἀλλήλοις, αὕτη ἄρα αἰτία αὐτοῖς ἐγένετο: *Lg.*931C μὴ δή τις ἀτιμαζομένῳ μὲν . . . ἡγείσθω . . . , τιμωμένῳ δὲ ἄρα . . . , οὐκ ἄρα τὰ τοιαῦτα ἀκούειν . . . ἡγησόμεθα; *Ep.*315D λέγειν . . . ὡς ἄρα σοῦ ποτε λέγοντος ἀκούσας . . . , ταῦτ' ἄρα σὲ μὲν τότε διεκώλυσα . . . , νῦν δὲ . . .

(3) In questions following an interrogative. Here, strictly speaking, ἄρα forecasts the effect of the enlightenment which the answer will bring : who, if one only knew . . . ?' But, in effect, the particle does little more than add liveliness to the question.

(i) Direct questions. Hom.*A*8 τίς τ' ἄρ σφωε θεῶν ἔριδι ξυνέηκε μάχεσθαι; Γ226 ἐρέειν' ὁ γεραιός· τίς τ' ἄρ' ὅδ' ἄλλος . . . ; Pi.*P.*11.22 πότερόν νιν ἄρ' Ἰφιγένει' ἐπ' Εὐρίπῳ σφαχθεῖσα τῆλε πάτρας ἔκνιξεν . . . ; A.*Th.*91 τίς ἄρα ῥύσεται, τίς ἄρ' ἐπαρκέσει . . . ; S.*Aj.*1185 Τίς ἄρα νέατος ἐς πότε λήξει πολυπλάγκτων ἐτέων ἀριθμός . . . ; *OT* 1099 τίς σ' ἔτικτε τῶν μακραιώνων ἄρα . . . ; *OC* 117 Ὅρα· τίς ἄρ' ἦν; E.*Ba.*556 πόθι Νύσας ἄρα . . . θυρσο-

φορεῖς . . .; 639 *τί ποτ' ἄρ' ἐκ τούτων ἐρεῖ*; *IT*492 *Πότερος ἄρ' ὑμῶν* . . . *Πυλάδης κέκληται*; *Ion* 324 *τίς ποτ' ἦν ἄρα*; *Ph.*1288 *δίδυμα τέκεα πότερος ἄρα πότερον αἱμάξει* . . .; *Or.*1269 *τίς ὅδ' ἄρ' ἀμφὶ μέλαθρον πολεῖ* . . .; Ar.*V.*273 *τί ποτ' οὐ πρὸ θυρῶν φαίνετ' ἄρ' ἡμῖν ὁ γέρων* . . .; *Av.*517 *τίνος οὕνεκα ταῦτ' ἄρ' ἔχουσιν*; 1498 *Πηνίκ' ἐστὶν ἄρα τῆς ἡμέρας*; *Ra.*461 *πῶς ἐνθάδ' ἄρα κόπτουσιν οὑπιχώριοι*; *Ec.*91 *τί γὰρ ἂν χεῖρον ἀκροῴμην ἄρα ξαίνουσα*; S.*Ant.*1285,1296: *OC*1715: E.*Ph.*1515: *IA*6, 790,1036: Ar.*V.*143,266: *Pax* 1045,1048: *Av.*310,311,314: Eup.*Fr.*206: Pl.*Euthd.*279A *ἀγαθὰ δὲ ποῖα ἄρα* . . . *τυγχάνει ἡμῖν ὄντα*; *Lg.*895A *εἰ σταίη πως τὰ πάντα* . . ., *τίν' ἄρα ἐν αὐτοῖς ἀνάγκη πρώτην κίνησιν γενέσθαι* . . .; 944D *ζημία δὴ* . . . *τίς ἄρα γίγνοιτ' ἂν πρόσφορος*; *Plt.*290A *Τί δὲ ἄρα τοὺς τὰ τοιάδε διακονοῦντας* . . .; *Euthd.*279B: *Sph.*243E.

Preceding the interrogative. S.*Tr.*504 *ἀλλ' ἐπὶ τάνδ' ἄρ' ἄκοιτιν τίνες ἀμφίγυοι κατέβαν πρὸ γάμων* . . .;

(ii) Indirect questions. Hom.*H*415 *ποτιδέγμενοι ὁππότ' ἄρ' ἔλθοι*: A.*Pers.*144 *φροντίδα* . . . *θώμεθα* . . . *πῶς ἄρα πράσσει Ξέρξης*: *Pr.*594 *εἰπέ μοι* . . . *τίς ὤν, τίς ἄρα* . . .: S.*Ph.*689 *τόδε θαῦμά μ' ἔχει* . . . *πῶς ἄρα* . . . *βιοτὰν κατέσχεν*: E.*Rh.*135 *κατόπταν μολεῖν* . . . *ὅ τί ποτ' ἄρα* . . .: Ar.*Eq.*119 *φέρ' ἴδω τί ἄρ' ἔνεστιν αὐτόθι*: *Ra.*1253 *φροντίζειν* . . . *τίν' ἄρα μέμψιν ἐποίσει*: *Ec.*231: Pi.*O.*10.57: Pl.*Prt.*343C *ἐπισκεψώμεθα* . . . *εἰ ἄρα* . . .: *Phdr.*228D *δείξας* . . . *τί ἄρα* . . . *ἔχεις ὑπὸ τῷ ἱματίῳ*: *Phd.*78B *δεῖ ἡμᾶς ἀνερέσθαι ἑαυτούς, τῷ ποίῳ τινὶ ἄρα προσήκει*: 95B *πειρώμεθα εἰ ἄρα τι λέγεις*: *Cra.*424B *ἴδωμεν πότερον ἄρα* . . .: D.xx 68 *πρῶτον τοίνυν Κόνωνα σκοπεῖτε, εἰ ἄρα ἄξιον* . . . .

The use of *ἄρα* after *ὅστις* is essentially similar. E.*Hec.*1119 *ὅστις ἦν ἄρα*: *Ba.*894 *ἰσχὺν τόδ' ἔχειν, ὅ τι ποτ' ἄρα τὸ δαιμόνιον*: Pl.*Lg.*692B *καὶ τοῖς τότε νομοθέταις, οἵτινες ἄρα ἦσαν νομοθετοῦντες*: Hp.*Epid.*ii 2.15 (reading uncertain).

(4) Logical. A particle which marks realization or enlightenment is half-way to becoming a logical connective particle, since enlightenment naturally results from something which has just been said or done: 'Hullo, you're here': 'So you're here!' In some of the examples given above a logical force is plainly discernible: more plainly in the following: S.*Aj.*269 *Τό τοι δίπλαζον, ὦ γύναι, μεῖζον κακόν.—Ἡμεῖς ἄρ' οὐ νοσοῦντος ἀτώ-*

μεσθα νῦν: E.*Ion* 312 Οὐκ οἶδα πλὴν ἕν· Λοξίου κεκλήμεθα.—Ἡμεῖς σ' ἄρ' αὖθις, ὦ ξέν', ἀντοικτίρομεν: *HF* 581: *IT* 542: Gorg.*Fr.* 11a.12 ἀλλὰ διελὼν τοῦ τείχους; ἅπασιν ἄρα φανερὰ γένοιτ' ἄν: *ib.* πάντως ἄρα καὶ πάντῃ πάντα πράττειν ἀδύνατον ἦν μοι.

The connective use of ἄρα is rare in early Greek prose. Th.iii 113.4 (introducing an answer in a conversation): cf. v 100 Ἠ που ἄρα (Melian Dialogue). It is not till we come to Plato that we find ἄρα used practically as a variant for οὖν and δή, though even in Plato ἄρα perhaps conveys a slightly less formal and more conversational connexion than those particles: 'so', instead of 'therefore' or 'then'.[1] *Chrm.* 161A Ἔστιν ἄρα, ὡς ἔοικεν, αἰδὼς οὐκ ἀγαθόν: 171B: *La.* 186A: *Ly.* 220D. In Demosthenes connective ἄρα has always a colloquial tone. v 24 τὰ κελευόμεν' ἡμᾶς ἄρα δεῖ ποιεῖν ταῦτα φοβουμένους; καὶ σὺ ταῦτα κελεύεις; πολλοῦ γε καὶ δέω: xxiv 203 τοῦτον . . . οὐκ ἀποκτενεῖτε; δόξετ' ἄρα . . . κρίσεις βούλεσθαι καὶ πράγματ' ἔχειν: xxix 40 καὶ δὴ λέγει. διὰ τοῦτ' ἄρ' οὐκ ἔχει; xx 57: xxiii 96,174,197: xlv 70. But in Aristotle[2] the particle has become completely devitalized, and is a pure connective. (In its occasional apodotic use it must be regarded as connective, not emphatic: *PA* 642a13 ἐπεὶ . . ., ἀνάγκη ἄρα . . .)

IV. Position. Connective ἄρα, like most connectives, is usually the second word of clause or sentence. But a later position is by no means infrequent. Pl.*Chrm.* 171B Ἐν τοῖς ὑγιεινοῖς ἄρα: *La.* 193B Καὶ τὸν μετ' ἐπιστήμης ἄρα ἱππικῆς καρτεροῦντα: *Ly.* 219B Τὸ οὔτε κακὸν οὔτε ἀγαθὸν ἄρα: *Phd.* 58A Οὐδὲ τὰ περὶ τῆς δίκης ἄρα ἐπύθεσθε . . .; *Cra.* 387A Κατὰ τὴν αὐτῶν ἄρα φύσιν: 394E Καὶ τῷ ἐκ τοῦ εὐσεβοῦς ἄρα γενομένῳ ἀσεβεῖ: *R.* 426B: Lycurg. 78 ῥᾴδιον ἔσται παρ' ὑμῖν ἄρα μεγάλα ἀδικεῖν.

When ἄρα is not a connective, though here too it tends to an early position, there is naturally greater freedom. E.*Ion* 790 τὸν δ' ἐμὸν ἄτεκνον ἄτεκνον ἔλακεν ἄρα βίοτον; *IT* 886 ἀλλὰ ποδῶν

[1] Des Places (p. 229): 'Chez Platon . . . alors même que la particule marque une conclusion ou une inférence, elle indique la surprise de la découverte'. But Dr. Chapman is, perhaps rightly, sceptical as to this distinction.

[2] For statistics of the relative frequency of ἄρα in various Aristotelian works, see Eucken, pp. 50–1

ῥιπᾷ θανάτῳ πελάσεις ἄρα βάρβαρα φῦλα: *Fr.*54 κακόν τι παίδευμ' ἦν ἄρα: *Fr.*377 μάτην δὲ θνητοὶ τοὺς νόθους φεύγουσ' ἄρα: Pl.*Grg.*524D ταὐτὸν δή μοι δοκεῖ τοῦτ' ἄρα . . . εἶναι: *Sph.*235A Γόητα μὲν δὴ καὶ μιμητὴν ἄρα θετέον: *Lg.*803D τὸ δὲ ἦν ἐν πολέμῳ μὲν ἄρα: 889D αἳ δέ τι καὶ σπουδαῖον ἄρα γεννῶσι τῶν τεχνῶν: *Alc.II*145D Δοκεῖ οὖν· σοι ἀναγκαῖον εἶναι τὸν περὶ τούτων τι ἐπιστήμονα ὄντα ἄρα καὶ ἄνδρα φρόνιμον εἶναι . . .; *Clit.*408B (see II.1 above): *R.*598E (I above): *Grg.*519B: *Lg.* 840C, 906B.

V. Ἄρα combined with other particles. Few of these combinations have any very particular significance. But they are perhaps worth illustrating. Sometimes ἄρα is connective, sometimes not.

ἀλλ' ἄρα, ἀλλ' . . . ἄρα. Hom.*N*716 οὐδ' ἔχον ἀσπίδας . . . ἀλλ' ἄρα τόξοισιν . . . ἅμ' ἕποντο πεποιθότες: *T*96: *Ω*699: Hes.*Th.*899: *Op.*132: *Sc.*259: Thgn.711: Phoc.*Fr.*16: Pl.*Lg.* 905E ἄρχοντας μὲν ἀναγκαῖόν που γίγνεσθαι . . .—Οὕτως.—Ἀλλ' ἄρα τίσιν προσφερεῖς τῶν ἀρχόντων; ('Well then'): X.*Hier.* 1.13 εἴποις οὖν ἂν ἴσως σύ, ἀλλ' ἄρα ἔρχεται αὐτοῖς τὰ τοιαῦτα καὶ οἴκοι μένουσιν ('But after all'): Pl.*R.*374B. Following on the rejection of a suggestion: ἀλλά marks the new departure, while ἄρα connects it logically with the preceding rejection. 'Well then'. Pl.*Euthd.*290E 'The boy can't have said that.'—Ἀλλ' ἄρα . . . μὴ ὁ Κτήσιππος ἦν ὁ ταῦτ' εἰπὼν . . .; ('Well then perhaps it was Ctesippus?'): 293E ἀλλ' οὐδὲν ἄρα ἐπίστασθον; 300C: *Ap.*25A: *Alc.I*130B: *Hp.Ma.*296D: X.*Mem.*iii 3.2: iv 2.22.

εἴτε ἄρα. We may perhaps compare ὅστις ἄρα (II.3 above): 'whether, if one knew the truth . . .'. Hom.*A*65 εἴτ' ἄρ' ὅ γ' εὐχωλῆς ἐπιμέμφεται εἴθ' ἑκατόμβης: S.*Ph.*345 λέγοντες, εἴτ' ἀληθὲς εἴτ' ἄρ' οὖν μάτην: Ar.*Nu.*272 εἴτ . . . εἴτ' . . . εἴτ' ἄρα: Th.vi 60.2 ἀναπείθεται εἷς τῶν δεδεμένων . . . εἴτε ἄρα καὶ τὰ ὄντα μηνῦσαι εἴτε καὶ οὔ: Pl.*Phd.*70C εἴτε ἄρα . . . εἴτε καὶ οὔ: *Lg.*932E εἴτε τις ἄρα πώμασιν ἢ καὶ βρώμασιν ἢ . . . πημαίνει: X.*Cyr.*vii 2.29 εἴτε ἄρα καὶ . . . εἴτε καί.

οὔτε (μήτε) ἄρα. Hom.*A*93 οὔτ' ἄρ' ὅ γ' εὐχωλῆς ἐπιμέμφεται οὔθ' ἑκατόμβης: *Υ*8 οὔτε τις οὖν ποταμῶν . . . οὔτ' ἄρα νυμφάων: Hes.*Op.*489 μήτ' ἄρ' ὑπερβάλλων . . . μήτ' ἀπολείπων: 784 οὔτε γενέσθαι πρῶτ'—οὔτ' ἂρ γάμου ἀντιβολῆσαι: Phoc.*Fr.*2.5 ἡ δὲ συὸς βλοσυρῆς οὔτ' ἂρ κακὴ οὐδὲ μὲν ἐσθλή: Emp.*Fr.*17.30 οὔτ' ἄρ τέ τι γίνεται οὔτ' ἀπολήγει: Hom.*O*72: δ605: Hes.*Sc.*217: Emp.*Fr.*142.

αὐτὰρ ἄρα. Hom.*B*103 αὐτὰρ ἄρα Ζεὺς δῶκε διακτόρῳ ἀργεϊφόντῃ: *h.Merc.*69.

γε ἄρα. Hom.*M*305 ἀλλ' ὅ γ' ἄρ' ἢ ἥρπαξε...: Hes.*Th.* 466,532: Ar.*Lys.*31 ἐπ' ὀλίγου γ' ἄρ' εἴχετο (γάρ *al.*): *Ec.*558 μακαρία γ' ἄρ' ἡ πόλις ἔσται (cf. *Av.*1542 γ' ἆρ'): Democr.*Fr.*191 ταύτης γ' ἄρ' ἐχόμενος τῆς γνώμης εὐθυμότερόν τε διάξεις... (γάρ *vulgo*): Pl.*Phlb.*46A Συμμεικτὸν τοῦτό γ' ἄρα, ὦ Σώκρατες, ἔοικε γίγνεσθαί τι κακόν (γ' ἄρ' *B*: γε *T*): *Tht.*171C ἄδηλον εἰ καὶ παραθέομεν τὸ ὀρθόν. εἰκός γε ἄρα ἐκεῖνον πρεσβύτερον ὄντα σοφώτερον ἡμῶν εἶναι (γάρ *W*): *Chrm.*159D (ἄρα *T*: γ' ἄρα *B*): *Phlb.*35B (ἄρα *T*: γ' ἄρα *B*).

ἄρα γε. X.*Oec.*1.8 Κἂν ἄρα γέ τις ... μὴ ἐπίστηται ... οὐ ...; *ibid.* οὐδ' ἄρα γε (γε *om.* some MSS.): Arist.*EN*1130a22 ἔστιν ἄρα γε ἄλλη τις ἀδικία (suspected by Bonitz: γάρ K^b).

δ' ἄρα is too common, particularly in Homer, to need illustration. Examples are to be found under I above.

δὴ ἄρα. Hom.η18 ἀλλ' ὅτε δὴ ἄρ' ἔμελλε: Demod.*Fr.*5.4 ἦν δ' ἄρα ... δή ῥα τότ': Hes.*Th.*58,883,888: Pl.*R.*369C Οὕτω δὴ ἄρα: 425A: *Phdr.*273E οὐ γὰρ δὴ ἄρα.

καί ῥα. Hom.*A*360: ξ233: Hes.*Th.*177,1000: *Sc.*453: Pi.*O.* 7.59: *P.*4.134,189.

μὲν ἄρα. Hom.*E*48 τὸν μὲν ἄρ' Ἰδομενῆος ἐσύλευον θεράποντες: *N*301: Σ79: κ403: λ139: Hes.*Th.*289: Pl.*Phdr.*258D: *R.* 467D.

οὖν ἄρα. Pl.*Chrm.*160E Οὐ μόνον οὖν ἄρα καλόν: *Tht.*149B μὲν οὖν ἄρα ... δὲ ... (the only instances in Plato: see des Places): X.*Oec.*6.2 Τί οὖν, ἔφη ὁ Σωκράτης, ἄρα, εἰ ... ἐπανέλθοιμεν ...;

τ' ἄρα, common in surprised questions in Homer. *Λ*838 Πῶς τ' ἄρ' ἔοι τάδε ἔργα; *M*409: *N*307.

With an exclamation. Βαβαῖ ἄρα: Pl.*Phlb.*23B: *Alc.I*118B: *Hp.Ma.*294E: *Sph* 249D (text uncertain).

(For ἦ ἄρα, ἦ ῥα, see ἦ, III.1. For γὰρ ἄρα, see γάρ. For τοι ἄρα, ἄρα τοι, see τοι, VI.8–9.)

Ἆρα

Ἆρα is used (1) in poetry only, as a substitute for ἄρα, in various uses of that particle: (2) as an interrogative particle. In both uses, ἆρα is almost confined to Attic. Of (1), which is the first to appear, there are three examples in Archilochus (*Frs.*45,81.5,89.2). The first instances of interrogative ἆρα are in Aeschylus (who almost always uses the particle interrogatively). In Pindar ἆρα is read by Boeckh in five places where the MSS. give ἄρα: in four of these Schroeder reads ἦρα, in one ἄρα. In none of them has the particle an interrogative force (*O.*8.46: *P.*4.78: *N.*5.30: *I.*6.55,8.59). In Sophocles, Euripides, and Aristophanes, the two meanings are found side by side: but the interrogative use strongly predominates, and it is the only use to be found in prose.

According to Apollonius (Bekker's *Anecdota* ii p. 490) ἆρα is formed by crasis from ἦ ἄρα. This view, which has been generally accepted, certainly suits (2) above, though it has to face the objection, perhaps not necessarily insuperable, that ἦ is almost always placed at, or near, the beginning of a sentence, while ἆρα is not infrequently postponed. On the other hand (1) diverges markedly from the usage of ἦ, and coincides markedly with the usage of ἄρα: and (1), as we have seen, is found earlier than (2). It seems conceivable that in (1) ἆρα is merely a *metri gratia* lengthening of ἄρα (that it should be a phonological lengthening appears hardly possible): while in (2), which is in origin quite distinct, ἆρα does represent ἦ ἄρα, replacing in Attic writers the Epic and Lyric ἦ ῥα, ἦ ἄρα, ἦ ἄρ, ἦρα.[1] At the same time, Attic poets continue, for metrical reasons, to avail themselves of (1), for which the prose writers have no need.[2]

I. Equivalent in sense to ἄρα.

(1) Adding liveliness. Archil. *Fr.*81.5 πίθηκος ᾔει . . . τῷ δ'

[1] See ἦ, III.1, and Schroeder's Pindar, *Prolegomena* II §39.

[2] Ahrens (*De Crasi et Aphaeresi*), accepting the crasis, rejects the *metri gratia* view, and holds that ἆρα 'extra interrogationem ubique gravem affirmationem continet'.

ἆρ' ἀλώπηξ κερδαλῇ συνήντετο. (Pi.*O*.8.46: *P*.4.78: *I*.6.55: if Boeckh's ἆρα, for ἄρα, is right.)

(2) Marking realization of the truth, or drawing a conclusion. (The two usages are not to be sharply distinguished in drama: cf. ἄρα, III.4.) A.*Pers*.348 θεοὶ πόλιν σῴζουσι Παλλάδος θεᾶς.—Ἔτ' ἆρ' Ἀθηνῶν ἔστ' ἀπόρθητος πόλις; S.*Aj*.738 Οὐκ ἔνδον ...—Ἰοὺ ἰού. βραδεῖαν ἡμᾶς ἆρ' ὁ τήνδε τὴν ὁδὸν πέμπων ἔπεμψεν: *OC*408–9 Οι. Ἦ καὶ κατασκιῶσι Θηβαίᾳ κόνει;—Ισ. Ἀλλ' οὐκ ἐᾷ τοὔμφυλον αἷμά σ', ὦ πάτερ.—Οι. Οὐκ ἆρ' ἐμοῦ γε μὴ κρατήσωσίν ποτε.—Ισ. Ἔσται ποτ' ἆρα τοῦτο Καδμείοις βάρος: *Ph*.106 Ἰοὺς ἀφύκτους καὶ προπέμποντας φόνον (ἔχει).—Οὐκ ἆρ' ἐκείνῳ γ' οὐδὲ προσμεῖξαι θρασύ; 114 Αἱρεῖ τὰ τόξα ταῦτα τὴν Τροίαν μόνα.—Οὐκ ἆρ' ὁ πέρσων, ὡς ἐφάσκετ', εἴμ' ἐγώ; E.*Hipp*. 1086 Κλαίων τις αὐτῶν ἆρ' ἐμοῦ τεθίξεται (cf. *Andr*.758 κλαίων ἄρα ψαύσει): *Andr*.1114 τῷ δὲ ξιφήρης ἆρ' ὑφειστήκει λόχος (ἄρα *codd.* 'as he found to his cost'): Ar.*Nu*.1301 ἔμελλόν σ' ἆρα κινήσειν ἐγώ (cf. *Ra*.268 ἔμελλον ἄρα παύσειν): *Av*.161 Ὑμεῖς μὲν ἆρα ζῆτε νυμφίων βίον: 1688 Ἐς καιρὸν ἆρα κατεκόπησαν οὑτοιί: S.*Aj*. 980,1238,1368: *El*.1179: *OC*858,1400: *OT*1395: *Fr*.845 (= Pearson 931: see his note): E.*Cyc*.638: *Heracl*.116,268,895: *Hipp*.1012: *El*.374,1229: *Ph*.566,1675: *Or*.190,1207: *IA*311: *Fr*.36 (ἄρα *codd.*): Ar.*Av*.91,1530: *V*.3, 839: *Lys*.933: *Pl*.579,920. (Pi.*I*.8.59, ἆρα Boeckh.)

(3) εἰ ἆρα. E.*Rh*.118 πῶς δ' αὖ γεφύρας διαβαλοῦσ' ἱππηλάται, ἢν ἆρα μὴ θραύσαντες ἀντύγων χνόας; (ἄρα *codd.* But the text seems doubtful: see Paley.)

(4) ὡς ἆρα. Archil.*Fr*.89.2 αἶνός τις ἀνθρώπων ὅδε, ὡς ἆρ' ἀλώπηξ καἰετὸς ξυνωνίην ἔμειξαν. (Pi.*N*.5.30 λόγον, ὡς ἆρα νυμφείας ἐπείρα (ἆρα Boeckh).)

(5) Following an interrogative pronoun. S.*Aj*.905 'Ajax is dead'.—Τίνος ποτ' ἆρ' ἔπραξε χειρὶ δύσμορος; E.*Ion* 563 Ὦ φίλη μῆτερ, πότ' ἆρα καὶ σὸν ὄψομαι δέμας; *Tr*.247 Τοὐμὸν τίς ἆρ' ἔλαχε τέκος ...; (ἄρ' *P*: *om. V*): 293 τὰς δ' ἐμὰς τύχας τίς ἆρ' Ἀχαιῶν ... ἔχει; *IT*472 τίς ἆρα μήτηρ ἡ τεκοῦσ' ὑμᾶς ποτε πατήρ τ'; Ar.*Pax* 1240 Τί δ' ἆρα τῇ σάλπιγγι τῇδε χρήσομαι ...; ('And what, I should like to know, ...?'). But

in *V*.893 ἆρα is better taken as a connective. *Τίς ἆρ' ὁ φεύγων*; ('Who's the defendant, then?'). S.*Fr*.790: E.*IA*1228: *Fr*.403.1: Philem.*Fr*.108.1 (*ἄρα codd.*).

II. *Ἆρα* as an interrogative particle. Strictly speaking, *ἆρα* does not imply any expectation of a positive or of a negative answer. Practically, however, in Greek as in English, the mere putting of a proposition in an interrogative form implies, in certain contexts, a doubt of its truth, and *ἆρα*, by itself, often has a sceptical tone. *Per contra*, *ἆρ' οὐ* more definitely and more frequently expects a positive answer. (For the widespread, but erroneous, view that *ἆρα μή* expects a negative answer, see (5) below.) A rigid separation of questions expecting a positive from those expecting a negative answer would be misleading. But an approximate grouping must be attempted.

(1) Leaving the question open. S.*OC*316 *ἆρ' ἔστιν; ἆρ' οὐκ ἔστιν; ἢ γνώμη πλανᾷ; καὶ φημὶ κἀπόφημι κοὐκ ἔχω τί φῶ*: E.*El*.229 *Ὦ φίλτατ', ἆρα ζῶντος ἢ τεθνηκότος*; S.*OC*1486: Pl. *Smp*.212E *ἆρα καταγελάσεσθέ μου ὡς μεθύοντος*; D.xxiii.82 *ἆρά τις ἡμῖν ἔτι λοιπός ἐστι νόμος; δεῖξον. οὑτοσί*: i 12: viii 18: xviii 195: lii 5.

(2) Expecting a negative answer. S.*El*.816 *ἤδη δεῖ με δουλεύειν . . . ἆρά μοι καλῶς ἔχει*; S.*El*.804: And.i 102 *ἆρ' ἂν οἴεσθε, ὦ ἄνδρες, ἄλλων τινῶν τυχεῖν με δι' ὑμᾶς, εἰ ἐλήφθην ὑπ' αὐτῶν*; D.vi 20,22: viii 75 *ἆρ' ἂν ἦν γεγονὸς . . .; οὐχ οἷόν τε* (the expected negative answer following: cf. xix 141: xxi 115, 224: xxiii 31: Lys.xxvi 7).

(3) Expecting a positive answer. But whereas *ἆρ' οὐ* definitely forecasts an affirmative reply, *ἆρα* ostensibly leaves the issue open to the person addressed, and the appeal for confirmation is the more confident because less obviously stressed.* A.*Pr*.735 *ἆρ' ὑμῖν δοκεῖ ὁ τῶν θεῶν τύραννος ἐς τὰ πάνθ' ὁμῶς βίαιος εἶναι*; ('Are you satisfied now that . . .'?): *Ch*.297 *τοιοῖσδε χρησμοῖς ἆρα χρὴ πεποιθέναι*; S.*OT*822 *ἆρ' ἔφυν κακός; ἆρ' οὐχὶ πᾶς ἄναγνος*; (Jebb well observes that 'the transition from *ἆρα* to *ἆρ' οὐχί* is from bitter irony to despairing earnest'): *El*.614 *ἆρά σοι δοκεῖ χωρεῖν ἂν ἐς πᾶν ἔργον αἰσχύνης ἄτερ*;

(where again see Jebb): E.*Alc.*341 ἆρά μοι στένειν πάρα τοιᾶσδ' ἁμαρτάνοντι συζύγου σέθεν; A.*Ch.*495–6 (the sense approaches '*nonne*', though Tucker's 'Dost not' is a little too strong): S.*Aj.*1282: *OC*753: E.*Alc.*771: Ar.*Av.*797: Th.i75.1 ἆρ' ἄξιοί ἐσμεν . . . ἀρχῆς . . . μὴ οὕτως ἄγαν ἐπιφθόνως διακεῖσθαι; (the only example of ἆρα in Thucydides): Pl. *Euthphr.*5A Ἆρ' οὖν μοι . . . κράτιστόν ἐστι μαθητῇ σῷ γενέσθαι . . .; X.*Cyr.*iv6.4 καὶ εἶπεν· Ἆρα βέβληκα δὶς ἐφεξῆς καὶ καταβέβληκα θῆρα ἑκατεράκις; (ἆρα *D*: ἄρα *cett.*: ὅρα Naber, but ἆρα is perhaps right: 'I ask you, have I . . .?')[1]: vii5.40 (ἄρα *codd.*: ὥρα Cobet): Lys.x28: xxxi21: D.lv15. With the expected positive answer following. Pl.*Phlb.*33D ἆρ' ὀρθότατα ἐροῦμεν;—Πῶς γὰρ οὔ; *R.*566A ἆρα τῷ τοιούτῳ ἀνάγκη . . .;—Πολλὴ ἀνάγκη: *Plt.*296D,309D: *Cra.*430C: *Phd.*64E: X.*Mem.*iii6.4: 10.1.

(4) ἆρ' οὐ. S.*OC*791 ἆρ' οὐκ ἄμεινον ἢ σὺ τὰν Θήβαις φρονῶ; Ar.*V.*620 ἆρ' οὐ μεγάλην ἀρχὴν ἄρχω . . .; Pl.*Grg.*453C ἆρ' οὐκ ἂν δικαίως σε ἠρόμην . . .; Lys.xxvi13: D.xix130: *et saep.*

(5) ἆρα μή. It is commonly, but wrongly, said that ἆρα μή expects a negative answer. Now the questions which, *par excellence*, expect an answer of a particular kind, positive or negative, are rhetorical questions: and it is significant that the orators never use ἆρα μή, though they use ἆρ' οὐ very freely. ἆρα μή is in fact exceedingly rare altogether. In classical Greek, there are two doubtful examples in Aeschylus, two in Sophocles, eight in Plato, four in Xenophon (three of them in Socratic writings): none in any other author. The force of ἆρα μή is, not *num*, but 'Can it be that . . .?' ('Doch nicht etwa', Stallbaum on Pl.*Ly.*213D). It does not necessarily imply the expectation of a negative reply, but merely that the suggestion made is difficult of acceptance (though the alternative may be even more difficult, or actually impossible). It expresses, in fact, an antinomy, a dilemma, an *impasse* of thought, or, at the least, a certain hesitancy. This interpretation is excluded in none of the passages, and is imperiously demanded in some. As a

[1] On second thoughts, I believe that ἄρα should be retained, punctuating καὶ εἶπεν ἄρα· Βέβληκα . . . Cf. X.*Ap.*28: *Ages.*7.5: and, for the position of ἄρα, Hdt.iii64.

cautious and tentative form of expression, ἆρα μή questions, like μή questions, are naturally commoner in Plato than elsewhere.

A.*Th.*208 *Τί οὖν; ὁ ναύτης ἆρα μὴ 's πρῷραν φυγὼν πρύμνηθεν ηὗρε μηχανὴν σωτηρίας ...;* (but here, though *M* gives ἆρα μή, the ἆρά γ' of inferior MSS. may well be right): *Fr.*62 is unintelligible: †*μακροσκελὴς μὲν ἄρα* (*sic*) *μὴ χλούνης τις ᾖ*†: S.*El.* 446 *ἆρα μὴ δοκεῖς λυτήρι' αὐτῇ ταῦτα τοῦ φόνου φέρειν;* ('Canst thou believe ...?', Jebb: it is incredible that Chrysothemis should believe this: but her conduct shows that she does): *Ant.*632 *ὦ παῖ, τελείαν ψῆφον ἆρα μὴ κλύων τῆς μελλονύμφου πατρὶ λυσσαίνων πάρει; ἢ σοὶ μὲν ἡμεῖς πανταχῇ δρῶντες φίλοι;* ('Can it be that ...?', Jebb): Pl.*Cri.*44E *ἆρά γε μὴ ἐμοῦ προμηθῇ ...;* ('Can it be that you are thinking of *me?*'): *Chrm.*174A (the sequel implies that an affirmative reply has been given): *Ly.* 213D *Ἆρα μὴ ... τὸ παράπαν οὐκ ὀρθῶς ἐζητοῦμεν;* (the context clearly envisages an affirmative reply as conceivable): *Prm.* 163C *ἆρα μή τι ἄλλο σημαίνει ἢ ...;—Οὐδὲν ἄλλο*: *Phd.*64C, *bis*: 103C: *R.*405A: X.*Mem.*ii 6.34: iv 2.10: *An.*vii 6.5: *Oec.*4.4.[1]

III. Position. In I the particle is normally placed second or third, or at any rate early in the sentence.[2] In II it is normally placed first: but there are many exceptions. In drama, it is often difficult to determine whether the interrogative force resides in the particle or is independent of it, in which case the force of

[1] Long after writing this section, I find confirmation both of the extreme relative rarity of ἆρα μή, and of the failure of scholars to observe this, in Prof. J. E. Harry's '*Indicative questions with μὴ and ἆρα μή*'. I had collected all except one of his examples which can be assigned with certainty to the classical period. Add Pl.*Phlb.*27C (ἆρα μὴ *T*: ἆρα *B*): [Pl.] *Virt.*376D Ἀλλ' ἆρα μή: *Amat.*135C. Harry omits X.*Oec.*4.4 Ἆρ', ἔφη ὁ Σωκράτης, μὴ αἰσχυνθῶμεν ...; This (though it has been suspected, e.g. by Marchant) seems sound: the cutting in half of the combination by ἔφη ὁ Σ. is paralleled by X.*An.*vii 6.5 Ἆρ' οὖν, ἔφασαν, μὴ καὶ ἡμῖν ἐναντιώσεται ...; and by the usage of other particles. (In the second of the two examples from Pl.*Phd.*64C ἆρα μή is followed by a subjunctive: in *Cri.*44E προμηθῇ is, I think, indicative: in X.*Oec.*4.4 αἰσχυνθῶμεν is deliberative (Goodwin, *M. T.* § 287), and the subjunctive has nothing to do with ἆρα μή: elsewhere the verb is in the indicative, or is omitted).

[2] In New Comedy ἆρα = ἄρα sometimes stands first, in a sentence of gnomic or reflective character, marking the realization of a universal truth. Men.*Fr.*164 ἆρ' ἐστὶ πάντων ἀγρυπνία λαλίστατον. ἐμὲ γοῦν ἀναστήσασα δευρὶ προάγεται λαλεῖν ...: 281,408,427: Diph.*Fr.*99: Philem.*Fr.*112.

the particle is as in I. (The point is of some literary importance, as it affects the tone of the words.) The following examples illustrate the precariousness of interpretation:

A.*Pers.*639 νέρθεν ἆρα κλύει μου; (presumably interrogative: cf. 633 ἦ ῥ' ἀίει μου . . .;): *Eu.*745 Ὦ Νὺξ μέλαινα μῆτερ, ἆρ' ὁρᾷς τάδε; (clearly interrogative; the early position of the apostrophe is common in the case of other particles: cf. E.*El.* 229): *Th.*208 (see under ἆρα μή): *Ag.*1646 'Ορέστης ἆρά που βλέπει φάος . . .; (ἆρα perhaps meaning 'after all', or 'I wonder'): E.*IT*932 Ταῦτ' ἆρ' ἐπ' ἀκταῖς κἀνθάδ' ἠγγέλης μανείς; (perhaps to be read as a statement: cf. ταῦτ' ἄρα): *Or.* 1512 ἀξιώτερος γὰρ εἶ.—'Ενδίκως ἡ Τυνδάρειος ἆρα παῖς διώλετο; (ironical. 'So Helen deserved all she got, did she?'): *IA*876 Ὦ τάλαιν' ἐγώ. μεμηνὼς ἆρα τυγχάνει πόσις; ('So my husband is mad, it seems?'): 1228 πρεσβὺν ἆρ' ἐσδέξομαι . . .; *Hec.*469 ἢ Παλλάδος ἐν πόλει . . . ζεύξομαι ἆρα πώλους . . .; *HF*1127 Ὦ Ζεῦ, παρ' Ἥρας ἆρ' ὁρᾷς θρόνων τάδε; *Heracl.*640 Ὦ φίλταθ', ἥκεις ἆρα . . .; *Alc.*477 Ἄδμητον ἐν δόμοισιν ἆρα κιγχάνω; Ar.*Th.*1 Ὦ Ζεῦ χελιδὼν ἆρά ποτε φανήσεται; *Ach.*238 Εὐφημεῖτε, εὐφημεῖτε.—Σῖγα πᾶς. ἠκούσατ' ἄνδρες ἆρα τῆς εὐφημίας; *V.*234 ὦ Στρυμόδωρε . . . Εὐεργίδης ἆρ' ἐστί που 'νταῦθ' . . .; *Ec.*462 Οὐδὲ στένειν τὸν ὄρθρον ἔτι πρᾶγμ' ἆρά μοι; (cf. 460 Οὐδ' ἐς δικαστήριον ἄρ' εἶμ' ἀλλ' ἡ γυνή;): 672 Οὐδὲ κυβεύσουσ' ἆρ' ἄνθρωποι; (cf. 668 Οὐδ' ἀποδύσουσ' ἄρα τῶν νυκτῶν,).

There are, then, not a few cases in the dramatists where interrogative ἆρα is placed late. Prose writers are, on the whole, far stricter, and the particle almost invariably opens the sentence: with this important exception, that Plato postpones ἆρα far more freely than the poets.

Hp.*Prorrh.*i 63 τὸ καρῶδες ἆρά γε πανταχοῦ κακόν; Pl.*Grg.* 467E Τὰ δὲ μήτε ἀγαθὰ μήτε κακὰ ἆρα τοιάδε λέγεις . . .; *Prt.* 358C ἀμαθίαν ἆρα τὸ τοιόνδε λέγετε . . .; *Phd.*67C Κάθαρσις δὲ εἶναι ἆρα οὐ τοῦτο συμβαίνει . . .; *Lg.*807A τοῖς δὴ ταύτῃ κεκοσμημένοις ἆρα . . .; *Prm.*156A Τὸ δὴ οὐσίας μεταλαμβάνειν ἆρά γε οὐ γίγνεσθαι καλεῖς; *ib.* Τὸ δὲ ἀπαλλάττεσθαι οὐσίας ἆρα οὐκ ἀπόλλυσθαι; 160B εἰ δὲ . . ., τί χρὴ συμβαίνειν ἆρ' οὐ σκεπτέον μετὰ τοῦτο; *Phlb.*27B τὴν δὲ τῆς μείξεως αἰτίαν καὶ γενέσεως τετάρτην λέγων ἆρα μὴ πλημμελοίην ἄν τι; *R.*437D οἷον δίψα ἐστὶ δίψα ἆρά γε θερμοῦ ποτοῦ . . .; Lys.*Fr.*11 ποιήσαντι δ' ἆρ' οὐ δώσετε; Pl.*Euthphr.*6B: *Cra.*410B,414A: *Lg.*832E: *Alc.II* 138C,139A: *Grg.*472D,476A: *R.*405A(*bis*),436C,476B,487A: *Smp.*201B.

Repeated interrogative ἆρα. Pl.*Cra.*429D: *R.*565E–566A.

Occasionally ἆρα introduces an indirect question. Pl.*Phd.* 70E τοῦτο οὖν σκεψώμεθα, ἆρα ἀναγκαῖον: *Grg.*512E σκεπτέον τίν' ἂν τρόπον τοῦτον ὃν μέλλοι χρόνον βιῶναι ὡς ἄριστα βιοίη, ἆρα ἐξομοιῶν αὑτὸν τῇ πολιτείᾳ...: Arist.*Pol.*1276a1 καίτοι καὶ τοῦτό τις ἔτι προσαπορήσειεν, ἆρα, εἰ μὴ δικαίως πολίτης, οὐ πολίτης: Pl.*R.*462A,526C: *Grg.*459C: Arist.*Ph.*204b3.

IV. ἆρα combined with other particles.

(1) ἆρά γε, ἆρα ... γε. γε adds liveliness and emphasis to the question. In verse, probably for metrical convenience,[1] the particles are sometimes separated, while still cohering in thought. Cf. δέ γε, δὲ ... γε. E.*Hec.* 745 Ἆρ' ἐκλογίζομαι γε...; Ar.*V.*4 ἆρ' οἶσθά γ' οἷον κνώδαλον φυλάττομεν; (contrast *Av.*668 Ἆρά γ' οἶσθ'...; (1221): *V.*1336 ἆρά γ' ἴσθ'...;): *Av.*307 ἆρ' ἀπειλοῦσίν γε νῷν; *Pl.*546 ἆρά γε πολλῶν ἀγαθῶν ... ἀποφαίνω σ' αἴτιον οὖσαν; (ironical): *Nu.*465: *Pax* 114: Cratin.*Fr.*360: Alex. *Fr.*270.4. Often in prose. Pl.*Euthphr.*6A Ἆρά γε τοῦτ' ἔστιν οὕνεκα τὴν γραφὴν φεύγω...; *Cri.*44E: And.i 41 ἆρά γε σὲ οἵδε περιμένουσι; D.iii 27 ἆρά γ' ὁμοίως ἢ παραπλησίως; xxiii 43 ἆρά γε μικρὸν ἢ τὸ τυχόν ἐστιν...; Pl.*R.*328A,422C: *Lg.*830C (late position: *R.*437D: *Prm.*156A: Hp.*Prorrh.*i 63): X.*Mem.* i 5.4: iii 2,1: 2,2: 8,3: 8,8: D.xxiii 122: Lycurg.119.

(2) ἀλλ' ἆρα. Each particle retains its separate force. Pl. *Euthd.*292C Ἆρ' οὖν ἡ βασιλικὴ σοφοὺς ποιεῖ...;—Τί γὰρ κωλύει...;—Ἀλλ' ἆρα πάντας καὶ πάντα ἀγαθούς; *Euthphr.* 9D ὥστε τούτου μὲν ἀφίημί σε ... ἀλλ' ἆρα τοῦτο...; *Phlb.*51D ἀλλ' ἆρα μανθάνομεν, ἢ πῶς; (ἀλλά here seems to convey a summons to attention: 'Come, do we grasp that?'): X.*Cyr.*i 4.11. After the rejection of a suggestion. Pl.*Tht.*188B: *Prm.*138C, 146C.

(3) ἆρα δή. [X.] *Ath.* 3.2 ἆρα δή τι θαυμαστόν ἐστιν...;

(4) ἆρ' οὖν. Pl.*R.*545A (342 times in Plato, according to J. E.

[1] The distinction drawn by Hartung (i 377) and Klotz (i 191) that in ἆρά γε, γε applies to the whole question, in ἆρα ... γε to the word it follows, is not of much practical importance.

Harry, *Studies in honor of B. L. Gildersleeve*, Baltimore, 1902, pp. 428–30): D.xviii 140,282: *id. saep.*

(5) καὶ ἆρα . . .; Pl.*Alc.I* 126D: *R.*376C,480A.

Ἀτάρ

The particle has often been connected, like ἄτερ, with Old High German 'suntar',[1] which is used both as an adverb, 'separately', and as a conjunction, 'but'. Brugmann, however (p. 623), prefers to connect it with the Latin *at*, with the addition of ἄρ (cf. αὐτάρ).

Homer uses ἀτάρ and αὐτάρ indifferently, according to metrical convenience. In later Greek, while αὐτάρ practically vanishes, ἀτάρ is used freely by some writers, by others rarely, by others not at all. There are five examples in Pindar, three apiece in Aeschylus and Sophocles, considerably more in Euripides and Aristophanes. In prose, ἀτάρ is common in Hippocrates, fairly common in Herodotus, Plato, and Xenophon, unknown in the orators, Thucydides, and Aristotle. (Eucken, p. 36, cites Theophrastus, *HP* ix 20.3.) It would appear that in post-Homeric Greek, at any rate in Attic, ἀτάρ was felt to be colloquial in tone, and was consequently avoided in formal language. Hence its frequency in Aristophanes, in Euripides (who aimed at realistic expression), and in those prose-writers whose style approximates most closely to every-day conversation. Like αὐτάρ, ἀτάρ may be either adversative or progressive in sense. The latter is the commoner in Hippocrates, but the former predominates strongly in Attic.

(1) Adversative. Hom.*A* 506 Ζεῦ πάτερ, . . . τίμησόν μοι υἱὸν . . . ἀτάρ μιν . . . Ἀγαμέμνων ἠτίμησεν: *E* 131 μή τι σύ γ' ἀθανάτοισι θεοῖς ἀντικρὺ μάχεσθαι τοῖς ἄλλοις· ἀτὰρ εἴ κε Διὸς θυγατὴρ . . .: *Z* 429 (in an impassioned appeal, like ἀλλά) Ἕκτορ, ἀτὰρ σύ μοί ἐσσι πατὴρ καὶ πότνια μήτηρ: Ψ 104 ἦ ῥά τίς ἐστι καὶ εἰν Ἀΐδαο δόμοισι ψυχὴ καὶ εἴδωλον, ἀτὰρ φρένες οὐκ

[1] See Neil on Ar.*Eq.* 111.

ἔνι πάμπαν: β240 ἧσθ' ἄνεῳ, ἀτὰρ οὔ τι . . . μνηστῆρας κατερύκετε: γ138 μάψ, ἀτὰρ οὐ κατὰ κόσμον: Callin.*Fr.*1.4 ἐν εἰρήνῃ δὲ δοκεῖτε ἧσθαι, ἀτὰρ πόλεμος γαῖαν ἅπασαν ἔχει: A.*Pr.*1011 ὡς νεοζυγὴς πῶλος βιάζει καὶ πρὸς ἡνίας μάχει. ἀτὰρ σφοδρύνει γ' ἀσθενεῖ σοφίσματι: E.*Hipp.*728 πικροῦ δ' ἔρωτος ἡσσηθήσομαι. ἀτὰρ κακόν γε χἀτέρῳ γενήσομαι: 1398 Οὐκ ἔστι σοι κυναγὸς...— Οὐ δῆτ'· ἀτάρ μοι προσφιλής γ' ἀπόλλυσαι: Ar.*Eq.*111 Ταῦτ'· ἀτὰρ τοῦ δαίμονος δέδοιχ' ὅπως μὴ τεύξομαι κακοδαίμονος: 427 Εὖ γε ξυνέβαλεν αὔτ'· ἀτὰρ δῆλόν γ' ἀφ' οὗ ξυνέγνω: *Nu.*403 Οὐκ οἶδ'· ἀτὰρ εὖ σὺ λέγειν φαίνει: *V.*981 καίτοι τὸ κατάβα τοῦτο πολλοὺς δὴ πάνυ ἐξηπάτηκεν. ἀτὰρ ὅμως καταβήσομαι: 1141 μὰ τὸν Δί' οὐ τοίνυν (γιγνώσκω)· ἀτὰρ δοκεῖ γέ μοι ἐοικέναι . . .: Hom.*Υ*348: β122: γ298: δ236: Pi.*P.*3.98: *Fr.* 116(131).3: E.*Ba.*516: Ar.*Nu.*761: *Pl.*572: Hdt.ii 135 μεγάλα ἐκτήσατο χρήματα ὡς εἶναι Ῥοδῶπιν, ἀτὰρ οὐκ ὥς γε ἐς πυραμίδα τοιαύτην ἐξικέσθαι. (In Hom.*X*331 ἀτάρ expresses the contrast between Hector's boast and his fate. ὁ δ' ἐπεύξατο δῖος Ἀχιλλεύς· Ἕκτορ, ἀτάρ που ἔφης Πατροκλῆ' ἐξεναρίζων σῶς ἔσσεσθ'. In δ236 the particle is most naturally taken as marking a contrast with ἐσθλῶν: it has also been explained as looking forward to δαίνυσθε: see Merry and Riddell.)

In particular, Attic writers employ ἀτάρ to express a break-off, a sudden change of topic. This is the prevailing sense in Euripides, Aristophanes, Plato, and Xenophon.

A.*Pers.*333 κακῶν ὕψιστα δὴ κλύω τάδε . . . ἀτὰρ φράσον μοι τοῦτ' ἀναστρέψας πάλιν: E.*Hel.*86 Οὐ τἄρα σ' Ἑλένην εἰ στυγεῖς θαυμαστέον. ἀτὰρ τίς εἶ πόθεν; *Ph.*1643 εἰς ἅπαντα δυστυχὴς ἔφυς, πατέρ. (Turning to Creon) ἀτὰρ σ' ἐρωτῶ, τὸν νεωστὶ κοίρανον: *Supp.*750 (after a digression on human folly) ἀτὰρ τί ταῦτα; κεῖνο βούλομαι μαθεῖν, πῶς ἐξεσώθης: *Ion* 433 'What does the woman mean by her hints? ἀτὰρ θυγατρὸς τῆς Ἐρεχθέως τί μοι μέλει;' Ar.*Pax* 177 ὦ μηχανοποιὲ πρόσεχε τὸν νοῦν ὡς ἐμὲ . . . ἀτὰρ ἐγγὺς εἶναι τῶν θεῶν ἐμοὶ δοκῶ: *Av.* 144 τῶν κακῶν οἵων ἐρᾷς. ἀτὰρ ἔστι γ' ὁποίαν λέγετον εὐδαίμων πόλις: E.*Heracl.*661,879: *Hec.*258,671: *Hel.*860,1076: *Ph.*382: *Or.*861: *Ba.*248,453: *HF*1353: *Tr.*266: *IT*672,719: Ar.*Ach.* 412,448: *Nu.*30,187,382,677,801,1220: *V.*15,28,147,150,530,815, 1514: *id.saep.*: Pl.*Phdr.*227B καλῶς γὰρ . . . λέγει. ἀτὰρ Λυσίας ἦν, ὡς ἔοικεν, ἐν ἄστει: 230A ἀτάρ, ὦ ἑταῖρε, μεταξὺ τῶν λόγων . . . : *Men.*72A σμῆνός τι ἀνηύρηκα ἀρετῶν παρὰ σοὶ κείμενον. ἀτάρ, ὦ Μένων, κατὰ ταύτην τὴν εἰκόνα τὴν περὶ τὰ σμήνη . . . : *Tht.*142C 'I am not surprised that he is brave. ἀτὰρ πῶς οὐκ αὐτοῦ Μεγαροῖ κατέλυεν;' *Prt.*339C Φαίνεται ἔμοιγε (καὶ ἅμα μέντοι ἐφοβούμην μή τι λέγοι). ἀτάρ, ἔφην ἐγώ, σοὶ οὐ φαίνεται; Pl.*Phdr.*238C: *Euthd.*304D,305B: *Tht.*142D, 147C,154D: *Sph.*226B: *Lg.*702E: X.*Mem.*iii 1.5: 1.11: 10.10: 11.5: *An.*iv 6.14: vii 7.10: *Cyr.*ii 1.3: *Vect.*4.16.

(2) Progressive, with little or no idea of contrast. Hom.*B*313 ὀκτώ, ἀτὰρ μήτηρ ἐνάτη ἦν: *Δ*448 σύν ῥ' ἔβαλον ῥινοὺς . . . ἀτὰρ ἀσπίδες ὀμφαλοέσσαι ἔπληντ' ἀλλήλῃσι: α181 Ἀγχιάλοιο δαΐφρονος εὔχομαι εἶναι υἱός, ἀτὰρ Ταφίοισι φιληρέτμοισιν ἀνάσσω: ν358 νῦν δ' εὐχωλῇς ἀγανῇσι χαίρετ'. ἀτὰρ καὶ δῶρα διδώσομεν: π151 ἀλλὰ σύ γ' ἀγγείλας ὀπίσω κίε . . . ἀτὰρ πρὸς μητέρα εἰπεῖν: τ443 ὣς ἄρα πυκνὴ ἦεν, ἀτὰρ φύλλων ἐνέην χύσις ἤλιθα πολλή: χ373 ὄφρα γνῷς κατὰ θυμόν, ἀτὰρ εἴπῃσθα καὶ ἄλλῳ: Sol.*Fr.*1.24 λάμπει δ' ἠελίοιο μένος κατὰ πίονα γαῖαν καλόν, ἀτὰρ νεφέων οὐδὲν ἔτ' ἔστιν ἰδεῖν: Pi.*N.*4.47 Κύπρῳ, ἔνθα Τεῦκρος ἀπάρχει ὁ Τελαμωνιάδας· ἀτὰρ Αἴας Σαλαμῖν' ἔχει πατρῴαν· ἐν δ' Εὐξείνῳ πελάγει φαεννὰν Ἀχιλεὺς νᾶσον: Hes. *Th.*198: *Sc.*470: Hp.*Art.*9 πολλῶν ἔμπειρον δεῖ εἶναι τὸν ἰητρόν, ἀτὰρ δὴ καὶ ἀνατρίψιος: *Carn.*1 ἑτέρων τε τῶν ἔμπροσθεν, ἀτὰρ καὶ ἐμεωυτοῦ: *Epid.*ii 3.1 μάλιστα δὲ . . . ἀτὰρ καὶ . . . ἀτὰρ καὶ . . . : *Hum.*14 ἀτὰρ ἀνύδριαι . . . : *Art.*7 ἀτὰρ τὸν ἄνθρωπον καθίσαι: *Mul.*17 οὔτε ἡ ὑγρηδόνα ἔχουσα, ἀτὰρ οὐδὲ ἡ αὐαινομένη (ἀτὰρ οὐδέ, *Art.*1: *Acut.*1,18). ἀτὰρ καί is a common form of connexion in Hippocrates: *Art.*5,6,7: Pl.*Phlb.*66C "Ἕκτῃ δ' ἐν γενεᾷ", φησὶν Ὀρφεύς, "καταπαύσατε κόσμον ἀοιδῆς·" ἀτὰρ κινδυνεύει καὶ ὁ ἡμέτερος λόγος ἐν ἕκτῃ καταπεπαυμένος εἶναι κρίσει: *Phd.*60D καὶ ('both') ἄλλοι τινές με ἤδη ἤροντο, ἀτὰρ καὶ Εὔηνος πρῴην: *Mi.*319C πολλαχοῦ καὶ ἄλλοθι δηλοῖ, ἀτὰρ καὶ ἐνταῦθα: *Hp.Ma.*296A τά τε γοῦν ἄλλα . . . ἀτὰρ οὖν καὶ τὰ πολιτικά. In *Tht.*144E ἀτάρ may be simply 'Now': but it is probably more strongly adversative. (Hom. M144 should be included among the above. The apodosis is introduced, not by ἀτάρ, as L. & S. suggest, but by δέ in 145: so Ebeling.)

(3) *μὲν . . . ἀτάρ.* This combination, like *μὲν . . . δέ*, may denote either strong opposition, or little more than mere addition, or anything between the two.

(i) Strong adversative force. Hom.A166 *ἀλλὰ τὸ μὲν πλεῖον πολυάϊκος πολέμοιο χεῖρες ἐμαὶ διέπουσ᾽· ἀτὰρ ἤν ποτε δασμὸς ἵκηται, σοὶ τὸ γέρας πολὺ μεῖζον*: Thgn.1038 *ἤδεα μὲν καὶ πρόσθεν, ἀτὰρ πολὺ λώιον ἤδη*: A.*Pr.*343 *Τὰ μέν σ᾽ ἐπαινῶ . . . ἀτὰρ μηδὲν πόνει*: S.*OT*1052 *Οἶμαι μὲν . . . ἀτὰρ ἥδ᾽ ἂν . . . λέγοι*: *Tr.*54 *πῶς παισὶ μὲν τοσοῖσδε πληθύεις, ἀτὰρ . . .*: E.*Med.*84 *ὄλοιτο μὲν μή . . . ἀτὰρ κακός γ᾽ ὢν . . . ἁλίσκεται*: *Hipp.*1250 *δοῦλος μὲν οὖν ἔγωγε . . . ἀτὰρ τοσοῦτόν γ᾽ οὐ δυνήσομαί ποτε . . . πιθέσθαι*: Ar.*Ach.*513 *ἐγὼ δὲ μισῶ μὲν Λακεδαιμονίους σφόδρα . . . ἀτὰρ . . . τί ταῦτα τοὺς Λάκωνας αἰτιώμεθα;* Hom.Z86,125: E.*Tr.*344, 416: Hdt.iv 178 *λωτῷ μὲν καὶ οὗτοι χρεώμενοι, ἀτὰρ ἧσσόν γε τῶν πρότερον λεχθέντων*: v 66.1 *οἰκίης μὲν ἐὼν δοκίμου, ἀτὰρ τὰ ἀνέκαθεν οὐκ ἔχω φράσαι*: Pl.*Plt.*269D *πολλῶν μὲν καὶ μακαρίων . . . μετείληφεν, ἀτὰρ οὖν δὴ κεκοινώνηκέ γε καὶ σώματος*: *Sph.*225C *ταῦτα θετέον μὲν εἶδος . . . ἀτὰρ ἐπωνυμίας οὔτε ὑπὸ τῶν ἔμπροσθεν ἔτυχεν . . .*: Hdt.vi 35.1: 133.1: vii 50.1: viii 144.1.

(ii) Weaker adversative force. Hom.*I* 217 *Πάτροκλος μὲν σῖτον ἑλὼν ἐπένειμε τραπέζῃ . . . ἀτὰρ κρέα νεῖμεν Ἀχιλλεύς*: Pi.*P.*4.169 *οἱ μὲν κρίθεν· ἀτὰρ Ἰάσων αὐτὸς ἤδη ὤρνυεν κάρυκας*: Parm.*Fr.*8.58: Emp.*Fr.*109: S.*Tr.*761: Hdt.ii 175 *ταῦτα μὲν τὰ μέτρα ἔξωθεν . . . ἀτὰρ ἔσωθεν*: Pl.*Tht.*172C *καὶ πολλάκις μέν γε δὴ . . . καὶ ἄλλοτε κατενόησα, ἀτὰρ καὶ νῦν . . .*: *R.*367E *ἀεὶ μὲν δὴ . . . ἀτὰρ οὖν καὶ τότε . . .*: Meliss.*Fr.*8: Hdt.iv 18: Hp. *Fract.*6: *Epid.*iii 5: Pl.*Prt.*335D: *Alc.I* 124D: X.*HG* v 3.7: Archyt.*Fr.*4.

(4) Position. Normally first in sentence or clause: but in Homer occasionally postponed after apostrophe: Z86: X331.

(5) *ἀτάρ* combined with other particles. (For *ἀτὰρ καί, ἀτὰρ οὐδέ*, see (2) above). *ἀτὰρ δή.* E.*Cyc.*84: *Andr.*883: *Tr.*63: Hp.*Art.*9,14: Pl.*Sph.*232E. *ἀτὰρ οὖν.* Pl.*R.*367E: *Hp.Ma.* 296A: X.*Oec.*18.1. *ἀτὰρ οὖν δή.* Pl.*Chrm.*154B: *Plt.*269D. *ἀτάρ τε.* Thgn.597 *δὴν δὴ καὶ φίλοι ὦμεν· ἀτάρ τ᾽ ἄλλοισιν ὁμίλει ἀνδράσιν.* *ἀτὰρ μέν.* See *μέν.* *ἀτάρ τοι.* Hdt.iii 29.

Αὐτάρ

αὐτάρ seems to represent *αὖτε + ἄρ*. If so, the evolution of 'on the contrary' from 'again' is paralleled in the Latin *rursus*. The particle is virtually confined to Epic (and, later, Pastoral) poetry, its place elsewhere being taken by *ἀτάρ*. The only example in drama seems to be Hermipp.*Fr*.63.17 (in hexameters, mock-epic.) *M*'s *αὐτάρ* in E.*Ph*.1643 is clearly a slip. In Hp.*Morb*.iii 15 some MSS. read *αὐτάρ*, but the *ἀτάρ* of others is no doubt right. L. & S. cite *ἀϝυτάρ* from *IG*.1². 1012, and *αὐτάρ* from *Inscr.Cypr*.57H. There appears to be no distinction in sense between *αὐτάρ* and *ἀτάρ*. Like *ἀτάρ*, *αὐτάρ* often answers *μέν*: Hom.*A*51,127: *id. saep.*

(1) Strongly adversative. Hom.*A*118 *ἀλλὰ καὶ ὣς ἐθέλω δομέναι πάλιν . . . αὐτὰρ ἐμοὶ γέρας αὐτίχ' ἑτοιμάσατ'*: 333 *οὐδέ τί μιν προσεφώνεον οὐδ' ἐρέοντο· αὐτὰρ ὁ ἔγνω*: *δ*259 *ἔνθ' ἄλλαι Τρῳαὶ λίγ' ἐκώκυον· αὐτὰρ ἐμὸν κῆρ χαῖρε*. *μὲν . . . αὐτάρ*, *T*63.

(2) Weakly adversative, or purely progressive. (A commoner use.) Hom.*B*218 *τὼ δέ οἱ ὤμω κυρτὼ . . . αὐτὰρ ὕπερθε φοξὸς ἔην κεφαλήν*: 465 *ἐς πεδίον προχέοντο Σκαμάνδριον· αὐτὰρ ὑπὸ χθὼν . . . κονάβιζε*: *E*729 *τοῦ δ' ἐξ ἀργύρεος ῥυμὸς πέλεν· αὐτὰρ ἐπ' ἄκρῳ δῆσε . . . ζυγόν*: *Z*243 *ξεστῇς αἰθούσῃσι τετυγμένον—αὐτὰρ ἐν αὐτῷ πεντήκοντ' ἔνεσαν θάλαμοι*: *ι*335 *τέσσαρες, αὐτὰρ ἐγὼ πέμπτος μετὰ τοῖσιν ἐλέγμην*: *φ*290. *αὐτὰρ ἐπεί* often marks the successive stages of a narrative. *A*458 *αὐτὰρ ἐπεί ῥ' εὔξαντο*: 464 *αὐτὰρ ἐπεὶ κατὰ μῆρ' ἐκάη*: 467 *αὐτὰρ ἐπεὶ παύσαντο πόνου*: 469 *αὐτὰρ ἐπεὶ πόσιος καὶ ἐδητύος ἐξ ἔρον ἕντο*.

(3) Apodotic. Hom.*Γ*290 *εἰ δ' . . ., αὐτὰρ ἐγὼ καὶ ἔπειτα μαχήσομαι*: *X*390 *εἰ δὲ θανόντων περ καταλήθοντ' εἰν Ἀΐδαο, αὐτὰρ ἐγὼ καὶ κεῖθι φίλου μεμνήσομ' ἑταίρου*. If *αὐτάρ* is *αὖτε + ἄρ*, these examples perhaps illustrate the original, adverbial, sense of the particle. Cf. also Hom.*A*133 *ἦ ἐθέλεις, ὄφρ' αὐτὸς ἔχῃς γέρας, αὐτὰρ ἔμ' αὔτως ἧσθαι δευόμενον . . .*; But the interpretation is uncertain (see Leaf).

Γάρ

The derivation of *γάρ* from *γε* and *ἄρ*, though occasionally challenged (as, e.g., by H. Weber in *Phil.Rundsch.*iv 1078), has been pretty generally accepted by scholars. It is adopted in the Brugmann-Thumb grammar, Boisacq's *Dictionnaire Étymologique*, and the new edition of Liddell and Scott. There appears little reason to doubt this etymology, though it may be remarked (1) that the form *γάρα* is nowhere found; (2) that the combinations *γὰρ ἄρα*, *γάρ ῥα*, are tolerated. (Pl.*Prt.*315C *ἐπεδήμει γὰρ ἄρα Πρόδικος*: *R.*438A: *Smp.*205B: *Grg.*469D: *γάρ ῥα*, Hom.*A*113: *id. saep.*) The fusion, if it occurred, must have occurred at an early date.

Hartung and his successors base their theories of *γάρ* on the supposed meaning of the supposed component parts: and divergent views of *γε* and *ἄρα* beget divergent views of *γάρ* in bewildering multiplicity. To pursue these various theories through all their ramifications would be unprofitable. It need only be said that the tendency of nineteenth-century research has been to question the old view that 'for' is the only, or at any rate the original, meaning of *γάρ*, all apparent deviations being explained by ellipse; and to give prominence to two other uses: (1) affirmative, adverbial, 'beziehungslos' (Bäumlein); (2) inferential, in exclamations and questions (a use affirmed by Hartung and Klotz, but denied by Bäumlein). More recently, however, a reaction has set in. Sernatinger and Prof. Misener (see her admirable dissertation) derive all uses of *γάρ* from the causal, and freely assume ellipse, where necessary. The latter scholar points out that the so-called 'affirmative' uses are commoner in the later Greek authors than in the earlier, from which she argues that they are derivative, not primary. Further, they are commoner in dramatic dialogue, which is, in general, highly compressed and elliptical, than in other literature.

The truth lies, I believe, somewhere between the two extremes. On the one hand, many peculiarities which *γάρ* exhibits, especially in dialogue, can be reasonably explained as elliptical variants of the 'for' sense; on the other, any attempt to confine *γάρ* everywhere to that sense breaks down finally at some point or other.

To begin with, etymological considerations apart, it is unlikely that 'for' is the primary meaning; and it would still, perhaps, be unlikely if *γάρ* undeniably meant 'for' in every single passage in which it occurred in extant Greek literature. Probably few Greek connecting particles started their careers as conjunctions. And the analogy of *δή* and *μήν* (the case of *οὖν* is more complicated) would suggest that an earlier, asseverative force lay behind the causal sense of *γάρ*. This supposition accords well with the derivation from *γε* and *ἄρα*, particularly if *γε* is regarded here as limitative in force. The combination would then mean 'this, at any rate (*γε*) is true, as I realize (*ἄρα*)'; and the development of a connective force, 'for', would be closely paralleled by the quasi-connective force of *γοῦν* (and, more rarely, simple *γε*), to which *γάρ* sometimes, as we shall see (III.8), comes very near in significance. Further, as with *δή* and *μήν*, so with *γάρ*, the original asseverative force remains in existence after the development of the connective, and side by side with it, at any rate in combinations (just as the asseverative force of *μήν* persists in *ἀλλὰ μήν*, *καὶ μήν*, and *ἦ μήν*): *καὶ γάρ*, *καὶ γὰρ οὖν*, *καὶ γάρ τοι*, *τοιγάρ*, *τοιγαροῦν*, *τοιγάρτοι*, and sometimes, perhaps, *ἀλλὰ γάρ* (*q.v.*, III. 8). That *γάρ* is asseverative anywhere except in these combinations (and perhaps in *εἰ γάρ*) is highly doubtful. (But cf. Plautus, *Bacchides* 1162: An amas?—*Ναὶ γάρ*). Some scholars regard explanatory, anticipatory, and assentient *γάρ*, and *γάρ* in *ἀλλὰ γάρ*, as affirmative. But these uses are nothing more than particular aspects of the causal. Little importance can be attached to the heterogeneous passages quoted in X (*ad init.*).

'Asseverative' *γάρ* must, then, be admitted, but probably only within narrowly defined limits. On the other hand 'inferential' *γάρ* (with *ἄρα* predominating) has little or no claim to recognition. An inferential force is, it is true, appropriate enough in interrogative answers. But a causal force fits interrogative and categorical answers alike with equal ease. (*Θανοῦμαι.—Νοσεῖς γάρ*; ('I shall die'.—'Because you're ill, are you?') *Νοσεῖς ἄρα*; ('So you're ill, are you?') gives a totally different, but equally appropriate, connexion.) The case for the 'inferential' explanation is certainly much stronger in progressive *γάρ* questions (VI). But I shall give reasons for believing that this use also is ultimately derived from the causal sense.

I. Confirmatory and causal, giving the ground for belief, or the motive for action. This usage may be illustrated from any page of any Greek author. It is, however, commoner in writers whose mode of thought is simple than in those whose logical faculties are more fully developed. The former tend to state a fact before investigating its reason, while the latter more frequently follow the logical order, cause and effect, whether they employ subordination or co-ordination of clauses. Broschmann calls attention to the commonness of γάρ in Homer and Herodotus, and to the comparative rarity in Herodotus of the syntactical conjunctions, ἐπεί, ἐπειδή, ὅτι, ὡς. He gives examples from these two writers of successions of γάρ clauses or sentences, each clause dependent on the preceding one: Hom.*B*12–14 (three): *Ω*66–70 (four): Hdt.iii 80–82 (γάρ used eighteen times in all): iv 1 six sentences opening with γάρ, consecutive except for an intermediate one opening with δέ). For a similar accumulation, cf. Pl.*Ap*.39E–40A (in a work marked by conscious naïveté of style: see 17B–C): Arist.*Pol*.1261a24-6. In Sophocles, γάρ not infrequently introduces successive clauses in successive lines: *Aj*.20, 215,514,1262: *OT*317: *Ant*.1255: *Ph*.1158: E.*Ion* 373: *El*.368: *IA* 1422. See Jebb on S.*El*.180 (III.6 below). γάρ twice in a line, S.*OT*1117: E.*IT*1325: *IA*425: *Hel*.1430: Callias*Fr*.12.

II. Explanatory. This usage, as Hartung (i 469) and Bäumlein (p. 86) rightly observe, is nearly related to the confirmatory. (There is no need, with Kühner, to regard the particle as 'adverbial' here.) It is rare in Homer, where some apparent examples are probably better explained as anticipatory (*N*736: *P*221: ι319: κ190: ψ362: see IV.2 below), or as ordinary causal (δ722: λ508). While the use of γάρ in explanations is regular, asyndeton is very often employed (Kühner, II ii 344).

Explanatory γάρ is most commonly found:—

(1) After τεκμήριον δέ, σημεῖον δέ, and similar expressions. S.*OC*146 δηλῶ δ'· οὐ γὰρ . . .: 1145 δείκνυμι δ'· ὧν γὰρ . . .: Hdt.viii 120 μέγα δὲ καὶ τόδε μαρτύριον· φαίνεται γὰρ Ξέρξης . . .: Th.i 3.1 δηλοῖ δέ μοι τόδε τῶν παλαιῶν ἀσθένειαν οὐχ ἥκιστα· πρὸ γὰρ τῶν Τρωικῶν . . .: i 143.5 σκέψασθε δέ· εἰ γὰρ ἦμεν νησιῶται . . .: Lys.i 37 σκέψασθε δέ, ὦ ἄνδρες· κατηγοροῦσι γάρ μου:

Isoc.vii 35 κεφαλαῖον δὲ τοῦ καλῶς ἀλλήλοις ὁμιλεῖν· αἱ μὲν γὰρ κτήσεις ἀσφαλεῖς ἦσαν: iv 87 σημεῖον δὲ τοῦ τάχους καὶ τῆς ἁμίλλης· τοὺς μὲν γὰρ . . .: X.*Mem.*i 2.32 ἐδήλωσε δέ· ἐπεὶ γὰρ οἱ τριάκοντα . . .: *Smp.*4.17 τεκμήριον δέ· θαλλοφόρους γὰρ . . .: Th.i 2.6.: 8.1: X.*HG*vi 4.13: Isoc.vii 17.

(2) After an expression denoting the giving or receiving of information, or conveying a summons to attention. Hom.μ59 ἐρέω δέ τοι ἀμφοτέρωθεν· ἔνθεν μὲν γὰρ πέτραι . . .:Pi.*P.*4.70 ἀπὸ δ' αὐτὸν ἐγὼ Μοίσαισι δώσω . . . τίς γὰρ ἀρχὰ δέξατο ναυτιλίας; A.*Pers.*255 ὅμως δ' ἀνάγκη πᾶν ἀναπτύξαι πάθος, Πέρσαι· στρατὸς γὰρ πᾶς ὄλωλε βαρβάρων: *Ag.*267 πεύσει δὲ χάρμα μεῖζον ἐλπίδος κλύειν· Πριάμου γὰρ ᾑρήκασιν Ἀργεῖοι πόλιν: S.*Tr.*475 πᾶν σοι φράσω τἀληθὲς . . . ἔστιν γὰρ οὕτως: Ar.*Pl.*78 ἀκούετον δή . . . ἐγὼ γάρ εἰμι Πλοῦτος: S.*OT*346,711,994: *Ph.*915,1049, 1326: E.*Cyc.*313: *Heracl.*800: *Hec.*1181: Th.i 73.4 ἀνάγκη λέγειν . . . ῥηθήσεται δὲ . . . φαμὲν γὰρ . . .: ii 49.1 λέξω . . . δηλώσω . . . τὸ μὲν γὰρ ἔτος . . .: Pl.*Smp.*217B προσέχετε τὸν νοῦν, καὶ εἰ ψεύδομαι, Σώκρατες, ἐξέλεγχε· συνεγιγνόμην γὰρ . . .: *Phlb.*37A διορισώμεθα δὴ σαφέστερον . . . ἔστιν γάρ πού τι δοξάζειν ἡμῖν; *Prt.*318D χαίρω ἀποκρινόμενος· Ἱπποκράτης γὰρ . . .: 320C δοκεῖ . . . χαριέστερον εἶναι μῦθον ὑμῖν λέγειν. ἦν γάρ ποτε χρόνος ('Well, once upon a time'): *Phd.*86E λέγω δή . . . ἐμοὶ γὰρ φαίνεται . . .: *Ap.*20D πᾶσαν ὑμῖν τὴν ἀλήθειαν ἐρῶ. ἐγὼ γὰρ . . .: *R.*329A ἐρῶ . . . πολλάκις γὰρ συνερχόμεθα: Isoc.iv 28 ὅμως αὐτῷ (τῷ λόγῳ) καὶ νῦν ῥηθῆναι προσήκει. Δήμητρος γὰρ ἀφικομένης . . .: Pl.*Euthphr.*12D: *R.*451C: *Lg.*626E,695C: *Phlb.* 29D: Lys.iii 5,6: ix 13: xiii 19.

(3) After a forward-pointing pronominal adjective or adverb. Hom.Θ148 ἀλλὰ τόδ' αἰνὸν ἄχος κραδίην καὶ θυμὸν ἱκάνει· Ἕκτωρ γάρ ποτε φήσει . . .: S.*OT*779 πρίν μοι τύχη τοιάδ' ἐπέστη . . . ἀνὴρ γὰρ . . .: E.*HF*1295 ἐς τοῦτο δ' ἥξειν συμφορᾶς οἶμαί ποτε· φωνὴν γὰρ ἥσει χθών: S.*Tr.*572: E.*IT*352: Hdt.i 191 ἐποίεε . . . τοιαῦτα . . . τὸν γὰρ ποταμὸν . . .: Lys.xii 19 εἰς τοσαύτην ἀπληστίαν . . . ἀφίκοντο . . . τῆς γὰρ Πολεμάρχου γυναικὸς . . .: Pl. *Prt.*349D ὧδε δὲ γνώσῃ ὅτι ἐγὼ ἀληθῆ λέγω· εὑρήσεις γὰρ πολλοὺς . . .: X.*Mem.*i 1.6 ἐποίει καὶ τάδε . . . τὰ μὲν γὰρ ἀναγκαῖα συνεβούλευε: Pl.*Ap.*31B: Lys. xvi 6: Isoc.iii 31.

(4) After a neuter superlative adjective. Ar.*Av.*514 ὁ δὲ δεινότατόν γ' ἐστὶν ἁπάντων, ὁ Ζεὺς γὰρ ὁ νῦν βασιλεύων . . . : Hdt. iii 80 ἀναρμοστότατον δὲ πάντων· ἤν τε γὰρ . . . : Isoc.iii 21 τὸ δὲ μέγιστον· τοῖς γὰρ κοινοῖς . . . : viii 53 ὃ δὲ πάντων σχετλιώτατον· οὓς γὰρ . . .

(5) Other examples do not fall under any of the above headings. S.*OC*1161 Οὐκ οἶδα πλὴν ἕν· σοῦ γὰρ . . . βραχύν τιν' αἰτεῖ μῦθον : E.*Tr.*688 ἐπίσταμαι (life on board ship). ναύταις γὰρ . . . : Hdt.i 59 Ἱπποκράτεϊ . . . τέρας ἐγένετο μέγα· θύσαντος γὰρ αὐτοῦ . . .: ix 50 ἄλλα γὰρ τούτων τοιούτων ἐόντων μᾶλλόν σφεας ἐλύπεε. οὔτε γὰρ σιτία εἶχον ἔτι : Pl.*Ap.*40A ἐμοὶ . . . θαυμάσιόν τι γέγονεν. ἡ γὰρ εἰωθυῖά μοι μαντικὴ . . . : Lys.xiii 79 : ἀλλ' ἕτερον· οὔτε γὰρ . . . : Pl.*Ti.*21B,82A. (In some of these examples the explanatory sense merges in the confirmatory.) See further γὰρ οὖν (5).

III. Peculiarities in the use of causal and explanatory γάρ.

(1) Γάρ gives the motive for saying that which has just been said : 'I say this because . . .'. S.*OT*559 δέδρακε ποῖον ἔργον ; οὐ γὰρ ἐννοῶ ('I ask you, because I don't understand' : cf. *Ph.* 28) : *Aj.*1265 Εἴθ' ὑμὶν ἀμφοῖν νοῦς γένοιτο σωφρονεῖν· τούτου γὰρ οὐδὲν σφῷν ἔχω λῷον φράσαι : *Tr.*289 φρόνει νιν ὡς ἥξοντα· τοῦτο γὰρ λόγου πολλοῦ καλῶς λεχθέντος ἥδιστον κλύειν : 817 ('γάρ justifies his unfilial language', Jebb) : E.*Med.*465 Ὦ παγκάκιστε, τοῦτο γάρ σ' εἰπεῖν ἔχω γλώσσῃ μέγιστον εἰς ἀνανδρίαν κακόν : 663 Μήδεια, χαῖρε· τοῦδε γὰρ προοίμιον κάλλιον οὐδεὶς οἶδε προσφωνεῖν φίλους : 1370 Οἴδ' οὐκέτ' εἰσί· τοῦτο γάρ σε δήξεται ('Aye, that will sting thee!') : *Tr.*983 Κύπριν δ' ἔλεξας—ταῦτα γὰρ γέλως πολύς—ἐλθεῖν ('I refer to it because it is so absurd') : *Heracl.*134 : *Ion*1022 : *Or.*75 : Ar.*Ec.*607 : Hdt. vi 111.2 τελευταῖοι δὲ ἐτάσσοντο . . . Πλαταιέες. ἀπὸ ταύτης γάρ σφι τῆς μάχης Ἀθηναίων θυσίας ἀναγόντων . . . κατεύχεται ὁ κῆρυξ ὁ Ἀθηναῖος ἅμα τε Ἀθηναίοισι λέγων γίνεσθαι τὰ ἀγαθὰ καὶ Πλαταιεῦσι (introducing a particular reason for mentioning the Plataeans here) : Pl.*Smp.*215B ὑβριστὴς εἶ· ἢ οὔ ; ἐὰν γὰρ μὴ ὁμολογῇς, μάρτυρας παρέξομαι (the motive for demanding a voluntary confession is that, failing it, witnesses will have to be produced) : *Phdr.*229A Εἰς καιρὸν . . . ἀνυπόδητος ὢν ἔτυχον· σὺ μὲν γὰρ δὴ ἀεί (γάρ explains why Phaedrus says ἔτυ-

χον, not ἐτύχομεν : cf. *Lg*.629B ὅδε μὲν γάρ explains the use of the singular σύ, instead of ὑμεῖς) : *Euthphr*.12C ἕπῃ γάρ που νῦν γε ; ('I think you can follow me now' : 'I put it like that because in that form it ought to be intelligible to you'. Cf. *R*.413B,491C (the etcetera is intelligible, because it adequately denotes the type)) : D.xliv20 χρόνῳ δ' ὕστερον οὐ πολλῷ—τοῖς γὰρ μετὰ ταῦτα λόγοις ἤδη σφόδρα τὸν νοῦν προσέχετε ('I mention these facts, because they are particularly deserving of attention') : Pl. *Smp*.192D : *Ap*.20B : *R*.347A,590A : *Lg*.711A.

Conversely, in S.*Ph*.1054, the use of the words contained in the γάρ clause forms a confirmation of what precedes : νῦν δὲ σοί γ' ἑκὼν ἐκστήσομαι. (To the attendants) ἄφετε γὰρ αὐτόν ('For I say, release him'). Converted into the form of the examples given above, this would run : ἄφετε αὐτόν· σοὶ γὰρ ἑκὼν ἐκστήσομαι.

(2) The connexion of thought is sometimes lacking in logical precision. Verrall well observes, on E.*Med*.573, that 'the use of γάρ is regulated by the substance of the thought, and not by its form'. Compression of thought is often the source of difficulty, and formal exactitude can then be achieved by supposing an ellipse, as in the passages quoted in the previous section. But this, though a convenient method of exposition, is psychologically somewhat misleading.

Hom.*O*612 ὅς μιν . . . τίμα καὶ κύδαινε. μινυνθάδιος γὰρ ἔμελλεν ἔσσεσθ' ('gave him glory', *sc*. 'but not long life' : cf. *Z*447, 'aiming at glory, not the preservation of Troy') : α411 οὐδ' ὑπέμεινε γνωμέναι ('as we would gladly have done')· οὐ μὲν γάρ τι κακῷ εἰς ὦπα ἐῴκει : S.*OT* 317 (see Jebb) : 569 Οὐκ οἶδ' ('and will not guess')· ἐφ' οἷς γὰρ μὴ φρονῶ σιγᾶν φιλῶ : *OC*1301 ('the connexion shows that the μάντεις are the soothsayers of his new army', Campbell : see also Jebb) : *Ph*.91 ('and we can easily force him, for . . .') : 1167 ('and it is worth escaping, for . . .') : E.*Med*.122 ('for they lack the salutary effects of an equal status') : 573 ('for woman is nothing but a badly contrived machine for reproduction', Verrall : ἄρ' Porson : cf.*Or*.755 (*M* γάρ for ἄρ') : perhaps τἄρ') : *El*.1068 ('Your excuse carries some conviction, because other people do not know you as I do') : *Ph*.961 ('Yet I am not surprised at your silence : for I too am dumbfounded'): Ar.*Av.*1220 *Ποίᾳ γὰρ ἄλλῃ χρὴ πέτεσθαι τοὺς θεούς;—Οὐκ οἶδα μὰ Δί' ἔγωγε· τῇδε μὲν γὰρ οὔ* ('I don't know: (but it must be *some* other way) for it isn't *this*'): *Lys.* 636 (*Οὐ γάρ* seems impossible, and Dobree's *Οὐκ ἄρ'* right): Th.i 120.1 *τοὺς μὲν Λακεδαιμονίους . . . οὐκ ἂν ἔτι αἰτιασαίμεθα ὡς οὐ καὶ αὐτοὶ ἐψηφισμένοι τὸν πόλεμόν εἰσι . . . χρὴ γὰρ τοὺς ἡγεμόνας . . . τὰ κοινὰ προσκοπεῖν* (*γάρ* substantiates the legitimacy, in principle, of such a grievance): Pl.*R.*328A *παννυχίδα ποιήσουσιν, ἣν ἄξιον θεάσασθαι·* ('and we can conveniently do so') *ἐξαναστησόμεθα γὰρ μετὰ τὸ δεῖπνον καὶ τὴν παννυχίδα θεασόμεθα*: *Thg.*127A (his rejection of the so-called *καλοὶ κἀγαθοί* is motivated by his conviction that Socrates, who is just as *καλὸς κἀγαθός* as they, is good enough for him): *Phd.*64C (*γάρ* introduces, not the individual sentence *εἴπωμεν . . . ἐκείνοις*, but the whole argument in support of *λέληθεν . . . φιλόσοφοι*): *Smp.* 173D: 'I don't know why you are called *μανικός* (but you have some right to the title)'—*μανικός*, not *μαλακός*, must be right—'you are *μανικός* enough *ἐν τοῖς λόγοις*'. *γάρ* approximates to *γοῦν* here (cf. III.8: Badham's *γε* is possible): *Lg.*794D (two thoughts are blended here. The speaker lays stress on this branch of education (1) because of its importance: (2) because he has original views on the subject. *γάρ* explains (2)): Ant.v36 *μὲν γάρ* (*μὲν* *om. N*: *γάρ* is very difficult: read perhaps *μὲν* [*γάρ*], or *μέν γε*): 56 ('they could not now get rid of the document (as they would gladly have done), for . . .'). On Arist.*Pol.*1270a15 see Susemihl-Hicks and Newman.*

In other cases the *γάρ* clause explains the tone of the preceding words, rather than their content. S.*Ph.*624 *ἦ κεῖνος . . . ἐμ' εἰς Ἀχαιοὺς ὤμοσεν πείσας στελεῖν; πεισθήσομαι γὰρ ὧδε κἀξ Ἅιδου θανὼν πρὸς φῶς ἀνελθεῖν* (Philoctetes justifies the indignant incredulity of his question: 'Why, in that case . . .' To suppose, with Jebb, an ellipse of *οὔτοι στελεῖ* is unnecessary): Ar. *Ach.*588 *Οὗτος τί δράσεις; τῷ πτίλῳ μέλλεις ἐμεῖν; πτίλον γάρ ἐστιν . . .* ('Why, its a feather . . .': 'you mustn't, for . . .').

(3) A *γάρ* clause supports the truth of an assertion by the argument that, were it untrue, something else known to be true would also be untrue: 'for otherwise'. See Jebb, Appendix to S.*OT*, p. 221.

Hom.*A*232 ἐπεὶ οὐτιδανοῖσιν ἀνάσσεις· ἦ γὰρ ἄν, Ἀτρεΐδη, νῦν ὕστατα λωβήσαιο : A.*Eu.*607 : S.*Aj.*1330 : *El.*1448 : *OT*82,318 : *Tr.*1118 : E.*HF*274 : *IT*666,1201 : *IA*1256 : Hdt.i124 Ὦ παῖ Καμβύσεω, σὲ γὰρ θεοὶ ἐπορῶσι, οὐ γὰρ ἄν κοτε ἐς τοσοῦτο τύχης ἀπίκευ : ii49 : iii38 : iv32 : ix45.2 : Pl.*Smp.*222C : *Cra.*413E, 436C : *R.*554B : Arist.*Metaph.*1038b29 : *Pol.*1280a32,b8,1283a1 : D.xix293.

(4) Γάρ refers, not to the immediately preceding sentence, but to something further back. This looseness of structure is characteristic of Homer and Herodotus : the Attic examples are few, and not remarkable. The Herodotean passages are discussed by Broschmann, pp. 17–18.

Hom.*B*119 αἰσχρὸν γὰρ τόδε γ' ἐστί (referring to δυσκλέα in 115) : α392 οὐ μὲν γάρ τι κακὸν βασιλευέμεν (referring to 390) : ρ400 δός οἱ ἑλών· οὔ τοι φθονέω· κέλομαι γὰρ ἐγώ γε : υ273 οὐ γὰρ Ζεὺς εἴασε (referring to 271) : Hes.*Sc.*357 (referring to 350–3 : unless γάρ is adverbial : cf. X) : A.*Ag.* 272 Τί γὰρ τὸ πιστόν ; (referring to 269) : 555 μόχθους γὰρ εἰ λέγοιμι (referring to 553 τὰ δ' αὖτε κἀπίμομφα) : S.*Aj.*25 (referring to 21–2) : *OC*25 τὰς γοῦν Ἀθήνας οἶδα, τὸν δὲ χῶρον οὔ.—Πᾶς γάρ τις ηὔδα τοῦτό γ' ἡμὶν ἐμπόρων (referring to the former of two paratactic clauses) : E.*HF.*1176 (referring to 1174, with ellipse: 'They cannot have been killed in battle, for . . .') : *Med.*1228 (referring to 1224: but see Verrall) : Hdt.i71 (Sandanis has been contrasting Persian asceticism with Lydian luxury) ταῦτα λέγων οὐκ ἔπειθε τὸν Κροῖσον. Πέρσῃσι γάρ, πρὶν Λυδοὺς καταστρέψασθαι, ἦν οὔτε ἁβρὸν οὔτε ἀγαθὸν οὐδέν : iii89 (Δαρεῖος) ἐτάξατο φόρους. Then details of the tribute. ἐπὶ γὰρ Κύρου ἄρχοντος καὶ αὖτις Καμβύσεω ἦν κατεστηκὸς οὐδὲν φόρου πέρι : iii102 αἱ γάρ σφι κάμηλοι . . . : vii22.2 ὁ γὰρ Ἄθως . . . : 106.1 κατέστασαν γὰρ . . . : 170.1 λέγεται γὰρ Μίνων . . .

(5) In dramatic dialogue, a speaker continues his own train of thought with γάρ, ignoring the intervening speech of another person. S.*OC*837 Εἴργου.—Σοῦ μὲν οὔ, τάδε γε μωμένου.—Πόλει μαχῇ γάρ, εἴ τι πημανεῖς ἐμέ : E.*Or.*1516 Ἐνδικώτατα (διώλετο) . . .—Δειλίᾳ γλώσσῃ χαρίζῃ . . .—Οὐ γάρ ; ἥτις Ἑλλάδ' . . . διελυμήνατο ; 1616 Πόνους πονήσας μυρίους.—Πλήν γ' εἰς ἐμέ.—Πέπονθα δεινά.—Τότε γὰρ ἦσθ' ἀνωφελής : *Hel.*348 πότερα δέρ-

κεται φάος (πόσις) . . . ;—Ἐς τὸ φέρτερον τίθει τὸ μέλλον . . .— Σὲ γὰρ . . . κατόμοσα, τὸν . . . Εὐρώταν ('that if he is dead I will kill myself'): Ar. *V.*300 'I won't give you figs'.—Μὰ Δί' οὐ τἄρα προπέμψω σε τὸ λοιπόν.—Ἀπὸ γὰρ τοῦδέ με τοῦ μισθαρίου τρίτον αὐτὸν ἔχειν ἄλφιτα δεῖ: *Pax* 1088 'You must not make peace yet.'—Ἆρα φενακίζων ποτ' Ἀθηναίους ἔτι παύσει;—Ποῖον γὰρ κατὰ χρησμὸν ἐκαύσατε μῆρα θεοῖσιν; *Pl.*418 τί φεύγετον; οὐ μενεῖτον;—Ἡράκλεις.—Ἐγὼ γὰρ ὑμᾶς ἐξολῶ κακοὺς κακῶς (the prospect of immediate destruction is humorously given as a reason for not running away: 'Dilly dilly duckling, come and be killed').

(6) Successive γάρ's have the same reference (Broschmann, pp. 32–3. Some of his examples are better explained otherwise. I add others of my own). A.*Ag.*559–60 τὰ δ' αὖτε χέρσῳ καὶ προσῆν πλέον στύγος· εὐναὶ γὰρ ἦσαν δαΐων πρὸς τείχεσιν. ἐξ οὐρανοῦ γὰρ κἀπὸ γῆς λειμώνιαι δρόσοι κατεψάκαζον (but see Verrall's punctuation, below: δέ Pearson): S.*El.* 179–80 (the healing effect of time, and the possibility of future retribution, are both urged as reasons for calmness. Jebb makes the second γάρ clause refer to the first: but his notes are evasive): *Aj.* 182–5 (a negative argument reinforced by a positive one): *Ant.* 659–61 ἀλλὰ κτενῶ. πρὸς ταῦτ' ἐφυμνείτω Δία ξύναιμον· εἰ γὰρ δὴ τά γ' ἐγγενῆ φύσει ἄκοσμα θρέψω, κάρτα τοὺς ἔξω γένους. ἐν τοῖς γὰρ οἰκείοισιν ὅστις ἔστ' ἀνὴρ χρηστός, φανεῖται κἀν πόλει δίκαιος ὤν (the same argument twice, in differing forms): E.*Hel.* 477–9, *IA* 1423–4 (see England): Hdt.vii 51.2 τούτους ὦν τοὺς ἄνδρας συμβουλεύω τοι μηδεμιῇ μηχανῇ ἄγειν ἐπὶ τοὺς πατέρας. καὶ γὰρ ἄνευ τούτων οἷοί τέ εἰμεν τῶν ἐχθρῶν κατυπέρτεροι γίνεσθαι. ἢ γάρ σφεας, ἢν ἕπωνται, δεῖ ἀδικωτάτους γίνεσθαι καταδουλουμένους τὴν μητρόπολιν, ἢ δικαιοτάτους συνελευθεροῦντας ('Their help is not needed: and they cannot be relied upon'): Th. i 40.5–6 δικαιοί γ' ἐστὲ . . . τὸν νόμον μὴ καθιστάναι ὥστε τοὺς ἑτέρων ἀφισταμένους δέχεσθαι. οὐδὲ γὰρ ἡμεῖς Σαμίων ἀποστάντων ψῆφον προσεθέμεθα ἐναντίαν ὑμῖν . . . εἰ γὰρ τοὺς κακόν τι δρῶντας δεχόμενοι τιμωρήσετε, φανεῖται καὶ ἃ τῶν ὑμετέρων οὐκ ἐλάσσω ἡμῖν πρόσεισι (a passage exactly parallel to Hdt.vii 51.2: two independent arguments—here, gratitude and self-interest—are urged in favour of a course of action): X.*An.*v 6.4 (the solemn

oath is motivated by two considerations: that giving counsel is, in general, a 'holy thing'; and that, in the present case, the reputation of the counsellor is deeply involved): D.xx 117 (οὐ γάρ and εἰ μὲν γάρ both look back to the last sentence of §116. The passage, therefore, lends no support to Stahl's view (*Rh.M.* 1902,1–7) that γάρ is sometimes concessive). Perhaps, Ant.v 6 ('malim δέ', for the second γάρ, Thalheim): 86–7 (a repetition of the trial is to be desired (1) because that is the best way of arriving at the truth (τοσούτῳ γὰρ ἄμεινον κ.τ.λ.): (2) because the consequences of condemnation are irreparable (φόνου γὰρ δίκη κ.τ.λ.): φόνου δέ, Reiske). Cf. also Arist.*Pol.* 1265a29–31.*

We must distinguish from the above passages others in which the first γάρ clause is parenthetical, and the references in the two γάρ clauses are therefore not parallel. Hom.υ305–6 Κτήσιππ', ἦ μάλα τοι τόδε κέρδιον ἔπλετο θυμῷ· οὐκ ἔβαλες τὸν ξεῖνον· ἀλεύατο γὰρ βέλος αὐτός. ἦ γάρ κέν σε μέσον βάλον ἔγχεϊ ὀξυόεντι (the first γάρ explaining οὐκ ἔβαλες, the second, κέρδιον ἔπλετο): S.*OC* 980–2 γάμους . . . οἵους ἐρῶ τάχ'· οὐ γὰρ οὖν σιγήσομαι . . . ἔτικτε γάρ μ' ἔτικτεν (the first γάρ being causal, the second explanatory): Pi.*P.*4.68–70: Th.i 91.3: ii 5.4: Pl.*Chrm.*174A: X.*An.*v 6.6: Lys.ii 3–4: D.lvi 4–5: Hyp.*Epit.*10. In A.*Ag.* 558–61, if Verrall's punctuation is adopted, the first γάρ clause is in a parenthesis which reaches from καὶ προσῆν to τείχεσιν: the second γάρ explains τὰ δ' αὖτε χέρσῳ. (Similarly, in E.*Or.* 1091–4 I should make καὶ τῆδ' . . . δάμαρτα a parenthesis: see *C.R.*xliv(1930)215.) In Th.iii 2.2–3 τῶν τε γὰρ λιμένων κ.τ.λ. explains ἀναγκασθέντες and πρότερον ἢ διενοοῦντο: Τενέδιοι γὰρ κ.τ.λ. explains ἀπέστη. We may, perhaps, include here a curious use of repeated γάρ in anaphora: Hp.*Art.*14 τοῦτο γὰρ ἔχει κίνησιν, τοῦτο γάρ ἐστι καὶ τὸ ἀποστὰν ἀπὸ τῆς φύσιος.

(7) Γάρ refers, not to the main idea of the preceding sentence, but (i) to a single clause, or (ii) to an individual word or phrase. Here, again, the force of the argument may be brought out by supposing an ellipse.[1]

(i) Hom.*A*342 εἴ ποτε δὴ αὖτε χρειὼ ἐμεῖο γένηται ἀεικέα λοιγὸν ἀμῦναι τοῖς ἄλλοις· ἦ γὰρ ὅ γ' ὀλοιῇσι φρεσὶ θύει ('and

[1] This section should be read in conjunction with III.2. Some of the examples there given might well have been grouped here. Cf. also V.7.

they may well need me, for . . .'): A.*Pr*.149 φοβερὰ δ' ἐμοῖσιν ὄσσοις ὁμίχλα προσῆξε . . . σὸν δέμας εἰσιδοῦσαν πέτραις προσαυαινόμενον . . . νέοι γὰρ οἰακονόμοι κρατοῦσ' Ὀλύμπου: Hom. *Ω*421: X.*An*.v 2.9 ἐσκοπεῖτο πότερον εἴη κρεῖττον ἀπαγαγεῖν καὶ τοὺς διαβεβηκότας ἢ καὶ τοὺς ὁπλίτας διαβιβάζειν . . . ἐδόκει γὰρ τὸ μὲν ἀπαγαγεῖν . . . (γάρ introduces the reason for preferring the second alternative).

(ii) Hom.*κ*437 σὺν δ' ὁ θρασὺς εἶπετ' Ὀδυσσεύς· τούτου γὰρ καὶ κεῖνοι ἀτασθαλίῃσιν ὄλοντο ('I call him θρασύς, because . . .'): A.*Ag*.422 φέρουσαι χάριν ματαίαν. μάταν γὰρ . . .: 1226 τῷ μολόντι δεσπότῃ ἐμῷ· φέρειν γὰρ χρὴ τὸ δούλιον ζυγόν (reference to δεσπότῃ): *Supp*.707: *Th*.742: S.*OC*110 οἰκτίρατ' ἀνδρὸς Οἰδίπου τόδ' ἄθλιον εἴδωλον· οὐ γὰρ δὴ τό γ' ἀρχαῖον δέμας: E.*Ba*.206 ἐρεῖ τις ὡς τὸ γῆρας οὐκ αἰσχύνομαι, μέλλων χορεύειν . . .; οὐ γὰρ διῄρηχ' ὁ θεὸς . . . ('I am going to dance, because . . .'): *IA*394a: *Rh*.609 φθέγματος γὰρ ᾐσθόμην τοῦ σοῦ συνήθη γῆρυν· ἐν πόνοισι γὰρ παροῦσ' ἀμύνεις τοῖς ἐμοῖς ἀεί ποτε (reference to συνήθη): Ar. *Av*.97 Μῶν με σκώπτετον ὁρῶντε τὴν πτέρωσιν; ἦν γάρ, ὦ ξένοι, ἄνθρωπος ('I have plumage like this because I was once a man'): Th.ii 77.4: X.*An*.iv 8.3 λίθους εἰς τὸν ποταμὸν ἔρριπτον· ἐξικνοῦντο γὰρ οὔ ('*into* the river, not *over* it'). Broschmann (pp. 28–9) gives many instances from Herodotus, pointing out that the word to which γάρ refers is often repeated: i 193.5 ψῆνας γὰρ . . .: iii 91.3: vii 165 τιμωρέων τῷ πενθέρῳ· Τηρίλλου γὰρ εἶχε θυγατέρα. (In Ar. *V*.253 Τί δὴ μαθὼν τῷ δακτύλῳ τὴν θρυαλλίδ' ὠθεῖς . . .; οὐ γὰρ δάκνει σ', ὅταν δέῃ τίμιον πρίασθαι, γάρ explains, not the emphatic τί μαθών, but the less emphatic main verb, ὠθεῖς: 'you do it because . . .'.)

(8) An example of a proposition constitutes an element in the explanation of it, or (if we like to put it so) in the inductive proof of it. Hence γάρ, instead of γοῦν, may introduce an instance.

Hom.*Ω*68 Ἕκτωρ φίλτατος ἔσκε θεοῖσι . . . ὣς γὰρ ἔμοιγ': S.*Aj*.650 ἁλίσκεται χὼ δεινὸς ὅρκος χαὶ περισκελεῖς φρένες. κἀγὼ γάρ, ὃς τὰ δείν' ἐκαρτέρουν τότε . . . ἐθηλύνθην στόμα: *El*.698 ὅταν δέ τις θεῶν βλάπτῃ, δύναιτ' ἂν οὐδ' ἂν ἰσχύων φυγεῖν. κεῖνος γὰρ . . .: A.*Pers*.603: E.*Heracl*.303: *IA*451: *Ph*.503 (where Pearson—'γάρ is explicative—"now"'—is wrong): *Rh*.267: Th.i 12.3 ἀφ' ὧν ἐκπίπτοντες τὰς πόλεις ἔκτιζον. Βοιωτοί τε γὰρ . . . τὴν

. . . Καδμηίδα γῆν καλουμένην ᾤκισαν: Pl.*R.*564A (the transition from ἄγαν ἐλευθερία to ἄγαν δουλεία is an example of the general tendency of excess to produce a violent reaction): *Lg.*953D ('for example', Jowett): Hdt.i 140.2: Arist.*Rh.*1362a4: Lys.i 50.

(9) The appositional use of γάρ, discussed by K. Hude in *Herm.*xxxvi 313–15, xxxix 476–7, is an extension of the explanatory: the particle now ceases to be a conjunction, though the meaning is still explanatory, 'that is to say', 'to wit'. The usage is commoner in Aristotle than elsewhere. I group Hude's most convincing examples, and a few others, under the following heads:—

(i) With μέν and δέ. Arist.*Po.*1448a31 διὸ καὶ ἀντιποιοῦνται τῆς τε τραγῳδίας καὶ τῆς κωμῳδίας οἱ Δωριεῖς, τῆς μὲν γὰρ κωμῳδίας οἱ Μεγαρεῖς . . . καὶ τῆς τραγῳδίας ἔνιοι τῶν ἐν Πελοποννήσῳ (μὲν γάρ A^cB^c: μέν *cett.*): *Somn.Vig.*460a21 (μὲν γὰρ τό *EMUY*): *EN*1098a30: *id. saep.*: Hdt.vii 2.3 ἐόντες δὲ μητρὸς οὐ τῆς αὐτῆς ἐστασίαζον, ὁ μὲν γὰρ Ἀρταβαζάνης . . . Ξέρξης δὲ . . . (γάρ *om. PRSVB*^c): ix 41.2 βουλευομένων δὲ αἵδε ἦσαν αἱ γνῶμαι, ἡ μὲν γὰρ Ἀρταβάζου . . . (γάρ *om. ABCP*): Th.vi 24.3 καὶ ἔρως ἐνέπεσε τοῖς πᾶσιν ὁμοίως ἐκπλεῦσαι· τοῖς μὲν γὰρ πρεσβυτέροις . . . τοῖς δ' ἐν τῇ ἡλικίᾳ . . .: Lys.ii 70 ἐτελεύτησαν δὲ τὸν βίον ὥσπερ χρὴ τοὺς ἀγαθοὺς ἀποθνῄσκειν, τῇ μὲν γὰρ πατρίδι τὰ τροφεῖα ἀποδόντες, τοῖς δὲ θρέψασι λύπας καταλιπόντες (γάρ *om. Fg.*): Aeschin.i 97 τούτῳ γὰρ κατέλιπεν ὁ πατὴρ οὐσίαν, ἀφ' ἧς . . . ἐδυνήθη· οἰκίαν μὲν γὰρ ὄπισθεν τῆς πόλεως, ἐσχατιὰν δὲ Σφηττοῖ: Hdt.i 92: Pl.*Ly.*215E.

(ii) With disjunctive ἤ. E.*Ion*844 δεῖ σε δὴ γυναικεῖόν τι δρᾶν· ἢ γὰρ ξίφος λαβοῦσαν ἢ δόλῳ τινὶ ἢ φαρμάκοισι σὸν κατακτεῖναι πόσιν: Pl.*Ap.* 40C δυοῖν γὰρ θάτερόν ἐστιν τὸ τεθνάναι· ἢ γὰρ οἷον μηδὲν εἶναι . . . ἢ . . . μεταβολή τις τυγχάνει οὖσα: And.i 20 ἐν ᾧ δυοῖν τοῖν μεγίστοιν κακοῖν οὐκ ἦν αὐτῷ ἁμαρτεῖν; ἢ γὰρ . . . μηνῦσαι . . . ἢ . . . ἀποκτεῖναι (*primum* ἤ *a corr. habet A*): Arist. *Po.*1447a17: 1457a28.

(iii) Other cases. Hdt.i 82 Λακεδαιμόνιοι δὲ τὰ ἐναντία τούτων ἔθεντο νόμον, οὐ γὰρ κομῶντες πρὸ τούτου ἀπὸ τούτου κομᾶν: vi 53 τάδε δὲ κατὰ τὰ λεγόμενα ὑπ' Ἑλλήνων ἐγὼ γράφω, τούτους γὰρ δὴ τοὺς Δωριέων βασιλέας . . . καταλεγομένους (γὰρ δή *om. PRSV*): ix 41.4 Μαρδονίου δὲ (ἡ γνώμη) ἰσχυροτέρη . . .· δοκέειν τε γὰρ πολλῷ κρέσσονα εἶναι τὴν σφετέρην στρατιὴν τῆς Ἑλληνικῆς, συμβάλλειν τε τὴν ταχίστην: 60.2 νῦν ὧν δέδοκται τὸ ἐνθεῦτεν τὸ ποιητέον ἡμῖν, ἀμυνομένους γὰρ τῇ δυνάμεθα ἄριστα περιστέλλειν ἀλλήλους: Arist.*deAn*.410b4 πολλὰ δ' ἀγνοήσει. πάντα γὰρ τἆλλα: *Ph*.200b5 ἴσως δὲ καὶ ἐν τῷ λόγῳ ἐστὶ τὸ ἀναγκαῖον· ὁρισαμένῳ γὰρ τὸ ἔργον: *GC*318b35: 325b6.

(For appositional καὶ γάρ, see καὶ γάρ, I.3.)

These examples are certainly remarkable, and in hardly any of them is it possible to suppose an ellipse of a verb. Hude's other instances are less impressive, and some of them can be otherwise explained (Th.i25.3: vii28.3). Vahlen (*Poetics*, Ed. 3, 1885, pp. 128–32) compares Aristotle's use of γάρ meaning 'in fact', 'that is to say', with conjunctions. *Po*.1450b18 ὡς γάρ (ὡς A^cB^c: ἢ *cett.*): *EN*1159b11 ἐπὶ πλεῖον διαμένουσιν· ἕως γὰρ ἂν πορίζωσιν ἡδονὰς ἢ ὠφελείας ἀλλήλοις ('as long, that is, as . . .'): 1157b2: οἱ δ' ἀγαθοὶ δι' αὐτοὺς φίλοι· ᾗ γὰρ ἀγαθοί: *Rh*.1402b26 ἐπεὶ γάρ. ἐπειδὴ γάρ is similarly used by Aristodemus and Philo.

IV. Anticipatory γάρ. Here the γάρ clause, instead of following the clause which it explains, precedes it, or is inserted parenthetically within it. Many authorities, denying that such an order of ideas is possible, interpret γάρ as asseverative, taking the γάρ clause as independent, and the next sentence as following asyndetically. Thus Hartung, Klotz, Bäumlein, and Kühner render 'ja', 'nämlich', 'profecto', and the like. But this procedure, as Misener points out, severs the logical connexion between ideas which plainly are so connected. It seems clear that γάρ here bears its normal force, and that the early position of the γάρ clause is to be explained, as Misener suggests, on stylistic and rhetorical grounds.

(1) Parenthetical. (Parenthesis approximates to anticipation where nothing of substantial import precedes the parenthesis.) Hom.*Ω*223 νῦν δ', αὐτὸς γὰρ ἄκουσα θεοῦ καὶ ἐσέδρακον ἄντην, εἶμι: E.*Tr*.998 εἶεν· βίᾳ γὰρ παῖδα φῄς σ' ἄγειν ἐμόν· τίς Σπαρτιατῶν ᾔσθετ'; Hom.α301: A.*Ag*.1069: *Eu*.230: E.*Med.* 80: *IT* 95: Ar.*Ach*.513: *Ec*.610: Pl.*Phlb*.16A ὅμως δέ, μανθάνομεν γὰρ ὃ λέγεις, εἴ τις τρόπος ἔστι . . . ἀνευρεῖν, σύ τε προθυμοῦ τοῦτο.

In the above passages the parenthesis is brief: in the following it is longer, and there is rather more ground for regarding the γάρ clause as independent. Pl.*Grg.*449C Φέρε δή· ῥητορικῆς γὰρ φῄς ἐπιστήμων τέχνης εἶναι καὶ ποιῆσαι ἂν καὶ ἄλλον ῥήτορα· ἡ ῥητορικὴ περὶ τί τῶν ὄντων τυγχάνει οὖσα; A.*Ch.*75 (where see Tucker).

Where a vocative precedes the γάρ clause, γάρ may either give a reason for addressing the person in question, or an anticipatory reason for what follows.* In most cases both factors are present. In the following the former predominates: Hom. Ψ156 Ἀτρεΐδη, σοὶ γάρ τε μάλιστά γε λαὸς Ἀχαιῶν πείσονται μύθοισι, γόοιο μὲν ἔστι καὶ ἆσαι, νῦν δ' ἀπὸ πυρκαϊῆς σκέδασον (the request is addressed to Agamemnon because he is capable of carrying it out. But there is, as Misener points out, a forward reference as well): Pi.*O.*4.2: E.*Rh.*608: Ar.*Ach.*1020: *V.*389: Pl.*Phd.*117A Εἶεν, ὦ βέλτιστε, σὺ γὰρ τούτων ἐπιστήμων, τί χρὴ ποιεῖν;

In the following, the latter: Hom.ρ78 Πείραι', οὐ γὰρ ἴδμεν ὅπως ἔσται τάδε ἔργα, εἴ κεν ... δάσωνται, ... βούλομ': Ω334: ε29: Hdt.i8 Γύγη, οὐ γάρ σε δοκέω πείθεσθαί μοι λέγοντι περὶ τοῦ εἴδεος τῆς γυναικὸς ... ποίει ὅκως ἐκείνην θεήσεαι γυμνήν. (In E.*El.*82ff., after Πυλάδη, σὲ γὰρ δὴ πρῶτον ἀνθρώπων ἐγὼ πιστὸν νομίζω, the sentence loses itself in the sand. The γάρ no doubt motivates in general both the narration which follows and the appeal for common action in 102 ff.)

In Herodotus a sentence often opens with καί, followed at once by the γάρ clause: iv125 καὶ οὐ γὰρ ἀνίει ἐπιὼν ὁ Δαρεῖος, οἱ Σκύθαι ... ὑπέφευγον: iv152: v33.2: vi61.2. There are also examples in Thucydides: i31.2 καὶ (ἦσαν γὰρ οὐδενὸς Ἑλλήνων ἔνσπονδοι ...) ἔδοξεν αὐτοῖς: iii107.3 καὶ (μεῖζον γὰρ ἐγένετο ...) ὁ Δημοσθένης ...: vii48.2. (Whether, or not, in such cases, we should put a bracket (or comma) after καί, is a question to be determined by considering whether our punctuation is to be based on logical grounds, or is only to reproduce the pauses actually made in speaking or reading.)

(2) Anticipatory, in the strict sense. The sentence opens with the γάρ clause, the whole of the main clause being postponed. γάρ would here naturally be rendered 'since' or 'as'. Hom.ψ362 σοὶ δέ, γύναι, τάδ' ἐπιτέλλω πινυτῇ περ ἐούσῃ· αὐτίκα γὰρ φάτις εἶσιν ...· εἰς ὑπερῷ' ἀναβᾶσα ... ἧσθαι (to take γάρ as

explanatory would assume an unlikely asyndeton at 364): E.*Ba.*477 Τὸν θεὸν ὁρᾶν γὰρ φῂς σαφῶς, ποῖός τις ἦν; S.*Ph.*852 (reading uncertain): Hdt.iv79 Ἡμῖν γὰρ καταγελᾶτε, ὦ Σκύθαι, ὅτι βακχεύομεν καὶ ἡμέας ὁ θεὸς λαμβάνει· νῦν οὗτος ὁ δαίμων καὶ τὸν ὑμέτερον βασιλέα λελάβηκε (δέ, for γάρ, *PRSV*): i97: iv162: vi11.2. (See also II, Explanatory, *ad init.*)

(3) The resumption or inception (for the examples to be given fall under both headings given above, (1) and (2)) of the main clause is often marked by a particle or demonstrative pronoun. Analysis here is complicated by various factors. (*a*) It is often difficult, particularly in Homer, to determine whether γάρ looks forward or backward. (*b*) The ensuing particle, where it is inferential, and therefore expresses a logical relationship inverse to that of γάρ, brings out the reciprocal interdependence of the two clauses (though here, as elsewhere, οὖν and δή may possibly be explained as apodotic): where it is copulative or adversative, it supplements a causal relationship by one of a different kind: where it is hortative ἀλλά, it bears no relationship whatever to the γάρ clause. Most of the examples are from Homer and Herodotus. There are very few in Attic: with the exception that in Plato an inferential particle, or its equivalent, not infrequently follows the γάρ clause, which is often preceded by νῦν δέ. In Plato, the γάρ clause, as modern punctuation implies, often tends to acquire independence, by anacoluthon. This is clearly illustrated in *Ap.*38B, where τοσούτου οὖν τιμῶμαι refers to the afterthought εἰ μὴ . . . ἀργυρίου, not to οὐ γὰρ ἔστιν. Cf. also *Chrm.* 175B.

(i) δέ (copulative or adversative). Hom.τ350 Ξεῖνε φίλ'. οὐ γάρ πώ τις ἀνὴρ πεπνυμένος ὧδε . . . ἐμὸν ἵκετο δῶμα . . . . ἔστι δέ μοι γρηῦς . . . ἥ σε πόδας νίψει (γάρ explains both the epithet φίλε and the granting of Odysseus' request): 407 τίθεσθ' ὄνομ' ὅττι κεν εἴπω· πολλοῖσιν γὰρ ἐγώ γε ὀδυσσάμενος τόδ' ἱκάνω . . . · τῷ δ' Ὀδυσεὺς ὄνομ' ἔστω ἐπώνυμον (where γάρ might, less well, be taken as explanatory): μ320: Th.iv132.2: And.i27 ἐπειδὴ αἱ μηνύσεις ἐγένοντο, περὶ τῶν μηνύτρων, ἦσαν γὰρ . . . χίλιαι δραχμαί . . ., περὶ δὲ τούτων ἠμφισβήτουν . . . .

(ii) ἀλλά, hortative. Hom.κ176 Ὦ φίλοι, οὐ γάρ πω καταδυσόμεθ' . . . εἰς Ἀΐδαο δόμους . . ., ἀλλ' ἄγετ': χ70 Ὦ φίλοι, οὐ γὰρ σχήσει ἀνὴρ ὅδε χεῖρας ἀάπτους . . . ἀλλὰ μνησώμεθα χάρμης: *N*736: *P*475: Ψ890: κ190,226: ψ248.

ἀλλά, adversative. Hom.μ154 Ὦ φίλοι, οὐ γὰρ χρὴ ἕνα ἰδμέναι οὐδὲ δύ' οἴους θέσφαθ' . . . ἀλλ' ἐρέω μὲν ἐγών, ἵνα εἰδότες ἤ κε θάνωμεν ἤ κεν . . . φύγοιμεν: E.*IT*646 Κατολοφύρομαι σὲ . . .—Οἶκτος γὰρ οὐ ταῦτ', ἀλλὰ χαίρετ', ὦ ξέναι ('Since this is no matter for lamentation, do ye rather rejoice': a fusion of οὐκ οἶκτος ταῦτα, ἀλλὰ χαίρετε and χαίρετε, οὐ γὰρ οἶκτος ταῦτα): Hdt.ix93.3 καὶ οὐ γὰρ ἔλαθε τοὺς Ἀπολλωνιήτας ταῦτα γενόμενα, ἀλλ' ὡς ἐπύθοντο, ὑπαγαγόντες μιν ὑπὸ δικαστήριον κατέκριναν (ἀλλά κως Stein). (In Pl.Com.*Fr.*168 the text is perhaps rightly thus emended: ὁ δ' οὐ γὰρ ἠττίκιζεν, ὦ Μοῖραι φίλαι, ἀλλ' ὁπότε μὲν χρείη 'διῃτώμην' λέγειν, ἔφασκε 'δῃτώμην'.)

(iii) τῷ. Hom.*H*328 Ἀτρεΐδη τε καὶ ἄλλοι . . . πολλοὶ γὰρ τεθνᾶσι . . . τῷ σε χρὴ πόλεμον . . . παῦσαι: *N*228 ἀλλά, Θόαν, καὶ γὰρ τὸ πάρος μενεδήϊος ἦσθα . . . τῷ νῦν μήτ' ἀπόληγε: σ259 Ὦ γύναι, οὐ γὰρ ὀΐω . . . τῷ οὐκ οἶδ'.

(iv) νυν. Hdt.i124 Ὦ παῖ Καμβύσεω, σὲ γὰρ θεοὶ ἐπορῶσι . . . σύ νυν . . . τεῖσαι: i85: iii83: iv97.

(v) οὖν (οὖν δή). Ar.*Eq.*1278 νῦν δ' Ἀρίγνωτον γὰρ οὐδεὶς ὅστις οὐκ ἐπίσταται . . . ἔστιν οὖν ἀδελφὸς αὐτῷ: Hdt.iii63 Ὤνθρωπε, φῂς γὰρ ἥκειν . . . νῦν ὦν εἴπας τὴν ἀληθείην ἄπιθι: i30,69,121,166: v19.2: vi11.2: 87: ix17.4 (ὦν *om. ABCP*): Hp. *deArte*3 περὶ δὲ ἰητρικῆς, ἐς ταύτην γὰρ ὁ λόγος, ταύτης οὖν τὴν ἀπόδειξιν ποιήσομαι: Pl.*La.*200E νῦν δὲ ὁμοίως γὰρ πάντες ἐν ἀπορίᾳ ἐγενόμεθα· τί οὖν . . .; *Smp.*180C νῦν δὲ οὐ γάρ ἐστιν εἷς· μὴ ὄντος δὲ ἑνὸς ὀρθότερόν ἐστι πρότερον προρρηθῆναι ὁποῖον δεῖ ἐπαινεῖν· ἐγὼ οὖν πειράσομαι: *Prm.*137A ὅμως δὲ δεῖ γὰρ χαρίζεσθαι . . . πόθεν οὖν δὴ ἀρξόμεθα; *Chrm.*157C ἐγὼ οὖν—ὀμώμοκα γὰρ αὐτῷ, καί μοι ἀνάγκη πείθεσθαι—πείσομαι οὖν: *Alc.*II147E: *Amat.*132B: X.*An.*i5.14.*

(vi) δή (δὴ οὖν). Hdt.i129 Ἅρπαγος δὲ ἔφη, αὐτὸς γὰρ γράψαι, τὸ πρῆγμα ἑωυτοῦ δὴ δικαίως εἶναι: v124.1 ἁλισκομένων δὲ τῶν πολίων, ἦν γὰρ . . . πρὸς ταῦτα δὴ ὦν . . .: Pl.*Tht.*143D νῦν δὲ ἧττον γὰρ ἐκείνους ἢ τούσδε φιλῶ . . . ταῦτα δὴ αὐτός τε σκοπῶ: *Ti.*32B νῦν δὲ στερεοειδῆ γὰρ αὐτὸν προσῆκεν εἶναι . . . οὕτω δὴ . . .: *La.*184D: *Euthphr.*11C,14C. Add perhaps Ar.*Ach.*450, but there δή is more probably emphatic.

(vii) διὰ ταῦτα, διὸ δή. Pl.*Prt.*347A νῦν δὲ σφόδρα γὰρ καὶ περὶ τῶν μεγίστων ψευδόμενος δοκεῖς ἀληθῆ λέγειν, διὰ ταῦτά σε ἐγὼ ψέγω: *Lg.*875D νῦν δὲ οὐ γάρ ἐστιν ... διὸ δὴ ....

(viii) καί (doubtful). Hdt.iii 105 τοὺς μέν νυν ἔρσενας τῶν καμήλων, εἶναι γὰρ ἥσσονας θέειν τῶν θηλέων, [καὶ] παραλύεσθαι ἐπελκομένους (καί *om. PRSV*). Perhaps τε is similarly used in Hdt.viii 101.4 (see p. 536(3)).

(ix) A demonstrative pronoun referring back to some idea contained in the γάρ clause (very common in Herodotus). Hom. *B*803 Ἕκτορ, σοὶ δὲ μάλιστ' ἐπιτέλλομαι, ὧδε δὲ ῥέξαι· πολλοὶ γὰρ κατὰ ἄστυ ... ἐπίκουροι ... τοῖσιν ἕκαστος ἀνὴρ σημαινέτω οἷσί περ ἄρχει: α337: ι432: Hdt.i 8 ὥστε δὲ ταῦτα νομίζων, ἦν γάρ οἱ τῶν αἰχμοφόρων Γύγης ὁ Δασκύλου ἀρεσκόμενος μάλιστα, τούτῳ τῷ Γύγῃ ...: i 119,126: iii 78: v 67,111: *id. saep.*

(In X.*An.*iii 2.11 an anticipatory γάρ is exceptionally answered by an explanatory γάρ: ἔπειτα δ' ἀναμνήσω γὰρ ὑμᾶς καὶ τοὺς τῶν προγόνων τῶν ἡμετέρων κινδύνους, ἵνα εἰδῆτε ... ἐλθόντων μὲν γὰρ Περσῶν ... There is an anacoluthon here, and Xenophon forgets that ἀναμνήσω was introduced parenthetically.)

(4) Fusion of clauses. A closer connexion is sometimes established between the γάρ clause and the main clause, by attracting the subject (or other element) of the latter into a case which suits the former.[1] Hdt.i 24 καὶ τοῖσι ἐσελθεῖν γὰρ ἡδονὴν εἰ μέλλοιεν ἀκούσεσθαι ... ἀναχωρῆσαι: 27 καί οἱ προσφυέως γὰρ δόξαι λέγειν, πειθόμενον παύσασθαι τῆς ναυπηγίης (for punctuation, see Broschmann, p. 63): 155 τὰ δὲ νῦν παρεόντα Πακτύης γάρ ἐστι ὁ ἀδικέων ... οὗτος δότω τοι δίκην (for τῶν παρεόντων): ii 101 τῶν δὲ ἄλλων βασιλέων οὐ γὰρ ἔλεγον οὐδεμίαν ἀπόδεξιν, κατ' οὐδὲν εἶναι λαμπρότητος: iv 149.2 τοῖσι δὲ ἐν τῇ φυλῇ ταύτῃ ἀνδράσι οὐ γὰρ ὑπέμειναν τὰ τέκνα, ἱδρύσαντο ... ἱρόν: 200 τῶν δὲ πᾶν γὰρ ἦν τὸ πλῆθος μεταίτιον, οὐκ ἐδέκοντο τοὺς λόγους: vii 142.1 ταῦτά σφι ἠπιώτερα γὰρ ... ἐδόκεε εἶναι, συγγραψάμενοι ἀπαλλάσσοντο (object attracted): viii 94: ix 109.2. (Th.i 115.4 is a little different: τῶν δὲ Σαμίων ἦσαν γάρ τινες οἳ οὐχ ὑπέμειναν ... ξυνθέμενοι ... διέβησαν. Here there is fusion, but no attraction, τινές, the subject of the main verb,

[1] For full discussion of Herodotean passages, and references to earlier authorities, see Broschmann, pp. 62 ff.

being contained in the *γάρ* clause. Cf. Th.i 51.2, with Steup's note.) In two passages an object from the main clause, having been attracted into the nominative as the subject of the *γάρ* clause, is picked up by *αὐτόν*: Hdt.i 114 *εἷς δὴ τούτων τῶν παίδων . . . οὐ γὰρ δὴ ἐποίησε . . . ἐκέλευε αὐτὸν τοὺς ἄλλους παῖδας διαλαβεῖν*: iv 149.1 *ὁ δὲ παῖς οὐ γὰρ ἔφη οἱ συμπλεύσεσθαι, τοιγαρῶν ἔφη αὐτὸν καταλείψειν.* Occasionally, perhaps, the main clause is introduced by a connecting particle. (Cf. (3) above.) Hdt.iv 149.1 (above: but see *τοιγαροῦν*, n. 1): Th.i 72.1 *τῶν δὲ Ἀθηναίων ἔτυχε γὰρ πρεσβεία . . . παροῦσα, καὶ ὡς ᾔσθοντο τῶν λόγων, ἔδοξεν αὐτοῖς* (*καί del.* Krüger). But in viii 30.1 *καί* probably means 'also': *τοῦ δ' αὐτοῦ χειμῶνος τοῖς ἐν τῇ Σάμῳ Ἀθηναίοις προσαφιγμέναι γὰρ ἦσαν . . . νῆες . . . καὶ τὰς ἀπὸ Χίου καὶ τὰς ἄλλας πάσας ξυναγαγόντες ἐβούλοντο . . . ἐφορμεῖν.*

Fusion of clauses is, as Sernatinger remarks, an idiom characteristic of Herodotus and (in a less degree) Thucydides, who no doubt adopted it from Herodotus. There is, however, an isolated instance of it in Homer, if, as seems probable, *δ' ἐν γάρ* is the right reading: H73 *ὑμῖν δ' ἐν γὰρ ἔασιν ἀριστῆες Παναχαιῶν· τῶν νῦν ὅν τινα θυμὸς ἐμοὶ μαχέσασθαι ἀνώγῃ, δεῦρ' ἴτω.*

V. In answers.

(1) Frequently in dialogue, after one speaker has made a statement (or asked a question which suggests its own answer), another speaker supports his implied assent by a *γάρ* clause: 'Yes, for': 'No, for': whereas in English it is the assent that is expressed, while the logical connexion is left implied. This elliptical form of answer is rare in Homer.

Hom.o545 "*τὸν ξεῖνον ἄγων . . . ἐνδυκέως φιλέειν . . .*" *τὸν δ' αὖ Πείραιος δουρικλυτὸς ἀντίον ηὔδα·* "*Τηλέμαχ', εἰ γάρ κεν σὺ πολὺν χρόνον ἐνθάδε μίμνοις, τόνδε τ' ἐγὼ κομιῶ*": S.*Aj.*593 *Πόλλ' ἄγαν ἤδη θροεῖς.—Ταρβῶ γάρ*: 1357 *ἐχθρὸν ὧδ' αἰδῇ νέκυν;—Κινεῖ γὰρ ἀρετή με τῆς ἔχθρας πολύ* ('Aye: worth moves me far more than enmity'): E.*Alc.*42 *Καὶ τοῖσδέ γ' οἴκοις ἐκδίκως προσωφελεῖν.—Φίλου γὰρ ἀνδρὸς συμφοραῖς βαρύνομαι*: 147 *Ἐλπὶς μὲν οὐκέτ' ἐστὶ σῴζεσθαι βίον;—Πεπρωμένη γὰρ ἡμέρα βιάζεται* ('No, for'): Ar.*Ra.*662 *Ξα. Ἤλγησεν· οὐκ ἤκουσας;—Δι. Οὐκ ἔγωγ' . . .—Ξα.* (to Aeacus) *Οὐδὲν ποιεῖς γάρ* ('No, you're not doing any good': lit. '(He did not suffer pain,) for you are doing nothing'): *Ec.*603 *Τοῦτ' ἐς τὸ μέσον καταθήσει. καὶ μὴ καταθεὶς ψευδορκήσει.—Κἀκτήσατο γὰρ διὰ τοῦτο* (here a new turn is given to the idiom, by the second speaker's giving primary importance to a suggestion made incidentally by the first). Very common in stichomythia: E.*Or.*410, 430, 444, 490, 794, 798. Hdt.vii 46.2 *μακαρίσας γὰρ σεωυτὸν δακρύεις. ὁ δὲ εἶπε· Ἐσῆλθε γάρ με λογισάμενον κατοικτῖραι*: Pl.*Smp.*194A *νῦν δὲ ὅμως θαρρῶ. τὸν οὖν Σωκράτη εἰπεῖν· Καλῶς γὰρ αὐτὸς ἠγώνισαι, ὦ Ἐρυξίμαχε* ('That's because you've performed so well yourself'): *R.*337A *καὶ ταῦτ' ἐγὼ ἤδη τε καὶ τούτοις προὔλεγον, ὅτι . . .—Σοφὸς γὰρ εἶ, ἦν δ' ἐγώ, ὦ Θρασύμαχε· εὖ οὖν ᾔδησθα ὅτι . . .* ('Ah, you're a clever fellow, Thrasymachus': 'Your foreknowledge springs from cleverness'): 509C *Ἄπολλον, ἔφη, δαιμονίας ὑπερβολῆς.—Σὺ γάρ, ἦν δ' ἐγώ, αἴτιος, ἀναγκάζων τὰ ἐμοὶ δοκοῦντα περὶ αὐτοῦ λέγειν* ('Why, that's your fault': 'I exaggerate, for you cause me to do so'): 531C *ἀλλ' οὐκ εἰς προβλήματα ἀνίασιν . . .—Δαιμόνιον γάρ, ἔφη, πρᾶγμα λέγεις* (*sc. τὸ εἰς προβλήματα ἀνιέναι*: 'No, that's a formidable task'): X.*An.*ii 5.40 *Ὦ κάκιστε ἀνθρώπων Ἀριαῖε καὶ . . . οὐκ αἰσχύνεσθε . . . οἵτινες . . . ξὺν τοῖς πολεμίοις ἐφ' ἡμᾶς ἔρχεσθε; ὁ δὲ Ἀριαῖος εἶπε· Κλέαρχος γὰρ πρόσθεν ἐπιβουλεύων φανερὸς ἐγένετο . . . ἡμῖν* ('We act so, because Clearchus has given us provocation': or, perhaps, 'No, we are not ashamed, for . . .'): *Cyr.* iv 2.46 *συνεῖπε δ' αὐτῷ Ὑστάσπας . . . Δεινὸν γάρ τἂν εἴη . . . εἰ . . .* ('Yes, it would be monstrous if . . .'): Pl.*Euthphr.*14D: *Tht.*142A: *R.*351C: *id. saep.*

(2) Less frequently, it is dissent, not assent, that is implied. S.*OC*864 *Αὐδῶ σιωπᾶν.—Μὴ γὰρ αἵδε δαίμονες θεῖέν μ' ἄφωνον*: E.*Hel.*446 *μήδ' ὤθει βίᾳ.—Πείθῃ γὰρ οὐδὲν ὧν λέγω* ('Yes, I will, for . . .'): Ar.*Nu.*1366 *ἐκέλευσ' αὐτὸν . . . τῶν Αἰσχύλου λέξαι τί μοι· κᾆθ' οὗτος εὐθὺς εἶπεν· ἐγὼ γὰρ Αἰσχύλον νομίζω πρῶτον ἐν ποιηταῖς ψόφου πλέων ἀξύστατον* ('No, I won't, for . . .': 'Why, I think Aeschylus the greatest wind-bag ever'): 1440 *Σκέψαι δὲ χἀτέραν ἔτι γνώμην.—Ἀπὸ γὰρ ὀλοῦμαι* ('No, for a second *γνώμη*, like the first, will be the end of me.' Schol., less probably, *ἐὰν μὴ πρόσσχω γάρ, ἀπολοῦμαι*. Perhaps *τἄρ*'). Here, again, neither assent nor dissent is in question, the first

speaker having given no lead: X.*Cyr*.viii 3.30 *Καὶ πῶς, ἔφη, οὐδὲ μεταστρέφεται; καὶ ὁ Κῦρος ἔφη· Μαινόμενος γάρ τις ἐστιν, ὡς ἔοικεν* ('Because, said Cyrus . . .'): Arist.*Pol*.1281a16.

(3) In other passages *γάρ* does not express assent or dissent but provides a motive for the language used, or the tone adopted, by the previous speaker. 'You say this (or talk like this) because . . .'. This use is closely analogous to that described above in III.1. The force of the particle can often be brought out by 'Ah!' or 'Yes'.

E.*Hel*.311 *Χο. Πόλλ' ἂν γένοιτο καὶ διὰ ψευδῶν ἔπη.—Ελ. Καὶ τἄμπαλίν γε τῶνδ' ἀληθείᾳ σαφῆ.—Χο. Ἐς ξυμφορὰν γὰρ ἀντὶ τἀγαθοῦ φέρῃ* ('You say so because you are inclined to pessimism'): Pl.*R*.337D *καὶ ἐγὼ οὖν τοῦτο ἀξιῶ παθεῖν* (*sc. μαθεῖν παρὰ τοῦ εἰδότος*).—*Ἡδὺς γὰρ εἶ, ἔφη* ('Yes, you talk like that in your charming innocence'): 338D *Βδελυρὸς γὰρ εἶ, ἔφη, ὦ Σώκρατες, καὶ ταύτῃ ὑπολαμβάνεις ᾗ ἂν κακουργήσαις μάλιστα τὸν λόγον*: 340C *Ἔγωγε, εἶπον, ᾤμην σε τοῦτο λέγειν . . .—Συκοφάντης γὰρ εἶ, ἔφη, ὦ Σώκρατες, ἐν τοῖς λόγοις*: *Hp.Ma*.282D 'Gorgias, Prodicus and Protagoras have made more money as sophists than anyone in another profession.'—*Οὐδὲν γάρ, ὦ Σώκρατες, οἶσθα τῶν καλῶν περὶ τοῦτο. εἰ γὰρ εἰδείης ὅσον ἀργύριον εἴργασμαι ἐγώ, θαυμάσαις ἄν* ('Ah, Socrates, you've no standard in these matters').

(4) The *γάρ* clause sometimes presupposes only a partial and qualified agreement with the previous speaker's words. Hom.*A* 293 Agamemnon protests against Achilles' intolerably autocratic behaviour. Achilles answers: *Ἦ γάρ κεν δειλὸς . . . καλεοίμην, εἰ δὴ σοὶ πᾶν ἔργον ὑπείξομαι* ('I agree I won't stand browbeating at your hands: I should be a poor creature if I did'): Ar.*Nu*.655 Strepsiades has made a long nose at Socrates. *Σω. Ἀγρεῖος εἶ καὶ σκαιός.—Στ. Οὐ γάρ, ᾠζυρέ, τούτων ἐπιθυμῶ μανθάνειν οὐδέν* ('Why, confound you, I don't want to learn *this*': 'I *have* given you some excuse for saying that: but it's because I don't want to be pestered with all this useless knowledge'): E.*Alc*.715 (where Admetus ironically implies that 713 is a *εὐχή*, not an *ἀρά*): Ar.*Ach*.598.

(5) The connexion of thought is sometimes obscured by compression. Cf. III.2. Hom.θ355 Poseidon has offered to go bail for Ares. Hephaestus answers: Impossible. *πῶς ἂν ἐγώ σε δέοιμι μετ' ἀθανάτοισι θεοῖσιν, εἴ κεν Ἄρης οἴχοιτο χρέος καὶ δεσμὸν ἀλύξας; τὸν δ' αὖτε προσέειπε Ποσειδάων ἐνοσίχθων· Ἥφαιστ', εἴ περ γάρ κεν Ἄρης χρεῖος ὑπαλύξας οἴχηται φεύγων, αὐτός τοι ἐγὼ τάδε τίσω* ('You need not fear, for ...'): S.*Ph.* 1280 *εἰ δὲ μή τι πρὸς καιρὸν λέγων κυρῶ, πέπαυμαι.—Πάντα γὰρ φράσεις μάτην* ('Yes, you will avail nothing by your words': 'You are right to stop, for ...'): Ar.*Ach.*71 *Καὶ δῆτ' ἐτρυχόμεσθα ... μαλθακῶς κατακείμενοι, ἀπολλύμενοι.—Σφόδρα γὰρ ἐσῳζόμην ἐγώ* ('Yes, *I* was in clover, wasn't I'? Happiness is relative, and therefore the private soldier's supposed luxury is ironically represented as a ground for admitting the ambassador's supposed privations. A much, but needlessly, discussed passage): Pl.*Phd.*69A *τοῦτο δ' ὅμοιόν ἐστιν ᾧ νυνδὴ ἐλέγετο, τῷ τρόπον τινὰ δι' ἀκολασίαν αὐτοὺς σεσωφρονίσθαι.—Ἔοικε γάρ.—Ὦ μακάριε Σιμμία, μὴ γὰρ οὐχ αὕτη ᾖ ἡ ὀρθὴ πρὸς ἀρετὴν ἀλλαγή* (*γάρ om. T.* 'We have been led to this *reductio ad absurdum* by the adoption of a wrong standard of exchange'. Cf. *Cra.*432A): D.viii 68 *αὐτοὶ δ' οὐ δύνανται παρ' ὑμῖν ἡσυχίαν ἄγειν οὐδενὸς αὐτοὺς ἀδικοῦντος. εἶτα φησὶν ὃς ἂν τύχῃ παρελθών "οὐ γὰρ ἐθέλεις γράφειν, οὐδὲ κινδυνεύειν, ἀλλ' ἄτολμος εἶ καὶ μαλακός"* ('Yes, because you won't ...'. Demosthenes' opponents offer his inactivity as an excuse for their own excessive activity).

(6) The answer is in the form of a question. The following types are to be distinguished:

(i) The question is rhetorical, and virtually constitutes a statement, which gives the grounds for an implied assent. The connexion of thought is that illustrated in V.1 above.

Pl.*La.*184D *τούτοις μέλλεις χρῆσθαι;—Τί γὰρ ἄν τις καὶ ποιοῖ ...;* (= *Οὐδὲν γὰρ ἂν ἄλλο τις ποιοῖ*: 'Well, what *can* one do?'): *Euthphr.*9D *ἆρ' οὕτω βούλει ...;—Τί γὰρ κωλύει;* ('Why not?'): Ar.*Nu.*1359 *ἀρχαῖον εἶν' ἔφασκε τὸ κιθαρίζειν ...—Οὐ γὰρ τότ' εὐθὺς χρῆν σ' ἄρα τύπτεσθαι ...;* ('Your request deserved a beating as well as a snub'): *Av.*1219 *διαπέτει διὰ τῆς πόλεως ...;—Ποίᾳ γὰρ ἄλλῃ χρὴ πέτεσθαι τοὺς θεούς;* ('Why, where else ...?): D.ix 68 'Unless you take precautions against

Philip, you will share the fate of Eretria and other cities. *καὶ μὴν ἐκεῖνό γ' αἰσχρὸν ὕστερόν ποτ' εἰπεῖν· "τίς γὰρ ἂν ᾠήθη ταῦτα γενέσθαι;"* ('Why, who would have expected this to happen?' 'We took no precautions against these disasters, because no one could have believed them possible'): Pl.*La.* 193C: *R.*564E, 578D: *Sph.*253C.

For elliptical answers of this type, *Πῶς γὰρ οὔ;* &c., see VII.

(ii) The question is rhetorical, or, at least, surprised and incredulous, often ironical; and implies that the speaker throws doubt on the grounds of the previous speaker's words. The tone is dissentient. We may often render 'why', 'what?' (or 'what!') Frequently the second speaker echoes, with contempt, indignation, or surprise, a word or words used by the first. Hom. *A*122 *γέρας αὐτίχ' ἑτοιμάσατ'* . . .—*Πῶς γάρ τοι δώσουσι γέρας μεγάθυμοι Ἀχαιοί;* (Agamemnon's request assumes that there is a possible way in which it can be granted: this possibility is called in question by Achilles): *O*201 'Let Zeus threaten his children. I care nothing for him.'—*Οὕτω γὰρ δή τοι . . . τόνδε φέρω Διὶ μῦθον ἀπηνέα τε κρατερόν τε;* (the specific terms of Poseidon's message presuppose the advisability or propriety of sending a message of such a kind: this Iris calls in question): A.*Ch.*909 *σὺν δὲ γηράναι θέλω.*—*Πατροκτονοῦσα γὰρ ξυνοικήσεις ἐμοί;* ('What! Live with me, after killing my father?'): S.*Aj.* 1126 *Ἡ γλῶσσά σου τὸν θυμὸν ὡς δεινὸν τρέφει.*—*Ξὺν τῷ δικαίῳ γὰρ μέγ' ἔξεστιν φρονεῖν.*—*Δίκαια γὰρ τόνδ' εὐτυχεῖν κτείναντά με;* *El.*1221–2 *ψεῦδος οὐδὲν ὧν λέγω.*—*Ἦ ζῇ γὰρ ἀνήρ;*—*Εἴπερ ἔμψυχός γ' ἐγώ.*—*Ἦ γὰρ σὺ κεῖνος;* *OT*1029 *ποιμνίοις ἐπεστάτουν.*—*Ποιμὴν γὰρ ἦσθα . . .;* *OC*1583 . . . *Οἰδίπουν ὀλωλότα.*—*Ὄλωλε γὰρ δύστηνος;* ('What? Dead, unhappy man?'): *Ant.*734 *Οὔ φησι . . . λεώς.*—*Πόλις γὰρ ἡμῖν ἁμὲ χρὴ τάσσειν ἐρεῖ;* 744 *Ὦ παγκάκιστε, διὰ δίκης ἰὼν πατρί.*—*Οὐ γὰρ δίκαιά σ' ἐξαμαρτάνονθ' ὁρῶ.*—*Ἁμαρτάνω γὰρ τὰς ἐμὰς ἀρχὰς σέβων;*—*Οὐ γὰρ σέβεις, τιμάς γε τὰς θεῶν πατῶν*: E.*Hipp.*328 *Κάκ', ὦ τάλαινα, σοὶ τάδ', εἰ πεύσῃ, κακά.*—*Μεῖζον γὰρ ἢ σοῦ μὴ τυχεῖν τί μοι κακόν;* *Andr.*590 *Με. Ψαυσόν γ', ἵν' εἰδῇς, καὶ πέλας πρόσελθέ μου.*—*Σὺ γὰρ μετ' ἀνδρῶν . . .;* (Menelaus's threat presupposes the manliness to carry it out): *Or.*483 *φίλου μοι πατρός ἐστιν ἔκγονος.*—*Κείνου γὰρ ὅδε πέφυκε τοιοῦτος γεγώς;* ('What!

that villain *his* son?'): 1071 *εἰ ζῆν με χρῄζειν σοῦ θανόντος ἤλπισας.—Τί γὰρ προσήκει κατθανεῖν σ' ἐμοῦ μέτα;* Ar.*V*.1159 *†ὑπόδυθι† τὰς Λακωνικάς.—Ἐγὼ γὰρ ἂν τλαίην ὑποδήσασθαί ποτε ἐχθρῶν παρ' ἀνδρῶν δυσμενῆ καττύματα;* Antiph.*Fr*.207.8 *ὡς ἔφασκ' Εὐριπίδης.—Εὐριπίδης γὰρ τοῦτ' ἔφασκεν;* ('What! Euripides say that?'): Hom.*κ*337,383,501 (cf. 490): E.*Hipp*. 702: Ar.*Pl*.429: Hdt.iii 120 *κρινομένων δὲ περὶ ἀρετῆς εἰπεῖν τὸν Μιτροβάτεα τῷ Ὀροίτῃ προφέροντα· Σὺ γὰρ ἐν ἀνθρώπων λόγῳ, ὃς . . .;* X.*Mem*.iv 8.4 *ὡς χρὴ σκοπεῖν ὅ τι ἀπολογήσεται. τὸν δὲ . . . εἰπεῖν· Οὐ γὰρ δοκῶ σοι τοῦτο μελετῶν διαβεβιωκέναι;* *Oec*.19.2 *οὐκ ἐπίσταμαι.—Οὐ γὰρ σύ, ἔφη . . . ἐπίστασαι;* *Cyr*.v 1.9 *δέδοικα μὴ . . . ἀναπείσῃ καὶ πάλιν ἐλθεῖν θεασόμενον . . . καὶ ὁ νεανίσκος ἀναγελάσας εἶπεν· Οἴει γάρ, ἔφη, ὦ Κῦρε, ἱκανὸν εἶναι κάλλος ἀνθρώπου ἀναγκάζειν . . .;* D.viii 27 *τοῦτ' εἰσὶν οἱ λόγοι· "μέλλει πολιορκεῖν", "τοὺς Ἕλληνας ἐκδίδωσιν". μέλει γάρ τινι τούτων τῶν τὴν Ἀσίαν οἰκούντων Ἑλλήνων;* Aeschin.iii 167 "*ὁμολογῶ τὰ Λακωνικὰ συστῆσαι . . .*" *σὺ γὰρ ἂν κώμην ἀποστήσαις;* Pl.*R*.341C,504D: *La*.185C: X.*Mem*.ii 3.16: iii 11.17: *Smp*.4.23: *An*.i 7.9: *Cyr*.i 3.4.

(iii) Rarely, the *γάρ* clause gives the cause of what precedes, and, by putting it in question form, the speaker asks why the cause has been brought into operation. Ar.*Nu*.57 *Ἔλαιον ἡμῖν οὐκ ἔνεστ' ἐν τῷ λύχνῳ.—Οἴμοι· τί γάρ μοι τὸν πότην ἧπτες λύχνον;* ('That's because you lit the thirsty lamp: and why did you?'): 1506 *κατακαυθήσομαι.—Τί γὰρ μαθόντες τοὺς θεοὺς ὑβρίζετε . . .;* ('Well, what put it into your heads to insult the gods?'). In the following two passages the logical connexion is not at first sight obvious: E.*Med*.689 *Μη. Ἀλλ' εὐτυχοίης καὶ τύχοις ὅσων ἐρᾷς.—Αι. Τί γὰρ σὸν ὄμμα χρώς τε συντέτηχ' ὅδε;* (Medea's words, and the tone in which they are uttered, imply that she is unhappy. This is corroborated by her haggard face. Aegeus notes the corroboration, and asks for an explanation of it. 'A curious example of elliptical compression', Verrall): *El*.64 The farmer, finding Electra drawing water, breaks in upon her soliloquy. *Τί γὰρ τάδ', ὦ δύστην', ἐμὴν μοχθεῖς χάριν;* (Her action is explained by her desire to save her husband trouble. He enquires the cause of that desire.)

(iv) Sometimes a *γάρ* question, forming the answer to a preceding question, conveys a surprised recognition of the grounds which occasioned that question. S.*El.*1477 *Τίνων . . . ἐν μέσοις ἀρκυστάτοις πέπτωχ' ὁ τλήμων ;—Οὐ γὰρ αἰσθάνῃ πάλαι ζῶντας θανοῦσιν οὕνεκ' ἀνταυδᾷς ἴσα*; (if Aegisthus had realized that Orestes was alive, not dead, he would not have asked his question): *Ph.*249–50 *Οὐ γὰρ δὴ σύ γ' ἦσθα ναυβάτης ἡμῖν κατ' ἀρχὴν τοῦ πρὸς Ἴλιον στόλου.—Ἦ γὰρ μετέσχες καὶ σὺ τοῦδε τοῦ πόνου ;—Ὦ τέκνον, οὐ γὰρ οἶσθά μ' ὅντιν' εἰσορᾷς ;—Πῶς γὰρ κάτοιδ' ὅν γ' εἶδον οὐδεπώποτε*; Pl.*Phdr.*234D *Εἶεν· οὕτω δὴ δοκεῖ παίζειν ;—Δοκῶ γάρ σοι παίζειν καὶ οὐχὶ ἐσπουδακέναι* ; ('What? Do you think I'm joking?'): X.*Smp.*3.12 *ἐπὶ τίνι μέγα φρονεῖς ; καὶ ὃς ἔφη· Οὐ γὰρ ἅπαντες ἴστε, ἔφη, ὅτι ἐπὶ τούτῳ τῷ υἱεῖ* ; ('Why, don't you all know . . .?'): D.iv 10 *ἢ βούλεσθ' . . . περιιόντες αὐτῶν πυνθάνεσθαι, "λέγεταί τι καινόν;" γένοιτο γὰρ ἄν τι καινότερον ἢ Μακεδὼν ἀνὴρ Ἀθηναίους καταπολεμῶν . . .*; ('Why, *could* there be anything more novel . . . ?'): Pl.*R.*344E : X.*Cyr.*i 4.12 : *Smp.*4.50.

(v) In other passages an *οὐ γάρ* question gives, in rhetorically interrogative form, the answer to the preceding question, and *γάρ* denotes that that question need never have been put, had not the questioner overlooked an answer rhetorically presented as obvious. 'Why?' 'Why, of course'. ('You ask that because, I suppose, so-and-so did'nt notoriously happen.') This highly colloquial idiom is almost confined to Aristophanes and Xenophon. (These passages are essentially distinct from those given under (iv), because here the question does really convey the required information. Hence Jebb, on S.*Ant.*21, is misleading when he cites in comparison S.*Ph.*249, and renders 'What, has not...?' Such translations are misleading in these cases, because they imply that the first speaker already knew the answer.)

S.*Ant.*21 *Τί δ' ἔστι ; . . .—Οὐ γὰρ τάφου νῷν τὼ κασιγνήτω Κρέων τὸν μὲν προτίσας τὸν δ' ἀτιμάσας ἔχει*; Ar.*Eq.*1392 *Πῶς ἔλαβες αὐτὰς ἐτεόν ;—Οὐ γὰρ ὁ Παφλαγὼν ἀπέκρυπτε ταύτας ἔνδον . . .*; ('Why, of course, the Paphlagonian was keeping them hid'): *Ach.*576 *Ὦ Λάμαχ', οὐ γὰρ οὗτος ἄνθρωπος πάλαι...*; (referring to the questions in 572–4): *V.*1299 *Τί δ' ἔστιν, ὦ παῖ . . .;—Οὐ γὰρ ὁ γέρων . . .*; X.*Mem.*i. 3.10 *Καὶ τί δή, ἔφη . . ., ἰδὼν ποιοῦντα τοιαῦτα κατέγνωκας αὐτοῦ ;—Οὐ γὰρ οὗτος, ἔφη, ἐτόλμησε . . .*; *Cyr.*iii 1.38 *ποῦ δὴ ἐκεῖνός ἐστιν . . . ;—Οὐ γάρ, ἔφη, ἀπέκτεινεν αὐτὸν οὑτοσὶ ὁ ἐμὸς πατήρ* ; *Mem.*iii 4.1

Τίνες . . . στρατηγοὶ ᾕρηνται ; καὶ ὅς, Οὐ γάρ, ἔφη, . . . τοιοῦτοί εἰσιν Ἀθηναῖοι, ὥστε ἐμὲ μὲν οὐχ εἵλοντο . . . ;

(7) The statement or question sometimes refers to a subordinate clause, or individual word, in the preceding speech. Cf. III.7. S.*Aj.*1320 *τηλόθεν γὰρ ᾐσθόμην βοὴν Ἀτρειδῶν . . .—Οὐ γὰρ κλύοντές ἐσμεν αἰσχίστους λόγους . . . ;* (referring to *βοήν*): *OT*324 *οὔτ' ἔννομ' εἶπας . . . τήνδ' ἀποστερῶν φάτιν.—Ὁρῶ γάρ οὐδὲ σοὶ τὸ σὸν φώνημ' ἰὸν πρὸς καιρόν* (referring to participial clause): 433 *οὐδ' ἱκόμην ἔγωγ' ἄν, εἰ σὺ μὴ 'κάλεις.—Οὐ γάρ τί σ' ᾔδη μῶρα φωνήσοντ'* (referring to protasis): 1151 (*ἁμαρτάνεις*) *Οὐκ ἐννέπων τὸν παῖδ' ὃν οὗτος ἱστορεῖ.—Λέγει γὰρ εἰδὼς οὐδέν* (referring to *οὐκ ἐννέπων*): E.*Med.*59 *ἵμερός μ' ὑπῆλθε . . . λέξαι . . . δεσποίνης τύχας.—Οὔπω γὰρ ἡ τάλαινα παύεται γόων ;* S.*Aj.*1128: *El.*837.

(8) Sometimes an exclamation, apostrophe, or question is interposed before the *γάρ* clause. A.*Pers.*798 *Πῶς εἶπας ; οὐ γὰρ . . . ;* S.*OT*1017 *Πῶς εἶπας ; οὐ γὰρ Πόλυβος . . . ; Tr.*1124 *Ὦ παγκάκιστε, καὶ παρεμνήσω γὰρ αὖ . . . ; OC*863 *Ὦ φθέγμ' ἀναιδές, ἦ σὺ γὰρ ψαύσεις ἐμοῦ ;* E.*Alc.*1089 *Τί δ' ; οὐ γαμεῖς γὰρ . . . ; Med.*670 *Πρὸς θεῶν—ἄπαις γὰρ δεῦρ' ἀεὶ τείνεις βίον ; El.*969 *Φεῦ· πῶς γὰρ κτάνω νιν . . . ;* Ar.*Eq.*32 *†Ποῖον βρέτας† ; ἐτεὸν ἡγεῖ γὰρ θεούς ;* 858 *Οἴμοι τάλας· ἔχουσι γὰρ πόρπακας ; Av.*815 *Ἡράκλεις· Σπάρτην γὰρ ἂν θείμην . . . ;* 1049 *Ἄληθες οὗτος ; ἔτι γὰρ ἐνταῦθ' ἦσθα σύ ; Ra.*116 *Ὦ σχέτλιε, τολμήσεις γὰρ . . . ; Pl.*124 *Ἄληθες, ὦ δειλότατε πάντων δαιμόνων ; οἴει γὰρ εἶναι τὴν Διὸς τυραννίδα . . . ;* Hom.κ337: S.*El.*930: *Ph.*249: E.*El.*243: Ar.*Ach.*576: *Nu.*57,200,1470: *V.*1126: *Pl.*429: Pl.*Euthd.*284C *Πῶς λέγεις . . ., ὦ Κτήσιππε ; εἰσὶν γάρ τινες . . . ; Phlb.*13B: X.*Mem.*ii 3.16: *Cyr.*i 3.4.

Sometimes, on the other hand, *γάρ* explains the exclamation, apostrophe, or question. E.*HF*1140 *Αἰαῖ· στεναγμῶν γάρ με περιβάλλει νέφος : Rh.*608 *Δέσποιν' Ἀθάνα, φθέγματος γὰρ ᾐσθόμην τοῦ σοῦ συνήθη γῆρυν : Hel.*857. Cf., in mid-speech, E.*Tr.*106. (In Ar.*Pax* 566 *γάρ* is extremely doubtful.)

On a review of the above evidence, there appears no reason to doubt that *γάρ* in answers means 'for'. This explanation, formerly accepted without question, was challenged by Hartung and Klotz, but has recently again been upheld by Sernatinger and Misener. The transition from the use in continuous speech to the use in affirmative answers, and then to the use in answers of interrogative form, is easily made: and the postulated ellipse is of a type very common in Greek dialogue. Alternative explanations are far less natural. Hartung (i 473–8) says that *γάρ* in answers serves to connect the answer closely with the preceding speech, which it takes up and continues: while in questions he attributes a conclusive meaning to the particle. Bäumlein (p. 73) shrinks from ever regarding *γάρ* as conclusive, and holds that its effect in a question is to ask whether something is decidedly and undoubtedly so. But this has the disadvantage of leaving a logical gulf between two speeches which clearly are connected logically.

VI. Progressive use, in answer-questions. In answers which take the form of a question *γάρ* sometimes marks a transition to a fresh point, when a speaker either (1) proffers a new suggestion after the elimination of a previous hypothesis, or (2), having been satisfied on one subject, wishes to learn something further. In both idioms there is a parallel use of *ἀλλά*.

(1) This presents no difficulty. The rejection of the previous hypothesis is founded on, or explained by, the fact that something else is true instead. The second speaker asks what that something is. The passages here noticed are to be distinguished from those cited under V.6 above, in so far as the note of incredulity or surprise is absent or less prominent, the force of the particle being 'well' rather than 'why', though it is impossible to draw this distinction rigidly.

S.*OC*581 *Χρόνῳ μάθοις ἄν, οὐχὶ τῷ παρόντι που.—Ποίῳ γὰρ ἡ σὴ προσφορὰ δηλώσεται;* ('Why, when ...?' or 'Well, when ...?'): 598 *Ἦ τὴν παλαιὰν ξυμφορὰν γένους ἐρεῖς;—Οὐ δῆτ'· ἐπεὶ πᾶς τοῦτό γ' Ἑλλήνων θροεῖ.—Τί γὰρ τὸ μεῖζον ἢ κατ' ἄνθρωπον νοσεῖς;* *El.*942 *Οὐκ ἐς τόδ' εἶπον ...—Τί γὰρ κελεύεις ...;* E.*Heracl.*656 *οὐκ Ἀργόθεν κῆρυξ ἀφῖκται πολεμίους λόγους ἔχων.—Τί γὰρ βοὴν ἔστησας ἄγγελον φόβου;* Ar.*Pax*.41 *Ἀφροδίτης μὲν γὰρ οὔ μοι φαίνεται ...—Τοῦ γάρ ἐστ';* ('Well, whose *is* it?'): *Nu.*403 *τί γάρ ἐστιν δῆθ' ὁ κεραυνός;* ('Well, what *is* the thunderbolt then (if it doesn't come from Zeus)?'): E.*Hipp*.322: *Ion* 971. With ellipse of verb. S.*OC* 539 Ἔρεξας—Οὐκ ἔρεξα—Τί γάρ; ("'Why, what else?' if not ἔρεξα", Jebb.)

(2) is more puzzling. (i)[1] In cases where the further information required concerns the cause or origin of the facts already known, we have again, perhaps, simply a variety of the ordinary causal γάρ. 'So-and-so happened.'—'Because it was caused by—what?' S.*Aj*.282 Ὡς ὧδ' ἐχόντων τῶνδ' ἐπίστασθαί σε χρή. —Τίς γάρ ποτ' ἀρχὴ τοῦ κακοῦ προσέπτατο; *Ph*.327 'May I be revenged on the Atridae.'—Εὖ γ', ὦ τέκνον· τίνος γὰρ ὧδε τὸν μέγαν χόλον κατ' αὐτῶν ἐκκαλῶν ἐλήλυθας; E.*Supp*.647 'The Athenian army is safe and victorious.'—Πῶς γὰρ τροπαῖα Ζηνὸς Αἰγέως τόκος ἔστησεν . . .; A.*Ag*.634: E.*Supp*.108: *Ion* 954: *Ph*.1086: *IT* 936: Ar.*Eq*.1002.

(ii) But in other passages the supplementary information required is in no sense explanatory. A.*Pers*.239 πλοῦτος ἐξαρκὴς δόμοις;—Ἀργύρου πηγή τις αὐτοῖς ἐστι . . .—Πότερα γὰρ τοξουλκὸς αἰχμὴ . . .; *Ag*.630 'Agamemnon was caught by a storm, as you guessed.'—Πότερα γὰρ αὐτοῦ ζῶντος ἢ τεθνηκότος φάτις . . . ἐκλῄζετο; S.*Aj*.101 'I have killed the Atreidae.'—Εἶεν· τί γὰρ δὴ παῖς ὁ τοῦ Λαερτίου; 983 'Ajax is dead.'—Φεῦ τάλας. τί γὰρ τέκνον τὸ τοῦδε, ποῦ . . . κυρεῖ . . .; *Ph*.161 Οἶκον μὲν ὁρᾷς . . .—Ποῦ γὰρ ὁ τλήμων αὐτὸς ἄπεστιν; (Jebb misunderstands γάρ here): 421 (if Badham's Τί γάρ is right): 433 'Ajax and Antilochus are dead.'—Φέρ' εἰπὲ πρὸς θεῶν, ποῦ γὰρ ἦν ἐνταῦθά σοι Πάτροκλος . . .; 651 Ἀλλ' ἔκφερ' αὐτό. τί γὰρ ἔτ' ἄλλ' ἐρᾷς λαβεῖν; 1405 Αἰτίαν δὲ πῶς Ἀχαιῶν φεύξομαι;—Μὴ φροντίσῃς.—Τί γάρ, ἐὰν πορθῶσι χώραν τὴν ἐμήν; ('And what of their hostile *acts*'?): E.*IT* 533 'Calchas is dead.'—Ὦ πότνι', ὡς εὖ. τί γὰρ ὁ Λαρτίου γόνος; Ar.*Nu*.191 Ζητοῦσιν οὗτοι τὰ κατὰ γῆς.—Βολβοὺς ἄρα ζητοῦσι . . . τί γὰρ οἵδε δρῶσιν . . .; ('And what are these doing?'): 218 Strepsiades (after having the map explained to him) φέρε τίς γὰρ οὗτος οὑπὶ τῆς κρεμάθρας ἀνήρ; 351 κᾆτ' ἢν μὲν ἴδωσι κομήτην . . . κενταύροις ἤκασαν αὑτάς.—Τί γὰρ ἢν ἅρπαγα τῶν δημοσίων κατίδωσι Σίμωνα, τί δρῶσιν; *Pax* 838 Καὶ τίς ἐστιν ἀστὴρ νῦν ἐκεῖ;—Ἴων ὁ Χῖος . . .—Τίνες γάρ εἰσ' οἱ διατρέχοντες ἀστέρες . . .; *Av*.299 ἐκεινηὶ δέ γ'

[1] Here again it is difficult to draw a sharp line between (i) and (ii).

ἀλκυών.—Τίς γάρ ἐσθ' οὔπισθεν αὐτῆς; 1501 Τί γὰρ ὁ Ζεὺς ποιεῖ; (Prometheus, having, as he imagines, been told the time, goes on to ask about the weather): E.*Alc.*1143: *HF* 1198: *Hel.*111: *Rh.*540. (Merry seems to take γάρ in Ar. *V.*538 in this way, since he compares *Ec.*72 Ὑμεῖς δὲ τί φατε; More probably γάρ looks back to 532–6, 537 being an aside.) It will be observed that in some of the above passages an exclamation, or even a substantial part of the speech, precedes the γάρ clause.

Both the above forms, (i) and (ii), admit of ellipse, leaving only interrogative and particle expressed. (i) Asking for a more detailed explanation. S.*OC*545 Ἔκανον. ἔχει δέ μοι—Τί τοῦτο;—Πρὸς δίκας τι.—Τί γάρ; E.*Cyc.*686 Οὔ· ταύτῃ λέγω.—Πῇ γάρ; ('Well, and what way is that?'). (ii) Purely transitional. A.*Eu* 211 Χο. Τοὺς μητραλοίας ἐκ δόμων ἐλαύνομεν.—Απ. Τί γάρ; γυναικὸς ἥτις ἄνδρα νοσφίσῃ; ('And what of women who kill their husbands?'): 678 Athena, after obtaining the Erinyes' assent to the taking of the vote, turns to Apollo and Orestes. Τί γάρ; πρὸς ὑμῶν πῶς τιθεῖσ' ἄμομφος ὦ; (Verrall's 'Of course' is surely wrong): S.*OC*542 Δύστανε, τί γάρ; ἔθου φόνον . . . πατρός; ('Marking the transition from the topic of the marriage to that of the parricide', Jebb, who rightly remarks that τί γάρ; is tame if taken with δύστανε, meaning 'of course' (cf. VII below). 'And then, unhappy man . . .?'): E.*IT*820 Καὶ λούτρ' . . . ἀνεδέξω . . .;—'Yes'.—Τί γάρ; κόμας σὰς μητρὶ δοῦσα σῇ φέρειν; *Ion* 212 Λεύσσω Παλλάδ', ἐμὰν θεόν.—Τί γάρ; κεραυνὸν ἀμφίπυρον . . .; ('And the thunderbolt . . .?'). Often in Xenophon: *Mem.*ii 6.2–3 Τί γάρ; ἔφη, ὅστις δαπανηρὸς ὢν . . .; ('Well, he said, and what of the spendthrift?') . . . Τί γάρ; ὅστις χρηματίζεσθαι μὲν δύναται . . .; (the two following questions are introduced, for variety, by Τί δέ;): iii 10.3 'Do you select in painting?'—'Yes'.—Τί γάρ; ἔφη, τὸ πιθανώτατον . . . ἀπομιμεῖσθε τῆς ψυχῆς ἦθος; *Smp.*3.7 τί γὰρ σὺ . . . ἐπὶ τίνι μέγιστον φρονεῖς; *Cyr.*i 6.5 μέμνημαι ἀκούσας ποτέ σου . . .—Τί γάρ, ἔφη, ὦ παῖ, μέμνησαι ἐκεῖνα . . .; *Mem.*iii 3.6: *Oec.*17.7: 17.14: *Smp.* 3.8: 3.9: *Cyr.*i 6.12: v 2.27: 5.18: 5.19: *Hier.*1.22. (I give the Oxford Text punctuations: perhaps we should uniformly put a question mark after γάρ. At the opening of Plato's *Hipparchus*, if, as seems likely, γάρ is of this kind, we should perhaps punctuate, with Boeckh, Τί γάρ; τὸ φιλοκερδὲς . . .;)

The use of purely progressive *γάρ* in questions is probably confined to drama, with the exception of elliptical *τί γάρ*; in Xenophon. Its absence in Plato is noticeable. There are a few apparent, but textually uncertain, examples in Homer. *K*61 Agamemnon has told Menelaus to summon Ajax and Idomeneus. Menelaus answers, asking for supplementary instructions: *Πῶς γάρ μοι μύθῳ ἐπιτέλλεαι ἠδὲ κελεύεις; αὖθι μένω μετὰ τοῖσι δεδεγμένος εἰς ὅ κεν ἔλθῃς, ἦε θέω μετὰ σ' αὖτις* . . .; 424 *πολύκλητοι ἐπίκουροι εὕδουσι* . . .—*Πῶς γὰρ νῦν, Τρώεσσι μεμιγμένοι ἱπποδάμοισιν εὕδουσ', ἦ ἀπάνευθε*; (In both passages *τάρ*, found in some MSS., is perhaps to be preferred, with Leaf.) *π*222 is different (206 *ἤλυθον εἰκοστῷ ἔτεϊ ἐς πατρίδα γαῖαν*): Telemachus, after weeping on his father's neck, says *Ποίῃ γὰρ νῦν δεῦρο* . . . *νηΐ σε ναῦται ἤγαγον εἰς Ἰθάκην*; Here the explanatory force is still present, in spite of the interval. The same is true of *ξ* 115, where *τίς γάρ σε πρίατο* looks back to Eumaeus's preceding speeches in general, and 96 ff. in particular.

In E.*Ph.*376 (see Pearson) progressive *γάρ* is used in a question in the middle of a speech: (371) *ἀλλ' ἐκ γὰρ ἄλγους ἄλγος αὖ σὲ* (Jocasta) *δέρκομαι ἔχουσαν* . . . *τί γὰρ πατήρ μοι πρέσβυς ἐν δόμοισι δρᾷ* . . .; ('Well, and what of my old father?'). This is perhaps an instance of the occasional transference of the idioms of dialogue to continuous speech, as in certain uses of *γε*, *δῆτα*, and *μὲν οὖν*. We might perhaps compare Pi.*O.*13.20 *ταὶ Διονύσου πόθεν ἐξέφανεν σὺν βοηλάτᾳ χάριτες διθυράμβῳ*; *τίς γὰρ ἱππείοις ἐν ἔντεσσιν μέτρα* . . . *ἐπέθηκ'*; (*τίς δ' ἄρ'*, Hermann, 'probabiliter', Christ). *I.*5.41 might also be cited in support of *γάρ* here, were it not that the metre requires a short syllable before the particle (C. M. Bowra, *C.Q.* 1930, p. 178). Schmid's *ἄρ'* is almost certain. See, further, on *γὰρ δή*, p. 244(5).

This use of progressive *γάρ* in questions, which has not, on the whole, been sufficiently recognized, is difficult to explain, particularly in the passages cited under 2.ii. Misener (pp. 50–1) analyses it as originating in the omission of *ἀλλά* in *ἀλλὰ γάρ*. 'The interrogative . . . besides arresting the attention, has associated with it that slightly contrasting sense which makes an *ἀλλά* unnecessary . . . *γάρ* gives the reason for the intention to change the topic or pass to a new item in the same. . . . Possibly, in conversation, where most of the instances occur, facial expression and gesture were effective aids in indicating transition.' This explanation can hardly be called satisfactory. The idiom under discussion bears no resemblance to ἀλλὰ γάρ. It is difficult both to find a 'contrasting sense' in the examples given above, and to account for the omission of its explicit expression, if felt by the speaker. For 'facial expression and gesture', though they play some part in Greek drama (cf. E.*Med.*689: *Ion* 241), are hardly important enough to form the basis of a grammatical idiom, particularly an idiom not normally associated with strong emotion. Nor is Wecklein's supposed ellipse (in E.*IT* 533) convincing ('Stop, another person occurs to me, for ...'). Neil may perhaps be right (Ar.*Eq.*p.201) in seeing here an instance of the 'original' sense of γάρ (γ' ἄρα, 'well, then': for which see above, *ad init.*). But I would suggest, tentatively, another explanation: that γάρ is originally explanatory here, as in the examples quoted in (1) and 2.i: but that, owing to the frequency with which supplementary questions are requests for explanation, the explanatory sense becomes forgotten, and γάρ is used in questions as a purely transitional particle. If this is so, we can trace here the stereotyping of an idiom in a sense alien to its original significance; a process not without parallel in the history of language.

VII. The elliptical questions, τί γάρ;—ἦ γάρ;—οὐ γάρ;—πῶς γάρ;—πῶς γὰρ οὔ;—deserve special notice.

τί γάρ; We have seen above (VI.1) that a γάρ question, which may be elliptical in form, sometimes follows upon the rejection of an hypothesis. (Since in such cases 'what?' implies 'what else?', we may, if we like, speak of an ellipse of ἄλλο also. ἄλλο is, in fact, not invariably omitted: Pl.*R.*392D ἆρ' οὐ πάντα ... διήγησις οὖσα τυγχάνει ...;—Τί γάρ, ἔφη, ἄλλο;) Hence τί γάρ;, like τί μήν;, when the question is rhetorical, comes to mean 'of course'. A.*Ag.*1139 οὐδέν ποτ' εἰ μὴ ξυνθανουμένην. τί γάρ; 1239 καὶ τῶνδ' ὅμοιον εἴ τι μὴ πείθω· τί γάρ; S.*OC* 1679 Βέβηκεν.—Ὡς μάλιστ' ἂν ἐν πόθῳ λάβοις. τί γάρ; ὅτῳ μήτ' Ἄρης μήτε πόντος ἀντέκυρσεν: *Fr.*90 βοτῆρα νικᾶν ἄνδρας ἀστίτας. τί γάρ; E.*Or.*482 προσφθέγγῃ νιν ...;—Τί γάρ; φίλου μοι πατρός ἐστιν ἔκγονος: *Supp.*51: Pl.*R.*393C Φήσομεν· τί γάρ; *Plt.*259C Οὐκοῦν ... φανερὸν ...;—Τί γάρ; In

A.*Ch.*880 τί γάρ;, following a negative statement, bears the opposite meaning, 'for how so?', 'of course not': οὐχ ὥστ' ἀρῆξαι διαπεπραγμένῳ· τί γάρ; cf. *Fr.*94 οὔτοι γυναιξὶ ⟨δεῖ⟩ κυδάζεσθαι· τί γάρ;

Introducing an example: Arist.*Pol.*1281a14 ἀλλὰ ταῦτα πάντα ἔχειν φαίνεται δυσκολίαν. τί γάρ; ἂν οἱ πένητες . . . (*quid enim*?).

(For the various progressive uses of τί γάρ; see VI above. The diverse shades of meaning expressed by the phrase are well illustrated in S.*OC*539–46.)

ἦ γάρ; 'Is not that so?': an appeal for confirmation, common in Plato. See ἦ.

οὐ γάρ; This is identical in meaning with ἦ γάρ; Pl.*Tht.*163A: *Grg.*480A: D.xviii 136 ὅμοιόν γε, οὐ γάρ; xix 253: xxi 209: xxii 73: xxiii 161,162,186. The Demosthenic instances are all ironical.

(In Epich.*Fr.*171.4 οὐ γάρ; is curiously fused with ἦ οὔ; τίς εἶμέν τοι δοκεῖ; ἄνθρωπος, ἦ οὐ γάρ;).

πῶς γάρ; confirms a negative statement. S.*El.*911 οὐδ' αὖ σύ· πῶς γάρ; Pl.*R.*379B οὐδ' ἄν τινος εἴη κακοῦ αἴτιον.—Πῶς γάρ; *Lg.*640C Ἔστιν δέ γε . . . οὐκ ἀθόρυβος. ἦ γάρ;—Πῶς γάρ; ἀλλ' οἶμαι πᾶν τοὐναντίον: Lys.i 27 οὐκ εἰσαρπασθεὶς ἐκ τῆς ὁδοῦ, οὐδ' ἐπὶ τὴν ἑστίαν καταφυγὼν . . . πῶς γὰρ ἂν (*sc.* κατέφυγε) . . .; Pl.*R.*425B,515A: D.xviii 312. (In S.*Aj.*279 πῶς γάρ is curiously used in the sense of πῶς γὰρ ἄλλως;)

πῶς γὰρ οὔ; confirms a positive statement. A.*Ch.*754: S.*El.*865, 1307: Pl.*Grg.*487B: *Euthphr.*10A: *id. saep.*: X.*Mem.*iv 4.13. Also τί γὰρ οὔ; Pl.*R.*425C,558D: *Prm.*134D. τί δὴ γὰρ οὔ; *Prm.* 138B,140E.

VIII. Assentient. We have seen above that γάρ, in answers, often introduces the reason for an assent which is left unexpressed. From this it is but a short step to the use of γάρ as an assentient particle *per se*. The transitional stage occurs where that which is a reason is almost identical with that of which it is a reason. Thus, in the common Platonic formulae εἰκὸς γάρ, ἔοικε γάρ, seeming is not sharply distinguished from being, and the force of γάρ here is very much what it is in the less equivocal ἔστι γάρ. *Phd.*69A ὅμοιόν ἐστιν . . .—Ἔοικε γάρ: *R.*445E οὔτε γὰρ . . . κινήσειεν ἂν . . .—Οὐ γὰρ εἰκός, ἔφη. Thus assentient *γάρ*, while originating in an ellipse, shakes itself free from its elliptical origin, and acquires an independent existence. (To suppose an actual ellipse everywhere, and to fill up with such words as 'You are right, for' (cf. Jebb on S.*OT* 1117), is unnecessary and artificial.) Those scholars who are in general disinclined to accept ellipse in interpreting *γάρ* naturally explain this usage differently. Hartung (i 474) derives it from affirmatory *γε*: Bäumlein (pp. 68–72) from *ἄρα* denoting that which is directly obvious and needs no proof.

Assentient *γάρ*, as a fully developed idiom, rarely appears before the fourth century. Earlier examples are less striking, and some of them (as my suggested renderings below indicate) admit of a different explanation.

(1) In general. A.*Ag.* 271 Χαρά μ' ὑφέρπει δάκρυον ἐκκαλουμένη.—Εὖ γὰρ φρονοῦντος ὄμμα σοῦ κατηγορεῖ ('Aye, truly.' Clytaemnestra agrees both that the man is weeping, and that he is weeping tears of loyal joy): S.*OT* 731 Ἔδοξ' ἀκοῦσαι σοῦ τόδ', ὡς . . .—Ηὐδᾶτο γὰρ ταῦτ' ('Aye, 'twas said so': better than 'I said so because it was the common report'): 1117 τῇ δ' ἐπιστήμῃ σύ μου προὔχοις τάχ' ἄν που, τὸν βοτῆρ' ἰδὼν πάρος.—Ἔγνωκα γάρ, σάφ' ἴσθι ('Aye, I know him, sure enough'): E.*IT* 520 Φασίν νιν . . . οἴχεσθαι δορί.—Ἔστιν γὰρ οὕτως: 539 Οὐκ ἔστιν· ἄλλως λέκτρ' ἔγημ' ἐν Αὐλίδι.—Δόλια γάρ (not, probably, 'It was ἄλλως because it was δόλια'): *Hel.* 565 Ἔγνως γὰρ ὀρθῶς (ἄρ' *codd.* Ar.*Th.* 911): Pl.*R.* 426A ἰατρευόμενοι γὰρ οὐδὲν περαίνουσιν, πλήν γε . . . μείζω ποιοῦσι τὰ νοσήματα . . .—Πάνυ γάρ, ἔφη, τῶν οὕτω καμνόντων τὰ τοιαῦτα πάθη ('Yes, that is their condition, exactly'): 465B 'Fear and shame will deter the young from assaulting the old'.—Συμβαίνει γὰρ οὕτως, ἔφη: 490A ἡγεῖτο δ' αὐτῷ, εἰ νῷ ἔχεις, . . . ἀλήθεια . . .—Ἦν γὰρ οὕτω λεγόμενον: X.*Cyr.* ii 4.12 μέμνημαι ἀκούσας ὡς ὁ Ἀρμένιος καταφρονοίη σου . . .—Ποιεῖ γὰρ ταῦτα, ἔφη: vi.13 ἀλλὰ καὶ φυλάττουσι . . .—Ποιοῦσι γάρ, ἔφη, ταῦτα. In A.*Ag.* 551 Εὖ γὰρ πέπρακται, *γάρ* seems to be assentient: 'Aye, 'tis well done'. The Herald returns to the reflections of his opening speech 503–37. (In S.*OC* 1426 *γάρ* seems to be causal: *v.* Jebb *ad loc.*). The following also may perhaps be classed

as assentient: Pl.*Phdr*.228C *ὥς μοι δοκεῖς σὺ οὐδαμῶς με ἀφήσειν ...—Πάνυ γάρ σοι ἀληθῆ δοκῶ* (cf. *R*.567E): *Grg*. 506D *ἆρα ἔστιν ταῦτα;—Ἐγὼ μὲν γάρ φημι* (*γάρ BPF*: *γὰρ δή T*). (In Is.viii 33 *γάρ* after *δῆλον* may be classed as assentient, the expected alternative being selected; 'I need not ask, for ....')

(2) Very frequently in Plato, sometimes in the Socratic works of Xenophon, and occasionally elsewhere, the answer echoes a word from the preceding speech. Epich.*Fr*.170b4 *Οὐδὲ μὰν οὐδ' ...;—Οὐ γάρ*: S.*Ph*.756 *Δεινόν γε τοὐπίσαγμα τοῦ νοσήματος.—Δεινὸν γάρ, οὐδὲ ῥητόν*: Ar.*Av*.611 *πολλῷ κρείττους οὗτοι ...—Οὐ γὰρ πολλῷ*; ('Yes, aren't they? Much.'): *Ec*. 773–6 *Λέγουσι γοῦν ἐν ταῖς ὁδοῖς.—Λέξουσι γάρ.—Καί φασιν οἴσειν ἀράμενοι.—Φήσουσι γάρ.—Ἀπολεῖς ἀπιστῶν πάντ'.—Ἀπιστήσουσι γάρ.—Ὁ Ζεὺς σέ γ' ἐπιτρίψειεν.—Ἐπιτρίψουσι γάρ* ('Aye, they'll say it', etc.): Alex.*Fr*.95.3 *ἆρ' ἦν ...;—Νὴ τὸν Δί', ἦν γάρ*: Pl.*Chrm*.164A *Οὐκ ... ἐλέγετο ...;—Ἐλέγετο γάρ*: 168A *φαμέν τινα εἶναι τοιαύτην ...;—Φαμὲν γάρ*: *R*.397D *ἥδιστος ...—Ἥδιστος γάρ*: 432D *ἰτέον.—Ἰτέον γάρ*: 353E,376B, 445B,502B: *Men*.85A: *Euthphr*.7B: *Phd*.90B: *Tht*.147B: *Prm*. 138B,145B: *Lg*.680D: *id.saep.*: X.*Mem*.ii 1.2 *Οὐκοῦν ... εἰκὸς ...;—Εἰκὸς γάρ*: iii 5.2 *οἶσθα ...;—Οἶδα γάρ*: *Oec*.16.11 *Οὐκοῦν ... οἶσθα ...;—Οἶδα γάρ*. The nonsensical string in Ar.*Ec*.773–6 is suggestive. It looks as though this idiom was coming into prominence in certain circles early in the fourth century.

A slightly different turn is given to the idiom in the following:—

Ar.*Lys*.55 *Ἆρ' οὐ παρεῖναι τὰς γυναῖκας δῆτ' ἐχρῆν;—Οὐ γὰρ μὰ Δί' ἀλλὰ πετομένας ἥκειν πάλαι* ('No, more than that, they ought to have flown here on wings long ago'. *ἆρ' οὐ* expects an affirmative answer: it gets a negative answer, which rejects the expected affirmative in favour of a stronger one. *οὐ γὰρ ... ἀλλά* thus corresponds to *μὲν οὖν* (cf. S.*El*.1453). I do not think this is an instance of *οὐ γὰρ ἀλλά* (*q.v.*)): Pl.*R*.509C *ἑκὼν οὐκ ἀπολείψω.—Μὴ γάρ, ἔφη* ('No, don't').

(3) *Γάρ τοι*, following a demonstrative pronoun, sometimes conveys assent, while adding something to it. (A colloquial idiom.) E.*Heracl*.716 *Οἶδ' οὐ προδώσουσίν σε ...—Τοσόνδε γάρ*

τοι θάρσος, οὐδὲν ἄλλ' ἔχω (' Aye, therein is my trust ; and in naught beside '): Ar.*Th.*81 τρίτη 'στὶ Θεσμοφορίων ἡ μέση.—Τοῦτ' αὐτὸ γάρ τοι κἀπολεῖν με προσδοκῶ (' Yes, that 's what 'll be the ruin of me '): 171 ' A man's poetry resembles his personal appearance '.—Ἄπασ' ἀνάγκη· ταῦτα γάρ τοι γνοὺς ἐγὼ ἐμαυτὸν ἐθεράπευσα (' that 's why I've got myself up so fine '): X.*Mem.*ii 3.6 ἢ ἔστιν οἷς καὶ πάνυ ἀρέσκει;—Διὰ τοῦτο γάρ τοι, ἔφη, ὦ Σώκρατες, ἄξιόν ἐστιν ἐμοὶ μισεῖν αὐτόν, ὅτι ἄλλοις μὲν ἀρέσκειν δύναται, ἐμοὶ δὲ . . .: iii 5.19: Ar.*Lys.*46: *Ra.*73. (Ar. *V.*588 is slightly different, approval rather than assent being conveyed, as in (4) below: Τουτὶ γάρ τοι σεμνόν, ' Yes, that 's fine '). (For γάρ τοι in general, see τοι, VI. 3.)

(4) Approval is closely allied to assent, and γάρ, like ἀλλά, can be used to signify the one as well as the other. S.*Ant.*639 ' I am your obedient son.'—Οὕτω γάρ, ὦ παῖ, χρὴ διὰ στέρνων ἔχειν: E.*IA* 1355 Ἀπεκρίνω δὲ τί;—Τὴν ἐμὴν μέλλουσαν εὐνὴν μὴ κτανεῖν.—Δίκαια γάρ (' A proper answer '): Ar.*Nu.*679 Τὴν καρδόπην θηλεῖαν (χρὴ καλεῖν);—'Ορθῶς γὰρ λέγεις: Pl.*R.*440D Πάνυ μὲν οὖν, ἔφη, ἔοικε τοῦτο ᾧ λέγεις· καίτοι γ' . . . τοὺς ἐπικούρους ὥσπερ κύνας ἐθέμεθα . . .—Καλῶς γάρ, ἦν δ' ἐγώ, νοεῖς ὃ βούλομαι λέγειν (' You get my meaning admirably '): *Alc.I* 134E ὑμᾶς ἐθέλω ἐγγυήσασθαι ἦ μὴν εὐδαιμονήσειν.—Ἀσφαλὴς γὰρ εἶ ἐγγυητής (' Well, you 're a guarantor one can trust '): X.*Mem.* iii 6.2 προστατεύειν διανενόησαι τῆς πόλεως;—Ἔγωγε, ἔφη . . .—Νὴ Δί', ἔφη, καλὸν γάρ (' And a very noble ambition,' he said).

(5) Plato often echoes a word from the preceding speech, when the second speaker endorses a view put forward by the first. *La.*180B οἶμαι δὲ . . .—Ἀληθῆ γὰρ οἴει: *Phd.*85E οὐ πάνυ φαίνεται . . . Καὶ ὁ Σωκράτης, Ἴσως γάρ, ἔφη, . . . ἀληθῆ σοι φαίνεται: *Tht.*187A τοῦτό γε καλεῖται, ὡς ἐγᾦμαι, δοξάζειν.—'Ορθῶς γὰρ οἴει (196B): *R.*327C δοκεῖτέ μοι . . .—Οὐ γὰρ κακῶς δοξάζεις: 506A μαντεύομαι δὲ . . .—Καλῶς γάρ, ἔφη, μαντεύῃ: *Phlb.*25E φαίνῃ . . .—'Ορθῶς γὰρ φαίνομαι: *Phdr.*227B φησὶ . . .—Καλῶς γάρ, ὦ ἑταῖρε, λέγει.

IX. In wishes: εἰ γάρ, αἲ γάρ. In post-Homeric Greek, εἰ γάρ is mostly found in the exalted style of tragedy, occurring but seldom in comedy and prose. We have two problems here: (1) the use of εἰ (αἴ): (2) the use of γάρ.

(1) The natural supposition is that an εἰ wish is a conditional protasis with suppressed apodosis, an ellipse paralleled in Latin, English, and other languages. A contrary view has been maintained by Lange, Monro (*H.G.*§321), Kühner, and Liddell and Scott, that εἰ in wishes is interjectional, and that from this primary use the conditional is, at least partly, derived. This theory certainly makes it easier to connect εἰ in wishes with εἰ in εἰ δ' ἄγε: and it accords with the development of hypotactic from paratactic forms of construction in other cases. But it is difficult to doubt that in practice (etymological history apart) even Homer, not to speak of later writers, regarded εἰ in wishes as conditional. The distinction between wish and condition is, in fact, hard to draw, as the variation in editors' punctuation shows. The difference between 'If only James were here! He would help me', and 'If only James were here, he would help me', is merely the difference between an apodosis at first vaguely conceived, and then clearly defined, and an apodosis clearly envisaged at the outset. (i) Condition, and (iii) Wish are bridged by an intermediate stage (ii) Wish-Condition.

(i) Condition. Hom.*N*276 Οἶδ' ἀρετὴν οἷός ἐσσι . . . εἰ γὰρ νῦν παρὰ νηυσὶ λεγοίμεθα πάντες ἄριστοι ἐς λόχον . . . (287) οὐδέ κέν ἔνθα τεόν γε μένος καὶ χεῖρας ὄνοιτο: ο545 εἰ γάρ κεν σὺ πολὺν χρόνον ἐνθάδε μίμνοις, τόνδε τ' ἐγὼ κομιῶ, ξενίων δέ οἱ οὐ ποθὴ ἔσται.

(ii) Wish-Condition (especially εἰ γὰρ . . . τῷ κε). Hom.*B*371 ἀγορῇ νικᾷς . . . αἲ γὰρ . . . τοιοῦτοι δέκα μοι συμφράδμονες εἶεν Ἀχαιῶν· τῷ κε τάχ' ἠμύσειε πόλις Πριάμοιο: *H*132 αἲ γὰρ . . . ἡβῷμ' ὡς ὅτε . . . (157) εἴθ' ὡς ἡβώοιμι . . . τῷ κε τάχ' . . . : ρ496 Εἰ γὰρ ἐπ' ἀρῇσιν τέλος ἡμετέρῃσι γένοιτο· οὐκ ἄν τις τούτων γε ἐΰθρονον Ἠῶ ἵκοιτο: *Δ*288: δ732: ο536: π99: φ372: ω376. These mixed wish-conditionals are characteristic of the fluidity of Homeric structure: they are rarely found in later Greek, where condition and wish crystallize as distinct modes of thought. A.*Ch*.345 εἰ γὰρ ὑπ' Ἰλίῳ . . . κατηναρίσθης·[1] λιπὼν ἂν εὔκλειαν . . . πολύχωστον ἂν εἶχες τάφον: *Th*.550.

(iii) Pure wish-clauses. εἰ γάρ and αἰ γάρ are often used in Homer when a speaker confirms the certainty of a fact by ex-

[1] Tucker, whose note well expresses the difficulty of analysing such constructions, prints a colon here: Sidgwick, a comma.

pressing the wish that something desired by him might be as certainly fulfilled: εἰ γὰρ . . . ὡς . . .: 'Would that . . . as surely as . . .'. (See Misener, '*The* εἰ γάρ *wishes*'.) Hom.*N*825 εἰ γὰρ ἐγὼν οὕτω γε Διὸς πάϊς αἰγιόχοιο εἴην . . . ὡς νῦν ἡμέρη ἥδε κακὸν φέρει Ἀργείοισι: Σ464 αἲ γάρ μιν θανάτοιο δυσηχέος ὧδε δυναίμην νόσφιν ἀποκρύψαι . . . ὥς οἱ τεύχεα καλὰ παρέσσεται: Θ538: Χ346: ι523: ρ251: σ235: φ402 (with an ironical ὡς clause). Without a following ὡς clause: γ205: ο156: Pi.*P*.1.46 εἰ γὰρ ὁ πᾶς χρόνος ὄλβον μὲν οὕτω καὶ κτεάνων δόσιν εὐθύνοι (where see schol.).

Apart from the above idiom, Homer appears to use only αἲ γάρ (never εἰ γάρ) in pure wish-clauses: though the distinction has not been noticed. In post-Homeric Greek, the almost complete disappearance of αἴ (αἲ γάρ in Hdt.i 27) makes differentiation no longer possible. Δ189: Π97: Σ272: Χ454: δ697: ζ244: η311.

(2) The function of γάρ in εἰ γάρ wishes has been variously explained. Hartung and Klotz connect it with a supposed use of γάρ in exclamations, while Bäumlein and Kühner regard it as adding emphasis or liveliness (though the latter adds that 'originally γάρ served here too to mark a thought as the direct result of the existing situation'). Liddell and Scott merely say that 'γάρ is used to strengthen a wish'. Prof. Misener, however, has recently argued that γάρ in εἰ γάρ wishes is causal. It will be well to review the evidence, and to discover what logical relationships, if any, are present where εἰ γάρ wishes are found, before attempting to solve the difficult question, whether, or not, these relationships are expressed by the particle γάρ.

(i) In many passages in Homer a causal relationship is admitted, or even required, by the context. Θ538 κείσεται οὐτηθείς, πολέες δ' ἀμφ' αὐτὸν ἑταῖροι . . . εἰ γὰρ ἐγὼν ὣς εἴην ἀθάνατος . . . ὡς νῦν ἡμέρη ἥδε κακὸν φέρει Ἀργείοισιν: Σ465 Θάρσει· μή τοι ταῦτα . . . μελόντων. αἲ γὰρ . . . δυναίμην . . . ὥς οἱ τεύχεα καλὰ παρέσσεται (the certainty that the arms will be forthcoming is a ground for the encouragement given): *B*371: Δ288: *H*132: Π97: Χ346: δ341: η311: ο156: σ235.

In the following passages also γάρ can be taken as causal, if we assume an elliptical answer, '(No,) for'. ι523 αὐτὸς δ' . . .

ἰήσεται (ἐννοσίγαιος) . . .—Αἲ γὰρ δὴ . . . δυναίμην, ὥς οὐκ ὀφθαλμόν γ' ἰήσεται οὐδ' ἐνοσίχθων: σ366 οὐκ ἐθελήσεις ἔργον ἐποίχεσθαι . . .—Εὐρύμαχ', εἰ γὰρ νῶϊν ἔρις ἔργοιο γένοιτο ('You are wrong to call me idle, for I could beat you at work'): φ402 'He looks like an archer'.—Αἲ γὰρ δὴ τοσσοῦτον ὀνήσιος ἀντιάσειεν, ὡς οὗτός ποτε τοῦτο δυνήσεται ἐντανύσασθαι (ironical).

There are few examples in post-Homeric Greek. Pi.*P.*1.46: A.*Ch.*345 (reference to 338–9). In the last case the intervening words of another speaker are ignored in the logical connexion.* Cf. III.5.

(ii) In dialogue, a wish is expressed that something stated or wished by the previous speaker may come true or might have come true. This type of connexion is not infrequent in Homer, and is almost invariably present in post-Homeric εἰ γάρ wishes. γάρ seems here to have an assentient or approving force: 'Aye, truly'.[1]

Hom.τ309 τοῦδ' αὐτοῦ λυκάβαντος ἐλεύσεται ἐνθάδ' Ὀδυσσεὺς . . .—Αἲ γὰρ τοῦτο, ξεῖνε, ἔπος τετελεσμένον εἴη: ρ496 Αἴθ' οὕτως αὐτόν σε βάλοι κλυτότοξος Ἀπόλλων. . . .—Εἰ γὰρ ἐπ' ἀρῇσιν τέλος ἡμετέρῃσι γένοιτο: Δ189: θ339: ο536: ρ163,513: υ236: φ200. A.*Th.*550 ἀπειλεῖ . . . ἃ μὴ κραίνοι θεός.—Εἰ γὰρ τύχοιεν ὧν φρονοῦσι πρὸς θεῶν ('Aye, in sooth'): E.*Or.*1209 ἢ ζῶν μακάριον κτήσει λέχος—Εἰ γὰρ γένοιτο ('Would God I might'): 1100 ὡς ἂν Μενέλεως συνδυστυχῇ.—Ὦ φίλτατ', εἰ γὰρ τοῦτο κατθάνοιμ' ἰδών ('Oh, could I but see that before I die!'): 1580 Ἑλένην φονεύσας ἐπὶ φόνῳ πράσσεις φόνον.—Εἰ γὰρ κατέσχον μὴ θεῶν κλεφθεὶς ὕπο: 1614 Σὲ σφάγιον ἔκομισ' ἐκ Φρυγῶν— —Εἰ γὰρ τόδ' ἦν: *Alc.*1072 (1066 δοκῶ γὰρ αὐτὴν εἰσορῶν γυναῖχ' ὁρᾶν ἐμὴν . . .) Εἰ γὰρ τοσαύτην δύναμιν εἶχον ὥστε σὴν ἐς φῶς πορεῦσαι . . . γυναῖκα: *Cyc.*437 σώθητι μετ' ἐμοῦ . . .—Ὦ φίλτατ', εἰ γὰρ τήνδ' ἴδοιμεν ἡμέραν: *IT*1221 Τὰ

[1] It is to be noted that εἰ γάρ is in drama almost confined to answers. In E.*Supp.*1145, with Murray's text, the speaker himself answers his own suggestion: ἆρ 'ἀσπιδοῦχος ἔτι=ποτ' ἀντιτάσσομαι σὸν φόνον—εἰ γὰρ γένοιτο—τεκνῶν; But τεκνῶν is difficult, and *L* and *p* mark a new speaker at εἰ γὰρ γένοιτο. In *Alc.* 90 the mark Ἡμιχ. in *VBL* (for which see Murray's *App. Crit.*) hardly justifies the supposition of a change of speaker (the connexion of thought here seems to be as in 2. iii: 86–90 'Alcestis is not yet dead': 90–2 'And may Apollo come to save her from dying'). *Rh.* 464.

τῆς θεοῦ πρᾶσσ' . . . καλῶς.—Εἰ γὰρ ὡς θέλω καθαρμὸς ὅδε πέσοι: *Ion* 979 παῖδα (τόλμησον κτανεῖν) . . .—Πῶς; εἰ γὰρ εἴη δυνατόν: Ar.*Ec*.380 Τὸ τριώβολον δῆτ' ἔλαβες;—Εἰ γὰρ ὤφελον: Com.Nov.Adesp.13Dem.: E.*Supp*.369: *El*.663: *Ion* 410: *Or*.1582: Ar.*Pax* 346: Pl.*Cri*.44D οἷοί τ' εἰσὶν οἱ πολλοὶ οὐ τὰ σμικρότατα τῶν κακῶν ἐξεργάζεσθαι . . .—Εἰ γὰρ ὤφελον . . . οἷοί τ' εἶναι οἱ πολλοὶ τὰ μέγιστα κακὰ ἐργάζεσθαι: *Prt* 310D ποιήσει καὶ σὲ σοφόν.—Εἰ γάρ, ἦ δ' ὅς . . . ἐν τούτῳ εἴη: Hdt.i 27.3: Pl.*R*.432C: X.*Cyr*.vi 1.38. In E.*Hipp*.1410 Theseus echoes, and amplifies, the wish suggested by his own last words, οὐδέ μοι χάρις βίου, which imply τεθναίην: 'Aye, would I were a corpse in thy stead!'

(iii) In other passages the wish is for something supplementary to, and usually similar to, a fact just stated as true. Hom.K536 ἵππων μ' ὠκυπόδων ἀμφὶ κτύπος οὔατα βάλλει. αἲ γὰρ δὴ 'Οδυσεύς τε καὶ ὁ κρατερὸς Διομήδης ὧδ' ἄφαρ ἐκ Τρώων ἐλασαίατο μώνυχας ἵππους ('I hear horses: and I hope they are the horses of O. and D.'): γ205 καὶ λίην κεῖνος μὲν ἐτίσατο . . . αἲ γὰρ ἐμοὶ τοσσήνδε θεοὶ δύναμιν περιθεῖεν, τίσασθαι μνηστῆρας ('I wish *I* could punish the suitors like that'): φ372 βίηφι δὲ φέρτερός εἰμι. αἲ γὰρ πάντων τόσσον . . . μνηστήρων . . . φέρτερος εἴην: ω376 Ὦ πάτερ, ἦ μάλα τίς σε θεῶν . . . ἀμείνονα θῆκεν ἰδέσθαι . . .—Αἲ γὰρ . . . οἷος Νήρικον εἷλον . . . τοῖος ἐών τοι χθιζὸς . . . ἀμύνειν ἄνδρας μνηστῆρας ('I wish I had been rejuvenated like that for yesterday's fight'): Pi.*N*.7.98 δύνασαι δὲ βροτοῖσιν ἀλκὰν . . . διδόμεν. εἰ γάρ σφισιν ἐμπεδοσθενέα βίοτον ἁρμόσαις: S.*El*.1416 Κλ. Ὤμοι μάλ' αὖθις.—Ηλ. Εἰ γὰρ Αἰγίσθῳ θ' ὁμοῦ: *OT* 80 Κρέοντα προσστείχοντα σημαίνουσί μοι.—Ὦναξ Ἄπολλον, εἰ γὰρ ἐν τύχῃ γέ τῳ σωτῆρι βαίη ('Creon is coming.'—'And may he bring good news.').

It will be noticed that in (i), (ii), and (iii) an exclamation or apostrophe sometimes precedes the wish. Cf. V.8.

(iv) In other Homeric passages the logical connexion does not fall under any of the above heads. Σ272 πολλοὺς δὲ κύνες καὶ γῦπες ἔδονται Τρώων· αἲ γὰρ δή μοι ἀπ' οὔατος ὧδε γένοιτο: X454 ἐγγὺς δή τι κακὸν Πριάμοιο τέκεσσιν. αἲ γὰρ ἀπ' οὔατος εἴη ἐμεῦ ἔπος: δ697 'The suitors are devouring my substance.'—Αἲ γὰρ δή, βασίλεια, τόδε πλεῖστον κακὸν εἴη: ζ244 νῦν δὲ θεοῖσιν ἔοικε, τοὶ οὐρανὸν εὐρὺν ἔχουσιν. αἲ γὰρ ἐμοὶ τοιόσδε πόσις κεκλημένος εἴη.

Hom.*h.Ap.*51 stands apart from all other examples of εἰ γάρ, in that the particles occur at the opening of a conversation, without any obvious logical connexion. (ἦ ἄρ κ', Matthiae: cf. σ 357.) In Alcm.*Frs.*16,17 the absence of context makes it impossible to determine the connexion, if any. So, too, Ar.*Fr.*109.

On reviewing the above evidence, it is not easy to say whether γάρ in εἰ γάρ wishes has (1) a connective force, or (2) a merely adverbial or emphatic one. In favour of (1) we may remark: (*a*) that, in the great majority of cases, those grouped under (i), (ii), and perhaps (iii) above, εἰ γάρ is used in contexts which admit of, or even require, a causal or assentient γάρ: (*b*) that there does not appear to be very much evidence, in general, for the supposed 'adverbial' use of the particle. On the other hand it may be pleaded in favour of (2): (*a*) that, in a not inconsiderable minority of cases, γάρ in εἰ γάρ cannot reasonably be interpreted as causal or assentient: (*b*) that simple εἰ wishes are relatively rare (see Kühner,II i 226): a consideration which may suggest that γάρ, like -θε, reinforces εἰ, converting 'if' into 'if only'. A decision between the rival views is perhaps not possible: but, on the whole, the 'adverbial' view seems preferable.

In A.*Th.*566 εἴθε γάρ, the reading of the later manuscripts, is a form not otherwise attested, and no doubt unsound.

(Hartung and Kühner cite E.*Cyc.*261 as indicating a distinctive use of γάρ, apart from εἰ, in wishes; ἐπεὶ κατελήφθη σοῦ λάθρᾳ πωλῶν τὰ σά.—'Εγώ; κακῶς γὰρ ἐξόλοι'. But one swallow does not make a summer. I should assign κακῶς γὰρ ἐξόλοιο to Odysseus, which removes all difficulty in the use of the particle (see *C.R.*xliv(1930)214–15). A few other passages in which γάρ might at first sight appear to have an optative force are better explained otherwise, or emended. In S.*OC*864 γάρ has nothing to do with the wish: Αὐδῶ σιωπᾶν.—Μὴ γὰρ αἵδε δαίμονες θεῖέν μ' ἄφωνον ('No, for . . .' Cf. V.2). The same is true of A.*Ag.*215 εὖ γὰρ εἴη. (Here the γάρ in 214 and the γάρ in 215 perhaps both look back to the question πῶς λιπόναυς γένωμαι; The reasonable anger of the army, and the hope that all may yet be well, are both reasons for not offending the army by refusing to sacrifice Iphigeneia. Cf. III. 6.) E.*Hipp.*640 'I don't like clever women: they're a bit *too* clever.' Harry's 'surely then (γε + ἄρ)' is unnecessary. *Ph.*1604: Pearson explains σῳζόμεσθα as 'I was so unfortunate as to be saved': but δ' ἄρ' is tempting. *Hel.*1201: Pearson is probably right in accepting Dobree's δ' ἄρ'. D.xix285 μὴ γὰρ οὕτω γένοιτο (γάρ is connective).

X. Special difficulties. There remains a certain residue of passages which are difficult to interpret on any of the lines suggested above. Few of them can be regarded as textually certain.

The following passages might appear to lend some support to the theory of an 'adverbial' γάρ. (In any of them δή would be natural enough.) Hom.K127 ἐν φυλάκεσσ', ἵνα γάρ σφιν ἐπέφραδον ἠγερέθεσθαι (γ' ἄρ has been suggested, though γε is rare after relatives in Homer: also τ' ἄρ, which violates the general, but not unbroken, principle that Epic (non-connective) τε has a universalizing force: a variation between γάρ and τ' ἄρ is found elsewhere, as Leaf points out: e.g. K61: Σ182,188: perhaps Peppmüller's ἄρα is right): *h.Ap.* 464 Ξεῖν', ἐπεὶ οὐ μὲν γάρ τι καταθνητοῖσιν ἔοικας (Allen and Sikes suppose a fusion of ἐπεὶ οὐ μέν and οὐ μὲν γάρ, which appears scarcely probable): Hp.*Morb.Sacr.*1 κῆν μὲν γὰρ αἶγα μιμῶνται . . . ἢν δὲ . . . (but this seems to stand for καὶ γὰρ ἢν μὲν . . . ἢν δέ). In Th.vii58.4 γάρ, read by *B* after ὅτι, cannot stand. Hp.*deArte*5 τὰ γὰρ τῷ ὠφελῆσθαι κ.τ.λ. has been adduced by Stahl (*Rh.M.*1902,1–7) as evidence for a concessive use of γάρ, 'freilich', with other passages which can all be otherwise explained. γάρ is normal if the sentence is read as a rhetorical question (see *C.R.*xliii (1929) 125). In A.*Eu.*747 Wecklein's 'allerdings' is inappropriate ('γάρ explains their cry l. 745', Sidgwick: but 747 clearly answers 746: perhaps δ' ἄρ'). In Hp.*Off.*15 the alternative reading δέ must be right.

XI. Position. *Γάρ* normally comes second in its clause. But:—

(1) *Μέν* takes precedence over it in this position.

(2) Certain words coalesce closely enough with the following word to be regarded as forming a unity with it: e.g. article, prepositions, and καί in the sense of 'also' or 'both'. Thus, in

tragedy, we sometimes find γάρ third or fourth word in such cases as the following:—

A.*Ch.*641 τὸ μὴ θέμις γάρ: S.*Ant.*1096 τό τ' εἰκαθεῖν γάρ: *Ph.* 1268 καὶ τὰ πρὶν γάρ: E.*Alc.*365 ἐν ταῖσιν αὐταῖς γάρ: *El.*68 ἐν τοῖς ἐμοῖς γάρ: *Tr.*1020 ἐν τοῖς Ἀλεξάνδρου γάρ (but S.*Ant.*661 ἐν τοῖς γὰρ οἰκείοισιν): *HF*309 τὰς τῶν θεῶν γάρ: *IT*676 καὶ δειλίαν γάρ: *Ion* 1022 καὶ σὺ γάρ: *Fr.*252 ἐκ τῶν δικαίων γάρ (ἐκ Meineke, for εἰ): *Fr.*502 τῆς γυναικὸς γάρ: *HF*1396 καὶ τοὺς σθένοντας γάρ: *Or.*684 καὶ χρὴ γάρ: 706 καὶ ναῦς γάρ: 1089 καὶ συγκατέκτανον γάρ.

(3) But the postponement of γάρ in tragedy is not confined to the above limits.

3rd. A.*Ag.*222 βροτοὺς θρασύνει γάρ: 758 τὸ δυσσεβὲς γὰρ ἔργον (δυσσεβὲς γάρ, for γὰρ δυσσεβές, Pauw: τὸ δυσσεβὲς γάρ, substantival, would be normal): S.*Aj.*522 χάρις χάριν γάρ: *El.* 492 ἄλεκτρ' ἄνυμφα γάρ: *Ant.*141 ἕπτα λοχαγοὶ γάρ: 732 Οὐχ ἥδε γὰρ ...; *OT*255 οὐδ' εἰ γὰρ ἦν: 277 οὔτ' ἔκτανον γάρ: *OC* 837 πόλει μαχῇ γάρ: *Tr.*338: *Ph.*209 διάσημα θροεῖ γάρ (Triclinius: γὰρ θροεῖ MSS.): E.*Andr.*764 πολλῶν νέων γάρ: *Tr.*621 κακῷ κακὸν γάρ: *Ion* 690 ἄτοπος ἄτοπα γὰρ παραδίδωσί μοι: *Supp.* 99 προσδοκῶ τι γάρ: *IT*1036: *Hec.*865: *HF*1126 ἀρκεῖ σιωπὴ γάρ: *Med.*1268 ἀμείβεται χαλεπὰ γάρ: *Or.*1244 τρισσοῖς φίλοις γάρ: *IA*1560 σιγῇ παρέξω γάρ: *Rh.*17 (anap.) τί σὺ γὰρ ...; *Fr.*1063.1 (? Euripides) δεῖ πυνθάνεσθαι γάρ.

4th. S.*Ph.*884 ὡς οὐκέτ ὄντος γάρ: *OT*1520 ἃ μὴ φρονῶ γάρ: *Aj.*867 πᾷ πᾷ πᾷ γάρ; E.*Ba.*477: *IA*122: *Fr.*142.

5th and 6th. In E.*Or.*314 κἂν μὴ νοσῇς γάρ, *Supp.*303 τἄλλ' εὖ φρονῶν γάρ (Marchant), crasis helps to mitigate the postponement. S.*Ph.*1451 stands alone in classical Greek, with the exception of Middle and New Comedy: καιρὸς καὶ πλοῦς ὅδ' ἐπείγει γάρ. (For B.3.22 see Jebb. In A.*Th.*114 Tucker reads κῦμα περὶ πτόλιν δοχμολόφων γὰρ ἀνδρῶν, for κῦμα γάρ κ.τ.λ., comparing Diph.*Fr.*60.3 (below), where two MSS. read ταλαιπωρότερον γάρ.)

In Aristophanes the postponement of γάρ is rather commoner and more violent:—

3rd. *Eq.*32 ἐτεὸν ἡγεῖ γάρ: 777 κἀγὼ γάρ: 789 καὶ σὺ γάρ: *V.*653 εἰ μὴ γάρ: 814 αὐτοῦ μένων γάρ: *Lys.*119 οὐ δεῖ γάρ: 144 δεῖ τᾶς γὰρ εἰράνας (a curious order, perhaps adopted *metri* *gratia*: cf. Alex.*Fr.*146.6 ἡ τῶν γάρ): *Av.*342 πῶς κλαύσει γάρ: 1546 μόνον θεῶν γὰρ διὰ σέ: *Ra.*634 εἴπερ θεὸς γάρ ἐστιν: *Pl.* 1188 καλῶς ἔσται γάρ: Archipp.*Fr.*15.1.

4th. *Ach.*581 ὑπὸ τοῦ δέους γάρ: 1076 ὑπὸ τούς Χοᾶς γάρ: 1087 ὁ τοῦ Διονύσου γάρ: *Nu.*1198 ὅπερ οἱ προτένθαι γάρ: *Av.* 1545 ἀεί ποτ' ἀνθρώποις γάρ: *Lys.*595 ὁ μὲν ἥκων γάρ: *Ra.* 867 οὐκ ἐξ ἴσου γάρ: 1434 ὁ μὲν σοφῶς γὰρ εἶπεν: *Ec.*984 τὰς ἐντὸς εἴκοσιν γάρ: *Pl.*65 εἰ μὴ φράσεις γάρ: 146 ἅπαντα τῷ πλουτεῖν γάρ.

5th. *Lys.*489 διὰ τἀργύριον πολεμοῦμεν γάρ; *Pl.*1189 ὁ Ζεὺς ὁ σωτὴρ γάρ. In *Ra.*340 γάρ may possibly come 5th: but the text is almost certainly corrupt.

Late position after φέρ' ἴδω *V.*563: after φέρε, Ar.*Nu.*218 (cf. δέ E.*Hel.*1043): for similar postponement of γάρ in answers, etc., see V.8.

In Middle and New Comedy:—

4th. Xenarch.*Fr.*7.2 οὐδὲ ἓν καινὸν γὰρ εὑρίσκουσιν: Diph.*Fr.* 60.3 ταλαιπωρότερον οὐδέν ἐστι γάρ.

5th. Philem.*Fr.*56.2 μετέχειν ἀνάγκη τῶν κακῶν γὰρ γίγνεται: *Fr.*79.17 οἱ μὲν ἥρπασάν τι γάρ: *Fr.*106.2 διὰ λύπην καὶ μανία γὰρ γίγνεται: Diph.*Fr.*102.1 ἀνδρὸς φίλου καὶ συγγενοῦς γὰρ οἰκίαν: Antiph.*Fr.*163.4 οὗ μὲν ἦμεν ἄρτι γάρ.

6th. Antiph.*Fr.*26.22 ἐπὶ τὸ τάριχός ἐστιν ὡρμηκυῖα γάρ: *Fr.* 164 ταῖς εὐτελείαις οἱ θεοὶ χαίρουσι γάρ.

7th and 8th. Alex.*Fr.*36 ὁ δεσπότης οὑμὸς περὶ λόγους γάρ ποτε διέτριψε: Philem.*Fr.*60.2 τοὺς ἐν τῇ πόλει μάρτυρας ἔχω γάρ: Alex.*Fr.*136.2 οὐκ εὐψυχία τοῦτ' ἔσθ' ὃ ποιεῖς νῦν γάρ, ἀλλ' ἀνανδρία.

9th. Antiph.*Fr.*212.7 αἱ μὲν ἄλλαι τοὔνομα βλάπτουσι τοῖς τρόποις γὰρ ὄντως ὂν καλόν.

The position of γάρ as first word in the line (lyr.), Ar.*Ec.*299, 913 is remarkable: cf. S.*OT*1103: *OC*1723. At end of iambic line: S.*OT*231 (without stop): E.*IT*1036 (before full stop).

In prose we, for the most part, find only the less violent types of postponement mentioned under (2). Hdt.i 194.5 ἀνὰ τὸν ποταμὸν γάρ: ix 49.3: v 92 δ1 ἡ Λάβδα γάρ: Th.iii 58.2 οὐκ ἐχθροὺς γάρ: Pl.*R.*431A ὁ αὐτὸς γάρ[1]: 518D τῷ ὄντι

[1] Dr. Chapman cites fourteen instances of ὁ αὐτὸς γάρ (&c.) in Plato, and only one of γάρ placed between article and αὐτός: *Phlb.*23A τὰ γὰρ αὔτ' ἔπαθεν ἄν.

γάρ[1]: 620A *κατὰ συνήθειαν γάρ*: *Alc.I*115C *κατὰ τὴν ἀνδρείαν γάρ*: 124E *παρὰ τοὺς ἱππικοὺς γάρ* (but *Smp.*209B *ἐν τῷ γὰρ αἰσχρῷ*: for this splitting of an integral phrase by *γάρ*, cf. *Ap.* 22B *ὡς ἔπος γὰρ εἰπεῖν*): *Sph.*238E *τὸ μὴ ὂν γάρ*: *Lg.*728E *τὰ μὲν ὑπέρογκα γάρ*: *Cra.*389C *τὸ φύσει γὰρ . . . πεφυκός*: X.*Cyr.* VI.16 *καὶ πυρὸς γάρ τοι.*

More violent transpositions are: Hp.*Cord.*9 *βέβλαπται ἔς τι γὰρ τὸ θερμόν*: Pl.*Sph.*255E *ἓν ἕκαστον γάρ*: *Lg.*681E "*κτίσσε δὲ Δαρδανίην*" *γάρ πού φησιν*: D.xxiii 136 *οὐδ' ὁτιοῦν ἐστι γάρ* (*ἐστι γάρ SF*: *γάρ ἐστι al.*): lix 55 *οὐ πολλῷ χρόνῳ γὰρ ὕστερον* (*γὰρ χρόνῳ r*).

In earlier Greek postponement of *γάρ* is rare: Hom.*P*363 *οὐδ' οἱ γάρ*: *Φ*331 *ἄντα σέθεν γάρ.* Semon.*Fr.*7.106 *ὅκου γυνὴ γάρ.*

Ἀλλὰ γάρ: ἀλλὰ . . . γάρ

The two forms must be considered together, as their uses overlap to a considerable extent. Both are used in two ways. Either *ἀλλά* goes with the main clause, and *γάρ* with a dependent clause: or both go with the main clause. The first use I will style 'complex', the second 'simple': preferring this nomenclature to Prof. Misener's 'complete' and 'elliptical', since the latter term begs the question with regard to the explanation of the idiom. We thus have four forms: (1) *ἀλλὰ . . . γάρ*, complex: (2) *ἀλλὰ . . . γάρ*, simple: (3) *ἀλλὰ γάρ* complex: (4) *ἀλλὰ γάρ*, simple. (3) is exceedingly rare. For the complex construction compare, in general, what has been said above regarding anticipatory *γάρ*.

I. *ἀλλὰ . . . γάρ*, complex. Here *ἀλλά* and *γάρ* fulfil their normal functions independently. But in cases where only one or two words intervene, the particles may rightly be regarded as forming a unity. This form is mainly found in Sophocles, Euripides, and Herodotus. It seldom occurs in Attic prose.

Hom.*ξ*355 *ἀλλ' οὐ γάρ σφιν ἐφαίνετο κέρδιον εἶναι μαίεσθαι προτέρω, τοὶ μὲν πάλιν αὖτις ἔβαινον*: Tyrt.*Fr.*8.1 Ἀλλ'—

[1] Dr. Chapman cites four other instances of this order from *Phdr.*, *R.*, and *Hp.Ma*: but *τῷ γὰρ ὄντι Tht.*146B, 174B: *Sph.*217E (late dialogues).

Ἡρακλῆος γὰρ ἀνικήτου γένος ἐστέ—θαρσεῖτ': Pi.*Paean* 6.54 ἀλλὰ παρθένοι γὰρ ἴστε Μοῖσαι πάντα . . . κλῦτε νῦν: A *Ch.*375 ἀλλὰ διπλῆς γὰρ τῆσδε μαράγνης δοῦπος ἱκνεῖται, τῶν μὲν ἀρωγοὶ κατὰ γῆς ἤδη (see Tucker): S.*Ph.*81 ἀλλ' ἡδὺ γάρ τι κτῆμα τῆς νίκης λαβεῖν, τόλμα: *OC*797 ἀλλ' οἶδα γάρ σε ταῦτα μὴ πείθων, ἴθι: E.*IT*118 ἀλλ' εὖ γὰρ εἶπας, πειστέον: *El.*1245 ἀλλ' ἄναξ γάρ ἐστ' ἐμός, σιγῶ: Ar.*Nu.*798 ἀλλ' οὐκ ἐθέλει γὰρ μανθάνειν, τί ἐγὼ πάθω; (rightly so punctuated, I think): *Th.*264 ἀλλ' ἔχεις γὰρ ὧν δέει, εἴσω τις ὡς τάχιστά μ' ἐσκυκλησάτω: S.*El.*256: *Ph.*874,1020: *OC*624,755,1267: *Ant.*392: E.*Alc.*422: *Heracl.* 80: *Hipp.*923: *El.*391: *Ph.*371,891: *Tr.*706: Hdt.vi 135.3 ἀλλὰ δεῖν γὰρ Μιλτιάδεα τελευτᾶν μὴ εὖ, φανῆναί οἱ: vii 209.1 ἀλλ' αὐτῷ γελοῖα γὰρ ἐφαίνοντο ποιέειν, μετεπέμψατο: i 14, 191: ii 116: iv 83: vii 214: ix 27.6: 109.3: X.*An.*iii 1.24. (Hom. **H**242 must count as an example of the complex construction, the act of throwing, as Hentze observes, really constituting the main clause.)

In passages where the ἀλλὰ . . . γάρ clause is followed by a clause introduced by τῷ (τῶ), οὖν or δή, we may hesitate whether to regard the ἀλλὰ . . . γάρ construction as self-contained, or to take the οὖν or δή as apodotic, and the construction as 'complex'. These cases are, in fact, on the borderline between 'simple' and 'complex'. Cf. γάρ, IV.3.

Hom.*O*739 ἀλλ' ἐν γὰρ Τρώων πεδίῳ . . . ἥμεθα . . . τῶ ἐν χερσὶ φόως: *P*338: *Ψ*607: Hdt.viii 108.4 ἀλλὰ δοκέειν γὰρ . . . οὐ μενέειν . . . τὸν Πέρσην· ἐατέον ὦν εἶναι φεύγειν: Pl.*Chrm.*165B τὸ δ' οὐχ οὕτως ἔχει, ἀλλὰ ζητῶ γὰρ . . . σκεψάμενος οὖν . . .: *Cra.* 406B.

II. Ἀλλὰ γάρ, complex. Of this there are very few examples. S.*Ant.*148 Ἀλλὰ γὰρ ἁ μεγαλώνυμος ἦλθε Νίκα τᾷ πολυαρμάτῳ ἀντιχαρεῖσα Θήβᾳ, ἐκ μὲν δὴ πολέμων τῶν νῦν θέσθαι (imperatival infinitive) λησμοσύναν ("γάρ introduces the reason given by ἦλθε", Jebb): E.*Ph.*1308 (see III.4 below). To these we should probably add Ar.*V.*318 τήκομαι . . . ὑπακούων. ἀλλὰ γὰρ οὐχ οἷός τ' εἴμ' ᾄδειν, τί ποιήσω; (where a stronger stop after ᾄδειν produces a harsh asyndeton): conceivably also Pl.*Phdr.* 228A εἰ ἐγὼ Φαῖδρον ἀγνοῶ, καὶ ἐμαυτοῦ ἐπιλέλησμαι. ἀλλὰ γὰρ οὐδέτερά ἐστι τούτων· εὖ οἶδα ὅτι . . . οὐ μόνον ἅπαξ ἤκουσεν . . .

(Prof. Misener here reads only a comma after *τούτων*: but in this case the asyndeton appears to me less objectionable: *εὖ δ'*, *T*).

III. Ἀλλὰ γάρ, ἀλλὰ . . . γάρ, simple. The explanation of these uses, which go back to Simonides and Pindar, has been much discussed. Most earlier writers on the particles suppose an ellipse of the ἀλλά clause, and Jebb, in his Sophocles, everywhere supplies the missing sense. Wilamowitz (on E.*HF* 138) says that the missing sense must always be completed explicitly or implicitly 'in good Greek': but that later (first in Isocrates) ἀλλὰ γάρ becomes 'practically a strong adversative particle'. (It is difficult, however, to draw any distinction between the usage of Pindar and Hippocrates, and that of the later fourth century.) On the other hand, Bäumlein, Kühner, and others deny that γάρ in ἀλλὰ γάρ is ever causal, and interpret it everywhere as 'adverbial'. Hartung admits ellipse, but only 'within reasonable limits'. The earlier theory has, however, been revived by Sernatinger, followed by Broschmann and Prof. Misener in their valuable analyses. But the latter, when she speaks of ellipse, does not mean an ellipse which can be supplied by certain definite words: and she has an alternative way of putting her view, which perhaps expresses it more clearly, when she says that γάρ explains 'the ἀλλά feeling'. This is substantially the same as Wilamowitz's 'aber das tut nichts: denn . . .'. Misener conjecturally supposes three stages of development: (1) normal order, ἀλλά clause followed by γάρ clause (e.g. Ar.*Lys.* 1107): (2) γάρ clause inserted in main sentence: (3) omission of main clause, the purport of which is made plain by the context. This explanation is, on the face of it, a likely one, though its proposer admits that we are dealing with linguistic developments so remote that certainty is unattainable. Certainly the 'adverbial' theory of γάρ, here as in most other places, has little to recommend it.[1] In the complex construction, unless we are to tolerate unnatural asyndeta,[2] γάρ must be causal: and the complex construction, as we have seen (I, *ad fin.*), merges so insensibly into the simple, that the explanation of γάρ must, surely, be the same in both

[1] Except in (8) below. [2] Though similar asyndeta occur in A.*Pers.* 150–2, S.*Ph.* 1153, E.*Alc.* 136–7, *IT* 65, *Ph.* 99. (In *HF* 1202 the εἰς συναλγοῦντ' of the MSS. cannot be right.)

cases. We are driven, then, to assume either ellipse of some kind, or the petrifaction of the particles into a set formula, a tendency setting in at an early stage of Greek literature, and progressing with the passage of time, but never becoming so complete as to disallow the occasional use (though very rarely when the particles are juxtaposed) of the complex construction in which each particle plays its full part.

Linguistic theory apart, 'aber das tut nichts: denn . . .', 'but, as a matter of fact,' is the meaning in the great majority of cases (though, as we shall see, there are certain marked deviations). The sense conveyed is that what precedes is irrelevant, unimportant, or subsidiary, and is consequently to be ruled out of discussion, or at least put in the shade.

Between the uses of *ἀλλὰ γάρ* and *ἀλλὰ . . . γάρ* there is no essential distinction of meaning. But *ἀλλὰ . . . γάρ* predominates in verse, *ἀλλὰ γάρ* (very strongly) in prose.

(1) In general, marking the contrast between what is irrelevant or subsidiary and what is vital, primary, or decisive.

(i) *ἀλλὰ . . . γάρ.* Hom.*κ*202 *κλαῖον δὲ λιγέως . . . ἀλλ' οὐ γάρ τις πρῆξις ἐγίγνετο μυρομένοισιν*: *λ*393 *ὀρέξασθαι μενεαίνων· ἀλλ' οὐ γάρ οἱ ἔτ' ἦν ἲς ἔμπεδος*: Pi.*I.*4.16 'They were glorious in prowess. *ἀλλ' ἁμέρᾳ γὰρ ἐν μιᾷ τραχεῖα νιφὰς πολέμοιο τεσσάρων ἀνδρῶν ἐρημῶσεν μάκαιραν ἑστίαν*': 7.16 (after describing the ancient glories of Thebes) *ἀλλὰ παλαιὰ γὰρ εὕδει χάρις*: B.5.162 *ἀλλ' οὐ γάρ τίς ἐστιν πρᾶξις τάδε μυρομένοις*: S.*El.*223 *οὐ λάθει μ' ὀργά ἀλλ' ἐν γὰρ δεινοῖς οὐ σχήσω ταύτας ἄτας*: 619 *Εὖ νυν ἐπίστω τῶνδέ μ' αἰσχύνην ἔχειν . . . ἀλλ' ἡ γὰρ ἐκ σοῦ δυσμένεια . . . ἐξαναγκάζει με ταῦτα δρᾶν*: Ar.*Eq.*328 *Ἆρα δῆτ' οὐκ ἀπ' ἀρχῆς ἐδήλους ἀναίδειαν . . .; . . . ἀλλ' ἐφάνη γὰρ ἀνὴρ ἕτερος πολὺ σοῦ μιαρώτερος*: Hom.*τ*591: Archil.*Fr.*7.5: Pi.*N.*7.30: *O.*6.54: Ar.*V.*1271: Hdt.viii 8.1 *ἐν νόῳ εἶχε καὶ πρότερον . . . ἀλλ' οὐ γάρ οἱ παρεῖχε ἐς τότε*: Pl.*Prt.*336A *πολὺ σοῦ μᾶλλον ἐγὼ ἐμαυτοῦ δέομαι . . . ἀλλ' οὐ γὰρ δύναμαι*: Arist.*Pol.* 1275b13 *ἀλλ' ἔχει γὰρ διόρθωσιν ὁ τοῦ πολίτου διορισμός*: Lys. vi 50 *Ἀθηναῖοι, μνήσθητε . . . ἀλλ' ἐστὲ γὰρ ὑπὸ τῶν τούτου ἁμαρτημάτων ἤδη καταπλῆγες*: D.xix 181 *ἀλλ' ἔτι γὰρ τότ', ὦ ἄνδρες Ἀθηναῖοι* (in this, the sole example of *ἀλλὰ . . . γάρ* in Demosthenes, the order is perhaps dictated by a desire to avoid a sequence of short syllables): Hdt.vii 158.3: Pl.*Lg*.636A,655A: X.*Cyr*.i 4.3: ii 1.13.

(ii) ἀλλὰ γάρ. Simon.*Fr*.140 Ἄνθρωπ', οὐ Κροίσου λεύσσεις τάφον· ἀλλὰ γὰρ ἀνδρὸς χερνήτεω· μικρὸς τύμβος, ἐμοὶ δ' ἱκανός (perhaps ἔμοιγ', with no stop between ἀλλά and ἱκανός): Pi.*O*.1.56 'Tantalus was honoured by the gods. ἀλλὰ γὰρ καταπέψαι μέγαν ὄλβον οὐκ ἐδυνάσθη': *P*.4.32 φιλίων δ' ἐπέων ἄρχετο, ξείνοις ἅτ' ἐλθόντεσσιν εὐεργέται δεῖπν' ἐπαγγέλλοντι πρῶτον. ἀλλὰ γὰρ νόστου πρόφασις γλυκεροῦ κώλυεν μεῖναι: E.*Med*.1085 πρὸς ἁμίλλας ἦλθον μείζους ἢ χρὴ γενεὰν θῆλυν ἐρευνᾶν. ἀλλὰ γὰρ ἔστιν μοῦσα καὶ ἡμῖν: Ar.*V*.1114 πάντα γὰρ κεντοῦμεν ἄνδρα κἀκπορίζομεν βίον. ἀλλὰ γὰρ κηφῆνες ἡμῖν εἰσιν ἐγκαθήμενοι ('But our efforts are rendered nugatory by the drones'): Hp.*Fract*.9 συμφέρει δὲ κατακεῖσθαι τοῦτον τὸν χρόνον. ἀλλὰ γὰρ οὐ τολμέωσιν ὑπερορῶντες τὸ νόσημα ('But expediency goes for nothing, for . . .'): *Aër*.22 'People try to win health from heaven by bribes. ἀλλὰ γὰρ diseases are not caused supernaturally': Hdt.vii 4 Δαρεῖος ὁρμᾶτο στρατεύεσθαι. ἀλλὰ γὰρ μετὰ ταῦτα . . . συνήνεικε Δαρεῖον . . . ἀποθανεῖν: ix 46 3 ἐν νόῳ ἐγένετο εἰπεῖν . . . ἀλλὰ γὰρ ἀρρωδέομεν μὴ ὑμῖν οὐχ ἡδέες γένωνται οἱ λόγοι: Pl.*Grg*.517B (the crux of the matter): *Tht*.144B Ἀκήκοα μὲν τοὔνομα, μνημονεύω δ' οὔ. ἀλλὰ γάρ ἐστι τῶνδε τῶν προσιόντων ὁ ἐν τῷ μέσῳ: *Ti*.53C ἐπιχειρητέον . . . ἀήθει λόγῳ πρὸς ὑμᾶς δηλοῦν, ἀλλὰ γὰρ ἐπεὶ μετέχετε . . . συνέψεσθε: *R*.432C δύσβατος ὁ τόπος φαίνεται . . . ἀλλὰ γὰρ ὅμως ἰτέον: *Tht*.148E: *Smp* 172B,199A,220E: *Phd*.95C,102B: *R*.467D,607C: *Lg*.751D: *Prt*.310E: *Grg*.448D: Lys.ix 17: D.lvii 33.

μὲν . . . ἀλλὰ γάρ (ἀλλὰ . . . γάρ). S.*OC* 1615 σκληρὰν μέν, οἶδα, παῖδες· ἀλλ' ἓν γὰρ μόνον τὰ πάντα λύει ταῦτ' ἔπος μοχθήματα: Ar.*Th*.384 Φιλοτιμίᾳ μὲν οὐδεμιᾷ . . . λέξουσ' ἀνέστην, ὦ γυναῖκες· ἀλλὰ γὰρ βαρέως φέρω: Ar.*V*.316: X.*Cyr*.vii 1.49 καὶ χρήσιμον μὲν ἐδόκει εἶναι (the use of camels against cavalry). ἀλλὰ γὰρ οὔτε τρέφειν οὐδεὶς ἐθέλει καλὸς κἀγαθὸς κάμηλον: Pl.*Plt*.262B: *Lg*.839C: *R*.487B.

(2) Breaking off (a very common prose usage).

(i) ἀλλὰ . . . γάρ. S.*El*.595 ἀλλ' οὐ γὰρ οὐδὲ νουθετεῖν ἔξεστί σε: *Tr*.552 ἀλλ' οὐ γάρ, ὥσπερ εἶπον, ὀργαίνειν καλόν: E.*Med*.1301 'Where is Medea? ἀλλ' οὐ γὰρ αὐτῆς φροντίδ' ὡς τέκνων ἔχω': S.*OC*988: E.*Cyc*.432: *Med*.252,1344: *Ion* 144: *IA* 511: Ar.*Eq*.1063: *Ach*.738: *Lys*.286: Hdt.ix 27.4 ἀλλ' οὐ γάρ τι προέχει τούτων ἐπιμεμνῆσθαι.

(ii) ἀλλὰ γάρ. Pi.*N*.7.52 θράσυ μοι τόδ' εἰπεῖν ... ἀλλὰ γὰρ ἀνάπαυσις ἐν παντὶ γλυκεῖα ἔργῳ: E.*Tr*.444 ἀλλὰ γὰρ τί τοὺς Ὀδυσσέως ἐξακοντίζω πόνους; Ar.*Eq*.1086 'You have interpreted the oracle wrongly. ἀλλὰ γάρ ἐστιν ἐμοὶ χρησμὸς ...': E.*Andr*.264: *Ph*.1762: Pl.*Phdr*.261C Ἴσως· ἀλλὰ γὰρ τούτους ἐῶμεν: *Men*.92C ἀλλὰ γὰρ οὐ τούτους ἐπιζητοῦμεν: Lys.vii 9 ἀλλὰ γάρ, ὦ βουλή, ... ἱκανὰ νομίζω τὰ εἰρημένα: D.xv 34 (after strictures on the Athenian politicians) ἀλλὰ γὰρ οὐχ ὅ τι τις κατηγορήσῃ τούτων ... χαλεπὸν εὑρεῖν: xviii 42 ἀλλὰ γὰρ ἐμπέπτωκ' εἰς λόγους, οὓς αὐτίκα μᾶλλον ἴσως ἁρμόσει λέγειν: Pl. *Ap*.19C,D,25B,26A,28A,42A: *Plt*.257C: *Lg*.707C: *Hp.Ma*.295C: X.*Oec*.11.11: 12.1: *An*.v 7.11: *Cyr*.v 5.13: viii 7.26: *Ages*.10.3: Lys.vii 42: xii 99: xxiv 21: D.xviii 211,263: xxiv 49.

(3) Resuming after a digression.

(i) ἀλλὰ ... γάρ. Ar.*Th*.531 (resumption of the main topic, after the general reflections in ἀλλ' ἅπαν ... ἀθρεῖν).

(ii) ἀλλὰ γάρ. Pl.*Grg*.525E 'Homer made his chief criminals in Hades kings. (No private individual has the chance to be incurably bad.) ἀλλὰ γὰρ ... ἐκ τῶν δυναμένων εἰσὶ καὶ οἱ σφόδρα πονηροὶ γιγνόμενοι' ('Well, anyhow'): *Smp*.180A 'The gods rewarded Achilles for avenging his lover Patroclus. (Achilles was not Patroclus's lover.) ἀλλὰ γὰρ τῷ ὄντι μάλιστα μὲν ... μᾶλλον μέντοι θαυμάζουσιν ... ὅταν ὁ ἐρώμενος τὸν ἐραστὴν ἀγαπᾷ': *Phlb*.43A (line 6): *R*.530C: *Sph*.229D: *Ion* 541E: X.*HG*.vii 3.4: And.i 73,130,132.

(4) Marking the appearance of a new character on the stage. The particles are here almost invariably separated.

(i) ἀλλὰ ... γάρ. S.*Ant*.155 ἀλλ' ὅδε γὰρ δὴ βασιλεὺς ... χωρεῖ: E.*HF* 138 ἀλλ' εἰσορῶ γὰρ ... Λύκον περῶντα: Ar.*Ach*. 40 ἀλλ' οἱ πρυτάνεις γὰρ οὑτοιὶ μεσημβρινοί: E.*Or*.725: *HF* 442: Ar.*Ach*.175: *Av*.1168: *Lys*.1239: *Ec*.951.

(ii) ἀλλὰ γάρ. A.*Th*.861 ἀλλὰ γὰρ ἤκουσ' αἴδ'.

In some cases the construction is complex (a further indication of the close relation existing between the simple and complex constructions).

(i) ἀλλὰ . . . γάρ. A.*Pr*.941 ἀλλ' εἰσορῶ γὰρ τόνδε τὸν Διὸς τρόχιν . . . πάντως τι καινὸν ἀγγελῶν ἐλήλυθεν (perhaps to be classed as 'simple'): E.*Hipp*.51: *Hec*.724: *El*.107: *Hel*.1385.

(ii) ἀλλὰ γάρ. E.*Ph*.1308 ἀλλὰ γὰρ Κρέοντα λεύσσω τόνδε δεῦρο συννεφῆ πρὸς δόμους στείχοντα, παύσω τοὺς παρεστῶτας γόους.

(5) Marking the non-fulfilment of a condition (while ἀλλὰ μήν (*q.v.* (3)) marks its fulfilment).

(i) ἀλλὰ . . . γάρ. Hdt.ii 120 εἰ ἦν Ἑλένη ἐν Ἰλίῳ, ἀποδοθῆναι ἂν αὐτὴν τοῖσι Ἕλλησι . . . ἀλλ' οὐ γὰρ εἶχον Ἑλένην ἀποδοῦναι: Pl.*Ap*.20C εἰ ἠπιστάμην ταῦτα· ἀλλ' οὐ γὰρ ἐπίσταμαι.

(ii) ἀλλὰ γάρ. Hdt.ix 113.2 τά περ ἂν καὶ ἐγένετο . . . εἴ περ ἔφθη . . . ἀλλὰ γὰρ Ξέρξης πυθόμενος . . .: Pl.*La*.200D εἰ ἐθέλοι οὗτος· ἀλλὰ γὰρ ἄλλους μοι ἑκάστοτε συνίστησιν . . . αὐτὸς δὲ οὐκ ἐθέλει: *Men*.94E εἴπερ ἦν τοῦτο διδακτὸν . . . ἀλλὰ γὰρ . . . μὴ οὐκ ᾖ διδακτὸν ἀρετή: Hdt.v 3.1: vii 143.2: Pl.*Phlb*.43A (line 1: cf. 42E, line 7): *Euthphr*.14B.

Marking the non-fulfilment of a wish. E.*Rh*.106 Εἴθ' ἦσθ' ἀνὴρ εὔβουλος ὡς δρᾶσαι χερί. ἀλλ' οὐ γὰρ αὐτὸς πάντ' ἐπίστασθαι βροτῶν πέφυκεν.

(6) In dialogue, introducing an objection.

(i) ἀλλὰ . . . γάρ. Ar.*Pl*.425 Ἴσως Ἐρινύς ἐστιν ἐκ τραγῳδίας . . —Ἀλλ' οὐκ ἔχει γὰρ δᾷδας.

(ii) ἀλλὰ γάρ. Ar.*Ach*.338 Οὐδ' ἐμοῦ λέγοντος ὑμεῖς ἀρτίως ἠκούσατε.—Ἀλλὰ γὰρ νῦν λέγ', εἴ σοι δοκεῖ ('Yes, but you can speak now, if you like'): Pl.*Euthphr*.6D 'You have only told me one particular ὅσιον'.—Καὶ ἀληθῆ γ' ἔλεγον.—Ἴσως. ἀλλὰ γὰρ καὶ ἄλλα πολλὰ φῂς εἶναι ὅσια ('But the point is . . .'): *Plt*.263A Ὀρθότατα· ἀλλὰ γὰρ τοῦτο αὐτὸ . . . πῶς ἄν τις γένος καὶ μέρος ἐναργέστερον γνοίη . . .; *R*.471C: *Hp.Ma*.301B (Ἀλλὰ γὰρ δή).

(7) Introducing an imaginary objection (Hypophora). (It is sometimes said, incorrectly, that ἀλλὰ γάρ is here equivalent to ἀλλὰ νὴ Δία. Actually the two idioms differ in so far that νὴ Δία marks[1] the objection *as* imaginary, while γάρ marks it as fundamental or important. 'But (it may be urged) the essential point

[1] Usually, but not invariably: see ἀλλά, I. 3. iii.

is that . . .' Where ἴσως follows ἀλλὰ γάρ, it to some extent replaces νὴ Δία.)

(i) ἀλλὰ . . . γάρ. Lys.vi 40 δεινὸν ἂν εἴη, εἰ περὶ Ἀνδοκίδου . . . ἐπεμελήθημεν . . . ἀλλὰ Λακεδαιμόνιοι γὰρ ἐν ταῖς πρὸς αὐτοὺς συνθήκαις ἐπεμελήθησαν Ἀνδοκίδου . . . · ἀλλ' ὑμεῖς ἐπεμελήθητέ γε αὐτοῦ; vi 48 (46 εἰς τί σκεψαμένους χρὴ ὑμᾶς Ἀνδοκίδου ἀποψηφίσασθαι; πότερον ὡς στρατιώτης ἀγαθός; ἀλλ' οὐδεπώποτε . . . ἐστρατεύσατο . . .) ἀλλὰ πλουτῶν γὰρ . . . ⟨εἰσέφερε⟩— ποίαν εἰσφοράν;

(ii) ἀλλὰ γάρ. Hdt.vi 124.1 ἀλλὰ γὰρ ἴσως τι ἐπιμεμφόμενοι . . . : Gorg.*Fr.*11a,32 ἀλλὰ γὰρ οὐκ ἐμὸν ἐμαυτὸν ἐπαινεῖν : Pl.*Men.*94D ἀλλὰ γὰρ ἴσως ὁ Θουκυδίδης φαῦλος ἦν : *Phd.*87D ἀλλὰ γὰρ ἂν φαίη . . . : *R.*365C ἀλλὰ γάρ, φησί τις, οὐ ῥᾴδιον ἀεὶ λανθάνειν : 366A ἀλλὰ γὰρ ἐν Αἵδου δίκην δώσομεν: Ant.v 62 'He did not ruin him on that occasion. ἀλλὰ γὰρ ἐνταῦθα μὲν ἀφῆκεν αὐτόν· οὗ δ' ἔδει . . . ἐνταῦθα δ' ἐπεβούλευεν' : And.iv 37 ἀλλὰ γὰρ ἴσως μετὰ μικρᾶς διαβολῆς . . . ἐκινδύνευον : Isoc.iv 175 ἀλλὰ γὰρ ἴσως διὰ τὰς συνθήκας ἄξιον ἐπισχεῖν (ἀλλὰ γὰρ ἴσως also vi 80,xi 48, xvii 49,xix 36) : X.*An.*vii 7.35 ἀλλὰ γὰρ Ἡρακλείδῃ . . . πάμπολυ δοκεῖ τοῦτο τὸ ἀργύριον εἶναι (an actual, quoted objection.)

(8) Progressive.

In (1)–(7) ἀλλὰ γάρ (ἀλλὰ . . . γάρ) is strongly adversative: it not only opposes what precedes, but rules it out of court as non-existent or inessential. In a few passages, however (proportionately numerous in Andocides i), ἀλλὰ γάρ appears to be weakly adversative or merely progressive. It simply adds something new and important, and is found in contexts where καὶ μήν or ἀλλὰ μήν would be natural.

Analysis is difficult here. It might, theoretically, be maintained that here too ἀλλὰ γάρ is, at bottom, strongly adversative, and means 'but that does not matter, for . . .'; and that the new matter is presented as so far outstripping the old in importance as to contrast with it and supplant it (cf. οὐ μὴν ἀλλά, (ii)). But this is an artificial explanation: and it certainly seems preferable to regard the adversative force of ἀλλά as weakened in ἀλλὰ γάρ (as in simple ἀλλά (sometimes), ἀλλὰ καί and ἀλλὰ μήν), and γάρ as purely ancillary or 'adverbial'. If it be objected that it is equally artificial to posit two quite different meanings for ἀλλὰ γάρ, 'but that does not matter, for . . .', and 'further indeed', we may reply, in general, that the Greek particles present many such ambiguities: and, in particular, that *καὶ γάρ* (cf. *οὐδὲ γάρ*) similarly bears two distinct meanings, 'for also (even)' and 'and indeed'. The line between adversative and progressive cannot, of course, be rigidly drawn, either here or in other similar cases. Many passages may reasonably be grouped under either heading.

(i) *ἀλλὰ . . . γάρ*. There is no certain instance of the separation of the particles in this usage. Anaxandr.*Fr*.33.9 is textually doubtful. 'What other art causes such excitement as cookery? *ἀλλ' οὐ μόνη γὰρ τὰς συνουσίας ποιεῖ εὔοψος ἀγορά*;' 'Again, does not a good cuisine . . .?'

(ii) *ἀλλὰ γάρ*. Hp.*Cord*.5 *περίβολον δὲ ἔχει παχύν, καὶ βόθρον ἐμβεβόθρωται τὸ εἶδος εἴκελον ὅλμῳ. ἀλλὰ γὰρ ἤδη καὶ τοῦ πνεύμονος ἐνδύεται μετὰ προσηνίης* ('Further'): X.*Lac*.8.1 'Money-hoarding is punished in Sparta. *ἀλλὰ γὰρ ὅτι μὲν ἐν Σπάρτῃ μάλιστα πείθονται ταῖς ἀρχαῖς . . . ἴσμεν ἅπαντες*': 10.8 'Lycurgus honoured the law-abiding and punished the lawless. *ἀλλὰ γὰρ ὅτι μὲν παλαιότατοι οὗτοι οἱ νόμοι εἰσὶ σαφές . . . οὕτω δὲ παλαιοὶ ὄντες ἔτι καὶ νῦν τοῖς ἄλλοις καινότατοί εἰσι*' ('Now'): And.i 22 (*ἀλλὰ γὰρ καί* introduces a fourth argument, the second and third being introduced by *καὶ μὲν δή* and *φέρε δὴ τοίνυν*): 101 'This man, who has led a shameful life, accuses others, when he is not legally entitled to defend himself. *ἀλλὰ γάρ, ὦ ἄνδρες, καθήμενος ἡνίκα μου κατηγόρει, βλέπων εἰς αὐτὸν οὐδὲν ἄλλο ἢ ὑπὸ τῶν τριάκοντα συνειλημμένος ἔδοξα κρίνεσθαι*' (for *καὶ μήν*): 103 'Is it not monstrous if, whereas the Thirty would have condemned me for my patriotism, you refuse to save me for it? *ἀλλὰ γάρ, ὦ ἄνδρες, τὴν μὲν ἔνδειξιν ἐποιήσαντό μου κατὰ νόμον κείμενον, τὴν δὲ κατηγορίαν κατὰ τὸ ψήφισμα*' ('Again'): 124 (perhaps rather to be regarded as resumptive): 128 'He divorced the daughter in favour of her mother, and now wants to divorce the mother in favour of her grand-daughter. *ἀλλὰ γὰρ τῷ παιδὶ αὐτοῦ τί χρὴ τοὔνομα θέσθαι; . . . Οἰδίπους, ἢ Αἴγισθος*;' (here *καίτοι* would be more regular ('Now what is the son to be called?'). So also in X.*HG*. vii 2.1 *διεκαρτέρουν (οἱ Φλειάσιοι) ἐν τῇ συμμαχίᾳ. ἀλλὰ γὰρ* the exploits of great cities are celebrated, but those of small ones are even more meritorious. *Φλειάσιοι τοίνυν. . . .* ('Now')): Lys.*Fr*.1.5.

The two following usages differ widely from those discussed in (1)–(7), in that *γάρ* here substantiates, not the suppressed *ἀλλά* clause, or the '*ἀλλά* feeling', but the preceding clause or sentence. The two particles independently express distinct connexions of thought, and either might stand without the other.

(9) Following a negative clause. *ἀλλά* contrasts what is affirmed with what has just been denied: *γάρ* substantiates the denial: 'for, on the contrary.'

(i) *ἀλλὰ . . . γάρ.* Alcm.*Fr.*49.7 *οὔτι γὰρ ἠὺ τετυγμένον ἔσθει, ἀλλὰ τὰ κοινὰ γάρ, ὥσπερ ὁ δᾶμος, ζατεύει* ('He doesn't eat dainty food, for he prefers common food instead'): Pi.*O.*6.54 *οὔτ' ἰδεῖν εὔχοντο πεμπταῖον γεγενημένον. ἀλλ' ἐν κέκρυπτο γὰρ σχοίνῳ* ('They couldn't find him, but (for) he was hidden'): A.*Eu.*797 *ἀλλ' ἰσόψηφος δίκη ἐξῆλθ' ἀληθῶς, οὐκ ἀτιμίᾳ σέθεν· ἀλλ' ἐκ Διὸς γὰρ λαμπρὰ μαρτύρια παρῆν*: Ar.*Lys.*1023 *Ἀλλὰ τὴν ἐξωμίδ' ἐνδύσω σε προσιοῦσ' ἐγώ.—Τοῦτο μὲν μὰ τὸν Δί' οὐ πονηρὸν ἐποιήσατε· ἀλλ' ὑπ' ὀργῆς γὰρ πονηρᾶς καὶ τότ' ἀπέδυν ἐγώ*: Pl.*R.*455E *ἦ οὖν ἀνδράσι πάντα προστάξομεν, γυναικὶ δ' οὐδέν;—Καὶ πῶς;—Ἀλλ' ἔστι γὰρ οἶμαι . . . καὶ γυνὴ ἰατρική* ('We won't assign everything to men, because, on the contrary, women are good at things like medicine'). In E.*Fr.*555 the correct text is irrecoverable. †*οὐ δῆκταί πως κύνες οἱ θεοί,*† *ἀλλ' ἡ Δίκη γὰρ καὶ διὰ σκότου βλέπει.*

(ii) *ἀλλὰ γάρ.* Hdt.ii 139 *οὐκ ὦν ποιήσειν ταῦτα, ἀλλὰ γάρ οἱ ἐξεληλυθέναι τὸν χρόνον ὁκόσον κεχρῆσθαι ἄρξαντα Αἰγύπτου ἐκχωρήσειν*: Hp.*Morb.Sacr.*3 'This disease is not sacred. *ἀλλὰ γὰρ αἴτιος ὁ ἐγκέφαλος τούτου τοῦ πάθεος*': Pl.*Chrm.*166C *καὶ ταῦτά σε πολλοῦ δεῖ λεληθέναι, ἀλλὰ γὰρ οἶμαι . . . τοῦτο ποιεῖς· ἐμὲ γὰρ ἐπιχειρεῖς ἐλέγχειν, ἐάσας περὶ οὗ ὁ λόγος ἐστίν* ('Your conduct is not due to forgetfulness, but (for) it is due to design'): X.*An.*v 7.8 *τοῦτ' οὖν ἔστιν ὅπως τις ἂν ὑμᾶς ἐξαπατήσαι ὥστε ἐμβαίνειν ὁπόταν νότος πνέῃ; ἀλλὰ γὰρ ὁπόταν γαλήνη ᾖ ἐμβιβῶ* ('No, for'): D.xliv 35 *οὐκ ἐπιλογισάμενος οὐθ' ὅτι . . . οὐθ' ὅτι . . . ἀλλὰ γὰρ οἶμαι ἁπλοῦν τι διελογίσατο, δεῖν αὐτὸν. . . .* (We may mention here Eup.*Fr.*68, though it is clearly different: *ἀναρίστητος ὢν κοὐδὲν βεβρωκώς, ἀλλὰ γὰρ στέφανον ἔχων*: Bekk.*Anecd.* 377.8, and Suidas: *ἀλλὰ γάρ· ἀντὶ τοῦ δέ· Εὔπολις Βάπταις.* In spite of the gloss, the sense seems to be 'but for all that'.)

(10) ἀλλὰ . . . γάρ in questions. Ar.*Ach.*594 Ἐγὼ γάρ εἰμι πτωχός;—Ἀλλὰ τίς γὰρ εἶ; ('Well, what are you?' We may illustrate the connexion between (9) and (10) by imagining a sentence like: οὔκ εἰμι πτωχός, ἀλλὰ πλούσιος γάρ εἰμι): *Pax*222 οὐκ οἶδ' εἴ ποτ' Εἰρήνην ἔτι τὸ λοιπὸν ὄψεσθ'.—Ἀλλὰ ποῖ γὰρ οἴχεται; ('Why, where has she gone, then?': 'For, on the contrary, she has gone—where?' Cf. γάρ, VI.1): *Lys.*463 Οἴμ' ὡς κακῶς πέπραγέ μου τὸ τοξικόν.—Ἀλλὰ τί γὰρ ᾤου; ('Well, what did you expect?'): Pl.*Hp.Ma.*287D Ὄντι γέ τινι τούτῳ;—Ὄντι· ἀλλὰ τί γὰρ μέλλει; ('For what else on the contrary is likely to be true?').

γάρ in ἀλλὰ γάρ is sometimes strengthened by δή or οὖν. For ἀλλὰ γὰρ δή, ἀλλὰ . . . γὰρ δή, see γὰρ δή. For ἀλλὰ . . . γὰρ οὖν, see γὰρ οὖν.

Καὶ γάρ: καὶ . . . γάρ

I. Normally γάρ is the connective, and καί means either (1) 'also' or 'even': or (2) 'in fact': or (3) 'both', being answered by another καί.

(1) It is sometimes hard to say whether καί refers to a single word, or to the clause or sentence as a whole (as it clearly does, e.g., in Ar.*Eq.*250 πολλάκις γὰρ αὔτ' ἐρῶ. καὶ γὰρ οὗτος ἦν πανοῦργος πολλάκις τῆς ἡμέρας). 'Also' and 'even' are often hard to distinguish. Clear examples of the sense 'also' are:—Hom.N228 ἀλλά, Θόαν, καὶ γὰρ τὸ πάρος μενεδήϊος ἦσθα: E.*Rh.*267 καὶ γὰρ σὺ . . . ('You are as stupid as the rest'): Ar.*Eq.*252 καὶ βδελύττου, καὶ γὰρ ἡμεῖς ('For so do we'). 'Even': S.*Aj.*669 καὶ γὰρ τὰ δεινὰ καὶ τὰ καρτερώτατα . . .: *OC*1698 καὶ γὰρ ὃ μηδαμὰ δὴ φίλον, ἦν φίλον: E.*Med.* 314 καὶ γὰρ ἠδικημένοι σιγησόμεσθα: *Heracl.*998 καὶ γὰρ ἐχθρὸς ὢν ἀκούσεται 'μοί γ' ἐσθλὰ χρηστὸς ὢν ἀνήρ: *Ion*1277 καὶ γὰρ εἰ τὸ σῶμά μοι ἄπεστιν αὐτῆς, τοὔνομ' οὐκ ἄπεστί πω: S.*OT*334: *Tr.*92 (where see Jebb): *Fr.*85.9: E.*Med.*463,1249: *Ba.*317: D.xix22 καὶ γὰρ νῦν φθονεῖν τινὰς αὐτῷ.

(2) S.*Tr.*416 καὶ γὰρ οὐ σιγηλὸς εἶ: *OC*547 ἐγὼ φράσω. καὶ γὰρ ἄνους ἐφόνευσ' (explanatory): E.*HF.*632 καὶ γὰρ οὐκ ἀναίνομαι

θεράπευμα τέκνων: *Ion* 276 καὶ γὰρ οὐ κάμνω σχολῇ: Ar.*Eq.* 253 καὶ γὰρ οἶδε τὰς ὁδούς: Hdt.vi 108.1 (καὶ γὰρ καί): Pl.*Smp.* 192A μέγα δὲ τεκμήριον· καὶ γὰρ ... (explanatory): *Euthphr.* 12A καὶ γὰρ οὐδὲ χαλεπὸν κατανοῆσαι ὃ λέγω: Pl.*Phd.* 57A, 86D: *R.* 441 A: D.xviii 138, 269: xix 198. Isocrates, as R. W. Chapman points out, often uses καὶ γάρ 'in sentences which disclaim an absurdity, inconsistency, or the like; the absurdity being expressed by εἰ or by μὲν ... δέ': iv 181 καὶ γὰρ αἰσχρὸν ἰδίᾳ μὲν ... δημοσίᾳ δέ: xi 41 καὶ γὰρ ἄλογον, εἰ ...: iv 160: xii 64: xiv 52, 53: *id.saep.* Cf. D.xix 267 καὶ γὰρ ἂν καὶ ὑπερφυὲς εἴη.

Often in answers, in Plato. *Cri.* 43B Καὶ γὰρ ἂν πλημμελὲς εἴη: *R.* 431B Καὶ γὰρ ἔοικεν: 433C Καὶ γὰρ ἀνάγκη: *Grg.* 459A Ἔλεγες ...—Καὶ γὰρ ἔλεγον (assentient: 'Yes, I did say so'): *Chrm.* 165C: *Euthd.* 287B: *R.* 377E.

(3) (It is not always easy to determine whether the two καί's are really correlative.) S.*El.* 1167 καὶ γὰρ ἡνίκ' ἦσθ' ἄνω ... καὶ νῦν ποθῶ: Pl.*Phd.* 66C καὶ γὰρ πολέμους καὶ στάσεις καὶ μάχας οὐδὲν ἄλλο παρέχει ἢ τὸ σῶμα: *Cra.* 395B καὶ γὰρ κατὰ τὸ ἀτειρὲς καὶ κατὰ τὸ ἄτρεστον καὶ κατὰ τὸ ἀτηρόν: *R.* 450C καὶ γὰρ ὡς δυνατὰ λέγεται, ἀπιστοῖτ' ἄν, καὶ ... ὡς ἄριστ' ἂν εἴη ταῦτα: X.*Mem.* iii 1.6 καὶ γὰρ παρασκευαστικὸν τῶν εἰς τὸν πόλεμον τὸν στρατηγὸν εἶναι χρή, καὶ ποριστικὸν ... καὶ μηχανικὸν καὶ ἐργαστικόν: D.xviii 171 εἰ δὲ τοὺς ἀμφότερα ταῦτα, καὶ εὔνους τῇ πόλει καὶ πλουσίους, οἱ μετὰ ταῦτα τὰς μεγάλας ἐπιδόσεις ἐπιδόντες· καὶ γὰρ εὐνοίᾳ καὶ πλούτῳ τοῦτ' ἐποίησαν: Isoc.ii. 18: viii 19: xv 168: D.i 23: xviii 144: xix 36.

In Hdt.vi 86β2 γάρ is appositional (cf. γάρ, III.9): βούλομαι ... ποιέειν πᾶν τὸ δίκαιον, καὶ γὰρ εἰ ἔλαβον, ὀρθῶς ἀποδοῦναι, καὶ εἴ γε ἀρχὴν μὴ ἔλαβον, νόμοισι ... χρήσομαι: probably καὶ ... καί is 'both ... and ...', and there is anacoluthon.

II. But sometimes, in answers, καί is the connective, and καὶ γάρ means 'yes, and', or 'and further'. Usually, the particles are followed by a pronoun, or by a word repeated from the preceding speech: sometimes by both. There is often ellipse of the verb. A.*Ag.* 1255 Καὶ μὴν ἄγαν γ' Ἕλλην' ἐπίσταμαι φάτιν.—Καὶ γὰρ τὰ πυθόκραντα· δυσμαθῆ δ' ὅμως ('Aye, and so are Pytho's oracles (spoken in Greek)'): E.*Ph.* 611 Ὦ πάτερ, κλύεις ἃ πάσχω;—Καὶ γὰρ οἷα δρᾷς κλύει: *IA*641 Ὦ πάτερ, ἐσεῖδόν σ' ἀσμένη πολλῷ χρόνῳ.—Καὶ γὰρ πατὴρ σέ: Ar.*Eq.*1088 ἀλλὰ γάρ ἐστιν ἐμοὶ χρησμὸς . . .—Καὶ γὰρ ἐμοί: 1092 Ἀλλ' ἐγὼ εἶδον ὄναρ . . .—Νὴ Δία καὶ γὰρ ἐγώ: *Lys.*12 νενομίσμεθα εἶναι πανοῦργοι—Καὶ γάρ ἐσμεν νὴ Δία: 1181 Τοῖσι γῶν ναὶ τὼ σιὼ ἁμοῖσι.—Καὶ γὰρ ναὶ μὰ Δία Καρυστίοις: Pl.*Grg.*467B Οὐκ ἄρτι ὡμολόγεις . . .;—Καὶ γὰρ νῦν ὁμολογῶ: *Tht.*145D Προθυμοῦμαί γε δή (μανθάνειν).—Καὶ γὰρ ἐγώ, ὦ παῖ ('Why, so do I': *La.*191A: *R.*473B): *Smp.*214B χαῖρε.—Καὶ γὰρ σύ: *R.*430C Ἀποδέχομαι τοίνυν τοῦτο ἀνδρείαν εἶναι.—Καὶ γὰρ ἀποδέχου, ἦν δ' ἐγώ, πολιτικήν γε: 465A Ὀρθῶς, ἔφη.—Καὶ γὰρ τόδε ὀρθὸν ἔχει, ἦν δ' ἐγώ, οὗτος ὁ νόμος: 506D ἀρκέσει γὰρ ἡμῖν ...—Καὶ γὰρ ἐμοὶ ... καὶ μάλα ἀρκέσει: *Euthphr.* 14A Πολλὰ καὶ καλὰ (οἱ θεοὶ ἀπεργάζονται) . . .—Καὶ γὰρ οἱ στρατηγοί, ὦ φίλε: *Euthd.* 298D Καὶ γὰρ σύ, ἔφη. . .—Καὶ γὰρ σοί, ἔφη: *Hp.Ma.*285A Ἔστι δέ γε Λακεδαιμονίοις, ὡς σὺ φῄς, ὠφελιμώτερον . . .—Καὶ ἀληθῆ γε λέγω.—Καὶ γὰρ ὅτι τὰ ὠφελιμώτερα νομιμώτερά ἐστι, καὶ τοῦτο λέγεις . . .; *Prm.*148C Ἔχει . . . καὶ τοιοῦτον λόγον.—Καὶ γὰρ τόνδε ἔχει: X.*An.*v8.11 ἧττόν τι ἀπέθανεν . . .;—Καὶ γὰρ ἡμεῖς . . . πάντες ἀποθανούμεθα: Pl.*Grg.* 495B: *Chrm.*161E: *La.*195C: *Sph.*231A: *R.*333A,340A: X.*Mem.* iii 7.8.

Whether καὶ γάρ (as distinct from καὶ γὰρ οὖν, καὶ γάρ τοι, for which see below) is ever so used in continuous speech, may be questioned. In And.i101 καὶ γὰρ νῦν seems to mean 'For that is what he is doing *now*' (καί going closely with νῦν, and emphasizing it): not 'And that . . .' D.xxxiv33 λέγει δ' ὡς ἡ συγγραφὴ . . . αὐτὸν ἀποδοῦναι κελεύει τὰ χρήματα. καὶ γὰρ ἐνθέσθαι τἀγοράσματα εἰς τὴν ναῦν κελεύει σε. But virtually speaking this is dialogue (παρενθέσθαι, for γὰρ ἐνθέσθαι, *SD*), and so is Arist.*Pol.*1280a13. In Lys.xxxi10 καίτοι, or καίτοι γε, for καὶ γάρ, seems pretty certainly right.

καὶ . . . γάρ. Where the particles are separated, καί usually goes closely with the following word or words. E.*Ba.*333 κεἰ μὴ γὰρ ἔστιν . . . παρὰ σοὶ λεγέσθω: Ar.*Lys.*801 Τὴν λόχμην πολλὴν φορεῖς.—Καὶ Μυρωνίδης γὰρ ἦν τραχὺς ἐντεῦθεν ('Yes, for Myronides too . . .'): Pi.*O.*7.48: Ar.*Eq.*1201. But sometimes there is a closer connexion between the particles. Hom.ρ317 καὶ ἴχνεσι γὰρ περιῄδη (where the sense, in the context, must be 'for in fact he was a skilled tracker', not 'for he was skilled at tracking too'): Ar.*V.*781 καὶ λέγεται γὰρ τουτογί ('for in fact they say this'): S.*Ph.*527 (I think, but see Jebb).

In the following καί is answered by καί: E.*Fr.*365 καὶ δεῖ γὰρ αὐτῆς κἄστιν αὖ κακὸν μέγα ('for she is both a necessity and a plague'): *Or.*1089 καὶ συγκατέκτανον γὰρ... καὶ πάντ' ἐβούλευσ' (where, however, the two καί's are perhaps not co-ordinated).

For καὶ γὰρ δή see γὰρ δή.

Οὐδὲ γάρ: οὐδὲ . . . γάρ

This is the negative counterpart of καὶ γάρ. Here again either (I) the second particle, or, more rarely, (II) the first, may be the connective.

I. Hom.ψ266 οὐ μέν τοι θυμὸς κεχαρήσεται· οὐδὲ γὰρ αὐτὸς χαίρω (though this might conceivably be classed under II): X.*An.* v 5.9 ἀξιοῦμεν . . . ἀγαθὸν μέν τι πάσχειν, κακὸν δὲ μηδέν· οὐδὲ γὰρ ἡμεῖς ὑμᾶς οὐδὲν πώποτε ὑπήρξαμεν κακῶς ποιοῦντες: Isoc. v 27 'The written word suffers in comparison with the spoken. ἅπερ καὶ τὸν νῦν ἐπιδεικνύμενον (λόγον) μάλιστ' ἂν βλάψειε . . . οὐδὲ γὰρ ταῖς περὶ τὴν λέξιν εὐρυθμίαις . . . κεκοσμήκαμεν αὐτόν' ('for I haven't ornamented it, either'. An added reason: cf. vii 53): v 114 λέγω δ' οὐχ ὡς δυνησόμενον . . . σε . . . οὐδὲ γὰρ ἂν τῶν θεῶν ἔνιοι δυνηθεῖεν: viii 137 ('for no other city will wrong them, any more than you will'): xii 245: xvi 36: Pl.*R.*506B.

II. Like the corresponding use of καὶ γάρ, this is confined to answers,[1] and is associated with ἐγώ, and with word-echoes. E.*El.* 580 Οὐδέποτε δόξασ'.—Οὐδ' ἐγὼ γὰρ ἤλπισα: Ar.*Lys.*130 Οὐκ ἂν ποιήσαιμ'. . .—Μὰ Δί' οὐδ' ἐγὼ γάρ: *Ec.*344 Οὔκουν λαβεῖν γ' αὐτὰς ἐδυνάμην οὐδαμοῦ.—Μὰ τὸν Διόνυσον οὐδ' ἐγὼ γὰρ τὰς ἐμάς: Pl.*Phlb.*22C τήν γε Φιλήβου θεὸν οὐ δεῖ διανοεῖσθαι ταὐτὸν καὶ τἀγαθόν . . .—Οὐδὲ γὰρ ὁ σὸς νοῦς . . . ἔστι τἀγαθόν ('Well, and your "Mind" isn't the Good, either'): *Euthphr.*13C Μὰ Δί' οὐκ ἔγωγε (συγχωρήσαιμ' ἄν).—Οὐδὲ γὰρ ἐγὼ . . . οἶμαί σε τοῦτο λέγειν: *R.*424D ὡς . . . κακὸν οὐδὲν ἐργαζομένη.—Οὐδὲ γὰρ ἐργάζεται: X.*Mem.*i 4.9 οὐ γὰρ ὁρῶ τοὺς κυρίους . . .—Οὐδὲ γὰρ τὴν σαυτοῦ σύ γε ψυχὴν ὁρᾷς: Pl.*Euthd.*292A: *Hp.Mi.*376B.

[1] In E.*Hipp.*1005 γάρ can be taken as causal.

(In Hom.*θ*159 it might appear that *οὐ γὰρ . . . οὐδέ* introduces a new point: 'I am too depressed to join in the games'.—'And you don't look like an athlete, either' (cf. the relationship between *οὐ μὴν οὐδέ* and *οὐδὲ μήν*). But far more probably there is a loose causal connexion.)

For *οὐδὲ γὰρ οὐδέ*, see *οὐδέ*.

It will be convenient to examine *καὶ γὰρ οὖν* and *καὶ γάρ τοι* in this place, since a division of senses analogous to that observed in *καὶ γάρ* and *οὐδὲ γάρ* obtains here also.

Καὶ γὰρ οὖν

I. Connective *γάρ*. A.*Ag.*524 *ἀλλ' εὖ νιν ἀσπάσασθε, καὶ γὰρ οὖν πρέπει*: S.*Ant.*489: E.*Heracl.*202: Pl.*R.* 495C **Καὶ γὰρ οὖν**, *ἔφη, τά γε λεγόμενα ταῦτα* (assentient): Democr.*Fr.*182: Pl.*Phd.* 86B: *Sph.*223C: *Lg.*711C: *Prt.*340A: *Smp.*221D: *La.*184B.

II. In Xenophon (there are no examples of this use in any other author), *καὶ γὰρ οὖν* appears always to be nearly equivalent to *τοιγαροῦν*: 'and in consequence'. Six out of the eight instances come from the *Anabasis*.

*An.*i.9.8 *ἐπέδειξεν αὐτὸν ὅτι περὶ πλείστου ποιοῖτο . . . μηδὲν ψεύδεσθαι. καὶ γὰρ οὖν ἐπίστευον μὲν αὐτῷ αἱ πόλεις*: 12 'He rewarded both injuries and benefits. *καὶ γὰρ οὖν πλεῖστοι δὴ αὐτῷ . . . ἐπεθύμησαν . . . τὰ ἑαυτῶν σώματα προέσθαι*': 17 'He rewarded just-dealing. *καὶ γὰρ οὖν ἄλλα τε πολλὰ δικαίως αὐτῷ διεχειρίζετο καὶ στρατεύματι ἀληθινῷ ἐχρήσατο*' (here *καὶ γὰρ οὖν* is precisely parallel to *τοιγαροῦν* in 15): vii 6.37 'I have done my best to save you from the enmity of the Greeks. *καὶ γὰρ οὖν νῦν ὑμῖν ἔξεστιν ἀνεπιλήπτως πορεύεσθαι ὅπῃ ἂν ἔλησθε*' ('and, as a result of what I have done . . .'): *Cyr.*vii 3.10: *An.*ii 6.13: v 8.17.

In an answer. *Smp.*2.20 *ἐχειρονόμουν δὲ . . .—Νὴ Δί', ἔφη ὁ Φίλιππος, καὶ γὰρ οὖν οὕτω τὰ σκέλη τοῖς ὤμοις φαίνει ἰσοφόρα ἔχειν, ὥστε . . .* ('and, as a result of your exercises . . .').

(The form *καὶ γὰρ οὖν δή* is not attested by Pl.*Hp.Ma.*297E, where *δή* coheres with the following *τι*.)

Καὶ γάρ τοι

This combination is almost confined to the Attic orators:[1] it is fairly common in Lysias, Isocrates, and Demosthenes: and there is one instance in Aeschines.

I. Connective γάρ. (Some of these passages might possibly be classed under II.[2]) D.xix 56 ὑποσχέσεσιν . . . αἷσπερ οἱ Φωκεῖς πιστεύσαντες ἀπώλοντο. καὶ γάρ τοι παραδόντες αὑτοὺς Φιλίππῳ . . . ἁπάντων τῶν ἐναντίων ὧν πρὸς ὑμᾶς οὗτος ἀπήγγειλ' ἔτυχον: Lys.xxvii 10 (confirming §9 οὗτοι . . . πένητες): D.xiii 22: xix 325: xxiii 198,200: li 14,22: Aeschin.iii 191.

II. 'And in consequence': or 'and in fact', 'and further'. It is sometimes difficult to decide between the two renderings. But the notion of 'consequence' is almost always appropriate, and is sometimes demanded by the context. R. W. Chapman observes that in Isocrates καὶ γάρ τοι 'rather states a consequence than assigns a reason'. Hesychius glosses καὶ γάρ τοι by τοιγαροῦν.

Lys.ii 26 'The arrival of the barbarians and the victory of our ancestors were announced simultaneously. καὶ γάρ τοι οὐδεὶς τῶν ἄλλων ἔδεισεν ὑπὲρ τοῦ μέλλοντος κινδύνου, ἀλλ' ἀκούσαντες ὑπὲρ τῆς αὑτῶν ἐλευθερίας ἥσθησαν' ('And, as a result'): Isoc.v 108 'Philip the Great knew how to treat Hellenes and barbarians. καὶ γάρ τοι συνέβη διὰ τὸ γνῶναι περὶ τούτων αὐτὸν ἰδίως καὶ τὴν βασιλείαν γεγενῆσθαι πολὺ τῶν ἄλλων ἐξηλλαγμένην': vii 30 (καὶ γάρ τοι καί) 'Your ancestors knew what true piety means. καὶ γάρ τοι καὶ τὰ παρὰ τῶν θεῶν οὐκ ἐμπλήκτως οὐδὲ ταραχωδῶς αὐτοῖς συνέβαινεν ἀλλ' εὐκαίρως': D.ix 58 οἱ ταλαίπωροι . . . Ἐρετριεῖς τελευτῶντες ἐπείσθησαν τοὺς ὑπὲρ αὑτῶν λέγοντας ἐκβαλεῖν. καὶ γάρ τοι πέμψας Ἱππόνικον ὁ σύμμαχος αὐτοῖς Φίλιππος καὶ ξένους χιλίους, τὰ τείχη περιεῖλε τοῦ Πορθμοῦ καὶ τρεῖς κατέστησε τυράννους: xix 137 'The King of Persia bribed

[1] Thgn.525: X.*Cyr.*i 1.4. In A.*Ag.*1040 καὶ παῖδα γάρ τοι: Pl.*Euthphr.*3B καὶ ἐμοῦ γάρ τοι: *Grg.*498E καὶ δὶς γάρ τοι καὶ τρίς: X.*Cyr.*v 1.16 καὶ πυρὸς γάρ τοι there is no cohesion between καί and γάρ. The negative form οὐδὲ γάρ τοι in Pl.*Grg.*488C,506A: *R.*595C.

[2] Decision is, in fact, often very difficult. Tournier (*Rev. de Phil.* vii (1883) 33–44) discusses all the Demosthenic examples, citing the renderings of Voemel and Schaefer, and concluding that in all of them καὶ γάρ τοι means 'therefore': in xix 56 he suggests καὶ γὰρ οὗτοι.

Timagoras, but afterwards found he had backed the wrong horse. *καὶ γάρ τοι* he restored Amphipolis to you, and never bribed anyone again': xxiv 140 'The Locrians make the proposer of a new law speak with a halter round his neck. *καὶ γάρ τοι καινοὺς μὲν οὐ τολμῶσι τιθέναι, τοῖς δὲ πάλαι κειμένοις ἀκριβῶς χρῶνται*': Lys. ii 20,63,79,80: xxx 4: Isoc. ii 4: vii 35,69: x 37: xv 286: D. iv 6: viii 66: xviii 99: xix 141: xx 69,91: xxi 150: xxiii 104,206: lxi 29.

It is exceedingly difficult to account for the idea of consequence so often contained in *καὶ γὰρ οὖν* and *καὶ γάρ τοι.* In *τοιγαροῦν* and *τοιγάρτοι*, to which these combinations approximate closely in their usage, the initial *τοι-* (= *τῷ* or *τώ*) gives the connexion.[1]

Γε

Γε has been connected with the Sanskrit particles *gha* and *ha*, and the Gothic *k* in *mi-k*. (Kühner, II ii 171, and authorities there quoted: Neil, Appendix I to Aristophanes, *Knights*, p. 185: Brugmann § 613.)

(1) The essential force of the particle appears to be concentration. It serves to focus the attention upon a single idea, and place it, as it were, in the limelight: differing thus from *δή*, which emphasizes the reality of a concept (though in certain respects the usages of the two particles are similar). From this original use, to describe which we may borrow Hartung's term 'determinative', two others are easily derived.

(2) Concentration entails limitation. Hence *γε* frequently has a restrictive force. The speaker or writer confines the applicability of his statement within certain limits. In some contexts he implies that its applicability beyond those limits is conceivable: and then the common rendering 'at least' is on

[1] It would be a counsel of despair to suggest that *καὶ γὰρ οὖν* and *καὶ γάρ τοι* express, in certain passages, a double connexion, 'and therefore', *τοι* being here really equivalent to *τῷ* (*τώ*), as in *τοιγάρτοι*, but losing its accent under the influence of the other usage, in which *τοι* is an enclitic auxiliary.

the right lines, though it gives excessive weight to the particle, which should rather be rendered in English by an inflexion of the voice, or by italics. In others, he implies the impossibility of such an extension, and has in mind a contrasted case: 'We don't do this in *Oxford* (but you evidently do in *Cambridge*)'. γε then approximates to μέν in force, *quidem* covering both in Latin. But the view-point of γε and μέν is not quite the same. γε shuts itself up in the house, while μέν, even when it is termed 'solitary', looks at a neighbour, real or imaginary, over the garden wall.

(3) We naturally tend, in describing anything, to concentrate our attention on those of its qualities which are present in a marked degree. Hence, in the case of adjectives and adverbs, and, to a lesser extent, of verbs, the idea of intensification accompanies that of concentration.

γε thus bears three forces, which may be illustrated by the varying inflexion given to the adjective in the following sentences. (1) Determinative. 'He is a *good* man'. (I am not concerned with his non-ethical qualities.) (2) Limitative. 'He is a *good* man.' (But not, or perhaps not, a clever one.) (3) Intensive. 'He is a *good* man.' (A very good man.) The stress is the same, or approximately so, in the three instances. But the pitch varies. To take another example: 'Have you been to those places I recommended?' (1) Determinative. 'I've been to *Paris*.' (This interests me so much that I can't bother to talk about the rest.) The pitch is high. (2) Limitative. 'I've been to *Paris*.' (Quite apart from whether I've been to the rest, and you may guess that I haven't.) The pitch is lower.

The test of pitch is, I think, of value in classifying the uses of γε. But γε is one of the subtlest and most elusive of particles, and any classification must necessarily be approximate. It will be convenient to adopt a two-fold division, between Determinative and Intensive γε (which may be grouped together as Emphatic) on the one hand, and Limitative γε on the other.

I. Emphatic (Determinative and Intensive). This use plays a bigger part than some scholars allow: hence they (and the copyists have sometimes been before them) often eject this γε summarily from the texts, or force it down upon the Procrustean bed of limitation. It therefore needs fuller illustration than the more familiar limitative γε. To illustrate it adequately, we must go to drama and prose dialogue. R. W. Chapman remarks of γε in general (and the observation is peculiarly true of emphatic γε) that it is a particle of conversation, of question and reply. Thus it tends to come near the beginning of the first sentence of a speech. In the Republic Myth (614B–621B) there is only one γε, and that in the first sentence. On the whole, γε is frequent in rapid dialogue, rare in long speeches.

Emphatic γε is but rarely to be met with in historians and orators, except in combination with other particles (and sometimes, in the livelier passages of oratory, in the particular 'exclamatory' form: see (10)). We have here one among many instances of a lively, conversational particle tending to be restricted in formal prose within certain stereotyped limits.

(1) General use. (i) In general, unsupported by a connecting particle.[1]

Hom.*E*446 *Περγάμῳ εἰν ἱερῇ, ὅθι οἱ νηός γ' ἐτέτυκτο* ('where his *temple* was'): *Z*479 *καί ποτέ τις εἴποι "πατρός γ' ὅδε πολλὸν ἀμείνων"* (where γε almost means 'even': a limitative force would attribute undue humility to Hector): *K*59 *τοῖσιν γὰρ ἐπετράπομέν γε μάλιστα*: *ι*458 *τῷ κέ οἱ ἐγκέφαλός γε . . . ῥαίοιτο*: *ξ*325 *καί νύ κεν ἐς δεκάτην γενεὴν ἕτερόν γ' ἔτι βόσκοι* ('support even another'): *ρ*244 *τῷ κέ τοι ἀγλαΐας γε διασκεδάσειεν ἁπάσας*: Thgn.1274 *ἐκ δὲ θυελλῶν ἧκά γ' ἐνωρμίσθην*: Simon. *Fr.*13.16 *εἰ δέ τοι δεινὸν τό γε δεινὸν ἦν*: S.*Aj.*476 *προσθεῖσα κἀναθεῖσα τοῦ γε κατθανεῖν* (where δή *patheticum* would be more natural): *Tr.*945 *οὐ γάρ ἐσθ' ἥ γ' αὔριον, πρὶν εὖ παρῇ τις τὴν παροῦσαν ἡμέραν*: *Ph.*584 *πόλλ' ἐγὼ κείνων ὕπο δρῶν ἀντιπάσχω χρηστά γ', οἷ' ἀνὴρ πένης* (θ' Dobree): 895 *τί δῆτ' ἂν δρῷμ' ἐγὼ τοὐνθένδε γε;* ('*next*': concentration on the future. Text uncertain): *OC*79 *οἵδε γὰρ κρινοῦσί γε εἰ χρή σε μίμνειν* ('they shall *judge*': σοι (for γε) L^{ac}): E.*Cyc.*195 *ποῖ χρὴ φυγεῖν;—Ἔσω πέτρας τῆσδ' οὗπερ ἂν λάθοιτέ γε* ('where you won't be *seen*'): 566 *Λαβών, ξέν', αὐτὸς οἰνοχόος γέ μου γενοῦ* (λάβ', ὦ . . . τε Dobree): *Med.*124 *ἐμοὶ γοῦν ἐν μὴ μεγάλοις ὀχυρῶς γ' εἴη καταγηράσκειν* (γ' Reiske, τ' *codd.*):

[1] In many of these passages a connecting particle occurs shortly before: but I do not trace any coherence, as in (ii), between the connective and the γε.

1132 Ἔχω τι κἀγὼ τοῖς γε σοῖς ἐναντίον λόγοισιν εἰπεῖν: *Hec.*602 δίδαξιν ἐσθλοῦ· τοῦτο δ' ἤν τις εὖ μάθῃ, οἶδεν τό γ' αἰσχρόν, κανόνι τοῦ καλοῦ μαθών ('he knows the bad as well'): 848 φίλους τιθέντες τούς γε πολεμιωτάτους ('their *bitterest foes*': cf. the use of δή with superlatives): *Supp.*206 ὡς τά γ' ἐκ γαίας τρέφῃ: *El.*101 ὡς συγγένωμαι καὶ φόνου ξυνεργάτιν λαβὼν τά γ' εἴσω τειχέων σαφῶς μάθω (Paley makes γε limitative: wrongly, I think): *HF*631 ὧδ' ἔβητ' ἐπὶ ξυροῦ; ἄξω λαβών γε τούσδ' ἐφολκίδας χεροῖν: *IT*200 ἔνθεν τῶν πρόσθεν δμαθέντων Ταντα-λιδᾶν ἐκβαίνει ποινά γ' εἰς οἴκους: 414 φίλα γὰρ ἐλπίς γ', ἐπί τε πήμασιν βροτῶν ἄπληστος (γ' ἐπί τε Murray: γένετ' ἐπί *LP*): *Hel.*1038 ἐσφέρεις γὰρ ἐλπίδας ὡς δή τι δράσων χρηστὸν ἐς κοινόν γε νῷν ('to *both* of us'): *IA*900 Οὐκ ἐπαιδεσθήσομαί γε προσπεσεῖν τὸ σὸν γόνυ (*fortasse* κοὐκ Murray): Ar.*Eq* 384 Ἦν ἄρα πυρός γ' ἕτερα θερμότερα: 413 ἢ μάτην γ' ἂν ... ἐκτρα-φείην: *Nu.*295 νυνί γ' ἤδη ('this very *moment*'): 1217 ὅτε τῶν ἐμαυτοῦ γ' ἕνεκα νυνὶ χρημάτων ... ('my *own* money': γε should not, I think, be taken closely with ὅτε): *V.*833 αὐτὸς κομιοῦμαι τό γε παραυτίκ' ἔνδοθεν ('right now'): *Pax* 625 κᾆτα τἀκείνων γε κέρδη τοῖς γεωργοῖς ἦν κακά ('*their* gains'): 894 Ἔπειτ' ἀγῶνά γ' εὐθὺς ἐξέσται ποιεῖν: 1074 Τοῖσδ' ἁλσί γε παστέα ταυτί: *Av.*378 αὐτίχ' αἱ πόλεις παρ' ἀνδρῶν γ' ἔμαθον ἐχθρῶν κοὐ φίλων (emphasis on ἐχθρῶν): 642 πρῶτον δέ γε εἰσέλθετ' ἐς νεοττίαν γε τὴν ἐμήν: Hp.*Epid.*i.1 τὸ ξύνολον ἔς γε χειμῶνα ὁκοῖον ἦρ γίγνεται: *Art.*50 καὶ μὴ εὖ ἐξιποῦται τῇ γε ἀλθέξει: *Aff.*11 ἡ γλῶσσα ... μέλαινα γίγνεται τοῦ πνεύματος ὑπό γε θερμότητος: *Vict.*80 καὶ τῶν βοτρύων ... ἐμφορεῖσθαι ἔν γε τοῖσι σιτίοισι: Philol.*Fr.*6 ἁ φύσις θείαν γα καὶ οὐκ ἀνθρω-πίνην ἐνδέχεται γνῶσιν: Pl.*Grg.*504E 'The true orator will try to implant justice in his hearers' souls'.—'Yes'.—Τί γὰρ ὄφελος ... σώματί γε κάμνοντι καὶ μοχθηρῶς διακειμένῳ σιτία πολλὰ διδόναι καὶ τὰ ἥδιστα ...; ('For in the case of *bodily* sick-ness ...': γε emphasizes the appositeness of the comparison): 515B Φιλόνικος εἶ ...—Ἀλλ' οὐ φιλονικίᾳ γ' ἐρωτῶ, ἀλλ' ὡς ἀληθῶς βουλόμενος εἰδέναι (here γε stresses the denied idea, in contrast with the affirmed. Distinguish *Tht.*165C, where γε is limitative: Οὐ φήσω οἶμαι τούτῳ γε (τῷ ὀφθαλμῷ ὁρᾶν), τῷ μέντοι ἑτέρῳ: the denial of vision is limited to the case of the one eye): *Grg.* 517E τέχνη ... ἢ δὴ τῷ ὄντι γέ ἐστιν σώματος θεραπεία ('an art which is *really*...': contrasted with δόξαι... θεραπευτὴν εἶναι σώματος just before): *Tht.*187D ἄρτι γὰρ οὐ κακῶς γε . . . ἐλέγετε: *Smp* 185A δοκεῖ γὰρ ὁ τοιοῦτος τό γε αὑτοῦ ἐπιδεῖξαι ('A man like that reveals his *own* character'. The light that the incident throws on the other party's character does not concern us): 220D τοῦτο γὰρ δὴ δίκαιόν γε αὐτῷ ἀποδοῦναι ('It's only *fair* to grant him that): *Chrm.*163B οὐκ οἴεσθαί γε χρή ('Don't you believe it!' cf. *Cri.*53D,54B): *La.* 189E δῆλον ὅτι αὐτό γε ἴσμεν τοῦτο ('If we know how to produce anything, we must, *ex hypothesi*, know the thing *itself*.' Cf.190A δῆλον ὅτι ὄψιν γε ἴσμεν αὐτὴν ὅτι ποτ' ἔστιν. In neither case is γε limitative, *sc.* 'whatever else we don't know'. Here again, in English, the stress is accompanied by a high, not a low pitch): *Men.*71B ὃ δὲ μὴ οἶδα τί ἐστιν, πῶς ἂν ὁποῖόν γέ τι εἰδείην; ('How can I know what it is *like*?'): *Euthd.*302D Ἀλλ' ἀρκεῖ γε ('Well, that's good *enough*'): *Alc.I*105A ᾧ καὶ γνώσῃ ὅτι προσέχων γέ σοι τὸν νοῦν διατετέλεκα ('that I have throughout paid much *attention* to you'): *Phlb.*19D φῂς . . . τὸ προσρηθησόμενον ὀρθῶς ἄμεινον ἡδονῆς γε ἀγαθὸν εἶναι νοῦν ('what may correctly be called *better than pleasure*): X.*Oec.*21.7 πρὸς ὅντινα . . ., οὗτοι δὴ ἐρρωμένοι γε ἄρχοντες γίγνονται: *Lac.*2.7 καὶ ὡς μὲν οὐκ ἀπορῶν ὅ τι δοίη ἐφῆκεν αὐτοῖς γε μηχανᾶσθαι τὴν τροφήν, οὐδένα οἶμαι τοῦτο ἀγνοεῖν ('left it to the boys *themselves*': τό (for γε) Weiske): Lys.xxxi 23 ὅστις γὰρ περὶ τοὺς ἑαυτοῦ ἀναγκαίους τοιαῦτα ἁμαρτάνει ἁμαρτήματα, τί ἂν περί γε τοὺς ἀλλοτρίους ποιήσειεν; ('what is he likely to do in the case of *strangers*?' *A fortiori*: cf. *ib.* 10[1]): D.xviii 190 ἦν . . . ἐκεῖνος ὁ καιρὸς τοῦ γε φροντίζοντος ἀνδρὸς τῆς πόλεως: xix 191 οἱ

[1] Here we have a positive *a fortiori* statement of the form 'if A is true, B will certainly be true'. For γε in negative *a fortiori* statements, see II. 5: 'if A is not true, certainly B will not be true' (there γε is restrictive, the implication being that B anyhow can be denied, even if, contrary to expectation, A *might* be true. ('Certainly', like γε, can be either purely emphatic or restrictive.) Lys.xxxi 23 can be converted into a negative *a fortiori* statement thus: 'If he does not refrain from such actions in the case of his relatives, he certainly won't refrain from them in the case of *strangers*'.

This distinction may appear pedantic: but it is based on a real difference in the thought, as can be seen from the different pitch given to 'strangers' in the two sentences: high in the positive, where γε is emphatic, low in the negative, where it is restrictive (cf. p. 115).

ἀδικοῦντες δηλονότι τὰς ὅλης γε τῆς πατρίδος σπονδὰς . . . οὐ μόνον τὰς ἰδίας: Pl.*R.*529A: *Prm.*132B,158B: *Lg.*645C (line 6), 746E,805D.

(ii) Determinative γε is most commonly found after connecting particles. Whether these express disjunction, opposition, progression, or inference, γε serves to define more sharply the new idea introduced: 'this, and nothing else.' I reserve καὶ . . . γε and δέ γε, δὲ . . . γε for separate treatment. For further examples of the combinations illustrated below, see the various connectives in question, and also V below.

ἢ (ἤτοι) . . . γε (in either limb of a disjunction). Hom.δ546 ἢ γάρ μιν ζωόν γε κιχήσεαι, ἢ . . .: S.*Aj.*1312 μᾶλλον ἢ τῆς σῆς ὑπὲρ γυναικός, ἢ τοῦ σοῦ γ' ὁμαίμονος λέγω (γ' Bothe: θ' *codd.*): E.*Med.*1296 (Elmsley's γε for σφε is probably right): *Ion* 431 ἤτοι φιλοῦσά γ' . . . ἢ καί τι σιγῶσ': *Rh.*623 ἢ σὺ κτεῖνε . . . ἢ 'μοὶ πάρες γε ('or leave it to *me*'): 817 ἤτοι μάραγνά γ' ἢ καρανιστῆς μόρος: Pl.*Grg.*467E ἤτοι ἀγαθόν γ' ἐστὶν ἢ κακόν: *Prt.* 331B ὅτι ἤτοι ταὐτόν γ' ἐστιν . . . ἢ ὅτι ὁμοιότατον: *Tht.*182D ἆρά ποτε οἷόν τέ τι προσειπεῖν χρῶμα . . .;—Καὶ τίς μηχανή, ὦ Σώκρατες; ἢ ἄλλο γέ τι τῶν τοιούτων . . .; ('or anything *else* of the kind'): *Hp.Ma.*301A ἢ σοφοὶ ἢ τίμιοι ἢ γέροντές γε ἢ νέοι: *Phd.*76A: *Tht.*189E.

ἀλλὰ . . . γε. Ar.*Nu.*401 ἀλλὰ τὸν αὑτοῦ γε νεὼν βάλλει ('but he strikes his *own temple*'): 676 ἀλλ' ἐν θυείᾳ στρογγύλῃ γ' ἂν ἐμάττετο: Pl.*Euthphr.*8E 'They agree on the general principle'.—'Yes.'—'Ἀλλ' ἕκαστόν γε, οἶμαι, . . . τῶν πραχθέντων ἀμφισβητοῦσιν ('but they differ about the *individual action*'): 12B Οὐ δοκεῖ μοι εἶναι "ἵνα δέος ἔνθα καὶ αἰδώς" . . . Ἀλλ' ἵνα γε αἰδὼς ἔνθα καὶ δέος εἶναι (stressing the correct view, as opposed to the incorrect: cf. 12C ἀλλ' ἵνα μὲν αἰδὼς ἔνθα καὶ δέος, οὐ μέντοι ἵνα γε δέος πανταχοῦ αἰδώς: stressing the incorrect as opposed to the correct): *Cra.*417D Ἀλλὰ "βλαβερόν" γε καὶ "ζημιῶδες": *Phd.*74A,81C,103D,107C: *Cra.*391A: *Tht.* 200A: X.*Mem.*i2.49: D.xlv48.

ἀτὰρ . . . γε. Ar.*Ach.*448 ἀτὰρ δέομαί γε πτωχικοῦ βακτηρίου: *V.*1514 ἀτὰρ καταβατέον γ': *Eq.*427: *Nu.*801: *Ec.*1067: X.*Oec.*21.1.

ἀλλὰ μὴν . . . γε. D.i23 ἀλλὰ μὴν τόν γε Παίονα . . . ἡγεῖσθαι χρή: Pl.*Cra.*386D,412B.

καὶ μὴν . . . γε. E.*Alc.*713 Καὶ μὴν Διός γε μείζονα ζῴης χρόνον: *Hipp.*862 καὶ μὴν τύποι γε . . . ('And look, the *seal*!'): *ib.*589: Ar.*Ra.*1198: Pl.*Cra.*412A,414A: *R.*328D.

καίτοι . . . γε. Pl.*Lg.*663E καίτοι μέγα γ' ἐστὶ νομοθέτῃ παράδειγμα: *Clit.*407C καίτοι διά γε ταύτην . . . ἀλλ' οὐ διὰ τὴν . . .

ἀλλὰ μὲν δὴ . . . γε. Pl.*Phd.*75A. καὶ μὲν δὴ . . . γε. Pl. *Cra.*396D. οὐ μὲν δὴ . . . γε. X.*An.*ii 4.6. οὐκοῦν . . . γε. Pl.*Phd.*67D Οὐκοῦν τοῦτό γε θάνατος ὀνομάζεται . . .; *Cra.*414B: *Grg.*494B: *Phlb.*54C,55A: *Hp.Mi.*367E: *Alc.II* 138B.

ἄρα . . . γε. Pl.*Phd.*93A Οὐκ ἄρα ἡγεῖσθαί γε προσήκει . . . ἀλλὰ ἕπεσθαι. For ἄρα γε, γε ἄρα see ἄρα, *V*.

Particular uses. (2) With adjectives and adverbs expressing number, size, and intensity, corresponding to the far more frequent use of δή. (This is not a striking or homogeneous class, and many of the examples can be grouped under other heads.)

Ar.*Ach.*127 τοὺς δὲ ξενίζειν οὐδέποτέ γ' ἴσχει θύρα: *Pl.*892 διαρραγείης μηδενός γ' ἐμπλήμενος: Hdt.ix 57.1 Ἀμομφάρετος δὲ ἀρχήν γε οὐδαμὰ δοκέων Πανσανίην τολμήσειν (τε *L*: γε Schweighaeuser): Pl.*Tht.*178E Νὴ Δί', ὦ μέλε· ἢ οὐδείς γ' ἂν αὐτῷ διελέγετο: Ar.*Av.*1542 Ἅπαντά γ' ἆρ' αὐτῷ ταμιεύει; ('Does she manage *everything* for him, then?'): Pl.*Smp.*185B οὕτω πᾶν πάντως γε καλὸν ἀρετῆς ἕνεκα χαρίζεσθαι: *Phd.*89D καὶ ἡγήσασθαι παντάπασί γ' ἀληθῆ εἶναι (τε *B*): *Euthphr.*15B αὐτὸς ὢν πολύ γε τεχνικώτερος (γε *om. T*): X.*Cyr.*ii 2.3 ὁ δὲ μάλα γε τοῦτο εὐτάκτως ὑπήκουσεν: Hom.*O*383 ἡ γάρ τε μάλιστά γε κύματ' ὀφέλλει: Ψ156 σοὶ γάρ τε μάλιστά γε λαὸς Ἀχαιῶν πείσονται μύθοισι: θ453 τόφρα δέ οἱ κομιδή γε θεῷ ὣς ἔμπεδος ἦεν: E.*IT*580 τὸ δ' εὖ μάλιστά γ' οὕτω γίγνεται: Pl. *Phdr.*246E τούτοις δὴ τρέφεταί τε καὶ αὔξεται μάλιστά γε τὸ τῆς ψυχῆς πτέρωμα (γε *b*: τε *B*: *om. T*): S.*El.*1437 Δι' ὠτὸς ἂν παῦρα γ' ὡς ἠπίως ἐννέπειν . . . συμφέροι: Ar.*Ra.*1136 Ἀλλ' ὀλίγον γέ μοι μέλει: A.*Ag.*1656 πημονῆς δ' ἅλις γ' ὑπάρχει.

Rarely with numerals. Pi.*O.*2.93 τεκεῖν μή τιν' ἑκατόν γε ἐτέων πόλιν . . . ἄνδρα: Ar.*V.*680 Μὰ Δί' ἀλλὰ παρ' Εὐχαρίδου καὐτὸς τρεῖς γ' ἄγλιθας μετέπεμψα: *Lys.*589 Καὶ μὴν ὦ παγκατάρατε πλεῖν ἤ γε διπλοῦν αὐτοὶ (τὸν πόλεμον) φέρομεν ('our share in it is more than *double*'): *Pl.*1083 διεσπλεκωμένῃ ὑπὸ μυρίων ἐτῶν γε καὶ τρισχιλίων (order remarkable): Din.i 74 τότε διὰ τρεῖς γ' ἀνθρώπους οὓς εἶπον...

(3) With ἄλλος, in negative or virtually negative sentences. 'Nothing *else*': 'What *else*?'. S.*Tr*.630 Τί δῆτ' ἂν ἄλλο γ' ἐννέποις; Hdt.i 49 οὐκ ἔχω εἰπεῖν ... ἄλλο γε ἢ ὅτι ...: iii 37 ἐς τὸ οὐ θεμιτόν ἐστι ἐσιέναι ἄλλον γε ἢ τὸν ἱρέα: Pl.*Prt*.311E τί ὄνομα ἄλλο γε λεγόμενον περὶ Πρωταγόρου ἀκούομεν; Hdt.vi 86δ: vii 152.1: ix 8.2.

So also in set phrases: οὐδὲν ἄλλο γ' ἤ ...: A.*Pers*.209 ὁ δ' οὐδὲν ἄλλο γ' ἢ πτήξας δέμας παρεῖχε. τί δ' ἄλλο γ' ἤ ...; A.*Th*.852 τί φῶ; τί δ' ἄλλο γ' ἢ πόνοι πόνων ...; Ar.*Nu*.1287, 1495: *Pax* 103,923: *Av*.25: *Ra*.198: *Ec*.395: Pl.*Phdr*.268B: *Phd*.63D. τί δ' ἄλλο γ' εἰ μὴ ...; Ar.*Eq*.615: X.*Cyr*.ii 2.11. τί γὰρ ἄλλο γ' ἤ ...; Ar.*Ec*.771. τί ἄλλο γ' ἤ ...; Pl.*Euthd*. 287E: *Men*.73C. (In Ar.*Nu*.1447 Kock's Τί δ' ἄλλο γ' ἢ ταῦτ' ἢν ποιῇς is clearly right.)

Alternatively, the emphasis may fail, not on ἄλλος, which is understood, but on its correlative. And so we get, in Xenophon, τί δέ, εἰ μὴ ... γε in questions. *Oec*.9.1 ἡ γυνὴ ἐδόκει σοι ... πώς τι ὑπακούειν ὧν σὺ ἐσπούδαζες διδάσκων;—Τί δέ, εἰ μὴ ὑπισχνεῖτό γε ἐπιμελήσεσθαι καὶ φανερὰ ἦν ἡδομένη ἰσχυρῶς ('Why, of course she said she'd be careful'): 9.2: 9.18: 10.9: *Cyr*.i 4.13.

The curious Aristophanic εἰ μὴ ... γε ('merely') is probably derived, by a further ellipse, from the above. Ar. *Eq*.186 μῶν ἐκ καλῶν εἶ κἀγαθῶν:—Μὰ τοὺς θεούς, εἰ μὴ 'κ πονηρῶν γ' ('Good gracious, no, I'm just a poor low-born fellow'): *Lys* 943 Οὐχ ἡδὺ τὸ μύρον ... τουτογί, εἰ μὴ διατριπτικόν γε: *Th*.898 Αὕτη Θεονόη Πρωτέως.—Μὰ τὼ θεὼ εἰ μὴ Κρίτυλλά γ' Ἀντιθέου ('it's only *Critylla*'). For other possible instances in Aristophanes, see Neil on *Eq*.186. (For εἰ μή, without γε, meaning 'just', cf. Philostr.*Imag*.i 24.2.)

(4) With pronouns. Neil remarks (Appendix to *Knights*, p. 186) that 'in Homer γε occurs after pronouns much oftener than in other combinations. It is not very often second in the Homeric sentence or line: for here the favourite use is to have γε with the second of two pronouns ... or with a pronoun

preceded by a particle or particles'. *B*55 τοὺς ὅ γε συγκαλέσας: *E*301 τὸν κτάμεναι μεμαώς, ὅς τις τοῦ γ' ἀντίος ἔλθοι: *A*116 εἰ τό γ' ἄμεινον: 286 ναὶ δὴ ταῦτά γε πάντα . . . ἔειπες: 320 ἀλλ' ὅ γε . . .: 342 ἦ γὰρ ὅ γ' ὀλοιῇσι φρεσὶ θύει: ζ120 ἦ ῥ' οἵ γ' ὑβρισταί τε καὶ ἄγριοι. The formulae ἀλλ' ὅ γε, ἔνθ' ὅ γε are common. In Hesiod also γε is predominantly used with pronouns. *Th.*523 αὐτὰρ ὅ γ' ἧπαρ ἤσθιεν: 621 ἔνθ' οἵ γ' ἄλγε' ἔχοντες . . . ἧατ': *Op.*206 τὴν ὅ γ' ἐπικρατέως πρὸς μῦθον ἔειπεν: *Th.*532 ταῦτά γ' ἄρ' ἁζόμενος: 605 ὅ γ' οὐ βιότου ἐπιδευὴς ζώει: *Op.*265 οἷ γ' αὐτῷ κακὰ τεύχει ἀνήρ.

In later Greek, particularly in dialogue (dramatic, especially comic, and Platonic), this tendency of γε to attach itself to pronouns still persists, though to a less extent. Naturally, in many cases γε is limitative: but in many others it is determinative: often it seems to be otiose, the pronoun apparently requiring no stress, or at most a secondary stress. The same tendency occasionally shows itself in English, as when we say 'Not *I*', meaning 'I certainly did *not*'.

Mimn.*Fr.*13.6 εὖθ' ὅ γ' ἀνὰ προμάχους σεύαιθ': Thgn.560 ὥστε σε μήτε . . . μήτε σέ γ' . . .: 1031 τόλμα, θυμέ, . . . μηδὲ σύ γ' . . .: Simon.*Fr.*30.3 ἔτικτε δ' Ἄτλας ἑπτὰ ἰοπλοκάμων φιλᾶν θυγατρῶν τάν γ' ἔξοχον εἶδος: B.11.23 οὐκ εἶδέ νιν ἀέλιος κείνῳ γε σὺν ἄματι πρὸς γαίᾳ πεσόντα: A.*Pr.*934 Ἀλλ' ἆθλον ἄν σοι τοῦδέ γ' ἀλγίω πόροι ('even than this': τοῦδ' ἔτ' Elmsley, perhaps unnecessarily): S.*Aj.*519 ἐν σοὶ πᾶσ' ἔγωγε σῴζομαι: 529 πάντ' ἔγωγε πείσομαι: *Tr.*321 καὶ συμφορά τοι μὴ εἰδέναι σέ γ' ἥτις εἶ: *El.*1146 οὔτε γάρ ποτε μητρὸς σύ γ' ἦσθα μᾶλλον ἢ κἀμοῦ φίλος: *Ant.*789 καί σ' οὔτ' ἀθανάτων φύξιμος οὐδεὶς οὔθ' ἁμερίων σέ γ' ἀνθρώπων: *Ph.*1117 πότμος σε δαιμόνων τάδ', οὐδὲ σέ γε δόλος ἔσχ' ὑπὸ χειρὸς ἐμᾶς: E.*Med.*1056 μὴ δῆτα, θυμέ, μὴ σύ γ' ἐργάσῃ τάδε (μὴ σύ γε is common: S.*OC*1441: E.*Ph.*532: *Hec.*408: *Ion* 439,1335: *Ba.*951: Pl.*R.*345B. So also μὴ 'μοί γε: Ar.*Eq.*18: *Nu.*84,433: *V.*1179,1400): *Or.* 1528 οὔτε γὰρ γυνὴ πέφυκας οὔτ' ἐν ἀνδράσιν σύ γ' εἶ: 1617 Σαυτὸν σύ γ' ἔλαβες: *Supp.*771 Δοκῶ μέν, αὐταί γ' εἰσὶν αἱ διδάσκαλοι: Ar.*Ach.*108 Οὐκ, ἀλλ' ἀχάνας ὅδε γε χρυσίου λέγει: 1192 Ἀτταταῖ ἀτταταῖ στυγερὰ τάδε γε κρυερὰ πάθεα: *Nu.*785 Ἀλλ' εὐθὺς ἐπιλήθει σύ γ': 1275 Οὐκ ἔσθ' ὅπως σύ γ' αὐτὸς ὑγιαίνεις: *V.*144 Κάπνος ἔγωγ' ἐξέρχομαι ('*I'm* the *smoke* going up'): 371 Διατέτρωκται τοῦτό γ': 518 Οὐ σύ γε ('Not *you*!'): 940 ἀλλ' ἔτι σύ γ' οὐρεῖς...; 953 Κλέπτης μὲν οὖν οὗτός γε: *Av.*85 Κακῶς σύ γ' ἀπόλοι': 357 Τί δὲ χύτρα νώ γ' ὠφελήσει; ('And what good 'll a pot be to *us*?'): 1391 Οὐ δῆτ' ἔγωγε.—Νὴ τὸν Ἡρακλέα σύ γε ('Not I.'—'Yes, by Heracles, you do'): *Th.*1004 Οἴμοι κακοδαίμων, μᾶλλον ἐπικρούεις σύ γε: 1224 's τοὔμπαλιν τρέχεις σύ γε: S.*OT*432,815: *Ant.*930: *Tr.*328, 1208: *Ph.*330,904: *OC*1134: E.*Alc.*719: Ar.*Ach.*769: *Eq.*6, 275: *V.*945,1371,1502: *Pax* 913: *Th.*518: *Ec.*776: *Pl.*74: Hdt.i 117 φὰς σέ γε εἶναι τὸν κελεύοντα: ii 173 ἤτοι μανεὶς ἢ ὅ γε ἀπόπληκτος γενόμενος: v 53 εἰ ... ὁ παρασάγγης δύναται τριήκοντα στάδια ὥσπερ οὗτός γε δύναται ταῦτα (where we might expect ὥσπερ γε (see I.5), or rather, perhaps, ὥσπερ οὖν): vi 12.3 πρό τε τούτων τῶν κακῶν ἡμῖν γε κρέσσον καὶ ὅ τι ὦν ἄλλο παθεῖν ἐστι: vii 108 3 ἤ κου ἐν γῇ τῇ Ἀθηναίων ἢ σέ γε ἐν τῇ Λακεδαιμονίων: Pl.*Phdr.*243D Τοῦτόν γε τοίνυν ἔγωγε αἰσχυνόμενος...: *Euthd.*271C πάσσοφοι ἀτεχνῶς τώ γε: 278C δῆλον ὅτι τούτω γέ σοι αὐτὼ τὰ σπουδαῖα ἐνδείξεσθον: 302B Ταλαίπωρος ἄρα τις σύ γε ἄνθρωπος εἶ: *Amat.*132B ἀδολεσχοῦσι μὲν οὖν οὗτοί γε: X.*HG.*i 7.29 μὴ ὑμεῖς γε, ὦ Ἀθηναῖοι: *Cyr.*iv 1.19 τὸ μὲν γὰρ πλῆθος ἡμεῖς γε τῶν πολεμίων οὐδὲ διωξόμεθα: *Hier.*i 7 ἔξω τούτων ὧν εἴρηκας σύ γε: D.xix 242 μὴ σύ γε: Pl.*Chrm.* 154A: *Cra.*393B,400D.

(5) With relatives. (For limitative γε with relatives, see II.2.) Except for ὥσπερ γε, for which see below, this is not a well-defined usage. The particle which normally stresses a relative relation is δή, and γε but rarely takes over this function.

Hom.τ511 κοίτοιο τάχ' ἔσσεται ἡδέος ὥρη, ὅν τινά γ' ὕπνος ἕλοι: Emp.*Fr.*12.3 αἰεὶ γὰρ τῇ γ' ἔσται, ὅπῃ γέ τις αἰὲν ἐρείδῃ (γε in both limbs, as often καί: 'just there, precisely where...': θήσεσθαι *codd.*): S.*Ph.* 559 φράσον δ' ἅπερ γ' ἔλεξας (so *A*: 'just those things which...', Jebb): E.*Ion* 942 ἆρ' ἦν ταῦθ' ἅ γ' ᾐσθόμην ἐγώ; *El.*910 οὔποτ' ἐξελίμπανον θρυλοῦσ' ἅ γ' εἰπεῖν ἤθελον κατ' ὄμμα σόν ('those same words which...'): Ar.*Pax* 479 Ἆρ' οἶσθ' ὅσοι γ' αὐτῶν ἔχονται τοῦ ξύλου, μόνοι προθυμοῦντ' ('just those who ... alone...'. But in Hom.η214 it is δή that stresses the relative, while γε rather picks up πλείονα epexegetically (cf. I. 12. iii): πλείον' ἐγὼ κακὰ μυθησαίμην, ὅσσα γε δὴ . . . μόγησα : 'even all that . . .') : Pl.*Cra*.422B Ἆρ' οὖν καὶ νῦν ἅ γ' ἐρωτᾷς τὰ ὀνόματα στοιχεῖα ὄντα τυγχάνει . . . ; ('Perhaps those very names you are asking about are elements?') : D.liv 33 ἀλλ' ὑφ' οὗ γε πρώτου ἐπλήγην . . . τούτῳ καὶ δικάζομαι (ἀλλὰ . . . γε) : Pl.*Alc.II* 146D.

In the following, with a word intervening, γε is completely detached from the relative. S.*Ant*.323 ἦ δεινόν, ᾧ δοκῇ γε, καὶ ψευδῆ δοκεῖν ('when a man *does* harbour suspicions', Jebb) : *Ph*.1276 μὴ λέξῃς πέρα. μάτην γὰρ ἂν εἴπῃς γε πάντ' εἰρήσεται ('anything you *do* say will be said in vain': Jebb, less probably, 'all thy *words* . . . (though I cannot resist force)'). καί is more commonly used in such cases (*q.v.* II.C.7). In Hp.*Nat. Hom*.1 γε seems to have little force : μαρτύριά τε καὶ τεκμήρια, ἅ γε ἔστιν οὐδέν (γε *om. AC*).

γε not infrequently strengthens ὥσπερ in Aristophanes, Plato and Xenophon : 'precisely as'. Ar.*Eq*.716 ὥσπερ αἱ τίτθαι γε : *Ra*.1158 : Pl.*Grg*.484E καταγέλαστοι γίγνονται, ὥσπερ γε οἶμαι οἱ πολιτικοί : Pl.*Cra*.427A : X.*Oec*.1.10 : *Smp*.4.17 : *Cyr*.vi 2.21. ὥσπερ γε καί. Ar.*Nu*.673 ὥσπερ γε καὶ Κλεώνυμον : Pl.*La*. 183A : *Cra*.394E : X.*Cyr*.i 6.34 : ii 1.27 : 3.9 : *Hier*.1.24 : 6.15 : Arist.*Pol*.1276b4.

(6) After interrogatives. On the whole there is little trace of this usage, δή being the particle normally used to strengthen an interrogative. S.*Ph*.441 ἀναξίου μὲν φωτὸς ἐξερήσομαι, γλώσσῃ δὲ δεινοῦ . . .—Ποίου δὲ τούτου πλήν γ' Ὀδυσσέως ἐρεῖς ; (γε some later MSS. : but δέ is no doubt right) ; *OC* 977 εἰ δ' . . . πῶς γ' ἂν τό γ' ἆκον πρᾶγμ' ἂν εἰκότως ψέγοις ; (πῶς ἄν Elmsley) : E.*Hec*.774 Θνῄσκει δὲ πρὸς τοῦ . . . ;—Τίνος γ' ὑπ' ἄλλου ; Θρῄξ νιν ὤλεσε ξένος ('Whom *else*'?) : *Ion* 999 (ἦ τί γ' οὐ *suprascr. L* is no doubt wrong) : Ar.*Nu*.689 ἐπεὶ πῶς γ' ἂν καλέσειας ἐντυχὼν Ἀμυνίᾳ ; (γ' *R* : *om. cett.* : 'a curious error', Starkie) : *Ra*.138 Εἶτα πῶς περαιωθήσομαι ; (πῶς *V* : πῶς γε *RAM*, but the stress is inappropriate) : 515 Πῶς λέγεις ; ὀρχηστρίδες ; (πῶς γε *RM*) : 936 Σὺ δ' ὦ θεοῖσιν ἐχθρὲ ποῖ' ἄττ' ἐστὶν ἅττ' ἐποίεις ; (ποῖ' ἄγ' *R* : ποῖά γ' *AM*) : *Pl*. 485 Οὐκ ἂν φθάνοιτον τοῦτο πράττοντ', ἢ τί γ' ἂν ἔχοι τις ἂν δίκαιον ἀντειπεῖν ἔτι ; (τί γ' ἄν *AAld.* : *al.al.*) : 583 εἰ γὰρ ἐπλούτει, πῶς ἂν ποιῶν . . . ; (πῶς γ' ἄν one inferior MS.).

In the following, where another particle precedes, γε seems to adhere to the interrogative, rather than to that particle. Ar.*Ach.*307 εἰ καλῶς ἐσπεισάμην.—Πῶς δέ γ' ἂν καλῶς λέγοις ἂν . . .; ('And *how* can you say καλῶς . . .?'): Aeschin.ii 163 ἐν δὲ τούτοις, ὡς ἔοικεν, ἐγὼ διαφανὴς ἦν . . . καὶ τῷ γε δῆλος ἦν . . .; ('And *whose* notice did I attract . . .?')

These instances are not impressive, and are for the most part textually doubtful. But it is perhaps significant that the majority are from Aristophanes, where we should expect to find a lively idiom of this type. For instances in later Greek, see Klotz i 292.

In indirect questions. Ar.*V.*310 μὰ Δί' οὐκ ἔγωγε νῷν οἶδ' ὁπόθεν γε δεῖπνον ἔσται ('where on earth our dinner's coming from': τό Cobet): Hdt.i 111 ἀναλαβὼν ἔφερον, δοκέων τῶν τινος οἰκετέων εἶναι· οὐ γὰρ ἄν κοτε κατέδοξα ἔνθεν γε ἦν (but the stress is different here: 'where he *did* come from': γενεήν for γε ἦν *RSV*).

In Ar.*Ach.*5 the subordinate clause is relative rather than interrogative: ἐγῷδ' ἐφ' ᾧ γε το κέαρ ηὐφράνθην ἰδών.

(I have dealt above with γε following an interrogative. In general, γε can of course emphasize a word or phrase in a question, just as well as in a statement: E.*Cyc.*207 ἦ πρός γε μαστοῖς εἰσι . . .; X.*Cyr.*viii 4.23 Ἔπειτ' οὐκ ἂν πρίαιό γε παμπόλλου . . .; Elmsley's attempt (on E.*Med.*1367: 1334 in his edition), to banish γε from the texts in such cases, is mistaken. In Pl. *Lg.*781C γε seems suspicious.)

(7) In commands. γε occasionally sharpens the tone of an imperative. The usage seems established, though few examples of it are critically above suspicion. S.*El.*345 ἔπειθ' ἑλοῦ γε θάτερ': 411 Ὦ θεοὶ πατρῷοι, συγγένεσθέ γ' ἀλλὰ νῦν: *Ph.*1003 Ξυλλάβετέ γ' αὐτόν (γ' *A*: *om. L*): E.*Andr.*589 Ψαῦσόν γ', ἵν' εἰδῇς (γ' *A*: δ' *L*: *om. V*): *Supp.*842 εἰπέ γ' ὡς σοφώτερος (πέ γ' *in rasura L²*: *fort.* εἰπόν, Murray): *IA*817 δρᾶ γ', εἴ τι δράσεις (δρᾶ γ' *P²*: δρᾶ *LP*): Pl.*R.*336E οἴου γε σύ, ὦ φίλε (γε Bekker: τε *AFDM*: cf. οἴεσθαί γε χρή *Cri.*53D, 54B). In E.*Alc.* 1127 read perhaps Ὁρῶ γε for Ὅρα γε (*C.R.*xliii 119).

With jussive subjunctive. Pl.*Tht.*201A Ὀρθῶς λέγεις· ἀλλ' ἴωμέν γε καὶ σκοπῶμεν (τε *W*).

In negative commands. E.*IT* 912 *Μηδέν μ' ἐπίσχῃ γ'* (*μηδέν* Murray: *οὐδέν codd.*): Ar.*V.*922 *Μή νυν ἀφῆτέ γ' αὐτόν* ('Don't you let him off!'). S.*OC* 1409 is different: *μή μ' ἀτιμάσητέ γε* ('at least do not *dishonour* me').

In wishes. E.*Ion* 632 *εἴη γ' ἐμοὶ ⟨μὲν⟩ μέτρια μὴ λυπουμένῳ* (*εἴη δ' ἔμοιγε* Lenting): S.*OT* 80 *εἰ γὰρ ἐν τύχῃ γέ τῳ σωτῆρι βαίη* (but the particle adheres to *τύχῃ σωτῆρι*).

(8) In a conditional protasis, usually following a negative, 'even if' (perhaps colloquial in tone). Contrast *εἴ γε* limitative, 'if, but not unless'. Hom.γ115 *τίς κεν ἐκεῖνα πάντα γε μυθήσαιτο . . . ; οὐδ' εἰ πεντάετές γε . . . παραμίμνων ἐξερέοις*: cf. **E**258 (p. 448): E.*Or.*1513 *'Ενδικώτατ'* (*διώλετο*), *εἴ γε λαιμοὺς εἶχε τριπτύχους θανεῖν*: Ar.*Ach.*968 *Οὐκ ἂν μὰ Δί' εἰ δοίη γέ μοι τὴν ἀσπίδα*: Pl.*Lg.*886E *Χαλεπόν γε λόγον . . . εἰρηκὼς τυγχάνεις, εἴ γε εἷς ἦν μόνον· νῦν δὲ ὅτε πάμπολλοι τυγχάνουσιν, ἔτι χαλεπώτερον ἂν εἴη*: X.*Ages.*5.5 *Οὐ τὼ σιώ, οὐδ' εἰ μέλλοιμί γε . . .*: Ar. *Nu.*108: *V.*298: *Pl.*924. Stressing a participial clause within the protasis. D.xix 172 *ἐξώλης ἀπολοίμην . . . εἰ προσλαβών γ' ἂν ἀργύριον πάνυ πολὺ μετὰ τούτων ἐπρέσβευσα.*

(9) Apodotic. (See Neil, pp. 199–200; Pearson, *Fragments of Sophocles*, ii. 27.) The opening of an apodosis is seldom stressed by *γε* (normally by *δή*). Hes.*Th.*800 *αὐτὰρ ἐπεὶ . . ., ἄλλος γ' ἐξ ἄλλου δέχεται*: S.*Ant.*6,7 *ἐπεὶ γὰρ . . ., ψευδῆ γ' ἐμαυτὸν οὐ καταστήσω πόλει*: E.*Tr.*388 *οὓς δ' ἕλοι δόρυ, νέκροι γ' ἐς οἴκους φερόμενοι . . . περιβολὰς εἶχον χθονός* (*γ' V*: *δ' P*): *HF* 861 *εἰ δὲ δὴ . . . ἀναγκαίως ἔχει . . ., εἰμί γ'*: *Hipp.*472 *εἰ . . ., κάρτα γ' εὖ πράξειας ἄν* (*κάρτ' εὖ L*: *corr. l*): *Ba.*445 *ἃς δ' αὖ σὺ Βάκχας εἶρξας . . ., φροῦδαί γ' ἐκεῖναι*: Ar.*Lys.*658 *εἰ δὲ λυπήσεις τί με, τῷδέ γ' ἀψήκτῳ πατάξω τῷ κοθόρνῳ τὴν γνάθον*: E.*Hel.*1323: Hdt.ix 42.2 (*γε* Gomperz): X.*An.*vii 7.54. (In Pl. *R.*453D *γε* seems to give a limitative stress to *νεῖ*, in spite of the order: 'he *swims* all the same.)

Resumptive. (Here, again, *δή* is normally used.) D.xviii 261 *ἐπειδὴ δ' εἰς τοὺς δημότας ἐνεγράφης ὁπωσδήποτε* (*ἐῶ γὰρ τοῦτο*), *ἐπειδή γ' ἐνεγράφης* (*δ' O*).

(10) Exclamatory. The tendency in Greek is for emphatic

words to be placed early. Emphatic γε similarly gravitates to the opening of sentence and speech (see above, I, *ad init.*). Often when following an adjective or adverb, less frequently after verbs and nouns, it has a force which may fairly be described as exclamatory.

(i) Adjectives. (Ellipse of ἐστι is common). A.*Pers.*286 *Στυγναί γ' Ἀθᾶναι δᾴοις*: *Ch.*777 *Οὔπω· κακός γε μάντις ἂν γνοίη τάδε*: S.*El.*341 *Δεινόν γε* (*Ph.*755,1225): E.*Cyc.*148 *Καλήν γε κρήνην εἶπας*: 283 *Αἰσχρὸν στράτευμά γ'* (order exceptional): 670 *Αἰσχρός γε φαίνῃ*: *Hec.*846 *Δεινόν γε, θνητοῖς ὡς ἅπαντα συμπίτνει*: *Ba.*800 *Ἀπόρῳ γε τῷδε συμπεπλέγμεθα ξένῳ*: *Supp.*426 *Κομψός γ' ὁ κῆρυξ*: *Ion* 381 *Πολλαί γε πολλοῖς εἰσι συμφοραὶ βροτῶν*: Ar.*Ach.*115 *Ἑλληνικόν γ' ἐπένευσαν ἄνδρες*: 909 *Μικκός γα μᾶκος οὗτος*: *Eq.*124 *Πολλῷ γ' ὁ Βάκις ἐχρῆτο τῷ ποτηρίῳ*: 1377 *Σοφός γ' ὁ Φαίαξ*: *Nu.*135 *Ἀμαθής γε νὴ Δί'*: 984 *Ἀρχαῖά γ'*: A.*Pr.*953: E.*Andr.*909: *Hel.*808: *Supp.*151,296: *HF*1116: Ar.*Ach.*1105,1106: *Eq.* 609,616,1368: *Av.*158,1208,1269: *Ra.*1370,1482: Pl.*Grg.*467B *Σχέτλιά γε λέγεις*: 470C *Χαλεπόν γέ σε ἐλέγξαι*: *Prt.*361A *Ἄτοποί γ' ἐστέ*: *Phdr.*242A *Θεῖός γ' εἶ*: *Ap.*25A *Πολλήν γέ μου κατέγνωκας δυστυχίαν*: *Cra.*409C *Διθυραμβῶδές γε τοῦτο τοὔνομα*: 417E *Ποικίλα γέ σοι ... ἐκβαίνει τὰ ὀνόματα*: *Tht.*161A *Φιλόλογός γ' εἶ ἀτεχνῶς*: X.*Mem.*ii 3.9 *Θαυμαστά γε λέγεις*: Pl.*Grg.*473A: *Phdr.*257C: *Euthd.*288A: *Ly.*204C: *Men.*92A: *Smp.*175A: *Prm.*136C: *Phlb.*34C,65D.

(ii) Adverbs. (Here, again, ellipse of verb is frequent.) A.*Pr.* 696 *Πρῴ γε στενάζεις*: S.*Aj.*589 *Ἄγαν γε λυπεῖς* (*Ant.*573): *Ant.*241 *Εὖ γε στιχίζῃ*: *Ph.*327 *Εὖ γ', ὦ τέκνον* (the only example in tragedy of this colloquial εὖ γε without a verb, Jebb): E.*Or.*99 *'Οψέ γε φρονεῖς εὖ*: 386 *Εὖ γ' εἶπας* (*Ba.*824): *IT*1212 *Εὖ γε κηδεύεις πόλιν*: Ar.*Ach.*952 *Μόλις γ' ἐνέδησα*: *Eq.*1180 *Καλῶς γ' ἐποίησε*: *Nu.*773 *Σοφῶς γε*: *V.*46 *'Ορθῶς γε*: *Pax* 856 *Εὐδαιμονικῶς γε*: *Eq.*1402: *Av.*1442: Pl.*Grg.*492D *Οὐκ ἀγεννῶς γε ... ἐπεξέρχῃ*: *Tht.*146D *Γενναίως γε καὶ φιλοδώρως ... πολλὰ δίδως*: 148B *Ἄριστά γ' ἀνθρώπων, ὦ παῖδες*: 205A *Ἀνδρικῶς γε ... μάχῃ*: *R.*472A: *La.*181A: *Tht.*151E, 154D,163C: *Phlb.*24B,25B: X.*An.*vii 1.22.

With repetition. Ar.*Pax* 285 *Εὖ γ', εὖ γε* (*Eq.*470): *Ec.*213 *Εὖ γ', εὖ γε, νὴ Δί', εὖ γε.*

(iii) Verbs. E.*Ion* 1290 *Οὐκ εὐσεβεῖς γε*: Ar.*Ach.*836 *Εὐδαιμονεῖ γ' ἄνθρωπος*: *V.*1162 *Ἀδικεῖς γέ με*: 1387 *Νὴ τὸν Δί' ἐξέμαθές γε* ('you *have* learned ...'): 1450 *Ζηλῶ γε*: *Pax* 1127 *Ἥδομαί γ', ἥδομαι*: *Av.*177 *Νὴ Δία, ἀπολαύσομαί τί γ'.* In Pl.*Lg.*886A *Φοβοῦμαί γε* the tone of γε is quieter. (Pl.*Smp.* 189B is difficult to class: *Βαλών γε, φάναι, ὦ Ἀριστόφανες, οἴει ἐκφεύξεσθαι.*)

(iv) Nouns. Pl.*Men.*76A *Ὑβριστής γ' εἶ*: X.*HG* vii 1.37 *Νὴ Δία, ὦ Ἀθηναῖοι, ὥρα γε ὑμῖν ... ζητεῖν*: *Smp.*4.54 *Νὴ τὴν Ἥραν ... εὐτύχημά γέ σου μέγα.* (In E.*Hipp.*1070 read perhaps *δακρύων γ' ἐγγὺς τόδε*, for *τ'*.)

The exclamation is sometimes sarcastic in tone, especially with *καλός, καλῶς.* S.*OT* 1035 *Καλόν γ' ὄνειδος σπαργάνων ἀνειλόμην*: *Ant.*739 *Καλῶς ἐρήμης γ' ἂν σὺ γῆς ἄρχοις μόνος*: E.*Cyc.*551 *Καλόν γε τὸ γέρας τῷ ξένῳ δίδως, Κύκλωψ*: 664 *Καλός γ' ὁ παιάν*: Ar.*Nu.*647 *ταχύ γ' ἂν δύναιο μανθάνειν περὶ ῥυθμῶν*: 1064 *Μάχαιραν; ἀστεῖόν γε κέρδος ἔλαβεν ὁ κακοδαίμων*: *Av.*1401 *χαρίεντά γ' ὦ πρεσβῦτ' ἐσοφίσω καὶ σοφά* (a whipping): E.*Med.*504,514,588: *IA* 305: Ar.*Eq.*344: *Av.* 139: Pl.*Prm.*131B *Ἡδέως γε ... ἓν ταὐτὸν ἅμα πολλαχοῦ ποιεῖς*: *R.*574C *Σφόδρα γε μακάριον ... ἔοικεν εἶναι τὸ τυραννικὸν ὑὸν τεκεῖν.* (For examples from the orators see p. 129 below.)

The word stressed by γε is sometimes preceded :—

(*a*) By an exclamation or oath, with or without apostrophe. A.*Pers.*739 *Φεῦ, ταχεῖά γ' ἦλθε χρησμῶν πρᾶξις*: S.*OT* 1169 *Οἴμοι, πρὸς αὐτῷ γ' εἰμὶ τῷ δεινῷ λέγειν*: E.*Cyc.*572 *Παπαῖ, σοφόν γε τὸ ξύλον τῆς ἀμπέλου*: *Andr.*184 *Φεῦ φεῦ· κακόν γε. .*: *IA* 1132 *Ἔα· τλήμονά γ' ἔλεξας*: *Fr.*636.2 *ἔα, ἔα· ὁρῶ γ' ἐπ' ἀκταῖς*: Ar.*Nu.*102 *Αἰβοῖ, πονηροί γ'*: 1462 *Ὤμοι, πονηρά γ'...*: Ar.*Ach.*811 *Νὴ τὸν Δί', ἀστείῳ γε...*: 860 *Ἴττω Ἡρακλῆς ἔκαμόν γα τὰν τύλαν*: 867 *Νεὶ τὸν Ἰόλαον ἐπεχαρίττα γ' ὦ ξένε*: E.*Hel.*777: *IA* 710: *Ion* 1312: Ar.*Eq.*1035: *V.*1474: *Av.* 135,1370: *Lys.* 403,1033: *Th.*20: *Ra.*1433: *Ec.*1045: *Pl.*220: Pl.*Phd.* 88C *Νὴ τοὺς θεούς, ὦ Φαίδων, συγγνώμην γ' ἔχω ὑμῖν*: *Phdr.*230B *Νὴ τὴν Ἥραν, καλή γε ἡ καταγωγή*: 273C *Φεῦ, δεινῶς γ'...*: X.*Cyn.*6.17 *Ἰὼ κύνες, ἰώ, καλῶς, σοφῶς γε, ὦ κύνες*: Pl.*Grg.*449D: *Prt.*340E: *Euthd.*292E: *Phd.*60C: *Hp.Ma.*285E: X.*HG* vii 1.37: *Oec.*11.19: *Smp.*4.54.

So, too, after ἦ θην, ἦ μέν, ἦ μήν. Hom.*Α*365: *τ*235: Ar. *Ra*.104.

Less frequently, γε is attached to the exclamation or oath itself (especially Ἰδού γε, followed by a contemptuous repetition of the previous speaker's words). Ar.*Eq*.87 ἄκρατον . . .—Ἰδού γ' ἄκρατον: *Nu*.818 μὰ τὸν Δία τὸν Ὀλύμπιον.—Ἰδού γ' ἰδού, Δί' Ὀλύμπιον: *Av*.11 Οὐδ' ἂν μὰ Δία γ' ἐντεῦθεν Ἐξηκεστίδης: *Th*.225 οὐ γὰρ μὰ τὴν Δήμητρά γ' ἐνταυθοῖ μενῶ: *Ec*.748 μὰ τὸν Ποσειδῶ γ' οὐδέποτ': *Eq*.698 (γ' in *R* only): *Nu*.1469: *Lys*. 441: *Ec*.93,136.

(*b*) By an apostrophe alone. E.*El*.971 Ὦ Φοῖβε, πολλήν γ' ἀμαθίαν ἐθέσπισας: Ar.*Eq*.421 Ὦ δεξιώτατον κρέας, σοφῶς γε προὐνοήσω: 1111 Ὦ Δῆμε, καλήν γ' ἔχεις ἀρχήν.

(*c*) By a shocked, contemptuous, or surprised repetition of the previous speaker's words. S.*Aj*.1127 κτείναντά με;—Κτείναντα; δεινόν γ' εἶπας: Ar.*V*.1336 προσκαλούμενοι.—Ἰὴ ἰεῦ, καλούμενοι. ἀρχαῖά γ' ὑμῶν: *Av*.1691 ὀπτῶ τὰ κρέα . . .—Ὀπτᾷς τὰ κρέα; πολλήν γε τενθείαν λέγεις: *Eq*.344: *Nu*.667,1064(*v.l.*): *Ec*. 190: Pl.*R*.328A ἀφ' ἵππων . . .—Ἀφ' ἵππων; ἦν δ' ἐγώ· καινόν γε τοῦτο. Cf. E.*El*.275 Ἥρου τόδ'; αἰσχρόν γ' εἶπας.

Occasionally this exclamatory note can also be detected in γε in the middle of a speech. E.*El*.374 πλούτῳ (κρινεῖ); πονηρῷ γ' ἆρα χρήσεται κριτῇ (τἄρα *Π*: γ' ἄρα *LP*): *Supp*.458 κλαίων γ' ἂν ἦλθες: 547 σκαιόν γε τἀνάλωμα: *Andr*.220 αἰσχρόν γε: *Rh*.837 μακροῦ γε δεῖ σε . . . λόγου: *Tr*.1191 αἰσχρὸν τοὐπίγραμμά γ' Ἑλλάδι (order remarkable): *Hipp*.480 ἦ τἄρ' ἂν ὀψέ γ' ἄνδρες ἐξεύροιεν ἄν: *Ion* 128 (in Ion's monody): *IA* 596: Ar.*Ach*.447 (second line): *Nu*.647 (second line): 1349 δῆλόν γε τἀνθρώπου 'στὶ τὸ λῆμα: *Pax* 618 πολλά γ' ἡμᾶς λανθάνει ('What a lot of things we don't know!'): 1272 ἀμαθές γ' εἶ: *Ec*.95 οὐκοῦν καλά γ' ἂν πάθοιμεν: Pl.*Alc.II* 150A πολλῷ γε μᾶλλον, οἶμαι. Exclamatory γε may even, exceptionally, occur late in the sentence: Ar.*Pl*.1043 Ἀρχαία φίλη, πολιὰ γεγένησαι ταχύ γε νὴ τὸν οὐρανόν ('You *have* gone grey quickly!').

There are also examples of this lively usage in the orators (almost all in Demosthenes). Lys.iv 1 (opening of speech) Θαυμαστόν γε, ὦ βουλή, τὸ διαμάχεσθαι περὶ τούτου: Isoc.v 103 ἦ πάντων γ' ἂν εἴη σχετλιώτατος: D.ix 66 δουλεύουσί γε: xxxix 33 ἦ δεινόν γ' ἂν εἴη. Ironical: D.vii 32 σφόδρα γε βούλεται τοὺς Ἕλληνας ἐλευθέρους εἶναι: ix 65 καλήν γε (66): xxiv 181 ὅμοιόν γε, οὐ γάρ; τοῦτο τοῖς προτέροις: Din. i 79 δημοτικός γ': D. xviii 136, 266: xix 253: xxi 209: xxii 73: xxiii 161, 162, 186: xxiv 106: xxv 62 (*bis*), 95 (apodotic: cf. xxiii 121): xxviii 6: xliii 72: xlv 56: lviii 15, 18, 29.

The idiom is even occasionally transplanted to reported speech. A. *Ag.* 1241 ἄγαν γ' ἀληθόμαντιν οἰκτείρας ἐρεῖς ('You will say ἄγαν γ' ἀληθόμαντις'): Pl. *Chrm.* 172E κἀνταῦθα καὶ ἄρτι ἀποβλέψας ἄτοπά γ' ἔφην μοι προφαίνεσθαι (a free quotation of 172C ὅτι μοι ἄτοπ' ἄττα καταφαίνεται). In both these passages editors have needlessly excised γε: both are rightly explained by Neil on Ar. *Eq.* 667 (though I do not agree with the rest of his note).

The use of γε in indignant questions is a branch of the exclamatory. Ar. *Ach.* 120 ὦ ..., τοιόνδε γ', ὦ πίθηκε, τὸν πώγων' ἔχων ... ἦλθες ...; *Nu.* 1378 οὐκ Εὐριπίδην ἐπαινεῖς σοφώτατον; —Σοφώτατόν γ' ἐκεῖνον ...; (In E. *HF* 557, if Scaliger's Αἰδῶ γε is right, which it probably is not, it must be taken as a question.) With οἷος: Eup. *Fr.* 314 οἷόν γέ πού 'στι γλῶσσα.

(ii) In answers. This extremely common and diversified use is an off-shoot of emphatic γε. It is not strictly true to say, as has often been said, that γε here means 'yes', though 'yes' is sometimes a convenient rendering. (Often, if anything, it stands for 'no'.) More accurately, it gives an air of liveliness, interest, or intensity to the opening of an answer. The Greek for 'yes' is ναί: but ναί is much rarer than 'yes', because the lively Greek mind was seldom satisfied with the baldness of an unqualified answer: and where ναί does occur it is often followed by a γε which gives additional detail. An answer may, of course, be limited in its content. And in what follows it is often difficult to distinguish between the limitative and intensive forces of γε.

(i) Affirmative answers to a question or statement. E. *Alc.* 149 Οὔκουν ἐπ' αὐτῇ πράσσεται τὰ πρόσφορα;—Κόσμος γ' ἕτοιμος: 201 Ἦ που στενάζει ...;—Κλαίει γε ('Aye, he weeps'): *Cyc.* 250 ὡς ἔκπλεώς γε δαιτός εἰμ' ὀρεσκόου· ... χρόνιος δ' εἴμ' ἀπ' ἀνθρώπων βορᾶς.—Τὰ καινά γ' ἐκ τῶν ἠθάδων ... ἡδίον' ἐστίν ('Aye, change is sweet'): Ar. *Eq.* 1388 Μακάριος ἐς τἀρχαῖα δὴ καθίσταμαι.—Φήσεις γ', ἐπειδὰν ... (cf. *Pax* 1351, D. xxx 30: not limitative, I think. In Pl. *R.* 457C the tone is *dissentient*: οὐ σμικρὸν κῦμα διαφεύγεις.—Φήσεις γε, ἦν δ' ἐγώ, οὐ μέγα αὐτὸ εἶναι, ὅταν τὸ μετὰ τοῦτο ἴδῃς): *Ec.* 933 Σοὶ γὰρ φίλος τίς ἐστιν ἄλλος ἢ Γέρης;—Δείξει γε καὶ σοί (Δείξει *Ald.*: Δόξει *codd.*): Pl. *Thg.* 122E οὐκ ἐδιδάξατό σε ὁ πατὴρ ...;—'Εμέ γε ('Yes, he did'): *Prm.* 131C Μεριστὰ ἄρα ... ἔστιν αὐτὰ τὰ εἴδη ...—Φαίνεται οὕτω γε ('It appears that that *is* so'): *R.* 575C κακὰ δρῶσι σμικρὰ πολλὰ ...—Σμικρά γ', ἔφη, κακὰ λέγεις: 610E ... σχολῇ ...—Σχολῇ γ', ἔφη: *Phlb.* 36D τοῦτο σκεπτέον.—Ἴσως τοῦτό γε ('Yes, perhaps that *is* the problem'). But normally, where a word is echoed in agreement, δῆτα or μέντοι is the particle used.

Answering a command or wish. No certain case; in E. *Alc.* 420 γε is *v.l.* and τε is inappropriate. Wilamowitz read γε for τε in *Rh.* 219, and γε is worth considering in S. *OC* 113, 494. Headlam (on A. *Ag.* 539) objected to the idiom; but it is artificial to distinguish 'answering a command' from 'answering a statement'.

In combination with other particles. Pl. *Phd.* 58D εἰ μή τίς σοι ἀσχολία τυγχάνει οὖσα.—Ἀλλὰ σχολάζω γε (γε *B*: τε *T*: 'Well, I *have* leisure'): 96A ἐὰν βούλῃ ...—Ἀλλὰ μὴν βούλομαί γε (τε *T*): Ar. *Av.* 144.

(ii) Negative answers. E. *Ion* 404 μῶν χρόνιος ἐλθών σ' ἐξέπληξ' ὀρρωδίᾳ;—Οὐδέν γε: *IT* 564 ἔστι τις λόγος;—Οὐδείς γε, πλὴν ...: *IA* 1440 ἀπολέσασά σε;—Οὐ σύ γε· σέσωσμαι: Ar. *Ach.* 176 χαῖρ' Ἀμφίθεε.—Μήπω γε πρίν γ' ἂν στῶ τρέχων: *Nu.* 734 Οὐδὲν πάνυ (ἔχεις);—Οὐδέν γε πλὴν ...: *V.* 518 ὅστις ἄρχω των ἀπάντων.—Οὐ σύ γ', ἀλλ' ὑπηρετεῖς: *Av.* 1360 Ἀπέλαυσά τἄρα ... ἐλθὼν ἐνθαδὶ ...—Οὐδέν γε ('Not at all'): Pl. *Prt.* 310B μή τι νεώτερον ἀγγέλλεις;—Οὐδέν γ', ἦ δ' ὅς, εἰ μὴ ἀγαθά γε: *Phlb.* 38A προθύμως ἀμύνεις τῷ τῆς ἡδονῆς ... λόγῳ τὰ νῦν.—Οὐδέν γε, ἀλλ' ἅπερ ἀκούω λέγω ('Not at all: I'm just saying what I hear'): S. *Ph.* 999 μεθ' ὧν Τροίαν σ' ἑλεῖν δεῖ ...—Οὐδέποτέ γ' ('*Never!*': Ar. *V.* 486): Pl. *Phd.* 74C Οὐδεπώποτέ γ': Ar. *Nu.* 688 Οὐδαμῶς γ' (*V.* 76, 1393: Pl. *Grg.* 462E: *Prm.* 144A): *Pax* 1260 Ἀπίωμεν, ὦ δορυξέ.—Μηδαμῶς γ': X. *Mem.* iii 9.4 προσερωτώμενος δὲ εἰ ... νομίζοι, Οὐδέν γε μᾶλλον, ἔφη, ἢ ...: Pl. *Euthd.* 272B Ἥκιστά γε (*Chrm.* 162B: X. *Mem.* iv 6.10): Pl. *Alc. I* 130B Πάντων γε ἥκιστα: X. *Mem.* iv 6.10 Ἔτι γε νὴ Δί' ἧττον. Similarly Ar. *Ach.* 295 Μάλλ' ἀκούσατε—Σοῦ γ' ἀκούσωμεν;

With exclamations (cf. (10) above) Ar.*V.*163 ἔκφρες με . . .—Μὰ τὸν Ποσειδῶ, Φιλοκλέων, οὐδέποτέ γε: 1507 ὠψώνηκ' ἄρα.—Μὰ τὸν Δί' οὐδέν γ' ἄλλο πλήν γε καρκίνους.

After rhetorical questions. S.*OT* 1386 ὀρθοῖς ἔμελλον ὄμμασιν τούτους ὁρᾶν; ἥκιστα γ': E.*Hipp.*1014 ἀλλ' ὡς τυραννεῖν ἡδύ; τοῖσι σώφροσιν ἥκιστα γ': Ar.*Nu.*1215 Εἶτ' ἄνδρα τῶν αὑτοῦ τι χρὴ προιέναι; οὐδέποτέ γ': *Ec.*748: D.xix 221 ἡδὺ . . .; οὐδέ γ' ἀσφαλές (γε marks the answer: οὐδέ goes closely with ἀσφαλές): lv 13 τίς . . .; οὐδείς γε: lvi 15 ἡμεῖς ἀναιρώμεθα; οὐδέν γε μᾶλλον ἢ ὁτιοῦν. A.*Pr.*961 μή τί σοι δοκῶ ταρβεῖν . . .; πολλοῦ γε καὶ τοῦ παντὸς ἐλλείπω: Ar.*Ach.*543 καθῆσθ' ἂν ἐν δόμοισιν; ἦ πολλοῦ γε δεῖ: Pl.*Tht.*166B αὐτίκα γὰρ δοκεῖς . . .; πολλοῦ γε δεῖ: D.v 24 καὶ σὺ ταῦτα κελεύεις; πολλοῦ γε καὶ δέω: xviii 47. πολλοῦ γε δεῖ interrogative: Pl.*Lg.*790A . . . γράφωμεν; ἢ πολλοῦ γε δεῖ; (γε *L*: τε *AO*).

(iii) Affirmative answers contradicting a denial: cf. German 'doch', French 'si'. E.*Heracl.*257 ἀλλ' οὐ σοὶ βλάβος.—Ἐμοί γε ('Yes, it is'): *IA* 364 ὡς φονεὺς οὐκέτι θυγατρὸς σῆς ἔσῃ. μάλιστά γε ('Yes, you will'): *Hec.*396: *Ba.*484: Ar.*Ach.*794 Οὐ χοῖρος Ἀφροδίτᾳ; μόνᾳ γα δαιμόνων ('To her *alone!*'): *V.*27 .οὐδὲν γὰρ ἔσται δεινὸν οὐ μὰ τοὺς θεούς.—Δεινόν γέ πού 'στ' ἄνθρωπος ἀποβαλὼν ὅπλα ('It *is* an awful thing'): *Eq.*411 Οὔτοι μ' ὑπερβαλεῖσθ' ἀναιδείᾳ...—Ἔγωγε νὴ τοὺς κονδύλους... ὑπερβαλεῖσθαί σ' οἴομαι: *Av.*1391: Pl.*Cri.*53D καὶ οὐκ οἴει . . .; οἴεσθαί γε χρή (cf. *ib.* 54B: *R.*336E: X.*Cyr.*viii 3.29 Ναὶ μὰ Δί', ἔφη ὁ Κῦρος, σύ γε ('Yes, you did'): Pl.*Grg.*491E (perhaps: reading and interpretation are disputed: see Thompson). Answering a rhetorical question: Pl.*Smp.*216D ὡς τὸ σχῆμα αὐτοῦ τοῦτο οὐ σιληνῶδες; σφόδρα γε: D.xxiii 197 οὐκ ἄρα . . . χάριν εἶχον; σφόδρα γε.

Sometimes the γε seems to do double duty, both affirming and limiting. E.*Or.*1074 Οὐκ ἔκτανες σὴν μητέρ', ὡς ἐγὼ τάλας.—Σὺν σοί γε κοινῇ ('Yes, I did: I *shared* the deed'): *Ba.*484 Φρονοῦσι γὰρ κάκιον Ἑλλήνων πολύ.—Τάδ' εὖ γε μᾶλλον ('*Better* in *this*'): *Heracl.*272 Μὴ πρὸς θεῶν κήρυκα τολμήσῃς θενεῖν.—Εἰ μή γ' ὁ κῆρυξ σωφρονεῖν μαθήσεται ('Yes I will, unless the Herald *behaves* himself'): *IT* 555: Ar.*Nu.*930: Pl.*Cri.*54A πότερον . . . οὐχὶ ἐπιμελήσονται; εἴπερ γέ τι ὄφελος αὐτῶν ἐστιν τῶν σοι φασκόντων ἐπιτηδείων εἶναι, οἴεσθαί γε χρή.

(On 'corrective' γε see Jebb on S.*Ph.*33.35. But I doubt whether γε should be regarded as corrective there.)

(iv) In answers to questions which give the answerer no lead (those, that is, which suggest, without prejudice, alternative answers, and those which contain interrogative pronouns or adverbs.) Slightly colloquial in tone, I think.

S.*Ph.*1385 Λέγεις δ' Ἀτρείδαις ὄφελος, ἢ 'π' ἐμοὶ τόδε;—Σοί που φίλος γ' ὤν ('I speak as *your* friend'. Jebb puts a comma after που, wrongly, I think): E.*Cyc.*107 Πόθεν . . . πάρει;—Ἐξ Ἰλίου γε κἀπὸ Τρωικῶν πόνων ('From *Ilium*': τε Hermann): *Hel.*1521 τίς δέ νιν ναυκληρία . . . ἀπῆρε . . . ;—Ἣν γε ξένῳ δίδως σύ (τῷ ξένῳ Wilamowitz). *Or.*398 Πῶς φῄς; . . .—Λύπη μάλιστά γ' ἡ διαφθείρουσά με: Ar.*V.*816 τί τὸν ὄρνιν ὡς ἔμ' ἐξηνέγκατε;—Ἵνα γ' . . .: *Pax* 675 Ποῖός τις οὖν εἶναι δοκεῖ τὰ πολεμικὰ ὁ Κλεώνυμος;—Ψυχήν γ' ἄριστος πλήν γ' ὅτι . . . ('A very stout *fellow*'): *Ec.*455 Τί δῆτ' ἔδοξεν;—Ἐπιτρέπειν γε τὴν πόλιν ταύταις: *Lys.* 1167 Κᾆτα τίνα κινήσομεν;—Ἕτερόν γ' ἀπαιτεῖτ' ἀντὶ τούτου χωρίον: Pl.*Ly.*204A διδάσκει δὲ τίς αὐτόθι;—Σὸς ἑταῖρός γε, ἦ δ' ὅς, καὶ ἐπαινέτης, Μίκκος (γε *scr. recc.*: τε *BTW* ('A *friend* of yours')): *Phdr.*260D ποῖόν τιν' ἂν οἴει . . . καρπὸν . . . θερίζειν; —Οὐ πάνυ γε ἐπιεικῆ ('Not a very *good* one': γε *B*: *om. T*): *Phlb.*34E ἐκ τῶν αὐτῶν πάλιν ἀναλάβωμεν.—Πόθεν δή;—Διψῆ γέ που λέγομεν ἑκάστοτέ τι; (γέ που *B*: που *T*): *R.*569A. (In view of these examples, Heath's ⟨γε⟩ νεαρᾶς in S.*OC* 475 is unexceptionable, and Jebb's objections to it are not valid.)

The following are only formally different. S.*Tr.*590 Ἀλλ' εἴ τις ἐστὶ πίστις ἐν τοῖς δρωμένοις, δοκεῖς παρ' ἡμῖν οὐ βεβουλεῦσθαι κακῶς.—Οὕτως ἔχει γ' ἡ πίστις ('My confidence amounts to *this*'): Ar.*Th.*1218 εἶδες αὐτό;—Ταύτῃ γ' οἴχεται. It is as though in the former passage τίς πίστις;, in the latter, πῇ; had preceded.

In reported speech. Pl.*Smp.*199D ὥσπερ ἂν εἰ . . . ἠρώτων, ἆρα ὁ πατήρ ἐστι πατήρ τινος ἢ οὔ; εἶπες ἂν . . . ὅτι ἔστιν υἱέος γε ἢ θυγατρὸς ὁ πατὴρ πατήρ.

(v) In affirmative answers to questions or statements, adding something to the bare affirmation, which is not expressed but implied. This form of ellipse is exceedingly common in tragic and comic dialogue, especially in stichomythia, where economy of space is an important consideration: it is but rarely found in the less compressed style of the Platonic dialogue, except in the formulae πάνυ γε, σφόδρα γε, etc., where the addition is merely one of degree, and in cases where the addition expresses a limitation.

S.*OT* 365 *Εἴπω τι δῆτα κἄλλ' . . . ;—Ὅσον γε χρῄζεις* ('Yes, all you wish'): 563 *Τότ' οὖν ὁ μάντις οὗτος ἦν ἐν τῇ τέχνῃ ;—Σοφός γ' ὁμοίως κἀξ ἴσου τιμώμενος*: *Ant.*404 *λέγεις ὀρθῶς ἃ φῄς ;—Ταύτην γ' ἰδὼν θάπτουσαν* ('Aye, I saw her . . .'): E.*Hipp.* 1053 *ἀλλά μ' ἐξελᾷς χθονός ;—Πέραν γε πόντου*: *Andr.*247 *Ὁρᾷς ἄγαλμα Θέτιδος εἰς σ' ἀποβλέπον ;—Μισοῦν γε πατρίδα σήν*: 912–18 (γε in four consecutive answers): *Ba.*835 *Ἦ καί τι πρὸς τοῖσδ' ἄλλο προσθήσεις ἐμοί ;—Θύρσον γε χειρί*: 966 *κεῖθεν δ' ἀπάξει σ' ἄλλος.—Ἡ τεκοῦσά γε*: *Ion* 552 *Ἐθιάσευσ' . . . ;—Μαινάσιν γε Βακχίου*: 560 *Ἢ θίγω . . . ;—Πιθόμενός γε τῷ θεῷ*: Ar.*Ach.*900 *ἢ φορτί' . . . ἄξεις ἰών ;—Ὅ τί γ' ἔστ' Ἀθάναις, ἐν Βοιωτοῖσιν δὲ μή*: *Eq.*797 *τὰς πρεσβείας τ' ἀπελαύνεις ἐκ τῆς πόλεως . . .—Ἵνα γ' Ἑλλήνων ἄρξῃ πάντων*: 1231 *χρησμός ἐστι Πυθικὸς φράζων ὑφ' οὗ . . .—Τοὐμόν γε φράζων ὄνομα*: *V.*421 *καὶ κέντρ' ἔχουσιν . . .—Οἷς γ' ἀπώλεσαν Φίλιππον*: 904 *Ἕτερος οὗτος αὖ Λάβης.—Ἀγαθός γ' ὑλακτεῖν*: S.*OT* 1011,1175: *OC* 479: E.*Cyc.*379: *Alc.*62: *Hipp.*1404: *Andr.*898: *El.*240: *IT* 919: *Hel.*104: *Ph.*723,1081,1647: *Or.*795,1596: Ar.*Eq.*258: *Nu.* 1180: Pl.*Grg.*449A *Ῥήτορα ἄρα χρή σε καλεῖν ;—Ἀγαθόν γε* ('Yes, a good one').

In Euripides the addition often takes the form of a consecutive ὥστε clause. *El.*667 *Ἔπειτ' ἀπαντῶν μητρὶ τἀπ' ἐμοῦ φράσον.—Ὥστ' αὐτά γ' ἐκ σοῦ στόματος εἰρῆσθαι δοκεῖν*: *Hel.*108 *Ἤδη γὰρ ἧπται καὶ κατείργασται πυρί ;—Ὥστ' οὐδ' ἴχνος γε τειχέων εἶναι σαφές*: E.*Cyc.*159,217: *Hec.*246,248: *Ph.*1344: *Or.*1122: *El.*273: *IA* 326: A.*Ag.*541: Ar.*Nu.*469. (Contrast S.*OT* 361, limitative: *Οὐχὶ ξυνῆκας πρόσθεν ; . . .—Οὐχ ὥστε γ' εἰπεῖν γνωστόν.*)

Euripides, again, likes to echo a word from the preceding speech, an abstract substantive, in the accusative, being governed by a cognate verb supplied from that speech. *Hel.*1633 *Ἥ με προὔδωκεν——Καλήν γε προδοσίαν*: *Ba.*970 *τρυφᾶν μ' ἀναγκάσεις.—Τρυφάς γε τοιάσδ'*: *Or.*1582: *IA* 1364. These parallels tell in favour of punctuating after ἔρωτα in *Med.*698. Cf. *HF* 716 *ἱκέτιν . . . θάσσειν . . .—Ἀνόνητά γ' ἱκετεύουσαν.*

Addition of degree only. E.*Hipp.*96 *ἔστι τις χάρις ;—Πλείστη* γε: S.*Tr*.669 Οὐ δή τι τῶν σῶν Ἡρακλεῖ δωρημάτων;—Μάλιστά γ': Ar.*V*.293 Ἐθελήσεις...;—Πάνυ γ' ὦ παιδίον. S.*OT*994: *Aj*.983: E.*HF*1414: Ar.*Nu*.253: *V*.521: *Lys*.81: Pl.*Grg*.491E Πάνυ γε σφόδρα: *Hp.Ma*.283D Πάντως γέ που... καὶ Λακεδαιμόνιοι: *Grg*.498B: *Phd*.81A: *Cra*.394E. πάνυ γε, σφόδρα γε, etc., are regular Platonic formulae of assent. So also εἰκός γε, εἰκότως γε, where γε seems to be assentient rather than limitative. (In *Cra*. 406D Οὐδὲ εἰκός γε, γε marks the answer, and οὐδὲ goes closely with εἰκός.)

In rhetorical questions. S.*OC*792 ἆρ' οὐκ ἄμεινον... φρονῶ; πολλῷ γ': E.*Hel*.851.

Less frequently, there is no ellipse, and the answer is grammatically (though not logically) self-sufficing. Pl.*Euthd*.274A τοσόνδε δέ μοι εἴπετον, εἰ ἐν νῷ ἔχετον ἐπιδεικνύναι ταύτην τὴν σοφίαν...—Ἐπ' αὐτό γε τοῦτο πάρεσμεν... ὡς ἐπιδείξοντε ('Yes, that's just what we've *come* for': with ellipse, this would be: Ἐπ' αὐτό γε τοῦτο παρόντες (ἐν νῷ ἔχομεν ἐπιδεικνύναι): X.*Cyr*.iv 2.7 Ἔχετε οὖν ὧν λέγετε πιστόν τι ἡμᾶς διδάσκειν ὡς ἀληθεύετε;—Ὁμηρούς γ', ἔφασαν, ἐθέλομεν... ἀγαγεῖν ('Yes, we're ready to bring *hostages*'). Such passages approximate to those grouped under (i) above. But there the actual fact of assent is conveyed: here, the reason for implied assent. '(We intend...) because we've come for that purpose': '(we can give a pledge,) for we are ready to bring hostages'.

Often the addition takes the form of a limitative qualification. We may then, perhaps, say that γε does double duty (cf. (iii) above): by emphasis implying assent, and by limitation qualifying that assent. S.*OT*680 τί μέλλεις κομίζειν...;—Μαθοῦσά γ' ἥτις ἡ τύχη (*sc*. κομιῶ. 'I will when I've learned... (but not before)'): Pl.*Phdr*.228D ἕκαστον ἐφεξῆς δίειμι...—Δείξας γε πρῶτον, ὦ φιλότης, τί ἄρα ἐν τῇ ἀριστερᾷ ἔχεις ὑπὸ τῷ ἱματίῳ ('Yes, when you've first shewn me...'): E.*Hel*.1634: Pl.*Tht*. 183D, 188D.

In imaginary dialogue. D.xliv 33 ὅτι νὴ Δία πατὴρ ἦν τοῦ τετελευτηκότος. ἀπεληλυθώς γ' εἰς τὸν πατρῷον οἶκον ('Yes, but a father who had gone back...'): Hyp.*Ath*.13 ἐρεῖ δὲ... ὡς ὁ νόμος λέγει, ὅσα ἂν ἕτερος ἑτέρῳ ὁμολογήσῃ κύρια εἶναι. τά γε δίκαια, ὦ βέλτιστε: D.xxi 147: xxxv 48: xliv 50. A further development of this usage is the epexegetic: see (12) below.

(vi) Often, too, though less often, γε adds detail to an assent already expressed. S.*OC*65 Καὶ κάρτα, τοῦδε τοῦ θεοῦ γ' ἐπώνυμοι: E.*Cyc.*586 Ναὶ μὰ Δί', ὃν ἁρπάζω γ' ἐγώ: *HF* 1061 Εὕδει;—Ναί, εὕδει, ὕπνον γ' ἄυπνον ὀλόμενον: *Hec.*1004 Μάλιστα, διὰ σοῦ γ': *Hel.*136 Οὔ πού νιν Ἑλένης αἰσχρὸν ὤλεσεν κλέος;—Φασίν, βρόχῳ γ' ἅψασαν εὐγενῆ δέρην: *Ba.*816 Σάφ' ἴσθι, σιγῇ γ' ὑπ' ἐλάταις καθήμενος: 937 Κἀμοὶ δοκοῦσι, παρά γε δεξιὸν πόδα: *IA* 1459 Ἐγώ, μετά γε σοῦ: Ar.*Ach.*187 Ἔγωγέ φημι, τρία γε ταυτὶ γεύματα: *Eq.*282 Νὴ Δί', ἐξάγων γε τἀπόρρηθ': *Pax* 1234 Ἔγωγε νὴ Δία, ἵνα μή γ' ἁλῶ (after oaths in *V.*146,*Pax* 963,*Ra.*128): E.*Ba.*812: Ar.*Ec.*1063: Pl.*Phd.*59C Ξένοι δέ τινες παρῆσαν;—Ναί, Σιμμίας τέ γε...: *Tht.*193A Ναί, ἀληθῆ γε: *Cra.*421A Μαίεσθαι οὖν καλεῖς τι;—Ἔγωγε, τό γε ζητεῖν: *Tht.*185C ἀλλά τι ἄλλο (φαίνεται).—Τί δ' οὐ μέλλει, ἥ γε διὰ τῆς γλώττης δύναμις; *Grg.*476D Οὐκοῦν ὑπό τινος ποιοῦντος;—Πῶς γὰρ οὔ; ὑπό γε τοῦ κολάζοντος: *R.*543B ... εἰ μνημονεύεις ...—Ἀλλὰ μνημονεύω, ἔφη, ὅτι γε ...: 575E καὶ τοῦτο δὴ τὸ τελος ἂν εἴη ...—Τοῦτο, ἦ δ' ὅς, παντάπασί γε: *Cra.*434E: *Alc.I* 135A: *La.*185E,195E: *R.*477D,578D.

Sometimes, in assenting, the second speaker echoes a word from the previous speaker (characteristic of Euripides). S.*Tr.* 1192 Οἶσθ' ...;—Οἶδ', ὡς θυτήρ γε: E.*Alc.*376 δέχου.—Δέχομαι, φίλον γε δῶρον: *Heracl.*792 φόβος γὰρ εἴ μοι ζῶσιν οὓς ἐγὼ θέλω.—Ζῶσιν, μέγιστόν γ' εὐκλεεῖς: *Hec.*995 Χρυσὸς δὲ σῶς ...;—Σῶς, ἐν δόμοις γε τοῖς ἐμοῖς φρουρούμενος: *Ba.*796 Θύοιμ' ἂν αὐτῷ μᾶλλον ἢ ...—Θύσω, φόνον γε θῆλυν: *IT* 522 ἀφῖκται ...;—Ἥκει, κακῶς γ' ἐλθοῦσα: 562: cf. Ar.*Eq.*671 ἀφῖκται γὰρ περὶ σπονδῶν ...—Νυνὶ περὶ σπονδῶν; ἐπειδή γ', ὦ μέλε, ᾔσθοντο τὰς ἀφύας παρ' ἡμῖν ἀξίας (ironical assent: 'Yes, now that they know sardines are cheap here!'): E.*Alc.*524: *Hipp.*1394: *IT* 568: *El.*673: *Med.* 1373: Ar.*V.*182 (cf. 1181): Hdt.i 159.4 κελεύεις ...;—Ναί, κελεύω, ἵνα γε ... ἀπόλησθε: Pl.*Phd.*74B φῶμεν ...;—Φῶμεν μέντοι νὴ Δία ... θαυμαστῶς γε.

(vii) A particular variety of the elliptical use of γε in answers are the formulae of assent, καλῶς γε ποιῶν, etc. Ar.*Ach.*1050 Ἔπεμψέ τίς σοι νυμφίος ταυτὶ κρέα ἐκ τῶν γάμων.—Καλῶς γε ποιῶν ὅστις ἦν ('Very kind of him'): *Lys.*521 ἔφασκε ...—Ὀρθῶς γε λέγων νὴ Δί' ἐκεῖνος: Pl.*Cra.*431A Καλῶς γε σὺ ποιῶν: *Ly.*204A Καλῶς γε, ἦν δ' ἐγώ, ποιοῦντες: *Cra.*399A Ὀρθῶς γε σὺ πιστεύων: *Tht.*181D Ὀρθῶς γε λέγων: *R.*399E Σωφρονοῦντές γε ἡμεῖς: *R.*474A: *Prt.*352D. Without the participle, Ὀρθῶς γε: E.*Hipp.*94: Pl.*Prt.*359E: *Tht.*197B: D.xxxvii 36. Without ellipse: Ar.*Pax* 271 Εὖ γ' . . . ποιῶν ἀπόλωλ' ἐκεῖνος.

(viii) In drama, the speech of one character is sometimes completed by a second, who either (*a*) interrupts, or (*b*) carries on a sentence which is already complete in itself, often giving a new and malicious turn to the thought. (The assignment of some passages to (*a*) or to (*b*) is precarious.)

(*a*) Ar.*Pl.*180 Ὁ Τιμοθέου δὲ πύργος— —Ἐμπέσοι γέ σοι: *Pax* 446 Κεἴ τις . . . φθονεῖ . . . ἐν ταῖσιν μάχαις— —Πάσχοι γε τοιαῦθ' οἷάπερ Κλεώνυμος: 452 Κεἴ τις . . . μὴ ξυλλάβοι, ἢ δοῦλος αὐτομολεῖν παρεσκευασμένος— —Ἐπὶ τοῦ τροχοῦ γ' ἕλκοιτο: Pl.Com.*Fr.*173.21 σκορπίος αὖ— —Παίσειέ γέ σου τὸν πρωκτὸν ὑπελθών.

Neil, who cites the above passages (*Equites*, pp. 189–90) suggests, perhaps over-ingeniously, that this form of expression may have been used in religious services, the priest beginning each prayer and the congregation finishing it. He observes that the distribution of the lines between the speakers is attested by the scholia, and suggests that in *Pax* 443 and 449 we should read Ἐκ τῶν ⟨γ'⟩ ὀλεκράνων and Ληφθείς ⟨γ'⟩. He also cites E.*Supp.* 805 Ἰὼ ἰώ— —Τῶν γ' ἐμῶν κακῶν ἐγώ: and *Ph.*1741 Φεῦ τὸ χρήσιμον φρενῶν— —Ἐς πατρός γε συμφορὰς εὐκλεᾶ με θήσει. In the latter passage again the scholiast divides the words between the speakers. Add the following: S.*OC* 535 Σαί τ' εἴσ' ἄρ' ἀπόγονοί τε καί— —Κοιναί γε πατρὸς ἀδελφεαί: 1109 Ὦ σκῆπτρα φωτός— —Δυσμόρου γε δύσμορα: E.*Ion* 271 Δίδωσι δ', ὥσπερ ἐν γραφῇ νομίζεται— —Κέκροπός γε σῴζειν παισὶν οὐχ ὁρώμενον: 562 Χαῖρέ μοι, πάτερ.—Φίλον γε φθέγμ' ἐδεξάμην τόδε.—Ἡμέρα θ' ἡ νῦν παροῦσα— —Μακάριόν γ' ἔθηκέ με (instead of the expected Χαιρέτω): Ar.*Ach.*598 Ἐχειροτόνησαν γάρ με— —Κόκκυγές γε τρεῖς: *V.*1227 Οὐδεὶς πώποτ' ἀνὴρ ἔγεντ' Ἀθήναις— —Οὐχ οὕτω γε πανοῦργος οὐδὲ κλέπτης. Ar.*Eq.*1151 is somewhat similar: Ἄπαγ' ἐς μακαρίαν ἐκποδών.—Σύ γ', ὦ φθόρε ('Go to hell (you)—'—'*You*').

(*b*) S.*El.*164 μολόντα τάνδε γᾶν Ὀρέσταν.—Ὅν γ' ἐγὼ ἀκάματα προσμένουσ' ἄτεκνος . . . ('Orestes, whom I . . .'): *Aj.*876 Ἔχεις οὖν;—Πόνου γε πλῆθος ('Have you found anything?'):

E.*Cyc.*683 *Ἔχεις;—Κακόν γε πρὸς κακῷ* ('Have you got them?'): *Supp.* 818 *Ἔχεις ἔχεις (sc. τὰ τέκνα).—Πημάτων γ' ἅλις βάρος*: *Alc.*49 *οὐ γὰρ οἶδ' ἂν εἰ πείσαιμί σε.—Κτείνειν γ' ὃν ἂν χρῇ; τοῦτο γὰρ τετάγμεθα* ('To kill those I ought, do you mean? Yes, that is my office.' This might be read differently, and classed under (*a*). *γ' om. LPB*). Perhaps Ar.*Ach.*92 is to be similarly explained: *ἄγοντες ἥκομεν Ψευδαρτάβαν, τὸν βασιλέως ὀφθαλμόν.—Ἐκκόψειέ γε κόραξ πατάξας, τόν τε σὸν τοῦ πρέσβεως*: *ὀφθαλμόν* being governed *ἀπὸ κοινοῦ* by both the old and the new verb: if, that is, *A*'s *τε* is right.

(ix) The first speaker, after the second has expressed agreement, amplifies his original statement. (Plato only.) Pl.*Grg.* 450A *περὶ λόγους ἐστίν.—Ναί.—Τούς γε περὶ τὰ νοσήματα* ('Words about *diseases*'): *Cra.*414B *ἐπίλοιπα δ' ἡμῖν ἔτι συχνὰ ...;—Ἀληθῆ λέγεις.—Ὧν γ' ἔστιν ἓν καὶ "τέχνην" ἰδεῖν*: *Tht.*186E *Σύμπαν ἄρ' αὐτὸ καλεῖς αἴσθησιν;—Ἀνάγκη.—Ὧι γε, φαμέν, ...*: *Phdr.*258B *πενθεῖ αὐτός τε καὶ οἱ ἑταῖροι.—Καὶ μάλα.—Δῆλόν γε ὅτι οὐχ ὡς ὑπερφρονοῦντες*: *Cra.*385C,435A: *Tht.*208B: *Grg.*479B.

In E.*Ph.*608 the first speaker ignores an interruption by the second. *Ἐξελαυνόμεσθα πατρίδος——Καὶ γὰρ ἦλθες ἐξελῶν.—Ἀδικίᾳ γ', ὦ θεοί.*

(12) Epexegetic. (See *C.R.*xliii (1929),59–60.) *γε* gives force and urgency to an addition or supplement. This idiom is closely connected with the use of *γε* in answers (see especially 11. v. *ad fin.*: *ib.* ix): perhaps, indeed, derived from it, the speaker reaffirming and supplementing his own preceding words: 'Yes.' (Cf. *μὲν οὖν*, 'No', and *δῆτα*, 'Yes', in continuous speech.) Epexegetic *γε*, which is common in drama, but extremely rare in prose, has considerable stylistic importance, though it has not been adequately recognized. Hence in some passages the particle has been suspected or altered, though in others editors have, with a true instinct, restored *γε* for *τε*. The epexegesis takes various forms:—

(i) A substantive or pronoun in apposition. (As *τε* also is employed in apposition (*q.v.*I.1.*e*) the decision between *γε* and *τε* is sometimes difficult.) A.*Ch.*94 *ἐσθλ' ἀντιδοῦναι ... δόσιν γε τῶν κακῶν ἐπαξίαν* (*γε* Stanley: *τε M*: 'even a gift worthy of ...'):

S.*Ph.*977 'Ὀδυσσέως, σάφ' ἴσθ', ἐμοῦ γ', ὃν εἰσορᾷς: *OC* 1278 ὡς μή μ' ἄτιμον, τοῦ θεοῦ γε προστάτην, οὕτως ἀφῇ ('me, the suppliant of the god'): E.*Heracl.*856 δισσὼ γὰρ ἀστέρ' . . . ἔκρυψαν ἅρμα λυγαίῳ νέφει· σὸν δὴ λέγουσι παῖδά γ' οἱ σοφώτεροι Ἥβην θ': *Ion* 1429 δώρημ' Ἀθάνας . . . Ἐριχθονίου γε τοῦ πάλαι μιμήματα (where γε is sound, even without the assumption of a break in the lines: 'nämlich', Wilamowitz): *Ba.*926 οὐχὶ τὴν Ἰνοῦς στάσιν, ἢ τὴν Ἀγαύης ἑστάναι, μητρός γ' ἐμῆς (μητρός γ' *p*: μητρὸς *P*): *IA* 252 Παλλάδ' ἐν μωνύχοις ἔχων πτερωτοῖσιν ἅρμασιν θετόν, εὔσημόν γε φάσμα ναυβάταις (γε Musgrave: τε *LP*): 1454 Πατέρα τὸν ἀμὸν μὴ στύγει, πόσιν γε σόν (γε Elmsley: τε *LP*): Ar.*Ach.*1185 πανύστατόν σ' ἰδὼν λείπω, φάος γε τοὐμόν: *Nu.*1190 ἐς δύ' ἡμέρας ἔθηκεν, ἔς γε τὴν ἕνην τε καὶ νέαν: *Pl.* 309 Οὐκοῦν σὲ τὴν Κίρκην γε . . . (not σε, surely): Pl.Com.*Fr.* 46.8 τίθημι κοττάβεια σφῷν ἐγώ, τασδί γε τὰς κρηπῖδας ἃς αὕτη φορεῖ, καὶ τὸν κότυλον τὸν σόν (τε Elmsley): S.*Ph.*1214: E. *Andr.*25: *IA* 85: Pl.*Cra.*438E ἆρα δι' ἄλλου του ἢ οὗπερ εἰκός τε καὶ δικαιότατον, δι' ἀλλήλων γε (τε Heindorf).

(ii) A participial clause. Sol.*Fr.*2.4 εἴην δὴ τότ' ἐγὼ Φολεγάνδριος ἢ Σικινίτης, ἀντί γ' Ἀθηναίου πατρίδ' ἀμειψάμενος: A. *Pers.*847 μάλιστα δ' ἥδε συμφορὰ δάκνει, ἀτιμίαν γε παιδὸς ἀμφὶ σώματι ἐσθημάτων κλύουσαν (Paley calls this γε 'intolerable'): E.*HF* 756 ἀντίποινα δ' ἐκτίνων τόλμα, διδούς γε τῶν δεδραμένων δίκην ('aye, paying the penalty . . .'): *IA* 1376 τοῦτο δ' αὐτὸ βούλομαι εὐκλεῶς πρᾶξαι, παρεῖσά γ' ἐκποδὼν τὸ δυσγενές: *Cyc.* 163 Δράσω τάδ', ὀλίγον φροντίσας γε δεσποτῶν: *HF* 770 ὁ δὲ παλαίτερος κρατεῖ, λιμένα λιπών γε τὸν Ἀχερόντιον (γε *L*: τε *P*: 'Aye, he hath left . . .'): Ar.*Pax* 483 ἕλκουσιν . . . ὥσπερ κυνίδια, ὑπὸ τοῦ γε λιμοῦ νὴ Δί' ἐξολωλότες (Yes, by Jove, they're *starving*'): A.*Pr.*948 read, perhaps, γ' for τ', which edd., following Elmsley, delete): S.*El.*1075 (Pearson): E.*Ion* 1138 (but 1138–9 are doubtful, and the γε, which troubled Paley, is here unnatural, and comes curiously late: 'A square, aye, of 10,000 square feet'): *Hel.*955: *IA* 1514: Hp.*Art.*32 κατορθῶσαι μὲν χρὴ τὸ ὀστέον, παρά γε τὴν γλῶσσαν πλαγίην ὑπείραντα τοὺς δακτύλους: 74 μοχλεύειν χρὴ . . . κατά γε αὐτὸν τὸν γλουτὸν τιθέμενον τὸν μοχλόν (reading doubtful). See also δέ, I.A.3.

(iii) A relative clause. E.*Med.*1340 οὐκ ἔστιν ἥτις τοῦτ' ἂν Ἑλληνὶς γυνὴ ἔτλη ποθ', ὧν γε πρόσθεν ἠξίουν ἐγὼ γῆμαι σέ ('those Greek women whom I rejected for *you*'): *IA* 1572 δέξαι τὸ θῦμα τόδ', ὅ γέ σοι δωρούμεθα ('even that which we offer to thee'): Ar.*V.*150 ἀτὰρ ἄθλιός γ' εἴμ', ὡς ἕτερός γ' οὐδεὶς ἀνήρ: 1268 Ἀμυνίας . . . οὗτος ὅν γ' ἐγώ ποτ' εἶδον: Pl.*Tht.*170E μάλα μυρίοι δῆτα . . . οἵ γέ μοι τὰ ἐξ ἀνθρώπων πράγματα παρέχουσιν ('And they are the people who . . .'): X.*Hier.*1.11 (γ' ἅ Marchant: τά *codd.*). In E.*HF* 850 οὗ γε can hardly be right.

(iv) Rarely, a repeated word. E.*Alc.*218 Δῆλα μέν, φίλοι, δῆλά γ' ('Aye, plain': δ' *V*): Ar.*Pax* 280 Οἴμοι τάλας, οἴμοι γε.

(v) An adverb or adverbial phrase. S.*OC* 1416 Στρέψαι στράτευμ' εἰς Ἄργος, ὡς τάχιστά γε: E.*Or.*212 ὡς ἡδύ μοι προσῆλθες, ἐν δέοντί γε ('Aye, in my hour of need': more forcible than τε Stob.): Ar.*Ra.*1135 Εὐθὺς γὰρ ἡμάρτηκεν, οὐράνιόν γ' ὅσον.

(vi) A consecutive or final clause. Ar.*Nu.*1342 Ἀλλ' οἴομαι μέντοι σ' ἀναπείσειν ὥστε γε οὐδ' αὐτὸς . . . ἀντερεῖς (cf. I.11.v): X.*Cyr.*i 6.29 οὐδ' ἀκοντίζειν ἄνθρωπον ἐπετρέπομεν ὑμῖν, ἀλλ' ἐπὶ σκοπὸν βάλλειν ἐδιδάσκομεν, ἵνα γε νῦν μὲν μὴ κακουργοίητε τοὺς φίλους. (But in Pl.*Phd.*67B (ὥστε ἥ γ' ἀποδημία . . .) γε goes rather more closely with the substantive.)

In Pl.*Sph.*217B γε, while not falling under any of the above categories, may be regarded as epexegetic: φθόνος μὲν γὰρ οὐδεὶς . . . εἰπεῖν ὅτι γε τρί' ἡγοῦντο (γε gives the effect of a slight pause after εἰπεῖν: 'I do not grudge the answer, that they considered them to be three'.)

II. Limitative. This, as I have observed, is the predominating use of γε, in prose at any rate, except in certain well-marked idioms. Classification can only be approximate, and the reader may often disagree with my assignment of examples to I or II.

(1) In general. As remarked above, we must distinguish[1] between (i) cases where an extension of application is not excluded (here γε means 'at least'): (ii) cases where it is, at any rate for the purpose in hand, excluded (here γε often approximates to μέν).

(i) Hom.K 556 ῥεῖα θεός γ' ἐθέλων καὶ ἀμείνονας . . . ἵππους δωρήσαιτο: S.*Aj.*469 ἀλλ' ὧδέ γ' Ἀτρείδας ἂν εὐφράναιμί που

[1] This distinction once stated and illustrated, I shall not complicate classification by observing it in the particular types (2) &c. below.

('by doing *that*' ('whatever effect on them another action might have')): 1342 ὥστ' οὐκ ἂν ἐνδίκως γ' ἀτιμάζοιτό σοι ('though he might be *wrongfully* dishonoured'): *El.*137 Ἀλλ' οὔτοι τόν γ' ἐξ Ἀΐδα παγκοίνου λίμνας πατέρ' ἀνστάσεις οὔτε γόοις οὔτε λιταῖσιν ('whether or not prayer is likely to be successful in other cases'): Ar.*Av.*816 οὐδ' ἂν χαμεύνῃ πάνυ γε κειρίαν γ' ἔχων: S.*El.*387, 518: *OT* 357,361: Pl.*Grg.*505A συγχωρεῖς τοῦτό γε καὶ σύ: *Phdr.*243B σοφώτερος ἐκείνων γενήσομαι κατ' αὐτό γε τοῦτο ('just in *this* respect'): *Phd.*65B ἢ τά γε τοιαῦτα καὶ οἱ ποιηταὶ ἡμῖν ἀεὶ θρυλοῦσιν: 69D ὧν δὴ καὶ ἐγὼ κατά γε τὸ δυνατὸν οὐδὲν ἀπέλιπον ἐν τῷ βίῳ: 85B ἀλλὰ τούτου γ' ἕνεκα λέγειν τε χρή: D.viii 28,44,49,53.

(ii) Hom.*Δ*372 **Τυδέος υἱὲ** . . . τί πτώσσεις . . .; οὐ μὲν **Τυδέϊ** γ' ὧδε φίλον πτωσκαζέμεν ἦεν ('*Tydeus* didn't skulk (but *you do*')): ***H***142 δόλῳ, οὔ τι κράτεΐ γε: 393 οὔ φησιν δώσειν· ἦ μὴν **Τρῶές** γε κέλονται ('I warrant the *Trojans bid* him'): *N*325 ἐν γ' αὐτοσταδίῃ· ποσὶ δ' οὔ πως ἔστιν ἐρίζειν: λ264 πύργωσάν τ', ἐπεὶ οὐ μὲν ἀπύργωτόν γ' ἐδύναντο ναιέμεν εὐρύχορον Θήβην: S.*Aj.*1067 εἰ γὰρ βλέποντος μὴ 'δυνήθημεν κρατεῖν, πάντως θανόντος γ' ἄρξομεν: *El.*319 **Φησίν** γε· φάσκων δ' οὐδὲν ὧν λέγει ποεῖ: E. *Andr.*5 ζηλωτὸς ἔν γε τῷ πρὶν Ἀνδρομάχῃ χρόνῳ, νῦν δ' . . . δυστυχεστάτη: *Hel.*432 ἐλπὶς δ' ἔκ γε πλουσίων δόμων λαβεῖν τι ναύταις· ἐκ δὲ μὴ ἐχόντων βίον . . .: 829 **Κοινῇ** γ' ἐκείνῃ ῥᾳδίως, λάθρᾳ δ' ἂν οὔ: *Ion* 414 **Ἡμεῖς** τά γ' ἔξω, τῶν ἔσω δ' ἄλλοις μέλει: Ar.*Ec.*985 ἐπὶ τῆς προτέρας ἀρχῆς γε . . . νυνὶ δὲ . . .: S.*Aj.*182: *El.*520,561,1023: *OT* 105,363,712: *Ant.*456,771: *Tr.*1211: *Ph.*907: E.*Ion* 1353: *El.*36–7: Ar.*Pax* 327: Pl.*Grg.* 517B οὐδ' ἐγὼ ψέγω τούτους ὥς γε διακόνους εἶναι πόλεως ('but in another respect I do blame them'): *Smp.*187A . . . βούλεται λέγειν, ἐπεὶ τοῖς γε ῥήμασιν οὐ καλῶς λέγει: *Phd.*60E ἔν γε τῷ πρόσθεν χρόνῳ . . . νῦν δὲ . . .: *Ly.*205D: *Men.*72C: *Phd.*117C: *Cra.*392D,420B: *Tht.*144D,165B.

(2) An important branch of the limitative use of γε is its use with relative pronouns, and with conditional and causal conjunctions. γε denotes that the speaker or writer is not concerned with what might or might not be true apart from the qualification laid down in the subordinate clause.

(i) With relative pronouns, *ut qui*, *quippe qui*. S.*El.*911 πῶς γάρ; ᾗ γε μηδὲ πρὸς θεοὺς ἔξεστ' ἀκλαύτῳ τῆσδ' ἀποστῆναι στέγης ('since I am one who ...'): 923 Πῶς δ' οὐκ ἐγὼ κάτοιδ' ἅ γ' εἶδον ἐμφανῶς; *Ph.*1282 οὐ γάρ ποτ' εὔνουν τὴν ἐμὴν κτήσῃ φρένα, ὅστις γε ...: Ar.*Ach.*1152 Ἀντίμαχον ... κακῶς ἐξολέσειεν ὁ Ζεύς· ὅς γ' ... ('a man who ...'): S.*OT* 35,853: *Ph.* 663,1364,1386: E.*Alc.*620: Pl.*Grg.*471B ἐπεὶ τὰ μέγιστα ἠδίκηκεν· ὅς γε ...: 487B πῶς γὰρ οὔ; ὥ γε εἰς τοσοῦτον αἰσχύνης ἐληλύθατον ...: *Phd.*96E: *R.*343A,349C,396B,402E,404A.

(ii) With conditional and causal conjunctions, *si quidem*, *quippe cum*, etc. Hom.*Λ*762 ὣς ἔον, εἴ ποτ' ἔον γε, μετ' ἀνδράσιν: η315 εἴ κ' ἐθέλων γε μένοις· ἀέκοντα δέ σ' οὔ τις ἐρύξει: S.*El.*1105 Ἥδ', εἰ τὸν ἄγχιστόν γε κηρύσσειν χρεών: *OT* 1015 Πῶς δ' οὐχί, παῖς γ' εἰ τῶνδε γεννητῶν ἔφυν; (order remarkable): Ar.*Eq.*276 Ἀλλ' ἐὰν μέντοι γε νικᾷς τῇ βοῇ, τήνελλος εἶ (ἀλλά goes with μέντοι and ἐάν with γε): S.*OT* 294,383,583: *OC* 648: E.*Med.*88,512: Ar.*Av.*1571: Hp.*Int.*50 εἶτα ἐξέρχεται μελετωμένη καλῶς ἐν χρόνῳ, ἤν γε καὶ μὴ καταρχὰς ἰηθῇ (this combination of εἴ γε, 'if, that is', with εἰ καί, 'even if', is easily intelligible, though, strictly speaking, illogical: γε καί *om.* *EHKθ*): Hdt.viii 140α2 ἢν δὴ βούλωνταί γε ('if, that is, they really wish'): Th.vi 18.2 ἐπεὶ εἴ γε ἡσυχάζοιεν ...: Pl.*Euthd.*272D Ἀλλ' οὐδὲν κωλύει ... ἐάν γε σοὶ δοκῇ ('if, that is, you want it to be so'): *Phd.*106D σχολῇ γὰρ ἄν τι ἄλλο φθορὰν μὴ δέχοιτο, εἰ τό γε ἀθάνατον ... φθορὰν δέξεται: Hdt.iii 73: Pl.*Phd.*115C: *La.*192C.

S.*Aj.*716 κοὐδὲν ἀναύδατον φατίσαιμ' ἄν, εὖτέ γ' ἐξ ἀέλπτων Αἴας μετανεγνώσθη: *OC* 1699 καὶ γὰρ ὃ μηδαμὰ δὴ φίλον, ἦν φίλον, ὁπότε γε καὶ τὸν ἐν χεροῖν κατεῖχον: Ar.*Pax* 1251 ὥς μ' ἀπώλεσας, ὅτ' ἀντέδωκά γ' ἀντὶ τῶνδε μνᾶν ποτέ (γ' *om.* *RV*): S.*El.*631 Οὔκουν ἐάσεις ... θῦσαί μ', ἐπειδὴ σοί γ' ἐφῆκα πᾶν λέγειν; E.*Hipp.*946 δεῖξον δ', ἐπειδή γ' ἐς μίασμ' ἐλήλυθας ...: Ar.*Th.*145 ἀλλὰ δῆτ' ἐκ τοῦ μέλους ζητῶ σ', ἐπειδή γ' αὐτὸς οὐ βούλει φράσαι; E.*Cyc.*181 ἐπεί γε πολλοῖς ἥδεται γαμουμένη (Pearson remarks, on E.*Hel.* 556, that γε, when it follows ἐπεί immediately, 'emphasizes the whole of the subordinate clause': but that 'it is far more commonly attached to a single member of the clause'. But such distinctions, particularly as regards verse, must not be unduly pressed):[1] S.*Ph.*1098: E.*Cyc.*220: *Med.*495: *Heracl.*562: *HF* 141: *Hipp.*955: *Ph.*554: Ar.*Nu.*

[1] See also Radermacher, *Obs. in Eur. Misc.*, p. 37.

1412: *Pax* 628: Pl.*Cri.*49B ἐπειδή γε οὐδαμῶς δεῖ ἀδικεῖν: *Phd.* 114D ἐπείπερ ἀθάνατόν γε ἡ ψυχὴ φαίνεται οὖσα: *Cra.*410A Οὐ τοίνυν δεῖ ταῦτα προσβιάζεσθαι, ἐπεὶ ἔχοι γ' ἄν τις εἰπεῖν: Hdt. i 60.3: Pl.*Phd.*77D,84E: *Smp.*208C: *Tht.*158B,167C.

(3) ὡς (' for ') . . . γε is especially common in Euripides and Aristophanes, and seems to become almost a stereotyped idiom, in which γε often retains little force. When ὡς is first word in an answer, γε does double duty, both assenting and qualifying ὡς.

S.*OC* 45 τὸν ἱκέτην δεξαίατο· ὡς οὐχ ἕδρας γε τῆσδ' ἂν ἐξέλθοιμ' ἔτι: E.*Cyc.*164 ὡς ἐκπιεῖν γ' ἂν κύλικα μαινοίμην μίαν: A.*Pers.*260: *Pr.*77: S.*Ant.*1312: *Ph.*117,812: E.*Cyc.*168,247, 336,439: *Alc.*800: *Hipp.*651: *Andr.*923: *Hec.*346,433: *Supp.* 294: *El.*901: *IT* 1035: *Ion* 759,935,1416: *Or.*93,1212: *Ba.* 1272: *IA* 1005,1010: Ar.*Ach.*327,346: *V.*218: *Pax* 942: *Av.* 540,605,798: *Lys.*865,1029,1241,1246: *Ra.*955: *Ec.*838. Rare in prose. X.*Cyr.*i 4.13 ὡς βουλεύομαί γε ὅπως . . .: viii 3.27 ὡς βαλῶ γε ταύτῃ τῇ βώλῳ: Pl.*Alc.I* 131E: Aen.Tact.28.4.

(4) Similarly, γε in a participial clause denotes that the main clause is only valid in so far as the participial clause is valid: whether or not the participial clause is in fact known to be valid. (Hence the sense may, according to context, be either *quippe cum*, or *dummodo, si quidem*: and σώφρων γ' οὖσα can either mean ' since you are wise ' or ' if you are wise '.)

S.*OT* 326 Μὴ πρὸς θεῶν φρονῶν γ' ἀποστραφῇς (' if you are in your right mind '): 930 Ἀλλ' ὀλβία . . . γένοιτ', ἐκείνου γ' οὖσα παντελὴς δάμαρ (' quippe quae sit . . . '): E.*HF* 1302 τί κέρδος ἕξομεν, βίον γ' ἀχρεῖον ἀνόσιον κεκτημένοι; S.*El.*365: *Ant.*745: *Ph.*587: Hdt.vii 129.1 εἶναι λίμνην, ὥστε γε συγκεκλῃμένην . . . ὄρεσι (γε *om. ABC*): Pl.*Chrm.*154E πρέπει δέ που . . . τοιοῦτον αὐτὸν εἶναι τῆς γε ὑμετέρας ὄντα οἰκίας: *Cra.*407E Ἀλλὰ ποιήσω ταῦτα, ἔτι γε ἓν ἐρόμενός σε (' but not before asking you one further question '): D.xxvii 27 ἐπίτροπόν γ' ὄντα (in his capacity of guardian): xxxvii 25 οὔτε γὰρ καθίστην ἐγώ, ὅ γ' ὢν ἐν τῷ Πόντῳ: Pl.*Phd.*94C,98A,103D: *Cra.*406D: *Chrm.*162A: *Tht.* 197A: D.xxvii 37.

(5) *A fortiori*, negative. (See I.1, p. 118, note 1). Pl.*Cra.*426A

καίτοι ὅτῳ τις τρόπῳ τῶν πρώτων ὀνομάτων τὴν ὀρθότητα μὴ οἶδεν, ἀδύνατόν που τῶν γε ὑστέρων εἰδέναι. So also μή τί γε, μή τι . . . γε. D.xxi 148 ἀλλ' οὐδὲ καθ' αὑτὸν στρατιώτης οὗτος οὐδενός ἐστ' ἄξιος, μή τί γε τῶν ἄλλων ἡγεμών ('certainly not, anyway . . .'): viii 27: xix 137: xxii 45, 53: xxiv 165. μή τί γε δή D.ii 23: liv 17. Cf. δή, I.10.vi.

(6) Duplication of γε. Emphatic and limitative γε are sometimes found in close proximity. S.*OC* 387 (the first γε marks the affirmative answer, the second is limitative): 977 (if the first γε is sound): E.*Ph.* 554 (the first γε closely with ἐπεί): Hdt.i 187: X.*Cyr.* ii 2.3: Lys.xxxi 29 (both limitative). In S.*OT* 1030 the double γε cannot be defended on the ground that the first γε means 'yes', and the second stresses σωτήρ: the γε which we render 'yes' is really emphatic (see I.11, *ad init.*), and a doubled emphasis on a single idea, σοῦ σωτήρ, is unthinkable (whereas σοῦ γε σωτήρ, ἔν γε τῷ τότε χρόνῳ would be perfectly possible Greek, '*your deliverer, once*'). In Ar.*Ach.* 93 τε is certainly right.

III. Quasi-connective use. Strictly speaking, γε is never, in classical Greek at any rate, a connecting particle. (Wilamowitz, on E.*HF* 631, points out that it is used for τοίνυν in an inscription of Gordian's time, apparently a mistaken attempt at reviving a particle then already obsolete.) In a few passages, however, γε appears to approach a connective sense, and to soften the harshness of an asyndeton (as μέν γε does more frequently). As Wilamowitz puts it (*loc. cit.*), though I doubt whether his interpretation is appropriate in this particular case: 'Gleichwol bewirkt die hervorhebung des begriffs ἄξω λαβὼν den eindruck einer gewissen verbindung.'

(1) Quasi-connective γε usually stands where we should expect γοῦν or γάρ. (γοῦν, which is, after all, only a strengthened γε, and not in essence a connective, often comes near to γάρ in sense, since it constitutes a partial confirmation. See γοῦν I.1.ii.)

Hom.*A* 174 οὐδέ σ' ἔγωγε λίσσομαι εἵνεκ' ἐμεῖο μένειν· πάρ' ἔμοιγε καὶ ἄλλοι οἵ κέ με τιμήσουσι: E.*Heracl.* 987 ἐγὼ δὲ νεῖκος οὐχ ἑκὼν τόδ' ἠράμην· ᾔδη γε σοὶ μὲν αὐτανέψιος γεγώς: *Cyc.* 270 Αὐτὸς ἔχ' ('Keep the curse for yourself'). ἔγωγε τοῖς ξένοις τὰ χρήματα περνάντα σ' εἶδον: *IA* 449 τῷ δὲ γενναίῳ φύσιν ἄνολβα ταῦτα. προστάτην γε τοῦ βίου τὸν ὄγκον ἔχομεν (δέ Plut.*Nic.*5: γάρ *suprascr. p*): 1394 οὐ δεῖ τόνδε . . . γυναικὸς εἵνεκα . . . κατθανεῖν. εἷς γ' ἀνὴρ κρείσσων γυναικῶν μυρίων ὁρᾶν φάος: 1424 (read, no doubt, γάρ, Hermann): Ar.*V.*707 εἰ γὰρ ἐβούλοντο βίον πορίσαι τῷ δήμῳ, ῥᾴδιον ἦν ἄν. εἰσίν γε πόλεις χιλίαι αἳ νῦν τὸν φόρον ἡμῖν ἀπάγουσι: *Lys.*82 ὡς δ' εὐχροεῖς, ὡς δὲ σφριγᾷ τὸ σῶμά σου. κἂν ταῦρον ἄγχοις.—Μάλα γ' οἰῶ ναὶ τὼ σιώ· γυμνάδδομαί γα καὶ ποτὶ πυγὰν ἅλλομαι (if γα is right: *R*'s γε is impossible on Lampito's Spartan lips: 'I should think so! I take plenty of exercise, anyhow': the conjecture γάρ is perhaps unnecessary): 822 Τὴν γνάθον βούλει θένω;—Μηδαμῶς· ἔδεισά γε ('Don't! I'm *frightened*!'): Pl.*Tht.* 200E 'The best definition of ἐπιστήμη is τὴν ἀληθῆ δόξαν ἐπιστήμην εἶναι. ἀναμάρτητόν γέ πού ἐστιν τὸ δοξάζειν ἀληθῆ': D.xix 234 φέρε δή, περὶ . . . εἴπω· μικροῦ γ', ἃ μάλιστά μ' ἔδει πρὸς ὑμᾶς εἰπεῖν, παρῆλθεν: xix.148 (γ' *S* only).

At the opening of a statement forecast by the preceding words (cf. explanatory γάρ). E.*Or.*531 ἐν δ' οὖν λόγοισι τοῖς ἐμοῖς ὁμορροθεῖ· μισῇ γε πρὸς θεῶν καὶ τίνεις μητρὸς δίκας: Ar.*Ach.*628 τοῖς ἀναπαίστοις ἐπίωμεν. ἐξ οὗ γε . . .: 916 Ἐγὼ φράσω σοι . . . ἐκ τῶν πολεμίων γ' εἰσάγεις θρυαλλίδας: Pl.*Alc.II* 139D Ἐγὼ δὴ σοί γε ἐρῶ. ὑπολαμβάνομέν γε . . .: cf. *Prt.*350C. But in such cases asyndeton is quite normal in Greek, and there is little ground for attributing a connective force to the particle.

In restating or illustrating something already stated in other words. Cf. γοῦν. X.*Mem.*iv 2.5 ἁρμόσειε δ' ἂν οὕτω προοιμιάζεσθαι καὶ τοῖς βουλομένοις . . . ἐπιτήδειόν γ' ἂν αὐτοῖς εἴη τοῦ λόγου ἄρχεσθαι ἐντεῦθεν (γάρ Weiske: *totam sententiam om.* Bessario). ἐπιτηδεῖον εἴη is perhaps not quite so strong as ἁρμόσειεν ἄν, and γε, like γοῦν, implies a reservation. So, more clearly, Ar.*Av.*720 ὄρνιν τε νομίζετε πάνθ' . . .· φήμη γ' ὑμῖν ὄρνις ἐστί: X.*Mem.*i 2.54 ἕκαστος ἑαυτοῦ . . . τοῦ σώματος ὅ τι ἂν ἀχρεῖον ᾖ . . . αὐτός τε ἀφαιρεῖ καὶ ἄλλῳ παρέχει. αὐτοί τέ γε αὑτῶν ὄνυχάς τε καὶ τρίχας . . . ἀφαιροῦσι: Th.iii 63.2 ἱκανή γε ἦν . . . ('The asyndeton is softened by γε', H.F.Fox *ad loc.*). Add D.ii 28, if γ' ἄν, for κἄν, is right.

(2) In ἔπειτά γε, the particle gives emphasis to an added point.

Pl.*Tht.*147C,171A: *R.*550E,591C: *Phdr.*263C: *Amat.*138E. In the last five passages πρῶτον μέν precedes. πρῶτον μὲν ... ἔπειτα (without δέ) is of course normal Greek. But in all these six passages ἔπειτά γε opens a continuation after an interpolation by another speaker, and perhaps Plato felt the need of a particle to carry on the flow. The emphasis has a connective tinge, and γε almost replaces δέ. (So also Εἶτά γε, Pl.*R.*528D: D.xxxvi 50 ποτ' εἶχεν ἀγρόν, εἶτά γε νῦν πολλοί.) The use of γε in Ar.*Av.* 297 is similar: Οὑτοσὶ πέρδιξ, ἐκεινοσί γε νὴ Δί' ἀτταγᾶς, οὑτοσὶ δὲ πηνέλοψ (Elmsley's δέ takes all the variety out of the passage). In the following, γε may perhaps, to some extent, soften the asyndeton: Hom.κ208 βῆ δ' ἰέναι, ἅμα τῷ γε δύω καὶ εἴκοσ' ἑταῖροι: Hp.*Loc.Hom.*47 τῆς γε κλίνης τὰ πρὸς ποδῶν ὑψηλότερα εἶναι. (For X.*Hier.*6.6, see τοι, VI.4.iii.)

IV. Position. γε normally follows the word which it stresses. (And, since emphatic words normally come early in a Greek clause or sentence, γε usually comes early too: but not always: Pl.*Phd.* 87A: *La.*193E: *Smp.*182B: *Lg.*625C,666D: Lys.xxvii 14 (last word in sentence): Demosthenes sometimes ends a sentence with τοῦτό γε.) When γε follows a conjunction, εἰ, ἐπεί, &c., we may, if we like, say that it stresses the whole clause: but it is perhaps more accurate to say that it stresses the logical relationship expressed by the conjunction: thus, εἴ γε emphasizes the hypothetical nature of a statement: 'I assert a truth subject to the validity of a hypothesis, but not independently of it.'

There are, however, certain exceptions:

(1) (First and foremost). Where the emphatic word is preceded by the article, or by a preposition, γε is normally placed after the article or preposition, and before the stressed word. As Dr. Chapman observes (in an analysis of the Platonic examples), 'the tendency of the particle to come early resists its tendency to follow the important word'.

E.*Ph.*554 τοῖς γε σώφροσιν: Ar.*V.*84 ὅ γε Φιλόξενος: Pl.*Clit.* 407D τό γε τοιοῦτον: *ib.* τό γε ἀδικεῖν: 410C τό γε ἐμόν. E.*Hel.* 432 ἔκ γε πλουσίων δόμων: Pl.*Tht.*170E ἔκ γε τοῦ λόγου: 171B ὑπό γε ἐκείνου: 183C κατά γε τὴν ... μέθοδον: 183D περί γε ὧν κελεύει: 185A διά γε τοῦ ἑτέρου: 197A ἔν γε τῷ παρόντι.

But the alternative order, article-substantive-particle or preposition-substantive-particle, is not infrequent, even in prose. Chapman suggests various reasons which may have influenced the postponement of the particle:

(*a*) Unified phrases, such as ὁ αὐτός, κατὰ φύσιν, resist intrusion. Pl.*Prm.*139B Οὐδὲ μὴν ταὐτόν γε . . . ἔσται : *id.saep.* : τό γε αὐτό (*R.*439B) is much rarer : *R.*545C Κατὰ λόγον γέ τοι ἂν . . . γίγνοιτο.

(*b*) Position after the important word gives more emphasis, and is peculiarly adapted to replies, where the emphasis is often strong. Pl.*R.*563D Τὸ ἐμόν γ', ἔφη, ἐμοὶ λέγεις ὄναρ : *Hp.Mi.*374A Ἐν δρόμῳ μὲν ἄρα πονηρότερος ὁ ἄκων κακὰ ἐργαζόμενος ἢ ὁ ἑκών ;—Ἐν δρόμῳ γε : *R.*354A : *Grg.*469B : *Hp.Mi.*375B.

(With what I have called 'exclamatory' γε postponement is, I believe, obligatory. Pl.*Prt.*340E Νὴ τὸν Δία, εἰς καιρόν γε παρατετύχηκεν : *Phlb.*19A Οὐκ εἰς φαῦλόν γε ἐρώτημα . . . ἡμᾶς ἐμβέβληκε Σωκράτης : *Euthd.*292E : *R.*435C,498D : X.*Smp.*1.4 Εἰς καλόν γε ὑμῖν συντετύχηκα.)

(*c*) Intrusion of γε is sometimes perhaps avoided because it would disturb balance. Pl.*Sph.*249A Ἀλλὰ ταῦτα μὲν ἀμφότερα ἐνόντ' αὐτῷ λέγομεν, οὐ μὴν ἐν ψυχῇ γε φήσομεν αὐτὸ ἔχειν αὐτά; cf. *Hp.Mi.*374A, (*b*) above : also *Smp.*187B ἐκ διαφερομένων πρότερον . . . οὐ γὰρ δήπου ἐκ διαφερομένων γε ἔτι. . . .

(*d*) Ἀλλὰ μήν and καὶ μήν have a certain tendency to cause postponement.[1] Pl.*Prt.*359D Ἀλλὰ μὴν ἐπὶ ἅ γε θαρροῦσι πάντες αὖ ἔρχονται : *R.*381B,400D,603A.

(*e*) With καὶ . . . γε (negative, οὐδὲ . . . γε), in cases where καί is emphatic ('also' (non-connective), or 'and also'), γε is regularly, perhaps invariably,[2] postponed. Pl.*Phd.*58D Ἀλλὰ μὴν . . . καὶ τοὺς ἀκουσομένους γε τοιούτους ἑτέρους ἔχεις : *R.*540C Παγκάλους, ἔφη, τοὺς ἄρχοντας . . . ἀπείργασαι.—Καὶ τὰς ἀρχούσας γε : *Phd.*72E : *Cra.*386D. (Chapman has noted 11 cases of postponement of γε with the article after emphatic καί, and 8 with a preposition. He observes that, even when καί is unemphatic, or less definitely emphatic (e.g. *Prt.*345C), there is still a tendency to postpone γε : and has noted 7 such cases where it is postponed

[1] Postponement after these combinations may be slightly more frequent than elsewhere : but, judging by my own incomplete statistics, it is very far indeed from being normal.

[2] But *R.*431B Καὶ μὴν καὶ τάς γε πολλὰς . . . ἐπιθυμίας (τε Stob.).

with the article, and 8 where it is postponed with a preposition, against 11 and 2, respectively, where it is not postponed.)

(*f*) Where γε is postponed with a prepositional phrase which also contains the article, it is ordinarily placed after the word with which the article agrees, not after the article itself. Thus the alternative to the regular *κατά γε τὸν λόγον* is not *κατὰ τόν γε λόγον*, but *κατὰ τὸν λόγον γε*. Pl.*Cra.*435A *Ἀπὸ τοῦ ἀνομοίου γε*: *Grg.*449E,460E. The only exception noted by Chapman is *Smp.* 200D *ἐπεὶ ἐν τῷ γε νῦν παρόντι . . . ἔχεις* (influenced, probably, by by the intrusion of *νῦν*: the order *ἐν τῷ νῦν παρόντι γε* would entail excessive postponement: contrast *Tht.*197A (IV.1, above)).

(*g*) The juxtaposition of *οὐ* (*μή*) and γε is avoided. *οὐ* (*μή*) and the following word form a unity, and γε follows both. Pl.*Cri.* 53A *καὶ οὐ καταγέλαστός γε ἔσῃ*: *Ly.*204A: *Prm.*149E: *Ap.*27B: D.xlvii 60: Hence I suspect E.*Ion* 361 *καὶ μή γ' ἐπ' οἶκτόν μ' ἔξαγε.*

Chapman observes that the number of cases in which γε is postponed with article and with preposition is relatively not large. Apart from *καὶ . . . γε*, *οὐδὲ . . . γε*, he has counted 39 such places with article, and 42 with preposition. I add a few further Platonic examples: with article, *Prt.*331B: *Tht.*165B: with preposition, *Men.*89E: *Grg.*449E,477D: *Phdr.*243B: *Euthd.*274A: *Ti.*56D: *Cra.*438D,E: *Tht.*170D: *Phd.*74C,79B: *Sph.*226E: with article and preposition, *Alc.I* 115C: *Grg.*460E.

Of other prose-writers, I have examined Demosthenes alone with some care in this matter. Of the order article-substantive-particle I find no instance, except xxii 57 *ἀλλὰ τὸ πρᾶγμά γ' οὐκ ἐπιτήδειον γίγνεσθαι*: and lvii 70, where a preposition precedes: *ὥστε ἐν τῇ πατρίδι γε . . . ταφῆναι.* The order preposition-article-particle, noted above (*f*) as exceptional in Plato, occurs in xxiii 193 *καὶ μὴν περὶ τοῦ γε μὴ μνησικακεῖν*: (but xxxvi 43 *ἀλλὰ μὴν περί γε τῆς εὐπορίας*). In xxix 38 *F* alone gives *περὶ τοῦ γ'*: in xxxvii 55 *S* alone gives *περὶ τοῦ ἐμοῦ γε βαδίσματος.* The great majority of cases in which γε is postponed after a preposition concern disyllabic prepositions, and examination of the passages suggests that avoidance of *tres breves* often perhaps influenced the order. ix 30: xiii 26: xvi 24: xviii 113,251,273: xix 150,249 (*ἀλλ' οὖν ἐν ταύτῃ γ' ἔζη*, where Demosthenes may have wished to balance *ταύτης ἔπι* above (besides avoiding hiatus): cf. (*c*)): xx 94: xxi 41: xxiii 153: xxix 32: xxx 10: xxxvii 13:

xxxix 28 : xliv 56 (*bis*) : lii 24. But in xviii 113 the tribrach is tolerated, καὶ διά γε τοῦτο : cf. xix 179 : xxiii 193 : xliv 59 : lvii 1 : lix 8.

In Isocrates, according to Chapman, the only example of postponed γε is xii 202 δι' ἐκεῖνό γε : from Xenophon I note *An*.vii 6.21 εἰ ὑπὸ πολεμίου γε ὄντος ἐξηπατήθην : *Hier*.3.9 ὑπ' ἄλλου γέ τινος.

In verse postponement is far commoner.

With article. S.*OT* 1007 : *Ant*.217,648 : *OC*.387,1278 : E. *Hipp*.412 : *Ion* 532,547,957 : *IT* 120 : *Ba*.966 : Ar.*Nu*.431,1217 : *V*.917 : *Pax* 625,628,966 : *Th*.207 : *Ra*.1393 : *Pl*.309.

With preposition. S.*El*.1029 : *Ant*.322,556 : *OT* 80,1169 : *Ph*.1403 : *OC* 966 : E.*Alc*.524,718 : *Hec*.1004 : *Ion* 270,550 : *Hel*. 1038 : *Or*.212,1074 : *Ph*.1741 : *IA* 515,1368 : *El*.37 : Ar.*Ach*.5, 60 : *Eq*.258,1310 : *Nu*.1180,1379 : *Pax* 386 : *Av*.642 : *Ra*.1198.

With article and preposition. Ar.*Ach*.916 : *V*.416. Preposition-article-particle-substantive : Ar.*Pax* 483 ὑπὸ τοῦ γε λιμοῦ.

(2) Other divergencies from normal order are seldom found.

(i) Occasionally the less important of two closely connected words (e.g. substantive and adjective in agreement) precedes γε, while the more important word follows it, instead of vice versa. Metrical convenience is probably a factor in most cases.

Hom.K403 ἀνδράσι γε θνητοῖσι : θ139 οὐ . . . κακώτερον ἄλλο θαλάσσης ἄνδρα γε συγχεῦαι : S.*OT* 712 οὐκ ἐρῶ Φοίβου γ' ἀπ' αὐτοῦ : *El*.1221 Ἦ ζῇ γὰρ ἀνήρ ;—Εἴπερ ἔμψυχός γ' ἐγώ : *OT* 80 εἰ γὰρ ἐν τύχῃ γέ τῳ σωτῆρι βαίη : *Aj*.84 εἴπερ ὀφθαλμοῖς γε τοῖς αὐτοῖς ὁρᾷ : 812 σῴζειν θέλοντες ἄνδρα γ' ὃς σπεύδει θανεῖν (where γε emphasizes the whole phrase ἄνδρα ὃς σπεύδει θανεῖν : cf. S.*El*.1506) : *Tr*.425 ταῦτά γ' εἰσήκουσ' ὄχλος.—Ναί· κλύειν γ' ἔφασκον ('Aye, *said* they heard') : *OC* 27 εἴπερ ἐστί γ' ἐξοικήσιμος ('if it is *inhabited*' : but γε goes rather with εἴπερ, 'if, that is') : *OT* 1066 Καὶ μὴν φρονοῦσά γ' εὖ τὰ λῷστά σοι λέγω : *Ant*.747 γυναικὸς ὕστερον.—Οὔ τἂν ἕλοις ἥσσω γε τῶν αἰσχρῶν ἐμέ : E.*El*.647 Ἐγὼ φόνον γε μητρὸς ἐξαρτύσομαι (as opposed to that of Aegisthus) : *Ba*.501 οὐ γὰρ φανερὸς ὄμμασίν γ' ἐμοῖς : Ar.*Av*.378 παρ' ἀνδρῶν γ' ἔμαθον ἐχθρῶν κοὐ φίλων (metrical consideration absent) : *Lys*.1024 Πρῶτα μὲν φαίνει γ' ἀνήρ, εἶτ' οὐ καταγέλαστος εἶ.*

There are very few prose examples. Pl.*Lg.*901B ᾧ δὴ προσήκει μὲν . . . ἐπιμελεῖσθαι . . ., ὁ δὲ τούτου γε νοῦς τῶν μὲν μεγάλων ἐπιμελεῖται, τῶν σμικρῶν δὲ ἀμελεῖ ('when a man's *duty* is to look after . . ., but his *mind* neglects the details'): *Phd.*116C οὐ καταγνώσομαί γε σοῦ ('I won't accuse *you*': γε *om. B*): Aeschin.iii 132 οὐ γὰρ βίον γε ἡμεῖς ἀνθρώπινον βεβιώκαμεν. But in the two latter passages γε perhaps leans back on the negative: 'at any rate not.' See p. 151, note 1. For Pl.*R.*453D see I.9.

(ii) Rarely the important word comes first and γε at the end, instead of in the middle, of the phrase. Hom.Ξ196 τελέσαι δέ με θυμὸς ἄνωγεν, εἰ δύναμαι τελέσαι γε: E.*Cyc.*283 Αἰσχρὸν στράτευμά γ': *Ion*221 (text uncertain): *IT*587 (Markland's σφε is probably right): *Hel.*837 Ταὐτῷ ξίφει γε: Ar.*Pl.*21 στέφανον ἔχοντά γε: 1083: Pl.*Ly.*214E καίτοι δυσχεραίνω τί γε (γέ τι H. Richards). In *ib.*204A Σὸς ἑταῖρός γε (γε *scr. recc.*: τε *BTW*) both words have equal value.

To some extent the emphatic and the unemphatic word form a unity which γε emphasizes. This is clearly the case where two words virtually form a compound. Ar.*V.*218 ὡς ἀπὸ μέσων νυκτῶν γε παρακαλοῦσ' ἀεί ('midnight'): *Nu.*676: D.xix250 καὶ θεοῖς ἐχθρός γε ('god-forsaken').

V. Γε combined with other particles. (See also I.1.ii.)

(1) The following observations are drawn from an unpublished paper of Dr. R. W. Chapman on the Platonic use of particles. They hold good, I think, for Greek in general.

γε is very frequently found, with intervening word or words, after certain other particles and combinations of particles: notably after ἀλλ' οὖν, ἀλλὰ μέντοι, ἀλλὰ μὲν δή, ἀλλὰ μήν, καὶ μήν, καίτοι, οὐ μήν, οὐ μέντοι, οὐ γάρ που, οὐ γὰρ δή, οὐ γὰρ δήπου. That γε in such cases forms an integral part of a combination is indicated by the fact that in later Greek μέντοιγε, καίτοιγε, and even μενοῦνγε coalesce into single words, and by the frequency with which γε follows the combinations enumerated above. Thus in Plato ἀλλὰ μήν is followed by γε in probably 75 per cent. of the cases, or more: καὶ μήν in about 50 per cent. (see Neil, *Knights*, p. 193): καίτοι in perhaps 30 per cent. ἀλλὰ μήν without γε is often ἀλλὰ μὴν καί, ἀλλὰ μήν που.

Moreover, γε is absent from certain phrases where it might be expected to be present. Thus γε regularly follows οὐ γὰρ δή, but rarely οὐ γὰρ οὖν: commonly καὶ μήν, rarely καὶ δή (p. 249). Again, γε tends to follow negatives. Thus γάρ που and γὰρ ... που occur more than 130 times in Plato, and γε follows in only one or two places. οὐ γάρ που, οὐ γὰρ ... που occur about 17 times without γε, about 39 times with γε. The case with γὰρ δή is similar. Again: οὐ μήν 3, οὐ μὴν ... γε 18: οὐ μὴν οὐδέ 2, οὐ μὴν οὐδὲ ... γε 3: οὐδὲ μήν 13, οὐδὲ μὴν ... γε 13: οὐ μὴν ἀλλά 4, οὐ μὴν ἀλλὰ ... γε 6. The reason for this tendency of γε to follow negatives is clearly that in a positive sentence the emphatic word will naturally come first, and position will of itself give the due emphasis: τοῦτο γάρ που λέγεις (but for the avoidance of γε γάρ see Introd.III.2): whereas, when the negative claims first place, and denies it to the emphatic word, a particle is needed to give the emphasis: οὐ γάρ που τοῦτό γε λέγεις. It is of course true that the word before γε is normally the emphatic word: and that, in οὐ γάρ που τοῦτό γε λέγεις, γε does emphasize τοῦτο. But that does not exclude the possibility that γε also attaches itself to the preceding particles: and that this is in fact so, follows from the consideration of passages in which γε is preceded by an unemphatic word.[1] *Grg.*489D οὐ γὰρ δήπου σύ γε τοὺς δύο βελτίους ἡγῇ τοῦ ἑνός (emphasis on τοὺς δύο): *R.*509A (emphasis on ἡδονήν): *La.*195A Οὔκουν φησί γε Νικίας (emphasis on Νικίας): *Ap.*20C. (As against this, however, it must be admitted that in three of these four passages γε follows the second person pronoun singular, which in general tends to attract it. See I.4.)

The conclusion would appear to be somewhat as follows. In such combinations as ἀλλὰ μὴν ... γε, οὐ γάρ που ... γε, γε usually emphasizes both the combination (I emphasize that I am adding something, or ruling something out), and also the most important word in the clause: but sometimes it only emphasizes the combination.

[1] E.g. in Pl.*Smp.*205E ἐὰν μὴ τυγχάνῃ γέ που ... ἀγαθὸν ὄν, where the stress is on ἀγαθόν, not on τυγχάνῃ, γε really belongs to ἐάν. Chapman notes the tendency of γε to attach itself to ὡς, εἰ, ἐάν, ὅταν: cf. II.2, 3, above. In prose, where γε is preceded by an unemphatic word, it always seems to have an earlier particle to lean back upon. See IV.2.i, *ad fin.*

(2) Juxtaposition of γε and (i) a preceding or (ii) a following particle.

(i) Except in the case of δέ γε, μέν γε, and (far less frequently) τέ γε, this is very rare. For ἀλλά γε, δή γε, καίτοι γε, μέντοι γε,[1] see ἀλλά, δή, καίτοι, μέντοι.* I treat δέ γε (δὲ . . . γε), καί γε (καὶ . . . γε), μέν γε, τέ γε separately below. It seems that καίπερ γε (though supported by εἴπερ γε) is only found, in some MSS., in Hdt.iii 42.2: while μήν γε does not occur at all. οὖν γε is highly doubtful (see οὖν II.2.i: ἀλλ' οὖν γε, see ἀλλ' οὖν *ad init.*: οὔκουν γε, see οὖν, II.5: for post-classical examples, see Headlam's note on Herondas 6.90). In Ar.*Ec*.577 *R* has γάρ τοί γε.

(ii) γε may precede δή, μέν, μέντοι, μήν, που, οὖν, τοι: see those particles. But when a negative precedes those particles, γε follows after a short interval: thus οὐ μὴν . . . γε is the negative form of γε μήν, οὔκουν . . . γε of γοῦν. According to Chapman, γε does not immediately follow οὐ in Plato, and μή γε is rare. (See IV.1.g.)

Δέ γε, δὲ . . . γε: οὐδέ γε, οὐδὲ . . . γε: καί γε, καὶ . . . γέ: μέν γε: τέ γε.

γε, in combination with δέ, καί, μέν and τε, usually has a force approximating to that of δή, but more lively and colloquial in tone.

Δέ γε: δὲ . . . γε

(No examples earlier than Aeschylus, unless Carm.Pop.17 is early or ἔπη δέ γε (for ἐπηγε δέ) is right in Alcm.*Fr*.92.)

In verse the particles are often separated by an intervening word or words. (The interval is rarely a wide one: rather wider than usual in Ar.*Eq*.713,1226: *Nu*.1277: *Ec*.728.) The choice between δέ γε and δὲ . . . γε is a mere matter of metrical convenience, entailing no difference of meaning, as the following passage shows: Ar.*Eq*.363–5 Ἐγὼ δ' ἐπεσπηδῶν γε τὴν βουλὴν βίᾳ κυκήσω.—Ἐγὼ δὲ κινήσω γέ σου τὸν πρωκτὸν ἀντὶ φύσκης.—Ἐγὼ δέ γ' ἐξέλξω σε τῆς πυγῆς θύραζε κύβδα. Cf. *Pl*.164–8. In prose, the particles are rarely separated when they are connected

[1] Chapman points out the curious fact that μέντοι γε, ἀλλά γε, καίτοι γε all occur near the opening of the *Republic* (329E,331B,332A), two out of the three in the mouth of Cephalus.

in thought. Th.v 109 τὸ δ' ἐχυρόν γε: Pl.*Ly.*215B 'Ὁ δὲ μὴ φιλῶν γ' οὐ φίλος: *Lg.*694E,731E. (In some cases there is no such connexion between the particles. S.*Ph.*1037 θεοῖσιν εἰ δίκης μέλει. ἔξοιδα δ' ὡς μέλει γε (probably, as Jebb says, γε emphasizes μέλει, 'and I know they *do* care': ὡς καὶ μέλει would be more normal. If δέ and γε went together, the force would be 'And I *know* that they care'): E.*IT* 580 (γε emphasizes μάλιστα): Pl.*Clit.*410B (γε goes closely with βλάπτειν): D.xviii 153 (τό γ' ἐξαίφνης is self-contained).) Separation in thought is possible even when the particles are juxtaposed: Ar.*Ach.*307 εἰ καλῶς ἐσπεισάμην.—Πῶς δέ γ' ἂν καλῶς λέγοις ἂν . . .; (δέ is *indignantis*: γε stresses πῶς, 'how?': cf. γε, I.6).)

(1) In retorts and lively rejoinders. In drama, the commonest use of δέ γε, δὲ . . . γε, is in retorts: particularly frequent in Aristophanes. A.*Ch.*921 Ἄλγος γυναιξὶν ἀνδρὸς εἴργεσθαι, τέκνον.—Τρέφει δέ γ' ἀνδρὸς μόχθος ἡμένας ἔσω: S.*Aj.*1150 Ἤδη ποτ' εἶδον ἄνδρ' ἐγὼ . . .—Ἐγὼ δέ γ' ἄνδρ' ὄπωπα: *Ant.*1056 Τὸ μαντικὸν γὰρ . . .—Τὸ δέ γε τυράννων . . .: *OT* 372 τυφλὸς . . . εἶ.—Σὺ δ' ἄθλιός γε: 1030 ('a gentle reproof', Jebb): E.*Heracl.* 109 Ἄθεον . . . μεθεῖναι . . .—Καλὸν δέ γ' ἔξω πραγμάτων ἔχειν πόδα: *Andr.*579 Χαλᾶν κελεύω δεσμὰ . . .—Ἐγὼ δ' ἀπαυδῶ γ': Ar.*Nu.*915 Θρασὺς εἶ πολλοῦ.—Σὺ δὲ γ' ἀρχαῖος: 920 Αὐχμεῖς αἰσχρῶς.—Σὺ δέ γ' εὖ πράττεις: *Av.*55 τῷ σκέλει θένε τὴν πέτραν.—Σὺ δὲ τῇ κεφαλῇ γ': A.*Th.*1031: *Ag.*939,941: *Supp.*746: S.*Ph.*1293: E.*Ion* 368,518,1330: *Med.*818: *HF* 1249: *Andr.*584: *Cyc.*538,637: Ar.*Eq.*356,432,443,700,744,906,908,967,1154,1156, 1257: Hdt.viii 59 ὁ Κορίνθιος στρατηγὸς . . . εἶπε· Ὦ Θεμιστόκλεες, ἐν τοῖσι ἀγῶσι οἱ προεξανιστάμενοι ῥαπίζονται. ὁ δὲ ἀπολυόμενος ἔφη· Οἱ δέ γε ἐγκαταλειπόμενοι οὐ στεφανοῦνται: Th.v. 109 (Melian Dialogue): Pl.*Phdr.*230C ἄριστά σοι ἐξενάγηται . . .—Σὺ δέ γε . . . ἀτοπώτατός τις φαίνῃ ('You've been an excellent guide'.—'And you're a very strange creature'): X.*An.*iv 6.9.

In lively rejoinders. E.*IT* 749 'By whom will you swear?'—Ἄρτεμιν . . .—Ἐγὼ δ' ἄνακτά γ' οὐρανοῦ, σεμνὸν Δία: E.*Supp.* 940: *Cyc.*708: *Hel.*564: Ar.*Pax* 50. In an antiphonal response: E.*Or.* 1239.

In imaginary dialogue: Ar.*Nu.*1417 φήσεις . . . ἐγὼ δέ γ' ἀντείποιμ' ἂν ὡς . . .: Th.iii 63.3 λέγετε ὡς αἰσχρὸν ἦν προδοῦναι τοὺς εὐεργέτας· πολὺ δέ γε αἴσχιον τοὺς πάντας Ἕλληνας καταπροδοῦναι: D.xix279 "καὶ ἠλέγχθησάν τινες αὐτῶν ἐν τῇ βουλῇ. . . ." οὗτοι δέ γε κἂν τῷ δήμῳ: xxii8: xxxiv32: xliv55: xlvi6: liv35.

(2) In Aristophanic and Platonic dialogue δέ γε often picks up the thread after a remark interpellated by another speaker. It thus connects, whether adversatively or continuatively, the speaker's words with his own previous words, not with those of the other person: 'Yes, and . . .': 'Yes, but. . . .' This use appears to be foreign to tragedy, except that in E.*Alc.*890 some MSS. give δέ γ'.

Ar.*Nu.*169 Πρώην δέ γε γνώμην μεγάλην ἀφῃρέθη: 175 Ἐχθὲς δέ γ' ἡμῖν δεῖπνον οὐκ ἦν ἑσπέρας: 211 Ἐνταῦθ' ἔνεισιν· ἡ δέ γ' Εὔβοι' . . .: *Ra.*565–7 (Καὶ . . . γ' in 564) Νὼ δὲ δεισάσα γέ που . . . ὁ δ' ᾤχετ' ἐξᾴξας γε: *Eq.*1347: *V.*605,776. Pl.*Grg.* 453D ὅτι καὶ ἄλλοι εἰσὶ ζωγράφοι . . .;—Ναί.—Εἰ δέ γε μηδεὶς ἄλλος ἢ Ζεῦξις ἔγραφε . . .: *Phdr.*265A μανίαν γάρ τινα ἐφήσαμεν εἶναι τὸν ἔρωτα. ἦ γάρ;—Ναί.—Μανίας δέ γε εἴδη δύο: *Euthphr.*13B Ἡ γάρ που κυνηγετική κυνῶν θεραπεία.—Ναί.—Ἡ δέ γε βοηλατικὴ βοῶν.—Πάνυ γε.—Ἡ δὲ δὴ (the crucial instance) ὁσιότης τε καὶ εὐσέβεια θεῶν . . .: *Phd.*81B οὕτω μὲν ἔχουσα . . . —Οὕτω νὴ Δία . . .—Ἐὰν δέ γε οἶμαι μεμιασμένη. . . .: *Prt.*340C: *Prm.*126B: *Phd.*74C,81C: 82A: *Cra.*390D,395A,418D: *Tht.*144E, 150B.

In Plato, δέ γε (δὲ . . . γε) in an answer often introduces the second (major or minor) premise of a syllogism. *Chrm.*159D Φαίνεται ἄρα . . . κατά γε τὸ σῶμα οὐ τὸ ἡσύχιον, ἀλλὰ τὸ τάχιστον . . . κάλλιστον ὄν. ἦ γάρ;—Πάνυ γε.—Ἡ δέ γε σωφροσύνη καλόν τι ἦν;—Ναί.—Οὐ τοίνυν κατά γε τὸ σῶμα ἡ ἡσυχιότης ἂν ἀλλ' ἡ ταχύτης σωφρονέστερον εἴη, ἐπειδὴ καλὸν ἡ σωφροσύνη: 159E: *Grg.*497A,498E,506E: *Euthd.*301D,302E: *Men.*96C: *Ly.* 215B.

(3) δέ γε (δὲ . . . γε) is occasionally used in answers otherwise than as in (1) and (2) above. Continuing the train of thought started by the other speaker. A.*Ch.*490 Ὦ γαῖ', ἄνες μοι πατέρ' . . .—Ὦ Περσέφασσα, δὸς δέ τ' εὔμορφον κράτος (δέ γ' Hermann: δ' ἔτ' Paley and Tucker, rightly, I think): E.*Supp.*936 Ἡ χωρὶς ἱερὸν ὡς νεκρὸν θάψαι θέλεις;—Ναί· τοὺς δέ γ' ἄλλους πάντας ἐν μιᾷ πυρᾷ: *IT*918 Στρόφιος ὁ Φωκεὺς τοῦδε κλῄζεται πατήρ.—Ὁ δ'

ἐστί γ' Ἀτρέως θυγατρὸς . . .; *HF* 1239 Κλαίω χάριν σὴν ἐφ' ἑτέραισι συμφοραῖς.—Ηὗρες δέ γ' ἄλλους ἐν κακοῖσι μείζοσιν; (I believe Fix's δ' ἔτ' is right).

(4) In continuous speech δέ γε (δὲ . . . γε) is much rarer.

(i) Strongly adversative. In the few instances from tragedy there is usually, I think, a sense of imaginary dialogue: the speaker counters his own words: cf. μὲν οὖν. E.*Or.*547 ἐγᾠδ' ἀνόσιός εἰμι μητέρα κτανών, ὅσιος δέ γ' ἕτερον ὄνομα, τιμωρῶν πατρί ('I know I am impure . . . Aye, but on another count I am pure.' I should print a stronger stop after κτανών): *Andr.*462 ἐπεὶ σὺ μὲν πέφυκας ἐν Σπάρτῃ μέγας, ἡμεῖς δὲ Τροίᾳ γ' ('Aye, but we in Troy'): *Hipp.*700: *Hec.*1248: *Ba.*1209 (γ' αὐτῇ Kirchhoff: but I believe ταύτῃ to be sound): *IA* 392.* In S.*El.*1367 δὲ . . . γε marks a break off, like ἀτάρ. Ar.*Pax* 20,150 (turning to audience).

In prose, examples are more numerous: here, again, I think there is often some tinge of repartee about δέ γε. Th.ii 54.3 ἢν δέ γε οἶμαί ποτε ἄλλος πόλεμος καταλάβῃ . . .: Pl.*Cra.*394A ὥσπερ ἡμῖν τὰ τῶν ἰατρῶν φάρμακα . . . πεποικιλμένα ἄλλα φαίνεται τὰ αὐτὰ ὄντα, τῷ δέ γε ἰατρῷ . . . τὰ αὐτὰ φαίνεται: And.i 68 οὗτοι μὲν ἔφυγον δι' ἐμέ, ὁμολογῶ· ἐσώθη δέ γε ὁ πατήρ: D.ix 31 εἰ υἱὸς . . . εἰ δέ γε δοῦλος: xxi 27 φεύγοντος μὲν . . ., δικαστῶν δέ γε . . .: 95 πένης μὲν ἴσως ἐστίν, οὐ πονηρὸς δέ γε: xxiv 129: Hdt.viii 142.5: Pl.*Grg.*483C,484A,502E: *Ap.*22D: *Chrm.*170D: X.*An.*iii 1.35: *Cyr.*ii 3.14: Arist.*Pol.*1277b28: D.v 23: xx 28: xxi 220: lvii 35. Isocrates never uses δέ γε. No doubt he found it too colloquial.

(ii) Weakly adversative, or purely continuative. There are a few apparent examples in tragedy, almost all of them suspicious.

A.*Th.*283 ἐγὼ δέ γ' ἄνδρας ἓξ . . . τάξω (δ' ἐπ' *codd.*, which Tucker keeps, taking ἐπί as adverbial): S.*Aj.*1409 παῖ, σὺ δὲ πατρός γ' . . . πλευρὰς . . . ἐπικούφιζ': *El.*548 φαίη δ' ἂν ἡ θανοῦσά γ', εἰ φωνὴν λάβοι ('Aye, and the dead maid would say so'): E.*Med.*318 τόσῳ δέ γ' ἧσσον ἢ πάρος πέποιθά σοι (τοσῷδε δ' *AVB* is, I believe, right): *IT* 113 ὅρα δέ γ' εἴσω τριγλύφων ὅποι κενὸν δέμας καθεῖναι (δὲ γεῖσα Blomfield): 1010 ἄξω δέ γ' (σ' Canter): *El.*582 (some doubt as to text).

But there is no doubt about the Aristophanic examples: *Eq.* 667 οἱ δ' ἐθορύβουν . . . ὁ δ' ἠντεβόλει γ' αὐτούς (where Neil's elaborate explanation is unnecessary): *V.*94,134: *Pax* 262,904: *Av.*641 (δέ τε *codd.*): *Th.*987: *Ec.*273: *Pl.*540. There are a few examples in prose: Hdt.viii 60γ: Ant.v 67: Pl.*Prt.*334A ἀλλ' ἔγωγε πολλὰ οἶδ' ἃ ἀνθρώποις μὲν ἀνωφελῆ ἐστι . . . τὰ δέ γε ὠφέλιμα . . . τὰ δέ γε τούτων μὲν οὐδενὶ . . . : *La.*191E: *Thg.*126A (in parenthesis): *R.*451B: *Cra.*417A: X.*An.*v 8.16. The only instance I can find in Demosthenes is lviii 44: 'They ought to prosecute Demosthenes. εἰσὶ δέ γε δεινοὶ καὶ οὗτοι' (δέ γε *AFQD*: δέ *S*).

(Ar.*Eq.*1204 is rightly divided between speakers by Neil: 'Εγὼ δ' ἐκινδύνευσ'.—'Εγὼ δ' ὤπτησά γε.)

Οὐδέ γε: οὐδὲ . . . γε (μηδέ γε: μηδὲ . . . γε)

These are the negative counterparts of δέ γε, δὲ . . . γε.

(1) Connective: 'Nor yet', 'and not . . . either'.

(i) In answers. S.*OC*1743 "Οπως μολούμεθ' ἐς δόμους οὐκ ἔχω.—Μηδέ γε μάτευε: E.*IT*570 Ψευδεῖς ὄνειροι, χαίρετ'· οὐδὲν ἦτ' ἄρα.—Οὐδ' οἱ σοφοί γε δαίμονες κεκλημένοι πτηνῶν ὀνείρων εἰσὶν ἀψευδέστεροι: *IA*308 Οὐ χρῆν σε λῦσαι δέλτον . . .—Οὐδέ γε φέρειν σὲ πᾶσιν "Ελλησιν κακά: Ar.*Pax* 457 "Αρει δὲ μή.—Μή.—Μηδ' 'Ενυαλίῳ γε: *Eq.*1309,1373: *Pax* 475: *Ra.*559: Pl.*Euthphr.*13A ἵππους οὐ πᾶς ἐπίσταται θεραπεύειν . . . Οὐδέ γε κύνας πᾶς ἐπίσταται θεραπεύειν: *Grg.*505C (ignoring Socrates' criticism): *Euthd.*299A: *Chrm.*171C.

(ii) In continuous speech. Ar.*Pax* 350 οὐδὲ δύσκολον, οὐδὲ τοὺς τρόπους γε δήπου σκληρόν: S.*OT*1378: Ar.*V.*62,1029: Pl.*Chrm.*165E οὐ γὰρ ὁμοία αὕτη πέφυκεν ταῖς ἄλλαις ἐπιστήμαις, οὐδέ γε αἱ ἄλλαι ἀλλήλαις: *R.*608B οὔτε . . . οὔτε . . . οὔτε . . . οὐδέ γε ποιητικῇ (the crucial case): D.xlvii 72 οὔτε γένει προσῆκεν ἡ ἄνθρωπος οὐδὲν . . . οὐδ' αὖ θεράπαινά γε: Pl.*Chrm.*163B: *Clit.*407B: *Phd.*97A,106B(*bis*): *Tht.*175E,180A,207E: X.*Cyr.*i 5.11 (*bis*): vii 1.48: D.v 16: xix 184: xx 138,161,162.

(2) (Rarely) non-connective, 'not . . . either', 'not even'. (Cf. καὶ . . . γε.) S.*El.*1347 Οὐχὶ ξυνίης;—Οὐδέ γ' ἐς θυμὸν φέρω (where Jebb's interpretation seems right): *OC*1702 (οὐδέ γ' Wecklein): Ar.*V.*917 Οὐδὲν μετέδωκεν οὐδὲ τῷ κοινῷ γ' ἐμοί: *Nu.*425 Οὐδ' ἂν διαλεχθείην γ' ἀτεχνῶς τοῖς ἄλλοις: D.xli 11 σκηνὴν δ' ἣν ἔχουσιν, οὐδέ γε ταύτην λαβόντες ἀναφέρουσιν.

In Pl.*R.*461C the reading μηδ' εἰς φῶς ἐκφέρειν κύημα μηδέ γ' ἕν is doubtful.

More frequently after ἀλλὰ μήν, καὶ μήν (cf. καὶ . . . γε, 2.i). Pl. *Prm.*147A Ἀλλὰ μὴν οὐδὲ τοῦ ἑνός γε μετέχει: *Lg.*728E καὶ μὴν οὐδὲ τὰ τούτων γ' ἐναντία: *Cra.*386D: D. vii 5.

Καί γε: καὶ . . . γε

Καί γε. The MSS. give καί γε, juxtaposed, in Hp. *Septim.* 9: καί γε ὁ θάνατος διὰ τὴν μοίρην ἔλαχεν: [Lys.]xi (*in Theomnestum B*, a composition of uncertain date and authorship) 7 καί γε τοῦτον μὲν ἑόρακα ποιοῦντα (καίτοι γε Contius). This is not sufficient to guarantee καί γε as a classical form, though it is not infrequent in post-classical Greek (Galen, Lucian, Libanius, Septuagint: Longin.13.2): nor does the fact that Hesychius glosses καί γε by καίτοι prove that he found it in a classical author. (So we say in English 'and . . . too', not 'and too').

καὶ . . . γε. (1) With connective καί. Connective καὶ . . . γε, coupling single words, phrases, clauses, and sentences, is first found in Aeschylus: *Supp.*296,313,468: *Pers.*1035: *Pr.*931. It is common throughout Attic[1] prose and verse literature, occurring either in the middle of a sentence, or at the opening of a sentence or speech. The effect of γε in καὶ . . . γε is to stress the addition made by καί. καὶ . . . γε is thus barely distinguishable from καὶ . . . δή, though perhaps in καὶ . . . γε it is the mere making of an addition ('yes, and more . . .'), in καὶ . . . δή the particular thing added ('and, in particular . . .') that is emphasized.

Normally only a single word intervenes between the particles, or at most two. S.*Aj.*1376 Καὶ νῦν γε: E.*Ph.*417 κᾆτά γε: *Hel.* 1417 Αὖθις κελεύω καὶ τρίτον γ': Ar.*Nu.*1067–8 Καὶ τὴν Θέτιν γ' ἔγημε διὰ τὸ σωφρονεῖν ὁ Πηλεύς.—Κᾆτ' ἀπολιποῦσά γ' αὐτὸν ᾤχετ': *Ra.*562 κἀμυκᾶτό γε: 564 Καὶ τὸ ξίφος γ' ἐσπᾶτο (Tucker well notes the effect of 'feminine underlining' given by γε throughout this passage): Pl.*Grg.*450D ἡ ἀριθμητικὴ καὶ λογιστικὴ καὶ γεωμετρικὴ καὶ πεττευτική γε καὶ ἄλλαι πολλαὶ τέχναι: *Smp.*219B

[1] It is not, however, confined to Attic, as Hartung (i 397) supposed. Hdt. i 120,146: ii 83,111,146,155: iii 12.

τετρῶσθαι αὐτὸν ᾤμην· καὶ ἀναστάς γε . . .: *La.*189B: Anaxag. *Fr.*12: Isoc.vii 72: D.ii 10: iii 12.

Sometimes, however, the number of intervening words is greater. S.*Ph.*438 *καὶ κατ' αὐτὸ τοῦτό γε*: *OT* 771 *Κοὐ μὴ στερηθῇς γ'*: *OC* 1432 *Καὶ μή μ' ἐπίσχῃς γ'*: E.*Cyc.*343 *πῦρ καὶ πατρῷον τό"δε λέβητά γ'*: *El.*986 *καὶ δεινὰ δράσω γ'*: Ar. *Eq.*423 *Καὶ ταῦτα δρῶν ἐλάνθανόν γ'*: Pl.*Grg.*456C *καὶ εἰ πρὸς ἄλλον γε δημιουργὸν ὁντιναοῦν ἀγωνίζοιτο*: *R.*554D. (Ar.*Pl.* 771 *Καὶ προσκυνῶ γε* looks strange, but Plutus enters continuing a speech which he has begun off the stage.)

(2) With adverbial *καί*. (A much rarer use.)

(i) *καί* meaning 'also' 'even'. Hom.π 309 *ἦ τοι ἐμὸν θυμὸν καὶ ἔπειτά γ', ὀΐω, γνώσεαι*: S.*Tr.*1236 *κρεῖσσον κἀμέ γ', ὦ πάτερ, θανεῖν*: *OT* 931 *Αὔτως δὲ καὶ σύ γ'*: E.*IA* 1244 *αἴσθημά τοι κἀν νηπίοις γε τῶν κακῶν ἐγγίγνεται*: Ar.*Nu.*1235 *Νὴ Δία κἂν προσκαταθείην γ' . . .*: *Th.*865 *Ὤφελες δὲ καὶ σύ γε*: *Ra.*116 *τολμήσεις γὰρ ἰέναι καὶ σύ γε*; *V.*6 *ἐπεὶ καὐτοῦ γ' ἐμοῦ . . .*: Pl.*Tht.*200A *ψευδῆ . . . δοξάσει . . .—Οὐ δήπου καὶ ἡγήσεταί γε ψευδῆ δοξάζειν*: *Grg.*496A: *La.*181A,*

Especially after *ἀλλὰ μήν, καὶ μήν*, etc. Pl.*Phd.*72E *Καὶ μὴν . . . καὶ κατ' ἐκεῖνόν γε τὸν λόγον . . .*: 58D *Ἀλλὰ μὴν . . . καὶ τοὺς ἀκουσομένους γε τοιούτους ἑτέρους ἔχεις*: *R.*464B *Καὶ μὲν δὴ καὶ τοῖς πρόσθεν γε ὁμολογοῦμεν*: *Euthd.*276E *Ὦ Ζεῦ . . . ἦ μὴν καὶ τὸ πρότερόν γε καλὸν ἡμῖν ἐφάνη τὸ ἐρώτημα*: *R.*582D: X.*Ages.*5.1: D.xxi 173: xliv 39,54.

(ii) *καί* meaning 'both'. Pl.*Hp.Ma.*302D *καὶ ἀμφοτέραις γε . . . καὶ ἑκατέρᾳ* (*γε TW*: *τε F*).

(iii) *καί* meaning 'actually'. Ar.*Ra.*1384 *Κόκκυ, μέθεσθε· καὶ πολύ γε κατωτέρω χωρεῖ τὸ τοῦδε* ('*far* lower'): Pl.*Tht.*144C *ὁ . . . Εὐφρονίου ἐστίν, καὶ πάνυ γε, ὦ φίλε, ἀνδρὸς οἷον καὶ σὺ τοῦτον διηγῇ* ('*καί* is intensive', Campbell): *Thg.*122B *Ἀλλὰ μὲν δὴ . . . καὶ λέγεταί γε* ('They do say'). In elliptical answers: Pl.*Prm.*144A *Καὶ πάνυ γε*: *Phlb.*24B *Καὶ σφόδρα γε*: 36B *Καὶ μάλα γε*. (Such answers seem distinguishable from other elliptical answers in which *καί* is connective: Pl.*Tht.*147E *Καὶ εὖ γε*: *Phd.*109A *Καὶ ὀρθῶς γε*: 'And rightly'.) Not elliptical: Pl. *Phd.*74D *ἐνδεῖ τι . . .;—Καὶ πολύ γε, ἔφη, ἐνδεῖ*: *Phdr.*266D *Καὶ καλῶς γε ὑπέμνησας* (*καί secl.* Hirschig).

(iv) In the following, the two particles are independent of one another. S.*Ph.*29 *Τόδ' ἐξύπερθε (ἄντρον εἰσορῶ)· καὶ στίβου γ' οὐδεὶς κτύπος* (γε goes closely with *στίβου*: see Jebb on line 38: but his parallels are not very apposite): *Ant.*577 *Δεδογμέν', ὡς ἔοικε, τήνδε κατθανεῖν.—Καὶ σοί γε κἀμοί* (γε assents, with amplification, and καί answers καί): E.*Ph.*1212 *Μεῖζόν τι χρῄζεις παῖδας ἢ σεσῳσμένους;—Καὶ τἀπίλοιπά γ' εἰ καλῶς πράσσω κλύειν* ('Yes (γε), to hear also (καί) ...': so, rightly, Pearson): Hdt.i 60 *μηχανῶνται δὴ ἐπὶ τῇ κατόδῳ πρῆγμα εὐηθέστατον ... μακρῷ ... εἰ καὶ τότε γε οὗτοι ἐν Ἀθηναίοισι ... μηχανῶνται τοιάδε* (this is difficult to analyse, but I think that γε goes with εἰ, 'siquidem', while καί stresses τότε): Pl.*Euthd.* 298D *Ἦ καὶ μήτηρ (πάντων ζῴων) ἡ μήτηρ;—Καὶ ἡ μήτηρ γε* ('Yes (γε), my mother too (καί)'. Contrast, a few lines below, *Καὶ ἡ σή γε*, 'Yes, and yours too').

(For καὶ ... γε δή see γε δή (5).)

Μέν γε

This combination is a natural one, the effect of γε being to concentrate attention momentarily on the μέν clause, with a deliberate temporary exclusion of the δέ clause. (The effect is the same when the particles are separated, but in close proximity: Pl.*Phlb.*37E *τὴν μὲν δόξαν γε*: *Phd.*91D *τοῦτο μὲν ἐμοὶ συγχωρεῖν, πολυχρονιώτερόν γε εἶναι ψυχὴν σώματος*: *Lg.* 662A.) μέν is sometimes *solitarium.*

μέν γε is probably entirely absent from serious poetry, and is rather rare in comedy. In Hom.*O* 211 there can be no doubt that μέν κε is the right reading. E.*Fr.*909.4 *πρῶτα μέν γε τοῦθ' ὑπάρχει*[1] (but the whole fragment, in which Clement of Alexandria found σεμνότης, seems to me incredibly lame, and Dobree has stigmatized certain lines as unworthy of Euripides). In *IA* 654 only P^2 reads μέν γ'. In *Med.*1094 μέν γ' has been proposed for μέν τ' (defended by Verrall), but Porson's μέν [τ'] is probably right (τ' *in rasura l*).

Epich.*Fr.*124 (Kaibel) *πρωὶ μέν γ' ... ἀφύας ἀπεπυρίζομες*: Ar.*Ach.*154 *Τοῦτο μέν γ' ἤδη σαφές*: *Ra.*80 *κἄλλως ὁ μέν γ'*

[1] Starkie (on Ar.*V.*564) and Neil (*Knights*, p. 192) confirm me in my belief that there is no other example in tragedy.

Εὐριπίδης . . . ὁ δ' εὔκολος . . .: *Lys.*589,1165,1236: *Ra.*290,907 (*Ald.*): Hdt.i 129 σκαιότατόν τε καὶ ἀδικώτατον . . . σκαιότατον μέν γε, εἰ . . . ἀδικώτατον δέ, ὅτι . . .: ii 97 ἐς μέν γε Μέμφιν . . . ἐς δὲ Ναύκρατιν . . .: i 145,173: iii 29,107,142: vi 109.3: viii 10.1: 65.3: Pl.*R.*475E: *Cra.*423A,437D: *Tht.*147A: *Smp.*180D: X. *Cyr.*ii 1.2: D.xxi 74: lvii 62. (Ar.*Pl.*665 is different: here γε assents with an addition: Ἦσαν δέ τινες κἄλλοι . . .;—Εἷς μέν γε Νεοκλείδης . . . ἕτεροί τε πολλοί: 'Yes, Neocleides for one.' Cf. καὶ . . . γε, 2.iv.)

The commonest (in Demosthenes almost the only) use of μέν γε is at the beginning of a sentence, as a quasi-connective, introducing a reason, explanation, or instance, and approximating to μὲν γάρ or μὲν γοῦν in force. (Thus in Ant. v 14 μέν γε, in the duplication of the passage in vi 2 μὲν γάρ.)

Ar.*Av.*1608 οὐ γὰρ μεῖζον . . . ἰσχύσετ', ἢν ὄρνιθες ἄρξωσιν κάτω; νῦν μέν γ' . . . ἐπιορκοῦσιν ὑμᾶς οἱ βροτοί· ἐὰν δὲ . . .: *Nu.*1172 ὡς ἥδομαί σου πρῶτα τὴν χρόαν ἰδών· νῦν μέν γ' ἰδεῖν εἶ πρῶτον ἐξαρνητικός: Alex.*Fr.*146.7 ἡ τῶν γὰρ ἀνδρῶν ἐστὶ πρὸς ἐκείνην μέλι· οἱ μέν γε συγγνώμην ἔχουσ' ἀδικούμενοι, αὗται δ' . . .: Ar.*Nu.*1382: *V.*564: *Th.*804 (γ' *add.* Dobr.): *Ec.*60: *Lys.*720: *Av.*612 (γ' *add.* Bentl.), 1136: Hdt.iii 72 τοῦ γὰρ αὐτοῦ γλιχόμεθα οἵ τε ψευδόμενοι καὶ οἱ τῇ ἀληθείῃ διαχρεώμενοι. οἱ μέν γε ψεύδονται . . . οἱ δ' ἀληθίζονται: Th.i 40.4 καίτοι δίκαιοί γ' ἐστὲ . . . ἐπὶ τούτους μεθ' ἡμῶν ἰέναι (Κορινθίοις μέν γε ἔνσπονδοί ἐστε, Κερκυραίοις δὲ . . .): Pl.*Smp.*215C ἀλλ' οὐκ αὐλητής; πολύ γε θαυμασιώτερος ἐκείνου. ὁ μέν γε δι' ὀργάνων ἐκήλει τοὺς ἀνθρώπους . . . σὺ δὲ . . .: *Lg.*896E: X.*Cyr.*ii 2.2 δύσκολοι . . . φαίνονται. πρῴην μέν γε . . . (an illustration): *Smp.*1.9 τῶν ὁρώντων οὐδεὶς οὐκ ἔπασχέ τι τὴν ψυχὴν ὑπ' ἐκείνου. οἱ μέν γε σιωπηρότεροι ἐγίγνοντο, οἱ δὲ καὶ ἐσχηματίζοντό πως: Ant.i 21 σκέψασθε οὖν ὅσῳ δικαιότερα ὑμῶν δεήσομαι ἐγὼ ἢ ὁ ἀδελφός. ἐγὼ μέν γε . . . οὗτος δὲ . . .: D. xviii 180 σοῦ πλείονος ἄξιος ὢν ἐφάνην τῇ πατρίδι. σὺ μέν γ' . . . ἐγὼ δὲ . . .: 160 τῶν οἰκείων μοι πραγμάτων τοιούτων συμβεβηκότων ἐν τῷ τότε καιρῷ, ὥστε ὑμᾶς ἂν ἀκούσαντας ἐλεῆσαι. ἡ μέν γε μήτηρ ἔκαμνε . . . ἡ δὲ γυνὴ . . . ἀσθενῶς διέκειτο: Th.i 70.2: 74.1: X.*Cyr.*ii 1.16: iv 3.18: *Smp.*6.7: *Hier.* 1.11: 8.9: And.ii 2,19: Isoc.iv 153: D.xiv 29,30,40: xvi 10: xviii 200: xix 252: xx 23: xxi 73: xxii 1: *id. saep.*

Pl.*Men.*86C is curious: *Εὖ μοι δοκεῖς λέγειν . . . Καὶ τοῦτο μέν γε δοκεῖς μοι εὖ λέγειν* ('That, too': an odd blend of *καὶ τοῦτό γε* and *τοῦτο μέν γε*: unless *καί* is simply 'and', which, in the context, seems most unlikely: *μέν* certainly looks suspicious.)

The stronger forms *μέν γε δή*, *μέν γε οὖν* are occasionally found. Pl.*Tht.*172C *καὶ πολλάκις μέν γε δὴ . . . ἀτὰρ καὶ νῦν . . .*: *Plt.*257D *κινδυνεύετον . . . ἄμφω ποθὲν ἐμοὶ συγγένειαν ἔχειν τινά. τὸν μέν γε οὖν . . . τοῦ δὲ . . . .*

Τέ γε (εἴτε γε: οὔτε γε)

The combination of *τε* and *γε*, especially in juxtaposition, seems to have been rather disliked by Greek writers, except perhaps Plato. Why, it is difficult to say, since the combination is a perfectly natural[1] one, *τε* meaning either 'both' or 'and', and *γε* stressing the word before *τε* (or, where the particles are separated, a word lying between the two). *δή* however largely supplants *γε* in this connexion. (See Introd.IV).

E.*Alc.*647 *ἥν ἐγὼ καὶ μητέρα πατέρα τέ γ' ἐνδίκως ἂν ἡγοίμην* (*γ' om. VB*): Pl.*Phd.*59C *Ναί, Σιμμίας τέ γε . . .* (*τε om.W*): 106D *Παρὰ πάντων . . . ἀνθρώπων τέ γε καὶ . . . θεῶν* (*γε om. TW*): *Grg.*454E *Ἀλλὰ μὴν οἵ τέ γε μεμαθηκότες πεπεισμένοι εἰσὶν καὶ οἱ πεπιστευκότες* (*τε om. F*): X.*Mem.*i2.54 *αὐτοί τέ γε αὑτῶν . . . ἀφαιροῦσι καὶ τοῖς ἰατροῖς παρέχουσι . . .* (*γε* for *γοῦν*). It will be noticed that only in the last passage are the MSS. unanimous. Ar.*Av.*823 *ἵνα καὶ τὰ Θεογένους τὰ πολλὰ χρήματα τά τ' Αἰσχίνου γ' ἅπαντα*: Pl.*Plt.*293D *Καὶ ἐάντε γε . . . εἴτε καὶ . . .*: *Alc.I* 107B *Ἐάν τέ γε . . . ἐάν τε . . .*: Ar.*Lys.* 939 *ἤν τε βούλῃ γ' ἤν τε μή*: D.xix 188 *εἴτε βούλομαί γ' εἴτε μή*: Hdt.ii 14 *εἰ μήτε γε . . . μήτε* (*ib.* 16: *μήτι CRSV*): viii 142.2 *οὔτε γὰρ δίκαιον οὐδαμῶς οὔτε κόσμον φέρον οὔτε γε ἄλλοισι Ἑλλήνων οὐδαμοῖσι, ὑμῖν δὲ δὴ . . . ἥκιστα* (*γε om. RSV*: reading uncertain): Pl.*R.*556A *Καὶ οὔτε γ' ἐκείνῃ . . . οὔτε τῇδε* (*γ' om. F*): 611B *μήτε . . . μήτε γε αὖ*: S.*Aj.*1075 *οὔτ' ἂν . . . οὔτ' ἂν στρατός γε.*

[1] Hartung (i 400) calls it an 'unnatural combination', and proposes to alter Ar.*Av.*823: the remaining instances he ignores. Neil's list (*op. cit.*, p. 192) is also far from complete.

γε occasionally follows 'adverbial' τε. Hdt.vii 129.1 ὥστε γε συγκεκληιμένην (γε *om.ABC*): Pl.*Lg*.770B εἴπερ οἷοί τέ γ' ἐσμέν: X.*Mem*.iv 2.11 καὶ οὐχ οἷόν τέ γε: 5.2 Ὡς οἷόν τέ γε μάλιστα (Pl.*R*.412B).

For τέ γε δή, see γε δή (7).

Δέ

The derivation of δέ is entirely obscure.[1]

Except in the apodotic use, δέ is always a connective. Whether the apodotic use is derived from the connective, or whether it harks back to an earlier, 'adverbial', sense, is a matter which concerns only the history of language. (A similar problem confronts us in the case of καί.) Both uses are already present in the earliest extant Greek literature.

As a connective, δέ denotes either pure connexion, 'and', or contrast, 'but', with all that lies between. (Modern languages are here less equivocal than Greek and Latin. Cf. *at*.) The former sense preponderates where no μέν precedes, and in such cases there is no essential difference[2] between δέ and καί: though it is to be noticed that δέ usually couples sentences, clauses, or phrases, single words[3] being normally joined by καί, and (in some styles) τε.

I. Connective. (**A**) Continuative, and (**B**) Adversative: though, as I have suggested above, no sharp line can be drawn between the two.

A. Continuative. δέ is the normal equivalent of 'and' at the beginning of a sentence. Cf. Pl.*R*.614B–*fin*. (Vision of Er), where καί is only occasionally used at the beginning of a sentence. In

[1] See Brugmann, § 630.

[2] Hartung's distinction, that δέ expresses duality, τε and καί unity, can hardly be of practical importance.

[3] Adversative δέ may couple single words, e.g. Ar.*Nu*.1462; continuative δέ hardly ever, if at all. Cf. A.*Supp*.287: S.*OT* 347 (*v.l.*): E.*HF* 1098. In A.*Pr*.502 τε *recc*. is read for δέ *M*: E.*Hel*.1550 τ' Ludv.Dindorf. δέ coupling clauses is often altered by editors, sometimes perhaps needlessly, to τε: E.*Hel*. 1566,1655. Conversely τε after a strong stop has been changed to δέ: S.*Aj*. 687,1182 (see Jebb): cf. τε, I.1. The delimitation of the functions of connective δέ and τε is a difficult matter, requiring further investigation.

Lys.i 6–27 (narrative) the openings are more varied. Cf. other passages in which δέ preponderates: Hom.*A* 1–5: 43–9: 345–51: E.*Rh.*762–803 (Messenger's speech): X.*Cyr.*i 2.1.

It is unnecessary to multiply instances of so familiar a use. But the following points may be noticed:

(1) Expressions standing in apposition to one another are sometimes linked by δέ. In English we use a connective only where the expressions are *eiusdem generis*: 'his brother, and my cousin' (cf. Hdt.vii 10α2 πατρὶ τῷ σῷ, ἀδελφεῷ δὲ ἐμῷ), but not 'his brother, and the Governor of Malta': in Greek, δέ is admissible in either case. τε and γε are similarly used, and the manuscripts cannot perhaps always be trusted.

A.*Ag.*1405 οὗτός ἐστιν Ἀγαμέμνων, ἐμὸς πόσις, νεκρὸς δέ ('my husband, dead'): *Ch.*190 ἀλλ' οὐδὲ μήν νιν ἡ κτανοῦσ' ἐκείρατο, ἐμὴ δὲ μήτηρ: 841 νέαν φάτιν . . . οὐδαμῶς ἐφίμερον, μόρον δ' Ὀρέστου (γ' Portus: but δέ may mark a contrast with ἐφίμερον): *Th.*277 (see Tucker (his 265): *sed*?): E.*Andr.*248 Ἑλένη νιν ὤλεσ', οὐκ ἐγώ, μήτηρ δὲ σή (Paley prints a colon before οὐκ: read perhaps γε): S.*OC* 1275 ὦ σπέρματ' ἀνδρὸς τοῦδ', ἐμαὶ δ' ὁμαίμονες: A.*Pers.*152: Hdt.i 114 ὑπὸ τοῦ σοῦ δούλου, βουκόλου δὲ παιδός: vii 8β3 Ἀρισταγόρῃ τῷ Μιλησίῳ, δούλῳ δὲ ἡμετέρῳ.

(2) In Anaphora, when δέ is in the second limb, μέν is usually in the first (see p. 370). But there are numerous exceptions to this principle in serious poetry. Hom.*Ω*483 ὡς Ἀχιλεὺς θάμβησεν . . . θάμβησαν δὲ καὶ ἄλλοι: A.*Fr.*70 Ζεύς ἐστιν αἰθήρ, Ζεὺς δὲ γῆ, Ζεὺς δ' οὐρανός: *Eu.*656 (clauses not co-ordinated): S *OT* 312 ῥῦσαι σεαυτὸν καὶ πόλιν, ῥῦσαι δ' ἐμέ, ῥῦσαι δὲ πᾶν μίασμα τοῦ τεθνηκότος: E.*Or.*709 μισεῖ γὰρ ὁ θεὸς . . . μισοῦσι δ' ἀστοί: S.*OT* 1490: *Tr.*517,1148: *Ph.*633,827: *OC* 1343: E.*Med* 99,131,767,961, 1071: *Andr.*1168: *Supp.*1149: *HF* 915,1062,1359,1374: *El.*312: *IT* 984: *Ph.*564,686,1034: *Or.*1135: *Ba.*142: 370 Ὁσία πότνα θεῶν, Ὁσία δ' ἃ κατὰ γᾶν χρυσέαν πτέρυγα φέρεις: *IA* 17,559, 1258.

Very rare in comedy: Hermipp.*Fr.*82.8 (mock-epic) ὄζει ἴων, ὄζει δὲ ῥόδων, ὄζει δ' ὑακίνθου. For Ar.*Av.*586 see p. 164.

In prose, there are a few examples in Herodotus and Plato: Hdt.vii 9α1 τί δείσαντες; κοίην πλήθεος συστροφήν; κοίην δὲ χρημάτων δύναμιν; ix 16.1 ἔφη . . . κληθῆναι καὶ αὐτὸς . . .

κληθῆναι δὲ καὶ Θηβαίων ἄνδρας πεντήκοντα: vii 10ε: Pl.*Lg.*649 B πάσης ... παρρησίας ... μεστοῦται καὶ ἐλευθερίας, πάσης δὲ ἀφοβίας: 914E. *Tht.*191B and *Min.*313C are of course different, since here the repetition of the word is compulsory, not voluntary, and we can hardly speak of anaphora. Different, again, are certain passages in Herodotus, where a main verb is repeated with added detail: i 114 ἔπαιζε ἐν τῇ κώμῃ ταύτῃ ... ἔπαιζε δὲ μετ' ἄλλων ἡλίκων ἐν ὁδῷ: ii 158: iii 1.4: vi 43.4: 89. In such cases the use of a connective is natural enough in English too, in leisurely and garrulous style: 'He was playing in this village ... and he was playing with boys of his own age'. Less natural to us is Herodotus' habit of repeating a substantive: v 113.2 καὶ ὁ Σολίων βασιλεὺς Ἀριστόκυπρος ὁ Φιλοκύπρου, Φιλοκύπρου δὲ τούτου τὸν Σόλων ... αἴνεσε τυράννων μάλιστα ('the Philocyprus whom Solon ..'): vi 127.3: vii 121.1: ix 73.1 ἐκ δήμου Δεκελεῆθεν, Δεκελέων δὲ τῶν κοτε ἐργασαμένων ... (the locality implies its inhabitants: conversely, vii 80: ix 92.2). Cf. καί, I.4, and see Stein on Hdt. i 52.

In some cases, connexion is varied with asyndeton. Hom.θ323 ἦλθε ... ἦλθ' ... ἦλθεν δὲ ...: Simon.*Fr.*13 18 εὗδε, βρέφος, εὑδέτω δὲ πόντος, εὑδέτω ἄμετρον κακόν (εὑδέτω δ' *B*): S.*OT* 1305 ἐθέλων πόλλ' ἀνερέσθαι, πολλὰ πυθέσθαι, πολλὰ δ' ἀθρῆσαι: *El.* 1151–3 (an astonishingly fine effect): E.*Rh.*311 πολλοὶ μὲν ἱππῆς, πολλὰ πελταστῶν τέλη, πολλοὶ δ' ἀτράκτων τοξόται (δ' *LP*: τ' *VO*): Ar *Av.*586 Ἢν δ' ἡγῶνται σὲ θεὸν σὲ βίον σὲ δὲ γῆν σὲ Κρόνον σὲ Ποσειδῶ: *Lys.*545–6, 962–4.

(3) In two passages in Euripides a participial addition is joined to an understood main verb by δέ: *Heracl.* 794 Μάλιστα (ἔστιν), πράξας δ' ἐκ θεῶν κάλλιστα δή: *Ba.*816 Σάφ' ἴσθι (ἴδοιμ' ἄν), σιγῇ δ' ὑπ' ἐλάταις καθήμενος. The more normal epexegetic γε (see γε, I.12.ii) has been suggested by Elmsley in the former passage, by Musurus in the latter.[1] In the former, Paley assumes a break in sense at the end of the line. In both, particularly the second, δέ seems rather unnatural.

(4) In Ar.*Eq.*79 only the second and third of three units are coupled by δέ, after asyndeton between the first and second. This and Lycurg.150 are the only instances I have noticed (except those given above under (2), *ad fin.* For A.*Pr.*502 see n. 3, p. 162): but there may be others. (Van Leeuwen's ingenious

[1] See Verrall on A.*Ch.*126.

emendation of Ar.*Pax* 758 is made less probable by the fact that the line = *V.*1035 (where *V* reads Λαμίας δ').) Cf. καί (I.1), τε (I.1.iii.*c*, p. 501), οὐδέ (I.2.iv), καὶ . . . δέ (iii). Two linked units in the middle of an otherwise asyndetic series: X.*Cyr.*viii 2.6. Cf. also (2), *ad fin.*, above.

B. Adversative.

(1) Normally, while ἀλλά is a strong adversative, eliminating, or almost eliminating, the opposed idea, δέ (like μήν and μέντοι) balances two opposed ideas.

(i) Examples of δέ as a balancing adversative preceded by μέν are given under μέν. But μέν is sometimes omitted, particularly in verse, even when the idea of balance is clearly present.[1] A.*Eu.*650: S.*Tr* 198 οὕτως ἐκεῖνος οὐχ ἑκών, ἑκοῦσι δὲ ξύνεστιν: *Ph.*971 Οὐκ εἶ κακὸς σύ πρὸς κακῶν δ' ἀνδρῶν μαθὼν ἔοικας ἥκειν αἰσχρά: E.*Ph.*1680 Γενναιότης σοι, μωρία δ' ἔνεστί τις: *Or* 100 Ὀρθῶς ἔλεξας, οὐ φίλως δ' ἐμοὶ λέγεις: Ar.*Nu.*1462 πονηρά γ', ὦ Νεφέλαι, δίκαια δέ: Hom.*I* 415: Hes.*Op.*472: E.*Or.*424: Ar.*Th.* 737: *Ra.*1461: and even when the close connexion between coordinated clauses implies logical subordination: E.*El.*920: *Hel.* 588: cf. p. 370(ii).

In prose such omission of μέν, though rarer than in verse, is not infrequent. Th.i 86.1 πρὸς τοὺς Μήδους ἐγένοντο ἀγαθοὶ τότε, πρὸς δ' ἡμᾶς κακοὶ νῦν: Pl.*Prt.*329E ἐπεὶ πολλοὶ ἀνδρεῖοί εἰσιν, ἄδικοι δέ, καὶ δίκαιοι αὖ, σοφοὶ δὲ οὔ: *Grg.*513C τῷ αὐτῶν . . . χαίρουσι, τῷ δὲ ἀλλοτρίῳ ἄχθονται: *Tht.*150C μαιεύεσθαί με ὁ θεὸς ἀναγκάζει, γεννᾶν δὲ ἀπεκώλυσεν: 192D ἐνίοτε μὲν ὁρῶ αὐτούς, ἐνίοτε δὲ οὔ, καὶ ἅπτομαί ποτ' αὐτῶν, τότε δ' οὔ: 202B ἄλογα καὶ ἄγνωστα εἶναι, αἰσθητὰ δέ: 208B ἀνεπιστήμων ὤν, ὀρθὰ δὲ δοξάζων: *Ti.*91D ἐκ τῶν ἀκάκων ἀνδρῶν, κούφων δέ, καὶ μετεωρολογικῶν μέν, ἡγουμένων δὲ . . .: *Lg.*691A οὖσα ἀμαθία μεγίστη, δοκοῦσα δὲ σοφία: 744C τῷ ἀνίσῳ, συμμέτρῳ δέ: Lys.iii 37 οὐ τοίνυν ταῦτα εἰκότα, ἄλλως δὲ περὶ αὐτῶν πέπρακται: D.viii 67 τῇ τῶν ὠνίων ἀφθονίᾳ λαμπροί, τῇ δ' ὧν προσῆκε παρασκευῇ καταγέλαστοι: Th.i 56.2: Pl.*Chrm.*170E: *Ap.*21C,31D: *Phd.*81B,112E: *Tht.*160A,B,174D,181E: *R.*398A, 548E,552C,598A,616B: *Lg.*728C: *Ep.*355A: Lys.xiii 85: xxvi 15: D.vi 11: ix 33: xxiv 87. The missing μέν has sometimes

[1] See Rehdantz, *Index*, Frohberger, *Philol.* xv 342, and other authorities cited by Kühner (II ii 273, n. 1).

been added by editors whose ideas on this subject are too unbending: Lys.i 38: v 4: x 31 (*coll.* xi 12): xii 79: xviii 17.

(ii) Occasionally ὁ μέν, etc., has to be understood before ὁ δέ, etc. Hom.*X* 157 τῇ ῥα παραδραμέτην, φεύγων, ὁ δ' ὄπισθε διώκων (a striking example, because of the discrepancy in number): Pi.*N.*8.37 χρυσὸν εὔχονται, πεδίον δ' ἕτεροι ἀπέραντον: E.*Hel.*1605 σπουδῆς δ' ὕπο ἔπιπτον, οἱ δ' ὠρθοῦντο: *Or.*1489 νεκροὶ δ' ἔπιπτον, οἱ δ' ἔμελλον, οἱ δ' ἔκειντ': *IT* 1350 κοντοῖς δὲ πρῷραν εἶχον, οἱ δ' ἐπωτίδων ἄγκυραν ἐξανῆπτον: S.*Tr.*117 (*ib.* 135 is more complicated: see Jebb): Hom.*Ω* 528: Pi.*I.*6.61: Xenoph.*Fr.*1.3: E.*HF* 636 (where see Wilamowitz): Pl.*Sph.* 221E νευστικοῦ μέρους, τὸ δὲ πεζοῦ τέμνοντες: *Phlb.*36E ψευδεῖς, αἱ δ' ἀληθεῖς οὐκ εἰσὶν ἡδοναί; *Ti.*22E πλέον, τότε δὲ ἔλαττον: *Lg.*629D ποτέρους . . . οὕτως ὑπερεπῄνεσας, τοὺς δὲ ἔψεξας τῶν ἀνδρῶν; *Epin.*983D ἔμφρον μέν που, τὸ δὲ ἄφρον θήσομεν, ἄρχον δέ, τὸ δὲ ἀρχόμενον: X.*HG* i 2.14 ἀποδράντες νυκτὸς ᾤχοντο εἰς Δεκέλειαν, οἱ δ' εἰς Μέγαρα: *Cyr.*iv 5.46 ὁρᾶτε . . . ἵπποι ὅσοι ἡμῖν πάρεισιν, οἱ δὲ προσάγονται: Arist.*EN* 1132a6 καὶ εἰ ἔβλαψεν ὃ δὲ βέβλαπται: *HA* 573b32: Pl.*Cra.*385B: *Ti.*63E,84C: *Sph.*248A,267B: *R.*451E,455E.456A: *Lg.*648C: *Plt.*291E: D.ix 64 εἰσφέρειν ἐκέλευον, οἱ δ' οὐδὲν δεῖν ἔφασαν: Arist.*PA* 654a28: *Po.*1447b14: Aen.Tact.10 (*ad fin.*). In Pl.*Ti.*63A, Lys.xix 59 τὸν δέ, τοὺς δέ answer τινα, τισι. In some of the above the ὁ δέ, etc., is more or less of an afterthought, and it is hardly necessary to suppose an ellipse of ὁ μέν: cf. S.*El.*1291: *OT* 1229: Ar.*Nu.*396. Most of the Platonic examples are from his later works. L. & S. cite *IG* 2².1388.45 σφραγῖδε . . . χρυσοῦν ἔχουσα τὸν δακτύλιον, ἡ δ' ἑτέρα ἀργυροῦν (see further Meisterhans, p. 250). Cf. τε E.*IT* 1238 ἐν κιθάρᾳ σοφόν, ἅ τ' ἐπὶ τόξων εὐστοχίᾳ γάνυται.

(2) But, just as ἀλλά sometimes is, or appears to be, a weak adversative, so δέ is at times a strong one: particularly in Sophocles, who not infrequently uses δέ in answers, to introduce a protest or objection.

S.*OT* 379 Κρέοντος, ἢ σοῦ ταῦτα τἀξευρήματα;—Κρέων δέ σοι πῆμ' οὐδέν, ἀλλ' αὐτὸς σὺ σοί ('Nay, Creon harms thee not')*: *El.*400 Πεσούμεθ', εἰ χρή, πατρὶ τιμωρούμενοι.—Πατὴρ δὲ τούτων, οἶδα, συγγνώμην ἔχει: *Tr.*536 κόρην γάρ, οἶμαι δ' οὐκέτ', ἀλλ' ἐζευγμένην (correcting, for μὲν οὖν): 729 Τοιαῦτα δ' ἂν λέξειεν οὐχ ὁ τοῦ κακοῦ κοινωνός, ἀλλ' . . . (rejecting comfort: 'Nay'): *Ant.*92 Οὐκοῦν, ὅταν δὴ μὴ σθένω, πεπαύσομαι.—Ἀρχὴν δὲ θηρᾶν οὐ πρέπει τἀμήχανα ('Aye, but ...'): 518 Οὐ γάρ τι δοῦλος, ἀλλ' ἀδελφὸς ὤλετο.—Πορθῶν δὲ τήνδε γῆν (δέ *L*: γε *A*): *OC* 395 Νῦν γὰρ θεοί σ' ὀρθοῦσι, πρόσθε δ' ὤλλυσαν.—Γέροντα δ' ὀρθοῦν φλαῦρον ὃς νέος πέσῃ: 592 Ὦ μῶρε, θυμὸς δ' ἐν κακοῖς οὐ ξύμφορον: 1443 Δυστάλαινά τἄρ' ἐγώ, εἴ σου στερηθῶ.—Ταῦτα δ' ἐν τῷ δαίμονι καὶ τῇδε φῦναι χἀτέρᾳ: E.*Hipp.* 911 σιγᾷς· σιωπῆς δ' οὐδὲν ἔργον ἐν κακοῖς: *Alc.*710 οὐ χρῆν σ' εἰς ἔμ' ἐξαμαρτάνειν.—Σοῦ δ' ἂν προθνῄσκων μᾶλλον ἐξημάρτανον ('Nay': for μὲν οὖν): 985: *IA* 956 πικροὺς ... χέρνιβάς τ' ἐνάρξεται Κάλχας ὁ μάντις. τίς δὲ μάντις ἔστ' ἀνήρ, ὃς ὀλίγ' ἀληθῆ, πολλὰ δὲ ψευδῆ λέγει ...; (for καίτοι: 'Yet how call him a prophet ...?'): 411: A.*Supp.*784 (perhaps: text uncertain) 1034 (δ' *add.* Pauw): E.*HF* 557 (δ' *P*: γ' *L*: δ' gives a stronger sense): Ar.*Ach.*292: *Ra.*1396: *V.*1188.)

(Contrast the weaker δέ in an answer in E.*IA* 1457: Ἄκων μ' ὑπὲρ γῆς Ἑλλάδος διώλεσεν.—Δόλῳ δ', ἀγεννῶς Ἀτρέως τ' οὐκ ἀξίως ('Unwillingly, perhaps, but unworthily'). Cf. S.*Ant.* 518 (δέ *L*: γε *A*).)

Expressing a break-off, like ἀτάρ. A.*Pers.*478 σὺ δ' εἰπὲ ... (Atossa turns to the messenger, after her soliloquy): E.*Cyc.*286, 597: *Hec.*868,1237: *El.*292: *Hel.*143: *Ba.*657.

In prose δέ only very rarely bears the stronger force normally conveyed by καίτοι or ἀλλά. Pl.*Smp.*212E ἆρά καταγελάσεσθέ μου ὡς μεθύοντος; ἐγὼ δέ, κἂν ὑμεῖς γελᾶτε, ὅμως εὖ οἶδ' ὅτι ἀληθῆ λέγω: *Ap.*38B 'I assess my penalty at a mina fine. Πλάτων δὲ ὅδε ... καὶ Κρίτων ... κελεύουσί με τριάκοντα μνῶν τιμήσασθαι ... τιμῶμαι οὖν τοσούτου' (for ἀλλὰ γάρ): *Lg.*727B καὶ οὐ τιμᾷ (τὴν αὐτοῦ ψυχήν)· δεῖ δέ, ὥς φαμεν (for καίτοι: cf. 732E): *Hp.Ma.*298B ('Yes, but': an objection to the previous speaker's words: δ' *TF*: δή *W*). The common μᾶλλον δέ, in a correction, is less brusque than μὲν οὖν: Pl.*Cri.*46A: *Phd.* 77E: Ar.*Eq.*429 οἶμαι δὲ μᾶλλον ἄμφω.

(3) So too after a preceding negative clause. Hom.ι 145 οὐδὲ σελήνη οὐρανόθεν προὔφαινε, κατείχετο δὲ νεφέεσσιν: A.*Supp.* 1026 μηδ' ἔτι Νείλου προχοὰς σέβωμεν ὕμνοις, ποταμοὺς δ' οἳ διὰ χώρας θελεμὸν πῶμα χέουσιν: *Pr.*1075 μὴ δῆτα (μέμψησθε τύχην), αὐταὶ δ' ὑμᾶς αὐτάς: S.*Ant.*85 προμηνύσῃς γε τοῦτο

μηδενὶ τοὔργον, κρυφῇ δὲ κεῦθε: *Ph.*334 Τέθνηκεν, ἀνδρὸς οὐδενός, θεοῦ δ' ὕπο: *OC*637 οὔποτ' ἐκβαλῶ . . . χώρᾳ δ' ἔμπολιν κατοικιῶ: E.*Or.*846 ἀφώρμηται . . . λύσσῃ δαμείς;—Ἥκιστα· πρὸς δ' Ἀργεῖον οἴχεται λεών: Ar. *Ra.*625: Hdt.vii.2 οὐ τύραννος, δημότης δὲ ἐών (δέ Bekker: τε *L*): vii 8α2 οὐδὲ φλαυροτέρην, παμφορωτέρην δέ: Th.i 5 οὐκ ἔχοντός πω αἰσχύνην τοῦ ἔργου, φέροντος δέ τι καὶ δόξης μᾶλλον: iv 86 αὐτὸς δὲ οὐκ ἐπὶ κακῷ, ἐπ' ἐλευθερώσει δὲ τῶν Ἑλλήνων παρελήλυθα: Arist.*Pol.* 1326a12 μὴ εἰς τὸ πλῆθος εἰς δὲ δύναμιν ἀποβλέπειν: Hdt.i 123: viii 79.2: Pl.*Tht.*182B: *Sph.*217C: *Lg.*637D,714B,718D,723D.

Sometimes an illusory effect of balance is produced by a μέν in the negative clause. S.*El.*1036 ἐπίστω γ' οἷ μ' ἀτιμίας ἄγεις.—Ἀτιμίας μὲν οὔ, προμηθίας δὲ σοῦ (in *Ant.*78 μέν and δέ are not correlated: see Jebb): E.*Heracl.*194 τῇ δίκῃ μὲν οὔ, τὸ δ' Ἄργος ὀγκῶν: *Supp.*747 φίλοις μὲν οὐ πείθεσθε, τοῖς δὲ πράγμασιν: Ar *Th.*1035 γαμηλίῳ μὲν οὐ ξὺν παιῶνι δεσμίῳ δὲ γοᾶσθέ με: Hdt.i 107.2 Μήδων μὲν . . . οὐδενὶ διδοῖ γυναῖκα, ὁ δὲ Πέρσῃ διδοῖ: iv 111.2: Th.i 125.2 ἐνιαυτὸς μὲν οὐ διετρίβη, ἔλασσον δέ: 131.1: Pl.*R.*543B: *Ti.*86E: Lys.ix 20. (For μὲν . . . οὐδέ, see pp. 191, 194).

Such cases are to be distinguished from others, in which (with or without a preceding μέν) the ideas expressed in the two clauses are not mutually exclusive, and μὲν . . . δέ is regular: S.*El.*906 δυσφημῶ μὲν οὔ, χαρᾷ δὲ πίμπλημ' εὐθὺς ὄμμα δακρύων: E.*Hec.*386 τήνδε μὲν μὴ κτείνετε, ἡμᾶς δ' ἄγοντες πρὸς πυρὰν Ἀχιλλέως κεντεῖτε: Th.ii 98.3 πορευομένῳ δὲ αὐτῷ ἀπεγίγνετο μὲν οὐδὲν τοῦ στρατοῦ εἰ μή τι νόσῳ, προσεγίγνετο δέ: Pl.*Lg.* 660C οὐδαμῶς ἡδύ, ἀναγκαῖον δ' ἐνίοτέ ἐστιν ('not at all pleasant, though sometimes necessary'): *R.*359D: *Ap.*32A: *Lg.*923E. (Two women can be killed as easily as one, and an army can receive drafts while suffering casualties: but nine months cannot equal twelve, nor a respectable monarch marry his daughter to two suitors at once.) [1]

[1] Cf. T. S. Evans, *Latin and Greek Verse, Memoir*, p. l: 'On being told that Bishop Ellicott had pointed out an incorrectness in his well-known definition of an ellipse in the Μαθηματογονία,—κύκλος μὲν οὔ, κύκλου δὲ φιλτάτη κάσις, which, the Bishop said, should have run οὐ κύκλος, ἀλλὰ φιλτάτη κύκλου κάσις, he smiled and said: "If an ellipse had been as different from a circle as a square is, the Bishop's remark might hold water, but inasmuch as it is μόνον οὐ κύκλος, all but a circle, I think my line is correct."' The defence is valid, but superfluous.

C. Particular uses of connective δέ. (It will be convenient to drop the distinction between continuative and adversative henceforward.)

(1) δέ for γάρ, οὖν (or δή), ἤ. δέ is not infrequently used where the context admits, or even appears to demand, γάρ (or, occasionally, οὖν or ἤ). In such cases the writer is content with merely adding one idea to another, without stressing the logical connexion between the two, which he leaves to be supplied.

(i) For γάρ. This is quite common, not only in Homer, where we might expect to find it, but also in later, and logically more developed, style. The Scholia often observe: ὁ δέ ἀντὶ τοῦ γάρ. (See Tucker on A.*Ch.* 32.)[1]

Hom.*H* 48 ἦ ῥά νύ μοί τι πίθοιο, κασίγνητος δέ τοί εἰμι: K240 ὣς ἔφατ', ἔδεισεν δὲ περὶ ξανθῷ Μενελάῳ: *M*412 ἀλλ' ἐφομαρτεῖτε· πλεόνων δέ τοι ἔργον ἄμεινον: ο540 Πείραιε Κλυτίδη, σὺ δέ μοι τά περ ἄλλα μάλιστα πείθῃ: Scol.Anon.20.2 (Diehl) ὑπὸ παντὶ λίθῳ σκορπίος . . . φράζευ μή σε βάλῃ· τῷ δ' ἀφανεῖ πᾶς ἕπεται δόλος: A.*Supp.*190 ἄμεινόν ἐστι . . . πάγον προσίζειν τόνδ' ἀγωνίων θεῶν. κρείσσων δὲ πύργου βωμός: E.*Ph.*689 ἄμυνε τᾷδε γᾷ· πάντα δ' εὐπετῆ θεοῖς: Ar.*Av.*584 εἶθ' ὅ γ' Ἀπόλλων ἰατρός γ' ὢν ἰάσθω· μισθοφορεῖ δέ: 935 ἔχε τὴν σπολάδα· πάντως δέ μοι ῥιγῶν δοκεῖς: *Ra.*857 πρᾳόνως ἔλεγχ' ἐλέγχου· λοιδορεῖσθαι δ' οὐ πρέπει ἄνδρας ποιητάς: Hom.*N*237: *O*563: *Π*90: *Σ*188: *T*27: *Φ*498: δ468: ε450: μ393: π401: ρ347: τ25: Hes.*Op.*697: Thgn.359: Melanipp.*Fr.*2.4: A.*Supp.* 651: *Th.*120,249: *Eu.*62,579: S.*Ph.*741: E.*Alc.*61: *Med.*717: *Hipp.*94: *Heracl.*70: *Andr.*1084: *Supp.*1233: *HF* 1394: *Ion* 1061: *Tr.*1046: *IT* 723,1401: *Hel.*138,417,544,1099: *Ph.*86,745: *Ba.*365: Ar.*Pax* 1118.

There are few instances in prose. Hdt.ii 100 νόῳ δὲ ἄλλα μηχανᾶσθαι· καλέσασαν δὲ . . . πολλοὺς ἱστιᾶν (editors omit δέ, or emend it to γάρ): Th.i 86.2 τοὺς ξυμμάχους, ἢν σωφρονῶμεν, οὐ περιοψόμεθα ἀδικουμένους οὐδὲ μελλήσομεν τιμωρεῖν· οἱ δ' οὐκέτι μέλλουσι κακῶς πάσχειν: Pl.*Cra.*428A εὐεργέτει καὶ Σωκράτη τόνδε—δίκαιος δ' εἶ—καὶ ἐμέ: X.*Mem.*iii 6.14 πῶς οὐχ ἕνα τὸν τοῦ θείου (οἶκον) πρῶτον ἐπειράθης αὐξῆσαι; δεῖται δέ ('it needs it'): *An.*vii 7.54 ἆρ' οὐκ . . . ἀπιόντα γε ἄμεινον φυλάτ-

[1] δέ is sometimes corrupted to γάρ: the converse also occasionally happens. See Pearson, *Index to Sophocles.*

τεσθαι πέτρους; ἤκουες δὲ τὰς ἀπειλάς: *Mem.*ii 1.1 *'Εδόκει... τοιαῦτα λέγων προτρέπειν τοὺς συνόντας ἀσκεῖν ἐγκράτειαν... γνοὺς δέ τινα τῶν συνόντων ἀκολαστοτέρως ἔχοντα... Εἰπέ μοι, ἔφη*... (*γάρ* Mücke: *δέ* can hardly stand, either here or in Hdt.ii 100 above, for explanatory *γάρ* of the type discussed in *γάρ*, II): Lys.xii 68 *φάσκων πρᾶγμα ηὑρηκέναι μέγα καὶ πολλοῦ ἄξιον* (*ὑπέσχετο δὲ εἰρήνην ποιήσειν μήτε ὅμηρα δοὺς*...): Pl. *Chrm.*153B (in an explanatory parenthesis): Aen.Tact.31.33 (introducing an example: *δή* and *γοῦν* have been suggested): Lys.xxi 14 (*γάρ* Reiske).

(ii) For *οὖν* or *δή*. In general, there are few examples, and none are striking. Hom.*A*83 *ἦ γὰρ ὀΐομαι ἄνδρα χολωσέμεν... σὺ δὲ φράσαι εἴ με σαώσεις*: *Θ*204 *οἱ δέ τοι... δῶρ' ἀνάγουσι πολλά τε καὶ χαρίεντα· σὺ δέ σφισι βούλεο νίκην* (but *βούλεο* may be an imperfect, not an imperative: see Leaf): *φ*259 *νῦν μὲν γὰρ κατὰ δῆμον ἑορτὴ τοῖο θεοῖο ἁγνή· τίς δέ κε τόξα τιταίνοιτ'*; E.*Ba.*1120 *ἐγὼ... εἰμι παῖς σέθεν... οἴκτιρε δ' ὦ μῆτέρ με*: *Rh.*165 *πονοῦντα δ' ἄξιον μισθὸν φέρεσθαι...—Ναί, καὶ δίκαια ταῦτα κοὐκ ἄλλως λέγω. τάξαι δὲ μισθόν*: *Hel.*710 *'Η δ' οὖσ' ἀληθῶς ἐστιν ἥδε σὴ δάμαρ;—Αὕτη· λόγοις δ' ἐμοῖσι πίστευσον τάδε* (*δ' secl.* Herwerden): Hdt.iv 154.1 *Ταῦτα δὲ Θηραῖοι λέγουσι* ('Well, that is what the Theraeans say': looking back to 150): Pl.*Lg.*903A ('Well, I think that is a pretty complete answer').

But two idioms emerge here with some distinctness:—

(*a*) A new suggestion, proffered on the rejection of a previous suggestion, is sometimes introduced by *δέ*. We might expect an inferential particle, 'then' or 'Well, then.' But the writer prefers to stress merely the difference between the suggestions (*δέ*). In such cases *δ' οὖν* (emphasizing the essential importance of the new suggestion), or *δ' ἀλλά* (further emphasizing the difference) are normal. E.*El.*532 (after the rejection of the hair-test) *Σὺ δ' εἰς ἴχνος βᾶσ' ἀρβύλης σκέψαι βάσιν*: *Alc.*1112: *Heracl.*257: *HF* 722 (*δ' add.* Nauck). (In E.*Ph.*1749 *δ'* perhaps goes with *ἀλλά* in 1751: see *ἀλλά*, II.1.iii.)

(*b*) *Δέ* sometimes marks the transition from the introduction to a speech to the opening of the speech proper: especially *ἐγὼ δέ*. 'Well.' Hom.*δ*400 *Τοιγὰρ ἐγώ τοι ταῦτα μάλ' ἀτρεκέως ἀγορεύσω. ἦμος δ' ἠέλιος μέσον οὐρανὸν ἀμφιβεβήκῃ*...: S.*Ant.*1196 *'Εγώ,* φίλη δέσποινα, . . . ἐρῶ . . . ἐγὼ δὲ σῷ ποδαγὸς ἑσπόμην πόσει: E.*Ph.*473 Ἁπλοῦς ὁ μῦθος τῆς ἀληθείας ἔφυ . . . ἐγὼ δὲ πατρὸς δωμάτων προὐσκεψάμην . . .: *Alc.*681,1010: *Supp.*301,467: *El.* 1018 (Dawes). E.*Rh.*424 is similar: so, perhaps, is S.*Tr.*252, where κεῖνος δὲ πραθεὶς . . . seems to open the promised λόγος, rather than to 'resume after the parenthetic apology' (Jebb). Cf. Ar.*Ec.* 555 ('Well, they say . . .').

The following prose passages, in which δέ introduces a disquisition predicted in advance, are broadly similar: Hdt.i 15 Ἄρδυος δὲ . . . μνήμην ποιήσομαι. οὗτος δὲ Πριηνέας τε εἷλε . . .: 140.3 ἄνειμι δὲ ἐπὶ τὸν πρότερον λόγον. Ἴωνες δὲ . . . (cf. vii 138.1): Th.iii 61.2: vi 89.2: Pl.*Smp.*215A Σωκράτη δ' ἐγὼ ἐπαινεῖν, ὦ ἄνδρες, οὕτως ἐπιχειρήσω (Alcibiades begins his encomium, after some preliminary observations): Ant.v 20 πειράσομαι ἐμαυτὸν ἀναίτιον ἐπιδεῖξαι . . . ἐγὼ δὲ τὸν μὲν πλοῦν ἐποιησάμην . . . ('Well'): Isoc.vii 72 τάχ' οὖν ἄν τις θαυμάσειεν, τί βουλόμενος . . . ἐγὼ δὲ . . .: here δέ opens the answer to the question just propounded: so, again, D.xviii 297 εἶτά μ' ἐρωτᾷς ἀντὶ ποίας ἀρετῆς ἀξιῶ τιμᾶσθαι; ἐγὼ δέ σοι λέγω ὅτι . . . (δέ *SL*: δή *vulg.*).

(iii) For ἤ. E.*Hipp.*145 Ἦ σύ γ' ἔνθεος, ὦ κούρα, εἴτ' ἐκ Πανὸς εἴθ' Ἑκάτας, ἢ . . .;—Σὺ δ' ἀμφὶ τὰν πολύθηρον Δίκτυνναν ἀμπλακίαις . . . τρύχῃ; *Ba.*560 Πόθι Νύσας . . . θυρσοφορεῖς . . . ἢ κορυφαῖς Κωρυκίαις; τάχα δ' ἐν ταῖς πολυδένδρεσσιν Ὀλύμπου θαλάμαις: A.*Supp.*781 (see Tucker). We may notice here the common εἰ δὲ βούλει, suggesting an alternative, 'or, if you like', where the English 'or' is perhaps more logical. Elliptical, Pl.*R.*432A εἰ μὲν βούλει . . ., εἰ δὲ βούλει . . ., εἰ δέ, . . .

(2) Apparently superfluous δέ. (i) In dialogue, when one question has been answered, and a second question asked (introduced by δέ or some other connecting particle), the second answer is sometimes introduced by δέ. The use of a connective in such a case, though not necessary, is natural enough, in Greek as in English.

Hom.*Γ*229 τὸ τρίτον αὖτ' Αἴαντα ἰδὼν ἐρέειν' ὁ γεραιός· "Τίς τ' ἄρ' ὅδ' ἄλλος Ἀχαιὸς ἀνὴρ . . .;" τὸν δ' Ἑλένη . . . ἀμείβετο . . .· "Οὗτος δ' Αἴας ἐστὶ πελώριος . . ." ('And who is this other?'—'And that is Ajax'.): A.*Pers.*480 σὺ δ' εἰπέ, ναῶν αἳ πεφεύγασιν μόρον, ποῦ τάσδ' ἔλειπες; . . .—Ναῶν δὲ ταγοὶ τῶν λελειμμένων . . . αἴρονται φυγήν (δέ marks the continuation of the Messenger's speech, as the Scholiast and Paley observe: the conjecture γε is unnecessary): Ar.*Nu.*192 τί ποτ' ἐς τὴν γῆν βλέπουσιν οὑτοιί;—Ζητοῦσιν οὗτοι τὰ κατὰ γῆς.—. . . τί γὰρ οἵδε δρῶσιν . . .;—Οὗτοι δ' ἐρεβοδιφῶσιν ('And these are probing Erebus'): Pl.*Cra.*398C ὁ δὲ δὴ "ἥρως" τί ἂν εἴη;—Τοῦτο δὲ οὐ πάνυ χαλεπὸν ἐννοῆσαι: 409A Τί δὲ ἡ "σελήνη";—Τοῦτο δὲ τὸ ὄνομα φαίνεται τὸν Ἀναξαγόραν πιέζειν.

(ii) δέ is occasionally found in passionate or lively exclamations, where no connexion appears to be required. In some cases γε would be appropriate, and should perhaps be read: in others a connective or adversative force is perhaps after all to be felt. There is little ground for assuming a specifically exclamatory use of δέ.

Hom.*O*90 "Ηρη, τίπτε βέβηκας; ἀτυζομένῃ δὲ ἔοικας: A.*Ag.* 1078 ὤπολλον ὤπολλον.—Ἡ δ' αὖτε δυσφημοῦσα τὸν θεὸν καλεῖ: 1256 Παπαῖ, οἷον τὸ πῦρ· ἐπέρχεται δέ μοι: *Pr.*67 Σὺ δ' αὖ κατοκνεῖς (cf. 743 Σὺ δ' αὖ κέκραγας κἀναμυχθίζει ('indignantis est interrupta per lamenta narratione', Wilamowitz). Neither passage should be read as a question, I think): S.*Tr.*1027 ἓ ἕ, ἰὼ δαῖμον. θρῴσκει δ' αὖ, θρῴσκει δειλαία . . . νόσος: 1091 (δε κείνοι (*sic*) *L*): *El.*593 ἢ καὶ ταῦτ' ἐρεῖς . . .; αἰσχρῶς δ', ἐάν περ καὶ λέγῃς (δ' *om. Γ*: γ' Hartung: but δέ may be 'nay', protesting): Ar.*Eq.*175 Εὐδαιμονήσω δ' εἰ διαστραφήσομαι (here and in the similar line, *Av.*177, only *R* reads δ', the rest, perhaps rightly, γ'): *Pax* 33 οἷον δὲ κύψας ὁ κατάρατος ἐσθίει (a connective is more natural in 524 οἷον δ' ἔχεις τὸ πρόσωπον, ὦ Θεωρία).

(iii). Inceptive. Herodotus and Xenophon occasionally place δέ at the opening of a speech, although in the nature of the case no connexion seems to be required. Sometimes δέ marks a contrast with the preceding speech: Hdt.v 109.3 (δέ *om. PSVU*): viii 142.1: X.*An.*v 5.13: vi 6.12. But in other places there is no obvious sense of contrast: X.*Cyr.*iv 5.23 ἐπεὶ δὲ ταῦτα ποιήσας ὁ Ὑρκάνιος προσῆλθε, λέγει ὁ Κῦρος· Ἐγὼ δ', ἔφη, ὦ Ὑρκάνιε, ἥδομαι . . .: vii 1.21 ἐπεὶ δὲ . . . ἐγένετο κατὰ τὸν ἄρχοντα . . . πρὸς τοῦτον ἔλεξεν· Ἐγὼ δὲ ἔρχομαι. . . . The object is, no doubt to give a conversational turn to the opening ('Well'), and to avoid formality. Cf. the corresponding use of ἀλλά (II.8).

In an answer to a question: Pl.*Chrm.*172C ἆρα ...;—Τάχα δ' ἄν, ἔφη οὕτως ἔχοι ('And perhaps that may be so'). At the opening of an oracle: Hdt.i 174.5. Mr. E. Harrison, *Studies in Theognis*, p. 211, observes that 'of the twenty-eight oracles given by Herodotus, eight begin with δέ, four with ἀλλά, one with καί': quoting the explanation of von Leutsch, that the seer directs his words against a popular, prevailing idea.

For the free use of δέ, and other connectives, at the opening of sections of Theognis, see again E. Harrison, *loc. cit.*: Reitzenstein suggests that the elegy was intended for use at the symposium, where you 'took up' the song (δέχεσθαι τὰ σκόλια): hence the connectives, δέ, γάρ, etc. Cf. Scol.Anon.9.1 ὁ δὲ καρκίνος ὧδ' ἔφα.

There are a few examples in Tragedy: A.*Ag.*717 ἔθρεψεν δὲ λέοντος ἶνιν (passing from the destruction of Troy to the fable of the lion's cub): E.*Ba.*272 οὗτος δ' ὁ δαίμων ὁ νέος ... οὐκ ἂν δυναίμην μέγεθος ἐξειπεῖν ὅσος καθ' Ἑλλάδ' ἔσται ('Now let me tell you about this god . . .').*

(3) In questions.

(i) δέ often follows (less frequently precedes) an interrogative at the opening of a question in dialogue. Though in some cases an adversative force would be appropriate enough, it seems clear, on the analogy of καὶ τίς . . . ; (and τίς τε . . . ; in Homer) that δέ is purely connective here. The speaker proceeds from the known to the unknown, and δέ denotes that the information he already possesses is inadequate.

The connective sense is found more or less unadulterated in the following: E.*Or.*435 Orestes has explained that Oeax is one of his persecutors. Menelaus: Τίς δ' ἄλλος; *Ion* 308 Σὺ δ' εἶ τίς; (contrast *Heracl.*638 Τίς δ' εἶ σύ;) *Hel.*459 Menelaus (ignoring the Beldame's unsympathetic comment): Τίς δ' ἥδε χώρα; *Heracl.*114 ... τυράννῳ τῆσδε γῆς . . .—Τίς δ' ἐστὶ χώρας τῆσδε καὶ πόλεως ἄναξ; Pl.*Lg.*664D Λέγεις δέ, ὦ ξένε, τίνας τούτους τοὺς χορούς . . . ; 676A,686D: *Clit.*409A: *Plt.*261C. But usually there is a note of surprise, impatience, or indignation in the question, as in καὶ τίς . . . ; and our 'And who . . . ?', 'And what . . . ?'. Hom.*K*82 Agamemnon comes in the night to Nestor, who awakes and says: Τίς δ' οὗτος κατὰ νῆας ἀνὰ στρατὸν ἔρχεαι οἷος . . . ; *Φ*481 Πῶς δὲ σὺ νῦν μέμονας, κύον ἀδεές, . . . ; *ζ*276 'Someone will say, "Τίς δ' ὅδε Ναυσικάᾳ ἕπεται . . . ;"': S.*Tr.*403 Σὺ δ' ἐς τί δή με τοῦτ' ἐρωτήσας ἔχεις; E.*HF*1114 εἶ γὰρ καὶ κακῶς πράσσων ἐμός.—Πράσσω δ' ἐγὼ τί λυπρὸν . . .; *Hel.*1635 Τοῖς γε κυριωτέροις.—Κύριος δὲ τῶν ἐμῶν τίς; Ar.*Eq.*1339 οὐκ οἶσθ' . . . οἷ' ἕδρας . . .—Τί δ' ἕδρων . . . ; *Av.*357 μένοντε δεῖ μάχεσθαι λαμβάνειν τε τῶν χυτρῶν.—Τί δὲ χύτρα νώ γ' ὠφελήσει ; *Nu.*1286 Τοῦτο δ' ἔσθ' ὁ τόκος τί θηρίον ; S.*OT*739,977 : *Tr.*314 : *Ph.*751,1001 : *OC*46 : Ar.*Ra.*630 : Hdt. v.33.4 Σοὶ δὲ καὶ τούτοισι τοῖσι πρήγμασι τί ἐστι ; Pl.*Men.*92B Πότερον δέ, ὦ Ἄνυτε, ἠδίκηκέ τίς σε τῶν σοφιστῶν . . . ; Is.viii 24 Σὺ δὲ τίς εἶ; σοὶ δὲ τί προσήκει θάπτειν ; D.ix 16 καὶ μηδεὶς εἴπῃ, "Τί δὲ ταῦτ' ἐστίν . . . ;" xlv 26 εὐθὺς ἂν εἶπε, "Τί δ' ἡμεῖς ἴσμεν . . . ,"

In E.*Rh.*844 the dialogue is imaginary : μὴ γάρ τι λέξῃς ὥς τις Ἀργείων μολὼν διώλεσ' ἡμᾶς· τίς δ' ὑπερβαλὼν λόχους Τρώων ἐφ' ἡμᾶς ἦλθεν, ὥστε καὶ λαθεῖν ;

(ii) Not infrequently, the δέ question does not stand at the exact opening of the speech, but is preceded by an apostrophe, an exclamation, an instigatory imperative such as εἰπέ or φέρε, or in general by any short phrase.[1] (For similar postponement in non-interrogative sentences, see III.B.2.)

Hom.*O*244 Ἕκτορ, υἱὲ Πριάμοιο, τιὴ δὲ σὺ . . . ; S.*OC*332 Τέκνον, τί δ' ἦλθες ; Hom.*P*170 : *τ*500 : S.*OC*1459 : Hdt.i32 Ὦ ξεῖνε Ἀθηναῖε, ἡ δ' ἡμετέρη εὐδαιμονίη οὕτω τοι ἀπέρριπται ἐς τὸ μηδὲν . . . ; Pl.*Lg.*890E Ὦ προθυμότατε Κλεινία, τί δ' ; (the postponement of elliptical τί δέ ; is remarkable) : X.*Mem.*ii 1.26 Ὦ γύναι, ἔφη, ὄνομα δέ σοι τί ἐστιν ; 1.30 Ὦ τλῆμον, τί δὲ σὺ ἀγαθὸν ἔχεις ; Pl.*Lg.*963B.

E.*Med.*116 Ἰώ μοί μοι, ἰὼ τλήμων. τί δέ σοι . . . ; Ar.*Av.*997 Πρὸς τῶν θεῶν σὺ δ' εἶ τίς ἀνδρῶν ; Pl.*R.*602C.

Ar.*Av.*89 Εἰπέ μοι, σὺ δὲ τὴν κορώνην οὐκ ἀφῆκας καταπεσών ; 812 Φέρ' ἴδω, τί δ' ἡμῖν τοὔνομ' ἔσται τῇ πόλει ; E.*Hel.* 832 : Ar.*V.*524 : *Av.*999 : *Pl.*1107 : Pl.*Thg.*126C Λέγε δή μοι· ἐπεὶ δὲ δὴ . . . ; *Sph.*229B Φέρε δή· διδασκαλικῆς δὲ . . . ; *Euthphr.*13E : X.*Mem.*ii 9.2.

[1] I include here some examples of questions containing no interrogative pronoun : see (vi) below.

S.*OT*437 γονεῦσι δ', οἵ σ' ἔφυσαν, ἔμφρονες.—Ποίοισι; μεῖνον. τίς δέ μ' ἐκφύει βροτῶν; *Ph.*1225 Δεινόν γε φωνεῖς· ἡ δ' ἁμαρτία τίς ἦν; E.*Or.*1072 Τί γὰρ προσήκει κατθανεῖν σ' ἐμοῦ μέτα;—Ἥρου; τί δὲ ζῆν σῆς ἑταιρίας ἄτερ; 1327 Εὔφημος ἴσθι· τί δὲ νεώτερον λέγεις; *Hel.*1043 Ἀδύνατον εἶπας. φέρε, τί δ' εἰ . . .; Ar.*Ach.*785 Σά μάν; πᾶ δ' οὐχὶ θύσιμός ἐστι; E.*El.*657: *IT* 1300: Pl.*Plt.*304B Τί δέ; τὸ δ' αὖ . . .; *R.*568E.

Even when the δέ question is very considerably postponed, the particle still often seems to look back to the preceding speech, rather than to mark a connexion with the present speaker's opening words. Hom.ψ184 Ὦ γύναι, ἦ μάλα τοῦτο ἔπος θυμαλγὲς ἔειπες. τίς δέ μοι ἄλλοσε θῆκε λέχος; Ar.*Eq.*88 Ἰδού γ' ἄκρατον. περὶ πότου γοῦν ἐστί σοι; πῶς δ' ἂν μεθύων χρηστόν τι βουλεύσαιτ' ἀνήρ; A.*Pers.*334 (and even 693, last line of speech, if δ' is sound): E.*Andr.*1083: Pl.*Ap.*24E. But sometimes the connexion is with the speaker's own words: Pl. *Cra.*392E οὐ . . . μανθάνω· ὦ Ἑρμόγενες, σὺ δὲ μανθάνεις; Ar. *Ach.*4.

(iii) The indignant tone which δέ often has in a question is present in an exclamation in the following: D.xxi 209 οὐκ ἂν εὐθέως εἴποιεν "τὸν δὲ βάσκανον, τὸν δ' ὄλεθρον, τοῦτον δ' ὑβρίζειν, ἀναπνεῖν δέ." ('And to think that . . .!' (question-mark in O.C.T.)).

(iv) τί δ' ἔστι; is a frequent expression in drama, conveying surprise. S.*Aj.*897: *El.*921,1237: *OT* 319: E.*Heracl.*795: *Hel.* 600,1514: Ar.*Ach.*178: *V.*836,1297: *et saep.*

The elliptical τί δέ; is also very common, in prose as well as in verse. There are several distinct types:

(*a*) (The commonest.) Expressing surprise or incredulity, and usually introducing a further question ('What?!'). E.*Hel.* 1240 θάψαι θέλω.—Τί δ'; ἔστ' ἀπόντων τύμβος; *El.*1008 Τί δ'; αἰχμάλωτόν τοί μ' ἀπῴκισας δόμων: S.*El.*1041: *OT* 941: *Ant.* 1281: *OC* 1175: E.*Heracl.*685: *Hipp.*784: *Hec.*886: *El.*406,963: *Ba.*654: Ar.*Nu.*481: *Ec.*135,525,762: *Pl.*1150: Pl.*Phdr.*234E: *Phd.*61C,D: *Cra.*427E: *Euthd.*272B: *R.*413A,450B: *Thg.*130B: *Alc.I* 114E. (E.*Hipp.*1413, rather differently: 'And why (do you blame the curse)?')

(*b*) With the connective force of δέ more prominent: 'And

what of that?' 'Well': 'Of course': 'Que voulez-vous?' A shrug of the shoulders. E.*Hec.*1256 Ἀλγεῖς· τί δ'; ἢ 'μὲ παιδὸς οὐκ ἀλγεῖν δοκεῖς; ('Well, do you not think that *I* grieve?'): *Or.*672 ὦ μέλεος ἐμῶν κακῶν, ἐς οἷον ἥκω. τί δέ; ταλαιπωρεῖν με δεῖ: 1326 κλύω βοήν.—Τί δ'; ἄξι' ἡμῖν τυγχάνει στεναγμάτων.

(*c*) As a formula of transition: 'And what (of this that follows)?' Cf. τί γάρ; *Quid? Quid igitur?* Mainly a prose use. S.*Ph.*421 (text uncertain, and Badham's τί γάρ; is perhaps right): E.*IT* 563 Λέλοιπεν Ἠλέκτραν γε παρθένον μίαν.—Τί δέ; σφαγείσης θυγατρὸς ἔστι τις λόγος; Ar.*Pl.*172 (after various instances of the power of Plutus) Τί δέ; τὰς τριήρεις οὐ σὺ πληροῖς; E.*Ph.*1078: *Or.*1275: And.iii 6 ἔστιν ὅπου ... ὁ δῆμος κατελύθη; τί δέ; πράττοντές τινες δήμου κατάλυσιν ἐλήφθησαν; Pl.*Prm.* 130C 'There is an εἶδος of τὸ καλόν, etc. ... Τί δέ; ἀνθρώπου εἶδος ...;' *Cra.*386A ἐξηνέχθην εἰς ...—Τί δέ; ἐς τόδε ἤδη ἐξηνέχθης ...; D.xix 104–9 ἔστιν οὖν ὅστις ὑμῶν φωνὴν ἀκήκοεν Αἰσχίνου κατηγοροῦντος Φιλίππου; τί δέ; ἐξελέγχοντα ἢ λέγοντά τι τοῦτον ἑόρακεν; 294 ἦσαν ἐν Ἤλιδι ... τί δέ; ἦσαν, ὅτ' ἦν Ὄλυνθος ...: Pl.*Grg.*503B (probably, while 503C is to be classed under (*a*)): *R.*410E, 459B: *Cra.*400A: *Phd.*74C,D,93A, 94B,101B: D.xix 309.

τί δὲ δή; is similarly used in Pl.*R.*470E,523E: *Ap.*24E: *Grg.* 452C. In continuous speech, Pl.*Lg.*935D.

(*d*) In E.*Supp.*124 τί δέ; represents a quoted question: Τί γὰρ λέγουσιν ...;—Τί δ'; εὐτυχοῦντες οὐκ ἐπίστανται φέρειν ('"What?"?'). πῶς δ' in *Ion* 959, where δέ has been suspected, is exactly similar: Καὶ πῶς ... ἔτλης;—Πῶς δ'; οἰκτρὰ πολλὰ στόματος ἐκβαλοῦσ' ἔπη ('Do you ask how?'). Add perhaps *HF* 1232: Τί δῆτά μου κρᾶτ' ἀνεκάλυψας ἡλίῳ;—Τί δ'; οὐ μιαίνεις θνητὸς ὢν τὰ τῶν θεῶν (though here τί δ'; might be taken as an ordinary surprised question).

(v) Other elliptical questions. πῶς δέ; πῶς δ' οὔ; In contrast with the very free use of elliptical τί δέ; elliptical πῶς δέ; is almost unknown: X.*Cyr.*vii 2.16 (δέ *om.DF*): and cf. E.*Ion* 959 above (iv.*d*). πῶς δ' οὔ; on the other hand is not rare in prose (there are few verse instances), denoting that the speaker not only assents, but characterizes his assent as inevitable. S.*OT* 567 Παρέσχομεν, πῶς δ' οὐχί; 937 ἥδοιο μέν, πῶς δ' οὐκ ἄν; Pl. *Euthphr.*13C:

*Phd.*67E: *Cra.*388C: *R.*457A,486C (cf. Καὶ πῶς; just above). Cf. A.*Fr.*310 λευκός, τί δ' οὐχί; (In S.*OT* 1015 πῶς δ' οὐχί; calls in question, not the possibility of denying the preceding words, but the validity of a denial contained in those words: Ἆρ' οἶσθα δῆτα πρὸς δίκης οὐδὲν τρέμων;—Πῶς δ' οὐχί (*sc.* πρὸς δίκης τρέμω), παῖς γ' εἰ τῶνδε γεννητῶν ἔφυν;)

Parallel cases without ellipse of verb. Pl.*R.*583A Πῶς δ' οὐ μέλλει; *Lg.*665A Πῶς δ' οὐ μεμνήμεθα; *Tht.*159C Τί δ' οὐ μέλλει; (185C: *R.*494B,530A,566D): *R.*469A Τί δ' οὐ μέλλομεν; X.*HG* iv 1.6 Τί δ' οὐ μέλλω;

ποῦ δέ; E.*Hec.*1015 Σκύλων ἐν ὄχλῳ ταῖσδε σῴζεται στέγαις.—Ποῦ δ'; αἵδ' Ἀχαιῶν ναύλοχοι περιπτυχαί.

τί δ' ἄλλο; E.*Or.*188 Θανεῖν, θανεῖν· τί δ' ἄλλο; Ar.*Nu.*1088 Σιγήσομαι· τί δ' ἄλλο; Pl.*R.*484B Τί δ' ἄλλο, ἦν δ' ἐγώ, ἢ τὸ ἑξῆς; X.*Cyr.* vi 1.47 Τί δ' ἄλλο, ἔφη, . . . ἢ πειρώμενος . . .;

(For the common Aristophanic τί δ' ἄλλο γ' ἢ . . .; and Xenophontine τί δέ, εἰ μὴ . . . γε . . .; see γε I.3.)

(vi) The use of δέ in questions which do not contain an interrogative is similar. Ironical in tone: E. *Heracl.*968 Καὶ ταῦτα δόξανθ' Ὕλλος ἐξηνέσχετο;—Χρῆν δ' αὐτόν, οἶμαι, τῇδ' ἀπιστῆσαι χθονί; ('And he should, I suppose, . . .?'): Ar.*Ra.*103 Σὲ δὲ ταῦτ' ἀρέσκει; ('And you really like that sort of thing?'). Purely continuative, without ironical colour: X.*Cyr.* v 1.4 Ἑώρακας δ', ἔφη, ὦ Κῦρε, τὴν γυναῖκα, ἥν με κελεύεις φυλάττειν; *Mem.* ii 9.2 Εἰπέ μοι, ἔφη, ὦ Κρίτων, κύνας δὲ τρέφεις . . .; (late position).

II. Non-connective.

(1) Apodotic. According as we regard δέ as originally 'adverbial' or as originally connective, we may explain apodotic δέ either as a survival of the adverbial use, or as an adaptation of paratactic expression to hypotactic structure.[1] Only in Homer and Herodotus is apodotic δέ really at home. Among other authors, Sophocles uses it, though rarely, more often than Aeschylus and Euripides, who eschew it almost entirely. Thucy-

[1] The latter view is certainly supported by such passages as those quoted from Herodotus in (iv), especially when compared with Hom.I 301 (see μέν, III.4.ii) and λ387: see p. 379.

dides, Plato, and Xenophon use it occasionally; Aristophanes, I think, never, and the orators hardly ever, if at all. (I exclude the duplication of δέ, which I reckon as a distinct idiom, though probably derived from apodotic δέ. See (4) below.) The Attic examples of apodotic δέ, though few in number, differ widely in character.[1]

(i) Relative protasis. Most of the examples are from Homer and Herodotus. The apodosis normally opens with a demonstrative (ὁ, οὗτος), or personal pronoun. Hom.*Z*146 οἵη περ φύλλων γενεή, τοίη δὲ καὶ ἀνδρῶν: *I*167 εἰ δ' ἄγε, τοὺς ἂν ἐγὼ ἐπιόψομαι, οἱ δὲ πιθέσθων: Hes.*Op*.363 ὃς δ' ἐπ' ἐόντι φέρει, ὁ δ' ἀλέξεται αἴθοπα λιμόν: Hom.*B*718: *K*490: *N*779: Hes.*Th*. 974: Hdt.iv 204 τοὺς δὲ ἠνδραποδίσαντο . . . τούτους δὲ . . .: vii 188.3 ὅσοι μὲν . . . οἱ δ' ἔφθησαν: Th.i 37.5 ὅσῳ ἀληπτότεροι ἦσαν τοῖς πέλας, τόσῳ δὲ . . . (τόσῳ δέ Hertlein: τοσῷδε *codd.*): ii 46.1 ἆθλα γὰρ οἷς κεῖται ἀρετῆς μέγιστα, τοῖς δὲ . . .: Pl.*Amat*. 137C πότερον ἥπερ . . . κολάζει ὀρθῶς, ἡ αὐτὴ δὲ καὶ γιγνώσκει τοὺς χρηστούς (ἡ αὐτὴ δέ *B*: αὕτη *T*: αὐτή Schanz): *Ep*.357B ἃ γὰρ . . . τυγχάνει . . . ταῦτα δὲ . . .: X.*Cyr*.iii 3.36 οὓς γὰρ . . . τούτους δὲ . . .: vii 5.6 ὅσῳ δὲ . . . τόσῳ δὲ . . . (τόσῳ δέ *F*: τοσῷδε *cett.*): Hdt. ii 61: vi 58.3: Hp.*Nat.Hom*.13. (In S.*Tr*.23, *Ph*.87 ὅδ', τούσδε should be read.)

In a few passages the pronoun opening the apodosis does not refer to the relative of the protasis: Hdt.iii 37 ὃς δὲ τούτους μὴ ὄπωπε, ἐγὼ δὲ σημανέω: iv 99 ὃς δὲ . . . μὴ παραπέπλωκε, ἐγὼ δὲ ἄλλως δηλώσω: Pl.*Lg*.878C ὅσα δέ τις . . . τοῦτον δὲ . . .: X.*An*. v 5.22 ἃ δ' ἠπείλησας ὡς . . . ἡμεῖς δὲ . . . πολεμήσομεν. Sometimes the apodosis does not open with a pronoun at all: Hom. *I*511 ὃς δέ κ' ἀναίνηται . . . λίσσονται δ' ἄρα ταί γε: *Ψ*321 ἀλλ' ὃς μὲν . . . ἵπποι δὲ πλανόωνται: Hes.*Th*.604 ὅς κε γάμον φεύγων . . . ὀλοὸν δ' ἐπὶ γῆρας ἵκοιτο: X.*An*.v 7.7 ὡς ἥλιος ἔνθεν μὲν ἀνίσχει, δύεται δὲ ἐνταῦθα, ἔνθα δὲ δύεται, ἀνίσχει δ' ἐντεῦθεν.

[1] Buttmann's attempt to confine apodotic δέ in Attic to cases 'cum sermo, extra protaseos et apodoseos formam spectatus, oppositionem contineat per μέν et δέ enuntiandam' imposes a restriction not warranted by the facts. Again, Jebb (on S.*Ph*.87) seeks to limit apodotic δέ after ὁ and οὗτος in 'good' Attic prose rather too narrowly, to cases where it is used 'to mark some proportion which exists between the two things'.

(ii) Temporal protasis. This is by far the commonest form of apodotic δέ in Homer, occurring more than seventy times.[1] Occasionally both protasis and apodosis begin within the same line. Hom.*O*343 ὄφρ' οἱ τοὺς ἐνάριζον ἀπ' ἔντεα, τόφρα δ' Ἀχαιοὶ . . .: ω205 οἱ δ' ἐπεὶ ἐκ πόλιος κατέβαν, τάχα δ' ἀγρὸν ἵκοντο. But the protasis usually begins in an earlier line, and usually fills at least one line. Hom.*A*193 ἧος ὁ ταῦθ' ὥρμαινε κατὰ φρένα καὶ κατὰ θυμόν, ἕλκετο δ' ἐκ κολεοῖο μέγα ξίφος, ἦλθε δ' Ἀθήνη: Ψ65 εὖτε . . . ἦλθε δ' ἐπὶ ψυχή: *Δ*221 ὄφρα . . . τόφρα δ' . . .: *N*779 ἐξ οὗ . . . ἐκ τοῦ δ' . . .: *A*58: *Δ*212,221: λ592: Hes.*Op*.681 ἦμος δὴ τὸ πρῶτον . . . τότε δ' ἄμβατός ἐστι θάλασσα: Thgn.724 ὅταν δέ κε τῶν ἀφίκηται ὥρη, σὺν δ' ἥβη γίνεται ἁρμοδία. I know of only three apparent instances in Attic Tragedy (A.*Ag*.205 S.*OT* 1267: E.*Ph*.47) and these have δέ in the protasis as well: hence we should perhaps regard them as instances of duplicated δέ (see p. 183).

Prose (Herodotus and Thucydides only). The commonest Herodotean form has μέν in the protasis, answered by another δέ in a second protasis: Hdt.ii 149 καὶ ἐπεὰν μὲν ἐκρέῃ ἔξω, ἡ δὲ τότε τοὺς ἓξ μῆνας ἐς τὸ βασιλήιον καταβάλλει ἐπ' ἡμέρην ἑκάστην τάλαντον ἀργυρίου ἐκ τῶν ἰχθύων, ἐπεὰν δὲ ἐσίῃ τὸ ὕδωρ ἐς αὐτήν, εἴκοσι μνέας: iii 133: iv 3,123,165: ix 6: 63.1: 70.2. Otherwise: i 163 τὰ μὲν πρῶτα . . . μετὰ δέ, ὡς . . . ὁ δὲ . . . ἐδίδου: iii 108 ἐπεὰν ὁ σκύμνος . . . ἄρχηται διακινεόμενος, ὁ δὲ . . .: vi 86.1 ὡς δὲ . . . οἱ δ' Ἀθηναῖοι . . . (δ' *om. PRSV*): in ii 52 ἔπειτα (*PRSV*) is probably the right reading: Th.iii 98.1 (in the normal Herodotean form) μέχρι μὲν οὖν οἱ τοξόται εἶχον . . . οἱ δὲ ἀντεῖχον . . . ἐπειδὴ δὲ . . . οὕτω δὴ τραπόμενοι ἔφευγον: otherwise: i 11.1 ἐπειδὴ δὲ ἀφικόμενοι μάχῃ ἐκράτησαν (δῆλον δὲ . . .) φαίνονται δ' οὐδ' ἐνταῦθα . . . (perhaps anacoluthon): ii 65.5 ὅσον τε γὰρ χρόνον προύστη τῆς πόλεως ἐν τῇ εἰρήνῃ, μετρίως ἐξηγεῖτο . . . ἐπειδή τε ὁ πόλεμος κατέστη, ὁ δὲ φαίνεται καὶ ἐν τούτῳ προγνοὺς τὴν δύναμιν: v 16.1 ἐπειδὴ δὲ . . . τότε δὲ . . . (δή *recc.*: δέ *codd.*).

It will be observed that, except in Homer and the normal Herodotean form, a δέ almost invariably follows the temporal relative in the protasis.

(iii) Comparative protasis. Hom.η109 ὅσσον Φαίηκες περὶ

[1] See the conspectus at the end of Lahmeyer's thesis.

πάντων ἴδριες ἀνδρῶν . . . ὣς δὲ γυναῖκες . . . : Thgn.357 ὥς δέ περ ἐξ ἀγαθῶν ἔλαβες κακόν, ὣς δὲ καὶ αὖτις ἐκδῦναι πειρῶ: Emp.*Fr*.84 ὡς δ' ὅτε τις . . . ὣς δὲ τότ' . . . : S.*El*.27 ὥσπερ γὰρ ἵππος εὐγενὴς . . . ὡσαύτως δὲ σὺ . . . : Hom.Ψ91 (perhaps anacoluthon): S.*Tr*.116: Hp.*VM*1 ἀλλ' ὥσπερ καὶ τῶν ἄλλων τεχνέων . . . οὕτω δὲ καὶ ἐπὶ ἰητρικῆς (δέ one MS.: δή the rest): Pl.*Prt*.326D ὥσπερ . . . ὣς δὲ . . . : X.*Cyr*.viii 5.12 ἐκάθευδον δὲ αὐτῷ ἐν τάξει ὥσπερ οἱ ὁπλῖται, οὕτω δὲ καὶ οἱ πελτασταί (text uncertain): Arist.*Mete*.355b15 ὥσπερ οὖν κἀκεῖ . . . ὁμοίως δὲ καὶ ἐν τούτοις: Hp.*Genit*.4,40. In both the following anacoluthon is a possible explanation: Pl.*Prt*.328A: *Alc.II* 151B.

(iv) Causal protasis (exceedingly rare). Hdt.i 112 ἐπεὶ τοίνυν οὐ δύναμαί σε πείθειν μὴ ἐκθεῖναι, σὺ δὲ ὧδε ποίησον: v 40.1 ἐπεὶ τοίνυν περιεχόμενόν σε ὁρῶμεν τῆς ἔχεις γυναικός, σὺ δὲ ταῦτα ποίεε: vii 51.1 (in these three closely similar passages the force of δέ is as in I.C.1.ii.*a*: cf. Hdt.iii 68, viii 22.2, under (v) below): Arist.*Rh*. 1355a10 ἐπεὶ δὲ . . . δῆλον δ' ὅτι . . . (some MSS. omit δ'): *Pol*.1278a32 (δή Susemihl). δέ cannot be defended in X.*An*.vii 7.7 ἐπεὶ δὲ . . . νῦν δὴ . . . (δέ *dett*.).

(v) Conditional protasis. Here again (at any rate in Homer, Herodotus, and Xenophon) the apodosis usually opens with a pronoun. Hom.*A*137 ἀλλ' εἰ μὲν δώσουσι . . . εἰ δέ κε μὴ δώωσιν, ἐγὼ δέ κεν αὐτὸς ἕλωμαι: *E*261 αἴ κέν μοι πολύβουλος Ἀθήνη κῦδος ὀρέξῃ ἀμφοτέρω κτεῖναι, σὺ δὲ . . . ἐρυκακέειν: Ψ559 εἰ μὲν δή με κελεύεις οἴκοθεν ἄλλο Εὐμήλῳ ἐπιδοῦναι, ἐγὼ δέ κε καὶ τὸ τελέσσω: *Φ*560 (perhaps: but see Leaf): δ832: μ163: π274.

Herodotus, who uses δέ in a conditional apodosis more often than any other writer, mainly has it in the first, or in the second, of two alternative hypotheses.

(*a*) In the first. iii 36 ὥστε, εἰ μὲν μεταμελήσῃ τῷ Καμβύσῃ . . . οἱ δέ ἐκφήναντες αὐτὸν δῶρα λάμψονται . . . ἢν δὲ μὴ μεταμέληται . . . τότε καταχρᾶσθαι: i 13: iv 65,68,94: v 1.2: 73.2: vi 52.6. Cf. iii 49 εἰ μέν νυν . . . φίλια ἦν πρὸς τοὺς Κερκυραίους, οἱ δὲ οὐκ ἂν συνελάβοντο τοῦ στρατεύματος . . . νῦν δὲ. . . .

(*b*) In the second. iii 69 ἢν μὲν φαίνηται ἔχων ὦτα, νόμιζε . . . ἢν δὲ μὴ ἔχων, σὺ δὲ . . . : iv 172 ἐκ τῆς χειρὸς διδοῖ πιεῖν . . . ἢν δὲ μὴ ἔχωσι ὑγρὸν μηδέν, οἱ δὲ . . . (the former hypothesis, ἢν μὲν ἔχωσι, is implied: cf. viii 115.2): iv 61: vii 157.2: 159: ix 60.3. In the second and third. viii 22.2 ἀλλὰ μάλιστα μὲν πρὸς ἡμέων γίνεσθε· εἰ δὲ ὑμῖν ἐστι τοῦτο μὴ δυνατὸν ποιῆσαι, ὑμεῖς δὲ . . . ἕζεσθε . . . εἰ δὲ μηδέτερον τούτων οἷόν τε γίνεσθαι . . . ὑμεῖς δὲ . . . ἐθελοκακέετε (the first protasis is implied in μάλιστα μέν).

(*a*) and (*b*) combined. iv 126 εἰ μὲν γὰρ . . . σὺ δὲ στὰς . . . εἰ δὲ . . . σὺ δὲ . . .: ix 48.4 καὶ ἢν μὲν δοκῇ . . . οἱ δ' ὦν . . . εἰ δὲ καὶ μὴ δοκέοι . . . ἡμεῖς δὲ διαμαχεσώμεθα.

A few Herodotean examples fall outside these categories. iii 68 εἰ μὴ αὐτὴ Σμέρδιν . . . γινώσκεις, σὺ δὲ παρὰ Ἀτόσσης πυθεῦ: vii 103.2 εἰ γὰρ κείνων ἕκαστος δέκα ἀνδρῶν . . . ἀντάξιός ἐστι, σὲ δέ γε δίζημαι εἴκοσι εἶναι ἀντάξιον (δέ *om. PRSV*).

Other authors. Verse. Timocr.*Fr.*1.2 ἀλλ' εἰ τύ γα Παυσανίαν . . . αἰνεῖς . . . ἐγὼ δ' Ἀριστείδαν ἐπαινέω: Pi.*O.*3.43 εἰ δ' ἀριστεύει μὲν ὕδωρ, κτεάνων δὲ χρυσὸς αἰδοιέστατος, νῦν δὲ πρὸς ἐσχατιὰν Θήρων ἀρεταῖσιν ἱκάνων ἅπτεται οἴκοθεν Ἡρακλέος σταλᾶν (δέ *AD*Thom.: γε *vulgo*): S.*OT* 302 πόλιν μέν, εἰ καὶ μὴ βλέπεις, φρονεῖς δ' ὅμως οἵᾳ νόσῳ σύνεστιν: *Ant.*234 κεἰ τὸ μηδὲν ἐξερῶ, φράσω δ' ὅμως: A.*Ag.*1061: *Eu.*887 (δ' οὖν). Prose. Hp.*Morb.*ii 54 καὶ ἢν μὴ νῆστις ᾖ, διδόναι δὲ . . .: Pl.*Phdr.*255A ἐὰν ἄρα καὶ ἐν τῷ πρόσθεν . . . διαβεβλημένος ᾖ . . . προϊόντος δὲ ἤδη τοῦ χρόνου . . .: *Ap.*38A ἐάντε γὰρ λέγω ὅτι . . . οὐ πείσεσθέ μοι . . . ἐάντε αὖ λέγω ὅτι . . . ταῦτα δ' ἔτι ἧττον πείσεσθέ μοι λέγοντι: *Prt.*353D ἢ κἂν εἰ . . ., ὅμως δ' ἂν κακὰ ἦν . . .; X.*HG* iv 1.33 εἰ οὖν ἐγὼ μὴ γιγνώσκω . . . ὑμεῖς δὲ διδάξατέ με: vi 3.6 εἰ δ' ἄρα . . . ἡμᾶς δὲ χρὴ ἄρχεσθαι: *Cyr.*v 5.21 ἀλλ' εἰ μηδὲ τοῦτο βούλει ἀποκρίνασθαι, σὺ δὲ τοὐντεῦθεν λέγε: *Vect.* 4.40 εἰ δ' αὖ . . . ὑμεῖς δὲ . . . (δή Bake): Aen.Tact.28.3 καὶ ἐάν τι δέῃ εἰσενέγκασθαι . . . ταῦτα δὲ χρὴ . . . κομίζειν: Arist.*Pol.* 1287b13 εἴπερ ὁ ἀνὴρ ὁ σπουδαῖος, διότι βελτίων, ἄρχειν δίκαιος, τοῦ δὲ ἑνὸς οἱ δύο ἀγαθοὶ βελτίους: [Pl.]*Sis.*388E: Arist.*Ph.* 215b15 (δέ *om. I*): *Rh.*1368b15 (some MSS. omit δέ).

(vi) After πλήν. Hdt.iv 189 πλὴν γὰρ ἢ ὅτι . . . τὰ δὲ ἄλλα πάντα κατὰ τὠυτὸ ἔσταλται: Hdt.i 164: vii 95.2: Pl.*Lg.*824A, 873E.

(2) After a participial clause. This idiom, analogous to apodotic δέ, is, I believe, confined to prose, except for Semon.7.110 κεχηνότος γὰρ ἀνδρός—οἱ δὲ γείτονες χαίρουσ' ὁρῶντες and a doubtful

passage in E.*Hyps.Fr.*60.11 Arn. ὃν ἐπ' ἐμαῖσιν ἀγκάλαις πλὴν οὐ τεκοῦσα τἄλλα δ' ὡς ἐμὸν τέκνον στέργουσ' ἔφερβον (γ' Hunt). Few examples are textually above suspicion.*

Hdt.v 50.2 χρεὸν γάρ μιν μὴ λέγειν τὸ ἐόν . . . λέγει δ' ὦν . . . : Hp.*Int.*1 εἶτα βρέξας . . ἐφ' ἑκάστην δὲ ἡμέρην ἀποχέειν: *Nat. Mul.*107 ταῦτα ἐγχέας . . . τοῦ δὲ ἐχίνου τρυπῆσαι τὸ ἐπίθεμα: *Mul.*162 μετὰ δὲ τοῦτο ἀμφιελίξασα εἴριον μαλθακόν, στρογγύλον δὲ ποιέειν: *Haem.*9 πολλῷ ὕδατι θερμῷ αἰονήσας, σύνεψε δέ: Pl.*Smp.*220B καί ποτε ὄντος πάγου . . . οὗτος δὲ ἐν τούτοις ἐξῄει: *R.*505E Ὃ δὴ διώκει μὲν ἅπασα ψυχὴ . . . ἀποροῦσα δὲ . . . διὰ τοῦτο δὲ ἀποτυγχάνει . . . περὶ δὴ τὸ τοιοῦτον . . . : X.*Mem.*iii 7.8 θαυμάζω σου εἰ, ἐκείνους, ὅταν τοῦτο ποιῶσι, ῥᾳδίως χειρούμενος, τούτοις δὲ μηδένα τρόπον οἴει δυνήσεσθαι προσενεχθῆναι (δέ in some MSS. only): *HG* iii 3.7 πάλιν οὖν ἐρωτώντων . . . τὸν δ' εἰπεῖν: *An.*vi 6.16 χαλεπὸν εἰ οἰόμενοι . . . τεύξεσθαι ἀντὶ δὲ τούτων οὐδ' ὅμοιοι τοῖς ἄλλοις ἐσόμεθα (δέ *om. det.*): Ant.i 12 εἰ γὰρ τούτων ἐθελόντων διδόναι εἰς βάσανον ἐγὼ δὲ μὴ ἐδεξάμην (δέ in *A* only): Isoc.xv 71 δέον αὐτοὺς τὴν φρόνησιν ἀσκεῖν μᾶλλον τῶν ἄλλων, οἱ δὲ χεῖρον παιδεύονται τῶν ἰδιωτῶν (MSS. vary between χεῖρον and οἱ δὲ χεῖρον): D.xliv 61 τὸ γὰρ σύνολον, ὄντες Ἀρχιάδῃ . . . κατὰ γένος ἐγγυτάτω, καὶ τῆς ποιήσεως . . . , τούτων δ' οὕτως ἐχόντων ἀξιοῦμεν κληρονομεῖν.

δέ can hardly stand in the following passages, where it follows the participle at a very short interval: Pl.*R.*393E ἐκείνοις μὲν τοὺς θεοὺς δοῦναι, ἑλόντας τὴν Τροίαν αὐτοὺς δὲ σωθῆναι (αὐτούς *AFM*: αὐτοὺς δέ *Df*): *Alc.I* 120B πρὸς τούτους σε δεῖ, οὕσπερ λέγω, βλέποντα σαυτοῦ δὲ ἀμελεῖν (δέ *BT*: *om. al.*: δή Madvig).

(3) Resumptive. This usage, akin to the apodotic, closely resembles in its limitations the resumptive use of δή (see δή, I.13). Usually a word (or words) at the beginning, or in the middle, of a clause is picked up by repetition. More often than not the clause is opened, as well as resumed, by a δέ. (Cf. 1.ii, *ad fin.*, above.) Often the insertion of δέ seems due to anacoluthon.

S.*El.*786 νῦν δ'—ἡμέρᾳ γὰρ . . .—νῦν δ' . . . : *OT* 258 νῦν δ' ἐπεὶ κυρῶ τ' ἐγὼ . . .—νῦν δ' . . . : Hdt.i 28 χρόνου δὲ ἐπιγενομένου καὶ κατεστραμμένων σχεδὸν πάντων . . . κατεστραμμένων δὲ τούτων . . . : vii 141.2 πειθομένοισι δὲ ταῦτα τοῖσι Ἀθηναίοισι καὶ λέγουσι . . . ταῦτα δὲ λέγουσι ἡ πρόμαντις χρᾷ δεύτερα τάδε: Hp. *Morb.*ii 5 ὁκόταν ᾗ ὑπερθερμανθῇ ᾗ . . . ὅταν δέ τι τούτων πάθῃ: X.*Cyr.*vii 2.23 νῦν δ' αὖ πάλιν ὑπό τε πλούτου τοῦ παρόντος διαθρυπτόμενος καὶ ὑπὸ . . . ὑπὸ τοιούτων δὲ λόγων ἀναφυσώμενος . . .: Arist.*deAn.*406a10 διχῶς δὲ κινουμένου παντὸς . . . διχῶς δὲ λεγομένου τοῦ κινεῖσθαι . . .: *Metaph.*1026b2: (without repetition) A.*Th.*745 Ἀπόλλωνος εὖτε Λάιος βίᾳ, τρὶς εἰπόντος . . . θνᾄσκοντα γέννας ἄτερ σῴζειν πόλιν, κρατηθεὶς δ' ἐκ φίλων ἀβουλίαν ἐγείνατο μὲν μόρον αὐτῷ.

In the following, δέ stands next to a demonstrative in a participial clause picking up the content of a temporal protasis: Hdt.ii 120 ἐπεὶ . . ., τούτων δὲ τοιούτων συμβαινόντων . . .: Pl. *Phdr.*272A ὅταν δὲ . . ., ταῦτα δ' ἤδη πάντα ἔχοντι . . . (πάντα δὴ ταῦτ' Galenus): *Smp.*183D ἐπειδὰν δὲ . . ., εἰς δὲ ταῦτά τις αὖ βλέψας . . . .

(4) Duplication of δέ. When apodotic δέ follows a relative protasis, the protasis itself is often introduced by δέ. Where this is the case, it is possible, and even natural, to regard the second δέ as a repetition of the first, and as looking back, not to the protasis, but to what precedes the protasis: the logical connexion being given twice over, in the main clause as well as in the subordinate clause, for the sake of clearness and emphasis. This is probably the origin of that duplication of δέ which is common even in Attic writers, who almost entirely eschew the strictly apodotic δέ. The duplication of μέν, not found before Empedocles, naturally follows, and we now have, as the full form, μὲν . . . μὲν . . . δὲ . . . δέ. Often, however, circumstances may make it desirable, or necessary, to duplicate one only of the two particles. We shall discuss later, under μέν (IV), the forms μὲν . . . μὲν . . . δὲ . . . δέ, and μὲν . . . μὲν . . . δέ. We have here to consider the duplication of δέ alone, preceded either by a single μέν or by no μέν at all.

It is often difficult to decide whether δέ is to be taken as apodotic or as duplicated (see p. 179). But (*a*) in Herodotus we should probably talk of duplication only where the two δέ's mark a sharp antithesis with what precedes. Hdt.ii 50 is a border-line case: 'Most names of Gods came to Greece from Egypt. τῶν δ' οὔ φασι (Αἰγύπτιοι) θεῶν γινώσκειν τὰ οὐνόματα, οὗτοι δέ μοι δοκέουσι ὑπὸ Πελασγῶν ὀνομασθῆναι.' (Cf. iv 66.

In both passages 'and' would be a possible translation of the first δέ.) In ii 111 δέ is more sharply antithetical. 'He burned all the other women. τῆς δὲ νιψάμενος τῷ οὔρῳ ἀνέβλεψε, ταύτην δὲ ἔσχε αὐτὸς γυναῖκα.' (*b*) Examples from Epic and Elegiac are perhaps best explained as apodotic, since they date from a time when duplicated δέ, as a distinct idiom, had not yet been developed. Hes.*Th.*609 ᾧ δ' . . . τῷ δέ τ' . . . : *Op.*239 οἷς δ' ὕβρις τε μέμηλε . . . τοῖς δὲ δίκην Κρονίδης τεκμαίρεται : *Op.*284,297 : Tyrt.*Fr.*9.27. And see, in general, (1) above.

Duplicated δέ is mainly found in two cases: (i) with a demonstrative pronoun (or pronominal adverb) answering a preceding relative: (ii) with a demonstrative pronoun standing in apposition to a preceding substantival phrase: very rarely (iii) in the protasis and apodosis of the second half of an antithetically bipartite conditional sentence. Of these (i) alone has a firm footing in the orators. Normally μέν precedes, but not always: but the δέ always expresses a fairly strong contrast, and is never purely continuative. In (i) the clause preceding the δέ complex usually opens with a contrasting relative.

(i) Hdt.i 171 τούτοισι μὲν δὴ μέτεστι, ὅσοι δὲ . . . ἐγένοντο, τούτοισι δὲ οὐ μέτα : Ant.v 62 ἐνταῦθα μὲν ἀφῆκεν αὐτόν· οὗ δὲ ἔδει κινδυνεύειν . . . , ἐνταῦθα δὲ ἐπεβούλευεν : Thrasym.*Fr.*1 ὁπόσα μὲν οὖν . . . , ἀκούειν ἀνάγκη . . . , ὁπόσα δὲ . . . , ταῦτα δὲ παρὰ τῶν εἰδότων πυνθάνεσθαι : Pl.*Prt.*325C τὰ μὲν ἄλλα ἄρα τοὺς ὑεῖς διδάσκονται, ἐφ' οἷς . . . , ἐφ' ᾧ δὲ . . . , ταῦτα δ' ἄρα οὐ διδάσκονται : *Phd.*113E καὶ οἳ μὲν ἂν δόξωσι . . . ἀφικνοῦνται . . .· οἳ δ' ἂν δόξωσιν . . . τούτους δὲ . . . οἳ δ' ἂν δόξωσι . . . , τούτους δὲ . . . : *Smp.*196B ἀνανθεῖ γὰρ . . . σώματι . . . οὐκ ἐνίζει Ἔρως, οὗ δ' ἂν εὐανθής τε καὶ εὐώδης τόπος ᾖ, ἐνταῦθα δὲ καὶ ἵζει καὶ μένει : X.*Eq.*10.6 ἵνα . . . τῇ μὲν λειότητι αὐτοῦ ἥσθῇ, ἃ δ' ἂν ὑπὸ τοῦ τραχέος παιδευθῇ, ταὐτὰ δὲ καὶ ἐν τῷ λείῳ ποιῇ (ταὐτὰ δέ *AB* : ταῦτα *cet.*) : Hdt.i 196 : ii 39,102 : ix 63.1 : 85.3 : Pl.*R.*431B : Arist. *Metaph.*1059b31 : Isoc.iv 98 : D.viii 3 : xx 80 : xlviii 39 : lvi 23.

(ii) Hdt.vi 54 αὐτὸς ὁ Περσεὺς . . . ἐγένετο Ἕλλην . . . τοὺς δὲ Ἀκρισίου γε πατέρας . . . τούτους δὲ εἶναι . . . Αἰγυπτίους : Hp. *VC* 13 τὰ μὲν ἄλλα τῆς κεφαλῆς ἀσφαλείην ἔχει ταμνόμενα· ὁ δὲ κρόταφος, καὶ ἄνωθεν ἔτι τοῦ κροτάφου . . . , τοῦτο δὲ τὸ χωρίον μὴ τάμνειν (anacoluthon) : Pl.*Phd.*78C οὐκοῦν ἅπερ . . . ταῦτα μάλιστα εἰκὸς εἶναι τὰ ἀσύνθετα, τὰ δὲ . . . ταῦτα δὲ σύνθετα :

X.*Eq.Mag.*8.3 οἱ δέ γε δεδιδαγμένοι . . . οὗτοι δ' αὖ . . . : Ant.v 42 τοῖς μὲν πρώτοις . . . λόγοις . . . συνεφέρετο . . . τοῖς δ' ἐπὶ τοῦ τροχοῦ λεγομένοις . . . τούτοις δὲ διεφέρετο: And.i 149 μὴ βούλεσθε Θετταλοὺς . . . πολίτας ποιεῖσθαι . . . τοὺς δὲ ὄντας πολίτας . . . τούτους δὲ ἀπόλλυτε: Hdt.i 146.2: Pl.*Phd.*80D,81B: *Phlb.* 30B,34A: *R.*475C,580C: *Ap.*32D: *Phdr.*278B: Arist.*HA* 524a8: *Metaph.* 1036a5.

We may also consider as appositional those passages in which a neuter demonstrative picks up an indirect statement or question. Hdt.vii 153.3 ὅθεν δὲ αὐτὰ ἔλαβε . . . τοῦτο δὲ οὐκ ἔχω εἰπεῖν: And.iii 1 ὅτι μὲν . . . δοκεῖτε . . . γιγνώσκειν· ὅτι δὲ . . . τοῦτο δὲ οὐ πάντες αἰσθάνεσθε: X.*Cyr.*i 6.43 ὅπως δὲ . . . ταῦτα δὲ πάντα τί ἂν ἐγὼ λέγοιμί σοι; Pl.*Chrm.*173D: X.*Cyr.*vi 2.14.

(iii) Hdt.vii 159 ἀλλ' εἰ μὲν βούλεαι . . . ἴσθι ἀρξόμενος . . . εἰ δ' ἄρα μὴ δικαιοῖς ἄρχεσθαι, σὺ δὲ . . . : Lys.xiv 21 ἀξιῶ δὲ . . . ἐὰν μέν τινες . . . ἐξαιτῶνται, ὀργίζεσθαι . . . ἐὰν δέ τινες . . . βοηθῶσιν . . . ὑμᾶς δὲ χρὴ ὑπολαμβάνειν (δέ *del.* Cobet): Pl.*Grg.* 502B διαμάχεσθαι, ἐάν τι αὐτοῖς ἡδὺ μὲν ᾖ . . . πονηρὸν δέ, ὅπως τοῦτο μὲν μὴ ἐρεῖ, εἰ δέ τι τυγχάνει ἀηδὲς καὶ ὠφέλιμον, τοῦτο δὲ καὶ λέξει καὶ ᾄσεται. Cf. D.xxi 100.

The following passages are remarkable for the shortness of the interval at which the particle recurs: Pl.*La.*194D ἃ δὲ ἀμαθής, ταῦτα δὲ κακός: X.*HG* ii 4.13 ὅτι εἰσὶ τῶν προσιόντων οἱ μὲν τὸ δεξιὸν ἔχοντες οὓς ὑμεῖς . . . ἐδιώξατε, οἱ δ' ἐπὶ τοῦ εὐωνύμου ἔσχατοι, οὗτοι δὲ οἱ τριάκοντα (δή *D*: δέ *cett.*): Tim.*Fr.*6d.230 τοὺς δὲ μουσοπαλαιολύμας, τούτους δ' ἀπερύκω.

III. Position. δέ is normally placed second in sentence or clause.

A. But certain types of postponement are common, in prose as well as in verse.

(1) When a clause opens with a preposition governing a substantive without the article (or governing a pronoun), δέ normally follows the substantive (Kühner II ii 268). Hom.*A* 461 ἐπ' αὐτῶν δ': *B* 194 ἐν βουλῇ δ': Hdt.i 31 μετὰ ταύτην δέ: Th.ii 98 ἐν ἀριστερᾷ δέ: Pl.*R.*564D ἐν δημοκρατίᾳ δέ: *Thg.*127C πρὸς σὲ δέ: X.*Mem.*i 2.24 διὰ μὲν κάλλος . . . διὰ δύναμιν δέ: D.xliv 5 ὑπὲρ αὐτῆς δέ. (Cf. Ar.*Eq.*1238 ἐν παιδοτρίβου δέ.) Less frequently, δέ is inserted between preposition and substantive (διὰ δὲ φρό-

νησιν): this position is regular, for δέ as for μέν, in the case of substantival ὁ governed by a preposition: X.*Mem*.iii 1.8 ἵνα ὑπὸ μὲν τῶν ἄγωνται, ὑπὸ δὲ τῶν ὠθῶνται. See Kühner, *loc. cit.*, citing Strange, *Lpz. Jhrb. Suppl.*i 345.

(2) Following article and substantive (or adjective). Hom.*A* 54 τῇ δεκάτῃ δέ: ρ14 ὁ ξεῖνος δέ: S.*OT* 389 τὴν τέχνην δ᾽: Hdt. i 121 τῇ σεωυτοῦ δέ: iv 137 τῆς Δαρείου δὲ δυνάμιος: Th.i 70.6 τῇ γνώμῃ δέ (*ABEFM*): Pl.*Prm*.128C τοὺς ἀνθρώπους δέ: *R*. 571E τὸ ἐπιθυμητικὸν δέ: *Grg*.521E ὁ αὐτὸς δέ (postponement after αὐτός seems normal: but Dr. Chapman quotes several examples of ὁ δὲ αὐτός: e.g. Pl.*Cra*.390C): X.*Smp*.2.17 τὰ σκέλη μὲν . . . τοὺς ὤμους δέ (followed immediately by τοὺς μὲν ὤμους . . . τὰ δὲ σκέλη): D.xviii 3 τοῖς ἐπαινοῦσι δέ: 315 τοὺς τεθνεῶτας δέ: 321 τοῦ δύνασθαι δέ: Pl.*Phdr*.257C: *Phlb*.63A. Cf. Hdt.iv 117 τὰ περὶ γάμων δέ: Pl.*R*.417A τὸ παρ᾽ ἐκείνοις δέ: *Cra*.388D Τῷ τίνος δὲ ἔργῳ . . . ; (but just below τῷ δὲ τίνος ἔργῳ). τὰ νῦν δέ is, I think, normal: but Pl.*Phdr*.266C τὰ δὲ νῦν (*B*).

(3) Following preposition, article, and substantive. A.*Pr*.323 πρὸς τοῖς παροῦσι δ᾽: E.*Alc*.603 ἐν τοῖς ἀγαθοῖσι δέ: A.*Pr*.383: *Th*.516: E.*El*.390: Hp.*Epid*.v 61 μετὰ τὰς πέντε δὲ ἐτελεύτησεν: Hdt.i 31 ἐπὶ τῆς ἁμάξης δέ: iv 192 κατὰ τοὺς νομάδας δέ: Th.i 6.3 ἐν τοῖς πρῶτοι δέ: iii 11.4 ἐν τῷ αὐτῷ δέ: X.*An*.v 4.13 ἐπὶ τῇ κεφαλῇ δέ (ἐν δὲ τῇ δεξιᾷ precedes): D.xviii 112 εἰς τοὺς συκοφάντας δ᾽ ἄγειν (so *AY*): Pl.*Cra*.389A: *R*.601A: *Cri*.47D. The order preposition, article, particle, substantive seems to be rare. Ar.*Lys*.593 περὶ τῶν δὲ κορῶν: *V*.94: Hdt.ii 159 ἐν τῇ δὲ ἐσθῆτι: Pl.*Grg*.490C: *Lg*.816C.

(4) Following two definite articles and substantive. A.*Th*.193 τὰ τῶν θύραθεν δ᾽: E.*Tr*.742 ἡ τοῦ πατρὸς δέ: Ar.*Ec*.49 τὴν τοῦ καπήλου δ᾽. But E.*Tr*.848 τὸ τᾶς δὲ λευκοπτέρου (τᾶσδε *codd.*).

(5) Late position after a negative. A.*Th*.411 αἰσχρῶν γὰρ ἀργός, μὴ κακὸς δ᾽ εἶναι φιλεῖ: S.*OC* 1360 οὐ κλαυτὰ δ᾽ ἐστίν: E.*Or*.100 οὐ φίλως δέ: Hdt.i 143 οὐδ᾽ ἐδεήθησαν δέ: Hp.*Vict*.26 οὐκ ἐν ἴσῳ δὲ χρόνῳ: *Jusj*. οὐ δώσω δέ: Pl.*Phdr*.227C οὐχ ὑπ᾽ ἐραστοῦ δέ: 242C οὐ πάνυ δέ (D.xliii 81): *Euthphr*.7A οὐ ταὐτὸν δέ: X.*Mem*.iv 1.3 οὐ τὸν αὐτὸν δὲ τρόπον (D.viii.67): Lys.vii 7 οὐ θαυμαστὸν δ᾽ (δ᾽ *C solus*): Is.iv 7 οὐκ ἐκ τούτων δὲ μόνον: D.xxii 16 οὐ πεποιημένης δέ: xlvi 17 μὴ πρὸς ἄλλο δέ τι: Hdt.i 91: v 71.1: ix 18.2: Pl.*Grg*.487A: *La*.194B: *Chrm*.174D: *Tht*.164A:

*Lg.*658B,693B,727A: *Epin.*990D: *id. saep.*: Lys.xii 59: xiii 85. In Hdt.i 71 the negative does not immediately precede the word to which it refers: *οὐ σῦκα δὲ ἔχουσι τρώγειν, οὐκ ἄλλο ἀγαθὸν οὐδέν* (for *οὐκ ἔχουσι δέ*).

The order is no doubt dictated by a desire to avoid the juxtaposition *οὐ δέ*: but that end is more usually obtained by transposition (*δὲ . . . οὔ, δὲ οὔ*), or by the substitution of another particle (*μέντοι, μήν*, etc.) for *δέ*. Nor is the juxtaposition entirely eschewed: but it is admitted only, I think, when the writer desires to convey the precise opposition between a positive idea and its negative counterpart, with a consequent heavy stress on the negative particle.[1] So normally with a conditional participle expressed or understood, a word or words being repeated. Hdt.v 35.4 *ἀποστάσιος ὧν γινομένης . . . μὴ δὲ νεώτερόν τι ποιεύσης τῆς Μιλήτου*: ii 70.2,177.2: iii 65.7: vii 149.1: viii 60 γ: Pl.*Plt.*284D *τούτου τε γὰρ ὄντος . . . μὴ δὲ ὄντος*: *Phlb.*17C: *Lg.*881D,916C, 930B.* With ellipse of verb: Pl.*R.*412D *ἐκείνου μὲν εὖ πράττοντος . . . μὴ δέ, . . .*: *Lg.*813D. With infinitive understood: Pl.*Sph.*262E *λόγον ἀναγκαῖον . . . τινὸς εἶναι λόγον, μὴ δέ τινος ἀδύνατον.*

B. The above limits are rarely overstepped in prose. (Such mild postponements as Pl.*Grg.*482E *ὡς τὰ πολλὰ δέ*: *Lg.*838A *ὡς οἷόν τε δέ*: *Phlb.*37C *ποιώ τινε δέ* can be reckoned under the categories enumerated above.) Poets go much further in the postponement of *δέ*, more, probably, as a matter of metrical convenience than from a reluctance to separate words closely united in sense. In many of the examples no such unity exists.

(1) In general.

Verse. Hom.*h.Merc.*510 *δεδαὼς ὁ δ' ἐπωλένιον κιθάριζεν*: Hes. *Op.*46 *ἔργα βοῶν δ' ἀπόλοιτο*: Thgn.992 *δύναται ἄλλοτε δ' ἄλλος ἀνήρ*: Xenoph.*Fr.*1.17 *οὐχ ὕβρις πίνειν δ'* (*δ' del. B*): Pi.*O.*10.99, *παῖδ' ἐρατὸν δέ*: A.*Pers.*719 *Πεζὸς ἢ ναύτης δέ*: 749: *Ag.*653 *ἐν νυκτὶ δυσκύμαντα δ' ὠρώρει κακά*: 606: *Th.*41 *αὐτὸς κατόπτης δ' εἰμ' ἐγώ*: 199: *Eu.*531 *ἄλλ' ἄλλᾳ δ' ἐφορεύει* (but Hermann's correction of *Pr.*400–1, approved by Paley and by Jebb on S *Aj.*116, goes

[1] I am confirmed in this supposition by an examination of Dr. Chapman's examples, some of which I had missed. For Hdt.viii 100.3, see p. 192.

too far): S.*Aj*.116 τοῦτο σοὶ δ' ἐφίεμαι: 169 μέγαν αἰγυπιὸν δ' ὑποδείσαντες (δ' *add.* Dawes): 1419 πρὶν ἰδεῖν δ': *OT* 486 ὅ τι λέξω δ' ἀπορῶ: 528 Ἐξ ὀμμάτων ὀρθῶν δέ (*lect. dub.*): 1282 ὁ πρὶν παλαιὸς δ': *Ph*.574 ἂν λέγῃς δέ: 618 εἰ μὴ θέλοι δ', ἄκοντα: 959 φόνον φόνου δὲ ῥύσιον τείσω: *Fr*.195 ἀρετῆς βέβαιαι δ' εἰσὶν αἱ κτήσεις: *Fr*.672: E.*Alc*.98 πυλῶν πάροιθε δ': *Andr*.617 κάλλιστα τεύχη δ': *Hipp*.835 πολλῶν μετ' ἄλλων δ' (δ' *om. LPV*): *Supp*.614 δίκα δίκαν δ' ἐκάλεσε (δ' *om. P*): *Ion* 1187 ἐν χεροῖν ἔχοντι δέ: 261,816: *El*.928: *Or*.88 Πόσον χρόνον δέ: 610 καλὸν πάρεργον δ': *IA* 1006 ψευδῆ λέγων δέ: *Hel*.331 βᾶτε βᾶτε δ' ἐς δόμους (following a repeated word: cf. *ib*.370 βοὰν βοὰν δ' Ἑλλὰς κελάδησε: Ar.*Av*.856): 688 Τίς μοι θυγατρὸς δ' (ὤμοι *codd.*: τίς μοι, Badham, defended by Pearson *ad loc.*): Ar.*Ach*.80 Ἔτει τετάρτῳ δ': *Pax* 186 Ποδαπὸς τὸ γένος δ' εἶ: *Lys*.160 ἐὰν λαβόντες δ': Theophil.*Fr*.6 τὸ πεῖσμ' ἀπορρήξασα δέ (δέ *om. A*): A.*Supp*. 786: *Pers*.446,729,818: *Th*.155,546,599,1015,1029: *Ag*.296,745, 1099,1277,1291,1320: *Ch*.266,519,761,839: *Eu*.19,21,68,176,197, 281,615: *Fr*.446: S.*Fr*.98: E.*Heracl*.39: *Alc*.469: *Supp*.783: *Fr*. 163,296,382.6,413,502,776 (several of the Euripidean fragments are textually doubtful): Ar. *V*.1351: *Pax* 1311: *Lys*.160: *Th*.746: *Ra*. 344,1007,1169: *Ec*.195.

Aeschylus was clearly far laxer than Sophocles or Euripides in this matter: and they, in turn, rather laxer than Aristophanes. T. W. Allen in *Rev. Phil.* 1937, pp. 280–1 lists thirteen examples of postponed δέ in the fragments of Middle and New Comedy,[1] which also took surprising liberties with γάρ. Porson corrected Alex.*Fr*.274–6 ὃς ἂν εἰς ἑτέραν ληφθῇ δ' ἀποστέλλων πόλιν (ὃς δ' ἂν *codd.*). Epig.*Fr*.7, even if δέ is sound, is inconclusive, in the absence of context. For references to authorities, see Ellendt, *Lex. Soph.*, *s.v.* δέ.

Prose. Hp.*Morb*.ii 12 τὰς φλέβας καίειν δέ: *Mul*.125 ἣν σφόδρα δὲ εὐημὴς ᾖ (δέ *om. Cθ*): Th.vi 10.4 τάχ' ἂν δ' ἴσως (so *ABEFM*): Pl.*Amat*.135C ἄκρον ἀρχιτέκτονα δέ: *Phlb*.50A ἅμα γίγνεσθαι δέ (δὲ γίγνεσθαι *T*): X.*Eq*.11.8 ἐπὶ τῶν τοιούτων ἤδη δὲ ἱππαζόμενοι ἵππων (so most MSS.: a surprising reading, which Kühner apparently defends): Lys.vii 4 δημευθέντων τῶν

[1] Add Apollod.Gel.*Fr*.27.2: Anaxipp.*Fr*.1.41,44: Philippid.*Fr*.6.2, 15.4.

ὄντων δέ (Bekker's δὲ τῶν is surely right): Isoc.viii 8 ὅ τι ἂν τύχῃ δὲ γενησόμενον: Hdt.v 79.2: vii 8δ1: ix 33.4: Pl.*Smp.*205A: *Prt.*311C: *Plt.*289B: *Lg.*669E,720A,721B,805B,929E,966A: *Ep.* 346B.

Most of these postponements are pretty mild. In contrast, Burnet's punctuation at Pl.*Lg.*785A goes beyond all reasonable bounds.

(2) In particular, when a sentence opens with a vocative, δέ is often postponed,[1] and follows the first word in the main body of the sentence. Except in questions (see I. C. 3. ii), this type of postponement is mainly confined to serious poetry: it is hardly found in comedy (Ar.*Ach.*259,1119), and it is rare in Attic prose (whereas the types of postponement described in I. C. 3. ii are appropriate enough to colloquial style: 'Good heavens! And what . . . ?' 'Come now, and what . . . ?').

Hes.*Th.*549 Ζεῦ κύδιστε μέγιστε θεῶν αἰειγενετάων, τῶν δ' ἕλε (δ' *om. L*): *Op.*213 ὦ Πέρση, σὺ δ' ἄκουε: 248 ὦ βασιλῆες, ὑμεῖς δὲ καταφράζεσθε: Thgn.817 Κύρν', ἔμπης δέ: Pi.*P.*4.59 ὦ μάκαρ υἱὲ Πολυμνάστου, σὲ δ': A.*Pr.*3 Ἥφαιστε, σοὶ δὲ χρὴ μέλειν ἐπιστολάς: S.*El.*150 ἰὼ παντλάμων Νιόβα, σὲ δ' ἔγωγε νέμω θεόν: *OT* 1096 ἰήιε Φοῖβε, σοὶ δὲ . . .: E.*Hec.*1287 Ἑκάβη, σὺ δ', ὦ τάλαινα . . .: Hom *A.*282: *B* 344,802: *Φ* 498: *γ* 247: *id. saep.*: Pi.*P.*1.67: 5.45: B.3.92: S.*Ant.*1087: *OC* 507,592: E.*Hec.*372, 415: *Hel.*1392: *Or.*622: Hdt.i 115.2 Ὦ δέσποτα, ἐγὼ δέ: vii 141.4 ὦ θείη Σαλαμίς, ἀπολεῖς δὲ σύ (in verse oracle): Pl.*Phlb.*48D Ὦ Πρώταρχε, πειρῶ δέ: Hdt.viii 68α1: Pl.*Thg.*127C: X.*Mem.*ii 1.26.

Postponement after an exclamation (for such postponement in questions see I.C.3.ii): E.*Andr.*1200 Ὀττοτοτοτοῖ . . .— Ὀττοτοτοτοῖ, διάδοχα δ' . . . (reading doubtful).

[1] According to L. & S., this happens 'when the speaker turns from one person to another'. That is probably true of most cases where δέ is postponed: but not of all, cf. S.*OC* 1459: E.*Hec.*415. On the other hand, Pearson (on E.*Hel.*1392) is hardly right in saying that δέ here is 'in its regular position with vocative outside the clause'.

Οὐδέ, μηδέ

We have seen that δέ is both connective (either continuative, 'and', or adversative, 'but') and responsive or 'adverbial' (apodotic). The same varieties of meaning are found in the negative form.

I. Connective. In Attic prose connective οὐδέ hardly ever occurs except when a negative clause precedes.* But Th.vii 77.1 καὶ ἐκ τῶν παρόντων . . . ἐλπίδα χρὴ ἔχειν μηδὲ καταμέμφεσθαι ὑμᾶς ἄγαν αὐτούς: Pl.*La.*198E προμηθεῖται . . . οὐδὲ τῇ μαντικῇ οἴεται δεῖν ὑπηρετεῖν: and perhaps *Lg.*889C ὡρῶν πασῶν ἐκ τούτων γενομένων, οὐδὲ διὰ νοῦν, φασίν, οὐδὲ διά τινα θεὸν οὐδὲ διὰ τέχνην (though here it would be easy to read οὔτε (or οὐ, Eusebius) for the first οὐδέ: to read οὐ δέ *separatim* (Burnet) does not help (see p. 187)). In Lys.xxiv 21–2 ἐγὼ δ' ὑμῶν . . . δέομαι . . . τὴν αὐτὴν ἔχειν περὶ ἐμοῦ διάνοιαν ἥνπερ καὶ πρότερον· μηδ' οὗ μόνου μεταλαβεῖν ἔδωκεν ἡ τύχη μοι . . . ἀποστερήσητέ με editors have generally, and no doubt rightly, altered μηδέ.

Where no negative clause precedes, Attic prose uses οὐ μήν, οὐ μέντοι, etc., or δ' οὔ, δ' . . . οὔ, as balancing adversatives: ἀλλ' οὐ as an eliminating adversative, and καὶ οὐ as a pure connective. ἀγαθὸς μέν, οὐ μέντοι συνετός: ἀγαθὸς μέν, συνετὸς δ' οὔ: κακός, ἀλλ' οὐκ ἀγαθός: κακὸς καὶ οὐ συνετός. (For the distinction between ἀλλ' οὐ and καὶ οὐ, see ἀλλά, I.1.ii.)

In poetry and Ionic prose the preceding clause is often positive. But H. Kallenberg has pointed out that Herodotus and Aristophanes are more restricted than Homer and the tragedians in this use of οὐδέ. In the case of Herodotus (1) there is almost always a sharp contrast between the ideas coupled (as in 1.ii below): (2) the ideas coupled are seldom (as often in poetry) 'nominale Begriffe': the following are exceptional: vii 174 οὕτω δὴ ἐμήδισαν προθύμως οὐδ' ἔτι ἐνδοιαστῶς: ix 87 σὺν γὰρ τῷ κοινῷ καὶ ἐμηδίσαμεν οὐδὲ μοῦνοι ἡμεῖς: (3) οὐδέ is seldom so used, more often μηδέ with the infinitive. Aristophanes, who stands far nearer than Herodotus to Attic prose usage in this respect (as in many others), *only* so uses μηδέ (*Av.*63 is obviously no exception): mostly in commands (*Pl.*448 in a conditional protasis).

(1) Without preceding negative clause.

(i) *Οὐδέ* as a balancing adversative, which sets a negative idea in the scale against a preceding positive idea, which may, or may not, be introduced by *μέν*. Hom.*Ω* 25 *ἔνθ' ἄλλοις μὲν πᾶσιν ἑήνδανεν, οὐδέ ποθ' Ἥρῃ οὐδὲ Ποσειδάων' οὐδὲ γλαυκώπιδι κούρῃ* ('on the one hand, he pleased the rest: on the other, he did not please these three'): *α* 369 *δαινύμενοι τερπώμεθα, μηδὲ βοητὺς ἔστω* (on the one hand, there is to be conviviality: on the other, absence of disorder): *γ* 141 *ἔνθ' ἦ τοι Μενέλαος ἀνώγει πάντας Ἀχαιοὺς νόστου μιμνήσκεσθαι ... οὐδ' Ἀγαμέμνονι πάμπαν ἑήνδανε*: *Ω* 418: *β* 182: Hes.*Sc.*368,415: Simon.121.3: Thgn.1070 *νήπιοι, οἵτε θανόντας κλαίουσ' οὐδ' ἥβης ἄνθος ἀπολλύμενον* ('who weep for the dead but not for the passing of youth': Theognis cannot mean that mourning the dead is in itself foolish: so that we cannot take *οὐδέ* as 'instead of': the precise interpretation of the particle is here a vital matter). Cf.S.*El.*132 *οὔ τί με φυγγάνει (τάδε), οὐδ' ἐθέλω προλιπεῖν τόδε* ('I realize you are trying to console me, but I cannot cease mourning'): A.*Ag.*263; S.*OC.*481: E.*Ba.*756,758.*

(ii) *οὐδέ* for *ἀλλ' οὐ*, holding apart incompatibles. Hom.*Z* 180 *ἡ δ' ἄρ' ἔην θεῖον γένος, οὐδ' ἀνθρώπων*: *ι* 408 *δόλῳ οὐδὲ βίηφιν*: *h.Ap.*1 *μνήσομαι οὐδὲ λάθωμαι Ἀπόλλωνος*: A.*Pr.*716 *ἀνήμεροι γὰρ οὐδὲ πρόσπλατοι ξένοις*: S.*El.*929 *ἡδὺς οὐδὲ μητρὶ δυσχερής*: *Ph.*996 *ἡμᾶς μὲν ὡς δούλους σαφῶς πατὴρ ἄρ' ἐξέφυσεν οὐδ' ἐλευθέρους*: *OT* 1434 *πρὸς σοῦ γάρ, οὐδ' ἐμοῦ, φράσω*: E.*Cyc.*376 *μύθοις εἰκότ', οὐδ' ἔργοις*: Ar.*Ra.*1020 *Αἰσχύλε λέξον, μηδ' αὐθάδως σεμνυνόμενος χαλέπαινε*: *V.*729 *πιθοῦ πιθοῦ λόγοισι, μηδ' ἄφρων γένῃ*: *Pl.*448 *εἰ ... φευξούμεθα ... μηδὲ διαμαχούμεθα*: Crates*Fr.*29 Dem.: S.*OT* 398: *Ant.*1269: *OC* 124: *El.*429, 997: *Fr.*624: E.*Fr.*87 418: Hdt.i 32.7 *ἐπισχεῖν μηδὲ καλέειν κω ὄλβιον*: iv 11.3 *δόξαι ἐν τῇ ἑωυτῶν κεῖσθαι ἀποθανόντας μηδὲ συμφεύγειν τῷ δήμῳ*: vi 96 *οἴχοντο φεύγοντες οὐδὲ ὑπέμειναν*: vii 206.1 *στρατεύωνται μηδὲ καὶ οὗτοι μηδίσωσι*: viii 60α *ἢν ἐμοὶ πείθῃ ναυμαχίην αὐτοῦ μένων ποιέεσθαι μηδὲ πειθόμενος τούτων τοῖσι λόγοισι ἀναζεύξῃς πρὸς τὸν Ἰσθμὸν τὰς νέας*: i 97.3 (rightly explained by Fritzsche): iii 76 2: vii 174.

Exceptionally, with the full force of a strong *ἀλλά*: Hom. *Π* 721 *Ἕκτορ, τίπτε μάχης ἀποπαύεαι; οὐδέ τί σε χρή* ('Nay, thou shouldst not'): A.*Ag.*1498.

(iii) *οὐδέ* for *καὶ οὐ*, simply adding a negative idea to a positive one. Hom.*A*330 *τὸν δ' εὗρον . . . ἥμενον· οὐδ' ἄρα τώ γε ἰδὼν γήθησεν Ἀχιλλεύς*: A.*Pr*.586 *ἅδην με πολύπλανοι πλάναι γεγυμνάκασιν, οὐδ' ἔχω μαθεῖν ὅπα πημονὰς ἀλύξω*: 769 *Ἦ τέξεταί γε παῖδα φέρτερον πατρός.—Οὐδ' ἔστιν αὐτῷ τῆσδ' ἀποστροφὴ τύχης*; S.*Aj*.1307 *οὓς . . . ὠθεῖς ἀθάπτους, οὐδ' ἐπαισχύνῃ λέγων*; *OT*731 *Ηὐδᾶτο γὰρ ταῦτ' οὐδέ πω λήξαντ' ἔχει*: 872 *μέγας ἐν τούτοις θεός, οὐδὲ γηράσκει*: *OC*663 *μακρὸν τὸ δεῦρο πέλαγος οὐδὲ πλώσιμον*: E.*Fr*.495.9 *εἶπόν θ'· εἶα συλλάβεσθ' ἄγρας, καιρὸν γὰρ ἥκετ'· οὐδ' ὑπώπτευον δόλον*: Hom.*A*97: Hes.*Op*. 488: S.*OC*685: Hdt.i45 *λέγων τὴν . . . συμφορήν, καὶ ὡς ἐπ' ἐκείνῃ τὸν καθήραντα ἀπολωλεκὼς εἴη, οὐδέ οἱ εἴη βιώσιμον*: viii52.2 *ἠμύνοντο . . . . οὐδὲ λόγους . . . ἐνεδέκοντο*: 60β *ὁμοίως αὐτοῦ τε μένων προναυμαχήσεις Πελοποννήσου καὶ πρὸς τῷ Ἰσθμῷ, οὐδέ σφεας, εἴ περ εὖ φρονέεις, ἄξεις ἐπὶ τὴν Πελοπόννησον*: 100.3 . . . *μηδὲ δυσθύμει* (*μὴ δέ* O.C.T.): ix8.2 . . . . *οὐδ' ἔχω εἰπεῖν τὸ αἴτιον* (contrast ix18.2 *οὐκ ἔχω δ' ἀτρεκέως εἰπεῖν*).

The line between (ii) and (iii) must not be too sharply drawn (any more than the line between *ἀλλ' οὐ* and *καὶ οὐ*). Some passages could be equally well assigned to either group: Hom. *A*95 (here I think *οὐδέ* stands for *καὶ οὐ*: the 'dishonour' consists not so much in the mere refusal to give back Chryseis as in the insult which accompanied that refusal, cf. 26–32): *A*542: A.*Pr*.326.

Nor, again, can we always distinguish sharply between (1) and (2). In Hdt.ii15 the question *τί περιεργάζοντο . . .*; virtually constitutes a negative ('there was no need for them to take so much trouble'). The same may be said of *ἄτλατον* in S.*Aj*.224 (a passage which may be plausibly explained in several ways).

Occasionally, in the positive clause preceding, *τε* prepares the way for *οὐδέ* (*τε . . . οὔτε* being hardly ever found: see *τε*, I.4.ii) Hom.*φ*310 *πῖνέ τε μηδ' ἐρίδαινε*: S.*OC*368 *πρὶν μὲν γὰρ αὐτοῖς ἦν ἔρως Κρέοντί τε θρόνους ἐᾶσθαι μηδὲ χραίνεσθαι πόλιν*: E.*IT* 697 *ὄνομά τ' ἐμοῦ γένοιτ' ἄν, οὐδ' ἄπαις δόμος . . . ἐξαλειφθείη ποτ' ἄν*. Cf. the irregular responsions mentioned under (2) below.

(2) With a preceding negative clause *οὐδέ*, in the sense 'and

not', is common in all styles. (For the rare sense 'but not', see S.*El.*132 quoted under 1.i.) Hom.*A*132 ἐπεὶ οὐ παρελεύσεαι οὐδέ με πείσεις: S.*Ph.*1006 ὦ μηδὲν ὑγιὲς μηδ' ἐλεύθερον φρονῶν: Th.iii 20.1 οὐδεμία ἐλπὶς ἦν τιμωρίας, οὐδὲ ἄλλη σωτηρία ἐφαίνετο. With a sense of climax, 'nor even' (cf. καί, I.5): Pl.*R.*347D οὐκ ἔχοντες ἑαυτῶν βελτίοσιν ἐπιτρέψαι οὐδὲ ὁμοίοις.

Irregular responsions. For τε ... οὐδέ, see (1) above, last paragraph.

(i) οὔτε ... οὐδέ, giving the effect of climax in the second limb: 'neither ... nor yet ...'. Pi.*I.*2.45 μὴ νῦν ... μήτ' ἀρετάν ποτε σιγάτω πατρῴαν, μηδὲ τούσδ' ὕμνους: S.*OC* 1141 οὔτ' εἰ ... οὐδ' εἰ (οὔτ' εἰ Elmsley, unnecessarily): Pi.*P.*8.85: Archil.*Fr.*7.1–2: Alcm.*Fr.*1.64–73 οὔτε ... οὔτε ... οὐδὲ ... οὐδὲ καὶ ... ἀλλ' οὐδ' ... οὐδὲ ... οὐδέ. In prose the οὐδέ is usually reinforced by αὖ. Pl.*Lg.*840A οὔτε τινὸς πώποτε γυναικὸς ἥψατο οὐδ' αὖ παιδός: (I am inclined to defend, with Burnet against Kühner, *R.*382E οὔθ' ὕπαρ οὐδ' ὄναρ (though the shortness of interval makes the irregularity harsher)): *Phlb.*22E: *Lg.*949C: *Ap.*19D (οὐδέ γε): D.xlvii 72: Lys.viii 7 οὔτε ... οὐ μὴν οὐδὲ ... οὐδ' αὖ ....

But in the commoner οὔτε ... οὔτε ... οὐδέ we need not necessarily regard οὐδέ as answering οὔτε. Th.vi 20.2: Pl.*R.*426B, 492E, 499B, 608B: X.*An.*vii 6.22: *Cyr.*i 6.6: *Mem.*ii 2.5: And.i 10, 29: Isoc.xii 259: Aeschin.i 47.

(ii) τε ... οὐ ... οὐδέ. Pi.*P.*8.36 Ὀλυμπίᾳ τε Θεόγνητον οὐ κατελέγχεις, οὐδὲ Κλειτομάχοιο νίκαν Ἰσθμοῖ. Th.ii.22.1 τε οὐκ ... οὐδὲ ... τε, and Pl.*Grg.*500B μήτε ... μηδὲ ... μήτε, are only apparent sequences. In each case there is true responsion between the τε clauses alone.

Kühner (II ii 294) observes that, when one οὐδέ is followed by another, the two never stand in a reciprocal relation,[1] like οὔτε ... οὔτε: but that either (*a*) the first is adverbial, the second connective: or (*b*) both are connective. (*a*) X.*An.*iii 1.27 σύ γε οὐδὲ ὁρῶν γιγνώσκεις οὐδὲ ἀκούων μέμνησαι (*ne videns quidem cernis, neque audiens meministi*): Pl.*R.*391C: (*b*) Hes.*Op.*715–7. Further instances in Kühner. (Ar.*Lys.*212–13, 249 are rightly

[1] In the sense, I should add, that οὐδέ is never, like οὔτε, a preparatory particle. For reciprocally related οὐδὲ ... οὐδέ, see II. 1. iii (especially X.*An.*i 8.20, where οὐδὲ ... οὐδέ comes near to οὔτε ... οὔτε in sense: though the distinction is obvious enough.

corrected by Bekker. Pl.*Phd.*93D (ll. 6, 7), altered by Stallbaum, is in any case no exception, being covered by (*a*).) (Hp.*Epid.* vii 93 is curious, and the text cannot stand: ἀποχρέμψιες ὑπόχολοι οὐδὲ ἐγένοντο οὐδὲ πολλαί.)

(iii) Occasionally the negative is omitted in the preceding clause, and has to be understood from the οὐδέ. (Cf. οὔτε = οὔτε . . . οὔτε: see τε, I. 4. v.) Jebb (on S.*Ph.*771) says that, where οὐδέ is retrospective, 'another negative, such as οὐδέν, is usually joined to the verb': 'usually' perhaps goes a little too far, in general: but in the orators a second negative seems always to be added.

(*a*) Without following negative. E.*Hec.*373 σὺ δ' ἡμῖν μηδὲν ἐμποδὼν γένῃ, λέγουσα μηδὲ δρῶσα (where the preceding negative, as in Th.v 47.2 below, certainly makes the omission easier: putting the comma after λέγουσα would, in fact, make the sentence perfectly normal): Ar.*Av.*694 γῆ δ' οὐδ' ἀὴρ οὐδ' οὐρανὸς ἦν: E.*Tr.*477 οὓς Τρῳὰς οὐδ' Ἑλληνὶς οὐδὲ βάρβαρος γυνὴ τεκοῦσα κομπάσειεν ἄν ποτε: Hdt.v 92β2 ἐκ δέ οἱ ταύτης τῆς γυναικὸς οὐδ' ἐξ ἄλλης παῖδες ἐγίνοντο: Th.viii 99 ὡς τροφήν τε οὐδεὶς ἐδίδου . . . καὶ αἱ Φοίνισσαι νῆες οὐδὲ ὁ Τισσαφέρνης τέως που ἧκον: Arist.*HA* 503b34 χεῖρας δὲ οὐδὲ πόδας προσθίους ἔχει.

(*b*) With following negative. Hdt.i 215.2 σιδήρῳ δὲ οὐδ' ἀργύρῳ χρέωνται οὐδέν: ii 52.1: iv 28.4: Th.v 47.2 ὅπλα δὲ μὴ ἐξέστω ἐπιφέρειν ἐπὶ πημονῇ μήτε Ἀργείους . . . μήτε Ἀθηναίους . . . τέχνῃ μηδὲ μηχανῇ (cf. 47.8): vi 55.1 Θεσσαλοῦ μὲν οὐδ' Ἱππάρχου οὐδεὶς παῖς γέγραπται: Isoc.iv 151 ὁμαλῶς μὲν οὐδὲ κοινῶς οὐδὲ πολιτικῶς οὐδεπώποτ' ἐβίωσαν: D.xxii 4 ἁπλοῦν μὲν οὐδὲ δίκαιον οὐδὲν ἂν εἰπεῖν ἔχοι. (In S.*Ph.*771 it is, as Jebb says, needless to read μηδ', μηδέ for μήτ', μήτε. See τε I.4.v.)

(iv) In Ar.*Ec.*452 only the last two of three units are connected: Οὐ συκοφαντεῖν, οὐ διώκειν, οὐδὲ τὸν δῆμον καταλύειν.: cf. E.*Cyc.*626: in Ar.*Fr.*317, the last two of five. Cf. δέ, I.A.4.

II. Responsive.

(1) Simply adding a negative idea, usually to a negative idea either expressed or implied:* 'not . . . either'.

(i) S.*Tr.*280 ὕβριν γὰρ οὐ στέργουσιν οὐδὲ δαίμονες ('any more than men'): *OC* 590 κεῖνοι κομίζειν κεῖσ' ἀναγκάσουσί με.—Ἀλλ' εἰ θέλοντ' ἄν γ', οὐδὲ σοὶ φεύγειν καλόν[1]: Pl.*R.*396A 'They must not imitate κακηγοροῦντας . . . ἀλλήλους καὶ αἰσχρολογοῦντας . . . οἶμαι δὲ οὐδὲ μαινομένοις ἐθιστέον ἀφομοιοῦν αὐτούς': *Phdr.*261A πείθετε ὡς ἐὰν μὴ ἱκανῶς φιλοσοφήσῃ, οὐδὲ ἱκανός ποτε λέγειν ἔσται περὶ οὐδενός: *Phd.*113C καὶ οὐδὲ τὸ τούτου ὕδωρ οὐδενὶ μείγνυται (looking back to 113B οὐ συμμειγνυμένους τῷ ὕδατι): *R.*372E ἴσως οὖν οὐδὲ κακῶς ἔχει ('Perhaps that's not a bad thing, either'): X.*Mem.*i 4.9 οὐ γὰρ ὁρῶ . . .—Οὐδὲ γὰρ τὴν σαυτοῦ σύ γε ψυχὴν ὁρᾷς: Ant.v 19.

The following are difficult. A.*Th.*1040 τούτου δὲ σάρκας οὐδὲ κοιλογάστορες λύκοι πάσονται ('And, as for his flesh, wolves shall not tear it, either', Tucker. The particle seems to look back to 1033 ἐγώ σφε θάψω. οὔτι Blomfield): E.*Ion* 1388 τὰ γὰρ πεπρωμέν' οὐδ' ὑπερβαίην ποτ' ἄν (οὐχ Nauck: Hartung, rightly I think, 'Dem, was mir bestimmt ist, kann ich auch nicht entgehen'). A.*Ag.*1523 is very curious: οὐδὲ γὰρ οὗτος δολίαν ἄτην οἴκοισιν ἔθηκ'; This means, of course, 'Did *he* not, too . . . ?' not 'Did *he* not, either . . . ?'. It is difficult to find a parallel. Jebb suggests, but rejects, the view that in S.*OT* 325 ὡς μηδ' ἐγώ stands for ὡς μὴ καὶ ἐγώ, and means 'lest I too': I believe that this interpretation is correct.

(ii) By a process of inversion frequently found in the case of καί (see καί, II.B.1.iii), οὐδέ, especially in a clause or sentence giving a reason, sometimes represents a negative idea which, logically speaking, is prior to another idea, as posterior to it. E.*Supp.* 523 πόλεμον δὲ τοῦτον οὐκ ἐγὼ καθίσταμαι, ὃς οὐδὲ σὺν τοῖσδ' ἦλθον ἐς Κάδμου χθόνα ('I was not bellicose on a former occasion, nor am I bellicose now, either'): S.*OT* 1409 ἀλλ' οὐ γὰρ αὐδᾶν ἔσθ' ἃ μηδὲ δρᾶν καλόν: *Tr.*126: Hdt.i 3.1 ἐπιστάμενον πάντως ὅτι οὐ δώσει δίκας· οὐδὲ γὰρ ἐκείνους διδόναι: i 141.2: Pl.*Prm.*137E Οὔτε ἄρα εὐθὺ οὔτε περιφερές ἐστιν, ἐπείπερ οὐδέ μέρη ἔχει ('Since it has no parts, it cannot have shape, either'): *Alc.II* 132D 'Εγώ σοι φράσω, ὅ γε ὑποπτεύω λέγειν . . . τοῦτο τὸ γράμμα. κινδυνεύει γὰρ οὐδὲ πολλαχοῦ εἶναι παράδειγμα αὐτοῦ, ἀλλὰ κατὰ τὴν ὄψιν μόνον ('There is not much evidence, and so I cannot be sure, either').

(iii) Further (again as in the case of καί: *q.v.*III.2) the addition

[1] Jebb is scarcely right in saying that 'οὐδέ is here the negative counterpart of δέ in apodosis'. The function of οὐδέ in this idiom is purely adverbial: that of apodotic δέ is structural.

may be conceived as reciprocal. In such cases οὐδέ, appearing in both limbs, takes over, as Hartung well remarks, the function of corresponsive καί. Hdt.i 2 τοὺς δὲ ὑποκρίνασθαι ὡς οὐδὲ ἐκεῖνοι . . . ἔδοσάν σφι δίκας τῆς ἁρπαγῆς· οὐδὲ ὦν αὐτοὶ δώσειν ἐκείνοισι: Pl.*Alc.II* 141A ὥσπερ οὐδ' ηὔχετο, οὐδ' ᾤετο: X.*Cyr.* i 6.18 ὥσπερ οὐδὲ γεωργοῦ . . . οὕτως οὐδὲ στρατηγοῦ: *An.*i 8.20 καὶ οὐδὲν μέντοι οὐδὲ τοῦτον παθεῖν ἔφασαν, οὐδ' ἄλλος δὲ τῶν Ἑλλήνων . . . ἔπαθεν οὐδεὶς οὐδέν (the first οὐδέ meaning both 'not either' and 'not even', the second simply 'not either'): D.xviii 140: Lys.xxvi 15 (perhaps: text doubtful).

(2) With sense of climax, 'not even'.

(i) In general. S.*El.*285 οὐδὲ γὰρ κλαῦσαι πάρα: X.*Smp.*6.2 οὐδ' ἂν τρίχα, μὴ ὅτι λόγον: *et saep.* In various set phrases, οὐδ' ὥς, οὐδ' ὁτιοῦν, οὐδὲ γρῦ, etc.

(ii) In the following, οὐδέ (μηδέ) negatives the succeeding idea *in toto*, passing beyond the mere negation of it in some qualified form. Pl.*R.*394D πότερον ἐάσομεν τοὺς ποιητὰς μιμουμένους ἡμῖν τὰς διηγήσεις ποιεῖσθαι ἢ τὰ μὲν μιμουμένους, τὰ δὲ μή, καὶ ὁποῖα ἑκάτερα, ἢ οὐδὲ μιμεῖσθαι ('not to imitate at all': τὴν ἀρχὴν οὐ, *omnino non*): 420D μὴ οἴου δεῖν ἡμᾶς οὕτω καλοὺς ὀφθαλμοὺς γράφειν, ὥστε μηδὲ ὀφθαλμοὺς φαίνεσθαι: *Smp.*202C πῶς ἂν . . . ὁμολογοῖτο μέγας θεὸς εἶναι παρὰ τούτων, οἵ φασιν αὐτὸν οὐδὲ θεὸν εἶναι; Pl.*Tht.*189A: *Cra.*436C: *R.*329A, 352B, 466B, 488B, 609C: *Lg.*809E: Arist.*Pol.*1261a17, 1275a27: *Rh.*1360a 29: D.xv 12. Cf. καί, II.A.2.

(3) Duplication of negative.

(i) In conformity with the Greek tendency to duplicate negatives, we often find οὐδέ reinforced by another negative. Thus οὐ is followed by responsive οὐδέ, and οὐδέ, connective or responsive, is followed by a negative. The great majority of my instances are from Kühner, II ii 204.

Hom.*P*641 οὔ μιν ὀΐομαι οὐδὲ πεπύσθαι: ε212 ἐπεὶ οὔ πως οὐδὲ ἔοικε: θ280 τά γ' οὔ κέ τις οὐδὲ ἴδοιτο: λ554 οὐκ ἄρ' ἔμελλες οὐδὲ θανὼν λήσεσθαι (but in λ613 μὴ . . . μηδέ represents a double wish, and neither negative is otiose): S.*Aj.*1334 μηδ' ἡ βία σε μηδαμῶς νικησάτω: *Tr.*280 ὕβριν γὰρ οὐ στέργουσιν οὐδὲ δαίμονες: *OT* 287: *El.*595: *Aj.*1242: Ar.*V.*448 Οὐκ ἀφήσεις οὐδὲ νυνί μ', ὦ κάκιστον θηρίον . . . ; Th.ii 97.6 οὐδ' ἐν τῇ Ἀσίᾳ ἔθνος ἓν πρὸς ἓν οὐκ ἔστιν ὅτι δυνατὸν Σκύθαις . . . ἀντιστῆναι: Pl.*Smp.*204A οὐδ' εἴ τις ἄλλος σοφός, οὐ φιλοσοφεῖ: X.*Cyr.*ii 1.8 οὐδ' εἰ πάντες ἔλθοιεν Πέρσαι, πλήθει γ' οὐχ ὑπερβαλοίμεθ' ἂν τοὺς πολεμίους: *An.*i 8.20 καὶ οὐδὲν μέντοι οὐδὲ τοῦτον παθεῖν ἔφασαν, οὐδ' ἄλλος δὲ . . . ἔπαθεν οὐδεὶς οὐδέν: D.xxii 32 ἐν γὰρ ταῖς ὀλιγαρχίαις, οὐδ' ἂν ὦσιν ἔτ' Ἀνδροτίωνός τινες αἴσχιον βεβιωκότες, οὐκ ἔστι λέγειν κακῶς τοὺς ἄρχοντας: Aeschin.iii 78 οὐδέ γε ὁ ἰδίᾳ πονηρὸς οὐκ ἂν γένοιτο δημοσίᾳ χρηστός.

(ii) In combination with other particles. οὐ μέντοι οὐδέ: Hdt.vi 45.1 (*ABCP*: οὐ μὲν οὐδέ *cett.*): Pl.*Prt.*331E. For οὐ μὴν οὐδέ, οὐ μὲν οὐδέ, see μήν (III.2.ii) and μέν (I.A.9: cf. III below). οὐ γὰρ οὐδέ: E.*Hipp.*1416: *El.*295 (here read probably καὶ γὰρ οὐδέ, Stob.: see Paley): Pl.*Lg.*821A.

Sometimes, again, the whole particle οὐδέ, not merely the negative, is duplicated: the first οὐδέ being either connective or adverbial. Hom.*I* 379–86 (the passionate emphasis with which οὐδέ recurs through the whole passage 369–91 adds great force): Hp.*VC* 9 οὐδὲ ἕδρη . . . οὐδὲ αὐτή: *ib.* οὐδὲ ἡ διακοπὴ . . . οὐδὲ αὐτή: X.*Cyr.*viii 7.20 οὐδέ γε ὅπως ἄφρων ἔσται ἡ ψυχὴ . . . οὐδὲ τοῦτο πέπεισμαι: Hdt.vii 196: Pl.*Ap.*19E: *Grg.*510C: Ant.v 48: Lys. xxxi 9. (In all the last five cases the second οὐδέ is followed by some part of οὗτος).

οὐδὲ ὦν οὐδέ: Hdt.ii 134.2: v 98.1.

οὐδὲ γὰρ οὐδέ: Hom.E22: Z130: Σ117: θ32: κ327: Hdt.i 215.2: iv 16.1: Pl.*Phdr.*278E: D.xiv 6.

For οὐδὲ μὴν οὐδέ, οὐδὲ μὲν οὐδέ, see μήν (III.2.iii) and μέν (I.A.8).

III. *Οὐδέ* as an emphatic negative, 'not at all'. In certain passages in Herodotus, where οὐδέ is clearly not connective, the sense 'not even', 'not either', is also inappropriate, and the particle appears merely to signify an emphatic negative.*

i 75.6 ἀλλὰ τοῦτο μὲν οὐδὲ προσίεμαι (οὐ *ABCP*: 'But this I do not at all accept': unless the meaning can be 'do not even consider'): vii 16β2 φῄς τοι . . . ἐπιφοιτᾶν ὄνειρον θεοῦ τινος πομπῇ . . . ἀλλ' οὐδὲ ταῦτά ἐστι, ὦ παῖ, θεῖα ('but this is *not* a supernatural occurrence': 'οὐδέ, als sollte zunächst folgen:

"auch hiervon ist deine Ansicht nicht richtig"', Stein, a very forced interpretation): viii. 25.2 *οὐ μὲν οὐδ' ἐλάνθανε τοὺς διαβεβηκότας Ξέρξης ταῦτα πρήξας περὶ τοὺς νεκροὺς τοὺς ἑωυτοῦ* (*sc.* 'though he *did* deceive them about the enemy dead'. It is, I take it, quite impossible that *οὐ οὐδ' ἐλάνθανε* should mean 'did not also deceive' (cf. II.1.i, *ad fin.*): 'jedoch auch nicht', Stein, but it should surely be, if anything, 'jedoch nicht auch')*: ix 7α2 *ἡμεῖς δὲ . . . οὐ καταινέσαμεν ἀλλ' ἀπειπάμεθα, καίπερ . . . ἐπιστάμενοί τε ὅτι κερδαλεώτερόν ἐστι ὁμολογέειν τῷ Πέρσῃ μᾶλλον ἤ περ πολεμέειν· οὐ μὲν οὐδὲ ὁμολογήσομεν ἑκόντες εἶναι* (where the repetition suggests that the last words mean 'nevertheless we will *not* come to terms': otherwise it might be possible to look back to *οὐ καταινέσαμεν*, and render 'we did not consent . . . nor will we in the future, either, come to terms': though this would perhaps require *οὐδὲ ἐς ὕστερον ὁμολογήσομεν*, or the like).

IV. The interpretation of a few other passages is doubtful. Hom.*I* 372 (probably adversative: 'he may try to fool some one else, but he will never dare to look *me* in the face again.' Or perhaps *οὐδέ* for *οὐ γάρ*, as *δέ* for *γάρ*: 'some one else, for it won't be me': *οὐκ ἄν, οὐκ ἄρ'*, for *οὐδ' ἄν, al.*): Ar.*Eq.*1302 *καὶ μίαν λέξαι τιν' αὐτῶν (τῶν τριηρῶν) . . . 'οὐδὲ πυνθάνεσθε ταῦτ' ὦ παρθένοι τἀν τῇ πόλει;'* (here *οὐδέ*, like *δέ*, *q.v.* I.C.3.vi, seems to introduce an indignant question: 'And haven't you heard . . . ?': though 'not even' is perhaps not impossible): Pl.*R.*328C *Ὦ Σώκρατες, οὐδὲ θαμίζεις ἡμῖν καταβαίνων εἰς τὸν Πειραιᾶ* (here *οὐδέ* is generally considered corrupt: *οὔ τι* Ast. Schneider supposes an ellipse, '"Tu neque alia facis, quae debebas, neque nostram domum frequentas". Simili ellipsi nostrates: "Du kommst *auch* nicht oft zu uns"'. There is certainly no very obvious implicit reference for *οὐδέ*, but Adam may be right in retaining it, comparing *R.*587C ('And it isn't very easy, either, to say . . .') as a (not easily analysed) colloquialism. See also Tucker on A.*Th.*1040 (his 1026)). In Lys.xx 8 *οὐδέ* is perhaps purely emphatic: 'And he did *not* make a single proposal' (cf. *καί*, II.C.7): *οὐδέποτε* Reiske (*οὐδέ* can hardly go closely with *οὐδεμίαν*): xx 36 seems similar, if Dobree's emendation is right: 'were saved by our enemies, but shall *not* find safety at your hands.' Cf. D.ix 48.

V. Position. Normally responsive *οὐδέ* immediately precedes the word with which it is most closely connected (unless a connecting particle claims precedence: *οὐδὲ γὰρ τοῦτο λέγω*). But a short interval between *οὐδέ* and the affiliated word is sometimes found. Hom.*A*354 *νῦν δ' οὐδέ με τυτθὸν ἔτεισεν*: E.*Supp.* 1068 *Ἀλλ' οὐδέ τοι σοὶ πείσομαι* (where it seems necessary to accent *σοί*: Iphis will not give way to Evadne any more than she to him): S.*El.*1304 (a more violent dislocation) *κοὐδ' ἂν σε λυπήσασα δεξαίμην βραχὺ αὐτὴ μέγ' εὑρεῖν κέρδος* (*οὐδὲ βραχύ*): *OT* 325 *ὡς οὖν μηδ' ἐγὼ ταὐτὸν πάθω* (Jebb takes *μηδέ* with *ταὐτὸν πάθω*: if this is correct, the order is dislocated: but see II.1.i). In Th.vi 21.2 *οὐδέ* does not go with *ἄγγελον* (see Marchant).

Connective *οὐδέ* is invariably first word in sentence, clause, or word-group.

Καὶ δέ: καὶ . . . δέ

This is a natural enough combination, the former particle denoting that something is added, the latter that what is added is distinct from what precedes.[1] In Homer the particles are always juxtaposed, in later Greek always separated by an intervening word or words. (In Hp.*VC* 13 *καὶ δ' αὖτε, δέ* may stand for *δή* (see *δή*, II.2): if, indeed, the text is sound.)

(1) *καὶ δέ.* Hom.*H*113 . . . *τόν τε στυγέουσι καὶ ἄλλοι. καὶ δ' Ἀχιλεὺς τούτῳ γε . . . ἔρριγ' ἀντιβολῆσαι*: *I*709 *καρπαλίμως πρὸ νεῶν ἐχέμεν λαὸν . . . καὶ δ' αὐτὸς ἐνὶ πρώτοισι μάχεσθαι*: *Ψ*494 *ἐπεὶ οὐδὲ ἔοικε. καὶ δ' ἄλλῳ νεμεσᾶτον, ὅτις τοιαῦτά γε ῥέζοι*: *Ω*370 *ἀλλ' ἐγὼ οὐδέν σε ῥέξω κακά, καὶ δέ κεν ἄλλον σεῦ ἀπαλεξήσαιμι*: *ν*302 . . . *ἥ τέ τοι αἰεὶ ἐν πάντεσσι πόνοισι παρίσταμαι ἠδὲ φυλάσσω, καὶ δέ σε Φαιήκεσσι φίλον πάντεσσιν ἔθηκα*: *Ω*563: *η*213: *φ*110,113. Preceded by *μέν*: *Ψ*80 *ἀλλ' ἐμὲ μὲν κὴρ ἀμφέχανε στυγερὴ . . . καὶ δὲ σοὶ αὐτῷ μοῖρα . . . ἀπολέσθαι.*

καὶ δέ is sometimes used where *καὶ γάρ* would be logically

[1] Jebb, on S.*Ph.*1362, argues for the view that, in *καὶ . . . δέ*, *καί* is the conjunction, while *δέ* means 'on the other hand', 'also'. This is, I think, the right explanation of most of the passages. But there are others (see (2) below) in which *δέ* seems to be the conjunction, while *καί* means 'also'. Here, as with other combinations, a different analysis is required in different cases.

more appropriate. Cf. δέ for γάρ. Hom.X420 λίσσωμ' ἀνέρα τοῦτον . . . καὶ δέ νυ τῷ γε πατὴρ τοιόσδε τέτυκται: Υ105. (π418 is remarkable: Ἀντίνο', ὕβριν ἔχων, κακομήχανε, καὶ δέ σέ φασιν ἐν δήμῳ Ἰθάκης μεθ' ὁμήλικας ἔμμεν ἄριστον . . . σὺ δ' οὐκ ἄρα τοῖος ἔησθα. The apparently superfluous connective seems to be *indignantis*: 'and they say, forsooth . . .'. Cf. καί in indignant questions (*q.v.* II.B.10.ii.*b*): in fact there may be an interrogative tinge in the present passage.)

(2) καὶ . . . δέ. The combination is relatively rare in verse, and some critics wrongly seek to exclude it altogether from tragedy. (See Paley on A.*Pr.*973, his 994.) In Sophocles, *Ph.*1362 is the only example: καὶ σοῦ δ' ἔγωγε θαυμάσας ἔχω τόδε (here I should regard δέ as the connective: 'And in thee also . . .': so too in A.*Pr.*973: *Ch.*879 πύλας μοχλοῖς χαλᾶτε· καὶ μάλ' ἡβῶντος δὲ δεῖ: E.*El.*1117 Τρόποι τοιοῦτοι· καὶ σὺ δ' αὐθάδης ἔφυς: *Ion* 1608 πείθομαι δ' εἶναι πατρὸς Λοξίου καὶ τῆσδε. καὶ πρὶν τοῦτο δ' οὐκ ἄπιστον ἦν (if δ' is right): 1327 Ἤκουσα· καὶ σὺ δ' ὠμὸς ὢν ἁμαρτάνεις: and perhaps this analysis is correct in other cases too).

A.*Pers.*153 προσπίτνω· καὶ προσφθόγγοις δὲ χρεὼν αὐτὴν πάντας μύθοισι προσαυδᾶν: 546 αἱ δ' ἁβρόγοοι Περσίδες . . . πενθοῦσι . . . κἀγὼ δὲ μόρον τῶν οἰχομένων αἴρω δοκίμως πολυπενθῆ: *Eu.*65 ἐγγὺς παρεστὼς καὶ πρόσω δ' ἀποστατῶν ('aye, and from afar'): E.*IT* 1206 ἴτ' ἐπὶ δεσμά, πρόσπολοι.—Κἀκκομιζόντων δὲ δεῦρο τοὺς ξένους: Ar.*Eq.*711 Ἕλξω σε πρὸς τὸν δῆμον . . . —Κἀγὼ δὲ σ' ἕλξω (like δέ γε: cf. Pl.Com.*Fr.*69.3 ἐγὼ δὲ νίπτρον παραχέων ἔρχομαι.—Κἀγὼ δὲ παρακορήσων): *Pax* 523 ὦ χαῖρ' Ὀπώρα, καὶ σὺ δ' ὦ Θεωρία ('and you too, Theoria'): 632 Κᾆτα δ' ὡς ἐκ τῶν ἀγρῶν ξυνῆλθεν οὑργάτης λεώς (proceeding with a narrative, after comments from the listeners): Antiph.*Fr.*140 Τρώγοιμι καὶ | ᾠὸν δὲ καταπίνοιμ' ἄν (καί and δέ in different lines): A.*Pers.*261,779 (τ' *recc.*): *Fr.*43.1: E.*Fr.*388,518: Ar.*Pax* 250, 1149: *Lys.*1320: *Pl.*764,838. (A.*Supp.*809–10 is corrupt: so, probably, is *Eu.*406.)

In prose καὶ . . . δέ appears early. Heraclit.*Fr.*5 καὶ τοῖς ἀγάλμασι δὲ τουτέοισιν εὔχονται: *Fr.*12 καὶ ψυχαὶ δὲ . . .: Anaxag.*Fr.*6 καὶ ὅτε δὲ ἴσαι μοῖραί εἰσι: Pherecydes*Fr.*18a καὶ ὅτε δὲ ἦν ἐν τῷ πελάγει: Democr.*Fr.*191 ἐπικαινουργεῖν ἀναγκάζεται καὶ ἐπιβάλλεσθαι δ' ἐπιθυμίην τοῦ τι πρήσσειν ἀνήκεστον: Gorg. *Fr.*11.11 ὅσοι δὲ ὅσους περὶ ὅσων καὶ ἔπεισαν καὶ πείθουσι δέ. It is found rarely in Herodotus (ii 44.1,44.5,127.1: iv 105.2 (some MSS.): in ix 79.1 κἀκείνοισι δὲ ἐπιφθονέομεν, καί means 'also'), Hippocrates (*Fract.*1,26,30: *Art.*48: *VM* 6: *Acut.*15: *Morb.Sac.*3: *Genit.*20), and Thucydides (i 132.4 ἐπυνθάνοντο δὲ καὶ ἐς τοὺς Εἵλωτας πράσσειν τι αὐτόν, καὶ ἦν δὲ οὕτως: ii 36.1 δίκαιον γὰρ αὐτοῖς καὶ πρέπον δὲ ἅμα: iv 24.2: vi 71.2: vii 56.3: viii 67.3). It is common in Plato, Aristotle, and the orators, and (as has often been observed) particularly common in Xenophon.[1]

(i) In general. Pl.*Grg.*475A Ὅταν ἄρα . . . Καὶ ὅταν δὲ δὴ . . . : *Prt.*331B ἐγὼ μὲν γὰρ αὐτὸς ὑπέρ γ' ἐμαυτοῦ φαίην ἂν . . . καὶ ὑπὲρ σοῦ δὲ . . . ταὐτὰ ἂν ταῦτα ἀποκρινοίμην: 361E οὐκ ἂν θαυμάζοιμι εἰ τῶν ἐλλογίμων γένοιο ἀνδρῶν ἐπὶ σοφίᾳ. καὶ περὶ τούτων δὲ εἰς αὖθις . . . διέξιμεν: *Cri.*51A ἐάν σε ἐπιχειρῶμεν ἡμεῖς ἀπολλύναι . . καὶ σὺ δὲ ἡμᾶς . . . : *Phlb.*40C εἰσὶν δὴ . . . ψευδεῖς . . . ἡδοναὶ . . . καὶ λῦπαι δὲ ὡσαύτως: X.*HG* v 1.16 'You must endure hardships. καὶ ἡ πόλις δέ τοι . . . τἀγαθὰ καὶ τὰ καλὰ ἐκτήσατο οὐ ῥᾳθυμοῦσα' (καὶ ἡ πόλις perhaps together): *An.*iii 2.25 ἐν ἀφθόνοις βιοτεύειν, καὶ Μήδων δὲ . . . παρθένοις ὁμιλεῖν: v 3.9 παρεῖχε δὲ ἡ θεὸς . . . τραγήματα, καὶ τῶν θυομένων ἀπὸ τῆς ἱερᾶς νομῆς λάχος, καὶ τῶν θηρευομένων δέ: D.ix 70 ἐγὼ νὴ Δί' ἐρῶ, καὶ γράψω δέ: xxi 189 οἵους ἐνίους τῶν λεγόντων ἐγὼ καὶ ὑμεῖς δ' ὁρᾶτε: Pl.*Lg.*637B,665B,682C, 696A,699B,964A: *Grg.*513A: *R.*335A,436E: *Phlb.*13B: X.*HG* v 4.25: Lys.i 12 (καὶ πρότερον closely together): xix 5: D.xviii 43,215: xxi 26,126: xxiii 51: xlv 41: xlvii 5: lvii 4: Aeschin. i 23,69: ii 51: iii 126.

Usually καὶ . . . δέ is taken in the writer's stride, like καὶ . . . δή, and follows a weak stop. Occasionally, however, it marks a completely new start after a stronger break, like καὶ μήν. Pl. *Lg.*921A 'Work must be punctually completed. καὶ ἀναιρουμένῳ δ' ἔργον συμβουλευτὴς νόμος . . . μὴ πλέονος τιμᾶν δια-

[1] Also in Lucian, according to Sikes and Willson on A.*Pr.*973. Rehdantz (*Index*, p. 92) gives information regarding the distribution of καὶ . . . δέ: it is commoner in Demosthenes than in the other orators. (Rehdantz is wrong in saying that καὶ . . δέ occurs 'seldom' in Plato, 'more often' in Thucydides. Krüger (apparently aiming at completeness) gives six examples from Thucydides: I have counted thirty-five in Plato (fourteen from the *Laws*).

πειρώμενον': X.*An*.ii 6.7 οὕτω μὲν φιλοπόλεμος ἦν . . . καὶ ἀρχικὸς δ' ἐλέγετο εἶναι. See also (ii).

(ii) Introducing a new instance. Pl.*Clit*.409B ἰατρική πού τις λέγεται τέχνη· ταύτης δ' ἐστὶν διττὰ τὰ ἀποτελούμενα . . . καὶ τεκτονικῆς δὲ κατὰ ταὐτὰ . . . : *Alc.I* 118D, 126B : X.*Oec*.8.8.

(iii) Introducing the last item of a series. Pl.*Tht*.171E πᾶν γύναιον καὶ παιδίον καὶ θηρίον δέ : *Lg*.833B πρῶτος δὲ . . . δεύτερος δὲ . . . καὶ τρίτος . . . καὶ δὴ καὶ τέταρτος . . . καὶ πέμπτος δέ : X.*An*.v 6.15 πελταστὰς πολλοὺς καὶ τοξότας καὶ σφενδονήτας καὶ ἱππέας δέ : D.lii 11 πρὸς τὸν Ἀρχεβιάδην καὶ τὸν Ἀριστόνουν καὶ πρὸς αὐτὸν δὲ τὸν Κηφισιάδην : Aeschin.i 50 πρῶτον μὲν κάλει . . . ἔπειτα τὴν Φαίδρου μαρτυρίαν ἀναγίγνωσκε. καὶ τελευταίαν δέ μοι λαβὲ τὴν . . . μαρτυρίαν : iii 115 Μειδίαν τε . . . καὶ . . . καὶ τρίτον δὲ μετὰ τούτων ἐμέ : Pl.*Lg*.637C : X.*Cyr*.ii 1.29 : D.iii 15 : Aeschin.i 61.

The last item may take the form of an etcetera. D.xlii 1 τί πρῶτον δεῖ ποιεῖν . . . καὶ τί δεύτερον καὶ τἆλλα δ' ἐφεξῆς : Pl. *Lg*.674B, 943B : *Phdr*.229D : *Sph*.244C : X.*Cyr*.i 1.2: 1.4. Introducing the penultimate item : Pl.*Ly*.215E (the last before the comprehensive καὶ τἆλλα οὕτω) : *Lg*.908D.

After an asyndetic series : X.*Lac*.13.4.

Xenophon is fond of using καὶ . . . δέ with the repetition of a word.[1] *An*.i 8.18 ἐφθέγξαντο πάντες . . . καὶ πάντες δὲ ἔθεον : ii 6.10 ἐκόλαζέ τε ἰσχυρῶς . . . καὶ γνώμῃ δ' ἐκόλαζεν : *Smp*.8.42 κατεθεᾶτο τὸν Καλλίαν. καὶ ὁ Καλλίας δὲ . . . : *HG* v 2.40 : 3.22 : vii 2.11 : *An*.i 8.22 : 9.11 : *Cyr*.vii 1.30. Cf. *HG* v 4.3.

Cf. Hom.*H* 173 οὗτος γὰρ δὴ ὀνήσει ἐϋκνήμιδας Ἀχαιούς, καὶ δ' αὐτὸς ὃν θυμὸν ὀνήσεται : 375 εἰπέμεν . . . καὶ δὲ τόδ' εἰπέμεναι πυκινὸν ἔπος : D.xix 40 μεμαρτύρηται δὲ . . . καὶ νῦν δὲ μαρτυρηθήσεται.

Usually only one word, or at most two, intervenes between καί and δέ. The number is only increased in order to avoid separating words which naturally go together. Pl.*Thg*.121A κἂν εἰ ἀσχολία δὲ μὴ πάνυ τις μεγάλη . . . : X.*An*.i 1.5 καὶ τῶν παρ' ἑαυτῷ δὲ βαρβάρων : *Cyr*.ii 1.29 καὶ πρὸς τὸ ἀλλήλοις δὲ πραοτέρους εἶναι : 31 καὶ τοὺς ἀμφὶ τὸ στράτευμα δὲ ὑπηρέτας.

καί ('both') . . . καὶ . . . δέ. Pl.*Alc.II* 147B καὶ οὗτος καὶ

[1] See W. Horn, 'Quaestiones ad Xenophontis elocutionem pertinentes', *Diss. Halis Saxonum*, 1926.

ἄλλοι δὲ ποιηταὶ σχεδόν τι πάντες: 151B ἀλλὰ δέχομαι καὶ τοῦτο καὶ ἄλλο δέ: D.vii 5 ὑπὸ τῶν τἀνταῦθα διοικήσειν . . . καὶ πρὶν ὑπεσχημένων καὶ νῦν δὲ πραττόντων.

τε . . . καὶ . . . δέ. Pl.*Cri.*48B οὗτός τε ὁ λόγος . . . δοκεῖ . . .· καὶ τόνδε δὲ αὖ σκόπει (δέ *T*: *om. B*): *Criti.*118E: *Lg.*708A: X.*HG* v 2.37.

μὲν . . . καὶ . . . δέ. Pl.*Lg.*721D ζημιούσθω μὲν . . . καὶ μὴ μετεχέτω δὲ τῶν τιμῶν: D.lix 126 ἐγὼ μὲν οὖν . . . καὶ ὑμᾶς δὲ χρὴ . . .: X.*HG* v 3.26 καὶ τὰ μὲν περὶ Φλειοῦντα οὕτως αὖ ἐπετετέλεστο . . . καὶ ὁ Πολυβιάδης δὲ δὴ . . . (a strong break): *An.*vi 3.23: 3.25: vii 1.30: *Cyr.*vii 1.30.

In X.*Oec.*11.22 καὶ . . . δέ, if the text is sound, means 'also': Ἀλλὰ καὶ ἔμελλον δὲ ἐγώ, ἔφην, ὦ Ἰσχόμαχε, τοῦτο ἐρήσεσθαι (but Richards' σε, for δέ, is a probable emendation).

οὐδὲ . . . δέ may be regarded as the negative counterpart of καὶ . . . δέ. Here δέ is clearly the connective, and οὐδέ is adverbial. X.*An.*i 8.20 (see οὐδέ, II.1.iii, and note the repetition, παθεῖν . . . ἔπαθεν, characteristic of Xenophontine καὶ . . . δέ): Arist.*EN* 1120a31 ὁ δὲ διδοὺς οἷς μὴ δεῖ . . . οὐκ ἐλευθέριος . . . οὐδὲ λήψεται δὲ ὅθεν μὴ δεῖ (cf. 1120b30 καὶ λήψεται δ' ὅθεν δεῖ): *Metaph.*1066b34: *de An.*427b11. See Eucken, pp. 32–3.

Δή

The derivation of δή, of which widely divergent views have been held, remains entirely obscure. It has often been held that the primary sense of δή is temporal. Thus Brugmann says that the particle combines a temporal sense with that of obviousness, notoriousness, actuality, certainty: the temporal element being stronger in Homer than in later Greek. Hence δή denotes 'that which lies, clear to see, before the speaker's eyes at the moment.' The evidence for this supposed temporal sense is, however, exceedingly weak: and I doubt whether any such view would have gained currency without the support of precarious etymologies. The essential meaning seems clearly to be 'verily', 'actually', 'indeed'. δή denotes that a thing really and truly is so: or that it is very much so (in cases where δή is attached to words, such as adjectives, which ἐνδέχονται μᾶλλον καὶ ἧττον: πολλοὶ δή, 'really many', or 'very many'). These meanings run through all the non-connective usages of the particle: and the connective use is easily derived from them.

I. Emphatic. We shall find here not a few points of contact with γε, though in the main each particle runs its own course. Like γε, δή normally emphasizes the preceding word (for exceptions, see I.6 and II): but δή is bound to the relevant word by a looser bond, and is more able to spread its influence over a whole clause.[1] As a corollary to this, it has greater structural importance than γε (for example, in its apodotic use).

The word emphasized by δή may be an adjective, an adverb, a noun, a pronoun, or a verb. But in prose, especially the formal prose of history and oratory, there is a marked tendency to restrict emphatic δή to certain well-defined types of word. Pathetic δή (found particularly with verbs) is almost confined to poetry. Plato uses it, with economy and rare beauty, in *Phd.* 89B *Αὔριον δή, ἔφη, ἴσως, ὦ Φαίδων, τὰς καλὰς ταύτας κόμας ἀποκερῇ.* In X.*Cyr.*vii 3.8 it adds a touch of mawkishness to a sentimental passage: *Φεῦ, ὦ ἀγαθὴ καὶ πιστὴ ψυχή, οἴχῃ δὴ ἀπολιπὼν ἡμᾶς;*

(1) With adjectives. In poetry, without restriction: in prose, almost confined to certain classes of adjective.

(i) In general. Hom.*A* 295 *ἄλλοισιν δὴ ταῦτ' ἐπιτέλλεο*: *O* 711 *ὀξέσι δὴ πελέκεσσι*: *Σ* 95 *ὠκύμορος δή μοι, τέκος, ἔσσεαι*: *θ* 209 *ἄφρων δὴ κεῖνός γε . . . πέλει ἀνήρ*: *ο* 451 *παῖδα . . . ἀτιτάλλω, κερδαλέον δὴ τοῖον*: Thgn.608 *ἐς δὲ τελευτὴν αἰσχρὸν δὴ κέρδος*: 962 *ἄλλης δὴ κρήνης πίομαι*: Pi.*P*.4.273 *ἀλλ' ἐπὶ χώρας αὖτις ἔσσαι δυσπαλὲς δὴ γίνεται*: A.*Pers.*1013 *δυσπόλεμον δὴ γένος τὸ Περσᾶν*: *Ag.*1610 *οὕτω καλὸν δὴ καὶ τὸ κατθανεῖν ἐμοί*: S.*Tr.* 223 *τάδ' ἀντίπρῳρα δή σοι βλέπειν πάρεστι*: *OC* 721 *νῦν σὸν τὰ λαμπρὰ ταῦτα δὴ φαίνειν ἔπη* (with a touch of bitterness: δή *L*:

[1] This consideration renders precarious, however practically convenient, the principle of classification formulated in the next paragraph, and carried out in the following sections.

δεῖ A): E.*Alc.*408 ὦ σχέτλια δὴ παθών: *Hipp.*193 δυσέρωτες δὴ φαινόμεθ' ὄντες: *Hec.*1135 ὕποπτος ὢν δὴ Τρωικῆς ἁλώσεως (with a half sneer): *Supp.*195 Ἄλλοισι δὴ 'πόνησ' ἁμιλληθεὶς λόγῳ τοιῷδ': *Fr.*911.1 χρύσεαι δή μοι πτέρυγες περὶ νώτῳ: Ar.*Eq.*1387 Μακάριος ἐς τἀρχαῖα δὴ καθίσταμαι: Pl.*La.*183D δορυδρέπανον, διαφέρον δὴ ὅπλον: *Lg.*861E ἄδικα . . . διπλᾶ, τὰ μὲν ἑκούσια δή, τὰ δ' ἀκούσια (emphasizing the first of two contrasted ideas: whereas τὰ μὲν δὴ ἑκούσια would have emphasized the form of the contrast): *Ep.*343B τὰ νῦν στρογγύλα καλούμενα εὐθέα κεκλῆσθαι τά τε εὐθέα δὴ στρογγύλα.

With adjectival phrases. Pl.*Lg.*779E τὸ δὴ τῶν νῦν εἰρημένων ἐχόμενον (in parenthesis): 805E ἢ τὸ τούτων δὴ διὰ μέσου φῶμεν . . .; X.*An.*v 2.26 οἱ δὲ κατὰ στόμα δὴ ἔτι μόνοι ἐλύπουν.

With comparative adjectives and adverbs. Hom.*I* 202 Μείζονα δὴ κρητῆρα . . . καθίστα: Ξ4 μείζων δὴ παρὰ νηυσὶ βοή: Ar.*V.* 1064 κύκνου τ' ἔτι πολιώτεραι δὴ αἵδ' ἐπανθοῦσιν τρίχες: Hp. *Acut.*9 σφῶν αὐτῶν δυσφορώτερον δὴ τὰ τοιαῦτα φέρουσιν.

With special classes of adjective.

(ii) With δῆλος (common in Plato). Pl.*Grg.*502A Δῆλον δὴ τοῦτό γε: *R.*412B σχεδὸν γάρ τι δῆλα δὴ ὅτι . . .: *Men.*91B ἦ δῆλον δὴ . . . ὅτι . . .: *Cri.*48B Δῆλα δὴ καὶ ταῦτα: *Grg.*478A: *Smp.*204B: *Euthphr.*4B: *Prt.*309A. *Plt.*264E δῆλον δὴ γὰρ παντί (where Burnet ejects δή, and others place it after γάρ) illustrates the tendency of δή to coalesce particularly closely with this adjective. In the adverb δηλαδή the fusion is so complete that the adjective loses its accent: Epich.*Fr.*149: S.*OT* 1501: E.*Or.*789: *IA* 1366: Ar.*V.*442: *Ec.*1157: Alex.*Fr.*173.6: Epigen.*Fr.*6: Hdt.iv 135.2: v 118.3: vi 39.2.

(iii) With adjectives expressing indefinite quantity or number (πολύς, πᾶς, etc.).

πολύς. Hom.τ 379: Pi.*O.*6.79: S.*El.*603,1377: E.*Ion* 1394: Ar.*Ach.*693: *Av.*539 πολὺ δὴ πολὺ δὴ χαλεπωτάτους λόγους ἤνεγκας: Hdt.i 143: Th.vi 61.1: Pl.*Prt.*361E: *Phd.*68A: Isoc. v 42.

πᾶς. E.*Med.*278 ἐξιᾶσι πάντα δὴ κάλων: Ar.*Av.*451 κατὰ πάντα δὴ τρόπον: S.*El.*764: Th.vii 55.1 ἐν παντὶ δὴ ἀθυμίας ἦσαν: Hdt.iii 157 (*bis*): vii 152.3: X.*HG* vi 2.24.

μόνος. B.5.156 φασὶν ἀδεισιβόαν Ἀμφιτρύωνος παῖδα μοῦνον δὴ τότε . . .: S.*Ant.*58,821: *Tr.*1063: E.*Tr.* 1092: Th.v 26.3 μόνον δὴ τοῦτο: Hdt.i 25: ii 156: iv 15: Th.ii 64.1: vii 44.1: Ant.v 15: Isoc.iv 109.

οἷος. Hom.θ 219: μ 69. ὀλίγος. Th.i 33.2 ἃ ... ὀλίγοις δὴ ἅμα πάντα ξυνέβη: Pl.*Ep*.316A. βραχύς. S.*OC* 586 Ἀλλ' ἐν βραχεῖ δὴ τήνδε μ' ἐξαιτῇ χάριν: E.*Hipp*.1246. μακρός. *E.Or*. 72 παρθένε μακρὸν δὴ μῆκος Ἠλέκτρα χρόνου: *Fr*.821. μέγας. X.*Cyr*.viii 3.7 Μέγας δὴ σύ γε: Ar.*Ach*.988. Pl.*R*.373D ἡ χώρα ... σμικρὰ δὴ ἐξ ἱκανῆς ἔσται: E.*Andr*.319 μυρίοισι δὴ βροτῶν: Pl.*Smp*.220B ἠμφιεσμένων θαυμαστὰ δὴ ὅσα.

(iv) With numerals. Hom.*B* 134 ἐννέα δὴ βεβάασι ... ἐνιαυτοί: *Θ* 297 ὀκτὼ δὴ προέηκα ... ὀϊστούς: Anacr.*Fr*.21.1 δέκα δὴ μῆνες: Pi.*O*.13.99 ἑξηκοντάκι δή: *P*.9.91 τρὶς δή: *N*.8.48 δὶς δὴ δυοῖν: E.*Med*.1282 Μίαν δὴ κλύω, μίαν τῶν πάρος ...: Hom.*I* 328: *Ω* 107: Pl.*Epin*.978B τὸ γὰρ ἓν δὴ καὶ δύο γέγονε πόθεν ἡμῖν ...; ('the concept of unity'): Hdt.v.76 τέταρτον δὴ τοῦτο ἐπὶ τὴν Ἀττικὴν ἀπικόμενοι Δωριέες. (For οὐδεὶς δή, see 10.i below.)

(2) With adverbs. Here again, as in the case of adjectives, δή is mainly used with certain types.

(i) In general. Hom.*N* 120 τάχα δή: *T* 401 ἄλλως δὴ φράζεσθε: *γ* 357 Εὖ δή: Ar.*Av*.1313 Ταχὺ δή: X.*HG* vii 4.34 τάχα δή: Ar. *Lys*.1102 Καλῶς δὴ λέγετε (Pl.*Hp.Ma*.299B): Th.vii 81.2 δίχα δὴ ὄντας: X.*An*.v 4.25 ἐπεὶ δὲ ... ἐνταῦθα οἱ πολέμιοι ὁμοῦ δὴ πάντες γενόμενοι.... (but in Pl.*R*.458D δή is to be regarded rather as apodotic).

(ii) With adverbs expressing frequency, intensity, distance of space or time, and so forth. Hom.*T* 85 πολλάκι δή: *M* 430 πάντῃ δή: 323 αἰεὶ δή: *N* 374 περὶ δή: *θ* 487 ἔξοχα δή: *h.Merc*. 126 δηρὸν δή (Emp.*Fr*. 112.12): S.*Ph*.1456 πολλάκι δή: Pl.*Smp*. 215E πολλάκις δή: *Ap*.40B πολλαχοῦ δή: Pi.*N*.1.17 θάμα δή: S.*Ph*.806 πάλαι δή (*OC* 1628: A.*Pr*.998: Ar.*Av*.921 Πάλαι πάλαι δή: X.*Cyr*.viii 7.1: Pl.*Alc.II* 139D): Th.i 13.5 αἰεὶ δή ποτε: Pl.*Lg*.836D ἀεὶ δή: Hdt.iv 113 πρόσω δή: Sapph.*Fr*.143 μάλα δὴ κεκορημένας: X.*An*.vii 7.16 μάλα δὴ ὑφειμένως: *Ap*.27 μάλα ὁμολογουμένως δή.

(iii) With temporal and local adverbs. νῦν. E.*Heracl*.873 ὦ τέκνα, νῦν δὴ νῦν ἐλεύθεροι πόνων ('now at last'): Ar.*Ra*.412 νῦν δὴ κατεῖδον ('just now'): *Pax* 5: *Av*.923: Th.vi 24.2 ἔδοξε ἀσφάλεια νῦν δὴ καὶ πολλὴ ἔσεσθαι: Pl.*Ly*.217E τοῦτο τοίνυν ἐρωτῶ νῦν δή: *La.*179A μὴ ... ἐπειδὴ μειράκια γέγονεν, ἀνεῖναι αὐτοὺς ὅτι βούλονται ποιεῖν, ἀλλὰ νῦν δὴ καὶ ἄρχεσθαι αὐτῶν ἐπιμελεῖσθαι ('precisely now'): *Phdr.*250C: Lys.xiii 93 ὑμεῖς τοίνυν ... νυνὶ δή, ἐπεὶ ἐν τῷ τότε χρόνῳ ... οὐχ οἷοί τε ἦστε ... νυνί, ἐν ᾧ δύνασθε, τιμωρήσατε. δή coalesces closely with νῦν. Hence the order in the following: E.*Hipp.*233 νῦν δὴ μὲν ... νῦν δ' αὖ: Ar.*Lys.*327 νῦν δὴ γάρ (Pl.*R.*528A). The words are, in fact, often written as one, νυνδή (cf. δηλαδή).

τότε. E.*El.*726 τότε δὴ τότε: D.xviii 47.

εἶτα. Ar.*Nu.*259 Εἶτα δὴ τί κερδανῶ; 750 Γυναῖκα φαρμακίδ' εἰ πριάμενος Θετταλὴν καθέλοιμι νύκτωρ τὴν σελήνην, εἶτα δὴ αὐτὴν καθείρξαιμ' (δή has been suspected here, but cf. Anaxil.*Fr.* 22.26 εἶτα τετράπους μοι γένοιτο ... εἶτα δὴ τρίπους τις, εἶτα ...).

αὐτίκα. Hyp.*Phil.*9 αὐτίκα δὴ μάλα: Ar.*Pl.*942: Pl.*R.*338B: D.xix 39,42,171: *id. saep.*

ἔνθα, ἐνταῦθα. Pl.*Prt.*324A ἔνθα δὴ πᾶς παντὶ θυμοῦται: *Phdr.* 247B ἔνθα δὴ πόνος τε καὶ ἀγὼν ἔσχατος ψυχῇ πρόκειται: Th.ii 58.2 ἐνταῦθα δή (X.*HG* i 2.15).

Other temporal and local adverbs. E.*Heracl.*484 οὐ νεωστὶ δή: *El.*653 Πότερα πάλαι τεκοῦσαν ἢ νεωστὶ δή; X.*An.*i 9.25 οὔπω δή: Pl.*Phd.*89B αὔριον δή: E.*Ion* 393 πέλας δή: Pl.*Lg.*811C ἐξ ἕω μέχρι δεῦρο δή (for δεῦρο δή with imperative, expressed or understood, see I.8.iii): S.*OT* 968 ὁ δὲ θανὼν κεύθει κάτω δὴ γῆς: Ar. *Ec.*733 πολλοὺς κάτω δὴ θυλάκους στρέψασ' ἐμούς: Hp.*Epid.* ii 4.1 καὶ πεφύκασιν ἄνωθεν δὴ φρενῶν.

(3) With superlative adjectives and adverbs. This is a favourite use of Thucydides: I have counted about thirty-six instances in him. Hom.*A* 266 κάρτιστοι δή: S.*Aj.*858 πανύστατον δή: *El.*202 ἐχθίστα δή: *Ant.*895 κάκιστα δὴ μακρῷ: E.*Heracl.*794 πράξας δ' ἐκ θεῶν κάλλιστα δή: Hom.*Z* 185: *μ* 258: Th.i 1.2 μεγίστη δή: 138.3 βεβαιότατα δή: vi 31.1 πολυτελεστάτη δή: 33.4 κάλλιστον δή: viii 106.1 ἐπικαιροτάτην δή: X.*HG* iv 8.24 ὑπεναντιώτατα δή: v 1.3 μακαριώτατα δή: Pl.*Lg.* 899D ὦ ἄριστε δή, φῶμεν: Hdt.ii 111,177: iii 10: v 82: Pl.*Phd.* 60A: D.xviii 298.

(4) With pronouns and pronominal adverbs. Particularly in the case of σύ (especially in questions), the emphasis is often ironical, contemptuous, or indignant in tone.

(i) Ἐγώ. Cratin.*Fr.*16 ἐν Καρὶ τὸν κίνδυνον ἐν ἐμοὶ δὴ δοκεῖ πρώτῳ πεπειρᾶσθαι: Ar.*Lys.*684 εἰ ... με ζωπυρήσεις, λύσω τὴν ἐμαυτῆς ὗν ἐγὼ δή: Hdt.iii 155 τῷ ἐστὶ δύναμις τοσαύτη ἐμὲ δὴ ὧδε διαθεῖναι: Pl.*Grg.*469C Ὦ μακάριε, ἐμοῦ δὴ λέγοντος τῷ λόγῳ ἐπιλαβοῦ.

(ii) Σύ. S.*Aj.*1226 Σὲ δὴ τὰ δεινὰ ῥήματ' ἀγγέλλουσί μοι τλῆναι ... χανεῖν: *El.*954 ἐς σὲ δὴ βλέπω: *Ant.*441 Σὲ δή, σὲ τὴν νεύουσαν ἐς πέδον κάρα, φῂς ...; E.*Hipp.*948 σὺ δὴ θεοῖσιν ὡς περισσὸς ὢν ἀνὴρ ξυνεῖ; *Andr.*324 σὺ δὴ στρατηγῶν ... Τροίαν ἀφείλου Πρίαμον, ὧδε φαῦλος ὤν; *Rh.*686 Ἦ σὺ δὴ Ῥῆσον κατέκτας; Ar.*Ra.*841 σὺ δή με ταῦτ' ὦ στωμυλιοσυλλεκτάδη ...; Hom.*Η* 24: A.*Pr.*300: E.*Hel.*464: Ar.*Lys.*146: Hdt.i 115 Σὺ δὴ ἐὼν τοῦδε τοιούτου ἐόντος παῖς ἐτόλμησας ...; vii 17.2 Σὺ δὴ κεῖνος εἶς ὁ ἀποσπεύδων ...; Pl.*R.*506B ἀλλὰ σὺ δή, ὦ Σώκρατες, πότερον ... φῂς ...; *Grg.*487E περὶ τούτων ὧν σὺ δή μοι ἐπετίμησας: *Euthphr.*9D: *R.*337E.

(iii) Νῷν. Hom.*Λ* 347 Νῶϊν δὴ τόδε πῆμα κυλίνδεται: S.*OC* 1670 ἔστιν ἔστι νῷν δὴ οὐ τὸ μέν, ἄλλο δὲ μή.

(iv) Ὑμεῖς. Hdt.ix 48.1 Ὦ Λακεδαιμόνιοι, ὑμεῖς δὴ λέγεσθε εἶναι ἄνδρες ἄριστοι: Pl.*Phd.*63E Ἔα αὐτόν, ἔφη. ἀλλ' ὑμῖν δὴ τοῖς δικασταῖς βούλομαι ἤδη τὸν λόγον ἀποδοῦναι.

(v) Ὁ (demonstrative). Hom.*Σ* 549 τὸ δὴ περὶ θαῦμα τέτυκτο: *δ* 819.

(vi) Ἐκεῖνος. Hom.*χ* 165 κεῖνος δὴ αὖτ' ἀΐδηλος ἀνὴρ ... ἔρχεται: S.*Tr.*1091 ὦ φίλοι βραχίονες, ὑμεῖς ἐκεῖνοι δὴ καθέσταθ', οἳ ....

(vii) Ὅδε. Hom.*τ* 571 ἥδε δὴ ἠὼς εἶσι δυσώνυμος: S.*OC* 111 πορεύονται γὰρ οἵδε δή τινες: 886 ἐπεὶ πέρα περῶσ' οἵδε δή: E.*Hipp.*1342 Καὶ μὴν ὁ τάλας ὅδε δὴ στείχει: *Alc.*233: *Supp.* 980, 1114: *Ion* 393: *Or.*348. (But καὶ δή is more frequently used than simple δή in announcing a new character on the stage.)

(viii) Οὗτος (often contemptuous in tone). Hom.*η* 48 Οὗτος δή τοι, ξεῖνε πάτερ, δόμος, ὅν με κελεύεις πεφραδέμεν: A.*Pers.* 159 Ταῦτα δὴ λιποῦσ' ἱκάνω χρυσεοστόλμους δόμους: S.*El.*385 Ἦ ταῦτα δή με καὶ βεβούλευνται ποεῖν; E.*Tr.*1272 Οἲ 'γὼ τάλαινα· τοῦτο δὴ τὸ λοίσθιον ... τῶν ἐμῶν ἤδη κακῶν: S.*Ph.* 565: Hp.*Fract.*47 τὸ δὲ σχῆμα τοῦ ἀγκῶνος ἐν τούτοισι δὴ καὶ παντάπασι χρὴ τοιοῦτον ποιέεσθαι (in some MSS. only): Th. vi 92.5 γνόντας τοῦτον δὴ τὸν ὑφ' ἁπάντων προβαλλόμενον λόγον:

Pl.*Grg.*511B *Οὐκοῦν τοῦτο δὴ καὶ τὸ ἀγανακτητόν*; ('Isn't that just what is so unpleasant?' In this common use ('just that', 'precisely that') *δή* is often followed by *καί*: *q.v.* II.B.8: cf. *αὐτὸ δὴ τοῦτο*, (xiii) below): *Chrm.*170E *ἀλλὰ τοῦτο δὴ τῇ σωφροσύνῃ μόνῃ ἀπέδομεν*: *R.*338B *Αὕτη δή, ἔφη, ἡ Σωκράτους σοφία*: *Tht.* 166A *Οὗτος δὴ ὁ Σωκράτης ὁ χρηστός*: X.*Cyr.*viii 4.9 *Τοῦτο δὴ πάντων ἥκιστα, ἔφη ὁ Κῦρος*: *Oec.*18.6 *Οὐκοῦν . . . ἐκ τούτου δὴ καθαροῦμεν τὸν σῖτον*: Hdt.iii 82: iv 20: Pl.*Ly.*206B,212A: *Phd.* 114C: *R.*485A,569B.

(ix) In Herodotus *δή* after *οὗτος* often emphasizes the fact that a person has already been mentioned some little way back. i 43 *ἔνθα δὴ ὁ ξεῖνος, οὗτος δὴ ὁ καθαρθεὶς τὸν φόνον* . . . : 45 *Ἄδρηστος δὲ . . . οὗτος δὴ ὁ φονεὺς . . . γενόμενος*: 110 *ἔνθα τὰς νομὰς τῶν βοῶν εἶχε οὗτος δὴ ὁ βουκόλος*: 114 *εἵλοντο . . . τοῦτον δὴ τὸν τοῦ βουκόλου ἐπίκλησιν παῖδα*: iii 2 *φάμενοί μιν ἐκ ταύτης δὴ τῆς Ἀπριέω θυγατρὸς γενέσθαι*: ii 129: iii 6: iv 151: vi 61.5: 63.1. Sometimes *δή* precedes the demonstrative: i 1 *ἀπικομένους δὲ τοὺς Φοίνικας ἐς δὴ τὸ Ἄργος τοῦτο* . . . : v 41.1 *τίκτει τὸν δὴ Κλεομένεα τοῦτον*.

(x) *Οὕτως, ὧδε.* Hdt.i 189 *οὕτω δή μιν ἀσθενέα ποιήσειν*: iii 3 *τὸν δὲ διαμνημονεύοντα οὕτω δή, ἐπείτε ἀνδρώθη καὶ ἔσχε τὴν βασιληίην, ποιήσασθαι τὴν ἐπ' Αἴγυπτον στρατηίην*: Pl.*Men.*88E *Οὐκοῦν οὕτω δὴ κατὰ πάντων εἰπεῖν ἔστιν* . . . ; *Tht.*156D *καὶ οὕτω δὴ γεννᾷ, τὰ δὲ γεννώμενα οὕτω δὴ θάττω ἐστίν*: *Phdr.*237B *ἦν οὕτω δὴ παῖς* (at the opening of a narrative).

(xi) Often in Homer in surprised or indignant questions (cf. III.8). *B* 174 *οὕτω δὴ . . . φεύξεσθ'* . . . ; *Ξ* 88: *O* 553: *ε* 204: E.*Tr.*1060 *Οὕτω δὴ τὸν ἐν Ἰλίῳ ναὸν . . . προύδωκας Ἀχαιοῖς, ὦ Ζεῦ* . . . ; (which should surely be printed as a question): Pl.*Phdr.* 234D *Εἶεν· οὕτω δὴ δοκεῖ παίζειν*;

(xii) Herodotus often uses *δή τι* after *οὕτω* and *ὧδε* with an adjective, usually placing it before the adjective: i 184 *οὕτω δή τι ἐποίησε σκολιόν*: iv 52 *οὕτω δή τι ἐοῦσα πικρή*: iii 120 *ὧδε δή τι ἐοῦσαν εὐπετέα χειρωθῆναι*: ii 71,135: iii 12,108,130,145. Sometimes after the adjective: i 163 *προσφιλέες . . . οὕτω δή τι ἐγένοντο*: ii 11 *μακρὸς οὕτω δή τι*: iv 184 *ὑψηλὸν δὲ οὕτω δή τι λέγεται*: iii 23: iv 28. So too with verbs: iv 58 *οὕτω δή τι οἱ Σκύθαι ἐσκευάδαται*: viii 99.1 *ἔτερψε οὕτω δή τι Περσέων τοὺς ὑπολειφθέντας*.

Herodotus similarly uses *δή τις* after *τοιοῦτος, τοιόσδε, τοσοῦτος*. v 92 ε 2 *τοιοῦτος δή τις ἀνὴρ ἐγένετο*: vi 23.1 *τοιόνδε δή τι*: i 192 *τοσοῦτο δή τι πλῆθος*: i 178: iv 5: vi 132. These uses of *δή τι, δή τις* are peculiar to Herodotus.

(xiii) *αὐτός*. Hom.*Θ* 243 *αὐτοὺς δή περ ἔασον*: E.*Alc.*371 *ὦ παῖδες, αὐτοὶ δὴ τάδ' εἰσηκούσατε*: *Hel.*646 *Ὄναιο δῆτα. ταὐτὰ δὴ ξυνεύχομαι* (*ταῦτά* (*sic*) *L*: *ταῦτα P*): Pl.*R.*473C *Ἐπ' αὐτῷ δὴ . . . εἰμὶ ὃ τῷ μεγίστῳ προσῃκάζομεν κύματι*: *Phlb.*12B *Πειρατέον, ἀπ' αὐτῆς δὴ τῆς θεοῦ*: D.xix 136 *οἷον αὐτὸς δή*. *αὐτὸ δὴ τοῦτο* is common: S.*Tr.*600 *Ἀλλ' αὐτὰ δή σοι ταῦτα καὶ πράσσω*: Ar.*V.*1062 *καὶ κατ' αὐτὸ δὴ τοῦτο μόνον ἄνδρες ἀλκιμώτατοι*: Pl.*Phdr.*227C *ἀλλ' αὐτὸ δὴ τοῦτο καὶ κεκόμψευται*: *Lg.*892C *Οὐκοῦν τὰ μετὰ ταῦτα ἐπ' αὐτὸ δὴ τοῦτο στελλώμεθα*; D.li 2 *καὶ κατ' αὐτὸ δὴ τοῦτο δικαίως ἂν ἔχοιτ' εὐνοϊκωτέρως ἐμοί*: Pl.*R.* 379A, 405B: D.xx 47. Cf. Ar.*Lys.*888 *ταῦτ' αὐτὰ δή 'σθ' ἃ* . . . .

(xiv) With possessive pronominal adjectives. E.*Heracl.*856 *δισσὼ γὰρ ἀστέρ' . . . ἔκρυψαν ἅρμα λυγαίῳ νέφει· σὸν δὴ λέγουσι παῖδα . . . Ἥβην θ'*: Cratin.*Fr.*198 *ὦ λιπερνῆτες πολῖται, τἀμὰ δὴ ξυνίετε ῥήματ'* (cf. Ar.*Pax* 603): Pl.*La.*189C *Ἀλλ' ἡμέτερον δὴ ἔργον* (perhaps to be classed under *ἀλλὰ . . . δή*): *Grg.*522C *Δικαίως πάντα ταῦτα ἐγὼ λέγω, καὶ πράττω τὸ ὑμέτερον δὴ τοῦτο* ('and I do this in *your* interests'). See further III.7.

(5) With interrogatives. (In many passages *δή* may equally well be regarded as connective. Cf. *δαί, δῆτα*.)

(i) Direct. (*a*) In general. Hom.*Ω* 201 *Ὤ μοι, πῇ δή τοι φρένες οἴχονθ'* . . .; *φ* 362 *Πῇ δή* (*κ* 281): *υ* 191 *Τίς δή* (*Α* 540: *Β* 225): *χ* 231 *πῶς δή* (*Σ* 364): Anacr.*Fr.*88.1 *πῶλε Θρῃκίη, τί δή με λοξὸν ὄμμασιν βλέπουσα νηλεῶς φεύγεις* . . . ; Pi.*O.*10.60 *τίς δή* (*N.*10.76): A.*Pr.*118 *πόνων ἐμῶν θεωρός, ἢ τί δὴ θέλων*; S.*El.*1184 *Τί δή ποθ'* . . . *ὧδ' ἐπισκοπῶν στένεις*; 1400 *Πῶς δή*: *Tr.*403 *Σὺ δ' ἐς τί δή με τοῦτ' ἐρωτήσας ἔχεις*; E.*Med.*516 *ὦ Ζεῦ, τί δὴ* . . .; *El.*566 *ἢ τί δὴ λέγεις, γέρον*; *Hec.*930 *Ὦ παῖδες Ἑλλάνων, πότε δὴ πότε* . . . *ἥξετε*; ('when, oh when . . .?'): Ar.*Nu.*673 *Πῶς δή*; (1442: *V.*21): *V.*1155 *Τιὴ τί δή*; *Pl.*1111 *ἀτὰρ διὰ τί δὴ* . . .; Hdt.i 30 *Κοίῃ δὴ κρίνεις Τέλλον εἶναι ὀλβιώτατον*; 117 *Ἅρπαγε, τέῳ δὴ μόρῳ τὸν παῖδα κατεχρήσαο* . . .; vii 135.2 *Ἄνδρες Λακεδαιμόνιοι, τί δὴ φεύγετε* . . .; Pl.*Tht.*176E *Τίνα δὴ λέγεις*; *Grg.*448E *Τί δή*; *Men.*80C *Τίνος δὴ οἴει*; *Phd.*89A *Πῶς δή*; *Grg.*454A *ἐπανε-*

ροίμεθα ἂν τὸν λέγοντα· *Ποίας δὴ πειθοῦς . . .*; *Phdr.*227A *Ὦ φίλε Φαῖδρε, ποῖ δὴ καὶ πόθεν*; *Phd.*81E *Τὰ ποῖα δὴ ταῦτα λέγεις* ; *La.* 193E: *Prm.*138B *Τί δὴ γὰρ οὔ*; ('Why ever not?': *ib.* 140E: E.*Or.* 1602): *R.*357D ἀλλὰ τί δή; (elliptical: 'But what do you *mean?*')

Late in clause. S.*Ant.*159 ἀλλ' ὅδε γὰρ δὴ βασιλεὺς χώρας . . . χωρεῖ τίνα δὴ μῆτιν ἐρέσσων . . . ; E.*Hipp.*250 τὸ δ' ἐμὸν πότε δὴ θάνατος σῶμα καλύψει ;

Sometimes δή precedes the interrogative (though in some of these cases δή might be taken with the word it follows). Ar.*Av.* 417 *Τί φῄς* ; λέγουσι δὴ τίνας λόγους; *Ec.*604 *Κατὰ δὴ τί* ; Pl.*R.* 556A *Κατὰ δὴ τίνα* ; *Sph.*251A *Οἷον δὴ τί* ; *Lg.*705D *Εἰς δὴ τί* τῶν εἰρημένων βλέψας εἶπες ὃ λέγεις; *Hp.Mi.*371A λέγεις δὴ τί . . . ; Add perhaps Pl.*Lg.*810A μανθάνειν δὲ ἐν τούτοις τοῖς χρόνοις δὴ τί ποτε δεῖ τοὺς νέους . . . μάνθανε : here the emphasis seems to be on τί rather than on μανθάνειν, certainly not on τούτοις τοῖς χρόνοις : 'they are to learn for so many years: and *what* are they to learn ?'

(*b*) καί before the interrogative (usually expressing surprise : cf. καί II.B.10.i.*b*: καὶ δή, I.ii) is characteristic of Xenophon. E.*Rh.*688 *Καὶ τί δὴ τὸ σῆμα* ; Ar.*V.*665 *Καὶ ποῖ τρέπεται δὴ . . .*; D.xix 336 καὶ τί δὴ . . . ἐπαινεῖς ; X.*Mem.*iv 4.10 *Καὶ ποῖος δὴ . . .*; *Oec.*1.18 : 7.16 : *An.*vii 6.20 : *Cyr.*i 3.5 : 3.10 (*bis*) : 6.16 : 6.22.

(*c*) In subordinate clauses. With ὡς ('as') and participle: E.*IT* 557 παῖς νιν . . . ὤλεσεν.— . . . ὡς τί δὴ θέλων ; ('He killed him, as wishing what?' Perhaps not to be sharply distinguished from *Alc.*537 *Ὡς δὴ τί δράσων . . .*; for which see III.1.ii). With ὡς (final), ἵνα, or ὅτι, and ellipse of subjunctive or indicative: E.*Or.* 796 *Ὡς τί δὴ* (*sc.* γένηται) τόδε ; *Ion* 525 *Ὡς. τί δὴ φεύγεις με* ; *HF* 1407 *Ὡς δὴ τί*; (this punctuation seems right: but one cannot be certain): *IA* 1342 *Ὡς τί δή*; Ar.*Nu.*755 *Ὁτιὴ τί δή*; *Pax* 409 *Ἵνα δὴ τί τοῦτο δρᾶτον* ; (*Nu.*1192: *Ec.*791) : Pl.*R.*343A *Ὅτι δὴ τί μάλιστα* ; *Chrm.*161C. It is characteristic of Euripides that he, alone of the tragedians, admits this obviously colloquial idiom.

(ii) Indirect. Hom.*Γ*317 κλήρους . . . πάλλον ἑλόντες, ὁππότερος δὴ πρόσθεν ἀφείη χάλκεον ἔγχος : *μ* 57 διηνεκέως ἀγορεύσω ὁπποτέρη δή τοι ὁδὸς ἔσσεται : *ψ* 37 νημερτὲς ἐνίσπες . . . ὅππως δὴ μνηστῆρσιν ἀναιδέσι χεῖρας ἐφῆκε : Pi.*N.*5.15 εἰπεῖν . . . πῶς δὴ . . . : S.*OT* 493 οὔτε . . . ἔμαθον πρὸς ὅτου δὴ βασάνῳ . . . ; Ar.*Ra.*1162 δίδαξον γάρ με καθ' ὅτι δὴ λέγεις : Hdt.ii 121ε λέγειν αὐτῇ ὅ τι δὴ ἐν τῷ βίῳ ἔργασται αὐτῷ σοφώτατον: vi 138.3 δεινόν τι ἐσέδυνε . . . τί δὴ ἀνδρωθέντες δῆθεν ποιήσουσι: Hp.*Int.*3 μελετᾶν, ὁκοίων δή τινων δοκέει σοι δεῖσθαι: Pl.*La.*186E εἴπετον . . . τίνι δὴ δεινοτάτῳ συγγεγόνατον . . .: *Men.*97D θαυμάζω . . . ὅτι δή ποτε . . .: *Tht.*206C ἰδεῖν ὅτι δή ποτε καὶ λέγεται: *R.*429E οἶσθ' οἷα δὴ γίγνεται: 545D εἰπεῖν ὅπως δὴ . . .: *Phd.*85E ἀλλὰ λέγε ὅπῃ δὴ οὐχ ἱκανῶς (*Alc.I* 105A should probably be punctuated as a direct question): X.*An.*vi 5.23 ἀναμιμνήσκεσθε ὅσας δὴ μάχας . . . νενικήκατε: Lys.xxv 9 σκέψασθε . . . ὁσάκις δὴ μετεβάλλοντο: Hdt.iii 14: viii 136.1: Pl.*Lg.*810A (i.*a* above).

In exclamations. Hom.*E* 601 Ὦ φίλοι, οἷον δὴ θαυμάζομεν Ἕκτορα δῖον: E.*Ion* 616 ὅσας σφαγὰς δὴ . . . γυναῖκες ηὗρον: Ar.*Ach.*1 Ὅσα δὴ δέδηγμαι: *Lys.*83 Ὡς δὴ καλὸν τὸ χρῆμα τιτθίων ἔχεις. But in Hom.*N* 633, *P* 587, *Φ* 57, ε 183, λ 429, οἷον is of course relative, and δή is indignant.

(6) With indefinite pronouns and pronominal adverbs. Here δή regularly precedes the word it qualifies. (For exceptions see below.) It may at first sight seem surprising that an enclitic, and therefore presumably weak, word should be capable of being stressed at all. But τις and ποτέ are enclitics in a different category from σε and με. The former, unlike the latter, have no parallel accented forms (τίς and πότε being interrogatives, and the occasional oxytone accentuation of disyllabic enclitics being purely phonetic). Originally, perhaps, δή was regarded as going with the preceding word. Hom.*X* 453 ἐγγὺς δή τι κακόν: δ 26 Ξείνω δή τινε τώδε: ζ 162 Δήλῳ δή ποτε τοῖον ... ἔρνος ἀνερχόμενον ἐνόησα. Such passages would naturally give rise to the use of δή τις, δή ποτε in association.

(i) δή τις is used in two senses. (*a*) The speaker cannot, or does not trouble to, particularize (*aliquis*, *nonnulli*): (*b*) he can, and does, particularize in his own mind, but keeps the particularization to himself (*quidam*).

(*a*) Carm.Pop.32.19 ἂν δὴ φέρῃς τι, μέγα δή τι φέροις: E.*Hipp.* 513 δεῖ δ' ἐξ ἐκείνου δή τι τοῦ ποθουμένου σημεῖον, ἢ λόγον τιν' ἢ πέπλων ἄπο λαβεῖν: Hdt.iii 69.5 ἐπ' αἰτίῃ δή τινι οὐ σμικρῇ ('some or other'): viii 106.1: Pl.*Phd.*107D ἄγειν ἐπιχειρεῖ εἰς δή τινα τόπον: 108C: *Plt.*306B: *R.*498A ἐκτὸς δή τινων ὀλίγων: 521C ὥσπερ ἐξ Ἅιδου λέγονται δή τινες . . . ἀνελθεῖν: *Phlb.*50E: *Lg.*

885B. With a comparative, in Hippocrates: *Epid.*iv 30 ἡσυχωτέρα δή τι σμικρὸν ἦν ('the condition was rather quieter'): *Acut.*14 διαχωρητικώτερος δή τι.

(*b*) S.*Ph.*573 Ἦν δή τις: E.*Hec.*978 Ἴδιον ἐμαυτῆς δή τι πρός σε βούλομαι . . . εἰπεῖν: *IT* 526 Ἀπέλαυσα κἀγὼ δή τι τῶν κείνης γάμων: 578 Ἀκούσατ'· ἐς γὰρ δή τιν' ἥκομεν λόγον: *IA* 661 Καὶ νῦν γέ μ' ἴσχει δή τι μὴ στέλλειν στρατόν. There is a meaning air of mystery about most of these.

But such a classification must not be unduly pressed. In many cases it is impossible to determine whether δή τις expresses vagueness or conceals definiteness. So in English 'a certain' often means that one is uncertain.

Δή τις is mainly found in the poets, and in Herodotus, Hippocrates, and Plato. In Thucydides I can find only iii 104.1 κατὰ χρησμὸν δή τινα and I cannot find it in the orators. Further examples are: E.*IT* 545: *Supp.*970: Ar.*Av.*652: Hdt.viii 53.1: Pl.*Phd.*115D: *R.*561B: *Lg.*630B,701B,706C: *Plt.*299C.

Occasionally the particle follows the pronoun. S.*Ach.Conv* 9 Diehl τίκτει ναύταν σύν τινι δὴ θεῶν: E.*IT* 946 ἔκ του δὴ χερῶν μιάσματος: Pl.*Lg.*803E παίζοντά ἐστιν διαβιωτέον τινὰς δὴ παιδιάς. (But in S.*Ant.*158 *L*'s τίνα is no doubt right.)

For τοιοῦτος δή τις, etc., see 4.xii above.

(ii) δή ποτε, sometimes written as one word, has several meanings:—(*a*) *Olim.* Pi.*I.*8.65 ἐπεὶ περικτίονας ἐνίκασε δή ποτε: Sapph.*Fr.*105 φαῖσι δή ποτα Λήδαν . . . : Alc.*Fr.*101 ὡς γὰρ δή ποτ' Ἀριστόδαμόν φαισ' . . . εἴπην: E.*Hec.*484 τὴν ἄνασσαν δή ποτ' οὖσαν Ἰλίου (cf.891): *Tr.*506 τὸν ἁβρὸν δήποτ' ἐν Τροίᾳ πόδα: 1277 ὦ μεγάλα δή ποτ' ἀμπνέουσα: *HF* 444: Hp.*Art.*47 ἐπειρήθην δὲ δή ποτε. (*b*) *Aliquando*: 'at last'. E.*Hipp.*1181 χρόνῳ δὲ δήποτ' εἶπ' ἀπαλλαχθεὶς γόων: *Hel.*855 Ὦ θεοί, γενέσθω δή ποτ' εὐτυχὲς γένος: Hdt.ii 32 ἰδεῖν δή κοτε δένδρεα: v 80.1. (*c*) *Unquam.* X.*Cyr.*iii 2.26 ὅσον τις καὶ ἄλλος πλεῖστον δήποτε ἔδωκε. With inverted order: E.*Tr.*149 οὐ τὰν αὐτὰν οἵαν ποτὲ δὴ . . . ἐξῆρχον.

(7) With substantives, and other parts of speech used substantivally (rare in prose). Hom.*B* 340 ἐν πυρὶ δὴ βουλαί τε γενοίατο: *Γ* 150 γήραϊ δὴ πολέμοιο πεπαυμένοι: *Θ* 470 ἠοῦς δὴ καὶ μᾶλλον ὑπερμενέα Κρονίωνα ὄψεαι: *K* 509 Νόστου δὴ μνῆσαι:

Λ 319 ἐπεὶ νεφεληγερέτα Ζεὺς Τρωσὶν δὴ βόλεται δοῦναι κράτος: *N* 123 Ἕκτωρ δὴ παρὰ νηυσὶ . . . πολεμίζει: *Ω* 243 ῥηΐτεροι γὰρ μᾶλλον Ἀχαιοῖσιν δὴ ἔσεσθε . . . ἐναιρέμεν: Carm.Pop.50.2 τρίπολον δή: A.*Pers*.433 Αἰαῖ, κακῶν δὴ πέλαγος ἔρρωγεν μέγα: *Th*.655 πατρὸς δὴ νῦν ἀραὶ τελεσφόροι: E.*Alc*.51 Ἔχω λόγον δὴ καὶ προθυμίαν σέθεν (contemptuous): 393 μαῖα δὴ κάτω βέβακεν (pathetic): *Heracl*.395 δόκησιν δὴ τόδ' ἂν λέγοιμί σοι: *Hec*.909 δορὶ δὴ δορὶ πέρσαν: *IT* 459 τὰ γὰρ Ἑλλήνων ἀκροθίνια δὴ ναοῖσι πέλας τάδε βαίνει: *Supp*.815 Δόθ', ὡς περιπτυχαῖσι δὴ χέρας προσαρμόσασ' . . .: *Ph*.337 γάμοισι δὴ κλύω ζυγέντα: *Rh*.535 ἀὼς δὴ πέλας, ἀὼς γίγνεται: Ar.*Ach*.693 ἀπομορξάμενον ἀνδρικὸν ἱδρῶτα δὴ καὶ πολύν: *Th*.1228 ὥσθ' ὥρα δή 'στι βαδίζειν: *Ec*. 1163 ὦ ὦ ὥρα δή: Pepl.Arist.56 ἐνθάδε Ῥῆσον Τρῶες δὴ θάψαν: Hdt.i 4 τὸ δὲ ἀπὸ τούτου Ἕλληνας δὴ μεγάλως αἰτίους γενέσθαι: ii 122 ἀπὸ δὲ τῆς Ῥαμψινίτου καταβάσιος . . . ὁρτὴν δὴ ἀνάγειν Αἰγυπτίους ἔφασαν: Pl.*R*.566A ἆρα τῷ τοιούτῳ ἀνάγκη δὴ τὸ μετὰ τοῦτο . . . ἀπολωλέναι: *Sph*.267E ὁ γὰρ σοφιστὴς οὐκ ἐν τοῖς εἰδόσιν ἦν ἀλλ' ἐν τοῖς μιμουμένοις δή: *Cra*.408A τὸ δὲ λέγειν δή ἐστιν εἴρειν: *Lg*.834B τὸ δὲ μετὰ ταῦτα ἵππων δὴ περὶ ἀγῶνος γίγνοιτο ἑξῆς ἂν νομοθετούμενα: X.*Cyr*.iii 3.24 Ὦ Κυαξάρη, ὥρα δὴ ἀπαντᾶν: iv 5.1 Ὥρα δή, ὦ Μῆδοι . . ., δειπνεῖν.

(8) With verbs. δή is freely used by the tragedians (perhaps rather too freely by Euripides) to emphasize verbs: not infrequently by Plato: and occasionally by other writers. In the austerer style of Thucydides and the orators this usage is hardly to be found. The emphasis conveyed by δή with verbs is for the most part pathetic in tone, and it is peculiarly at home in the great crises of drama, above all at moments when death or ruin is present or imminent, though its use is not confined to such moments. Often, in the nature of the case, δή standing in close relation to a verb might be taken as having temporal force. But to take it so, as some writers have done, is to miss an emotional factor of great importance.

(i) At moments of strong emotion. Thgn.511 ἦλθες δή, Κλεάριστε: Hippon.*Fr*.39.4 ὁ μὲν γὰρ . . . κατέφαγε δὴ τὸν κλῆρον (indignant): Anacr.*Fr*.52 ἀναπέτομαι δὴ πρὸς Ὄλυμπον πτερύγεσσι κούφαις: Crates Theb.*Fr*.11 στείχεις δή, φίλε κυρτών: Pi.*N*.8.19 ἵσταμαι δὴ ποσσὶ κούφοις: A.*Pr*.13 σφῷν μὲν ἐντολὴ

Διὸς ἔχει τέλος δή: 57 *πασσάλευε πρὸς πέτραις.—Περαίνεται δὴ κοὐ ματᾷ τοὔργον τόδε*: *Ch.*1057 *Ἄναξ Ἄπολλον, αἵδε πληθύουσι δή*: *Fr.*58 *ἐνθουσιᾷ δὴ δῶμα, βακχεύει στέγη*: S.*Aj.*1271 *ἀλλ' οἴχεται δὴ πάντα ταῦτ' ἐρριμμένα*: *El.*1482 *Ὄλωλα δὴ δείλαιος*: *Ant.*823 *Ἤκουσα δὴ λυγροτάταν ὀλέσθαι . . .*: 939 *ἄγομαι δὴ κοὐκέτι μέλλω*: *OT* 66 *ἴστε πολλὰ μέν με δακρύσαντα δή*: *Tr.* 1145 *οἴμοι, φρονῶ δὴ ξυμφορᾶς ἵν' ἕσταμεν*: *OC* 1216 *ἐπεὶ πολλὰ μὲν αἱ μακραὶ ἁμέραι κατέθεντο δὴ λύπας ἐγγυτέρω*: E.*El.*768 *δυσγνωσίαν εἶχον προσώπου· νῦν δὲ γιγνώσκω σε δή*: *Med.*1021 *σφῷν μὲν ἔστι δὴ πόλις*: 1024 *ἐς ἄλλην γαῖαν εἶμι δὴ φυγάς*: 1035 *νῦν δ' ὄλωλε δὴ γλυκεῖα φροντίς*: *Hipp.*688 *ἀλλὰ δεῖ με δὴ καινῶν λόγων*: 789 *ἤδη γὰρ ὡς νεκρόν νιν ἐκτείνουσι δή*: 1093 *φευξόμεσθα δὴ κλεινὰς Ἀθήνας*: 1401 *Ὤμοι· φρονῶ δὴ δαίμον' ἥ μ' ἀπώλεσεν*: *Heracl.*442 *ὀλούμεθ', ὦ τέκν'· ἐκδοθησόμεσθα δή*: *Hec.*413–14 *τέλος δέχῃ δὴ τῶν ἐμῶν προσφθεγμάτων. ὦ μῆτερ, ὦ τεκοῦσ', ἄπειμι δὴ κάτω*: 681 *Οἴμοι, βλέπω δὴ παῖδ' ἐμὸν τεθνηκότα*: *HF* 1245 *Γέμω κακῶν δή* (emphasis on *γέμω*): *Ion* 843 *ἐκ τῶνδε δεῖ σε δὴ γυναικεῖόν τι δρᾶν*: *Supp.*1012 *Ὁρῶ δὴ τελευτάν*: *Hel.* 134 *οἴχεται θανοῦσα δή*: 279 *οὐκέτ' ἔστι δή*: *Andr.*510 *Κείσῃ δή, τέκνον ὦ φίλος*: *Or.*1076 *σοὶ μὲν γὰρ ἔστι πόλις, ἐμοὶ δ' οὐκ ἔστι δή*: 1081 *κῆδος δὲ τοὐμὸν καὶ σὸν οὐκέτ' ἔστι δή*: *IA* 751 *Ἥξει δὴ Σιμόεντα*: X.*Cyr.*vii 3.8 *Φεῦ, ὦ ἀγαθὴ καὶ πιστὴ ψυχή, οἴχῃ δὴ ἀπολιπὼν ἡμᾶς*;

(ii) With less emotional force, or with a purely intellectual emphasis.

(*a*) Not infrequently with *ὁρᾶν*, especially in Plato. Th.vii 77.2 *ἀλλ' ὁρᾶτε δὴ ὡς διάκειμαι ὑπὸ τῆς νόσου*: Pl.*Grg.*461A *ὕστερον δ' ἡμῶν ἐπισκοπουμένων ὁρᾷς δὴ καὶ αὐτὸς . . .*: *Ap.*31B *νῦν δ' ὁρᾶτε δὴ καὶ αὐτοὶ . . .*: *Euthphr.*13B *ὥσπερ ὁρᾷς δὴ ὅτι . . .*: *Cri.*44D *Ἀλλ' ὁρᾷς δὴ ὅτι ἀνάγκη . . .*: *R.*421A *φύλακες δὲ νόμων . . . ὁρᾷς δὴ ὅτι . . . πόλιν ἀπολλύασιν*: X.*Cyr.*iii 2.12 *νῦν δὲ ὁρᾶτε δή*. For *ὅρα δή* see iii.*b* below.

(*b*) With other verbs. Hom.*Λ* 733 *ἀτὰρ μεγάθυμοι Ἐπειοὶ ἀμφίσταντο δὴ ἄστυ*: *N* 226 *ἀλλά που οὕτω μέλλει δὴ φίλον εἶναι ὑπερμενέϊ Κρονίωνι*: *Π* 127 *λεύσσω δὴ παρὰ νηυσὶ . . .*: *δ* 138 *Ἴδμεν δή, Μενέλαε*: S.*Ph.*241 *οἶσθα δὴ τὸ πᾶν*: *Euryp.Fr.*5.39 *οὐ γὰρ ἐκτὸς ἑστὼς σύρει δὴ φύρδαν*: E.*Heracl.*665 *Τοῦδ' οὐκέθ' ἡμῖν τοῦ λόγου μέτεστι δή*: *Ba.*934 *σοὶ γὰρ ἀνακείμεσθα δή*: Ar.*Nu.*1209 "*χοῖον τὸν υἱὸν τρέφεις*" *φήσουσι δή μ' οἱ φίλοι*:

*Lys.*1108 χαῖρ' ὦ πασῶν ἀνδρειοτάτη· δεῖ δὴ νυνί σε γενέσθαι...: Hp.*Salubr.*2 τοῖσι δὲ ... ξυμφέρει δὴ ...: Hdt.i 63 Ἀθηναῖοι δὲ οἱ ἐκ τοῦ ἄστεος πρὸς ἄριστον τετραμμένοι ἦσαν δὴ τηνικαῦτα: Pl.*Lg.*813B τοὺς γὰρ παῖδάς τε καὶ τὰς παῖδας ὀρχεῖσθαι δὴ δεῖ: *Phd.*99B ὁ μέν τις δινὴν περιτιθεὶς τῇ γῇ ὑπὸ τοῦ οὐρανοῦ μένειν δὴ ποιεῖ τὴν γῆν: *R.*387C καὶ ἄλλα ὅσα ... φρίττειν δὴ ποιεῖ: 461E ὡς δὲ ἑπομένη ... δεῖ δὴ τὸ μετὰ τοῦτο βεβαιώσασθαι: *Plt.* 286C Λέγω τοίνυν ὅτι χρὴ δὴ ...: *Phdr.*258A ἔπειτα λέγει δὴ μετὰ τοῦτο: *Hp.Ma.*303E "Τοῦτ' ἄρα", φήσει, "λέγετε δὴ τὸ καλὸν εἶναι ...;" (δή *Tf*: δέ *F*: *om.W*): *Prt.*341C Ἀκούεις δή, ἔφην ἐγώ, ... Προδίκου τοῦδε: *Plt.*258A ὦ Σώκρατες, ἀκούεις δὴ Σωκράτους; *Lg* 965C Σοὶ πιστεύων, ὦ ξένε, συγχωρῶ δή: *Ep.*330A τὸ δ' εἶχεν δὴ πῶς; X.*An.*v 8.13 ὁμολογῶ παῖσαι δὴ ἄνδρας: vii 1.26 οἷος δὲ πόλεμος ἂν γένοιτο εἰκάζειν δὴ πάρεστιν: *Cyr.*i 5.14 ἐγὼ δ' ἐπανελθὼν πρὸς τὸν πατέρα πρόειμι δή: Pl.*Lg.*684D ὡς ἐπιχειροῦντι δὴ νομοθέτῃ κινεῖν τῶν τοιούτων τι πᾶς ἀπαντᾷ (probably *indignantis*: 'when he tries, forsooth ...').

(iii) With imperatives, usually, but not always, directly following the verb. This use is exceedingly common in Aristophanes, and not infrequent in Homer (especially in the formula ἀλλ' ἄγε δή). It is rare in tragedy, and, though not wholly foreign to the grand style, appears to have been mainly colloquial in the fifth and fourth centuries. δή may usually here be rendered 'come' or 'now'. It sometimes implies a connexion, logical or temporal, the command either arising out of, or simply following upon, a previous action or speech. This usage may, in fact, have contributed to the growth of connective δή. Cf. A.*Supp.*625: *Pr.*630: Ar.*Eq.*21,152: *Nu.*340: *Ra.*888.

(*a*) In general. Hom.*Z* 306 ἆξον δὴ ἔγχος: 476 δότε δή: *Υ* 115 Φράζεσθον δὴ σφῶϊ: *μ* 378 Ζεῦ ... τῖσαι δή: *ο* 167 Φράζεο δή: *τ* 97 Εὐρυνόμη, φέρε δὴ δίφρον: *υ* 18 Τέτλαθι δή, κραδίη: *φ* 176 Ἄγρει δή: Sapph.*Fr.*123.1 ἴψοι δὴ τὸ μέλαθρον ὑμήναον ἀέρρατε: S.*El.*534 εἶεν· δίδαξον δή με τοῦτο: 634 Ἔπαιρε δὴ σὺ θύμαθ': *Fr.*760.1 βᾶτ' εἰς ὁδὸν δὴ πᾶς ὁ χειρῶναξ λεώς: Ar.*Ach.* 103 λέγε δή (*Av.*587: *Lys.*503): *Eq.*8 Δεῦρο δὴ πρόσελθ': *Nu.* 683 Εἰπὲ δή (778,1410): *Ach.*777 Φώνει δή: *Pax* 1099 Φράζεο δή: *Ach.*733 ἀκούετε δή (*Pl.*76): 1143 Ἴτε δὴ χαίροντες: *Pax* 458 Ὑπότεινε δὴ πᾶς: 1102 ἔγχει δή (1105): *Av.*1512 ὑπόδυθι ταχὺ δή: *Lys.*1295 Πρόφαινε δή: *Th.*982 ἔξαιρε δή: *Ra.*190 ἔσβαινε δή:

207 Κατακέλευε δή: 270 Ἔχε δὴ τὠβολώ: 498 Φέρε δὴ ταχέως αὔτ': 641 ἀποδύεσθε δή: 885 Εὔχεσθε δή: *Ec.*131 Περίθου δή: *Nu.*700 Φρόντιζε δή: *Av.*675 Ἴωμεν.—Ἡγοῦ δὴ σὺ νῷν τὐχἀγαθῇ: Antid. *Fr.*2.1 κατὰ τὴν στάσιν δὴ στάντες ἀκροάσασθέ μου: Nicostr.Com.*Fr.*19.3 Λαβὲ τῆς ὑγιείας δὴ σύ: Pl.*Prt.*353C Ἀκούετε δή: 330C Ὦ Πρωταγόρα τε καὶ Σώκρατες, εἴπετον δή μοι: X.*Cyr.*v 2.13 Πρὸς τῶν θεῶν . . . δεῖξον δή μοι.

(*b*) Particularly common in connexion with certain verbs. Ὅρα δή. Pl.*Phlb.*11A Ὅρα δή, Πρώταρχε: *Phd.*105A ἀλλ' ὅρα δή (*Tht.*163C: *R.*596B: *Sph.*241B): *Cri.*48E ὅρα δὲ δή. Ἔχε δή. Pl.*Grg.*490B Ἔχε δὴ αὐτοῦ: *Hp.Ma.*296A Ἔχε δὴ ἠρέμα: *Prt.*349E: *Grg.*460A: *La.*198B: *Tht.*186B: *R.*353B: Eup.*Fr.*276.5 Ἴσχε δή. Φέρε δή: φέρε . . . δή. With 2nd or 3rd person imperative. S.*El.*376 Φέρ' εἰπὲ δή (*Ant.*534): Ar.*Nu.* 1088: Ant.Soph.*Fr.*49 (*ter*): D.xix 251 φέρε δὴ . . . σκέψασθε. With jussive subjunctive. E.*Andr.*333 Μενέλαε, φέρε δὴ διαπεράνωμεν λόγους: Pl.*Grg.*464B Φέρε δὴ . . . ἐπιδείξω: Lys.xii 62 φέρε δὴ . . . διδάξω: D.xviii 267 φέρε δὴ καὶ τὰς . . . μαρτυρίας . . . ἀναγνῶ: Gorg.*Fr.*11.10. In questions. Ar.*Ach.*1058 Φέρε δή, τί σὺ λέγεις; *Nu.*940: Ant.*Fr.*1a φέρε δή, πῶς εἰκός ἐστιν . . .; Lys.vi 46 φέρε δή, εἰς τί . . .; xii 34 φέρε δή, τί . . .; Pl.*Amat.*136C. Absolute. Pl.*Phlb.*60A Φέρε δή, πρὸς Διός· οἶμαι γάρ . . . .

Ἄγε δή. With imperative. Hom.Κ 479 ἀλλ' ἄγε δὴ πρόφερε: Φ 221 ἀλλ' ἄγε δὴ καὶ ἔασον: β 178 Ὦ γέρον, εἰ δ' ἄγε δὴ μαντεύεο: 349 Μαῖ', ἄγε δή μοι οἶνον . . . ἄφυσσον: Anacr.*Fr.*43.1 ἄγε δὴ φέρ' ἡμίν, ὦ παῖ, κελέβην: Ar.*Ach.*98 Ἄγε δὴ σὺ . . . φράσον: Hom Θ 139: μ 112: τ 16: Thgn. 829: Ar.*Ach.*111: *Eq.* 155,634: *Nu.*478,775: *Th.*778: *Ra.*1500: Cephisod.*Fr.*12: Pl. *Phlb.*33A Ἄγε δὴ τοίνυν, ταύτης προθυμοῦ μεμνῆσθαι: *Phdr.*237A Ἄγετε δή, ὦ Μοῦσαι . . . "ξύμ μοι λάβεσθε": *Lg.*893B: X.*An.*ii 2.10 Ἄγε δὴ . . . εἰπέ: vii 6.3 ἄγετε δὴ πρὸς θεῶν καὶ τὰ ἐμὰ σκέψασθε ὡς ἔχει: v 4.9. With jussive subjunctive. Hom.Δ 418 ἀλλ' ἄγε δὴ καὶ νῶϊ μεδώμεθα: A.*Supp.*625 Ἄγε δή, λέξωμεν: Hom.Ε 249: A.*Eu.*307: Pl.*Phd.*116D ἀλλ' ἄγε δή, ὦ Κρίτων, πειθώμεθα αὐτῷ. With future indicative. Hom.Υ 351 ἀλλ' ἄγε δὴ . . . πειρήσομαι: Φ 60 ἀλλ' ἄγε δὴ . . . γεύσεται. With present indicative understood. E.*Cyc.*590 Ἄγε δὴ . . . ἔνδον μὲν ἀνήρ. In questions. A.*Ag.* 783 ἄγε δή, βασιλεῦ . . . πῶς σε προσείπω; Ar.*Eq.*482 Ἄγε δὴ σὺ τίνα νοῦν . . . ἔχεις; *Nu.*636: *Ra.*460.

Ἴθι δή, with imperative. Ar.*Eq.*152 Ἴθι δὴ κάθελ': *Pax* 405, 1238: *Ra.*569: Pl.*Phdr.*262D Ἴθι δή μοι ἀνάγνωθι: *Prt.*352A.

We may include here εἶα δή and δεῦρο δή (the latter with or without ellipse: 'Here!': 'Come here'). A.*Ag.*1650 Εἶα δή, φίλοι λοχῖται, τοὔργον οὐχ ἑκὰς τόδε: Ar.*Th.*659: Hom.χ 395 Δεῦρο δὴ ὄρσο: Ar.*Ec.*952 δεῦρο δή, δεῦρο δή, φίλον ἐμὸν . . . πρόσελθε: E.*IA* 630 καὶ—δεῦρο δή—πατέρα πρόσειπε: 1377: Pl.*Ly.*203B Δεῦρο δή, ἦ δ' ὅς, εὐθὺ ἡμῶν: *R.*477D. Cf. X.*Cyn.*6.18 ἀναβοᾶν δ' ἐκεῖνον αὐτῷ Παισάτω παῖς· παῖ δή, παῖ δή (παῖε δή, παῖε δή *A*).

δή νυν (δὴ νῦν) expresses an increased urgency in command or appeal. Hom.ω 454 Κέκλυτε δὴ νῦν (β 25,161,229): S.*El.*947 Ἄκουε δή νυν (a favourite Euripidean formula: E.*Cyc.*441: *Hec.* 833: *Supp.*857: *HF* 1255: *Ion* 1539: *IT* 753: *Ph.*911,1427: *Hel.*1035: *Or.*237,1181: *IA* 1009,1146: Ar.*Eq.*1014: *Av.*1513. Pl.*Lg.*693D Ἄκουσον δή νυν): Ar.*Nu.*500 Εἰπὲ δή νύν μοι (748): Cratin.*Fr.*222 ἔγειρε δὴ νῦν, Μοῦσα, Κρητικὸν μέλος. χαῖρε δή, Μοῦσα: Pl.*Sph.*239B ἀλλ' εἶα δὴ νῦν ἐν σοὶ σκεψώμεθα: D.ix 16 φέρε δὴ νῦν . . . τί ποιεῖ; (In Pl.*Sph.*224C ἴθι δὴ νῦν συναγάγωμεν (Burnet) is probably the right reading.)

(iv) With jussive subjunctives. S.*Ph.*1469 Χωρῶμεν δὴ πάντες ἀολλεῖς: E.*Heracl.*344 ἐζώμεσθα δή.

(v) In wishes. Alcm.Fr.94.2 βάλε δή, βάλε κηρύλος εἴην: A.*Pers.*228 ἐκτελοῖτο δὴ τὰ χρηστά: S.*Aj.*384 Ἴδοιμι δή νιν: Ar.*Pl.*891 Ὡς δὴ . . . διαρραγείης.

Hitherto δή has emphasized individual words, though in many cases, as we have seen, the emphasis is to some extent distributed over the whole clause or sentence. We have now to consider passages in which it emphasizes structural words, which affect the whole architecture of the sentence.

(9) With relatives, usually stressing the importance of the antecedent, or its exact identification with the consequent (though sometimes the particle has a more independent force). A very common use throughout Greek literature.

(i) Relative pronouns. Hom.*B* 117 οὕτω που Διὶ μέλλει ὑπερμενέϊ φίλον εἶναι, ὃς δὴ πολλάων πολίων κατέλυσε κάρηνα ('Zeus, who . . .'): *K* 27 Ἀργεῖοι, τοὶ δὴ . . . ἤλυθον: S.*Aj.*995 ὁδὸς . . .

ἣν δὴ νῦν ἔβην: *OT* 399 ὃν δὴ σὺ πειρᾷς ἐκβαλεῖν (indignant): E.*Hipp.* 347 Τί τοῦθ', ὃ δὴ λέγουσιν ἀνθρώπους, ἐρᾶν; ('this unknown thing that men call love': δή expresses Phaedra's remoteness from love): Hom.*B* 436: *Z* 98: *O* 131: ψ339: S.*Tr.* 1011: *Aj.* 1029: E.*Alc.* 102: *IA* 933: Hdt.i 214.1 ταύτην τὴν μάχην, ὅσαι δὴ . . . ἐγένοντο, κρίνω ἰσχυροτάτην γενέσθαι ('of absolutely all which . . .'): v 56.2 ἔπεμπε τὴν πομπήν, ἐν τῇ δὴ τελευτᾷ: Pl.*Tht.* 144A ὧν δὴ πώποτε ἐνέτυχον . . . οὐδένα πω ᾐσθόμην . . .: *Grg.* 461B τοῦτο ὃ δὴ ἀγαπᾷς (contemptuous): *Smp.* 184A ἵνα χρόνος ἐγγένηται, ὃς δὴ δοκεῖ . . . ('time . . . time which . . .'): *Euthd.* 289D τὴν ἐπιστήμην ἣν δὴ πάλαι ζητοῦμεν ('precisely that knowledge which . . .'): *Hipparch.* 231A ὅ τι δή ('in virtue of just which': not, of course, to be grouped under III.2): D.xv 29 ταύτας ὧν δὴ κατηγοροῦσι (ironical): Hdt.vii 8β: ix 58.4: Th.ii 29.4: vi 18.2: Pl.*R.* 579B: X.*An.* iv 7.23: *Hier.* 7.12: Aeschin.iii 56.

With word repeated from main clause. Hdt.iii 16.1 ποιῆσαι τὰ δὴ καὶ ἐποίησε: Pl.*Phd.* 107E τυχόντας δὲ ἐκεῖ ὧν δὴ τυχεῖν: *Lg.* 902A: D.viii 63 πεπόνθασιν ἃ δὴ πεπόνθασιν (reading uncertain: cf. x 65): xvi 23 μισοῦσιν οὓς δὴ μισοῦσιν.

With depreciatory or sceptical colour. X.*Cyr.* viii 2.14 εὐδαίμονα . . . ᾗ δὴ προβάτων εὐδαιμονία ('as far as sheep can be said to be happy'): *Hier.* 1.1 Καὶ ποῖα ταῦτ' ἐστὶν . . . ὁποῖα δὴ ἐγὼ βέλτιον ἂν εἰδείην σοῦ οὕτως ὄντος σοφοῦ ἀνδρός; Semon.*Fr.* 1.4: S.*Aj.* 1043 κακοῖς γελῶν ἃ δὴ κακοῦργος ἐξίκοιτ' ἀνήρ: Pl.*La.* 181E: *Phdr.* 244D. Cf. οἷα δή, ἅτε δή (see v.*b* below).

(ii) Relative local adverbs. Hom.*K* 199 ὅθι δή: η281 τῇ δή: Mimn.*Fr.* 10.9 ἵνα δὴ θοὸν ἅρμα καὶ ἵπποι: S.*OT* 1263 οὗ δὴ κρεμαστὴν τὴν γυναῖκ' εἰσείδομεν: E.*Med.* 68 πεσσοὺς προσελθών, ἔνθα δὴ παλαίτατοι θάσσουσι: *IA* 547 ὅθι δή: E.*Tr.* 435: *IA* 97: Ar.*Pax* 901: *Th.* 1150: Pl.*Phd.* 72A ὅθεν δή (*Cra.* 401D: X.*HG* vi 5.33): X.*An.* vii 6.37 καὶ πλεῖτε ἔνθα δὴ ἐπεθυμεῖτε: Hdt.ii 152, 156: X.*An.* vii 6.9.

δή is here often followed by καί (*q.v.* II.B.1): Pl.*Grg.* 488D οἳ δὴ καὶ τοὺς νόμους τίθενται: *Smp.* 180A ὅθεν δὴ καὶ ὑπεραγασθέντες οἱ θεοὶ . . .: Th.i 128.1: ii 21.1: 42.1.

(iii) Relative temporal adverbs, 'precisely when', 'just when'. Hom.*A* 6 ἐξ οὗ δὴ τὰ πρῶτα διαστήτην ἐρίσαντε: *E* 65 ὅτε δὴ κατέμαρπτε διώκων: Θ229 πῇ ἔβαν εὐχωλαί, ὅτε δή φαμεν εἶναι ἄριστοι . . . ; (with irony): *Π*453 ἐπὴν δή: υ386 δέγμενος αἰεί, ὁππότε δὴ μνηστῆρσιν ἀναιδέσι χεῖρας ἐφήσει ('waiting for when': but perhaps an indirect question): S.*Ant.*91 Οὐκοῦν ὅταν δὴ μὴ σθένω πεπαύσομαι (*sc.* 'but not before'): E.*Hel.*534 ἥξειν δ' ὅταν δὴ πημάτων λάβῃ τέλος: Ar.*Ach.*10 ὅτε δὴ 'κεχήνη: *Pl.*688 ὡς ᾔσθετο δή: Ar.*Ach.*16,535: *Eq.*658: *Ra.*771,789,1090: Hdt.iii 156 ἐπείτε δή: 158 ἐς ὃ δή: i67 ἐς οὗ δή: Th.ii 102.5 ὅτε δὴ ἀλᾶσθαι: iii 54.5 ὅτεπερ δὴ μέγιστος φόβος περιέστη . . . : Pl. *Phdr.*260B Οὔπω γε· ἀλλ' ὅτε δὴ σπουδῇ σε πείθοιμι: *Grg.*518D ὅταν δὴ αὐτοῖς ἥκῃ ἡ πλησμονή: *Ly.*217D ἀλλ' ὅταν δὴ . . . τότε . . . : *R.*405A,568E: *Tht.*160C.

ὅτε δὴ δέ (Ar.*Lys.*523: *Ec.* 315,827) illustrates the completeness with which the particle sometimes fuses with the relative. This fusion is normal in the case of ἐπειδή, which is scarcely distinguishable in sense from ἐπεί.

πρὶν δή. E.*Andr.*1147 ἔστη . . . πρὶν δή τις . . . ἐφθέγξατο: *Rh.*294: Hdt.i 13: iv 157: Th.i 118.2: iii 29.1: 104.6. ἕως δή. X.*HG*ii 3.13: iv 4.9. ἔστε δή. A.*Pr.*457,656.

(iv) Comparative modal adverbs. E.*Hyps.Fr.*64.10 Arn. ἡμεῖς δ' ὥσπερ ὡρμήμεσθα δή, στράτευμ' ἄγοντες ἥξομεν: Hdt.i 193 ψῆνας γὰρ δὴ φέρουσι ἐν τῷ καρπῷ οἱ ἔρσενες, κατά περ δὴ οἱ ὄλονθοι: X.*An.*vii 4.17 φεύγουσιν, ὥσπερ δὴ τρόπος ἦν αὐτοῖς: iii 1.29.

(v) With οἷος. (*a*) Adjectival. The note of disparagement, irony, or contempt is rarely quite absent. (See below.) Hom. ε183 ἀλιτρός γ' ἐσσὶ . . . οἷον δὴ τὸν μῦθον ἐπεφράσθης ἀγορεῦσαι (*quippe cum talem*): υ393 δόρπου δ' οὐκ ἄν πως ἀχαρίστερον ἄλλο γένοιτο, οἷον δὴ τάχ' ἔμελλε θεὰ καὶ καρτερὸς ἀνὴρ θησέμεναι: E.*Heracl.*632 Πάρεσμεν, οἵα δή γ' ἐμοῦ παρουσία: *Andr.*911 Μῶν εἰς γυναῖκ' ἔρραψας οἷα δὴ γυνή; *El.*870 φέρ' οἷα δὴ 'χω . . . ἐξενέγκωμαι: Ant.Soph.*Fr.*53 ἥδονται οἷα δή τις ἂν εἰκάσειεν ἥδεσθαι: Th.vi 63.2 οἷον δὴ ὄχλος φιλεῖ θαρσήσας ποιεῖν: Pl. *Ap.*32C οἷα δὴ καὶ ἄλλοις ἐκεῖνοι πολλοῖς πολλὰ προσέταττον, βουλόμενοι ὡς πλείστους ἀναπλῆσαι αἰτιῶν: *Cri.*53D ἢ διφθέραν λαβὼν ἢ ἄλλα οἷα δὴ εἰώθασιν ἐνσκευάζεσθαι οἱ ἀποδιδράσκοντες: *R.*372C καὶ λάχανά γε, οἷα δὴ ἐν ἄγροις ἑψήματα: *Phd.*60A: *R.*420A,565E: *Alc.I* 106B: X.*Cyr.*ii 1.24.

Without irony. Hom.*Ω*376 τοιόνδ' . . . οἷος δὴ σὺ δέμας . . . ἀγητός: *h.Ven.*179 ὁμοίη . . . οἵην δή με τὸ πρῶτον . . . νοήσας:

E.*Ba.*291 Ζεὺς δ' ἀντεμηχανήσαθ' οἷα δὴ θεός: Pl.*R.*467B σφαλεῖσιν, οἷα δὴ ἐν πολέμῳ φιλεῖ: *Lg.*944A οἷον δὴ μυρίοις συνέπεσεν: Hdt.i 132: X.*Cyr.*i 2.6.

(*b*) Adverbial accusative, οἷα δή (rarely οἷον δή). Here there is seldom any tinge of irony. Archil.*Fr.*78.3 οὐδὲ μὲν κληθεὶς ... ἦλθες, οἷα δὴ φίλος ('as a friend would'): E.*Or.*32 Κἀγὼ μετέσχον, οἷα δὴ γυνή, φόνου (depreciatory): Hdt.i 122 οἷα δὴ ἐπιστάμενοι (*ut qui scirent*): vi 26.2 οἷα δὴ κεκακωμένων: Th.viii 84.3 οἷα δὴ ναῦται (contemptuous): Pl.*Smp.*219E ἀποληφθέντες που, οἷα δὴ ἐπὶ στρατείας ('as will happen on active service'): *Criti.*113E οἷα δὴ θεὸς εὐμαρῶς διεκόσμησεν: X.*HG* iv 5.4 ἔχοντες οἷα δὴ θέρους σπειρία ('as they would, in summer'): v 2.9: 4.39: vi 4.26: *Cyr.*i 3.2: Pl.*Smp.*203B οἷον δὴ εὐωχίας οὔσης. Introducing an example: Pl.*Lg.*667B (in *Ap.*30E οἷον is perhaps masculine). For indignant οἷον δή in Homer, see above, (5) *ad fin.*

ἅτε δή, in the same sense. Hdt.ii 172 ἅτε δὴ δημότην τὸ πρὶν ἐόντα: Hp.*Genit.*12 ἅτε δὴ ἐν θερμῷ ἐοῦσα: *Fract.*7 ἅτε δὴ καὶ ἐλινύοντας (ἤδη *al.*): X.*HG* iv 2.21 καὶ ἅτε δὴ ἀπαθεῖς ὄντες: Pl.*Tht.* 182D.

(vi) With universalizing relatives, ὅστις, ὁποῖος, etc.[1] Thgn. 1173 ὦ μάκαρ, ὅστις δή μιν ἔχει φρεσίν: Hdt.vii 16γ2 ὅ τι δή κοτέ ἐστι τὸ ἐπιφαινόμενον: Hp.*VC* 16 ὀστέον δέ, ὅ τι δὴ ἀποστῆναι δεῖ ..., ἀφίσταται: Pl.*Tht.*160E ὅτι δή ποτε τυγχάνει ὄν: *R.*438C μαθήματος ... ἢ ὅτου δὴ δεῖ θεῖναι τὴν ἐπιστήμην: Hdt.v 109.2: vi 62.2: Pl.*Tht.*200D.

With ellipse of verb in the relative clause. Pl.*Grg.*512E τὸ ζῆν ὁποσονδὴ χρόνον: *Phd.*100D ὅπῃ δὴ ... προσγενομένη: *Alc.II* 143C ἔστι γὰρ ὁτιοῦν πρᾶγμα ὅτῳ δὴ ὁπωσοῦν ἔχοντι ἄμεινον ἀγνοεῖν ἢ γιγνώσκειν;

In the above, δή makes the relative comprehensive: *quivis, quicunque.* In the following, it denotes indifference of choice: *aliquis,*

[1] Cf. οὖν, II. 4. iii. I have not the materials for a systematic comparison of these corresponding uses of δή and οὖν: the matter requires a more thorough examination than it has yet received. In general there is a tendency, I think, to employ οὖν in the elliptical construction, δή in the non-elliptical. Thus the self-contained *quidvis* ('anything') is regularly ὁτιοῦν, not ὅτι δή. (In Pl.*Alc.II* 143C (see below, ὅτῳ δή) δή alternates with οὖν, for the sake of variety.) But self-contained ὁστισδήποτε is frequent: D.viii 1: xix 167: xxi 32.

nescioquis. This latter use is absent from strict Attic composition.[1] It is perhaps rather colloquial, like our 'whoever it was'.

Hdt.i 86 *θεῶν ὅτεῳ δή*: iii 129 *ὅκου δὴ ἀπημελημένον* ('somewhere or other'): vi 134.2 *ὅ τι δὴ ποιήσοντα ἐντός, εἴτε κινήσοντα . . . εἴτε ὅ τι δή κοτε πρήξοντα*: i 86 *ἔλεγε ὡς ἦλθε ὁ Σόλων . . . καὶ θεησάμενος πάντα τὸν ἑωυτοῦ ὄλβον ἀποφλαυρίσειε (οἷα δὴ εἴπας)*... ('saying this and that'): iv 151 *σιτία παρακαταλιπόντες ὅσων δὴ μηνῶν* ('for so many months'): Ant.Soph.*Fr.*54 *φέρων δ' ἀπέθετο ὅποι δή*: X.*HG* v 4.58 *ῥήγνυται ὁποία δὴ φλέψ*: Aen. Tact.31.31 *τίθεσθαι ὅ τι δή* (*ὅ τι δή* Haase: *τί δαί M*): Hdt.i 157, 160: ii 103,126: iii 121,159: X.*An.*iv 7.25: v 2.24.

The sole example in strict Attic is Ar.*Ach.*753 *τί δ' ἄλλο πράττεθ' οἱ Μεγαρῆς νῦν;—Οἷα δή* ('One thing and another.' *πράττετε* means 'do', not 'fare', as is plain from *τί δ' ἄλλο* (not *πῶς δ' ἄλλως*), and from 754–6: and *οἷα* is not 'euphemistic', as has been supposed. The use is perhaps Doric as well as Ionic. See *C.R.*xliii (1929) 119.)

(vii) In the following, *δή* is approximative, 'about': Hp.*Mul.* 75 *σιδήρου σκωρίην ὅσην δὴ παλαστὴν τὰ θρύμματα*: 200 *στέαρ ὅσον δὴ τῷ δακτύλῳ λαβεῖν.*

(10) With negatives.

(i) In general. Except in a few well-defined types of phrase, *δή* is not very often used to strengthen negatives, its place being taken by *δῆτα* or *τοι*: or *οὐδαμῶς*, *οὐ πάνυ* are used. Hom.*υ*322 *Ὦ φίλοι, οὐκ ἂν δή τις ἐπὶ ῥηθέντι δικαίῳ . . . χαλεπαίνοι*: S.*OC*1698 *καὶ γὰρ ὃ μηδαμὰ δὴ φίλον ἦν φίλον*: E.*Alc.* 94 *Οὐ δὴ φρουδός γ' ἐξ οἴκων*: *El.*36 *πατέρων μὲν Μυκηναίων ἄπο γεγῶσιν—οὐ δὴ τοῦτό γ' ἐξελέγχομαι*: 57 *μετέρχομαι—οὐ δή τι χρείας ἐς τοσόνδ' ἀφιγμένη*: *Hec.*202 *οὐκέτι σοι παῖς ἅδ' οὐκέτι δὴ . . . συνδουλεύσω*: Ar.*Th.*567 *Οὐ δὴ μὰ Δία σύ γ' ἄψει*: Hdt.ii 162 *οὐδένα δὴ χρόνον ἐπισχόντες*: iii 143 *νόῳ λαβὼν ὡς, εἰ . . ., οὐ δή τι ἐν νόῳ εἶχε μετιέναι*: ix 111.5 *Δέσποτα, οὐ δή κώ με ἀπώλεσας*: Hp.*Prorrh.*ii 12 *τοῦ τρώματος οὐδὲν δή τι δεινοῦ ἐόντος*: Th.vii 71.7 *οὐδεμιᾶς δὴ τῶν ξυμπασῶν ἐλάσσων*

[1] In D.xix 167 (*cum cuius*, not *cum alicuius*), xxi 32 (*quodcunque est nomen*, not *aliquod nomen*), *ὁστισδήποτε* denotes, not indifference of choice, but the inclusion of all cases: 'any', not 'some': while in the passages quoted below the idea of inclusion ('whatever it was') has passed into the idea of indifference ('some or other').

ἔκπληξις: Pl.*Lg.*921B ἐν ἐλευθέρων οὖν πόλεσιν οὐ δή ποτε χρὴ . . . . (In *Lg.*890A δή seems to go with τινι.)

(ii) Sophocles eight times has οὐ δή, usually followed by που or ποτε, to introduce a surprised or incredulous question. (The idiom seems to be peculiar to him. The tone of Arete's question in Hom.η239 is of course different: οὐ δὴ φῇς ἐπὶ πόντον ἀλώμενος ἐνθάδ' ἱκέσθαι; 'Did you not say . . . ?')

S.*El.*1108 Οἴμοι τάλαιν', οὐ δή ποθ' ἧς ἠκούσαμεν φήμης φέροντες ἐμφανῆ τεκμήρια; ('Surely not . . . ?'): *Ph.*900 Οὐ δή σε δυσχέρεια τοῦ νοσήματος ἔπεισεν . . .; *El.*1180,1202: *OT* 1472: *Ant.*381: *Tr.*668,876.

(iii) In Homer οὐκ ἂν δή often introduces a polite request, in the form of a question. *E*32 οὐκ ἂν δὴ Τρῶας μὲν ἐάσαιμεν καὶ Ἀχαιοὺς μάρνασθ' . . .; 456: ζ57 Πάππα φίλ', οὐκ ἂν δή μοι ἐφοπλίσσειας ἀπήνην . . .; ('Couldn't you . . . ?'): *Γ*52 (Hector to Paris, with ironical courtesy) οὐκ ἂν δὴ μείνειας ἀρηΐφιλον Μενέλαον; ('Could you not oblige me by not running away?'): *Ω*263 (Priam's tone is impatient).

(iv) Μὴ δή in negative commands. Hom.*A*131 Μὴ δὴ οὕτως . . . κλέπτε νόῳ: λ488 Μὴ δή μοι θάνατόν γε παραύδα, φαίδιμ' Ὀδυσσεῦ: Thgn.352 μὴ δή μ' οὐκ ἐθέλοντα φίλει: S.*OT* 1505 μή σφε δὴ παρῇς: Hom.*E*684: *P*501: X.*Cyr.*v 5.41 Μὴ δὴ σὺ κέλευε.

(v) Μὴ δή in dependent clauses. Hom.*Ξ*44 δείδω μὴ δή μοι τελέσῃ ἔπος ὄβριμος Ἕκτωρ: *Π*81 ἔμπεσ' ἐπικρατέως, μὴ δὴ πυρὸς αἰθομένοιο νῆας ἐνιπρήσωσι: σ10.

(vi) *A fortiori*, μή τι δή. Pl.*Plt.*292E ἄκροι πεττευταὶ τοσοῦτοι . . . οὐκ ἂν γένοιντό ποτε, μή τι δὴ βασιλῆς γε: *Ep.*321A (315C *coni.* Burnet). μὴ ὅτι δή: Pl.*Phdr.*240E ἃ καὶ λόγῳ ἐστὶν ἀκούειν οὐκ ἐπιτερπές, μὴ ὅτι δὴ ἔργῳ . . . μεταχειρίζεσθαι. For μή τί (ὅτι) γε δή see γε δή (4): for μὴ ὅτι δή γε (Pl.*Phlb.*60D) see δή γε. Cf. μή τί γε (γε, II.5.)

(11) In conditional protases, εἰ (ἐὰν) δή, εἰ . . . δή: 'if indeed', 'if really'. We often find εἰ δή where εἰ ἄρα, 'if after all', or εἴ γε, 'if, but not unless', might have been used instead.[1]

[1] Jebb remarks on S.*Tr.*27 that 'the tone of εἰ δή is sceptical, as that of εἴπερ is usually confident'. This is for the most part true, but not invariably. εἰ δή is clearly confident, for example, in Hom.Σ120: Ar.*Ra.*242 Μᾶλλον μὲν οὖν φθεγξόμεσθ', εἰ δή ποτ' εὐηλίοις ἐν ἁμέραισιν ἡλάμεσθα διὰ κυπείρου. See also περ, p. 488, note 1.

Hom.*A*574 Ἦ δὴ λοίγια ἔργα τάδ' ἔσσεται . . . εἰ δὴ σφὼ ἕνεκα θνητῶν ἐριδαίνετον ὧδε: N111 ἀλλ' εἰ δὴ καὶ πάμπαν ἐτήτυμον αἴτιός ἐστιν ἥρως Ἀτρεΐδης . . . ἡμέας γ' οὔ πως ἔστι μεθιέμεναι πολέμοιο ('even if in reality'): S.*Ph.*818 Καὶ δὴ μεθίημ', εἴ τι δὴ πλέον φρονεῖς: E.*Alc.*386 Ἀπωλόμην ἄρ', εἴ με δὴ λείψεις, γύναι: *Heracl.*739 Εἰ δή ποθ' ἥξομέν γε· τοῦτο γὰρ φόβος: *El.*911 ἅ γ' εἰπεῖν ἤθελον κατ' ὄμμα σόν, εἰ δὴ γενοίμην δειμάτων ἐλευθέρα: *IT*43 λέξω πρὸς αἰθέρ', εἴ τι δὴ τόδ' ἔστ' ἄκος: Hom.*M*79: *Π*66: *Φ*463: E.*Heracl.*437,592: *IT*494: *IA*794: *Hipp.*1071: Hdt.i 112 εἰ δὴ πᾶσά γε ἀνάγκη . . .: ii 160 ἀλλ' εἰ δὴ βούλονται δικαίως τιθέναι: Pl.*Grg.*481B εἰ δὴ καὶ ἔστιν τις χρεία: *Euthd.*296D εἰ δὴ τῷ ὄντι ἀληθῆ λέγεις: *Chrm.* 165B ὡς φάσκοντος ἐμοῦ εἰδέναι περὶ ὧν ἐρωτῶ προσφέρῃ πρός με, καὶ ἐὰν δὴ βούλωμαι, ὁμολογήσοντός σοι ('if I really want to'): *Lg.*638C (with ironical colour): D.vi 23 ἀπεύχεσθε, εἰ σωφρονεῖτε δή, ἰδεῖν: Hdt.v 60: vi 123.2: Pl.*Ap.*29B: *R.*470A: *Tht.*166C: *Alc.I* 119E.

Sometimes with a word repeated from the apodosis. S.*Tr.* 27 τέλος δ' ἔθηκε Ζεὺς ἀγώνιος καλῶς, εἰ δὴ καλῶς: E.*Or.*17 ὁ κλεινός, εἰ δὴ κλεινός, Ἀγαμέμνων: 744 Ἐν δόμοις ἐμοῖσιν, εἰ δὴ τούσδ' ἐμοὺς καλεῖν χρεών: *HF*41 κἀμ'—εἴ τι δὴ χρὴ κἀμ' ἐν ἀνδράσιν λέγειν γέροντ' ἀχρεῖον: D.viii 36 ὑγιαινόντων, εἰ δὴ τοὺς τὰ τοιαῦτα ποιοῦντας ὑγιαίνειν φήσαιμεν.

(12) *In apodosi.* The use of δή, with or without a temporal or modal adverb, to mark the opening of the apodosis after a temporal, causal, relative, or conditional protasis, is exceedingly common in Homer and frequent throughout Greek literature.

(i) After temporal protasis. Without adverb. S.*Ant.*173 ὅτ' οὖν ἐκεῖνοι . . . ὤλοντο . . . ἐγὼ κράτη δὴ πάντα . . . ἔχω: Pl.*Cra.* 435D ὡς ἐπειδάν τις εἰδῇ τὸ ὄνομα . . . εἴσεται δὴ καὶ τὸ πρᾶγμα: *Phd.*89D ὅταν . . . τελευτῶν δὴ . . .: *Euthd.*293D ἐπεὶ δὲ . . . κἀκείνην δὴ . . .: Lys.xxiii 6 ἐπειδὴ . . . ἠρώτων δὴ . . . . With adverb. Hom.*A*476 ἦμος δ' ἠέλιος κατέδυ . . . δὴ τότε κοιμήσαντο: S.*Tr.*37 νῦν δ' ἡνίκ' . . . ἔφυ, ἐνταῦθα δὴ μάλιστα ταρβήσασ' ἔχω: E.*Hipp.*38 ἐπεὶ δὲ . . . ἐνταῦθα δὴ . . .: Ar.*Eq.*199 (oracle) ἀλλ' ὁπόταν . . . δὴ τότε . . .: *Nu.*62 ὅπως νῷν ἐγένεθ' υἱὸς οὑτοσὶ . . . περὶ τοὐνόματος δὴ 'ντεῦθεν ἐλοιδορούμεθα: Pl. *Smp.*184E ὅταν . . . εἰς τὸ αὐτὸ ἔλθωσιν . . . τότε δὴ . . .: *Lg.*948C ὅτε . . . οὐκέτι δὴ . . . : Ant.vi 38 ἐπειδὴ δὲ . . . τότε δὴ . . . : Hdt.i 5,62 : ii 2 : Th.ii 70.1 : iii 51.4 : iv 127.2 : Pl.*Chrm.*155D.

Sometimes (frequently in Homer) both protasis and apodosis are strengthened by δή. Hom.*X*74–6 : α293–4 : ω71–2 : Pl.*R.* 573A ὅταν δὴ . . . τότε δή.

(ii) After causal protasis. Thrasym.*Fr.*1 ἐπειδὴ δ' . . ., ἀνάγκη δὴ λέγειν : Pl.*Lg.*876D ἐπειδὴ δὲ . . ., ἐπιτρεπτέον δή : *Men.*99A ἐπειδὴ . . ., οὐδ' ἐπιστήμη δὴ . . . : *Euthd.*282A,293D : *Phd.*93E : *Lg.*906A,948C.

(iii) After relative protasis. A.*Pr.*229 ὃ δ' οὖν ἐρωτᾶτ' . . . τοῦτο δὴ σαφηνιῶ : Hp.*Int.*17 τὸν αὐτὸν τρόπον ὥσπερ ἀφῄρει, οὕτω δὴ προστιθείς : Pl.*Smp.*184B ἔστι γὰρ ἡμῖν νόμος, ὥσπερ ἐπὶ τοῖς ἐρασταῖς ἦν . . . οὕτω δὴ . . . : *Criti.*113C καθάπερ . . ., οὕτω δὴ . . . : *R.*484D,556E.

(iv) After conditional protasis. Hom.*O*163 εἰ δὲ . . ., φραζέσθω δὴ ἔπειτα : E.*Or.*511 εἰ . . ., πέρας δὴ ποῖ κακῶν προβήσεται ; Hdt.viii 80.2 ἢν μὲν πείθωνται, ταῦτα δὴ τὰ κάλλιστα : Pl.*Prm.* 127E εἰ ἀδύνατον . . . ἀδύνατον δὴ καὶ . . . : *Smp.*209B ἂν ἐντύχῃ ψυχῇ καλῇ . . . πάνυ δὴ ἀσπάζεται : *R.*524E εἰ δὲ . . ., τοῦ ἐπικρινοῦντος δὴ δέοι ἂν ἤδη : *Grg.*514C εἰ δὲ μήτε διδάσκαλον εἴχομεν . . . οὕτω δὴ ἀνόητον ἦν : Hdt.i 39,108 : Pl.*Phdr.*273B : *Euthd.*290D : *Men.*75D : *Chrm.*162D.

(v) After final clause. Pl.*Lg.*893A μὴ δὴ σκοτοδινίαν . . . ὑμῖν ἐμποιήσῃ . . . δοκεῖ δή μοι χρῆναι . . . .

(vi) After participial clause. E.*Alc.*176 ἐσπεσοῦσα . . . ἐνταῦθα δὴ 'δάκρυσε : Hdt.i 60 ἐνδεξαμένου δὲ . . . μηχανῶνται δή : 116 ὁ δὲ ἀγόμενος ἐς τὰς ἀνάγκας οὕτω δὴ ἔφαινε τὸν ἐόντα λόγον : Pl.*Phd.*82D ἡγούμενοι . . . ταύτῃ δὴ τρέπονται : 97C ἀλλὰ ἀκούσας . . . ταύτῃ δὴ τῇ αἰτίᾳ ἥσθην : *R.*458D οἱ δέ, ἅτε . . ., ὁμοῦ δὴ ἔσονται : X.*Mem.*iii 7.2 εἴ τις, δυνατὸς ὢν . . . ὀκνοίη δὴ τοῦτο πράττειν : *Cyr.*iv 2.30 πυθόμενοι τὸ γιγνόμενον ἔφευγον δή.

(13) Resumptive. Closely allied to the apodotic use is the resumptive, where δή emphasizes a pronoun or repeated word, usually one which picks up the thread of a train of thought that is beginning to wander. This rather rare use is mainly confined to the more naive style of Herodotus, Xenophon, and the private speeches of the orators, and to the awkward and involved style of Plato's *Laws*. The appearance of an example (apparently

sound textually) in a formal speech like the *Aristocrates* is remarkable. The following varieties may be distinguished:

(i) δή stresses a demonstrative pronoun standing in apposition to a preceding substantival phrase. Hdt.vi 58.3 φάμενοι τὸν ὕστατον αἰεὶ ἀπογενόμενον τῶν βασιλέων, τοῦτον δὴ γενέσθαι ἄριστον: Pl.*Grg.*490E οἷον γεωργικὸν ἄνδρα . . . τοῦτον δὴ ἴσως δεῖ πλεονεκτεῖν (with a tinge of irony): X.*HG* ii 4.13 ὅτι εἰσὶ τῶν προσιόντων οἱ μὲν . . . οἱ δ' ἐπὶ τοῦ εὐωνύμου ἔσχατοι, οὗτοι δὴ οἱ τριάκοντα (indignant): *Oec.*20.20 τὸ δὲ . . . ἐπιμελεῖσθαι, τοῦτο δὴ . . .: Ant.vi 34 τῇ δὲ τρίτῃ ἡμέρᾳ ᾗ ἐξεφέρετο ὁ παῖς, ταύτῃ δὴ . . .: D.xxiii 17 τῶν δ' ἡμετέρων μὲν φίλων, ἐκείνου δὲ . . . ἐχθρῶν, τούτων δή τίς ἐστιν ὁ τοῦτο τὸ ψήφισμα φοβηθεὶς ἄν (δή τις S γρ.: ἄν τις *codd.* We can scarcely take δή τις together, as δή appears not to attach itself to τις in the orators): Pl.*R.*565D ὁ γευσάμενος . . . ἀνάγκη δὴ τούτῳ λύκῳ γενέσθαι (with anacoluthon): *Lg.*714A εἰ δ' ἄνθρωπος εἷς ἢ ὀλιγαρχία τις . . . ἄρξει δὴ πόλεως ἢ τινος ἰδιώτου καταπατήσας ὁ τοιοῦτος τοὺς νόμους (where, exceptionally, the particle does not follow the appositional pronoun).

In the following a repeated substantive takes the place of a pronoun in apposition: D.xliii 24 τῆς Φυλομάχης δὲ . . . καὶ Φιλάγρου . . . τοῦ δὴ Φιλάγρου . . . καὶ τῆς Φυλομάχης . . . ἐγένετο υἱός ('Well, Philagrus . . . had a son . . .').

(ii) The essence of a subordinate (usually participial) clause is repeated, and δή, again usually following a demonstrative pronoun, marks the opening of the recapitulation, the verb being either repeated or replaced by a synonym. Hdt.i 102 ἐς ὃ στρατευσάμενος ἐπὶ τοὺς Ἀσσυρίους . . . ἐπὶ τούτους δὴ στρατευσάμενος . . . (Herodotus is fond of this chiastic form: iv 76 καταδὺς ἐς τὴν καλεομένην Ὑλαίην . . . ἐς ταύτην δὴ καταδύς: i 189 (one temporal clause picked up by another): vii 43.1 (a participial clause picked up by a temporal one)): Pl.*Lg.*642C ἀκούων γὰρ . . . ταῦτα δὴ ἀκούων: X.*Cyr.*ii 3.19 ταῦτα δ' ἀγασθεὶς . . . τούτοις δὴ ἡσθείς: vii 5.58 ἐννοῶν δὲ . . . ταῦτα δὴ λογιζόμενος: D.xlviii 32 νικήσας δὲ καὶ διαπραξάμενος . . . καὶ ἀπολαβὼν . . . ταῦτα δὴ πάντ' ἔχων (summing up the preceding participles).

With repetition of a conjunction. Meliss.*Fr.*8 εἰ γὰρ ἔστι γῆ καὶ ὕδωρ . . . εἰ δὴ ταῦτα ἔστι: Pherecyd.Syr.*Fr.*2 ἐπεὶ δὲ ταῦτα ἐξετέλεσαν πάντα . . . ἐπεὶ δὴ πάντα ἑτοῖμα γίγνεται.

In the following, the resumption is of a different type: Pl.*Lg.* 801A *Τρίτος δ' οἶμαι νόμος, ὅτι γνόντας δεῖ τοὺς ποιητὰς ὡς εὐχαὶ . . . εἰσίν, δεῖ δὴ τὸν νοῦν αὐτοὺς σφόδρα προσέχειν.*

(14) Assentient. We have seen (γε, I.11) that γε, though not in itself denoting assent, frequently emphasizes affirmative answers, and, in so doing, itself acquires an affirmative or assentient colour. The same thing happens occasionally, but to a far lesser extent, in the case of *δή*.

Hom.*A*286 *Ναὶ δὴ ταῦτά γε πάντα, γέρον, κατὰ μοῖραν ἔειπες*: S.*Aj.*278 *Ξύμφημι δή σοι*: Pl.*Prt.*359C *Πότερον . . . ;—Λέγεται δή, ὦ Σώκρατες, οὕτως ὑπὸ τῶν ἀνθρώπων*: *Ap.*27C *οὐχ οὕτως ἔχει ;—Ἔχει δή*: *R.*381A *Ἔστι δὴ ταῦτα*: *Lg.*695C *Λέγεται δὴ ταῦτά γε.*

So, often, in practical consent, answering a command or request. Ar.*Th.*1209 *φεῦγε . . .—Ἐγὼ δὴ τοῦτο δρῶ*: Pl.*Grg.*448B *Ἐρώτα.—Ἐρωτῶ δή*: 507A *Λέγ', ὠγαθέ.—Λέγω δὴ ὅτι . . .*: *R.*523A *Δείκνυ', ἔφη.—Δείκνυμι δὴ . . . .* So *ταῦτα δή* ('Very good'): Ar. *Ach.*815 *Περίμεν' αὐτοῦ.—Ταῦτα δή*: *V.*851 *Κάλει νυν.—Ταῦτα δή.*

It would be theoretically possible to take *δή* as connective in the passages cited in the last paragraph: 'then'. But this explanation cannot be seriously entertained.

Very occasionally *δή* is used, instead of *δῆτα*, in echoing a word or thought. A.*Pers.*1070 *Ἰὼ ἰὼ . . .—Ἰωὰ δὴ κατ' ἄστυ.—Ἰωὰ δῆτα, ναί, ναί*: E.*Alc.*222 *ἔξευρε μηχανὰν . . .—Πόριζε δή, πόριζε*: Ar.*Pax* 973 *εὐχώμεθ'.—Εὐχώμεσθα δή.*

II. Position of emphatic *δή*. It has been observed above (I, *ad init.*) that *δή* normally emphasizes the word it immediately follows: but that it is less rigidly tied down than γε to this position. In poetry, particularly, the freedom with which *δή* is used makes it difficult to determine the precise reference of the particle in all cases. There are two types of deviation from the normal order.

(1) *δή* emphasizes a preceding, but not the immediately preceding, word. E.*Hec.*480 *ἐγὼ δ' ἐν ξείνᾳ χθονὶ δὴ κέκλημαι δούλα* (emphasis on *ξείνᾳ*: but *ξείνᾳ χθονί* is practically a single word): *Andr.*1247 *τῶν ἀπ' Αἰακοῦ μόνον λελειμμένον δή*: *Hel.* 1171 *ἐγὼ δ' ἐμαυτὸν πόλλ' ἐλοιδόρησα δή*: Hdt.ix 27.5 *οἵτινες μοῦνοι Ἑλλήνων δή*: E.*Supp.*573 *πολλοὺς ἔτλην δὴ . . . πόνους*:

1118 πολλοῦ τε χρόνου ζώσης μέτρα δή: S.*Tr.*460 οὐχὶ χἀτέρας πλείστας ἀνὴρ εἷς Ἡρακλῆς ἔγημε δή;

(2) δή precedes the emphatic word. E.*Heracl.*331 πόνους δὴ μυρίους: *Hipp.*835 Οὐ σοὶ τάδ', ὦναξ, ἦλθε δὴ μόνῳ κακά: *Ion* 417 Καλῶς· ἔχω δὴ πάνθ' ὅσων ἐχρῄζομεν: S.*Aj.*994 ὁδός θ' ὁδῶν πασῶν ἀνιάσασα δὴ μάλιστα: *Tr.*464 ἐπεί σφ' ἐγὼ ᾤκτιρα δὴ μάλιστα: E.*Hel.*563 Ἑλένῃ σ' ὁμοίαν δὴ μάλιστ' εἶδον: X.*HG* v.4.24 καὶ πολλοῖς ἔδοξεν αὕτη δὴ ἀδικώτατα ἐν Λακεδαίμονι ἡ δίκη κριθῆναι.

Preceding temporal adverbs. Thgn.853 ἀτὰρ πολὺ λώια δὴ νῦν: Sol.*Fr.*2.3 εἴην δὴ τότ' ἐγὼ Φολεγάνδριος: Pi.*N.*8.51 ἦν γε μὰν ἐπικώμιος ὕμνος δὴ πάλαι: Pl.*Epigr.*6.2 Δάκρυα ... γυναιξὶ Μοῖραι ἐπέκλωσαν δὴ τότε γεινομέναις. At the opening of an apodosis. Pi.*Fr.*78-9(88).10 ἀλλ' ἁ Κοιογενὴς ὁπότ' ... ἐπέβα νιν, δὴ τότε ...: Ar.*Av.*985 (in hexameter oracle). See also I.12.i. At the opening of a sentence. Hom.**E**136 δὴ τότε μιν τρὶς τόσσον ἕλεν μένος: A.*Th.*214 (lyr.) δὴ τότ' ἤρθην φόβῳ: Hom.α424: ι193: *id. saep.*: Hes.*Th.*542,643: *Op.*452: Pi.*O.*3.25: E.*Or.*1483 (lyr.: *coni.* Murray). δὴ αὖτε often in Homer (for the crasis, see Monro, *HG*§350): **A**340 εἴ ποτε δὴ αὖτε χρειὼ ἐμεῖο γένηται: **H**448 οὐχ ὁράᾳς ὅτι δὴ αὖτε.... δηὖτε often in Lyric: Sapph.*Fr.*154 δεῦρο δηὖτε, Μοῖσαι: Anacr.*Fr.*5.1,17.1 (Herwerden, p. 200). δαὖτε: Sapph.*Fr.*137.1: Alcm.*Fr.*101: A. *Ch.*410 (perhaps: see Wilamowitz's edition, p. 199). (Murray assumes a similar elision, or crasis, in E.*Hec.*1211 τί δ' οὐ. Burnet prints δἄν (= δὴ ἄν) in Pl.*Smp.*199B,214B: in S.*El.*314 ἦ δἄν (= ἦ δὴ ἄν) is perhaps right.) In Democr.*Fr.*172 δή goes rather with καί: ὕδωρ βαθὺ εἰς πολλὰ χρήσιμον καὶ δαὖτε κακόν.

The position of δή before a temporal adverb which it stresses is very rare in the lyrics of tragedy, and unknown to iambic verse and to prose. In Pl.*Hp.Ma.*291E ἀλλ' ἡμῶν δὴ νῦν καὶ πλεῖστον καταγελάσεται, where the context shows that νῦν, not ἡμῶν, is the emphatic word, νῦν δή (*W*) must be right.

Homer never opens a sentence or clause with δή, except when it precedes a temporal adverb or γάρ (for δὴ γάρ see γὰρ δή): but he occasionally places the particle immediately after an apostrophe at the opening of a speech: *O*437 Τεῦκρε πέπον, δὴ νῶϊν ἀπέκτατο πιστὸς ἑταῖρος: *T*342 Τέκνον ἐμόν, δὴ πάμπαν ἀποίχεαι.

The interposition of emphatic δή between a preposition and the word which the preposition governs is not infrequent in Herodotus and Plato. Ar.*Ec.*604 Κατὰ δὴ τί; Hdt.i 98 ἐν δὴ τῷ τελευταίῳ: iii 7 κατὰ δὴ τὰ εἰρημένα: 9 διὰ δὴ τούτου: vii 148.3 ἐς δὴ τὸ Ἄργος: vi 42: viii 5.1: Th.i 24.2 κατὰ δὴ τὸν παλαιὸν νόμον: Pl.*R.*458D ἀλλὰ μετὰ δὴ ταῦτα: *Ti.*38E κατὰ δὴ τὴν θατέρου φοράν: 44A: *Lg.*692A: *Plt.*270A (Stallbaum, for δέ): Isoc.xv 190 ἐν δὴ πᾶσι. Between article and adjective. Pl.*Plt.*292B Τῷ δὴ ποίῳ λέγεις; (contrast Τὸ ποῖον δὴ . . .; *La.* 193E and often): *Phdr.*272E. Cf. III.7.

In tmesis: Hdt.vii 12.2 Μετὰ δὴ βουλεύεαι. Cf. the common Herodotean use of οὖν in tmesis.

(For δή preceding interrogatives see I.5: preceding τις, I.6.)

III. Ironical. In discussing emphatic δή, we have seen that the emphasis which the particle gives is often ironical in tone. This use is so important and widespread that it demands separate treatment. The task of classification is difficult, since many uses have an ironical tinge in some contexts but not in others. It must be understood, then, that in the following pages we are dealing with uses which are largely or predominantly, but not wholly, ironical.

(1) Comparative clauses with ὡς, etc. Nearly always δή immediately follows ὡς.

(i) With finite verb: *quasi vero*. Grammatically, the main clause has to be supplied from the preceding words or from the general context: for practical purposes, the comparative clause forms an independent sentence.[1] (Cf. p. 552, ὡς δή τοι).

A.*Ag.*1633 Ὡς δὴ σύ μοι τύραννος Ἀργείων ἔσει ('You speak on the assumption that you will be king of Argos'): S.*OC*809 Ὡς δὴ σὺ βραχέα, ταῦτα δ' ἐν καιρῷ λέγεις: E.*Cyc.* 674 Ὡς δὴ σύ — (broken by interruption): Pl.*Grg.*468E Ὡς δὴ σὺ . . . οὐκ ἂν δέξαιο . . . ('As though you wouldn't choose . . .'): 499B ὡς δὴ σὺ οἴει ἐμὲ . . . οὐκ ἡγεῖσθαι . . . With ellipse of verb: Pl.*R.*337C ὡς δὴ ὅμοιον τοῦτο ἐκείνῳ (see Adam).

(For ὥσπερ δή, κατά περ δή, without irony, in dependent clauses, see I. 9. iv above: for ὡς δὴ λέγεται, etc., see (5) below.)

[1] Jebb, on S.*OC*809, assumes an ellipse of 'do you mean . . .?': but Hartung and Kühner are more probably right in rendering ὡς 'wie', 'als ob', *quasi vero*.

(ii) With participle, far commoner than (i): almost always ironical, sceptical, or indignant in tone. E.*Alc.*1014 ἀλλά μ' ἐξένιζες ἐν δόμοις, ὡς δὴ θυραίου πήματος σπουδὴν ἔχων; *Andr.* 594 ἄκληστ' ἄδουλα δώμαθ' ἑστίας λιπών, ὡς δὴ γυναῖκα σώφρον' ἐν δόμοις ἔχων: *Hel.*1057 Ὡς δὴ θανόντα σ' ἐνάλιον κενῷ τάφῳ θάψαι . . . αἰτήσομαι: Ar.*Eq.*693 προσέρχεται . . . ὡς δὴ καταπιόμενός με: Antiph.*Fr.*5 ὡς δὴ σύ τι ποιεῖν δυνάμενος ὀρτυγίου ψυχὴν ἔχων: E.*Hel.*1378: *Ph.*873,1416: *IT*682,1338: *HF* 998: *Ion*654,1183: Hdt.i66 οἱ δὲ πέδας φερόμενοι ἐπὶ Τεγεήτας ἐστρατεύοντο, χρησμῷ κιβδήλῳ πίσυνοι, ὡς δὴ ἐξανδραποδιούμενοι τοὺς Τεγεήτας: Pl.*Prt.*342C ὡς δὴ τούτοις κρατοῦντας τῶν Ἑλλήνων τοὺς Λακεδαιμονίους: *Smp.*222C ὡς ἐν παρέργῳ δὴ λέγων: *Phdr.*228C ἐθρύπτετο ὡς δὴ οὐκ ἐπιθυμῶν λέγειν: 242C φωνὴν . . . ἥ με οὐκ ἐᾷ ἀπιέναι πρὶν ἂν ἀφοσιώσωμαι, ὡς δή τι ἡμαρτηκότα εἰς τὸ θεῖον (incredulous): *Lg.*778E ὡς δὴ τῶν ὅρων τῆς χώρας οὐκ ἐάσοντας ἐπιβαίνειν (which cannot be the case if a wall is needed): *Ep.*344E ὡς παιδείας δὴ μέτοχος ὤν: X.*HG* v4.3 πρὸς τὰς πύλας ἦλθον, ὡς δὴ ἐξ ἀγροῦ ἀπιόντες: D.xxii 70 ὡς δὴ δίκαιος ὤν (xxiv178): Hdt.iii143.1: vii17.2: ix59.1: Pl.*Cra.*418C: *R.*545E: *Thg.*123A: X.*Cyr.*i4.23: v4.4: *Smp.*8.4.

In other passages δή does not throw doubt on the facts, but suggests that they constitute an unworthy or inadequate cause or motive. Cf. ὅτι δή, ἵνα δή, (2) and (3) below. E.*Supp.*477 τοῖς ἐμοῖς θυμούμενος λόγοισιν, ὡς δὴ πόλιν ἐλευθέραν ἔχων ('just because'): *El.*947 ὕβριζες, ὡς δὴ βασιλικοὺς ἔχων δόμους: *Alc.*537 Εἴθ' ηὕρομέν σ', Ἄδμητε, μὴ λυπούμενον.—Ὡς δὴ τί δράσων τόνδ' ὑπορράπτεις λόγον; (δή marks Admetus' suspicion of Heracles' intentions): Pl.*Euthphr.*3B καὶ ὡς διαβαλῶν δὴ ἔρχεται εἰς τὸ δικαστήριον, εἰδὼς ὅτι εὐδιάβολα τὰ τοιαῦτα πρὸς τοὺς πολλούς: X.*Cyr.*vii4.3 (describing a piece of sharp practice).

Sometimes there is little or no trace of irony or scepticism. S.*Ph.*1065 Μή μ' ἀντιφώνει μηδέν, ὡς στείχοντα δή (*quippe cum iturus sim*): E.*Hel.*1037 ἐσφέρεις γὰρ ἐλπίδας ὡς δή τι δράσων χρηστόν (perhaps faintly sceptical): Pl.*Chrm.*164D οὕτω μοι δοκεῖ τὸ γράμμα ἀνακεῖσθαι, ὡς δὴ πρόσρησις οὖσα. . . .

In a depreciatory sense. Hp.*Art.*34 ἐγγὺς γάρ τι τοῦ ἰσορρόπου ἐστίν, ὡς δὴ μὴ ἰσόρροπον ἐόν (as far as τὸ μὴ ἰσόρροπον can be said to be ἐγγὺς τοῦ ἰσορρόπου).

With ellipse of participle. E.*Hec.*1152 ὡς δὴ παρὰ φίλῳ: *Ba.*224 πρόφασιν μὲν ὡς δὴ μαινάδας θυοσκόους: Ar.*V.*1315 ὡς δὴ δεξιός: Hdt.iii 156 ὡς δὴ ἀληθέως αὐτόμολος: Th.iv 46.5 καὶ διδάξαντες ὡς κατ' εὔνοιαν δὴ λέγειν: vi 54.4 ὡς οὐ διὰ τοῦτο δή. Exceptionally, with genitive absolute without participle: X.*An.* vii 8.11 ὡς ἑτοίμων δὴ χρημάτων.

Equivalent in sense to οἷα δή. S.*Tr.*889 Ἐπεῖδον, ὡς δὴ πλησία παραστάτις ('as a bystander naturally would'): X.*Cyr.* vi 2.4 ὡς δὴ ἀνὴρ οὐδὲν μικρὸν ἐπινοῶν πράττειν.

In Pl.*Ep.*330B ὡς δή can hardly stand.

(2) In causal clauses, usually ὅτι δή, implying that the reason given is inadequate ('just because'), or is not the true reason. Hom.τ72 τί μοι ὧδ' ἐπέχεις κεκοτηότι θυμῷ; ἦ ὅτι δὴ ῥυπόω, κακὰ δὲ χροῒ εἵματα εἷμαι . . .; Pl.*Phdr.*244A Οὐκ ἔστ' ἔτυμος λόγος ὃς ἂν . . . τῷ μὴ ἐρῶντι μᾶλλον φῇ δεῖν χαρίζεσθαι, διότι δὴ ὁ μὲν μαίνεται, ὁ δὲ σωφρονεῖ: 268D οἰομένῳ ἁρμονικῷ εἶναι, ὅτι δὴ τυγχάνει ἐπιστάμενος ὡς οἷόν τε ὀξυτάτην καὶ βαρυτάτην χορδὴν ποιεῖν: *Cra.*418D καίτοι τινὲς οἴονται, ὡς δὴ ἡ ἡμέρα ἥμερα ποιεῖ, διὰ ταῦτα ὠνομάσθαι αὐτὴν οὕτως (marking an erroneous explanation): *Tht.*197C εἴ τις ὄρνιθας ἀγρίας . . . θηρεύσας οἴκοι . . . τρέφοι, τρόπον μὲν ἄν πού τινα φαῖμεν αὐτὸν αὐτὰς ἀεὶ ἔχειν, ὅτι δὴ κέκτηται. ἦ γάρ;—Ναί.—Τρόπον δέ γ' ἄλλον οὐδεμίαν ἔχειν ('merely on the ground that': the inadequacy of the reason becomes apparent in the δέ clause): X.*Cyr.*ii 3.13 μέγα φρονοῦσιν ὅτι πεπαίδευνται δὴ καὶ πρὸς λιμὸν . . . καρτερεῖν: Hdt.vi 41.3.

Or expressing indignation at the fact presented as a cause. Hdt.i 44 τὸν μὲν ἐπίστιον καλέων, διότι δὴ οἰκίοισι ὑποδεξάμενος τὸν ξεῖνον φονέα τοῦ παιδὸς ἐλάνθανε βόσκων: i 141.

Or presenting that fact subjectively, without irony or indignation. X.*HG* v 4.20 προσποιησάμενος τὸν Πειραιᾶ καταλήψεσθαι, ὅτι δὴ ἀπύλωτος ἦν ('because, he said').

ὅτε δή, causal. Ar.*Ra.*1189 πῶς γάρ (ἀθλιώτατος ὢν ἐπαύσατο); ὅτε δὴ πρῶτον μὲν αὐτὸν γενόμενον χειμῶνος ὄντος ἐξέθεσαν: Hdt.iv 120 οἱ Σκύθαι ἐβουλεύοντο ἰθυμαχίην μὲν μηδεμίαν ποιέεσθαι ἐκ τοῦ ἐμφανέος, ὅτε δή σφι οὗτοί γε σύμμαχοι οὐ προσεγίνοντο (ὅτι *CP*). There is obvious contempt in the first passage, and also, I think, in the second, from the Scythians' point of view: and in neither is ὅτε δή quite equivalent to the commoner ὅτε γε.

(3) In final clauses, usually after ἵνα. (Sometimes after ὡς or μή, or with infinitive of purpose.) Mainly a prose use, and commonest in Herodotus and Plato, (i) being markedly characteristic of Plato, (ii) of Herodotus.

(i) Denoting that the object is a trivial or unworthy one, or that it is not to be attained by the means in question. Pl.*Euthd.* 286D Λόγου ἕνεκα λέγεις τὸν λόγον, ἵνα δὴ ἄτοπον λέγῃς ('just in order to be paradoxical'): *Chrm.*165A εἶθ' ἵνα δὴ καὶ σφεῖς μηδὲν ἧττον συμβουλὰς χρησίμους ἀναθεῖεν, ταῦτα γράψαντες ἀνέθεσαν (vainly hoping to rival Apollo in this department): *Men.*82A ἐρωτᾷς ... ἵνα δὴ εὐθὺς φαίνωμαι αὐτὸς ἐμαυτῷ τἀναντία λέγων: 86D σὺ σαυτοῦ μὲν οὐδ' ἐπιχειρεῖς ἄρχειν, ἵνα δὴ ἐλεύθερος ᾖς (*R.*562E): *Plt.*264A μηδὲ σπεύσαντες, ἵνα δὴ ταχὺ γενώμεθα πρὸς τῇ πολιτικῇ: *R.*374B τὸν μὲν σκυτοτόμον διεκωλύομεν μήτε γεωργὸν ἐπιχειρεῖν εἶναι ἅμα ... ἵνα δὴ ἡμῖν τὸ τῆς σκυτικῆς ἔργον καλῶς γίγνοιτο ... τὰ δὲ δὴ περὶ τὸν πόλεμον ... (cobblery is a small matter compared with war): X.*HG* iv 1.26 ἀφείλετο ἅπαντα ... ἵνα δὴ πολλὰ ἀπαγάγοι τὰ αἰχμάλωτα τοῖς λαφυροπώλαις: *Smp.*1.14 γελοῖόν τι εὐθὺς ἐπεχείρει λέγειν, ἵνα δὴ ἐπιτελοίη ὧνπερ ἕνεκα ἐκαλεῖτο: Pl.*Chrm.*175C: *Tht.*176B, 183A: *R.*420E,563B,D,610C: *Plt.*277B: *Ep.*324E,354E: Hyp. *Ath.*23.

(ii) Describing an ingenious stratagem or device: often, but not always, indignant or contemptuous in tone. Hes.*Th.*900 ἑὴν ἐσκάτθετο νηδύν, ὡς δή οἱ φράσσαιτο θεὰ ἀγαθόν τε κακόν τε: E. *IT* 1025 Τί δ' εἴ με ναῷ τῷδε κρύψειας λάθρα;—Ὡς δὴ σκότον λαβόντες ἐκσωθεῖμεν ἄν; 1184 'They said Orestes was living'.—Ὡς δή σφε σῴσαις ἡδοναῖς ἀγγελμάτων: 1336 χρόνῳ δ', ἵν' ἡμῖν δρᾶν τι δὴ δοκοῖ πλέον, ἀνωλόλυξε: Hdt.i 29 κατὰ θεωρίης πρόφασιν ἐκπλώσας, ἵνα δὴ μή τινα τῶν νόμων ἀναγκασθῇ λῦσαι τῶν ἔθετο: 94 τὴν μὲν ἑτέρην τῶν ἡμερέων παίζειν πᾶσαν, ἵνα δὴ μὴ ζητέοιεν σιτία: ii 93 ψαύοντες (τῆς γῆς) ὡς μάλιστα, ἵνα δὴ μὴ ἁμάρτοιεν τῆς ὁδοῦ: v 87.3 μετέβαλον ἐς τὸν λίνεον κιθῶνα, ἵνα δὴ περόνῃσι μὴ χρέωνται: ix 74.1 'Sophanes used to anchor himself ἵνα δή μιν οἱ πολέμιοι ἐκπίπτοντες ἐκ τῆς τάξιος μετακινῆσαι μὴ δυναίατο': i 22 τῶνδε εἵνεκεν, ὅκως ἂν δὴ ὁ κῆρυξ ... ἰδών τε σωρὸν μέγαν σίτου κεχυμένον ... ἀγγείλῃ Ἀλυάττῃ: Th.v85 ἐπειδὴ οὐ πρὸς τὸ πλῆθος οἱ λόγοι γίγνονται, ὅπως δὴ μὴ ξυνεχεῖ ῥήσει οἱ πολλοὶ ἐπαγωγὰ ... ἀκούσαντες ἡμῶν ἀπατηθῶσιν: X. *Cyr.*i 3.9 οἱ τῶν βασιλέων οἰνοχόοι, ἐπειδὰν διδῶσι τὴν φιάλην, ἀρύσαντες ... καταρροφοῦσι, τοῦ δὴ εἰ φάρμακα ἐγχέοιεν μὴ λυσιτελεῖν αὐτοῖς: Hdt.ii 161: v68.1: vii 149.1: viii 7.1: 76.2: Th.iv67.3: vii 26.2: Pl.*Ep.*333C.

(iii) Introducing a pretended object. Aen.Tact.10.26 ἵνα δὴ †πρός τι κοιτασθῶσιν: D.vii 32 φρουρὰν ἐν τῇ ἀκροπόλει κατέστησεν, ἵνα δὴ αὐτόνομοι ὦσιν.

(iv) In general. Hom.*H*26 ἦ ἵνα δὴ Δαναοῖσι ... νίκην δῷς; (indignant): σ10 Εἶκε, γέρον, προθύρου, μὴ δὴ τάχα καὶ ποδὸς ἕλκῃ (contemptuous): Th.vii 18.1 ὅπως δὴ ἐσβολῆς γενομένης διακωλυθῇ (a frustrated intention: cf. Is.ii 30 καὶ ἡμεῖς, ἵνα δὴ πραγμάτων ἀπαλλαγῶμεν, ὥς γε δὴ ᾠόμεθα, οὕτως ἐπιτρέπομεν).

Occasionally with little apparent significance except added emphasis. Hom.*E*24 ὡς δή.οἱ μὴ πάγχυ γέρων ἀκαχήμενος εἴη: Anacr.*Fr.*27 ὡς δὴ πρὸς Ἔρωτα πυκταλίζω: Hdt.i 32 εἰ ἐθελήσει τοὔτερον τῶν ἐτέων μηνὶ μακρότερον γίνεσθαι, ἵνα δὴ αἱ ὧραι συμβαίνωσι.

(4) After verbs of saying, thinking, hoping, and fearing: implying, at most, that what follows is false: at least, that it is not unquestionably true. Hom.*A*110 Μάντι κακῶν ... καὶ νῦν ... ἀγορεύεις ὡς δὴ τοῦδ' ἕνεκά σφιν ἑκηβόλος ἄλγεα τεύχει: E. *Andr.*235 τί σεμνομυθεῖς ... ὡς δὴ σὺ σώφρων ...; *El.*919 ἤλπισας ὡς ἐς σὲ ἐμὴν δὴ μητέρ' οὐχ ἕξοις κακήν; *Hipp.*962 μισεῖν σε φήσεις τήνδε καὶ τὸ δὴ νόθον τοῖς γνησίοισι πολέμιον πεφυκέναι: Hdt.ix 48.3 προσδεκόμενοι γὰρ κατὰ κλέος ὡς δὴ πέμψετε ἐς ἡμέας κήρυκα: Th.iv23.1 ἰσχυριζόμενοι ὅτι δὴ εἴρητο, ἐὰν καὶ ὁτιοῦν παραβαθῇ, λελύσθαι τὰς σπονδάς: v 105.3 τῆς δ' ἐς Λακεδαιμονίους δόξης, ἣν διὰ τὸ αἰσχρὸν δὴ βοηθήσειν ὑμῖν πιστεύετε αὐτούς: Pl.*La.*198A ἀπεκρίνω ὡς μόριον, ὄντων δὴ καὶ ἄλλων μερῶν: *Phdr.*235E Φίλτατος εἶ ... εἴ με οἴει λέγειν ὡς Λυσίας τοῦ παντὸς ἡμάρτηκεν, καὶ οἷόν τε δὴ παρὰ πάντα ταῦτα ἄλλα εἰπεῖν: *Ep.*324D ᾠήθην γὰρ αὐτοὺς ἔκ τινος ἀδίκου βίου ἐπὶ δίκαιον τρόπον ἄγοντας διοικήσειν δὴ τὴν πόλιν: *Phdr.*272E καὶ (φασὶ) πάντως λέγοντα τὸ δὴ εἰκὸς διωκτέον εἶναι.

Th.vii 86.4 δείσαντες ... μὴ χρήμασι δὴ πείσας τινάς, ὅ

πλούσιος ἦν, ἀποδρᾷ (here δή seems to mark the indignation felt by the fearers: cf. Pl.*Prt.*320A δεδιὼς περὶ αὐτοῦ, μὴ διαφθαρῇ δὴ ὑπὸ Ἀλκιβιάδου: *Ep.*330B). In Hom.Σ125 δή marks the speaker's indignation: γνοῖεν δ' ὡς δὴ δηρὸν ἐγὼ πολέμοιο πέπαυμαι.

The note of scepticism or reserve is occasionally absent. Hp. *Genit.*45 ἀναβήσομαι δ' αὖθις ὀπίσω περὶ τῆς ὑγιείης ἐρέων ὅτι δὴ ...: Pl.*Euthphr.*3B Μανθάνω ... ὅτι δὴ σὺ τὸ δαιμόνιον φῄς σαυτῷ ἑκάστοτε γίγνεσθαι: *Lg.*688B λέγω ... ὅτι δή φημι ('that I say, in point of fact'): *La.*196D Τοῦτο δὲ (φῄς) οὐ παντὸς δὴ εἶναι ἀνδρὸς γνῶναι.

(5) Again, the particle may be attached to the verb of saying or thinking. A.*Pr.*955 νέον νέοι κρατεῖτε καὶ δοκεῖτε δὴ ναίειν ἀπενθῆ πέργαμ' ('you think, forsooth'): Hdt.ix11.1 ἐπῆλθον ἐπὶ τοὺς ἐφόρους, ἐν νόῳ δὴ ἔχοντες ἀπαλλάσσεσθαι: Th.i39.1 καὶ φασὶ δὴ δίκῃ πρότερον ἐθελῆσαι κρίνεσθαι: viii48.5 τάς τε ξυμμαχίδας πόλεις, αἷς ὑπεσχῆσθαι δὴ σφᾶς ὀλιγαρχίαν, ὅτι δὴ καὶ αὐτοὶ οὐ δημοκρατήσονται...: Pl.*Phdr.*236B καὶ οἴει δή με ὡς ἀληθῶς ἐπιχειρήσειν εἰπεῖν: *Plt.*284E ὃ γὰρ ἐνίοτε οἰόμενοι δή τι σοφὸν φράζειν πολλοὶ τῶν κομψῶν λέγουσιν: *Alc.I*113E οἴει δὴ καινὰ ἄττα δεῖν ἀκούειν.

With the verb of saying or thinking in a parenthesis. Hdt.ii 45 ἔτι δὲ ἕνα ἐόντα τὸν Ἡρακλέα καὶ ἔτι ἄνθρωπον, ὡς δή φασι, κῶς φύσιν ἔχει πολλὰς μυριάδας φονεῦσαι; iii105 ὡς δὴ λέγεται ὑπὸ Περσέων: iv191 ὡς δὴ λέγονταί γε ὑπὸ Λιβύων: Th.viii87.1 ὡς ἐδόκει δή: Pl.*Plt.*301D ὡς δή φαμεν (with no trace of irony): *Lg.*727B τιμῶν τὴν αὑτοῦ ψυχήν, ὡς δὴ δοκεῖ.

(6) δή, without a verb of saying, thinking, etc., often denotes that words are not to be taken at their face value, objectively, but express something merely believed, or ironically supposed, to be true. Hence δή often gives the effect of inverted commas.

Hdt.v72.3 ὡς γὰρ ἀνέβη ἐς τὴν ἀκρόπολιν μέλλων δὴ ('as he thought') αὐτὴν κατασχήσειν: Th.iii10.5 αὐτόνομοι δὴ ὄντες καὶ ἐλεύθεροι τῷ ὀνόματι ξυνεστρατεύσαμεν: iv59.4 τὰ ἴδια ... εὖ βουλευόμενοι δὴ θέσθαι: vi10.5 ἡμεῖς δὲ Ἐγεσταίοις δὴ οὖσι ξυμμάχοις ὡς ἀδικουμένοις ὀξέως βοηθοῦμεν: 80.1 τὸ μηδετέροις δὴ ... βοηθεῖν ('the blessed word "neutrality"'): 80.2 τοὺς Ἀθηναίους φίλους δὴ ὄντας μὴ ἐᾶσαι ἁμαρτεῖν ('our "friends" the Athenians'): viii 9 Ἆγις δὲ αὐτοῖς ἑτοῖμος ἦν ἐκείνους μὲν μὴ λύειν δὴ τὰς Ἰσθμιάδας σπονδάς, ἑαυτοῦ δὲ τὸν στόλον ἴδιον ποιήσασθαι: Pl.*La*.197C ὡς εὖ ὅδε ἑαυτὸν δή, ὡς οἴεται, κοσμεῖ (with verb of thinking in parenthesis): *Ap*.27A Σωκράτης ὁ σοφὸς δή ('Socrates the "Wise"'): *Lg*.636D τοῦτον τὸν μῦθον προστεθηκέναι κατὰ τοῦ Διός, ἵνα ἑπόμενοι δὴ τῷ θεῷ καρπῶνται καὶ ταύτην τὴν ἡδονήν (not a case of ἵνα δή): 962E τῶν δ' ἡ προθυμία πρὸς τὸν ἐλεύθερον δὴ βίον ὡρμημένη ('the so-called "free" life'): 963B σὺ δ' ὢν δὴ διαφέρων, ὡς φαίης ἄν: X.*HG* ii 3.18 καταλέγουσι τρισχιλίους τοὺς μεθέξοντας δὴ τῶν πραγμάτων; v 4.6 εἰσήγαγε τὰς ἑταίρας δή ('the "courtesans"', i.e. men disguised as such): Lys.viii 3 ἵνα μή τις ὑμῶν τάχα δὴ βοηθῶν οἷς ἐξημάρτηκε ('thinking to palliate his offences': but the text is dubious): D.xix 150 ἀντὶ δὲ τούτων δὴ τὰ θαυμάσι' ἀγάθ' ἡμῖν ἔμελλεν ἔσεσθαι: 167 διὰ ταῦτ' ἐδίδοτο, ξένια δὴ πρόφασιν.

(7) So also in definite quotations. Pl.*Grg*.515D Ἴσως.—Οὐκ ἴσως δή, ὦ βέλτιστε, ἀλλ' ἀνάγκη ἐκ τῶν ὡμολογημένων ('not "perhaps", but necessarily'): 500C τὰ τοῦ ἀνδρὸς δὴ ταῦτα πράττοντα (glancing at Callias' frequent references to ἀνήρ).

Attached to a formula of quotation, τὸ σὸν δή, etc. A.*Ag*.550 Ὡς νῦν, τὸ σὸν δή, καὶ θανεῖν πολλὴ χάρις (referring to 539): Pl.*Smp*.221B τὸ σὸν δὴ τοῦτο (*Sph*.233B). None of these are ironical. Pl.*Grg*.508D ἄντε τύπτειν βούληται, τὸ νεανικὸν δὴ τοῦτο τὸ τοῦ σοῦ λόγου, ἐπὶ κόρρης (ironical: 'to quote your vigorous phrase').

With τὸ λεγόμενον, etc., the particle being attached either to the words quoted or to the formula of quotation. Th.vii 87.6 πανωλεθρίᾳ δὴ τὸ λεγόμενον: Pl.*Grg*.514E τὸ λεγόμενον δὴ τοῦτο ἐν τῷ πίθῳ τὴν κεραμείαν ἐπιχειρεῖν μανθάνειν: *Phdr*.242A μεσημβρία ἵσταται ἡ δὴ καλουμένη σταθερά: *Sph*.241D Πῶς γὰρ οὐ φαίνεται καὶ τὸ λεγόμενον δὴ τοῦτο τυφλῷ; (the formula splits καὶ τυφλῷ): *Phlb*.46C τὸ δὴ λεγόμενον πικρῷ γλυκὺ μεμειγμένον: *Amat*.134A ᾤμην τὸ λεγόμενον δὴ τοῦτο κἂν ὗν γνῶναι ὅτι . . .: *Euthd*.293D τὸ γὰρ λεγόμενον, καλὰ δὴ πάντα λέγεις: *Phd*.112C εἰς τὸν τόπον τὸν δὴ κάτω καλούμενον: X.*An*.i 8.10 ἅρματα . . . τὰ δὴ δρεπανηφόρα καλούμενα.

(8) The ironical use of δή is not confined to the above categories. The following examples illustrate the various shades of irony, scorn, and indignation which δή can express. Hom.Φ472 Φεύγεις δή, ἑκάεργε: E.*Supp*.521 ἄνω γὰρ ἂν ῥέοι τὰ πράγμαθ' οὕτως, εἰ 'πιταξόμεσθα δή: *Heracl*.269 Πειρώμενος δὴ τοῦτό γ' αὐτίκ' εἴσομαι: *El*.951 τὰ δ' εὐπρεπῆ δὴ κόσμος ἐν χοροῖς μόνον: *HF*1303 χορευέτω δὴ Ζηνὸς ἡ κλεινὴ δάμαρ: *Ba*.652 'Ωνείδισας δὴ τοῦτο Διονύσῳ καλόν: Ar.*Ra*.1261 Πάνυ γε μέλη θαυμαστά· δείξει δὴ τάχα: Pl.*Ap*.31C ἴσως ἂν οὖν δόξειεν ἄτοπον εἶναι ὅτι δὴ ἐγὼ ἰδίᾳ μὲν ταῦτα συμβουλεύω . . . δημοσίᾳ δὲ οὐ τολμῶ . . . συμβουλεύειν τῇ πόλει: *Phdr*.258A τὸν αὐτὸν δὴ λέγων μάλα σεμνῶς καὶ ἐγκωμιάζων ὁ συγγραφεύς (contrast *Grg*.493B, not ironical: ἐν Αἵδου—τὸ ἀϊδὲς δὴ λέγων): *Phdr*.273C ὁ δ' οὐκ ἐρεῖ δὴ τὴν ἑαυτοῦ κάκην: *Tht*.195C Ὦ Σώκρατες, ηὕρηκας δὴ ψευδῆ δόξαν . . .; ('You've discovered false opinion, have you?') X. *Cyr*.v5.33 καὶ νῦν ἃ ἔλαβες τῇ ἐμῇ δυνάμει ἄγεις δή μοι: [X.] *Ath*.1.18 δίκην δοῦναι . . . ἐν τῷ δήμῳ, ὅς ἐστι δὴ νόμος Ἀθήνησι.

In indignant questions. S.*Ph*.1071 Ἦ καὶ πρὸς ὑμῶν . . . λειφθήσομαι δὴ . . .; 1235 Πρὸς θεῶν, πότερα δὴ κερτομῶν λέγεις τάδε; *Ant*.726 Οἱ τηλικοίδε καὶ διδαξόμεσθα δὴ φρονεῖν . . .; E. *Andr*.262 Ὦ βάρβαρον σὺ θρέμμα . . . ἐγκαρτερεῖς δὴ θάνατον; *Fr*.711 εἶτα δὴ θυμούμεθα παθόντες οὐδὲν μεῖζον ἢ δεδρακότες; Ar.*Ach*.311 ταῦτα δὴ τολμᾷς λέγειν . . .; *Eq*.1224 Ὦ μιαρέ, κλέπτων δή με ταῦτ' ἐξηπάτας; *Ra*.1476 Ὦ σχέτλιε, περιόψει με δὴ τεθνηκότα; (For οὕτω δή introducing surprised or indignant questions, see I.4.xi.)

IV. Connective.

(1) We have seen that γε, while it never, in classical Greek at any rate, attains to the position of a connective, yet seems in some passages to mitigate the harshness of an asyndeton, and to be invested with a certain quasi-connective force. Unlike γε, but like μήν (the case of οὖν is more complicated), δή does develop into a full-blown connective. The evolution is helped by the commonness of such openings to sentences as οὕτω δή, ἐνταῦθα δή. Here the demonstrative adverb is in itself a sufficient link, as is shown, for example, by Xenophon's free use of ἔνθα, ἐνταῦθα, and so on, at the beginning of the sentence without a connecting particle. But the employment of δή to strengthen

the adverb may well have tended to give the particle a measure of connective force. Again, in μὲν δή, δή no doubt originally merely strengthened μέν. We see this in Homer, and in later Greek in places where μὲν δή comes in the middle of a sentence. And it is possible that μὲν δή at the opening of a sentence in Herodotus, and even in Thucydides, is to be taken in this way. But there can be little doubt that in the middle and late fourth century δή was here felt to be a connective. (The same problem of analysis presents itself in the case of μὲν οὖν.)

The connective use of δή can be derived, then, without difficulty from its emphatic use: it cannot legitimately be adduced to support the theory that δή originally had a temporal force, and that the senses 'then', 'moreover', therefore' developed out of the senses 'now', 'next'. This connective use plays a big part in Greek literature, though scholars have often been inclined to push it into the background.[1] δή here, like οὖν, expresses *post hoc* and *propter hoc*, and anything between the two, tending on the whole to denote a less strictly logical sequence than οὖν. Examples are hardly to be found before the Attic period. In tragedy, owing to the free employment of emphatic δή, and the less stringent need for connexion between sentences, it is often difficult to determine whether δή is connective or emphatic. But in passages like the following a connective is clearly required. S.*Tr.*1221 Ἰόλην ἔλεξας . . .—Ἔγνως. τοσοῦτον δή σ' ἐπισκήπτω, τέκνον· ταύτην . . . προσθοῦ δάμαρτα: *Ph.* 276 λιπόντες ᾤχονθ' . . . σὺ δή, τέκνον, ποίαν μ' ἀνάστασιν δοκεῖς . . . στῆναι τότε; *OC* 23 Κάθιζέ νύν με . . .—Χρόνου μὲν οὕνεκ' οὐ μαθεῖν με δεῖ τόδε.—Ἔχεις διδάξαι δή μ' ὅποι καθέσταμεν; E.*Hipp.*1008 τὸ σῶφρον τοὐμὸν οὐ πείθει σ'· ἴτω· δεῖ δή σε δεῖξαι τῷ τρόπῳ διεφθάρην: *Ion* 1181 ἔλεξ'· Ἀφαρπάζειν χρεὼν οἰνηρὰ τεύχη σμικρά, μεγάλα δ' ἐσφέρειν . . . ἦν δὴ φερόντων μόχθος . . . φιάλας. In prose, connective δή gains ground rapidly during the fourth century. Herodotus has it, but not very often. Sometimes δή follows a demonstrative adverb, which, as remarked above, constitutes a sufficient connexion in itself: i 3 οὕτω δή (83, 87): 43 ἔνθα δή (59): iii 78 ἐνθαῦτα δή. In vii 49.4 (. . . ἔρχομαι ἐρέων. γῆ δὴ . . .) a connecting particle is unnecessary (for γε in

[1] Bäumlein, indeed (p. 103), almost denies its existence.

a similar context, see γε, III.1). But in other passages δή is unmistakably connective, usually conveying temporal rather than logical sequence: i 11 *αἱρέεται αὐτὸς περιεῖναι. ἐπειρώτα δὴ λέγων τάδε*: i 85,98,114,179. In Thucydides connective δή is still proportionately rare, including less than ten per cent. of the examples of the particle. But in him we already begin to find δή with full logical force: i 142.7 *οὐδὲ γὰρ ὑμεῖς μελετῶντες αὐτὸ εὐθὺς ἀπὸ τῶν Μηδικῶν ἐξείργασθέ πω· πῶς δὴ ἄνδρες γεωργοὶ . . . ἄξιον ἄν τι δρῷεν*; ii 89.5 *ἐπεὶ οὐκ ἄν ποτε ἐνεχείρησαν ἡσσηθέντες παρὰ πολὺ αὖθις ναυμαχεῖν. μὴ δὴ αὐτῶν τὴν τόλμαν δείσητε*. There is a slight proportionate increase in Lysias and Isocrates, and in Plato examples are numerous. Finally, in Demosthenes the connective sense is far the commonest: δή occurs twenty-five times in the *Olynthiacs* and first three *Philippics*, and in every case it is connective.

(2) I have said that the connective sense of δή can be either temporal or logical, or something between the two. It is clearly temporal when it marks a new stage in a narrative ('Well': 'Now') in such passages as these: E.*Heracl.*853 *ἠράσαθ' Ἥβη . . . ἡμέραν μίαν νέος γενέσθαι . . . κλύειν δὴ θαύματος πάρεστί σοι*: ('Well, after that something astonishing happened'): Pl.*Ly.* 207B *προσῆλθον δὴ καὶ οἱ ἄλλοι*: 207D *ἐπεχείρουν δὴ μετὰ τοῦτο ἐρωτᾶν*: *Smp.*222C *εἰπόντος δὴ ταῦτα τοῦ Ἀλκιβιάδου γέλωτα γενέσθαι* (the following sentence is connected by οὖν): *Phd.* 91D *συνωμολογείτην δὴ ταῦτ' εἶναι ἄμφω*: *Prm.*136E *ταῦτα δὴ εἰπόντος τοῦ Ζήνωνος . . .*: *R.*350C *ὁ δὴ Θρασύμαχος ὡμολόγησε μὲν πάντα ταῦτα*. (Cf. οὖν, III.1 for closely similar passages where οὖν is used.)

In other passages δή has full logical force. E.*El.*71 *Ἐγώ σ' ἴσον θεοῖσιν ἡγοῦμαι φίλον . . . δεῖ δή με . . . συνεκκομίζειν σοι πόνους*: Pl.*Euthd.*275B *ἔστι δὲ νέος· φοβούμεθα δὴ περὶ αὐτῷ*: *Phdr.*239A,245C. D.xviii 108 affords an instructive instance of the convertibility of connective δή and οὖν: *ἐν τοῖς πένησιν ἦν τὸ λῃτουργεῖν· πολλὰ δὴ τἀδύνατα συνέβαινεν. ἐγὼ δ' ἐκ τῶν ἀπόρων εἰς τοὺς εὐπόρους μετήνεγκα τὰς τριηραρχίας· πάντ' οὖν τὰ δέοντ' ἐγίγνετο*. Eucken (p. 41) observes that in many formulae Aristotle uses δή, ἄρα, τοίνυν, and οὖν indifferently: *λείπεται δή* (*τοίνυν, οὖν*): *φανερὸν δή* (*τοίνυν*): *δῆλον δή* (*τοίνυν, ἄρα*).

Often, again, connective δή expresses something intermediate between temporal and logical connexion, and marks the progression from one idea to a second of which the consideration naturally follows. We may render variously, 'now', 'well', 'again'. Verse. A.*Th.*631 Τὸν ἕβδομον δὴ . . . λέξω (the last of the seven chieftains): E.*Hel.*1033 Μενέλαε, πρὸς μὲν παρθένου σεσῴσμεθα· τοὐνθένδε δὴ σὲ τοὺς λόγους φέροντα χρὴ κοινὴν ξυνάπτειν μηχανὴν σωτηρίας: *Heracl.*132: *HF* 151. At the opening of an answer: E.*El.*618: *IT* 1051. At the opening of an interrogative answer: E.*Hel.*1218: *Ph.*927,983: *IA* 1447: *Rh.*496: Ar.*Pax* 929. Prose. Pl.*Grg.*450C εἰσὶν ἡμῖν τέχναι. ἦ γάρ;—Ναί.—Πασῶν δὴ οἶμαι τῶν τεχνῶν . . .: 457A ὁ αὐτὸς δὴ λόγος καὶ περὶ τῆς ῥητορικῆς: 457E τοῦ δὴ ἕνεκα λέγω ταῦτα; ('Now why do I say that?' After saying something it is natural to justify it): *Euthd.*279A Εἶεν, ἦν δ' ἐγώ· τὸ δὴ μετὰ τοῦτο . . . πῶς ἂν εὖ πράττοιμεν; *Prm.*134C Ὅρα δὴ ἔτι τούτου δεινότερον τόδε ('Now consider . . .'): *Alc.II* 141E (after considering the fate of Archelaus) ὁρᾷς δὴ καὶ τῶν ἡμετέρων πολιτῶν . . . ὅσοι . . .: *Ti.*67C τέταρτον δὴ λοιπὸν ἔτι γένος (66D δὲ δή: 67A τρίτον δέ): X.*Hier.* 8.4 κάμνοντα θεραπευσάτωσαν ὁμοίως· οὐκοῦν τοῦτο σαφὲς . . .; δότωσαν δὴ τὰ ἴσα· οὐ καὶ ἐν τούτῳ σαφὲς . . .; ('Again'): *An.* v 1.9 Ἐννοεῖτε δὴ καὶ τόδε.

Ἔτι δή, like ἔτι τοίνυν: Pl.*Sph.*224E Ἔτι δὴ σκοπῶμεν: *Plt.* 290C: *Prt.*324D.

Progressive δή in these intermediate cases is often almost synonymous with the commoner καὶ μήν and τοίνυν. (As we shall see later, τοίνυν, like δή and οὖν, combines the notions of inference and pure progression.) Like καὶ μήν and τοίνυν, δή usually marks the opening of a new section of the discourse, the broaching of a new topic. In lighter transitions δέ is used instead. Thus δή in the following passage is somewhat exceptional: Pl.*R.*369D Ἀλλὰ μὴν πρώτη γε . . . —Παντάπασί γε.—Δευτέρα δὴ οἰκήσεως, τρίτη δὲ ἐσθῆτος καὶ τῶν τοιούτων. In *Lg.*960C δέ should perhaps be read: Τὸ Λάχεσιν μὲν τὴν πρώτην εἶναι, Κλωθὼ δὲ τὴν δευτέραν, τὴν Ἄτροπον δὴ τρίτην σώτειραν τῶν λεχθέντων (δή *ALO*: δέ *vulg.*). In Hippocrates, however, where progressive δή is common, this restriction hardly applies: *Acut.*11 προστεκμαρτέα δή: *Int.*49 τῇ ὑστεραίῃ . . . τῇ δὲ τρίτῃ αἰγείῳ ἐφθῷ, ὡσαύτως δὴ καὶ τῇ τετάρτῃ (δέ *al.*): *Epid.*vii 11 ἐνάτῃ . . . ὡσαύτως δὴ καὶ ἐνδεκάτῃ:

*Septim.*9 ἄλλη δὴ τεσσαρακοντὰς . . . τρίτη δὲ . . . : *Acut.*18 οὐδὲ δὴ . . . .

Exceptionally, proceeding from major to minor premise: Pl. *Sph.*238A.

V. Position of connective δή. Where δή is a connective, it normally, like other connectives, comes second in the sentence: but, like them, yields precedence to τε, μέν, and γάρ. Where several words coalesce closely, the particle is not infrequently postponed to the third or fourth place. S.*Ant.*908 τίνος νόμου δὴ . . . ; *OC* 23 Ἔχεις διδάξαι δή μ' . . . ; Th.v43.1 κατὰ τοιαύτην δὴ διαφοράν (contrast viii85.1 κατὰ δὴ τοιαύτην διαφοράν: Pl.*R.*334D Κατὰ δὴ τὸν σὸν λόγον): Pl.*Ap.*37B ἀντὶ τούτου δή (contrast *Grg.*482D διὰ δὴ ταύτην): *Phd.*104D Ἐπὶ τὸ τοιοῦτον δή: *Grg.*508A ἢ ἐξελεγκτέος δή: *Sph.*263A Σὸν ἔργον δή: 263C Ὃν ὕστερον δὴ λόγον εἴρηκα: *Chrm.*171A Καὶ ἡ ἰατρικὴ δή: *Phdr.*261D Καὶ ἐν δημηγορίᾳ δή: *R.*589B Κατὰ πάντα τρόπον δή (δὴ τρόπον Stob.): *Lg.*701E Τούτων ἕνεκα δή: 898E νῷ μόνῳ δή.

Ἀλλὰ δή: ἀλλὰ . . . δή

Here δή reinforces ἀλλά in various meanings of that particle. Most of the examples are Platonic. The two particles sometimes form a unity even when separated by intervening words.

(1) General adversative sense. Diph.*Fr.*32.18 Ὀρθῶς γε νὴ Δί'. ἀλλὰ δὴ τί τοῦτ' ἐμοί; Pl.*Tht.*164E οὐδ' οἱ ἐπίτροποι . . . βοηθεῖν (τῷ λόγῳ) ἐθέλουσιν . . . . ἀλλὰ δὴ αὐτοὶ κινδυνεύσομεν τοῦ δικαίου ἕνεκ' αὐτῷ βοηθεῖν: *R.*352C οἱ δὲ ἄδικοι οὐδὲ πράττειν μετ' ἀλλήλων οἷοί τε—ἀλλὰ δὴ καὶ οὕς φαμεν . . . μετ' ἀλλήλων κοινῇ πρᾶξαι ἀδίκους ὄντας, τοῦτο οὐ παντάπασιν ἀληθὲς λέγομεν ('but in fact'): 365D 'We must try to conceal our misdeeds'.—Ἀλλὰ δὴ θεοὺς οὔτε λανθάνειν οὔτε βιάσασθαι δυνατόν ('Ah, but'): *Lg.*835D οὐ γάρ πω μανθάνομεν.—Εἰκότως γε· ἀλλὰ δὴ πειράσομαι ἐγὼ φράζειν ὑμῖν ἔτι σαφέστερον: X.*An.*vi3.16 εἰς Κάλπης δὲ λιμένα . . . ἐλαχίστη ὁδός. ἀλλὰ δὴ ἐκεῖ μὲν οὔτε πλοῖά

ἐστιν . . . ('but the difficulty is that'): Gorg.*Fr.*11a.7,8: Pl.*R.* 453D: *Lg.*858E (ἀλλὰ . . . δή).

(2) Like ἀτάρ or ἀλλὰ γάρ, brushing aside a digression or irrelevancy, and coming to the point. Pl.*Euthphr.*2B 'My accuser is Meletus.'—Οὐκ ἐννοῶ, ὦ Σώκρατες· ἀλλὰ δὴ τίνα γραφήν σε γέγραπται; *Phd.* 95B μὴ μέγα λέγε, μή τις ἡμῖν βασκανία περιτρέψῃ τὸν λόγον . . . ἀλλὰ δὴ ταῦτα μὲν τῷ θεῷ μελήσει, ἡμεῖς δὲ . . .: *Grg.*502A ἢ πρὸς τὸ βέλτιστον βλέπων ἐδόκει σοι κιθαρῳδεῖν; ἢ ἐκεῖνος μὲν οὐδὲ πρὸς τὸ ἥδιστον; ἠνία γὰρ ᾄδων τοὺς θεατάς. ἀλλὰ δὴ σκόπει· οὐχὶ ἥ τε κιθαρῳδικὴ δοκεῖ σοι . . .; *Phdr.*269C 'That is a fair description of pseudo-rhetoric. ἀλλὰ δὴ τὴν τοῦ τῷ ὄντι ῥητορικοῦ . . . τέχνην . . .;' Arist.*SE* 171a12 ἀλλὰ δὴ ὅθεν ὁ λόγος ἦλθε . . . (resumptive): Antiph.*Fr.*196.16: Pl.*R.*500E,568D: *Men.*92D: *Ti.*21A: *Tht.*206C: *Lg.*723D,891B, 965E: *Plt.*258B,268E,271C: *Phlb.*12B,33B.

(3) Progressive. Cf. ἀλλά, II.9, and the much commoner ἀλλὰ μήν, (4). 'Well now': 'Further': 'Again'. S.*OT* 1492 ποίας γὰρ ἀστῶν ἥξετ' εἰς ὁμιλίας . . .; ἀλλ' ἡνίκ' ἂν δὴ πρὸς γάμων ἥκητ' ἀκμὰς . . .; Pl.*R.*502B Ἄρχοντος γὰρ . . . τιθέντος τοὺς νόμους . . . οὐ δήπου ἀδύνατον ἐθέλειν ποιεῖν τοὺς πολίτας.—Οὐδ' ὁπωστιοῦν. —Ἀλλὰ δή, ἅπερ ἡμῖν δοκεῖ, δόξαι καὶ ἄλλοις . . . ἀδύνατον; *Phlb.*26E ἀλλὰ τρίτον φάθι με λέγειν . . . —Ἔμαθον.—Ἀλλὰ δὴ πρὸς τρισὶ τέταρτόν τι τότε ἔφαμεν εἶναι γένος σκεπτέον: *Cra.* 400B 'The derivation of ψυχή is satisfactory . . .'—Ἀλλὰ δὴ τὸ μετὰ τοῦτο πῶς φῶμεν ἔχειν; *R.*351C Σοὶ γάρ, ἔφη, χαρίζομαι.—Εὖ γε σὺ ποιῶν· ἀλλὰ δὴ καὶ τόδε μοι χάρισαι . . .: Arist.*GC* 334a25 λέγω δ' οἷον ἔστιν ἐκ πυρὸς ὕδωρ καὶ ἐκ τούτου γίγνεσθαι πῦρ . . . ἀλλὰ δὴ καὶ σὰρξ ἐξ αὐτῶν γίγνεται καὶ μυελός: Pl.*Cra.* 407A,418A: Arist.*Ph.*214a28: 237b34: 249b15: D.xix 200.

(4) After a rejected suggestion. S.*OT* 1021 Ἀλλ' οὔ σ' ἐγείνατ' οὔτ' ἐκεῖνος οὔτ' ἐγώ.—Ἀλλ' ἀντὶ τοῦ δὴ παῖδά μ' ὠνομάζετο; ('Well, then, why . . .?'): E.*HF* 1286 ἀλλ' Ἄργος ἔλθω; πῶς, ἐπεὶ φεύγω πάτραν; φέρ' ἀλλ' ἐς ἄλλην δή τιν' ὁρμήσω πόλιν; Gorg. *Fr.*11a.18 καὶ μὴν οὐδ' ἀσφαλείας οὕνεκά τις ἂν ταῦτα πράξαι . . . ἀλλὰ δὴ φίλους ὠφελεῖν βουλόμενος . . .; Th.vi 38.5 πότερον

ἄρχειν ἤδη (βούλεσθε); ἀλλ' οὐκ ἔννομον· . . . ἀλλὰ δὴ μὴ μετὰ πολλῶν ἰσονομεῖσθαι; Pl.*Ap.*37C πότερον δεσμοῦ; . . . ἀλλὰ χρημάτων . . .; . . . ἀλλὰ δὴ φυγῆς τιμήσωμαι; *R.*600A 'Is Homer known as a legislator?'—'No'.—Ἀλλὰ δή τις πολέμος ἐπὶ Ὁμήρου ὑπ' ἐκείνου ἄρχοντος . . . εὖ πολεμηθεὶς μνημονεύεται;—Οὐδείς.—Ἀλλ' οἷα δὴ εἰς τὰ ἔργα σοφοῦ ἀνδρὸς πολλαὶ ἐπίνοιαι . . . λέγονται . . .;—Οὐδαμῶς τοιοῦτον οὐδέν.—Ἀλλὰ δὴ εἰ μὴ δημοσίᾳ, ἰδίᾳ . . .; *Ion* 540B Οὐκ ἄρα πάντα γε γνώσεται ἡ ῥαψῳδικὴ . . . ἀλλὰ ποῖα δὴ γνώσεται, ἐπειδὴ οὐχ ἅπαντα; X.*HG* ii 4.41 σκέψασθε εἰ ἄρα ἐπ' ἀνδρείᾳ ὑμῖν μέγα φρονητέον . . . ἀλλὰ γνώμῃ φαίητ' ἂν προέχειν . . .; ἀλλ' ἐπὶ Λακεδαιμονίοις δὴ οἴεσθε μέγα φρονητέον εἶναι; *Smp.* 2.4 οὐ παρὰ τῶν μυροπωλῶν.—Ἀλλὰ πόθεν δή; D.xliii 77 τὸ δ' ὄνομα, ὅ ἐστιν αὐτῷ, μὴ ὅτι ἐκ . . . ἀλλ' οὐδ' . . . οὐδ' . . . ἀλλὰ πόθεν δή ἐστι τὸ ὄνομα ὁ Μακάρτατος; Pl.*R.*333B,335C,531E: *Prt.*338C: *Ly.*215A: *Cri.*54A: *Prm.*138D.

(5) Assentient (very rare). Pl.*Tht.*169D τήρει τὸ τοιόνδε, μὴ . . .—Ἀλλὰ δὴ πειράσομαί γε ('Well, I'll try'): *La.*189C 'You are clearly ready to help in the investigation.'—Ἀλλ' ἡμέτερον δὴ ἔργον, ὦ Σώκρατες.

ἀλλὰ δή, in all its senses, almost invariably follows a strong stop. The following are exceptional:—Adversative: Pl.*Lg.* 689B μηδὲν ποιῶσιν πλέον ἀλλὰ δὴ τούτοις πᾶν τοὐναντίον. Progressive: Hp.*Virg.*1 ἄλλα τε πολλὰ ἀλλὰ δὴ καὶ τὰ πουλυτελέστατα τῶν ἱματίων καθιεροῦσι (καὶ τὰ ἱμάτια τὰ πουλυτελέστατα *C*): cf. Pseud-Arist. *de Plant.* 828b15 καὶ τοῦτο εὑρίσκεται ἐν πάσαις ταῖς βοτάναις ταῖς λεπταῖς, ἀλλὰ δὴ καὶ ἔν τισι λαχάνοις.

Ἀλλά γε δή: ἀλλὰ δή γε

These combinations are extremely doubtful. Pl.*Phdr.*262A ἀπάτη πότερον ἐν πολὺ διαφέρουσι γίγνεται μᾶλλον ἢ ὀλίγον;—Ἐν τοῖς ὀλίγον.—Ἀλλά γε δὴ κατὰ σμικρὸν μεταβαίνων μᾶλλον λήσεις ἐλθὼν ἐπὶ τὸ ἐναντίον ἢ κατὰ μέγα (γε δή *B*: δή *T*: μήν Galenus): *Hp.Ma.*304A Ἀλλὰ δή γ', ὦ Σώκρατες, τί οἴει ταῦτα εἶναι συνάπαντα; (protesting: γ' *om. F*).

Γὰρ δή

Δή emphasizing *γάρ* is already found in Homer: *Ω*54 *κωφὴν γὰρ δὴ γαῖαν ἀεικίζει μενεαίνων*. The reverse order, *δὴ γάρ*, which gives an even stronger emphasis, is also frequently found in him: *Λ*314 *δὴ γὰρ ἔλεγχος ἔσσεται*: *N*122,517.

In later Greek *γὰρ δή* is exceedingly common. Tyrt.*Fr*.7.21 *αἰσχρὸν γὰρ δὴ τοῦτο*: Xenoph.*Fr*.1.1 *νῦν γὰρ δὴ ζάπεδον καθαρόν*: S.*Aj*.807 *ἔγνωκα γὰρ δὴ φωτὸς ἠπατημένη*: *OC*1613 *ὄλωλε γὰρ δὴ πάντα τἀμά*: E.*Med*.722 *ἐς τοῦτο γὰρ δὴ φροῦδός εἰμι πᾶς ἐγώ*: *Hel*.329 *γυναῖκα γὰρ δὴ συμπονεῖν γυναικὶ χρή*: Archil.*Fr*.67b: A.*Ch*.874: Ar.*Nu*.397: Hdt.i34 *διέφθαρτο, ἦν γὰρ δὴ κωφός*: ii60 *ποιεῦσι τοιάδε· πλέουσί τε γὰρ δή* (explanatory: cf. vi137.3): Pl.*Cri*.53D *ἐκεῖ γὰρ δὴ πλείστη ἀταξία*: *Phd*.115A *ὥρα τραπέσθαι πρὸς τὸ λουτρόν· δοκεῖ γὰρ δὴ βέλτιον εἶναι λουσάμενον πιεῖν τὸ φάρμακον*: *Tht*.156C.

Certain idiomatic uses may be noted.

(1) Arresting attention at the opening of a narrative. Pl. *Euthd*.291C *Ἐγὼ φράσω. ἔδοξε γὰρ δὴ ἡμῖν ...*: *La*.179B *χρὴ ἀκοῦσαι ... συσσιτοῦμεν γὰρ δὴ ἐγώ τε καὶ Μελησίας*: *Phd*.59D *πάντα πειράσομαι διηγήσασθαι. ἀεὶ γὰρ δὴ ... εἰώθεμεν φοιτᾶν*: *R*.358E,415A,453E,615C.

(2) *οὐ γὰρ δή, μὴ γὰρ δή*. (Usually, though not invariably, these combinations, particularly when followed by *γε*, are used for clearing the ground by ruling out at least one possibility: 'certainly not', 'certainly not, at any rate'.) S.*OC*110 *τόδ' ἄθλιον εἴδωλον· οὐ γὰρ δὴ τό γ' ἀρχαῖον δέμας*: 265 *ὄνομα μόνον δείσαντες; οὐ γὰρ δὴ τό γε σῶμ'*: E.*Ion*954 *Τίς γάρ νιν ἐξέθηκεν; οὐ γὰρ δὴ σύ γε*: *Tr*.210 *Τὰν κλεινὰν εἴθ' ἔλθοιμεν Θησέως εὐδαίμονα χώραν.—Μὴ γὰρ δὴ δίναν γ' Εὐρώτα*: S.*OT*576: *El*.1020: *Ant*.46: *Ph*.246: Ar.*Nu*.402: *Ec*.157: Th.i122.4 *οὐκ ἴσμεν ὅπως τάδε τριῶν τῶν μεγίστων ξυμφορῶν ἀπήλλακται, ἀξυνεσίας ἢ μαλακίας ἢ ἀμελείας. οὐ γὰρ δὴ πεφευγότες αὐτὰ ἐπὶ τὴν πλείστους δὴ βλάψασαν καταφρόνησιν κεχωρήκατε* ('Surely you have not avoided these three errors only to fall into a fourth': see, however, Steup): Pl.*Chrm*.161C *Ἔοικεν ... ἄλλου. οὐ γὰρ δὴ ἐμοῦ γε*: *Phd*.76C *Πότε ...; οὐ γὰρ δὴ ἀφ' οὗ γε ...*: Hdt.ii120: Th.i81.6: iv87.4: v111.3: vi69.1:

76.2: Pl.*Phd.*76D,92B: *R.*336E,613A: Arist.*Pol.*1264b23,1280b 24: Isoc.xv24,34.

(3) δή reinforcing assentient γάρ in answers. This is rarer than γὰρ οὖν. Pl.*Tht.*187E ψευδῆ φαμεν . . .;—Φαμὲν γὰρ δή: *R.*454A Ἔστι γὰρ δή, ἔφη, περὶ πολλοὺς τοῦτο τὸ πάθος: 562C Λέγεται γὰρ δή, ἔφη, καὶ πολὺ τοῦτο τὸ ῥῆμα: *Prm.*141C.

(4) With elliptical γάρ in an answer-question. X.*Oec.*11.9 Μέλει γὰρ δή σοι, ὦ Ἰσχόμαχε, ὅπως . . .; ('Why, do you really care . . . ?').

S.*OT* 582 is difficult: Οὔκουν ἰσοῦμαι σφῷν ἐγὼ δυοῖν τρίτος;—Ἐνταῦθα γὰρ δὴ καὶ κακὸς φαίνῃ φίλος. ('Yes, that is just where your treachery manifests itself.' It is just because Creon is Oedipus' equal, not his inferior, that he is able to manifest his spite. Hence the manifestation of his spite is evidence for his equality. Jebb, less well, I think: 'for otherwise your guilt would be less glaring.')

(5) Reinforcing progressive γάρ. S.*Aj.*101 Τεθνᾶσιν ἄνδρες . . .—Εἶεν· τί γὰρ δὴ παῖς ὁ τοῦ Λαερτίου; ('Well, and what of Laertius' son?'). Cf. Theocr.22.115, Ap.Rhod.2.851,1090: 4.450.

γὰρ . . . δή, separated, can hardly be regarded as a distinctive idiom: but in E.*IA* 637 ποθῶ γὰρ ὄμμα δὴ σόν there is a certain coherence between the particles.

καὶ γὰρ δή. Hom.*Π*810: Hdt.i135: Pl.*Tht.*203B: *Cra.*412C: *Prt.*314A: X.*HG*vi3.14: 5.41: 5.52: Lys.xxviii3.

ἀλλὰ γὰρ δή. Pl.*Hp.Ma.*301B. ἀλλὰ . . . γὰρ δή. S.*Aj.* 167: E.*Med.*1067: *Fr.*573,773.59: Th.vi77.1.

Γε δή

We have seen that γε and δή, as emphatic particles, share a good deal of common ground. The usages of γε δή correspond closely with those of its component parts in different idioms. (It makes little difference whether we regard the two particles as exercising their force independently, or δή as strengthening γε.) Only in *a fortiori* statements (4) does the combination acquire any noticeable individuality.

While fairly common in prose (e.g. 43 examples in Plato,

according to R. W. Chapman), γε δή hardly ever occurs in verse. Hom.*H*281 τό γε δὴ καὶ ἴδμεν ἅπαντες: η214: ξ198: π136: ρ281: S.*Ant.*923: E.*Hel.*1176: *IT* 512 Φεύγω τρόπον γε δή τιν' οὐχ ἑκὼν ἑκών (but here δή really coalesces with τινα): Ar.*V.*857. In A.*Pr.*42 the MSS. τε is quite possibly sound.

(1) Emphatic limitative. E.*Hel.*1176 θανεῖται δ', ἢν γε δὴ ληφθῇ μόνον: Hdt.i 114 ὥς γε δὴ ἀνάξια ἑωυτοῦ παθών: ii 120 μέλλοντά γε δὴ . . . ἀπαλλαγήσεσθαι: iii 9 ἐπεί γε δή (S.*Ant.* 923: Th.i 132.3): Hdt.vi 79.2 πρίν γε δή (82.1: 110: vii 239.4: Th.vii 71.5): Th.vii 56.4 πλήν γε δή (Pl.*Phd.*57B: *Plt.*305A): Pl.*Tht.*182C εἴπερ γε δή (*Prm.*138D elliptical, in answer): *Phd.* 84C εἴ γε δή (*Lg.*672A: *Alc.I* 106B): *Lg.*834B κατά γε δὴ Κρήτην: *Phdr.*268A ἔν γε δὴ πλήθους συνόδοις: *R.*389C ἀλλὰ πρός γε δὴ τοὺς τοιούτους ἄρχοντας: *Cri.*45D χρὴ δὲ . . . ταῦτα αἱρεῖσθαι, φάσκοντά γε δὴ ἀρετῆς . . . ἐπιμελεῖσθαι: X.*Eq.Mag.*4.6 ἢν δ' ἄρα αὐτὸς ἀπείρως ἔχῃ, τῶν ἄλλων γε δὴ τοὺς ἐπιστημονεστάτους . . . παραλαμβάνειν (for γοῦν: δεῖ *B*): Is.ii 30 ὥς γε δὴ ᾠόμεθα (ὥστε δηώμεθα *codd.*): D.vi 17 νῦν γε δή: xxi 161 καίτοι τόν γε δὴ φιλότιμον πανταχοῦ προσῆκεν ἐξετάζεσθαι: 199 τόν γε δὴ μέχρι τῆς κρίσεως χρόνον, εἰ καὶ μὴ πάντα (for γοῦν): Pl.*R.*445C, 517C, 533A: *Ti.*27C: *Tht.*164D: *Hp.Ma.*290B: *Lg.*842A: *Epin.* 983D: *Ep.*350E: X.*HG* iii 2.16: vii 4.39.

(2) Purely emphatic. Hom.η214 καὶ πλείον' ἐγὼ κακὰ μυθησαίμην, ὅσσα γε δὴ . . . μόγησα (γε epexegetic, and δή strengthening ὅσσα): Th.ii 62.1 ἐν οἷς ἄλλοτε πολλάκις γε δὴ . . . ἀπέδειξα: viii 41.2 ὃς αὐτοῖς ἔτυχε μέγιστός γε δὴ ὧν μεμνήμεθα γενόμενος (for the last two examples cf. the common uses of δή, I.2.ii and 3): Pl.*Ap.*40A συμβέβηκέ μοι . . . ταυτὶ ἅ γε δὴ οἰηθείη ἄν τις . . . ἔσχατα κακῶν εἶναι: X.*An.*iv 6.3 τοῦτό γε δὴ Χειρισόφῳ καὶ Ξενοφῶντι μόνον διάφορον ἐν τῇ πορείᾳ ἐγένετο: *Cyr.*v 5.8 ὅτι . . . δοκῶν γε δὴ . . . πατρὸς βασιλέως πεφυκέναι . . . ἐμαυτὸν μὲν ὁρῶ οὕτω ταπεινῶς καὶ ἀναξίως ἐλαύνοντα.

(3) In answers, sometimes purely emphatic, but usually limitative. Pl.*Smp.*172C εἰ νεωστὶ ἡγῇ . . .—Ἐγώ γε δή, ἔφη ('I certainly did think so'): *Phdr.*242D τὸν Ἔρωτα οὐ . . . θεόν τινα ἡγῇ;—Λέγεταί γε δή ('He is *said* to be, certainly': *R.*557B): *Grg.*449B Ἐπαγγέλλομαί γε δή ('Yes, I profess to do that': not, on the lips of a Gorgias, 'Anyhow I *profess* to do that'): *Plt.*261D Φαίνεταί γε δὴ ῥηθὲν νῦν (*Prm.*157D): *Tht.*155B Δοκεῖ

γε δή: 204B Δεῖ γε δή: *Euthd.*275A Οἰόμεθά γε δή: X.*Oec.*13.4 Ἦ...παιδεύεις...;—Πειρῶμαί γε δή ('I *try* to, anyhow': contrast *Grg.*449B above): Pl.*R.*526E: *Prm.*138D: *Phdr.*277B: *Tht.*145D.

(4) *A fortiori*, '*praesertim*', '*nedum*': Hdt.iii11 ἐγὼ μὲν γὰρ ἔλπομαί γε καὶ μυρίων ἐντὸς χωσθῆναι ἄν. κοῦ γε δὴ ἐν τῷ προαναισιμωμένῳ χρόνῳ... οὐκ ἂν χωσθείη κόλπος καὶ πολλῷ μέζων...; Hp.*Art.*37 εἰ... πῶς γε δὴ οὐκ...; Th.iv78.2 ἄλλως τε οὐκ εὔπορον... καὶ μετὰ ὅπλων γε δή: vi37.2 μόλις..., εἰ..., ἦ πού γε δὴ ἐν πάσῃ πολεμίᾳ Σικελίᾳ: D.ii23 οὐκ ἔνι... οὐδὲ τοῖς φίλοις ἐπιτάττειν... μή τί γε δὴ τοῖς θεοῖς: liv17 ἃ πολλὴν αἰσχύνην ἔχει καὶ λέγειν, μὴ ὅτι γε δὴ ποιεῖν ἀνθρώπους μετρίους.

For μή τι δή, μὴ ὅτι δή in *a fortiori* statements, see δή, I.10.vi. For μὴ ὅτι δή γε (Pl.*Phlb.*60D) see δή γε.

(5) καὶ... γε δή. Th.i11.2 τά τε πρὸ τούτων ἀσθενῆ ἦν καὶ αὐτά γε δὴ ταῦτα: Pl.*Sph.*237B παρ' ἐκείνου τ' οὖν μαρτυρεῖται, καὶ μάλιστά γε δὴ πάντων...: *Tht.*156B καὶ καύσεις καὶ ἡδοναί γε δὴ καὶ λῦπαι: *Smp.*173E Ὦ φίλτατε, καὶ δῆλόν γε δὴ ὅτι... μαίνομαι καὶ παραπαίω; (ironical, 'So it's obvious, is it...?' For καί in indignant questions, *v.s.v.* II.B.10.ii.*b.*: καί does not cohere closely with γε δή here): X.*Oec.*5.20 καὶ ὑπὲρ ὑγρῶν καί... καὶ... καὶ... καὶ... καὶ ὑπὲρ πάντων γε δή: Th.iv78.2 (see (4)): Pl.*Phlb.*26B,47B: *Epin.*978B: X.*Mem.*i2.53: *Cyr.*i6.43.

(6) μέν γε δή, Pl.*Tht.*172C καὶ πολλάκις μέν γε δὴ... καὶ ἄλλοτε κατενόησα, ἀτὰρ καὶ νῦν.

(7) τέ γε δή, τε... γε δή. Pl.*Lg.*709D Οἵ τε ἄλλοι γε δὴ πάντες... εἴποιεν ἄν: 722E ἡ νῦν διατριβὴ γεγονυῖα, ὡς ἐμοὶ δοκεῖ, σημαίνει ὡς ὄντος, οἵ τέ γε δὴ διπλοῖ ἔδοξαν... νόμοι οὐκ εἶναι ἁπλῶς οὕτω πως διπλοῖ.

In Ant.v57 δή is connective (cf. δή, IV.2) after **ΜΑΡΤΥΡΕΣ**: τίνος γε δὴ ἕνεκα τὸν ἄνδρα ἀπέκτεινα; ('Again, *why* did I kill the man?'), and apparently inferential in iii δ9: οὐκ ἀτιμώρητος ὁ φόνος ἐστίν. ἔχοντός γε δὴ (δή *om. A*) τὴν δίκην τοῦ φονέως,... ἐὰν καταλάβητε, ἐνθύμιον ὑπολείψεσθε: but the punctuation is in doubt. In Pl.*Ly.*219C γε marks the amplification of a preceding statement (see γε, I.11.ix), while δή stresses φίλου: Εἰ ἄρα φίλον, ἕνεκά του.—Ναί.—Φίλου γέ τινος δή.

For ἀλλά γε δή see p. 242, *ad fin.*

Δή γε

On this very rare combination, seldom textually above suspicion, see Neil, Appendix to *Knights*, p. 196, and Paley on E.*IT* 943 ('generally, if not always, an indication of a grammarian's patchwork').

A few instances seem to be certain. In most of them δή and γε clearly do not coalesce. E.*Supp.*162 *εὐψυχίαν ἔσπευσας . . .—Ὃ δή γε πολλοὺς ὤλεσε στρατηλάτας* ('Yes, the very thing that . . .': γε marks the answer: δή goes closely with the relative): *Heracl.*632 *Πάρεσμεν, οἵα δή γ' ἐμοῦ παρουσία* (γε adding a restrictive sense to the closely cohering *οἵα δή*): Ar. *Th.*934 *Νὴ Δί', ὡς νῦν δή γ' ἀνὴρ ὀλίγου μ' ἀφείλετ' αὐτόν* (δή γ' Dobree: δῆτ' *R*: ὡς . . . γε is common, and νῦν δή is practically one word): Pl.*Phlb.*60D *καὶ ὁτιοῦν . . . μὴ ὅτι δή γε ἡδονήν* (*a fortiori*): *Plt.*294E *Διὸ δή γε καὶ* . . . (διὸ δή closely together: γε marks a new stage in the thought).

The following are more than doubtful, and are almost universally emended: E.*IT* 943 *ἔνθεν μοι πόδα ἐς τὰς Ἀθήνας δή γ' ἔπεμψε Λοξίας* (δῆτ' Scaliger: but the corruption is probably wider spread): *HF* 1146 *Οἴμοι· τί δή γε φείδομαι ψυχῆς ἐμῆς* (δῆτα Schaefer, with much probability: or perhaps *τί δὴ 'γώ*, 'Why, then, do I spare my *own* life'): *IA* 1207 *εἰ δ' εὖ λέλεκται, † νῶι μὴ δή γε κτάνῃς †*. In Ar.*Nu.*681,786 the textual authority for δή γε is slight. In X.*Oec.*17.2 δή γε is a most unlikely emendation of δέ γε. The combination ἀλλὰ δή γε in Pl.*Hp.Ma.*304A (see p. 242, *ad. fin.*) is equally suspicious. In Hdt.vii 10θ1 *RSV* read ἀλλ' εἰ δή γε δεῖ, *CP* ἀλλ' εἰ δεῖ δή γε (ἀλλ' εἰ δὴ δεῖ γε Hude). The reading of *RSV* may possibly be right, εἴ γε, 'if, but not otherwise', being combined with εἰ δή, 'if really': and the order δή γε being preferred to the stereotyped γε δή as giving more independent force to the two particles. Cf. Pl.*Prm.*135B εἴ γέ τις δή *B* Proclus: εἰ δή γέ τις *T*.

Καὶ δή

This combination is sometimes connective, 'and indeed', sometimes non-connective, 'also indeed', 'actually indeed'. Some cases admit of classification under either head.

(1) Connective. *Καί δή* as a connecting particle, linking either sentences or clauses, is not infrequent in Homer, and common in Ionic prose (Herodotus and Hippocrates). It is occasionally found in Plato, but is on the whole rare in Attic,[1] where *καὶ ... δή* or *καὶ δὴ καί* is normally used in adding something *eiusdem generis*, and *καὶ μήν* in introducing a new departure.

In Homer connective *καὶ δή* usually corresponds to the later *καὶ δὴ καί*. It introduces something similar in kind to what has preceded, but stronger in degree, and marks a kind of climax. *A*161 *οὐδ' ἀλεγίζεις· καὶ δή μοι ... ἀπειλεῖς*: *E*175 *ὅς τις ὅδε κρατέει, καὶ δὴ κακὰ πολλὰ ἔοργε*: *I*349 *μάλα πολλὰ πονήσατο νόσφιν ἐμεῖο, καὶ δὴ τεῖχος ἔδειμε*: *O*251 *οὐκ ἀΐεις ὅ με ... βάλεν Αἴας ... ἔπαυσε δὲ θούριδος ἀλκῆς; καὶ δὴ ἔγωγ' ἐφάμην νέκυας ... ἵξεσθαι*: *X*457 *δείδω μὴ ... Ἀχιλλεὺς ... δίηται, καὶ δή μιν καταπαύσῃ*: *Z*52: *β*315: *ε*409: *ι*496: *κ*30: *φ*377: *χ*10: Even.*Fr*.9.1.

Herodotus uses *καὶ δή* in a less restricted manner. With him, though the sense of climax is frequently present, *καὶ δή* is often merely a lively connective, denoting that something important or interesting is to follow. i 66 ... *καὶ εὐθενήθησαν. καὶ δή σφι οὐκέτι ἀπέχρα ἡσυχίην ἄγειν*: ii 87 *τὰς δὲ σάρκας τὸ λίτρον κατατήκει, καὶ δὴ λείπεται τοῦ νεκροῦ τὸ δέρμα μοῦνον*: vi 61.3 *ἐλίσσετο τὴν θεὸν ἀπαλλάξαι τῆς δυσμορφίης τὸ παιδίον. καὶ δή κοτε ἀπιούσῃ ...*: vii 12.1 *κατύπνωσε, καὶ δή κου ἐν τῇ νυκτὶ εἶδε ὄψιν*: 38.2 *ἔφη τε ὑποργήσειν καὶ δὴ ἀγορεύειν ἐκέλευε ὅτευ δέοιτο*: 149.2 *ὑποκρίνασθαι, καὶ δὴ λέγειν*: vi 12.3: 128.2: vii 34: 224.2: viii 88.2.

Hippocrates contains many examples: *Vict*.25 *ἅτε βραδέης ἐούσης τῆς κινήσιος καὶ δὴ ψυχροῦ τοῦ σώματος*: *VC*2 *καὶ δὴ ὅτι οὕτω ταῦτα ἔχει ...*: *ib*.2,6,12.

[1] The scarcity of *connective* καὶ δή in Attic has hardly been noticed. Eucken (p. 44), not distinguishing between (1) and (2), observes that the juxtaposition of the particles, without a second *καί*, is not to be found in the genuine works of Aristotle.

Attic instances are few and far between. Pl.*Ap.*41B θαυμαστὴ ἂν εἴη ἡ διατριβὴ αὐτόθι, ὁπότε . . . καὶ δὴ τὸ μέγιστον (καὶ δὴ καί *T*): *Ti.*74E ἃ δὲ (τῶν ὀστῶν) ἀψυχότατα ἐντός, πλείσταις καὶ πυκνοτάταις (συνέφραττε σαρξίν), καὶ δὴ κατὰ τὰς συμβολὰς τῶν ὀστῶν . . . βραχεῖαν σάρκα ἔφυσεν (καὶ κατά *F*): *Lg.*682E καὶ δὴ ταῦτά γε ἤδη πάνθ' ὑμεῖς, ὦ Λακεδαιμόνιοι, τἀντεῦθεν μυθολογεῖτε: X.*An.*i5.7 καὶ δή ποτε στενοχωρίας καὶ πηλοῦ φανέντος . . . (elsewhere Xenophon expresses lively connexion by καὶ μέντοι): And.i41 ἥκειν ἔφη τῇ ὑστεραίᾳ, καὶ δὴ κόπτειν τὴν θύραν: Pl.*Tht.*158D: *Ep.*311A. (For D.xlviii15, see καὶ δὴ καί, *ad init.*: καὶ δὴ ὅ τι, in Lys.xiii4, is a rather rash conjecture.) Sometimes introducing a new point, like καὶ μήν: Pl.*R.*490C: *Lg.*677B,964A.

In the following, καὶ δή seems to combine the ideas of connexion and immediacy: 'And lo, straightway'. E.*Cyc.*423 ἄλλην ἔδωκα κύλικα . . . καὶ δὴ πρὸς ᾠδὰς εἷρπε: Pl.*Phdr.*255E καὶ δή, οἷον εἰκός, ποιεῖ τὸ μετὰ τοῦτο ταχὺ ταῦτα. (Cf. Hom. B135 ἐννέα δὴ βεβάασι . . . ἐνιαυτοί, καὶ δὴ δοῦρα σέσηπε νεῶν: Thgn.1316 ἐκ πάντων σ' ἐδόκουν θήσεσθαι ἑταῖρον πιστόν· καὶ δὴ νῦν ἄλλον ἔχεισθα φίλον.)

In three places where, with the accepted punctuation, καὶ δή must be taken as connective, it is perhaps better to put a colon or full-stop before the particles, and assume an asyndeton. Ar.*Pax* 178 ἀτὰρ ἐγγὺς εἶναι τῶν θεῶν ἐμοὶ δοκῶ, καὶ δὴ καθορῶ τὴν οἰκίαν τὴν τοῦ Διός: *Lys.*925 κατάκεισο, καὶ δὴ 'κδύομαι ('Look! I'm taking off my clothes'): E.*Hipp.*1447 Ὄλωλα καὶ δὴ νερτέρων ὁρῶ πύλας.

In a few passages καὶ δή expresses the secondary sense of καὶ δὴ καί (*q.v.*, (2)), marking the transition from general to particular. Hdt.v67.5 τά τε δὴ ἄλλα . . . ἐτίμων . . . καὶ δὴ . . . ἐγέραιρον: Pl.*Lg.*674C τακτὰ δὲ τά τ' ἄλλα ἂν εἴη . . . καὶ δὴ τά γε περὶ οἶνον: 722D λόγων πάντων . . . προοίμιά τέ ἐστιν . . . καὶ δή που κιθαρῳδικῆς ᾠδῆς λεγομένων νόμων . . . προοίμια . . . πρόκειται: 794D πρὸς δὲ τὰ μαθήματα τρέπεσθαι χρεὼν ἑκατέρους . . . καὶ δὴ τά γε μάλιστα πρὸς τὴν τῶν ὅπλων χρείαν: D.lv11 τηνικαῦτα τοῦτο (τὸ ὕδωρ) εἰς τὰ χωρία ὑπεραίρειν ἀναγκαῖον ἤδη. καὶ δὴ κατὰ τοῦτο τὸ χωρίον . . . συνέβη τὸ ὕδωρ ἐμβαλεῖν (καὶ δὴ καί *A*). For D.xlviii14, see καὶ δὴ καί, *ad init.*

In the following a second καί follows at a short interval, in close connexion with the word or words which come after it. Pl.*R*.344D ἠνάγκασαν ὑπομεῖναι (οἱ παρόντες) . . . καὶ δὴ ἔγωγε καὶ αὐτὸς πάνυ ἐδεόμην: *Thg*.121A καὶ ἄλλως . . . καὶ δὴ σοῦ γ' ἕνεκα καὶ πάνυ: *Ap*.21A ἴστε οἷος ἦν Χαιρεφῶν, ὡς σφοδρὸς ἐφ' ὅτι ὁρμήσειεν. καὶ δή ποτε καὶ εἰς Δελφοὺς ἐλθὼν ἐτόλμησε. . . . In *R*.361E the sense perhaps indicates that the καί in κἄν, in spite of the crasis, goes with the preceding καὶ δή: λεκτέον οὖν· καὶ δὴ κἂν ἀγροικοτέρως λέγηται, μὴ ἐμὲ οἴου λέγειν.

I have left two special usages to the last.

(i) In two passages, elsewhere unparalleled, καὶ δή introduces an argument from precedent: 'Before now . . .'. (καί here is perhaps not connective). A.*Supp*.499 φύλαξαι μὴ θράσος τέκῃ φόβον· καὶ δὴ φίλον τις ἔκταν' ἀγνοίας ὕπο: Ar.*Av*.1251 πέμψω δὲ πορφυρίωνας ἐς τὸν οὐρανόν . . . πλεῖν ἑξακοσίους τὸν ἀριθμόν. καὶ δή ποτε εἷς Πορφυρίων αὐτῷ παρέσχε πράγματα. (Cf. ἤδη Th.ii 77.4).

(ii) Euripides four times introduces a surprised question with καὶ δή, instead of the simple καί often so used: cf. δή, I.5.i.*b*. *Hec*.758 Καὶ δὴ τίν' ἡμᾶς εἰς ἐπάρκεσιν καλεῖς; *Hel*.101 Καὶ δὴ τί τοῦτ' Αἴαντι γίγνεται κακόν; *El*.655: *Or*.1188. X.*Cyr*.iv 3.5 is perhaps analogous: ἔχομεν . . . ὅπλα οἷς δοκοῦμεν ἂν τρέπεσθαι τοὺς πολεμίους ὁμόσε ἰόντες· καὶ δὴ τρεπόμενοι ποίους . . . δυναίμεθ' ἂν . . . κατακανεῖν; Perhaps, however, καὶ δὴ τρεπόμενοι means 'supposing we do rout', a participial use analogous to the finite use described in 2.v below.

(2) Non-connective. (Usually, but by no means invariably, at opening of sentence. Sometimes combined, and even juxtaposed, with connecting particles, ἀλλά, ἀτάρ, μὲν οὖν, μέντοι, οὖν, γάρ, δέ, τοίνυν.) καὶ δή here signifies, vividly and dramatically, that something is actually taking place at the moment. This use is already found in Homer: Φ421 Ὢ πόποι . . . Ἀτρυτώνη, καὶ δὴ αὖθ' ἡ κυνάμυια ἄγει . . . ('See now!'): μ116 Σχέτλιε, καὶ δὴ αὖ τοι πολεμήϊα ἔργα μέμηλε: ν169: χ249. In an indignant question: Ξ364 Ἀργεῖοι, καὶ δὴ αὖτε μεθίεμεν Ἕκτορι νίκην . . .; Examples of the apodotic use (see (vi) below) are also to be found in Homer. This vivid use of καὶ δή occurs several times in Demosthenes but not in the other orators.

(i) In general, marking vivid perception by mind, ear, or eye:

'lo!', 'hark!', 'see there!'. (Cf. *καὶ μήν*, (7).) Thgn.1107 *ὤ μοι ἐγὼ δειλός· καὶ δὴ κατάχαρμα μὲν ἐχθροῖς . . . γενόμην*: S.*Fr.* 465.1 *τειχέων καὶ δὴ τοὺς Ποσιδείους . . . θριγκοὺς ἀποσεισαμένη*: E.*HF* 867 *ἦν ἰδού· καὶ δὴ τινάσσει κρᾶτα*: Ar.*Th.*769 *οἶδ' ἐγὼ καὶ δὴ πόρον*: 1092 *Ποῦ 'στ' ἡ μιαρά; καὶ δὴ πεύγει*: *V.*492 *ὥστε καὶ δὴ τοὔνομ' αὐτῆς (τυραννίδος) ἐν ἀγορᾷ κυλίνδεται*: *Nu.* 906 *τουτὶ καὶ δὴ χωρεῖ τὸ κακόν* (*V.*1483: *Ra.*1018): *V.*1484 *Κλῇθρα χαλάσθω τάδε. καὶ δὴ γὰρ σχήματος ἀρχή*: Antiph. *Fr.*237.1 *ἄλλοι δὲ καὶ δὴ βακχίου παλαιγενοῦς . . . δέπας μεστὸν . . . ἕλκουσι*: Carm.Pop.43.4 *ἁμέρα καὶ δή*: Hdt.vii 14 *Ὦ παῖ Δαρείου, καὶ δὴ φαίνεαι . . . ἀπειπάμενος τὴν στρατηλασίην*: Pl.*Cra.*416A *Τὸ μὲν τοίνυν "αἰσχρὸν" καὶ δὴ κατάδηλόν μοι φαίνεται.*

(ii) Sometimes used (as, far more often, *καὶ μήν*: *q.v.* (6)) to mark the entrance of a character on the stage. S.*Aj.*544 *Καὶ δὴ κομίζει προσπόλων ὅδ' ἐγγύθεν*: E.*Med.*1118 *καὶ δὴ δέδορκα τόνδε . . . στείχοντα*: *Cyc.*488 *Σίγα σίγα. καὶ δὴ μεθύων . . . χωρεῖ πετρίνων ἔξω μελάθρων*: *Supp.*1114 *Τάδε δὴ παίδων καὶ δὴ φθιμένων ὀστᾶ φέρεται* (the text has been suspected, but may be sound. Paley keeps it): Ar.*Av.*268 *ἀλλ' εἷς οὑτοσὶ καὶ δή τις ὄρνις ἔρχεται*: *Ra.*604 *ὡς ἀκούω τῆς θύρας καὶ δὴ ψόφον*: *V.* 1324: *Lys.*65,77: *Ec.*500.

(iii) Marking the provision or completion of something required by the circumstances. Ar.*Pax* 942 *ὁ γὰρ βωμὸς θύρασι καὶ δή*: *Lys.*601 *σορὸν ὠνήσει· μελιτοῦτταν ἐγὼ καὶ δὴ μάξω* (*μάζω R*): 909 *ἰδοὺ τὸ μέν σοι παιδίον καὶ δὴ 'κποδών*: *Th.*266 *Ἀνὴρ μὲν ἡμῖν οὑτοσὶ καὶ δὴ γυνὴ τό γ' εἶδος*: Pl.*Grg.*523D *παυστέον ἐστὶν προειδότας αὐτοὺς τὸν θάνατον . . . τοῦτο μὲν οὖν καὶ δὴ εἴρηται τῷ Προμηθεῖ ὅπως ἂν παύσῃ αὐτῶν*: [X.]*Ath.* 2.11 *ἐξ αὐτῶν μέντοι τούτων καὶ δὴ νῆές μοί εἰσι* ('Well, there are my ships!').

So too in response to a definite command, often with a word of the command echoed. The answer is usually in the present tense, sometimes in the perfect, rarely in the future: action here being normally regarded as preceding, or synchronizing with, speech. A.*Pr.*54 *Οὔκουν ἐπείξει τῷδε δεσμὰ περιβαλεῖν . . .;—Καὶ δὴ πρόχειρα ψάλια*: 75 *Καὶ δὴ πέπρακται τοὔργον*: *Th.*473 *πέμπε . . .—Πέμποιμ' ἂν ἤδη τόνδε, σὺν τύχῃ δέ τῳ καὶ δὴ πέπεμπται*: S.*OC* 173 *Πρόσθιγέ νύν μου.—Ψαύω καὶ* δή: E.*Alc.*1118 *Τόλμα προτεῖναι χεῖρα . . .—Καὶ δὴ προτείνω*: *Ph.*387 (the rarity of this use of *καὶ δή* in Euripides is remarkable): Ar.*Pax* 327 *παῦε . . .—Ἢν ἰδοὺ καὶ δὴ πέπαυμαι*: *Av.* 175 *βλέψον κάτω.—Καὶ δὴ βλέπω*: 550 *σὺ δίδασκε . . .—Καὶ δὴ τοίνυν πρῶτα διδάσκω*: *Th.*214 *ἀπόδυθι τουτὶ θοἰμάτιον.—Καὶ δὴ χαμαί*: *Ra.*1205 *σὺ δείξεις;—Φημί.—Καὶ δὴ χρὴ λέγειν*: Pl.Com.*Fr.*69.9 *νεοκρᾶτά τις ποιείτω.—Καὶ δὴ κέκραται*: Anaxil. *Fr.*9 *ἀπόδος.—Καὶ δὴ φέρουσ' ἐξέρχομαι*: A.*Supp.*438,507: S.*Tr.*345: *El.*317,558,892,1436,1464: *Ant.*245: *Ph.*818: Ar. *Eq.*22: *Nu.*778,1097: *Ec.*1014: *Pl.*227,414: Pl.*Phdr.*236D *Μηδαμῶς τοίνυν εἴπῃς.—Οὔκ, ἀλλὰ καὶ δὴ λέγω* (refusal to obey command).

(iv) The line between 'actually happening' and 'happening now' is often difficult to draw. Hence *καὶ δή* frequently approximates in sense (particularly in the historians) to *ἤδη*, though it is always more vivid and dramatic in tone.

S.*Aj.*49 *Ἦ καὶ παρέστη κἀπὶ τέρμ' ἀφίκετο;—Καὶ δὴ 'πὶ δισσαῖς ἦν στρατηγίσιν πύλαις*: *OC* 31 *Ἦ δεῦρο προσστείχοντα . . .;—Καὶ δὴ μὲν οὖν παρόντα*: E.*Med.*1065 *πάντως πέπρακται πάντα κοὐκ ἐκφεύξεται. καὶ δὴ 'πὶ κρατὶ στέφανος . . . σάφ' οἶδ' ἐγώ*: *Heracl.*671 *Ἴσασι· καὶ δὴ λαιὸν ἕστηκεν κέρας*: 673 *Καὶ δὴ παρῆκται σφάγια*: Ar.*Ra.*647 *πατάξω.—Πηνίκα;—Καὶ δὴ 'πάταξα* (the approximation to *ἤδη* is remarkably close here. *καὶ δή* cannot mean 'there!', since the blow precedes the question *Πηνίκα;*): *Ec.*581 *ἀλλ' οὐ μέλλειν, ἀλλ' ἅπτεσθαι καὶ δὴ χρῆν ταῖς διανοίαις*: 786 *Ὄντως γὰρ οἴσεις;—Ναὶ μὰ Δία, καὶ δὴ μὲν οὖν τωδὶ ξυνάπτω τὼ τρίποδε*: E.*Or.*1108,1214: *Supp.*1070: Hdt.iv 102.1 *τῶν δὲ καὶ δὴ οἱ βασιλέες συνελθόντες ἐβουλεύοντο*: ix 66.3 *ὥρα καὶ δὴ φεύγοντας τοὺς Πέρσας*: vii 196 *ἐσβεβληκὼς ἦν καὶ δὴ τριταῖος ἐς Μηλιέας*: ix 6 *ὁ δὲ ἐπιὼν καὶ δὴ ἐν τῇ Βοιωτίῃ ἐλέγετο εἶναι*: 11.2 *εἶπαν ἐπ' ὅρκου καὶ δὴ δοκέειν εἶναι ἐν 'Ορεσθείῳ*: X.*Cyr.*iii 1.2 *λέγοντες ὅτι καὶ δὴ αὐτὸς ὁμοῦ*: iv 4.11 *ὁπόσοι δ' ἂν τὰ πολεμικὰ μὴ ἀποφέρωσιν ὅπλα, ἐπὶ τούτους ἡμεῖς καὶ δὴ στρατευσόμεθα*: vi 3.14 *ἀπαντᾷ δ' αὐτοῖς καὶ δὴ ἐντὸς τῶν σκοπῶν*: D.iv 13 *τὸν δὲ τρόπον τῆς παρασκευῆς . . . καὶ δὴ πειράσομαι λέγειν, δεηθεὶς ὑμῶν . . . τοσοῦτον* (perhaps to be classed as quasi-apodotic, in spite of the order): xx 65 *τὰς δὲ δωρειάς . . . καὶ δὴ λελυμένας*: Hdt.viii 94.3: ix 48.2: 89.1: 102.1: X.*Cyr.*ii 4.17: iii 3.43: *HG* iv 2.13.

(v) From καὶ δή denoting actual realization it is an easy transition to καὶ δή denoting imaginary realization, 'suppose that so-and-so happens'. As a general rule the clause introduced by καὶ δή is not linked to what follows by a connective. A.*Ch.*565 ἥξω . . . ἐφ' ἑρκείους πύλας . . . καὶ δὴ θυρωρῶν οὔτις ἂν φαιδρᾷ φρενὶ δέξαιτ' . . .· μενοῦμεν . . . : *Eu.*894 δέχου δὲ σύ. —Καὶ δὴ δέδεγμαι· τίς δέ μοι τιμὴ μένει; E.*Med.*386 καὶ δὴ τεθνᾶσι· τίς με δέξεται πόλις; *Hipp.*1007 καὶ δὴ τὸ σῶφρον τοὐμὸν οὐ πείθει σ'· ἴτω: *Hel.*1059 θάψαι τύραννον τῆσδε γῆς αἰτήσομαι.—Καὶ δὴ παρεῖκεν· εἶτα πῶς . . . ; ('Suppose he agrees. Then how . . . ?'): Ar.*V.*1224 καὶ δὴ γάρ εἰμ' ἐγὼ Κλέων ('Suppose I'm Cleon'): Philyll.*Fr.*3.1: E.*Med.*1107: Gorg.*Fr.*11a6 συνουσία δὲ τίνα τρόπον γένοιτ' ἂν . . . ; ἀλλὰ δὴ τοῦτο τῷ λόγῳ δυνατὸν γενέσθαι. καὶ δὴ τοίνυν σύνειμι ('Suppose, then . . .'): *Fr.*11a11 καὶ δὴ τοίνυν γενέσθω καὶ τὰ μὴ γενόμενα: D.xxix 40 τί μάλιστ' ἂν αὐτὸν εὔξαιτο λέγειν σκοπῶμεν. οὐχ ὅτι . . . ; καὶ δὴ λέγει (Well, suppose he says it'): X.*An.*v 7.9: D.xxxix 8. Add, possibly, Hdt.vii 186.2: but it is perhaps more natural to take καὶ δή as connective there.*

(vi) *In apodosi*, καὶ δή denotes the instant and dramatic following of the apodosis upon the protasis. There are three Homeric instances, all in the *Odyssey*: ε401 ἀλλ' ὅτε τόσσον ἀπῆν . . ., καὶ δὴ δοῦπον ἄκουσε: μ330: τ533. X.*An.*i 10.10 ἐν ᾧ δὲ ταῦτα ἐβουλεύοντο, καὶ δὴ βασιλεὺς . . . κατέστησεν ἀντίαν τὴν φάλαγγα: D.ii 13 κἂν ταῦτ' ἐθελήσηθ' ὡς προσήκει καὶ δὴ περαίνειν . . . : v 9 καὶ μόνον ἓν τοῦτ' εἰπὼν ἔτι καὶ δὴ περὶ ὧν παρελήλυθ' ἐρῶ ('I shall speak, without further ado'): xviii 276 ὡς, ἐὰν πρότερός τις εἴπῃ . . ., καὶ δὴ ταῦθ' οὕτως ἔχοντα ('that it is *ipso facto* so'): Hdt.ix 7 β1: D.xxiii 77: Arist.*MM* 1187b24: 1191b8: 1208a32.

Καὶ . . . δή

We have observed above that καὶ δή is seldom used in Attic as a connective, its place being taken by καὶ . . . δή or καὶ δὴ καί. These combinations signify that the addition made by καί is an important one. They thus differ slightly from καὶ . . . γε, which merely stresses the fact that an addition is made. The difference is, however, a barely perceptible one, and the choice between καὶ . . . γε and καὶ . . . δή is largely a matter of stylistic preference. Thus the dramatists prefer καὶ . . . γε. When they write καὶ . . . δή, it is difficult, in view of the freedom with which emphatic δή is used in drama, to say whether the two particles should be taken in combination. S.*Tr.*31 κἀφύσαμεν δὴ παῖδας: *Ph.*878 τοῦ κακοῦ δοκεῖ λήθη τις εἶναι κἀνάπαυλα δή, τέκνον. On the other hand, in prose writers, who are more sparing of emphatic δή, we can usually be fairly certain that the two particles, occurring in the same clause, and separated by only a short interval, are to be taken together, particularly where δή follows a type of word (e.g. substantive or verb) with which it is not normally associated in prose.

(1) *Καὶ* . . . δή joins sentences, clauses, and single words. Hence it may be preceded by a heavy or a light stop, or by no stop at all. (See, however, καὶ δὴ καί, *ad init.*)

(i) After a full stop. Pl.*Ap.*21A καὶ ἴστε δὴ οἷος ἦν Χαιρεφῶν: *Cra.*389C Καὶ περὶ τῶν ἄλλων δὴ ὀργάνων: D.xxi 135 καὶ τὸ δὴ σχετλιώτατον: Pl.*Tht.*156E,159C,187A: X.*HG*iii 1.9: *An.*i 8.23. (ii) After a colon. Pl.*Chrm.*167A καὶ ἔστιν δὴ τοῦτο τὸ σωφρονεῖν: 172B καὶ τοὺς ἄλλους δὴ κάλλιον ἐξετάσει. (iii) After a comma, or no stop at all. Pl.*Phd.*101B πρῶτον μὲν . . . ἔπειτα . . . εἶναι, καὶ τοῦτο δὴ τέρας εἶναι: 115D οἴεται . . ., καὶ ἐρωτᾷ δή: X.*Cyr.*ii 2.6 καὶ στήσας τὸν λοχαγὸν πρῶτον καὶ τάξας δὴ ἐπ' αὐτῷ . . .: D.xix 246 ἀλλὰ Μόλων ἠγωνίζετο καὶ εἰ δή τις ἄλλος . . .: xxi 20 καὶ πλοῦτον καὶ τἆλλα ὅσα δὴ πρόσεστι τούτῳ: Pl.*Ly.*215D: *Tht.*156E: *Euthphr.*9A. At the end of a catalogue: Pl.*Men.*87E ὑγίεια, φαμέν, καὶ ἰσχὺς καὶ κάλλος καὶ πλοῦτος δή: *Euthd.*302E ὅσα ἄν σοι ἐξῇ καὶ δοῦναι καὶ ἀποδόσθαι καὶ θῦσαι δὴ θεῷ: *Cri.*45E: X.*HG*vii 3.6.

In X.*Ages.*3.5 καὶ . . . δή is exceptionally used in the secondary sense of καὶ δὴ καί, marking a transition from general to particular: τοῖς τε ἄλλοις ἅπασι καὶ ἀνδρὶ δὴ στρατηγῷ.

(2) Occasionally καὶ in καὶ . . . δή means, not 'and', but 'even', 'actually', 'both'. (Cf. καὶ . . . γε (2).) Pl.*Men.*96D ὥστε καὶ θαυμάζω δή ('I am absolutely astonished'): *Phlb.*63A Εἰ δέ γε καί, καθάπερ . . ., καὶ νῦν δὴ ταὐτὰ λέγομεν: *Alc.I* 108D καὶ σὺ δὴ οὖν: *Ep.*362D τὰ γὰρ ἀναλώματα . . . καὶ σὺ δὴ

φῇς ἀγαθὸν εἶναι: *Lg.*645B οὕτω καὶ κακία δὴ καὶ ἀρετή: X. *Cyr.*i 5.6 ἐπεὶ δὲ προσείλοντο καὶ οὗτοι δὴ τοὺς τέτταρας: Pl.*La.* 190D Καὶ μάλα δὴ οὕτω δοκεῖ: *Phd.*76A Καὶ μάλα δὴ οὕτως ἔχει.*

When the particles are used with dramatic effect, 'lo there!', they are hardly ever separated. Hom.*h.Merc.*270 καί κεν δὴ μέγα θαῦμα μετ' ἀθανάτοισι γένοιτο.

In Pl.*R.*371A δή is connective and καί means also: Καὶ ἐμπόρων δὴ δεησόμεθα ('We shall need merchants, then, as well'): cf. *R.*516E, and *Chrm.*171A, *Phdr.*261D (see δή, V).

Καὶ δὴ καί

In its primary significance (1), καὶ δὴ καί does not differ essentially from καὶ . . .δή: though perhaps there is a certain tendency to use καὶ . . . δή after light stops, καὶ δὴ καί after heavy ones. From (1) is easily developed the secondary meaning (2), 'and in particular', the generality of the preceding clause being often marked by ἄλλος, ἀεί, etc. Both meanings are perhaps found close together in D.xlviii 14–15: οὗτος ὁ οἰκέτης σχεδόν τι ᾔδει τά τ' ἄλλα τοῦ Κόμωνος ἅπαντα καὶ δὴ καὶ τὸ ἀργύριον οὗ ἦν, τὸ ἔνδον κείμενον τῷ Κόμωνι. καὶ δὴ καὶ ἔλαθεν τὸν Κόμωνα . . . (in the first case *S* and *D*, in the second *A*, omit the second καί: see Rennie's *apparatus*). In both usages καὶ δὴ καί is common throughout Greek prose literature, though far commoner in some authors than in others. No writer uses it proportionately more than Herodotus, while Xenophon and Aristotle have it very seldom. Its avoidance in verse, apparently absolute, cannot be explained on metrical grounds alone.

(1) Democr.*Fr.*253 κίνδυνος κακῶς ἀκούειν καὶ δὴ καὶ παθεῖν τι: Hdt.ii 33 καὶ 'Ετέαρχος συνεβάλλετο εἶναι Νεῖλον, καὶ δὴ καὶ ὁ λόγος οὕτω αἱρέει: 115 ὁ δέ οἱ καὶ τὸ γένος κατέλεξε καὶ τῆς πάτρης εἶπε τὸ οὔνομα καὶ δὴ καὶ τὸν πλόον ἀπηγήσατο: 146 κατά περ 'Ηρακλέης . . . καὶ δὴ καὶ Διόνυσος . . . καὶ Πάν: Pl. *Chrm.*169B ἐπιστήμην ἐπιστήμης καὶ δὴ καὶ ἀνεπιστημοσύνης: *Ly.*218C συνεχωρείτην οὕτω τοῦτ' ἔχειν. καὶ δὴ καὶ αὐτὸς ἐγὼ πάνυ ἔχαιρον: *Phd.*111B τὰς δὲ ὥρας αὐτοῖς κρᾶσιν ἔχειν . . . καὶ δὴ καὶ θεῶν ἄλση . . . αὐτοῖς εἶναι: *R.*328B Λυσίαν τε αὐτόθι

κατελάβομεν καὶ Εὐθύδημον . . . καὶ δὴ καὶ Θρασύμαχον καὶ . . . καὶ . . .: *Phdr.*274D *τοῦτον ἀριθμόν τε καὶ λογισμὸν εὑρεῖν καὶ γεωμετρίαν καὶ ἀστρονομίαν, ἔτι δὲ πεττείας τε καὶ κυβείας, καὶ δὴ καὶ γράμματα*: *Sph.*265C *Ζῷα δὴ πάντα θνητὰ καὶ δὴ καὶ φυτά*: Hdt.iii 61 : Pl.*R.*419A.

Normally the addition introduced by *καὶ δὴ καί* is of the same nature as what precedes. The idea conveyed is one of climax, 'and actually', 'and in fact'. Occasionally, however, the particles mark a new departure, a sense normally expressed in Attic by *καὶ μήν, ἀλλὰ μήν, τοίνυν*. Pl.*Smp.*182A After explaining how certain persons have brought love into disrepute, Plato goes on to discuss the laws regarding love in various cities: *καὶ δὴ καὶ ὁ περὶ τὸν ἔρωτα νόμος . . .*: *Cra.*419B (after discussing the etymology of various words) *καὶ δὴ καὶ τὸ "ζημιῶδες" . . .*: *R.*371A *Πλειόνων δὴ γεωργῶν . . . Καὶ δὴ καὶ τῶν ἄλλων διακόνων . . .*: D.xlv 13. This transitional use of *καὶ δὴ καί* is particularly common in Plato's later work: *Ti.*79E,80D,90E,92C: *Criti.*111C, 114E, 115D.

(2) Hdt.i 1 *τῇ τε ἄλλῃ . . . καὶ δὴ καὶ ἐς Ἄργος*: 129 *κατεκερτόμεε, καὶ ἄλλα λέγων . . . καὶ δὴ καὶ εἴρετό μιν*: Pl.*La.*182D *πάντα ἐπίστασθαι ἀγαθὸν δοκεῖ εἶναι. καὶ δὴ καὶ τὸ ὁπλιτικὸν τοῦτο . . .*: *Prt.*345E *οὐδεὶς τῶν σοφῶν ἀνδρῶν ἡγεῖται . . . καὶ δὴ καὶ ὁ Σιμωνίδης . . .*: *Phd.*59D *ἀεὶ . . . καὶ δὴ καὶ τότε*: 113A *ὃς δι' ἐρήμων τε τόπων ῥεῖ ἄλλων καὶ δὴ καὶ ὑπὸ γῆν ῥέων . . .*: *Phdr.*260A "*Οὔτοι ἀπόβλητον ἔπος*" *εἶναι δεῖ, ὦ Φαῖδρε, ὃ ἂν εἴπωσι σοφοὶ . . . καὶ δὴ καὶ τὸ νῦν λεχθὲν οὐκ ἀφετέον*: *R.*328E *χαίρω διαλεγόμενος τοῖς σφόδρα πρεσβύταις . . . καὶ δὴ καὶ σοῦ ἡδέως ἂν πυθοίμην*: D.viii 26 *πάντες ὅσοι πώποτ' ἐκπεπλεύκασι . . . χρήματα λαμβάνουσιν . . . καὶ δὴ καὶ νῦν τῷ Διοπείθει . . . δῆλον ὅτι δώσουσι χρήματα*: Hdt.i 29: Pl.*Prt.*343B: *R.*357A: Lys.xiii 40: D.liv 14. Followed by a third *καί*: Pl.*Lg.*888D *παρά τε τῶν ἄλλων καὶ δὴ καὶ μάλιστα καὶ παρὰ τοῦ νομοθέτου.*

Far less frequently the transition is from the particular to the general. Pl.*R.*527C *Ἅ τε δὴ σὺ εἶπες . . . τὰ περὶ τὸν πόλεμον, καὶ δὴ καὶ πρὸς πάσας μαθήσεις*: *Euthphr.*16 *ὡς . . . καὶ* ('both') *τῆς πρὸς Μέλητον γραφῆς ἀπαλλάξομαι . . . καὶ δὴ καὶ τὸν ἄλλον βίον ἄμεινον βιωσοίμην*: *Plt.*268B *καὶ δὴ καὶ τῶν ἄλλων πέρι νομέων ὁ αὐτὸς τρόπος*: *Phlb.*62A,63E: *Lg.*686D,722A (cf. 890D).

Other uses of *καὶ δὴ καί* are less normal.

(3) Apodotic (as, more frequently, *καὶ δή*). This usage is perhaps more apparent than real. Some instances are textually uncertain, others can be explained as anacoluthon, or by the consideration that the second *καί* goes closely with the word that follows it. Hdt.vii 1.1 *ἐπεὶ δὲ ἡ ἀγγελίη ἀπίκετο . . . παρὰ βασιλέα Δαρεῖον . . . καὶ πρὶν μεγάλως κεχαραγμένον . . . καὶ δὴ καὶ τότε πολλῷ τε δεινότερα ἐποίεε* . . . (perhaps anacoluthon): 164.2 *ἀλλ' ἐπεὶ οἱ Ἕλληνες ἐπεκράτησαν τῇ ναυμαχίῃ καὶ Ξέρξης οἰχώκεε ἀπελαύνων, καὶ δὴ καὶ ἐκεῖνος ἀπίκετο* (*καὶ ἐκεῖνος* together: *καὶ δή C*): Pl.*Ap.*18A *ὥσπερ οὖν ἄν, εἰ . . ., καὶ δὴ καὶ νῦν τοῦτο ὑμῶν δέομαι* (*καὶ νῦν* together. *R.*420D is similar, but the sentence is so long that there is a sort of anacoluthon): X. *HG* vi 4.13 *πρῶτον μὲν πρὶν καὶ αἰσθέσθαι τὸ μετ' αὐτοῦ στράτευμα ὅτι ἡγοῖτο, καὶ δὴ καὶ οἱ ἱππεῖς συνεβεβλήκεσαν* (*καὶ δή CF*: *καὶ οἱ ἱππεῖς* together: 'straightway the cavalry also').

(4) In Hdt.vii 10β1 *καὶ δὴ καί* exceptionally introduces an hypothesis (cf. *καὶ δή*, 2.v): *καὶ δὴ καὶ συνήνεικε . . . ἑσσωθῆναι* (*καὶ συνήνεικε* together).

(5) Pl.*Ap.*26D is curious: *καὶ οὕτω . . . οἴει αὐτοὺς ἀπείρους γραμμάτων εἶναι ὥστε οὐκ εἰδέναι ὅτι τὰ Ἀναξαγόρου βιβλία . . . γέμει τούτων τῶν λόγων; καὶ δὴ καὶ οἱ νέοι ταῦτα παρ' ἐμοῦ μανθάνουσιν . . .*; This appears to be analogous to *καὶ δή* in surprised questions (cf. *καὶ δή*, 1.ii).

καὶ δὴ . . . καί: Pl.*Sph.*251C *τεθαυμακόσι, καὶ δή τι καὶ πάσσοφον οἰομένοις* (S.*Fr.*305: cf. *καί*, II.A.3).

καὶ δὴ οὖν καί: Pl.*R.*619B.

Μὲν δή: δὲ δή

In a *μέν* and *δέ* antithesis either of the opposed particles may be strengthened by *δή*, *δέ* the more frequently, owing to the tendency in Greek to put emphasis on the second of two coordinated clauses rather than on the first. Sometimes both clauses are stressed: E.*Supp.*457 *καὶ ταῦτα μὲν δὴ πρὸς τὰ σὰ ἐξηκόντισα. ἥκεις δὲ δὴ τί τῆσδε γῆς κεχρημένος*; Pl.*Tht.*170D *σοὶ μὲν δὴ . . . ἡμῖν δὲ δὴ . . .*: *R.*456C *Καὶ ὅτι μὲν δὴ δυνατά, διωμολόγηται;—Ναί.—Ὅτι δὲ δὴ βέλτιστα . . .*;

Μὲν δή

Hom.*Ω*599 *Υἱὸς μὲν δή τοι λέλυται . . . νῦν δὲ μνησώμεθα δόρπου*: Anacr.*Fr*.6.1 *μεὶς μὲν δὴ Ποσιδηϊὼν ἕστηκεν, νεφέλαι δ' ὕδει βρίθονται*: A.*Pr*.500 *τοιαῦτα μὲν δὴ ταῦτ'· ἔνερθε δὲ χθονὸς . . .*: S.*Ph*.350 *μάλιστα μὲν δὴ . . . ἔπειτα μέντοι . . .*: E.*Alc*.156: *Hel*.761: *Or*.19: Ar.*Ach*.523: Pl. *Smp*.216C *καὶ ὑπὸ μὲν δὴ τῶν αὐλημάτων . . . ἄλλα δὲ . . .*: *Ti*.83E *καὶ ταῦτα μὲν δὴ . . .* (without answering *δέ*): X.*An*.ii 6.28 *καὶ τὰ μὲν δὴ ἀφανῆ . . . ἃ δὲ πάντες ἴσασι . . .*: Hdt.ii 152: Pl.*Cri*.43B: *et saep.*

It is a peculiarity of Xenophon's to use *μὲν δή* in anaphora, where the absence of any real antithesis seems to make the emphasis unnecessary. *An*.vii 6.36 *πολλὰ μὲν δὴ πρὸ ὑμῶν ἀγρυπνήσαντα, πολλὰ δὲ σὺν ὑμῖν πονήσαντα*: *Cyr*.i 3.9 *οὕτω μὲν δὴ εὖ κλύσαι τὸ ἔκπωμα . . . οὕτω δὲ στήσαντα τὸ πρόσωπον . . . προσενεγκεῖν*: *Oec*.1.15. Cf. Gorg.*Fr*.6 *πολλὰ μὲν δὴ . . . πολλὰ δὲ . . . .*

Μὲν δή is frequently used by the historians as a formula of transition, the *μέν* clause often summing up the preceding section of the narrative. Hdt.vi 60–1 *ταῦτα μὲν δὴ οὕτω γίνεται. τότε δὲ τὸν Κλεομένεα . . .*: 94 *Ἀθηναίοισι μὲν δὴ πόλεμος συνῆπτο πρὸς Αἰγινήτας, ὁ δὲ Πέρσης . . .*: Th.i 46.1 *αἱ μὲν δὴ νῆες ἀφικνοῦνται ἐς τὴν Κέρκυραν, οἱ δὲ Κορίνθιοι . . .*: Hdt.vi 117.3: vii 105,121,124,201: Th.i 53.3: ii 4.8: iii 24.3: iv 39.3: X.*An*. vi 3.9.

It is not always easy to say in such cases whether we are to regard *δή* as a connective, or as strengthening *μέν*. On the one hand, there is the analogy of transitional *μὲν οὖν*, where (at any rate in Thucydides and subsequent writers) it can hardly be doubted that *οὖν* is connective: Th.i 55.2 *ἡ μὲν οὖν Κέρκυρα οὕτω περιγίγνεται*: iii 24.3 *οἱ μὲν οὖν Πελοποννήσιοι . . . .* On the other hand, the historians did not regard a connecting particle at the beginning of each sentence as absolutely indispensable in narrative, particularly where a demonstrative (which in itself constitutes a connexion) occurs early in the sentence. Hdt.vii 11.1 *Ἀρτάβανος μὲν ταῦτα ἔλεξε*: 41 *ἐξήλασε μὲν οὕτως*: 100.1 *ἐς μὲν τοσόνδε*: X.*An* vi 5.1 *τὴν μὲν νύκτα οὕτω διήγαγον.* It is possible that originally *δή* was regarded as strengthening *μέν*:

but that subsequently, as connective δή grew commoner, δή came to be regarded as having a connective force here also. The problems presented by transitional μὲν δή and transitional μὲν οὖν are precisely similar, and the two combinations must be considered together.

For δή strengthening affirmative and adversative μέν, see μὲν δή, *s.v.* μέν.

Δὲ δή

This combination is found both with and without a preceding μέν: and δέ may be definitely adversative, or almost purely connective. (For the distinction between δὲ δή and δ' οὖν, see δ' οὖν.) Thgn.53 πόλις μὲν . . . λαοὶ δὲ δὴ ἄλλοι: Archil.*Fr*.88.3 τίς . . . φρένας, ἧς τὸ πρὶν ἠρήρεισθα; νῦν δὲ δὴ . . . : E.*El*.37 λαμπροὶ γὰρ ἐς γένος γε, χρημάτων δὲ δὴ πένητες: *Or*.56 τὴν δὲ δὴ πολύστονον Ἑλένην . . . : Hom.Σ 20,290,291: Pl.*Chrm*.154C ἐμοὶ θαυμαστὸς ἐφάνη . . . οἱ δὲ δὴ ἄλλοι πάντες ἐρᾶν ἔμοιγε ἐδόκουν αὐτοῦ . . . πολλοὶ δὲ δὴ ἄλλοι ἐρασταὶ . . . εἵποντο: *Prt*.311D παρὰ δὲ δὴ Πρωταγόραν νῦν ἀφικόμενοι . . . (marking the case in point as distinct from other parallel cases): *Thg*.126C Λέγε δή μοι· ἐπεὶ δὲ δὴ τὰ πολιτικὰ βούλει σοφὸς γενέσθαι . . . ; Hdt.iii 129: vii 201: Pl.*La*.179D: *Grg*.496D: *et saep*.

In Euripides and Aristophanes, often in surprised, or emphatic and crucial questions. E.*Heracl*.963 Εἴργει δὲ δὴ τίς . . . νόμος; *Ph*.1277 Δράσω δὲ δὴ τί; ('And what shall I *do*?'): *Or*.101 Αἰδὼς δὲ δὴ τίς σ' ἐς Μυκηναίους ἔχει; Ar.*Av*.112 Πράγους δὲ δὴ τοῦ δεομένω δεῦρ' ἤλθετον; *Ra*.805 Κρινεῖ δὲ δὴ τίς ταῦτα; ('And who's the *judge* to be?'): E.*Ph*.709: *Or*.425: *El*.237, 974: *HF*206,1246: Ar.*Nu*.1178: *V*.858: *Pax* 227: *Av*.67,155: Pl.*Euthphr*.3E Ἔστιν δὲ δὴ σοὶ . . . τίς ἡ δίκη;

In Pl.*Phd*.80D δή is exceptionally attached to a duplicated δέ: Ἡ δὲ ψυχὴ ἄρα . . . αὕτη δὲ δὴ . . . ;

Τε δή (εἴτε δή, οὔτε δή)

In this combination δή is probably always emphatic (never connective: see (3) below), stressing either τε or the word or phrase which precedes τε: the latter distinction is one which cannot be pressed. The frequency of τε δή in Herodotus is a remarkable instance of an individual writer's preference for a particular particle or combination of particles. There are some sixty examples in him (Hammer, p. 36) as against three in Thucydides, perhaps none in Xenophon, and one in Demosthenes.[1] On the whole, τε δή is rarer than one would expect, particularly in verse. In Tragedy and Plato εἴτ' οὖν, οὔτ' οὖν are preferred to εἴτε δή, οὔτε δή.

(1) τε = 'both'. A.*Pr.*42 *Αἰεί τε δὴ νηλὴς σὺ καὶ θράσους πλέως* (where γε δή is usually read: *q.v.*): *Pers.*735 *Πῶς τε δὴ καὶ ποῖ τελευτᾶν*; Ar.*Nu.*61 *ὅπως νῷν ἐγένεθ' υἱὸς οὑτοσί, ἐμοί τε δὴ καὶ τῇ γυναικὶ τἀγαθῇ* (the explicitness of garrulity: 'us, my wife and me, that is'): Hdt.ii 121δ *τὸν δὲ πεισθῆναί τε δὴ καὶ καταμεῖναι*: Th.vii 13.2 *ἐπειδὴ παρὰ γνώμην ναυτικόν τε δὴ καὶ τἆλλα . . . ἀνθεστῶτα ὁρῶσιν*: Isoc.vi 3 *ἄλλως τε δὴ καὶ . . .* (xv 81: Hyp.*Lyc.*14): Hdt.ii 116: vi 49.2: 131.2 (τε δή picks up τε): Pl.*R.*330C,465C,561D: *Ti.*18B: *Phd.*59B: *Tht.*142C: *Phdr.*240E, 248B: *Plt.*307C: D.xix 139.

(2) τε = 'and'. (i) Joining words, phrases, or clauses. S.*Aj.*414 *πολὺν πολὺν δαρόν τε δὴ . . . χρόνον*: Hdt.i 77 *ἐπαγγείλας δὲ καὶ Λακεδαιμονίοισι . . . ἁλίσας τε δὴ τούτους*: iii 108 *ἀμύσσει τὰς μήτρας, αὐξόμενός τε δὴ . . . ἐσικνέεται*: 146 *οὔτε προσδεκομένους . . . δοκέοντάς τε δή*: iv 111 *ἐδόκεον δὲ αὐτὰς εἶναι ἄνδρας . . . μάχην τε δὴ πρὸς αὐτὰς ἐποιεῦντο*: Pl.*Ly.*206E *κατελάβομεν . . . τεθυκότας τε τοὺς παῖδας καὶ τὰ περὶ τὰ ἱερεῖα σχεδόν τι ἤδη πεποιημένα, ἀστραγαλίζοντάς τε δὴ καὶ κεκοσμημένους ἅπαντας*: *Lg.*967D: *Ti.*32B: *R.*563C (*om.F*).

(ii) Joining sentences. Th.iv 40.1 *παρὰ γνώμην τε δὴ μάλιστα τῶν κατὰ τὸν πόλεμον τοῦτο τοῖς Ἕλλησιν ἐγένετο*: 63.2 *τὸ ξύμπαν τε δὴ γνῶμεν*: Hdt.v 69.2: vi 56 (δὲ δή *RSV*: opening of a paragraph): viii 103: Pl.*Ti.*47C: Arist.*EN* 1156a17 (see Eucken, p. 21: perhaps δή has come in from 1156a14).

(3) Doubtful cases. Whereas in (1) and (2) above the senses 'and' and 'both' are respectively excluded (either absolutely or

[1] I am not certain how many Platonic examples there are. I only know of 17, but there may be more.

beyond all reasonable doubt), there remain a number of passages, almost all Herodotean, which might be assigned with some degree of plausibility to either class: here τε might mean either (i) 'and' or (ii) 'both', and on the latter supposition we might either take δή as giving the connexion, or assume asyndeton. But although δή would be a not unsuitable connective in these passages, and although the analogy of μὲν δή removes any difficulty in the view that δή in τε δή is sometimes emphatic, sometimes connective, the two particles seem to cohere closely, and the supposition of asyndeton is, I think, to be preferred.[1]

(i) In some passages, though καί or δέ follows, it does not appear to answer τε, and τε is probably connective. Hdt.iii 36 εἰ μὲν μεταμελήσῃ . . . ἢν δὲ μὴ μεταμέληται μηδὲ ποθῇ μιν, τότε καταχρᾶσθαι. ἐπόθησέ τε δὴ ὁ Καμβύσης τὸν Κροῖσον . . . καὶ οἱ θεράποντες μαθόντες τοῦτο ἐπηγγέλλοντο αὐτῷ ὡς περιείη ('and Cambyses did in fact miss Croesus'): ii 32,163: v 77.2: vi 39.2: viii 42: ix 26.5.

(ii) In others, a closer connexion between τε and καί is indicated. (*a*) τε δὴ . . . καὶ δὴ καί. Hdt.i 214 ἥ τε δὴ πολλὴ τῆς Περσικῆς στρατιῆς αὐτοῦ ταύτῃ διεφθάρη καὶ δὴ καὶ αὐτὸς Κῦρος τελευτᾷ: vi 49.1 οἵ τε δὴ ἄλλοι . . . καὶ δὴ καὶ Αἰγινῆται: iii 61: iv 118: viii 105.2. (*b*) τε δὴ . . . καὶ . . . , meaning 'when . . . then', 'while . . . meantime'. Herodotus allows asyndeton in analogous cases of simple τε . . . καί (iv 181: vi 41.1: 134.2: viii 56: cf. τε, I.7): this tells for the assumption of asyndeton here, and against regarding δή as connective. Hdt.iii 108 πέλας τε δὴ ὁ τόκος ἐστὶ καὶ τὸ παράπαν λείπεται αὐτέων ὑγιὲς οὐδέν: vi 49.1 οὗτοί τε δὴ παρεσκευάζοντο ταῦτα καὶ . . . : iii 76: vii 23.3: 217.1.

In the following I should, with greater or less confidence, render τε 'both': Hdt.ii 154: vi 89: ix 22.2 (τε δή only in *RV*): in the following, 'and': Hdt. i 214 χρόνον τε δὴ . . . (though just below τε δή seems to be 'both': *v. supr.*): ii 46: Pl.*Criti.*117A.

(4) εἴτε δή, οὔτε δή.

εἴτε δή. Hdt.i 19 εἴτε δὴ . . . εἴτε καί (i 86: iii 33: iv 147: ix 5.2): i 191 εἴτε δὴ ὦν . . . εἴτε καί: iii 24 εἴτε δὴ . . . εἴτε ἄλλως

[1] It must, however, be admitted that in Pl.*R.*465D it is very tempting to take δή as connective.

κως: Pl.*Ap.*40C καὶ εἴτε δὴ . . . εἰ δ' αὖ: *R.*493D εἴτ' ἐν γραφικῇ εἴτ' ἐν μουσικῇ εἴτε δὴ ἐν πολιτικῇ.

οὔτε δή. Pl.*Ti.*62D οὔτε δὴ μέσος οὔτε . . . : *Chrm.*171C Οὐδέ γ' ἄλλος οὐδεὶς . . . οὔτε δὴ ὁ σώφρων: *Phlb.*58B οὔτε σοὶ οὔτε δὴ ἐκείνῳ.

(5) τε δὴ ὦν. Hdt.i82,124: iii62. εἴτε δὴ ὦν. Hdt.i191.

τε . . . δή. Pl.*Lg.*961B τοῖς τε ἄλλοις δὴ καὶ μάλιστ' αὐτῷ τῷ ἀποκριθέντι.

Δαί

Δαί may perhaps stand in the same relation to δή as ναί to νή (Brugmann, p. 628). It is thrice found in MSS. of Homer,[1] and is recognized by Aristarchus: α225 τίς δαίς, τίς δαὶ ὅμιλος ὅδ' ἔπλετο; ω299 τίς πόθεν εἷς ἀνδρῶν; πόθι τοι πόλις ἠδὲ τοκῆες; ποῦ δαὶ νηῦς ἕστηκε θοὴ . . .; K408 (see (1) below). Cf. Apollonius Dyscolus, *Synt.* 78.2. But it is nowhere read unanimously by all MSS.: and Hartung banishes it from Homer, confining it to the Attic dialect. That it is a colloquial particle is clear from its frequency in Aristophanes and its complete absence from formal prose. In Aeschylus and Sophocles it is found only in *Pr.*933, *Ch.*900, *Ant.*318 (see Tucker and Jebb on the last two). There may be some justification for emending these passages, but the eight Euripidean examples present a solid front against attack (though the MSS. often vary; see D. L. Page on *Med.*339): *Cyc.*450: *Med.*1012: *Hel.*1246: *IA* 1443,1447: *El.* 244,1116: *Ion* 275. In this case, as in others, Euripides draws his expressions from everyday speech. The frequency of δαί in Plato is uncertain, as the MSS. often vary. Kühner holds that for transitional τί δαί; in Plato, τί δέ; should everywhere be read (e.g. *Phd.*71D).

δαί always follows an interrogative, τί; τίς; πῶς; ποῦ; The particle may be either emphatic or connective, and the assignment of some passages is doubtful. Cf. δή, δῆτα. The elliptical

[1] See Leaf on K 408.

forms (e.g. *τί δαί*; 'What?', 'Why?': 'Well, what (why)?') are common, and Kühner will allow no others in Plato.

(1) Emphatic, in a lively or surprised question. Hom.*α* 225 (*L*[4] Ar.: *δέ cett.*): *ω* 299 (the MSS. vary): (in **K** 408, where a connective seems required, *δ' αἰ* is probably right): Pherecr.*Fr.* 93.1 *τί δαί; τί σαυτὸν ἀποτίνειν τῷδ' ἀξιοῖς;* Ar.*Pax* 1224 ***Τί δαὶ*** *δεκάμνῳ τῷδε θώρηκος κύτει . . . χρήσομαι* (the first words of a character who has just entered: 'What ever shall I do with . . .?'): *Eq.* 28 *δέδοικά τουτονὶ τὸν οἰωνόν;*—***Τί δαί;***—*'Οτιὴ . . .* (*Eq.* 493: *Nu.* 491,1275: *Av.* 225): Pl.*Phd.* 61C ***Τί δαί;*** *ἦ δ' ὅς, οὐ φιλόσοφος* ***Εὔηνος;*** *Grg.* 461D ***Τί δαί;*** *οὐκ ἐξέσται μοι λέγειν . . .;* 477B.

(2) Connective, in a question motivated by what precedes. E.*Med* 1012 ***Ἤγγειλας*** *οἷ' ἤγγειλας· οὐ σὲ μέμφομαι.*—***Τί δαὶ*** *κατηφεῖς ὄμμα καὶ δακρυρροεῖς; El.* 244 'What is dearer to me than father and brother?'—***Φεῦ*** *φεῦ· τί δαὶ σὺ σῷ κασιγνήτῳ, δοκεῖς;* ('Well, and what do *you* mean to your *brother*?'): Ar.*Nu.* 1266 *ὦ Παλλὰς ὥς μ' ἀπώλεσας.*—***Τί δαί*** *σε Τληπόλεμός ποτ' εἴργασται κακόν;* ('Why, what has T. been doing to you?'): E.*Med.* 339 (Housman). Especially:—(i) After the rejection of an idea: 'Well, what . . .?'. E.*Hel* 1246 ***Οὐχ*** *ὧδε ναύτας ὀλομένους τυμβεύομεν;*—***Πῶς δαί;*** ('Well, how *do* you bury them?'): Ar.*Ach.* 764 'I have no garlic'.—***Τί δαὶ*** *φέρεις; Pax* 925 ***Τί δαὶ*** *δοκεῖ; βούλεσθε . . .; Eq.* 351 ***Τί δαὶ*** *σὺ πίνων τὴν πόλιν πεποίηκας . . .;* (the preceding speech implies that a water-drinking politician is no good): *Av.* 64 *Ἀλλ' οὐκ ἐσμὲν ἀνθρώπω.*—***Τί δαί;*** ('Well, what *are* you?'): E.*Cyc.* 450: Ar.*V.* 1212: *Av.* 832,1451,1640: *Nu.* 656.

(ii) Transitional, proceeding to a new point. E.*El.* 1116 Clytaemnestra has defended her killing of Agamemnon and her keeping of Orestes in banishment. ***Ηλ.*** ***Τί δαὶ*** *πόσιν σὸν ἄγριον εἰς ἡμᾶς ἔχεις;* ('Well, why do you . . .?'): *Ion* 275 ***Εἶεν·*** *τί δαὶ τόδ';* ('Now what of this?'): Ar.*Ach.* 612 (after discussing Marilades' fate) *τί δαὶ Δράκυλλος . . .;* 802–3 ***Τρώγοις*** *ἂν ἐρεβίνθους;*—***Κοῒ*** *κοΐ κοΐ.*—***Τί δαί;*** *φιβάλεως ἰσχάδας;*—***Κοῒ*** *κοΐ.*—***Τί*** *δαὶ σύ; τρώγοις ἄν; Th.* 140 *τί λήκυθος καὶ στρόφιον; ὡς οὐ ξύμφορον. τίς δαὶ κατόπτρου καὶ ξίφους κοινωνία;* ('Then again'): *Eq.* 171: *Pax* 700: *Av.* 136,826,1153,1615: Pl.*Phd.* 71D ***'Εξ οὖν*** *τοῦ ζῶντος . . . .*—***Τί δαί,*** *ἦ δ' ὅς, ἐκ τοῦ τεθνεῶτος;*

τί δαὶ δή; is occasionally found in Plato: *Cri.*49C Τί δαὶ δή; κακουργεῖν δεῖ . . . ; *Sph.*234C: *Cra.*407C: *Tht.*204B.

In Ar.*Lys.*372 δ' αὖ should perhaps be read. For a possible converse corruption, cf. E.*Med.*339. In Ar.*Ach.*912 Bentley's δέ (confirmed by the papyrus) is necessary for metre.

Δῆθεν

Δῆθεν is usually thought to be formed from δή and the suffix -θεν. But Wackernagel (*Ztschr. f. vergl. Sprachf.* xxxiii 23) thinks that it has originally nothing to do with δή, but is a 'Nebenform' of Homeric δηθά, subsequently associated with δή, and assimilated to it in function: 'schon lange' becomes 'augenscheinlich'.[1] The form δῆθε (cf. δήπουθε) only occurs in E.*El.*268 (conjectured in Eup.*Fr.*7 Demiańczuk, *Supp. Com.*). δῆθεν is never found in Homer, Hesiod, or Lyric. It is occasionally met with in tragedy (though not in comedy), and is not infrequent in Ionic prose. Apart from Thucydides, who uses it five times, it is almost entirely absent from Attic prose. It never, I think, occurs in the orators: never in Aristotle (but see (6), *ad fin.*): and only once in Plato and once in Xenophon.

Whether or not δῆθεν is etymologically derived from δή, it resembles it in function. But the nuance of pretence or unreality, and the ironical colour, which, though often present in δή, do not dominate that particle, are in δῆθεν but rarely absent (more rarely, I think, than some authorities recognize). Suidas says: προσποίησιν ἀληθείας ἔχει, δύναμιν δὲ ψεύδους.

(1) After final conjunctions, implying, like δή, that the desired object is undesirable or contemptible, or not genuinely desired.

[1] Some old lexicographers explain δῆθεν as = ἐντεῦθεν, ἔκ τινος τόπου. Navarre accepts this as the original sense, 'depuis lors'. But *Anacreont.*i 16, which he quotes, is from an Anacreontic of late date: καὶ δῆθεν ἄχρι καὶ νῦν ἔρωτος οὐ πέπαυμαι. No doubt the lexicographers were misled by -θεν. It is possible, as Hartung suggests (i 317), that when later writers occasionally used δῆθεν for '*inde ab eo tempore*', they were artificially following this mistaken etymology.

A.*Pr.*204 θέλοντες ἐκβαλεῖν ἕδρας Κρόνον, ὡς Ζεὺς ἀνάσσοι δῆθεν: E.*El.*268 Ὡς δῆθε παῖδας μὴ τέκοις ποινατόρας; Hp.*Art.*53 'The Amazons are said to dislocate the joints of their male children, ὡς δῆθεν χωλὰ γίνοιτο': Aen.Tact.23.10 ἵνα δῆθεν προαγάγοιεν τοὺς πολεμίους ('ostensibly that').

(2) With causal conjunctions, implying that the supposed cause is untrue as a fact, or inadequate as a cause. E.*Ion* 831 καινὸν δὲ τοὔνομ' ἀνὰ χρόνον πεπλασμένον Ἴων, ἰόντι δῆθεν ὅτι συνήντετο: X.*Cyr.*iv 6.3 μέγα φρονῶν ὅτι δῆθεν τῆς βασιλέως θυγατρὸς ὀψοίμην τὸν ἐμὸν υἱὸν γαμέτην (but he was killed, and never married the girl).

(3) With ὡς and participle (or, very occasionally, substantive or prepositional phrase) implying that a supposition is mistaken. E.*Or.*1320 ὡς δῆθεν οὐκ εἰδυῖα τἀξειργασμένα: *HF* 949 κἄθεινε, κέντρον δῆθεν ὡς ἔχων, χερί: Hdt.i 73 φέροντες ὡς ἄγρην δῆθεν: iii 74 ὡς πιστοτάτου δῆθεν ἐόντος: ix 66.3 ὡς ἐς μάχην ἦγε δῆθεν τὸν στρατόν: Hp.*Acut.*15 ὡς τοιούτῳ δῆθεν ἐόντι: Hdt.vi 1.1: 39.1: viii 5.1. (In Hdt.ix 99.3 the ὡς clause contains a true statement, but one which is not the real reason for the action described in the main clause: τὰς διόδους . . . προστάσσουσι τοῖσι Μιλησίοισι φυλάσσειν ὡς ἐπισταμένοισι δῆθεν μάλιστα τὴν χώρην· ἐποίευν δὲ τούτου εἵνεκεν, ἵνα ἐκτὸς τοῦ στρατοπέδου ἔωσι ('ostensibly because').)

ἅτε . . . δῆθεν. Hdt.ix 80.3 οἳ τὸν χρυσὸν ἅτε ἐόντα χαλκὸν δῆθεν παρὰ τῶν εἱλωτέων ὠνέοντο ('as if it had been bronze').

(4) In general, conveying that the words used are untrue. E.*Ion* 656 τῆς δ' Ἀθηναίων χθονὸς ἄξω θεατὴν δῆθεν, ὡς οὐκ ὄντ' ἐμόν: Hdt.i 59 ὡς ἐκπεφευγὼς τοὺς ἐχθρούς, οἵ μιν . . . ἠθέλησαν ἀπολέσαι δῆθεν ('as he said'): vii 211.3 ἀλέες φεύγεσκον δῆθεν ('pretended to flee'): Th.i 92 οὐδὲ γὰρ ἐπὶ κωλύμῃ, ἀλλὰ γνώμης παραινέσει δῆθεν τῷ κοινῷ ἐπρεσβεύσαντο: iii 68.1 διότι τόν τε ἄλλον χρόνον ἠξίουν δῆθεν αὐτοὺς κατὰ τὰς . . . σπονδὰς ἡσυχάζειν (Thucydides implies 'dass er an der Aufrichtigkeit der hier erwähnten Ermahnungen zweifelt', Steup): 111.1 ἅμα ξυλλέγοντες ἐφ' ἃ ἐξῆλθον δῆθεν (pretended object).

(5) Expressing, not incredulity, but contempt or indignation: 'forsooth'. Hdt.vi 138.3 καί σφι βουλευομένοισι δεινόν τι ἐσέδυνε, εἰ δὴ διαγινώσκοιεν σφίσι τε βοηθέειν οἱ παῖδες . . ., τί δὴ ἀνδρωθέντες δῆθεν ποιήσουσι: viii 6.2 'The Persians did not make

a frontal attack, lest the Greeks should escape under cover of darkness. καὶ ἔμελλον δῆθεν ἐκφεύξεσθαι, ἔδει δὲ μηδὲ πυρφόρον τῷ ἐκείνων λόγῳ ἐκφυγόντα περιγενέσθαι': Hp.*Fract.*1 οἱ δὲ ἰητροὶ σοφιζόμενοι δῆθεν ἐστὶν ἄρα ἐφ' οἷς ἁμαρτάνουσιν: *Art.*48 καὶ μὴν αἱ μεγάλαι σικύαι προσβαλλόμεναι ἀνασπάσιος εἵνεκα δῆθεν (implies that the treatment is a foolish one).

(6) δῆθεν is seldom devoid of all trace of scepticism, irony, or indignation. Hdt.iii 136 τοὺς Πέρσας εἶρξε ὡς κατασκόπους δῆθεν ἐόντας (the men *were* spies: but δῆθεν may convey the indignation felt by the arrester): Hp.*Art.*14 οἵ τε ἰητροὶ προθυμέονται δῆθεν ὀρθῶς ἰῆσθαι (for δήπου: 'are presumably anxious'): 58 τί γὰρ δῆθεν δεῖ περὶ τῶν ἤδη ἀνηκέστων γεγονότων ἔτι προσξυνιέναι; Pl.*Plt.*297C Πῶς τί τοῦτ' εἴρηκας; οὐδὲ γὰρ ἄρτι δῆθεν κατέμαθον τὸ περὶ τῶν μιμημάτων ('I suppose', Campbell, who says that the non-ironical use of δῆθεν is commoner in later Greek (Schol. Ap.Rhod.: τὸ δῆθεν ποτὲ μὲν πληρωματικόν, ποτὲ δὲ ἀντὶ τοῦ δηλαδὴ ἢ ὡς δή): ῥηθέν, Badham).

In E.*Fr.*900.1 Nauck's δῆθεν is by no means certain. In Arist. *Pol.*1264b9 Goettling conjectures ᾗ που δῆθεν for ἤπουθεν δή.

(7) Position. δῆθεν, like most particles of nuance, normally, at any rate, follows the word it qualifies. Whether it can ever precede that word is a disputed question, answered (in the main) negatively by Jebb on S.*Tr.*382. But see A.*Pr.*986 'Εκερτόμησας δῆθεν ὥστε παῖδά με: S.*Tr.*382 'Ιόλη 'καλεῖτο, τῆς ἐκεῖνος οὐδαμὰ βλαστὰς ἐφώνει δῆθεν οὐδὲν ἱστορῶν (here δῆθεν certainly seems to go with οὐδὲν ἱστορῶν, and many editors place a comma after ἐφώνει): E.*Or.*1119 Ἔσιμεν ἐς οἴκους δῆθεν ὡς θανούμενοι (in this passage, which Jebb does not cite, δῆθεν clearly goes closely with ὡς θανούμενοι): *Rh.*719 πολλὰ τὰν ἑστίαν Ἀτρειδᾶν κακῶς ἔβαζε δῆθεν ἐχθρὸς ὢν στρατηλάταις: Th.i 127.1 τοῦτο δὴ τὸ ἄγος οἱ Λακεδαιμόνιοι ἐκέλευον ἐλαύνειν δῆθεν τοῖς θεοῖς πρῶτον τιμωροῦντες, εἰδότες δὲ Περικλέα ... ('in seltener Weise vorangestellt', Steup, comparing vi 10.5 ἡμεῖς δὲ 'Εγεσταίοις δὴ οὖσι ξυμμάχοις ... βοηθοῦμεν). Th.iv 99 can be taken in different ways: see Jebb, *loc. cit.*

Δήπου

This combination is already found in Homer, but it is probable that the words do not coalesce as closely in him as in later writers. *Φ*583 *ἦ δή που μάλ' ἔολπας ἐνὶ φρεσί* ('in truth, methinks'): *Ω*736 *τις Ἀχαιῶν . . . ᾧ δή που ἀδελφεὸν ἔκτανεν Ἕκτωρ* ('even one, I ween, whose . . .'): *Π*746: *δ*739. For *δή κου* in Herodotus, see *που*.

δήπου is rare in tragedy, frequent in comedy and prose (though in Thucydides only in viii 87.4: 87.5). It is found in subordinate, as well as in independent, clauses (e.g. Pl.*Euthd.*276A: *R.*345D: *Chrm.*161D). Strictly speaking, the certainty of *δή* is toned down by the doubtfulness of *που*. But often the doubt is only assumed, *μετ' εἰρωνείας* (not always 'ironically' in the modern sense of the word), 'presumably', 'I believe', 'I imagine' being virtually equivalent to 'of course'.

(1) In statements. A.*Pr.*1064 *οὐ γὰρ δή που τοῦτό γε τλητὸν παρέσυρας ἔπος*: S.*OT*1042 *Τῶν Λαΐου δήπου τις ὠνομάζετο* (where the hesitation is, ostensibly, genuine): Ar.*Nu.*369 *Ἀλλὰ τίς ὕει; . . .—Αὗται δήπου* ('*They* do, of course'): *Ec.*661 *κλέπτων δήπου 'στ' ἐπίδηλος*: *Pl.*497 *κᾆτα ποιήσει πάντας χρηστοὺς καὶ πλουτοῦντας δήπου τά τε θεῖα σέβοντας*: 523 *Ἀλλ' οὐδ' ἔσται . . . κατὰ τὸν λόγον ὃν σὺ λέγεις δήπου*: Th.viii 87.4 *ἐμοὶ μέντοι δοκεῖ . . ., ἐπεί, εἴ γε ἐβουλήθη, διαπολεμῆσαι ἂν ἐπιφανεὶς δήπου οὐκ ἐνδοιαστῶς*: Pl.*Lg.*647D *ἄπειρος δὲ δήπου . . . ὢν τῶν τοιούτων ἀγώνων ὁστισοῦν οὐδ' ἂν ἥμισυς ἑαυτοῦ γένοιτο πρὸς ἀρετήν*: X.*HG* vii 3.11 *πρὸς δὲ τούτοις ἀναμνήσθητε ὅτι καὶ ἐψηφίσασθε δήπου τοὺς φυγάδας ἀγωγίμους εἶναι*: *Smp.*5.5 *Πάντως δήπου, ἔφη* (in answer): Isoc.iv 63 *εἰ δὲ δεῖ . . . οὐ δήπου πάτριόν ἐστιν ἡγεῖσθαι*: D.ii 25 *ἴστε γὰρ δήπου τοῦτο.*

(2) In questions. S.*Tr.*418 *Τὴν αἰχμάλωτον . . . κάτοισθα δήπου;* ('You know, I suppose . . .?'): Ar.*Av.*179 *Οὐχ οὗτος οὖν δήπου 'στὶν ὀρνίθων πόλος; Pl.*261 *Οὔκουν πάλαι δήπου λέγω; Eq.*900.

(3) Particularly *οὐ δήπου* in surprised or incredulous questions. S.*Ant.*381 *οὐ δή που σέ γ' . . . ἄγουσι . . .;* Ar.*Av.*269 *τίς ποτ' (ὄρνις) ἐστίν; οὐ δήπου ταὼς;* ('It can't be a peacock, can it?'): *Ec.*327 *Τίς ἔστιν; οὐ δήπου Βλέπυρος ὁ γειτνιῶν;* ('Not

neighbour Blepyrus?'): Pl.*Smp.*194B *Τί δέ, ὦ Σώκρατες; τὸν Ἀγάθωνα φάναι, οὐ δήπου με οὕτω θεάτρου μεστὸν ἡγῇ . . .*; ('Surely you don't think me so stage-struck . . .?'): X.*Mem.*iv 2.11 *Οὐ δήπου, ὦ Εὐθύδημε, ταύτης τῆς ἀρετῆς ἐφιέσαι . . .*;

(4) Certain common Platonic uses deserve notice. (I am indebted here to Dr. Chapman's notes.)

(i) In replies, particularly:—(*a*) Selecting one of two alternatives offered. *Euthd.*300A: *Tht.*159B, 163E. (*b*) In formulae of assent. *Πάντως δήπου*: *Euthd.*285E: *id. saep.* (rarely *Μάλα δήπου*: *Euthd.*299C. *Μάλιστα δήπου*: *Euthd.*284E). (*c*) *Οὐ δήπου*: *Men.*78D: *R.*501E.

(ii) *οὐ γὰρ δήπου . . . γε*, supporting a positive statement by an appeal to the impossibility of its opposite. *Grg.*459A: *Chrm.*171B: *Smp.*187B.

(5) Position. While *δήπου*, like all other particles, tends to an early place in the sentence, postponement is by no means rare, and *δήπου* is often found in the apodosis: Pl.*Grg.*468D, 496D, 510B, 514C. Last word in sentence: D.xviii 117.

(6) *δήπου* combined with other particles. Few of the combinations are conspicuous by their occurrence or non-occurrence. But it is perhaps not entirely fortuitous that, while *γὰρ δήπου* is exceedingly common in Plato, *δὲ δήπου* is far less frequent (e.g. *Ly.*214A: *R.*433A, 439A: *Lg.*647D, 766D), while *καὶ δήπου* (or *καὶ δή που*) is exceedingly rare: *Sph.*251B: *Lg.* 662C (*καὶ δήπου καί*), 722D: for *καὶ δή κου* in Herodotus, see *που*.

γε δήπου. Ar.*Pax* 350 *οὐδὲ τοὺς τρόπους γε δήπου σκληρόν*: Pl.*Grg.*459B *Ὁ δὲ μὴ ἰατρός γε δήπου . . .*: *Phd.*94A *Οὐδέ γε δήπου. οὐ δήπου γε*: D.xx 167: lvii 65. *οὖν* (connective) *δήπου*: Pl. *Lg.*801C. In Lys. xxix 4 read, I think, *οὔκουν δήπου* (*C.R.* xliv (1930), 214). *μὲν οὖν δήπου*: Pl.*Prt.*309D *σοφῷ. . . .—Σοφωτάτῳ μὲν οὖν δήπου τῶν γε νῦν. τε δήπου*: Pl.*Prm.*157D.

Δήπουθεν

Here *δήπου* is usually supposed to be reinforced by the suffix -*θεν*, as in *δῆθεν*. But Wackernagel (*op. cit.*, see p. 264) thinks that *δήπου*–*δήπουθεν* is a mere analogue of *δή*–*δῆθεν*. Ar.*Av.*187 *Ἐν μέσῳ δήπουθεν ἀήρ ἐστι γῆς*: *Pl.*140 *οὐκ ἔσθ' ὅπως ὠνήσεται δήπουθεν*: *V.*296: *Pax* 1019: Antiph.*Fr.*207.9: Lys.vi 36 (*οὐ* δήπουθεν, in an answer to a rhetorical question): Pl.*Ion* 534A: *Phlb.*62E: X.*Cyr.*iv 3.20 (some MSS. only): Is.viii 33: xi 13: D.xiv 34: xviii 127. δήπουθε: Bato, *Fr.*7.3 (cf. δῆθε).

Δῆτα

Δῆτα is usually described as a 'combination of δή and the suffix -τα', or as a 'lengthened form of δή'. (Wackernagel (*op. cit.*) regards the etymology as uncertain.) Its uses are analogous to those of δή, though they are more restricted, and are developed on individual lines.

δῆτα is not found in epic or lyric poets. It is very rare in Herodotus, and not common in the orators, but frequent in Plato, and exceedingly frequent in drama. There are only 9 examples in Demosthenes (Preuss): Dr. Chapman cites 92 from Plato: there are 28 in Aeschylus (Dindorf), and I have collected 89 in Sophocles, and 117 in Euripides: Todd cites over 230 from Aristophanes. δῆτα is a lively particle, far more at home in question and answer than elsewhere.

I. In questions. Δῆτα in questions always has a logical connective force, analogous to that of δή or οὖν. Moreover, as we shall see, this connective force is almost wholly confined to questions: a restriction which, though it may appear curious, finds a parallel in the early history of οὖν. δῆτα denotes that the question springs out of something which another person (or, more rarely, the speaker himself) has just said. In passages such as the following the logical connexion is vital, and could not be left unexpressed. A.*Pr.*627 Ἀλλ' οὐ μεγαίρω τοῦδέ σοι δωρήματος.—Τί δῆτα μέλλεις μὴ οὐ γεγωνίσκειν τὸ πᾶν; Ar.*Nu.* 180 Strepsiades, after hearing of a Socratic *tour de force*: Τί δῆτ' ἐκεῖνον τὸν Θαλῆν θαυμάζομεν; 904 Φέρε γὰρ ποῦ 'στιν (δίκη);—Παρὰ τοῖσι θεοῖς.—Πῶς δῆτα δίκης οὔσης ὁ Ζεὺς οὐκ ἀπόλωλεν . . .;

Sometimes δῆτα expresses *post hoc* rather than *propter hoc* (cf. δή and οὖν). E.*Ba.*925 νῦν δ' ὁρᾷς ἃ χρή σ' ὁρᾶν.—Τί φαίνομαι δῆτ'; (doubt of his eyesight having been removed, Pentheus proceeds to ask for information about his appearance:

'Well now, what do I *look* like?'): 1273–7 Cadmus' three questions to Agave: *Ἐς ποῖον ἦλθες οἶκον ...; ... Τίς οὖν ἐν οἴκοις παῖς ἐγένετο σῷ πόσει; ... Τίνος πρόσωπον δῆτ' ἐν ἀγκάλαις ἔχεις;*

Although in some places it would be possible to take *δῆτα* in questions as merely emphatic, a connective sense is nowhere inappropriate, and is, I think, everywhere intended.

(1) *δῆτα* in questions most frequently follows an interrogative pronoun or pronominal adverb (*πῶς*, *τί*, etc.) at the opening of a speech. This use is extremely common in tragedy and comedy.

A.*Ag*.1211 *Πῶς δῆτ' ἄνατος ἦσθα Λοξίου κότῳ;* S.*Aj*.42 *Τί δῆτα ποίμναις τήνδ' ἐπεμπίπτει βάσιν;* Ar.*Nu*.193 *Τί δῆθ' ὁ πρωκτὸς ἐς τὸν οὐρανὸν βλέπει;* A.*Ag*.622: S.*Aj*.537.540,879 (lyr.): E.*Supp*.937,946: Ar.*Nu*.1087,1098,1102,1273,1430,1456. Following an apostrophe. S.*OC*1734 (lyr.) *Αἰαῖ, δυστάλαινα, ποῦ δῆτ' ...;* E.*Supp*.734 *Ὦ Ζεῦ, τί δῆτα ...;* Elliptical. Ar.*Nu*.1105 *Τί δῆτα;* (1290: *Eq*.439): E.*IT* 1042 *Ποῖ δῆτα;*

Less frequent in prose. Hdt.iii 6 *Κοῦ δῆτα, εἴποι τις ἄν, ταῦτα ἀναισιμοῦται;* Pl.*Phdr*.236E *ὡς εὖ ἀνηῦρες τὴν ἀνάγκην ... ποιεῖν ὃ ἂν κελεύῃς.—Τί δῆτα ἔχων στρέφῃ;* *Grg*.469B *Πῶς δῆτα, ὦ Σώκρατες;* (one of the passages in which the connective sense is least apparent): *Sph*.218E,240A: *Plt*.279A,B: *Phlb*.64C: *Lg*. 753A: *Hp.Ma*.283D: *Mi*.313C: X.*Smp*.4.22: *Lac*.2.8: *Vect*.4. 28. Elliptical: Pl.*Ap*.25D: *Lg*.789A,830A.

(2) Less frequently, but still commonly, *τί δῆτα; πῶς δῆτα;* etc., are used in the middle of a speech. A.*Ag*.1264 *τί δῆτ' ἐμαυτῆς καταγέλωτ' ἔχω τάδε ...;* *Ch*.1075 (anap.) *νῦν δ' αὖ τρίτος ἦλθέ ποθεν σωτήρ, ἢ μόρον εἴπω; ποῖ δῆτα κρανεῖ ...;* E.*Alc*.689 *πατρὸς γὰρ ταῦτ' ἐδεξάμην πάρα. τί δῆτά σ' ἠδίκηκα;* *Hel*.56 *τί δῆτ' ἔτι ζῶ;* S.*Ph*.428,1060: E.*Alc*.960: *Heracl*.162, 433: *Hec*.313,828: *HF*1301: *Ion*253: *Tr*.505,1012: *Or*.275: *Ph*.1615: *Hel*.293,753: Ar.*Nu*.79,1423: Thrasym.*Fr*.1 *τί δῆτα μέλλοι τις ἂν ...;* Pl.*Smp*.211D *τί δῆτα, ἔφη, οἰόμεθα, εἰ ...;* Hdt.vii 147.3: X.*Cyr*.vi 1.13: 2.15: Lys.viii 3.

(3) Sometimes, in verse, *δῆτα* does not immediately follow the interrogative word. S.*OT*558 *Πόσον τιν' ἤδη δῆθ' ὁ Λάιος*

χρόνον . . . ; *OC* 52 Τίς ἔσθ' ὁ χῶρος δῆτ' . . . ; E.*Hec.*828 ποῦ τὰς φίλας δῆτ' εὐφρόνας δείξεις . . . ; *Ion* 1253 Ποῖ φύγω δῆτ'; *Ph.*420 Τί θηρσὶν ὑμᾶς δῆτ' Ἄδραστος ᾔκασεν; Ar.*V.*191 Περὶ τοῦ μαχεῖ νῷν δῆτα; S.*OT* 765: *Tr.*400: E.*Alc.*380,960: *Hel.* 1248: Ar.*Nu.*1051,1196: *Ra.*1399. (The order in E.*Fr.*231 is otherwise irregular: ἡμῶν τί δῆτα τυγχάνεις χρείαν ἔχων;)

(4) δῆτα not infrequently follows interrogative particles (ἦ, ἆρα, πότερον), while retaining its own logical force. A.*Th.*93 (lyr.) πότερα δῆτ' . . . ; S.*OT* 429 Ἦ ταῦτα δῆτ' ἀνεκτὰ . . . ; 1014 Ἆρ' οἶσθα δῆτα . . . ; (*Tr.*76): *Tr.*342 Πότερον ἐκείνους δῆτα . . . καλῶμεν . . . ; E.*Ion* 547 Ἆρα δῆτ' . . . ; 560 Ἦ θίγω δῆθ' . . . ; Ar.*Nu.*1094 Ἆρα δῆτ' ἔγνωκας . . . ; *Lys.*54 Ἆρ' οὐ παρεῖναι τὰς γυναῖκας δῆτ' ἐχρῆν; E.*Alc.*1051: *IT* 1176: *Fr.* 552: Ar.*Eq.*324 (lyr.): *V.*463 (lyr.): Hdt.ii 114 κότερα δῆτα τοῦτον ἐῶμεν . . . ; X.*Cyr.*v 2.27 Πότερα δῆτα . . . εἰς σὲ μόνον τοιοῦτος ἐγένετο . . . ;

(5) δῆτα is also used in questions in which the interrogative note is conveyed by tone of voice alone. Unlike most connecting particles, it frequently comes as late as third or fourth word in the sentence.

S.*Aj.*985 Οὐχ ὅσον τάχος | δῆτ' αὐτὸν ἄξεις δεῦρο (the unparalleled position of δῆτα, first word in the line, is characteristic of Sophoclean synaphea): 1360 Τοιούσδ' ἐπαινεῖς δῆτα σὺ κτᾶσθαι φίλους; *El.*1037 Τῷ σῷ δικαίῳ δῆτ' ἐπισπέσθαι με δεῖ; *Tr.*1219 Τὴν Εὐρυτείαν οἶσθα δῆτα παρθένον; E.*Hel.*103 Σὺ τοῖς ἐκείνου δῆτα πήμασιν νοσεῖς; 812 Σιγῇ παράσχω δῆτ' . . . ; *Or.* 92 Πρὸς θεῶν, πίθοι' ἂν δῆτα . . . ; *El.*834 ὁ δ' εἶπε· Φυγάδος δῆτα δειμαίνεις δόλον . . . ; *Hec.*247 (progressive rather than logical): *Supp.*1104 οὐχ ὡς τάχιστα δῆτά μ' ἄξετ' ἐς δόμους; *Ion* 538 Πρῶτα δῆτ' ἐμοὶ ξυνάπτεις πόδα σόν; 1303 Σὺ τῶν ἀτέκνων δῆτ' ἀναρπάσεις δόμους; Ar.*Nu.*486 Ἔνεστι δῆτα μανθάνειν ἐν τῇ φύσει; *V.*350 Ἔστιν ὀπῇ δῆθ' . . . ; 354 (surely a question): S.*OT* 364: *Ph.*108,761: E.*Ph.*722,901,909: *IA* 867: *Fr.*286.1: Ar.*Ach.*1127: *Pax* 1233: Eup.*Fr.*210: Pl. *Phlb* 28E Βούλει δῆτα . . . συμφήσωμεν . . . ; (Βούλει δῆτα . . . ; also Pl.*Phlb.*62C: *Sph.*218D: *Plt.*272B. The only other Platonic example of δῆτα in a question without a preceding interrogative seems to be *Plt.*301E.)

The note of surprise or indignation present in some of the above examples is accentuated when ταῦτα, εἶτα, ἔπειτα precedes the particle, as often in Aristophanes. S.*Ph.*987 Ὦ Λημνία χθὼν . . . ταῦτα δῆτ' ἀνασχετά, εἰ . . . ; E.*Alc.*822 Τί φῄς; ἔπειτα δῆτά μ' ἐξενίζετε; *Hec.*623 εἶτα δῆτ' ὀγκούμεθα . . . ; (surely a question): Ar.*Ach.* 125–6 Ταῦτα δῆτ' οὐκ ἀγχόνη; κἄπειτ' ἐγὼ δῆτ' ἐνθαδὶ στραγγεύομαι; 618 Ὦ δημοκρατία, ταῦτα δῆτ' ἀνασχετά; 917 Ἔπειτα φαίνεις δῆτα διὰ θρυαλλίδας; *Nu.*1299 Ταῦτ' οὐχ ὕβρις δῆτ' ἐστίν; *Av.*1217 Κἄπειτα δῆθ' οὕτω σιωπῇ διαπέτει . . . ; 1585 Εἶτα δῆτα σίλφιον ἐπικνῇς πρότερον αὐτοῖσιν; ('So you grate *silphium* on them, then?'): *V.*417,441: *Lys.* 914,985: *Ra.*950: *Th.*563,705: *Pl.*794: Antiph.*Fr.*159.1.

(6) δῆτα in questions sometimes follows other particles. See also (4) above.

(i) οὖν . . . δῆτα, οὔκουν . . . δῆτα. Almost confined to Aristophanes. Compare οὖν δή, οὔκουν δή. The interval between the particles is sometimes a wide one. Ar.*Eq.*18 πῶς ἂν οὖν ποτε εἴποιμ' ἂν αὐτὸ δῆτα κομψευριπικῶς; 810 Οὔκουν δεινὸν ταυτί σε λέγειν δῆτ' ἔστ' ἐμὲ . . ; *Nu.*87 Τί οὖν πίθωμαι δῆτά σοι; *V.*172 Οὔκουν κἂν ἐγὼ αὐτὸν ἀποδοίμην δῆτ' ἄν; 985 Οὔκουν ἀποφεύγει δῆτα; *Av.*969 Τί οὖν προσήκει δῆτ' ἐμοὶ Κορινθίων; *Eq.*878: *V.*1148: *Pax* 200,274: *Th.*211,226: *Ec.*1144: *Ra.*193, 200: Eup.*Fr.*211 ὡς οὖν τίν' ἔλθω δῆτά σοι τῶν μάντεων; (In Ar. *Pl.*845 Μῶν ἐνεμυήθης δῆτ' . . .; is no doubt the true reading.)

Juxtaposition of the particles is less common. Ar.*Eq.*871 Ἔγνωκας οὖν δῆτ' αὐτὸν . . .; 875: *Nu.*791: *Av.*27: Hdt.ii 22 κῶς ὦν δῆτα ῥέοι ἂν . . . ; Pl.*Tht.*164C Τί οὖν δῆτα . . . ; οὔκουν δῆτα: Ar.*Av.*477,1177.

The particles are reversed in E.*Med.*1290 (lyr.) τί δῆτ' οὖν γένοιτ' ἂν ἔτι δεινόν; Ar.*Nu.*423 Ἄλλο τι δῆτ' οὖν νομιεῖς ἤδη θεὸν οὐδένα . . . ;

The combination of δῆτα with its (presumed) parent δή is remarkable, and seems only to occur in Ar.*Pax* 929 Τῷ δὴ δοκεῖ σοι δῆτα τῶν λοιπῶν;

(ii) καὶ . . . δῆτα, expressing sometimes mere liveliness, sometimes indignation. Cf. καὶ δή, (1), *ad fin.* Each particle perhaps preserves its own force, καί connective, δῆτα logical, 'and ... then'. (Cf. γὰρ ... δῆτα: Ar.*Nu*.403 τί γάρ ἐστιν δῆθ' ὁ κεραυνός; 'Well, what *is* the thunderbolt then?') For κἄπειτα δῆτα see (5) above.

A.*Ch*.218 Καὶ πρὸς τί δῆτα τυγχάνω κατευγμάτων; *Eu*.206 Καὶ τὰς προπομποὺς δῆτα τάσδε λοιδορεῖς; E.*Andr*.1279 κᾆτ' οὐ γαμεῖν δῆτ' ἔκ τε γενναίων χρεὼν ...; *Heracl*.516 κοὐκ αἰσχυνοῦμαι δῆτ' ...; (surely a question): Ar.*Nu*.724 Καὶ τί δῆτ' ἐφρόντισας; *Lys*.912 Καὶ πῶς ἔθ' ἁγνὴ δῆτ' ἂν ἔλθοιμ' ἐς πόλιν; *Pl*.44 Καὶ τῷ ξυναντᾷς δῆτα πρώτῳ; 868 Καὶ τίνα δέδρακε δῆτα τοῦτ'; X.*Cyr*.v 4.35 τάχ' οὖν εἴποι τις ἄν· Καὶ τί δῆτα ...;

The position of δῆτα, first word of the resumed apodosis, in Ar.*Nu*.398 is remarkable: Καὶ πῶς ... εἴπερ βάλλει τοὺς ἐπιόρκους, δῆτ' οὐχὶ Σίμων' ἐνέπρησεν ...; Third word of apodosis: S.*Ant*.230 κεἰ τάδ' εἴσεται Κρέων ... πῶς σὺ δῆτ' οὐκ ἀλγυνῇ;

The only instance of juxtaposed καὶ δῆτα in a question (except for Th.vi 38.5, which is different: see IV.1) seems to be S.*Ant*.449 Ἤιδη (κηρυχθέντα μὴ πράσσειν τάδε) ...—Καὶ δῆτ' ἐτόλμας τούσδ' ὑπερβαίνειν νόμους; (Jebb: '"And you *indeed* dared ...?" Not, "And *then*" (i.e. with that knowledge), which would be κᾆτα.' In view of the interrogative use of δῆτα in general, and καὶ ... δῆτα in particular (e.g. Ar.*Lys*.912), the rejected interpretation seems the correct one.)

(7) Since ἀλλὰ δῆτα (ἀλλὰ ... δῆτα) is predominantly, though not exclusively, used in questions, and since it is often difficult to say whether a question-mark should be printed or not, it will be convenient to consider here all examples of this combination.

(i) The commonest use is in questions which follow a rejected suggestion (including hypophora). Cf. ἀλλά (II.1), ἀλλὰ δή (4). S.*Aj*.466 πότερα πρὸς οἴκους ...; ... ἀλλὰ δῆτ' ἰὼν πρὸς ἔρυμα Τρώων ... εἶτα λοίσθιον θάνω; ('Well, then, shall I go ...?'): *El*.537 πότερον Ἀργείων (χάριν) ἐρεῖς; ἀλλ' ... ἀλλ' ἀντ' ἀδελφοῦ δῆτα ...; Ar.*Pax* 1279 Ἀλλὰ τί δῆτ' ᾄδω; ('Well, what *shall* I sing, then?': the boy's first attempt at song having been suppressed): *Th*.143–4 πότερον ὡς ἀνὴρ τρέφει; ... ἀλλ' ὡς γυνὴ δῆτ'; εἶτα ποῦ τὰ τιτθία; τί φῄς; τί σιγᾷς; ἀλλὰ δῆτ' ἐκ τοῦ μέλους ζητῶ σ' ...; (γυνὴ δῆτ'· *OCT*): S.*OT* 1375: *Ph.*

1352: *Indag.*300 Diehl: E.*Or.*781 (read *Οὔκουν . . . μένειν*; and *ἔλθω*; see Paley): Pl.*Sph.*249A *Ἀλλὰ . . .*; *. . . Ἀλλὰ . . .*; *. . . Ἀλλὰ δῆτα . . .*; *Hp.Ma.*283C *πότερον . . .*; *. . . Ἀλλὰ . . .*; *. . . Ἀλλὰ δῆτα . . .*; 285C *Ἀλλὰ . . .*;—*Οὐδαμῶς . . .*—*Ἀλλὰ δῆτα . . .*;

(ii) Other uses of *ἀλλὰ δῆτα*, *ἀλλὰ . . . δῆτα* are much rarer. S.*Tr.*1245 *Ἀλλ' ἐκδιδαχθῶ δῆτα δυσσεβεῖν, πάτερ*; (protesting): Crates Com.*Fr.*14.2 *ἔπειτα δοῦλον οὐδὲ εἷς κεκτήσετ' οὐδὲ δούλην, ἀλλ' αὐτὸς αὑτῷ δῆτ' ἀνὴρ γέρων διακονήσει*; (indignant: 'but, forsooth'): Ar.*Av.*375 *Ἀλλ' ἀπ' ἐχθρῶν δῆτα πολλὰ μανθάνουσιν οἱ σοφοί* (an objection): *Pl.*1098 *Τίς ἔσθ' ὁ κόπτων τὴν θύραν*; *τουτὶ τί ἦν*; *οὐδεὶς ἔοικεν· ἀλλὰ δῆτα τὸ θύριον φθεγγόμενον ἄλλως κλαυσιᾷ* (probably to be classed under (i) as a question: 'Well, then, is it just the door creaking?'. Van Leeuwen's objection to Blaydes' insertion of the question-mark is not convincing): Pl.*Cra.*410E *Ἀλλὰ δῆτα, ὦ Σώκρατες, πολὺ ἐπιδίδως* (surprised approval: cf. *ἀλλά*, II.6.iii.*b*: 'Why, you *are* getting on'): D xix287 *ἀλλὰ δῆτ' ἄνω ποταμῶν ἐκείνῃ τῇ ἡμέρᾳ πάντες οἱ περὶ πορνείας ἐρρύησαν λόγοι.*

Pl.*Lg.*858D is a difficult and debatable passage: *Ἀλλὰ δῆτα οὐ χρὴ τὸν νομοθέτην μόνον τῶν γραφόντων . . . συμβουλεύειν . . . .* England is probably right in taking the sentence as ironical, 'whether interrogative or not'.

II. Emphatic. In this sphere *δή* and *δῆτα* carry out separate functions, which rarely overlap.

(1) In negative statements, *οὐ δῆτα*. Contrast the rarity of *οὐ δή*. Mostly in dialogue, in emphatic negative answers. About two-thirds of the Platonic examples of *δῆτα* come under this head.

(i) An expected denial, expressing agreement with the previous speaker's negative statement. S.*Ph.*419 *οὐ μὴ θάνωσι . . .* —*Οὐ δῆτ'*: Ar.*Eq.*1307–9 *Ἀποτρόπαι' οὐ δῆτ' ἐμοῦ γ' ἄρξει ποτ' . . .*—*Οὐδὲ Ναυφάντης γε τῆς Ναύσωνος, οὐ δῆτ' ὦ θεοί* (the first speaker perhaps corroborates *οὐκ ἀνασχετόν* (1305): 'No, he shan't rule *me*!'): S.*Tr.*1127: *OC*810: E.*Hel.*1228 (1227 is ironically affirmative in form): *Hipp* 324 (probably: the interpretation is doubtful): Pl.*R.*387D *Οὐκ ἄρα . . . ὀδύροιτ' ἄν.*—*Οὐ δῆτα*: 436A: *Cri.*49B.

(ii) An expected denial, answering a question anticipating a negative answer. Ar.*Ach.*619 *ταῦτα δῆτ' ἀνασχετά*;—*Οὐ δῆτ'*:

*Eq.*870: Pl.*Ap.*25D ἔσθ' ὅστις . . .;—Οὐ δῆτα: *R.*472E: X. *Mem.*ii 2.9.

(i) and (ii) are exceedingly common in Plato, and embrace almost all the Platonic examples of οὐ δῆτα: naturally enough, since the answers given in the dialogues are usually the expected ones. In *Grg.*453D οὐ δῆτα rejects, as expected, the second of two alternatives: πότερον ὃ διδάσκει πείθει ἢ οὔ;—Οὐ δῆτα, ὦ Σώκρατες, ἀλλὰ πάντων μάλιστα πείθει.

(iii) Answering a neutral question. S.*OT* 758 Ἦ κἀν δόμοισι τυγχάνει ταννῦν παρών;—Οὐ δῆτ': *Ph.*735: *OC* 597: Ar.*Nu.* 733: *V.*396: Pl.*Lg.*962C ἔχομεν φράζειν;—Οὐ δῆτα . . . σαφῶς γε: And i 101 (an imaginary cross-examination).

(iv) Giving the lie to a positive statement. S.*OT* 1161 Ἁνὴρ ὅδ' . . . ἐς τριβὰς ἐλᾷ.—Οὐ δῆτ' ἔγωγ': *Tr.*1208: E.*Heracl.*61: *Alc.*389: Ar.*Eq.*1110: *Nu.*913: *V.*169: Pl.*Grg.*473B (substituting a stronger form of expression, almost like μὲν οὖν).

(v) Refusing to obey a command or follow a suggestion. 'No, I will not'. E.*Hipp.*334 Ἄπελθε πρὸς θεῶν δεξιᾶς τ' ἐμῆς μέθες.—Οὐ δῆτ': *Med.*1378: *Ph.*1661: *Cyc.*198 (197 is virtually a suggestion): Ar.*Eq.*1229: *V.*989.

(vi) A negative answer to a question which either definitely expects a positive answer, or recognizes with reluctance or surprise that a negative answer may be given. S.*El.*403 Σὺ δ' οὐχὶ πείσῃ . . .;—Οὐ δῆτα: *OT* 942 Τί δ'; οὐχ ὁ πρέσβυς Πόλυβος ἐγκρατὴς ἔτι;—Οὐ δῆτ': Ar.*V.*1496 οὐκ εὖ;—Μὰ Δί' οὐ δῆτ' ἀλλὰ μανικὰ πράγματα: A.*Pr.*770: S.*El.*1198: Pl.*Grg.* 470E: X.*Cyr.*i 6.28: Arist.*Pol.*1313a33: *Rh.*1419a34 (the only examples of δῆτα in Aristotle).

(Cf. Pl.*Euthd.*298C, a positive answer (with δῆτα) where a negative one is expected.)

(vii) Strengthened with an oath, Μὰ (τὸν) Δί' οὐ δῆτα: Ar. *Nu.*733: *V.*169,396,1496: *Ra.*914: Pl.*Grg.*470E.

(viii) Rarely in continuous speech. (*a*) Answering a rhetorical question: E.*Med.*1048: *Heracl.*507: *Hipp.*1062: Aeschin.i 88. (*b*) Answering a supposed objection: S.*OC* 433 (εἴποις ἂν ὡς . . .): D.lviii 64 (νὴ Δία). (*c*) Picking up and reinforcing a preceding negative: A.*Pr.*349: Ant.vi 15. Here too, as in (*a*) and (*b*), δῆτα gives the impression of dialogue: the speaker answers himself.

οὐ δῆτα is almost always elliptical. For Ar.*Eq.*1307 see (i) above. S.*Ant.*762 is another apparent exception: but the construction of 762 is perhaps to be regarded as self-contained in inception, the sequel, containing the verb, being added as the thought develops. *οὐ* ... *δῆτα* in Ar.*Ach.*323 perhaps has an assentient tinge (cf. (3) below): *οὐκ ἀκούσεσθ'* ...;—*Οὐκ ἀκουσόμεσθα δῆτα* ('That's it, we *won't* listen': not 'No, we won't', which would be *Οὐ δῆτα*).

(2) Passionate negative commands or wishes, *μὴ δῆτα*.

In answers. S.*Aj.*111 *Μὴ δῆτα τὸν δύστηνον ὧδέ γ' αἰκίσῃ*: Ar.*Eq.*960 *Μὴ δῆτά πώ γ', ὦ δέσποτ'*: S.*El.*1206: *OT* 1153: *Ph.*762: *OC* 174: E.*Med.*336: *Or.*1329: *Ph.*735: Ar.*Lys.*36: *Nu.*696.

In continuous speech. A.*Pr.*1075 *μηδὲ* ... *μέμψησθε τύχην* ... *μὴ δῆτ', αὐταὶ δ' ὑμᾶς αὐτάς*: S.*OT* 830 *μὴ δῆτα, μὴ δῆτ', ὦ θεῶν ἁγνὸν σέβας, ἴδοιμι* ...: E.*Med.*644 (lyr.) *ὦ πατρὶς* ... *μὴ δῆτ' ἄπολις γενοίμαν*: S.*Ph.*1367: E.*Alc.*308: *Med.*1056: *Hel.*939: *Supp.*320: *IA* 1183: D.xxi 183 *μὴ τοίνυν* ... *δεῖγμα τοιοῦτον ἐξενέγκητ'* ... *ὡς* .... *μὴ δῆτα· οὐ γὰρ δίκαιον*: xxxii 23 *μὴ δῆτ', ὦ Ζεῦ καὶ θεοί*: And.i 149: D.xviii 324: xxi 188: Lycurg.116.

(3) In affirmative answers, echoing a word, or words, of the previous speaker. (Cf. *μέντοι*, II.1.ii.*b*.) Common in verse and prose dialogue, particularly in Aristophanes, where the particle is often reinforced by an oath. For the very rare similar use of *δή*, see *δή* I.14, *ad fin.*

A.*Supp.*359 (lyr.) *εἴη δ' ἄνατον πρᾶγμα* ...—*Ἴδοιτο δῆτ' ἄνατον φυγάν**: S.*El.*844 (lyr.) *Φεῦ* ...—*Φεῦ δῆτ'*: *OT* 445 *κόμιζέ με.*—*Κομιζέτω δῆθ'*: Ar.*Av.*1548 *Μισῶ δ' ἅπαντας τοὺς θεοὺς* ...—*Νὴ τὸν Δί' ἀεὶ δῆτα θεομισὴς ἔφυς*: A.*Th.*879,933,985: S.*El.*1455: *OC* 536: E.*Med.*1373: *El.*673,676: *HF* 901: *Hel.* 646: *Ph.*161,1702: *Tr.*584,1231: Ar.*Ach.*1228: *Eq.*6,726,749: *Av.*275: *Lys.*848,882,930: *id. saep.*: Antiph.*Fr.*58.3: Pl.*R.*333A, 381B,563E: *Phd.*90D: *Cra.*422B: *Phlb.*30C: *Lg.*658D: (reinforced by preceding oath: Ar.*Av.*269: *Lys.*836: Pl.*Tht.*170E: *Thg.*125B: followed by oath, Ar.*Lys.*972).

(But in Pl.*Lg.*636A the second speaker virtually dissents: *ἔοικεν γὰρ τά τε συσσίτια καὶ τὰ γυμνάσια καλῶς ηὑρῆσθαι πρὸς ἀμφοτέρας.*—'*Ἔοικεν δῆτα* that all political institutions, including these, have defects as well as merits'. Perhaps there is a sort of *παρὰ προσδοκίαν*: 'It seems . . .'—'Yes, it seems—that the matter is not quite as simple as that'. 'It does seem difficult', England: but this is not in line with any usage of *δῆτα*: and the echo of *ἔοικεν* cannot be left out of account.)

Sometimes the second speaker merely endorses and restates the purport of the words of the first, without verbal echo. A.*Pers.*988 (lyr.) 'Did you leave behind you trusted henchmen?' —*Ἰυγγά μοι δῆτ' ἀγαθῶν ἑτάρων ὑπορίνεις*: E.*Or.*219 *βούλῃ θίγω σου κἀνακουφίσω δέμας;—Λαβοῦ λαβοῦ δῆτ'*: 1231 *σὺ δ' ἡμῖν τοῦδε συλλήπτωρ γενοῦ.—Ὦ πάτερ, ἱκοῦ δῆτ'*: Ar.*Lys.*96 *Μύσιδδέ τοι ὅ τι λῇς ποθ' ἁμέ.—Νὴ Δί', ὦ φίλη γύναι, λέγε δῆτα.* In Pl.*Alc.I*130B there is, exceptionally, endorsement without restatement: *Ἀλλ' ἄρα . . .;—Ἴσως δῆτα* ('Yes, perhaps that is so').

Sometimes a speaker echoes or endorses his own words. A.*Th.*890 (lyr.) *δι' εὐωνύμων τετυμμένοι, τετυμμένοι δῆθ'*: S.*El.* 1164 *ὥς μ' ἀπώλεσας· ἀπώλεσας δῆτ', ὦ κασιγνητὸν κάρα* ('Aye, undone me'): *Ph.*760 *Ἰὼ ἰὼ δύστηνε σύ, δύστηνε δῆτα . . .*: 1348 *Ὦ στυγνὸς αἰών, τί με, τί δῆτ' ἔχεις ἄνω . . . ;* Ar.*Nu.*269 *Σω. . . . ἄρθητε, φάνητ'* . . . (interruption by Strepsiades).—*Σω. Ἔλθετε δῆτ'*: *Ec.*1122 *ὥστ' ἐστὶ πολὺ βέλτιστα, πολὺ δῆτ' ὦ θεοί*: Pl.*Prt.*310C *ἑσπέρας γε . . . ἑσπέρας δῆτα* ('Yes, in the evening'). For *δῆτα* with a resumed negative see II. (1) and (2) above.

(4) Outside the above limits emphatic *δῆτα* is very rare. A.*Th.*814 *Αὐτὸς δ' ἀναλοῖ δῆτα δύσποτμον γένος*: Cratin.*Fr.*188 *ἀτὰρ ἐννοοῦμαι δῆτα τῆς μοχθηρίας* (*δή τι* Nauck): Ar.*V.*796 *Ὁρᾷς ὅσον καὶ τοῦτο δῆτα κερδανεῖς*: *Pl.*697 *μετὰ τοῦτο δ' ἤδη καὶ γέλοιον δῆτά τι ἐποίησα*: D.xlv 76 *ὡς δῆτα πονηρὸν . . . ἐπιδείξων* (ironical).

In exclamations and imprecations. E.*Andr.*514 (lyr.) *Ὤμοι μοι, τί πάθω; τάλας δῆτ' ἐγὼ σύ τε, μᾶτερ*: X.*HG*ii 4.17 *ὦ μακάριοι δῆτα, οἳ ἂν ἡμῶν νικήσαντες ἐπίδωσι τὴν πασῶν ἡδίστην ἡμέραν*: Ar.*Nu.*6 *ἀπόλοιο δῆτ', ὦ πόλεμε, πολλῶν οὕνεκα.*

After relatives. S.*Ph.*130 *ἐκπέμψω πάλιν τοῦτον τὸν αὐτὸν ἄνδρα . . . οὗ δῆτα, τέκνον, ποικίλως αὐδωμένου δέχου . . .*: A.*Th.* 829: *Eu.*399.

III. Connective. There are very few examples of this use, outside questions. Ar.*V*.121 ὅτε δῆτα ταύταις ταῖς τελεταῖς οὐκ ὠφέλει, διέπλευσεν εἰς Αἴγιναν: *Nu*.1058 ἄνειμι δῆτ' ἐντεῦθεν ἐς τὴν γλῶτταν: Hdt.iv 69 δέδοκται . . . ἀπόλλυσθαι. ἀπολλῦσι δῆτα αὐτοὺς τρόπῳ τοιῷδε (δῆτα *ABCP*: δέ *cett.* δῆτα, though it has the support of the two best MSS., *A* and *B*, seems highly improbable, in continuous prose narrative): Pl.*Grg*.452C μετὰ δὲ τὸν παιδοτρίβην εἴποι ἂν ὁ χρηματιστὴς . . . "Σκόπει δῆτα, ὦ Σώκρατες . . ." (but δῆτα is probably emphatic here): *Tht*.208E Νῦν δῆτα . . . .

IV. Combined with other particles. (For ἀλλὰ δῆτα, and for οὖν . . . δῆτα, οὔκουν . . . δῆτα, καὶ . . . δῆτα in questions, see I.6 and 7.)

(1) καὶ δῆτα. This is not uncommon in colloquial Greek (Aristophanes, Plato, and Xenophon). It closely resembles καὶ δή and καὶ δὴ καί in force, but is more lively and picturesque. Ar.*Ach*.68 Καὶ δῆτ' ἐτρυχόμεσθα: 142 καὶ δῆτα φιλαθήναιος ἦν ὑπερφυῶς: *V*.13 καὶ δῆτ' ὄναρ θαυμαστὸν εἶδον ἀρτίως: *Av*.511, 1670: *Ra*.52: *Ec*.378,385: Th.vi 38.5 (in speech) καὶ δῆτα . . . τί καὶ βούλεσθε, ὦ νεώτεροι; Pl.*Prt*.310C ὁ γάρ τοι παῖς με ὁ Σάτυρος ἀπέδρα· καὶ δῆτα μέλλων σοι φράζειν . . . ἐπελαθόμην: *Euthphr*.11D: *Tht*.142C: X.*Oec*.11.4: *Cyr*.v1.4: D.xxiv 159: xxxvi 45. (Pl.*Tht*.171D καὶ δῆτα καὶ νῦν, exactly like καὶ δὴ καί, after a general statement.)

In Pherecr.*Fr*.45.2 καί is not, as elsewhere, connective, and καὶ δῆτα is used like καὶ δή (2): Ὅπως παρασκευάζεται τὸ δεῖπνον εἴπαθ' ἡμῖν.—Καὶ δῆθ' ὑπάρχει τέμαχος.

(2) δῆτα very occasionally replaces δή in combination with other particles. S.*Ant*.551 Ἀλγοῦσα μὲν δῆτ': E.*El*.926 ᾔδησθα γὰρ δῆτ': *Supp*.1098 ἥδιστα πρίν γε δῆθ', ὅτ' ἦν παῖς ἥδε μοι (δῆθ' ὅτ' Canter, probably rightly, for δήποτ'): *Ph*.1717 (lyr.) σύ μοι ποδαγὸς ἀθλία γενοῦ—Γενόμεθα γενόμεθ', ἄθλιαί γε δῆτα (here there is little cohesion between the particles, γε marking the assent, δῆτα the repetition: 'Aye, wretched indeed'): *Hyps. Fr*.20–21.6 Arn. Τί δῆτά γ' ἐξεύρηκας; (δῆτά γε looks suspicious): A.*Th*.670 †ἤδητ'† ἂν εἴη πανδίκως ψευδώνυμος Δίκη (the decision between ἤ δῆτ' and ἦ δῆτ' is difficult: Tucker prefers the latter, as 'a more natural and accepted (*sic*) combination. ἤ would

require a different position of δῆτ', e.g. ἦ εἴη ἂν δῆτα'. But see next example): Ar.*V*.332 (lyr.) εἰς ὀξάλμην ἔμβαλε θερμήν· ἢ δῆτα λίθον με ποίησον: *Ec*.853 Οὐκοῦν βαδιοῦμαι δῆτα (but the much commoner Οὔκουν . . . δῆτα . . .; is just possible here). For ἀτὰρ . . . δῆτα, see Cratin.*Fr*.188 (II.4).

V. Textually uncertain cases. In E.*Hipp*.716 δή τι (*LPB*) seems more probable than δῆτα (*cett.*), though supported by inferior textual authority: but the context is corrupt. In *IT* 943 δή γ' (*LP*) seems very doubtful (see p. 247): Scaliger δῆτ': the whole passage is uncertain. In *Hel*.1374, if we assume a lacuna before the line, κάλλιστα δῆτα is apparently used for κάλλιστα δή (an 'improper use', Paley observes: an unparalleled one at all events: κάλλιστα δὴ τάδ' ἥρπασ', Fix). In *Ba*.202, *IA* 84, δῆτα is a poor conjecture. In Hp.*Septim*.9 ἐφάνη ἰσχύοντα δῆτα μᾶλλον for δῆτα read probably δή τι.

Ἦ

Boisacq connects ἦ with Sanskrit emphatic *ā́*. ἦ is used both as an affirmative and as an interrogative particle. The latter use is no doubt derived from the former: the transition being an easy one, from ἦ in a pure statement to ἦ in a statement with an interrogative inflexion, and hence to ἦ as an interrogative proper.

The distinction between ἦ and other affirmative particles has been variously formulated. Kühner regards the difference between ἦ and μήν or δή as merely one of strength, pointing out that ἦ is (usually) placed at the beginning of the sentence, and that it always retains its adverbial nature, never sinking to the rank of a conjunction (though in ἐπεὶ ἤ, τιή, ὁτιή it sinks to the rank of a mere suffix). Bäumlein maintains that ἦ expresses subjective certainty, a view borne out by the fact (noticed by Ebeling) that Homer never (except χ31 ἐπεὶ ἦ) uses ἦ *in propria persona*, but only in speeches, and that in prose, except in certain combinations (notably ἦ μήν, ἦ που) the particle is almost confined to dialogue. If this view is correct, ἦ μήν, ἦ δή mean, strictly speaking, 'I am certain that really . . .'.*

I. Affirmative, mostly with adjectives and adverbs. This is mainly a verse idiom, and is hardly found at all in oratory, except for ἦ μήν (*q.v.*), and the common use of ἦ που in *a fortiori* argument.

(1) In general. Hom. *Γ*204 *Ὦ γύναι, ἦ μάλα τοῦτο ἔπος νημερτὲς ἔειπες*: *E*800 *Ἦ ὀλίγον οἷ παῖδα ἐοικότα γείνατο Τυδεύς*: *I*197 *Χαίρετον· ἦ φίλοι ἄνδρες ἱκάνετον*: *O*105 *ἦ ἔτι μιν μέμαμεν καταπαυσέμεν*: *X*356 *Ἦ σ' εὖ γιγνώσκων προτιόσσομαι*: Simon. *Fr.*76.1 *ἦ μέγ' Ἀθηναίοισι φόως γένεθ'*: 142.1 *ἦ σεῦ καὶ φθιμένας λεύκ' ὀστέα . . . ἴσκω ἔτι τρομέειν θῆρας*: A.*Pr.*752 *Ἦ δυσπετῶς ἂν τοὺς ἐμοὺς ἄθλους φέροις*: *Th.*838 *ἦ δύσορνις ἅδε ξυναυλία δορός*: *Ag.*1064 *Ἦ μαίνεταί γε*: 592 *ἦ κάρτα* (1252: *Ch.*929: S.*Aj.*1359: *El.*312 ('only here as an independent affirmative, which is elsewhere *καὶ κάρτα* [*OC*65, 301]', Jebb): *El.*1279): *Aj.*1366 *Ἦ πάνθ' ὅμοια*: *Ant.*484 *ἦ νῦν ἐγὼ μὲν οὐκ ἀνήρ*: E.*Tr.*383 *ἦ τοῦδ' ἐπαίνου τὸ στράτευμ' ἐπάξιον*: *Alc.*865 *ἦ βαρυδαίμονα μήτηρ μ' ἔτεκεν*: Ar.*Nu.*167 *ἦ ῥᾳδίως φεύγων ἂν ἀποφύγοι δίκην* (ironical): *Av.*13 *Ἦ δεινὰ νὼ δέδρακεν*: 162 *ἦ μέγ' ἐνορῶ βούλευμ' ἐν ὀρνίθων γένει*: Hom.*Z* 441: *P*143: *Υ*94: Thgn.1173: Pi.*O.*1.28: *P.*1.47: A.*Pers.* 262,647,843: *Ag.*1481: *Eu.*34: E.*Med.*579: *Andr.*274: *Tr.* 424,446: *El.*483: *Ph.*798: *Rh.*245: Ar.*Lys.*1031: Hdt. vii 159 *Ἦ κε μέγ' οἰμώξειε . . . Ἀγαμέμνων* (a reminiscence of Hom.*H* 125): Pl.*Euthd.*271A *ἦ πολὺς ὑμᾶς ὄχλος περιειστήκει* (*ἦ B* (*sed in ras.*) Demetrius: 'There *was* a crowd round you!': *ᾗ T*): *Phdr.* 264A *ἦ πολλοῦ δεῖν ἔοικε ποιεῖν*: *R.*454A *Ἦ γενναία, ἦν δ' ἐγώ, ἡ δύναμις τῆς ἀντιλογικῆς τέχνης*: ('There's really something noble about the faculty of argument'): 530C *Ἦ πολλαπλάσιον, ἔφη, τὸ ἔργον . . . προστάττεις*: *Sph.*246B *Ἦ δεινοὺς εἴρηκας ἄνδρας*: *Ti.* 21D *Τίς δ' ἦν ὁ λόγος . . .;—Ἦ περὶ μεγίστης . . . πράξεως* (*ἦ* in *A* only: 'In truth it was about . . .'): X.*Cyr.*vii 5.48 *Ἦ καλῶς, ἔφη, ἐποίησας*: Lys.ii 40 *ἦ πολὺ πλεῖστον ἐκεῖνοι κατὰ τὴν ἀρετὴν ἁπάντων ἀνθρώπων διήνεγκαν*: xx 19 *ἦ δεινά τἂν πάθοιμεν . . . εἰ . . .* ('Really it *would* be hard'): Pl.*Smp.*176B: *Prt.*327D,355D: *R.*567E: *Tht.*175C (*ἦ* Burnet, for *εἰ*).

(2) Position. Affirmative ἦ is occasionally placed later than first word in the sentence.

(i) After a vocative. Hom.*Γ*204 Ὦ γύναι, ἦ μάλα τοῦτο ἔπος νημερτὲς ἔειπες: *Δ*441 Ἆ δείλ', ἦ μάλα δή σε κιχάνεται αἰπὺς ὄλεθρος: ω351 Ζεῦ πάτερ, ἦ ῥα ἔτ' ἐστὲ θεοί: A.*Th.*979 μέλαιν' Ἐρινύς, ἦ μεγασθενής τις εἶ: S.*El.*622 Ὦ θρέμμ' ἀναιδές, ἦ σ' ἐγὼ καὶ τἄμ' ἔπη . . . ποεῖ: E.*Tr.*1182 Ὦ μῆτερ, ηὔδας, ἦ πολύν σοι βοστρύχων πλόκαμον κεροῦμαι: Hdt.iii 72 Ὀτάνη, ἦ πολλά ἐστι . . .: vi 80 Ὦ Ἄπολλον χρηστήριε, ἦ μεγάλως με ἠπάτηκας: Pl.*Hp.Ma.*291E Ἰοὺ ἰού, ὦ Ἱππία, ἦ θαυμασίως τε καὶ μεγαλείως . . . εἴρηκας: X.*Cyr.*v 4.13 Ὦ Γαδάτα, ἦ πολὺ μεῖζον παρεὶς θαῦμα ἐμὲ νῦν θαυμάζεις.

(ii) After an exclamation or oath. Hom.φ249 Ὢ πόποι, ἦ μοι ἄχος (A.*Pers.*852): Ar.*V.*209 νὴ Δί' ἦ μοι κρεῖττον ἦν . . .: *Av.*1397 Νὴ τὸν Δί' ἦ 'γώ σου καταπαύσω τὰς πνοάς.

(iii) At the opening of an apodosis. Hom.ψ108 εἰ δ' . . . ἦ μάλα . . . (E.*Alc.*464 (lyr.)): E.*Rh* 476 (iamb.): X.*An.*vii 6.27 εἰ οὖν . . . ἦ κακῶς ἂν ἐδόκουν . . . (In Hp.*VM* 15 *M* gives εἰ δὲ δὴ τυγχάνει . . . ἦ διοίσει τι . . .) Apodotic ἦ τε occurs several times in Homer: *Π*687, *Χ*49, etc. See further (4) below.

(iv) Outside the above limits, postponement of affirmative ἦ is exceedingly rare. Hom.*P*34 Νῦν μὲν δή, Μενέλαε διοτρεφές, ἦ μάλα τείσεις: Pi.*O.*13.63 ὃς τᾶς ὀφιώδεος υἱόν ποτε Γοργόνος ἦ πόλλ' ἀμφὶ κρουνοῖς Πάγασον ζεῦξαι ποθέων ἔπαθεν: Ar.*V.*1464 ἕτερα δὲ νῦν ἀντιμαθὼν ἦ μέγα τι μεταπεσεῖται. At opening of parenthesis: A.*Eu.*144 ἐπάθομεν, φίλαι—ἦ πολλὰ δὴ παθοῦσα καὶ μάτην ἐγώ—. Epexegetic: E.*Rh.*899 οἵαν ἔκελσας ὁδὸν ποτὶ Τροίαν· ἦ δυσδαίμονα καὶ μελέαν, ἀπομεμφομένας ἐμοῦ πορευθείς.

(3) Repetition of ἦ. Very occasionally, ἦ is repeated, and followed by another repeated word. A.*Pr.*887 Ἦ σοφός, ἦ σοφός, ὃς . . .: E.*Ph.*320 ἰὼ τέκος . . . ἔλιπες . . . ἦ ποθεινὸς φίλοις, ἦ ποθεινὸς Θήβαις: *IA* 1330 ἦ πολύμοχθον ἄρ' ἦν γένος, ἦ πολύμοχθον ἁμερίων. (In A.*Pers.*647 the second ἦ is unmetrical.) S.*Aj.*172–6 ἦ ῥα . . . ἦ που.

(4) A particular use of ἦ (almost always ἦ που . . . γε) is in *a fortiori* argument. E.*Hipp.*412 ὅταν γὰρ . . . δοκῇ, ἦ κάρτα δόξει.

X.*HG*vi 5.48 ὁπότε . . ., ἦ πού ὑμῖν γε . . .: Ant.v 91 καίτοι ὅπου . . ., ἦ καὶ πάνυ τοι χρῆν τούς γε ἐξαπατῶντας ἀπολωλέναι: And.i 86 ὅπου οὖν ἀγράφῳ νόμῳ . . ., ἦ που ἀγράφῳ γε ψηφίσματι . . .: Lys.xiii 57 καίτοι εἰ ἐκεῖνος ἀπέθανεν, ἦ που Ἀγόρατός γε δικαίως ἀποθανεῖται: xxvii 15 καίτοι εἰ . . ., ἦ που σφόδρα χρὴ . . .: Lycurg.71 (with the *a fortiori* clause ironically negatived) ὅπου δὲ καὶ τοῦ λόγου τιμωρίαν ἠξίουν λαμβάνειν, ἦ που τὸν ἔργῳ παραδόντα τὴν πόλιν . . . οὐ μεγάλαις ἂν ζημίαις ἐκόλασαν: Lys.vi 12: vii 8: xxv 17: Isoc.iv 138: viii 24: D. xxiii 76,79: lv 18 (ironical): Aeschin.ii 88: (all of these ἦ που.)

Less frequently, the *a fortiori* clause comes first. (This order of clauses is, in general, less rhetorically effective. See Dissen, *De structura periodorum oratoria*.) S.*Aj*.1229 ἦ που τραφεὶς ἂν μητρὸς εὐγενοῦς ἄπο ὑψήλ' ἐκόμπεις . . . ὅτ' οὐδὲν ὢν τοῦ μηδὲν ἀντέστης ὕπερ: Hdt.i 68.2 Ἦ κου ἂν . . . εἴ περ εἶδες τό περ ἐγώ, κάρτα ἂν ἐθώμαζες, ὅκου νῦν οὕτω τυγχάνεις θῶμα ποιεύμενος . . .: Pl.*Phd*.84E ἦ που χαλεπῶς ἂν τοὺς ἄλλους ἀνθρώπους πείσαιμι . . . ὅτε γε μηδ' ὑμᾶς δύναμαι πείθειν: Th.v 100 (Ἦ που ἄρα): Pl.*Alc.II* 147E (without που: but read, perhaps, ἤ): And.iv 27 (ἦ που).

Three times, in Thucydides, the two clauses are paratactically, not hypotactically, related (*nedum*): i 142.3 τὴν μὲν γὰρ (ἐπιτείχισιν) χαλεπὸν καὶ ἐν εἰρήνῃ πόλιν ἀντίπαλον κατασκευάσασθαι, ἦ που δὴ ἐν πολεμίᾳ τε . . . ('far *more* difficult'): vi 37.2: viii 27.3 (ἦ που Lindau: ποῦ *codd.*).

In Ar.*Th*.63 ἦ που νέος γ' ὢν ἦσθ' ὑβριστής, ὦ γέρον the *a fortiori* relationship is implied, the second clause being unexpressed.

II. Interrogative.[1] In prose almost confined to the combinations ἦ που, ἦ γάρ, ἦ καί.

(1) In general. Hom.*Γ*46 ἦ τοιόσδε ἐὼν . . . γυναῖκ' εὐειδέ' ἀνῆγες . . .; A.*Eu*.949 Ἦ τάδ' ἀκούετε . . .; S.*OT* 993 Ἦ ῥητόν; ἢ οὐχὶ θεμιτὸν ἄλλον εἰδέναι; E.*Ba*.1300 Ἦ πᾶν ἐν ἄρθροις συγκεκλῃμένον καλῶς (φέρεις); Ar.*Ach*.776 ἦ λῇς ἀκοῦσαι φθεγγομένας; Hom.*O* 504,506: A.*Pr*.773: *Ag*.269: S.*El*.385: *OT* 943,1120: *OC* 30: E.*Hipp*.97: *Supp*.145,935: *Cyc*.280: *IT*

[1] Prof. J. E. Harry, *Indirect Questions with* μή *and* ἆρα μή, remarks that interrogative ἦ is much commoner in tragedy than in comedy: 'Aeschylus 25, Sophocles 61, Euripides 74, Aristophanes hardly a dozen'.

1176: Ar.*Pl.*869: Pl.*Grg.*479B *ἦ οὐ δοκεῖ καὶ σοὶ οὕτω;* (*ἤ* Burnet): 479C *ἦ βούλει συλλογισώμεθα αὐτά;* (*ἤ* Burnet): X.*Cyr.*i4.19.

(2) Often introducing a suggested answer, couched in interrogative form, to a question just asked. Hom.*A*203 *Τίπτ' αὖτ' ... εἰλήλουθας; ἦ ἵνα ...;* A.*Ag.*1542 *τίς ὁ θάψων νιν; τίς ὁ θρηνήσων; ἦ σὺ τόδ' ἔρξαι τλήσει ...;* S.*OT*622 *Τί δῆτα χρῄζεις; ἦ με γῆς ἔξω βαλεῖν;* E.*Cyc.*129 *Αὐτὸς δὲ Κύκλωψ ποῦ 'στιν; ἦ δόμων ἔσω;* Hom.*Υ*17: *κ*330: E.*IT* 1168: *Ba.*828 (*ἤ codd.*): 1290: Pl.*Cri.*43C *Τίνα ταύτην* (*ἀγγελίαν φέρεις χαλεπήν*); *ἦ τὸ πλοῖον ἀφῖκται ἐκ Δήλου, οὗ δεῖ ἀφικομένου τεθνάναι με;* *Ap.*37B *τί δείσας; ἦ μὴ πάθω τοῦτο ...;* *Smp.*173A *ἀλλὰ τίς σοι διηγεῖτο; ἦ αὐτὸς Σωκράτης;* (*ᾗ B*: *ἢ ᾗ T*: *ἦ* Ast: *ἤ* Schanz). (On the question of accent, see Herodian, *Gramm.*2.112.)

(3) Position. (i) Like affirmative *ἦ*, interrogative *ἦ* normally opens the sentence, but sometimes follows a vocative. Hom. *E*421 *Ζεῦ πάτερ, ἦ ῥά τί μοι κεχολώσεαι ...;* S.*Ph.*369 *ὦ σχέτλι', ἦ 'τολμήσατ' ...;* *OC* 863 *Ὦ φθέγμ' ἀναιδές, ἦ σὺ γὰρ ψαύσεις ἐμοῦ;* 1102 *Ὦ τέκνον, ἦ πάρεστον;* E.*Or.*844 *Γυναῖκες, ἦ που ... ἀφώρμηται ...;* Ar.*Ach.*749 *Δικαιόπολι, ἦ λῇς πρίασθαι χοιρία;* Hom.*E*762: *δ*632. (For similar postponement of *ἀλλ' ἦ* v.s.v., p. 27.)

(ii) Otherwise, postponement of interrogative *ἦ* is very rare, and there is usually some doubt about reading or punctuation. Hom.*Batr.*174 *Ὦ θύγατερ μυσὶν ἦ ῥα βοηθήσουσα πορεύσῃ;* In S.*Ant.*1281 *Τί δ' ἔστιν αὖ; κάκιον ἦ κακῶν ἔτι;* is the reading nearest the MSS. (Pearson even punctuates before *ἔστιν*.) But Jebb observes that interrogative *ἦ* occurs about fifty times in Sophocles, and is always placed first, except that a vocative sometimes precedes it. (*ἦ που*, however, is not infrequently postponed by Sophocles: see below, III,9.) E.*Hec.*1013 *πέπλων ἐντὸς ἦ κρύψασ' ἔχεις* (here Valckenaer's *ἦ*, adopted by Porson, is perhaps unnecessary): *El.*967 *Τί δῆτα δρῶμεν μητέρ'; ἦ φονεύσομεν;* (this punctuation is probably right; though, apart from the difficulty in the position of *ἦ*, we might be inclined to put the question-mark after *δρῶμεν*): *Ion* 962 (Bruhn's *ἦ* seems impossible: see Wilamowitz, *ad loc.*). Paley prints E.*Supp.*106 as a single sentence: but it is usually, and rightly, divided.

There are, however, a few indubitable instances of postponed interrogative *ἦ* in Plato: *Lg.*935D *τὴν τῶν κωμῳδῶν προθυμίαν* τοῦ γελοῖα εἰς τοὺς ἀνθρώπους λέγειν ἦ παραδεχόμεθα ...; *R.* 469C. At opening of apodosis: *R.*552A,581B.

(4) Indirect questions: Homer only. Θ111 εἴσεται ἦ καὶ ἐμὸν δόρυ μαίνεται ἐν παλάμῃσιν: *A*83: ν415: τ325. (The MSS. read everywhere ἤ or εἰ. L. & S., doubtfully, prefer ἦ. Kühner (II ii 526) denies that ἦ is ever used in indirect questions.) In π138 (MSS. ἤ or εἰ) the question may be direct.

(Homeric ἦ, ἦε, in the sec nd limb of a disjunctive interrogative or deliberative sentence (direct or indirect) stands for the disjunctive ἤ, ἠέ. See L. & S., ἤ, A.ii.)

III. Combinations. Most of these are used both affirmatively and interrogatively.

(1) ἦ ἄρα, ἦ ἄρ, ἦ ῥα: mainly Homeric.

(i) Affirmative. Hom.*Γ*183 ἦ ῥά νύ τοι πολλοὶ δεδμήατο: *Δ*82 Ἦ ῥ' αὖτις πόλεμος ... ἔσσεται: ω28 ἦ τ' ἄρα: 193 ἦ ἄρα σὺν μεγάλῃ ἀρετῇ ἐκτήσω ἄκοιτιν: S.*Aj.*955 Ἦ ῥα κελαινώπαν θυμὸν ἐφυβρίζει πολύτλας ἀνήρ.

(ii) Interrogative. Hom.*E*421 Ζεῦ πάτερ, ἦ ῥά τί μοι κεχολώσεαι ...; N446 Δηΐφοβ', ἦ ἄρα δή τι ἐΐσκομεν ...; υ166 Ξεῖν', ἦ ἄρ τί σε μᾶλλον Ἀχαιοὶ εἰσορόωσιν ...; B.5.165 ἦ ῥά τις ἐν μεγάροις ... ἔστιν ... σοὶ φυὰν ἀλιγκία; A.*Pers.*633 (lyr.) ἦ ῥ' ἀίει μου ... βασιλεὺς ...; S.*Aj.*172 (lyr.) ἦ ῥά σε ... Ἄρτεμις ... ὥρμασε ...; Hom.Ξ190: *T*56.

(iii) The contracted form ἦρα is often found in dialects other than Attic. (The decision between ἦρα and ἦ ῥα is difficult.) Sapph.*Fr.*53: Alc.*Fr.*40: Alcm.*Fr.*31: Pi.*P.*4.57: 9.37: 11.38: *I.*7.3: Hp.*Prorrh.*i 117,120,121: *Epid.*iv 25,27: v 77: vi 2.5: 2.20: 3.7. (In Ar.*Th.*260 *R* reads ἦρ, but ἆρ' is no doubt right.) See further *s.v.* ἆρα.

(2) ἦ γάρ, ἦ ... γάρ. (The split form even in prose, [Pl.] *Sis.*387D.)

(i) Affirmative. Hom.*A*78 ἦ γὰρ ὀΐομαι ἄνδρα χολωσέμεν: π199 ἦ γάρ τοι νέον ἦσθα γέρων: S.*Aj.*1330 ἦ γὰρ εἴην οὐκ ἂν εὖ φρονῶν: Hom.*A*232,293: Thgn.524: E.*Cyc.*150: *Hipp.*90, 756: Ar.*Pax* 1292: X.*An.*i 6.8.

(ii) Interrogative. A.*Pr.*745 Ἦ γάρ τι λοιπὸν τῇδε πημάτων ἐρεῖς; 974 Ἦ κἀμὲ γάρ τι συμφοραῖς ἐπαιτιᾷ; S.*Aj.*1133 Ἦ σοὶ γὰρ Αἴας πολέμιος προὔστη ποτέ; *Ant.*44 Ἦ γὰρ νοεῖς θάπτειν σφ' . . .; *Ph.*654: E.*Heracl.*729 Ἦ παιδαγωγεῖν γὰρ . . . χρεών; A.*Pr.*757: *Ag.*1366: S.*OT* 1000: E.*Hipp.*702: *Or.*739,1595,1600: X.*Cyr.*ii 2.11 Ἦ γὰρ οἴει . . .; *Oec.*4.23 Τί λέγεις . . .; ἦ γὰρ σὺ . . . ἐφύτευσας; Elliptical (*Nonne* ?, *nicht wahr* ?): Pl.*Cra.*390A, 421C: *Prm.*153B: *Tht.*160E: *Grg.*449D,468C,D: *Phd.*93D: *Euthphr.*10E,13A: *Phdr.*266D: *id. saep.*

(3) ἦ δή. Hom.*A*518 Ἦ δὴ λοίγια ἔργ' ὅ τέ μ' ἐχθοδοπῆσαι ἐφήσεις Ἥρῃ: *B*272 Ὢ πόποι, ἦ δὴ μυρί' Ὀδυσσεὺς ἐσθλὰ ἔοργε: *E*422 ἦ μάλα δή (Hes.*Sc.*103: Pi.*P.*4.64): *Ξ*53 Ἦ δὴ ταῦτά γ' ἑτοῖμα τετεύχαται: *P*538 Ἦ δὴ μάν: *Φ*583 Ἦ δή που: A.*Ch.* 742 ἦ δὴ κλύων ἐκεῖνος εὐφρανεῖ νόον: S.*El.*314 Ἦ δὴ ἂν ἐγὼ θαρσοῦσα μᾶλλον ἐς λόγους τοὺς σοὺς ἱκοίμην (but the text is uncertain): E.*Supp.*423 ἦ δὴ νοσῶδες τοῦτο τοῖς ἀμείνοσιν: *Ion* 711 ἦ δὴ πέλας δείπνων κυρεῖ: Hom.*B*337: *O*467: *Ω*518: *α*253: ε182: Hdt.v 92α1 Ἦ δὴ ὅ τε οὐρανὸς ἔνερθε ἔσται τῆς γῆς . . . ὅτε γε . . . .

(4) ἦ δῆτα. For this very doubtful combination in A.*Th.*670, see δῆτα, IV.2.

(5) ἦ θην. See θην. (6) ἦ καί. (i) Affirmative. The only example known to me is Ar.*Lys.*1226 ἦ καὶ χαρίεντες ἦσαν οἱ Λακωνικοί: and there is no close coherence between the particles here (cf. Lawson on A.*Ag.*942).

(ii) Interrogative (common). Sometimes ἦ καί, 'inquires with a certain eagerness' (Jebb on S.*El.*314): sometimes καί means 'also', and goes closely with an individual word. A.*Ag.* 1207 Ἀλλ' ἦν παλαιστὴς κάρτ' ἐμοὶ πνέων χάριν.—Ἦ καὶ τέκνων εἰς ἔργον ἠλθέτην νόμῳ; ('Did you also (or 'actually') . . . ?'): 1362: *Ch.*526: *Pers.*978: S.*Aj.*38,44,48,97: *OT* 368, 757,1045: E.*HF* 614: *El.*278,351: Pl.*Phd.*94A: *Tht.*149A: *Euthd.*285E: *R.*534B: X.*Cyr.*i 3.6: ii 2.20: 3.23: *Oec.*7.35: 8.1: 19.12.

(7) ἦ νυ. Hom.*X*11 ἦ νύ τοι οὔ τι μέλει Τρώων πόνος.

(8) ἦ οὖν. Pl.*R.*484C,485C (*bis*), 493C,580C.

ἦ . . . οὖν. E.*Supp.*574 Ἦ πᾶσιν οὖν σ' ἔφυσεν ἐξαρκεῖν πατήρ; *Or.*787 Ἦ λέγωμεν οὖν ἀδελφῇ ταῦτ' ἐμῇ; X.*Oec.*14.3 Ἦ καὶ ταύτην οὖν . . . τὴν δικαιοσύνην σὺ ὑποδύει διδάσκειν; Pl.*R.*605E: *Prm.*142A: *Sph.*250D: *Amat.*137D.

(9) ἦ που (see also I.4 above), ἦ . . . που (in Homer the particles sometimes seem to form a unity even when separated).

Here the hesitation implied by *που* imposes a slight check on the certainty implied by *ἦ*. Cf. *δήπου*.

(i) Affirmative (in the lyrics of Sophocles sometimes late in the sentence. But in Lys.xii 88 *ἦπου* is corrupt). Hom.*Γ*43 *ἦ που καγχαλόωσι . . . Ἀχαιοί*: *Π*830 *Πάτροκλ', ἦ που ἔφησθα . . .*: *ζ*278 *ἦ τινά που πλαγχθέντα κομίσσατο*: Hes.*Sc.*92 *ἦ που πολλὰ μετεστοναχίζετ' ὀπίσσω . . .*: A.*Pr.*521 *Ἦ πού τι σεμνόν ἐστιν ὃ ξυναμπέχεις*: S.*Aj.*382 *Ἰὼ πάντα δρῶν . . . ἦ που πολὺν γέλωθ' ὑφ' ἡδονῆς ἄγεις*: 1008 *ἦ πού με Τελαμὼν . . . δέξαιτ' ἂν εὐπρόσωπος* (ironical): *Tr.*846–7 *τὰ δ' . . . ἦ που ὀλοὰ στένει, ἦ που . . . τέγγει*: *Ph.*1130 *ὦ τόξον φίλον . . . ἦ που ἐλεινὸν ὁρᾷς*: Ar.*V.*725 *Ἦ που σοφὸς ἦν, ὅστις ἔφασκεν . . .*: S.*Aj.*624,850: E.*Heracl.*55: *Ba.*939: *Hel.*1465: Ar.*Lys.*28: *Th.*63: *Ra.*803: *Pl.*700,832: Pl.*Grg.*448A *Ἦ που ἄρα ῥᾳδίως ἀποκρινῇ*: *R.*595C *Ἦ που ἄρ', ἔφη, ἐγὼ συννοήσω*: Lycurg.71 *ἦ που ταχέως ἂν ἠνέσχετό τις . . . τοιοῦτον ἔργον* (ironical): Pl.*Euthphr.*4A. In conjuring up an historical scene: Lys.ii 37 *ἦ που . . . πολλάκις μὲν ἐδεξιώσαντο ἀλλήλους* ('I can imagine them . . .'): ii 39.

(ii) Interrogative: 'I expect . . . ?' (Here, as often, the line between questions and statements cannot be sharply drawn.) Hom.*O*245 *ἦ πού τί σε κῆδος ἱκάνει; ζ*125 *ἦ νύ που ἀνθρώπων εἰμὶ σχεδὸν αὐδηέντων*; 200 *ἦ μή πού τινα δυσμενέων φάσθ' ἔμμεναι ἀνδρῶν*; S.*Aj.*176 *ἦ ῥά σε . . . Ἄρτεμις . . . ὥρμασε . . . ἦ πού τινος νίκας ἀκάρπωτον χάριν . . .*; E.*Med.*1308 *Τί δ' ἔστιν; ἦ που κἄμ' ἀποκτεῖναι θέλει*; *Or.*435 *Τίς δ' ἄλλος; ἦ που τῶν ἀπ' Αἰγίσθου φίλων*; E.*Alc.*199: *Tr.*59: Ar.*Lys.*1089: *Pl.*970: Pl. *R.*450D *Ὦ ἄριστε, ἦ που βουλόμενός με παραθαρρύνειν λέγεις*; *Ly.*207D *Ἦ που . . . σφόδρα φιλεῖ σε ὁ πατήρ*; ('I suppose your father is very fond of you?'): Din.57 *ἦ που ἄρα ἡ βουλή, Δημόσθενες, τὰ ψευδῆ ἀπέφηνεν*; *οὐ δήπου.*

(10) *ἦ τε, ἦ τοι.* See *τε*, II.2.xiii: *τοι*, VI.8.

(11) *ἐπεὶ ἦ, τί ἦ, ὅτι ἦ.* (On the question of accentuation, see Kühner II ii 145, Anm.1, and L. & S. *ἦ*, I.2. According to Eustathius, the Attic accentuation is *τιή, ὁτιή*.) In these forms *ἦ* has sunk to the level of a mere suffix, and is used in a manner similar to *δή*.

ἐπεὶ ἦ is used by Homer in the combinations *ἐπεὶ ἦ πολύ, ἐπεὶ ἦ μάλα, ἐπεὶ ἦ καί.* Hom.*A*156,169: *Υ*437: *id. saep.*: Xenoph.*Fr.*6.4 *ἐπεὶ ἦ φίλου ἀνέρος ἐστὶν ψυχή.*

τί ἦ, τιή (Homer, Hesiod, and Attic Comedy): Hom.O244 τί ἦ δὲ σὺ νόσφιν ἀπ' ἄλλων ἧσ' ὀλιγηπελέων; π421: Ar. *V*.1155 Τιὴ τί δή; (*Th*.84).

ὁτιή. Attic Comedy. In sense 'because': Ar.*Eq*.29,34,181, 236: *id saep*. *Nu*.784 'Ότιὴ τί; 755 'Ότιὴ τί δή; More rarely in sense 'that': Ar.*Eq*.360: *Nu*.331: *V*.1395: *Av*.1010.

(L. & S. observe that "this ἦ (or ἤ) is probably to be recognized in Hom.*B*289 (ὥς τε γὰρ ἦ), γ348, τ109 (ὥς τέ τευ ἦ), where *codd*. have ἤ".)

(12) ἠμέν, ἠδέ. These combinations are formed by adding μέν and δέ to affirmative ἦ: 'verily on the one hand', 'verily on the other'. ἠμέν is wholly, ἠδέ for the most part, confined to Epic.

(i) ἠμὲν ... ἠδέ. Hom.*Δ*258 περὶ μέν σε τίω ... ἠμὲν ἐνὶ πτολέμῳ ἠδ' ἀλλοίῳ ἐπὶ ἔργῳ ἠδ' ἐν δαίθ': *E*128 ὄφρ' εὖ γιγνώσκῃς ἠμὲν θεὸν ἠδὲ καὶ ἄνδρα. (ii) μὲν ... ἠδέ. Hom.μ168 αὐτίκ' ἔπειτ' ἄνεμος μὲν ἐπαύσατο ἠδὲ γαλήνη ἔπλετο νηνεμίη: 380 βοῦς ... ἧσιν ἐγώ γε χαίρεσκον μὲν ἰὼν εἰς οὐρανὸν ἀστερόεντα, ἠδ' ὁπότ' ἂψ ἐπὶ γαῖαν ἀπ' οὐρανόθεν προτραποίμην. (iii) ἠμὲν ... τε. Hom.θ575 ἠμὲν ὅσοι χαλεποί τε καὶ ἄγριοι οὐδὲ δίκαιοι, οἵ τε φιλόξεινοι. (iv) ἠμὲν ... καί. Hom.*O*664 ἠμὲν ὅτεῳ ζώουσι καὶ ᾧ κατατεθνήκασι: *O*670: Hes.*Op*.339 ἠμὲν ὅτ' εὐνάζῃ καὶ ὅτ' ἂν φάος ἱερὸν ἔλθῃ. (v) ἠμὲν ... δέ. Hom.*M*428 πολλοὶ δ' οὐτάζοντο ... ἠμὲν ὅτεῳ στρεφθέντι μετάφρενα γυμνωθείη μαρναμένων, πολλοὶ δὲ διαμπερὲς ἀσπίδος αὐτῆς. (vi) τε ... ἠδέ. Hom.*I*99 Ζεὺς ἐγγυάλιξε σκῆπτρόν τ' ἠδὲ θέμιστας: *A*400: *B*262,815: *M*61: *id. saep*: Hes.*Op*.767,813. (vii) ἠδέ alone. Hom.*A*251 ἅμα τράφεν ἠδ' ἐγένοντο: *B*27: Hes.*Th*.47,113.

There are a few instances of ἠδέ in the lyric and elegiac poets and tragedians. Ion Eleg.*Fr*.5 ἠνορέῃ τε κεκασμένος ἠδὲ καὶ αἰδοῖ: Simon.*Fr*.32 οὕτω γὰρ Ὅμηρος ἠδὲ Στασίχορος ἄεισε λαοῖς: Pi.*O*.13.43 ὅσσα τ' ἐν Δελφοῖσιν ἀριστεύσατε, ἠδὲ χόρτοις ἐν λέοντος: *Fr*.151(168).3 καὶ τότ' ἐγὼ σαρκῶν τ' ἐνοπὰν ἴδον ἠδ' ὀστέων στεναγμὸν βαρύν: Semon.18.1 ἠδέ Ahrens (καί *codd*.).

Aeschylus in his earlier plays uses ἠδέ in lyrics only, and far more frequently in the *Persae*, a play in which there are many Ionic forms, than elsewhere: (he uses it 'almost exclusively in catalogues of names, titles, etc.', Verrall on *Eu*. 188): *Th*.862 Ἀντιγόνη τ' ἠδ' Ἰσμήνη: *Pers.*16 οἵτε τὸ Σούσων ἠδ' Ἀγβατάνων καὶ τὸ παλαιὸν Κίσσιον ἕρκος προλιπόντες ἔβαν: 21,22,26: *ib.saep.* But in the trilogy all the examples, except *Ag.*42, are from dialogue: *Ch.*232 (a certain emendation for εἰς δέ): 1025 ᾄδειν ἕτοιμος ἠδ' ὑπορχεῖσθαι κότῳ: *Eu.*188,414 (doubtful). The five instances from Sophocles and Euripides are all in dialogue: S.*Fr.*354 Φερητίδης τ' Ἄδμητος ἠδ' ὁ Δωτιεὺς Λαπίθης Κόρωνος: *Fr* 505 κρημνούς τε καὶ σήραγγας ἠδ' ἐπακτίας αὐλῶνας: E.*Hec.*323 εἰσὶν παρ' ἡμῖν οὐδὲν ἧσσον ἄθλιαι γραῖαι γυναῖκες ἠδὲ πρεσβῦται σέθεν: *HF*30 Ἀμφίον' ἠδὲ Ζῆθον: *IA* 812 γῆν γὰρ λιπὼν Φάρσαλον ἠδὲ Πηλέα. (Add S.*Ant.*673 (doubtful): *Ph.*491 (*coni.* Jebb).)

Comedy. Eup.*Fr.*14 καὶ πρὸς τούτοισί γε θαλλόν, κύτισόν τ' ἠδὲ σφάκον εὐώδη: Alex.*Fr.*133 τυρῷ τε σάξον ἁλσί τ' ἠδ' ὀριγάνῳ (probably corrupt).

Prose. There are no examples in classical prose: but Galen τῶν Ἱπποκράτους γλωσσῶν ἐξήγησις (19.102, Kühn) testifies in the gloss ἠδέ: ἔτι δέ to Hippocrates' use of ἠδέ.

The shorter form ἰδέ is confined (except for S.*Ant.*969 ἀκταὶ Βοσπόριαι ἰδ' ὁ Θρῃκῶν ἠιών) to Epic: Hom.*Γ*194: *E*3: *id. saep.*: Hes.*Sc.*19: *id. saep.*

τε ... ἰδέ: Hom.*Z*469 χαλκόν τε ἰδὲ λόφον: Hes.*Th.*887 πλεῖστα θεῶν τε ἰδυῖαν ἰδὲ θνητῶν ἀνθρώπων: 11–21 (τε ... ἠδὲ ... ἰδὲ ... καί). Herwerden, p. 382, cites ἰδέ from an inscription.

Θην

This particle (the derivation of which is unknown) is almost confined to Homer and Sicilian literature (Sophron, Epicharmus, and Theocritus). The sole Attic example is A.*Pr.*928 Σύ θην ἃ χρῄζεις, ταῦτ' ἐπιγλωσσᾷ Διός.* It is equivalent in sense to δή, but perhaps rather weaker in force. It often follows οὐ, ἦ, ἐπεί, and γάρ.

Hom.*K*104 οὔ θην Ἕκτορι πάντα νοήματα μητίετα Ζεὺς ἐκτελέει: *N*620 Λείψετέ θην οὕτω γε νέας: *P*29 ὥς θην καὶ σὸν ἐγὼ λύσω μένος: *Φ*568 καὶ γάρ θην τούτῳ τρωτὸς χρώς: ε211 οὐ μέν θην κείνης γε χερείων εὔχομαι εἶναι: π91 Ὦ φίλ', ἐπεί θήν μοι καὶ ἀμείψασθαι θέμις ἐστὶν . . .. Sometimes with a note of contempt: Θ448: N813 (ἦ θην).

Sophr.*Fr.*24,36,56: Epich.*Fr.*34.2 τὸν ῥᾳδίως λαψῇ τυ κἀτ τὸ νῦν γά θην εὔωνον ἀείσιτον: *Fr.*173.5 ὄνος δ' ὄνῳ κάλλιστον, ὗς δέ θην ὑί.

Καί

The etymology of καί is uncertain (for a suggested derivation, see Boisacq), but its primary force is, beyond all reasonable doubt, addition. Like δέ, it is used both as a connective and as a responsive particle: and Kühner is perhaps right in regarding the responsive or 'adverbial' use as the original one in both particles. This includes the meanings 'also' and 'even'; while in some cases, the idea of responsion receding into a dim background (see II.C), καί conveys little more than pure emphasis, 'actually'. Lastly, the employment of καί in two or more clauses of a sentence (whether in co-ordination or in subordination) produces corresponsion, and the addition is regarded as reciprocal. We may conveniently consider the commoner, copulative, use first, even though it may be historically the later: proceeding then to discuss the responsive and corresponsive uses.

I. Copulative, joining single words, phrases, clauses, or sentences. (Joining sentences in, e.g. Hom.Ψ75: Pl.*Euthphr.*3A: *Grg.*462B: Lys.xiv 8: D.xviii 105.) This use is, in general, too common to need illustration. (For a comparison of καί with δέ, see δέ, *ad init.*) In a series of more than two items variety is sometimes sought by using now δέ, now καί. Pl.*Lg.*697B τιμιώτατα μὲν καὶ πρῶτα . . . δεύτερα δὲ . . . καὶ τρίτα: 925D μὲν . . . δὲ . . . δὲ . . . δὲ . . . καὶ . . . δέ. We may notice a few special points where English idiom often differs from Greek.

(1) In Greek, as in Latin, a series of words or phrases is normally either connected throughout, or not connected at all (asyndeton). Occasionally, however, as normally in English,

there is connexion between the last two units only. In some of these cases the last unit stands on a different footing from the rest, either because it is given special prominence, or because it takes the form of an etcetera. Pl.*R*.367D οἷον ὁρᾶν, ἀκούειν, φρονεῖν, καὶ ὑγιαίνειν δή, καὶ ὅσ' ἄλλα ἀγαθὰ . . . ἐστίν: *Phdr.* 246E καλόν, σοφόν, ἀγαθόν, καὶ πᾶν ὅτι τοιοῦτον (cf. *R*.395C): Is.xi 41 τῶν ἑαυτοῦ ἔδωκεν ἀγρὸν 'Ελευσῖνι δυοῖν ταλάντοιν, πρόβατα ἑξήκοντα, αἶγας ἑκατόν, ἔπιπλα, ἵππον λαμπρὸν ἐφ' οὗ ἐφυλάρχησε, καὶ τὴν ἄλλην κατασκευὴν ἅπασαν: Pl.*Lg*.649D: *Phd*.65D: *Plt*.260E: *R*.491B,580A: Arist.*Po*.1451a20 (some MSS.): Aeschin.i 18. In Hdt.vii 132.1 the length of the last unit, καὶ Θηβαῖοι κτλ., explains the insertion of καί: also the fact that the last unit is bipartite: cf.X.*Cyn*.4.4. In other cases there appears to be no very obvious reason for the irregularity: X.*HG*vii 2.2 ἦσαν δ' οὗτοι Κορίνθιοι, 'Επιδαύριοι... καὶ Πελληνεῖς (cf. *Ages*.2.6): Arist.*Rh*.1371b15 οἷον ἄνθρωπος ἀνθρώπῳ ἵππος ἵππῳ καὶ νέος νέῳ (καί before ἵππος in all MSS. but *A*, the best): Ar.*V*.659 (καί in *Aldine* only: here the last two units seem to cohere closely). In Pl.*Smp*.203D the link seems to be inserted in the middle of the series (καὶ φρονήσεως).*

(2) πολύς and a qualitative attribute applied to a single substantive (expressed or understood) are normally linked by καί. Hom.*I*330 πολλὰ καὶ ἐσθλά: E.*Andr*.953 πολλὰ καὶ κακά: A.*Ag*.63 πολλὰ παλαίσματα καὶ γυιοβαρῆ: Pl.*Smp*.175E πολλῆς καὶ καλῆς σοφίας: X.*An*.v 6.4 πολλά μοι καὶ ἀγαθὰ γένοιτο: D.xxviii 1 πολλὰ καὶ μεγάλα. Very rarely in reverse order. Lys. xxiv 19 συλλέγεσθαί φησιν ἀνθρώπους ὡς ἐμὲ πονηροὺς καὶ πολλούς (here perhaps καί may emphasize πολλούς): Isoc.xii 179 εἰς τόπους κατοικίσαι μικροὺς καὶ πολλούς: D.xxxvii 57 τόν γε δεινά σε καὶ πόλλ' εἰργασμένον (a variation on πολλὰ καὶ δεινά, just before.)

πολύς linked by καί to adverb. S.*OC*1565 πολλῶν γὰρ ἂν καὶ μάταν πημάτων ἱκνουμένων (but καί might be emphatic, and the text is very doubtful: in Pl.*Tht*.202D I agree with Campbell that καί is intensive.)

(3) There are few examples of καί linking qualitative attributes, and most of them are textually doubtful. In A.*Ag*.1452–3 φύλακος εὐμενεστάτου καὶ πολλὰ τλάντος, καί seems to me doubtful Greek. *Ch*.428: E.*Fr*.941 (καί usually emended): Pl.*Phdr*.235B. In

*Phdr.*250B μόγις αὐτῶν καὶ ὀλίγοι, καί may mean 'even' (but see Stallbaum). Cf. τε p. 501 (d).

(4) καί (unlike δέ: *q.v.* I.A.2) is not often used in anaphora. S.*Tr.*30 νὺξ γὰρ εἰσάγει καὶ νὺξ ἀπωθεῖ διαδεδεγμένη πόνον: *Ant.* 1158: Pl.*Grg.*496B ἐν μέρει λαμβάνει καὶ ἐν μέρει ἀπαλλάττεται: *Prt.*356B συνθεὶς τὰ ἡδέα καὶ συνθεὶς τὰ λυπηρά (συνθεὶς τὰ ἡδέα καὶ τὰ λυπηρά would be misleading): *R.*476A χωρὶς μὲν . . . καὶ χωρὶς αὖ: *Lg.*758E τίς ἐπιμέλεια καὶ τίς τάξις; 813E: 903C πᾶς γὰρ ἰατρὸς καὶ πᾶς ἔντεχνος δημιουργός: *R.*538D: Lys.xxxii 22 ἵνα . . . καὶ ἵνα. . . . Hp.*VM* 2 ἑτέρῃ ὁδῷ καὶ ἑτέρῳ σχήματι. With chiasmus: Hdt.iii 119.6 ἀνὴρ μὲν ἄν μοι ἄλλος γένοιτο . . . καὶ τέκνα ἄλλα: Pl.*R.*515A Ἄτοπον, ἔφη, λέγεις εἰκόνα καὶ δεσμώτας ἀτόπους: *Lg.*668A. Neither Pl.*Tht.*159B nor the repetitions instanced in (4) *ad fin.* can be described as anaphoric: cf. δέ, I.A.2.*

(5) Appositionally related ideas are occasionally linked by καί (as sometimes by δέ (I.A.1) and τέ (I.1.*e*)). A.*Th.*788 τέκνοις . . . ἐφῆκεν . . . πικρογλώσσους ἀράς, καί σφε σιδαρονόμῳ διὰ χερί ποτε λαχεῖν κτήματα (Tucker takes καὶ λαχεῖν as explaining ἀράς): E.*Ba.*919 δισσὰς δὲ Θήβας καὶ πόλισμ' ἑπτάστομον: *IA* 751 Σιμόεντα καὶ δίνας ἀργυροειδεῖς: *HF* 15. (In Hom.*h.Ap.*17 (κεκλιμένη πρὸς μακρὸν ὄρος καὶ Κύνθιον ὄχθον) καί means 'and in particular' (**E**398, in reverse order: πρὸς δῶμα Διὸς καὶ μακρὸν Ὄλυμπον): cf. Hdt.ix 25.2. With a partitive genitive. Hdt.iii 136.1 καταβάντες . . . ἐς Φοινίκην καὶ Φοινίκης ἐς Σιδῶνα πόλιν (i 52,102.2: iv 151.2): ii 32.4 παρήκουσι παρὰ πᾶσαν Λίβυες καὶ Λιβύων ἔθνεα πολλά ('Libyans, and many tribes of Libyans'): ix 21.3 Ἀθηναῖοι ὑπεδέξαντο καὶ Ἀθηναίων οἱ τριηκόσιοι λογάδες (in viii 17 καί is indispensable, as two distinct facts are stated: τῶν δὲ Ἑλλήνων . . . ἠρίστευσαν Ἀθηναῖοι καὶ Ἀθηναίων Κλεινίης). With addition of an adverbial qualification: i 124.3 ποίεε ταῦτα καὶ ποίεε κατὰ τάχος: iv 189.3 (Cf. δέ, I.A.2, and see Stein on Hdt.i 52.): X.*An.*vii 6.17 (καὶ . . . μέντοι).

(6) Καί with a sense of climax: cf. οὐδέ, I.2, *ad init.* (But here the particle is usually reinforced: καὶ . . . γε, καὶ δή, καὶ . . . δή, καὶ δὴ καί.) A.*Pers.*750 θεῶν ἁπάντων . . . καὶ Ποσειδῶνος ('and most of all Poseidon'): Th.iii 17.1 παραπλήσιαι καὶ ἔτι πλείους: vii 68.2: Pl.*Ti.*75B διπλοῦν καὶ πολλαπλοῦν: Arist.*Rh.*1374b32 χαλεπὸν καὶ ἀδύνατον. Preceding οὗτος: Hdt.vi 11.2 δούλοισι, καὶ

τούτοισι ὡς δρηπέτῃσι. Καὶ ταῦτα, 'and that too': X.*Cyr*.ii 2.16: *et saep*. (Introducing a finite clause, A.*Eu*.112.)

(7) After words expressing sameness, likeness, or contrast. S.*OT* 611 ἴσον καί: *et saep*.: Hdt.vii 50 γνώμῃσι ἐχρέωντο ὁμοίῃσι καὶ σύ: Th.vii 28.4 οὐχ ὁμοίως καὶ πρίν: 70.1 ναυσὶ παραπλησίαις τὸν ἀριθμὸν καὶ πρότερον: Pl.*Lg*.967A πᾶν τοὐναντίον ἔχει νῦν τε καὶ ὅτε . . .: X.*An*.vii 7.49 ἀνομοίως ἔχοντα . . . νῦν τε καὶ ὅτε . . .

(8) Linking alternatives, instead of ἤ. A.*Pr*.212 Θέμις, καὶ Γαῖα, πολλῶν ὀνομάτων μορφὴ μία: S.*Ph*.1082 πέτρας γύαλον θερμὸν καὶ παγετῶδες ('hot or icy, as the case may be': cf. Pl. *R*.411A Τοῦ δὲ ἀναρμόστου (ψυχὴ) δειλὴ καὶ ἄγροικος;): *Phdr*. 246B: Isoc. vii 78 ὁμοίας καὶ παραπλησίας (the weaker expression being alternative to the stronger: cf. Th.i 22.4: 143.3: v 74.1: vii 19.2: 42.2: 78.1: but in Pl.*R*.356B αὕτη τε καὶ τοιαύτη means 'this, *and* of such a nature').

In numerical approximations, where two alternative estimates are given. Th.i 82.2 διελθόντων ἐτῶν δύο καὶ τριῶν: X.*Eq*.4.4 ἁμάξας τέτταρας καὶ πέντε. (Cf. Pl.*Ap*.23A ὀλίγου τινὸς ἀξία καὶ οὐδενός ('little or nothing'): *Tht*.173E σμικρὰ καὶ οὐδέν. Perhaps these might rather be classed under (5) as examples of descending climax. Cf. also the common χθὲς καὶ πρώην.)

(In Pl.*La*.191E καὶ . . . ἢ . . . , 'both . . . or', can hardly stand (though Hartung keeps it): καὶ μένοντες ἢ ἀναστρέφοντες: καί is usually read for ἤ.)

(9) Sometimes used where the context implies an adversative sense, 'and yet': as we might say 'he is seventy years old, and he walks ten miles a day'. (Cf. p. 323, and see Jebb on S.*El*. 597.) A.*Th*.639 τοιαῦτ' ἀυτεῖ (such curses against his brother) καὶ θεοὺς γενεθλίους καλεῖ ('and withal', Tucker): E.*HF* 509 ὁρᾶτ' ἔμ' ὅσπερ ἦ περίβλεπτος βροτοῖς . . . καί μ' ἀφείλεθ' ἡ τύχη . . . ἡμέρᾳ μιᾷ: *Med*.1243 τί μέλλομεν τὰ δεινὰ κἀναγκαῖα μὴ πράσσειν κακά; A.*Eu*.110: S.*Ph*.385: *OT* 567: *Tr*.1048,1072: *OC* 6: E.*Andr*.657: *Heracl*.554,981: *Ph*.899: *Hipp*.284: *Ion* 1108: Pl. *Grg*.519D καὶ τούτου τοῦ λόγου τί ἂν ἀλογώτερον εἴη πρᾶγμα . . .; καίτοι Heindorf): Hdt.ix 37.3.

In Ar.*Eq*..1250 κεἰ is generally read, and in Lys.vi 31, 47 καίτοι: but in Lys.xxiv 9 (καὶ πῶς οὐ δεινόν ἐστι . . .;) καί may well stand. *καί* for *δέ*: Pl.*Alc.I* 106A *πῶς διὰ σοῦ μοι ἔσται καὶ ἄνευ σοῦ οὐκ ἂν γένοιτο*; *Lg.*767A,776C. Cf. *τε*, I.7.

(10) Of two clauses linked by *καί*, the first sometimes gives the time or circumstances in which the action of the second takes place. S.*OT*718: *Ph.*355: E.*Ba.*1077: Th.i50.5 *ἤδη δὲ . . . ἐπεπαίανιστο . . . καὶ οἱ Κορίνθιοι ἐξαπίνης πρύμναν ἐκρούοντο* (see Krüger's Index to Thucydides): Pl.*Phd.*116B. Cf.*μέν*, III. 1.i, *τε*, I.7.

II. Responsive. *καί* here marks an addition to the content of the preceding (less frequently, e.g. Pl.*R.*327A, of the following) context: 'also'. Further, when the addition is surprising, or difficult of acceptance, and when a sense of climax is present, 'also' becomes 'even'. (Greek does not, like English, express the distinction between these two ideas.)

A. In general. These uses of *καί* are too common in all periods and styles of Greek literature to need copious illustration.

(1) 'Also': 'even' (ascending climax). Hom.K556 *θεὸς καὶ ἀμείνονας ἵππους δωρήσαιτο*: A.*Pr.*59 *δεινὸς γὰρ εὑρεῖν κἀξ ἀμηχάνων πόρον*: Hdt.i2 *διαπρηξαμένους καὶ τἆλλα τῶν εἵνεκεν ἀπίκατο*: Th.i14.1 *φαίνεται δὲ καὶ ταῦτα . . . τριήρεσι μὲν ὀλίγαις χρώμενα*: Pl.*Euthphr.*2D *τῶν νέων πρῶτον . . . μετὰ δὲ τοῦτο καὶ τῶν ἄλλων.* Repeated. Lys.vii18 *ἀλλὰ καὶ περὶ ὧν ἀποκρυπτόμεθα μηδένα εἰδέναι, καὶ περὶ ἐκείνων πυνθάνονται*; whereas in X.*HG*iv8.5 the two *καί*'s have separate references: *καὶ ἐν τῇ Ἀσίᾳ, ἣ ἐξ ἀρχῆς βασιλέως ἐστί, καὶ Τῆμνος, οὐ μεγάλη πόλις . . . .* See also Thgn.1345 (II.B.2).

(2) Marking a minimum (descending climax). Hom.α58 *ἱέμενος καὶ καπνὸν ἀποθρῴσκοντα νοῆσαι ἧς γαίης* ('were it but the smoke'): Pi.*O.*2.28 *ἐν καὶ θαλάσσᾳ*: E.*IA* 1192 *τίς δὲ καὶ προσβλέψεται παίδων σ' . . .*; ('so much as look at'): Ar.*Nu.*528 *ἀνδρῶν οἷς ἡδὺ καὶ λέγειν*: S.*El.*1054: Pl.*Ap.*28B *ἄνδρα ὅτου τι καὶ σμικρὸν ὄφελός ἐστιν*: 35B: *Prt.*317A. Pl.*Lg.*853B *Αἰσχρὸν . . . καὶ νομοθετεῖν* ('to legislate at all': not only legislation of this or that kind, but the possibility of any legislation, is ruled out). Cf. *οὐδέ*, II.2.ii.

Between article and infinitive. E.*Hel.*748 *εὔηθες . . . τὸ καὶ δοκεῖν . . .*: Pl.*Lg.*853B *τὸ καὶ ἀξιοῦν . . . αἰσχρόν.* Also exclamatory, 'to think that . . .!': S.*Ph.*234 φεῦ τὸ καὶ λαβεῖν πρόσφθεγμα τοιοῦδ' ἀνδρός: E.*Med.*1052 τὸ καὶ προσέσθαι μαλθακοὺς λόγους φρενί.

(3) In καί τι καί (where τι is sometimes adverbial: Pi.*O.*1.28: Th.i 107.6) the first καί is copulative, the second adverbial. S.*Ph.*274 ῥάκη προθέντες βαιὰ καί τι καί βορᾶς ἐπωφέλημα σμικρόν: Ar.*Eq.*1242 Ἠλλαντοπώλουν καί τι καὶ βινεσκόμην ('and did a bit of *adultery*': I doubt Neil's statement here that καί τι καί was 'precious'): Th.i 107.6 καί τι καὶ τοῦ δήμου καταλύσεως ὑποψίᾳ: D.xix 194 κελεύσαντος δὲ . . . καί τι καὶ νεανιευσαμένου: 197 κατακλίνεσθαι καί τι καὶ ᾄδειν ('and give them a bit of a *song*'): Th.ii 17.1: Pl.*Cri.*43A. S.*Ph.*308 καί πού τι καί (Pi.*O.*1.28: Th.ii 87.2): *Fr.*305 καὶ δή τι καί (Pl. *Sph.*251C).

(In Ant.v 6, as the text stands, both καί's are adverbial: ἀνάγκη δὲ κινδυνεύοντα περὶ αὐτῷ καί πού τι καὶ ἐξαμαρτεῖν. But there is every ground for supposing that a verb of fearing has fallen out before περί.)

Cf. Th.i 107.4 τὸ δέ τι καὶ . . .: viii 80.4 καί τις καὶ ναυμαχία βραχεῖα γίγνεται: Pl.*R.*561A ἀλλά τι καί.

B. Under the heading 'Responsive' I group a number of clearly marked uses of καί in which the particle has a structural function: that is to say, it denotes the addition of the content of a subordinate clause (relative, causal, final, or consecutive) to that of the main clause: or vice versa (apodotic use).

(1) In relative clauses (cf. (8) below).

(i) In general. καί emphasizes the fact that the relative clause contains an addition to the information contained in the main clause: whereas δή (*q.v.* I.9) stresses the importance of the antecedent, or the closeness of the relation, and γε (*q.v.* I.5 and II.2) usually marks the relative clause as having a limiting force. καί is often combined with a preceding δή here: for ὥσπερ γε καί, see γε, I.5 *ad fin.*

Hom.*A* 249 Νέστωρ ἡδυεπὴς ἀνόρουσε . . . τοῦ καὶ ἀπὸ γλώσσης μέλιτος γλυκίων ῥέεν αὐδή ('even Nestor from whose tongue . . .'): A.*Th.*732,760: S.*OC*792 πολλῷ γ' (ἄμεινον φρονῶ), ὅσῳπερ καὶ σαφεστέρων κλύω: E.*Or.*920 αὐτουργός—οἵπερ καὶ μόνοι σῴζουσι γῆν: Ar.*Av.*822 Νεφελοκοκκυγία, ἵνα καὶ τὰ

Θεαγένους τὰ πολλὰ χρήματα: *Th.*621 Ἔσθ' ὁ δεῖν', ὅς καί ποτε . . .: Hom.*B* 827 : *Υ* 165 (combined with 'Epic' τε): Hes.*Th.*458: E.*El.* 984: Ar.*Ec.*338: Hdt.i 78 ἰδόντι δὲ τοῦτο Κροίσῳ, ὥσπερ καὶ ἦν, ἔδοξε τέρας εἶναι: Pl.*Phd.*59D εἰς τὸ δικαστήριον ἐν ᾧ καὶ ἡ δίκη ἐγένετο: Hdt.i 80,142: v76: Pl.*Phd.*110D,113B: *Ti.*20C.

The emphasis which καί gives to a relative clause can often be best brought out in English by the insertion of a new (pronominal) antecedent. S.*Ph.*297 ἔφην' ἄφαντον φῶς, ὃ καὶ σῴζει μ' ἀεί ('and that it is which preserves me'): Pl.*Phd.*81D ἀλλὰ τοῦ ὁρατοῦ μετέχουσαι, διὸ καὶ ὁρῶνται ('and that is why they are seen'): *Tht.*169D διαφέρειν τινάς, οὓς δὴ καὶ εἶναι σοφούς: *R.*408B ἰάσασθαι, ὅθεν δὴ καὶ κεραυνωθῆναι αὐτόν: *Men.*96E: *Tht.*194A: *R.*371B,432E.

(ii) καί following a relative (especially the universalizing ὅστις) often gives an effect of limitation, by imposing an additional qualification. A.*Pr.*1064 παραμυθοῦ μ' ὅ τι καὶ πείσεις: S.*Tr.* 726 οὐδ' ἐλπίς, ἥτις καὶ θράσος τι προξενεῖ (a hope which is not only a hope, but a hope warranting confidence): *OT* 1239 ὅσον γε κἀν ἐμοὶ μνήμης ἔνι, πεύσει . . .: *Aj.*917 οὐδεὶς ἄν, ὅστις καὶ φίλος, τλαίη βλέπειν: *OC* 1051 οὗ πότνιαι σεμνὰ τιθηνοῦνται τέλη θνατοῖσιν, ὧν καὶ χρυσέα κλῇς ἐπὶ γλώσσᾳ βέβακε: E.*Hel.* 1200 Ἥκει γὰρ ὅστις καὶ τάδ' ἀγγέλλει σαφῆ; *Or.*439 Τί δρῶντες ὅ τι καὶ σαφὲς ἔχεις εἰπεῖν ἐμοί; *Ion* 232 Πάντα θεᾶσθ', ὅ τι καὶ θέμις, ὄμμασι: Ar.*Ec.*350 ὅ τι κἄμ' εἰδέναι; Hdt.ii 85 ἄνθρωπος τοῦ τις καὶ λόγος ᾖ: Th.ii 49.6 καὶ τὸ σῶμα, ὅσονπερ χρόνον καὶ ἡ νόσος ἀκμάζοι, οὐκ ἐμαραίνετο: Pl.*R.*492A ὅτι καὶ ἄξιον λόγου: D.v 16 αἱ συμμαχίαι τοῦτον ἔχουσι τὸν τρόπον, ὧν καὶ φροντίσειεν ἄν τις: Hdt.i 171: iii 98: Th.ii 54.5: iv 48.5: Pl.*R.* 544A,C (*bis*): *Lg.*663D.

(iii) Not infrequently, by a kind of inversion, καί is attached to the relative where, in strict logic, it should be attached to the demonstrative: that which is really prior in thought being represented as posterior. (Cf. οὐδέ, II.1.ii.) Some of the examples given under (ii) might be grouped here. S.*OC* 53 Ὅσ' οἶδα κἀγὼ πάντ' ἐπιστήσῃ ('All that I know, thou too shalt learn'): 276 ὥσπερ με κἀνεστήσαθ' ὧδε σώσατε: Ar.*Nu.*1443 Τὴν μητέρ' ὥσπερ καὶ σὲ τυπτήσω ('I'll beat my mother, too, as I beat you'): S.*OC* 185,298: Pl.*Phd.*76D ἢ ἐν τούτῳ ἀπόλλυμεν ἐν ᾧπερ καὶ λαμβάνομεν; 83D δοξάζουσαν ταῦτα ἀληθῆ εἶναι ἅπερ ἂν καὶ τὸ σῶμα φῇ: *R.*599B εἴπερ ἐπιστήμων εἴη τῇ ἀληθείᾳ τούτων πέρι ἅπερ καὶ μιμεῖται: X.*HG* iii 1.28 ποῦ χρὴ οἰκεῖν . . . ;—Ἔνθαπερ καὶ δικαιότατον: Hdt.viii 143.2: ix 33.5: X.*An.*iii 5.18: v 7.28: *Cyr.*ii 3.23: viii 4.25: Ant.v 4: Lys.x 6.

(Cf. inversion between sentences: A.*Pr.*312 μεθάρμοσαι τρόπους νέους· νέος γὰρ καὶ τύραννος ἐν θεοῖς: S.*El.*62 τί γάρ με λυπεῖ τοῦθ', ὅταν λόγῳ θανὼν ἔργοισι σωθῶ . . . ; . . . ἤδη γὰρ εἶδον πολλάκις καὶ τοὺς σοφοὺς λόγῳ μάτην θνῄσκοντας (there is no point in 'even the wise', and the meaning appears to be, 'I, as well as they, will feign death'): Pl.*Prt.*351E Δίκαιος, ἔφη, σὺ ἡγεῖσθαι· σὺ γὰρ καὶ κατάρχεις τοῦ λόγου: *R.*328B.)

The illogicality of the inversion is particularly obvious where the main clause is negative. Ar.*Av.*728 κοὐκ ἀποδράντες καθεδούμεθ' ἄνω . . . ὥσπερ χὠ Ζεύς ('Zeus does it: we *won't* do it too'): *Pax* 350 οὐδὲ . . . σκληρὸν ὥσπερ καὶ πρὸ τοῦ: *Th.*398: Hdt.i 93 θώματα . . . οὐ μάλα ἔχει, οἷά γε καὶ ἄλλη χώρη: ii 20 οὐδὲν τοιοῦτο πάσχουσι οἷόν τι καὶ ὁ Νεῖλος: iv 187: Th.vi 68.2 πρὸς ἄνδρας . . . οὐκ ἀπολέκτους ὥσπερ καὶ ἡμᾶς: Pl.*R.*477C, 505E.

(iv) ὥσπερ καί, καθάπερ καί, οἷον καί, are often used in illustration and analogy. Pl.*Phd.*73D: *Cra.*420C: X.*Oec.*21.3. καί sometimes refers, not to the content of the main clause, but to other, unspecified, examples. A.*Ag.*399 οἷος καὶ Πάρις . . .: Th. i 32.1 τοὺς . . . ἥκοντας . . . ὥσπερ καὶ ἡμεῖς νῦν: Hp.*Prorrh.*i 99 κοιλίης περίτασις . . . ἔχει τι σπασμῶδες, οἷον καὶ τῷ Ἀσπασίου υἱῷ: Pl.*Cra.*400D περὶ δὲ τῶν θεῶν τῶν ὀνομάτων, οἷον καὶ περὶ τοῦ "Διὸς" νυνδὴ ἔλεγες: *Tht.*184C: *Phd.*62C μὴ πρότερον αὑτὸν ἀποκτεινύναι δεῖν, πρὶν ἂν ἀνάγκην τινὰ θεὸς ἐπιπέμψῃ, ὥσπερ καὶ τὴν νῦν ἡμῖν παροῦσαν: Arist.*Po.*1453b28 ὥσπερ οἱ παλαιοὶ ἐποίουν, εἰδότας καὶ γινώσκοντας, καθάπερ καὶ Εὐριπίδης ἐποίησεν ἀποκτείνουσαν τοὺς παῖδας τὴν Μήδειαν (here a misunderstanding of καί has led editors astray: see *C.R.*xliii(1929)60): Hp.*Prorrh.*ii 43: Pl.*Cra.*401C, 414D, 418B: Arist.*Rh.*1354a23, 1367a8: *Po.*1456a17: *Pol.*1259a6, 1277a17.

(2) In causal clauses. Mainly a prose idiom. We have seen that καί is sometimes placed in the relative clause when logically it belongs rather to the main clause. A similar inversion is not infrequent in causal clauses: ἐπεὶ καί, ἐπειδὴ καί, ἅτε καί. In other passages, again, καί marks an addition, not to the

content of the main clause, but to a general, unexpressed, concept: 'in addition to everything else'. Hence 'also' merging into 'even', 'actually', *καί* does little more than emphasize. Decision is often difficult, and the particle may adhere either to the causal conjunction or to the word or expression following *καί*.

Hom.*υ*156 ἀλλὰ μάλ' ἦρι νέονται, ἐπεὶ καὶ πᾶσιν ἑορτή: Thgn. 1345 παιδοφιλεῖν δέ τι τερπνόν, ἐπεί ποτε καὶ Γανυμήδους ἤρατο καὶ Κρονίδης ('since, in fact, the son of Kronos, too'): A.*Ag.*822 τούτων θεοῖσι χρὴ πολύμνηστον χάριν τίνειν, ἐπείπερ χἀρπαγὰς ὑπερκόπους ἐπραξάμεσθα: S.*OT*412 λέγω δ', ἐπειδὴ καὶ τυφλόν μ' ὠνείδισας: *Tr.*321 Εἴπ' . . . ἐπεὶ καὶ ξυμφορά τοι μὴ εἰδέναι σέ γ' ἥτις εἶ (καὶ with ξυμφορά, 'an actual misfortune'): E.*Andr.*57 Δέσποιν'—ἐγώ τοι τοὔνομ' οὐ φεύγω τόδε καλεῖν σ', ἐπείπερ καὶ κατ' οἶκον ἠξίουν (perhaps inversion: 'as I called you "mistress" in Troy, I will call you so now'): *Cyc.*9 τοῦτ' ἰδὼν ὄναρ λέγω; οὐ μὰ Δί', ἐπεὶ καὶ σκῦλ' ἔδειξα Βακχίῳ ('actually'): *Med.*526 ἐγὼ δ', ἐπειδὴ καὶ λίαν πυργοῖς χάριν, Κύπριν νομίζω . . .: Ar.*Nu.*1177 ὅπως σώσεις μ', ἐπεὶ κἀπώλεσας: *Lys.*442 ταύτην προτέραν ξύνδησον, ὁτιὴ καὶ λαλεῖ: *Ra.*509 οὐ μή σ' ἐγὼ περιόψομἀπελθόντ', ἐπεί τοι καὶ κρέα ἀνέβραττεν ὀρνίθεια ('she was actually boiling'): Hom.*γ* 197: S.*Ph.*380: E.*Hec.*1286; Ar.*Pax*401: Hdt.ix 68 ἔφευγον, ὅτι καὶ τοὺς Πέρσας ὥρων: Pl.*Prm.*159A πάντα τὰ ἐναντία πάθη . . . εὑρήσομεν πεπονθότα τἆλλα τοῦ ἑνός, ἐπείπερ καὶ ταῦτα ἐφάνη πεπονθότα: *Ly.*211B Ἀλλὰ χρὴ ποιεῖν ταῦτα, ἐπειδή γε καὶ σὺ κελεύεις: *Men.*71D Ἐκεῖνον μὲν τοίνυν ἐῶμεν, ἐπειδὴ καὶ ἄπεστιν ('as he's not *here*'): X.*HG* iii 4.26 Σὺ δ' ἀλλὰ . . . μεταχώρησον . . . ἐπειδὴ καὶ ἐγὼ τὸν σὸν ἐχθρὸν τετιμώρημαι: *An.*iii 2.37 Χειρίσοφος μὲν ἡγοῖτο, ἐπειδὴ καὶ Λακεδαιμόνιός ἐστιν ('since he's a *Lacedaemonian*'): vii 7.54 ἆρ' οὐκ, ἐπειδὴ καὶ ἐπικίνδυνόν μοί ἐστιν, ἀπιόντα γε ἄμεινον φυλάττεσθαι πέτρους; ('actually dangerous'): *Smp.*8.6 τὸν μὲν σὸν ἔρωτα κρύπτωμεν, ἐπειδὴ καὶ ἔστιν οὐ ψυχῆς ἀλλ' εὐμορφίας τῆς ἐμῆς: Pl.*Grg.* 454B: *Smp.*177D, 188E: *R.*349A, 474B, 612D: *Euthd.*285C, 287D: *Cri.*50C: *Cra.*407E: *Tht.*142B, 153A, 157A, 177B, 187B: *Clit.*406A: *Lg.*638E: *Prm.*137A: X.*An.*v 8.7: *Cyr.*i 5.13: iv 5.22: v 4.42: viii 4.16: *Oec.*19.16; *Smp.*5.5: *Vect.*2.6: *Eq.Mag.*1.8: *Eq.*7.11: D.xliv 65.

ἅτε καί. Pl.*R.*350D μετὰ ἱδρῶτος θαυμαστοῦ ὅσου, ἅτε καὶ θέ-

ρους ὄντος ('as was natural in *summer*'): X.*HG*v 2.37 *ἅτε καὶ Ἀγησιλάου ὄντος αὐτῷ ἀδελφοῦ*: vi 4.10 *ἅτε καὶ πεδίου ὄντος τοῦ μεταξύ*.

(3) In final clauses. Here, again, though the original function of the particle is to present the action described in the main clause as not standing alone, but accompanied by the intended result, it often merely adds emphasis. And here, again, *καί* sometimes adheres to the word or expression following it, rather than to the conjunction. This use (in so far, at least, as a close connexion between conjunction and particle is implied) is mainly colloquial and fourth century. It is common in Plato and Xenophon, but rather rare in drama (even in comedy), and apparently not found in the orators.

Hom.Θ110 *ὄφρα καὶ Ἕκτωρ εἴσεται* ('that Hector too may know'): θ461 *Χαῖρε, ξεῖν', ἵνα καί ποτ' ἐὼν ἐν πατρίδι γαίῃ μνήσῃ ἐμεῖ'* ('that you may be mindful of me in the future too'): S.*Ph.*534 *ἴωμεν . . . εἰς οἴκησιν, ὥς με καὶ μάθῃς ἀφ' ὧν διέζων* ('learn, as well as merely go'): E.*Alc.*779 *δεῦρ' ἔλθ', ὅπως ἂν καὶ σοφώτερος γένῃ*: *IA* 117 (*καί* closely with *γλώσσῃ*): Ar.*V.* 1252 *τὸ δεῖπνον . . . συσκεύαζε νῷν, ἵνα καὶ μεθυσθῶμεν*: *Ra.* 1210 *λέγ' ἕτερον αὐτῷ πρόλογον, ἵνα καὶ γνῶ πάλιν*: Hom.η164, 180: Hdt.iii 134 *φαίνεσθαί τι ἀποδεικνύμενον, ἵνα καὶ Πέρσαι ἐκμάθωσι*: Pl.*Grg.*501C *συγχωρῶ, ἵνα σοι καὶ περανθῇ ὁ λόγος*: *Ap.*22A *πόνους τινὰς πονοῦντος ἵνα μοι καὶ ἀνέλεγκτος ἡ μαντεία γένοιτο*: *Men.*75A *πειρῶ εἰπεῖν, ἵνα καὶ γένηταί σοι μελέτη* ('so that you may get *practice*'): Hdt.vii 11.4: ix 116.3: Th.vi 22: Pl. *Cra.*407E: *Tht.*163C: *R.*346A, 350E, 460B, 468C, 523A, 537A, 612D: *Sph.*250A: X.*Cyr.*iii 3.39: iv 1.20: v 2.21: 4.42.

Μὴ καί in negative final clauses, and after verbs of fearing. Here *καί* rather means 'even', 'actually'. S.*Ph.*13 *μὴ καὶ μάθῃ μ' ἥκοντα*: 46 *μὴ καὶ λάθῃ με*: Ar.*Th.*580 *τηρῆτε μὴ καὶ προσπέσῃ ὑμῖν*: *Ec.*29 *μὴ καί τις ὢν ἀνὴρ ὁ προσιὼν τυγχάνῃ*: 495 *μὴ καί τις . . . κατείπῃ*: Pl.*Tht.*145C *ἵνα μὴ καὶ ἀναγκασθῇ μαρτυρεῖν*: 173B *ἵνα μὴ καὶ . . . καταχρώμεθα*: X.*Cyr.*i 4.23 *δείσαντες μὴ καὶ ἐνέδρα τις μείζων ὑπείη*: vi 1.37 *ἐκποδὼν ἔχειν ἐμαυτόν, μή τι καὶ πάθω ὑπὸ σοῦ*.

In indirect questions. S.*Ant.*1253 *Ἀλλ' εἰσόμεσθα, μή τι καὶ κατάσχετον κρυφῇ καλύπτει*: Pl.*Thg.*122C (a further possibility, which must not be ignored).

(4) In consecutive clauses, *ὥστε καί*. Ar.*Nu*.613: Pl.*Tht*. 161D *σοφός, ὥστε καὶ ἄλλων διδάσκαλος ἀξιοῦσθαι δικαίως*: X. *HG* v 4.52 *τὰ δόρατα ἐξηκόντιζον, ὥστε καὶ ἀπέθανεν Ἀλύπητος*.

Sometimes the addition, following a negative or virtually negative expression, constitutes a limitative qualification. S.*Aj*. 1325 *Τί γάρ σ' ἔδρασεν, ὥστε καὶ βλάβην ἔχειν*; (such as to constitute, not merely an action, but an injurious action): E.*Hel*. 841 *Πῶς οὖν θανούμεθ' ὥστε καὶ δόξαν λαβεῖν*; (not merely die, but die gloriously): *Rh*.845 *τίς . . . ἦλθεν, ὥστε καὶ λαθεῖν*; Ar. *Th*.34 *οὔτοι γ' ὥστε καί μέ γ' εἰδέναι*: Pl.*Tht*.182D *ἆρά ποτε οἷόν τέ τι προσειπεῖν χρῶμα, ὥστε καὶ ὀρθῶς προσαγορεύειν*; Th.ii 51.6 *δὶς γὰρ τὸν αὐτόν, ὥστε καὶ κτείνειν, οὐκ ἐπελάμβανεν*: v 74.3.

(5) In comparative clauses, *ἤ καί*, following a negative. Two ideas are combined: (i) A is not more true than B: (ii) B is true as well as A. S.*El*.1146 *οὔτε γάρ ποτε μητρὸς σύ γ' ἦσθα μᾶλλον ἢ κἀμοῦ φίλος* ('You were not your mother's darling more than' (by implication, 'so much as') 'mine'): *Ant*.928: Hdt.iv 118.3 *ἥκει γὰρ ὁ Πέρσης οὐδέν τι μᾶλλον ἐπ' ἡμέας ἢ οὐ καὶ ἐπ' ὑμέας* (with a redundant negative in the *ἤ* clause: v 94.2: vii 16γ1 (*bis*)): Pl.*Chrm*.161B *αἰδὼς δὲ οὐδὲν μᾶλλον ἀγαθὸν ἢ καὶ κακόν*: Ant.v 23 *ἐζητεῖτο οὐδέν τι μᾶλλον ὑπὸ τῶν ἄλλων ἢ καὶ ὑπ' ἐμοῦ*: Pl.*R*.524E.

In S.*Aj*.1103 both ideas are denied, instead of both being affirmed: *οὐδ' ἔσθ' ὅπου σοὶ τόνδε κοσμῆσαι πλέον ἀρχῆς ἔκειτο θεσμὸς ἢ καὶ τῷδε σέ* (*καί* approximates to *αὖ* in sense: 'for him, on his part', Jebb).

ἤ καί without a preceding negative is of course quite different, and *καί* means 'even'. S.*OT* 94 *τῶνδε γὰρ πλέον φέρω τὸ πένθος ἢ καὶ τῆς ἐμῆς ψυχῆς πέρι*.

(6) In conditional clauses, *εἰ καί, καὶ εἰ*. The distinction between *εἰ καί* and *καὶ εἰ* is perhaps that, strictly speaking, *εἰ καί* merely represents the fulfilment of the condition as immaterial, without conveying any effect of climax: whereas *καὶ εἰ* represents the condition as an extreme case, and does convey an effect of climax.[1] *

[1] I adopt this distinction as a provisional basis for discussion more out of respect for authority, and inability to find an alternative solution, than

(i) *εἰ καί.* The distinction formulated above is most clearly observable in those cases where the conditional clause, in the present or past indicative, expresses an admitted fact: 'even though', 'obwohl'.[1]

Hom.*E*410 *τῶ νῦν Τυδεΐδης, εἰ καὶ μάλα καρτερός ἐστι, φραζέσθω μή τίς οἱ ἀμείνων σεῖο μάχηται* ('though he *is*, admittedly, *μάλα καρτερός*'): S.*OT* 408 *Εἰ καὶ τυραννεῖς, ἐξισωτέον τὸ γοῦν ἴσ' ἀντιλέξαι*: E.*Supp.*528 *εἰ γάρ τι καὶ πεπόνθατ' Ἀργείων ὕπο, τεθνᾶσιν* ('even if you *have* (as I admit) suffered'): *Med.*75 *Καὶ ταῦτ' Ἰάσων παῖδας ἐξανέξεται πάσχοντας, εἰ καὶ μητρὶ διαφορὰν ἔχει*; Ar.*Nu.*593 *εἴ τι κἀξημάρτετε, ἐπὶ τὸ βέλτιον τὸ πρᾶγμα τῇ πόλει συνοίσεται*: *Lys.*254 *ἡγοῦ βάδην, εἰ καὶ τὸν ὦμον ἀλγεῖς* ('even if your shoulder *does* hurt you'): Hom.*ζ*312: S.*OT* 302: *El.*547: Th.ii 64.1 *μήτε ἐμὲ δι' ὀργῆς ἔχετε . . . εἰ καὶ ἐπελθόντες οἱ ἐναντίοι ἔδρασαν ἅπερ εἰκὸς ἦν* ('even though the enemy *have* done what was to be expected'): X.*Cyr.*vi 1.14 *στέγαι δὲ εἰ καὶ ἡμῖν αὐτοῖς εἰσιν, ἀλλὰ μὰ Δί' οὐχ ἵπποις*: Ant.iv γ5 *εἰ δέ τοι καὶ ὑπὸ τοῦ ἰατροῦ ἀπέθανεν, ὡς οὐκ ἀπέθανεν, ὁ μὲν ἰατρὸς οὐ φονεὺς αὐτοῦ ἐστιν* (an admission for the sake of argument: cf. Pl.*R.* 337C): Lys.xx 8: Is.v 25: Th.ii 11.3.

In other cases, particularly, of course, those with *ἐάν* and subjunctive, *εἰ* and optative, *εἰ* and past indicative of unreal hypothesis, the validity of the hypothesis is less unequivocally admitted, or implicitly denied: 'even if', 'wenngleich'.

E.*Andr.*90 *οὐ περίβλεπτος βίος δούλης γυναικός, ἤν τι καὶ πάθω κακόν* ('even if I *do* meet with misfortune'): *HF* 1282 *οὔτ' ἐμαῖς φίλαις Θήβαις ἐνοικεῖν ὅσιον· ἢν δὲ καὶ μένω, ἐς ποῖον ἱερὸν . . . εἶμ'*; ('and if I *do* remain'): Ar.*Av.*508 *Ἦρχον δ' οὕτω σφόδρα τὴν ἀρχήν, ὥστ' εἴ τις καὶ βασιλεύοι ἐν ταῖς πόλεσιν . . . ἐπὶ τῶν σκήπτρων ἐκάθητ' ὄρνις*: Hom.*Π*748: S.*OT* 851: Ar.*Ra.*737: Antiph.*Fr.*217.26: Pl.*Tht.*146C *πάντως γάρ,*

because I have much confidence in it. See L. & S. *καί*, B.8: Hartung i 139–41: Kühner II ii 488–9: Jebb, Appendix to S.*OT*, p. 224. Kühner (II ii 489, Anm. 1) observes that *εἰ καί* and *καὶ εἰ* more frequently exchange meanings in verse (where metre is a factor in determining order). But there are many irregularities in prose also.

[1] But Jebb (*loc.cit.*) narrows the issue overmuch when he says that *εἰ καί* is only 'normal' where the 'speaker admits that a condition exists'. Kühner's 'wirklich oder möglich' is far nearer the mark.

ἄν τι καὶ ἁμάρτω, ἐπανορθώσετε ('even if I *do* make a mistake'): X.*HG*v1.20 ἐνόμισεν ἀμελέστερον μὲν ἔχειν τοὺς Ἀθηναίους . . . εἰ δὲ καὶ εἶεν τριήρεις ὁρμοῦσαι, ἀσφαλέστερον ἡγήσατο ἐπ' εἴκοσι ναῦς Ἀθήνησιν οὔσας πλεῦσαι ἢ ἄλλοθι δέκα ('and even if there *were* triremes . . .'): *An*.vi5.20 'Formidable dangers confront us. ἢν δὲ δὴ καὶ σωθῶμεν ἐπὶ θάλατταν . . .': Pl.*Prt*.323B: *Phd*.66D, 108D: *R*.411D,425A,498A: *Smp*.191C: *Lg*.663D: X.*Cyr*.v4.42: vi4.18: *HG*vi5.12: *Oec*.2.8: Lys. xx23: Isoc.xv33: D.xvi24.

(ii) καὶ εἰ. The sense of climax, of the presentation of an extreme hypothesis, is clearly discernible in such passages as the following. Hom.Δ347 νῦν δὲ φίλως κ' ὁρόῳτε καὶ εἰ δέκα πύργοι Ἀχαιῶν ὑμείων προπάροιθε μαχοίατο νηλέϊ χαλκῷ: Ε351 ἦ τέ σ' ὀΐω ῥιγήσειν πόλεμόν γε καὶ εἴ χ' ἑτέρωθι πύθηαι ('if you so much as hear the sound of it anywhere', Leaf): Υ371 τοῦ δ' ἐγὼ ἀντίος εἶμι, καὶ εἰ πυρὶ χεῖρας ἔοικεν: ν292 καὶ εἰ θεὸς ἀντιάσειε ('yea, though it were even a god'): S.*OC*306 κεἰ βραδὺς εὕδει, κλύων σου δεῦρ' ἀφίξεται ταχύς: E.*Med*.393 ξίφος λαβοῦσα, κεἰ μέλλω θανεῖν, κτενῶ σφε: *Andr*.266 καὶ γὰρ εἰ πέριξ σ' ἔχει τηκτὸς μόλυβδος, ἐξαναστήσω σ' ἐγώ: Pl.*Ap*.32A ἀναγκαῖόν ἐστι τὸν τῷ ὄντι μαχούμενον ὑπὲρ τοῦ δικαίου, καὶ εἰ μέλλει ὀλίγον χρόνον σωθήσεσθαι, ἰδιωτεύειν (καί with ὀλίγον, 'if he is to be safe even for a short time').

Much less clearly in the following. X.*HG*ii4.25 πιστὰ δόντες, οἵτινες συμπολεμήσειαν, καὶ εἰ ξένοι εἶεν, ἰσοτέλειαν ἔσεσθαι: *An*.iii2.24 καὶ ὁδοποιήσειέ γ' ἂν αὐτοῖς καὶ εἰ σὺν τεθρίπποις βούλοιντο ἀπιέναι: Sapph.*Fr*.1.21 καὶ γὰρ αἰ φεύγει, ταχέως διώξει: Isoc.iv28 καὶ γὰρ εἰ μυθώδης ὁ λόγος γέγονεν, ὅμως αὐτῷ καὶ νῦν ῥηθῆναι προσήκει.

(iii) The distinction between εἰ καί and καὶ εἰ is, in fact, one that cannot be very strongly pressed. Take, for example, these closely similar passages in which εἰ καί, καὶ εἰ are followed by an intensive adverb or adjective (μάλα, πάνυ, μέγας, etc.). Hom. Ε410 εἰ καὶ μάλα καρτερός ἐστι: Ν316 καὶ εἰ μάλα καρτερός ἐστιν: ζ312 εἰ καὶ μάλα τηλόθεν ἐσσί: θ139 εἰ καὶ μάλα καρτερὸς εἴη: π98 καὶ εἰ μέγα νεῖκος ὄρηται: S.*OT*669 κεἰ χρή με παντελῶς θανεῖν: *Tr*.1218 Εἰ καὶ μακρὰ κάρτ' ἐστίν: Pl.*Smp*.185E καὶ ἐὰν τοῦτο ποιήσῃς . . . καὶ εἰ πάνυ ἰσχυρά ἐστι, παύσεται. We might, it is true, take refuge in the subtlety that καὶ εἰ μάλα καρτερός ἐστιν means 'though he is even very brave' (though he reaches the extreme of bravery): εἰ καὶ μ. κ. ἐ. 'even though he is very brave' (the hypothesis of his bravery being immaterial). But the subtlety seems a trifle excessive.

Nor, in general, do εἰ καί and καὶ εἰ keep very closely to the provinces assigned to them by grammarians. Thus in Pl.*Sph.* 230D εἰ καί clearly gives a sense of climax: ἂν καὶ τυγχάνῃ βασιλεὺς ὁ μέγας ὤν. Contrariwise, καὶ εἰ not infrequently introduces an admitted fact, and there is no sense of climax whatever. S.*Aj.*692 καὶ τάχ' ἄν μ' ἴσως πύθοισθε, κεἰ νῦν δυστυχῶ, σεσωμένον: E.*Med.*463 καὶ γὰρ εἰ σύ με στυγεῖς, οὐκ ἂν δυναίμην σοὶ κακῶς φρονεῖν ποτε: S.*Aj.*962 ἴσως τοι, κεἰ βλέποντα μὴ 'πόθουν, θανόντ' ἂν οἰμώξειαν: *OT* 986,1516: *OC* 661,875: *El.*617: *Aj.* 563: E.*HF* 709.

Nor is there any sense of climax in the following. Pl.*Prt.* 333E Ἀρ' οὖν ... ταῦτ' ἐστὶν ἀγαθὰ ἅ ἐστιν ὠφέλιμα τοῖς ἀνθρώποις;—Καὶ ναὶ μὰ Δί', ἔφη, κἂν μὴ τοῖς ἀνθρώποις ὠφέλιμα ᾖ, ἔγωγε καλῶ ἀγαθά: *Men.*72C κἂν εἰ πολλαὶ καὶ παντοδαπαί εἰσιν, ἕν γέ τι εἶδος ταὐτὸν ἅπασαι ἔχουσιν δι' ὃ εἰσὶν ἀρεταί: S.*OT* 1077: *Ant.*461: Ar.*V.*813: Arist.*Pol.*1265b15,1277b17: D.xxi 102.

Two passages require separate treatment. Th.vi 64.1 εἰδότες οὐκ ἂν ὁμοίως δυνηθέντες (στρατόπεδον καταλαμβάνειν) καὶ εἰ ... ἐκβιβάζοιεν (καί seems to mean 'in addition to their power to take up a position if they pursued a different course: but καί, generally suspected, can hardly stand): X.*Cyr.*iii 3.69 δείσας μὴ καὶ εἰ βιάσαιντο εἴσω, ὀλίγοι ὄντες ὑπὸ πολλῶν σφαλεῖέν τι (if καὶ εἰ *HAG* is right, καί probably goes closely with μή (cf. (3) above): εἰ καί *CEDF*).

In S.*Ant.*234 κεἰ means 'and if'. (See Jebb.)

κἂν[1] (καὶ ἂν) εἰ: 'even if', Ar.*Ra.*585: Pl.*Men.*72C: *R.*408B, 473A,579D,612C: *Phd.*71B: *Sph.*247E. 'And if', only, apparently, Pl.*Phd.*72C: in *Lg.*872E κἂν εἰ (*in marg. O*[2]) is unlikely (see England).

κἄν (καὶ ἐάν): 'even if', S.*Aj.*15,1077: Ar.*V.*813: Pl.*Prt.* 319C: 'also if', Arist.*Rh.*1372a15. 'and if', Ar.*Ra.*736.

(iv) To return to εἰ καί. 'Even if' (representing the fulfilment of the condition as immaterial), and 'if even, actually'

[1] See Jebb, Appendix to Sophocles, *Electra* (on line 1482): Kühner II i 244, Anm.2.: Goodwin, *M.T.* §§ 195, 228: Bonitz, *Index Arist.* *s.v.* ἄν.

(climax: for καὶ εἰ) are by no means the only forces of the combination.

(*a*) εἰ καί often means 'if indeed', 'if really' ('though I should be surprised if it were so'). Cf. II.C.7, below. This force is often combined with 'even if' ('even if indeed'), and classification of examples is difficult. E.g. Pl.*Tht.*146C πάντως γάρ, ἄν τι καὶ ἁμάρτω, ἐπανορθώσετε (see (i) above), where we might render 'even if I do make a slip' (though, strictly speaking, ἐπανόρθωσις presupposes ἁμαρτία, and 'even' is illogical: but the general sense is 'I shall be all right whatever happens'). English is, in this matter, more finely shaded than Greek. 'I shall keep dry if it does rain': 'I shall keep dry even if it rains': 'I shall keep dry even if it does rain': all three represented in Greek by ἐὰν καὶ ὕσῃ. I group here those passages in which 'even if' is an impossible, or at least an unnatural, rendering: but this class shades off imperceptibly into (i).

A.*Pr.*345 μάτην . . . πονήσεις, εἴ τι καὶ πονεῖν θέλεις ('if you *want* to labour'): S.*OT* 305 Φοῖβος γάρ, εἰ καὶ μὴ κλύεις τῶν ἀγγέλων, πέμψασιν ἡμῖν ἀντέπεμψεν ('if indeed you haven't *heard*'): E.*Rh.*521 ξύνθημα δ' ἡμῖν Φοῖβος, ἥν τι καὶ δέῃ ('if we *need* it (but I don't think we shall)'): Pl.*Euthphr.*4D ἠμέλει ὡς ἀνδροφόνου καὶ οὐδὲν ὂν πρᾶγμα εἰ καὶ ἀποθάνοι ('if he *did* die': better than 'even if he died': καί slightly mitigates the callousness, by regarding death as improbable): Pl.*Chrm.*168A Οὐκοῦν ἄτοπον, εἰ ἄρα καὶ ἔστιν; ('if it really does exist'): E.*Andr.*1079 Ἄκουσον, εἰ καὶ σοῖς φίλοις ἀμυναθεῖν χρῄζεις, τὸ πραχθέν ('if you really *want* to help'). In the last two examples the sense 'even if' is directly excluded by the context. In E.*Hel.*698 εἰ καί, 'if indeed', indicates cautious reserve, not scepticism.

(*b*) The use of εἰ καί, εἰ καὶ . . . γε, in the sense of *siquidem*, in appealing to a single case for support of a general proposition (see Stein on Hdt.v 78), seems to be characteristically Herodotean. Hdt.v 78 εἰ καὶ Ἀθηναῖοι ... ('if the *Athenians* ...'): ix 68 δηλοῖ τέ μοι ὅτι πάντα τὰ πρήγματα τῶν βαρβάρων ἤρτητο ἐκ Περσέων, εἰ καὶ τότε οὗτοι . . . ἔφευγον, ὅτι καὶ τοὺς Πέρσας ὥρων: i 60: ix 100.2. Cf. Ar.*V.*503.

(*c*) In many other passages καί, meaning 'also', 'even', 'actually', although immediately following the conditional, does not cohere closely in sense with it, but with what follows.

Possibly pronunciation helped to make the distinction clear. Naturally the separation of *καί* and *εἰ* in sense is more marked where a word (or words) intervenes. In such cases *καί* sometimes approximates to *αὖ* in force.

Hom.*Π* 623 *εἰ καὶ ἐγώ σε βάλοιμι* ('if I, on my side, struck you'): S.*Ant*.90 *ἀρέσκουσ' οἷς μάλισθ' ἁδεῖν με χρή.—Εἰ καὶ δυνήσῃ γ'* ('Aye, if thou *canst*': if, besides having the will, you have also the power): *Aj*.816 *εἴ τῳ καὶ λογίζεσθαι σχολή* ('if one has leisure for thought as well as for action'): 1127 *Κτείναντα; δεινόν γ' εἶπας, εἰ καὶ ζῇς θανών* ('if, actually, though I cannot believe it'): *Tr*.71 *Πᾶν τοίνυν, εἰ καὶ τοῦτ' ἔτλη, κλύοι τις ἄν* ('even that'): Ar. *V*.556 *οἴκτιρόν μ' ... εἰ καὐτὸς πώποθ' ὑφείλου ἀρχὴν ἄρξας*: *Ra*.74 *Τοῦτο ... μόνον ἔτ' ἐστὶ λοιπὸν ἀγαθόν, εἰ καὶ τοῦτ' ἄρα* ('even that'): 339 *ὡς ἡδύ μοι προσέπνευσε χοιρείων κρεῶν.—Οὔκουν ἄτρεμ' ἕξεις, ἤν τι καὶ χορδῆς λάβῃς*; ('a dinner as well as a smell'): Hom.*Π* 746: *λ* 356: S.*Ph*.292: Th.ii 11.6 *εἰ μὴ καὶ νῦν ὥρμηνται* ('if they have not actually started *already*': cf. vi 60.3 *εἰ μὴ καὶ δέδρακεν* ('if he has not actually *done* it'). I do not think we should talk of 'transposition', *εἰ μὴ καί* for *εἰ καὶ μή*, in either passage): Pl.*R*.365B *ἐὰν μὴ καὶ δοκῶ* ('unless I also *seem* just'): 388D *ἐπιπλήξειεν (ἄν τις), εἰ καὶ ἐπίοι αὐτῷ τι τοιοῦτον ... ποιεῖν* ('if it so much as occurred to him'): *Ti*.44B *ἂν μὲν οὖν δὴ καὶ συνεπιλαμβάνηταί τις ὀρθὴ τροφή* ('if, further'): *Thg*.130C *φεύγω ἄν τινα καὶ αἰσθάνωμαι πεπαιδευμένον* ('at the mere realization that a man is educated'): X.*Mem*.i 6.12 *δῆλον δὴ ὅτι εἰ καὶ τὴν συνουσίαν ᾤου τινὸς ἀξίαν εἶναι* ... (*sc*. 'as well as a cloak or a house'): *Oec*.2.2 *Οὔκουν ἔγωγε ... εἰ καὶ περὶ ἐμοῦ λέγεις* ('if you mean *me*'): 8.5 'Such an army would be incapable of marching. *εἰ δὲ καὶ μάχεσθαι δέοι* ...' ('if, again'): D.xviii 317 *καὶ μὴν εἰ καὶ τοῦτ' ἄρα δεῖ μ' εἰπεῖν* ('this as well'): Pl.*R*.522E (*bis*), 540C: *Ti*.62D, 63A: *Lg*.947D: X.*Eq*.11.7. (For Pl.*Cra*.436E, see II.C.7 below.)

(v) By the process of inversion which we noted in the case of relative clauses, *καί* in the protasis sometimes logically refers to the apodosis. S.*Tr*.228 *χαίρειν δὲ τὸν κήρυκα προυννέπω ... χαρτὸν εἴ τι καὶ φέρεις*: *Ph*.1042 *τείσασθε ... αὐτούς, εἴ τι κἄμ' οἰκτίρετε*: E.*IT* 1010: X.*Cyr*.viii 7.17 *τιμᾶτε ἀλλήλους, εἴ τι καὶ τοῦ ἐμοὶ χαρίζεσθαι μέλει ὑμῖν.* Especially in the formula *εἴ τις καὶ ἄλλος*: X.*An*.i 4.15: *et saep*.

Plato often uses this inversion with *εἴπερ καί*. *Cra*.385C *Ἔστιν* ἄρα ὄνομα ψεῦδος καὶ ἀληθὲς λέγειν, εἴπερ καὶ λόγον; *Tht.*155C, 164B,204E: *R.*387D: *Prm.*138A,146B,C: *Lg.*896D: X.*Mem.*iv 3.14 ψυχή, ἥ, εἴπερ τι καὶ ἄλλο τῶν ἀνθρωπίνων .... Cf. Th.vi 38.4.

(7) In co-ordinated clauses καί is sometimes used in conjunction with other particles: with τε, to strengthen the idea of addition, 'and also': with δέ and ἤ, to supplement the adversative or disjunctive sense with the idea of addition.

(i) εἴτε καί (used also in disjunctive indirect questions). εἴτε ... εἴτε καί: E.*Tr.*942 εἴτ' Ἀλέξανδρον ... εἴτε καὶ Πάριν: Pl. *Phd.*70C σκεψώμεθα ... εἴτ' ἄρα ... εἴτε καὶ οὔ: D.xviii 20 εἴτε χρὴ κακίαν εἴτ' ἄγνοιαν εἴτε καὶ ἀμφότερα ταῦτ' εἰπεῖν: Hdt.ii 181: iii 65,121: Pl.*Cra.*394E,428C: *Tht.*168B: *R.*394D. ἄντε ... ἄντε καί: *Cra.*433E: X.*Oec.*21.9. εἴτε δή ... εἴτε καί: Hdt.i 19, 86 (εἴτε δή ... εἴτε καὶ ... εἴτε καί), 191: iii 33: iv 147: Pl. *Ti.*21B.

The corresponsive form εἴτε καὶ ... εἴτε καί may, for convenience, be included here: Th.vi 60.2: Pl.*R.*471D,557A: *Lg.* 845E: Lys.xii 59.

Examples of εἰ ... εἴτε καί, and εἴτε καί without preceding εἰ are given under τε, I.3.

(ii) δὲ καί (καί often approximating in sense to αὖ). Hom.σ 371 εἰ δ' αὖ καὶ ... (376): A.*Pers.*296 λέξον ... τίς οὐ τέθνηκε, τίνα δὲ καὶ πενθήσομεν ('and whom, again, ...'): *Ag.*848 τὸ μὲν καλῶς ἔχον ὅπως χρονίζον εὖ μενεῖ βουλευτέον· ὅτῳ δὲ καὶ δεῖ φαρμάκων παιωνίων ... ('and he, again, who needs ...'): Pi.*O.*10.30 λόχμαισι δὲ δοκεύσαις ... δάμασε καὶ κείνους Ἡρακλέης ('in his turn': they had defeated him before): *P.*6.44: *I.*1.40: B.16.58: S.*OT*682: Hdt.i 134.3 ἦρχε τὰ ἔθνεα ἀλλήλων, συναπάντων μὲν Μῆδοι καὶ τῶν ἄγχιστα οἰκεόντων σφίσι, οὗτοι δὲ καὶ τῶν ὁμούρων, οἱ δὲ μάλα τῶν ἐχομένων ('and these in their turn': δὲ αὖ Krueger): Pl.*R.*566E τοῖς μὲν καταλλαγῇ, τοὺς δὲ καὶ διαφθείρῃ: *Grg.*458B εἰ μὲν ... εἰ δὲ καὶ ...: X.*HG* iv 3.23 οἱ μὲν διὰ τὴν δυσχωρίαν ἔπιπτον, οἱ δὲ καὶ διὰ τὸ μὴ προορᾶν ... οἱ δὲ καὶ ὑπὸ τῶν βελῶν: *An.*v 1.17 οἱ μὲν ἐλάμβανον, οἱ δὲ καὶ οὔ: Hdt.i 26.3: viii 10.3: 100.3: ix 106.1: Th.vi 82.2: Pl.*Lg.*636A: X.*HG* iv 3.8: *Smp.*1.9: Arist.*Po.* 1447b20.

καί following a purely connective δέ: Pl.*R.*619D ὡς δὲ καὶ εἰπεῖν, οὐκ ἐλάττους ... ('and in fact pretty well half ...'). In

*R.*571C δὲ καί can hardly stand: *Λέγεις δὲ καὶ τίνας, ἔφη, ταύτας;* (δὲ καί *AM*: δέ *FD*: δή Stobaeus). *

By inversion, καί in the μέν clause. Hdt.iv 195 εἰσὶ μὲν καὶ πλεῦνες αἱ λίμναι αὐτόθι, ἡ δ' ὦν μεγίστη αὐτέων . . .: Pl.*Chrm.* 153A κατέλαβον πάνυ πολλούς, τοὺς μὲν καὶ ἀγνῶτας ἐμοί, τοὺς δὲ πλείστους γνωρίμους (' I knew most of them, but there were some, too, whom I didn't know'): X *Cyr.*viii 2.18 Εἷς μὲν τοίνυν καὶ οὗτος ἤδη θησαυρὸς ἡμῖν . . . τοὺς δ' ἄλλους . . .: *Oec.*20.10.

Corresponsive, καί in both clauses. Hdt.ii 174 πολλὰ μὲν δὴ καὶ ἡλίσκετο ὑπὸ τῶν μαντηίων, πολλὰ δὲ καὶ ἀπέφευγε (καὶ ἡλίσκετο Valckenaer: κατηλίσκετο or καταλίσκετο *codd.*): X.*HG* vii 1.46 τὰ μέν τι καὶ χρήμασι διεπράττετο, τὰ δὲ καὶ . . .: *Cyr.* iii 3.67 αἱ μὲν καὶ τέκνα ἔχουσαι, αἱ δὲ καὶ νεώτεραι (καί *post* δέ *om. CE*): Th.vii 12.1: 85.4: viii 47.2. Add perhaps Th.v 43.2 μὲν καὶ . . . οὐ μέντοι ἀλλὰ καὶ . . . . But in Pl.*Cra.*421D (see below, C.7) the two καί's probably do not correspond.

(iii) ἢ καί. In this combination ἤ separates two ideas objectively, in point of fact, while καί denotes that, subjectively, both must be kept before the mind. Render often 'or again': but sometimes καί means 'also', or marks a climax, 'even'. The greater part of the examples are Platonic.

Usually in the second clause of a disjunction. Hom.*A*63 μάντιν ἐρείομεν ἢ ἱερῆα, ἢ καὶ ὀνειροπόλον: Xenoph.*Fr.*2.4 εἴτε παλαίων ἢ καὶ πυκτοσύνην ἀλγινόεσσαν ἔχων: E.*Tr.*56 ἢ Ζηνὸς ἢ καὶ δαιμόνων τινός: *IT* 382 ἥν τις ἅψηται φόνου, ἢ καὶ λοχείας ἢ νεκροῦ θίγῃ χεροῖν: Hes.*Op.*710: *Sc.*43: E.*Med.*42: *Or.*1359: *Ion* 432: Ar.*Th.*346: Pl.*R.*395E αἰσχρολογοῦντας, μεθύοντας ἢ καὶ νήφοντας, ἢ καὶ ἄλλα ὅσα . . .: 599A ἐπισκέψασθαι πότερον . . . ἐξηπάτηνται . . . ἤ τι καὶ λέγουσιν: 602D ἀλλὰ τὸ λογισάμενον καὶ μετρῆσαν ἢ καὶ στῆσαν: *Lg.*656B Πότερον εἰκὸς ἢ καὶ ἀναγκαῖον . . .; ('actually necessary'): *Grg.*505D ἐὰν δὲ ἐμοὶ πείθῃ, ἐάσεις χαίρειν τοῦτον τὸν λόγον, ἢ καὶ ἄλλῳ τῳ διαλέξῃ (a further possibility): *Ion* 535C τοῖς πράγμασιν . . . ἢ ἐν Ἰθάκῃ οὖσιν ἢ ἐν Τροίᾳ ἢ ὅπως ἂν καὶ τὰ ἔπη ἔχῃ (in any other of the further possible circumstances): D.xlvii 68 ἤροντό με πότερον ἐξηγήσωνταί μοι μόνον ἢ καὶ συμβουλεύσωσιν ('or give me advice as well'): Hdt.vii 10β1: 103.3: Hp.*VC* 14,19: *Art.*7: Pl.*Phd.*88C: *Ti.*70B: *R.*437A: *Prm.*143A: *Phlb.*12A,36D: *Alc.I* 134E: *II* 144E: *Lg.*668C,789D,885C: X.*Oec.*19.9: Arist.*Pol.*1264a15.

Exceptionally in the first clause of a disjunction: E.*Fr.*273 πᾶσιν γὰρ ἀνθρώποισιν . . . ἢ καὶ παραυτίκ' ἢ χρόνῳ δαίμων βίον ἔσφηλε ("ἤτοι *malim*", Nauck, unnecessarily. 'Actually at the outset' is a possible explanation: and the same treatment may be applied to many passages in which καί comes in the second clause. But I think that καί everywhere has the other clause of the disjunction in particular view).

In both clauses of a disjunction: Th.i 35.4: here the καί's go closely with the following pronouns. In Pl.*Cri.*44E the first καί goes closely with πᾶσαν.

(iv) γὰρ καί. This can hardly be regarded as a combination, since καί adheres to what follows (whereas in καὶ γάρ the particles usually go more closely together). Th.i 91.3 ἤδη γὰρ καὶ ἧκον αὐτῷ οἱ ξυμπρέσβεις ('his fellow ambassadors also had arrived'): X.*Mem.*iii 6.10 ἴσως γὰρ καὶ διὰ τὸ μέγεθος αὐτῶν . . . οὔπω ἐξήτακας ('owing to the magnitude of the subject, as well as for other possible reasons'): Hdt.ii 99.

(8) Following demonstratives. The particle here denotes that the words following it add something, and something important, to the content of the demonstrative. Or, to look at it in another way, καί binds the demonstrative more closely to the following words. The connexion may be established by the demonstrative alone, or a connecting particle may precede or follow the demonstrative. This idiom is closely analogous to the use of καί with relatives ((1) above), ταῦτα καὶ ποιῶ being equivalent to ἃ καὶ ποιῶ. The former is used for connecting sentences, the latter (normally) for connecting clauses. καί following demonstratives is mainly found in dialogue: it is too lively an idiom to be common in formal oratory. The particle follows the pronoun immediately, or after a short interval. Often δή precedes καί, giving the tone 'of just this something else is to be said': see δή I.4.viii.

S.*OT* 148 τῶνδε γὰρ χάριν καὶ δεῦρ' ἔβημεν ('That is why we have *come*'): 582 Ἐνταῦθα γὰρ δὴ καὶ κακὸς φαίνῃ φίλος ('That is just where your treachery appears'): *Tr.*600 Ἀλλ' αὐτὰ δή σοι ταῦτα καὶ πράσσω, Λίχα: E.*Andr.*622 τοῦτο καὶ σκοπεῖτέ μοι, μνηστῆρες, ἐσθλῆς θυγατέρ' ἐκ μητρὸς λαβεῖν: 906 Τοῦτ' αὐτὸ καὶ νοσοῦμεν: *Hec.*1007 Καλῶς ἔλεξας· τῇδε καὶ σοφώτερον: *Or.* 1331 Ἦ τοῦδ' ἕκατι καὶ βοὴ κατὰ στέγας; *Ba.*616 Ταῦτα καὶ καθύβρισ' αὐτόν: *IA* 127 τόδε καὶ δεινόν ('There's the rub'): Ar.*Eq.*180 Δι' αὐτὸ γάρ τοι τοῦτο καὶ γίγνει μέγας ('That is the origin of your *greatness*'): S.*Tr.*490: E.*Ion* 346: Ar.*Nu.*856, 1499: *Pax* 892: *Lys.*46: *Th.*81,166: *Ra.*73: Hdt.i 18 οὗτος γὰρ καὶ ὁ τὸν πόλεμον ἦν συνάψας: Pl.*Prt.*310E ἀλλ' αὐτὰ ταῦτα καὶ νῦν ἥκω παρὰ σέ: 341C Διὰ ταῦτα ἄρα καὶ μέμφεται: *Chrm.* 156E ὅτι ... οὐ δεῖ ... ἀλλὰ τοῦτο καὶ αἴτιον εἴη ...: *La.*195A ταῦτά τοι καὶ ληρεῖ ('That's the rubbish he *talks*!'): *Euthphr.*13C ἀλλὰ τούτου δὴ ἕνεκα καὶ ἀνηρόμην: *Men.*71C ἀλλὰ ταῦτα περὶ σοῦ καὶ οἴκαδε ἀπαγγέλλωμεν; ('Is *that* the message ...?'): X. *Mem.*iii 5.19 Τοῦτο γάρ τοι, ἔφη, καὶ θαυμαστόν ἐστι: Ant.i 23 τούτου γε ἕνεκα καὶ δικασταὶ ἐγένεσθε ('That is precisely the reason why ...'): D.xli 27 τοῦτο δὴ καὶ μέλλω λέγειν ('That is just what I am going to tell you'): Hdt.i 73,194: ii 103: v 13.3: Pl.*Phd.*58C: *Phdr.*235B: *R.*497B: *Min.*319A: X.*Oec.*6.10: *An.* iv 6.17: *Cyr.*i 4.27: D.iv 28.

(9) Apodotic. Compare the far commoner apodotic δέ (*q.v.* II.1). Most of the true examples are from Homer and lyric.

(i) In general (Epic and Lyric). Hom.*A* 494 ἀλλ' ὅτε δὴ ... καὶ τότε δή: β 107 ἀλλ' ὅτε ... καὶ τότε δή: *A* 478 ἦμος δ' ... καὶ τότ' ἔπειτα: Ε 898 εἰ δὲ ... καί κεν δή: λ 111 εἰ ... καί κεν: ξ 112 αὐτὰρ ἐπεὶ ... καί: ν 79: σ 135: *h.Ap.*428 εὖτε ... καί: Hdt. i 55.2 (hexameter oracle) ἀλλ' ὅταν ... καὶ τότε: Simon.*Fr.*13.16 εἰ δέ τοι δεινὸν τό γε δεινὸν ἦν, καί κεν ἐμῶν ῥημάτων λεπτὸν ὑπεῖχες οὖας: Pi.*O.*10.91 ἀλλ' ὥτε ... καὶ ... (in a comparison: but there is a long interval, and a change from strophe to antistrophe: perhaps anacoluthon). After participial clause. Hom.*X* 247 ὣς φαμένη καὶ κερδοσύνῃ ἡγήσατ' Ἀθήνη.

Add probably Alc.*Fr.*70.18: 89.2 (but the text in both places is uncertain).

(ii) κᾆτα, κἄπειτα. Ar.*Lys.*560 ὅταν ἀσπίδ' ἔχων καὶ Γοργόνα τις κᾆτ' ὤνηται κορακίνους: *Eq.*392 Ἀλλ' ὅμως οὗτος τοιοῦτος ὢν ἅπαντα τὸν βίον, κᾆτ' ἀνὴρ ἔδοξεν εἶναι: *Av.*674 ἀπολέψαντα χρὴ ... τὸ λέμμα κᾆθ' οὕτω φιλεῖν: *Nu.*624 λαχὼν Ὑπέρβολος τῆτες ἱερομνημονεῖν, κἄπειθ' ὑφ' ἡμῶν ... τὸν στέφανον ἀφῃρέθη: *Av.* 536 (Comedy is fond of this idiom: cf. Plat.Com.*Fr.*23: in Ar. *Ec.*276 I suggest ἐπαναβάλησθε, κᾆτα being apodotic after the temporal clause: *C.R.*xlvii(1933)215)*: Pl.*Grg.*457B ἐὰν δὲ οἶμαι ῥητορικὸς γενόμενός τις κᾆτα ταύτῃ τῇ δυνάμει . . . ἀδικῇ . . .: X.*Cyr*.iv 3.14 ὅ γε μὴν μάλιστ' ἄν τις φοβηθείη, μή, εἰ δεήσει ἐφ' ἵππου κινδυνεύειν . . ., κἄπειτα μήτε πεζοὶ ἔτι ὦμεν μήτε πω ἱππεῖς ἱκανοί, ἀλλ' οὐδὲ τοῦτο ἀμήχανον. (Add, perhaps, E.*Cyc*.235: the text is uncertain. In S.*Fr*.579 κᾆθ' is highly probable. For a possibly similar use of εἶτα δέ, see van Leeuwen on Ar.*Ach*.24.)

(iii) There are hardly any prose examples of apodotic καί other than the two just quoted. Th.v 27.1 ἐπειδὴ γὰρ αἱ πεντηκοντούτεις σπονδαὶ ἐγένοντο καὶ ὕστερον ἡ ξυμμαχία, καὶ αἱ ἀπὸ τῆς Πελοποννήσου πρεσβεῖαι . . . ἀνεχώρουν ἐκ τῆς Λακεδαίμονος (αἱ καί *al*.): here, certainly, καί seems to belong to the whole apodosis ('it also happened that'): ii 21.1: vii 43.1: 75.1. But in other passages quoted by the authorities as apodotic, the particle is followed by an emphatic word, with which it goes closely in the normal sense 'also', 'in fact':[1] Hdt.i 79 ὡς δέ οἱ ταῦτα ἔδοξε, καὶ ἐποίεε κατὰ τάχος: Th.ii 93.4 ὡς δὲ ἔδοξεν αὐτοῖς, καὶ ἐχώρουν εὐθύς: Pl.*Tht*.190A ὅταν ἄρα τις . . . δοξάζῃ, καὶ φησίν: Th.iv 8.9: viii 1.4: 8.4: 27.5. The following are textually doubtful, and correct punctuation and analysis reveal that καί, if sound, is not apodotic: Hdt.ix 117: Pl.*Euthphr*.5B: *Plt*.257C. In E.*Ion* 1199 only the corrector of *L* (see Wecklein) reads κἀς. In Thgn.1101–2 the sense is clearly incomplete, and καί is not apodotic. (E. Harrison, *Studies in Theognis*, p. 157, takes 1101–2 in conjunction with 1103–4.)

(10) καί in questions. It is practically convenient to group under this heading various idioms which logically have little in common, and in which καί is sometimes copulative, sometimes adverbial.

(i) καί preceding an interrogative, usually at the opening of a speech in dialogue. The particle may either (*a*) simply denote that the speaker requires further information: or (*b*), more commonly, convey an emotional effect of surprise, contempt, and so

[1] All these passages are closely similar: a temporal protasis describing a thought is followed by an apodosis describing a corresponding action: and the verb describing that action immediately follows the καί: whereas in Th.vii 43.1, 75.1 the verb does not immediately follow the καί, which I therefore regard as applying to the whole apodosis, not merely to the following word. (The distinction seems perhaps, on reflexion, a trifle wiredrawn.)

forth. Both senses (to which the use of δέ and, more rarely, τε after interrogatives is closely parallel) are natural enough: just as we say 'I am going to London'.—'And when are you going?': or 'And what is the good of that?' There is no sharp dividing line between (*a*) and (*b*), which melt imperceptibly into each other.

(*a*) S.*El.*928 τοῦ τάδ' ἤκουσας βροτῶν;—Τοῦ πλησίον παρόντος, ἡνίκ' ὤλλυτο.—Καὶ ποῦ 'στιν οὗτος; *OT* 1435 πιθοῦ τί μοι ...—Καὶ τοῦ με χρείας ὧδε λιπαρεῖς τυχεῖν; Ar.*Eq.* 1322 Τὸν Δῆμον ἀφεψήσας ὑμῖν καλὸν ἐξ αἰσχροῦ πεποίηκα.—Καὶ ποῦ 'στιν νῦν ...; Pl.*Cra.*391D παρ' Ὁμήρου χρὴ μανθάνειν ...—Καὶ τί λέγει ... Ὅμηρος ...; X.*Cyr.*i6.16 τούτου σοι δεῖ μέλειν.—Καὶ τίνα δὴ ἐγώ, ἔφη, ὦ πάτερ, ὁδὸν ἰὼν τοῦτο πράττειν ἱκανὸς ἔσομαι; 6.22.

(*b*) (Where a strong degree of surprise is to be expressed, 'why' is often a better rendering than 'and'.) S.*El.*236 μὴ τίκτειν σ' ἄταν ἄταις.—Καὶ τί μέτρον κακότατος ἔφυ; 883 'Orestes is here'. —Οἴμοι τάλαινα· καὶ τίνος βροτῶν λόγον τόνδ' εἰσακούσασ' ὧδε πιστεύεις ἄγαν; E.*IT* 254 Ἄκραις ἐπὶ ῥηγμῖσιν ἀξένου πόρου.—Καὶ τίς θαλάσσης βουκόλοις κοινωνία; *Ion* 973 Τὸν πρῶτον ἀδικήσαντά σ' ἀποτίνου θεόν.—Καὶ πῶς τὰ κρείσσω θνητὸς οὖσ' ὑπερδράμω; Pl.*Tht.*182D Καὶ τίς μηχανή, ὦ Σώκρατες; A.*Ag.*280: *Eu.*94 (καί separated from τί): S.*El.*1189: *Tr.*187,1140: *Ant.* 548,1174: *OT*976: *OC*606,1439: E.*Ph.*900,1348: Ar.*Eq.*1044: *Nu.*398: Pl.*Ti.*26E: *Lg.*648A: X.*Oec.*2.3: *Smp.*4.62: *An.*iv6.19.

There is often an echo of a word from the previous speech. S.*OT* 1019 ἀλλ' ἴσον.—Καὶ πῶς ὁ φύσας ἐξ ἴσου τῷ μηδενί; E.*Or.* 1025 Οὐ σῖγ' ... στέρξεις ...;—Καὶ πῶς σιωπῶ; Ar.*Ach.*86 ἐκ κριβάνου βοῦς.—Καὶ τίς εἶδε πώποτε βοῦς κριβανίτας; S.*OC*73: Ar.*Eq.*178,792: *Nu.*1380: Hdt.iii 140 ἔφη Δαρείου εὐεργέτης εἶναι ... ὁ δὲ θωμάσας λέγει πρὸς αὐτόν· Καὶ τίς ἐστι Ἑλλήνων εὐεργέτης ...; Pl.*Tht.*196D ἀναισχυντεῖν ....—Καὶ τί τοῦτο ἀναίσχυντον; X.*Mem.*iii 11.10 ... εἰς τὰ σὰ δίκτυα.—Καὶ ποῖα, ἔφη, ἐγὼ δίκτυα ἔχω; *Oec.*7.5: 12.6: *Smp.*3.6: 4.4: *Cyr.*i3.11: *Hier.*1.1. Preceded by a request for an answer: Ar.*Eq.*178 Εἰπέ μοι, καὶ πῶς ...;

The elliptical form Καὶ πῶς; is common in Plato. E.*Or.*1110: Ar.*Eq.*128: *Nu.*717,1434: Pl.*Tht.*163D,188E: *R.*402E,485C,486C, 502B. Καὶ πῶς ἄν; Pl.*Tht.*188C: *R.*353C. καὶ τί; (Pl.*Phlb.*21B) is exceptional.

This idiom is occasionally found in mid speech: in Pl.*Phlb.*63D,

D.xix 120, introducing an imaginary objection: elsewhere a rhetorical question usually precedes, and there is always a suggestion of imaginary dialogue. S.*Aj.*462 πότερα πρὸς οἴκους ... περῶ; καὶ ποῖον ὄμμα πατρὶ δηλώσω φανεὶς Τελαμῶνι; *OT* 355 Οὕτως ἀναιδῶς ...; καὶ ποῦ τοῦτο φεύξεσθαι δοκεῖς; *OC* 263 'Athens is said to be chivalrous to strangers. κἄμοιγε ποῦ ταῦτ' ἐστιν ...;' (here an emphatic word intervenes between particle and interrogative): E.*HF* 297 ἥξειν νομίζεις παῖδα σὸν γαίας ὕπο; καὶ τίς θανόντων ἦλθεν ἐξ Ἅιδου πάλιν; *Tr.*1280 ἰὼ θεοί. καὶ τί τοὺς θεοὺς καλῶ (Hecuba pulls herself up): X.*Mem.*i 5.1 ἆρα ... τοῦτον ἂν αἱροίμεθα; καὶ πῶς ἂν οἰηθείημεν τὸν τοιοῦτον ...; D.xviii 282 οὐδὲν ἐξαίρετον οὐδ' ἴδιον πεποίημαι. ἆρ' οὖν οὐδὲ σύ; καὶ πῶς; ὃς εὐθέως μετὰ τὴν μάχην πρεσβευτὴς ἐπορεύου πρὸς Φίλιππον: Ant.v 57: Isoc.xii 23: Is.i 20,29: D.xviii 101: xix 232.

To embody so lively and conversational an idiom in reported speech is quite exceptional: X.*HG* v 3.10 λεγόντων δὲ τῶν κατεληλυθότων καὶ τίς αὕτη δίκη εἴη...: 3.15 ἐρωτώμενος δὲ καὶ τί τοῦτο ἂν εἴη, πάλιν ἀπεκρίνατο ... ('And when someone asked him, and what could that be ...').

(ii) καί, not followed by an interrogative, sometimes introduces surprised, indignant, or sarcastic questions.

(*a*) In particular, κᾆτα, κἄπειτα are so used by Euripides and Aristophanes. At the beginning of a speech: E.*Ph.*598 Κᾆτα σὺν πολλοῖσιν ἦλθες πρὸς τὸν οὐδὲν ἐς μάχην; *Or.*419 Κᾆτ' οὐκ ἀμύνει Λοξίας τοῖς σοῖς κακοῖς; *Supp.*1058 Κἄπειτα τύμβῳ ... φαίνῃ πέλας; Ar.*Th.*637 ἀπόδυσον αὐτὸν ...; —Κἄπειτ' ἀποδύσετ' ἐννέα παίδων μητέρα; E.*HF* 266: *Ion* 1286: *Or.*443: *IA* 894 (Κᾆτα πῶς ...;): Ar.*Pax* 369 (Κᾆτα τῷ τρόπῳ ...;): *Ra.*647 (Κᾆτα πῶς ...;). Also in mid-speech: E.*Alc.*831: *Andr.* 391: *Supp.*246: *HF* 1287: *Ion* 1408: *Ba.*1207: Ar.*Ach.*126.

(*b*) In general, καί sometimes introduces questions of the above types. It is often difficult to determine in such cases whether καί is copulative or adverbial ('actually'). S.*Ant.*554 Σῶσον σεαυτήν. οὐ φθονῶ σ' ὑπεκφυγεῖν.—Οἴμοι τάλαινα, κἀμπλάκω τοῦ σοῦ μόρου; 1102 κτίσον δὲ τῷ προκειμένῳ τάφον.—Καὶ ταῦτ' ἐπαινεῖς καὶ δοκεῖς παρεικαθεῖν; *El.*1046 Καὶ μὴν ποήσω γ' οὐδὲν ἐκπλαγεῖσά σε.—Καὶ τοῦτ' ἀληθές, οὐδὲ βουλεύσῃ πάλιν; 1481 οὐ γὰρ ἔσθ' ὅπως ὅδ' οὐκ Ὀρέστης ἔσθ' ὁ προσφωνῶν ἐμέ.—Καὶ μάντις ὢν ἄριστος ἐσφάλλου πάλαι; (some scholars take *καί* as = *καίπερ*, with *ὤν*: wrongly, I think): *OC*414 Καὶ ταῦτ' ἐφ' ἡμῖν Φοῖβος εἰρηκὼς κυρεῖ; E.*IA* 1358 Ἀλλ' ὅμως ἀρήξομέν σοί.—Καὶ μαχῇ πολλοῖσιν εἷς; Ar. *V*.1406 Philocleon has tried to put off the Ἀρτόπωλις with an anecdote. *Ap*. Καὶ καταγελᾷς μου; *Av*.325 Ἄνδρ' ἐδεξάμην ἐραστὰ τῆσδε τῆς ξυνουσίας.—Καὶ δέδρακας τοῦτο τοὔργον; 1033 οὐ δεινά; καὶ πέμπουσιν ἤδη 'πισκόπους ἐς τὴν πόλιν . . .; *Ra*.607 Οὐκ ἐς κόρακας; μὴ πρόσιτον.—Εἶεν, καὶ μαχεῖ; Pl.*Clit*.407B Ποῖ φέρεσθε, ὤνθρωποι; καὶ ἀγνοεῖτε οὐδὲν τῶν δεόντων πράττοντες . . .; (no question mark in *O.C.T.*): X.*Cyr*.vi 3.22 Καὶ δοκοῦμέν σοι, ἔφη, ὦ Κῦρε, ἱκανῶς ἕξειν . . .;

Different, of course, is the purely copulative *καί* in Ar.*Nu*.90 τί κελεύεις;—Καί τι πείσει; ('And you'll obey?').

(iii) *καί* following an interrogative (*τίς*, *ποῦ*, etc.) bears two[1] meanings not adequately distinguished by scholars, who talk vaguely of 'emphasis'. Though the border-line between the two meanings cannot be sharply drawn, the distinction seems to me a real and important one.

(*a*) The questioner asks for supplementary information, as in *καὶ τίς*;, but the placing of the particle after the interrogative gives stress to the addition. The effect is usually produced in English by an inflexion of the voice. The stress is sometimes on the interrogative, more often on the word which follows *καί*, or on a later word. (There is often both a main and a subsidiary stress.) A connecting particle other than *καί* may be either present or absent.

A.*Ag*.278 Ποίου χρόνου δὲ καὶ πεπόρθηται πόλις; ('And how *long* is it since the city was sacked?'): S.*OT*989 ἀλλὰ τῆς ζώσης φόβος.—Ποίας δὲ καὶ γυναικὸς ἐκφοβεῖσθ' ὕπερ; ('And *who* is the woman about whom you fear?'): *Ant*.772 Μόρῳ δὲ ποίῳ καί σφε βουλεύῃ κτανεῖν; ('by what *manner* of fate': not 'by what fate *do* you purpose', Jebb): E.*Hipp*.1171 'Poseidon has heard my prayer. πῶς καὶ διώλετ';' *Hec*.515 'Alas for my child. πῶς καί νιν ἐξεπράξατ';' ('And after what *manner* did ye slay her?'): 1066 ὦ κατάρατοι, ποῖ καί με φυγᾷ πτώσσουσι μυχῶν; *Fr*.403.3 τίς ἄρα μήτηρ ἢ πατὴρ . . . ἔφυσε . . .; ποῦ καί ποτ' οἰκεῖ . . .; Ar.*Pax* 1289 τοῦ καί ποτ' εἶ; *Lys*.836 τίς κἀστίν ποτε; S.*Ant*. 1314: E.*Alc*.834,1049: *Hipp*.92: *Hec*.1201: *Ph*.1354: Pl.

[1] For yet a third variety of *καί* following interrogatives, see p. 323, n. 1.

*Euthphr.*3A καί μοι λέγε, τί καὶ ποιοῦντά σέ φησι διαφθείρειν τοὺς νέους; *Tht.*144B τίνος δὲ καὶ ἔστι τῶν πολιτῶν; ('And whose *son* is he?'): 187E Socrates and Theaetetus have agreed to continue the investigation. Σω. Πῶς οὖν; τί δὴ καὶ λέγομεν; ('What do we *say*?' This and the next three examples, where a verb of saying follows καί, are differentiated from apparently similar examples grouped under *b*.ε below by the lower pitch (see (*b*) *ad init.*) on the stressed word): *Lg.*821E Ἀληθῆ λέγεις. ἀλλὰ τί καὶ φῂς τοῦτο τὸ μάθημα ...; *Min.*313A Ὁ νόμος ἡμῖν τί ἐστιν;—Ὁποῖον καὶ ἐρωτᾷς τῶν νόμων; (cf. *Euthd.*271A): *Epin.*977A τίνα δὴ καὶ σεμνύνων ποτὲ λέγω θεόν ...; D.liv 35 τί δὲ καὶ δεινόν ἐστιν ὧν παρέξεται κατὰ σοῦ; ('And what is the *danger* ...?').

Indirect questions. Ar.*Ec.*946 Old Woman (after cursing the Young Man, who has just taken himself off) ἀλλ' εἶμι τηρήσουσ' ὅ τι καὶ δράσει ποτέ ('to watch what he'll *do*'): 1014 Τοῦτο δ' ἔστι τί;—Ψήφισμα....—Λέγ' αὐτὸ τί ποτε κἄστι: Hdt.i 11 ἐπεί με ἀναγκάζεις δεσπότεα τὸν ἐμὸν κτείνειν οὐκ ἐθέλοντα, φέρε ἀκούσω, τέῳ καὶ τρόπῳ ἐπιχειρήσομεν αὐτῷ ('*how* we shall attack him'): ii 114 συλλαβόντες ἀπάγετε παρ' ἐμέ, ἵνα εἰδέω τί κοτε καὶ λέξει: Pl.*Euthd.*272D διήγησαι τὴν σοφίαν τοῖν ἀνδροῖν τίς ἐστιν, ἵνα εἰδῶ ὅτι καὶ μαθησόμεθα ('what it *is* that we're going to learn'): *Cra.*407E πειρώμεθα οὖν τὸν "Ἑρμῆν" σκέψασθαι τί καὶ νοεῖ τὸ ὄνομα: *Lg.*819E Τοῦ πέρι; λέγ' ὅτι καὶ φῂς: *Amat.* 136C Ὁ δὲ ὡμολόγει χρησίμους....—Φέρε δή γνῶμεν, εἰ σὺ ἀληθῆ λέγεις, ποῦ καὶ χρήσιμοι ἡμῖν εἰσιν οἱ ὕπακροι οὗτοι; ('*where* they are useful'): X.*HG* iii 3.6 ἐρωτώντων δὲ τῶν ἐφόρων πόσους φαίη καὶ τοὺς συνειδότας τὴν πρᾶξιν εἶναι ... ('how *many*': but perhaps καί stresses τοὺς συνειδότας): *An.*v 8.2 φάσκοντες παίεσθαι ... καὶ ὁ Ξενοφῶν ἐκέλευσεν εἰπεῖν ... ποῦ καὶ ἐπλήγη ('*where* he had been hit'): Pl.*Thg.*122D: *Ly.*214E: *Phdr.*266D: X.*Oec.*6.13.

(*b*) καί, following an interrogative, denotes that the question cuts at the foundations of the problem under consideration. A question is put which, it is implied, cannot be answered, or cannot be satisfactorily answered: so that the discussion of any further, consequential, question does not arise. καί here marks a descending climax, and is roughly equivalent to ἀρχήν, τὴν ἀρχήν, *omnino*, 'at all', 'to start with'. Whereas both in (*a*) and in (*b*) the effect of the particle is often best rendered in English by stress, the stress is stronger in (*b*) than in (*a*), and is accompanied by a higher pitch, as the following example shows: 'I will give you a motor-car'.—'Very nice: where can I *keep* it?' Contrast: 'Oh but, my dear man, where can I *keep* it?' In the first case a lively question proceeds with the discussion: in the second, the question erects a barrier against all further discussion. This use falls naturally into certain main subdivisions.

(α) The very possibility of something is by implication denied, so that further discussion of it is seen to be unnecessary. Hdt. ix 122.2 οἰκὸς δὲ ἄνδρας ἄρχοντας τοιαῦτα ποιέειν· κότε γὰρ δὴ καὶ παρέξει κάλλιον ἢ ὅτε . . .; ('When will there be a better *opportunity*?': *sc.* 'therefore we have no choice in the matter').

Usually with ἄν and optative, or past indicative, in a potential clause. Parm.*Fr*.8.9 τί δ' ἄν μιν καὶ χρέος ὦρσεν . . .; S.*OT* 772 'I will tell you. τῷ γὰρ ἂν καὶ μείζονι λέξαιμ' ἂν ἢ σοὶ . . .;' E.*Tr*.1188 τί καί ποτε γράψειεν ἄν σε μουσοποιὸς ἐν τάφῳ; ('What *could* he write?'): Ar.*Nu*.840 μάνθανε.—Τί δ' ἂν παρ' ἐκείνων καὶ μάθοι χρηστόν τις ἄν; *Lys*.910 σὺ δ' οὐ κατακλίνει.—Ποῦ γὰρ ἄν τις καὶ τάλαν δράσειε τοῦθ'; Pl.*La*.184D τί γὰρ ἄν τις καὶ ποιοῖ; (*Phd*.61E): *Tht*.202D τίς γὰρ ἂν καὶ ἔτι ἐπιστήμη εἴη . . .; ('What knowledge *could* there be?'): X.*Eq*.11.11 ἐκ δὲ ταύτης τῆς ὄψεως τί ἂν καὶ λαμπρὸν γένοιτ' ἄν; ('What possible brilliance *could* there be in such a spectacle?'): D.xlvii 29 τί γὰρ ἂν καὶ ἀντέλεγον αὐτῷ . . .; Lys.xxiv 23 μηδαμῶς, ὦ βουλή, ταύτῃ θῆσθε τὴν ψῆφον. διὰ τί γὰρ ἂν καὶ τύχοιμι τοιούτων ὑμῶν;

(β) With future indicative, the idea of futurity being tinged with the idea of (denied) possibility. And.i.148 τίνα γὰρ καὶ ἀναβιβάσομαι δεησόμενον ὑπὲρ ἐμαυτοῦ; ('whom *shall* I, or *can* I, bring forward to plead for me?'): Lys.xii 29 νῦν δὲ παρὰ τοῦ ποτε καὶ λήψεσθε δίκην, εἴπερ ἐξέσται . . .; Pl.*Euthphr*.6B ἀνάγκη . . . καὶ ἡμῖν συγχωρεῖν. τί γὰρ καὶ φήσομεν . . .; *R*.434D συγχωρησόμεθα ἤδη—τί γὰρ καὶ ἐροῦμεν; X.*Smp*.1.15 πρόσθεν μὲν γὰρ τούτου ἕνεκα ἐκαλούμην ἐπὶ τὰ δεῖπνα, ἵνα . . . νῦν δὲ τίνος ἕνεκα καὶ καλεῖ μέ τις; ('Why *will*, or *should*, anybody invite me?').

With deliberative subjunctive. D.xix 138 ταὐτὸν τοίνυν τοῦτ' ἂν ἐποίησε Φίλιππος, εἰ . . . . ἐπειδὰν δ' ἀκούῃ . . . τί καὶ ποιήσῃ; ('What *is* he to do?').

(γ) With δεῖ, χρή, etc. The very necessity or advisability of something is denied: hence it need not be further discussed.

Ar.*Lys*.526 μετὰ ταῦθ' ἡμῖν εὐθὺς ἔδοξεν . . . ποῖ γὰρ καὶ χρῆν ἀναμεῖναι ; Pl.*La*.182E τί καὶ δέοι ἂν αὐτὸ μανθάνειν ; ('what *need* could there be ?') : *Lg*.891B νόμοις οὖν . . . τίνα καὶ μᾶλλον προσήκει βοηθεῖν ἢ νομοθέτην ; (καί with προσήκει): X.*HG* ii 3.47 ἀποκαλεῖ δὲ κόθορνόν με . . . ὅστις δὲ μηδετέροις ἀρέσκει, τοῦτον . . . τί ποτε καὶ καλέσαι χρή (καί with χρή : 'what *are* we to call him?' : we can save ourselves the trouble of hunting for an appropriate nickname) : *Oec*.12.4 τί αὐτὸν καὶ δεῖ ἄλλο ἐπίστασθαι . . . ; *Smp*.2.4 μύρου μὲν τί καὶ προσδέονται ; ('what do they *want* with myrrh ?').

But sometimes καί adheres not so much to the verb of obligation as to another word. E.*Andr*.395 τί δέ με καὶ τεκεῖν ἐχρῆν ἄχθος τ' ἐπ' ἄχθει τῷδε προσθέσθαι διπλοῦν ; ('give birth as well') : D.iv 46 ὅταν γὰρ . . . τί καὶ χρὴ προσδοκᾶν ; ('what must one *expect* ?').

(δ) καί calls in question the ground or motive (usually expressed by a participle) of an action. Motive being absent, the further question of action does not arise. Ar.*Eq*.342 Τῷ καὶ πεποιθὼς ἀξιοῖς ἐμοῦ λέγειν ἔναντα ; Th.vi 38.5 τί καὶ βούλεσθε, ὦ νεώτεροι ; ('what do you *want* (whether or not your desires can be realized) ?') : Pl.*R*.365D τί καὶ ἡμῖν μελητέον τοῦ λανθάνειν ; (καί with μελητέον : 'why should we *trouble* at all ?') : X.*HG* i 7.26 τί δὲ καὶ δεδιότες σφόδρα οὕτως ἐπείγεσθε ; Ant.vi 34 τίνες οὖν ἦσαν οἱ πείσαντες αὐτούς ; καὶ τίνος ἕνεκα καὶ πρόθυμοι ἐγένοντο πεῖσαι αὐτούς ; And.i 4 τί γὰρ ἂν καὶ βουλόμενος . . . ὑπομείνειεν . . . ; D.xviii 24 τί γὰρ καὶ βουλόμενοι μετεπέμπεσθ' ἂν αὐτοὺς ἐν τούτῳ τῷ καιρῷ ;

(ε) In general. S.*Aj*.1290 δύστηνε, ποῖ βλέπων ποτ' αὐτὰ καὶ θροεῖς ; ('why *talk* like that at all ?' : you had better avoid the whole topic) : *OT* 1129 Τί χρῆμα δρῶντα ; ποῖον ἄνδρα καὶ λέγεις ; ('What sort of a man do you *mean*?' : I cannot answer your question until I know *that*) : *Tr*.314 Τί δ' οἶδ' ἐγώ ; τί δ' ἄν με καὶ κρίνοις ; ('Why should you *ask* me ?'. Not 'Why *should* you ask me ?', as in (α) above : the stress here is on the content of the verb, not on the modality) : E.*Or*.1093 τί γὰρ ἐρῶ κἀγώ ποτε . . . ; ('what shall I *say* (whether people believe me or not) ?' : the stress is on ἐρῶ : but the text is uncertain) : Pl.*Plt*.292A Τί γὰρ δὴ καὶ κωλύει ; ('What is the *difficulty*?') : 305A Τίν' οὖν ποτε καὶ ἐπιχειρήσομεν . . . δεσπότιν ἀποφαίνεσθαι . . . ; X.*HG* v 2.16

τί γὰρ δὴ καὶ ἐμποδὼν . . . ; *Ages.*10.3 ' This is an *ἐγκώμιον*, not a *θρῆνος*, though its subject is dead. *πρῶτον μὲν γὰρ . . . ἔπειτα δὲ τί καὶ πλέον θρήνου ἄπεστιν ἢ βίος τε εὐκλεὴς* . . . ;' (*καί* with *ἄπεστιν*: 'what *is* there further removed . . . ?'): Hyp.*Eux.*14 *τοῦτ' εἰ μὲν ὑπελάμβανες ἀληθὲς εἶναι . . . τί καὶ ἀδικεῖ* . . . ; ('what is his *crime*?').

In indirect questions. Ar.*Nu.*1344 *'Αλλ' οἴομαι μέντοι σ' ἀναπείσειν* . . .—*Καὶ μὴν ὅ τι καὶ λέξεις ἀκοῦσαι βούλομαι* ('what you'll *say*'): X.*HG* iii 3.11 *ἤροντο τί καὶ βουλόμενος ταῦτα πράττοι*: And.iii 13 *φασὶ δέ τινες ἀναγκαίως νῦν ἡμῖν ἔχειν πολεμεῖν. σκεψώμεθα οὖν πρῶτον . . . διὰ τί καὶ πολεμήσωμεν* ('why we *should* fight'): D.lix 118 *θαυμάζω δ' ἔγωγε τί ποτε καὶ ἐροῦσι*: Pl.*Ly.*214E *ἴδωμεν τί καὶ ὑποπτεύω* ('let us see *what* it is that I suspect'): *Cra.*428D.

(iv) *καί*, without an interrogative, and not opening a question, sometimes means 'actually', and conveys surprise or indignation. Cf. *καί* opening a question, 10.ii.*b* above. The particle coheres closely with the word that follows it.

S.*El.*385 *Ἦ ταῦτα δή με καὶ βεβούλευνται ποεῖν*; ('Are they actually resolved to do *that* to me?'): *Ant.*726 *Οἱ τηλικοίδε καὶ διδαξόμεσθα δὴ φρονεῖν* . . . ; E.*Med.*1367 *Λέχους σφε κἠξίωσας οὕνεκα κτανεῖν*; (*σφέ γ' ἠξίωσας AVB*): *Heracl.*498 *'Εν τῷδε κἀχόμεσθα σωθῆναι λόγῳ*; Ar.*Av.*74 *Δεῖται γὰρ ὄρνις καὶ διακόνου τινός*; ('Why, does a bird need a *servant*?'): 1446 *Λόγοισί τἄρα καὶ πτεροῦνται*; Cratin.*Fr.*314 *ταυτὶ καὶ τολμᾷς σὺ λέγειν*; Hdt.iii 36.3 *Σὺ καὶ ἐμοὶ τολμᾷς συμβουλεύειν* . . . ; (the sentence is interrogative, I think). S.*Ant.*1062 *Οὕτω γὰρ ἤδη καὶ δοκῶ τὸ σὸν μέρος* is best taken as affirmative: see Jebb, *ad loc.*

(v) The use of *καί* in exclamations is analogous. S.*Ph.*991 *Ὦ μῖσος, οἷα κἀξανευρίσκεις λέγειν* ('what *things* you invent!'): Ar.*V.*900 *Ὦ μιαρὸς οὗτος· ὡς δὲ καὶ κλέπτον βλέπει* ('And what a *thievish* look there is in his eye!'): *Ec.*125 *σκέψαι, τάλαν, ὡς καὶ καταγέλαστον τὸ πρᾶγμα φαίνεται.*

C. In the idioms which I have considered above *καί* everywhere denotes the connexion between two ideas, either expressed, or fairly clearly implied (the line between expression and implication cannot be sharply drawn), and bears the sense 'also' (addition) or 'even' (climax). Hence, by an easy transition, the sense of addition sometimes recedes into the background, while the sense of climax predominates, a ladder of which only the top rung is clearly seen. 'Even' then passes into 'actually', and *καί* is little more than a particle of emphasis, like *δή*. As such, it precedes, and emphasizes, various parts of speech (a convenient classification, which must not, however, be taken too seriously, since the words which follow the particle often coalesce into a single entity).

(1) With intensive and quantitative adverbs and adjectives. *Καί* is often used before intensive and quantitative adverbs and adjectives: for example, before *λίαν, κάρτα, μάλα, πάνυ*, etc.: before *πολύς, μόνος*, and *πᾶς*: and before comparatives and superlatives. The particle conveys a sense of climax, and denotes that something is not only true, but true in a marked degree: *καὶ μάλα*, 'even (actually) very much'. (It would nowhere, I think, be correct to say that *καί* e.g. with adverbs represents the adverbial qualification as something additional to the verbal action, so that *καὶ μάλα λέγει* would virtually = *λέγει, καὶ μάλα γε*.)

καὶ λίαν. Hom.*A* 553 *καὶ λίην σε πάρος γ' οὔτ' εἴρομαι οὔτε μεταλλῶ*: E.*Alc*.811 *Ἦ κάρτα μέντοι καὶ λίαν θυραῖος ἦν*: Hom. *α* 46. *καὶ ἄγαν*: Th.vii 50.4.

καὶ κάρτα. S.*Aj*.527 *Καὶ κάρτ' ἐπαίνου τεύξεται* (Jebb holds that *καί* is copulative here: but that when *καὶ κάρτα* replies to a question, as in *OC* 65,301, *καί* is adverbial. In view of the frequent appearance of *καί* before adverbs of this type, I should be inclined to believe that it is always adverbial): Ar.*Ach*.544 *ἦ πολλοῦ γε δεῖ· καὶ κάρτα μέντἂν εὐθέως καθείλκετε τριακοσίας ναῦς*: E.*Hipp*.90 *Καὶ κάρτα γ'*: Hdt.i 119 *φαμένου δὲ Ἁρπάγου καὶ κάρτα ἡσθῆναι*: ii 69,92. With article, *καὶ τὸ κάρτα*. Hdt. iii 104 *καὶ τὸ ἀπὸ τούτου ἀπιὼν ἐπὶ μᾶλλον ψύχει, ἐς ὃ ἐπὶ δυσμῇσι ἐὼν καὶ τὸ κάρτα ψύχει*: i 71,191: iv 181 (text uncertain): vi 52.4.

καὶ μάλα. Thgn.1294 *τέλος δ' ἔγνω καὶ μάλ' ἀναινομένη*: S.*El*.1455 *Πάρεστι δῆτα καὶ μάλ' ἄζηλος θέα* (Jebb takes *καί* as 'and' here, and in *El*.1178): Ar.*Ra*.412 *μειρακίσκης νῦν δὴ κατεῖδον καὶ μάλ' εὐπροσώπου . . . τιτθίον προκύψαν*: Hermipp. *Fr*.70.2 *εἶδον οὖν τὴν Ἡράκλειαν καὶ μάλ' ὡραίαν πόλιν*: E. *Heracl*.386: *Rh*.85: Hdt.vii 11.2 *ἀλλὰ καὶ μάλα στρατεύσονται*: Pl.*R*.592A *Νὴ τὸν κύνα . . . ἔν γε τῇ ἑαυτοῦ πόλει καὶ μάλα*: *Tht*. 142B *ζῶντι καὶ μάλα μόλις*: 152D *Ἐγὼ ἐρῶ καὶ μάλ' οὐ φαῦλον* λόγον: *Clit.*407E ταῦτ' οὖν . . . καὶ μάλα ἄγαμαι: *Phd.*117C καὶ μάλα εὐχερῶς καὶ εὐκόλως ἐξέπιεν: X.*HG* iv 7.2 ὁ δὲ ἀπεκρίνατο καὶ μάλα κατὰ ταὐτά: Pl.*Tht.*142D: *R.*457C (καί not connective, though at opening of answer: cf. *Lg.*627C: *Sph.*239C: *Phd.*76A: *Cra.*386B,418E): *R.*506D: X.*Cyr.*vi 1.36: D.iii 2: viii 48: xviii 16: xix 307. (In Hdt.iv 68.4 καί is of course connective.) Καὶ μάλα, as a self-contained answer. Ar.*Nu.*1326: *Ra.*890: Pl.*Ly.*208B: *Phd.*68D: *Tht.*152B,153C: *id. saep.* Pl. *Phd.*105D Καὶ μάλα σφόδρα: *Tht.*177A Καὶ μάλα δή.

καὶ σφόδρα. Pl.*Lg.*627A πάνυ γάρ ἐστι καὶ σφόδρα τὸ τοιοῦτον: D.i 11 διὸ καὶ σφόδρα δεῖ: lvii 4. Καὶ σφόδρα, as a self-contained answer. Pl.*La.*191E: X.*Cyr.*iii 2.20 Καὶ σφόδρ' ἄν, ἔφη: v 2.26 ἔφασαν καὶ σφόδρ' ἄν.

Καὶ πάνυ, πάγχυ. Ar.*Ec.*54 Καὶ πάνυ ταλαιπώρως . . . ἐκδρᾶσα παρέδυν: Th.iii 30.2 κατὰ μὲν θάλασσαν καὶ πάνυ: Pl.*Phd.*64B καὶ συμφάναι ἂν . . . καὶ πάνυ: *Tht.*150D ἔνιοι μὲν καὶ πάνυ ἀμαθεῖς: X.*Oec.*13.1: D.liii 4. Καὶ πάνυ, as a self-contained answer. X.*Oec.*14.3 Καὶ πάνυ, ἔφη. Hdt.vi 112.2 μανίην . . . ἐπέφερον καὶ πάγχυ ὀλεθρίην.

Καὶ πολύς, συχνός. Ar.*Lys.*501 Τοῦδ' οὕνεκα καὶ πολὺ μᾶλλον: Th.vi 24.2 ἀσφάλεια νῦν δὴ καὶ πολλὴ ἔσεσθαι: Pl.*R.*562C Λέγεται γὰρ δή, ἔφη, καὶ πολὺ τοῦτο τὸ ῥῆμα: X.*Cyr.*v.4.42 Εἰσὶ μὲν . . . καὶ πολλαὶ ὁδοί: Archyt.*Fr.*4: Pl.*Tht.*202D: *Alc.II* 142B: *Tht.* 152A 'Ανέγνωκα καὶ πολλάκις: *Grg.*455C ὡς ἐγώ τινας σχεδὸν καὶ συχνοὺς αἰσθάνομαι. In answers. Pl.*Phd.*74D Καὶ πολύ γε, ἔφη, ἐνδεῖ: *R.*478C Καὶ πολύ γε, ἔφη: X.*Mem.*iii 8.4 Καὶ πολλά, ἔφη.

Καὶ πᾶς. Pl.*Lg.*625C: D.xviii 279: Pl.*Tht.*177A ταῦτα δὴ καὶ παντάπασιν ὡς δεινοὶ . . . ἀκούσονται.

Καὶ μόνος. Lys.xxix 5 δύο εἶναι καὶ μόνας ἀπολογίας: D.vi 13 ἀλλὰ τοῦτον καὶ μόνον πάντων τῶν λόγων . . .: xvii 25. But in D.xix 141 καί before μόνα means 'also'.

Pi.*O.*6.20 καὶ μέγαν ὅρκον ὀμόσσαις: Hdt.i 117.1 καὶ μεγάλως (see (2)): D.xviii 3 δύο δὲ καὶ μεγάλα: Pl.*Phd.*59A εἷς δὲ ἡμῶν καὶ διαφερόντως: *Lg.*657D Μῶν οὖν οἰόμεθα καὶ κομιδῇ μάτην . . .;

With temporal adverbs denoting length of time. S.*Ant.*289 καὶ πάλαι (*OC* 1252: *Tr.*87: *Ph.*1218: Hdt.i 45: X.*Oec.*19.17): D.i 22 καὶ ἀεί.

(2) With comparatives. Hom.*Γ*168 ἤτοι μὲν κεφαλῇ καὶ μείζονες ἄλλοι ἔασι: Hdt.i65.3 (hexameter oracle) δίζω ἤ σε θεὸν μαντεύσομαι ἢ ἄνθρωπον· ἀλλ' ἔτι καὶ μᾶλλον θεὸν ἔλπομαι: 117.1 Ἀστυάγης δὲ τοῦ μὲν βουκόλου τὴν ἀληθείην ἐκφήναντος λόγον ἤδη καὶ ἐλάσσω ἐποιέετο, Ἁρπάγῳ δὲ καὶ μεγάλως μεμφόμενος . . . ('did not mind so *much*'): Pl.*Chrm.*175D τὸ μὲν οὖν ἐμὸν καὶ ἧττον ἀγανακτῶ· ὑπὲρ δὲ σοῦ . . . πάνυ ἀγανακτῶ ('not so *much*'): *Thg.*121D ἐμοὶ δὲ τῶν μὲν χρημάτων καὶ ἔλαττον μέλει (καί *secl.* Cobet): *Prm.*135C τοῦ τοιούτου μὲν οὖν μοι δοκεῖς καὶ μᾶλλον ᾐσθῆσθαι: *Lg.*752D τὰς μὲν οὖν ἄλλας καὶ βραχύτερον ἔργον: Th.vi46.2: Pl.*Phlb.*38E. (Distinguish from the above, where καί is emphatic, such passages as Hom.*Θ*470, where καὶ μᾶλλον means 'even more'.)

With superlatives. Ar.*Av.*1144 Τοῦτ' ὦγάθ' ἐξηυρῆτο καὶ σοφώτατα: X.*Mem.*iii4.11 Ἐνταῦθα δήπου καὶ πλεῖστον, ἔφη: *An.*vii3. 19 ἄξιον οὖν σοι καὶ μεγαλοπρεπέστατα τιμῆσαι Σεύθην: *Cyr.*i3.10 τότε γὰρ δὴ ἔγωγε καὶ πρῶτον κατέμαθον: D.xix239: xlv41.

(3) With other adjectives and adverbs. Ar.*Th* 259 Νὴ τὸν Δί' ἀλλὰ κἀπιτηδεία πάνυ ('Why, it's the very thing'): *Pl.*697 μετὰ τοῦτο δ' ἤδη καὶ γέλοιον δῆτά τι ἐποίησα ('something absolutely ridiculous'): Hdt.i187.3 Δαρείῳ δὲ καὶ δεινὸν ἐδόκεε εἶναι ('actually monstrous'): viii25.2: Pl.*Smp.*177B καὶ τοῦτο μὲν ἧττον καὶ θαυμαστόν ('less actually astonishing'): *Prm.*144B: *Lg.*708E: *Grg.*458C σκοπεῖν . . . μή τινας αὐτῶν κατέχομεν βουλομένους τι καὶ ἄλλο πράττειν ('wanting to do something *else*'): Hom.*X*322 τοῦ δὲ καὶ ἄλλο τόσον μὲν ἔχε χρόα χάλκεα τεύχεα . . . φαίνετο δ' ᾗ . . . ('the armour protected the *rest* of the body . . . but there was an opening where . . .').

S.*Ant.*1280 τὰ δ' ἐν δόμοις ἔοικας ἥκων καὶ τάχ' ὄψεσθαι κακά ('full soon'). E.*Alc.*796 καὶ σάφ' οἶδ' ὁθούνεκα . . . (not connective): Pl.*R.*445D ἐπονομασθείη δ' ἂν καὶ διχῇ: *Phd.*102D Ἔοικα, ἔφη, καὶ συγγραφικῶς ἐρεῖν: X.*Oec.*11.25 ἤδη δ', ἔφη, καὶ διειλημμένως πολλάκις ἐκρίθην: Pl.*Alc.I* 103A οὗ σὺ τὴν δύναμιν καὶ ὕστερον πεύσῃ ('you shall hear *afterwards*': 'there will be an opportunity later, as well as now': cf. *Smp.*175E: *R.*347E): Hdt. iii10 οὐ γὰρ δὴ ὕεται τὰ ἄνω τῆς Αἰγύπτου τὸ παράπαν· ἀλλὰ καὶ τότε ὕσθησαν αἱ Θῆβαι ψακάδι ('but *then*': perhaps, however, καὶ should be placed before αἱ).

With numerals. Hom.*N*236 αἴ κ' ὄφελός τι γενώμεθα καὶ δύ' ἐόντε ('being *two*'): Ψ833 ἕξει μιν καὶ πέντε περιπλομένους ἐνιαυτούς ('full five'): Pi.*I*.3.9 καὶ διδύμων: Hdt.ii68.2 αὐξανόμενος δὲ γίνεται καὶ ἐς ἑπτακαίδεκα πήχεας καὶ μέζων ἔτι: Th.i44.1 γενομένης καὶ δὶς ἐκκλησίας (v 10.9): vii 81.3 τὸ δὲ Νικίου στράτευμα ἀπεῖχεν ἐν τῷ πρόσθεν καὶ πεντήκοντα σταδίους ('as much as fifty': *post* πρόσθεν *add.* ἑκατόν *B*): Arist.*Pol*.1270a37 καί φασιν εἶναί ποτε τοῖς Σπαρτιάταις καὶ μυρίους: Hdt.viii 24.1. Hdt. ix 33.1 ἐθύοντο καὶ ἀμφότεροι.

(4) With substantives. Hom.*Π*746 εἰ δή που καὶ πόντῳ ἐν ἰχθυόεντι γένοιτο ('at *sea*'):* Thgn.1097 ἤδη καὶ πτερύγεσσιν ἐπαίρομαι ('I rise even upon wings'): Pi.*O*.6.25 ὄφρα . . ., ἵκωμαί τε πρὸς ἀνδρῶν καὶ γένος: E.*Med*.1396 Οὔπω θρηνεῖς· μένε καὶ γῆρας ('Wait until you are *old*': that is when you will have real cause for lamentation): Ar.*V*.420 Ἡράκλεις, καὶ κέντρ' ἔχουσιν ('They've actually got *stings*!'): Th.6.70.1 καὶ ὥρᾳ ἔτους, 'because of the *season*' (without any deeper cause): Pl.*La*.194A ἀλλά τίς με καὶ φιλονεικία εἴληφεν ('I am seized with an absolute zeal'): *Men*.95C οἱ σοφισταί σοι . . . δοκοῦσι διδάσκαλοι εἶναι ἀρετῆς.— Καὶ Γοργίου μάλιστα . . . ταῦτα ἄγαμαι, ὅτι οὐκ ἄν ποτε αὐτοῦ τοῦτο ἀκούσαις ὑπισχνουμένου ('That is just what I admire about *Gorgias*': a connective sense hardly seems appropriate here): *R*.400B λέγειν οὐκ ἔχω.—Ἀλλὰ ταῦτα μέν, ἦν δ' ἐγώ, καὶ μετὰ Δάμωνος βουλευσόμεθα ('We'll discuss that with *Damon*'): X.*An*. v6.10 ἐξ Ἡρακλείας δὲ οὔτε πεζῇ οὔτε κατὰ θάλατταν ἀπορία· πολλὰ γὰρ καὶ πλοῖά ἐστιν ἐν Ἡρακλείᾳ ('There are plenty of *boats* at Heraclea'): Lys.xxv13 μὴ τοῖς τούτων λόγοις πιστεύειν ἀλλὰ καὶ ἐκ τῶν ἔργων σκοπεῖν (almost = ἐξ αὐτῶν τῶν ἔργων: Emperius deletes καί, but it may perhaps stand. In Hdt.ix 27.5 καί, after ἀλλά, is easier: 'even on the score of Marathon alone'). In Hdt.ii 99 καί can hardly stand: ἀπογεφυρῶσαι καὶ τὴν Μέμφιν: καί *om. RSV*.

(5) With pronouns. Pl.*Phlb*.25B Σὺ καὶ ἐμοὶ φράσεις ('*You* shall tell *me*': instead of vice versa): X.*An* vii 7.10 ἀτὰρ τί καὶ πρὸς ἐμὲ λέγεις ταῦτα; ἔφη· οὐ γὰρ ἔγωγ' ἔτι ἄρχω. *

(6) With verbs. A.*Eu*.71 κακῶν δ' ἕκατι κἀγένοντ' ('for evil's sake were they even born'): S.*Ph*.807 Ἀλγῶ . . . .—Ἀλλ', ὦ τέκνον, καὶ θάρσος ἴσχ' ('Have *courage*': 'have good hope also'

(as well as ἄλγος), Jebb: but I doubt this explanation): *Ant.* 1192 Ἐγώ, φίλη δέσποινα, καὶ παρὼν ἐρῶ, κοὐδὲν παρήσω τῆς ἀληθείας ἔπος ('I will speak as one who was *present*': though Jebb is perhaps right in taking καὶ . . . καί as 'both . . . and'): *OC*1586 Τοῦτ' ἐστὶν ἤδη κἀποθαυμάσαι πρέπον: Hom.E685: P647: Φ274: Pl.*Grg.* 448A ἂν δέ γε βούλῃ . . . ἐμοῦ (πάρεστι πεῖραν λαμβάνειν). Γοργίας μὲν γὰρ καὶ ἀπειρηκέναι μοι δοκεῖ ('Gorgias seems to be *tired*'): *Tht.*143A πάντως ἔγωγε καὶ ἀναπαύσασθαι δέομαι: X.*Cyr.*iii 1.9 τούτου ἕνεκα καὶ γενέσθω ὅ τι βούλεται ('let it even happen'). In Ant.i 27 the text is doubtful.

Occasionally at the beginning of a sentence. S.*OT*415 ἆρ' οἶσθ' ἀφ' ὧν εἶ; καὶ λέληθας ἐχθρὸς ὢν τοῖς σοῖσιν αὐτοῦ ('Thou hast been unwittingly . . .': not connective, I think): *El.*680 Κἀπεμπόμην πρὸς ταῦτα καὶ τὸ πᾶν φράσω ('I was *sent* for that end': καὶ . . . καί, Jebb): E.*HF*577 καὶ δεῖ μ' ὑπὲρ τῶνδ' . . . θνῄσκειν ἀμύνοντ' ('It is my bounden duty . . .').

With a whole verbal phrase: Hom.Ω425 ἦ ῥ' ἀγαθὸν καὶ ἐναίσιμα δῶρα διδοῦναι ἀθανάτοις ('Whatever else one does, it is good to give the gods also their due', Leaf): In *Pi.N.*8.50 ἐπαοιδαῖς δ' ἀνὴρ νώδυνον καί τις κάματον θῆκεν, καί seems to mean something like 'ere now': cf. the use of καὶ δή illustrated on p. 250 (1.i.)

(7) Sometimes καί contrasts the objective reality of an idea with its subjective reality or with the unreality of something else, whereas in (1)–(6) above it is the content of an idea which is stressed: hence in translating examples of this class the stressed word is some part of the verb 'to be', or an auxiliary ('do', 'might', etc.). This use of καί has not been adequately recognized.

In relative clauses (here καί is virtually equivalent to the καί in εἰ καί, B.6.iv.*a*). S.*Tr.*1009 ἀνατέτροφας ὅ τι καὶ μύσῃ ('anything that *has* closed the eyes', Jebb): Ar.*Nu.*785 Ἀλλ' εὐθὺς ἐπιλήθει σύ γ' ἅττ' ἂν καὶ μάθῃς ('anything you *do* learn'): Hdt. ii 65.2 θεῖα πρήγματα, τὰ ἐγὼ φεύγω μάλιστα ἀπηγέεσθαι. τὰ δὲ καὶ εἴρηκα, . . . ἀναγκαίῃ καταλαμβανόμενος εἶπον: v 101.1 ἦσαν . . . οἰκίαι αἱ μὲν πλεῦνες καλάμιναι, ὅσαι δ' αὐτέων καὶ πλίνθιναι ἦσαν καλάμου εἶχον τὰς ὀροφάς ('those that *were* of brick': καλάμιναι implies 'not of brick'): Th.i 97.2 τοῖς πρὸ ἐμοῦ ἅπασιν ἐκλιπὲς τοῦτο ἦν τὸ χωρίον . . . τούτων δὲ ὅσπερ καὶ ἥψατο . . . Ἑλλάνικος, βραχέως . . . ἐπεμνήσθη ('the author who *did* touch on this topic'): Pl.*Tht*.186C παραγίγνεται οἷς ἂν καὶ παραγίγνηται (cf.Pl.*Smp*.181B: *Phdr*.276B): X.*HG* iii.2.17 οἱ μέν τινες . . . ἀπεδίδρασκον . . . ὅσοι δὲ καὶ ἔμενον, δῆλοι ἦσαν οὐ μενοῦντες (the context shows that καί goes, not with δέ, as in B.7.ii, 'and those again who remained', but with ἔμενον, 'and those who *did* remain').

Similarly with participles. Pl.*R*.497E οἱ καὶ ἁπτόμενοι.

In main clauses. Hom.*Ω*641 νῦν δὴ καὶ σίτου πασάμην καὶ αἴθοπα οἶνον λαυκανίης καθέηκα· πάρος γε μὲν οὔ τι πεπάσμην ('*Now* I *have* tasted': I do not think the two καί's correspond): S.*Aj*.1396 σὲ δ' . . . τάφου μὲν ὀκνῶ τοῦδ' ἐπιψαύειν ἐᾶν . . . τὰ δ' ἄλλα καὶ ξύμπρασσε, κεἰ . . . ('but in everything else *do* assist': Jebb, in his excellent note, rightly denies that the first καί is answered by the second): E.*Heracl*.526 οὐκ οὖν θανεῖν ἄμεινον ἢ τούτων τυχεῖν ἀναξίαν; ἄλλῃ δὲ κἂν πρέποι τινὶ μᾶλλον τάδ' ('This conduct *might* be rather more suitable to some other woman'): *Ion*.264 τοσαῦτα κεὐτυχοῦμεν ('Thus far I *am* fortunate'): *Rh*.849 τίς οὖν τέτρωται, τίς τέθνηκε συμμάχων τῶν σῶν . . .; ἡμεῖς δὲ καί τετρώμεθα ('but we *have* been wounded': δ' ἑκάς Murray for δὲ καί): Antiph.*Fr*.124.12 καὶ τοῦτο μὲν δὴ κἄστι συγγνώμην ἔχον· ἀλλ' οἷα λογοποιοῦσιν . . . ('And *that is* excusable: but what follows is not'): Hdt.iii 134.3 οἰκὸς δέ ἐστι ἄνδρα . . . φαίνεσθαί τι ἀποδεικνύμενον . . . νῦν γὰρ ἄν τι καὶ ἀποδέξαιο ἔργον ('*now* you *might* achieve something)': Th.vi.11.3 νῦν μὲν γὰρ κἂν ἔλθοιεν ἴσως . . ., ἐκείνως δ' οὐκ εἰκὸς ἀρχὴν ἐπὶ ἀρχὴν στρατεῦσαι ('as things are, they *might* perhaps attack us; but in the other case they are unlikely to'): 89 3 διότι καὶ τῷ δήμῳ προσεκείμην ('because I *was* in fact democratically inclined': not to be classed under II B.2): viii 91.3 ἃς (ναῦς) ἔφη Θηραμένης . . . ἦν δέ τι καὶ τοιοῦτον ἀπὸ τῶν τὴν κατηγορίαν ἐχόντων, καὶ οὐ πάνυ διαβολὴ μόνον τοῦ λόγου ('And there really *was* something in the accusation': καί stresses ἦν): Pl.*Cra*.421D Φάναι, ὃ ἂν μὴ γιγνώσκωμεν, βαρβαρικόν τι τοῦτ' εἶναι· εἴη μὲν οὖν ἴσως ἄν τι τῇ ἀληθείᾳ καὶ τοιοῦτον αὐτῶν, εἴη δὲ κἂν . . . ἀνεύρετα εἶναι ('may in fact *be* of that kind': καί really stresses εἴη): *Tht*.166D καὶ σοφίαν καὶ σοφὸν ἄνδρα πολλοῦ δέω τὸ μὴ φάναι εἶναι, ἀλλ' αὐτὸν καὶ λέγω σοφόν, ὃς ἂν . . . ('I *do* call wise that man, and that man only, who . . .': there is a double stress, on αὐτὸν τοῦτον and on λέγω: the sense is not, as in II.B.8, 'that is precisely the man whom': an instructive example): 172B φῆσαι, ἃ ἂν θῆται πόλις συμφέροντα οἰηθεῖσα αὑτῇ, παντὸς μᾶλλον ταῦτα καὶ συνοίσειν ('*will actually* benefit'): *R.*340C τοὺς ἄρχοντας ὡμολόγεις οὐκ ἀναμαρτήτους εἶναι ἀλλά τι καὶ ἐξαμαρτάνειν ('are not infallible, but *do* occasionally make mistakes'): *Ap.*34D Ἐμοί, ὦ ἄριστε, εἰσὶν μέν πού τινες καὶ οἰκεῖοι ('I *have* got relatives': καί with εἰσίν): *Phd.*62A οὐδὲν ἀκήκοα.—Ἀλλὰ προθυμεῖσθαι χρή, ἔφη· τάχα γὰρ ἂν καὶ ἀκούσαις ('perhaps you *may* hear'): 107C ὁ κίνδυνος νῦν δὴ καὶ δόξειεν ἂν δεινὸς εἶναι ('*would* appear formidable': under other circumstances it would not, Socrates goes on to say): *Grg.*493A 'Euripides may be right in saying that life is death and vice versa': ἤδη γάρ του ἔγωγε καὶ ἤκουσα τῶν σοφῶν ὡς νῦν ἡμεῖς τέθναμεν ('for I have in fact heard that ...'): *Prt.*329A τάχ' ἂν καὶ τοιούτους λόγους ἀκούσειεν: *Lg.* 805C εἰ μὲν ..., τάχα ἦν ἄν τι καὶ ἀντειπεῖν τῷ λόγῳ, νῦν δὲ ... ('it *might* have been possible to object'): Ant.v 91 ἐν δὲ τοῖς ἀνηκέστοις πλέον βλάβος τὸ μετανοεῖν ... ἤδη δέ τισιν ὑμῶν καὶ μετεμέλησεν ἀπολωλεκόσι ('*have*, in fact, so repented'): Lys.vi 20 ὁ δὲ θεὸς ὑπῆγεν αὐτόν, ἵνα ... δοίη δίκην. ἐλπίζω μὲν οὖν αὐτὸν καὶ δώσειν δίκην ('Well, I hope he *will* be punished'): 49 'Andocides has not done this and that for his country. σὺ δὲ τί καὶ ἀγαθὸν ποιήσας, ὦ Ἀνδοκίδη, ...;' ('what good *have* you done ...?'): D.xliii 52 (after mentioning those to whom the law does *not* grant inheritance) ἀλλὰ τίνι καὶ δίδωσιν; ('to whom *does* it grant it?')[1] (cf. also p. 314 (β)).*

III. Corresponsive καὶ ... καί.

(1) Normally the first καί is preparatory, the second connective: 'both ... and'. In Homer, according to Leaf (on *N*260), καὶ ... καί is found in correspondence only thrice: *N*260 (καὶ ἓν καὶ εἴκοσι, 'not only one but twenty'): 636 πάντων μὲν κόρος ἐστί, καὶ ὕπνου καὶ φιλότητος, μολπῆς τε γλυκερῆς καὶ ἀμύμονος

[1] Thus we have three varieties of καί following interrogatives. τίνα καὶ λέγεις; (1) 'Whom do you *mean*?' (moderate stress with low pitch, as in B.10.iii.*a*). (2) 'Whom do you *mean*?' (strong stress with high pitch, as in B.10.iii.*b*). (3) 'Whom *do* you mean (as you don't mean so-and-so)?'

ὀρχηθμοῖο (but the first *καί* may mean 'even'): *Ω*641 (the second *καί* is metrically anomalous (*ἠδ'* Brandreth), and the first is perhaps emphatic, not preparatory, 'I *have* tasted': see II.C.7). There is, to say the least, no need to assume corresponsion in *B*700, *Σ*419, *ψ*55. But in the *Hymns* *καὶ . . . καί* is beginning to establish itself: *h.Ap.*179–80 *καὶ . . . καὶ . . . καί* (a clear case, though lines 179–81 are probably a late addition): *h.Cer.*495 *αὐτὰρ ἐγὼ καὶ σεῖο καὶ ἄλλης μνήσομ' ἀοιδῆς* (a common formula in the *Hymns*). See further Ebeling, II.618*a*, *ad fin.*

In post-Homeric Greek this use is so common that a few examples will suffice.[1] S.*OT*413 *σὺ καὶ δέδορκας κοὐ βλέπεις ἵν' εἶ κακοῦ*: *OC*317 *καὶ φημὶ κἀπόφημι κοὐκ ἔχω τί φῶ*: 1444 ('whether . . . or . . .'): E.*Hec.*751 *τολμᾶν ἀνάγκη, κἂν τύχω κἂν μὴ τύχω*: Hdt.vi 98.1 *καὶ πρῶτα καὶ ὕστατα*: Pl.*Euthphr.*7D *καὶ ἐγὼ καὶ σὺ καὶ οἱ ἄλλοι ἄνθρωποι*: D.i 4 *κύριον καὶ ῥητῶν καὶ ἀπορρήτων*.*

(2) Far less frequently, both *καί*'s are adverbial, 'also' (cf. *οὐδέ*, II.1.iii). Particularly, *καί* both in subordinate and in main clause. This use is almost confined to prose, and is commonest in Plato and Xenophon. When the subordinate clause is placed first, as sometimes happens, it is often difficult to decide whether the first *καί* looks forward or back.

(i) Relative clauses. Hom.*Z*476 *δότε δὴ καὶ τόνδε γενέσθαι παῖδ' ἐμόν, ὡς καὶ ἐγώ περ . . .*: *σ*135 *ἀλλ' ὅτε δὴ καὶ . . . καὶ τὰ φέρει* (the second *καί* apodotic): Emp.*Fr.*16 *ἦ γὰρ καὶ πάρος ἔσκε, καὶ ἔσσεται*: S.*El.*1301 *ὧδ' ὅπως καὶ σοὶ φίλον καὶ τοὐμὸν ἔσται τῇδ'*: Pl.*Ly.*211A *ἅπερ καὶ ἐμοὶ λέγεις, εἰπὲ καὶ Μενεξένῳ*: *R.*544D *ὅτι καὶ ἀνθρώπων εἴδη τοσαῦτα ἀνάγκη τρόπων εἶναι ὅσαπερ καὶ πολιτειῶν*: X.*Cyr.*ii 2.6 *οὕτω δὴ καὶ ἐγώ, ὥσπερ καὶ οἱ ἄλλοι ἐποίουν*: D.xlii 31 *ὥσπερ καὶ κοινῇ . . . οὕτω καὶ ἰδίᾳ*: Hdt.vii 24: Pl.*R.*470B: *Ti.*65C: *Criti.*106B–C: *Thg.*128C: *Grg.* 458A: *Alc.I* 110D, 114C: X.*Oec.*9.17: 9.19: *Eq.*7.19: *Smp.*2.25: Lys.xxi 14: Is.xi 28.

(ii) Causal clauses. Ar.*Pl.*1084 *Ὅμως δ', ἐπειδὴ καὶ τὸν οἶνον ἠξίους πίνειν, συνεκποτέ' ἐστί σοι καὶ τὴν τρύγα*: Pl.*Smp.*199C *ἐπειδὴ καὶ τἆλλα . . . διῆλθες . . . καὶ τόδε εἰπέ*: *La.*195A *δοκεῖ . . . Λάχης ἐπιθυμεῖν κἀμὲ φανῆναι μηδὲν λέγοντα, ὅτι καὶ αὐτὸς ἄρτι τοιοῦτός τις ἐφάνη*: X.*Lac.*2.1 *ἐπεὶ καὶ περὶ γενέσεως ἐξήγημαι,*

[1] In prose inscriptions mostly in 'formelhaften Verbindungen' like *καὶ κατὰ γῆν καὶ κατὰ θάλατταν* (Meisterhans, p. 249).

βούλομαι καὶ τὴν παιδείαν ἑκατέρων σαφηνίσαι: Lys.xiv 24 ἐπειδὴ γὰρ καὶ τῶν ἀπολογουμένων ἀποδέχεσθε λεγόντων . . . εἰκὸς ὑμᾶς καὶ τῶν κατηγόρων ἀκροᾶσθαι: X.*Cyr.*vii 5.47.

(iii) Conditional clauses. Hdt.iii 2 εἰ γάρ τινες καὶ ἄλλοι, τὰ Περσέων νόμιμα ἐπιστέαται καὶ Αἰγύπτιοι: Pl.*Chrm.*166E Οὐκοῦν . . . καὶ ἀνεπιστημοσύνης ἐπιστήμη ἂν εἴη, εἴπερ καὶ ἐπιστήμης; *R.*444C: *Thg.*122B: X.*Smp.*2.6.

Corresponsion may also be recognized between adverbial καί's in independent clauses, such as the following. S.*OC* 1267–8 ἀλλ' ἔστι γὰρ καὶ Ζηνὶ σύνθακος θρόνων Αἰδὼς ἐπ' ἔργοις πᾶσι, καὶ πρὸς σοί, πάτερ, παρασταθήτω (' even Zeus '): E.*IT* 1401–2: Isoc.vii 72.3 ἐγὼ δὲ καὶ τῶν ἰδιωτῶν τοὺς . . . μέμφομαι . . . τὴν αὐτὴν οὖν γνώμην ἔχω καὶ περὶ τῶν κοινῶν. Cf. Pl.*Lg.*792D (V, *ad fin.*).

For μὲν καὶ . . . δὲ καί, see II.B.7.ii.

IV. I have left a few special difficulties to the last. In S.*El.* 1251 Jebb's explanation (on *Ph.*79) is perhaps satisfactory: ' your sorrows as well as your joys ': but read, perhaps, τοι. In E.*Andr.* 59 δὲ καί is difficult, and there is much to be said for Badham's δ' ἐκεῖ. In S.*Ph.*79 read, probably, παῖ: see Jebb. In Ant.v 16 ὡς καὶ τοῖς τότε δικασταῖς ἀπιστήσων makes no sense: a simple remedy is to transpose τότε and τοῖς (*C.R.*xlvii(1933)216). In Ar.*Av* 823 Καὶ λῷστον μὲν οὖν τὸ Φλέγρας πεδίον has been suspected: but it may well stand, καί stressing λῷστον: ' No, best of *all* ': cf. καὶ δὴ μὲν οὖν (μὲν οὖν, (3)).

In two passages καί appears to mark affirmation, ' Yes ' A.*Pers.*236 Ὧδέ τις πάρεστιν αὐτοῖς ἀνδροπλήθεια στρατοῦ;—Καὶ στρατὸς τοιοῦτος, ἔρξας πολλὰ δὴ Μήδους κακά: Pl.*Hp.Ma.* 302E διὰ τοῦτο ἐλέγετο καλὰς αὐτὰς εἶναι.—Καὶ ἐρρήθη οὕτως. In the first passage some MSS. give ναί written above καί: ὁ Wilamowitz: in the second, καί may be connective, ' And we did say so ': cf. Pl.*R.*548D Καὶ ὀρθῶς, ' And rightly '. The analogy of our ' Even so ' is tempting: but there is no ground for attributing to καί a specifically affirmative force in answers.

V. Position. When καί is copulative, it comes first in sentence or clause. A.*Pr.*51 is no exception: punctuate after τοῖσδε. When it is adverbial, it normally comes next before the emphatic word, except where that word is preceded by article or preposition. (But interposition of *καί* between preposition and substantive is not unknown. Pi.*O*.2.28 ἐν καὶ θαλάσσᾳ: 7.26: *P*.4.186.) For *καί* interposed between article and substantival infinitive see II.A.2. Between article and participle, Thgn.169 ὁ καὶ μωμεύμενος[1] (see E. Harrison, *Studies in Theognis*, p. 215). The position of *καί* at the end of a verse in S.*Ph*.312 is characteristic of Sophoclean synaphea: cf. Ar.*V*.1193.

There are, however, frequent exceptions, many of which are probably due to the writer's regarding two words as an indivisible unity, and placing *καί* before the first of the two, even when the less emphatic.

Verse. S.*Ant*.280 Παῦσαι, πρὶν ὀργῆς κἀμὲ μεστῶσαι λέγων (καὶ μεστῶσαι): 770 τὼ δ' οὖν κόρα τώδ' οὐκ ἀπαλλάξει μόρου.—Ἄμφω γὰρ αὐτὼ καὶ κατακτεῖναι νοεῖς (see Jebb); *OC*151 ἆρα καὶ ἦσθα φυτάλμιος . . .; (καὶ φυτάλμιος): E.*Hipp*.1326 Δείν' ἔπραξας, ἀλλ' ὅμως ἔτ' ἔστι καί σοι τῶνδε συγγνώμης τυχεῖν (καὶ τῶνδε): *Hel*.1069 Σὲ καὶ παρεῖναι δεῖ μάλιστα (καὶ μάλιστα, or καί δεῖ).

On the transposition of *καί* in drama, see Campbell's *Sophocles*, Introd. § 25: Wilamowitz on E.*Hipp*.391 and *HF*217: Starkie on Ar.*Nu*.1474: but these scholars sometimes suppose transposition where it is hardly necessary. E.*Hipp*.391 λέξω δὲ καί σοι τῆς ἐμῆς γνώμης ὁδόν (Wilamowitz and Harry take *καί* with ὁδόν: but probably Phaedra means that she will reveal to the chorus what she has hitherto kept to herself, and Murray's καὶ σοί is right): *HF*217 ὦ γαῖα Κάδμου, καὶ γὰρ ἐς σὲ ἀφίξομαι (Wilamowitz needlessly assumes transposition, for καὶ ἐς σὲ γάρ): Ar.*Nu*. 1474 οἴμοι δείλαιος ὅτε καὶ σὲ χυτρεοῦν ὄντα θεὸν ἡγησάμην (καὶ χυτρεοῦν together, Starkie: but why not καὶ σέ? Or ὅτε καί, *quippe cum*: cf.Hdt.iv195 ὅκου καί: Pl.*Tht*.158C ὅτε καί): E. *Hipp*.224 τί κυνηγεσιῶν καί σοι μελέτη; (καὶ κυνηγεσιῶν together, Wilamowitz and Starkie: but the sense surely is 'as well as Hippolytus', and Murray's καὶ σοί is again right.)

Prose. Hdt.i52 τὰ ἔτι καὶ ἀμφότερα ἐς ἐμὲ ἦν κείμενα (καί, though not inappropriate with ἀμφότερα, is almost indispensable with ἐς ἐμέ): ix 7 *init.*[2] ἅμα δὲ τὸ τεῖχος ... καὶ ἤδη ἐπάλξις ἐλάμβανε (ἤδη καὶ ἐ. ἐ.): Pl.*Grg*.461B οὕτω καὶ σὺ περὶ τῆς ῥητορικῆς δοξά-

[1] This, as Mr. Harrison points out, means 'he that even blames', and is not equivalent to καὶ ὁ μωμεύμενος. [2] *Ad init.*

ζεις ὥσπερ νῦν λέγεις; (καὶ δοξάζεις: 'Do you really think?'): 520B μόνοις δ' ἔγωγε καὶ ᾤμην τοῖς δημηγόροις . . . οὐκ ἐγχωρεῖν μέμφεσθαι τούτῳ τῷ πράγματι (καὶ μόνοις, 'actually the only people': the order is perhaps dictated by a desire to put the emphatic μόνοις at the beginning): *Phd.*66D ἐάν τις ἡμῖν καὶ σχολὴ γένηται ('if we *have* leisure': cf.*R.*425A ἐπανορθοῦσα εἴ τι καὶ πρότερον τῆς πόλεως ἔκειτο, 'if there *was* anything amiss in the city before): 96C ἐγὼ γὰρ ἃ καὶ πρότερον σαφῶς ἠπιστάμην . . . ἀπέμαθον (καὶ ἅ): *Cra.*392D (perhaps καὶ ἡγεῖτο: but more probably, 'Did not Homer, as well as ourselves, think. . . ?': cf. 392C): 398A τεκμήριον δέ μοί ἐστιν ὅτι καὶ ἡμᾶς φησιν σιδηροῦν εἶναι γένος (καί φησιν, 'he says also': but perhaps καὶ ἡμᾶς, '*us*'): *Euthd.*295D ἐπεὶ δὲ οὖν διενενοήμην καὶ παρὰ τοῦτον φοιτᾶν (καὶ φοιτᾶν, 'to *go* to him', with the implied contrast μήδ' ἀρχὴν φοιτᾶν: whereas ἐπεὶ δὲ οὖν καὶ διενενοήμην would mean 'but since I *had* decided'): *Chrm.*172D 'Let us grant that σωφροσύνη is of this nature. καὶ πάντα ταῦτα δόντες ἔτι βέλτιον σκεψώμεθα εἰ ἄρα τι καὶ ἡμᾶς ὀνήσει τοιοῦτον ὄν' (καὶ ὀνήσει, 'whether it will do us any *good*'): X.*An.*vi3.23 καὶ τὸ μὲν πρῶτον θαῦμα ἦν . . . ἔπειτα δὲ καὶ τῶν καταλελειμμένων ἐπυνθάνοντο (καὶ ἐπυνθάνοντο: καί *om. det.*): *Oec.*13.3 Ἦ . . . καὶ σὺ ἄρχειν ἱκανοὺς εἶναι παιδεύεις τοὺς ἐπιτρόπους; (for σὺ καὶ ἄρχειν, which Hertlein reads): *Eq.Mag.*8.7 μετέχει μὲν γάρ τι καὶ ἡ πόλις ταύτης τῆς δόξης (καὶ ταύτης).

That καί can *follow* the word it emphasizes seems doubtful. X.*An.*v1.4 Φίλος μοί ἐστιν, ὦ ἄνδρες, Ἀναξίβιος, ναυαρχῶν δὲ καὶ τυγχάνει (καί *om. det.*: Marchant suggests τυγχάνει δὲ καὶ ναυαρχῶν): in E.*Or.*1093 the text is doubtful: in Th.viii91.3, Pl.*Cra.*421D καί may go with τοιοῦτον 'actually of such a kind': in Pl.*Lg.*792D I suggest καὶ ἡμῶν τὸν μέλλοντα, or καὶ τὸν μέλλοντα ἡμῶν. But in *Lg.*891E it certainly seems that καί must go with λεκτέον.

In καὶ . . . καί, 'both . . . and', the particle stands each time at the opening of phrase or clause. Exceptions are very rare. E.*Alc.*329 ἐπεί σ' ἐγὼ καὶ ζῶσαν εἶχον καὶ θανοῦσ' ἐμὴ γυνὴ μόνη κεκλήσῃ (for καὶ ζῶσάν σ' ἐγὼ εἶχον καὶ . . .).

For other instances of irregular order, see II.B.6.ii (Pl.*Ap.*32A): 7.iv (Th.i91.3): 10.iii.*b*.γ (Pl.*Lg.*891B: X.*HG*ii3.47: D.iv46): 10.iii.*b*.δ(Pl.*R.*365D): 10.iii.*b*.ε (X.*Ages.*10.3): II.C.7 (Pl.*Cra.*436E: Arist. *Po.*1447b22).

Μάν, μήν, μέν

The etymology of μάν (μήν) is obscure.[1] Nor is its relation to μέν clear. Certainly the parallelism in the uses of μάν (μήν) and μέν is on the whole remarkably close. Thus we find οὐ μάν, οὐ μήν, οὐ μέν: ἦ μάν, ἦ μήν, ἦ μέν: καὶ μάν, καὶ μήν, καὶ μέν: γε μάν, γε μήν, γε μέν: and so forth: even μάντοι is found in Doric (Epidauros 3339, 37 Coll.). It is, at any rate, difficult to believe that in such combinations the Greeks (whether rightly or wrongly) did not regard the three words as merely differing dialectally.

Leaving Epic on one side for the moment, μάν, μήν, and μέν are, broadly speaking, confined respectively to Doric, Attic, and Ionic: with the exception that preparatory μέν is common to all three dialects. The few places where μήν appears in the MSS. of Herodotus (i 196,212: iii 2,74: vi 74.1: 129.4) must be altered. Wackernagel would also restore μέν everywhere in Hippocrates: in Anonymus *Κατὰ Αἰσχροκερδείας* 26 (Diehl, *Anth. Lyr. Gr.* i. 297) he regards καὶ μήν as an Atticism. γε μέν and γε μάν are, however, found side by side in the mixed dialect employed by Pindar.

In Epic the state of affairs is more complicated. Wackernagel holds that μήν in Homer is always due to Attic influence, being often a false form, for which μάν or μέν must be restored, though in some places he regards it as original, the passage being late and Attic: e.g. λ582,593 (καὶ μήν). μάν occurs 24 times (22 in the *Iliad* and 2 in the *Odyssey*). In 22 places it comes before a vowel. μέν, on the other hand, apart from preparatory μέν, usually precedes a consonant (though γε μέν always precedes a vowel). From this evidence Wackernagel concludes, with Monro *HG*², § 342, that 'an original μάν was changed into μέν whenever it came before a consonant,[2] and preserved when the metre made this corruption impossible'. He finds here a 'striking confirmation' of Fick's theory of an Aeolic *Iliad* translated into Ionic. Where

[1] See Wackernagel, *Glotta* vii (1916) pp. 177 ff.

[2] Of the two (*Iliad*) passages where μάν precedes a consonant, in E765 Wackernagel attributes the preference given to μάν to the fact that ἄγρει is Aeolic: in E895 he excises σ'.

μέν (= μάν) precedes a vowel, as in Ξ275, T261, Wackernagel regards the passage as representing the 'genuine Ionic element' in Epic. It is beyond my province to discuss Fick's theory [1] in general. But the facts as to μάν—μέν can also be explained on the supposition that Homer, or the Homeric poets, writing in a composite dialect which was predominantly Ionic but admitted an admixture of other forms, used μέν, as to them the more familiar and natural form, whenever metre demanded or allowed it, and only had recourse to μάν, which they borrowed from an earlier age [2] or from another region, when μέν would not scan.[3] It must be admitted, however, that the comparative rarity of affirmative μέν before vowels is not easy to explain on this hypothesis.

Μήν (μάν)[4]

Μήν fulfils three functions: (1) as an emphatic particle: (2) as an adversative connecting particle: (3) as a progressive connecting particle. Of these, we should expect (1) to be the earliest sense. (See Introd., II. 1.) And so, in fact, it turns out to be. See II, *ad init.* (2) and (3), widely as they differ from one another, follow when the need is felt for means of connexion. For the evolution of (2) from (1), we may compare the Latin particle *vero*: for that of (3) from (1), the history of δή (and perhaps οὖν).

Μήν (μάν) is pre-eminently a Doric particle. Its less restricted use in Plato's later writings may be due to Sicilian influence (see I.4.iii.*c*, *ad fin.*). In Attic it is generally associated with οὐ or with other particles. Thus, in drama, besides γε μήν, ἦ μήν, καὶ μήν (all frequent), we find οὐ μήν (frequent), οὐδὲ μήν, οὐδὲ . . . μήν, οὐ μὰν οὐδέ, οὐ μὴν . . . ἀλλά, ἀλλ' οὐ . . . μήν, ἀλλ'

[1] For which see C. M. Bowra, *Tradition and design in the Iliad*, pp. 138 ff.

[2] That μάν is an earlier form is suggested by its almost complete disappearance in the *Odyssey*. When the *Odyssey* was composed, μάν was perhaps almost entirely obsolete, but just admissible as an exceptional licence, like ἰδέ in the lyrics of tragedy.

[3] For parallels, see Bowra, *op. cit.*, pp. 136–7.

[4] For valuable information and statistics regarding μήν and its combinations, see W. Dittenberger, *Herm.* xvi (1881), 323–37, who points to the increasing frequency of the particle in the later works of Plato, Lysias, Isocrates, and Xenophon. I owe much to him as regards prose usage.

οὐδὲ μήν: τί μήν; (in the tragedians: Doric σά μάν; in Aristophanes): μάν following imperatives in tragic choruses and Aristophanic Doric: ἀλλὰ . . . μήν once in Sophocles: ἀλλὰ μήν twice in Aristophanes (and ἀλλὰ μάν twice). There only remain, I think, S.*Ant.*626 (I.1): E.*IT*889 (II.2). In early Attic prose μήν, excluding ἦ μήν, is not found in the pseudo-Xenophontine *Atheniensium Respublica* or in the genuine speeches of Andocides: in Antiphon and Thucydides (again excluding ἦ μήν) there are respectively five and nine examples (all καὶ μήν and οὐ μήν). With Lysias, the first orator to use ἀλλὰ μήν in positive sentences, μήν begins to grow commoner in Attic: but it continues, in the orators, to be restricted to the combinations οὐ μήν, οὐδὲ μήν, οὐ μὴν οὐδέ, οὐ μὴν ἀλλά, ἀλλὰ μήν, ἦ μήν, καὶ μήν.

I. Emphatic. It is difficult to grasp the exact difference in sense between μήν and the far commoner δή.[1] μήν almost invariably occurs near the opening of a sentence. Its uncompounded use is commoner in Doric and semi-Doric (Theocritus and Pindar) than in other dialects.[2]

(1) In statements. In Homer μήν (μάν), except when combined with other particles, perhaps emphasizes only negative, never positive, statements. (See, however, II, *ad init.*: for μήν (μάν) with imperatives see (2).) *E*895 ἀλλ' οὐ μάν σ' ἔτι δηρὸν ἀνέξομαι: *P*415 Ὦ φίλοι, οὐ μὰν ἧμιν ἐϋκλεὲς ἀπονέεσθαι: *N*414 οὐ μὰν αὖτ' ἄτιτος κεῖτ' Ἄσιος: *M*318: *Ξ*454: *O*16,508: *P*41: *Ψ*441: λ344: ρ470.

But this restriction does not hold in Pindar. *I.*3.15 ἴστε μὰν Κλεωνύμου δόξαν παλαιὰν ἅρμασιν: 4.35 ἴστε μὰν Αἴαντος ἀλκάν: *N.*11.33 συμβαλεῖν μὰν εὐμαρὲς ἦν (λίαν *codd.*: μάν Pauwius: see also III.1): *O.*9.49 'I will tell the tale of Pyrrha and Deucalion. (New songs deserve the greater praise.) λέγοντι μὰν χθόνα μὲν κατακλύσαι μέλαιναν ὕδατος σθένος' (at the beginning of a story: see also III.1.iii, *ad fin.*): *N.*10.29 Ζεῦ πάτερ, τῶν μὰν ἔραται φρενί, σιγᾷ οἱ στόμα· πᾶν δὲ τέλος ἐν τὶν ἔργων (where

[1] That μήν is subjective, δή objective, is a distinction unsupported by evidence, and rightly rejected by Kühner.

[2] Hartung, ii 386.

μάν perhaps approaches μέν in force: see IV): *O.*13.45 δηρίομαι πολέσιν περὶ πλήθει καλῶν· ὡς μὰν σαφὲς οὐκ ἂν εἰδείην λέγειν ποντιᾶν ψαφῶν ἀριθμόν (here the use of μάν after ὡς in a subordinate clause is quite exceptional): *O.*2.53.

In the dramatists and prose writers there is hardly a trace of uncompounded emphatic μήν, whether in positive or in negative statements: and the few instances which we do find are quite heterogeneous. S.*Ph.*811 Ἦ μενεῖς;—Σαφῶς φρόνει.—Οὐ μήν σ' ἔνορκόν γ' ἀξιῶ θέσθαι, τέκνον (Οὔτοι in the closely similar *OC*650)[1]: *Ant.*626 ὅδε μὴν Αἵμων (this instance of μήν, for the usual καὶ μήν, announcing the arrival of a new character on the stage, stands alone, so far as I know:[2] it occurs, as καὶ μήν not infrequently does (see *Addenda* to p. 356) at the opening of a short anapaestic system at the end of a chorus: we should perhaps regard the particle as adversative here, representing a break-off, like ἀτάρ or ἀλλά: 'But lo!'): Pl.*Grg.* 449C τοῦτο ἕν ἐστιν ὧν φημι, μηδένα ἂν ἐν βραχυτέροις ἐμοῦ τὰ αὐτὰ εἰπεῖν.—Τούτου μὴν δεῖ, ὦ Γοργία· καί μοι ἐπίδειξιν αὐτοῦ τούτου ποίησαι, τῆς βραχυλογίας (assentient or approving in force: cf. ἀλλὰ μήν (2), καὶ μήν (4): μέντοι (Olympiodorus) would be more normal here): *Sph.*248D Φασὶ μὴν τοῦτό γε (assentient): Hp.*Genit.*47 ὁκόσοι ἤδη . . . ἐφαρμακεύθησαν . . . οὗτοι οὐ μὴν ὑπερεκαθάρθησαν (the lateness of position is remarkable).[3] In Emp.*Fr.*76 ναὶ μήν can hardly stand: see καὶ μήν (1).

(2) With imperatives. This very rare use is confined to Epic, and the Doric (mainly choral) parts of drama. Hom.*A*302 εἰ δ' ἄγε μὴν πείρησαι: *E*765 ἄγρει μάν (*H*459): A.*Supp.*1018 ἴτε μὰν ἀστυάνακτας μάκαρας θεοὺς γανόοντες[4]: *Ch.*963 ἄναγε μὰν δόμοι (so Hermann: ἀναγεμὰν δόμοις *M*: ἄνα γε μὰν δόμοι Tucker): S.*OC*182 Ἕπεο μάν: Ar.*Lys.*183 Πάρφαινε μὰν τὸν ὅρκον (the

[1] Jebb's ellipse is far-fetched: 'I should prefer a promise on oath: however, I do not like to ask for it'. μέν Wilamowitz.

[2] Hartung (ii 387, 'etc.') and Klotz (ii 670, 'iis locis') imply the existence of parallels, but quote none.

[3] In Pl.*R.*520E, cited by Kühner, μήν is clearly adversative.

[4] Tucker, *ad loc.*, observes that 'in such use μήν is adversative'. I doubt this.

Spartan Lampito is talking in her native Doric): Sophr.*Fr.*26 ἴδε φίλα· θᾶσαι μάν.

(3) With optative, in the formula μὴ μὰν ἀσπουδί γε, three times in Homer. Θ512 μὴ μὰν ἀσπουδί γε νεῶν ἐπιβαῖεν ἕκηλοι: *O*476: *X*304. The wish is perhaps tinged with an asseverative force, and 'I swear they shan't' lurks beneath 'May they never'.[1]

(4) In questions. Of this usage there are several types, which, widely different as they are, may conveniently be grouped together.

(i) μήν simply emphasizing a question, or giving it liveliness. S.*OC* 1468 οὐράνια γὰρ ἀστραπὰ φλέγει πάλιν. τί μὰν ἀφήσει τέλος; E.*Rh.*955 ἐγὼ δὲ γῆς ἔφεδρον Ἑλλήνων στρατὸν λεύσσων τί μὴν ἔμελλον οὐ πέμψειν φίλοις κήρυκας ...; With ellipse of verb. S.*El.*1280 Ξυναινεῖς;—Τί μὴν οὔ; (μή *codd.*: μήν Seidler): E.*Rh.*706 Δοκεῖς γάρ;—Τί μὴν οὔ;

(ii) (*a*) ἀλλὰ τί (τίς, etc.) μήν, in elliptical and non-elliptical questions. ἀλλά follows the rejection, expressed or implied, of a supposition (see ἀλλά, II.1.i), while μήν adds liveliness to the ensuing question. Pl.*Smp.*202D θνητός;—Ἥκιστά γε.—Ἀλλὰ τί μήν; ('Well, what *is* he?'): *Ly.*208A Μὰ Δί' οὐ μέντοι ἂν ἐῷεν (με).—Ἀλλὰ τίνα μήν; 208E 'Have you wronged your parents?'—'No'.—Ἀλλ' ἀντὶ τίνος μὴν οὕτω σε δεινῶς διακωλύουσιν εὐδαίμονα εἶναι ...; *R.*348C,410C,422E.578B: X.*Smp.* 3.13: 4.23: *Cyr.*ii 2.11.

(*b*) Hence, from meaning 'Well, if not that, what?', elliptical ἀλλὰ τί μήν; comes to be virtually an emphatic affirmative answer, the elliptical form being almost equivalent to Πῶς γὰρ οὔ; 'Of course'. Pl.*Ly.*208B μισθωτῷ μᾶλλον ἐπιτρέπουσιν ἢ σοὶ ...;—Ἀλλὰ τί μήν; ἔφη: 208C Μῶν δοῦλος ὤν;—Ἀλλὰ τί μήν; *R.*362D Οὔ τί που οἴει ... ἱκανῶς εἰρῆσθαι ...;—Αλλὰ τί μήν; εἶπον.—Αὐτό, ἦ δ' ὅς, οὐκ εἴρηται ὃ μάλιστα ἔδει ῥηθῆναι (this is on the border-line between (*a*) and (*b*): ἀλλὰ τί μήν; here expects no answer, but gets one): *R.*438B,574A. Not elliptical. Pl.*Tht.*

[1] Leaf's explanations, on Θ512 and O476, are scarcely consistent, and the latter seems to me artificial.

162B Ἆρα κἂν . . . ἀξιοῖς ἂν . . . ;—Ἀλλὰ τί μὴν δοκεῖς, εἴπερ μέλλοιέν μοι ἐπιτρέψειν . . . ; ('Why, what do you imagine?').

(iii) The usage of τί μήν; ποῦ μήν; etc., is precisely parallel to that of ἀλλὰ τί μήν; It is not easy to determine the function of μήν here. Perhaps we may say that the idea of 'otherness', conveyed in ἀλλὰ τί μήν; by ἀλλά, is here understood from the context (though it is sometimes expressed: see X.*Cyr*.ii.1.9, (*a*) below), μήν being, here again, emphatic, and τί being equivalent to τί ἄλλο: cf. γάρ, VII. It is alternatively possible to regard μήν as an adversative connective, corresponding to the ἀλλά, not to the μήν, in ἀλλὰ τί μήν; 'But what?' To attribute different forces to μήν in two such closely similar idioms certainly seems an artificial procedure: but it gains some plausibility from the passages quoted under (*c*) below.

(*a*) Following the rejection of a supposition: either elliptical or not. Pl.*Tht*.142A Οὐ γὰρ ἦ κατὰ πόλιν.—Ποῦ μήν; ('Well, where *were* you?'): *R*.523B Οὐ πάνυ, ἦν δ' ἐγώ, ἔτυχες οὗ λέγω.—Ποῖα μήν, ἔφη, λέγεις; *Phlb*.44B οἳ τὸ παράπαν ἡδονὰς οὔ φασιν εἶναι.—Τί μήν;—Λυπῶν ταύτας εἶναι πάσας ἀποφυγάς ('Well, what *do* they say?': cf. *Plt*.263B: the rare occurrence in Plato of elliptical τί μήν; in this sense is in marked contrast with the commonness of the sense illustrated in (*b*) below: 'rarus hic est usus formulae', Stallbaum on *Phlb*.44B): X.*Cyr*.ii 1.9 πλήθει γε οὐχ ὑπερβαλοίμεθ' ἂν τοὺς πολεμίους.—Τί μὴν ἄλλο ἐνορᾷς ἄμεινον τούτου; viii 4.10 Various grounds of offence have been suggested and rejected. Τίνος μὴν ἕνεκα, ἔφη, . . . Χρυσάνταν ἔγραψας ὥστε εἰς τὴν τιμιωτέραν ἐμοῦ χώραν ἱδρυθῆναι; *HG*vi 3.13 'We have not come for the alleged reason. εἶεν· τί μὴν ἥκομεν;' vii 3.7 ὑπερορᾶν μὲν . . . οὐ δυνατὸν ὑμῶν . . . τίνι μὴν πιστεύων ἐνθάδε ἀπέκτεινα τὸν ἄνδρα;

(*b*) Elliptical τί μήν; practically equivalent to an emphatic affirmative, 'of course'. B.1.180 (perhaps: but see Jebb): A.*Supp*.999 θῆρες δὲ κηραίνουσι καὶ βροτοί, τί μήν; *Ag*.672 (τί μή *codd.*): *Eu*.203 Ἔχρησα ποινὰς τοῦ πατρὸς πρᾶξαι. τί μήν; S.*Aj*.668 ἄρχοντές εἰσιν, ὥσθ' ὑπεικτέον. τί μήν; E.*Rh*.705: Ar.*Ach*.757,784 (both Σὰ μάν;). Common in Plato: *Phdr*.229A, 267A: *Tht*.145E: *R*.410A,438D,441C,453C,455E,485D,501A, 505D: *id. saep.*

(*c*) In Xenophon sometimes introducing an objection in

interrogative form. *Cyr.*i 6.28 'One has to practice deceit in war'.—*Πῶς μήν, ἔφη, παῖδας ὄντας ἡμᾶς . . . τἀναντία τούτων ἐδιδάσκετε*; ('But why . . . ?'): *ib.* *ὅπως δέ γε τοὺς πολεμίους δύναισθε κακῶς ποιεῖν οὐκ οἶσθα μανθάνοντας ὑμᾶς πολλὰς κακουργίας*;—*Οὐ δῆτα* . . .—*Τίνος μὴν ἕνεκα, ἔφη, ἐμανθάνετε τοξεύειν*; (this might be classed under (*a*)): *Hier.*1.31 *τυράννῳ οὐ φῄς παιδικῶν ἔρωτας ἐμφύεσθαι*; *πῶς μὴν σύ, ἔφη, ἐρᾷς Δαϊλόχου* . . . ; ('Well, how is it that . . . ?').

Dittenberger believes *τί μήν*; to be a conversational idiom of the Sicilian Dorians, picked up by Plato on his first Sicilian journey, and hence not found in his earliest dialogues: he quotes Epich.*Fr.*149, Sophr.*Fr.*55 Kaibel (where punctuation and interpretation are uncertain).

(iv) In the two following passages, *οὐ μήν*, following a rejected suggestion, introduces, tentatively and half incredulously, an alternative suggestion. I regard *μήν* as emphatic here, in view of the closely parallel use of *οὐ δή* in questions: see *δή*, I.10.ii. (This seems far better than taking *μήν* as adversative, and comparing the use of *ἀλλά* in such cases.) E.*Alc.*518 'My children and father are alive'.—*Οὐ μὴν γυνή γ' ὄλωλεν Ἄλκηστις σέθεν*; ('Why, surely your *wife* is not dead?'): *Rh.*175 *οὔ σ' ἀπαιτῶ Μενέλεω σχέσθαι χέρα.*—*Οὐ μὴν τὸν Ἰλέως παῖδά μ' ἐξαιτῇ λαβεῖν*;

II. Adversative. An adversative sense of *μήν* (*μάν*) is hardly to be found in Homer. True, there are certain passages in which an adversative sense is appropriate. Θ373 *νῦν δ' ἐμὲ* (*Ἀθήνην*) *μὲν στυγέει, Θέτιδος δ' ἐξήνυσε βουλὰς* . . . *ἔσται μὰν ὅτ' ἂν αὖτε φίλον γλαυκώπιδα εἴπῃ* (where *μάν* probably means simply 'I warrant'): Π14: Ω52. In such passages *μήν* is, I think, still a particle of emphasis: though quite possibly the adversative force is to be seen here in embryo, especially in view of the fact that Homer does not elsewhere use *μήν* in positive statements (see I.1).

(1) As an adversative, *μήν* normally balances, denoting that a fact coexists with another fact opposed to it: 'yet', 'however'.

In positive statements: hardly ever in drama (*v. ad init.*), never in the orators, who use *μέντοι* instead. Pi.*P.*3.88 *αἰὼν δ'* ἀσφαλὴς οὐκ ἔγεντ' οὔτ' Αἰακίδᾳ παρὰ Πηλεῖ οὔτε παρ' ἀντιθέῳ Κάδμῳ· λέγονται μὰν βροτῶν ὄλβον ὑπέρτατον οἳ σχεῖν: Semon. *Fr.*29.3: Pi.*O.*7.45: *P.*2.82 (ὅμως μάν): *N.*1.69: 9.39: Pl.*R.* 528A ἀλλὰ σαυτοῦ ἕνεκα τὸ μέγιστον ποιῇ τοὺς λόγους, φθονοῖς μὴν οὐδ' ἂν ἄλλῳ: *Epin.*981D τὸ γὰρ πλεῖστον πυρὸς ἔχει, ἔχει μὴν γῆς τε καὶ ἀέρος: *Ep.*337D ἀδελφὰ . . . δεύτερα μήν: X. *Ages.*6.3 κρατήσας τρόπαιον ἐστήσατο . . . τρόπαια μὴν Ἀγησιλάου οὐχ ὅσα ἐστήσατο ἀλλ' ὅσα ἐστρατεύσατο δίκαιον νομίζειν ('though indeed'): Pl.*R.*520E: *Phdr.*244B: *Ep.*347C.

οὐ μήν. (γε almost always follows: hence οὐ μὴν . . . γε is the negative counterpart of γε μήν, as οὔκουν . . . γε of γοῦν.) A.*Ag.* 1279 ἀπήγαγ' ἐς τοιάσδε θανασίμους τύχας . . . οὐ μὴν ἄτιμοί γ' ἐκ θεῶν τεθνήξομεν: S.*OT* 810 διπλοῖς κέντροισί μου καθίκετο. οὐ μὴν ἴσον γ' ἔτεισεν: E.*Hipp.*285 Ἐς πάντ' ἀφῖγμαι κοὐδὲν εἴργασμαι πλέον· οὐ μὴν ἀνήσω γ' οὐδὲ νῦν προθυμίας: A.*Pr.*270: E.*Heracl.* 885: *Hipp* 914: *IT* 1004: *Rh.*958: Ar.*Nu.*53: *V.*268: Pl.*Tht.*164A ὑποπτεύω, οὐ μὴν ἱκανῶς γε συννοῶ: *Ly.*207C: *R.*530C: X.*An.*i 10.3: vii 6.38: *HG*iv 6.12: Isoc.iv 97: D.xiv 3: xix 22: xxi 179: xxxix 27: liv 6. Pl.*Grg.*526A οὐδὲν μήν κωλύει . . . .

In prose, often answering a preceding μέν.

Positive. (Plato only.) Pl.*Grg.*493C ταῦτ' ἐπιεικῶς μέν ἐστιν ὑπό τι ἄτοπα, δηλοῖ μὴν . . .: *R.*529E κάλλιστα μὲν ἔχειν ἀπεργασίᾳ, γελοῖον μὴν ἐπισκοπεῖν αὐτὰ σπουδῇ: *Ti.*43B ὥστε τὸ μὲν ὅλον κινεῖσθαι ζῷον, ἀτάκτως μὴν . . . προϊέναι: *Lg.*644D Μόγις μέν πως ἐφέπομαι, λέγε μὴν τὸ μετὰ ταῦτα ὡς ἑπομένου: 862A ἀδικεῖν μέν, ἄκοντα μήν: *Sph.*216B δοκεῖ θεὸς μὲν ἀνὴρ οὐδαμῶς εἶναι, θεῖος μήν: *Tht.*142B: *Ti.*24D,87B (adversative force slight): *Phlb.*51B: *Epin.*973B: *Ep.*326E.

Negative, μὲν . . . οὐ μήν. Isoc.iv 68: v 61: xii 183: D.i 16: xix 302: xxi 102.

(2) Less frequently, μήν is a strong adversative, often denoting, not merely contrast with what precedes, but the complete, or almost complete, negation of it: thus approximating in sense to ἀλλά or ἀτάρ, or even μὲν οὖν.

Sapph.*Fr.*116 λελάθοντο δὲ μαλοδρόπηες, οὐ μὰν ἐκλελάθοντ', ἀλλ' οὐκ ἐδύναντ' ἐπίκεσθαι (for μὲν οὖν, 'Nay, forgot it not'): A.*Ag.*1068 Ἦ μαίνεταί γε . . . οὐ μὴν πλέω ῥίψασ' ἀτιμασθήσομαι (for ἀλλά or ἀτάρ, breaking off impatiently): S.*Ach.Conv.*

16 (Οὐ μήν, objecting): E.*Cret.*(*Suppl.Eur.*p.23,l.16) ἐς τί γὰρ βοὸς βλέψασ' ἐδήχθην θυμὸν αἰσχίστῃ νόσῳ; ὡς εὐπρεπὴς μὲν ἐν πέπλοισιν ἦν ἰδεῖν . . .; οὐ μὴν δέμας γ' εὔρυθμόν ἐστι νυμφίου (for ἀλλά or μὲν οὖν: 'Nay'): *Hel.*571 Ὦ φωσφόρ' Ἑκάτη . . . – Οὐ νυκτίφαντον πρόπολον Ἐνοδίας μ' ὁρᾷς.—Οὐ μὴν γυναικῶν γ' εἷς δυοῖν ἔφυν πόσις (protesting: but perhaps this is better explained as progressive (III.2.i): 'Nor again am I a bigamist'): *Ph.*1622 οὐ μὴν ἑλίξας γ' ἀμφὶ σὸν χεῖρας γόνυ κακὸς φανοῦμαι (breaking away from her suppliant posture): *IT* 889 'Escape by land is difficult and dangerous. διὰ κυανέας μὴν στενοπόρου πέτρας μακρὰ κέλευθα ναΐοισιν δρασμοῖς' (objecting, like καίτοι: 'Yet'): X.*Mem.*i 2.26 'Is Socrates to get all the blame for the incontinence shown by Critias and Alcibiades after they had left him, and none of the credit for their continence while with him? οὐ μὴν τά γε ἄλλα οὕτω κρίνεται' (protesting).

III. Progressive. Here μήν, like other progressive particles and combinations of particles, either adds a fresh point ('again', 'further'), or marks a fresh stage in the march of thought ('well', 'now').

(1) In positive statements this use is almost confined to Plato's writings, in which it is often found, both at the opening of a speech and in continuous discourse. Hp.*Art.*7 πάνυ μὴν ἱκανῶς ἔχει καὶ . . . ('Again, a quite adequate method is . . .'): Pl.*R.*413C κλαπέντας μὲν γὰρ . . . λέγω . . . Τοὺς τοίνυν βιασθέντας λέγω . . . Τοὺς μὴν γοητευθέντας . . .: 465B εἰρήνην πρὸς ἀλλήλους οἱ ἄνδρες ἄξουσι;—Πολλήν γε.—Τούτων μὴν ἐν ἑαυτοῖς μὴ στασιαζόντων οὐδὲν δεινὸν μή ποτε ἡ ἄλλη πόλις . . . διχοστατήσῃ ('Well, if *they* don't disagree, the rest of the city won't'): 504B Ἀλλ' ἔμοιγε, ἔφη, μετρίως· ἐφαίνετο μὴν καὶ τοῖς ἄλλοις ('Moreover the others thought so as well'): *Euthd.* 283C 'Do you seriously wish the lad to be made wise'?—'Certainly'.—Σκόπει μὴν . . . ὅπως μὴ ἔξαρνος ἔσῃ ἃ νῦν λέγεις ('Well, see that you don't contradict that'): *Lg.*828A (opening of book) τούτων μὴν ἐχόμενά ἐστιν . . .: 920A δεύτερος μὴν νόμος . . .: *Phlb.*27B Τὸ δὲ δὴ πάντα ταῦτα δημιουργοῦν λέγομεν τέταρτον . . .; . . . Ὀρθῶς μὴν ἔχει, διωρισμένων τῶν τεττάρων . . . ἐφεξῆς αὐτὰ καταριθμήσασθαι: 38B Δόξα, φαμέν, ἡμῖν ἔστι μὲν ψευδής, ἔστι δὲ καὶ ἀληθής;—Ἔστιν.—Ἕπεται μὴν ταύταις . . .

ἡδονὴ καὶ λύπη πολλάκις ('Again'): 66B πρῶτον μὲν . . . Δεύτερον μὴν . . . : *R*.430C,465A,485E,524C: *Phlb*.40A(*bis*),48C,D,50B, 61B: *Sph*.224C,225D: *Lg*.863C(*bis*): *id. saep.* Perhaps a progressive sense is already to be found in Pi.*N*.11.33 (see I.1), where a new subject is introduced: *atqui*, Christ: the force of μάν here is difficult to determine.

Certain varieties of progressive μήν may be noted:

(i) Marking the fulfilment of a condition just stipulated (so, far more commonly, ἀλλά (II.7) and ἀλλὰ μήν (3)). Pl.*Ti*.20D *Ταῦτα χρὴ δρᾶν εἰ καὶ . . . Τιμαίῳ συνδοκεῖ.—Δοκεῖ μήν.*

(ii) Marking the transition from major to minor premise (so, far more commonly, ἀλλὰ μήν (6), καὶ μήν (2)). Pl.*R*.452A *Εἰ ἄρα ταῖς γυναιξὶν ἐπὶ ταὐτὰ χρησόμεθα καὶ τοῖς ἀνδράσι, ταὐτὰ καὶ διδακτέον αὐτάς.—Ναί.—Μουσικὴ μὴν ἐκείνοις γε καὶ γυμναστικὴ ἐδόθη.—Ναί.—Καὶ ταῖς γυναιξὶν ἄρα τούτω τὼ τέχνα* . . . ἀποδοτέον: *Euthd*.284A: *Prm*.146C,161D: *Phlb*.30C: *Lg*.640A.

(iii) Marking a transition from the statement of a problem to the discussion of it. μήν may then be termed 'inceptive', and rendered 'well'. The speaker rolls up his sleeves before addressing himself to the task. καὶ μήν (*q.v.* (5)) is commoner in this sense: see also ἀλλὰ μήν, 2.i, *ad fin*.

Pl.*Tht*.193D ὃ ἐν τοῖς πρόσθεν οὕτως ἔλεγον καί μου τότε οὐκ ἐμάνθανες.—Οὐ γὰρ οὖν.—Τοῦτο μὴν ἔλεγον, ὅτι . . . ('Well, this is what I meant'): *R*.521D 'What study will draw our citizens' souls to reality, and at the same time be suited to the training of warriors?'—'Yes, that is what we need'.—*Γυμναστικῇ μὴν καὶ μουσικῇ ἔν γε τῷ πρόσθεν ἐπαιδεύοντο ἡμῖν* (μήν marks the opening of the review of possible μαθήματα): *Sph*. 225D *Τὴν ἐπωνυμίαν τοίνυν . . . πειραθῶμεν εἰπεῖν.—Οὐκοῦν χρή.—Δοκῶ μὴν* . . . (μέν Heindorf): *Phlb*.17A τὰ δὲ ἔτι σαφέστερον δέομαι ἃ λέγεις ἀκοῦσαι.—Σαφὲς μὴν . . . ἐστιν ἐν τοῖς γράμμασιν ὃ λέγω: *Lg*.696A ἃ . . . τῷ νομοθέτῃ σκεπτέον, καὶ ἡμῖν δὲ ἐν τῷ νῦν παρόντι. δίκαιον μήν, ὦ Λακεδαιμόνιοι, τοῦτό γε τῇ πόλει ὑμῶν ἀποδιδόναι, ὅτι . . . : 810E διακελεύῃ με . . . τὴν νῦν . . . ὁδὸν τῆς νομοθεσίας πορεύεσθαι μηδὲν ἀνιέντα.—Τί μήν;—Οὐ τοίνυν ἀνίημι. λέγω μὴν ὅτι . . . . (In Ar.*Th*.804 μήν has been suggested for the unmetrical μέν: σκεψώμεθα δὴ κἀντιτιθῶμεν πρὸς ἕκαστον, παραβάλλουσαι τῆς τε γυναικὸς καὶ τἀνδρὸς τοὔνομ' ἑκάστου. Ναυσιμάχης μὲν ἥττων ἐστὶν Χαρμῖνος. μήν, if right here, should be taken as inceptive. But, in the absence of Aristophanic parallels, Dobree's μέν ⟨γ'⟩ is far more probable.) The germ of this use may perhaps be descried in Pi.*O*.9.49, where μάν marks the opening of a promised story, after a parenthetical apophthegm: see I.1.

(2) In negative statements the progressive use is far more extended. The three types are οὐ μήν, οὐ μὴν οὐδέ, and οὐδὲ μήν. In the last it is not easy to determine whether μήν or οὐδέ marks the connexion, 'Again, not . . . either' or 'Nor indeed': (In Homer (*Δ*512, see (ii) below) we can hardly, perhaps, regard μάν as connective.) Usually, though not invariably, a negative clause precedes.

(i) οὐ μήν, in the sense 'nor again', is rare. A.*Th.*538 ὁ δ' ὠμόν, οὔτι παρθένων ἐπώνυμον, φρόνημα, γοργὸν δ' ὄμμ' ἔχων, προσίσταται. οὐ μὴν ἀκόμπαστός γ' ἐφίσταται πύλαις ('Nor again is he without his blazon'):* E.*Alc.*658 ὥστ' οὐκ ἄτεκνος κατθανὼν ἄλλοις δόμον λείψειν ἔμελλες ὀρφανὸν διαρπάσαι. οὐ μὴν ἐρεῖς γέ μ' ὡς . . . (meeting an alternative plea: 'Nor again'): Ar.*Pax*41 Ἀφροδίτης μὲν γὰρ οὔ μοι φαίνεται (εἶναι ἡ προσβολή), οὐ μὴν Χαρίτων γε: Moschio Trag.*Fr.*6.9 οὐδέπω γὰρ ἦν οὔτε στεγήρης οἶκος οὔτε . . . πόλις. οὐ μὴν ἀρότροις ἀγκύλοις ἐτέμνετο . . . βῶλος: X.*Smp.*8.21 τί μᾶλλον στέρξει τὸν πριάμενον . . .; οὐ μὴν ὅτι γε . . . ὁμιλεῖ, φιλήσει αὐτόν: *Ages.*5.2 ποίας (ἡδονῆς) οἶδέ τις Ἀγησίλαον ἡττηθέντα; ὃς μέθης μὲν ἀποσχέσθαι ὁμοίως ᾤετο χρῆναι . . . διμοιρίαν γε μὴν λαμβάνων ἐν ταῖς θοίναις οὐχ ὅπως ἀμφοτέραις ἐχρῆτο . . . οὐ μὴν ὕπνῳ γε δεσπότῃ . . . ἐχρῆτο.

(ii) οὐ μὴν οὐδέ. Hom.*Δ*512 ἐπεὶ οὔ σφι λίθος χρὼς οὐδὲ σίδηρος . . . οὐ μὰν οὐδ' Ἀχιλεὺς . . . μάρναται: E.*Alc.*89 κλύει τις ἢ στεναγμὸν ἢ χειρῶν κτύπον . . .; οὐ μὰν οὐδέ τις ἀμφιπόλων στατίζεται ἀμφὶ πύλας: *Rh.*778 οἱ δ' οὐδέν· οὐ μὴν οὐδ' ἐγὼ τὰ πλείονα: Gorg.*Fr.*11a.21 'I could not have endured to live among barbarians: οὐ μὴν οὐδὲ παρὰ τοῖς βαρβάροις πιστῶς ἂν διεκείμην': Th.i 3.3 οὐδαμοῦ τοὺς ξύμπαντας (Ἕλληνας) ὠνόμασεν . . . οὐ μὴν οὐδὲ βαρβάρους εἴρηκε: 82.1 (an adversative sense of μήν would be appropriate here, but, in view of the general usage of οὐ μὴν οὐδέ, should hardly be held to be actually present in the particle:[1] simply, perhaps, 'Nor again'): Pl. *Lg*.906E ἀλλ' οὔτι μὴν ἡνιόχοισί γε (τοὺς θεοὺς ἀπεικάζοιμεν ἄν) . . .—'No'.—Οὐ μὴν οὐδὲ στρατηγοῖς γε: X.*Mem*.i 2.5 ἀλλὰ μὴν . . . ἀλλ' οὐ μὴν . . . οὐ μὴν οὐδέ: Ant.iiα4 οὐ μὴν οὐδὲ . . . οὐδὲ μὴν . . . οὐδὲ μήν: Lys.viii 7 οὔτε γὰρ . . . οὐ μὴν οὐδέ: D. xiv 32.

In the following without preceding negative: Isoc.xii 265 περιστάντες αὐτὸν ἐπῄνουν . . . οὐ μὴν οὐδ' ἐγὼ παρεστὼς ἐσιώπων: Th.vi 55.3: Pl.*R*.486C: *Lg*.634C,902D: X.*Lac*.6.4: Isoc.iv 75,139: D.iii 14.

Th.ii 97.6 is, on the face of it, quite different from the other examples, and it is difficult to interpret οὐδέ here in the sense 'not either'. Steup says that a negative statement, οὐχ ὁμογνωμονοῦσι, is implied in the conditional participle ὁμογνωμονοῦσι, which is just possible, as an example of τὸ τάχος τῆς σημασίας: Poppo explains 'nec vero (Scythae) in sollertia quoque . . . similes', i.e. here they are inferior, while in the former respect they are superior: which is, to say the least, highly artificial. Perhaps οὐδέ here simply strengthens οὐ ('but they are certainly not equal': cf. οὐ μὲν οὐδέ, *s.v.* μέν, I.**A**.9.iii), and the use of οὐδέ is an Ionic touch, taken perhaps from an Ionic original on which Thucydides is drawing here.

(iii) οὐδὲ μήν. Pi.*P*.4.87 οὔ τί που οὗτος Ἀπόλλων οὐδὲ μὰν χαλκάρματός ἐστι πόσις Ἀφροδίτας: 8.17 Τύφως . . . οὔ νιν ἄλυξεν, οὐδὲ μὰν βασιλεὺς Γιγάντων: A.*Eu*.471 Τὸ πρᾶγμα μεῖζον, εἴ τις οἴεται τόδε βροτὸς δικάζειν· οὐδὲ μὴν ἐμοὶ θέμις φόνου διαιρεῖν ὀξυμηνίτους δίκας: Ar.*Ec*.1075 οὐκ ἀφήσω σ' οὐδέποτ'.—Οὐδὲ μὴν ἐγώ: Ar.*Ra*.263,264: (S.*OT* 870, *lect. dub.*): Critias,*Fr*.44 οὔθ' ὅτι . . . οὔθ' ὅτι . . . οὔθ' ὅτι . . . οὐδὲ μὴν ὅτι: Pl.*Euthd*.289C πολλοῦ δεῖ ἡμᾶς λυροποιοὺς δεῖν εἶναι . . . Οὐδὲ μὴν αὐλοποιικῆς γε δῆλον ὅτι δεόμεθα: *R*.469E Ἐατέον ἄρα τὰς νεκροσυλίας . . . Οὐδὲ μήν που πρὸς τὰ ἱερὰ τὰ ὅπλα οἴσομεν: X.*Cyr*.iii 3.50 οὐκ ἂν οὖν τοξότας γε . . . οὐδὲ μὴν ἀκοντιστάς, οὐδὲ μὴν ἱππεάς, ἀλλ' οὐδὲ μὴν . . .: Pl.*Ly*.216E: *Chrm*.167E: *La*.194E: *Smp*.177E: *Phd*.93A: *Tht*.160A: *R*.395A,404C: X.

[1] An adversative sense is, however, clearly present in Pl.*Lg*.822C, as the μέν shows: γελοῖον μὲν οὐδαμῶς, οὐ μὴν οὐδὲ θεοφιλές γε (cf. X.*Ages*.2.12 καὶ κραυγὴ μὲν οὐδεμία παρῆν, οὐ μὴν οὐδὲ σιγή, φωνὴ δέ τις ἦν τοιαύτη . . .: Arist. *Pol*.1280b32). Cf. also D.xviii 124.

*Mem.*i2.63: *Oec.*12.14: *Smp.*7.3: *An.*ii4.20: vii6.22: *Cyr.*iv 5.27: *Lac.*7.4: *Vect.*4.3: Ant.iiα4,γ5. Answering μέν, Pl.*Prm.*165E.

οὐδὲ μὴν οὐδὲ: Epich.*Fr.*170b3 οὐκ ἐμίν γά κα (δοκεῖ).—Οὐδὲ μὰν οὐδ' . . .: Ar. *V.*480.

οὐδὲ . . . μήν: A.*Th.*668 ἀλλ' οὔτε νιν φυγόντα μητρόθεν σκότον, οὔτ' . . . οὔτ' . . . οὔτ . . . Δίκη προσεῖδε καὶ κατηξιώσατο· οὐδ' ἐν πατρῴας μὴν χθονὸς κακουχίᾳ οἶμαί νιν αὐτῷ νῦν παραστατεῖν πέλας: 808 Αγ. Οἰδίπου τόκω— —Χο. Οἳ 'γὼ τάλαινα, μάντις εἰμὶ τῶν κακῶν.—Αγ. Οὐδ' ἀμφιλέκτως μὴν κατεσποδημένω (no preceding negative): X.*Eq.Mag.*3.3 οὐδὲ δόρατα μὴν παραλείψω (no preceding negative).

IV. Supposed concessive use. Hartung (ii 385) finds traces of a concessive use of μήν in certain passages (*inter alia* in Ar.*Th.*804, Pl.*R.*521D, with both of which I have dealt above (III.1.iii)). He might with more plausibility have cited E.*Heracl.*556 (but μήν is here adversative, and the succession of clauses indicates Iolaus' bewildered uncertainty): Hp.*Acut.*15 μέγα μὴν διαφέρει (where μήν (one MS. reads μέν) might be taken as concessive, answered by δ' ὅμως: but it is probably affirmative, as in *Fract.* 27 (μέν in one MS.)). In fact a concessive sense, while in some passages (e.g. Hom.ρ470: Pi.*N.*10.29) not inappropriate, is nowhere required: and it seems clear that this sense was from the first, in all dialects, reserved for μέν.

V. Position of connective μήν. Like other connectives which normally occupy the second place, μήν after article and after preposition is sometimes postponed. Pl.*Phlb.*48D τοὐναντίον μήν: *Plt.*275B Διὰ ταῦτα μήν (but *Lg.*729D εἰς μὴν πόλιν): as late, perhaps, as seventh word in *Lg.*903C πρὸς τὸ κοινῇ συντεῖνον βέλτιστον μέρος μὴν . . . (see England): *R.*478C Μὴ ὄντι μήν.

The apparent postposition after an oath in D.liv6 must be altered: μὰ τοὺς θεοὺς οὐ μὴν ἔγωγ' ᾠόμην δεῖν (Rennie keeps this, citing Ar.*V.*231, X.*Smp.*4.33: but in neither of these passages is μέντοι connective).

VI. Μήν in combination with other particles. The principal combinations are ἀλλὰ μήν, γε μήν, ἦ μήν, καὶ μήν. Other combinations are very rare, δή, not μήν, being normally used to strengthen other particles. For οὐ μὴν ἀλλά see pp. 28 ff.

(1) δὲ μήν (to say the least, highly suspicious). Pl.*Lg*.782C Τὸ δὲ μὴν θύειν ἀνθρώπους ἀλλήλους ἔτι καὶ νῦν παραμένον ὁρῶμεν πολλοῖς (perhaps γε μήν): X.*An*.ii 4.6 ἡττωμένων δὲ μὴν οὐδένα οἷόν τε σωθῆναι (δὲ μήν *det.*: δέ *cett.*).

(2) δὴ μάν. Hom.*P*538 Ἦ δὴ μάν: Alc.*Fr*.89 (conjectured).

(3) ἦ μήν. Hp.*Epid*.ii 6.31 ἀναπαυέσθω εὐκόπως, ἦ μὴν ... ἐσθιέτω (ἡμῖν for ἦ μήν some MSS.).

(4) οὐδὲ ('not even') μήν. Hp.*Jusj*. οὐ τεμέω δὲ οὐδὲ μὴν λιθιῶντας. (But the whole sentence is much disputed.)

(5) τε μήν. Hp.*Mul*.2 τά τε μὴν τρίτα πονήματα πάντα μᾶλλον πονήσει, καὶ μάλιστα ἐν τῷ χρόνῳ τῶν καταμηνίων (reading doubtful). οὔτε μήν. Anacr.*Fr*.12 (*coni.* Cobet): X. *Cyr*.iv 3.12 οὔτε ... οὔτε μήν: v 4.11 οὔτε ... οὔτε μὴν ... οὔτε: *Smp*.1.15: *Eq*.9.11 μήτε ... μήτε μήν.

Ἀλλὰ μήν

This combination is rare in verse, but common in prose. The particles are sometimes separated in verse: hardly ever in prose, except ἀλλ' οὐ μήν, ἀλλ' οὐδὲ μήν. (For ἀλλὰ τί μήν; etc. see μήν, I.4.ii.)

(1) Adversative. A.*Pers*.233 'Where is Athens?'—'Far away'.—Ἀλλὰ μὴν ἵμειρ' ἐμὸς παῖς τήνδε θηρᾶσαι πόλιν ('And yet my son ...'): Ar.*Ach*.771 οὔ φατι τάνδε χοῖρον εἶμεν. ἀλλὰ μάν, αἰ λῇς, περίδου μοι ... αἰ μή 'στιν οὗτος χοῖρος Ἑλλάνων νόμῳ ('But come now'): Epich.*Fr*.78.1 (probably adversative): Pl.*Grg*.449E Οὐκ ἄρα περὶ πάντας γε τοὺς λόγους ἡ ῥητορική ἐστιν.—Οὐ δῆτα.—Ἀλλὰ μὴν λέγειν γε ποιεῖ δυνατούς ('But still'): 454E 'πίστις is not identical with ἐπιστήμη ... Ἀλλὰ μὴν οἵ τέ γε μεμαθηκότες πεπεισμένοι εἰσὶν καὶ οἱ πεπιστευκότες' ('And yet'): *R*.397D 'Shall we allow the mixed style as well?' —'No, only the unmixed'.—Ἀλλὰ μὴν ... ἡδύς γε καὶ ὁ κεκραμένος: X.*Mem*.iii 1.6 τὰ γὰρ τακτικὰ ἐμέ γε καὶ ἄλλ' οὐδὲν ἐδίδαξεν.—Ἀλλὰ μὴν ... τοῦτό γε πολλοστὸν μέρος ἐστὶ στρατηγίας: D.vi 22 'Do you think the Thessalians expected their fate? οὐκ ἔστι ταῦτα. ἀλλὰ μὴν γέγονεν ταῦτα' ('Nevertheless it happened'): Pl.*Euthd*.291A: *Ly*.222D: *Phd*.74C: *Sph*.

231A: X.*Mem.*i7.2: iii10.14: *An.*v8.26: D.xix65: xx130: xxi57: Hyp.*Ath.*16.

Breaking off, like ἀτάρ or ἀλλὰ γάρ. X.*An.*iii4.40 Ἀλλὰ μὴν ὥρα γ', ἔφη, βουλεύεσθαι: D.xviii192 ἀλλὰ μὴν τὸ μὲν παρεληλυθὸς ἀεὶ παρὰ πᾶσιν ἀφεῖται.

Marking the appearance of a new character on the stage, like καὶ μήν (6). E.*Or.*1549 ἀλλὰ μὴν καὶ τόνδε λεύσσω Μενέλεων.

ἀλλὰ . . . μήν. Epich.*Fr.*170a1 Ἀλλ' ἀεί τοι θεοὶ παρῆσαν . . . —Ἀλλὰ λέγεται μὰν χάος πρᾶτον γενέσθαι τῶν θεῶν: S.*Ph.*1273 Τοιοῦτος ἦσθα τοῖς λόγοισι χὤτε μου τὰ τόξ' ἔκλεπτες . . . —Ἀλλ' οὔ τι μὴν νῦν: *Indag.*109 Diehl Οὐκ εἰσακούω πω τορῶς τοῦ φθέγματος, ἀλλ' αὐτὰ μὴν ἴχνη . . . ἐναργῆ τῶν βοῶν ('but the tracks are clear enough'): S.*El.*817: *OC*153: Pl.*Phlb.*14A Ἀλλ' οὐ μὴν δεῖ τοῦτο γενέσθαι: *Phdr.*270E: *Lg.*960E (with echoed word: cf. (2) and (3) below): *Ion*541A Ἀλλ' ἐκεῖνο μὴν δοκεῖ σοι (μήν *F*: μέν *TW*).

(2) Assentient. Here ἀλλὰ μήν conforms closely to the corresponding uses of ἀλλά (II.6).

(i) In the sphere of action, expressing consent, willingness to act as required, readiness to accept a proposal. A.*Ag.*1652 ξίφος πρόκωπον πᾶς τις εὐτρεπιζέτω.—Ἀλλὰ μὴν κἀγὼ (ἀλλὰ κἀγὼ μήν *codd.*) πρόκωπος οὐκ ἀναίνομαι θανεῖν (Aegisthus accepts the challenge of the chorus): Pl.*Grg.*458D ἔμοιγε, κἂν τὴν ἡμέραν ὅλην ἐθέλητε διαλέγεσθαι, χαριεῖσθε.—Ἀλλὰ μὴν . . . τό γ' ἐμὸν οὐδὲν κωλύει ('Well, there is no objection on *my* part'): *Prt.*332A Ἀλλὰ μὴν . . . ἐπειδὴ δυσχερῶς δοκεῖς μοι ἔχειν πρὸς τοῦτο, τοῦτο μὲν ἐάσωμεν ('Very well'): *Smp.*176D: *Euthd.*295A ἐπιδείξω καὶ σὲ ταῦτα . . . ὁμολογοῦντα.—Ἀλλὰ μήν, ἦν δ' ἐγώ, ἥδιστα ταῦτα ἐξελέγχομαι: *Ly.*211D ἡμῖν δὲ οὐ μεταδίδοτον τῶν λόγων;—Ἀλλὰ μήν, ἦν δ' ἐγώ, μεταδοτέον ('Why, certainly'): *Phd.*110B εἰ γὰρ δὴ καὶ μῦθον λέγειν καλόν, ἄξιον ἀκοῦσαι . . .—Ἀλλὰ μὴν . . . ἡμεῖς γε τούτου τοῦ μύθου ἡδέως ἂν ἀκούσαιμεν: *Hipparch.*229E (I think this is assentient, 'Very well, I'll retract', rather than adversative, 'But I'll retract'). In Ar.*Ra.*258, Οἰμώζετ'· οὐ γάρ μοι μέλει.—Ἀλλὰ μὴν κεκραξόμεσθά γ' . . ., ἀλλὰ μήν marks the acceptance of the invitation implied in οὐ γάρ μοι μέλει: 'I don't care what you do'.—'All right, then'.

Or a speaker accedes in practice to a request to speak, by actually speaking. Inceptive-responsive, 'Well': cf. μήν, III.1.iii: καὶ μήν, (5). Pl.*Grg.*470C ἔλεγχε.—Ἀλλὰ μὴν . . . οὐδέν γέ σε δεῖ παλαιοῖς πράγμασιν ἐλέγχειν: *Cra.*407E πειρώμεθα οὖν τὸν "Ἑρμῆν" σκέψασθαι τί καὶ νοεῖ τὸ ὄνομα . . .—Ἀλλὰ μὴν τοῦτο γε ἔοικε περὶ λόγον τι εἶναι ὁ "Ἑρμῆς": *Cra.*402C: *Tht.* 187A: *Lg.*724A,842B: *Phlb.*41B: X.*Oec.*15.10.

(ii) In the sphere of thought, assent. Pl.*Chrm.*161A Ἀλλὰ μὴν οὕτω γε δοκεῖ μοι ἔχειν, ὡς σὺ λέγεις ('Why, yes'): *Tht.* 188A Οὐκοῦν τόδε γ' ἐσθ' ἡμῖν περὶ πάντα . . . ἤτοι εἰδέναι ἢ μὴ εἰδέναι; . . .—Ἀλλὰ μὴν . . . ἄλλο γ' οὐδὲν λείπεται περὶ ἕκαστον πλὴν εἰδέναι ἢ μὴ εἰδέναι: *Phd.*107A Οὐκοῦν ἔγωγε . . . ἔχω . . . ἀπιστεῖν τοῖς λόγοις.—Ἀλλὰ μὴν . . . οὐδ' αὐτὸς ἔχω ἔτι ὅπῃ ἀπιστῶ: X.*Mem.*ii 7.2 Ἔοικας . . . βαρέως φέρειν τι . . .—Ἀλλὰ μήν, ἔφη, . . . ἐν πολλῇ γέ εἰμι ἀπορίᾳ ('Well, certainly'): *An.*v 8.3 Ἀλλὰ μὴν . . . ὁμολογῶ: Pl.*Phdr.*269C: *R.*534B: *Phd.*63A: X.*Mem.*iv 2.36.

(iii) In general, indicating a favourable reaction to the previous speaker's words. A.*Pers.*226 Ἀλλὰ μὴν εὔνους γ' . . . τήνδ' ἐκύρωσας φάτιν: Ar.*Ach.*765 ἐπίδειξον (τὰς χοιρώς).—Ἀλλὰ μὰν καλαί ('Aye, they're fine'): *Av.*385 κἀμοὶ δεῖ νέμειν ὑμᾶς χάριν.—Ἀλλὰ μὴν οὐδ' ἄλλο σοί πω πρᾶγμ' ἐνηντιώμεθα ('Well, we never opposed you before'): Pl.*Phd.*58D τὸ μεμνῆσθαι Σωκράτους . . . ἔμοιγε ἀεὶ πάντων ἥδιστον.—Ἀλλὰ μὴν . . . καὶ τοὺς ἀκουσομένους γε τοιούτους ἑτέρους ἔχεις ('Well, certainly'): *R.*376A 'The dog likes acquaintances and hates strangers'.—Ἀλλὰ μὴν κομψόν γε φαίνεται τὸ πάθος αὐτοῦ ('Well, that *is* an attractive trait').

Ἀλλὰ . . . μήν. Pl.*Clit.*407A Ἀλλ' αἰσχρὸν μὴν σοῦ γε ὠφελεῖν με προθυμουμένου μὴ ὑπομένειν.

(3) Closely connected with (2), substantiating a condition: cf. ἀλλά, II.7, μήν, III.1.i, καὶ μήν, (3), ἀλλὰ μὲν δή, (3). Very frequent in Plato, often with an echoed word. S.*OC* 28 εἴπερ ἐστί γ' ἐξοικήσιμος.—Ἀλλ' ἔστι μὴν οἰκητός: Alex.*Fr.*167.2 γυναιξὶ δ' ἀρκεῖ πάντ', ἐὰν οἶνος παρῇ πίνειν διαρκής.—Ἀλλὰ μήν, νὴ τὼ θέω, ἔσται γ' ὅσον ἂν βουλώμεθ': Pl.*Cra.*391B εἴπερ ἐπιθυμεῖς εἰδέναι . . .—Ἀλλὰ μὴν ἐπιθυμῶ γε εἰδέναι ('And I *do* want to know'): *R.*508A εἴπερ μὴ ἄτιμον τὸ φῶς.—Ἀλλὰ μήν,

ἔφη, πολλοῦ γε δεῖ ἄτιμον εἶναι: *Phd.*100C ἃ εἴ μοι δίδως...—Ἀλλὰ μὴν ὡς διδόντος σοι οὐκ ἂν φθάνοις περαίνων: *Grg.*466B: *Chrm.*161E,176C: *La.*192C,193C: *Men.*73D,77A: *Euthphr.*6E: *Phd.*78B,96A: *Tht.*186A: *R.*400D,416B,509C,568A,576B,586E, 588A: *Lg.*966A: *Hp.Ma.*285A,301D: *Hp.Mi.*375D,376B. (E.*IA* 1368 is essentially similar. Ἀντέχου θυγατρός.—Ὡς τοῦδ' εἵνεκ' οὐ σφαγήσεται.—Ἀλλὰ μὴν ἐς τοῦτό γ' ἥξει ('If clinging can save her, she shall be saved'.—'And clinging will, in fact, be the only thing that *can* save her').)

(4) Progressive: proceeding to a new item in a series, introducing a new argument, or marking a new stage in the march of thought. We have seen that both ἀλλά and μήν (with certain restrictions) are sometimes used in this sense. The use of the combination ἀλλὰ μήν is far more extended, though very rare in verse. (In fact, except for ἀλλ' οὐδὲ μήν (see (ii) below), there seems to be no certain verse example. But in Nicostr.Com.*Fr.*8, which lack of precise context leaves somewhat doubtful, ἀλλὰ μήν seems to mean 'then again'.) γε usually follows at a short interval.

(i) Positive. Pl.*Euthd.*279B ἀγαθὰ δὲ ποῖα . . . τυγχάνει ἡμῖν ὄντα; . . . τὸ πλουτεῖν ἀγαθὸν . . . Οὐκοῦν καὶ τὸ ὑγιαίνειν . . .; . . . Ἀλλὰ μὴν εὐγένειαί γε ('Again'): X.*Mem.*iii 5.7 δοκεῖ δέ μοι ἀνδρὶ ἀγαθῷ ἄρχοντι νῦν εὐαρεστοτέρως διακεῖσθαι ἡ πόλις . . .—Ἀλλὰ μὴν . . . εἴ γε νῦν μάλιστα πείθοιντο, ὥρα ἂν εἴη λέγειν, πῶς ἂν αὐτοὺς προτρεψαίμεθα πάλιν ἀνερασθῆναι τῆς ἀρχαίας ἀρετῆς ('Well, now'): D.i 23 (after describing the disaffection of the Thessalians) ἀλλὰ μὴν τόν γε Παίονα καὶ τὸν Ἰλλυριὸν . . .: xix 7 (in discussing a series of points enumerated in § 4: δέ, καὶ μήν and δὲ δή have been used above) ἀλλὰ μὴν ὑπέρ γε τοῦ προῖκ' ἢ μὴ . . .: 279 "καὶ καταψευδόμενοι τῶν συμμάχων καὶ δῶρα λαμβάνοντες". ἀντὶ μὲν τοίνυν τοῦ καταψευδόμενοι παντελῶς ἀπολωλεκότες . . . ἀλλὰ μὴν ὑπέρ γε τοῦ δῶρ' εἰληφέναι . . .: xx 123 (in discussing two propositions enunciated in § 120) ἐγὼ δ' ὑπὲρ ὧν μὲν τῇ πόλει καταλείπειν φήσει, τοσοῦτο λέγω . . . ἀλλὰ μὴν ὑπὲρ ὧν γε τοῖς εὑρημένοις τὰς τιμὰς καταλείπειν φήσει . . .: X.*Mem.*iv 8.9 (new argument): *Cyr.*viii 8.11: 8.12: 8.15: 8.17 (successive points in description of Persians): Archyt.*Fr.*1 (four successive arguments each introduced by ἀλλὰ μὰν καί): Hp.*Art.*47,48: *Flat.*3 (*ter*): Gorg.*Fr.*11.18: 11a.24: Pl.*Prt.*359D: *Chrm.*160A: *Phdr.*240A,

244D: *Phd.*75A: *Cra.*412B,419E,422D: *R.*334A,370B,E,382B,387D, 389B,398E,429A: X.*HG* ii 3.40: iii 5.13: v 2.17: 2.34: vii 1.4: *An.*i 9.18: ii 5.14: iii 2.16: *Cyr.*i 6.19: iv 3.12: v 3.31: 5.23: Lys. xix 18,35,42: xx 28: Isoc.iii 16: v 37,53: D.xiv 29: xix 243: xxiv 109,192: xxix 38: xxxiii 30,31: xxxix 40: xlvi 6: Hyp. *Epit.*35.

Introducing an *a fortiori* argument. X.*Mem.*i 5.3: D.lvii 5.

(ii) Negative. (*a*) ἀλλ' οὐδὲ μήν (ἀλλ' οὐδὲ ... μήν). A.*Ch.*189 πῶς γὰρ ἐλπίσω ἀστῶν τιν' ἄλλον τῆσδε δεσπόζειν φόβης; ἀλλ' οὐδὲ μήν νιν ἡ κτανοῦσ' ἐκείρατο: E.*Or.*1117 δὶς θανεῖν οὐκ ἄζομαι.—Ἀλλ' οὐδ' ἐγὼ μήν ('No more do I'): *Hel.*1047 'It is impossible to kill Thoas'.—Ἀλλ' οὐδὲ μὴν ναῦς ἔστιν ᾗ σωθεῖμεν ἄν ('Nor, again'): *Hec.*401 τῆσδ' ἑκοῦσα παιδὸς οὐ μεθήσομαι.—Ἀλλ' οὐδ' ἐγὼ μὴν τήνδ' ἄπειμ' αὐτοῦ λιπών: *Andr.*256 κοὐ μενῶ πόσιν μολεῖν.—Ἀλλ' οὐδ' ἐγὼ μὴν πρόσθεν ἐκδώσω μέ σοι: Ar.*Pl.* 373 Μῶν οὐ κέκλοφας ἀλλ' ἥρπακας;—Κακοδαιμονᾷς.—Ἀλλ' οὐδὲ μὴν ἀπεστέρηκάς γ' οὐδένα; X.*Cyr.*iv 3.12 οὔτε ... οὔτε μὴν ... ἀλλ' οὐδὲ μήν.

(*b*) ἀλλὰ μὴν οὐδέ. Pl.*R.*388E 'Our guardians must not be prone to lamentation'.—'No'.—Ἀλλὰ μὴν οὐδὲ φιλογέλωτάς γε δεῖ εἶναι: Lys.xx 11 'I am not related to Phrynichus. ἀλλὰ μὴν οὐδ' ἐκ παιδείας φίλος ἦν αὐτῷ': Pl.*Cra.*386D,406D,439E: Hyp.*Phil.*5.

(*c*) ἀλλ' οὐ μήν. Pl.*Tht.*188C Ἀλλ' οὐ μήν, ἅ γέ τις οἶδεν, οἴεταί που ἃ μὴ οἶδεν αὐτὰ εἶναι: *Lg.*906E Ἀλλ' οὔτι μὴν ἡνιόχοισί γε: *R.*486D: *Plt.*290A: X.*Mem.*i 2.5. (But in Hom.**E** 895, **P** 448, **Ψ** 441 the particles do not, of course, cohere, and ἀλλ' οὐ μάν means 'but not, in sooth'.)

Rarely connecting phrases or clauses, after a comma. Hp.*Vict.* 76 τοῖσί τε περιπάτοισι πολλοῖσιν ἀπὸ τῶν γυμνασίων, ἀλλὰ μὴν καὶ ἀπὸ τοῦ δείπνου (reading doubtful): X.*Cyr.*iii 3.50 οὐκ ἂν οὖν τοξότας γε (μὴ ὄντας ἀγαθοὺς παραίνεσις ἀγαθοὺς ποιήσειε) ... οὐδὲ μὴν ἀκοντιστάς, οὐδὲ μὴν ἱππέας, ἀλλ' οὐδὲ μὴν τά γε σώματα ἱκανοὺς πονεῖν: Isoc.v 146 οὐθ' ὅτι ... οὐθ' ὅτι ... ἀλλὰ μὴν οὐδ' ὅτι. (In Pherecr.*Fr.*64.5 Kock conjectures ⟨ἀλλ⟩ οὐ μὴν οὐδ', which may be right, though Hom.**Ψ** 441, which he cites in support, is quite different: see above.)

Certain particular uses of progressive ἀλλὰ μήν deserve notice.

(5) Demosthenes and Isaeus (not, I think, any of the other orators, who prefer *καί*, *οὖν*, etc. in such cases) often use *ἀλλὰ μήν* to mark the transition from a statement to the calling of evidence in support of it. D.xix 146 *ἀλλὰ μὴν ὅτι ταῦτ' ἀληθῆ λέγω, κάλει μοι τοὺς 'Ολυνθίους μάρτυρας*: Is.iii 43,76: vii 32: viii 11: D.xix 161,165,233: xx 27: xxi 93,107,119,167: *id. saep.* (D.xix 303 is similar: *ἀλλὰ μὴν ὅτι ταῦθ' οὕτως ἔχει, αὐτὸς οὐχ οἷός τ' ἀντειπεῖν ἔσται*).

(6) In Plato *ἀλλὰ μήν* often marks the transition from the major premise of a syllogism to the minor premise, or vice versa. Cf. *ἀλλὰ μὲν δή*, (4). *Grg.*496E 'Pleasure and pain can be felt simultaneously'.—'Yes'.—*Ἀλλὰ μὴν εὖ γε πράττοντα κακῶς πράττειν ἅμα ἀδύνατον φῂς εἶναι . . . Οὐκ ἄρα τὸ χαίρειν ἐστὶν εὖ πράττειν οὐδὲ τὸ ἀνιᾶσθαι κακῶς*: *R.*464B *Ἆρ' οὖν τούτων αἰτία . . . ἡ τῶν γυναικῶν τε καὶ παίδων κοινωνία τοῖς φύλαξιν ;—Πολὺ μὲν οὖν μάλιστα, ἔφη.—Ἀλλὰ μὴν μέγιστόν γε πόλει αὐτὸ ὡμολογήσαμεν ἀγαθὸν . . .—Καὶ ὀρθῶς γε, ἔφη, ὡμολογήσαμεν.—Τοῦ μεγίστου ἄρα ἀγαθοῦ τῇ πόλει αἰτία ἡμῖν πέφανται ἡ κοινωνία τοῖς ἐπικούροις τῶν τε παίδων καὶ τῶν γυναικῶν*: *Grg.*477E,497D,498C, 506D,E,516C: *Prt.*360C: *Smp.*202D: *Men.*98E: *Phd.*79B: *Tht.* 189A: *R.*334D,342C,350C,354A.369D: *Prm.*139E.

(7) A use analogous to the above is not infrequently found in non-philosophical language, especially in Demosthenes, whereby the minor premise precedes the major, and the conclusion, as being self-evident, is left unexpressed. 'He is a murderer. *Ἀλλὰ μήν* all murderers should be put to death'. (*Sc.* 'Therefore he should be put to death'.) Thus used, *ἀλλὰ μήν* often proceeds to a consideration of the wider implications of a fact just posited, and puts a particular idea into a general setting.

X.*Mem.*iv 8.8 'If I live longer, my faculties will deteriorate. *ἀλλὰ μὴν ταῦτά γε μὴ αἰσθανομένῳ μὲν ἀβίωτος ἂν εἴη ὁ βίος, αἰσθανόμενον δὲ . . .*' (*sc.* 'Therefore to live longer is intolerable'): *Vect.* 6.1 '*ἀλλ' εἴ γε μήν* the course recommended has all these advantages, it should be adopted': D.xxi 42 'Meidias' crimes are crimes of deliberate *ὕβρις*. *ἀλλά μήν* the law enjoins particularly severe penalties for crimes of deliberate *ὕβρις*'. (*Sc.* 'Therefore Meidias should be punished with particular severity'): xxiv 95

'Timocrates' law makes effective military operations impossible. ἀλλὰ μὴν εἰ φαίνει τοιοῦτον τεθηκὼς νόμον ὃς τὰ τοιαῦτα λυμαίνεται . . . πῶς οὐχὶ δικαίως ὁτιοῦν ἂν πάθοις;' xxxvii 18 'Pantaenetus admitted that I was free of obligations to him. ἀλλὰ μὴν ὅτι γ' οὐκ ἐῶσιν οἱ νόμοι περὶ τῶν οὕτω πραχθέντων πάλιν λαγχάνειν, οἶμαι μὲν ὑμᾶς . . . γιγνώσκειν': i 15,27: iii 9: xviii 89,168: xxv 40: xxxiv 40: xlvi 3.

Less frequently, the major premise comes first (as regularly in formal reasoning: see (6) above). D.xxv 17 'The laws must be sacred. ἀλλὰ μὴν ὅτι νῦν Ἀριστογείτων τοῖς μὲν τῆς ἐνδείξεως δικαίοις ἅπασιν ἑάλωκεν . . . ῥᾴδιον διδάξαι': xlvi 12 'All agree that we must maintain the existing laws. ἀλλὰ μὴν οἵ γε νόμοι ἀπαγορεύουσι . . .': xxv 47.

(8) I have left two exceptional passages to the end. X.*Mem.* iii 8.3 Ἆρά γε, ἔφη, ἐρωτᾷς με εἴ τι οἶδα πυρετοῦ ἀγαθόν; . . . Ἀλλ' ὀφθαλμίας; . . . Ἀλλὰ λιμοῦ; . . . Ἀλλὰ μήν, ἔφη, εἴ γ' ἐρωτᾷς με εἴ τι ἀγαθὸν οἶδα ὃ μηδενὸς ἀγαθόν ἐστιν, οὔτ' οἶδα, ἔφη, οὔτε δέομαι (after the rejection of successive suggestions: 'Well'): *An.* ii 5.12 τίς οὕτω μαίνεται ὅστις οὐ βούλεται σοὶ φίλος εἶναι; ἀλλὰ μὴν ἐρῶ γὰρ καὶ ταῦτα ἐξ ὧν ἔχω ἐλπίδας καὶ σὲ βουλήσεσθαι φίλον ἡμῖν εἶναι (a combination of progressive ἀλλὰ μήν and ἀλλὰ γάρ).

Γε μήν

This combination affords a remarkable example of a particular author's predilection for a particular particle. γε μήν occurs several times as often in Xenophon as γε μήν, γε μάν, and γε μέν together in the whole of the rest of Greek classical literature. It is especially common in the *Opuscula* (34 times in the 30 pages (O.C.T.) of the *Agesilaus*, 39 in the 28 of the *Equitum magister*), where it is often used as a variant for ἀλλὰ μήν and καὶ μήν in proceeding to a new point. It is not to be found in Thucydides, the Orators, or Aristotle (it occurs in the pseudo-Aristotelian *de Mundo*). The earliest example is Hes.*Sc.* 139 (see (3): here only in Hesiod: some MSS. give, probably rightly, γε μέν, which Hesiod uses elsewhere: but verses 141–317 are regarded by Goettling as late work): the earliest Attic example is Phryn.Trag.*Fr.* 14.

The uses coincide with those of μήν, ἀλλὰ μήν, καὶ μήν. γε adheres closely to the preceding word.

(1) Affirmative (very rare). Pi.*N*.8.50 χαίρω δὲ πρόσφορον ἐν μὲν ἔργῳ κόμπον ἱεὶς . . . ἦν γε μὰν ἐπικώμιος ὕμνος δὴ πάλαι (in *P*.7.20 and *I*.3.18 also γε μήν is perhaps to be so explained, not as adversative): Pl.*Lg*.819D Ποίαν . . . λέγεις ταύτην;—Ὦ φίλε Κλεινία, παντάπασί γε μὴν καὶ αὐτὸς ἀκούσας ὀψέ ποτε τὸ περὶ ταῦτα ἡμῶν πάθος ἐθαύμασα (here the particles may perhaps be regarded as inceptive: 'Well': cf. μήν, III.1.iii): *Tht*.208E Φαμέν γε μὴν οὕτω (assentient: νῦν for μήν, *W*).

(2) Adversative, often answering μέν. Pi.*O*.13.104 νῦν δ' ἔλπομαι μέν, ἐν θεῷ γε μὰν τέλος: *P*.1.17 τόν ποτε Κιλίκιον θρέψεν πολυώνυμον ἄντρον· νῦν γε μὰν . . . (in Pi.*P*.1.50 νῦν γε μάν has only the mildest adversative force 'while now': 'rebus praeteritis praesentes opponit', Christ): Epich.*Fr*.3.11 οὐκ αὐτὸς εἴη κα τέχνα, τεχνικός γα μάν: A.*Pr*.871 μακροῦ λόγου δεῖ ταῦτ' ἐπεξελθεῖν τορῶς. σπορᾶς γε μὴν ἐκ τῆσδε φύσεται θρασύς (almost = ἀλλὰ γάρ): *Ag*.1378 ἐμοὶ δ' ἀγὼν ὅδ' οὐκ ἀφρόντιστος πάλαι νείκης παλαιᾶς ἦλθε, σὺν χρόνῳ γε μήν: *Eu*.51 οὐδ' αὖτε Γοργείοισιν εἰκάσω τύποις. εἶδόν ποτ' ἤδη Φινέως γεγραμμένας δεῖπνον φερούσας· ἄπτεροί γε μὴν ἰδεῖν αὗται ('But these are wingless'): S.*OC* 587 Ἀλλ' ἐν βραχεῖ δὴ τήνδε μ' ἐξαιτῇ χάριν.—Ὅρα γε μήν, οὐ σμικρός, οὔκ, ἀγὼν ὅδε ('Aye, but look you'): E.*Hipp*. 1340 τοὺς γὰρ εὐσεβεῖς . . . τούς γε μὴν κακοὺς . . .: *Or*.1083 χαῖρ'· οὐ γὰρ ἡμῖν ἔστι τοῦτο, σοί γε μήν ('but *thou mayest*'): *Rh*.196 Μέγας ἀγών, μεγάλα δ' ἐπινοεῖς ἑλεῖν· μακάριός γε μὴν κυρήσας ἔσῃ: 284 Οὐκ οἶδ' ἀκριβῶς· εἰκάσαι γε μὴν πάρα: *El*. 754 Μακρὰν γὰρ ἕρπει γῆρυς, ἐμφανής γε μήν: Ar.*Eq*.232 οὐδεὶς ἤθελεν τῶν σκευοποιῶν εἰκάσαι. πάντως γε μὴν γνωσθήσεται: *Nu*.631 ταῦτ' ἐπιλέλησται πρὶν μαθεῖν· ὅμως γε μὴν αὐτὸν καλῶ: A.*Th*.1062:* Ar.*Nu*.822: *Lys*.144 (γα μάν: 170): Pl. *Prm*.153A Οὐκ ἔχω λέγειν.—Τόδε γε μὴν ἔχεις λέγειν, ὅτι . . .: *Plt*.258D ἀλλ' οὐκ ἐμὸν γίγνεται (τὸ ἔργον).—Δεῖ γε μὴν . . . αὐτὸ εἶναι καὶ σόν: *Ti*.20D λόγου μάλα μὲν ἀτόπου, παντάπασί γε μὴν ἀληθοῦς: *Criti*.108B ὡς ὑπαρχούσης αὐτῷ συγγνώμης . . . λεγέτω. προλέγω γε μὴν . . . σοὶ τὴν τοῦ θεάτρου διάνοιαν . . . ὥστε τῆς συγγνώμης δεήσει τινός σοι παμπόλλης: X.*HG* vi 3.1 πολεμεῖν μὲν . . . κοινωνεῖν γε μὴν . . .: *Cyr*.vi 1.7 ἡμῖν ἐχρῶντο ὡς ἐκείνοις ἦν ἥδιστον, ἡμῖν γε μὴν ὡς χαλεπώτατον: Hp.*Fract*.

3,35,45: Pl.*R*.332E: *Ti*.41A,53B,63E,72D,77B: *Tht*.197B: *Lg*.628E: X.*Cyr*.viii 8.9: *Eq*.8.8.

(3) Progressive (in Xenophon far the commonest use). Hes. *Sc*.139 χερσί γε μὴν σάκος εἷλε παναίολον (γε *om. M*: δέ *Ω b*: μέν *BΨNO*): S.*El*.973 ἐλευθέρα καλῇ τὸ λοιπὸν . . . λόγων γε μὴν εὔκλειαν οὐχ ὁρᾷς ὅσην σαυτῇ . . . προσβαλεῖς . . . ; E.*Alc*. 516 'Have you lost a child?'—'No'.—Πατήρ γε μὴν ὡραῖος, εἴπερ οἴχεται ('Well, your *father* is full of years'): Epich. *Fr*.79: Philol.*Fr*.5 ὅ γα μὰν ἀριθμὸς ἔχει δύο μὲν ἴδια εἴδη (probably progressive): Pl.*R*.443A Οὐκοῦν καὶ . . . Καὶ μὴν οὐδὲ . . . Μοιχεῖαί γε μὴν . . .: 465B Οὐ γὰρ οὖν.—Τά γε μὴν σμικρότατα τῶν κακῶν δι' ἀπρέπειαν ὀκνῶ καὶ λέγειν: *Smp*.197A καὶ μὲν δὴ . . . ἀλλὰ . . . γε μήν: *Sph*.231E τὸ πρῶτον . . . Τὸ δέ γε δεύτερον . . . Τρίτον δὲ . . . Ναί, καὶ τέταρτόν γε . . . πέμπτον δὲ . . . Τό γε μὴν ἕκτον (last of series): 232D Ἀλλὰ μὴν . . . Τί δ' αὖ περὶ . . .; . . . Τά γε μὴν . . .: *Lg*.801E Κείσθω· τί μήν;—Μετά γε μὴν ταῦτα ὕμνοι θεῶν: X.*HG* vi 1.11 πλείους ἐκείνων ἱκανοὶ ἐσόμεθα ναῦς ποιήσασθαι. ἀνδρῶν γε μὴν ταύτας πληροῦν . . . τούς γε μὴν ναύτας τρέφειν . . .: vii 5.12 οὐκ ἀνέβαινεν εἰς τὴν πόλιν. τό γε μὴν ἐντεῦθεν γενόμενον ἔξεστι μὲν τὸ θεῖον αἰτιᾶσθαι: *An*.vii 6.41 (at the beginning of a speech, adding something to what has been said before): Hp.*Off*.9: *Art*.53: Pl.*Phdr*.267C: X.*HG* vi 3.14: *Mem*.iii 6.12: 8.10: 9.6: 11.10: *Cyr*.i 6.20: viii 8.17: *Smp*.8.3.

Unlike other writers, Xenophon freely uses progressive γε μήν after light stops, as a mere variant for δέ. *HG* v 2.16 ξύλα μὲν . . . χρημάτων δὲ πρόσοδοι . . . πολυανθρωπία· γε μὴν . . . : vi 1.19 ἱππεῖς μὲν . . . ὁπλῖται δὲ . . . πελταστικόν γε μὴν . . .: *HG*.iv 2.17: *Cyr*.ii 1.23: *Smp*.4.38: *Ages*.11.13.

Introducing an *a fortiori* argument. X.*Eq.Mag*.4.20 'Wolves do so-and-so. θηρίων γε μὴν δυναμένων τὰ τοιαῦτα φρονίμως λῄζεσθαι, πῶς οὐκ ἄνθρωπόν γε ὄντα εἰκὸς σοφώτερον τούτων φαίνεσθαι . . .;' *Hier*.8 7.

(4) Introducing the minor premise of a syllogism. Pl.*Lg*.628C Ἆρα οὖν οὐ τοῦ ἀρίστου ἕνεκα πάντα ἂν τὰ νόμιμα τιθείη πᾶς;—Πῶς δ' οὔ;—Τό γε μὴν ἄριστον οὔτε ὁ πόλεμος οὔτε ἡ στάσις: 654B τὸν δὲ πεπαιδευμένον ἱκανῶς κεχορευκότα θετέον.—Τί μήν;—

Χορεία γε μὴν ὄρχησίς τε καὶ ᾠδὴ τὸ συνολόν ἐστιν.—Ἀναγκαῖον.—Ὁ καλῶς ἄρα πεπαιδευμένος ᾄδειν τε καὶ ὀρχεῖσθαι δυνατὸς ἂν εἴη καλῶς: *Sph.*228C.

Introducing the major premise, after a preceding minor premise. (Cf. the Demosthenic use of ἀλλὰ μήν, (7).) X.*Eq.*5.1 πολλάκις ἂν ἕλκῃ ποιοίη. ἑλκουμένων γε μὴν τούτων ...: *HG*ii 3. 33: *Ap.*18: *Lac.*5.4.

(5) Combined with other particles (very rare). Epich.*Fr.*170b7 ὁ μὲν γὰρ αὔξεθ', ὁ δέ γα μὰν φθίνει: Philol.*Fr.*4 καὶ πάντα γα μὰν τὰ γιγνωσκόμενα ἀριθμὸν ἔχοντι: Pl.*Sph.*219E Τὴν δέ γε μὴν θηρευτικήν (δέ *om. W*): 240B Ἀλλ' ἔστι γε μήν πως.*

(6) Position. After preposition and substantive: Pl.*Plt.*265A, 269E (but between the two in *Lg.*801E). Other transpositions: Pl.*R.*332E Εἶεν· μὴ κάμνουσί γε μήν: *Lg.*819D Ὦ φίλε Κλεινία, παντάπασί γε μήν. Last words of sentence, Pl.*Lg.*832A.

Ἦ μήν

ἦ μήν introduces a strong and confident asseveration, being used both in direct and in indirect speech. It is most frequently employed in oaths and pledges: the wider use is very rare in prose and entirely absent from the orators. (According to Dittenberger (*l.c.*, p. 329, n. 4) ἦ μήν occurs fifteen times in the *Parmenides*, as often as in all the remaining dialogues of Plato put together.)

(1) General use. Hom.*B* 291 ἦ μὴν καὶ πόνος ἐστὶν ἀνιηθέντα νέεσθαι: *H* 393 ἦ μὴν Τρῶές γε κέλονται: *P* 429 ἦ μὰν Αὐτομέδων... ἐπεμαίετο: Sapph.*Fr.*96.6 Ψάπφ', ἦ μάν σ' ἀέκοισ' ἀπυλιμπάνω: Ibyc.*Fr.*7.5 ἦ μὰν τρομέω νιν ἐπερχόμενον: Pi.*N.*8.28 ἦ μὰν ἀνόμοιά γε δᾴοισιν ἐν θερμᾷ χροὶ ἕλκεα ῥῆξαν: *I.*1.63 ἦ μὰν πολλάκι καὶ τὸ σεσωπαμένον εὐθυμίαν μείζω φέρει: A.*Pr.*907 Ἦ μὴν ἔτι Ζεύς ... ἔσται ταπεινός: S.*OC* 816 Ἦ μὴν σὺ κἄνευ τοῦδε λυπηθεὶς ἔσῃ: E.*Alc.*692 ἦ μὴν πολύν γε τὸν κάτω λογίζομαι χρόνον: *Med.*1032 ἦ μήν ποθ' ἡ δύστηνος εἶχον ἐλπίδας: Ar.*V.* 258 Ἦ μὴν ἐγὼ σοῦ χἀτέρους μείζονας κολάζω: 280 ἦ μὴν πολὺ δριμύτατός γ' ἦν τῶν παρ' ἡμῖν: *Ra.*104 Ἦ μὴν κόβαλά γ' ἐστίν (but the Aristophanic examples are mostly with the future indicative, and threatening in tone: *Nu.*865,1242: *V.*643,1332: *Av.* 1259: *Ec.*1034: *Pl.*608): Hom.*B* 370: *N* 354: Hes.*Sc.*101: Pi.*P.*

4.40: A.*Pr.*73: E.*Alc.*64: Th.viii 33.1 πολλὰ ἀπειλήσας τοῖς Χίοις ἦ μὴν μὴ ἐπιβοηθήσειν: Pl.*Euthd.*276E Ὦ Ζεῦ, ἔφην ἐγώ, ἦ μὴν καὶ τὸ πρότερόν γε καλὸν ἡμῖν ἐφάνη τὸ ἐρώτημα: *R.*432D Ἦ μήν, ἦν δ' ἐγώ, βλακικόν γε ἡμῶν τὸ πάθος: *Phlb.*18D Ἦ μὴν ἐπ' αὐτῷ γε ἤδη γεγονότες ζητεῖτε: X.*An.*vii 7 35 ἦ μὴν πολύ γέ ἐστιν ἔλαττον: *Cyr.*viii 4.16 Ἦ μὴν . . . πολλά γέ μοί ἐστι τοιαῦτα συγγεγραμμένα.

(2) In oaths and pledges, usually in indirect speech. Hom.*h. Ap.*87 μέγαν ὅρκον ὄμοσσεν· ἴστω νῦν τάδε γαῖα ... ἦ μὴν Φοίβου τῇδε θυώδης ἔσσεται αἰεὶ βωμός: A.*Th.*531 ὄμνυσι . . . ἦ μὴν λαπάξειν ἄστυ Καδμείων: S.*Tr.*1186–7 Ὄμνυ Διὸς . . . κάρα.—Ἦ μὴν τί δράσειν; . . .—Ἦ μὴν . . . ἐκτελεῖν: *Ph.*593 διωμοτοὶ πλέουσιν ἦ μὴν . . . ἄξειν: E.*IA* 475: Ar.*Ra.*1470: Th.iv 118.14 σπείσασθαι . . . ἦ μὴν ἐμμενεῖν: Pl.*Phd.*115D ἠγγυᾶτο ἦ μὴν παραμενεῖν: *Ap.*22A καὶ νὴ τὸν κύνα ... ἦ μὴν ἐγὼ ἔπαθόν τι τοιοῦτον: X.*An.*vi 1.31 ὀμνύω ὑμῖν θεοὺς πάντας καὶ πάσας, ἦ μὴν ἐγὼ ... ἐθυόμην: *HG* iii 4.5 πίστιν λαβεῖν ἦ μὴν ...: *Cyr.* ii 3.12 σὺν θεῶν ὅρκῳ λέγω, ἦ μὴν ἐμοὶ δοκεῖ Κῦρος ...: vii 2.12 ὑπεσχόμην ... ἦ μὴν ...: And.i 31 ὅρκους μεγάλους ὀμόσαντες ... καὶ ἀρασάμενοι τὰς μεγίστας ἀρὰς ... ἦ μὴν ψηφιεῖσθαι: 126 ὤμοσεν ἦ μὴν μὴ εἶναι: Lys.vi 12 ἠντεδίκει ἦ μὴν τὸν Ἑρμῆν ὑγιᾶ τε καὶ ὅλον εἶναι: Isoc.xviii 53 μεμαρτυρηκὼς ἦ μὴν τεθνάναι τὴν ἄνθρωπον: D.xix 292 ὤμνυες ἦ μὴν ἀπολωλέναι Φίλιππον ἂν βούλεσθαι: xxiv 77 καταστήσαντι τοὺς ἐγγυητάς, ἦ μὴν ἐκτείσειν.

Καὶ μήν

In καὶ μήν we find many points of contact on the one hand with καὶ δή, on the other with μήν, γε μήν, ἀλλὰ μήν. Only in the adversative use (8) does καὶ μήν entirely part company with καὶ δή. Except for an isolated apodotic example (9), καί in καὶ μήν seems always to be copulative; though for purposes of idiomatic translation 'and' is often inappropriate. Hence in (7) καὶ μήν never comes late in the sentence, whereas καὶ δή, in a closely similar use (*q.v.*, 2.i), is often postponed.

(1) Progressive. This is a very common use, particularly in prose, where καὶ μήν often introduces a new argument, a new

item in a series, or a new point of any kind. In Attic, the emphatic word or phrase, following immediately upon the particles, is very frequently reinforced by γε. (See γε, I.1.ii: V.1. In Plato, in fact, γε is comparatively seldom absent, except from the form *καὶ μὴν καί*. On *καὶ μὴν . . . γε* in Sophocles, see Jebb on *Aj.* 531.) Normally *καὶ μήν* marks a new departure: it is mainly used after a strong stop, *καὶ δή*, *καὶ . . . δή*, or *καὶ δὴ καί* being used after weaker stops. There are, however, exceptions, mostly in verse and in Xenophon. Hom.Ψ410 *ὧδε γὰρ ἐξερέω, καὶ μὴν τετελεσμένον ἔσται*: Emp.*Fr.*76 *ἐν κόγχαισι θαλασσονόμων βαρυνώτοις, καὶ μὴν κηρύκων* (*καὶ μήν* Xylander (' and especially ', like *καὶ δὴ καί*): *ναὶ μήν codd.*): Pi.*P.*1.63 *θέλοντι δὲ Παμφύλου καὶ μὰν Ἡρακλειδᾶν ἔκγονοι*: 6.6 *ποταμίᾳ τ' Ἀκράγαντι καὶ μὰν Ξενοκράτει*: Hp.*Int.*27 *τά τε ἄλλα καὶ μὴν καὶ τὰ χλιάσματα*: X.*Smp.*4.15 *ἐλευθεριωτέρους μὲν . . . φιλοπονωτέρους δὲ . . ., καὶ μὴν αἰδημονεστέρους*: *Lac.*5.7 *περιπατεῖν τε γὰρ ἀναγκάζονται ἐν τῇ οἴκαδε ἀφόδῳ, καὶ μὴν τοῦ ὑπὸ οἴνου μὴ σφάλλεσθαι ἐπιμελεῖσθαι* (*μήν om. C*): *HG* iv 2.16: 2.17.

After strong stops. Hom.λ582 *καὶ μὴν Τάνταλον ἐσεῖδον* (cf. λ593: Crates Theb.*Fr.*3.1,5.1): Pi.*P.*4.289 (like *καὶ δὴ καί*, introducing an instance of a general proposition): A.*Pr.*459 *ἀντολὰς ἐγὼ ἄστρων ἔδειξα. . . . καὶ μὴν ἀριθμὸν . . . ἐξηῦρον αὐτοῖς*: *Supp.* 311 *ἐκ γῆς ἤλασεν μακρῷ δρόμῳ.— . . .—Καὶ μὴν Κάνωβον κἀπὶ Μέμφιν ἵκετο*: E.*Med.*1375 *πικρὰν δὲ βάξιν ἐχθαίρω σέθεν.—Καὶ μὴν ἐγὼ σήν* (a *tu quoque*): *Hec.*824,1224 (introducing new arguments): *Hel.*1053 *ἕτοιμός εἰμι μὴ θανὼν λόγῳ θανεῖν.—Καὶ μὴν γυναικείοις σ' ἂν οἰκτισαίμεθα κουραῖσι*: Ar.*Lys.*206 *Εὔχρων γε θαῖμα . . .—Καὶ μὰν ποτόδδει γ' ἀδύ*: Pi.*O.*10.34: *P.*4.90: B.13.182: A.*Pers.*406,992: *Ag.*931,1188: E.*Cyc.*141,151,541: *Alc.* 369,653: *Hipp.*862: *El.*1119: *Supp.*442 697: *Or.*1260: Ar.*V.* 521: Pl.*Grg.*450A *Ἀρ' οὖν . . . ἡ ἰατρικὴ . . .; . . . Οὐκοῦν καὶ ἡ γυμναστικὴ . . .; . . . Καὶ μὴν καὶ αἱ ἄλλαι τέχναι. . .*: *Prt.*310A *χάριν εἴσομαι, ἐὰν ἀκούητε.—Καὶ μὴν καὶ ἡμεῖς σοί, ἐὰν λέγῃς*: *Tht.*154E *ἔγωγε τοῦτ' ἂν βουλοίμην.—Καὶ μὴν ἐγώ*: *Smp.*179B *καὶ μὴν ὑπεραποθνῄσκειν γε μόνοι ἐθέλουσιν οἱ ἐρῶντες*: *Cra.*420A *καὶ μὴν "πόθος" αὖ καλεῖται*: *Phd.*72E (new argument): Gorg. *Fr.*11a.16,17: Th.i 70.4: vii 75.6: Pl *Grg.*474E,479D,504B: *Smp.* 179A: *Euthd.*306D: *Chrm.*166B: *Ly.*207C: X.*HG* iii 5.10: *Mem.* ii 7.1: Ant.v 91: D.ix 12: xviii 76,108,232,317.

(2) Plato sometimes uses *καὶ μήν* (though less frequently than *ἀλλὰ μήν*) to mark the transition from the major to the minor premise of a syllogism, or vice versa. *La.*199E *Οὐκ ἄρα . . . μόριον ἀρετῆς ἂν εἴη τὸ νῦν σοι λεγόμενον . . .—Ἔοικεν.—Καὶ μὴν ἔφαμέν γε τὴν ἀνδρείαν μόριον εἶναι ἓν τῶν τῆς ἀρετῆς . . . Οὐκ ἄρα ηὑρήκαμεν . . . ἀνδρεία ὅτι ἔστιν**: *Men.*87D: *Phlb.*37E: *Tht.*182E: *La.*193C: *Prm.*137D,145C,151B,153C: X.*Mem.*ii 3.19.

(3) Plato and Sophocles use *καὶ μήν*, usually with an echoed word, in substantiating a required condition (cf. *ἀλλὰ μήν*, (3)). Logically speaking, *καὶ μήν* here introduces the minor premise of an enthymeme, the conclusion being left unexpressed.* S.*Aj.* 794 *Αἴαντος . . . θυραῖος εἴπερ ἐστίν, οὐ θαρσῶ πέρι.—Καὶ μὴν θυραῖος* ('And he is, in fact, without'. Elmsley's *θυραῖός ⟨γ'⟩* is perhaps right, but unnecessary): *El.*556 *ἢν ἐφῇς μοι . . .—Καὶ μὴν ἐφίημ'*: 1045 *Ἀλλ' εἰ ποήσεις ταῦτ', ἐπαινέσεις ἐμέ.—Καὶ μὴν ποήσω γ'* ('And do it I will'): *OT*749 *ἢν ἐν ἐξείπῃς ἔτι.—Καὶ μὴν ὀκνῶ μέν, ἂν δ' ἔρῃ μαθοῦσ' ἐρῶ*: Pl.*Cra* 408E *εἴπερ σοι κεχαρισμένον ἔσται, ἐθέλω.—Καὶ μὴν χαριῇ*: *Phlb.*44A *εἴπερ χωρὶς τοῦ μὴ λυπεῖσθαι . . .—Καὶ μὴν χωρίς γε ἦν*: *Ion* 536D *εἴ μου ἀκούσαις λέγοντος . . .—Καὶ μὴν ἐθέλω γε ἀκοῦσαι.* (Pl.*Cra.* 427D is rather different: *αὕτη μοι φαίνεται . . . βούλεσθαι εἶναι ἡ τῶν ὀνομάτων ὀρθότης, εἰ μή τι ἄλλο Κρατύλος ὅδε λέγει.—Καὶ μὴν . . . πολλά γέ μοι πολλάκις πράγματα παρέχει Κρατύλος . . . φάσκων μὲν εἶναι ὀρθότητα ὀνομάτων, ἥτις δ' ἐστὶν οὐδὲν σαφὲς λέγων.* The speaker here is uncertain whether, in fact, Cratylus says *ἄλλο τι* or *τὸ αὐτό*: 'And C. has, in fact, views on the subject (whether your views or others, I do not know)'.)

S.*Ant.*221 is similar: *Οὐκ ἔστιν οὕτω μῶρος ὃς θανεῖν ἐρᾷ.—Καὶ μὴν ὁ μισθός γ' οὗτος* (no one is such a fool as to desire death: disobedience means death: (therefore no one should be such a fool as to disobey). 'In sooth, that is the meed', Jebb).

(4) In dialogue, expressing, directly or by implication, agreement or consent, or a generally favourable reaction to the words of the previous speaker. We sometimes use 'and' in English in such cases: 'And so it is', 'And I will, certainly': but often 'Yes', 'Indeed', will serve better as renderings.

A.*Pr.*248 *εἰσιδοῦσά τ' ἠλγύνθην κέαρ.—Καὶ μὴν φίλοις ἐλεινὸς* εἰσορᾶν ἐγώ ('Aye, truly': Wilamowitz, misunderstanding the sense of *καὶ μήν*, supposes a lacuna after 248: Wecklein's *φίλοις* ⟨γ'⟩ is possible, but unnecessary): *Ch.*510 Chorus (after Electra's final appeal): *Καὶ μὴν ἀμεμφῆ τόνδ' ἐτεινάτην λόγον . . . τὰ δ' ἄλλα . . . ἔρδοις ἂν ἤδη* ('Well, certainly, nobody can say you have scanted your prayer'): S.*Aj.*539 *Δός μοι προσειπεῖν αὐτὸν ἐμφανῆ τ' ἰδεῖν.—Καὶ μὴν πέλας γε προσπόλοις φυλάσσεται* ('*καὶ μήν* here announces a fact which favours the last speaker's wish . . . an expression of assent', Jebb): 990 Teucer: 'Bring the boy here, out of his enemies' hands: the dead are always insulted'.—*Xo. Καὶ μὴν ἔτι ζῶν, Τεῦκρε, τοῦδέ σοι μέλειν ἐφίεθ' ἁνὴρ κεῖνος, ὥσπερ οὖν μέλει* ('Yea', Jebb): *OT* 290 Cho.: 'We should consult Phoebus through Teiresias'.—Oed.: 'I have sent for him'.—Xo. *Καὶ μὴν τά γ' ἄλλα κωφὰ καὶ παλαί' ἔπη* ('Aye, truly'): 836 *ἕως δ' ἂν οὖν πρὸς τοῦ παρόντος ἐκμάθῃς, ἔχ' ἐλπίδα.—Καὶ μὴν τοσοῦτόν γ' ἐστί μοι τῆς ἐλπίδος, τὸν ἄνδρα τὸν βοτῆρα προσμεῖναι μόνον* ('Yes, that in truth is my hope, and that only'): 1004–5 *Τί δῆτ' ἐγὼ οὐχὶ τοῦδε τοῦ φόβου σε . . . ἐξελυσάμην;—Καὶ μὴν χάριν γ' ἂν ἀξίαν λάβοις ἐμοῦ.—Καὶ μὴν μάλιστα τοῦτ' ἀφικόμην, ὅπως . . . εὖ πράξαιμί τι* (the Messenger picks up Oedipus' *καὶ μήν* rather impudently, 'Well, truly', as Xanthias picks up *οὔ τί που* in Ar.*Ra.*526): *Ph.*660 *Σοί γ', ὦ τέκνον, καὶ τοῦτο κἄλλο τῶν ἐμῶν ὁποῖον ἄν σοι ξυμφέρῃ γενήσεται.—Καὶ μὴν ἐρῶ γε* ('I certainly long to touch it', Jebb): E.*Cyc.*176 *Ἄκου', Ὀδυσσεῦ· διαλαλήσωμέν τί σοι.—Καὶ μὴν φίλοι γε προσφέρεσθε πρὸς φίλον*: *Alc.*713 *Ψυχῇ μιᾷ ζῆν, οὐ δυοῖν, ὀφείλομεν.—Καὶ μὴν Διός γε μείζονα ζῴης χρόνον* ('All right, then: *have* a long life, and *too* long a one'): *Ba.*808 *Ξυνέθεσθε κοινῇ τάδ', ἵνα βακχεύητ' ἀεί.—Καὶ μὴν ξυνεθέμην—τοῦτό γ' ἔστι—τῷ θεῷ* ('Aye, I agreed on it—with the god'. 'Immo ego et deus', Murray: but *καὶ μήν* can scarcely be used for *μὲν οὖν*: see, however, (8) below): *El.* 670 *Στείχοιμ' ἄν, εἴ τις ἡγεμὼν γίγνοιθ' ὁδοῦ.—Καὶ μὴν ἐγὼ πέμποιμ' ἂν οὐκ ἀκουσίως*: *Ion* 985 *σὺ νῦν βούλευέ τι.—Καὶ μὴν ἔχω γε δόλια* ('Aye, truly'): Ar.*Nu.*1344 *Ἀλλ' οἴομαι μέντοι σ' ἀναπείσειν . . .—Καὶ μὴν ὅ τι καὶ λέξεις ἀκοῦσαι βούλομαι*: *V.* 537 Chorus (to Philocleon): 'Now for a really fine speech'.—Bdelycleon: *Καὶ μὴν ὅσ' ἂν λέξῃ γ' ἁπλῶς μνημόσυνα γράψομαι 'γώ* ('All right, I'll write down every word'): *Lys.*362 *Εἰ . . . τὰς γνάθους τούτων τις . . . ἔκοψεν . . . φωνὴν ἂν οὐκ ἂν εἶχον.*—

Καὶ μὴν ἰδοὺ παταξάτω τις ('All right, then': accepting the implied challenge: cf. *Pl.*928): *Ec.*523 *Οὔτοι παρὰ τοῦ μοιχοῦ γε φήσεις* (*ἥκειν με*).—*Οὐκ ἴσως ἑνός γε.*—*Καὶ μὴν βασανίσαι τουτί γέ σοι ἔξεστι* (the speaker, without accepting the previous speaker's statement, expresses her readiness to put it to the test: 'Very well, you can test it': cf. *Pl.*467,902): *Pl.*414 *μὴ νῦν διάτριβ', ἀλλ' ἄνυε πράττων ἕν γέ τι.*—*Καὶ μὴν βαδίζω* (*μήν R*: *δή cett.*, which would certainly be more regular): Pl.*R.*328D *δεῦρο παρ' ἡμᾶς φοίτα . . .*—*Καὶ μὴν . . . χαίρω γε διαλεγόμενος τοῖς σφόδρα πρεσβύταις*: *Smp.*172A *οὗτος Ἀπολλόδωρος. οὐ περιμένεις; κἀγὼ ἐπιστὰς περιέμεινα. καὶ ὅς, Ἀπολλόδωρε, ἔφη, καὶ μὴν καὶ ἔναγχός σε ἐζήτουν* ('Why, I was just looking for you, Apollodorus': the speaker greets the rencontre with pleasure): 222D *τὸν οὖν Ἀγάθωνα εἰπεῖν, Καὶ μήν, ὦ Σώκρατες, κινδυνεύεις ἀληθῆ λέγειν* ('Why, Socrates, I believe you're right'): *R.*427A *ἀγνοοῦντες ὅτι τῷ ὄντι ὥσπερ Ὕδραν τέμνουσιν.*—*Καὶ μήν, ἔφη, οὐκ ἄλλο γέ τι ποιοῦσιν* ('Why, certainly'): X.*Cyr.*vi 3.18 Cyrus asks Araspas for information regarding the enemy's strength. *Καὶ μήν, ἔφη ὁ Ἀράσπας, ὡς ἂν ἀσφαλέστατά γε εἰδείην ὁπόσον τὸ στράτευμά ἐστιν ἐποίουν* (ready response): v 1.1 (eager acceptance of an offer): 3.10: *Mem.*ii 6.30.

(5) A particular variety of the above is the use which we might call 'inceptive-responsive' (cf. *μήν*, III.1.iii, *ἀλλὰ μήν*, 2.i, *ad fin.*). A person who has been invited to speak expresses by the particles his acceptance of the invitation: 'Well', 'Very well', 'All right'. This use is common in Aristophanes and Plato, and is almost confined to them.

A.*Ag.*1178 *Χο. Τέρμα δ' ἀμηχανῶ.*—*Κα. Καὶ μὴν ὁ χρησμὸς οὐκέτ' ἐκ καλυμμάτων ἔσται δεδορκώς* (response to an implied appeal for plainer speaking): S.*OT* 345 *πρὸς τάδ', εἰ θέλεις, θυμοῦ δι' ὀργῆς ἥτις ἀγριωτάτη.*—*Καὶ μὴν παρήσω γ' οὐδέν, ὡς ὀργῆς ἔχω, ἅπερ ξυνίημ'. ἴσθι γὰρ . . .*: Ar.*Eq.*335 *νῦν δεῖξον . . .*—*Καὶ μὴν ἀκούσαθ'*: *Nu.*1036 *δεῖ σε λέγειν τι καινὸν . . .*—*Καὶ μὴν πάλαι γ' ἐπνιγόμην*: *Ra.*1249 *ἀλλ' ἐς τὰ μέλη . . . αὐτοῦ τραποῦ.*—*Καὶ μὴν ἔχω γ' οἷς αὐτὸν ἀποδείξω κακὸν μελοποιὸν ὄντα*: *Eq.*624: *Nu.*1353: *V.*548: *Av.*462,639: *Lys.*486: *Ra.* 907,1119: *Ec.*583: Pl.*Phd.*58E *πειρῶ . . . διεξελθεῖν πάντα.*—*Καὶ μὴν ἔγωγε θαυμάσια ἔπαθον παραγενόμενος* ('Well'): *R.*445C μόνον λέγε.—*Καὶ μήν, ἦν δ' ἐγώ, ὥσπερ ἀπὸ σκοπιᾶς μοι φαίνεται* . . .: 550D *Οὐκοῦν ὡς μεταβαίνει . . . ῥητέον ;—Ναί.—Καὶ μὴν . . . καὶ τυφλῷ γε δῆλον ὡς μεταβαίνει* (' Well, even a blind man can see . . . ') : *Tht.*158C *ἐρωτώντων, τί ἂν τις ἔχοι τεκμήριον ἀποδεῖξαι . . .—Καὶ μήν, ὦ Σώκρατες, ἄπορόν γε ὅτῳ χρὴ ἐπιδεῖξαι τεκμηρίῳ*: *Phd.*84D,88E : *Cra.*384C,411B: *Smp.*189C,199C: *Phdr.* 227C,262C : *Tht.*143E : *Sph.*221C : *Phlb.*33C : *Lg.*712D : *Hp.Mi.* 363A,373C.

The inceptive force, without the responsive, is seen in Pl.*Mx.* 234C : *Euthd.*304C (' Well, Socrates ' : not adversative, I think).

(6) Marking the entrance of a new character upon the stage (cf. *καὶ δή*, 2.ii) : opening a speech in dialogue, or a short anapaestic system (see *Addenda*). This use is scarcely to be found in Aeschylus. (In *Th.*372 *Καὶ μὴν ἄναξ ὅδ' αὐτὸς* . . . the second semichorus is announcing Eteocles after the first has announced the Messenger, and *καὶ μήν* is here more definitely and obviously connective than it elsewhere is in this usage.) But in Sophocles, Euripides, and Aristophanes it is extremely common. Normally some part of *ὅδε* follows.

S.*El.*1422 *καὶ μὴν πάρεισιν οἵδε*: *Ant.*526: E.*Hec.*216 *Καὶ μὴν Ὀδυσσεὺς ἔρχεται*: S.*Ant.*1180,1257: *Aj.*1168: *OC*549,1249: E.*Alc.*507,611 : *Andr.*494,879,1166: *Ion* 1257 (opening a speech in the middle of a trochaic tetrameter): Ar.*Ach.*908,1069: *Ec.*41. In S.*Aj.*1223 *καὶ μήν* is used by the entering character himself.

(7) Closely connected with (6), calling attention to something just seen or heard. ' See ! ' : ' Hark ! '. (Cf. *καὶ δή*, 2.i.) A.*Th.* 245 *Καὶ μὴν ἀκούω γ' ἱππικῶν φρυαγμάτων* (see Tucker) : *Pr.* 1080 *Καὶ μὴν ἔργῳ κοὐκέτι μύθῳ χθὼν σεσάλευται* : S.*El.*78 *Καὶ μὴν θυρῶν ἔδοξα προσπόλων τινὸς ὑποστενούσης ἔνδον αἰσθέσθαι* : E.*Alc.*385 *Καὶ μὴν σκοτεινὸν ὄμμα μου βαρύνεται*: *Andr.*820 *Καὶ μὴν ἐν οἴκοις προσπόλων ἀκούομεν βοήν* : *Ba.*918 *Καὶ μὴν ὁρᾶν μοι δύο μὲν ἡλίους δοκῶ* : 957 *Καὶ μὴν δοκῶ σφᾶς ἐν λόχμαις ὄρνιθας ὡς λέκτρων ἔχεσθαι* (of the mind's eye) : *El.*966 *καὶ μὴν ὄχοις γε καὶ στολῇ λαμπρύνεται* : *Rh.*546 *Καὶ μὴν ἀΐω* : Ar.*Ach* 247 *ἀνάδος δεῦρο τὴν ἐτνήρυσιν, ἵν' ἔτνος καταχέω . . .—Καὶ μὴν καλόν γ' ἔστ'*—(' There ! That 's splendid ') : *Av.*1462 *βέμβικος οὐδὲν διαφέρειν δεῖ.—Μανθάνω βέμβικα· καὶ μὴν ἔστι*

μοι νὴ τὸν Δία κάλλιστα Κορκυραῖα τοιαυτὶ πτερά ('See here'): *Pax* 513 *καὶ μὴν ὁμοῦ 'στιν ἤδη* (Peace appearing from the well): *Ra.*285 *Νὴ τὸν Δία καὶ μὴν αἰσθάνομαι ψόφου τινός*: 288 *Καὶ μὴν ὁρῶ νὴ τὸν Δία θηρίον μέγα*: *Pl.*1204 *οἴσω τὰς χύτρας.—Καὶ μὴν πολὺ τῶν ἄλλων χυτρῶν τἀναντία αὗται ποιοῦσι* ('Hullo!'): *Th.*568 *Οὐ δὴ μὰ Δία σύ γ' ἅψει.—Καὶ μὴν ἰδού.—Καὶ μὴν ἰδού.*

(8) Adversative (a use not yet to be found in Pindar). Since *καί* means 'and' and *μήν* often means 'yet', it might seem natural to regard *καὶ μήν* as combining two forms of connexion, copulative and adversative: 'and yet'. Such a fusion of two modes of connexion is perhaps not without parallel in Greek:[1] but it is no doubt preferable to derive adversative *καὶ μήν* from progressive *καὶ μήν*, and to regard *καί* alone as conveying the connexion, and *μήν* as ancillary. The adversative sense is, in origin at least, implied rather than expressed, as occasionally with *καί* (I.8), and frequently with *καίτοι*.

The objection may be urged by the speaker against another person, or against himself. A.*Pr.*982 *ἐκδιδάσκει πάνθ' ὁ γηράσκων χρόνος.—Καὶ μὴν σύ γ' οὔπω σωφρονεῖν ἐπίστασαι*: S.*Ant.* 1054 *Οὐ βούλομαι τὸν μάντιν ἀντειπεῖν κακῶς.—Καὶ μὴν λέγεις* ('Yet that is what you are doing'): E.*Hel.*554 *Οὐ κλῶπές ἐσμεν ...—Καὶ μὴν στολήν γ' ἄμορφον ... ἔχεις*: Ar.*Av.*1590 *Ἔλαιον οὐκ ἔνεστιν ἐν τῇ ληκύθῳ.—Καὶ μὴν τά γ' ὀρνίθεια λιπάρ' εἶναι πρέπει*: *Nu.*4 *οὐδέποθ' ἡμέρα γενήσεται; καὶ μὴν πάλαι γ' ἀλεκτρυόνος ἤκουσ' ἐγώ*: *Lys.*131 *Ταυτὶ σὺ λέγεις, ὦ ψῆττα; καὶ μὴν ἄρτι γε ἔφησθα ...*: *Pl.*93 *οὕτως ἐκεῖνος τοῖσι χρηστοῖσι φθονεῖ.—Καὶ μὴν διὰ τούς χρηστούς γε τιμᾶται μόνους*: A.*Ag.*1254: S.*OT*987,1066: *OC*396: *Ant.*558: *Aj.*531: *El.*321,1188: E.*Alc.* 1099: *Tr.*72: *Hipp.*589 (perhaps to be classed under (7)): Ar.*Nu.*1185,1414,1441: *Lys.*559: Pl.*Smp* 201C *Κινδυνεύω ... οὐδὲν εἰδέναι ὧν τότε εἶπον.—Καὶ μὴν καλῶς γε εἶπες*: *La.*199E *Οὐκ ἄρα ηὑρήκαμεν ... ἀνδρεία ὅτι ἔστιν.—Οὐ φαινόμεθα.—Καὶ μὴν ἔγωγε ... ᾤμην σε εὑρήσειν*: *Prt.*309A (where *καὶ μήν* seems to have *ἀνὴρ μέντοι*, rather than *καλὸς μὲν ἀνήρ*, in view): D. xviii 23 *ἔστιν ὅπου σὺ παρὼν ... ἐδίδαξας καὶ διεξῆλθες; καὶ μὴν εἰ ..., σοὶ τὸ μὴ σιγῆσαι λοιπὸν ἦν*: Pl.*Grg.*452C,511C:

[1] See Introduction, III.5.

*Smp.*202B: *Euthd.*304D: *Men.*89C: *Euthphr.*12A: *Phd.*92C: *R.*577C: *Lg.*664D.

Like μήν, ἀλλὰ μήν, and γε μήν, καὶ μήν is normally a balancing adversative. Very occasionally, however, it is as strong as ἀλλά or even μὲν οὖν. Ar.*Lys.*588 αἷς (ταῖς γυναιξὶ) οὐδὲ μετῆν πάνυ τοῦ πολέμου.—Καὶ μήν, ὦ παγκατάρατε, πλεῖν ἤ γε διπλοῦν αὐτὸν φέρομεν ('On the contrary'): *Pl.*67 Carion threatens Plutus with violence: Chremylus tries politeness, which fails. Κα. Καὶ μὴν ὃ λέγω βέλτιστόν ἐστ', ὦ δέσποτα. ἀπολῶ τὸν ἄνθρωπον κάκιστα τουτονί ('No, my idea's the best'): Pl.*Grg.* 471D καὶ ἐγὼ ὑπὸ σοῦ νῦν, ὡς σὺ οἴει, ἐξελήλεγμαι τούτῳ τῷ λόγῳ ...; πόθεν, ὠγαθέ; καὶ μὴν οὐδέν γέ σοι τούτων ὁμολογῶ ὧν σὺ φῄς ('On the contrary, I admit nothing that you say').

In X.*Mem.*iii 12.2–4 καὶ μήν is three times used in hypophora, instead of the more usual, and stronger, ἀλλά, in introducing objections. (Ant.v 44 is textually doubtful. If we retain the MSS. καὶ μὴν πολλῷ πλέον γε ἀγνοεῖν ἔστι, καὶ μήν introduces an imaginary objection, like ἀλλὰ νὴ Δία ('Mais, dira-t-on', Gernet), and the following καὶ μήν counters it, 'Yes, but'. With the emendation πολλῷ ἐπὶ πλέον γεγωνεῖν the first καὶ μήν means 'and yet', the second καὶ μήν 'moreover': there is, it is true, some awkwardness in the use of καὶ μήν in different senses at so short an interval.[1])

(9) Apodotic. (Cf. apodotic καί (II.B.9) and καὶ δή (2.vi).) Of this there appears to be but one example: Hom.*T*45 καί ῥ' οἵ περ ... μένεσκον ..., καὶ μὴν οἱ τότε γ' εἰς ἀγορὴν ἴσαν.

Καὶ ... μήν

Progressive καὶ μήν is occasionally split in Plato's later works. (Cf. the regular splitting of connective καὶ δή in Attic.) *Lg.* 644D Καὶ ἐν ἐμοὶ μὴν ταὐτὸν τοῦτο πάθος ἔνι: *Sph.*220B Καὶ τοῦ πτηνοῦ μὴν γένους ...: *Prm.*165A Καὶ ἴσος μὴν ... δοξασθήσεται. (But in A.*Ag.*1240 for καὶ σὺ μήν (which Verrall keeps) Auratus' καὶ σύ μ' ἐν has been generally, and rightly, adopted. For Philol.*Fr.*6 see καὶ μέν, *ad fin.*)

[1] See, however, Introduction, IV.

Μέν

The similarity between the uses of μήν (μάν) and μέν has been noted above. Nevertheless, the two particles have already begun to diverge in the earliest surviving Greek literature. The primary function of μέν, as of μήν, is emphatic, strongly affirming an idea or concentrating the attention upon it. But, as this process naturally entails the isolation of one idea from others, μέν acquires a concessive or antithetical sense, and serves to prepare the mind for a contrast of greater or lesser sharpness. (The same thing occurs in Latin, German, and English, with *sane*, *zwar*, 'certainly'.) The original, affirmative, sense of μέν nevertheless maintains some kind of precarious existence throughout classical Greek. Further, μέν shows some signs (especially with negatives) of developing the secondary senses of μήν, progressive and adversative. But these senses atrophy, except that adversative μέν becomes firmly established in the compounds μὲν δή, μέντοι, μὲν οὖν, and progressive μέν in μὲν δή, μέντοι.

I. Emphatic. The great majority of the examples are from Homer and Pindar (for οὐδὲ μέν in Ionic verse, see **A**.8): though survivals of this use are to be found in Aeschylus, Euripides, Xenophon, and other writers. Broadly speaking, preparatory μέν, already fully developed in Homer, ousts emphatic μέν from the field in the fifth and fourth centuries, and many cases which appear at first sight emphatic are really elliptically antithetical. It is often difficult to distinguish the one type from the other, μέν the bachelor from μέν the widower, particularly in Homer, where expression is reaching out tentatively towards logical relationships. Some authorities seem to go too far in making μέν emphatic wherever they possibly can: while, conversely, Hartung (ii 393) is perhaps wrong in refusing to recognize emphatic μέν at all (except in combination with other particles) in Attic Greek.

A. Homer, Hesiod, Pindar, Ionic verse (οὐδὲ μέν, see (8)). It will be convenient to take first the examples from these authors,[1] and

[1] I include a few cases in which μέν could conceivably be taken as preparatory, and would naturally be so taken in a later author.

to classify them according to the parts of speech preceding the particle, which usually, like other emphatic particles, immediately follows the emphasized word. Most frequently that word is a pronoun: less frequently a substantive, adjective, adverb, or verb.

(1) Substantives. Hom.*Γ*308 *Ζεὺς μέν που τό γε οἶδε καὶ ἀθάνατοι θεοὶ ἄλλοι*: *M*294 *αὐτίκα δ' ἀσπίδα μὲν πρόσθ' ἔσχετο* ('as though *δύο δὲ δοῦρε τίνασσε* (298) were to follow', Leaf): *P*336 *αἰδὼς μὲν νῦν ἥδε γ'*: *Υ*261 *Πηλεΐδης δὲ σάκος μὲν ἀπὸ ἕο χειρὶ παχείῃ ἔσχετο*: *Ω*237 *ὁ δὲ Τρῶας μὲν ἅπαντας αἰθούσης ἀπέεργεν*: *γ*317 *ἀλλ' ἐς μὲν Μενέλαον ἐγὼ κέλομαι . . . ἐλθεῖν.*

(2) Pronouns. Hom.*B*324 *ἡμῖν μὲν τόδ' ἔφηνε τέρας . . . Ζεύς* ('It is to *us* that Zeus has revealed this portent'): *I*69 *αὐτὰρ ἔπειτα, Ἀτρεΐδη, σὺ μὲν ἄρχε· σὺ γὰρ βασιλεύτατός ἐσσι*: K164 *Σχέτλιός ἐσσι, γεραιέ· σὺ μὲν πόνου οὔ ποτε λήγεις*: N47 *Αἴαντε, σφὼ μέν τε σαώσετε λαόν*: P556 *Σοὶ μὲν δή, Μενέλαε, κατηφείη καὶ ὄνειδος ἔσσεται*: *α*159 *τούτοισιν μὲν ταῦτα μέλει, κίθαρις καὶ ἀοιδή* (contemptuous): *ρ*595 *αὐτὸν μέν σε πρῶτα σάω*: Pi.*P*.4.174 *τάχα δὲ Κρονίδαο Ζηνὸς υἱοὶ τρεῖς ἀκαμαντομάχαι ἦλθον . . . τῶν μὲν κλέος ἐσλὸν . . . ἐκράνθη*: *I*.6.47 *νῦν σε . . . λίσσομαι παῖδα θρασὺν . . . ἀνδρὶ τῷδε . . . τελέσαι, τὸν μὲν ἄρρηκτον φυάν* (appositional, like *ille quidem*: an odd use): Hom.*Φ*437: *ε*23, 188: *id.saep.*: Pi.*P*.9.18: *I*.8.24,66.

Occasionally *μέν* stresses a pronoun which seems to need no stress. (Similarly *γε* (*q.v.* I.4) tends to attach itself to pronouns.) Hom.*E*656 *ὁ δ' ἀνέσχετο μείλινον ἔγχος Τληπόλεμος· καὶ τῶν μὲν ἁμαρτῇ δούρατα μακρὰ ἐκ χειρῶν ἤϊξαν*: *Σ*285 *Πουλυδάμα, σὺ μὲν οὐκέτ' ἐμοὶ φίλα ταῦτ' ἀγορεύεις*: *T*92 *Ἄτη . . . οὐλομένη· τῇ μέν θ' ἁπαλοὶ πόδες*: *α*166 *νῦν δ' ὁ μὲν ὣς ἀπόλωλε.*

When *μέν* follows a pronoun at the beginning of a sentence which is not introduced by a connecting particle proper, it seems to acquire a quasi-connective, progressive force (cf. *μήν*, III). Here, again, there often appears to be no need for stressing the pronoun. Hom.*ζ*13 *Ἀλκίνοος δὲ τότ' ἦρχε . . . τοῦ μὲν ἔβη πρὸς δῶμα . . . Ἀθήνη*: *λ*55 *πρώτη δὲ ψυχὴ Ἐλπήνορος ἦλθεν ἑταίρου . . . τὸν μὲν ἐγὼ δάκρυσα ἰδών*: *μ*234 *ἡμεῖς μὲν στεινωπὸν ἀνεπλέομεν γοόωντες*: Pi.*O*.1.75 *ὁ δ' αὐτῷ πὰρ ποδὶ σχεδὸν φάνη.*

τῷ μὲν εἶπε: Hom.μ134: Hes.*Th.*479: Pi.*O.*7.32: 13.60: *P.*3.72: 4.53: *I.*4.61.

Repeated. Hom.ι320 Κύκλωπος γὰρ ἔκειτο μέγα ῥόπαλον . . . τὸ μὲν ἔκταμεν, ὄφρα φοροίη αὐανθέν. τὸ μὲν ἄμμες ἐΐσκομεν . . . τοῦ μὲν . . . : τ459–62.

Essentially similar, though here the particle precedes the pronoun, are the following: Hom.Δ396 Τυδεὺς μὲν καὶ τοῖσιν . . . : Λ502 Ἕκτωρ μὲν μετὰ τοῖσιν . . . .

(3) Relatives (not sharply distinguishable from demonstratives, since ὁ is used for both). Hom.Α234 ναὶ μὰ τόδε σκῆπτρον, τὸ μὲν οὔ ποτε φύλλα καὶ ὄζους φύσει: Β101 ἔστη σκῆπτρον ἔχων, τὸ μὲν Ἥφαιστος κάμε τεύχων: Ο40: Π141: ε369: χ300: Pi.*P.*1.30.

With a relative bearing a causal force: Hom.υ377 Τηλέμαχ', οὔ τις σεῖο κακοξεινώτερος ἄλλος· οἷον μέν τινα τοῦτον ἔχεις ἐπίμαστον ἀλήτην ('quippe qui talem habeas mendicatorem': cf. ε183 οἷον δή, *s.v.* δή, I.9.v.*a.*).

(4) Adjectives. Hom.Α514 Νημερτὲς μὲν δή μοι ὑπόσχεο: δ100 ἀλλ' ἔμπης πάντας μὲν ὀδυρόμενος . . . : *h.Merc.*480 εὔκηλος μὲν ἔπειτα φέρειν εἰς δαῖτα θάλειαν.

(5) Adverbs. Hom.Δ257 Ἰδομενεῦ, περὶ μέν σε τίω Δαναῶν (ω24): ε290 ἀλλ' ἔτι μέν μίν φημι ἅδην ἐλάαν κακότητος: η259 ἔνθα μὲν ἑπτάετες μένον ἔμπεδον (δ87): ο220 οἱ δ' ἄρα τοῦ μάλα μὲν κλύον ἠδ' ἐπίθοντο (Hes.*Th.*474: Pi.*N.*10.54): σ79 Νῦν μὲν μήτ' εἴης, βουγάϊε (Pi.*O.*8.65): φ307 Ἔνδον μὲν δὴ ὅδ' αὐτὸς ἐγώ: Pi.*P.*4.1 σάμερον μέν: *N.*9.11 τότε μέν.

ὣς μέν, often in Homeric similes: Κ487: Μ436: Ρ740: ψ162: τὼς μέν, τ234.

(6) Verbs. Hom.Α216 Χρὴ μὲν σφωΐτερόν γε, θεά, ἔπος εἰρύσσασθαι (Ι309): β318 εἶμι μέν (the crucial decision): μ156 ἀλλ' ἐρέω μὲν ἐγών: Pi.*P.*3.77 ἀλλ' ἐπεύξασθαι μὲν ἐγὼν ἐθέλω (but see III.4.i): 4.279 ἐπέγνω μὲν Κυράνα.

With negatives. It will be practically convenient to group together, under the following three headings, the uses of μέν with negatives: though the force of the particle is not everywhere the same.

(7) *οὐ μέν.* (i) Most commonly *οὐ μέν* merely conveys an emphatic denial. Hom.*B*203 *οὐ μέν πως πάντες βασιλεύσομεν ἐνθάδ' Ἀχαιοί*: *Ξ*472 *οὐ μέν μοι κακὸς εἴδεται*: *B*233: *Z*326: *X*126: *Ψ*70: *ρ*415,483: *χ*462: Hes.*Sc.*357. In a subordinate clause, after *ἐπεί*: Hom.*K*79 *ἐπεὶ οὐ μὲν ἐπέτρεπε γήραϊ λυγρῷ*: *ε*364: *θ*585.

(ii) But in certain passages an adversative sense (for which, in general, see II) is at least appropriate. Hom.*Δ*158 *κατὰ δ' ὅρκια πιστὰ πάτησαν. οὐ μέν πως ἅλιον πέλει ὅρκιον*: 372 *Τυδέος υἱὲ . . . τί πτώσσεις . . .; οὐ μὲν Τυδέϊ γ' ὧδε φίλον πτωσκαζέμεν ἦεν*: *X*13 *σὺ δὲ δεῦρο λιάσθης. οὐ μέν με κτενέεις*: 283 *ὄφρα σ' ὑποδείσας μένεος ἀλκῆς τε λάθωμαι. οὐ μέν μοι φεύγοντι μεταφρένῳ ἐν δόρυ πήξεις*: *ω*251 *αὐχμεῖς τε κακῶς καὶ ἀεικέα ἕσσαι. οὐ μὲν ἀεργίης γε ἄναξ ἕνεκ' οὔ σε κομίζει.*

(iii) In other passages, again, *οὐ μέν*, following a negative sentence or clause, might conceivably be explained as progressive, 'nor again'. (Cf. *οὐ μήν*, *s.v. μήν*, III.2.i.) Hom.*A*603 *οὐδέ τι θυμὸς ἐδεύετο δαιτὸς ἐΐσης, οὐ μὲν φόρμιγγος περικαλλέος*: *ω*246 *οὐδέ τι πάμπαν, οὐ φυτόν, οὐ συκέη, οὐκ ἄμπελος, οὐ μὲν ἐλαίη, οὐκ ὄγχνη, οὐ πρασιή τοι ἄνευ κομιδῆς κατὰ κῆπον.* *O*738 might also be taken so, the preceding rhetorical question counting as a negative statement. But far more probably *μέν* is emphatic in all these passages, and asyndeton is to be assumed.

(8) At all events 'nor again' is normally *οὐδὲ μέν* in Epic and Ionic verse, corresponding to *οὐδὲ μήν* in Attic. Here, as with *οὐδὲ μήν*, it is difficult to say whether *οὐδέ* or *μέν* marks the connexion. (Ebeling prefers the former view.) Hom.*Z*489 *οὐ κακόν, οὐδὲ μὲν ἐσθλόν*: *A*154: *I*374: Hes.*Op.*785: Thgn.611,1080, 1142: Archil.*Fr.*78.3: Phoc.*Fr.*2.5: Xenoph.*Fr.*2.17: Emp. *Fr.*27.

Sometimes *οὐδὲ μέν* follows a positive statement, repeating or amplifying the same idea in a negative form. Hom.*O*688 *ὣς Αἴας . . . φοίτα . . . οὐδὲ μὲν Ἕκτωρ μίμνεν*: *M*82: *κ*447.

In Hom.*K*181, exceptionally, neither particle is connective, and *οὐδὲ μέν* means 'also not . . . indeed': *οἱ δ' ὅτε δὴ φυλάκεσσιν* ἐν ἀγρομένοισιν ἔμιχθεν, οὐδὲ μὲν εὕδοντας φυλάκων ἡγήτορας εὗρον ('The guards, too, were certainly not asleep, any more than their assailants.' 'An unusual form of the common δέ *in apodosi*', Leaf: but οὐδέ is adverbial here, not structural).

οὐδὲ μὲν οὐδέ. Hom.*K*299 βάν ῥ' ἴμεν ... οὐδὲ μὲν οὐδὲ Τρῶας ἀγήνορας εἴασεν Ἕκτωρ εὕδειν. The following admit, though they do not, perhaps, absolutely require, an adversative force in μέν: Hom.*B*703 'Protesilaus, their captain, was dead. οὐδὲ μὲν οὐδ' οἱ ἄναρχοι ἔσαν' ('Yet they, too, were not leaderless'[1]): *P*24: *T*295. Exceptionally, in a subordinate clause, neither particle being connective ('the repetition of the negative gives a rhetorical emphasis', Leaf): *M*212 ἐπεὶ οὐδὲ μὲν οὐδὲ ἔοικε ('Since it is indeed not seemly, either': φ319).

οὐδὲ μέν γ' οὐδ' cannot of course stand in Ar. *V*.480.

(9) οὐ μὲν οὐδέ is fairly common in Herodotus. Here μέν is clearly connective.

(i) Progressive, after preceding negative: ii 12 οὔτε τῇ Ἀραβίῃ ... οὔτε τῇ Λιβύῃ, οὐ μὲν οὐδὲ τῇ Συρίῃ: 49 οὐ γὰρ δὴ ... φήσω ... οὐ μὲν οὐδὲ φήσω ...: 142: iii 2: viii 130.3.

(ii) Introducing a new argument, with no preceding negative: ii 120.

(iii) Adversative:[2] iv 205 'Pheretime took a savage vengeance on the Barcaeans. οὐ μὲν οὐδὲ ἡ Φερετίμη εὖ τὴν ζόην κατέπλεξε'. Here οὐδέ has the force of οὐκ αὖ: 'However, Pheretime, on her side, came to a bad end'. vi 45.1 (οὐ μέντοι οὐδέ *ABCP*) and vi 71.2 are closely similar. viii 25.2 and ix 7α2 are quite different: here the meaning 'not, either', 'not, again' is inappropriate, and οὐδέ seems to be merely an emphatic negative, 'not at all'. For a discussion of these last two passages, see οὐδέ, III.

Herodotean οὐ μὲν οὐδέ is certainly puzzling. (Stein ignores the difficulties.) It seems artificial to assume such various explanations of the combination. But a more uniform treatment would, I think, do violence to the facts.

[1] This would follow naturally enough upon the description of other tribes and their chieftains: but it certainly comes awkwardly after the description of the leaderless contingent of Achilles, 681–94: whereas in 726 οὐδὲ μὲν οὐδέ is natural (as Leaf observes: but I cannot agree with his explanation).

[2] It would be possible to regard the first three examples as progressive. Cf. οὐ μὴν οὐδέ, *s.v.* μήν, III.2.ii.

B. In Attic the use of emphatic *μέν* is extremely limited. It is often difficult to decide whether *μέν* is to be taken as purely emphatic, or as suggesting an unexpressed antithesis (the so-called *μέν solitarium*: see III.5 below). The following list of possible examples could hardly be materially increased: as my observations show, it should probably be materially reduced. Most of the passages are from tragedy and Xenophon.

(1) In statements. A.*Pers.*548 *Νῦν δὴ πρόπασα μὲν στένει γαῖ' Ἀσὶς ἐκκεκενωμένα* (but very probably Paley's *δέ* in 558 is right, and answers this *μέν*, not, as Paley thought, the *μέν* in 554, which I believe to be *solitarium* (see III.5.i): there is everywhere a close connexion of thought between strophe and antistrophe in this chorus): 730 *Πρὸς τάδ' ὡς Σούσων μὲν ἄστυ πᾶν κενανδρίαν στένειν* (*μέγ'* Mayer: but the thought is completed by *Βακτρίων δ' ἔρρει πανώλης δῆμος* in 732): 1014 *Πῶς δ' οὔ; στρατὸν μὲν τοσοῦτον τάλας πέπληγμαι.—Τί δ' οὐκ ὄλωλεν . . . Περσᾶν*; (but here, again, as the answer suggests, the utterance may be incomplete): *Supp.*991 (but most editors emend here: and *μέν* may be answered by *δέ* in 996): *Ch.*400 *Ἀλλὰ νόμος μὲν φονίας σταγόνας . . . ἄλλο προσαιτεῖν αἷμα* ('*μέν* simply affirmative', Verrall: Tucker supposes the implication of a suppressed clause): *Fr.*99.2 *ταύρῳ τε λειμὼν ξένια πάμβοτος παρῆν. τοιόνδε μὲν Ζεὺς κλέμμα . . . ἤνυσεν λαβεῖν* (a clear case of emphatic *μέν*, if the text is sound: '*τοιόνδε δή malim*' Nauck): S.*El.*1307 *ἀλλ' οἶσθα μὲν τἀνθένδε, πῶς γὰρ οὔ*; (but *μέν* seems to look forward to a request for orders, which follows, after a digression, in 1319): *OC*702 *τὸ μέν τις οὐ . . . ἁλιώσει*: E.*El.*631 *Δμῶες μέν εἰσιν οἵ σέ γ' οὐκ εἶδόν ποτε* (I read no comma after *εἰσιν*: 'The *slaves* are people who have never seen you before': the suppressed thought is, I think, 'But there may be others, besides slaves, in the *οἰκεία χείρ*, who *have* seen you'): 649 *Ὑπηρετείτω μὲν δυοῖν ὄντοιν ὅδε* (*δ' εἷς* (for *μέν*), Weil, with much probability): *Supp.*767 *Κἄστρωσέ γ' εὐνὰς κἀκάλυψε σώματα.—Δεινὸν μὲν ἦν βάσταγμα κᾀσχύνην ἔχον* ('Well, certainly, it was a terrible task to perform' ('but perhaps he was right')): *Hel.* 664 *Λέγ'· ὡς ἀκουστὰ . . .—Ἀπέπτυσα μὲν λόγον, οἷον οἷον ἐσοίσομαι.—Ὅμως δὲ λέξον* (the unexpressed antithesis is expressed in the answer): *Hipp.*882 *Τόδε μὲν οὐκέτι στόματος ἐν πύλαις καθέξω* (there is no apparent implied contrast here: *τόδ' ἐμόν*

MOv): in E.*Heracl.*181 μέν (for which Wilamowitz reads γάρ) looks forward to δέ in 184: 'While Athenian law is impartial, there is here no case in law at all'.

Pl.*R.*403E *Τί δὲ δὴ σίτων πέρι; ἀθληταὶ μὲν γὰρ οἱ ἄνδρες τοῦ μεγίστου ἀγῶνος* (μέν perhaps implies that this is only one out of many aspects under which the guardians may be considered): 460B *ἀρχαὶ εἴτε ἀνδρῶν εἴτε γυναικῶν εἴτε ἀμφότερα—κοιναὶ μὲν γάρ που καὶ ἀρχαὶ γυναιξί τε καὶ ἀνδράσιν— —Ναί* (μὲν γάρ *AM*: γάρ *FD*): *Phdr.*228B *ἀπαντήσας δὲ τῷ νοσοῦντι περὶ λόγων ἀκοήν, ἰδὼν μέν, ἰδὼν ἥσθη ὅτι ἕξοι τὸν συγκορυβαντιῶντα* (the MSS. vary: but this text looks to me genuine: it is perhaps a poetical quotation or reminiscence: μέν is clearly not answered by δέ after δεομένου): *Lg.*953D *ἴτω μὲν νῦν κτλ.* (I should prefer νυν. Emphatic μέν here is perhaps a poetical reminiscence: England compares *R.*364B ('a semi-proverbial expression', Adam) and 489B): X.*Cyr.*i 6.2 *Ὦ παῖ, ὅτι μὲν οἱ θεοὶ . . . πέμπουσί σε . . . δῆλον* (where μέν is not answered by the following δέ: but it may be *solitarium*, '*this* is clear, though other things may be obscure'): ii 1.4 *Ἀγωνιστέον μὲν ἄρα ἡμῖν πρὸς τοὺς ἄνδρας*: vi 3.18 *Σὺ μὲν ἄρα . . . οἶσθα . . . .—Ἐγὼ μὲν ναὶ μὰ Δί', ἔφη* (the first μέν (*om. CE*) is rather different from the examples of σὺ μέν given under III.5.ii: the second seems to be assentient, for *Ἔγωγε*: cf. μέντοι, μὲν δή, μὲν οὖν).*

Ἀλλὰ . . . μέν in Xenophon[1] demands separate treatment. Krüger (on *An.*i 7.6) observes that in *Ἀλλὰ . . . μέν* at the opening of an answer μέν is often not balanced by a following δέ, and that in such cases μέν is equivalent to μήν in force, as (admittedly) in ἀλλὰ μὲν δή, καὶ μὲν δή, οὐ μὲν δή. *An.*vii 6.11 *Ἀλλὰ πάντα μὲν ἄρα ἄνθρωπον ὄντα προσδοκᾶν δεῖ, ὁπότε γε καὶ ἐγὼ νῦν ὑφ' ὑμῶν αἰτίας ἔχω . . .*: i 7.6 (μέν perhaps answered by δέ in §7): vii 1.9 (perhaps, in spite of the order, answered by οἱ δὲ στρατιῶται): *Mem.*i 2.2 (not formally at the opening of an answer, but rebutting a charge presented in a rhetorical question:

[1] A. Platt (*C.R.* xxv (1911), 14) rather light-heartedly assumes the equivalence of ἀλλὰ . . . μέν and ἀλλὰ μὲν δή, ἀλλὰ μήν in Pl.*R.*614B and other passages, where, as R. W. Chapman shows in his reply (*ib.* pp. 204–5), a contrasted idea *precedes* μέν (see III.4.i). Platt does not cite the most remarkable of the Xenophontine passages, and seems to be unaware that Krüger has anticipated him.

πῶς οὖν . . . ἄλλους ἂν ἢ ἀσεβεῖς ἢ παρανόμους . . . ἐποίησεν; ἀλλ' ἔπαυσε μὲν τούτων πολλοὺς ἀρετῆς ποιήσας ἐπιθυμεῖν: but this may stand for ἔπαυσε μὲν . . . ἐποίησε δὲ . . .: cf. III.4.ii.*b*).[1] I add the following: *HG* ii 3.35 Ἀλλὰ πρῶτον μὲν μνησθήσομαι, ὦ ἄνδρες, ὃ τελευταῖον κατ' ἐμοῦ εἶπε (not 'First of all I will mention', but 'I will mention first': μέν does not very definitely look forward here, as it does in III.5.iv): vii 3.7 Ἀλλ' ὑπερορᾶν μὲν . . . οὐ δυνατὸν ὑμῶν (μέν is perhaps answered by τίνι μὴν πιστεύων . . .;): *Mem.* ii 6.21 Ἀλλ' ἔχει μὲν . . . ποικίλως πως ταῦτα. In *Oec.* 7.3 μέν is really answered by οὐ γὰρ δὴ . . .: in *An.* vii 6.9, by εἰ μὴ Ξενοφῶν . . . .

What is the true explanation of this Xenophontine ἀλλὰ . . . μέν? "Ἔχει ποικίλως πως ταῦτα." Krüger's view is at first sight attractive, and it accounts adequately for some awkward passages. But on reflection it appears improbable. μέν (sometimes without a contrasted idea expressed or implied) often has a certain inceptive force. (See III.5.v.) Xenophon seems to combine this quasi-inceptive μέν with the inceptive ἀλλά which he uses so freely. (See ἀλλά, II.8.) Usually (I have counted about forty instances, and there are no doubt many more) μέν is answered explicitly or implicitly. Hence ἀλλὰ . . . μέν becomes for Xenophon a stereotyped opening formula, occasionally used even where no answer is readily to be found or imagined. There is, I think, a unity about the use of the formula that it would be artificial to disintegrate.

Pl. *La.* 182D resembles the Xenophontine examples: Ἀλλ' ἔστι μέν, ὦ Νικία, χαλεπὸν λέγειν . . . . Here I think μέν is answered by καὶ δὴ καί.

(2) In questions. The above examples are rather heterogeneous, and highly inconclusive. μέν in questions (with which we may perhaps compare interrogative μέντοι, though the tone is quite different, μέν being uncertain and tentative, μέντοι impatient or conversationally lively) has the appearance of a far more clear-cut idiom. Most of the examples are from Euripides, with one or two from Aristophanes and Plato. The force of μέν in

[1] Kühner (*ad loc.*) holds (wrongly, I think) that μέν looks forward to καίτοι.

questions is thus expressed by Verrall (on E.*Med.*676, following Hermann on Elmsley's *Med.*1098): 'μέν in an interrogative sentence as elsewhere marks the proposition as preliminary[1] and points to a sequel. It implies therefore that the speaker either wishes or feels bound to assume it true.'* Hadley (on E.*Hipp.* 316, which is, however, I think, rather different: see below) quotes Verrall, and adds: 'It [μέν] generally implies that unless the answer is "yes", the discussion cannot go on'.[2]

E.*Alc.*146 Ἐλπὶς μὲν οὐκέτ' ἐστὶ σῴζεσθαι βίον; (if there *is* hope, it is premature to discuss the misery of the bereaved Admetus, as in 144–5): *Med.*1129 Τί φῄς; φρονεῖς μὲν ὀρθὰ κοὐ μαίνῃ, γύναι . . .; (it is no good starting a conversation with a person, unless you can assume that they are sane: cf. *Ion*520 Εὖ φρονεῖς μέν; Ar.*Av.*1214 Ὑγιαίνεις μέν;): *E.Med.*676 Θέμις μὲν ἡμᾶς χρησμὸν εἰδέναι θεοῦ; (*sc.* 'If not, I will curb my inquisitiveness'): *Hel.*1226 Ὀρθῶς μὲν ἥδε συμφορὰ δακρύεται; (this is surely a question (so Pearson: not, as Murray takes it, an interrupted statement), *sc.* 'If Menelaus is not dead, we need not discuss what to do in view of his death'): Ar.*Th.*97 Ἀλλ' ἦ τυφλὸς μέν εἰμ'; ἐγὼ γὰρ οὐχ ὁρῶ ἄνδρ' οὐδέν' (certainly a question, with ἀλλ' ἦ read for ἀλλ' ἤ: see ἀλλ' ἦ, p. 28): Pl.*Chrm.*153C Παρεγένου μέν, ἦ δ' ὅς, τῇ μάχῃ; ('Were you *there*?' (*sc.* 'If not, there is no point in asking you questions')): *Men.*82B Ἕλλην μέν ἐστι καὶ ἑλληνίζει; (*sc.* 'If the boy cannot talk Greek, he is of no use to us'). E.*Hipp.*316 seems rather different: ἄλλῃ δ' ἐν τύχῃ χειμάζομαι.—Ἁγνὰς μέν, ὦ παῖ, χεῖρας αἵματος φορεῖς; (μέν shows that blood-guilt is only the first cause suggested for Phaedra's trouble and that other suggestions will follow, the question being not so much a preliminary, to clear the ground, as the first of an intended series: the interrogative force is, I think, slight: 'Your hands are free of blood, I suppose?'). *

Fundamentally distinct from all the above is Pl.*Tht.*161E τὸ γὰρ ἐπισκοπεῖν . . . οὐ μακρὰ μὲν καὶ διωλύγιος φλυαρία, εἰ ἀληθὴς ἡ Ἀλήθεια Πρωταγόρου, ἀλλὰ μὴ παίζουσα . . . ἐφθέγξατο; ('μέν points forward to the alternative implied in ἀλλὰ μὴ παίζουσα, κτλ. "But then perhaps he was in jest"', Campbell,

[1] Hence it would really be more logical to class this under III, as a 'preparatory' use.

[2] This explanation had occurred to me independently.

rightly, I am inclined to think). The new turn given to the sentence by μέν is merely an incidental afterthought. μέν *om. W*: certainly the particle is very difficult here.

II. Adversative. The existence of this use has often been denied, and the evidence for it is certainly not strong. But (not to mention μὲν δή, μὲν οὖν, μέντοι, γε μέν) we have seen above (I.A.7–9) that in certain places μέν following negatives is, or may be, adversative. And in two Homeric passages positive μέν seems to be adversative. (1) *M*344 αἶψα δ' ἐπ' Αἴαντα προΐει κήρυκα Θοώτην· "ἔρχεο, δῖε Θοῶτα, θέων Αἴαντα κάλεσσον, ἀμφοτέρω μὲν μᾶλλον" (where μὲν οὖν would be used in Attic: 'Nay, better, the twain of them'). There is, however, another reading Αἴαντε, and, if this is correct,[1] Leaf must be right in interpreting μὲν μᾶλλον as μάλιστα μέν. In giving the message, the herald repeats ἀμφοτέρω μὲν μᾶλλον, which (with Αἴαντε) can only mean μάλιστα μὲν α.: 354 Αἴαντ', Ἀργείων ἡγήτορε ... ἠνώγει ... κεῖσ' ἴμεν ... ἀμφοτέρω μὲν μᾶλλον. If, then, Αἴαντα is right in 343, μέν seems to bear different senses in the two passages. This would certainly be surprising, and γ195–203 (where μέν in Nestor's mouth is purely emphatic, while when repeated by Telemachus it has an antithetical tinge) is far less remarkable. (2) *Ω*92 τίπτε με κεῖνος ἄνωγε μέγας θεός; αἰδέομαι δὲ μίσγεσθ' ἀθανάτοισιν, ἔχω δ' ἄχε' ἄκριτα θυμῷ. εἶμι μέν, οὐδ' ἅλιον ἔπος ἔσσεται. μέν is clearly adversative here, as Leaf takes it, while in β318, εἶμι μέν, οὐδ' ἁλίη ὁδὸς ἔσσεται, it is clearly emphatic.

In Hp.*Iudic.*10 it is possible to take μέν as adversative: μάλιστα μὲν οὖν ταῦτα ποιέει κρίσιν ... ποιέει δὲ καὶ ἕτερα κρίσεις, ἧττον μὲν τουτέων: but μέν may equally be concessive, though looking back (as in III.4.i): 'to a less degree, certainly' (but still they do produce the effect). In *Fract.*37 and *Art.*55 Petrequin's μέν has no MS. authority: but *Fract.*6 μὴ μὲν πολλῷ *vulg.*, μήν *cett.* In X.*HG* iv 1.6 an adversative sense would suit the context: Τὸν δὲ υἱόν, ἔφη, ἑόρακας αὐτοῦ ὡς καλός ἐστι.—Τί δ' οὐ μέλλω; . . .—Τούτου μέν φασι τὴν θυγατέρα αὐτῷ καλλίονα εἶναι. But, in default

[1] It must be admitted, however, that the logical inconsequence of 'Call Ajax, both of them if possible' is not very startling: and, even with the singular, Leaf's interpretation may well be right.

of Attic parallels, we should regard *μέν* as affirmative here, or better, perhaps, read *μέντοι*.

III. Preparatory. (1) Normally preparatory *μέν* introduces the first limb of a grammatically co-ordinated antithesis,[1] the second limb being introduced by an adversative particle or combination of particles. But there are many exceptions to this principle. Viz.: (2) The second clause is introduced by a non-adversative particle (e.g. *τε, καί, τοίνυν*): (3) It is not introduced by any particle at all: (4) The contrasted idea is expressed, not in a following co-ordinated clause, but in what precedes; or one of the two clauses is subordinated to the other: (5) The contrasted idea is not expressed, either paratactically or hypotactically, but left to the imagination.

(1) Normal use. *δέ* is by far the commonest answer to *μέν*. But (*a*) *οὐ δέ* is almost entirely avoided (see *δέ*, III.A.5: for *μὲν . . . οὐδέ* see *οὐδέ*, I.1.i), either by inversion (*δὲ οὔ, δὲ . . . οὔ*),

[1] When a relative clause is divided into co-ordinated sub-clauses, of which the second demands a different case for the relative pronoun, the relative in the second sub-clause is omitted, or a demonstrative substituted for it. D.xviii 82 *οὓς ἡ μὲν πόλις . . . ἀπήλασε, σοὶ δ' ἦσαν φίλοι*: Hom.K244: E.*Supp.*862: Pl.*R.*533D: D.ix 47. In such cases *μέν* is usually omitted in the first sub-clause. Kühner II ii 267, 431–3.

A similar transition from participial to finite construction is often found. Hom.E145 *ἕλεν Ἀστύνοον καὶ Ὑπείρονα . . . τὸν μὲν . . . βαλὼν . . . τὸν δ' ἕτερον . . . πλῆξ'*: S.*Tr.*836 *πῶς ὅδ' ἂν ἀέλιον ἕτερον . . . ἴδοι, δεινοτάτῳ μὲν ὕδρας προστετακὼς νήματι; μελαγχαίτα τ' ἄμμιγά νιν αἰκίζει φόνια . . . κέντρ'*: Hom. E593: Σ173: S.*Tr.*265 (if Jebb is right): *OC* 522 *ἤνεγκ' ἀέκων μὲν . . . τούτων δ' αὐθαίρετον οὐδέν*: Ant.v 27 *κᾆτ' ἐγὼ συγχωρῶ τῷ τούτων λόγῳ, παρεχόμενος μὲν τοὺς μάρτυρας ὡς οὐκ ἐξέβην ἐκ τοῦ πλοίου; εἰ δὲ καὶ ὡς μάλιστα ἐξέβην ἐκ τοῦ πλοίου, οὐδενὶ τρόπῳ εἰκὸς ἦν . . .* (*μέν* has been suspected here: but, though the change of subject adds to the real difficulty, and modern punctuation to the apparent difficulty, of this and S.*Tr.*836, it is certainly not too harsh for Antiphon): S.*OC* 348: Th.iv 72.1: X.*Mem.*ii 1.30: D.lvii 11. Cf. S.*El.*190 (from prepositional phrase to independent construction): *OT* 1135 (from comitative dative to independent construction): E.*Ba.*224: X.*An.*i 10.12: ii 1.7 (all from appositional to independent construction): cf. also Lys.xii 15. For similar changes of construction without *μέν*, see Jebb, *ad locc.*, Kühner, *locc. cit.*

(Kühner (II ii 100) rightly distinguishes from such passages quite different ones (Th.i 52.2, 67.2) in which the *μέν* clause is *subordinated* to a main clause containing the contrasted idea. See III.4.ii.)

or by postponement of δέ (see δέ, III.A.5), or by the substitution of another particle (usually μήν or μέντοι): (β) μήν, μέντοι, ἀλλά, ἀτάρ, etc., are sometimes used instead of δέ where a stronger adversative is required. μὲν ... δέ is in itself too common to need illustration. But certain points should be noted.

(i) The strength of the antithesis varies within wide limits. Sometimes μὲν ... δέ conveys little more than τε ... καί. D. ii.11 τοῖς μὲν Ὀλυνθίοις βοηθεῖν ... πρὸς δὲ Θετταλοὺς πρεσβείαν πέμπειν: S.*Aj*.624: *Fr*.619.

This is particularly the case when the same word is repeated before μέν and δέ (the figure of anaphora, exceedingly common throughout Greek literature, verse and prose).[1] Hom.*A*288 πάντων μὲν κρατέειν ἐθέλει, πάντεσσι δ' ἀνάσσειν: S.*Tr*.229 Ἀλλ' εὖ μὲν ἵγμεθ', εὖ δὲ προσφωνούμεθα: Hdt.i 45.3 Ἄδρηστος δὲ ... οὗτος δὴ ὁ φονεὺς μὲν τοῦ ἑωυτοῦ ἀδελφεοῦ γενόμενος, φονεὺς δὲ τοῦ καθήραντος: Th.i 85.2: 126.12: vi 20.4: Pl.*Lg*.697D, 739C: Ant.v 62: Lys.xii 94: xiii 1: D.xix 84. With an unemphatic word repeated: E.*Heracl*.491 εἰ χρὴ μὲν ἡμᾶς, χρὴ δὲ τήνδ' εἶναι πόλιν. With a strong sense of contrast: S.*Ant*.616–7 ἐλπὶς πολλοῖς μὲν ὄνασις ἀνδρῶν, πολλοῖς δ' ἀπάτα κουφονόων ἐρώτων.

Similarly in passages where the μέν clause gives the time or circumstances in which the δέ clause takes place. E.*Supp*.650 Λαμπρὰ μὲν ἀκτὶς ἡλίου ... ἔβαλλε γαῖαν· ἀμφὶ δ' Ἠλέκτρας πύλας ἔστην: *Ba*.677: B.5.144.

(ii) Often, on the other hand, the antithesis carries an idea of strong contrast, so that in English we should make one of the clauses concessively dependent on the other. In such cases the weight is far more frequently on the δέ clause. (See Dissen, *De structura periodorum oratoria* (preface to ed. of *De Corona*).) D.ii 9 εἴ τις ὑμῶν ταῦτα μὲν οὕτως ἔχειν ἡγεῖται, οἴεται δὲ ... ('while thinking'): 24: iii 20: xix 267. Cases, however, are not lacking where the μέν clause bears the weight. D.xviii 125 ὅρα μὴ τούτων μὲν ἐχθρὸς ᾖς, ἐμοὶ δὲ προσποιῇ ('while pretending to be mine'): S.*OT* 673 (see Jebb): E.*Med*.726: *Or*.1076. In E.*Cyc*.199 the weight is on the first clause, but there is no μέν (see also p. 165).

(iii) In ὁ μὲν ... ὁ δέ, ὁ μέν normally refers to the first, ὁ

[1] For the relative frequency of anaphora in various prose authors, see Blass, *Att. Ber.*, Index, *s.v. anaphora*: Rehdantz, Index, *s.v. anaphora* (commonest in Xenophon).

δέ to the second substantive. But occasionally the order of reference is reversed. Th.iii 82.7 *ῥᾷον δ' οἱ πολλοὶ κακοῦργοι ὄντες δεξιοὶ κέκληνται ἢ ἀμαθεῖς ἀγαθοί, καὶ τῷ μὲν αἰσχύνονται, ἐπὶ δὲ τῷ ἀγάλλονται*: i 68.4: iv 62.2: X.*An.*i 10.4. (Kühner II ii 264, *Anm.*1.)

(iv) (*a*) Normally *μέν* and *δέ* stand second in their respective clauses, and everything between the last stop and the word preceding *μέν* applies to the whole *μὲν* . . . *δέ* complex. (Strictly speaking, one should say, not ' clause ' but ' word-group ', which does not necessarily coincide with punctuation.) Thus we often find *οὐ* negativing a whole *μὲν* . . . *δέ* complex.[1] D.xviii 13 *οὐ γὰρ δήπου Κτησιφῶντα μὲν δύναται διώκειν δι' ἐμέ, ἐμὲ δ', εἴπερ ἐξελέγξειν ἐνόμιζεν, αὐτὸν οὐκ ἂν ἐγράψατο* (' It is not the case that, while able to . . . he would not have . . . '): 288 *καὶ οὐχ ὁ μὲν δῆμος οὕτως, οἱ δὲ τῶν τετελευτηκότων πατέρες . . . ἄλλως πως*: E.*IT* 116: *Hel.*575: Pl.*Grg.*512A: Ant.v 63: Lys.xii 47. Or an adjectival or substantival expression applies to the whole complex: D.xviii 31 *τὸ μὲν τοίνυν ἐν τῇ πρεσβείᾳ πρῶτον κλέμμα μὲν Φιλίππου, δωροδόκημα δὲ τῶν ἀδίκων τούτων ἀνθρώπων*: xix 90 *ἡ δέ γε τῶν πραγμάτων κατασκευὴ . . . ἡ μὲν ἡμετέρα . . . ἡ δ' ἐκείνου* . . . . Cf. S.*Aj.*765.

(*b*) The words standing immediately before *μέν* and *δέ* are usually corresponding elements in the contrasted thoughts, and, further, the most important elements in the contrast: while the subsidiary elements in the contrast follow, often in symmetrical order, in the two clauses. That Isocrates favours this symmetrical arrangement goes without saying. But even Demosthenes, who was so free from a pedantic love of uniformity that a contemporary comic poet (Timocles, *Fr.*12) accused him of ' never uttering an antithesis in his life ', sometimes does the same: e.g. i 10,16: xviii 68: though he often varies the order, and deliberately avoids a too obvious symmetry, underlined by assonance.

But these principles, predominant though they are in the highly polished prose writing of the fourth century, are even then far from being hard and fast rules: while in earlier and less developed prose, and even more in verse, where order is partly

[1] Schoolboys and undergraduates often go astray here: but it is surprising to find mature scholars sometimes falling into the trap.

determined by metrical convenience, they are constantly subject to exception.[1]

Hom.*N*13 ἔνθεν γὰρ ἐφαίνετο πᾶσα μὲν Ἴδη, φαίνετο δὲ Πριάμοιο πόλις: *h.Ap.*488, *h.Merc.*509: A.*Ag.*759 τὸ δυσσεβὲς γὰρ ἔργον μέτα μὲν πλείονα τίκτει, σφετέρᾳ δ' εἰκότα γέννᾳ: *Ch.*554 Ἁπλοῦς ὁ μῦθος· τήνδε μὲν στείχειν ἔσω, αἰνῶ δὲ κρύπτειν τάσδε συνθήκας ἐμάς: S.*OT*15 ὁρᾷς μὲν ἡμᾶς . . . τὸ δ' ἄλλο φῦλον . . . θακεῖ: *Ph.*307 οὗτοί μ' . . . λόγοις ἐλεοῦσι μὲν . . . ἐκεῖνο δ' οὐδεὶς . . . θέλει: 919 Σῶσαι κακοῦ μὲν πρῶτα τοῦδ', ἔπειτα δὲ . . . πορθῆσαι: E.*Hel.*264 καὶ τὰς τύχας μὲν τὰς κακὰς . . . τὰς δὲ μὴ κακὰς . . .: *Fr.*291 ὦ παῖ, νέων τοι δρᾶν μὲν ἔντονοι χέρες, γνῶμαι δ' ἀμείνους εἰσὶ τῶν γεραιτέρων: Ar.*Ach.*117 καὶ τοῖν μὲν εὐνούχοιν τὸν ἕτερον τουτονὶ ἐγᾦδ' ὅς ἐστι . . . ὁδὶ δὲ τίς ποτ' ἐστίν; *Th.*266 Ἁνὴρ μὲν ἡμῖν οὑτοσὶ καὶ δὴ γυνὴ τό γ' εἶδος· ἢν λαλῇς δ', ὅπως τῷ φθέγματι γυναικιεῖς εὖ: *Pl.*1120 Πρότερον γὰρ εἶχον μὲν . . . πάντ' ἀγάθ' . . . νυνὶ δὲ πεινῶν ἀναβάδην ἀναπαύομαι: *Pax* 774 Μοῦσα σὺ μὲν . . . μετ' ἐμοῦ τοῦ φίλου χόρευσον . . ., ἤν δέ σε Καρκίνος ἐλθὼν ἀντιβολῇ . . . χορεῦσαι, μήθ' ὑπάκουε . . .: A.*Supp.*940: E.*Tr.* 1232.*

Prose (particularly Antiphon). Hdt.i 131 οἱ δὲ νομίζουσι Διὶ μὲν ἐπὶ τὰ ὑψηλότατα τῶν ὀρέων ἀναβαίνοντες θυσίας ἔρδειν . . . θύουσι δὲ ἡλίῳ τε καὶ σελήνῃ: Pl.*Ti.*21A ποῖον ἔργον τοῦτο Κριτίας οὐ λεγόμενον μέν, ὡς δὲ πραχθὲν ὄντως . . . διηγεῖτο . . .; 21D ἣν ἥδε ἡ πόλις ἔπραξε μέν, διὰ δὲ χρόνον . . . οὐ διήρκεσε δεῦρο ὁ λόγος: X.*Smp.*4.32 καὶ εἰμὶ νῦν μὲν τυράννῳ ἐοικώς, τότε δὲ σαφῶς δοῦλος ἦν: Ant.i 23 δεήσεται δ' ὑμῶν οὗτος μὲν ὑπὲρ τῆς μητρὸς . . . ἐγὼ δ' ὑμᾶς ὑπὲρ τοῦ πατρὸς . . . αἰτοῦμαι: ii α9 μάρτυρες δ' εἰ μὲν πολλοὶ παρεγένοντο, πολλοὺς ἂν παρεσχόμεθα· ἑνὸς δὲ τοῦ ἀκολούθου παραγενομένου . . .: ii γ9 ἡμεῖς δὲ ὑμῶν δεόμεθα μὲν οὐδέν, λέγομεν δ' ὑμῖν . . .: iii α2 τῷ δὲ ἀποθανόντι αὐτῷ μὲν οὐδὲν ἐνθύμιον, τοῖς δὲ ζῶσι προσέθηκεν: v 20 ἐγὼ δὲ τὸν μὲν πλοῦν ἐποιησάμην ἐκ τῆς Μυτιλήνης . . . ἐπλέομεν δὲ εἰς τὴν Αἶνον: vi 17 αἰτιῶνται δὲ οὗτοι μὲν ἐκ τούτων, ὡς . . . ἐγὼ δ' ἐξ αὐτῶν τούτων ὧν αἰτιῶνται οὗτοι ἀποφανῶ ὅτι οὐκ ἔνοχός εἰμι: Pl.*Cra.*385C: *R.*573E: *Lg.*761A, 874D, 902D.

[1] Demetrius (*De Eloc.* 53), in discussing τὸ μεγαλοπρεπές, deprecates excessive regularity: Χρὴ δὲ καὶ τοὺς συνδέσμους μὴ μάλα ἀνταποδίδοσθαι ἀκριβῶς, οἷον τῷ "μέν" συνδέσμῳ τὸν "δέ"· μικροπρεπὲς γὰρ ἡ ἀκρίβεια· ἀλλὰ καὶ ἀτακτοτέρως πως χρῆσθαι.

The above transpositions are all more or less violent. Far commoner is the postponement of μέν (paralleled in the case of other particles) to third or fourth place after article-substantive (etc.), preposition-substantive, article-preposition-substantive.[1]

S.*OT*620 τὰ τοῦδε μέν: *El.*1424 τὰν δόμοισι μέν: Hdt.i 93 ἡ κρηπὶς μέν: ix 18.3 τὰ περὶ Φωκέων μέν (77.3): Th.iii 22.1 ἀνὰ τὸ σκοτεινὸν μέν: X.*Smp.*2.17 τὰ σκέλη μὲν . . . τοὺς ὤμους δέ (directly afterwards τοὺς μὲν ὤμους . . . τὰ δὲ σκέλη): Timocl. *Fr.*9.3: Hdt.ii 20: Th.ii 98.2: iv 134.2: Pl.*Ti.*67B,88B: *Lg.*806C: X.*Smp.*2.2: And.i 99,106: D.xix 271,299: Pl.*Criti.*121A ἡ τοῦ θεοῦ μὲν μοῖρα: *R.*607E διὰ τὸν ἐγγεγονότα μὲν ἔρωτα.

Postponement after negatives: Pl.*Lg.*876B οὐκ εὐτυχὲς μέν: 928E μὴ κακοῦ μὲν πατρός: And.i 72 μὴ πείθων μέν: iii 26: Arist.*MM*1209a21 οὐχ αἱ αὐταὶ μέν, οὐ παντελῶς δὲ οὐδὲ ἀλλότριαι ἀλλήλων ('on the one hand, not the same'). After ὡς: Ant.ii β3 ὡς δεινὸν μὲν . . . ὡς δ' ἠλίθιον. After other closely cohering words: Hdt.i 87 τῇ σῇ μὲν εὐδαιμονίῃ: Pl.*Lg.*759D τρὶς φερέτωσαν μέν: 842E Διὸς ὁρίου μέν: 948C μέρος τι μέν.

Where the μὲν . . . δέ complex is joined to what precedes by a connecting particle μέν takes precedence over the connective (μὲν γάρ, μὲν δή, etc.). But τε ousts μέν from second place in Hp. *Morb.*ii 53: ἔς τε μὲν πεντεκαίδεκα ἡμέρας πάσχει τοιαῦτα· μετὰ δὲ πῦον πτύει. The juxtaposition of connective τε and μέν is strikingly avoided in Pl.*Phdr.*239A τοσούτων κακῶν . . . ἐραστὴν ἐρωμένῳ ἀνάγκη γιγνομένων τε καὶ φύσει ἐνόντων [τῶν] μὲν ἥδεσθαι, τὰ δὲ παρασκευάζειν.

μέν combined with καὶ . . . καί: Pl.*Lg.*655A ἀλλ' ἐν γὰρ μουσικῇ καὶ σχήματα μὲν καὶ μέλη ἔνεστιν: granted the order of the remaining words, that of the particles is inevitable. μέν combined with καί ('even'): Hp.*Fract.*32 γεγράφαται ἤδη οἱ τρόποι οἵως χρὴ ἰητρεύειν, ἥν τε ἐλπίζῃς ὀστέα ἀποστήσεσθαι, ἥν τε μή. χρὴ δέ, καὶ ἢν μὲν ἐλπίζῃς ὀστέα ἀποστήσεσθαι . . . (καί omitted in some MSS.: μέν (*solitarium*) denotes that this is only one of two possible alternatives): cf. *VC* 14 ἢν δὲ ὑποπτεύσῃς μὲν . . . .

In Ar.*Ec.*301 the position of μέν as first word in an acephalous glyconic is remarkable. In tmesis: Ar.*Lys.*263 κατὰ μὲν

[1] δέ in the answering clause is either postponed or normally placed: Pl.*R.*453A,571D: *Lg.*822B,890E,947C: *Tht.*153B (*bis*).

ἅγιον ἔχειν βρέτας. In Pl.*Alc.II* 148E φάναι oddly separates πλείστας from μέν.

(2) Second clause introduced by a non-adversative particle. We have seen above that the contrast conveyed by μέν and δέ may be so slight as hardly to be a contrast at all. It is therefore not surprising that, instead of δέ, we often find a particle expressing mere addition.[1] The great majority of the examples are poetical.

(i) μὲν . . . καί (The Homeric examples are not conclusive, as in them μέν may be purely emphatic.) Hom.*A*267 κάρτιστοι μὲν ἔσαν καὶ καρτίστοις ἐμάχοντο: *M*258 κρόσσας μὲν πύργων ἔρυον, καὶ ἔρειπον ἐπάλξεις: Tyrt.*Fr.*9.11–12: S.*Aj.*1 Ἀεὶ μὲν . . . καὶ νῦν: E.*Hel.*734 πολλὰ μὲν . . . καὶ νῦν: Ar.*Ach.*1164 τοῦτο μὲν αὐτῷ κακὸν ἕν, κᾆθ' ἕτερον νυκτερινὸν γένοιτο: *V.*552 πρῶτα μὲν . . . κἄπειτα: 607 πρῶτα μὲν . . . καί (*Nu.*1016): *Ra.*405 κατεσχίσω μὲν . . . κἀξηῦρες: Hom.*K*458: γ351: ι49: S.*Tr.*689: (in Pi.*P.* 2.58 μέν is answered by εἰ δέ τις): Pl.*R.*476B χωρὶς μὲν . . . καὶ χωρὶς αὖ: *Phdr.*258E Σχολὴ μὲν δή, ὡς ἔοικε· καὶ ἅμα . . . (the connexion is loose here, and μέν is almost *solitarium*): Anaxim. *Rh.Al.*36 ([Arist.]1442a8) αὐτοὺς μὲν συντόμως ἐπαινετέον καὶ τοὺς ἐναντίους κακολογητέον: X.*Cyr.*i4.3: *Mem.*ii6.22: *An.*v2. 21: Ant.vi14: (in Th.v60.1 οἱ μὲν ταῦτα εἰπόντες τῶν Ἀργείων is answered by οἱ δὲ Λακεδαιμόνιοι in § 2, not by καὶ ὁ Ἆγις: the negotiators of the treaty are contrasted with the army, which dislikes the treaty: see Graves and Steup) : Ant.*Fr.*50 ἡ ⟨μὲν⟩ γὰρ νῆσος, ἣν ἔχομεν, δήλη μὲν καὶ πόρρωθεν ὅτι ἐστὶν ὑψηλὴ καὶ τραχεῖα· καὶ τὰ μὲν χρήσιμα . . . μικρὰ αὐτῆς ἐστι, τὰ δὲ ἀργὰ πολλά: Demetrius (*De Eloc.*53) quotes this, with the curious explanation that one δέ answers three μέν's: it looks, though, as if the μέν after δήλη were answered by καὶ τὰ μὲν χρήσιμα: the μέν after ἡ is added by editors to make up the three.

(ii) μὲν . . . ἠδέ. See ἤ, III.12.ii.

(iii) μὲν . . . τε[2] (a good deal commoner than μὲν . . . καί,

[1] To style this slight inconsistency 'anacoluthon' (Hartung, ii 410) is surely going too far.

[2] J. B. Bury (Appendix A to edition of Pindar's Isthmian Odes, shows that many of the examples of μὲν . . . τε fall into two classes: (1) equivalent

but often needlessly altered by editors). Hom.*T*291 ἄνδρα μὲν . . . τρεῖς τε κασιγνήτους: χ475 τοῦ δ' ἀπὸ μὲν ῥῖνας . . . τάμνον, μήδεά τ' ἐξέρυσαν: Pi.*O*.6.88 πρῶτον μὲν . . . κελαδῆσαι, γνῶναί τ' ἔπειτ': 7.88 τίμα μὲν . . . δίδοι τε: A.*Supp*.410 ὅπως ἄνατα ταῦτα πρῶτα μὲν πόλει, αὐτοῖσί θ' ἡμῖν ἐκτελευτήσει καλῶς: *Th*.924 ὡς ἐρξάτην πολλὰ μὲν πολίτας, ξένων τε πάντων στίχας: *Ch*.585 Πολλὰ μὲν γᾶ τρέφει . . . πόντιαί τ' ἀγκάλαι . . . βρύουσι: 975 σεμνοὶ μὲν ἦσαν ἐν θρόνοις τόθ' ἥμενοι, φίλοι τε καὶ νῦν: S.*Ant*.963 παύεσκε μὲν γὰρ ἐνθέους γυναῖκας εὔιόν τε πῦρ, φιλαύλους τ' ἠρέθιζε Μούσας: *Tr*.1012 πολλὰ μὲν ἐν πόντῳ κατά τε δρία πάντα καθαίρων: 1233 ἥ μοι μητρὶ μὲν θανεῖν μόνη μεταίτιος, σοί τ' αὖθις ὡς ἔχεις ἔχειν: *Ph*.1424–6 πρῶτον μὲν νόσου παύσῃ λυγρᾶς, ἀρετῇ τε πρῶτος ἐκκριθεὶς στρατεύματος Πάριν μὲν . . . νοσφιεῖς βίου, πέρσεις τε Τροίαν: E.*Heracl*.337 πρῶτα μὲν σκοποὺς πέμψω . . . μάντεις τ' ἀθροίσας θύσομαι: *Cyc*.41 Παῖ γενναίων μὲν πατέρων, γενναίων τ' ἐκ τοκάδων: Ar. *Nu*.563 Ὑψιμέδοντα μὲν θεῶν Ζῆνα τύραννον ἐς χορὸν πρῶτα μέγαν κικλήσκω· τόν τε μεγασθενῆ . . .: *Pl*.665 Εἷς μέν γε Νεοκλείδης . . . ἕτεροί τε πολλοί: Pi.*O*.4.12: *P*.11.46: S.*Ant*. 1162: *Ph*.1056,1136: E.*Med*.11,125,430: *Heracl*.238: *Tr*.48, 134,647: *Ph*.55: *Or*.22,500,1318: *Rh*.912: *El*.146: *Ion* 402: Ar. *Nu*.612: (*Lys*.263: δέ Dindorf, rightly): Th.i 144.2 νῦν δὲ τούτοις ἀποκρινάμενοι ἀποπέμψωμεν, Μεγαρέας μὲν ὅτι ἐάσομεν . . . τάς τε πόλεις ὅτι αὐτονόμους ἀφήσομεν (τε *ABEF*: δέ *cett.* But Steup seems right in taking δέ after δίκας as answering μέν): ii 70.2 οἱ δὲ προσεδέξαντο, ὁρῶντες μὲν τῆς στρατιᾶς τὴν ταλαιπωρίαν . . . ἀνηλωκυίας τε ἤδη τῆς πόλεως δισχίλια τάλαντα (τε *ABEFM*: δέ *cett.*): iii 46.2 τίνα (πόλιν) οἴεσθε ἥντινα οὐκ ἄμεινον μὲν ἢ νῦν παρασκευάσεσθαι, πολιορκίᾳ τε παρατενεῖσθαι ἐς τοὔσχατον . . .; (Steup reads τε in the last two passages, while in iv 32.2 and 69.3, in both of which all MSS. give τε, he accepts

to anaphora with μέν and δέ: e.g. πολλὰ μὲν . . . τε = πολλὰ μὲν . . . πολλὰ δέ: (2) πρῶτον (πρῶτα) μὲν . . . τε = πρῶτον μὲν . . . ἔπειτα δέ. Certainly this explanation covers a number of cases (the treatment of Th.ii 65.12, where Bury keeps τρία μὲν ἔτη . . . Κύρῳ τε, as equivalent to τρία μὲν ἔτη . . . τρία δὲ ἔτη Κύρῳ, is particularly ingenious). But it by no means covers the whole field. (At the same time, while recognizing the true correspondence of μὲν . . . τε in some passages, we must not lose sight of the possibility that in others which have been cited as examples the τε clause is a mere supplement to the μέν clause, while the contrasting δέ clause comes later on.)

the emendation δέ, on the ground that the close connexion between the clauses makes μὲν . . . δέ essential (in iv 32.2, for example, it is obvious that the ships' crews are to be contrasted with other arms): rightly, I think): Pl.*Phdr.*266C σοφοὶ μὲν αὐτοὶ λέγειν γεγόνασιν, ἄλλους τε ποιοῦσιν: *Lg.*927B ὀξὺ μὲν ἀκούουσιν βλέπουσίν τε ὀξύ: 717E,857D,866E,950D: *Ti.*82D: *Alc. II* 148E (but οἱ . . . μέν here is perhaps answered by 149A Λακεδαιμονίοις δέ): X.*Cyr.*viii 1.3 (cited by Kühner, II ii 271.5, but the Oxford text does not record the reading ἀθρόοι τε: in any case ταχὺ μέν is answered by τῶν δ'): *Cyn.*13.10. In Pl.*Lg.*782C, if Schanz's ἐτόλμων μέν is right (which I doubt) μέν is perhaps answered by σαρκῶν δ' (not, I think, by πέλανοι δέ, as England says). In *Lg.*894C (τήν τε ἑαυτὴν κινοῦσαν picked up by ταύτην δέ) read δέ for τε.

(iv) μὲν . . . αὖτε. Hom.Ψ774 ἔνθ' Αἴας μὲν ὄλισθε θέων . . . κρητῆρ' αὖτ' ἀνάειρε . . . Ὀδυσσεύς (where μέν is not answered by δ' in 777): Pi.*P.*2.89 ὃς ἀνέχει τότε μὲν τὰ κείνων, τότ' αὖθ' ἑτέροις ἔδωκε μέγα κῦδος: *I.*6.3 ἐν Νεμέᾳ μὲν πρῶτον . . . νῦν αὖτεν Ἰσθμοῦ δεσπότᾳ: Hom.Γ241: χ5. μὲν . . . αὖ: Hom.Λ103, 108: δ210. (For S.*Ant.*165, μὲν . . . αὖθις, see below, (3) *ad fin.*)

(For μὲν . . . τοίνυν, see τοίνυν, II.2.)

In other cases, where the answering particle follows at a considerable interval, and particularly where a second speaker's words have intervened, the corresponsion is less direct, and we must assume some measure of anacoluthon. A.*Pr.*478–84: E. *Hel.*1255–61: Ar.*V.*807–11: Pl.*R.*396C–397A (οὐκοῦν), 398C–D (οὐκοῦν), 412B (δή), 491B–C (ἔτι τοίνυν), 544E–545A (οὖν): *Prm.* 138D (οὖν).

(3) Second clause not introduced by any particle. This mostly occurs when the μέν clause contains the ordinal πρῶτος (etc.), and (or) the answering clause contains either δεύτερος or ἔπειτα, εἶτα. Hes.*Th.*309 Ὄρθον μὲν πρῶτον κύνα γείνατο Γηρυονῆι· δεύτερον αὖτις ἔτικτεν . . . Κέρβερον: A.*Ch.*1068 παιδοβόροι μὲν πρῶτον ὑπῆρξαν . . . δεύτερον . . .: E.*Ion* 1590 γίγνεται κοινὸν γένος, Δῶρος μὲν . . . ὁ δεύτερος Ἀχαιός: *Ba.*681 ὧν ἦρχ' ἑνὸς μὲν Αὐτονόη, τοῦ δευτέρου μήτηρ Ἀγαύη σή: *Cyc.*383 ἀνέκαυσε μὲν πῦρ πρῶτον . . . ἔπειτα . . .: *Hec.*349 ἢ πατὴρ μὲν ἦν ἄναξ . . . τοῦτό μοι πρῶτον βίου· ἔπειτ' ἐθρέφθην: *Ion* 1579 Γελέων μὲν ἔσται πρῶτος· εἶτα δεύτερος . . .: Ar.*Nu.*553 Εὔπολις μὲν τὸν

Μαρικᾶν πρώτιστον παρείλκυσεν . . . εἶθ' Ἕρμιππος . . .: S.*Ph.* 1345 τοῦτο μὲν παιωνίας ἐς χεῖρας ἐλθεῖν, εἶτα . . . λαβεῖν: Ar. *Eq.*520 τοῦτο μὲν εἰδὼς ἄπαθε Μάγνης . . . εἶτα Κρατίνου μεμνημένος: A.*Pers.*522: S.*Aj.*311: E.*El.*890: *Supp.*506: Pl.*Lg.*774E πατρὸς μὲν πρῶτον, δευτέραν πάππου, τρίτην δὲ . . .: Ant.v14 ὑπάρχει μέν γε αὐτοῖς (τοῖς νόμοις) ἀρχαιοτάτοις εἶναι ἐν τῇ γῇ ταύτῃ, ἔπειτα τοὺς αὐτοὺς ἀεὶ περὶ τῶν αὐτῶν.

By far the commonest type is πρῶτον μὲν (πρῶτα μέν, πρώτιστα (-ον) μέν) . . . εἶτα (ἔπειτα). This is freely used both in prose and in verse. πρῶτα μὲν . . . εἶτα. S.*El.*261: E.*IA* 986: Ar.*Nu.*609,1117: *V.*1104: *Av.*114. πρῶτα μὲν . . . ἔπειτα. S.*Tr.*616: E.*Hec.*357. πρῶτον μὲν . . . ἔπειτα. E.*Cyc.*3 (ἔπειτά γε): *Hel.*270: Ar.*Ec.*60 (πρῶτον μέν γε . . . ἔπειτα): Pl.*R.*591C (ἔπειτά γε): Ant.v18: vi8,11,19: D.vi3: ix75: Lycurg.19,55, 118. πρῶτον μὲν . . . εἶτα. Ar.*Eq.*1340: *Nu.*963: X.*Mem.*i 2.1: D.xvi26: xviii176: lvii62,67. Cf. also E.*El.*664 Πρώτιστα μὲν . . . Ἔπειτα: Ar.*Lys.*589 πρώτιστον μέν γε . . . Εἶτα: *Eq.* 129 ὡς πρῶτα μὲν . . . Μετὰ τοῦτον αὖθις: Isoc.xv117–19 πρῶτον μὲν . . . δεύτερον. μάλιστα, priority in importance, is akin to πρῶτον, priority in time: S.*OT*647 μάλιστα μὲν . . . ἔπειτα (but in *OC*1298 μέν is *solitarium*: see Jebb).

In a few other passages ἄλλοτε, νῦν, οὗτος atone for the absence of an answering particle. Thgn.158 ἄλλοτε μὲν πλουτεῖν, ἄλλοτε μηδὲν ἔχειν: S.*Ant.*367 τότε μὲν κακόν, ἄλλοτ' ἐπ' ἐσθλὸν ἕρπει: A.*Supp.*506 Κλάδους μὲν αὐτοῦ λεῖπε . . . Λευρὸν κατ' ἄλσος νῦν ἐπιστρέφου τόδε: *Eu.*636 ἀνδρὸς μὲν ὑμῖν οὗτος εἴρηται μόρος . . . ταύτην τοιαύτην εἶπον: ('as for that woman there': 'the abruptness is calculated, and thrilling', Verrall): S.*OT*603 καὶ τῶνδ' ἔλεγχον τοῦτο μὲν Πυθώδ' ἰὼν πεύθου τά χρησθέντ' . . . τοῦτ' ἄλλ', ἐὰν . . .: *Ant.*165.

(4) The contrasted idea is not expressed in a following coordinated clause.

(i) The μέν clause is contrasted with what precedes, not with what follows. A.*Pr.*901 (894 μήποτέ με . . . λεχέων Διὸς εὐνάτειραν ἴδοισθε πέλουσαν· . . . ταρβῶ γὰρ ἀστεργάνορα παρθενίαν εἰσορῶσ' Ἰοῦς ἀμαλαπτομέναν) . . . ἐμοὶ δ' ὅτε μὲν ὁμαλὸς ὁ γάμος, ἄφοβος: S.*Tr.*350 σαφῶς μοι φράζε πᾶν ὅσον νοεῖς· ἃ μὲν γὰρ ἐξείρηκας ἀγνοίᾳ μ' ἔχει: Hom.*A*421: Pi.*N.*6.61: S.*OT*1251 (perhaps: cf. 1239–40): Pl.*Alc.I* 130C Εἰ δέ γε μὴ ἀκριβῶς ἀλλὰ καὶ μετρίως, ἐξαρκεῖ ἡμῖν· ἀκριβῶς μὲν γὰρ τότε εἰσόμεθα: *Thg.* 127B Ὦ Σώκρατες, οὐ μέντοι κακῶς λέγει, καὶ ἅμα μὲν ἐμοὶ χαριῇ: X.*Mem.*i 1.1 ἡ μὲν γὰρ γραφὴ κατ' αὐτοῦ τοιάδε τις ἦν (opposed to τίσι ποτὲ λόγοις Ἀθηναίους ἔπεισαν οἱ γραψάμενοι Σωκράτην, preceding): *Oec.*19.11 ἐπαμήσαιο δ' ἂν μόνον, ἔφη, τὴν γῆν, ἢ καὶ σάξαις ἂν . . . ;—Σαττοιμ' ἄν, ἔφην, . . . εἰ μὲν γὰρ μὴ σεσαγμένον εἴη . . . : D.ix 16 τί ἐποίει; εἰρήνην μὲν γὰρ ὠμωμόκει ('He had sworn to keep the peace: but what did he *do*?'): Th.vii 55.1: Pl.*Phd.*58A.

So, particularly, ἀλλὰ . . . μέν.[1] Hom.*A* 211 μηδὲ ξίφος ἕλκεο χειρί· ἀλλ' ἤτοι ἔπεσιν μὲν ὀνείδισον: ο405 (νῆσος) οὔ τι περιπληθὴς λίην τόσον, ἀλλ' ἀγαθὴ μέν: δ694: Ar.*Ach.*428 Οὐ Βελλεροφόντης· ἀλλὰ κἀκεῖνος μὲν ἦν χωλὸς προσαιτῶν: Pl.*Tht.* 201B ἢ σὺ οἴει δεινούς τινας οὕτω διδασκάλους εἶναι, ὥστε . . . δύνασθαι . . . διδάξαι . . . τὴν ἀλήθειαν;—Οὐδαμῶς ἔγωγε οἶμαι, ἀλλὰ πεῖσαι μέν: *R.*475E φιλοσόφους φήσομεν;—Οὐδαμῶς, εἶπον, ἀλλ' ὁμοίους μὲν φιλοσόφοις: *Phdr.*242C εἰμὶ δὴ οὖν μάντις μέν, οὐ πάνυ δὲ σπουδαῖος, ἀλλ' ὥσπερ οἱ τὰ γράμματα φαῦλοι, ὅσον μὲν ἐμαυτῷ μόνον ἱκανός (*posterius* μέν *B*: *om. T*: the δέ clause contrasts both with the preceding, and with the following, μέν): Lys.vi 20 οὔτε γὰρ ὁ θεὸς παραχρῆμα κολάζει (ἀλλ' αὕτη μέν ἐστιν ἀνθρωπίνη δίκη): Pl.*Men.*87A: *Grg.*462E: *R.*614B: *Tht.*197C: *Sph.*240B: *Euthd.*297E: *Prt.*344A:[2] *Alc.I* 106B: [Pl.]*Eryx.*398B: Is.v 36. Cf.Pi.*P.*3.77: 4.154.

(ii) One or other of the clauses is grammatically subordinated to the other.

(*a*) Μέν clause subordinate. Hom.*Ω*289 ἐπεὶ ἄρ σέ γε θυμὸς ὀτρύνει ἐπὶ νῆας, ἐμεῖο μὲν οὐκ ἐθελούσης ('*I* don't want to: but *you* apparently *do*'): Pi.*O.*3.19 ἤδη γὰρ αὐτῷ, πατρὶ μὲν βωμῶν ἁγισθέντων, διχόμηνις . . . ἀντέφλεξε Μήνα: A.*Th.*313 τοῖσι μὲν ἔξω . . . ἄταν ἐμβαλόντες ἄροισθε κῦδος τοῖσδε πολίταις: Pl.*La.* 186B ἢ εἴ τις ἡμῶν αὐτῶν ἑαυτῷ διδάσκαλον μὲν οὔ φησι γεγονέναι, ἀλλ' οὖν ἔργα αὐτὸν αὑτοῦ ἔχειν εἰπεῖν (δεῖ) (a blend of εἰ . . . οὔ φησι . . . ἀλλ' οὖν ἔχειν εἰπεῖν, and διδάσκαλον μὲν οὐ φάναι γεγονέναι, ἔργα δὲ ἔχειν εἰπεῖν. Add perhaps Th.i 52.2

[1] See R. W. Chapman, *C.R.*xxv(1911)204–5: Stallbaum on Pl.*Phdr.*242C. For a quite different use of ἀλλὰ . . . μέν, see I. B. 1.

[2] But μέν here is influenced by the quotation from Simonides.

(see Steup). In Pl.*Phd.*115B μέν after ὑμῶν (in *B* only) cannot be defended.

In the following passages both antithetical particles are retained, μέν in the subordinate, and δέ in the main, clause. Hom. *I* 300 εἰ δέ τοι Ἀτρεΐδης μὲν ἀπήχθετο . . . σὺ δ' ἄλλους περ Παναχαιοὺς τειρομένους ἐλέαιρε: λ387 αὐτὰρ ἐπεὶ ψυχὰς μὲν ἀπεσκέδασ' . . . ἦλθε δ' ἐπὶ ψυχὴ Ἀγαμέμνονος: Th.iii 82.1 ἐν μὲν εἰρήνῃ οὐκ ἂν ἐχόντων προφάσιν . . . πολεμουμένων δὲ καὶ ξυμμαχίας . . . ῥᾳδίως αἱ ἐπαγωγαὶ τοῖς νεωτερίζειν τι βουλομένοις ἐπορίζοντο: cf.i 67.2, vi 69.1: Pl.*Lg.*780B καὶ τοῦτο μὲν δὴ θαυμαστὸν ὄν, ὅτε κατ' ἀρχὰς πρῶτον ἐγένετο . . . γευσαμένοις δὲ . . . ἔδοξεν μέγα διαφέρειν εἰς σωτηρίαν τὸ νόμιμον: 898C εἰπεῖν ὡς, ἐπειδὴ ψυχὴ μέν ἐστιν ἡ περιάγουσα ἡμῖν πάντα, τὴν δὲ οὐρανοῦ περιφορὰν ἐξ ἀνάγκης περιάγειν φατέον . . . ἤτοι τὴν ἀρίστην ψυχὴν ἢ τὴν ἐναντίαν (England regards the speech as broken by an interruption): *Epin.*976A: *Cri.*44B ἀλλὰ χωρὶς μὲν τοῦ ἐστερῆσθαι τοιούτου ἐπιτηδείου . . . ἔτι δὲ καὶ πολλοῖς δόξω . . . ἀμελῆσαι (δέ *secl.* Schanz, probably rightly: if the text is sound, the μέν clause is a mere prepositional phrase). In E.*IT*419–20 Paley takes οἷς as relative. If so, μέν in the relative clause answers δέ in the main clause, since μέν can hardly be *solitarium* here. But the sense given is not satisfactory, and οἷς must be demonstrative (see Kühner, II ii 228) and the clauses co-ordinated (if the text is sound).

(*b*) δέ clause[1] subordinate. A.*Ag.*1412 Νῦν μὲν δικάζεις ἐκ πόλεως φυγὴν ἐμοὶ . . . οὐδὲν τότ' ἀνδρὶ τῷδ' ἐναντίον φέρων: S. *Aj.*1299 ὃς ἐκ πατρὸς μέν εἰμι Τελαμῶνος γεγώς (Teucer's mother is described in a relative clause): *OT* 302 πόλιν μέν, εἰ καὶ μὴ βλέπεις, φρονεῖς δ' ὅμως οἵᾳ νόσῳ σύνεστιν (but Jebb is perhaps right in holding that 'μέν is balanced by the thought of the expected healer (310)')*: *OC*1370 τοιγάρ σ' ὁ δαίμων εἰσορᾷ μὲν οὔ τί πω, ὡς αὐτίκ': E.*Ba.*1039 Συγγνωστὰ μέν σοι, πλὴν ἐπ' ἐξειργασμένοις κακοῖσι χαίρειν . . . οὐ καλόν: Ar.*Eq.*598 ἀλλὰ τὰν τῇ γῇ μὲν αὐτῶν οὐκ ἄγαν θαυμάζομεν, ὡς ὅτ' ἐς τὰς ἱππαγωγοὺς εἰσεπήδων ἀνδρικῶς: Hom.*Λ*277: Σ408. For X. *Mem.*i 2.2, see I.B.1, ἀλλὰ . . . μέν.

[1] By this I mean the clause contrasted with the μέν clause but not, in fact, containing a δέ.

(5) Contrasted idea not expressed (the so-called *μέν solitarium*). We may exclude (*a*) passages in dialogue where a second person intervenes before μέν has been answered: (*b*) passages in continuous speech where the speaker interrupts himself by a definite anacoluthon. E.g. (*a*) E.*HF* 555 Βίᾳ, πατὴρ μὲν ἐκπεσὼν στρωτοῦ λέχους— —Κοὐκ ἔσχεν αἰδῶ ...; Ar.*Lys.*1236 (the speaker breaks off on the entrance of new characters on the stage): (*b*) D.iv 20 ξένους μὲν λέγω—καὶ ὅπως μὴ ποιήσετε .... The explanation of μέν *solitarium*, in general, is either that the speaker originally intends to supply an answering clause, but subsequently forgets his intention (e.g. Pl.*R.*466E, where Περὶ μὲν γὰρ τῶν ἐν πολέμῳ is never answered at all), or, far more frequently, that he uses μέν, like γε, in contrast with something which he does not, even in the first instance, intend to express in words, or even (sometimes) define precisely in thought (see in particular (ii) and (iii)). Obviously there is no sharp line of demarcation, and many passages may be explained in either way. Apart from certain stereotyped idioms μέν *solitarium* is considerably commoner in verse than in prose.

(i) In general. A.*Supp.*338 Τίς δ' ἂν φίλους ὄνοιτο τοὺς κεκτημένους;—Σθένος μὲν οὕτως μεῖζον αὔξεται βροτοῖς ("Strength *at least* (whatever may be the case in other respects)", Tucker): *Pers.*554 τίπτε Δαρεῖος μὲν οὕτω τότ' ἀβλαβὴς ἐπῆν τόξαρχος πολιήταις ...; (in contrast with Xerxes): *Ag.*932 Καὶ μὴν τόδ' εἰπὲ μὴ παρὰ γνώμην ἐμοί.—Γνώμην μὲν ἴσθι μὴ διαφθεροῦντ' ἐμέ: *Eu.*418 Γένος μὲν οἶδα ... (completed by the Chorus, Τιμάς γε μὲν δὴ τὰς ἐμὰς πεύσει τάχα): 589 Ἓν μὲν τόδ' ἤδη τῶν τριῶν παλαισμάτων: S.*El.*1424 πῶς κυρεῖτε;—Τἀν δόμοισι μὲν καλῶς: *Tr.*380 Πατρὸς μὲν οὖσα γένεσιν Εὐρύτου ποτὲ Ἰόλη 'καλεῖτο (the Messenger meant, I think, to add further details: Jebb, less probably, takes this as equivalent to π.μ.ο.γ.Ε., Ἰόλη δὲ καλουμένη): *Ph.*159 Οἶκον μὲν ὁρᾷς (*sc.* 'but not its inhabitant'): E.*HF* 740 ἦλθες χρόνῳ μέν ('at last (but not quickly)'): cf. Pi.*O.*10.85): *El.*575 Πῶς φῄς; ὁρῶ μὲν πτώματος τεκμήριον ('I see the scar (but hesitate to draw the conclusion)'): 615 ἀλλὰ πῶς λάβω;—Τειχέων μὲν ἐλθὼν ἐντὸς οὐδ' ἂν εἰ θέλοις: *Hel.*1250 Ὦ ξένε, λόγων μὲν κληδόν' ἤνεγκας φίλην: *IA* 527 Ποικίλος ἀεὶ πέφυκε τοῦ τ' ὄχλου μέτα.—Φιλοτιμίᾳ μὲν ἐνέχεται ('He is certainly ambitious'): Ar.*Nu.*654 πρὸ τοῦ μέν ('in old days (whatever the case is now)'): *Pax* 125 Καὶ τίς πόρος σοι τῆς ὁδοῦ γενήσεται; ναῦς μὲν γὰρ οὐκ ἄξει σε ταύτην τὴν ὁδόν: *Av.*358 Γλαῦξ μὲν οὐ πρόσεισι νῷν.—Τοῖς δὲ γαμψώνυξι τοισδί; (the implied antithesis is expressed by the other speaker): 381 Ἔστι μὲν λόγων ἀκοῦσαι πρῶτον . . . χρήσιμον ('We'd better listen to what they say (we needn't agree to it)'): *Ec.*180 χαλεπὸν μὲν οὖν ἄνδρας δυσαρέστους νουθετεῖν ('Well, it's not very *easy* (but it must be done)'): A.*Ag.*1266: *Ch.*737 (see Tucker), 1016: S.*Ant.*551: *Tr.*6 (the antithesis does not come till 27): *OC* 22,44,1096: E.*Supp.*655: *Ion* 753: *HF* 982: *Tr.*1150: *Ph.*1683: *Or.*8: *Hel.*1258: *Ba.*970: Ar.*Ach.*754: *Pax* 673: *Av.*36: *Ra.*1184: *Pl.*422: Hdt.i 140 μάγους μὲν γὰρ ἀτρεκέως οἶδα ταῦτα ποιέοντας (*sc.* 'but I can't answer for the rest'): Th. vi 25.2 ὁ δὲ ἄκων μὲν εἶπεν (for ἄκων μὲν εἶπεν, εἶπε δέ. ἄκων μέν, εἶπε δ', Krueger, ingeniously): Pl.*Chrm.* 154A ἀνηρώτων τὰ τῇδε, περὶ φιλοσοφίας ὅπως ἔχοι τὰ νῦν, περί τε τῶν νέων . . . καὶ ὁ Κριτίας . . . Περὶ μὲν τῶν καλῶν, ἔφη, . . . αὐτίκα μοι δοκεῖς εἴσεσθαι: *Tht.*148D προθυμήθητι δὲ παντὶ τρόπῳ . . . λαβεῖν λόγον . . .—Προθυμίας μὲν ἕνεκα . . . φανεῖται: *R.*453C ὡς μὲν ἐξαίφνης . . .: 557C ἴσως μὲν . . .: *Alc.I* 112D Πῶς οὖν εἰκὸς . . .;—Ἐκ μὲν ὧν σὺ λέγεις οὐκ εἰκός: *Amat.*134E Τίνα . . . ἂν δικαίως ἐροίμεθα . . .;—Ὡμολογοῦμεν μὲν . . . ὅτι ἰατρόν: X.*Mem.*i 4.5 Πρέπει μὲν . . .: *Smp.*4.62 Καὶ τί μοι σύνοισθα . . .;—Οἶδα μέν, ἔφη, σε . . .: Hp.*Fract.*32: Th.i 10.1: Pl.*Phd.* 61D,80C: *Prt.*312A: *Lg.*663E: X.*Mem.*ii 6.21.

(ii) With personal and demonstrative pronouns, implicitly contrasted with other persons and things. ἐγώ, ἐμοῦ, ἐμοί. A.*Ag.* 924: S.*Aj.*80: *El.*372: E.*Hel.*496: Ar.*Ach.*59: Hdt.i 182: ii 120: iii 3: Pl.*Ap.*23B: *Grg.*506D: *Cra.*397A: *Tht.*158A: D.iii 8: viii 15,37: xx 4,12,23. σύ, σοῦ. S.*OT* 1062,1322: *Ant.*634: *OC* 836: Ar.*Ach.*109 Ποίας ἀχάνας; σὺ μὲν ἀλαζὼν εἶ μέγας ('*You're* a great big *charlatan* (whatever else is true)'): *Av.*12: Pl.*Alc.II* 138C Ἀλλὰ σὺ μέν, ὦ Σώκρατες, μαινόμενον ἄνθρωπον εἴρηκας: D.xliv 27 διὰ μὲν σέ. ἡμεῖς, ἡμῖν. A.*Pr.*1036: S.*Ant.* 681: *OT* 404: Ar.*Nu.*794. ὑμεῖς, ὑμᾶς. Ar.*Av.*161: *Pax* 497: Pl.*R.*595B ὡς μὲν πρὸς ὑμᾶς εἰρῆσθαι ('between you and me'). ἐμός, ἐμοῖς. E.*IA* 859 Τίνος; ἐμὸς μὲν οὐχί ('Not *mine*'): A. *Pers.*300. οὗτος, τοῦτο, etc. S.*Ph.*981: E.*Cyc.*146: *Or.*415: *IT* 501: *Supp.*939: Ar.*Ach.*196: *Eq.*777,1216: *Nu.*1188: *Pax* 244,1226,1256: Pl.*Ap.*21D: *Phd.*105E: *Cra.*402D 414D: *Phlb.*

49D: D.xviii 95: xix 86. οὕτω. Ar.*Av.*656,1503: Pl.*Hipparch.* 226D. ὅδε. Ar.*Th.*922: Pl.*R.*545C: *Lg.*629B: Ar.*Av.*1220 τῇδε μὲν γὰρ οὔ ('Not *this* way'). ἐκεῖνος. D.viii 59. τοιοῦτος. Pl.*Prm.*135C. (But in E.*Rh.*467 τοιαῦτα μέν is answered by ἐπεὶ δ' ἄν, which seems clearly the right reading.)

(iii) With words denoting opinion, appearance, or probability, implicitly contrasted with certainty or reality. οἶμαι. S.*Ph.* 339: E.*Alc.*781: Pl.*Cra.*438C: *R.*585A σφόδρα μὲν οἴονται: *R.* 423B,492E,548D: X.*HG* iv i.34: *Mem.*ii 6.5: Ant.iii α 1. δοκῶ. S.*El.*547: E.*Hel.*917: Ar.*Pax* 47: Hdt.vii 50.2: Pl.*Men.*94B. S. *Aj.*56 κἀδόκει μέν: Pl.*Cri.*43D ἀλλὰ δοκεῖν μέν μοι ἥξει. S.*OT* 82 εἰκάσαι μέν: *OC* 1677 Ἔστιν μὲν εἰκάσαι: Pl.*Cra.*390B εἰκὸς μέν: *R.*595B ἔοικε μέν: *Alc.I* 113B φαίνομαι μέν: Th.v 90 Ἧι μὲν δὴ νομίζομέν γε.

(iv) With πρῶτον, πρῶτα. The speaker either has, at the start, no clear idea of a definite antithesis to his μέν: or the development of the antithesis is broken by the intervention of another speaker, or from some other cause. A.*Supp.*917 Ξένος μὲν εἶναι πρῶτον οὐκ ἐπιστάσαι: *Pr.*447 οἳ πρῶτα μὲν βλέποντες ἔβλεπον μάτην, κλύοντες οὐκ ἤκουον: *Ch.*111 Τίνας δὲ τούτους τῶν φίλων προσεννέπω;—Πρῶτον μὲν αὑτὴν χὤστις Αἴγισθον στυγεῖ: E.*Supp.*403 Πρῶτον μὲν ἤρξω τοῦ λόγου ψευδῶς: Ar. *Nu.*649 Τί δέ μ' ὠφελήσουσ' οἱ ῥυθμοὶ πρὸς τἄλφιτα;—Πρῶτον μὲν εἶναι κομψὸν ἐν συνουσίᾳ: *Av.*164 Τί σοι πιθώμεσθ';—Ὅ τι πίθησθε; πρῶτα μὲν μὴ περιπέτεσθε πανταχῇ κεχηνότες: E.*IT* 467 (μέν not answered by δέ in 470): Ar.*Eq.*774: *Nu.*224: Pl. *Cra.*411D.

(Some examples of μέν γε *solitarium* are given under μέν γε.)

(v) Inceptive. There are signs of a tendency, at least in certain authors, to open a work, or a part of a work, with μέν, with or without an expressed or implied antithesis, perhaps in order to mitigate the harshness of the inevitable asyndeton. Bäumlein, who alone, I think, has said anything on this matter, observes that Aeschylus and Sophocles show a liking for μέν openings. But the observation is justified in the case of Aeschylus only. Five of his seven plays (all except *Septem* and *Choephori*) open with μέν. In *Supp.*1 μέν hardly seems to be answered by 4 Δίαν δὲ λιποῦσαι: and in *Ag.*1 the correspondence with 8 καὶ νῦν (Headlam), or 20 νῦν δέ (Verrall), is not very obvious. Sophocles has three μέν openings (*Aj.*, *Tr.*, *Ph.*). Of these, *Ph.*1 is scarcely answered by 11 ἀλλὰ ταῦτα μὲν τί δεῖ λέγειν (Jebb). But, on the whole, Sophocles, Euripides, and Aristophanes (who usually plunges at once *in medias res*) show no particular tendency to open their plays with μέν.

In early oratory the tendency to open with μέν is clearly marked. Antiphon opens with it ten times out of fifteen: so does Andocides in all three of the genuine speeches. From Lysias onwards the predominance of the μέν opening disappears (though it is often still used: in D.xliv 1 μέν has no answer, expressed or implied, for §3 δέομαι δ' ὑμῶν is too far off: Is.i 1).

Speeches in drama show a certain tendency to open with μέν. A.*Pers.*353 Ἦρξεν μέν, ὦ δέσποινα, τοῦ παντὸς κακοῦ . . .: *Ag.* 587 Ἀνωλόλυξα μὲν πάλαι χαρᾶς ὕπο (hardly answered by 590 καί τίς μ' ἐνίπτων εἶπε: while 598 καὶ νῦν, which Verrall and Headlam take to be the answer, seems too far off): S.*Aj.*815 Ὁ μὲν σφαγεὺς ἕστηκεν (823 ἐκ δὲ τῶνδε, where Jebb supposes the answer to begin, is rather too far off): *El.*516 Ἀνειμένη μέν, ὡς ἔοικας, αὖ στρέφῃ (where Jebb admits that there is no answer, expressed or implied): *OT* 1369: *Ant.*223: E.*Supp.*409. In other openings μέν is less distinctively inceptive. A.*Ag.*810 Πρῶτον μὲν Ἄργος, picked up and answered by 829–30 θεοῖς μὲν ἐξέτεινα φροίμιον τόδε, τὰ δ' ἐς τὸ σὸν φρόνημα . . .: *Pers.*598 Φίλοι, κακῶν μὲν ὅστις ἔμπειρος κυρεῖ (contrasted with the implied ὅστις δ' ἄπειρος): E.*HF* 1089 Ἔα· ἔμπνους μέν εἰμι ('I am alive at any rate': and this is not, of course, a formal opening).

The mock speeches in Aristophanes, modelled on the style of the assembly or the law-courts, almost always begin with μέν. *Ach.*136 Χρόνον μὲν οὐκ ἂν ἦμεν ἐν Θρᾴκῃ πολύν: *V.*907: *Av.* 1565 (broken off by the buffoonery of the Triballian): *Th.*383: *Pl.*489. It is difficult to resist the impression that the budding speaker, at the turn of the fifth and fourth centuries, was recommended, as a kind of stylistic convention, to start off with a μέν, and to trust more or less to luck that he would find an answer to it, and not to care greatly if he did not. And this impression is strengthened by the prevalence of the μέν opening in contemporary oratory, Antiphon and Andocides.

We may mention here two passages in which a chorus opens

with a μέν to which there is no answer, expressed or implied: A.*Ag*.40: E.*Rh*.342.

(For inceptive ἀλλὰ . . . μέν in Xenophon, see I.B.1.)

IV. Duplication of μέν. This is a convenient heading under which to group two distinct idioms.

(1) Resumption of clause. The content of the first of the two contrasted ideas proves too great to admit of compression into a single clause, particularly when the speaker or writer permits himself to wander somewhat from the precise point at issue. Hence a second μέν clause is necessary, before the δέ clause can follow. The force of the opening μέν has half evaporated, and must be resuscitated by a fresh μέν.

Hom.Σ 432–4 ὅσσ' ἐμοὶ ἐκ πασέων Κρονίδης Ζεὺς ἄλγε' ἔδωκεν. ἐκ μέν μ' ἀλλάων ἁλιάων ἀνδρὶ δάμασσεν . . . ὁ μὲν δὴ γήραϊ λυγρῷ κεῖται ἐνὶ μεγάροις ἀρημένος, ἄλλα δέ μοι νῦν (here the point of view shifts, Thetis emphasizing first the mortality of her consort, secondly the old age attendant on that mortality, in contrast with her other sorrows: to take the first μέν as affirmative is possible, but less likely): χ48–54 ἀλλ' ὁ μὲν ἤδη κεῖται . . . Ἀντίνοος . . . νῦν δ' ὁ μὲν ἐν μοίρῃ πέφαται, σὺ δὲ φείδεο λαῶν σῶν: A.*Th*.1012–17 Ἐτεοκλέα μὲν . . . θάπτειν ἔδοξε . . . οὕτω μὲν ἀμφὶ τοῦδ' ἐπέσταλται λέγειν· τούτου δ' ἀδελφὸν . . . : Pl.*Cra*.406D Οὐκοῦν τὸ μὲν ἕτερον ὄνομα αὐτῆς οὐ χαλεπὸν εἰπεῖν δι' ὃ κεῖται. . . . Τοῦτο μὲν τοίνυν . . . "Παλλάδα" μὲν τοίνυν ταύτῃ: *R*. 406D–E Τέκτων μὲν . . .—Καὶ τῷ τοιούτῳ μέν γ' . . .—Ὁ δὲ δὴ πλούσιος . . .: *Lg*.655A (both μέν's answered by δέ after εὔχρων: but perhaps Boeckh and Schanz are right in adding χρώματα δὲ οὐκ ἔνεστι after ἔνεστιν in line 5)*: D.ii 3–4 τὸ μὲν οὖν . . . τὴν Φιλίππου ῥώμην διεξιέναι . . . οὐχὶ καλῶς ἔχειν ἡγοῦμαι . . . ταῦτα μὲν οὖν παραλείψω . . . ἃ δὲ . . . ταῦτ' εἰπεῖν πειράσομαι: xix 25–7 τοῦ χάριν δὴ ταῦθ' ὑπέμνησα . . .; ἑνὸς μὲν . . . μάλιστα καὶ πρώτου, ἵνα . . . πρώτου μὲν τούτου καὶ μάλισθ', ὅπερ εἶπον, εἵνεκα ταῦτα διεξῆλθον, δευτέρου δὲ τίνος . . .; viii 39–43 πρῶτον μὲν (χρὴ) . . . τοῦτο . . . γνῶναι . . . πρῶτον μὲν δὴ τοῦτο δεῖ . . . δεύτερον δ' εἰδέναι . . .: xxii 13–14 τοῦτο μὲν . . . εἶεν· ἀλλ' ἐκεῖνα μὲν ἀρχαῖα καὶ παλαιά. ἀλλ' ἃ πάντες ἑοράκατε . . .: xlviii 56: Anaxim. *Rh. Al.* 36, ll. 17–18 ([Arist.]1442a6–8): Lys.x 12 (μέν after αὐτός is picked up by μέν after ὅταν in §13): Pl.*Phd.*80E–81A (anacoluthon): *Lg.*742E.

(2) Whereas in the passages quoted above there are two μέν clauses, the second of which supplements or resumes the first, in the following there is only one μέν clause, but it contains two μέν's, the second of which is added for clearness, as an extra sign-post, or, perhaps more often, for emphasis. Often δέ also is duplicated. Except for two examples in Empedocles, I can find no verse instances.[1]

(i) The first μέν goes with a substantive, the second with οὗτος in apposition.

(*a*) μέν alone duplicated. Hp.*Art.*45 ἀπὸ μὲν τοῦ ἱεροῦ ὀστέου ἄχρι τοῦ μεγάλου σπονδύλου . . . ἄχρι μὲν τούτου: Pl.*R.*510E (with anacoluthon) αὐτὰ μὲν ταῦτα ἃ πλάττουσιν . . . τούτοις μὲν ὡς εἰκόσιν αὖ χρώμενοι, ζητοῦντες δὲ αὐτὰ ἐκεῖνα ἰδεῖν ἃ . . .: And.i12 Ἀλκιβιάδην μὲν οὖν καὶ Νικιάδην καὶ Μέλητον, τούτους μὲν αὐτοὺς εἶναι τοὺς ποιοῦντας: Isoc.iv60 καὶ τῷ μὲν ὑπερενεγκόντι . . . τούτῳ μὲν . . .: D.viii44 τῶν μὲν ἐν Θρᾴκῃ κακῶν (. . .) τούτων μὲν ἐπιθυμεῖν: xliii56 τῆς μὲν ἐπικλήρου, ἣ ἦν Ἁγνίᾳ ἀνεψιοῦ παῖς πρὸς πατρός, ταύτης μὲν μηδεπώποτε ἀμφισβητῆσαι Θεόπομπον: Pl.*Phd.*108B: Lys.xiii54.

(*b*) μέν and δέ both duplicated. Hdt.i184 ἡ μὲν πρότερον ἄρξασα . . . αὕτη μὲν ἀπεδέξατο χρήματα . . . ἡ δὲ δὴ δεύτερον γενομένη . . . αὕτη δὲ . . .: X.*Hier.*9.2 τὸ μὲν γὰρ διδάσκειν . . . αὕτη μὲν ἡ ἐπιμέλεια . . . τὸ δὲ . . . ταῦτα δὲ . . . .

(ii) μέν following both relative and demonstrative: μέν both in conditional protasis and in apodosis.

(*a*) μέν alone duplicated. Hdt.ii121 (*ad init.*) τὸν μὲν καλέουσι θέρος, τοῦτον μὲν προσκυνέουσι: X.*Mem.*iv6.12 καὶ ὅπου μὲν . . . ταύτην μὲν . . .: Ant.vi9 ἵνα μὲν ἐξῆν αὐτοῖς . . . ἐνταῦθα μὲν . . .: D.xlv14 ὅσοις μὲν . . . ταῦτα μὲν . . .: xlviii54 ἃ μὲν . . . τούτων μὲν . . . (with no answering δέ): Lys.xiv11 ἐὰν μέν τις . . . τούτου μὲν . . . ἐὰν δέ τις . . . τούτῳ . . .: Hdt.iii65,75, 158: iv9: Lys.xxiv8.

(*b*) μέν and δέ both duplicated. Emp.*Fr.*9 οἱ δ' ὅτε μὲν . . . τότε μὲν . . . εὖτε δ' . . . τὰ δ' αὖ . . .: *Fr.*26 ᾗ μὲν . . . τῇ μὲν . . .

[1] For further examples, and full discussion, see Kühner, II ii 269–70.

ᾗ δὲ . . . ταύτῃ δὲ . . . : Hdt.ii 26 τῇ μὲν . . . ταύτῃ μὲν . . . τῇ δὲ . . . ταύτῃ δὲ . . . : 42 ὅσοι μὲν δὴ . . . οὗτοι μὲν . . . ὅσοι δὲ . . . οὗτοι δὲ . . . : Pl.*Men.*94C–D οὐκ ἄν ποτε, οὗ μὲν ἔδει . . . ταῦτα μὲν ἐδίδαξε . . . οὗ δὲ οὐδὲν ἔδει . . . ταῦτα δὲ οὐκ ἐδίδαξεν : *Ap.*28E εἰ ὅτε μὲν . . . τότε μὲν . . . τοῦ δὲ θεοῦ τάττοντος . . . ἐνταῦθα δὲ . . . : *Tht.* 152A λέγει, ὡς οἷα μὲν ἕκαστα ἐμοὶ φαίνεται, τοιαῦτα μὲν ἔστιν ἐμοί, οἷα δὲ σοί, τοιαῦτα δὲ αὖ σοί (cf.*Cra.*386A) : Hdt.ii 102,174 : Pl.*Grg.*512A : *Alc.I* 108E–109A : X.*Oec.*9.9–10 : Isoc.vii 47 : D. xvii 18.

(For δέ alone duplicated, see δέ, II.4.)

(3) In the three following remarkable, and doubtful, passages, which lend each other some measure of support, μέν is duplicated at a short interval, within the limits of a single indivisible clause. Hdt.iv 48 εἰσὶ δὲ οἵδε οἱ μέγαν αὐτὸν ποιεῦντες (ποταμοί), διὰ μέν γε τῆς Σκυθικῆς χώρης πέντε μὲν οἱ ῥέοντες, . . . οὗτοι μὲν αὐθιγενέες . . . ἐκ δὲ Ἀγαθύρσων . . . (μέν τε *V*, μέν τοι *S*, for μέν γε : μεγάλοι Koen, for μὲν οἱ : the μέν after πέντε is certainly remarkable : otherwise the passage falls normally under (1) : Pl.*Smp.*198B καὶ τὰ μὲν ἄλλα οὐχ ὁμοίως μὲν θαυμαστά· τὸ δὲ ἐπὶ τελευτῆς . . . (*posterius* μέν *BT*: *om. Vind.* 21) : X.*Oec.* 19.11 ὥστε τὰ φυτὰ κίνδυνος ὑπὸ μὲν τοῦ ὕδατος σήπεσθαι μὲν δι' ὑγρότητα (ὑπὸ . . . ὕδατος *del.* Schneider). In Pl.*R.*607E the interval is wider : ὥσπερ . . . , καὶ ἡμεῖς οὕτως διὰ τὸν ἐγγεγονότα μὲν ἔρωτα τῆς τοιαύτης ποιήσεως ὑπὸ τῆς τῶν καλῶν πολιτειῶν τροφῆς εὖνοι μὲν ἐσόμεθα . . . . Cf. also *R.*479A (μέν *post* ἀεί *om. FD*).

Γε μέν

Γε μέν is found in Homer, Hesiod, Theognis, Pindar, probably Bacchylides,[1] and Herodotus.[2] Its usage for the most part corresponds closely with that of γε μήν (μάν). As regards the authors just mentioned, γε μήν (μάν) is not to be found in Homer and Theognis, and it should be banished from the texts of Hesiod

[1] Restored, with great probability, in 3.63,90, both adversative. (The distinction drawn by Jebb on 63 seems needless.)

[2] In the Oxford text of X.*Ages.*9.3 γε μέν is a misprint for γε μήν.

(probably: see γε μήν, *ad init.*) and Herodotus (certainly: see **Μάν, μήν, μέν**, p. 328, and (3) below). But Pindar has both γε μάν and γε μέν (the latter only where metre demands a short syllable). Where γε μέν is used in the same way as γε μήν (μάν), i.e. in (1), (2), (3), there is no reason to suppose any difference in strength. (Kühner holds that γε μέν is 'rather weaker'.)

(1) Adversative.[1] Hom.*B*703 οὐδὲ μὲν οὐδ' οἳ ἄναρχοι ἔσαν, πόθεόν γε μὲν ἀρχόν: *Λ*813 αἷμα μέλαν κελάρυζε· νόος γε μὲν ἔμπεδος ἦεν: Hes.*Op.*772 (with Mair's interpretation of this difficult passage): *Sc.*50 οὐκέθ' ὁμὰ φρονέοντε· κασιγνήτω γε μὲν ἤστην: 300 μελάνθησάν γε μὲν αἵδε ('But the grapes, in contrast with the gold and silver, were coloured black': γε Triclinius: δέ *codd.*): Thgn.1095 σκέπτεο δὴ νῦν ἄλλον, ἐμοί γε μὲν οὔ τις ἀνάγκη τοῦθ' ἔρδειν (but this might be classed under (4), γε μέν being equivalent to μέν γε, and virtually to γοῦν): Pi.*N.*10.33 ὕπατον δ' ἔσχεν Πίσα Ἡρακλέος τεθμόν· ἀδεῖαί γε μὲν ἀμβολάδαν ἐν τελεταῖς δὶς Ἀθαναίων νιν ὀμφαὶ κώμασαν ('The Olympian prize is the highest: but he has won twice at the Panathenaea': so Christ, rightly: not 'Sweet, surely', Bury): Hdt.v 92ε2 (hexameter oracle) ὄλβιος οὗτος ἀνὴρ . . . αὐτὸς καὶ παῖδες, παίδων γε μὲν οὐκέτι παῖδες: Hom.*E*516: δ195: ε206: τ264: Hes.*Th.*363: *Sc.*171: Pi.*P.*4.50 (μάν *vett.*: *corr.* Byz.): Hdt.vii 234.2 οὗτοι πάντες εἰσὶ ὅμοιοι τοῖσι ἐνθάδε μαχεσαμένοισι· οἵ γε μὲν ἄλλοι Λακεδαιμόνιοι τούτοισι μὲν οὐκ ὅμοιοι, ἀγαθοὶ δέ (γε μήν *R*). In Pi.*N.*3.83 the connexion of thought is not obvious: 'μέν similem hic habet vim atque μήν, ut nomini, cui postponitur, pondus addat', Christ: 'Verily', Sandys: this would class the passage under (3): but Mr. C. M. Bowra points out to me that the thought really is: 'I, Pindar, am the real bird of song: there are, of course, also the chattering daws, my imitators: but for you (because of my song) a great light of glory shines'.

(2) Progressive (or weakly adversative). Hes.*Sc.*5 ἣ ῥα γυναικῶν φῦλον ἐκαίνυτο θηλυτεράων εἴδεΐ τε μεγέθει τε· νόον γε μὲν οὔ τις ἔριζε τάων, ἃς θνηταὶ θνητοῖς τέκον ('Aye, and in understanding ...'): *Sc.*139 (γε μήν *al.*): Thgn.1215 ('moreover').

(3) Affirmative (a very rare use, corresponding to the rare use

[1] Paley, in his notes on the Hesiodic passages, seems to imply that this is the only sense of γε μέν.

of γε μήν (*q.v.* (1)). Hes.*Op.*774 δύω . . . ἤματα μηνὸς ἔξοχ' ἀεξομένοιο βροτήσια ἔργα πένεσθαι, ἑνδεκάτη τε δυωδεκάτη τ', ἄμφω γε μὲν ἐσθλαί ('aye, both of them good': τε, not δέ, after ἑνδεκάτη, is necessary on what seems the best interpretation: but the passage is debatable): *Sc.*260 ἡ μὲν ὑφήσσων Ἄτροπος οὔ τι πέλεν μεγάλη θεός, ἀλλ' ἄρα ἥ γε τῶν γε μὲν ἀλλάων προφερής τ' ἦν πρεσβυτάτη τε:[1] Hdt.vi 129 4 Ὦ παῖ Τεισάνδρου, ἀπορχήσαό γε μὲν τὸν γάμον (μήν *L*: I doubt Stein's ellipse, 'You are certainly a good dancer, but . . .', 'Doch traun, vertanzt hast du die Heirat').

(4) Concessive. In other passages μέν is concessive, and γε μέν parts company from γε μήν, and is equivalent in sense to μέν γε. (But, as in the case of μέν, a sharp line can hardly be drawn between (3) and (4).) In the Homeric passages the contrasted idea is contained in what precedes, not in what follows (cf. μέν, III.4.i). θ134 τὸν ξεῖνον ἐρώμεθα εἴ τιν' ἄεθλον οἶδέ τε καὶ δεδάηκε· φυήν γε μὲν οὐ κακός ἐστι ('He *looks* a lusty fellow, and may be an athlete'): Ω642 νῦν δὴ καὶ σίτου πασάμην . . . πάρος γε μὲν οὔ τι πεπάσμην (cf. Σ386: in neither passage would it be right, I think, to take γε μέν as adversative). But in the following passages in Hesiod γε μέν is followed by δέ, and the equivalence with μέν γε is clearly marked: *Th.*871 οἵ γε μὲν ἐκ θεόφιν γενεή, θνητοῖς μέγ' ὄνειαρ· οἱ δ' ἄλλοι μαψαῦραι ἐπιπνείουσι θάλασσαν: *Sc.*282[2] τοί γε μὲν αὖ . . . τοὶ δ' αὖ: 288 οἵ γε μὲν . . . οἱ δ' ἄρ': 301 οἵ γε μὲν ἐτράπεον, τοὶ δ' ἤρυον: in *Op.* 774 ((3) above) μέν perhaps looks forward to δέ in 776: Thgn. 1160a (cf. 1095, (1) above: the text is doubtful: see E. Harrison, *Studies in Theognis*, p. 156): Pi.*O.*12.5 αἵ γε μὲν ἀνδρῶν . . . κυλίνδοντ' ἐλπίδες· σύμβολον δ' οὔ πώ τις ἐπιχθονίων πιστὸν . . . εὗρεν θεόθεν (but an adversative sense is possible here: 'Fortune controls all, while the hopes of man are tossed helplessly about'.)

γε μὲν ὦν is read by three late, but reputable, manuscripts in

[1] But γε μέν, in this position, is very odd: and there is much to be said for Paley's supposition that a line has been lost after ἥ γε, e.g. μικρὴ μὲν δέμας ἦεν, ἀφαυροτέρη δὲ τέτυκτο, γε μέν being adversative.

[2] Rzach rightly excises 283: to retain it, as several scholars have done, making τοί γέ μὲν αὖ answer τοί γέ μὲν αὖ ('some . . . others') is clearly impossible.

Hdt.vii 152.3: ὀφείλω λέγειν τὰ λεγόμενα, πείθεσθαί γε μὲν οὐ παντάπασιν ὀφείλω (γε μὲν ὦν οὐ *RSV*), and is perhaps right, as a stronger form of adversative γε μέν.

Ἦ μέν[1]

Like ἦ μήν, ἦ μέν is used in oaths, and in earnest asseverations which partake of an oath's solemnity.

(1) In oaths. (i) With fut. ind. Hom.ξ160 ἴστω νῦν Ζεὺς ... ἦ μέν τοι τάδε πάντα τελείεται ὡς ἀγορεύω: Hdt.i 212 ἐπόμνυμι ... ἦ μέν σε ἐγὼ ... κορέσω. (ii) With fut. inf. Hom.*Α*77 ὄμοσσον ἦ μέν μοι ... ἀρήξειν: Ξ275: Hdt.i 196 ἐγγυητὰς καταστήσαντα ἦ μὲν συνοικήσειν αὐτῇ: iii 74 πίστι τε λαβόντες καὶ ὁρκίοισι, ἦ μὲν ἕξειν: v 93.1 ἀμείβετο τοὺς αὐτοὺς ἐπικαλέσας θεοὺς ἐκείνῳ, ἦ μὲν Κορινθίους ... ἐπιποθήσειν: iii 133: vi 74.1: ix 91.2.

(2) In strong asseverations. (Almost confined to speeches. Very occasionally in narrative: Hom.*Π*362 (ἦ μὲν δή): Hes.*Sc.* 11.) (i) With fut. ind. Hom.τ167 ἦ μέν μ' ἀχέεσσί γε δώσεις. (ii) With past ind. Hom.τ235 ἦ μὲν πολλαί γ' αὐτὸν ἐθηήσαντο γυναῖκες: κ65: Hes.*Sc.*11. (iii) With pres. ind. Hom.*Ω*416 ἦ μέν μιν ... ἕλκει: ν425.

ἦ μὲν δή and ἦ τοι μέν are similarly used by Homer. *Η*97 ἦ μὲν δὴ λώβη τάδε γ' ἔσσεται: ξ216 ἦ μὲν δὴ θάρσος μοι Ἄρης τ' ἔδοσαν καὶ Ἀθήνη: *Β*798: *Γ*430: *Ι*348: δ33: *Λ*442 ἦ τοι μέν ῥ' ἐμ' ἔπαυσας: *Φ*372 ἀλλ' ἦ τοι μὲν ἐγὼν ἀποπαύσομαι: π129 ἀλλ' ἦ τοι μὲν ταῦτα θεῶν ἐν γούνασι κεῖται: τ560 Ξεῖν', ἦ τοι μὲν ὄνειροι ... γίγνοντ': *Α*140: *Υ*22: α307: ρ6. ἦ τοι μέν is also used with imperative and optative: *Π*451 ἀλλ' εἴ τοι φίλος ἐστὶ ... ἦ τοι μέν μιν ἔασον: *Ρ*509: *Δ*18 εἰ δ' αὖ ... γένοιτο, ἦ τοι μὲν οἰκέοιτο πόλις. (In certain passages the possibility that μέν is preparatory cannot, perhaps, be absolutely excluded: e.g. *Α*140: *Υ*67: ξ259.)

The negative form of ἦ μέν is μὴ μέν. (i) With infinitive. Hom.*Ψ*585 ὄμνυθι μὴ μὲν ἑκὼν ... πεδῆσαι: δ254: Hdt.ii 118 λέγειν ... καὶ ὀμνύντας καὶ ἀνωμοτί, μὴ μὲν ἔχειν Ἑλένην: iii 67 ἔξαρνος ἦν μὴ μὲν ἀποκτεῖναι: i 68 ὑπὸ ἀπιστίης μὴ μὲν γενέσθαι:

[1] For a full discussion of the Homeric uses of ἦ μέν, μὴ μέν, ἦ τοι μέν, καὶ μέν, ἀτὰρ μέν, with plentiful references to authorities, see Mutzbauer.

ii 179: iii 99: v 106.6. (ii) With indicative. Hom.*K* 329 *Ἴστω νῦν Ζεὺς . . . μὴ μὲν τοῖς ἵπποισιν ἀνὴρ ἐποχήσεται ἄλλος*: *T* 258.

Καὶ μέν

(The negative forms corresponding to (1) and (3) are *οὐ μέν, οὐδὲ μέν, οὐ μὲν οὐδέ*, for which see *μέν*, I.A.7,8,9.)

(1) Progressive. *Καὶ μέν*, like *καὶ μήν*, introduces a new point, or develops and amplifies an old one. Hom.*Z* 27 *βῆ δὲ μετ' Αἴσηπον καὶ Πήδασον . . . καὶ μὲν τῶν ὑπέλυσε μένος*: *Ω* 490 *Μνῆσαι πατρὸς σοῖο . . . τηλίκου ὥς περ ἐγών, ὀλοῷ ἐπὶ γήραος οὐδῷ· καὶ μέν που κεῖνον περιναιέται ἀμφὶς ἐόντες τείρουσ'*: *κ* 16 *ἐξερέεινεν ἕκαστα . . . καὶ μὲν ἐγὼ τῷ πάντα . . . κατέλεξα*: *Z* 194: *Ψ* 174: *τ* 244: Hdt.ii 43 *καὶ μὲν ὅτι γε οὐ παρ' Ἑλλήνων ἔλαβον τὸ οὔνομα Αἰγύπτιοι . . .*: viii 60 *β τοσάδε ἐν αὐτοῖσι χρηστὰ εὑρήσεις· πρῶτα μὲν . . . αὖτις δὲ . . . καὶ μὲν καὶ τόδε ἐν αὐτοῖσι ἔνεστι* (*μήν ABCP*). *καὶ μέν* is usually preceded by a strong stop: but Hom.*Ω* 732 *αἳ δή τοι τάχα νηυσὶν ὀχήσονται γλαφυρῇσι, καὶ μὲν ἐγὼ μετὰ τῇσι.*

(2) Affirmative (not connective) introducing a general proposition, which leads up to an *a fortiori* argument (Mutzbauer, p. 19): 'verily, even'. Hom.*Σ* 362 *ποῖον τὸν μῦθον ἔειπες. καὶ μὲν δή πού τις μέλλει βροτὸς ἀνδρὶ τελέσσαι, ὅς περ θνητός τ' ἐστὶ καὶ οὐ τόσα μήδεα οἶδε· πῶς δὴ ἔγωγ', ἥ φημι θεάων ἔμμεν ἀρίστη . . .*; ('Even a mortal . . . much more I, a goddess'): *υ* 45 *Σχέτλιε, καὶ μέν τίς τε χερείονι πείθεθ' ἑταίρῳ, ὅς περ θνητός τ' ἐστὶ καὶ οὐ τόσα μήδεα οἶδεν· αὐτὰρ ἐγὼ θεός εἰμι.*

The analogy of Hom.*ρ* 485 *καί τε* (p. 529) is in favour of rendering *καὶ μέν* 'verily', 'even', in the following also. Hom.*I* 499 *οὐδέ τί σε χρὴ νηλεὲς ἦτορ ἔχειν· στρεπτοὶ δέ τε καὶ θεοὶ αὐτοί, τῶν περ καὶ μείζων ἀρετὴ τιμή τε βίη τε. καὶ μὲν τοὺς θυέεσσι . . παρατρωπῶσ' ἄνθρωποι . . .* (513) *ἀλλ', Ἀχιλεῦ, πόρε καὶ σὺ Διὸς κούρῃσιν* (*Λιταῖς*) *ἕπεσθαι τιμήν* ('Even the gods respect prayers: you must do so too'): 632 ('A man (*καὶ μέν τις*) accepts recompense from the slayer of his brother or son: but you are irreconcilable because of a mere girl'): *ξ* 85–8 (*καὶ μέν* repeated with anacoluthon) *οὐ μὲν σχέτλια ἔργα θεοὶ μάκαρες φιλέουσιν . . . καὶ μὲν δυσμενέες καὶ ἀνάρσιοι, οἵ τ' ἐπὶ γαίης ἀλλοτρίης βῶσιν καί σφι Ζεὺς ληΐδα δώῃ, πλησάμενοι δέ τε νῆας ἔβαν οἶκόνδε νέεσθαι, καὶ μὲν τοῖς ὄπιδος κρατερὸν δέος ἐν φρεσὶ πίπτει. οἵδε δὲ . . . ('Even pirates have fear of divine wrath, but these men have none ').[1]

(3) [Adversative.] Mutzbauer is probably right in denying that καὶ μέν is ever adversative in Homer, though some have found an adversative sense in the following:[2] *A* 269 κάρτιστοι μὲν ἔσαν καὶ καρτίστοις ἐμάχοντο, φηρσὶν ὀρεσκῴοισι, καὶ ἐκπάγλως ἀπόλεσσαν. καὶ μὲν τοῖσιν ἐγὼ μεθομίλεον (cf. 273): η 325 Εὐβοίης, τήν περ τηλοτάτω φάσ' ἔμμεναι οἵ μιν ἴδοντο . . . καὶ μὲν οἱ ἔνθ' ἦλθον (cf. κ 13). Some of the passages grouped under (2) might also be taken as adversative (see n. 1). So, too, might Hdt. ii 43 Αἰγύπτιοι οὔτε Ποσειδέωνος οὔτε Διοσκόρων τὰ οὐνόματά φασι εἰδέναι . . . καὶ μὲν εἴ γε παρ' Ἑλλήνων ἔλαβον οὔνομά τευ δαίμονος, τούτων οὐκ ἥκιστα . . . ἔμελλον μνήμην ἕξειν. But, on the analogy of the other examples of καὶ μέν in Herodotus, it is far more probably progressive here, marking the transition from minor to major premise.

[καὶ . . . μέν.] In Philol.*Fr*.6, ἁ μὲν· ἐστὼ τῶν πραγμάτων ἀΐδιος ἔσσα καὶ αὐτὰ μὲν ἁ φύσις, the second μέν seems impossible and Usener's μάν highly probable.

Ἀτὰρ μέν. Five times in Homer (all in speeches): *Z* 125 τὸ πρίν· ἀτὰρ μὲν νῦν γε . . . : β 122: δ 32: σ 123: υ 200. 'But, in sooth.'

[Δὲ μέν.] In Hes.*Sc*.300–1 δὲ μέν is clearly a mere blunder: cf. δὲ μήν (μήν, VI.1).

[Ἀλλὰ μέν.] The particles are not found juxtaposed in Homer (see Mutzbauer, p. 22, *Anm*.13), nor, I believe, elsewhere. Where ἀλλὰ . . . μέν occurs in Homer (e.g. *A* 125, *B* 721, *Θ* 374, ε 290, μ 156), the particles do not cohere. For ἀλλὰ . . . μέν in Xenophon, see μέν, I.B.1.

Μὲν δή

The collocation of these two particles represents either (1) preparatory μέν strengthened by δή: (2) a μὲν . . . δέ complex

[1] In *I* 499, 632 Mutzbauer renders 'und fürwahr', 'und gewiss' (while others take καὶ μέν in both passages as adversative): in ξ 85–8 he puts a full stop at νέεσθαι: T. W. Allen (in *O.C.T.*) puts one at δώῃ: I prefer Monro's punctuation, given above.

[2] In such passages an adversative sense is appropriate, but is not, I think, expressed by the particles, which simply mean 'and verily'. See καὶ μήν (8).

introduced by connective δή: (3) affirmative, adversative, or progressive μέν strengthened by δή. We have discussed (1) and (2) above (under δή, pp. 258–9), and remarked on the difficulty, in certain cases, of distinguishing between them. (3) alone concerns us here.

In a few passages in epic and elegiac poetry δή strengthens an affirmative μέν. (For ἦ μὲν δή see under ἦ μέν, (2).) Hom.*I* 309 χρὴ μὲν δὴ τὸν μῦθον ἀπηλεγέως ἀποειπεῖν: *A* 514 (with imperative) Νημερτὲς μὲν δή μοι ὑπόσχεο: ο280 οὐ μὲν δή: (an adversative sense, though appropriate to the context, is probably not to be found in μὲν δή in Θ238, ε341, μ209): Thgn.1314 τούτοισ', οἷσπερ νῦν . . . φίλος ἔπλευ . . . οὐ μὲν δὴ τούτοις γ' ἦσθα φίλος πρότερον (οὐ . . . γ' Hermann: συ . . . τ' *A*): Mimn.*Fr.*13.1 οὐ μὲν δὴ κείνου γε μένος . . . πεύθομαι: Semon.*Fr.*20.1 ⟨ἦ⟩ πολλὰ μὲν δὴ προεκπονέαι (ἦ *add.* Bergk: but the lost sequel perhaps supplied an answer to μέν, as in A.*Eu.*106 (see n. 1)). In particular, εἰ μὲν δή in Homer always begins an answer, and means 'if, in very sooth, as you say': *I*434: *K*242: *O*49: *Ω*406: δ831: ι410: χ45: ψ286: ω328.

μὲν δή, in sense (3) above, now temporarily vanishes from Greek. Drama knows μὲν δή in compounds only, γε μὲν δή, ἀλλὰ . . . μὲν δή, καὶ μὲν δή[1]: while ἀλλὰ μὲν δή, καὶ μὲν δή are found in Attic prose. But sense (3) reappears, in certain limited usages, in Plato and Xenophon. The uses throughout correspond closely with those of μήν.

I. Affirmative (cf. the far commoner uses of μέντοι, II.1).

(1) Assent with echoed word. Pl.*Phlb.*55E φαῦλον τὸ καταλειπόμενον ἑκάστης ἂν γίγνοιτο.—Φαῦλον μὲν δή (μὲν δή *BT*: μέντοι *vulgo*): *Lg.*901A οὐκ ἐπιτρεπτέον.—Οὐ μὲν δή.

(2) Negative answer to a question, following μὰ Δία, μὰ τὸν Δία (Xenophon only). X.*Smp.*4.3 Ἦ καί σοι, ἔφη, ἀποδιδόασιν ὅ τι ἂν λάβωσι;—Μὰ τὸν Δί', ἔφη, οὐ μὲν δή ('I should think not!'): *Cyr.*vi 3.10 ἦ καὶ ἔχαιρον . . .;—Οὐ μὰ Δί', εἶπον ἐκεῖνοι, οὐ μὲν δὴ ἔχαιρον, ἀλλὰ καὶ μάλα ἠνιῶντο: *Smp.*4.52: *Cyr.*i 6.9: ii 2.22: v 5.19.

(Pl.*Phlb.*46B Οὐ μὲν δὴ Φιλήβου γε ἕνεκα παρεθέμην τὸν λόγον· ἀλλ' ἄνευ τούτων . . . . Here μὲν δή seems simply to give liveliness

[1] In A.*Eu.*106 μέν is answered by καί in 110, 'and yet'.

to the negation, like *μέντοι*, which one would expect here: 'This isn't a hit at Philebus, you know': *μέν* should not, I think, be taken as concessive, whether *solitarium* or answered by *ἀλλά*.)

II. Adversative, either (1) in an answer, protesting; or (2) answering *μέν*.

(1) Pl.*Phdr*.259B *ἀνήκοος γάρ, ὡς ἔοικε, τυγχάνω ὤν.—Οὐ μὲν δὴ πρέπει γε φιλόμουσον ἄνδρα τῶν τοιούτων ἀνήκοον εἶναι*: X.*Oec*.13.5 *ὥστε ἴσως ἂν καὶ καταγελάσαις ἀκούων.—Οὐ μὲν δὴ ἄξιόν γε . . . τὸ πρᾶγμα καταγέλωτος*. It would of course be possible to take *μέν* as concessive in both places: but the context rather suggests a protest, 'but really', and this interpretation gains support from the following passages, where *μὲν δή* is undoubtedly adversative.

(2) Pl.*Phdr*.266C *Βασιλικοὶ μὲν ἄνδρες, οὐ μὲν δὴ ἐπιστήμονές γε ὧν ἐρωτᾷς*: *Ti*.41B *ἀθάνατοι μὲν οὔκ ἐστὲ οὐδ' ἄλυτοι τὸ πάμπαν, οὔτι μὲν δὴ λυθήσεσθέ γε οὐδὲ τεύξεσθε θανάτου μοίρας* ('but, on the other hand, you shall not . . .'): with less adversative force, X.*An*.iii 2.14 *τοιούτων μέν ἐστε προγόνων. οὐ μὲν δὴ τοῦτό γε ἐρῶ ὡς ὑμεῖς καταισχύνετε αὐτούς* ('Nor will I say that you, on your side, are a disgrace to them').

III. Progressive.

(1) In negative statements, usually after a preceding negative. Pl.*Tht*.148E *οὔτε . . . οὔτε . . . οὐ μὲν δὴ αὖ οὐδέ*: X.*An*.i 9.13 'He rewarded those who did him good service. *οὐ μὲν δὴ οὐδὲ τοῦτ' ἄν τις εἴποι, ὡς τοὺς κακούργους καὶ ἀδίκους εἴα καταγελᾶν*' ('Nor, on the other hand'): ii 2.3 *ποταμὸς . . . ὃν οὐκ ἂν δυναίμεθα ἄνευ πλοίων διαβῆναι· πλοῖα δὲ ἡμεῖς οὐκ ἔχομεν. οὐ μὲν δὴ αὐτοῦ γε μένειν οἷόν τε* ('Nor, again'): ii 4.6 *τὸν δ' οὖν Εὐφράτην ἴσμεν ὅτι ἀδύνατον διαβῆναι κωλυόντων πολεμίων. οὐ μὲν δὴ ἂν μάχεσθαί γε δέῃ, ἱππεῖς εἰσιν ἡμῖν ξύμμαχοι* ('Again': a further objection: here *ἀδύνατον* is equivalent to a negative): *Hier*.7.11 *οὔτε σὺ οὔτε ἄλλος μὲν δὴ οὐδεὶς πώποτε* (oddly separated from the negative: read, perhaps, *οὔτε μὲν δὴ ἄλλος*: cf. *οὔτε μήν* (*μήν*, VI.5)).

(2) In positive statements. (Only) Pl.*Ly*.204D *ἡμῶν γοῦν . . . ἐκκεκώφωκε τὰ ὦτα καὶ ἐμπέπληκε Λύσιδος· ἂν μὲν δὴ καὶ ὑποπίῃ, εὐμαρία ἡμῖν ἐστιν καὶ ἐξ ὕπνου ἐγρομένοις Λύσιδος οἴεσθαι*

τοὔνομα ἀκούειν ('and if, besides, he is a bit drunk . . .': perhaps κἂν μὲν δή).

Ἀλλὰ μὲν δή

This combination is found in Antiphon, Lysias, Plato, and Xenophon: and, in the split form, ἀλλὰ . . . μὲν δή, in Sophocles, though not in the other dramatists. It conveys meanings more commonly expressed by ἀλλὰ μήν, ἀλλὰ μέντοι. In the split form it is sometimes alternatively possible to take μέν as *solitarium*.

(1) Adversative. Ant.*Fr.*1 a ἀλλὰ μὲν δὴ λέγουσιν οἱ κατήγοροι ὡς . . . (for ἀλλὰ νὴ Δία): Pl.*Cri.*48A Οὐκ ἄρα . . . φροντιστέον τί ἐροῦσιν οἱ πολλοὶ ἡμᾶς . . . "Ἀλλὰ μὲν δή", φαίη γ' ἄν τις, "οἷοί τέ εἰσιν ἡμᾶς οἱ πολλοὶ ἀποκτεινύναι": *Grg.*492E.

ἀλλὰ . . . μὲν δή. S.*El.*103 'I alone pity you. ἀλλ' οὐ μὲν δὴ λήξω θρήνων' ('Yet, for all that'): *OT* 294 τὸν δὲ δρῶντ' οὐδεὶς ὁρᾷ.—Ἀλλ' εἴ τι μὲν δὴ δείματός γ' ἔχει μέρος, τὰς σὰς ἀκούων οὐ μενεῖ τοιάσδ' ἀράς: 523 'I cannot bear Oedipus' reproaches'.—Ἀλλ' ἦλθε μὲν δὴ τοῦτο τοὔνειδος τάχ' ἂν ὀργῇ βιασθέν: Pl.*Tht.*187A Ἀλλ' οὔ τι μὲν δὴ τούτου γε ἕνεκα ἠρχόμεθα διαλεγόμενοι: X.*Oec.*11.2 ἵνα καὶ μεταρρυθμίσῃς με . . .—Ἀλλ' ἐγὼ μὲν δή, ἔφην, πῶς ἂν δικαίως μεταρρυθμίσαιμι . . .; (perhaps rather μέν *solitarium*): Lys.vi 39 ἀλλ' οὐ μὲν δὴ . . . .

(2) Assentient. Pl.*Tht.*143B ἀναπαύσασθαι δέομαι . . .—Ἀλλὰ μὲν δὴ καὶ αὐτὸς . . . οὐκ ἂν ἀηδῶς ἀναπαυοίμην: *Cra.*428B δοκεῖς μοι ἐσκέφθαι τὰ τοιαῦτα . . .—Ἀλλὰ μὲν δὴ . . . ὥσπερ σὺ λέγεις, μεμέληκέν μοι περὶ αὐτῶν ('Well, certainly, I *have* given some thought to the matter'): *Grg.*506B.

(3) Substantiation of condition, usually with echoed word (cf. μήν, III.1.i, ἀλλὰ μήν, (3), καὶ μήν, (3)). Pl.*Grg.*471A Ἄθλιος ἄρα οὗτός ἐστιν . . .; —Εἴπερ γε . . . ἄδικος.—Ἀλλὰ μὲν δὴ πῶς οὐκ ἄδικος; *R.*459C εἴπερ . . . ὡσαύτως ἔχει.—Ἀλλὰ μὲν δὴ ἔχει, ἔφη: *Euthd.*275C: *Thg.*122B (perhaps rather to be classed as assentient): *Prm.*126A: *Alc.I* 119E.

(4) Progressive. Pl.*R.*442D 'A man will become σώφρων by the harmony of these elements'.—'Yes.'—Ἀλλὰ μὲν δὴ δίκαιός γε . . . τούτῳ καὶ οὕτως ἔσται ('Again, he will become just . . .'): *Hipparch.*232C: *Phd.*75A: *R.*477E: Lys.xiii 27 ἀλλὰ μὲν δὴ οὐχ

ὅμοιά γε σοὶ καὶ ἐκείνοις ὑπῆρχεν (a new argument: cf. xiv44): xxvi22 ἀλλὰ μὲν δὴ οὐδὲ τὴν οὐσίαν ἡμᾶς ἐν τῷ πολέμῳ φήσει κτήσασθαι (a further charge refuted in advance).

Introducing minor premise (cf. ἀλλὰ μήν, (6)). Pl.*Grg.*506D ἀγαθοί ἐσμεν . . . ἀρετῆς τινος παραγενομένης.—'Yes.'—Ἀλλὰ μὲν δὴ ἥ γε ἀρετὴ ἑκάστου . . . τάξει (παραγίγνεται) . . . Κόσμος τις ἄρα ἐγγενόμενος . . . ἀγαθὸν παρέχει ἕκαστον τῶν ὄντων; *Euthphr.*10D.

ἀλλὰ . . . μὲν δή. S.*El.*913 κἀγὼ μὲν οὐκ ἔδρασα . . . οὐδ' αὖ σὺ . . . ἀλλ' οὐδὲ μὲν δὴ μητρὸς οὔθ' ὁ νοῦς φιλεῖ τοιαῦτα πράσσειν . . .: *Tr.*627 Ἐπίσταμαί τε (τἀν δόμοισι) καὶ φράσω σεσωμένα.—Ἀλλ' οἶσθα μὲν δὴ καὶ τὰ τῆς ξένης ὁρῶν προσδέγματ': *Aj.*877: *Tr.*1128 (both ἀλλ' οὐδὲ μὲν δή).

Γε μὲν δή

This rare combination is confined to tragedy, where it is commonest in Aeschylus, rarest in Euripides. In A.*Eu.*419 it is progressive, or only faintly adversative, in sense: Γένος μὲν οἶδα κληδόνας τ' ἐπωνύμους.—Τιμάς γε μὲν δὴ τὰς ἐμὰς πεύσει τάχα ('Aye, and . . .'). Elsewhere it is always definitely, and strongly, adversative:[1] A.*Ag.*661 ὁρῶμεν ἀνθοῦν πέλαγος Αἰγαῖον νεκροῖς . . . ἡμᾶς γε μὲν δὴ . . . ἐξέκλεψεν . . . θεός τις: S.*El.*1243 τόδε μὲν οὔ ποτ' ἀξιώσω τρέσαι, περισσὸν ἄχθος ἔνδον γυναικῶν ὂν αἰεί.—Ὅρα γε μὲν δὴ κἀν γυναιξὶν ὡς Ἄρης ἔνεστιν ('Aye, but mark you'): A.*Supp.*241 ('Your dress is foreign, but you have suppliant branches after Hellenic fashion'), 273: *Ag.*1213: S.*Tr.*484: E.*Hel.*1259 (the logical link is with 1257).

Καὶ μὲν δή

Καὶ μὲν δή[2] is not infrequent in Plato and Isocrates, less frequent in Xenophon (*Cyr.* only, five times), and notably common in

[1] A concessive sense would be appropriate in some places (cf. γε μέν, (4) and see Tucker on A.*Supp.*241 (his 215)), but should nowhere, I think, be posited.

[2] See Prof. P. Shorey in *C.Phil.*xxviii(1933),2, pp. 131–2. Our statistics tally almost exactly: I have taken an example or two from him, and added one or two to his list.

Lysias, who has it twenty-one times. (In the attack on love in the *Phaedrus*, a passage written either by Lysias or in imitation of his style, it occurs five times in four and a half pages: 231D, 232B,E, 233A,D). There are two examples apiece in Antiphon and Andocides, and one in Thucydides: hardly any in verse[1] (two only, in Aristophanes), or in the remaining orators (Is.x 12: [D.]lxi 13). The uses correspond closely to those of the far commoner *καὶ μήν*.

(1) Assentient. Pl.*Cra*.396D *τῆς σοφίας ταυτησὶ . . . ἥ ἐμοὶ ἐξαίφνης νῦν οὑτωσὶ προσπέπτωκεν . . .—Καὶ μὲν δή, ὦ Σώκρατες, ἀτεχνῶς γέ μοι δοκεῖς . . . ἐξαίφνης χρησμῳδεῖν* ('Yes, indeed, Socrates'): *R*.409B *εὐήθεις νέοι ὄντες οἱ ἐπιεικεῖς φαίνονται . . .—Καὶ μὲν δή, ἔφη, σφόδρα γε αὐτὸ πάσχουσι*: *Ti*.20C *συνωμολογήσατ' οὖν . . . εἰς νῦν ἀνταποδώσειν μοι τὰ τῶν λόγων ξένια . . .—Καὶ μὲν δὴ . . . οὔτε ἐλλείψομεν προθυμίας οὐδὲν . . .*: *R*.526B, 528D: X.*Cyr*.i 6.3: vi 2.23.

Somewhat similar are the following passages, in which *καὶ μὲν δή* conveys a lively response, rather after the manner of *μέντοι* (*q.v.* II.1). Pl.*Tht*.155E *εἰσὶν δὲ οὗτοι οἱ οὐδὲν ἄλλο οἰόμενοι εἶναι ἢ οὗ ἂν δύνωνται ἀπρὶξ τοῖν χεροῖν λαβέσθαι . . .—Καὶ μὲν δή, ὦ Σώκρατες, σκληρούς γε λέγεις καὶ ἀντιτύπους ἀνθρώπους* ('Why, they *are* a stubborn type!'): *Sph*.217B ('Why, that is just what we were asking him'). There seems to be little, if any, connective force in these.

(2) Inceptive (cf. *μήν*, III.1.iii: *ἀλλὰ μήν*, 2.i: *καὶ μήν*, (5)). Pl.*R*.428A *Οὐκοῦν καὶ περὶ τούτων, ἐπειδὴ τέτταρα ὄντα τυγχάνει, ὡσαύτως ζητητέον; —Δῆλα δή.—Καὶ μὲν δὴ πρῶτόν γέ μοι δοκεῖ ἐν αὐτῷ κατάδηλον εἶναι ἡ σοφία* ('Well').

(3) Adversative. Pl.*Hp.Ma*.290A *τὸ γὰρ ὀρθῶς λεγόμενον ἀνάγκη αὐτῷ ἀποδέχεσθαι . . .—Καὶ μὲν δὴ ταύτην γε τὴν ἀπόκρισιν οὐ μόνον οὐκ ἀποδέξεται . . .*: *R*.406A: *Plt*.287D.

(4) Progressive (by far the commonest use). Ar.*Th*.805 *Ναυσιμάχης μέν γ' ἥττων ἐστὶν Χαρμῖνος· δῆλα δὲ τἄργα. καὶ μὲν δὴ καὶ Κλεοφῶν χείρων πάντως δήπου Σαλαβακχοῦς*: 819 *καὶ μὲν δήπου καὶ τὰ πατρῷά γε χείρους ἡμῶν εἰσιν σώζειν* (*δή* goes more closely with *καὶ μέν*, which cannot stand without it in Attic, than with *που*, and we should perhaps write *καὶ μὲν δή*

[1] In Homer (Σ362, see *καὶ μέν*, (2)) the combination is not yet stereotyped.

που): Hp.*Art.*47 *καὶ μὲν δὴ καὶ κατὰ φύσιν γε ἀναγκάζουσι*: Th.iii 113.4 "*ἀλλ' ἡμεῖς γε οὐδενὶ ἐμαχόμεθα χθές, ἀλλὰ πρῴην ἐν τῇ ἀποχωρήσει*". "*καὶ μὲν δὴ τούτοις γε ἡμεῖς χθὲς . . . ἐμαχόμεθα*" (' And *we* fought yesterday against *these* men'): Pl.*Grg.*507B *τὸν δὲ τὰ δίκαια . . . πράττοντα ἀνάγκη δίκαιον . . . εἶναι.—Ἔστι ταῦτα.—Καὶ μὲν δὴ καὶ ἀνδρεῖόν γε ἀνάγκη*: *Prt.*315C ' I caught sight of Hippias. *καὶ μὲν δὴ καὶ Τάνταλόν γε εἰσεῖδον*' (where Homer λ582 has *καὶ μήν*): *Smp.*197A (a series, *πρῶτον μὲν . . . καὶ μὲν δὴ . . . ἀλλὰ . . . γε μήν*): *Chrm.*159C *Τί δ' ἀναγιγνώσκειν; ταχέως ἢ βραδέως (κάλλιστον);—Ταχέως.—Καὶ μὲν δὴ καὶ τὸ κιθαρίζειν ταχέως . . . κάλλιον τοῦ . . . βραδέως*; *Grg.*458D ' I should like more than anything to listen to the discussion'.—*Νὴ τοὺς θεούς, ὦ Χαιρεφῶν, καὶ μὲν δὴ καὶ αὐτὸς . . . οὐκ οἶδ' εἴ πώποτε ἥσθην οὕτως ὥσπερ νυνί* (preceded by oath: cf. X.*Cyr.* viii 4.8): Ant.v 51 *ἐκ τῶν λόγων τῶν τοῦ ἀνθρώπου μερὶς ἑκατέροις ἴση ἂν εἴη . . . καὶ μὲν δὴ τὰ ἐξ ἴσου γενόμενα τοῦ φεύγοντός ἐστι μᾶλλον ἢ τοῦ διώκοντος* (transition to major premise, with conclusion left unexpressed): And.i 20 (new argument): Pl.*Men.*88D: *Ly.*206B: *Cra.*428A: *Ti.*18C: *Lg.*712E: *R.*464B: X.*Cyr.*v 5.44: viii 4.17: Ant.v 63: And.i 140: Lys.xii 30,35,49,89: xiv 12,32, 34,43: Isoc.iii 36: iv 40 (in all the eleven Isocratean instances, except iii 16, a second *καί* follows immediately).

καὶ . . . μὲν δή. X.*Cyr.*iii 3.48 *ἔλεγον ὅτι ἐξίοιεν . . . καὶ παρατάττοι αὐτοὺς αὐτὸς ὁ βασιλεὺς ἔξω ὤν, καὶ παρακελεύοιτο μὲν δὴ τοῖς αἰεὶ ἔξω οὖσι πολλά τε καὶ ἰσχυρά*: if the text is sound, *καί*, though not juxtaposed, seems to go with *μὲν δή*, exceptionally without a strong stop preceding: *ἤδη* for *δή* (*HAG*) makes things worse, not better.

(For *μὲν οὖν*, with adversative or affirmative *μέν*, see *μὲν οὖν*, (3).)

Μέντοι

Μέντοι is formed of *μέν* and *τοι*. In Homer the fusion has not yet taken place, and the particles[1] are, rightly, written separately. In Attic they coalesce into one word, sometimes

[1] All the Homeric instances are in speeches, and *τοι* is perhaps everywhere in Homer to be regarded as dative singular: so L. & S.: see Ebeling, *s.v. μέν*, p. 1048 a.

μέν and sometimes, but less frequently, *τοι* being the preponderating element.[1] Some scholars read *μέν τοι separatim* in a few passages, in which they take *μέν* as preparatory: A.*Th.*515: *Ag.*644,943. It is certainly significant that all these are from Aeschylus, in whose time the fusion may not yet have been complete: but in the first two passages *μέντοι* follows *τοιόσδε*, with which it is often associated (see below): in the third, the interpretation is doubtful (see II.1.v.). *μέν τοι separatim* seems to have been avoided in Attic. Why, it is hard to say: not through fear of ambiguity, since a similar ambiguity is tolerated in *μὲν οὖν* and *μὲν δή*. In Ionic prose: Hp.*Acut.*5 *οἱ μέν τοι . . . οἱ δέ* (*μέν τι al.*, as often).

μέν in *μέντοι* has either a confirmatory or an adversative sense: sometimes, again (mainly in the fourth century), a progressive sense: occasionally, perhaps, in Epic (*μέν τοι*), a preparatory sense.

I. *μέν τοι, μέντοι* in Epic, Elegiac, and early Iambic. The instances are few.

(1) Epic, *μέν τοι*. Determination of the force of *μέν* is here, as often, difficult at this early stage in the development of logical thought.

(i) Affirmative. Hom.*δ*157 Menelaus recognizes Telemachus as Odysseus' son. Peisistratus answers: *Ἀτρεΐδη Μενέλαε . . . κείνου μέν τοι ὅδ' υἱὸς ἐτήτυμον, ὡς ἀγορεύεις* ('in very sooth'): *ξ*508 *Ὦ γέρον, αἶνος μέν τοι ἀμύμων, ὃν κατέλεξας*: *π*267 *Ἐσθλώ τοι τούτω γ' ἐπαμύντορε . . . —Οὐ μέν τοι κείνω γε πολὺν χρόνον ἀμφὶς ἔσεσθον φυλόπιδος κρατερῆς* ('Aye, truly'): *ω*321 *Κεῖνος μέν τοι ὅδ' αὐτὸς ἐγώ, πάτερ, ὃν σὺ μεταλλᾷς.* It will be noted that in these four passages (all from the *Odyssey*) *μέν τοι* occurs at the beginning of an answer. The first two forecast the Attic use of *μέντοι* in affirmative answers, 'Aye, truly'. In *Φ*370 *μέν τοι* might conceivably be adversative, but is better taken as affirmative: *Ἥρη, τίπτε σὸς υἱὸς ἐμὸν ῥόον ἔχραε κήδειν ἐξ ἄλλων; οὐ μέν τοι ἐγὼ τόσον αἴτιός εἰμι, ὅσσον οἱ ἄλλοι πάντες.*

(ii) Adversative. Hom.*σ*233 Penelope blames Telemachus for allowing the fight between Odysseus and Irus. Telemachus answers that he is powerless in face of the suitors: *οὐ μέν τοι*

[1] Interpretation is what matters here, not orthography. The Greeks very probably made some slight distinction in pronunciation between *μέν τοι* and *μέντοι*. (Cf. 'all right', 'all round'.)

ξείνου γε καὶ Ἴρου μῶλος ἐτύχθη μνηστήρων ἰότητι, βίῃ δ' ὅ γε φέρτερος ἦεν (doubt as to the precise interpretation (see Monro) does not affect the sense of μέν).

(iii) Preparatory (possibly). Hom.*Δ*318 Ἀτρεΐδη, μάλα μέν τοι ἐγὼν ἐθέλοιμι καὶ αὐτὸς . . . ἀλλ' . . . : δ411 φώκας μέν τοι πρῶτον ἀριθμήσει . . . αὐτὰρ ἐπὴν πάσας πεμπάσσεται . . . : Hes.*Op.*287 τὴν μέν τοι κακότητα καὶ ἰλαδὸν ἔστιν ἑλέσθαι . . . τῆς δ' ἀρετῆς ἱδρῶτα θεοὶ προπάροιθεν ἔθηκαν (μὲν γάρ Xenophon and Stobaeus).

μὲν γάρ τοι. Hom.*O*222: *Ω*172.

(2) Iambic and Elegiac, μέντοι. Semon.*Fr.*20.2 (with no context to define the sense): Thgn.661 (clearly corrupt). In Lyric I find no instances.

II. μέντοι in Ionic prose and in Attic. It is only when we reach the tragedians that μέντοι begins to be frequent. The earliest (apparent) prose example is Heraclit.*Fr.*28 καὶ μέντοι καὶ Δίκη καταλήψεται ψευδῶν τέκτονας: but Wilamowitz' καὶ μὲν πῦρ καί is almost certainly right. We can distinguish three broad classes: (1) Affirmative or emphatic: (2) Adversative: (3) Progressive.

(1) Emphatic. μέν denotes objective certainty, while τοι brings the truth home to another person: 'really, you know'. On the whole, perhaps, τοι preponderates, and μέντοι in this sense is mostly found in writers who use τοι freely. The particle is often associated with pronouns, σύ, οὗτος, τοιοῦτος.

(i) In general. Often there is a certain assentient force, 'yes', as, more clearly, in (ii). S.*Aj.*86 Ἐγὼ σκοτώσω βλέφαρα καὶ δεδορκότα.—Γένοιτο μέντἂν πᾶν θεοῦ τεχνωμένου ('Well, all is possible when a god contrives', Jebb): E.*Ph.*899 Φράσον πολίταις καὶ πόλει σωτηρίαν.—Βούλῃ σὺ μέντοι κοὐχὶ βουλήσῃ τάχα ('Yes, you wish it, but in a moment you won't': sarcastic): Ar.*Eq.* 1152 Ὦ Δῆμ', ἐγὼ μέντοι . . . τρίπαλαι καθῆμαι ('I've been sitting for ages, you know'): *Nu.*126 Ἀλλ' οὐδ' ἐγὼ μέντοι πεσών γε κείσομαι: 1338 Ἐδιδαξάμην μέντοι σε νὴ Δί', ὦ μέλε, τοῖσιν δικαίοις ἀντιλέγειν (bitterly sarcastic: '*I have* had you taught'): *V.*231 ὦ Κωμία, βραδύνεις· μὰ τὸν Δί' οὐ μέντοι πρὸ τοῦ γ': 426 Τοῦτο μέντοι δεινὸν ἤδη νὴ Δί', εἰ μαχούμεθα: Pl.*Grg.*466C Νὴ τὸν κύνα, ἀμφιγνοῶ μέντοι ('I swear I can't make up my mind, you know'): *La.*181B Ὦ Σώκρατες, οὗτος μέντοι ὁ ἔπαινός ἐστιν καλός, ὃν σὺ νῦν ἐπαινῇ: 195C Τί δοκεῖ Λάχης λέγειν, ὦ Νικία; ἔοικε μέντοι λέγειν τι ('There *seems* to be something in what he says, you know'): *Ly.*203B οὐ παραβάλλεις; ἄξιον μέντοι: *Phd.*117D Οἷα, ἔφη, ποιεῖτε, ὦ θαυμάσιοι. ἐγὼ μέντοι οὐχ ἥκιστα τούτου ἕνεκα τὰς γυναῖκας ἀπέπεμψα ('you know'): *Tht.*151E αἴσθησις, φῄς, ἐπιστήμη;—Ναί.—Κινδυνεύεις μέντοι λόγον οὐ φαῦλον εἰρηκέναι περὶ ἐπιστήμης (half-ironical approval: 'Well, that is no mere commonplace observation'): *R.*329C: *Euthd.*273C: *Thg.*129A: *Phlb.*36D: *Tht.*152B: X.*Mem.*ii 1.14: iii 1.2: *Cyr.*ii 2.5.

With τοιοῦτος, τοιόσδε, ὅδε, οὗτος, usually at the opening of an answer. A.*Pr.*964 Τοιοῖσδε μέντοι καὶ πρὶν αὐθαδίσμασιν ἐς τάσδε σαυτὸν πημονὰς καθώρμισας ('That is the sort of stubbornness which has brought you into *trouble*'): Ar.*Av.*100 Τὸ ῥάμφος ἡμῖν σου γέλοιον φαίνεται.—Τοιαῦτα μέντοι Σοφοκλέης λυμαίνεται ἐν ταῖς τραγῳδίαισιν ἐμὲ τὸν Τηρέα ('That's what *Sophocles* does to me in his tragedies'): A.*Pr.*1054: *Ag.*886: S *Aj.*952, 1246, 1358: E.*El.*1011: Ar.*Eq.*1221: *Nu.*1361: *Av.*1351: *Ra.*743, 971: *Lys.*968: *Th.*520: Pl.*Hp.Ma.*281B Hippias: 'I have been extremely busy lately'.—Τοιοῦτον μέντοι, ὦ Ἱππία, ἔστι τὸ τῇ ἀληθείᾳ σοφόν τε καὶ τέλειον ἄνδρα εἶναι ('Ah, that's what it means to be really *clever*'). A.*Th.*515 τοιάδε μέντοι προσφίλεια δαιμόνων: πρὸς τῶν κρατούντων δ' ἐσμέν, οἱ δ' ἡσσωμένων is, I think, different: the emphasis lies more on τοιάδε than on προσφίλεια.

With σύ, often in a parenthetical or quasi-parenthetical clause, giving the reason why this particular person is addressed in this particular way. Ar.*Av.*339 Ὡς ἀπωλόμεσθ' ἄρα.—Αἴτιος μέντοι σὺ νῷν εἶ τῶν κακῶν τούτων μόνος ('This is all *your* fault, you know'): 933 οὗτος, σὺ μέντοι σπολάδα καὶ χιτῶν' ἔχεις, ἀπόδυθι: *Th.*218 Ἀγάθων, σὺ μέντοι ξυροφορεῖς ἑκάστοτε, χρῆσόν τί νυν ἡμῖν ξυρόν ('Agathon, *you* always carry a *razor*'): *Ra.*171 οὗτος, σὲ λέγω μέντοι (a call to attention: cf. τοι, I.8): Pl.*Prt.*339E Ὦ Πρόδικε, ἔφην ἐγώ, σὸς μέντοι Σιμωνίδης πολίτης· δίκαιος εἶ βοηθεῖν τῷ ἀνδρί: *Phdr.*238D τὰ νῦν γὰρ οὐκέτι πόρρω διθυράμβων φθέγγομαι.—Ἀληθέστατα λέγεις.—Τούτων μέντοι σὺ αἴτιος ('Well, that's *your* fault': cf. *Grg.*447A Τούτων μέντοι . . . αἴτιος Χαιρεφῶν ὅδε): X.*Smp.*6.8 Σὺ μέντοι δεινὸς εἶ . . . εἰκάζειν· οὐ δοκεῖ σοι ὁ ἀνὴρ οὗτος λοιδορεῖσθαι βουλομένῳ ἐοικέναι;

Emphatic μέντοι almost invariably comes early in the sentence.

The following are exceptional. Hdt.viii 87.3 *εἰ μὲν καί τι νεῖκος πρὸς αὐτὸν ἐγεγόνεε . . . οὐ μέντοι ἔχω γε εἰπεῖν* (*ἔγωγε ἔχω S*: *ἔγωγε V*): Aeschin.i 98 *ὅτι δὲ ταῦτ' ἀληθῆ λέγω, ἐνταῦθα μέντοι νὴ Δία σαφῶς . . . μαρτυροῦντας ὑμῖν τοὺς μάρτυρας παρέξομαι.*

Emphatic *μέντοι* is hardly ever found (as in these last two passages) outside dialogue. And.i 41 is from a conversation: *Ἆρά γε σὲ οἵδε περιμένουσι; χρὴ μέντοι μὴ ἀπωθεῖσθαι τοιούτους φίλους* ('You oughtn't, you know, . . .').

(ii) A particular variety of emphatic *μέντοι* is the assentient use.

(*a*) Conveying a favourable opinion of the previous speaker's words (cf. *τοι*, I.7): Aristophanes and Plato. Ar.*Lys.*1095 *Νὴ τὸν Δί' εὖ μέντοι λέγεις*: *Th.*9 *Πῶς μοι παραινεῖς; δεξιῶς μέντοι λέγεις*: Pl.*La.*194D *Ἀληθῆ μέντοι νὴ Δία λέγεις*: *Cra.* 385A *Ἴσως μέντοι τι λέγεις*: *Lg.* 646B, 665B, 861A: *Smp.*176B: *Sph.*245B.

Naturally, the verb is normally in the second person. Pl.*Tht.* 187B is only formally an exception: *Οὕτω μέντοι χρὴ . . . λέγειν.* Elliptical: Pl.*R.*425A *Ἀληθῆ μέντοι, ἔφη.* But sometimes the assent is conveyed to a third party: Pl.*Phd.*86D *Δίκαια μέντοι, ἔφη, λέγει ὁ Σιμμίας*: *Thg.*127B *οὐ μέντοι κακῶς λέγει* ('There's something in what he says, you know'): *Phlb.*18A *Ὀρθῶς μέντοι τοῦθ' ἡμᾶς, ὦ Πρώταρχε, ἠρώτηκε Φίληβος*: *Tht.*152B. In Ar.*Pl.*1052 *Εὖ μέντοι λέγει* is an aside.

(*b*) Occasionally in Aristophanes, not seldom in Xenophon, and extremely often in Plato, marking assent by echoing a word, or words, of the previous speaker. (Cf. *μὲν δή*, I.1, p. 392.) Ar.*Eq.*895 *οἶσθα . . . ;—Οἶδα μέντοι*: *V.*665 *Οὐδὲ . . .—Μὰ Δί' οὐ μέντοι*: *Eq.*168 *Ἐγώ;—Σὺ μέντοι*: *Lys.*498 *Ὑμεῖς;—Ἡμεῖς μέντοι*: Pl.*Euthd.*291A *μή τις τῶν κρειττόνων . . . ἐφθέγξατο; . . .—Ναὶ μὰ Δία . . . τῶν κρειττόνων μέντοι τις*: *La.*190C *Φαμὲν ἄρα . . .—Φαμὲν μέντοι*: *R* 371B *συχνῶν . . .—Συχνῶν μέντοι*: *Ly.* 208A *οὐκ ἂν ἐῷεν . . . ;—Μὰ Δί' οὐ μέντοι ἄν, ἔφη, ἐῷεν*: X.*Cyr.* i 4.19 *Ἦ . . . πολέμιοί εἰσιν . . . ;—Πολέμιοι μέντοι, ἔφη.—Ἦ καὶ ἐκεῖνοι, ἔφη, οἱ ἐλαύνοντες;—Κἀκεῖνοι μέντοι*: *Oec.* 1.8 *Οὐδ' ἄρα γε ἡ γῆ ἀνθρώπῳ ἐστὶ χρήματα . . .—Οὐδὲ ἡ γῆ μέντοι χρήματά ἐστιν* (where the number of words repeated is remarkable): Pl.*R.*375E, 386C, 389A, 443A, 469E: X.*Mem.*ii 6.2: *Smp.*4.4.

μέντοι νὴ (*μὰ*) *Δία* is extremely common in Plato. Ar.*Pax*

1290 Ἐγώ;—Σὺ μέντοι νὴ Δία (*Av.*1651: *Ec.*1130): *Av.*1668 οὐδὲν ...;—Οὐ μέντοι μὰ Δία: Pl.*La.*195A Οὔκουν φησί γε Νικίας.—Οὐ μέντοι μὰ Δία: *Chrm.*154B: *Euthphr.*4B: *Phd.*65D, 68B, 73D, 74A. (οὐ μέντοι μὰ Δία adversative, answering μέν, D.iv 49.) With the oath preceding the particle and negative. Hermipp.*Fr.*76 μὰ τὸν Δί' οὐ μέντοι: Pl.*Euthd.*290E Οὐκ οἴει ...;—Μὰ Δί' οὐ μέντοι: X.*Smp.*3.13 Ἆρ' οἶσθα ...;—Μὰ Δί', ἔφη, τοῦτο μέντοι ἐγὼ οὐκ οἶδα: 4.33 Οὐκοῦν (*num*) θύεις;—Μὰ Δία τοῦτο μέντοι ... οὐ ποιῶ.

In reported speech. Pl.*Lg.*809E οὔπω διείρηκέ σοι πότερον ... ἢ τὸ παράπαν οὐδὲ προσοιστέον· ὣς δ' αὔτως καὶ περὶ λύραν. προσοιστέον μέντοι νῦν φαμεν (μέντοι νῦν Bekker: μὲν τοίνυν *codd.*).

(iii) In potential statements, with ἄν and optative or past indicative, by crasis, μέντἄν, expressing lively surprise or indignation. Common in Aristophanes and Plato, and not infrequent in Demosthenes (a mark of the liveliness of his style): surprisingly, absent from Xenophon. (In S.*Aj.*86 (see II.1.i) the tone is quiet, and quite different. Pl.*Smp.*206B also stands apart from the normal usage: so, of course, does *R.*415D.)

Ar.*Av.*1692 οὐκ εἶ μεθ' ἡμῶν;—Εὖ γε μέντἂν διετέθην (regretfully, 'I *should* have been in clover': γε, exclamatory, is clearly to be separated from μέντοι): *Ra.*743 Τὸ δὲ μὴ πατάξαι σ' ...—Ὤιμωξε μέντἄν ('He'd have caught it if he had!'): *Ach.* 906 συκοφάντην ἔξαγε ...—Νεὶ τὼ θιὼ λάβοιμι μέντἂν κέρδος ἀγαγὼν καὶ πολύ (ironical, 'That *would* pay me!'): *Ach.*162, 544: *Ec.*650: *Pl.*1062: Pl.*Cra.*391C Ἄτοπος μέντἂν εἴη μου ... ἡ δέησις: *Tht.*158E Γελοῖον μέντἂν εἴη: *R.*459B Ἄτοπον μέντἂν ... εἴη: *Smp.*194A Ἐπιλησμὼν μέντἂν εἴην: *Grg.*461E Δεινὰ μέντἂν πάθοις: *Lg.*669A Πάντες μέντἂν ... τὰ καλὰ τῶν ζῴων ἐγιγνώσκομεν: D.i 26 τῶν ἀτοπωτάτων μέντἂν εἴη: viii 27 ἀμείνους μέντἂν εἶεν: xviii 209 δικαίως μέντἂν ἀπέθανον: xix 138 μαίνοιτο μέντἄν: Pl.*Prt.*330D, 350B: *Smp.*194C: *Ap.*37C: *R.*382D: Is.x 13: D.xxi 196: xxxiv 45.

In apodosi: Pl.*Phd.*87E εἰ γὰρ ῥέοι τὸ σῶμα ... ἀναγκαῖον μέντἂν εἴη.

In Ar.*Ach.*710 ἀλλὰ ... μέντἄν is a perhaps rather improbable conjecture (for μέν or μὲν ἄν): perhaps μέν γ' ἄν (Bentley), or μέν τἄν, *separatim*.

(iv) In questions. (*a*) Impatient questions. Ar.*Nu.*787–8

Φέρ' ἴδω τί μέντοι πρῶτον ἦν; τί πρῶτον ἦν; τίς ἦν ἐν ᾗ 'ματτόμεθα μέντοι τἄλφιτα; ('Let's see, now what *was* it . . . what *was* it now . . . ?'): *Th.*630 Φέρ' ἴδω, τί μέντοι πρῶτον ἦν; ἐπίνομεν: Eub.*Fr.*116.13 ἀλλὰ νὴ Δία χρηστὴ τίς ἦν μέντοι, τίς; οἴμοι δείλαιος ('Who was good, oh, who *was* good?'): Pl.*Phdr.* 236D ὄμνυμι γάρ σοι—τίνα μέντοι, τίνα θεῶν; ('I swear by—now, whom *do* I swear by?').

(*b*) Questions of *nonne* form (common in Plato). Phryn.Com. *Fr.*2 οὐ τουτονὶ μέντοι σὺ κιθαρίζειν ποτὲ αὐλεῖν τ' ἐδίδαξας; ('Wasn't this the fellow, now . . . ?'): Pl.*Phdr.*229B Εἰπέ μοι, ὦ Σώκρατες, οὐκ ἐνθένδε μέντοι ποθὲν . . . ; *Chrm.*159C εἰπὲ γάρ μοι, οὐ τῶν καλῶν μέντοι ἡ σωφροσύνη ἐστίν; *Prt.*309A οὐ σὺ μέντοι Ὁμήρου ἐπαινέτης εἶ . . . ; *Phdr.*267C Πρωταγόρεια δέ, ὦ Σώκρατες, οὐκ ἦν μέντοι τοιαῦτ' ἄττα; *R.*584A Τὸ δὲ μήτε λυπηρὸν μήτε ἡδὺ οὐχὶ ἡσυχία μέντοι . . . ἐφάνη ἄρτι; *Phdr.*261C οἱ ἀντίδικοι τί δρῶσιν; οὐκ ἀντιλέγουσιν μέντοι; *Cra.*439A: *Tht.* 163E: *R.*339B,346A, 521D, 581A, 597A: *Ion* 537A: *Hp.Mi.*366C: X.*Cyr.*v 3.8: *Ap.*3.

In an indirect question: Pl.*Phdr.*266D λεκτέον δὲ τί μέντοι καὶ ἔστι τὸ λειπόμενον τῆς ῥητορικῆς. In an exclamation: X.*Smp.*8.5 Ὡς σαφῶς μέντοι σὺ . . . ἀεὶ τοιαῦτα ποιεῖς.

(v) In commands. An apparent, rather than a real, idiom. In Hdt.ix 79.2 there is apparently no connective force in μέντοι, which merely adds severity to the warning: but most of the examples group themselves more naturally under other headings. A.*Ag.*943 Πιθοῦ· κράτος μέντοι πάρες γ' ἑκὼν ἐμοί (Verrall takes μέν τοι separately: I believe Weil's κρατεῖς μέντοι παρείς to be the right reading: Headlam compares S.*Aj.*1353 κρατεῖς τοι τῶν φίλων νικώμενος): E.*Hipp.*304 ἀλλ' ἴσθι μέντοι (ἀλλὰ . . . μέντοι, *q.v.*): Ar.*Pax* 1100 (adversative: see below, 2.iii): *Av.*661 Ὦ τοῦτο μέντοι νὴ Δί' αὐτοῖσιν πιθοῦ (assentient: 'Yes, do agree'): *Ec.*509 (καὶ μέντοι: *q.v.* I.i): X.*Smp.*4.4 (καὶ . . . μέντοι).

(vi) *In apodosi.* A.*Ag.*644 ὅταν δὲ . . . τοιῶνδε μέντοι πημάτων σεσαγμένον πρέπει λέγειν παιᾶνα τόνδ' Ἐρινύων (μέν τοι *separatim*, Verrall): And.i 130 εἰ γὰρ μέμνησθε, ὅτε . . ., τότε μέντοι πάντες ἴστε ὅτι . . . ('If you remember, when . . ., well, then . . .').

(vii) Emphatic μέντοι is hardly to be found in a subordinate clause: in Ar.*Eq.*276 ἀλλὰ . . . μέντοι introduces the main clause, while γε goes with ἐάν: Ἀλλ' ἐὰν μέντοι γε νικᾷς τῇ βοῇ, τήνελλος εἶ.

(For (iii)–(vi) above, cf. the corresponding uses of τοι.)

(2) Adversative. This use makes its appearance rather later than the affirmative. Aeschylus affords at most one example:[1] *Pr.*320 ἀρχαῖ' ἴσως σοι φαίνομαι λέγειν τάδε· τοιαῦτα μέντοι τῆς ἄγαν ὑψηγόρου γλώσσης, Προμηθεῦ, τἀπίχειρα γίγνεται: Sophocles (*Ant.*687,897: *Tr.*413) and Euripides, not many.

Prose. Already in Herodotus, adversative μέντοι predominates over other uses: and this predominance is even more strongly marked in Thucydides and the orators (less strongly in Plato and Xenophon, where affirmative μέντοι, as we have seen, is common). Fuhr observes (*Rh.M.*xxxiii(1878) 593) that οὐ μέντοι is rare in Isocrates, who prefers οὐ μήν, but common in Thucydides, who never has οὐ μήν alone (but has οὐ μὴν οὐδέ). Demosthenes uses οὐ μήν and οὐ μέντοι indifferently. It is unnecessary to multiply instances, but the following points may be noted:

(i) The contrast may, or may not, be forecast by μέν in the preceding clause.

With preceding μέν. This is very rare in verse: E.*IT*1335. For S.*Ph.*352, see II.3.ii, *ad fin.*: for μὲν . . . γε μέντοι see γε μέντοι. Common in prose: Hdt.i 139 τὸ Πέρσας μὲν αὐτοὺς λέληθε, ἡμέας μέντοι οὔ: Th.i 142.4: D.iii 2: *et saep.*

Without preceding μέν. E.*Hec.*761 Ὁρῶ· τὸ μέντοι μέλλον οὐκ ἔχω μαθεῖν: 885: *Ion*812: *Ph.*272: Ar.*Nu.*588: *Ec.*646, 700: *Pl.*554: Hdt.i 13 καὶ ἐβασίλευσε οὕτω Γύγης. τοσόνδε

[1] But I am not at all certain that μέντοι is adversative here. The association of the particle with τοιαῦτα is here again important. (Aeschylus uses μέντοι nine times (excluding γε μέντοι), and in six cases it immediately follows τοιοῦτος, τοιόσδε). I am inclined to believe that μέντοι does not contrast the old-fashioned nature of Oceanus' remarks with their truth, but is self-contained, and means 'mark you', 'remember'. τάδε looks forward to the two following lines, which are virtually in inverted commas: they are proverbial in tone, as Paley points out, and indeed Oceanus' whole speech is a patchwork of tags: 'Do not think me an old fogey when I say, "Remember that the wages of pride is punishment"': cf. τοι in proverbs.

μέντοι εἶπε ἡ Πυθίη: vii 13.2: Th.i 111.3: Pl.*Men.*92E: *R.*408D.

(ii) The μέντοι clause, or a particular element in it, is often emphasized by γε: μέντοι γε, μέντοι . . . γε. Juxtaposition of the particles is not very common: Ar.*Th.*709 κοὔπω μέντοι γε: Ion.*Fr.*6: Hdt.i 187.2: ix 111.2 (γε *om. ABCP*): Pl.*Cra.*424C φωνήεντα μὲν οὔ, οὐ μέντοι γ' ἄφθογγα: *R.*329E (the only two instances of juxtaposition in Plato, according to R. W. Chapman): X.*HG*ii 4.42: *Cyr.*v 5.11: 5.24: Ant.v 19: vi 3: Lys.xxxi 2: D.iv 49 (γε *om. AY*): vii 26: xviii 112: xxii 56 γε *om. SLYO*): xxxiv 20,49: xxxvii 53: xlix 38 (γε only in *A*): lv 24 (γε only in *S*). μέντοι . . . γε: Hdt.i 104.2 οὐ μέντοι οἵ γε Σκύθαι ταύτῃ ἐσέβαλον: D.xxxv 40: xlix 21: *et saep.*

(iii) Like μήν, μέντοι is normally a balancing adversative, and seldom goes so far as to eliminate, or seriously invalidate, the opposed idea, like ἀλλά or μὲν οὖν. The difference in force between μέντοι and ἀλλά is illustrated in Th.viii 68.1 and 86.2. But, like μήν, μέντοι is occasionally stronger in force. E.*Alc.* 1103 εἴθ' ἐξ ἀγῶνος τήνδε μὴ 'λαβές ποτε.—Νικῶντι μέντοι καὶ σὺ συννικᾷς ἐμοί (protesting, 'And yet'): *HF* 1264 Ζεὺς . . . πολέμιόν μ' ἐγείνατο Ἥρᾳ—σὺ μέντοι μηδὲν ἀχθεσθῇς, γέρον (checking an impatient gesture, 'Nay, be not angry': *IT* 637 is similar: μέντοι here refers, not to the previous line, but to the general situation, the fact that Iphigeneia is about to compass Orestes' death: so, approximately, Wecklein): Ar.*Th.*714 λήψει δὲ κακόν.—Τοῦτο μέντοι μὴ γένοιτο μηδαμῶς ('No, no': for μὲν οὖν: cf., perhaps, *Pax* 1100 'No, *you* (the servant) look out for that': the kite threatens, not the state, but the dinner: but perhaps μέντοι is merely lively: 'Here, *you* look out for that'): *Av.*1071 (μέντοι has almost the force of ἀλλὰ γάρ: the Birds break off from the complacent contemplation of their own importance, to announce their list of rewards to tyrannicides and so forth): Pl.*Plt.*296B ἀπόκριναι, τί τοὔνομα τῆς βίας ἔσται; μὴ μέντοι πω, περὶ δὲ τῶν ἔμπροσθεν πρότερον (the speaker corrects himself: *Men.*86C might be similarly explained, but there I think οὐ μέντοι . . . ἀλλά go together: see οὐ μέντοι ἀλλά, p. 31).

(iv) With ellipse. Pl.*Grg.*517A σὺ δὲ ὡμολόγεις τῶν γε νῦν οὐδένα (ἄνδρα ἀγαθὸν γεγονέναι . . .), τῶν μέντοι ἔμπροσθεν: *Tht.*165C Οὔ, φήσω, οἶμαι τούτῳ γε, τῷ μέντοι ἑτέρῳ: *Prt.*350E: *R.*415D: *Tht.*197A. (Cf. δέ: Pl.*Phdr.*230D,243A,274B).

(v) The following instance of adversative μέντοι in a participial clause is exceptional: Th.iv51 Χῖοι τὸ τεῖχος περιεῖλον τὸ καινὸν κελευσάντων Ἀθηναίων . . . ποιησάμενοι μέντοι πρὸς Ἀθηναίους πίστεις . . . μηδὲν περὶ σφᾶς νεώτερον βουλεύσειν ('the Chians dismantled their wall, but only after securing a pledge'). So also, perhaps, Pl.*Lg*.783A, μέντοι answering μέν in the main clause: but the reading is doubtful (see England).

(3) Progressive. Like μήν (*q.v.*, III), μέντοι is used as a progressive connecting particle, denoting (i) temporal sequence, (ii) the transition to a new point, a new argument, or a new stage in the march of thought. (A rigid division between (i) and (ii) is hardly possible.) Whereas we have seen that progressive μήν, except with negatives, is almost peculiar to Plato, progressive μέντοι is commonest in Hippocrates and in Xenophon (who uses it very frequently). It is almost confined to prose. In the few verse examples there is usually some other factor which helps to establish the connexion: and this is often the case in prose as well.

(i) Purely temporal: most of the examples are from historical narrative. S.*OC*1653 ἄνακτα (ἐξαπείδομεν) . . . χεῖρ' ἀντέχοντα κρατὸς . . . ἔπειτα μέντοι . . . ὁρῶμεν αὐτὸν γῆν τε προσκυνοῦνθ': Hdt.viii85.1 κατὰ δὲ Λακεδαιμονίους Ἴωνες (ἐτετάχατο) . . . ἐθελοκάκεον μέντοι αὐτῶν . . . ὀλίγοι ('Now some of them . . .'): X.*HG*iii2.1 ἐρωτᾷ πότερον βούλεται εἰρήνην ἢ πόλεμον ἔχειν. ὁ μέντοι Φαρνάβαζος . . . σπονδὰς εἵλετο ('Well, Pharnabazus chose a truce'): iii4.15 ἄλοβα γίγνεται τὰ ἱερά. τούτου μέντοι φανέντος . . .: v2.20 ἐκέλευον συμβουλεύειν . . . ἐκ τούτου μέντοι πολλοὶ μὲν συνηγόρευον στρατιὰν ποιεῖν: *An*.iii1.5 ἦν δέ τις ἐν τῇ στρατιᾷ Ξενοφῶν Ἀθηναῖος . . . ὁ μέντοι Ξενοφῶν . . . ('Well, Xenophon . . .'): Pl.*Chrm*.155C ὁ δ' ἐλθὼν μεταξὺ ἐμοῦ τε καὶ τοῦ Κριτίου ἐκαθέζετο. ἐνταῦθα μέντοι, ὦ φίλε, ἐγὼ ἤδη ἠπόρουν: Hp.*Fract* 19 διατείνειν . . . χρὴ . . . ἐπὴν μέντοι ἱκανῶς κατατανύσῃς . . .: *Acut*.7 (μέν *al*.): Th.iv134.2: viii6.3: 106.3: Pl *Euthd*.303B: X.*HG*iii5.5.: vi4.25: *Smp*.4.59.

Less purely temporal. Th.ii65.3 ἰδίᾳ δὲ τοῖς παθήμασιν ἐλυποῦντο . . . οὐ μέντοι πρότερόν γε οἱ ξύμπαντες ἐπαύσαντο ἐν ὀργῇ ἔχοντες αὐτὸν πρὶν ἐζημίωσαν χρήμασιν (with a sense of climax, 'in fact'): X.*Cyr*.viii 3.7 νῦν γοῦν φέρω τώδε δύο κασᾶ . . .

σὺ μέντοι τούτων λαβὲ ὁπότερον βούλει ('Well, then': for οὖν or δή): *HG*vii 1.39.

(ii) Proceeding to a new item in a series, a new point. a new argument. 'Again', 'further'. A.*Pr*.254 Μέγ' ὠφέλημα τοῦτ' ἐδωρήσω βροτοῖς.—Πρὸς τοῖσδε μέντοι πῦρ ἐγώ σφιν ὤπασα: E.*Cyc*.160 'Did you like the wine?'—'Yes'.—Πρὸς τῷδε μέντοι καὶ νόμισμα δώσομεν: *El*.660 Ἥξει...—Ἐλθοῦσα μέντοι δῆλον ὡς ἀπόλλυται: X.*HG*ii 1.32 'He was accused on various counts. ᾐτιάθη μέντοι ὑπό τινων προδοῦναι τὰς ναῦς' ('further'): ii 4.12 ἐτάχθησαν μέντοι ἐπ' αὐτοῖς πελτοφόροι... οὗτοι μέντοι συχνοὶ ἦσαν (successive details of order of battle: cf. *Cyr*.vi 3.25: *Eq. Mag*.2.5-6): *Cyr*.viii 7.23 'Honour the gods. μετὰ μέντοι θεοὺς καὶ ἀνθρώπων τὸ πᾶν γένος... αἰδεῖσθε': *Mem*.i 4.18 (an empirical test supplementing an *a priori* argument): *Oec*.7.20 στεγῶν δεῖται δῆλον ὅτι. δεῖ μέντοι τοῖς μέλλουσιν ἀνθρώποις ἕξειν ὅ τι εἰσφέρωσιν εἰς τὸ στεγνόν: *Lac*.2.1 ἐγὼ μέντοι, ἐπεὶ καὶ περὶ γενέσεως ἐξήγημαι, βούλομαι καὶ τὴν παιδείαν ἑκατέρων σαφηνίσαι ('Well now'): Lys.xiii 73 (a fresh charge): Hdt.iii 96: Hp.*Art*.8,69(*ad init.*): *Acut*.9,12: *Morb*.iii 15: Th.v 36.2: X. *HG*.iv 1.8: *Eq.Mag*.7.13: 8.1.

Marking a new stage in the march of thought. In particular, μέντοι often follows a demonstrative at the opening of a sentence which expresses the importance or relevance of someone or something mentioned in the previous sentence: 'Well, that is the man who...': 'Well, that is what...'.

Ar.*Nu*.329 Strepsiades: 'I see the Clouds now.'—Σω. Ταύτας μέντοι σὺ θεὰς οὔσας οὐκ ᾔδησθ' οὐδ' ἐνόμιζες; ('Well, didn't you know they were goddesses?'): *Lys*.1016 Οὐδέν ἐστι θηρίον γυναικὸς ἀμαχώτερον...—Ταῦτα μέντοι σὺ ξυνιεὶς εἶτα πολεμεῖς ἐμοί...; ('Well, do you dare make war on me when you know *that*?'): S.*Ant*.913,1052: Ar.*Nu*.340: *Ra*.1325: Hdt.iii 3 A Persian woman admires Cassandane's children: Cassandane replies: Τοιῶνδε μέντοι ἐμὲ παίδων μητέρα ἐοῦσαν Κῦρος ἐν ἀτιμίῃ ἔχει ('Well, it is the mother of such children that Cyrus dishonours'): vii 8γ1 (after describing Athenian misdeeds) τούτων μέντοι εἵνεκα ἀνάρτημαι ἐπ' αὐτοὺς στρατεύεσθαι ('Well, that is why I am determined to march against them': μέντοι here has caused needless surprise): Hp.*Art*.67 ὅμως δέ τι ἄξιον ἐμβάλλειν... ἐμβάλλειν μέντοι ῥήϊστον... ('Well, the easiest way to reduce is . . .'): X.*Oec*.8.22 'A slave can always find you anything you want in the market. *τούτου μέντοι . . . οὐδὲν ἄλλο αἴτιόν ἐστιν ἢ ὅτι ἐν χώρᾳ κεῖται τεταγμένῃ*' ('Well, the reason for that is . . .'): *Lac*.9.3 'Courage is both safer and more honourable than cowardice. *ᾗ μέντοι ὥστε ταῦτα γίγνεσθαι ἐμηχανήσατο, καὶ τοῦτο καλὸν μὴ παραλιπεῖν*': *HG*v3.7 'A complete rout and massacre followed. *ἐκ μέντοι γε τῶν τοιούτων παθῶν ἐγώ φημι ἀνθρώπους παιδεύεσθαι . . . ὡς οὐδ' οἰκέτας χρὴ ὀργῇ κολάζειν*' (where the *γε* is remarkable): D.vii41 'The Chersonese extends as far as the *βωμὸς τοῦ Διός*. *ταύτην μέντοι τὴν χώραν . . . ὡς ἑαυτοῦ οὖσαν τὴν μὲν αὐτὸς καρποῦται, τὴν δ' ἄλλοις δωρειὰν δέδωκε*' ('Well, that country . . .'): Hp.*Art*. 7 (*ἐσκευάσθαι μέντοι*), 69 (*ἡ μέντοι κνήμη*): Pl.*Sph*.242A: *Alc.II* 140E: X.*Cyr*.vi2.20: And.i63: Is.ix26: D.v23: vii35: xli29; Aeschin.i22,74.

Not infrequently *μέντοι*, like *μήν* (III.1.ii) and *ἀλλὰ μήν* (6–7), is syllogistic or quasi-syllogistic in force. Used in enthymemes rather than in strict syllogisms, the particle leads from the first premise to the second, the conclusion being left, as obvious, to the imagination. But whereas in *ἀλλὰ μήν* enthymemes, as we have seen (*s.v.*(7)), the minor premise usually comes first, with *μέντοι* the reverse order obtains. D.xlv66 'Certain conduct is that of an enemy of mankind. *ταῦτα μέντοι τὰ τοσαύτην ἔχοντα αἰσχύνην . . . προῄρηται πράττειν*' (*sc.* 'Therefore he is an enemy of mankind'). Contrast D.xxi42 'Midias' crimes are crimes of deliberate *ὕβρις*. *ἀλλὰ μήν* the law enjoins particularly severe penalties for crimes of deliberate *ὕβρις*' (*sc.* 'Therefore Midias should be punished with particular severity').

Th.i74.1 'The naval defeat brought about the Persian retreat. *τοιούτου μέντοι τούτου ξυμβάντος . . . τρία τὰ ὠφελιμώτατα ἐς αὐτὸ παρεσχόμεθα*' (*sc.* 'Therefore we were the prime cause of the Persians' discomfiture'): X.*Cyn*.12.14 (after a description of certain evils) *τούτων μέντοι τῶν κακῶν οὐδεὶς ὅστις οὐκ ἀφέξεται ἐρασθεὶς ὧν ἐγὼ παραινῶ* (*sc.* 'Therefore take up hunting'): D.xix64 *τούτων . . . δεινότερ' οὐ γέγονεν οὐδὲ μείζω πράγματ' ἐφ' ἡμῶν . . . τηλικούτων μέντοι καὶ τοιούτων πραγμάτων κύριος εἷς ἀνὴρ γέγονεν διὰ τούτους*: xix84.

μέντοι, following an example or analogy, sometimes introduces a statement of its applicability to the present case. Here too *μέντοι* is often quasi-syllogistic, the example standing for the general truth which it illustrates. Cf. the closely similar use of *τοίνυν* (II.4).

S.*OC*781 *ὥσπερ τις εἴ σοι . . . ἆρ' ἂν ματαίου τῆσδ' ἂν ἡδονῆς τύχοις; τοιαῦτα μέντοι καὶ σὺ προσφέρεις ἐμοί* ('A friend in need is a friend in deed: you are not a friend in need: therefore you are not a friend in deed'): 997 *εἴ τίς σε . . . κτείνοι παραστάς, πότερα πυνθάνοι' ἂν . . .; δοκῶ μὲν . . . τὸν αἴτιον τίνοι' ἂν . . . τοιαῦτα μέντοι καὐτὸς εἰσέβην κακά* ('Well, that is the plight *I* was in'): Hdt.iii32 'Cambyses' sister asked him *κότερον περιτετιλμένη ἢ δασέα ἡ θρίδαξ ἐοῦσα εἴη καλλίων, καὶ τὸν φάναι δασέαν, τὴν δὲ εἰπεῖν· Ταύτην μέντοι κοτὲ σὺ τὴν θρίδακα ἐμιμήσαο, τὸν Κύρου οἶκον ἀποψιλώσας*: Pl.*Grg.*522B 'A doctor could not defend himself against a confectioner before a jury of children'.—'No'.—*Τοιοῦτον μέντοι καὶ ἐγὼ οἶδα ὅτι πάθος πάθοιμι ἂν εἰσελθὼν εἰς δικαστήριον*: X.*Cyr.*vi.1.14: 5.33: *Hier.*i25.

Pl.*R.*440A is different: here *μέντοι* leads from the example to the formulation of the general truth which the example illustrates: 'Well, that story shows . . .'.

Progressive *μέντοι* sometimes answers *μέν*. S.*Ph.*352 *μάλιστα μὲν δὴ τοῦ θανόντος ἱμέρῳ . . . ἔπειτα μέντοι χὠ λόγος καλὸς προσῆν* (faintly adversative): X.*HG*iii5.25 *αὕτη μὲν δὴ οὕτως ἡ στρατιὰ τῶν Λακεδαιμονίων διελύθη. ὁ μέντοι Παυσανίας . . .*: v4.34 *τοιούτῳ μὲν δὴ τρόπῳ Σφοδρίας ἀπέφυγε. τῶν μέντοι Ἀθηναίων οἱ βοιωτιάζοντες . . . .* Usually, of course, *μέντοι* following *μέν* is more definitely adversative.

III. *μέντοι* in combination with other particles. The commonest combinations are *ἀλλὰ μέντοι, γε μέντοι, καὶ μέντοι*. For these, see subsections below. For *οὐ μέντοι ἀλλά*, see pp. 30–1.

μέντοι γε: *μέντοι . . . γε*. For *γε* following (seldom immediately following) adversative *μέντοι*, see II.2.ii. Except when adversative, *μέντοι* is seldom followed by *γε*, either juxtaposed or separated. In A.*Ag.*943 (II.1.v) I think *παρείς*, without *γε*, is the correct reading: in Hdt.viii87.3 (II.1.i) I think *ἔγωγε ἔχω* (*S*) is right: for Th.ii65.3 see II.3.i: in X.*HG*v3.7 (II.3.ii) μέντοι γε, I doubt γε, which is quite out of place in this usage.

ἀλλὰ μέντοι is frequently followed, at an interval, by γε. (X. *Smp*.6.10 Ἀλλ' οὐ μέντοι γε, juxtaposed.) But in Ar.*Eq*.276 Ἀλλ' ἐὰν μέντοι γε νικᾷς I think γε goes rather with ἐάν (II.1.vii).

καὶ μέντοι, καὶ . . . μέντοι, in marked contrast with καὶ μήν, seem hardly ever to be followed by γε (often by another καί): but Ar.*Th*.709 Κοὔπω μέντοι γε πέπαυμαι (here I feel a close connexion between καί and γε, while μέντοι stands apart: 'Yes, and I haven't stopped yet, I tell you').

The following are all very rare:—

τε μέντοι. Ar.*Nu*.1269 ἄλλως τε μέντοι καὶ κακῶς πεπραγότι: Hp.*Art*.63 εἴτε ἔσω ῥέψαντα, εἴτε μέντοι καὶ ἔξω: Pl.*Ap*.35D ἄλλως τε μέντοι νὴ Δία πάντως καὶ ἀσεβείας φεύγοντα. μέντἄρα. Crates Com.*Fr*.8 οὐκ ἀσκίῳ μέντἄρ' ἐμορμολύττετο αὐτούς. ἦ . . . μέντοι. E.*Alc*.811 Ἦ κάρτα μέντοι καὶ λίαν θυραῖος ἦν. δὲ μέντοι. Hp *Fract*.8 φυλάσσεσθαι δὲ μέντοι χρή (δὲ μέντοι *FGI*: μέντοι *cett*.: γε μέντοι should perhaps be read. Cf. the similarly doubtful δὲ μήν (μήν, VI.1)). οὐδὲ μέντοι. X.*HG*iv1.36 οὐδὲ μέντοι τοῦτό σε κελεύομεν. οὐ μέντοι οὐδέ. Hdt.vi45.1 (*ABCP*): Pl.*Prt*.331E: D.xlix38.

Ἀλλὰ μέντοι: ἀλλὰ . . . μέντοι

The usages are closely analogous to those of ἀλλὰ μήν, though far less common. Ἀλλὰ μέντοι is practically confined to Plato and Xenophon, who seldom separate the particles. The dramatists use ἀλλὰ . . . μέντοι, but hardly ever the metrically intractable ἀλλὰ μέντοι. (Ar.*Av*.291 Ἀλλὰ μέντοι τίς ποθ' ἡ λόφωσις ἡ τῶν ὀρνέων;) Other authors do not seem to use either form of the combination.

(1) Adversative. ἀλλὰ μέντοι. Pl.*Grg*.517A 'The ancient politicians were no better than the modern'.—Ἀλλὰ μέντοι πολλοῦ γε δεῖ, ὦ Σώκρατες, μή ποτέ τις τῶν νῦν ἔργα τοιαῦτα ἐργάσηται ('But surely, Socrates'): *Prm*.135B 'It is difficult to discover εἴδη'.—'Yes'.—Ἀλλὰ μέντοι . . . εἴ γέ τις δὴ . . . αὖ μὴ ἐάσει εἴδη τῶν ὄντων εἶναι . . . τὴν τοῦ διαλέγεσθαι δύναμιν παντάπασι διαφθερεῖ ('Yet on the other hand, you know'): *Euthd*.304E: *Chrm*.173D: *Tht*.196D: X.*Ap*.30.

ἀλλὰ . . . μέντοι. S.*Ant.*567 Τί γὰρ μόνῃ μοι τῆσδ' ἄτερ βιώσιμον ;—Ἀλλ' ἥδε μέντοι μὴ λέγ'· οὐ γὰρ ἔστ' ἔτι ('Nay, say not "here"'): E.*Hipp.*304: Ar.*Nu.*1342: Pl.*R.*349A Ἀλλ' οὐ μέντοι . . . ἀποκνητέον γε τῷ λόγῳ ἐπεξελθεῖν: X.*An.*i 4.8 Ἀπολελοίπασιν ἡμᾶς Ξενίας καὶ Πασίων. ἀλλ' εὖ γε μέντοι ἐπιστάσθων ὅτι οὔτε ἀποδεδράκασιν . . . οὔτε ἀποπεφεύγασιν: *HG* ii 4.22.

(2) Assentient. ἀλλὰ μέντοι. Pl.*R.*331E δοκεῖ ἔμοιγε καλῶς λέγειν.—Ἀλλὰ μέντοι . . . Σιμωνίδῃ γε οὐ ῥᾴδιον ἀπιστεῖν ('Well, certainly'): *Prt.*331D Ἀλλὰ μέντοι, ἦ δ' ὅς, προσέοικέν τι δικαιοσύνη ὁσιότητι: X.*Smp.*1.12 Philip knocks at the door, and asks for admission. ὁ οὖν Καλλίας ἀκούσας ταῦτα εἶπεν· Ἀλλὰ μέντοι, ὦ ἄνδρες, αἰσχρὸν στέγης γε φθονῆσαι: Pl.*R.*451B: *Hp. Ma.*287D.

ἀλλὰ . . . μέντοι. S.*Ph.*524 The chorus begs Neoptolemus to take Philoctetes.—*Νε.* Ἀλλ' αἰσχρὰ μέντοι σοῦ γέ μ' ἐνδεέστερον ξένῳ φανῆναι πρὸς τὸ καίριον πονεῖν (conceding the point): *Aj.* 1370: Ar.*Pl.*1202: X.*Cyr.*iv 1.21: v 5.36.

(3) Inceptive-responsive (cf. ἀλλὰ μήν, 2.i, καὶ μήν, (5)). Pl. *Chrm.*163E σκοπῶμεν . . . ὃ σὺ λέγεις νῦν.—Ἀλλὰ μέντοι ἔγωγε, ἔφη, . . . οὔ φημι . . . ('Well'): *Phd.*108D: *Tht.*151D: *Hp.Ma.* 289D.

ἀλλὰ . . . μέντοι. Pl.*R.*614B Λέγοις ἄν, ἔφη, ὡς οὐ πολλὰ ἄλλ' ἥδιον ἀκούοντι.—Ἀλλ' οὐ μέντοι σοι, ἦν δ' ἐγώ, Ἀλκίνου γε ἀπόλογον ἐρῶ.

(4) Substantiating a condition (cf., much more commonly, ἀλλὰ μήν, (3)). Pl.*R.*430E εἰ ἔμοιγε βούλει χαρίζεσθαι, σκόπει . . .—Ἀλλὰ μέντοι, ἦν δ' ἐγώ, βούλομαί γε: 525A.

(5) Progressive. Almost confined to Xenophon: other authors use ἀλλὰ μήν, καὶ μήν, etc., although the particular variety (6) occurs several times in Plato.

ἀλλὰ μέντοι. Pl.*R.*433C (new argument): X.*Ap.*27 'Why do you weep for me now? From the moment I was born, I was destined to die. ἀλλὰ μέντοι life holds out no prospect of happiness for me' (new argument): *HG* vi 3.15 (new argument): *Cyr.* i 6.24: *Hier.*1.24: 4.8.

ἀλλὰ . . . μέντοι. E.*Heracl.*520 ἀλλ' οὐδὲ μέντοι (examining a fresh alternative): X.*Cyr.*viii 3.29 Οὐ μὰ τὸν Δί', ἔφη, οὐδενὸς τῶν παρόντων.—Ἀλλ' οὐ μέντοι, ἔφη ὁ νεανίσκος, τῶν γε ἀπόντων ('Nor yet'): *Smp.*4.17: *Ap.*26.

(6) Introducing minor, or major, premise (cf. ἀλλὰ μήν, (6)). ἀλλὰ μέντοι. Pl.*R*.398D τὴν ἁρμονίαν καὶ ῥυθμὸν ἀκολουθεῖν δεῖ τῷ λόγῳ.—Πῶς δ' οὔ;—Ἀλλὰ μέντοι θρήνων γε καὶ ὀδυρμῶν ἔφαμεν ἐν λόγοις οὐδὲν προσδεῖσθαι. Therefore the θρηνώδεις ἁρμονίαι must be eliminated': *R*.584C: *Chrm*.162A: *Ly*.221D: X.*Cyr*.iii 1.16.

Γε μέντοι

This combination is not infrequent in drama: it is common in Xenophon (not less than thirty-four examples): the orators hardly use it (And.ii 20 is the only example I know[1]), and it is surprisingly rare (three times only) in Plato, who freely uses μέντοι, ἀλλὰ μέντοι, and καὶ μέντοι.

(1) Adversative (the commonest sense). S.*Ant* 233 τοιαῦθ' ἑλίσσων ἤνυτον σχολῇ βραδύς . . . τέλος γε μέντοι δεῦρ' ἐνίκησεν μολεῖν: Ar.*Ra*.61 Οὐκ ἔχω φράσαι. ὅμως γε μέντοι σοι δι' αἰνιγμῶν ἐρῶ: *Ec*.410 παρῆλθε γυμνός, ὡς ἐδόκει τοῖς πλείοσιν· αὐτός γε μέντοὔφασκεν ἱμάτιον ἔχειν: A.*Pers*.386: *Fr*.266.4: S.*Aj*.483: *OT* 1292: *Ph*.93,1052: E.*Med*.95,534: *Heracl*.593,1016: *Hel*. 994: *Fr*.796 (no context): Trag.Adesp.*Fr*.384: Ar.*Eq*.885: *V*. 1344: *Lys*.1213: X.*HG* vi 5.5 ἀπῄει ὀργιζόμενος· στρατεύειν γε μέντοι ἐπ' αὐτοὺς οὐ δυνατὸν ἐδόκει εἶναι: Aen.Tact.2.3: Hdt.i 120: vii 103.5: Pl.*Chrm*.164A: *Tht*.165A.

Introducing an objection in dialogue. S.*El*.398 οὐκ ἐμοὺς τρόπους λέγεις.—Καλόν γε μέντοι μὴ 'ξ ἀβουλίας πεσεῖν ('Aye, but'): A.*Th*.716,1049: *Ag*.938: S.*OT* 442: E.*Alc*.725: *Heracl*. 267,637: *Hipp*.103: *Or*.106: *Rh*.589: Pl.*Tht*.164A.

Answering μέν. S.*OT* 778 τύχη . . . θαυμάσαι μὲν ἀξία, σπουδῆς γε μέντοι τῆς ἐμῆς οὐκ ἀξία: E.*Med*.725 (τοσόνδε μέντοι *B*): X. *Cyr*.iii 1.22 πέπονθε μὲν οὐδ' ὁτιοῦν πω κακόν· φοβεῖταί γε μέντοι: *HG* iv 8.16 τὸ μὲν . . . οὐκ ἀσφαλὲς αὐτῷ ἡγεῖτο εἶναι· λάθρᾳ γε μέντοι ἔδωκε.

γε μέντοι is normally a balancing adversative: in Ar.*Ec*.1008 it exceptionally stands for μὲν οὖν: Ἀλλ' οὐκ ἀνάγκη μοὔστὶν . . . —Νὴ τὴν Ἀφροδίτην δεῖ γε μέντοι ⟨σ'⟩ (here perhaps it is γε that provides the adversative (corrective) force, 'doch' (see γε, I.11.iii), while μέντοι adds liveliness: 'Yes you must, you know').

[1] Confirmed by Schmidt, p. 54.

(2) Progressive (in Xenophon only. In the following, γε μέντοι is better explained as adversative: A.*Eu.*591: S.*Ant.*495 (see Jebb): Ar *V.*1155: X.*HG* iii 5.15). X.*HG* vi 5.39 ἐγὼ μὲν οὐδὲν μᾶλλον Λακεδαιμονίοις ἂν ὑμᾶς ἡγοῦμαι στρατεύσαντας βοηθῆσαι ἢ καὶ ὑμῖν αὐτοῖς . . . συμφορώτερόν γε μέντἂν ὑμῖν αὐτοῖς βοηθήσαιτε ἐν ᾧ ἔτι εἰσὶν οἳ συμμαχοῖεν ἄν ('Further, it is to your advantage to defend yourselves *now*'): *Cyr.*vii 5.51.

In an enumerative series. X.*HG* v 2.14 εἰσὶν ὁπλῖται μὲν . . . πελτασταὶ δὲ . . . ἱππεῖς γε μέντοι . . . ἔσονται: *Oec.*17.1 Περὶ μὲν τῆς νεοῦ ὁρᾷς . . . Περί γε μέντοι τοῦ σπόρου ὥρας . . .: *Eq.*1.7 μηροί γε μέντοι (in a series with γε μήν and καὶ μήν).

(3) Like γέ τοι (see τοι, VI.4.i), approximating to γοῦν in force, giving a partial ground for the acceptance of a belief. This rare use seems to be established by the following three passages. A.*Supp.*347 Αἰδοῦ σὺ πρύμναν πόλεος ὧδ' ἐστεμμένην.—Πέφρικα λεύσσων τάσδ' ἕδρας κατασκίους.—Βαρύς γε μέντοι Ζηνὸς ἱκεσίου κότος (the grievousness of Zeus's anger is some justification for fear: 'Truly indeed'): E.*Hec.*600 ἆρ' οἱ τεκόντες διαφέρουσιν ἢ τροφαί; ἔχει γε μέντοι καὶ τὸ θρεφθῆναι καλῶς δίδαξιν ἐσθλοῦ (γε τοί τι *MBl*: γέ τοι *A*. 'Certainly τροφή (as well as birth, καί) counts for something'. 'Not but that', Paley, less well): X.*An.*iii 1.27 σύ γε οὐδὲ ὁρῶν γιγνώσκεις οὐδὲ ἀκούων μέμνησαι. ἐν ταὐτῷ γε μέντοι ἦσθα τούτοις ὅτε βασιλεὺς . . . (the inability of Apollonides to learn by experience is attested by the fact that he recommends a course which has proved disastrous in the past).

ἀλλὰ . . . γε μέντοι is only an apparent combination in X.*An.* i 4.8 ἀλλ' εὖ γε μέντοι ἐπιστάσθων: γε goes closely with εὖ: cf. Ar.*Av.*1692 (μέντοι, II.1.iii).

Καὶ μέντοι, καὶ . . . μέντοι

μέντοι gives liveliness and force to the addition. The combination is a favourite one of Xenophon's, and not uncommon in comedy and Plato, but rare elsewhere. It is almost always progressive in meaning (very rarely, if ever, adversative, καὶ μήν being used instead), and is commonest in narrative, though it sometimes introduces a new point or argument. It usually follows a strong stop, and opens a sentence. The split form καὶ . . .

μέντοι is a good deal the commoner in Xenophon, whereas Plato prefers the juxtaposed καὶ μέντοι. Plato usually reinforces the particles with a second καί.

(1) Progressive.

(i) Introducing sentence. *καὶ μέντοι.* Ar.*Ec.*509 βακτηρίας ἄφεσθε. καὶ μέντοι σὺ μὲν ταύτας κατευτρέπιζ' : Pl.*Smp.*222A εἶπον ἅ με ὕβρικεν. καὶ μέντοι οὐκ ἐμὲ μόνον ταῦτα πεποίηκεν : *Phdr.*266B ἐάν τέ τιν' ἄλλον ἡγήσωμαι δυνατὸν . . . τοῦτον διώκω . . . καὶ μέντοι καὶ τοὺς δυναμένους αὐτὸ δρᾶν . . . καλῶ μέχρι τοῦδε διαλεκτικούς : X.*Smp.*4.24 παρέδωκέ μοι αὐτόν, εἴ τι δυναίμην ὠφελῆσαι. καὶ μέντοι πολὺ βέλτιον ἤδη ἔχει : D.xix45 καὶ ὅπως γ' . . . , ἔφην, ἄν τι τούτων γίγνηται, τούτους ἐπαινέσεσθε . . . ἐμὲ δὲ μή· καὶ μέντοι κἄν τι τῶν ἐναντίων, ὅπως τούτοις ὀργιεῖσθε : Hp.*Coac.*528 (καὶ μέντοι καί) : Pl.*Plt.*291B : *Euthd.*289E : *Ap.* 17C (καὶ μέντοι καί : *R.*331D,588A : *Thg.*127B : *Alc.I* 113C) : *Ly.* 216A (καὶ μέντοι . . . καί) : X.*HG* v 4 61 : vii 1.16 : *Cyr.*iii 1.27 : iv 2.13. For Heraclit.*Fr.*28, see μέντοι, II, *ad init.*

καὶ . . . μέντοι. A.*Pr.*949 πατὴρ ἄνωγέ σ' . . . αὐδᾶν . . .· καὶ ταῦτα μέντοι μηδὲν αἰνικτηρίως, ἀλλ' αὔθ' ἕκαστ' ἔκφραζε : Ar. *Th.*709 . . . ὅδ' ἀναισχυντεῖ;—Κοὔπω μέντοι γε πέπαυμαι : S.*El.* 963 : E.*Heracl.*398 : Ar.*Ach.*1025 : *Eq.*540 : *Ra.*166 : Hdt.i 96 προθυμότερον δικαιοσύνην ἐπιθέμενος ἤσκεε· καὶ ταῦτα μέντοι ἐούσης ἀνομίης πολλῆς ἀνὰ πᾶσαν τὴν Μηδικὴν ἐποίεε : X.*HG* iv 8.39 ἀποθνήσκει. καὶ τὰ παιδικὰ μέντοι αὐτῷ παρέμεινε : vii 1.29 βοηθεῖν ἐκέλευε· κἀκεῖνος μέντοι ἐβοήθει : *Oec.*10.9–10 καθαρὰν . . . ἐπειρᾶτο ἑαυτὴν ἐπιδεικνύναι. καὶ ἐμὲ μέντοι ἠρώτα εἴ τι ἔχοιμι συμβουλεῦσαι . . . . καὶ ἐγὼ μέντοι . . . συνεβούλευον αὐτῇ : Hdt.vi 137.3 : Th.vi 38.2 : Pl.*Ep.*314D : *Alc.I* 135D · X.*HG* iii 1.1 : 5.15 : *Smp.*4.4 : 4.63 : *Cyr.*ii 2.26 : iii 3.38 : v 4.18 : 4.27 : And.ii 23.

(ii) Introducing phrase or clause. *καὶ μέντοι* (very rare). Hp. *Prorrh.*i 27 δυσφορίαι φρενιτικαὶ . . . καὶ μέντοι καὶ ὀλέθριαι : X.*Cyr.*vi 3.12 συχνὸν προελαύνουσι, καὶ μέντοι, ἔφη, κατ' αὐτοὺς ἡμᾶς : Pl.*Tht.*143A ἤκουσά σου καὶ πρότερον, καὶ μέντοι ἀεὶ μέλλων κελεύσειν ἐπιδεῖξαι διατέτριφα· δεῦρο : 144C.

καὶ . . . μέντοι. Hom.*h.Ap.*327 καὶ νῦν μέν τοι ἐγὼ τεχνήσομαι : Ar.*Eq.*189 οὐδὲ μουσικὴν ἐπίσταμαι πλὴν γραμμάτων, καὶ ταῦτα μέντοι κακὰ κακῶς : *V.*747 νῦν δ' ἴσως τοῖσι σοῖς λόγοις πείθεται καὶ σωφρονεῖ μέντοι : Hdt.vi 61.2 ἐοῦσα γυνὴ καλλίστη . . ., καὶ ταῦτα μέντοι καλλίστη ἐξ αἰσχίστης γενομένη (cf. Pl.*Ap.*26E) :

Hp.*Art.*60 δύνανται . . . ὀρθοὶ ὁδοιπορεῖν ἄνευ ξύλου, καὶ πάνυ μέντοι εὐθέες ('and quite upright too'): X.*An.*i 9.6 καὶ φιλοθηρότατος ἦν καὶ πρὸς τὰ θηρία μέντοι φιλοκινδυνότατος: 9.29 πολλοὶ πρὸς Κῦρον ἀπῆλθον . . ., καὶ οὗτοι μέντοι οἱ μάλιστα ὑπ' αὐτοῦ ἀγαπώμενοι: vii 6 17 ἀπαιτήσει με, καὶ ἀπαιτήσει μέντοι δικαίως: *Ap.*31 προσπεσεῖσθαί τινι αἰσχρᾷ ἐπιθυμίᾳ καὶ προβήσεσθαι μέντοι πόρρω μοχθηρίας: *An.*iv 6.16: *Oec.*4.2: *Eq.*7.18.

(2) Adversative. It is doubtful whether this sense should be recognized at all. In a few passages καὶ μέντοι, καὶ . . . μέντοι may be adversative (like καὶ μήν), but may equally well be explained as progressive.

Pl.*Prt.*339C Δοκεῖ οὖν σοι, ἔφη, . . .;—Φαίνεται ἔμοιγε (καὶ ἅμα μέντοι ἐφοβούμην μή τι λέγοι): X.*Cyr.*v 1.12 καὶ εὐχομένους . . . ἀπαλλαγῆναι, καὶ οὐ δυναμένους μέντοι ἀπαλλάττεσθαι: *ib.* καὶ μέντοι οὐδ' ἀποδιδράσκειν ἐπιχειροῦσι, τοιαῦτα κακὰ ἔχοντες: *An.*i 8.20 ('καὶ . . . μέντοι, *und jedoch*, drückt Verbindung und Gegensatz zugleich aus', Krüger, wrongly, I think).

X.*Mem.*iv 7.4 is different (μέντοι is clearly adversative here, but καί means 'also', and goes closely with ταύτης): ἐκέλευε δὲ καὶ ἀστρολογίας ἐμπείρους γίγνεσθαι, καὶ ταύτης μέντοι μέχρι τοῦ νυκτός τε ὥραν . . . δύνασθαι γιγνώσκειν ('but here, again, only so far . . .'). This close adherence of καί to the following word is perhaps paralleled in Ar.*Ec.*969: Καὶ ταῦτα μέντοι μετρίως πρὸς τὴν ἐμὴν ἀνάγκην εἰρημέν' ἐστίν. Here, again, καί seems to go closely with ταῦτα (the young man's song, as well as the girl's own, expresses her feelings adequately), while μέντοι adds liveliness: 'This song too, you know . . .'.

Οὖν (ὦν)

Epic and Attic, οὖν: Ionic, Aeolic, and Doric ὦν.[1] The derivation of οὖν and ὦν, and their etymological relationship, is

[1] Apollonius, *De Coni.* 228. 22. Wackernagel (*Glotta* vii (1916), 182) says that, where οὖν is found in inscriptions outside Attica, it can be attributed to 'Koinismos': and that the best MS. tradition always gives ὦν in all dialects but Attic. Aristarchus thought that οὖν in Homer proved that Homer came from Athens (Monro, *HG*² § 395).

obscure. The usages (in which there is no distinction between the two words) are consistent with the often suggested derivation from the participle of *εἰμί*.

The history of *οὖν* falls into three broad divisions. (1) In Homer, it almost invariably follows *ἐπεί* or *ὡς*, in a subordinate temporal clause, which refers to something previously described or implied. (2) In lyric poetry, and already occasionally in Homer, it follows *γάρ*, *οὔτε*, *εἴτε*, *μέν*, *δέ*, and other particles, giving the idea of actuality or essentiality, only rarely sinking, like *δή*, to the rank of a mere strengthening auxiliary. (3) Finally it attains its commonest, connective, meaning (inferential or progressive), which is not firmly established before about the middle of the fifth century: while (2), in certain combinations and in certain authors, continues to exist side by side with (3).

Of the above usages, (2) points to 'actuality' or 'essentiality' as the root-meaning of the particle. And this meaning, although in a restricted sphere, is already present in (1). When an occurrence is mentioned in a subordinate clause, its independent actuality is not *ipso facto* stressed. That stress is conveyed here by *οὖν*, which denotes that the event did actually happen, as previously described. As Brugmann puts it (§ 638: cf. Boisacq, p. 728): 'in der Tat, in Wahrheit, in Wirklichkeit, und zwar mit Hinweis auf etwas Vorangehendes'. *τὸν δ' ὡς οὖν ἐνόησε*, 'And when in actual fact he saw him (as I have described)'. Cf. the later use of *ὥσπερ οὖν* (II.4). The restriction of the Homeric use is very curious. It is in direct contradiction to the general principle according to which Homeric particles, like Homeric constructions, are characterized by a great freedom and variety, their diversity being later canalized in certain particular directions. But Homer is not the beginning of all things: and perhaps a wider usage lies behind the Homeric. In (2) the backward reference disappears, the idea of actuality or essentiality remaining: but with the restriction that *οὖν* is only employed in conjunction with other particles. The evolution of (2) from (1) was perhaps also helped by the analogy of *ὅτε δή*, *ἐπὴν δή*, etc., which made it natural to regard *οὖν* in *ἐπεὶ οὖν*, *ὡς οὖν* as merely ancillary. The evolution of (3) from (2) presents no difficulty. Other connecting particles (*δή*, *μήν*, and *μέντοι* quite clearly:

probably also γάρ) were originally adverbial in force, being later invested, for individual reasons which we usually cannot guess, with particular connective meanings, inferential, causal, adversative, or progressive. In the case of οὖν, the evolution of a connective force is aided by, and indeed foreshadowed in, the Homeric usage. We may even say that the backward reference in (1), after being dormant in (2), reappears in (3) in a more logically developed form. The stages of evolution are clearly seen in the case of μὲν οὖν: (i) in the *Iliad* and *Odyssey*, οὖν always retrospective: (ii) οὖν with no external reference, doing little more than strengthen μέν: (iii) οὖν as a fully developed connective particle.

I. Specifically Homeric use: ἐπεὶ οὖν, ὡς οὖν.

(1) Ἐπεὶ οὖν occurs 35 times in the *Iliad*, *Odyssey*, and Homeric *Hymns*. In 4 places ἐπεί is causal (Σ333: ρ226: σ362: *h.Merc.*475): in 31, temporal. In 33 places there is a reference to something already described or foreshadowed. *A*57 καλέσσατο λαὸν . . . οἱ δ' ἐπεὶ οὖν ἤγερθεν: *Λ*642 πινέμεναι δ' ἐκέλευσεν . . . τὼ δ' ἐπεὶ οὖν πίνοντ': *X*475 Andromache faints (466–7). ἡ δ' ἐπεὶ οὖν ἔμπνυτο: *Ω*329 Priam and his suite set out. οἱ δ' ἐπεὶ οὖν πόλιος κατέβαν: 349 οἱ δ' ἐπεὶ οὖν μέγα σῆμα πάρεξ Ἴλοιο ἔλασσαν: θ454 ἔς ῥ' ἀσάμινθον βάνθ' . . . τὸν δ' ἐπεὶ οὖν δμῳαὶ λοῦσαν. In two instances alone there is no such reference (*N*1, which Ebeling strangely adds, does refer back to the last lines of *M*): *Γ*4 ἠΰτε περ κλαγγὴ γεράνων πέλει . . . αἵ τ' ἐπεὶ οὖν χειμῶνα φύγον: *Δ*244 ἠΰτε νεβροί, αἵ τ' ἐπεὶ οὖν ἔκαμον. It may be noted that both these passages are in similes, and may possibly be abbreviated from longer passages (*loci communes* in the Epic tradition), in which οὖν did have a backward reference.

(2) Ὡς οὖν occurs 26 times, always (except for *B*321) with a verb of seeing, hearing, or ascertaining. *Γ*21 τὸν δ' ὡς οὖν ἐνόησεν (a common formula): 154 οἱ δ' ὡς οὖν εἴδονθ' Ἑλένην: Σ222 οἱ δ' ὡς οὖν ἄϊον ὄπα χάλκεον: θ272 Ἥφαιστος δ' ὡς οὖν θυμαλγέα μῦθον ἄκουσε: Σ530 οἱ δ' ὡς οὖν ἐπύθοντο πολὺν κέλαδον. In every case the object of the verb of seeing, etc., has been mentioned not long before. (In *B*321, if, with Leaf and *O.C.T.*, we print a full stop at the end of 320, οὖν is

practically a connecting particle. But punctuation and interpretation are disputed.)

'Επεὶ οὖν is used in Hesiod and later hexameter verse as in Homer. Hes.*Th.*853 (the only instance of οὖν in Hesiod) Ζεὺς δ' ἐπεὶ οὖν κόρθυνεν ἑὸν μένος (referring back to 838 ff.): Emp. *Fr.*23.3 ὡς δ' ὁπόταν γραφέες ἀναθήματα ποικίλλωσι . . . οἵ τ' ἐπεὶ οὖν μάρψωσι πολύχροα φάρμακα χερσίν.

II. Οὖν as an ancillary strengthening particle, in close association with other particles, negatives, and relatives. Apart from these associations, and ἐπεὶ οὖν, ὡς οὖν (above), οὖν never has an affirmative force, except in Hom. λ351 ξεῖνος δὲ τλήτω, μάλα περ νόστοιο χατίζων, ἔμπης οὖν ἐπιμεῖναι ἐς αὔριον. (In Ar.*Th.*755 οὖν coalesces with γε, as in γοῦν (see II.5.iv). In E.*Alc.*514 οὖν is connective (see III.1). In III.3,4,5 the use of οὖν is, I think, to be regarded as derived from the connective.)

Many of these uses are post-Homeric only. Where they occur in Homer, the retrospective force of οὖν is often discernible in him: whereas in later Greek the particle merely conveys emphasis. They continue to exist side by side with connective οὖν, but fall into decline in the fourth century, οὖν being here gradually replaced by δή.

(1) εἴτ' οὖν (ἄντ' οὖν). This combination, which first occurs in Pindar, is almost confined to the tragedians and Plato. (Des Places (p. 8) notes the frequency of εἴτ' οὖν, οὔτ' οὖν in the *Laws.*) It is not found in the other Attic prose writers or in comedy. Kühner holds that the function of οὖν in εἴτ' οὖν is to emphasize the clause in which it occurs: but Bäumlein's view, that οὖν denotes indifference, is better supported by the evidence: 'whether, in point of fact', the implication being that the fact does not greatly matter for immediate purposes.

(i) εἴτ' οὖν . . . εἴτε (far the commonest form). A.*Ag.*491 εἴτ' οὖν ἀληθεῖς εἴτ' ὀνειράτων δίκην τερπνὸν τόδ' ἐλθὸν φῶς ἐφήλωσεν φρένας: 843 εἴτ' οὖν θανόντος εἴτε καὶ ζῶντος πέρι λέγω: S.*OT* 1049 εἴτ' οὖν ἐπ' ἀγρῶν εἴτε κἀνθάδ' εἰσιδών: E.*IT* 272 εἴτ' οὖν ἐπ' ἀκταῖς θάσσετον Διοσκόρω, ἢ Νηρέως ἀγάλμαθ': S.*El.*199, 560: E.*Heracl.*149: *Rh.*722: Hdt.vi 137.1 εἴτε ὦν δὴ δικαίως εἴτε ἀδίκως: Pl.*Prt.*333C οὐδέν μοι διαφέρει . . . εἴτ' οὖν δοκεῖ σοι ταῦτα εἴτε μή: *Men*.92C: *Euthphr*.3D: *Ap*.27C: *Lg*.639B,808A, 859A: *id. saep.*

(ii) εἴτε . . . εἴτ' οὖν: εἰ . . . εἴτ' οὖν: . . . εἴτ' οὖν. Pi.*P*.4.78 ξεῖνος αἴτ' ὦν ἀστός: A.*Fr*.266 εἰ θέλεις εὐεργετεῖν εἴτ' οὖν κακουργεῖν (ὁ γοῦν *SMA*, εἴτ' οὖν Hermann): E.*Alc*.140 εἰ δ' ἔτ' ἐστὶν ἔμψυχος γυνή, εἴτ' οὖν ὄλωλεν εἰδέναι βουλοίμεθ' ἄν: Pl.*Lg*.738C εἴτε αὐτόθεν ἐπιχωρίους εἴτ' οὖν Τυρρηνικὰς εἴτε Κυπρίας εἴτε ἄλλοθεν ὁθενοῦν: 881D ἐάντε παῖς ἐάντε ἀνὴρ ἐάντ' οὖν γυνή: 933D.

(iii) εἴτ' οὖν . . . εἴτ' οὖν. Pl.*Ap*.34E καὶ τοῦτο τοὔνομα ἔχοντα, εἴτ' οὖν ἀληθὲς εἴτ' οὖν ψεῦδος: *Lg*.934D ἐάντ' οὖν δοῦλον ἐάντ' οὖν καὶ ἐλεύθερον περιορᾷ: Moschion, *Fr*.6.20–1. (In A.*Ch*.683 Paley and Tucker take the first οὖν as connective. But, apart from the rarity of connective οὖν in Aeschylus, for which see III below, it seems difficult to avoid co-ordinating the οὖν's as well as the εἴτε's. In the loose, colloquial style of this speech, we may perhaps put a comma after λάθῃ, and take the conditional clauses ἀπὸ κοινοῦ with what precedes and what follows, by a kind of anacoluthon: 'Tell them that Orestes is dead, whether it will be that they decide to convey his body home, or have it buried abroad, bring back their orders': τὸν δ' εἰ κομίζειν, Wilamowitz.)

(2) οὔτ' οὖν (μήτ' οὖν). This use is closely similar to εἴτ' οὖν. It is commoner, and is already found in Homer. Otherwise it is confined to the same authors as εἴτ' οὖν. οὖν emphasizes the duality, or plurality, of the ideas negatived. The particle is found with equal frequency in the first, and in the second, limb. In Homer a word occasionally intervenes between οὔτε and οὖν.

(i) οὔτ' οὖν . . . οὔτε (τε οὐ, δέ, οὐ). Hom.*P*20 οὔτ' οὖν παρδάλιος τόσσον μένος οὔτε λέοντος οὔτε συὸς κάπρου; *Υ*7 οὔτε τις οὖν ποταμῶν ἀπέην . . . οὔτ' ἄρα νυμφάων: ρ401 μήτ' οὖν μητέρ' ἐμὴν ἅζευ τό γε μήτε τιν' ἄλλον δμώων; *h.Cer*.236 οὔτ' οὖν σῖτον ἔδων, οὐ θησάμενος ⟨γάλα μητρός⟩: Pi.*O*.6.52 τοὶ δ' οὔτ' ὦν ἀκοῦσαι οὔτ' ἰδεῖν εὔχοντο: *N*.11.39 οὔτ' ὦν μέλαιναι καρπὸν ἔδωκαν ἄρουραι, δένδρεά τ' οὐκ ἐθέλει . . . ἄνθος εὐῶδες φέρειν: *P*.4.297 μήτ' ὦν τινι πῆμα πορών, ἀπαθὴς δ' αὐτὸς πρὸς ἀστῶν: E.*Andr*.329 οὐκ ἀξιῶ οὔτ' οὖν σὲ Τροίας οὔτε σοῦ Τροίαν ἔτι:

731 οὔτ' οὖν τι δράσω φλαῦρον οὔτε πείσομαι: *IA* 1437 μήτ' οὖν γε . . . μήτ' (οὖν γε is hardly possible: see γε, V.2.i: μήτ' οὖν σύ Elmsley): Hdt.ix 18.3 οὔτ' ὦν ἐμὲ οὔτε βασιλέα: 26.7 οὔτ' ὦν καινὰ οὔτε παλαιά: Pl.*Ti.*48C μήτ' οὖν ὑμεῖς οἴεσθε δεῖν ἐμὲ λέγειν, οὔτ' αὐτὸς αὖ πείθειν ἐμαυτὸν εἴην ἂν δυνατὸς ὡς ὀρθῶς ἐγχειροῖμ' ἂν τοσοῦτον ἐπιβαλλόμενος ἔργον: *Lg.*742C,778A, 792D,803D,944E.

(ii) οὔτε . . . οὔτ' οὖν. Hom.λ200 οὔτ' ἐμέ γ' ἐν μεγάροισιν ἐΰσκοπος ἰοχέαιρα . . . κατέπεφνεν, οὔτε τις οὖν μοι νοῦσος ἐπήλυθεν: Pi.*O.*6.19 οὔτε δύσηρις ἐὼν οὔτ' ὦν φιλόνικος ἄγαν: A.*Ag.*359 μήτε μέγαν μήτ' οὖν νεαρῶν τιν': 474 μήτ' εἴην πτολιπόρθης μήτ' οὖν αὐτὸς ἁλοὺς ὑπ' ἄλλων βίον κατίδοιμι: *Eu.*412: S.*OT* 90,271: E.*Hec.*1244: Hdt.iv 96 οὔτε ἀπιστέω οὔτε ὦν πιστεύω τι λίην: vii 140.2 οὔτε . . . οὔτε . . . οὔτε πόδες νέατοι οὔτ' ὦν χέρες (oracle): Pl.*Lg.*775B πίνειν δὲ εἰς μέθην οὔτ' ἄλλοθί που πρέπει . . . οὔτ' οὖν δὴ περὶ γάμους ἐσπουδακότα: 779C. (For οὐ . . . οὔτ' οὖν, see τε, I.4.iii.)

(3) τ' οὖν, οὐδ' οὖν. On the analogy of οὔτ' οὖν, εἴτ' οὖν, we should expect τ' οὖν ('both') to be fairly common. It is, in fact, surprisingly rare, its place being filled by τε δή, and S.*Aj.* 34 seems to be the only instance: πάντα γὰρ τά τ' οὖν πάρος τά τ' εἰσέπειτα σῇ κυβερνῶμαι χερί. (In A.*Eu.*567 οὖν seems (though the text is very doubtful) to reinforce a simple connective τε: στρατὸν κατειργαθοῦ, ἥ τ' οὖν . . . σάλπιγξ . . . γήρυμα φαινέτω στρατῷ (ἥ τ' *m*: εἴτ' *M*). For connective οὖν following prospective τε, see V.)

οὐδ' οὖν ('nor, in fact') is also not common. S.*OC* 1135 οὐκ ἔγωγέ σε (θέλω θιγεῖν μου), οὐδ' οὖν ἐάσω: (conjectured in Hom. ι147,[1] S.*Ach.Conv.*17 Diehl: see τε, I.4.iii): Hdt.ii 134.2 οὐδὲ ὦν οὐδὲ εἰδότες μοι φαίνονται λέγειν οὗτοι ἥτις ἦν ἡ Ῥοδῶπις: v 98.1 οὐδεμία ἔμελλε ὠφελίη ἔσεσθαι (οὐδ' ὦν οὐδὲ τούτου εἵνεκα ἐποίεε . . .): Pl.*R.*492E οὔτε γὰρ γίγνεται οὔτε γέγονεν οὐδὲ οὖν μὴ γένηται. (In Hdt.i 56.1 ὦν is the connective, and οὐδέ means 'not . . . either'.)

οὐδὲ . . . οὖν. Hom.ξ254 οὐδέ τις οὖν μοι νηῶν πημάνθη. In Pi.*O.*1.86 *Byz.* read οὐδ' ἀκράντοις ἐφάψατ' ὦν ἔπεσι.

[1] Mr. T. W. Allen prints οὐδ' οὖν, without comment, in his *O.C.T.* But he informs me that all MSS. read οὔτ' οὖν.

καὶ οὐδ' οὖν. Ar.*Av.*531 *κοὐδ' οὖν, εἴπερ ταῦτα δοκεῖ δρᾶν, ὀπτησάμενοι παρέθενθ' ὑμᾶς.*

(For *οὖν* combined with *ἀλλά, καί, γάρ, γε, δέ, δή, μέν*, see pp. 441–81.)

(4) With relatives. *οὖν*, following *περ*, is sometimes used after relative adjectives and adverbs (in particular, *ὥσπερ*), mostly by Aeschylus and Plato, occasionally by other writers. The function of the particle is (i) in general, to stress the closeness of the relation (like *δή*): (ii) in particular, to stress the correspondence between idea and fact, the objective reality of something which in the main clause is merely supposed.

(i) A.*Ag.*607 *γυναῖκα πιστὴν δ' ἐν δόμοις εὕροι μολὼν οἵανπερ οὖν ἔλειπεν* ('exactly as he left her'): 1427 (probably: but punctuation and interpretation are doubtful): *Ch.*96 *ἢ σῖγ' ἀτίμως, ὥσπερ οὖν ἀπώλετο πατήρ, τάδ' ἐκχέασα . . . στείχω* ('even as my father perished in dishonour'): 888 *δόλοις ὀλούμεθ', ὥσπερ οὖν ἐκτείναμεν* ('even as by guile we slew'). (In E.*Hipp.* 1307 the reading of *LP*, *ὥσπερ οὖν δίκαιον*, is adopted by almost all editors, and seems certainly right: 'in exact accordance with right': Artemis' mission is to establish the *δικαιοσύνη* of Hippolytus (cf.1298–9): *ὥσπερ ὢν δίκαιος* could only mean 'tamquam si iustus esset', not 'ut qui iustus esset': see Kühner II ii 98.)

(ii) A.*Ag.*1171 *ἄκος δ' οὐδὲν ἐπήρκεσαν τὸ μὴ πόλιν μὲν ὥσπερ οὖν ἔχει παθεῖν*: S.*Aj.*991 *τοῦδέ σοι μέλειν ἐφίεθ' ἀνὴρ κεῖνος, ὥσπερ οὖν μέλει* ('as you do, in fact, care'): Hdt.ii 2 *ταῦτα δὲ ἐποίεε . . . ὁ Ψαμμήτιχος θέλων ἀκοῦσαι τῶν παιδίων . . . ἥντινα φωνὴν ῥήξουσι πρώτην. τά περ ὢν καὶ ἐγένετο* ('And this did actually come about': viii 109.5): Pl.*Euthphr.*4D *ἠμέλει ὡς ἀνδροφόνου καὶ οὐδὲν ὂν πρᾶγμα εἰ καὶ ἀποθάνοι, ὅπερ οὖν καὶ ἔπαθεν* ('which is just what did happen to him'): *Euthd.*283A *ὡς αὐτίκα μάλα ἀκουσόμενοι θαυμασίους τινὰς λόγους. ὅπερ οὖν καὶ συνέβη ἡμῖν*: *Chrm.*155B *Ἀλλ' ἥξει, ἔφη. Ὃ οὖν καὶ ἐγένετο. ἧκε γάρ* (a prophecy fulfilled): *Prm.*130A (the inference from the smile is corroborated by Parmenides' actual words, *ὡς ἀγαμένους* by *ἄγασθαι*): *Phdr.*242E *εἰ δ' ἔστιν, ὥσπερ οὖν ἔστι, θεὸς . . . ὁ Ἔρως* ('as in fact he is'): *R.*564C *τριχῇ διαστησώμεθα τῷ λόγῳ δημοκρατουμένην πόλιν, ὥσπερ οὖν καὶ ἔχει*:

*Phd.*60C: *Cra.*404C,405C: *Ap.*21D. Pl.*Ti.*65C is rather different: φαίνεται δὲ καὶ ταῦτα, ὥσπερ οὖν καὶ τὰ πολλά, διὰ . . . γίγνεσθαι ('as in fact most things do').

(iii) οὖν is also used with indefinite relatives, especially with ellipse of verb in the relative clause, to emphasize the idea of universality. Kühner remarks that this use is not yet to be found in Aeschylus. It appears also to be absent from Sophocles and Euripides, and in fact hardly occurs in verse at all. The corresponding use of δή (I.9.vi) is to be compared. But οὖν never, like δή, denotes mere indifference of choice. (οὖν and δή together, Pl.*Lg.*789D ὁπωσοῦν δή.) Hdt.i 199.4 τὸ δὲ ἀργυρίου μέγαθός ἐστι ὅσον ὦν· οὐ γὰρ μὴ ἀπώσηται ('the sum is anything, however small; she will never refuse it'): ii 22 εἰ τοίνυν ἐχιόνιζε καὶ ὅσον ὦν: 113 Ἡρακλέος ἱρόν, ἐς τὸ ἢν καταφυγὼν οἰκέτης ὅτευ ὦν ἀνθρώπων ἐπιβάληται στίγματα ἱρὰ . . . οὐκ ἔξεστι τούτου ἅψασθαι: vi 56 προβάτοισι χρᾶσθαι . . . ὁκόσοισι ἂν ὦν ἐθέλωσι: Th.v 41.2 ἐξεῖναι δ' ὁποτεροισοῦν: vi 56.3 εἰ καὶ ὁποσοιοῦν τολμήσειαν ('however few'): X.*Cyr.*ii 4.10 ὁποίου τινὸς οὖν πράγματος: Pl.*Alc.II* 144C οὐδὲ τὴν ὁτουοῦν μητέρα διενοεῖτο ἀποκτεῖναι ('nec cuiusvis matrem in animo habuit occidere'): *Ly.*214E ὁτιοῦν ὅμοιον ὁτῳοῦν ὁμοίῳ τίνα ὠφελίαν ἔχειν . . . ἂν δύναιτο . . .; ('quidvis simile cuivis simili . . .?'): *Prt.*331D καὶ γὰρ ὁτιοῦν ὁτῳοῦν ἁμῇ γέ πῃ προσέοικεν: 313E,323A,328E: D.iv 29: xiv 2: xxiii 50. Without ellipse: Is.*Fr.*22 ὡς ἂν οὖν δυνώμεθα (οὖν *del.* Bekker): D.xxx 20.

Especially after negatives, οὐδ' ὁτιοῦν, οὐδ' ὁπωστιοῦν, etc. Ar.*Pl.*385 κοὐ διοίσοντ' ἀντίκρυς τῶν Ἡρακλειδῶν οὐδ' ὁτιοῦν: X.*An.*vii 6.27: D.ii 30: xx 158: xxxv 6.

(5) Emphasizing negatives. Probably always in Attic,[1] where οὖν strengthens a negative, γε follows at a short interval. (The juxtaposition of the particles in Pl.*Phd.*70B is exceptional.) The statement is emphatic, but the limits of its application are restricted. Thus οὔκουν . . . γε is the negative form of γοῦν (cf. οὔτοι δὴ . . . γε and γέ τοι δή, *s.v.* τοι, VI.6.ii). This relationship has often escaped notice, but it is well brought out by Paley (on E.*HF* 1251), in the new edition of Liddell and Scott (*s.v.* γοῦν), and by des Places (p. 156). (But γοῦν . . . οὐκ in Pl.*Lg.*666D,

[1] See (iii) below.

because here *οὐκ* goes closely with *ἄλλην*: 'We, at any rate, could sing no other song'. Cf. *Men.*89E: *R.*557E.)

(i) *οὔκουν . . . γε.* Particularly in dialogue, introducing an emphatic negative answer. A.*Pr.*518 **Τούτων** (Μοιρῶν) *ἄρα* **Ζεύς** *ἐστιν ἀσθενέστερος;—Οὔκουν ἂν ἐκφύγοι γε τὴν πεπρωμένην* ('At any rate, he cannot escape fate'): S.*OT* 565 **Ἐμνήσατ' οὖν ἐμοῦ** *τι . . .;—Οὔκουν ἐμοῦ γ' ἑστῶτος οὐδαμοῦ πέλας*: 1357 (answering his own preceding speech): *Ant.*993 *πιθοῦ.—Οὔκουν πάρος γε σῆς ἀπεστάτουν φρενός* ('Well, at any rate, I never disobeyed you in the *past*'): E.*IT* 516 **Καὶ** *μὴν ποθεινός γ' ἦλθες . . .—Οὔκουν ἐμαυτῷ γ'*: *Or.*1606 *Ὅστις δὲ τιμᾷ μητέρα;—Εὐδαίμων ἔφυ.—Οὔκουν σύ γε*: Ar.*Ra.*1065 **Τοῦτ'** *οὖν ἔβλαψά τι δράσας; —Οὔκουν ἐθέλει γε τριηραρχεῖν πλουτῶν οὐδεὶς διὰ ταῦτα* ('Well, anyhow, you did *this* much harm'): E.*Andr.*444: *Hel.* 1251: Ar.*V.*823: *Eq.*465: *Pl.*889: *Ec.*350,926: Pl.*Tht.*142D *ἔχοις ἂν διηγήσασθαι;—Οὐ μὰ τὸν Δία, οὔκουν οὕτω γε ἀπὸ στόματος*: *Sph.*241C *οὕτως ἀποστησόμεθα νῦν μαλθακισθέντες; —Οὔκουν ἔγωγέ φημι δεῖν*: 238B: *R.*536C,599E,611B: X.*Mem.* IV 5.7: *Cyr.*IV 1.23. On E.*IA* 9 *Τίς ποτ' ἄρ' ἀστὴρ ὅδε πορθμεύει; —Σείριος . . . ἔτι μεσσήρης.—Οὔκουν φθόγγος γ' οὔτ' ὀρνίθων οὔτε θαλάσσης* Paley explains: 'At all events there is no voice of birds, etc., i.e. whatever time of night is indicated by the stars'. (The relevance of *οὔτε θαλάσσης* is obscure: but Mr. D. L. Page suggests to me that Euripides means that two things would make a difference to Agamemnon: dawn would bring his daughter to be sacrificed, and a rising of the wind would make the sacrifice unnecessary. This is ingenious, and if it is right the second thought treads on the heels of the first, as the possibility of a wind occurs to Agamemnon).

Similarly, *οὔκουν δὴ . . . γε*, the negative form of *γοῦν δή*: Pl. *R.*407A: *Phdr.*276C: *Tht.*186D: *Plt.*291C: *Prm.*139B,141D (where, as Burnet subsequently admitted to R. W. Chapman, the comma after *δή* must certainly be omitted): 164B. *οὔκουν δήπου . . . γε* Pl.*Lg.*752A (mid-speech): *οὔκουν . . . γε δή* [Pl.] *Virt.*377A.

Less frequently, *οὔκουν . . . γε* is thus used in continuous speech. A.*Pr.*324 *οὔκουν ἔμοιγε χρώμενος διδασκάλῳ πρὸς κέντρα κῶλον ἐκτενεῖς*: Ar.*Ec.*343 'My wife has run off with my shoes. *οὔκουν λαβεῖν γ' αὐτὰς ἐδυνάμην οὐδαμοῦ*' ('Anyhow, I couldn't find 'em'): S.*Ph.*872 (see (iii) below): *OC* 924: Ar.*Pl.*342:

Pl.*R.*398C Ἐγὼ τοίνυν, ἔφη, ὦ Σώκρατες, κινδυνεύω ἐκτὸς τῶν πάντων εἶναι· οὔκουν ἱκανῶς γε ἔχω ἐν τῷ παρόντι συμβαλέσθαι (but here οὔκουν comes early in an answer: cf. *Cra.*408B): D.xviii 310 ἐν οἷς οὐδαμοῦ σὺ φανήσει γεγονὼς ... οὔκουν ἐπί γ' οἷς ἡ πατρὶς ηὐξάνετο ('not, at any rate, where ...'): Isoc. xv 313: xvii 32: D.xxiv 56.

In apodosi. Pl.*Epin.*974E εἰ καὶ κατ' ἀρχὰς ἔδοξέν τις εἶναί ποτε σοφός, οὔκουν νῦν γε οὔτε σοφὸς εἶναι δοξάζεται ...: *Lg.* 810D. Cf. Th.ii 43.1, viii 91.3 below.

(ii) *οὐκ οὖν, separatim* (*μὴ οὖν, οὐκ ... οὖν*) ... γε. There are a few examples, mostly in Thucydides and Xenophon. It is doubtful whether juxtaposed οὐκ οὖν should ever be written separately. Cf. IV.5 below.

E.*HF* 1251 Ὁ πολλὰ δὴ τλὰς Ἡρακλῆς λέγει τάδε;—Οὐκ οὖν τοσαῦτά γ': Th.ii 43.1 ἐνθυμουμένους ὅτι τολμῶντες ... ἄνδρες αὐτὰ ἐκτήσαντο, καὶ ὁπότε καὶ πείρᾳ του σφαλεῖεν, οὐκ οὖν καὶ τὴν πόλιν γε τῆς σφετέρας ἀρετῆς ἀξιοῦντες στερίσκειν: viii 91.3 μάλιστα μὲν ἐβούλοντο ὀλιγαρχούμενοι ἄρχειν καὶ τῶν ξυμμάχων, εἰ δὲ μή, ... αὐτονομεῖσθαι, ἐξειργόμενοι δὲ καὶ τούτου μὴ οὖν ὑπὸ τοῦ δήμου γε αὖθις γενομένου ... διαφθαρῆναι: X.*Cyr.*iii 3.50 οὐδεμία γάρ ἐστιν οὕτω καλὴ παραίνεσις ἥτις τοὺς μὴ ὄντας ἀγαθοὺς ... ἀγαθοὺς ποιήσει· οὐκ ἂν οὖν τοξότας γε ...: *Lac.* 5.9 καὶ ἐμοὶ μὲν οὐδ' ἐν τούτῳ σφαλῆναι δοκεῖ. οὐκ ἂν οὖν ῥᾳδίως γέ τις εὕροι Σπαρτιατῶν οὔτε ὑγιεινοτέρους ....

(iii) Without following γε. Hdt.ii 20 λέγει τοὺς ἐτησίας ἀνέμους εἶναι αἰτίους πληθύειν τὸν ποταμὸν ... πολλάκις δὲ ἐτησίαι μὲν οὐκ ὦν ἔπνευσαν, ὁ δὲ Νεῖλος τὠυτὸ ἐργάζεται ('do not, in fact, blow'): iii 137 ταῦτα λέγοντες τοὺς Κροτωνιήτας οὐκ ὦν ἔπειθον.[1]

Wherever, in Attic, γε is lacking after emphatic οὔκουν, it should probably be supplied. In E.*Ion* 356 (assuming the text to be otherwise in order) Badham's ἄλλον ⟨γ'⟩ springs from a sure instinct, as does Musgrave's ἐν Ἄργει ⟨γ'⟩ in *Hel.*124, and Reiske's τό γ', for τόδ', in S.*Ant.*321. In S.*Ph.*872 I have suggested γ' αὔτ' for τοῦτ', a change supported by other considera-

[1] Kühner (II ii 161) explains these passages as quasi-adversative: he also finds an adversative sense in other passages which can easily be taken as progressive. There is no adequate evidence for an adversative οὖν. Ὦν with negatives seems to have more independent force than οὖν.

tions (*C.R.*xliii (1929) 118). In A.*Supp.*392, where *οὖν* can scarcely be connective, we should perhaps read: *Μή τί ποτ' οὖν γενοίμαν ὑποχείριος κράτεσί γ' ἀρσένων* (for *κράτεσιν*): 'Whether I adopt the expedient you suggest, or another, may I at least not become subject to the males'. In Th.iii 113.4 read, perhaps, *οὔκουν τά ⟨γ'⟩ ὅπλα*. In S.*Aj.*1339 the reading is most uncertain. In A.*Pr.*520 *M*'s *οὐκ ἂν οὖν* can hardly be right. (See *C.R.* xliv (1930) 213–4.)

(iv) Just as *οὔκουν . . . γε* is the negative form of *γοῦν*, so, in one passage, *οὖν . . . γε* is equivalent to *γοῦν*: Ar.*Th.*755 *ἵν' οὖν τό γ' αἷμα τοῦ τέκνου τοὐμοῦ λάβω.* There is no parallel, but the explanation seems certain. (Cf. *ἀλλ' οὖν . . . γε*, p. 444.) The position of *οὖν* is perhaps *metri gratia* here: whereas in *οὔκουν . . . γε* it is due to sense, *οὖν* being naturally drawn to the negative which it strengthens.

III. *Οὖν* as a connecting particle.

(1) Normal use. The independent use of *οὖν* (*ὦν*) as a connecting particle is not firmly established before the second half of the fifth century, though it is faintly foreshadowed by the Homeric and Pindaric use of the particle, notably in the combination *μὲν οὖν*. Hecataeus *Fr.*30 is one of the earliest examples: *οὐ γὰρ ὑμῖν δυνατός εἰμι ἀρήγειν· ὡς μὴ ὦν . . . ἀπόλησθε . . . ἀποίχεσθαι.* Aeschylus, it is true, not infrequently uses connective *οὖν* in answer-questions. *Pr.*515 *Τίς οὖν ἀνάγκης ἐστὶν οἰακοστρόφος*; *Ch.*171 *Πῶς οὖν παλαιὰ παρὰ νεωτέρας μάθω*; *Supp.*314, 318: *Pr.*771: *Ch.*114: *Eu.*902. (In *Supp.*19, a question in the middle of the Parodos, the reading is not quite certain.) Apart from questions, there are only two certain examples of connective *οὖν* in Aeschylus: *Ch.*579: *Eu.* 219. For *Ch.*683, see II.1.iii: in *Ch.*931 *οὖν* probably strengthens *μέν*: for *Supp.*392, see II.5.iii. (The tendency to use *οὖν* particularly in questions (for which compare *δῆτα*), perhaps survives into the fourth century: in D.xviii and xix *οὖν* occurs 79 times, 63 times in questions. But there is no trace of this tendency in Herodotus or Thucydides.) From Sophocles onwards the connective use of *οὖν* predominates over others. The particle expresses *post hoc* and (more frequently) *propter hoc*, or anything between the two.

In narrative, almost purely temporal, marking a new stage in the sequence of events: 'Well', 'Now'. Hermipp.*Fr.*70.2 *εἰς τὸ Κυλικράνων βαδίζων † σπληνόπεδον † ἀφικόμην· εἶδον οὖν τὴν Ἡράκλειαν καὶ μάλ' ὡραίαν πόλιν*: Ar.*Pl.*733 *εἶθ' ὁ θεὸς ἐπόππυσεν. ἐξηξάτην οὖν δύο δράκοντ' ἐκ τοῦ νέω*: Pl.*Chrm.* 154D *Συνέφασαν οὖν καὶ οἱ ἄλλοι*: 155B: *Phd.*61D: *Smp.*175C, 176A,B: *R.*327A,B,C: *Prm.*136E.

Proceeding to a new point, or a new stage in the march of thought. E.*Hel.*1266 The offerings to the dead have been prescribed. *Πῶς οὖν; ἐς οἶδμα τίνι τρόπῳ καθίετε;* (a supplementary question): Ar.*Th.*67 ('He is going to compose: now he finds that difficult, except in the sun'): S.*Ph.*305: E.*Tr.* 968: *El.*912: *IT* 22: Hp.*Epid.*ii 2.18 *ἐπεὶ δὲ ἔτεκεν . . . αὖθις ἤλγησεν· ἔτεκεν οὖν ἄρσεν*: *Acut.*18 (we have been told what preparations are necessary for the bath, and what persons will benefit from it: *οὖν* introduces the next point, how often one should have a bath): Lys.xiii 19 *ἐδόκει αὐτοῖς οὗτος ἐπιτήδειος εἶναι μηνυτής. ἐβούλοντο οὖν ἄκοντα δοκεῖν αὐτὸν καὶ μὴ ἑκόντα μηνύειν*: Hdt.ii 10,49: vii 81: Th.ii 34.5.

The inferential use of *οὖν* is too common to need illustration. But we may notice two passages in which the sequence of thought is not at first sight obvious. E.*Alc.*514 (*οὖν* shows that the wish is prompted by the information received: 'I hope it's not one of your children, then'): *Or.*793 *Ορ. Δυσχερὲς ψαύειν νοσοῦντος ἀνδρός.—Πυ. Οὐκ ἔμοιγε σοῦ.—Ορ. Εὐλάβου λύσσης μετασχεῖν τῆς ἐμῆς.—Πυ. Τόδ' οὖν ἴτω.* In the rapid dialogue Pylades ignores Orestes' repeated protest: 'Not for me to touch thee . . . So let that pass'. Paley's ellipse of *οὐ μέλει μοι*, before *τόδ'*, is unnecessary and unlikely. His alternative suggestion, to read *τὸ δ' οὖν*, gives a wrong sense to *δ' οὖν*.

The use of *οὖν* in direct questions is transferred to an indirect question in Pl.*Prt.*322C *Ἑρμῆν πέμπει ἄγοντα εἰς ἀνθρώπους αἰδῶ τε καὶ δίκην . . . ἐρωτᾷ οὖν Ἑρμῆς Δία τίνα οὖν τρόπον δοίη δίκην καὶ αἰδῶ ἀνθρώποις* ('in what way, then'). In *Smp.* 219D *ὥστε οὔθ' ὅπως οὖν ὀργιζοίμην εἶχον*, des Places (p. 42) follows Stallbaum in explaining *ὅπως οὖν ὀργιζοίμην* as representing the direct *πῶς οὖν ὀργίζωμαι*; (*igitur*): but the sense *igitur* is singularly inappropriate here: the text is certainly difficult: perhaps *οὔτ' οὖν ὅπως*. (*R.*524C, which des Places (*loc. cit.*) cites as indirect, may equally well be direct.)

(2) Position. Connective οὖν, like most other connecting particles, is normally placed second in the sentence. But it not infrequently comes later. (Sophocles is much freer than the other tragedians in this respect.)

3rd. A.*Eu.*219 εἰ τοῖσιν οὖν κτείνουσιν ἀλλήλους χαλᾷς: S. *OT* 141 κείνῳ προσαρκῶν οὖν: 1520 Φῂς τάδ' οὖν: *Tr.*1247 Πράσσειν ἄνωγας οὖν: *Ph.*121 Ἦ μνημονεύεις οὖν: E.*Heracl.* 1021 πῶς τάδ' οὖν γενήσεται; Ar.*Ec.*1082 Ποτέρας προτέρας οὖν: 1157 σχεδὸν ἅπαντας οὖν: Pherecr.*Fr.*191: Hdt.i 85.1 ἐν τῇ ὦν παρελθούσῃ εὐεστοῖ: iii 127.3 πρίν τι ὦν: vii 150.2 οὕτω ἂν ὦν εἴημεν: 153.4 θῶμά μοι ὦν: Th.i 91.7 ἢ πάντας οὖν ἀτειχίστους ἔφη χρῆναι ξυμμαχεῖν ἢ . . .: Pl.*Phlb.*43E Τριῶν ὄντων οὖν: *Phdr.*258C Οἴει τινὰ οὖν: *La.*201B καὶ ἡμεῖς οὖν: *Men.*74E Τί ποτε οὖν: 96D παντὸς μᾶλλον οὖν: *R.*565D Τίς ἀρχὴ οὖν: *Chrm.*160E Οὐ μόνον οὖν: *Lg.*799A Ἔχει τις οὖν: D.xix 111 τῷ προσῆκεν οὖν: lvii 26 οἴεταί τις οὖν . . .;

4th. S.*OT* 1128 Τὸν ἄνδρα τόνδ' οὖν οἶσθα: 1517 Οἶσθ' ἐφ' οἷς οὖν εἶμι; *OC* 1424 Ὁρᾷς τὰ τοῦδ' οὖν: 1539 τὰ μὲν τοιαῦτ' οὖν: Ar.*V.*291 Ἐθελήσεις τί μοι οὖν: Hdt.ii 12 τὰ περὶ Αἴγυπτον ὦν: Pl.*Men.*86E εἰ μή τι οὖν: *Euthd.* 272A πρὸ τοῦ μὲν οὖν: *Cra.* 438E Διὰ τίνος ἄλλου οὖν: *Phlb.*56D Πῇ ποτε διορισάμενος οὖν: *Plt.*262C ἐν τῷ μὲν οὖν παρεστηκότι: *Hipparch.*230E Καὶ περὶ ποτοῦ οὖν: *Plt.*304C Εἶεν· τίνι τὸ πειστικὸν οὖν ἀποδώσομεν . . .; X.*Cyr.*iv 5.21 καὶ ἡ ὀργὴ οὖν αὕτη: Aen.Tact.24.7 ὡς ἀπήγαγέν τε οὖν αὐτούς: D.xlvii 23 ἐξ ἀνάγκης ἦν οὖν μοι: 135 τίς ἂν δύναιτ' οὖν.

5th. S.*Aj.*1215 τίς μοι, τίς ἔτ' οὖν τέρψις ἔπεσται; Ar.*Pl.*848 Καὶ ταῦτ' ἀναθήσων ἔφερες οὖν; in E.*Hec.*96 Bothe reads ἀπ' ἐμᾶς ἀπ' ἐμᾶς οὖν for ἀπ' ἐμᾶς οὖν ἀπ' ἐμᾶς: Pl.*R.*332C Ὦ Σιμωνίδη, ἡ τίσιν οὖν τί ἀποδιδοῦσα . . . τέχνη ἰατρικὴ καλεῖται; (postponement after vocative plus postponement after interrogative, which gravitates to an early position).

6th. Ar.*Av.*1405 Βούλει διδάσκειν καὶ παρ' ἡμῖν οὖν μένων: Pl.*Lg.*777D ὁ περὶ τὰ τῶν δούλων οὖν ἤθη.

Postponement after preposition, article, and noun (etc.) is in accordance with the usage of other particles: Pl.*Ti.*81B πρὸς τὸ συγγενὲς οὖν. But particle sometimes immediately follows preposition: S.*El* 307: E.*Alc.*514: Pl.*R.*456D Ἐν οὖν τῇ πόλει: *Lg.*782D Πρὸς οὖν δὴ τί ταῦτα . . .; 731C.

(3) *In apodosi.*[1] Like δή, though far less frequently, οὖν is used apodotically, after a temporal, causal, or conditional protasis. This use is perhaps best regarded as an offshoot of the connective, though Kühner (II ii 327) takes it as 'adverbial'. Apodotic οὖν is almost confined to Ionic prose and Plato.

Hdt.i 132.2 ἐπεὰν δὲ . . . ἑψήσῃ τὰ κρέα, ὑποπάσας ποίην . . ., ἐπὶ ταύτης ἔθηκε ὦν πάντα τὰ κρέα: vi 76.1 ἐπείτε δὲ Σπαρτιήτας ἄγων ἀπίκετο ἐπὶ ποταμὸν Ἐρασῖνον, ὃς λέγεται . . ., ἀπικόμενος ὦν ὁ Κλεομένης ἐπὶ τὸν ποταμὸν τοῦτον: ix 26.3 ἐπεὶ μετὰ Ἀχαιῶν . . . ἰζόμεθα ἀντίοι τοῖσι κατιοῦσι, τότε ὦν λόγος Ὕλλον ἀγορεύσασθαι: 87.1 ἄνδρες Θηβαῖοι, ἐπειδὴ οὕτω δέδοκται τοῖσι Ἕλλησι . . ., νῦν ὦν . . .: Hp.*Int.*8 ἣν . . . ἀναρραγῇ (ἀναρρήγνυται δὲ μάλιστα ὑπὸ ταλαιπωρίης), τάδε οὖν πάσχει (καὶ τάδε πάσχει *vulg.*): *Mul.*110: Pl.*Ly.*223B ἐπειδὴ δὲ οὐδὲν ἐφρόντιζον ἡμῶν . . ., ἡττηθέντες οὖν αὐτῶν διελύσαμεν τὴν συνουσίαν: *Cra.*420A ὅτι γὰρ ἱέμενος ῥεῖ . . ., ἀπὸ ταύτης οὖν πάσης τῆς δυνάμεως "ἵμερος" ἐκλήθη: *R.*367D ἐπειδὴ οὖν ὡμολόγησας τῶν μεγίστων ἀγαθῶν εἶναι δικαιοσύνην . . ., τοῦτ' οὖν αὐτὸ ἐπαίνεσον δικαιοσύνης: *Alc. I* 105B (οὖν *B*: δέ *T* Proclus): X.*Cyr.*i 2.11 ἐξέρχονται δὲ ἐπὶ τὴν θήραν ἄριστον ἔχοντες . . . ἣν δέ τι δεήσῃ . . . διατρῖψαι περὶ τὴν θήραν, τὸ οὖν ἄριστον τοῦτο δειπνήσαντες τὴν ὑστεραίαν αὖ θηρῶσι (οὖν *om. DFG*). Perhaps also *Cyr.*i 3.17: but the text is doubtful.

In some of these examples (e.g. Pl.*Cra.*420A) οὖν has a noticeable inferential force: 'for that reason'. So in three cases in Thucydides after an explanation of motives: iii 95.1 νομίσας . . ., ἄρας οὖν . . . παρέπλευσεν ἐς Σόλλιον: vi 64.1: vii 6.1.

οὐκῶν. Hdt.ix 55 ὡς γὰρ δὴ παρηγόρεον τὸν Ἀμομφάρετον . . ., οὐκῶν ἔπειθον (οὐκῶν Stein: οὔκουν *E*: οὔ κως *rell.*).

For apodotic οὔκουν . . . γε see II.5.i, *ad fin.*

(4) Resumptive. Allied to the above idiom, and not always to be rigidly distinguished from it, is the resumptive use of οὖν, mostly after a parenthesis, found in Herodotus and Plato, and occasionally in other writers. The resumption of the main thought is often marked by a demonstrative pronoun, or by a repeated word or synonym.

[1] On apodotic and resumptive οὖν in Plato, see des Places, pp. 52–4. In some passages anacoluthon is no doubt to be assumed.

Hdt.iii 97 Κόλχοι δὲ ⟨τὰ⟩ ἐτάξαντο ἐς τὴν δωρεὴν καὶ οἱ προσεχέες μέχρι Καυκάσιος ὄρεος (ἐς τοῦτο γὰρ τὸ ὄρος . . .), οὗτοι ὦν δῶρα τὰ ἐτάξαντο . . . ἀγίνεον : iv 72 λαβόντες τῶν λοιπῶν θεραπόντων τοὺς ἐπιτηδεοτάτους (οἱ δέ εἰσι . . .), τούτων ὦν τῶν διηκόνων ἐπεὰν ἀποπνίξωσι πεντήκοντα . . . : vii 137.2 τὸ δὲ συμπεσεῖν . . . , δῆλον ὦν μοι ὅτι θεῖον ἐγένετο τὸ πρῆγμα : Hp.*Septim.* 1 ἢν γὰρ . . . λογίσῃ . . . , οὕτως οὖν τουτέων ἐόντων . . . : Pl.*Chrm.* 157C ἐγὼ οὖν—ὀμώμοκα γὰρ αὐτῷ, καί μοι ἀνάγκη πείθεσθαι—πείσομαι οὖν : *R.*352B–D ὅτι μὲν γὰρ . . .— . . .—ταῦτα μὲν οὖν ὅτι οὕτως ἔχει μανθάνω : X.*An.*vi 6.15 ἐγὼ μὲν οὖν (καὶ γὰρ ἀκούω . . .), ἐγὼ μὲν οὖν ἀπολύω: Hdt.v 99.1 : vi 13.1 : Pl.*Lg.*713C,812E: *Ep.*348C: Aen.Tact.8.5: Lys.viii 3: D.xix 45: lix 99.

In almost all the above cases the parenthesis is of some considerable length, and actual anacoluthon may be assumed in some of them. The following is remarkable for the shortness of the parenthesis, if indeed it can be so styled: Hdt.i 144.1 κατά περ οἱ ἐκ τῆς πενταπόλιος νῦν χώρης Δωριέες, πρότερον δὲ ἑξαπόλιος τῆς αὐτῆς ταύτης καλεομένης, φυλάσσονται ὦν . . . (αἰνῶς Stein).

(5) In tmesis (cf. p. 460).* Frequently in Herodotus and certain works of the Hippocratic corpus, very occasionally elsewhere, ὦν (οὖν) is inserted between a preposition and a verb compounded with it. This usage, which Kühner (II i 537) associates with popular speech, is mainly found in apodoses, though the earliest examples are not apodotic: Epich.*Fr.*124 καὶ γλυκύν γ' ἐπ' ὦν ἐπίομες οἶνον : *Fr.*35.6 κἀπ' ὦν ἠχθόμαν. It may therefore derive from Homeric οὖν referring to something foreshadowed, 'accordingly'.

In Herodotus the verb is always an aorist, and (except in ii 172) always a gnomic aorist, usually describing some local custom or process. The expression for the most part occurs in an apodosis (not necessarily early in the apodosis) following either a protasis opening with ἐπεάν or a participial clause. i 194 ἐπεὰν ὦν ἀπίκωνται πλέοντες ἐς τὴν Βαβυλῶνα καὶ διαθέωνται τὸν φόρτον, νομέας μὲν τοῦ πλοίου καὶ τὴν καλάμην πᾶσαν ἀπ' ὦν ἐκήρυξαν : ii 39,40,47(*bis*) ; 70,85,86,87(*bis*),88,122 : iii 82 : iv 196 : vii 10ε. Not apodotic, ii 96.2,172.3.

In Hippocrates, also, the verb denotes an habitual occurrence, the tense being indicative present or gnomic aorist. Normally a general conditional or temporal protasis precedes (though not always immediately precedes). The idiom is common in *de Morbis* i (though it is read only in the good MS. θ: see Littré, vi 271): e.g. 14,15,18,19,21,22,30: *Morb.*ii 50 ἔπειτα καὶ πυρετοὶ ἰσχυροὶ ἐπιγινόμενοι κατ' οὖν ἔκτειναν (*E* only): 51 ὅταν . . ., ἀπ' οὖν ὤλετο: *Nat.Mul.*11 θ only).

Kühner cites Dorieus[1] *ap.* Athen.413A ὃν γὰρ ἐπόμπευσεν βοῦν ἄζυγον, εἰς κρέα τόνδε κόψας πάντα κατ' οὖν μοῦνος ἐδαίσατό νιν. Hartung gives two examples from late epigrams. In Hippon.*Fr.* 64.2 ἀπ' ὧν ἔδυσε was conjectured by Hermann for ἄπουν ἔδυσε: lack of context makes it impossible to say if ὦν would be apodotic there. The appearance of this tmesis in Ar.*Ra.*1047 is remarkable: ὥστε γε καὐτόν σε (Euripides) κατ' οὖν ἔβαλεν. I have little doubt that there is an intentional Ionism (or Dorism) here, and that Aristophanes is parodying some one, probably Euripides himself. Euripides used tmesis freely (Kühner II i 534: and cf. *Andr.*837 κατὰ μὲν οὖν στένω).

Οὔκουν, οὐκοῦν

IV. We have already dealt with οὔκουν denoting an emphatic negative (οὖν, II.5). It remains to consider those uses of οὔκουν, οὐκοῦν in which οὖν has a connective force. It is usually agreed that the ancient grammarians are right in saying that in οὔκουν the predominant element is οὐκ, in οὐκοῦν, οὖν. (Phrynichus, Bekk.*Anecd.*i 57: Apollonius, *ib.*ii 525: Joann. Charax, *ib.*iii 1155: Ammonius, *de differ. affin. vocal.* 105.)

οὔκουν and οὐκοῦν are found both in statements and in questions. We thus have four forms. The punctuation and accentuation of our MSS. are not to be trusted over-implicitly, and frequent changes should probably be made.[2] Editors have been rather haphazard in this matter.

[1] Perhaps a contemporary of Leonidas of Tarentum (Pauly-Wissowa, *s.v. Dorieus*).

[2] I cordially agree with Hermann (on Viger, *De Idiotismis*): 'Verum mirifice perturbatus est huius particulae usus, ita ut vix scias quo te vertas. Librorum auctoritati non multum tribui potest in tanta scripturae varietate'.

(1) *Οὔκουν* in questions, usually at the opening of an answer. This, as Kühner observes (II ii 166), is characteristic of the lively, emotional style of tragedy. Often, the logical starting-point is, not what the previous speaker has said, but the fact that he has said it. 'Why' or 'well' then brings out the force of the *οὖν*.

A.*Pr.*379 *ἐγὼ δὲ τὴν παροῦσαν ἀντλήσω τύχην, ἔς τ' ἂν Διὸς φρόνημα λωφήσῃ χόλου.—Οὔκουν, Προμηθεῦ, τοῦτο γιγνώσκεις, ὅτι ὀργῆς νοσούσης εἰσὶν ἰατροὶ λόγοι;* ('Why, Prometheus, don't you know ...?'): *Eu.*725 *Τοιαῦτ' ἔδρασας καὶ Φέρητος ἐν δόμοις ...—Οὔκουν δίκαιον τὸν σέβοντ' εὐεργετεῖν ...;* ('Well, isn't it right ...?' *Οὐκοῦν*, *codd.*, is clearly wrong): *Th.*217 *πύργον στέγειν εὔχεσθε πολέμιον δορύ.—Οὔκουν τάδ' ἔσται πρὸς θεῶν;* (*οὔκουν M*: *οὐκοῦν* m_1 *recc.*): S.*Ph.* 628 Exit *Ἔμπορος*. *Φι. Οὔκουν τάδ', ὦ παῖ, δεινά, τὸν Λαερτίου ἔμ' ἐλπίσαι ...;* ('Now, isn't it monstrous ...?'): Ar.*Eq.*1381 *συνερτικὸς γάρ ἐστι ....—Οὔκουν καταδακτυλικὸς σὺ ...;* ('Well, aren't *you* ...?'): *Nu.*1377 *κἄπειτ' ἔφλα με ...—Οὔκουν δικαίως, ὅστις οὐκ Εὐριπίδην ἐπαινεῖς σοφώτατον;* *V.*47 ('Well, now, isn't that odd?'): *Pl.*257 *ἴτ' ἐγκονεῖτε....—Οὔκουν ὁρᾷς ὁρμωμένους ἡμᾶς πάλαι προθύμως ...;* ('Why, don't you see we *are* hurrying?'): S.*El.*795: *OT* 440,973: *Aj.*79 (*οὐκοῦν sine interrogationis nota LA rec.*): E.*IT* 1190,1196: *Ph.*1690.

Far less frequently in mid-speech: E.*Alc.*794 (*B*'s division between speakers is clearly wrong): *Heracl.*1005 (perhaps an ironical statement, as Paley takes it): *Hec.*592.

Οὔκουν is often used, as Kühner (II ii 167) observes, with the second person future indicative (or optative with *ἄν*) in impatient questions, at the opening of a speech. A.*Pr.*52 *Ἔγνωκα τοῖσδε κοὐδὲν ἀντειπεῖν ἔχω.—Οὔκουν ἐπείξει τῷδε δεσμὰ περιβαλεῖν ...;* ('Well, then, won't you hurry ...?'): 616 *Ἀρμοῖ πέπαυμαι τοὺς ἐμοὺς θρηνῶν πόνους.—Οὔκουν πόροις ἂν τήνδε δωρεὰν ἐμοί;* S. *OT* 676 *Στυγνὸς μὲν εἴκων δῆλος εἶ ...—Οὔκουν μ' ἐάσεις κἀκτὸς εἶ;* *El.*631 *πρὸς ὀργὴν ἐκφέρῃ, μεθεῖσά μοι λέγειν ἃ χρῄζοιμ' ... —Οὔκουν ἐάσεις οὐδ' ὑπ' εὐφήμου βοῆς θῦσαί μ' ...;* *Aj.*1051: *Ant.*244: *OC* 897 (*οὐκοῦν L rec.*): E.*Or.*1238: Ar.*Ra.*201: *Pl.* 71. Cf. *Av.*1185 *Οὔκουν σφενδόνας δεῖ λαμβάνειν καὶ τόξα;*

Postponed after apostrophe: Ar.*Ra.*480 *Ὦ καταγέλαστ' οὔκουν ἀναστήσει ταχὺ ...;*

οὔκουν δῆτα, οὔκουν ... δῆτα (for which, in general, see *δῆτα*,

I.6.i) are sometimes similarly used by Aristophanes. *Av.*1177 Οὔκουν δῆτα περιπόλους ἐχρῆν πέμψαι κατ' αὐτὸν εὐθύς; *Ra.* 193 Οὔκουν περιθρέξει δῆτα τὴν λίμνην κύκλῳ; 200 Οὔκουν καθεδεῖ δῆτ' ἐνθαδὶ γάστρων; *Ec.*1144: *Pax* 274.

The above instances of interrogative οὔκουν are all from drama. If we trust our manuscripts, we must believe that interrogative οὔκουν is practically unknown to prose. But in many passages, where a surprised or indignant question is clearly required, there are strong grounds for restoring οὔκουν ...; for affirmative or interrogative οὐκοῦν.

Plato. Des Places observes (p.158) that *Smp.*175A is the only example of interrogative οὔκουν in Plato. Ἄτοπόν γ', ἔφη, λέγεις· οὔκουν καλεῖς αὐτὸν καὶ μὴ ἀφήσεις; (Cf. the examples with 2nd pers. fut. ind. quoted above.) And Kühner (II ii 166) says that interrogative οὐκοῦν, rather than οὔκουν, 'gehört der ruhigen und gemässigten Rede an, namentlich den Sokratischen Gesprächen bei Xenophon und Plato'. Broadly speaking, this is no doubt true; but even Socrates is capable, at times, of surprise, and the people with whom he converses are not invariably 'ruhig'. I suspect we should write οὔκουν in such passages as the following, where the particle introduces a lively, surprised, or indignant question of a type as closely similar to those quoted above as it is different *toto caelo* from the quieter οὐκοῦν questions considered below.

*Men.*81A ὁρᾷς τοῦτον ὡς ἐριστικὸν λόγον κατάγεις ...;—Οὐκοῦν καλῶς σοι δοκεῖ λέγεσθαι ὁ λόγος οὗτος, ὦ Σώκρατες; ('Why, don't you *like* the argument?'): *Grg.*459C 'Rhetoric only teaches you to *appear* to know things'.—Οὐκοῦν πολλὴ ῥᾳστώνη ... γίγνεται, μὴ μαθόντα τὰς ἄλλας τέχνας ἀλλὰ μίαν ταύτην, μηδὲν ἐλαττοῦσθαι τῶν δημιουργῶν; ('Well, isn't that a delightfully easy way of doing things?'): 466E οὐδὲν γὰρ ποιεῖν (φημὶ τοὺς ῥήτορας) ὧν βούλονται ὡς ἔπος εἰπεῖν, ποιεῖν μέντοι ὅτι ἂν αὐτοῖς δόξῃ βέλτιστον εἶναι.—Οὐκοῦν τοῦτο ἔστιν τὸ μέγα δύνασθαι; ('Well, *isn't* that having great power?'): *Euthd.* 291D σαφῶς οὖν ἐδόκει ἡμῖν ...—Οὐκοῦν καλῶς ἡμῖν ἐδόκει ...; *Grg.*511B: *Phdr.*260E.

In Demosthenes, the MSS. give interrogative οὔκουν in the following:—xx 28 οὔκουν ὅτε πολλῷ μείζονα βλάψει τῶν ὠφελειῶν ὧν ἔχει (ὁ νόμος), προσήκει λελύσθαι παρὰ τοῖσδ' αὐτόν; ἔγωγ' ἂν φαίην: lix 125 οὔκουν ἤδη δοκεῖ ὑμῖν . . .; In other passages various editors have restored interrogative οὔκουν for affirmative οὐκοῦν: xx 26,62,71,97: xxxiv 49 (for οὐκ οὖν *separatim*). We should probably further restore οὔκουν everywhere in οὐκοῦν δεινόν followed by an infinitive or conditional clause (cf. S.*Ph*.628, above). The tone clearly demands 'Now, is it not monstrous . . .?': not, 'Now it is monstrous, is it not?' xix 226: xxiii 56: xxxix 21,31: xl 42: xlv 73: lv 22: lvii 47: lix 107,117. The editions are chaotic in this respect. Thus Blass sometimes prints a question-mark after οὐκοῦν δεινόν, sometimes not: while Rennie prints οὔκουν for οὐκ οὖν in xxxiv 49, but retains οὐκοῦν in the closely similar xxxix 21,31. οὔκουν is at least probable in other passages: v 25: xix 285: xxxvii 57: xliv 56.

These passionate questions are especially characteristic of Demosthenes. But there are some examples in other prose writers where interrogative οὔκουν should probably be read. Lys. x 12 οὐκ οὖν ἄτοπον ἂν εἴη . . .; Isoc.xviii 21 οὐκ οὖν δεινὸν . . .; Th.v 107 (οὔκουν *BC*: οὐκοῦν *cett.*: οὐκ οὖν . . .; Steup: οὔκουν . . . Stuart Jones): Aeschin.i 85: iii 245.

(2) *Οὐκοῦν* in questions. *Οὐκοῦν* questions, less lively in tone than those introduced by οὔκουν, are pre-eminently suited to the even, unemotional character of intellectual discussion: hence their frequency in Plato. (See Kühner, quoted on p. 432.) Outside Plato and Xenophon they are probably extremely rare. In Plato, as des Places well observes, the boundary between οὐκοῦν questions and οὐκοῦν statements cannot be rigidly drawn. There is probably always some tinge of interrogation in the tone: and it is significant that, as des Places points out, Plato uses οὐκοῦν in dialogue only, never in continuous discourse. (In *R*.365D, *Sph*.251E, *Lg*.629E there is supposed question and answer.) I should be inclined, in fact, to go further than des Places, and actually insert the question-mark everywhere (the difficulty of finding a place for it in *Phd*.66B ff. is merely formal): e.g. in *R*.337D (see (3) below, p. 438), 565A,B: *Phdr*.271A: *Men*.99B: cf. X.*Mem*.iii 6.6: 6.8. The question of punctuation is, however, of subordinate importance. What is important is that we should

recognize the existence of an interrogative tinge, whether or not strong enough to call for a question-mark. In any case, des Places is certainly right in saying that the distinction between interrogative and affirmative cannot, in Plato, be made the basis of classification.

Οὐκοῦν is very common in Plato, being used both in the strictly inferential, and in the looser progressive, sense. The following grouping (in which I follow des Places pretty closely) illustrates the great variety of the Platonic usage.

(*a*) Strictly inferential, 'therefore', 'then'. *Ly.*219C *ἡ ἰατρική, φαμέν, ἕνεκα τῆς ὑγιείας φίλον.—Ναί.—Οὐκοῦν καὶ ἡ ὑγίεια φίλον*; *Euthd.*298E *ἔστι σοι κύων;—Καὶ μάλα πονηρὸς . . .—Ἔστιν οὖν αὐτῷ κυνίδια;—Καὶ μάλ' . . .—Οὐκοῦν πατήρ ἐστιν αὐτῶν ὁ κύων; . . . Τί οὖν; οὐ σός ἐστιν ὁ κύων;—Πάνυ γ', ἔφη.—Οὐκοῦν πατὴρ ὢν σός ἐστιν . . .;*

(*b*) Proceeding to introduction of minor or major premise, 'Now'. (α) Minor. *Phd.*105E *ὃ ἂν θάνατον μὴ δέχηται τί καλοῦμεν;—Ἀθάνατον, ἔφη.—Οὐκοῦν ψυχὴ οὐ δέχεται θάνατον;—Οὔ.—Ἀθάνατον ἄρα ψυχή* ('Now, the soul . . .?'): *Men.*96C. (β) Major. *Smp.*201B *ἄλλο τι ὁ Ἔρως κάλλους ἂν εἴη ἔρως, αἴσχους δὲ οὔ;—Ὡμολόγει.—Οὐκοῦν ὡμολόγηται, οὗ ἐνδεής ἐστι καὶ μὴ ἔχει, τούτου ἐρᾶν;—Ναί, εἰπεῖν.—Ἐνδεὴς ἄρ' ἐστὶ καὶ οὐκ ἔχει ὁ Ἔρως κάλλος.*

(*c*) In enumeration of details (sometimes in formal induction): 'Again'. *Men.*72E *Ἡ αὐτή μοι δοκεῖ ὑγίειά γε εἶναι καὶ ἀνδρὸς καὶ γυναικός.—Οὐκοῦν καὶ μέγεθος καὶ ἰσχύς*; *Chrm.*160A 'Speed is admitted to be good in various cases. *Οὐκοῦν καὶ τὸ συνιέναι τὰ λεγόμενα . . . οὐχ ὡς ἡσυχαίτατα ἀλλ' ὡς τάχιστά ἐστι κάλλιστα*;'

(*d*) In general, proceeding to a new point, or a new step in the argument: 'Now', 'Again'. *Chrm.*166A *οἷον ἡ λογιστική ἐστίν που τοῦ ἀρτίου καὶ τοῦ περιττοῦ . . .;—Πάνυ γε, ἔφη.—Οὐκοῦν ἑτέρου ὄντος τοῦ περιττοῦ καὶ ἀρτίου αὐτῆς τῆς λογιστικῆς*; *Prt* 330C–D *Ἔστιν ἄρα τοιοῦτον ἡ δικαιοσύνη οἷον δίκαιον εἶναι, φαίην ἂν ἔγωγε ἀποκρινόμενος τῷ ἐρωτῶντι· οὐκοῦν καὶ σύ;—Ναί, ἔφη.—Εἰ οὖν μετὰ τοῦτο ἡμᾶς ἔροιτο· "Οὐκοῦν καὶ ὁσιότητά τινά φατε εἶναι;" φαῖμεν ἄν, ὡς ἐγῷμαι.—Ναί, ἦ δ' ὅς.—" Οὐκοῦν* φατε καὶ τοῦτο πρᾶγμά τι εἶναι;" *Phd.*82A: *Tht.*144E. With ellipse of verb, *Ep.*319C.

(*e*) Introducing a disquisition for which the interlocutor has declared himself ready or eager: 'Well'. *Men.*76C Βούλει οὖν σοι κατὰ Γοργίαν ἀποκρίνωμαι . . .;—Βούλομαι . . .—Οὐκοῦν λέγετε ἀπορροάς τινας τῶν ὄντων κατὰ Ἐμπεδοκλέα; *R.*456C ὅτι δὲ δὴ βέλτιστα, τὸ μετὰ τοῦτο δεῖ διομολογηθῆναι;—Δῆλον.—Οὐκοῦν . . .; *Alc.II* 125C.

In Xenophon interrogative οὐκοῦν is common, particularly in the Socratic works: his usage closely follows Plato's. *Mem.*iii 8.9(*bis*), successive stages in an argument: *An.*i 6.7(*bis*) successive stages in a narration: *Hier.*1.21, a new argument.

In the orators interrogative οὐκοῦν should probably everywhere be replaced by οὔκουν. The tentative and intimate tone which attaches to interrogative οὐκοῦν does not suit the character of oratory, whether political, forensic, or epideictic.

In questions in drama, also, οὔκουν should perhaps everywhere be written. A.*Supp* 300 Βοῦν τὴν γυναῖκ' ἔθηκεν Ἀργεία θεός.—Οὐκοῦν πελάζει Ζεὺς ἐπ' εὐκραίρῳ βοΐ; (οὐκοῦν *M*: οὔκουν Schuetz. Though here, perhaps, the quieter οὐκοῦν would seem more in place. The king, who does not know the details of Io's story, hazards a guess at the next step. 'Then Zeus . . .?'): E. *Cyc.*632 Οὐκοῦν σὺ τάξεις . . .; (cf. p. 431: in *Cyc.*241, where Wecklein says the MSS. read οὐκοῦν, editors have tacitly made the change): *El.*357 Ἴσασιν, οὐδὲν τῶνδ' ἔχουσιν ἐνδεές.—Οὐκοῦν πάλαι χρῆν τοῖσδ' ἀνεπτύχθαι πύλας; (cf. Ar.*Av.*1185 οὔκουν): 662 Καὶ μὴν ἐπ' αὐτάς γ' εἶσι σῶν δόμων πύλας.—Οὐκοῦν τραπέσθαι σμικρὸν εἰς Ἅιδου τόδε; ('Well, is not that a short step to Hades?'): *Ba.*191.

οὐκοῦν οὐ, οὐκοῦν . . . οὐ, expecting a negative answer: Pl. *Phlb.*43D οὐκοῦν οὐκ ἂν εἴη . . .;—Πῶς γὰρ ἄν; *Tht.*204A: *Men.*89A.

In X.*Cyr.*iv 3.17 οὐκοῦν is rather curiously used in an interrogative main clause following a relative clause: ὧν δὲ δὴ μάλιστα δοκῶ ζῴων, ἔφη, ἐζηλωκέναι ἱπποκενταύρους . . . οὐκοῦν πάντα κἀγὼ ταῦτα ἱππεὺς γενόμενος συγκομίζομαι πρὸς ἐμαυτόν; (οὐκοῦν *om. D*). The livelier οὔκουν (Herwerden, Marchant) certainly seems more in place here.

(3) Οὐκοῦν (positive) in statements. Often in drama, where the texts give οὐκοῦν, as introducing a statement, the livelier interrogative οὔκουν seems more appropriate (as my translations indicate), while the quieter interrogative οὐκοῦν is also possible. (In some places editors have already substituted οὔκουν, with or without the support of inferior MSS.: e.g. A.*Eu.*725: S.*Aj.*79: *Ph.*1270.)

A.*Th.*248 Στένει πόλισμα γῆθεν, ὡς κυκλουμένων.—Οὐκοῦν ἔμ' ἀρκεῖ τῶνδε βουλεύειν πέρι ('Well, am *I* not capable of dealing with that?'): S.*OT* 342 Ἥξει γὰρ αὐτὰ ...—Οὐκοῦν ἅ γ' ἥξει καὶ σὲ χρὴ λέγειν ἐμοί: *Ant.*91 ἀλλ' ἀμηχάνων ἐρᾷς.—Οὐκοῦν, ὅταν δὴ μὴ σθένω, πεπαύσομαι: 817 Ἀχέροντι νυμφεύσω.—Οὐκοῦν κλεινὴ καὶ ἔπαινον ἔχουσ' ἐς τόδ' ἀπέρχῃ κεῦθος νεκύων ('Well, are you not dying a glorious death?' Jebb's 'therefore' is inappropriate): E.*Hipp.*332 (Οὐκ οὖν ...; Wil.): *Heracl.*111 Οὐκοῦν ... χρῆν (cf. E.*El.*357 (p. 435)): *Ph.*979 Ποῖ δῆτα φεύγω; ...;—Ὅπου χθονὸς τῆσδ' ἐκποδὼν μάλιστ' ἔσῃ.—Οὐκοῦν σὲ φράζειν εἰκός, ἐκπονεῖν δ' ἐμέ: 1653 Οὐκ ἔννομον γὰρ τὴν δίκην πράσσεσθέ νιν.—Εἴπερ γε πόλεως ἐχθρὸς ἦν οὐκ ἐχθρὸς ὤν.—Οὐκοῦν ἔδωκε τῇ τύχῃ τὸν δαίμονα ('Well, has he not paid his penalty already?'): *El.*239 'I have come to see how you are'.—Οὐκοῦν ὁρᾷς μου πρῶτον ὡς ξηρὸν δέμας: Ar.*Pl.*929 Καὶ μὴν προσελθέτω ... ὁ βουλόμενος.—Οὐκοῦν ἐκεῖνός εἰμ' ἐγώ ('Well, am I not the man?', echoing 918): E.*El.*355 (the Farmer speaks with a touch of bitterness): S.*OT* 342: E.*IT* 810: *Rh.*161: *Or.* 780,788: *Ba.*959: Ar.*Pl.*587,1087.

But in a few other passages in drama the more deliberate οὐκοῦν, with a statement, seems preferable. S.*El.*799 Οὐκοῦν ἀποστείχοιμ' ἄν: Ar.*Ec.*853 Οὐκοῦν βαδιοῦμαι δῆτα. In *Pax* 43 the force is 'now' (Rogers), going on to a new point, rather than 'then'.

In Plato, as I have observed above (2), οὐκοῦν always appears to have some measure of interrogative force. Two types are, at first sight. difficult to reconcile with this view:—

(*a*) Οὐκοῦν with the imperative. *Phdr.*274B Οὐκοῦν τὸ μὲν ...

ἱκανῶς ἐχέτω: 278B Οὐκοῦν ἤδη πεπαίσθω μετρίως ἡμῖν τὰ περὶ λόγων. Kühner (II ii 165) observes that οὐκοῦν is seen here at the furthest remove from its original significance: but des Places (p. 158) rightly detects an interrogative tone here also: 'nicht-wahr?'. (It is worth remarking that the instances occur with the third person imperative, the tone of which is less sharp than that of the second: hardly at all sharper, in fact, than that of the first person subjunctive: *La.*195A Οὐκοῦν διδάσκωμεν αὐτὸν . . .)*

(*b*) Occasionally, in Plato, οὐκοῦν, in the phrase οὐκοῦν χρή, seems to be assentient rather than logical: cf. τοίνυν, I.1. Des Places remarks (p. 207): 'L'idée introduite par οὐκοῦν suit de ce qui précède': and renders 'Eh bien alors, c'est ce qu'il faut faire'. As in the case of assentient γάρ, so here, the logical force merges insensibly in the assentient. Here, for example, is a border-line passage: *Sph.*246A τοὺς δὲ ἄλλως λέγοντας αὖ θεατέον . . .—Οὐκοῦν πορεύεσθαι χρὴ καὶ ἐπὶ τούτους. More purely assentient are the following: *Tht.*206C τὸ δὲ προκείμενον μὴ ἐπιλαθώμεθα δι' αὐτὰ ἰδεῖν . . .—Οὐκοῦν χρὴ ὁρᾶν: *Sph.* 229D ἔτι καὶ τοῦτο σκεπτέον . . .—Οὐκοῦν χρὴ σκοπεῖν: *Lg.*713A Ἆρ' οὖν μύθῳ σμικρά γ' ἔτι προσχρηστέον . . .;—Οὐκοῦν χρὴ ταύτῃ δρᾶν; (It is not easy to understand why Burnet differentiates this from the other passages by printing it as a question. But the inconsistency illustrates the fluidity of the distinction between question and statement.)

Οὐκοῦν χρή, elliptical. *R.*462E ὥρα ἂν εἴη ἐπανιέναι . . .—Οὐκοῦν χρή, ἔφη: 559A: *Sph.*225D,254D: *Plt.*282D,283C,289D: *Phlb.*55D,66D.

Des Places observes that all the instances of οὐκοῦν χρή are from Plato's later work.

Of this assentient force of οὐκοῦν there appear to be some slight traces in drama. S.*Ph.*639 ἴωμεν . . .—Οὐκοῦν ἐπειδὰν πνεῦμα τοὐκ πρῴρας ἀνῇ, τότε στελοῦμεν ('Aye, we will sail, when . . .': but perhaps, simply, 'We will sail, then, when . . .'): E.*Hel.*454 Αἰαῖ· τὰ κλεινὰ ποῦ 'στί μοι στρατεύματα;—Οὐκοῦν ἐκεῖ που σεμνὸς ἦσθ', οὐκ ἐνθάδε ('Aye, *there* thou *wast* in high estate'): *Ion* 1289 Ἀλλ' ἐγενόμεσθα πατρός· οὐσίαν λέγω.—Οὐκοῦν τότ' ἦσθα· νῦν δ' ἐγώ, σὺ δ' οὐκέτι.

But it is possible that in some, or all, of these passages οὔκουν . . .; should be read, with a strong stress on the temporal or local adverb. E.g. *Hel.*454 'Well, doesn't your *σεμνότης* show itself in *Troyland*, not here?'

In Ar.*Pax* 364 the absence of a verb is remarkable: *Ἀπόλωλας, ὦ κακόδαιμον.—Οὐκοῦν, ἢν λάχω* ('I suppose I shall, if my lot is drawn', Sharpley, who adds, 'Still, *οὐκοῦν*, standing alone with the verb understood, sadly needs confirmation'. *Οὐκ, ἢν μή*, Dobree). Pl.*R.*337D is only superficially similar: *ἀπότεισον ἀργύριον.—Οὐκοῦν ἐπειδάν μοι γένηται, εἶπον*: this is, I think, slightly interrogative, 'When I *get* some then, eh?' For the connexion, cf. *τοίνυν* in Pl.*Euthphr.*15E.

It remains to consider the use of *οὐκοῦν* in statements in prose writers other than Plato. In the earlier fourth-century prose, up to and including Isocrates, there are but few examples.

In Thucydides, our MSS. only give *οὐκοῦν* in iii 63.2, and here perhaps *οὔκουν χρῆν . . .*; should be read (*οὐκ οὖν . . .*; Steup). And.iii 10 *ἀναμνήσθητε, τί ὑμῖν ἐξ ἀρχῆς ὑπεθέμην τῷ λόγῳ. ἄλλο τι ἢ τοῦτο, ὅτι . . .; οὐκοῦν ἀποδέδεικται* ('Well, I have proved it'): iii 14 'Why should we go to war For this reason or for that? *ἀλλ' ὅπως τὰς νήσους κομισώμεθα . . .; οὐκοῦν διαρρήδην γέγραπται ταύτας Ἀθηναίων εἶναι*' ('Well': the previous answers are introduced by *ἀλλά*, or asyndetically. *οὔκουν . . .*; is possible here again and in the preceding example): Lys.iv 5 *οὐκοῦν ἦλθον* ('I came, then'): Isoc.iv 184 (introducing minor premise): xv 253 (marking new stage in argument: 'Now').

In Demosthenes and Aeschines, on the other hand, *οὐκοῦν* in statements is very common. The varieties of usage correspond pretty closely with those of Platonic interrogative or quasi-interrogative *οὐκοῦν*.

(i) With full logical force, 'therefore'. D.xix 179 *φαίνεται δ' οὗτος πάντα τἀναντία τοῖς νόμοις . . . πεπρεσβευκώς· οὐκοῦν ἑαλωκέναι προσήκει παρά γε νοῦν ἔχουσι δικασταῖς*: vi 14: Aeschin.i 73,164.

(ii) Less strictly logical, summing up what precedes, rather than drawing a formal inference from it: 'then', 'well'. D.xix 178 *συλλογίσασθαι δὴ βούλομαι τὰ κατηγορημέν' ἀπ' ἀρχῆς, ἵν' ὅσ' ὑμῖν ὑπεσχόμην ἀρχόμενος τοῦ λόγου δείξω πεποιηκώς. ἐπέδειξ' . . . οὐκοῦν ταῦθ' ὑπεσχόμην ἐν ἀρχῇ, ταῦτ' ἐπέδειξα*: xxiv

109: Aeschin.iii 172. Often after the reading of documents: D. xviii 119,136,218.

(iii) Progressive, going on to a new stage in narration or argument. D.xix 130 'What did Philip pray, but that . . . ? *οὐκοῦν ταῦτα συνηύχεθ' οὗτος*' ('Well, Aeschines joined in that prayer'): 279 "*οὐδ' ἐπιστέλλοντες*", *φησί*, "*τἀληθῆ*". *οὐκοῦν οὐδ' οὗτοι* ('Well, neither did they': whereas in xviii 117 there is a fuller logical force in *οὐκοῦν*): viii 15,75: xix 205,286: xxiii 17: lvi 40: Aeschin.i 75,153.

(iv) Introducing minor premise of enthymeme: 'well', 'now'. D.xxi 147 *τὸ δ' ὅλως ἀφανίζειν ἱερὰ ἔσθ' ὅ τι τοῦ κόπτειν διαφέρει· οὐκοῦν οὗτος ἐξελήλεγκται τοῦτο ποιῶν*: xviii 247 (conclusion introduced by *ὥστε*): xxiv 53 (conclusion introduced by *τοίνυν*).

(v) Inceptive, 'well', 'now'. D.xxxiv 5 *σκέψασθε . . . ὅ τι ὁμολογεῖται παρ' αὐτῶν τούτων καὶ τί ἀντιλέγεται . . . οὐκοῦν δανείσασθαι μὲν τὰ χρήματα ὁμολογοῦσι*: xvi 4: xxiv 108.

In an answer in hypophora. D.xxxv 48 *ἀλλὰ παρὰ τῷ ἄρχοντι* (*χρὴ λαβεῖν δίκην*); *οὐκοῦν ἐπικλήρων . . . τῷ ἄρχοντι προστέτακται ἐπιμελεῖσθαι* ('Well, the archon's business is . . .'. The answers are varied in form, as in And.iii 14: see above).

The negative form is *οὐκοῦν οὐ*: D.xvi 4 *οὐκοῦν οὐδ' ἂν εἷς ἀντείποι*: Hyp.*Phil.*10 *οὐκοῦν οὐκ ἄξιον*. In a negative command: Aeschin.i 159 *οὐκοῦν μὴ . . . αὐτομολήσῃς*.

(4) *Οὔκουν* (negative) in statements. E.*IT* 601 *οὔκουν δίκαιον ἐπ' ὀλέθρῳ τῷ τοῦδ' ἐμὲ χάριν τίθεσθαι*: *Med.*890: *Supp.*342: *HF* 168: *Hel.*917: *IA* 1430: Th.i 10.3 *οὔκουν ἀπιστεῖν εἰκός*: Pl.*Ap.* 35C *οὔκουν χρὴ οὔτε ἡμᾶς ἐθίζειν*: X.*Cyr.*v 5.41 *οὔκουν καλῶς ἂν πράττοιμι*: And.i 40 *λέγειν . . . ὡς ἴδοι ἡμᾶς ἐν ἐκείνῃ τῇ νυκτί· οὔκουν δέοιτο παρὰ τῆς πόλεως χρήματα λαβεῖν μᾶλλον ἢ παρ' ἡμῶν* (progressive: 'Well, he didn't want . . .'): D.viii 42 *οὔκουν βούλεται τοῖς ἑαυτοῦ καιροῖς τὴν παρ' ὑμῶν ἐλευθερίαν ἐφεδρεύειν*: Ant.v 67 (*οὐκοῦν NA pr., corr.* 2): And.iv 37: Lys.vi 14: D.xviii 281: xix 93: *et saep.*

(5) *οὐκ οὖν*, *separatim*. *οὐκ* and *οὖν* are sometimes (*οὐκ ὦν* customarily) found written separately, for *οὔκουν*, in questions

and (rarely) in statements. It is difficult to find any appreciable distinction in meaning accompanying the difference in orthography.

E.*IA* 528 Οὐκ οὖν δοκεῖς νιν . . . λέξειν . . . ; *Heracl.*255,262, 525,971 : *IA* 528 : *Rh.*481,543,585,633 : *Ph.*1589 : Hdt.ii 139 οὐκ ὦν ποιήσειν ταῦτα : v 92η5 οὐκ ὦν παύσεσθε . . . ; Pl.*Grg.*467B Οὐκ οὖν ποιοῦσιν ἃ βούλονται ; *Chrm.*172E Οὐκ οὖν, ἔφη, καλῶς ὡμολογήσαμεν ; Hdt.i 59,206,209 : iv 118 : v 79 : vii 206.2 : Lys. x 12 : Isoc.xviii 21 : Aeschin.iii 179 : D.xxxiv 49.

With word intervening. Pl.*R.*333E οὐκ ἂν οὖν . . . εἴη (οὐκ ἂν οὖν *in marg. A* : οὐκοῦν *ADFM*) : Th.i 9.4 οὐκ ἂν οὖν νήσων . . . ἐκράτει.

To determine the chronological sequence and evolution of the four forms examined above is not an easy task. Our difficulties are increased by the unsatisfactory nature of the manuscript tradition, which is, as I think I have shown, so often at fault that it cannot be made the basis of investigation (or only with great reserve). We have to remember that the invention of accents is attributed to Aristophanes of Byzantium : while the mark of interrogation first appears about the eighth or ninth century.[1]

To start with, we shall be fairly safe in assuming that one or other of the interrogative forms is the earliest. We have seen (III.1) that in Aeschylus connective οὖν is almost entirely limited to questions : and it is natural that the same limitation should have applied to the negative form. Further, of the two interrogative forms, everything points to the priority of οὔκουν. In the manuscripts of drama it predominates strongly over οὐκοῦν : and reasons have been given for substituting οὔκουν in the great majority of cases where interrogative οὐκοῦν is found. The evolution of a milder form of question, by shifting the accent on to the οὖν ('Then, is it not so . . . ?', for 'So then . . . ?'), is a natural development, though, perhaps by reason of the varying tone and content of Greek literature in its different stages, it is only seen fully developed in Plato and Xenophon. Finally, the appearance of οὐκοῦν as a connecting particle in pure state-

[1] Maunde Thompson, *Greek and Latin Palaeography*, pp. 60–1.

ments, divested of every shred of interrogative force, can hardly be put earlier than the middle of the fourth century.[1]

The remaining form, οὔκουν in statements, presumably originated independently when οὖν came into regular use as a connecting particle in statements. I know of no example earlier than E.*Med.*890.

V. οὖν combined with other particles. For εἴτ' οὖν, οὔτ' οὖν, τε οὖν (οὖν reinforcing τε, 'both, in fact', 'and, in fact'), οὐδ' οὖν, see II.1–3. For οὔκουν . . . γε, οὖν . . . γε, see II.5. For ἀλλ' οὖν, καὶ οὖν, γὰρ οὖν, γοῦν, δ' οὖν, οὖν δή, δὴ οὖν, μὲν οὖν, see below. For οὖν δῆτα, οὔκουν δῆτα, δῆτ' οὖν, see δῆτα, I.6, IV.2. For οὖν ἄρα, see ἄρα, V.

The collocation of prospective τε with connective οὖν, though no less natural than the common μὲν οὖν . . . δέ, appears in general to have been avoided, though Plato tolerates it, and even shows a certain liking for it. Thus *Ti.*20C πάρειμί τε οὖν δὴ κεκοσμημένος ἐπ' αὐτὰ καὶ πάντων ἑτοιμότατος ὢν δέχεσθαι (for π. ο. δ. κ. τε : 'Suivant une habitude de Platon, τε se trouve rapproché de οὖν', des Places, p 34) :[2] Hdt.i 70 τούτων τε ὦν εἵνεκεν . . . καὶ ὅτι . . . : vi 86α5 ταῦτά τε ὦν ἐπιλεγομένῳ καὶ βουλευομένῳ ἔδοξέ μοι . . . (here, again, the collocation appears to be sought) : Pl.*Phd.*112C : *Prt* 345C : *Smp.*191C,209B : *Phdr.*242E, 252D : *Euthd.*274D : *Sph.*237B : *Lg* 717D,943E : Aen.Tact.18.13. Collocation with adverbial τε : Pl.*R.*451E Οἷόν τ' οὖν.

In Pl.*Tht.*210B, *B*'s οὖν τοίνυν is clearly impossible.

'Αλλ' οὖν

In ἀλλ' οὖν (not found before Aeschylus) ἀλλά bears one or other of the shades of meaning expressed by simple ἀλλά: while οὖν adds the notion of essentiality or importance. Very

[1] The derivation of οὐκοῦν in statements from οὐκοῦν in questions is maintained by Kühner (II ii 163). Baümlein, with less probability, makes interrogative οὔκουν the father of affirmative οὐκοῦν, and the grandfather of interrogative οὐκοῦν: 'Isn't it, then . . .?': 'Then . . .': 'Then . . .?'

[2] Des Places only gives examples, not an exhaustive list: I add a few to his, but there are no doubt more.

frequently γε follows at a short interval, denoting that the idea is to be emphatically accepted in a limited sphere. ἀλλ' οὖν γε, juxtaposed, is read in Isoc.xx 14, ἀλλ' οὖν γ' ἐπειδὰν γνωρισθῶσι, προσήκει πᾶσι μισεῖν τοὺς τοιούτους (γ' *om. V*) : Lycurg. 141 ἀλλ' οὖν γε περὶ προδοσίας (περὶ προδοσίας γε Benseler). The juxtaposition of the words can hardly stand in classical Greek. ([Arist.] *Mu.*397b12, post-classical). Cf. ἀλλά γε (ἀλλά, IV.1) and see γε, V.2.i.

(1) In answers, introducing an objection, protest, or remonstrance. A.*Th.*217 Οὔκουν τάδ' ἔσται πρὸς θεῶν ;—Ἀλλ' οὖν θεοὺς τοὺς τῆς ἁλούσης πόλεος ἐκλείπειν λόγος ('Aye, but') : E.*Ion* 1325 μῆτερ, οὐ τεκοῦσά περ.—Ἀλλ' οὖν λεγόμεθ' : *Heracl.*689 Οὐκ ἔστιν, ὦ τᾶν, ἥ ποτ' ἦν ῥώμη σέθεν.—Ἀλλ' οὖν μαχοῦνταί γ' ἀριθμὸν οὐκ ἐλάσσοσι ('But anyway') : Ar.*Nu.*985 Ἀρχαῖά γε ...—Ἀλλ' οὖν ταῦτ' ἐστὶν ἐκεῖνα, ἐξ ὧν ἄνδρας Μαραθωνομάχας ἡμὴ παίδευσις ἔθρεψεν ('Well, anyhow, these are the ideas that produced the men of Marathon') : 1002 τοῖς Ἱπποκράτους υἱέσιν εἴξεις ...—Ἀλλ' οὖν λιπαρός γε ... διατρίψεις : *V.*1129 Philocleon refuses to give up his favourite coat. Βδ. Ἀλλ' οὖν πεπειράσθω γε ('Well, have a try, anyhow') : *Av.*1408 Καταγελᾷς μου, δῆλος εἶ. ἀλλ' οὖν ἔγωγ' οὐ παύσομαι ('But I *won't* stop': referring, perhaps, to 1397 ἦ 'γώ σου καταπαύσω τὰς πνοάς) : *Th* 710 : *Ra.*1298 : Pl.*Sph.*237C Χαλεπὸν ἤρου καὶ ... ἄπορον.—Ἀλλ' οὖν τοῦτό γε δῆλον, ὅτι ... : *Phlb.*13C.

(2) In continuous speech, a speaker countering his own words. More emphatic than the commoner καίτοι. E.*Tr.*1192 ἄθλιον θάπτω νεκρὸν ... ἀλλ' οὖν πατρῴων οὐ λαχὼν ἕξεις ὅμως ἐν ᾗ ταφήσῃ χαλκόνωτον ἰτέαν ('Still, you *shall* have your father's shield to be buried in') : *IA* 983 αἰσχύνομαι δὲ παραφέρουσ' οἰκτροὺς λόγους, ἰδίᾳ νοσοῦσα· σὺ δ' ἄνοσος κακῶν ἐμῶν. ἀλλ' οὖν ἔχει τοι σχῆμα, κἂν ἄπωθεν ᾖ ἀνὴρ ὁ χρηστός, δυστυχοῦντας ὠφελεῖν ('Still, it *does* look well ...') : Pherecr.*Fr.*145.6 'Melanippides was the origin of my woes. ἀλλ' οὖν ὅμως οὗτος μὲν ἦν ἀποχρῶν ἀνήρ' : *ib.*13,17 : And.ii.18.

(3) Following upon the rejection of a suggestion. Cf. ἀλλά, II.1. Ar.*V.*1190 Φι. 'I can't sing of my θεωρία, because I've

never been on one.'—*Βδ.* Ἀλλ' οὖν λέγειν χρή σ' ὡς ἐμάχετό γ' αὐτίκα Ἐφουδίων παγκράτιον ('Well, tell how . . .').

Usually in such cases ἀλλ' οὖν introduces a more moderate suggestion, made as a *pis aller* ('Well, at least'). A.*Pr.*1071 The chorus refuses to leave Prometheus at Hermes' bidding *Ερ.* Ἀλλ' οὖν μέμνησθ' ἁγὼ προλέγω ('Well, remember my *warning*'): S.*Ant.*84 Ismene has failed to dissuade Antigone. *Ισ.* Ἀλλ' οὖν προμηνύσῃς γε τοῦτο μηδενὶ τοὔργον: *Ph.*1305 Neoptolemus will not let Philoctetes shoot at Odysseus. *Φι.* Ἀλλ' οὖν τοσοῦτόν γ' ἴσθι, τοὺς πρώτους στρατοῦ . . . κακοὺς ὄντας πρὸς αἰχμήν (Philoctetes contents himself with a moral victory): *El.*233 ('Well, if you cannot heal your sorrows, at least forbear from making them worse'): 1035 ('Well, since you refuse to help me (1017–26), do at least realize what that refusal means').

(4) Approaching δ' οὖν or ἀλλὰ γάρ in sense, signifying an elimination of the secondary or irrelevant, a break-off in thought, a resumption of the main issue: 'Well, anyhow, however that may be.' S.*Aj.*535 'I removed the boy, fearing you might kill him'.—Πρέπον γέ τἂν ἦν δαίμονος τοὐμοῦ τόδε.—Ἀλλ' οὖν ἐγὼ 'φύλαξα τοῦτό γ' ἀρκέσαι ('Well, anyhow, whether πρέπον or not, I stopped *that* happening'): Ar.*Ach.*620 ταῦτα δῆτ' ἀνασχετά; —Οὐ δῆτ' ἐὰν μὴ μισθοφορῇ γε Λάμαχος.—Ἀλλ' οὖν ἐγὼ μὲν πᾶσι Πελοποννησίοις ἀεὶ πολεμήσω (impatiently brushing away the taunt): *V.*1434 *Βδ.* Ὅμοιά σου καὶ ταῦτα τοῖς ἄλλοις τρόποις.—*Κατήγορος.* Ἀλλ' οὖν σὺ μέμνησ' αὐτὸς ἀπεκρίνατο ('Well, you remember his *answer*'. The Accuser is not interested in Philocleon's ἄλλοι τρόποι): A.*Pr.*1058: E.*Alc.*363: Pl.*Prt.*310A Διπλῆ ἂν εἴη ἡ χάρις. ἀλλ' οὖν ἀκούετε (getting to business, after the interchange of compliments): *Phd.*102D Ἔοικα, ἔφη, καὶ συγγραφικῶς ἐρεῖν, ἀλλ' οὖν ἔχει γέ που ὡς λέγω (the essential point is the matter, not the style): *Cra.*411D φορᾶς γάρ ἐστι (ἡ "φρόνησις") καὶ ῥοῦ νόησις. εἴη δ' ἂν καὶ ὄνησιν ὑπολαβεῖν φορᾶς· ἀλλ' οὖν περί γε τὸ φέρεσθαί ἐστιν (the first part of the word is what matters): *Ep.*316A ἀλλ' οὖν, ὅπερ ἀρτίως εἶπον, οὐ διαβολῆς προσδέομαι: 319C ἀλλ' οὖν ὧν ἕνεκα πάντ' εἴρηται ταῦτ' ἐστί: *Euthd.*302D Οὐκοῦν καὶ οὗτοι σοὶ θεοὶ ἂν εἶεν; ἔφη.—Πρόγονοι, ἦν δ' ἐγώ, καὶ δεσπόται.—Ἀλλ' οὖν σοί γε, ἔφη ('Well, *yours*

anyhow'): *Ap*.27C οὐκοῦν δαιμόνια μὲν φῄς με καὶ νομίζειν καὶ διδάσκειν, εἴτ' οὖν καινὰ εἴτε παλαιά, ἀλλ' οὖν δαιμόνιά γε νομίζω: Aeschin.iii 11 μέτριοί εἰσιν, εἰ δή τις ἐστὶ μέτριος τῶν τὰ παράνομα γραφόντων· ἀλλ' οὖν προβάλλονταί γέ τι πρὸ τῆς αἰσχύνης (brushing aside the reservation implied in εἰ... γραφόντων): Pl.*Cra*.413D: *Prt*.327C: *Ly*.221A: *R*.501A,509D: *Lg*.770B: D. xix 249.

(5) μὲν... ἀλλ' οὖν. Pl.*Men*.84A (ἐννοεῖς) ὅτι τὸ μὲν πρῶτον ᾔδει μὲν οὔ..., ὥσπερ οὐδὲ νῦν πω οἶδεν, ἀλλ' οὖν ᾤετό γ' αὐτὴν τότε εἰδέναι... νῦν δὲ ἡγεῖται ἀπορεῖν ἤδη (the first μέν is answered by δέ: the second is answered by ἀλλ' οὖν, which also has a quasi-resumptive force after the parenthesis: 'just as he doesn't know now, either: but the point is that then he *thought* he knew'): D.lviii 26 ἔτι δὲ τῶν τοῦ ἐμπορίου μόλις μέν, ἀλλ' οὖν ταὐτὰ τούτοις μεμαρτυρηκότων ('They gave their evidence with reluctance, but they *did* give evidence to the same effect.')

(6) Apodotic, after concessive conditional clauses, or their equivalent: 'Even if..., still' (cf. ἀλλά, II.2): cf. (3): especially ἀλλ' οὖν... γε, 'still, at least'. Rare in verse. E.*Cyc*.652 χειρὶ δ' εἰ μηδὲν σθένεις, ἀλλ' οὖν ἐπεγκέλευέ γ': *Ph*. 498 'Εμοὶ μέν, εἰ καὶ μὴ καθ' Ἑλλήνων χθόνα τεθράμμεθ', ἀλλ' οὖν ξυνετά μοι δοκεῖς λέγειν: Hp.*Art*.14 εἰ δὲ μὴ τελέως ἱδρυνθείη, ἀλλ' οὖν τὸ ὑπερέχον γε... γίνεται: Pl.*Grg*.506B ἐπειδὴ... οὐκ ἐθέλεις συνδιαπερᾶναι τὸν λόγον, ἀλλ' οὖν ἐμοῦ γε ἀκούων ἐπιλαμβάνου: *Phd*.91B εἰ δὲ μηδέν ἐστι τελευτήσαντι, ἀλλ' οὖν τοῦτόν γε τὸν χρόνον... ἧττον τοῖς παροῦσιν ἀηδὴς ἔσομαι ὀδυρόμενος: Isoc.v 68 ἐν οἷς κατορθώσας μὲν... καταστήσεις... διαμαρτὼν δὲ τῆς προσδοκίας ἀλλ' οὖν τήν γ' εὔνοιαν κτήσει (after a participial clause equivalent to a conditional): D.ix 30 ὅσα μὲν ὑπὸ Λακεδαιμονίων... ἔπασχον... ἀλλ' οὖν ὑπὸ γνησίων γ' ὄντων τῆς Ἑλλάδος ἠδικοῦντο: Pl.*Sph*.254C: *Plt*.279B: *Lg*.885E: *La*.186B: *Alc.II* 148C: X.*Hier*.2.9: *Ages*.2.21: *Cyn*.2.1: Isoc iv 171: xi 33: D. xvi 31: xl 47.

(As ἀλλ' ὦν is not elsewhere found in Herodotus, it seems better in iii 140 to read ὦν: ἔδωκας, εἰ καὶ σμικρά, ἀλλ' ὦν ἴση γε ἡ χάρις.... Moreover this gives a smoother construction.)

(7) With ellipse of contrasted idea, 'at least' (cf. ἀλλά, II.3). Isoc.xv 314 τοὺς μὲν γὰρ ἄλλους ἀλλ' οὖν πειρᾶσθαί γε λανθάνειν ('do at any rate *try* to avoid detection'): Aeschin.iii 86 τοὺς μὲν πρώτους χρόνους ἀλλ' οὖν προσεποιοῦνθ' ὑμῖν εἶναι φίλοι: X.*Cyr*.i 4.19 'Are those the enemy?'—'Yes.'—Νὴ τὸν Δί', ἔφη, ὦ πάππε, ἀλλ' οὖν πονηροί γε φαινόμενοι καὶ ἐπὶ πονηρῶν ἱππαρίων ἄγουσιν ἡμῶν τὰ χρήματα. ('They're not much to *look* at, anyhow' (whatever hidden qualities they may possess), 'these people who are raiding us.' I think this is the force, rather than 'But, really'.)

(An assentient force of ἀλλ' οὖν (cf. ἀλλά, ἀλλὰ μέντοι) cannot, as I once thought, be established by Pl.*Phlb*.65E. If Stallbaum's ἀλλ' οὖν (for ἆρ' οὖν), adopted by Burnet, is right, it may be taken as combating the afterthought ἢ τοὐναντίον.)

A reinforced form ἀλλ' οὖν δή is occasionally found in Plato: *Phd*.100A: *R*.526D,544A (with a slight anacoluthon after the preceding μέν), 552E,602B.

Καὶ οὖν

This is a very rare combination, 'And, in fact'. Pl.*Prt*.309B καὶ γὰρ πολλὰ ὑπὲρ ἐμοῦ εἶπε βοηθῶν ἐμοί, καὶ οὖν καὶ ἄρτι ἀπ' ἐκείνου ἔρχομαι: *Phdr*.235A 'The style of the piece seemed to me inadequate. καὶ οὖν μοι ἔδοξεν . . . δὶς καὶ τρὶς τὰ αὐτὰ εἰρηκέναι' (καὶ οὖν Hermann: καὶ δὴ οὖν Stephanus: δικαιοῦν *B*: δίκαιον οὖν *T*).

καὶ . . . οὖν. Hp.*Morb*.ii 39 καὶ οἱ πυρετοὶ ἐπαύσαντο οὖν (οὖν in most MSS.): 53 καὶ ἐρράγη οὖν τὸ αἷμα.

Γὰρ οὖν

In Homer οὖν in γὰρ οὖν (usually τόφρα γὰρ οὖν) always has a backward reference. *B* 350 πρὶν καὶ Διὸς αἰγιόχοιο γνώμεναι εἴ τε ψεῦδος ὑπόσχεσις, εἴ τε καὶ οὐκί. φημὶ γὰρ οὖν κατανεῦσαι ὑπερμενέα Κρονίωνα ἤματι τῷ ('that Zeus did in fact promise'): *Λ* 754 τόφρα γὰρ οὖν ἑπόμεσθα διὰ σπιδέος πεδίοιο (as described above):

O232 σοὶ δ' αὐτῷ μελέτω, ἑκατηβόλε, φαίδιμος Ἕκτωρ· τόφρα γὰρ οὖν οἱ ἔγειρε μένος μέγα (221 ἔρχεο νῦν, φίλε Φοῖβε, μεθ' Ἕκτορα): β123 τόφρα γὰρ οὖν βίοτόν τε τεὸν καὶ κτήματ' ἔδονται (against which Telemachus has protested above): *h.Merc.*291 τοῦτο γὰρ οὖν . . . γέρας ἕξεις· ἀρχὸς φηλητέων κεκλήσεαι (282 ἠπεροπευτὰ δολοφραδὲ κ.τ.λ.).

In post-Homeric Greek οὖν adds to γάρ the idea of importance or essentiality. It seems, on the whole, to have greater independent importance than δή in γὰρ δή: though it is often hard to distinguish between γὰρ οὖν and γὰρ δή. γὰρ οὖν is never found in Thucydides, Aristotle, or the orators (in Isoc.v7 ὅπως γὰρ οὖν is for ὁπωσοῦν γάρ: cf. Arist.*EN* 1180b25), and it is rare in comedy (hence Kalinka's view, that it was revived from colloquial speech by Plato and Xenophon, lacks probability).

(1) In general. Pi.*I.*2.12 ἐσσὶ γὰρ ὦν σοφός· οὐκ ἄγνωτ' ἀείδω (looking forward): S.*Ant.*741 Ὅδ', ὡς ἔοικε, τῇ γυναικὶ συμμαχεῖ.—Εἴπερ γυνὴ σύ· σοῦ γὰρ οὖν προκήδομαι ('For it is thou, in truth, I care for'): 771 Ἄμφω γὰρ αὐτὼ καὶ κατακτεῖναι νοεῖς;—Οὐ τήν γε μὴ θιγοῦσαν· εὖ γὰρ οὖν λέγεις ('You are certainly right there': cf. 1255): *OC*980 γάμους . . . οἵους ἐρῶ ταχ'· οὐ γὰρ οὖν σιγήσομαι ('In sooth, I will not hold my peace'): E.*Med.*533 ὅπῃ γὰρ οὖν ὤνησας, οὐ κακῶς ἔχει ('Where you *have* helped me'): *Or.*1147 μὴ γὰρ οὖν ζῴην ἔτι, ἢν μὴ . . .: Ar.*V.*726 Ἦ που σοφὸς ἦν ὅστις ἔφασκεν πρὶν ἂν ἀμφοῖν μῦθον ἀκούσῃς, οὐκ ἂν δικάσαις. σὺ γὰρ οὖν νῦν μοι νικᾶν πολλῷ δεδόκησαι: *Av.*39 οἱ μὲν γὰρ οὖν τέττιγες . . . Ἀθηναῖοι δὲ . . . (simply sharpens antithesis): A.*Ag.*674: *Eu.*368 (lyr.): S.*Ph.*298,766: E.*Hipp.*666: *Ba.*922: *El.*290: *Ion* 1614: Ar.*Pax* 892 (οὖν *add.* Herm.): Hdt. i94.3 ἐξευρεθῆναι . . . τῶν ἀλλέων πασέων παιγνιέων τὰ εἴδεα, πλὴν πεσσῶν· τούτων γὰρ ὦν τὴν ἐξεύρεσιν οὐκ οἰκηιοῦνται Λυδοί: Pl. *Smp* 218B ἐπειδὴ γὰρ οὖν . . . ὅ τε λύχνος ἀπεσβήκει . . . (the climax of the story): *Sph.*261A ἔοικεν ἀληθὲς εἶναι τὸ περὶ τὸν σοφιστὴν κατ' ἀρχὰς λεχθέν, ὅτι δυσθήρευτον εἴη τὸ γένος. φαίνεται γὰρ οὖν προβλημάτων γέμειν ('He really does seem to be a mass of problems'): *R.*451A ἐλπίζω γὰρ οὖν ἔλαττον ἁμάρτημα ἀκουσίως τινὸς φονέα γενέσθαι ἢ ἀπατεῶνα καλῶν τε καὶ ἀγαθῶν καὶ δικαίων νομίμων πέρι (a daring assertion: 'I really do think'): Hdt.i182: ii127,131: iii131: v1.2: 34.1: vi58.2: ix31.5: 96.2:

99.2: Pl.*Ap.*30C: *Plt.*287D: *Ti.*22C,77B: *Lg.*647B,688C,738B, 792C,E.

(2) In parenthesis. Xenoph.*Fr.*1.16 *ταῦτα γὰρ ὦν ἐστι προχειρότερον* (*sc.* *εὔξασθαι*: 'for this, in truth . . .'): Ar.*Th.*164 *καὶ Φρύνιχος, τοῦτον γὰρ οὖν ἀκήκοας* ('You've heard of *him* (even if you've never heard of Ibycus and Anacreon)'): Hdt.i49 *οὐ γὰρ ὦν οὐδὲ τοῦτο λέγεται*: (cf. iii121 *οὐ γὰρ ὦν δή*): Pl.*Smp.*209A *οἱ δὲ κατὰ τὴν ψυχήν* (*εἰσὶ γὰρ οὖν, ἔφη, οἳ ἐν ταῖς ψυχαῖς κυοῦσιν*) ('for there are, in fact, . . .'): *Phdr.*247C *ἔχει δὲ ὧδε* (*τολμητέον γὰρ οὖν τό γε ἀληθὲς εἰπεῖν*): Hdt.viii128.1: 133: ix32.2: Pl. *Ti.*21C.

(3) As a stronger form of assentient *γάρ*: often in Platonic dialogue: *Grg.*466E *Φημὶ γὰρ οὖν* ('Yes, I do say so'): *Chrm.* 167E *Οὐ γὰρ οὖν* (elliptical: *Phd.*93E,104C: *R.*376D,394E): *Cra.*421D: *Tht.*199B: *R.*357D,388E,397E: X.*Oec.*19.1: *Cyr.*i6.22: 6.25: ii1.8: v5.17.

(4) *γὰρ οὖν δή* (Plato only, except Hdt.iii121 *οὐ γὰρ ὦν δή*). Pl.*Chrm.*169B *τὴν γὰρ οὖν δὴ σωφροσύνην ὠφέλιμόν τι καὶ ἀγαθὸν μαντεύομαι εἶναι*: *Ti.*84E *ὧν καὶ τὸ φάρμακον χαλεπόν· πυρετοὶ γὰρ οὖν δὴ τὰ τοιαῦτα ἐπιγιγνόμενοι μάλιστα λύουσιν*: *Lg.*682A, 686B: *Plt.*270B,306B: *R.*615D.

Assentient: Pl.*Tht.*189B,205D: *R.*389A,476B: *Prm.*148C: *Plt.*269A,303E.

(5) In a few passages in Plato's later works *γὰρ οὖν*, *γὰρ οὖν δή* are used where the context would appear rather to demand a forward-pointing connective, *οὖν* or *δή*. That is to say, the sequel is regarded as implicitly contained in, rather than as following from, the preceding thought: explanatory *γάρ* (see *γάρ*, II) being pushed almost beyond its proper limits.

*Plt.*270B *Λογισάμενοι δὴ συννοήσωμεν τὸ πάθος . . . ἔστι γὰρ οὖν δὴ τοῦτ' αὐτό.—Τὸ ποῖον*; (cf. *Phlb.*37A *Διορισώμεθα δὴ σαφέστερον . . . ἔστιν γάρ που . . .*;): *Lg.*637D *ἡμῖν δ' ἐστὶ νῦν . . . οὐ περὶ τῶν ἀνθρώπων τῶν ἄλλων ὁ λόγος, ἀλλὰ περὶ τῶν νομοθετῶν αὐτῶν κακίας τε καὶ ἀρετῆς. ἔτι γὰρ οὖν εἴπωμεν πλείω περὶ ἁπάσης μέθης* (explanatory of *ὁ λόγος*): 858C 'We can afford to be theoretical'.—*Γένοιτο γοῦν ἂν . . . κατὰ φύσιν μᾶλλον* ἡμῖν ἡ σύνοψις τῶν νόμων. ἴδωμεν γὰρ οὖν, ὦ πρὸς θεῶν, τὸ τοιόνδε περὶ νομοθετῶν ('Well, let us see ...'): 926E ἐμμελῆ τούτοις τε αὐτοῖς ... προοιμιασάμενοι καὶ τοῖς ἐπιτρόποις. εἴς τινα γὰρ οὖν μοι καιρὸν φαινόμεθα τοὺς ἔμπροσθεν λόγους διεξελθεῖν (explanatory of προοιμιασάμενοι).

(6) ἀλλὰ ... γὰρ οὖν. S.*OC*985.
For καὶ γὰρ οὖν, see καὶ γάρ, p. 112.

Γοῦν

(Negative normally οὔκουν ... γε: see οὖν, II.5.)

There can be no doubt that γοῦν is formed by the coalescence of γε and οὖν. But how far, and in what circumstances, γ' οὖν, *separatim*, should be retained in our texts, or imported into them, is a disputed question.[1]

The number of passages in which our texts give γ' οὖν is relatively small, and the following list is in all probability approximately complete. In both the Homeric examples the particles are written separately: *E*258 τούτω δ' οὐ πάλιν αὖτις ἀποίσετον ὠκέες ἵπποι ἄμφω ἀφ' ἡμείων, εἴ γ' οὖν ἕτερός γε φύγῃσιν (here εἴ γε has the rare force of 'even if': see γε, I.8: there is no parallel for such a use of εἰ γοῦν): *Π* 30 μὴ ἐμέ γ' οὖν οὗτός γε λάβοι χόλος (the familiar Attic restrictive γοῦν). In A. *Eu.*258 ὁ δ' αὖτέ γ' οὖν ἀλκὰν ἔχων περὶ βρέτει πλεχθεὶς θεᾶς ἀμβρότου ὑπόδικος θέλει γενέσθαι χερῶν neither γ' οὖν nor γοῦν is easy to explain: Verrall reads γοῦν: 'that Orestes has taken

[1] Klotz (i 351) holds that γ' οὖν should be written wherever γε appears to go closely with the preceding word: Bäumlein (p. 188), that the particles are best written separately 'where each preserves its separate meaning'. (He reads γ' οὖν in Ar.*Eq.*87, Pl.*Ap.*21D, *Prt.*324B, X.*HG*iv4.12; saying, quite wrongly, that οὖν denotes 'Folgerung' in *Prt.*324B, and is recapitulatory in X.*HG*iv4.12: in both passages γοῦν clearly bears its common 'part-proof' meaning.) Kühner (II ii 155–6) says that γ' οὖν is found in 'nachdrücklich bejahenden Erwiderungen', such as E.*El.*350, X.*Mem.*iii1.1: but adds, 'Doch schreibt man an diesen beiden Stellen richtiger γοῦν': he goes on, 'Aber häufig so, dass οὖν eine Folgerung bezeichnet', quoting, however, only Pl.*Ap.*21D, for which see below (II.1). Navarre, on the other hand, maintains that γ' οὖν should never be retained in classical (post-Homeric) texts. Des Places (pp. 134, 143) is also sceptical regarding the distinction.

sanctuary is a step towards a complete escape'. In Hdt.iv 76 μήτι γε ὦν (*sic*), the reading of L, is probably corrupt. In Thgn. 664 ἀπό γ' οὖν is a surprising conjecture of Diehl: πάντ' οὖν (*dett.*) may perhaps be right.

Our remaining examples are from Attic prose. They fall into two groups:

(*a*) γ' οὖν in 'part proof' (the commonest sense of γοῦν: see below, I.1.ii). Pl.*Lg*.649C Τό γ' οὖν εἰκός: *Plt*.257D κινδυνεύετον . . . ἐμοὶ συγγένειαν ἔχειν τινά. τὸν μέν γε οὖν . . . τοῦ δ' . . . : *Euthd*.299E: *Ion* 530C (γοῦν *WF*: γ' οὖν *T*): X.*Cyr*.ii 2.28 (γε οὖν *AEGH*).

(*b*) Passages where οὖν is connective, and separated in sense from γε, which is emphatic. (So, clearly, Pl.*Euthd*.292E, *Lg*.923A, ἔγωγε οὖν.) Pl.*R*.585A ῟Ωδέ γ' οὖν, εἶπον, ἐννόει ('Well, look at it *this* way'): *Hp.Ma*.292E καίτοι ἐγὼ αὐτὸν ἠρώτων οὕτως ὥσπερ σὺ ἐμέ, ὃ πᾶσι καλὸν καὶ ἀεί ἐστι . . .—Εὖ γ' οὖν οἶδα . . . ὅτι πᾶσι καλὸν τοῦτ' ἐστίν, ὃ ἐγὼ εἶπον ('Well, I know quite *well* . . .').

γ' . . . οὖν, separated by ἄν (though the collocation γοῦν ἄν also occurs: Pl.*R*.555B) is found in two senses:

(*α*) 'Part proof'. Th.i 76.4 (the implication that the Athenians have behaved well is supported by the statement that others, in their shoes, would behave worse): 77.6 (the proposition, τὸ παρὸν αἰεὶ βαρὺ τοῖς ὑπηκόοις, is supported by the statement that an imperial Sparta would soon become as unpopular as an imperial Athens): Pl.*R*.469C. Add, perhaps, Amips.*Fr*.1 (partial ground for assent).

(*β*) Ironical (see I.2.ii below). E.*Med* 504 καλῶς γ' ἂν οὖν δέξαιντό μ' οἴκοις ὧν πατέρα κατέκτανον (γ' ἂν οὖν *LPv*: τ' ἂν οὖν *VA*: τὰ νῦν *B*. Less probably, οὖν might be taken as connective): 588 Καλῶς γ' ἂν οὖν σὺ τῷδ' ὑπηρετεῖς λόγῳ (οὖν σύ *AV*: οὖν μοι *LP*: οὖν (*et* ἐξυπηρετεῖς) *B*: οἶμαι Nauck): Ar.*Ec*.806 Πάνυ γ' ἂν οὖν Ἀντισθένης αὔτ' εἰσενέγκοι: *Eq*.344 Ἰδοὺ λέγειν. καλῶς γ' ἂν οὖν σὺ πρᾶγμα . . . μεταχειρίσαιο.

It is certainly significant that the MSS. give evidence for the two forms γοῦν and γ' οὖν, while they show no trace of δοῦν And the distinction may well have been used to differentiate those passages in which οὖν has a connective force: if it was in fact so used, the copyists have frequently confused the forms. Our comparative ignorance of ancient Greek pronunciation makes it difficult to say how far γ' οὖν and γοῦν would have been differentiated in speech. γε in γοῦν, unlike τοί in τἄν, ceases to be enclitic.

γοῦν (γ' οὖν) is almost confined to Attic Greek. Homer provides (as we have seen) two examples: Herodotus another two (i 31: vii 104.5: I exclude iv 76 (see top of p. 449)). Most Attic writers use γοῦν freely, though for some reason or other there is no instance in Isocrates. The 'part proof' use is perhaps not precise enough for his formal style.[1] Aeschylus, as Wilamowitz points out (on *Ag.*676), first uses γοῦν in the *Agamemnon*.

I. With γε predominating, the normal use of γοῦν. γε is either limitative or emphatic: οὖν adds a sense of reality or essentiality, but often does little more than emphasize.

(1) With limitative γε.

(i) In general. With γοῦν, as with simple γε, the possibility that the statement may hold good outside the imposed limits is either included or excluded by the context. A.*Ag.*1425 ἐὰν δὲ τοὔμπαλιν κραίνῃ θεός, γνώσει διδαχθεὶς ὀψὲ γοῦν τὸ σωφρονεῖν: S.*Ant.*45 Ἦ γὰρ νοεῖς θάπτειν σφ', ἀπόρρητον πόλει;—Τὸν γοῦν ἐμὸν καὶ τὸν σὸν . . . ἀδελφόν ('One who is at least our *brother*'): 779 ἢ γνώσεται γοῦν ἀλλὰ τηνικαῦθ' ('*then*, at any rate'): *OC* 24 Ἔχεις διδάξαι δή μ' ὅποι καθέσταμεν;—Τὰς γοῦν Ἀθήνας οἶδα, τὸν δὲ χῶρον οὔ ('I know *Athens*'): E.*Ph.*1449 ὡς τοσόνδε γοῦν τύχω χθονὸς πατρῴας ('*this* much, at any rate'): *El.*350 ἀνὴρ ἔστι . . . ;—Ἔστιν λόγῳ γοῦν ('He lives in *report* at least'): *El.*770 Τέθνηκε· δίς σοι ταὔθ', ἃ γοῦν βούλῃ, λέγω ('I am repeating myself: but it's what you *want* to hear, anyhow'): *Med.*1408 ἀλλ' ὁπόσον γοῦν πάρα καὶ δύναμαι τάδε καὶ θρηνῶ: Ar.*Nu.*343 Φέρε ποῖαι γάρ τινές εἰσιν;—Οὐκ οἶδα σαφῶς· εἴξασιν γοῦν ἐρίοισιν ('they *look* like *wool*'): *Lys.*612 Μῶν ἐγκαλεῖς ὅτι οὐχὶ προὐθέμεσθά σε; ἀλλ' εἰς τρίτην γοῦν ἡμέραν . . . ἥξει παρ' ἡμῶν τὰ τρίτ' ἐπεσκευασμένα: 877 Μὴ δῆτ', ἀλλὰ τῷ γοῦν παιδίῳ ὑπάκουσον ('Listen to the *child* anyway, if you won't listen to *me*'): Hdt.i 31 δοκέων πάγχυ δευτερεῖα γῶν οἴσεσθαι: Th.iv 85.4 οἰόμενοί τε παρὰ συμ-

[1] Dr. Chapman comments: 'Isocrates had no use for "part proof": he always knows the whole truth'.

μάχους, καὶ πρὶν ἔργῳ ἀφίκεσθαι, τῇ γοῦν γνώμῃ ἥξειν: vii 49.1 καὶ ἅμα ταῖς γοῦν ναυσὶ μᾶλλον ἢ πρότερον ἐθάρσησε κρατήσειν: viii 59 καὶ ἐβούλετο παρασκευαζόμενος γοῦν δῆλος εἶναι: Pl.*Euthd.* 284D Κακῶς ἄρα λέγουσιν οἱ ἀγαθοὶ τὰ κακὰ . . . ;—Ναὶ μὰ Δία, σφόδρα γε, τοὺς γοῦν κακοὺς ἀνθρώπους ('Yes, they speak ill of *bad* men, certainly': here γε alone would be sufficient): *Hp.Mi.* 374D Βελτίω ἄρα ἥγησαι τῶν σαυτοῦ τὰ ἑκουσίως πονηρὰ ἐργαζόμενα ἢ τὰ ἀκουσίως ;—Τὰ γοῦν τοιαῦτα ('Yes, in cases like *that*' (defects of the senses): *sc.* 'but not in others'): X.*An.*vii 1.30 ἐὰν δὲ μὴ δύνησθε ταῦτα, ἡμᾶς δεῖ ἀδικουμένους τῆς γοῦν Ἑλλάδος μὴ στέρεσθαι: *Cyr.*i 1.4 τἆλλα . . . ἔθνη ἀκούομεν τὰ γοῦν ἐν τῇ Εὐρώπῃ ἔτι καὶ νῦν αὐτόνομα εἶναι: *Mem.*i 4.8 Σὺ δὲ σαυτῷ δοκεῖς τι φρόνιμον ἔχειν ;—Ἐρώτα γοῦν καὶ ἀποκρινοῦμαι ('*Ask* me, anyhow'): D.xx 16 παρὰ δ' ὑμῖν ἀδεῶς ἂν λάβῃ τις ἔχειν ὑπῆρχε τὸν γοῦν ἄλλον χρόνον: Pl.*Cra.*401B (γοῦν *om.G*: *R.*425B is an example of 'part proof'): *Prt.*334E: X.*Oec.*7.19: D. xxi 11.

The purely 'adverbial' γοῦν appears, as R. W. Chapman observes, to be rare in Plato: *Grg.*509A,*R.*576C are cited below, (ii) *ad fin.* and (iv).

In the following, γοῦν, like γε, seems to give causal force to a participle: Pl.*Phdr.*236A τίνα οἴει λέγοντα ὡς χρὴ μὴ ἐρῶντι μᾶλλον ἢ ἐρῶντι χαρίζεσθαι, παρέντα τοῦ μὲν τὸ φρόνιμον ἐγκωμιάζειν, τοῦ δὲ τὸ ἄφρον ψέγειν, ἀναγκαῖα γοῦν ὄντα, εἶτ' ἄλλα ἄττα ἕξειν λέγειν ('quippe quae necessaria sint').

(ii) 'Part proof'. Much the commonest use of γοῦν is to introduce a statement which is, *pro tanto*, evidence for a preceding statement. This has been well termed 'part proof'.

Erinna,*Fr.*4.3 Προμαθεῦ, ἐντὶ καὶ ἄνθρωποι τὶν ὁμαλοὶ σοφίαν. ταύταν γοῦν ἐτύμως τὰν παρθένον ὅστις ἔγραψεν, αἰ καὐδὰν ποτέθηκ', ἦς κ' Ἀγαθαρχὶς ὅλα: A.*Ag.*432 πένθεια τλησικάρδιος δόμων ἑκάστου πρέπει. πολλὰ γοῦν θιγγάνει πρὸς ἧπαρ: S.*OC*319 οὐκ ἔστιν ἄλλη. φαιδρὰ γοῦν ἀπ' ὀμμάτων σαίνει με: E.*Alc.*694 τὸ δὲ ζῆν . . . γλυκύ. σὺ γοῦν ἀναιδῶς διεμάχου τὸ μὴ θανεῖν ('The sweetness of life may be inferred from your determination to avoid death'): *IT* 73 Καὶ βωμός, Ἕλλην οὗ καταστάζει φόνος ;—Ἐξ αἱμάτων γοῦν ξάνθ' ἔχει τριχώματα: *Rh.*707 'Is this Odysseus' work?'—Θρασὺς γοῦν ἐς ἡμᾶς: Ar.*Nu.*1063 Πολλοῖς (διὰ τὸ σωφρονεῖν ἀγαθόν τι γενόμενον εἶδον). ὁ γοῦν Πηλεὺς ἔλαβε διὰ τοῦτο τὴν μάχαιραν: *V.*262 'It looks like rain. ἔπεισι γοῦν τοῖσιν λύχνοις οὑτοιὶ μύκητες': *Pax* 220 ἐλέγετ' ἂν ὑμεῖς...—Ὁ γοῦν χαρακτὴρ ἡμεδαπὸς τῶν ῥημάτων: 233 ἐξιέναι... μέλλει· θορυβεῖ γοῦν ἔνδον: E.*Cyc.*523: Ar.*Pax* 1152: *Ra.*1028, 1037: Hdt.vii 104.5 τὸν ὑποδειμαίνουσι... ποιεῦσι γῶν τὰ ἂν ἐκεῖνος ἀνώγῃ: Hp.*Fract.*19 'If a man is to have his leg badly set, he had better break both legs. ἰσόρροπος γοῦν ἂν εἴη αὐτὸς ἑωυτῷ': Pl.*Smp.*195B ταχὺ ὂν δῆλον ὅτι· θᾶττον γοῦν τοῦ δέοντος ἡμῖν προσέρχεται: *Phdr.*229B Ἆρ' οὐκ ἐνθένδε (ἡρπάσθη ἡ Ὠρείθυια); χαρίεντα γοῦν... τὰ ὑδάτια φαίνεται, καὶ ἐπιτήδεια κόραις παίζειν παρ' αὐτά: *Men.*71A κινδυνεύει... παρ' ὑμᾶς οἴχεσθαι ἡ σοφία. εἰ γοῦν τινα ἐθέλεις οὕτως ἐρέσθαι τῶν ἐνθάδε, οὐδεὶς ὅστις οὐ γελάσεται καὶ ἐρεῖ· "Ὦ ξένε, κινδυνεύω σοι δοκεῖν μακάριός τις εἶναι—ἀρετὴν γοῦν... εἰδέναι—": 93D ἱππέα ἐδιδάξατο ἀγαθόν. ἐπέμενεν γοῦν ἐπὶ τῶν ἵππων ὀρθὸς ἑστηκώς: Th.i 2.5: 20.2: 76.1: 77.5: 144.4: vi 59.3: Pl.*R.*522D, 583A: *Ti.*23B: *Grg.*516A, 517C: *Prt.*314D, 341B: *Men.*89E, 90B: D.xxiv 57: liv 25.

Repeated at a short interval: Pl.*R.*554B Ἐμοὶ γοῦν, ἔφη, δοκεῖ· χρήματα γοῦν μάλιστα ἔντιμα τῇ τε πόλει καὶ παρὰ τῷ τοιούτῳ.

In Pl.*R.*432C γοῦν is difficult, since 'the second pair of adjectives seems to go as far as the first' (R. W. C.): perhaps γοῦν refers mainly to δύσβατος.

Plato often uses γοῦν in answers conveying a qualified assent, and the following phrases are all more or less common:—ἔοικε γοῦν, εἰκὸς γοῦν, τὸ γοῦν εἰκός, δίκαιον γοῦν, ἔχει γοῦν λόγον, ὡς γοῦν ὁ λόγος σημαίνει, φασὶ γοῦν, λέγεται γοῦν, φαίνεται γοῦν, φιλεῖ γοῦν οὕτω γίγνεσθαι. Here, again, the negative form is οὔκουν... γε (R. W. C.). In some of these, confirmation of assent is verging into assent pure and simple, as in assentient γάρ (*q.v.* VIII). See further 2.i below.

Euripides (and other authors at times) uses γοῦν in the sphere of action to introduce a *pro tanto* reason for following a suggested course. *Cyc.*567 οἰνοχόος τέ μοι γενοῦ.—Γιγνώσκεται γοῦν ἡ ἄμπελος τήμῇ χερί ('Well, certainly, the vine is no stranger to my hand'): *IT* 1194 Θάλασσα κλύζει πάντα τἀνθρώπων κακά (*sc.* 'so the strangers must be cleansed with sea-water').—Ὁσιώτερον γοῦν τῇ θεῷ πέσοιεν ἄν: *Ion* 557 Πατέρα νυν δέχου, τέκνον.—Τῷ θεῷ γοῦν οὐκ ἀπιστεῖν εἰκός: 1027 Αὐτοῦ νυν αὐτὸν κτεῖν', ἵν' ἀρνήσῃ φόνους.—Προλάζυμαι γοῦν τῷ χρόνῳ τῆς ἡδονῆς: *Or.* 781 Ἀλλὰ δῆτ' ἔλθω;—Θανὼν γοῦν ὧδε κάλλιον θανῇ: 788: *Ba.*839: X.*Mem.*iii 1.10 ἆρα τοὺς φιλοτιμοτάτους προτακτέον;—Οὗτοι γοῦν εἰσιν, ἔφη, οἱ . . . κινδυνεύειν ἐθέλοντες: Pl.*Lg.*648C, 683B: X.*Oec.*6.3.

In a parenthesis. E.*Ba.*638 ὡς δέ μοι δοκεῖ—ψοφεῖ γοῦν ἀρβύλη δόμων ἔσω— . . . ἥξει: Pl.*R.*431A ὅταν μὲν τὸ βέλτιον φύσει τοῦ χείρονος ἐγκρατὲς ᾖ, τοῦτο λέγειν τὸ κρείττω αὑτοῦ—ἐπαινεῖ γοῦν—ὅταν δὲ . . .: Th.i 74.3: viii 87.3: Pl.*Hp.Ma.*284C: D.xxiii 89.

In a relative clause. Pl.*R.*334A Ὡς γοῦν ὁ λόγος, ἔφη, σημαίνει: 584A: *Grg.* 509A.

In a question. Ar.*Pax* 545 σκόπει τὰ πρόσωφ', ἵνα γνῷς τὰς τέχνας.—Αἴβοι τάλας.—Ἐκεινονὶ γοῦν τὸν λοφοποιὸν οὐχ ὁρᾷς . . .; ('Well, anyhow, don't you see . . .?').

(iii) *In apodosi.* (I include below only those passages in which γοῦν occurs early in the apodosis.) S.*OT* 408 Εἰ καὶ τυραννεῖς, ἐξισωτέον τὸ γοῦν ἴσ' ἀντιλέξαι: 1425 ἀλλ' εἰ τὰ θνητῶν μὴ καταισχύνεσθ' ἔτι γένεθλα, τὴν γοῦν . . . φλόγα αἰδεῖσθ': Ar. *Nu.*885 ὅπως δ' ἐκείνω τὼ λόγω μαθήσεται . . . ἐὰν δὲ μή, τὸν γοῦν ἄδικον πάσῃ τέχνῃ: *Ra.*736 ἐπ' ἀξίου γοῦν τοῦ ξύλου, ἤν τι καὶ πάσχητε, πάσχειν τοῖς σοφοῖς δοκήσετε (apodosis first): Th.v 40.2 ἐλπίζοντες . . . εἰ μὴ . . ., τοῖς γοῦν Ἀθηναίοις ξύμμαχοι ἔσεσθαι: Pl.*Alc.I* 112B καὶ εἰ μὴ ἑώρακας, ἀκήκοας γοῦν: *Hipparch.*232B εἴτε πέπεισαι εἴτε ὁπωσδὴ ἔχεις, σύμφῃς γοῦν ἡμῖν: Ant.vi 1 εἰ δ' ἄρα τις καὶ ἀναγκάζοιτο κινδυνεύειν, τοῦτο γοῦν ὑπάρχειν: Lys. xxx 6 καὶ ἐπειδὴ ἑνὸς ἑκάστου δίκην οὐκ εἰλήφατε, νῦν ὑπὲρ ἁπάντων γοῦν τὴν τιμωρίαν (χρὴ) ποιήσασθαι (γοῦν, *om. CO*, is not 'vix sanum' (Hude): it refers both to νῦν and to ὑπὲρ ἁπάντων: hence the order): D.xviii 306 ὡς ἑτέρως δὲ συμβάντων, τὸ γοῦν εὐδοκιμεῖν περίεστι: Pl.*Smp.*191C: *Phdr.*265D: *Phd.*85C: *Sph.*251A: *Plt.*264C: *Lg.*952C.

So also οὔκουν . . . γε: Pl.*Lg.*810D: εἰ δὲ ἐλάττοσιν, οὔκουν χείροσί γε. See further p. 424.

For apodotic ἀλλὰ . . . γοῦν, see III.1 below.

(iv) With pronouns. S.*Aj.*527 Καὶ κάρτ' ἐπαίνου τεύξεται πρὸς γοῦν ἐμοῦ: Pl.*R.*576C Ἀνάγκη, ἔφη, ταῦτα γοῦν οὕτως ἔχειν: D.xix 13 καὶ μέχρι τοῦ δεῦρ' ἐπανελθεῖν . . . ἐμὲ γοῦν . . . ἐλάνθανε. But most instances of γοῦν with pronouns come under the heading of 'part proof': Ar.*Nu.*408 *Νὴ Δί' ἐγὼ γοῦν ἀτεχνῶς ἔπαθον τουτί*: Pl.*Smp.*215D: *Ly.*204C. In general, *γοῦν* has probably no particular affinity with pronouns. But in Plato it is often attached to a personal pronoun in replies, 'the speaker giving his own assent for what it is worth' (R. W. C.) Pl.*R.* 335E *Μαχούμεθα . . . κοινῇ ἐγώ τε καὶ σύ . . .—'Εγὼ γοῦν, ἔφη, ἕτοιμός εἰμι κοινωνεῖν τῆς μάχης* ('Well, *I'm* ready enough to join in'): *Phd.*70B: *Tht.*171D. *'Εμοὶ γοῦν δοκεῖ* ('some twelve times in Plato', R. W. C.): *R.*476C,613B. Similarly *Οὔκουν . . . γε*: *Prm.*142A *Οὔκουν ἔμοιγε δοκεῖ.*

(2) With emphatic *γε*. On the whole, the uses of *γοῦν* here correspond with the far commoner uses of *γε*.

(i) In affirmative answers. E.*Cyc.*472 *Ἔστ' οὖν ὅπως ἂν . . . κἀγὼ λαβοίμην τοῦ τυφλοῦντος ὄμματα δαλοῦ; φόνου γὰρ τοῦδε κοινωνεῖν θέλω.—Δεῖ γοῦν· μέγας γὰρ δαλός· οὗ ξυλληπτέον* ('Yes, you *must*'): *Ph.*852 *συλλέξαι σθένος καὶ πνεῦμ' ἄθροισον, αἶπος ἐκβαλὼν ὁδοῦ.—Κόπῳ παρεῖμαι γοῦν* ('Yes, I *am* tired': but this might also be classified under I.ii above: 'I certainly *am* tired (and therefore I had better rest)': moreover the text is doubtful): Pl.*Phdr.*262B *Οὐκοῦν τοῖς . . . ἀπατωμένοις δῆλον ὡς τὸ πάθος τοῦτο δι' ὁμοιοτήτων τινῶν εἰσερρύη.—Γίγνεται γοῦν οὕτως* ('Yes, that *is* what happens'): *R.*442D *σώφρονα οὐ τῇ φιλίᾳ . . . τούτων (καλοῦμεν) . . .;—Σωφροσύνη γοῦν, ἦ δ' ὅς, οὐκ ἄλλο τί ἐστιν ἢ τοῦτο*: 461A 'The *ἀκμή* of a woman is 20–40, of a man 25–55'.—*Ἀμφοτέρων γοῦν, ἔφη, αὕτη ἀκμὴ σώματός τε καὶ φρονήσεως* ('Yes, certainly'): X.*Mem.*iii 1.1 *βούλει σκοπῶμεν, ἀρξάμενοι ἀπὸ τῆς τροφῆς ὥσπερ ἀπὸ τῶν στοιχείων;—Δοκεῖ γοῦν μοι ἡ τροφὴ ἀρχὴ εἶναι.*

It is difficult to draw a rigid line between this use of *γοῦν* and 'part proof'. In Pl.*R.*409C, for example, *γοῦν* might at first sight appear to convey unreserved assent. But *γενναιότατος* does not strictly imply the *ἀγαθός* of 409B. Similarly, in 410A, *ἄριστον* hardly, perhaps, conveys an unhesitating acceptance of the ruthless elimination of the unfit recommended by Socrates: 'That is certainly the *best* way. (But have we the nerve to take it?)'

It is perhaps reasonable, then, to regard this assentient *γοῦν* as derived from 'part proof'. Cf. assentient *γάρ* (*q.v.* VIII), and ἔοικε γοῦν, etc., in replies (1.ii). The rather inconclusive fifth-century examples do not militate strongly against this view.

(ii) Exclamatory (Aristophanes). *V.*795 ἀλεκτρυόνος μ' ἔφασκε κοιλίαν ἔχειν. "ταχὺ γοῦν καθέψεις τἀργύριον," ἦ δ' ὃς λέγων ('You *do* digest money quickly': though this might be part proof: 'anyhow'): *Ec.*872 (after the failure of a ruse) Νὴ τὸν Δία, δεῖ γοῦν μηχανήματός τινος: *Pax* 1344 Οἰκήσετε γοῦν καλῶς ('You *will* have a good time': '*sanequam.* Iocantium particula', van Leeuwen): *Th.*263 (perhaps).

In ironical or sarcastic exclamations (Euripides and Aristophanes). E.*Hel.*1227 'Ορθῶς μὲν ἥδε συμφορὰ δακρύεται;—'Εν εὐμαρεῖ γοῦν σὴν κασιγνήτην λαθεῖν ('Your sister is easily fooled, isn't she?'): *Ph.*618 Μῆτερ, ἀλλά μοι σὺ χαῖρε.—Χαρτὰ γοῦν πάσχω, τέκνον: *Or.*1602 Εὖ γοῦν θίγοις ἂν χερνίβων: Ar.*Eq.*87 'Ιδού γ' ἄκρατον. περὶ ποτοῦ γοῦν ἔστι σοι (best taken, with Neil, as a sarcastic statement, not as a question: 'So *drink*'s the matter in hand!'): *Th.*845 ἀλλ' ἀφαιρεῖσθαι βίᾳ τὰ χρήματ' εἰπόντας τοδί, "ἀξία γοῦν εἶ τόκου . . .": *Ec.*794 Χαρίεντα γοῦν πάθοιμ' ἄν: *Pl.*565 κοσμιότης οἰκεῖ μετ' ἐμοῦ . . .—Πάνυ γοῦν κλέπτειν κόσμιόν ἐστιν ('Thieving's a *most* respectable thing, isn't it?')

See also p. 449, γ' . . . οὖν separated by ἄν, (β).

II. With οὖν predominating, as a connective particle: 'well' or 'then'. (Cf. p. 449, γ' οὖν (*b*).) This usage is exceedingly rare in classical Greek, apart from Hippocrates (see below), though there are a few indubitable instances in Plato's later works. The topic is inadequately discussed by the authorities, who omit many of the real examples, and include others which come under the heading of 'part proof'. To clear the ground, I will deal with the latter first.

(1) Pl.*Prt.*324B. The practice of deterrent punishment supports (in the speaker's view) the assumption that virtue can be taught. 'Unstreitig ist diese Folgerung aus dem Vorhergehenden,' says Bäumlein, unaccountably. *Ap.*21D ἐλογιζόμην ὅτι τούτου μὲν τοῦ ἀνθρώπου ἐγὼ σοφώτερός εἰμι· κινδυνεύει μὲν γὰρ ἡμῶν οὐδέτερος οὐδὲν καλὸν κἀγαθὸν εἰδέναι, ἀλλ' οὗτος μὲν οἴεταί τι εἰδέναι οὐκ εἰδώς, ἐγὼ δέ, ὥσπερ οὖν οὐκ οἶδα, οὐδὲ οἴομαι· ἔοικα γοῦν τούτου γε σμικρῷ τινι αὐτῷ τούτῳ σοφώτερος εἶναι, ὅτι ἃ μὴ οἶδα οὐδὲ οἴομαι εἰδέναι. A logical sense is, it is true,

clearly appropriate in γοῦν here, and οὖν in such a context would not excite remark: 'I, unlike him, know that I know nothing much: I am consequently slightly wiser than he, in virtue of that knowledge.' But the ordinary force of γοῦν is at least equally suitable: κινδυνεύει μὲν γάρ κ.τ.λ. and ἔοικα γοῦν κ.τ.λ. both look back to τούτου . . . εἰμι. The two sentences are substantially identical in content, the former giving full proof by γάρ, the latter part proof by γοῦν. The use of the two particles with a common reference is paralleled by the similar use of successive γάρ's (see γάρ, III.6, and in particular S.*Ant.*659–61 there quoted). The looseness of the style is consonant with the naive, colloquial tone of the *Apology*. (Burnet's suggestion (in a private communication to Dr. Chapman) that the clause κινδυνεύει κ.τ.λ. is a sort of parenthesis, arrives at the same result, but appears to me less natural.)

(2) In the following passages, on the other hand, the context demands that the οὖν shall bear an inferential or progressive force, while the γε emphasizes the preceding word, the two particles playing independent roles: whether or not this is a reason for writing γ' οὖν, *separatim*.

Pl.*Cra.*432D. Cratylus has objected (431E) that, if the name of a thing is written wrongly, it ceases to *be* the name of the thing. Socrates answers: 'A name is a kind of image or copy (430A μίμημα: 431D εἰκών). Now exact correspondence with the original cannot be demanded in a copy. If Cratylus were imitated exactly, the result would be two Cratyluses, not Cratylus and his image. γελοῖα γοῦν ... ὑπὸ τῶν ὀνομάτων πάθοι ἂν ἐκεῖνα ὧν ὀνόματά ἐστιν τὰ ὀνόματα εἰ πάντα πανταχῇ αὐτοῖς ὁμοιωθείη. διττὰ γὰρ ἄν που πάντα γένοιτο'. The inferential force, marking the conclusion of what is almost a formal syllogism, is indispensable here. The γε is emphatic, almost exclamatory: 'It would be *ridiculous*, then.' *Prm.*147C Τὸ ἓν ἄρα, ὡς ἔοικεν, ἕτερόν τε τῶν ἄλλων ἐστὶν καὶ ἑαυτοῦ καὶ ταὐτὸν ἐκείνοις τε καὶ ἑαυτῷ.—Κινδυνεύει φαίνεσθαι ἔκ γε τοῦ λόγου.—Ἆρ' οὖν καὶ ὅμοιόν τε καὶ ἀνόμοιον ἑαυτῷ τε καὶ τοῖς ἄλλοις;—Ἴσως.—Ἐπειδὴ γοῦν ἕτερον τῶν ἄλλων ἐφάνη, καὶ τἆλλά που ἕτερα ἂν ἐκείνου εἴη.—Τί μήν;—Οὐκοῦν οὕτως ἕτερον τῶν ἄλλων, ὥσπερ καὶ τἆλλα ἐκείνου, καὶ οὔτε μᾶλλον οὔτε ἧττον; The successive stages of the argument are marked by οὖν, γοῦν, οὐκοῦν. The γε coalesces with ἐπειδή, '*quippe cum*'. *Lg.*633D 'Does courage merely consist in fighting fear, or in fighting desire as well?'—'The latter.'—*Εἰ γοῦν μεμνήμεθα τοὺς ἔμπροσθεν λόγους, ἥττω τινὰ ὅδε* (Cleinias in 626 D–E) *καὶ πόλιν ἔλεγεν αὐτὴν αὑτῆς καὶ ἄνδρα* . . .—'Yes.'—*Νῦν οὖν πότερα λέγομεν τὸν τῶν λυπῶν ἥττω κακὸν ἢ καὶ τὸν τῶν ἡδονῶν;* The γε goes closely with εἰ, '*if*': The οὖν marks a new step in the argument, 'now'. *Lg.*681C 'Family custom is the origin of law. *Ἀρχῇ δὴ νομοθεσίας οἷον ἐμβάντες ἐλάθομεν, ὡς ἔοικεν.—Πάνυ μὲν οὖν—Τὸ γοῦν μετὰ ταῦτα ἀναγκαῖον αἱρεῖσθαι τοὺς συνελθόντας τούτους κοινούς τινας ἑαυτῶν, οἳ . . . νομοθέται κληθήσονται*'. 'Well (οὖν) the *next* (γε) step.' (England takes γοῦν as 'explanatory'.) *Alc.II* 142E 'Men bring misfortunes on themselves by praying for the wrong things. *κινδυνεύει γοῦν . . . φρόνιμός τις εἶναι ἐκεῖνος ὁ ποιητής*, who asked Zeus to send him and his friends good things, whether they prayed for them or not' (γοῦν *B*: γάρ *T*). οὖν has its full logical force, 'therefore': γε limitatively stresses κινδυνεύει, 'the *probability* is'. *Alc.II* 149B *φησὶν ἂν βούλεσθαι αὐτῷ τὴν Λακεδαιμονίων εὐφημίαν εἶναι . . . τὴν γοῦν εὐφημίαν οὐκ ἄλλην τινά μοι δοκεῖ λέγειν ὁ θεὸς ἢ τὴν εὐχὴν αὐτῶν* (γ' οὖν Burnet: δ' οὖν Sauppe). 'Now by εὐφημία the god meant . . . .' *Lg.*629A is more difficult. The Stranger has asserted that war legislation must aim at peace, not peace legislation at war. Cleinias objects that Cretan and Spartan legislation is entirely devised for war. The Stranger replies: *Τάχ' ἂν ἴσως· δεῖ δὲ οὐδὲν σκληρῶς ἡμᾶς αὐτοῖς διαμάχεσθαι τὰ νῦν ἀλλ' ἠρέμα ἀνερωτᾶν, ὡς μάλιστα περὶ ταῦτα ἡμῶν τε καὶ ἐκείνων σπουδαζόντων. καί μοι τῷ λόγῳ συνακολουθήσατε. προστησώμεθα γοῦν Τύρταιον . . . ὃς δὴ μάλιστα ἀνθρώπων περὶ ταῦτα ἐσπούδακεν . . . ἴθι νυν ἀνερώμεθα κοινῇ τουτονὶ τὸν ποιητὴν οὑτωσί πως· "Ὦ Τύρταιε . . . ."* Here the connective force of οὖν would be appropriate enough. But γε, after προστησώμεθα, would not be as appropriate as γε always is in the passages considered above. I have no doubt that 'at any rate' ('par exemple', des Places, p. 135) is the sense here: 'We must gently cross-examine the Cretan and Spartan legislators. At any rate, let us take Tyrtaeus, and ask *him*' (ἀνερώμεθα in 629B looking back to ἀνερωτᾶν).[1]

[1] R. W. Chapman's suggestion, that γοῦν refers to σπουδαζόντων, seems to

The above sense of *γοῦν* is far commoner in Hippocrates, and in the post-classical pseudo-Aristotelian *de Plantis*, where Bonitz notes the frequency of the particle. *οὖν* and *δ' οὖν* are often found as *variae lectiones*.

Hp.*Art*.14 'Others do so-and-so. *ταῦτα γοῦν ἀπείρῳ μὲν ἀκοῦσαι φαίνεται ἐγγὺς τοῦ κατὰ φύσιν εἶναι*' (*γοῦν M* : *οὖν al.*): *Int*.18 *ἐρράγη . . . ἢν γοῦν ῥαγῇ* (*οὖν EHK*): *Nat.Mul*.45 (after describing symptoms and their causes) *ὁκόταν γοῦν ὧδε ἔχῃ, φάρμακον χρὴ πιπίσκειν*: *Genit*.47 'Those who were purged on the odd days died. *οἱ γοῦν πρόσθεν ἰητροὶ ἐν τούτῳ μάλιστα ἡμάρτανον· ἐφαρμάκευον γὰρ ἐν τῇσι περισσῇσιν ἡμέρῃσι καὶ ἀπώλλυον τοὺς ἀνθρώπους*' ('Now that is the great mistake the old doctors made'): *Epid*.v 95 *πρόρρησις ὅτι, σπασμοῦ γενομένου, ταχέως ἀπολεῖται. τῇ γοῦν ἐπιούσῃ νυκτὶ δύσφορος, ἄγρυπνος . . . τῇ τρίτῃ ἅμ' ἡμέρῃ ἐσπᾶτο, καὶ τηνικαῦτα ἐτελεύτησεν* ('Well, the following night . . .'): *Vict*.68 *διελεῖν τὸν χρόνον ἐς μέρεα ἓξ κατὰ ὀκτὼ ἡμέρας. ἐν γοῦν τῇ πρώτῃ μοίρῃ χρὴ . . .* (*οὖν EHI*): *Mul*.166,167,183: *Epid*.ii 3.8 : vii 1,2 : *Haem*.4 : *Vict*.36,56(*bis*), 80: [Arist.] *de Plantis* 815b22 '*ἐπιθυμία* can only come from *αἴσθησις. οὐχ εὑρίσκομεν γοῦν ἐν τοῖς τοιούτοις αἴσθησιν*': 815b29, 817a5,817a15: *ib. saep.*: Aen.Tact.*Fr*.51 (if Julius Africanus' excerpt can be relied on: but in *Fr*.56 Julius' *γοῦν* is not supported by the MS. reading of 39.2): *ἀναγκαῖον εἰδέναι πῶς ἐπιστολὰς δεῖ αὐτοὺς εἰσπέμπειν. ἀπόστελλε γοῦν οὕτως* ('Well, send them like this').

The resumptive use of *γοῦν*, like *δ' οὖν*, after a digression, is analogous. Hp.*Art*.9 *τὸν γοῦν τοιοῦτον ὦμον . . .* : *Int*.15 *ὁκόταν γοῦν ἔμπυος ᾖ ὁ νεφρὸς . . .* : *Vict*.1 *ἐγὼ γοῦν, ὥσπερ εἶπον, . . .* So also in Is.i 10, if Schoemann's *τότε γοῦν*, for *ὅτι γοῦν*, is right: but read, probably, *τότε δ' οὖν*.

III. In combinations. *γοῦν* is rarely found in close association with other particles.

(1) *ἀλλὰ . . . γοῦν, in apodosi* (for the commoner *ἀλλ' οὖν* . . .

me less probable: he renders 'It is right for both parties *σπουδάζειν περὶ ταῦτα* : Tyrtaeus at all events—one of the most prominent of our opponents—*μάλιστα ἀνθρώπων περὶ ταῦτα ἐσπούδακεν*.' In any case, *καὶ . . . συνακολουθήσατε* is virtually parenthetical: and minor difficulties of text and interpretation in the first sentence of 629A do not affect the main issue.

γε). E.*IA* 908 εἰ γὰρ μὴ γάμοισιν ἐζύγης, ἀλλ' ἐκλήθης γοῦν ταλαίνης παρθένου φίλος πόσις: Ar.*Th.*250 ἐπειδὴ . . . φθονεῖς, ἀλλ' ἱμάτιον γοῦν χρῆσον: Pl.*Phd.*71B κἂν εἰ μὴ . . ., ἀλλ' ἔργῳ γοῦν πανταχοῦ οὕτως ἔχειν ἀναγκαῖον. (Except *in apodosi*, ἀλλὰ . . . γοῦν need hardly be regarded as a combination. A few instances will be found in I.1.i.) S.*Ant.*779 γοῦν ἀλλά (see I.1.i).

(2) μὲν γοῦν.[1] Ar.*Pax* 497 Ὑμεῖς μὲν γοῦν οἱ κιττῶντες τῆς εἰρήνης σπᾶτ' ἀνδρείως (γοῦν Bentley: οὖν *codd.*): X.*Oec.*19.6 Ξηρὰ μὲν γοῦν μοι δοκεῖ. Pl.*Plt.*257D μέν γε οὖν.

(3) ἤγουν, a curious combination, meaning 'namely', 'that is to say', is to be found in Hippocrates and the pseudo-Aristotelian *de Plantis*. (Madvig's suggested ἤγουν at A.*Fr.*266 is unfortunate.) Hp.*Int.*50 μελετῇν δὲ χρὴ ταύτην ἐν τοῖσιν αὐτοῖσιν, οἷοισι καὶ τὸν ὑδεριῶντα, ἤγουν πυρίῃσι καὶ φαρμάκοισι καὶ ἐδέσμασι καὶ ταλαιπωρίῃσιν: *Mul.*119 κρέα δὲ ἀμείνω ἰχθύων, ἤγουν ὀρνίθια ἢ λαγῶα: *Ulc.*21 λιβανωτός, μολύβδαινα, ἤγουν τοῦ μὲν μοῖρα, καὶ τῆς δὲ μοῖρα: *Int.*17 τὰ σιτία διελών, ἃ μεμαθήκει ἐσθίειν, ἤγουν δέκα μερίδας ('par exemple', Littré): [Arist.]*de Plant.*817a1 ζητητέον . . . τοῦτό ἐστιν ὅπερ εἶπεν Ἐμπεδοκλῆς, ἤγουν εἰ εὑρίσκεται ἐν τοῖς φυτοῖς γένος θῆλυ καὶ γένος ἄρρεν: 817 b 15 διὰ τὰς δύο δυνάμεις ἃς ἔχει, ἤγουν διὰ τὴν τροφὴν . . . καὶ διὰ τὴν . . .: 818 a 9, 828 a 25. (Kühner, II ii 163, observes that ἤγουν is common in the glosses of grammarians. In X.*Oec.*19.11, αὐαίνεσθαι δὲ διὰ ξηρότητα, ἤγουν χαυνότητα τῆς γῆς, the last four words are almost certainly a gloss.)

IV. Textual questions. In Ar.*Eq.*1217 γοῦν (or γ' οὖν) of the MSS. is by common consent corrupt, and νυν is generally read. In *V.*217 γοῦν is a most unlikely emendation of the unmetrical γάρ, and Lenting's τἄρ' (or Porson's γ' ἆρ') is far more probable. In S.*Ant.*471 Blaydes' τὸ γοῦν λῆμα is not very attractive. In Hp.*VC* 19 the use of γοῦν (instead of οὖν) to emphasize ὅστις is peculiar, and perhaps suspicious: ἢ . . . ἢ . . . ἢ ὅτῳ γοῦν τρόπῳ κατεηγός (γ' οὖν *C*).

[1] The function of μὲν γοῦν is really fulfilled by μέν γε, where γε often nearly has the force of γοῦν. See p. 160.

Δ' οὖν

δέ and οὖν appear to coalesce less closely than γε and οὖν: at any rate δοῦν is nowhere found. Yet the particles are very rarely separated by an intervening word: but cf. S.*OT* 834 'Ἡμῖν μέν, ὦναξ, ταῦτ' ὀκνήρ'· ἕως δ' ἂν οὖν πρὸς τοῦ παρόντος ἐκμάθῃς, ἔχ' ἐλπίδα: Pl.*Smp*.202D Πῶς δ' ἂν οὖν θεὸς εἴη ...; (so *T*: Πῶς ἂν *B* Stobaeus): X.*Lac*.2.8 εἴποι δ' ἂν οὖν τις, τί δῆτα ...; (Stobaeus omits all the quoted words). In the last two passages δὲ ... οὖν is not in line with the normal usage of δ' οὖν. In the former we should expect ἀλλὰ μήν or the like, in the latter, ἀλλά or ἀλλὰ νὴ Δία.

δ' οὖν is found only once in Homer: *T*94 κατὰ δ' οὖν ἕτερόν γε πέδησε (the line is athetized by Aristarchus: it occurs in a passage showing 'many linguistic peculiarities', Leaf). Here there is no close connexion between the component parts, οὖν being used in tmesis between preposition and verb, as often in Herodotus (see pp. 429–30). In philosophical epic, Parm.*Fr*.8. 16: occasionally in Pindar. In Attic Greek and in Herodotus (δ' ὦν) δ' οὖν is common.

δ' οὖν differs from δὲ δή (though in many contexts either would be appropriate) in two respects. (1) In δ' οὖν, δὲ almost always, I think, has some contrasting force, and is hardly ever purely copulative, as sometimes in δὲ δή. (See, however, E.*Heracl*.310, II.3 below.) (2) Whereas δή added to δέ merely sharpens a contrast or stresses an addition, οὖν marks the opposed idea as essential. Thus, taking the examples of δὲ δή cited on p. 259: in Pl.*Chrm*.154C, πολλοὶ δὲ δὴ ἄλλοι ἐρασταὶ ... εἵποντο, δ' οὖν would be unsuitable: in *Prt*.311D παρὰ δὲ δὴ Πρωταγόραν νῦν ἀφικόμενοι ..., δ' οὖν would be equally possible, but it would emphasize the essential importance of this case, instead of sharpening the contrast between it and other cases. Contrast Pl.*R*.439A ποιοῦ μέν τινος πώματος ποιόν τι καὶ δίψος, δίψος δ' οὖν αὐτὸ οὔτε πολλοῦ οὔτε ὀλίγου, where δὲ δή might have been written. See further I.2, *ad fin.* For X.*Lac*.13.11, Hp.*Nat.Mul.* 10, see II.3. δ' οὖν is a more idiomatic combination than δὲ δή, and tends more to be canalized in certain well-defined usages.

I. In general.

(1) μὲν . . . δ' οὖν. S.*Tr.*1273 οἰκτρὰ μὲν ἡμῖν, αἰσχρὰ δ' ἐκείνοις, χαλεπώτατα δ' οὖν ἀνδρῶν πάντων τῷ τήνδ' ἄτην ὑπέχοντι (the consequences to Herakles are what really matters): Hdt.iii80 καὶ ἐλέχθησαν λόγοι ἄπιστοι μὲν ἐνίοισι Ἑλλήνων, ἐλέχθησαν δ' ὦν ('but the point is that they *were* said'): Pl.*Grg.* 458C Τοῦ μὲν θορύβου . . . αὐτοὶ ἀκούετε τούτων τῶν ἀνδρῶν βουλομένων ἀκούειν ἐάν τι λέγητε· ἐμοὶ δ' οὖν καὶ αὐτῷ μὴ γένοιτο τοσαύτη ἀσχολία, ὥστε τοιούτων λόγων καὶ οὕτω λεγομένων ἀφεμένῳ προὐργιαίτερόν τι γενέσθαι ἄλλο πράττειν ('what I can certainly do is to speak for myself'): *Prt.* 315D ὡς μὲν ἐγῷμαι καλόν τε κἀγαθὸν τὴν φύσιν, τὴν δ' οὖν ἰδέαν πάνυ καλός ('certainly handsome, whether good or not'): *Smp.*174E (the οὖν denotes that we are now approaching τὸ γελοῖον): 180E ἐπαινεῖν μὲν οὖν δεῖ πάντας θεούς, ἃ δ' οὖν ἑκάτερος εἴληχε πειρατέον εἰπεῖν (division of functions, not praise, being now the important thing): *R.*440A καὶ τέως μὲν μάχοιτο . . . κρατούμενος δ' οὖν ὑπὸ τῆς ἐπιθυμίας ('he resisted for a time, but *was* in the end conquered'): *Lg.*699B μίαν δὴ σωτηρίαν συνενόουν, λεπτὴν μὲν καὶ ἄπορον, μόνην δ' οὖν ('a poor one, I admit: but it *was* the only way'): 888C μεῖναι, πολλοῖσι μὲν οὔ, μεῖναι δ' οὖν τισιν: Th.i63.1: Pl.*La.*181C,184A: *Tht.*197B: *Plt.*306B: *Ti.*38B: *Ep.*327C,338A,342A: X.*Oec.*19.1.

Following an indirect question introduced by εἰ μέν, ὅτι μέν, the answer to which the speaker cannot, or does not trouble to give. Cf. II.2, *ad fin.* Hdt.iv187 εἰσι . . . οἱ Λίβυες ἀνθρώπων πάντων ὑγιηρότατοι τῶν ἡμεῖς ἴδμεν· εἰ μὲν διὰ τοῦτο, οὐκ ἔχω ἀτρεκέως εἰπεῖν, ὑγιηρότατοι δ' ὦν εἰσί ('but they certainly *are* the healthiest'): Pl.*Phdr.*266B εἰ μὲν ὀρθῶς ἢ μὴ προσαγορεύω, θεὸς οἶδε, καλῶ δὲ οὖν μέχρι τοῦδε διαλεκτικούς: *Ap.*17A ὅτι μὲν ὑμεῖς . . . πεπόνθατε ὑπὸ τῶν ἐμῶν κατηγόρων, οὐκ οἶδα· ἐγὼ δ οὖν καὶ αὐτὸς ὑπ' αὐτῶν ὀλίγου ἐμαυτοῦ ἐπελαθόμην: X.*An.*i3.5 εἰ μὲν δὴ δίκαια ποιήσω οὐκ οἶδα, αἱρήσομαι δ' οὖν ὑμᾶς: Pl.*Ap.*34E: X.*An.*ii4.6.

(2) δ' οὖν without preceding μέν. Pi.*P.*9.103 (breaking off and beginning a new story): A.*Th.*809 Ἐκεῖθι κεῖσθον; βαρέα δ' οὖν ὅμως φράσον: *Ag.*255 'The future cannot be foreseen. πέλοιτο δ' οὖν τἀπὶ τούτοισιν εὖ πρᾶξις': Fr.180/1.827–30 Mette (*Nachtrag*)

πολὺς ἦν αὐτῇ χρόνος ὃν χήρα . . . τείρετο· νῦν δ' οὖν ἐσορῶσ' ἥβην τὴν ἡμετέραν [: S.*Ant.*769 Δράτω, φρονείτω μεῖζον ἢ κατ' ἄνδρ' ἰών· τὼ δ' οὖν κόρα τώδ' οὐκ ἀπαλλάξει μόρου ('but *these maidens* he shall never save'): 890 μετοικίας δ' οὖν τῆς ἄνω στερήσεται ('in any case, whether she live or die'): E.*El.*508 ὃν . . . ἀνόνητ' ἔθρεψας . . .; —Ἀνόνηθ'· ὅμως δ' οὖν τοῦτό γ' οὐκ ἠνεσχόμην: *Ion* 408 Οὐκ ἠξίωσε τοῦ θεοῦ προλαμβάνειν μαντεύμαθ'. ἓν δ' οὖν εἶπεν ('but *one* thing he *did* say'): Ar.*Ach.*1195 διόλλυμαι δορὸς ὑπὸ πολεμίου τυπείς. ἐκεῖνο δ' οὖν αἰακτὸν ἂν γένοιτο, Δικαιόπολις εἴ μ' ἴδοι τετρωμένον ('But *this would* be dreadful, if . . .'): *Ec.*326 (breaking off): Pi.*O.*3.38: A.*Ag.*34,1568: S.*Ant.*1251: *OC*1444: E.*Alc.*73: Ar.*Lys.*717: Hdt.iii 46.1 οἱ δέ σφι . . . ὑπεκρίναντο τῷ θυλάκῳ περιεργάσθαι· βοηθέειν δ' ὦν ἔδοξε αὐτοῖσι ('Still, they *did* decide to help them'): Pl.*Euthd.*295D ἀνεμνήσθην οὖν τοῦ Κόννου, ὅτι μοι κἀκεῖνος χαλεπαίνει . . .· ἐπεὶ δ' οὖν διενενοήμην καὶ παρὰ τοῦτον φοιτᾶν, ᾠήθην δεῖν ὑπείκειν ('But after all, as I *had* decided to go to him for lessons . . .'): *Cra.*386B πάνυ χρηστοὶ οὔπω σοι ἔδοξαν εἶναι;—Καὶ μάλα ὀλίγοι.—"Εδοξαν δ' οὖν (brushing aside the question of number): Hdt.iii 115.2,116.3: ix 46.3: Pl.*Ti.*50C,53B,54A: *Cra.*433A: *R.*517B: *Tht.*179D: *Phdr.*260D: *Lg.*657A,839D: *Hipparch.*232B: X.*An.*i 2.12.

In some passages δ' οὖν appears to be little more than an emphasized connective adding something of peculiar weight or importance, like δὲ δή. But it can often be seen that the idea of essentiality underlies the thought.

E.*Med.*306 'People regard me in various ways. σὺ δ' οὖν φοβῇ με' (δ' οὖν *ALP*: δ' αὖ *VB* (for the variation cf. *Or.*1149, where *P* reads δ' οὖν, *F* δ' αὖ: in *Cyc.*251 Reiske's οὖν, for αὖ, may be right): 'it is *your* opinion with which I am now concerned': perhaps δ' οὖν has here a certain resumptive force also, looking back to Creon's δέδοικά σ' (282): σὺ δὲ δή would merely emphasize the contrast between Creon and other people). In Ar.*Av.*499 Hamaker has suggested αὖ for οὖν (for the confusion cf. E.*Hel.*1067): 'The cock once was king . . . Ἰκτῖνος δ' οὖν τῶν Ἑλλήνων ἦρχεν τότε': but the point of δ' οὖν is to dismiss the intervening foolery of Euelpides (see van Leeuwen). X.*HG* iv 3.8 φυγὴ τῶν Θετταλῶν ἐξαισία γίγνεται· ὥστε οἱ μὲν ἀπέθνῃσκον αὐτῶν, οἱ δὲ καὶ ἡλίσκοντο. ἔστησαν δ' οὖν οὐ πρόσθεν, πρὶν ἐν τῷ ὄρει τῷ Ναρθακίῳ ἐγένοντο (cf. *Ages*.2.4): the essential point is, not the number of casualties or prisoners, but where the routed army stopped: Parm.*Fr*.8.16 ἡ δὲ κρίσις περὶ τούτων ἐν τῷδ' ἔστιν· ἔστιν ἢ οὐκ ἔστιν· κέκριται δ' οὖν, ὥσπερ ἀνάγκη, τὴν μὲν ἐᾶν ἀνόητον ἀνώνυμον . . . τὴν δ' ὥστε πέλειν καὶ ἐτήτυμον εἶναι ('and the decision in fact is': rather than 'damit ist also notwendigerweise entschieden', Diels.)

II. Special uses.

(1) At the end of a series of details, δ' οὖν often marks the last and most important; or sums up the main import of details which have been either given or omitted as unnecessary. (Almost confined to prose.)

E.*Or*.15 τί τἄρρητ' ἀναμετρήσασθαί με δεῖ; ἔδαισε δ' οὖν νιν τέκν' ἀποκτείνας Ἀτρεύς: Ar.*Th*.477 ξύνοιδ' ἐμαυτῇ πολλὰ ⟨δεῖν'⟩. ἐκεῖνο δ' οὖν δεινότατον . . .: Hdt.iv 195 εἰσὶ μὲν καὶ πλεῦνες αἱ λίμναι αὐτόθι, ἡ δ' ὦν μεγίστη αὐτέων . . .: vii 145.1 ἦσαν δὲ πρός τινας καὶ ἄλλους ἐγκεκρημένοι (πόλεμοι), ὁ δὲ ὦν μέγιστος . . .: viii 36.2 οἱ μὲν πλεῖστοι ἀνέβησαν . . . οἱ δὲ . . . πάντες δὲ ὦν οἱ Δελφοί ἐξέλιπον τὴν πόλιν: Hp.*Epid*.vii 1 τῇ δ' οὖν ἑπτακαιδεκάτῃ . . . (marking the climax of the disease: the preceding stages are introduced by δέ): Pl.*R*.620D Details of the choice of lives. ἐπειδὴ δ' οὖν πάσας τὰς ψυχὰς τοὺς βίους ᾑρῆσθαι . . .: *Ti*.41A 'The various gods were born. ἐπεὶ δ' οὖν πάντες . . . θεοὶ γένεσιν ἔσχον . . .': X.*An*.v 6.11 ἐπεὶ δὲ ταῦτ' ἔλεξεν, οἱ μὲν ὑπώπτευον . . . οἱ δὲ . . . οἱ δὲ . . . οἱ δ' οὖν Ἕλληνες ἐψηφίσαντο: *Cyr*.i 4.15 τέλος δ' οὖν πολλὰ θηρία ἔχων ὁ Ἀστυάγης ἀπῄει: D.xviii 213 'They made all sorts of speeches. τὸ δ' οὖν κεφάλαιον . . .': xxi 79 (after describing the foul language used by Midias and his gang) ὃ δ' οὖν δεινότατον καὶ οὐ λόγος, ἀλλ' ἔργον ἤδη . . .: xxiii 65 πολλὰ μὲν δή παρ' ἡμῖν ἐστι τοιαῦθ' οἷ' οὐχ ἑτέρωθι, ἓν δ' οὖν ἰδιώτατον πάντων: Hyp.*Ath*.4 τέλος δ' οὖν, ἵνα μὴ μακρολογῶ . . .: Th.i 10.5: Pl.*R*.615A: *Alc.II* 140B: *Sph*.230A: *Prm*.130D: *Lg*. 957A: *Ep*.333B: D.xviii 214: xxii 13: lvi 10.

(2) Resumptive. δ' οὖν leads back to the main topic, which has temporarily been lost sight of. This usage, again, is rare in

verse. A.*Pr.*228 ὁ δ' οὖν ἐρωτᾶτ', αἰτίαν καθ' ἥντινα αἰκίζεταί με, τοῦτο δὴ σαφηνιῶ (looking back to 196, ποίῳ λαβών σε Ζεὺς ἐπ' αἰτιάματι οὕτως...αἰκίζεται;): *Ag.*224 ἔτλα δ' οὖν θυτὴρ γενέσθαι θυγατρός (resuming after general reflection in 222–3): S.*OT*971 on the sequence of thought here see *C.R.*xlvii (1933) 165: Hdt.v49.1 (resuming from 38, after a long digression about Cleomenes and Dorieus) ἀπικνέεται δὲ ὦν ὁ Ἀρισταγόρης: Th. i3.4 (looking back to 3.1): ii34.8 (looking back to 34.1): Pl.*Grg.* 513D οὐ πάνυ σοι πείθομαι.—Ὁ δήμου γὰρ ἔρως ... ἐνὼν ἐν τῇ ψυχῇ τῇ σῇ ἀντιστατεῖ μοι· ἀλλ' ἐὰν πολλάκις βέλτιον ταὐτὰ ταῦτα διασκοπώμεθα, πεισθήσῃ. ἀναμνήσθητι δ' οὖν ὅτι δύ' ἔφαμεν εἶναι ...: *Prt.*359B καὶ ἐγὼ εὐθὺς τότε πάνυ ἐθαύμασα τὴν ἀπόκρισιν ... ἠρόμην δ' οὖν τοῦτον: *Euthd.*275D 'How shall I describe the sequel? The Muses must come to my aid. ἤρξατο δ' οὖν ἐνθένδε ποθὲν ὁ Εὐθύδημος' ('Well'): *Cra.*426D τὸ ῥῶ ἔμοιγε φαίνεται ὥσπερ ὄργανον εἶναι πάσης τῆς κινήσεως. Digression on the etymology of κίνησις. τὸ δ' οὖν ῥῶ ...: X.*HG*v3.8 τοῖς δ' οὖν Λακεδαιμονίοις ... (resuming thread of narrative after general reflections in §7): Isoc.xv162 ὅτε γὰρ ἐπαμύνειν ἠρχόμην ... ὅτε δ' οὖν, ὥσπερ εἶπον, ἠρχόμην: D.xviii277 εὖ οἶδ' ὅτι τὴν ἐμὴν δεινότητα ... (then a digression to the effect that it is really popularity that counts, not eloquence) εἰ δ' οὖν ἐστι καὶ παρ' ἐμοί τις ἐμπειρία τοιαύτη ...: xxxv42 ταῦτα γὰρ ἐπαγγέλλεται δεινὸς εἶναι .... πῶς ἂν γένοιντο πονηρότεροι ἄνθρωποι ...; ἐπεὶ δ' οὖν δεινός ἐστιν ... κελεύσατε αὐτὸν διδάξαι ὑμᾶς ('Well, anyhow, since he *is* δεινός'): Hdt.v119.2: viii82.2: ix45.2: Pl.*Phdr.*230E,253E: *Chrm.*158B: *Ap.*36B: *R.*488A: *Ti.*48E.

Often in Herodotus, coming back to what is certain after a digression, long or short, about a debatable detail. iii122 Two possible motives for Oroetes' murder of Polycrates. ὁ δ' ὦν Ὀροίτης ...: vii35.2 'Xerxes ordered the Hellespont to be whipped. I have heard it said that he also ordered it to be branded. ἐνετέλλετο δὲ ὦν ῥαπίζοντας λέγειν ...': i140: ii125: iv180,194: v9.3: 10: vi82.1: vii153.3: 189.3: cf. Th.viii87.6 οὐδὲ ῥᾴδιον εἰδέναι τίνι γνώμῃ παρῆλθεν ἐς τὴν Ἄσπενδον ... ἐς δ' οὖν τὴν Ἄσπενδον ἥτινιδὴ γνώμῃ ὁ Τισσαφέρνης ἀφικνεῖται (looking back to §2): X.*Cyr.*iv1.13.

(3) εἰ δ' οὖν, which Hartung renders 'wenn einmal', and

Kühner 'wenn aber wirklich', is particularly used when a speaker hypothetically grants a supposition which he denies, doubts, or reprobates. It approximates in force to εἰ δὲ δή, 'but if, in reality': whereas εἰ δ' ἄρα means 'but if, contrary to expectation'. 'But if so-and-so *does* happen.'

A.*Ag*.1042 καὶ παῖδα γάρ τοι φασὶν Ἀλκμήνης ποτὲ πραθέντα τλῆναι δουλίας μάζης τυχεῖν. εἰ δ' οὖν ἀνάγκη τῆσδ' ἐπιρρέποι τύχης, ἀρχαιοπλούτων δεσποτῶν πολλὴ χάρις ('Slavery is unpleasant: but if one *must* be a slave . . .'. For the ellipse, *v. schol.*): *Ch*.571 'If the porter keeps me out, I will sit at Aegisthus' doors until people begin to ask why he excludes me. εἰ δ' οὖν ἀμείψω βαλόν ('while if I *do* cross the threshold . . .'): *Fr*. 190. 30–33 Mette ὡς ἐξέτριβες Ἰσθμιαστικήν [. . .] κοὐκ ἠμέλησας ἀλλ' ἐγυμνάζου καλῶς: εἰ δ' οὖν ἐσῴζου τὴν πάλαι παροιμίαν, τοὔρχημα μᾶλλον εἰκὸς ἦν σε [: S.*El*.577 ἀνθ' ὧν βιασθεὶς . . . ἔθυσεν αὐτήν, οὐχὶ Μενέλεω χάριν. εἰ δ' οὖν, ἐρῶ γὰρ καὶ τὸ σόν, κεῖνον θέλων ἐπωφελῆσαι ταῦτ' ἔδρα, τούτου θανεῖν χρῆν αὐτὸν οὕνεκ' ἐκ σέθεν; *OT*851 κοὐκ ἔστιν αὐτῷ τοῦτό γ' ἐκβαλεῖν πάλιν . . . . εἰ δ' οὖν τι κἀκτρέποιτο τοῦ πρόσθεν λόγου . . .: E.*Alc*.850 οὐκ ἔστιν ὅστις αὐτὸν ἐξαιρήσεται . . . . ἢν δ' οὖν ἁμάρτω τῆσδ' ἄγρας . . .: *Heracl*.310 (μὲν . . . ἢν δ' οὖν: as Paley observes, δέ is copulative here, not, as usually, adversative): 714 Παιδὸς μελήσει παισὶ τοῖς λελειμμένοις.—Ἢν δ' οὖν, ὃ μὴ γένοιτο, χρήσωνται τύχῃ: ('But if—and there's the rub— . . .'): *Rh*.572 Φυλάξομαί τοι κἂν σκότῳ τιθεὶς πόδα.—Ἢν δ' οὖν ἐγείρῃς, οἶσθα σύνθημα στρατοῦ; ('But if—which God forbid—you *do* wake anyone . . . ?'): Ar.*Eq*.423 Καὶ ταῦτα δρῶν ἐλάνθανόν γ'· εἰ δ' οὖν ἴδοι τις αὐτῶν . . .: E.*Andr*.163,338: *Or*.1149: *HF*213: *Fr*.460: Ar.*Pax*736: *V*.92: *Av*.577: Pl.*R*.337C ὡς δὴ ὅμοιον τοῦτο ἐκείνῳ.—Οὐδέν γε κωλύει . . .· εἰ δ' οὖν καὶ μὴ ἔστιν ὅμοιον . . .: D.xviii 277 (to be classed, perhaps, rather as resumptive: see (2) above): xlvii 4 μάλιστα μὲν οὖν ἂν ἠβουλόμην μὴ ἔχειν πράγματα· εἰ δ' οὖν ἀναγκάζοι τις . . .: Pl.*Chrm*.160C: *Lg*.664A,711E,840E,860C,917B, 932A: *Plt*.276B: *Phlb*.42E: *R*.388C,494D: *Ep*.336D: X.*Cyr*.v.4. 49: Lys.ix 11: D.lviii 16.

(A.*Ag*.676 is different: Μενέλεων γὰρ οὖν πρῶτόν τε καὶ μάλιστα προσδόκα μολεῖν. εἰ δ' οὖν τις ἀκτὶς ἡλίου νιν ἱστορεῖ . . . ἐλπίς τις αὐτὸν πρὸς δόμους ἥξειν πάλιν ('And, supposing the contrary, still if . . .', Verrall: if so, εἰ δ' οὖν stands for εἰ δ' οὖν ἤδη μὴ ἔμολεν, ὅμως, εἰ. . . . Perhaps, more simply, 'Anyhow he *will* come, if alive', δ' οὖν going with apodosis rather than with protasis.)

In X.*Lac.*13.11, if δ' οὖν is sound (δ' οὖν *AM*: δέ *C*), it comes near to δὲ δή in force (cf. *supr.* I.2), sharply contrasting the all-embracing initial authority of the king with the subsequent delegation of that authority to special officials: καὶ ἄρχονται μὲν πάντες ἀπὸ βασιλέως, ὅταν βούλωνται πρᾶξαί τι. ἢν δ' οὖν δίκης δεόμενός τις ἔλθῃ, πρὸς ἑλλανοδίκας τοῦτον ὁ βασιλεὺς ἀποπέμπει, ἢν δὲ χρημάτων, πρὸς ταμίας. In Pl.*R.*365E δ' οὖν brushes aside the possibility of disbelieving the poets: οἷς ἢ ἀμφότερα ἢ οὐδέτερα πειστέον. εἰ δ' οὖν πειστέον, ἀδικητέον.

Occasionally the εἰ clause is elliptical, and εἰ δ' οὖν virtually stands for εἰ δὲ μή. S.*Ant.*722 φήμ' ἔγωγε πρεσβεύειν πολὺ φῦναί τιν' ἄνδρα πάντ' ἐπιστήμης πλέων· εἰ δ' οὖν, φιλεῖ γὰρ τοῦτο μὴ ταύτῃ ῥέπειν, καὶ τῶν λεγόντων εὖ καλὸν τὸ μανθάνειν: E.*Hipp.*508 Εἴ τοι δοκεῖ σοι, χρῆν μὲν οὔ σ' ἁμαρτάνειν· εἰ δ' οὖν, πιθοῦ μοι· δευτέρα γὰρ ἡ χάρις: Hp.*Vict.*89 οἶνον δὲ μὴ πίνειν· εἰ δ' οὖν, λευκόν (some MSS.): Pl.*Ap.*34D οὐκ ἀξιῶ μὲν γὰρ ἔγωγε, εἰ δ' οὖν.

Hp.*Nat.Mul.*10 is different: καὶ ἢν μὴ δάκνῃ, ἀπὸ τοῦ ἐγκεφάλου φάναι (χρὴ) εἶναι τὸ ῥεῦμα· εἰ δ' οὖν, ἀπὸ τῆς κοιλίης (some MSS.): here οὖν simply stresses the contrast between positive and negative suppositions: 'Whereas if it *does* . . .'.

(4) Permissive. δ' οὖν is often used in the dialogue of drama (there is no trace of this idiom in prose dialogue: see, however, Hdt.ix48.4, under (5) below) to denote that the speaker waives any objection that he has, or might be supposed to have, to something being done, or contemplated, by another person. The verb is in the imperative, 2nd or 3rd person. The particles are almost invariably preceded by σύ or ὁ (ἡ, οἱ), and the expression nearly always forms the opening of a speech. The tone is usually defiant or contemptuous.

A.*Pr.*935 Ἀλλ' ἆθλον ἄν σοι τοῦδ' ἔτ' ἀλγίω πόροι.—Ὁ δ' οὖν ποιείτω: *Eu.*226 Τὸν ἄνδρ' ἐκεῖνον οὔ τι μὴ λίπω ποτέ.—Σὺ δ' οὖν δίωκε: S.*OC*1205 Τέκνον, βαρεῖαν ἡδονὴν νικᾶτέ με λέγοντες· ἔστω δ' οὖν ὅπως ὑμῖν φίλον: E.*Andr.*258 Πῦρ σοι προσοίσω . . .—Σὺ δ' οὖν κάταιθε: Ar.*Ach.*186 οἱ δ' ἐδίωκον κἀβόων.—Οἱ δ' οὖν βοώντων ('Well, *let* them shout'): *Nu.*39 Ἔασον . . . καταδαρθεῖν τί με.—Σὺ δ' οὖν κάθευδε: *V.*764 (the concession takes the form of a compromise): *Av.*56 *Πι.* . . . τῷ σκέλει θένε τὴν πέτραν.—*Ευ.* Σὺ δὲ τῇ κεφαλῇ γ', ἵν' ᾖ διπλάσιος ὁ ψόφος.—*Πι.* Σὺ δ' οὖν λίθῳ κόψον λαβών (Peithetaerus admits that Euelpides has held his own in the contest of wits: 'missis iocis', van Leeuwen: 'All right then, seriously, knock with a stone'): *Ra.*31 *Δι.* (abandoning his thesis that the donkey, not Xanthias, is carrying the load) Σὺ δ' οὖν, ἐπειδὴ τὸν ὄνον οὐ φῄς σ' ὠφελεῖν, ἐν τῷ μέρει σὺ τὸν ὄνον ἀράμενος φέρε ('All right, then'). (In the last three examples δ' οὖν, while making a concession, goes on to make a fresh suggestion, thus trenching on the province of δ' ἀλλά.) Exceptionally, in mid speech: Ar.*Lys.*491 ἀεί τινα κορκορυγὴν ἐκύκων. οἱ δ' οὖν τοῦδ' οὕνεκα δρώντων ὅ τι βούλονται. S.*Tr.*329,1157: *Aj.*114,961: *El.*891: *OT*669: E.*HF*726: *Rh.* 336,868: Ar.*V.*6: *Th.*612.

In S.*Ant.*751 Ἡ δ' οὖν θανεῖται καὶ θανοῦσ' ὀλεῖ τινα, Hartung's ἡ δ' οὖν is adopted in the *O.C.T.*, against MSS. and scholia: 'Very well, then, she shall die'. If correct, this is a solitary instance of permissive δ' οὖν with the indicative: but see Jebb. The interpretation of Ar.*V.*1154 is uncertain.

(5) Apodotic. δ' οὖν is very occasionally found *in apodosi*, like the far commoner apodotic δέ. Hdt.v 50.2 χρεὸν γάρ μιν μὴ λέγειν τὸ ἐόν, βουλόμενόν γε Σπαρτιήτας ἐξαγαγεῖν ἐς τὴν Ἀσίην, λέγει δ' ὦν τριῶν μηνῶν φὰς εἶναι τὴν ἄνοδον: ix 48.4 καὶ ἢν μὲν δοκῇ καὶ τοὺς ἄλλους μάχεσθαι, οἱ δ' ὦν μετέπειτα μαχέσθων ὕστεροι: A.*Eu.*887 ἀλλ' εἰ μὲν ἁγνόν ἐστί σοι Πειθοῦς σέβας . . ., σὺ δ' οὖν μένοις ἄν (where Verrall and other editors deny that the sense is continuous). In the last two examples apodotic and permissive are perhaps blended.

In the following, δ' οὖν is hardly to be regarded as apodotic, since we may reasonably assume an anacoluthon after the parenthesis. Pl.*Men.*98B ἀλλ' εἴπερ τι ἄλλο φαίην ἂν εἰδέναι—ὀλίγα δ' ἂν φαίην—ἓν δ' οὖν καὶ τοῦτο ἐκείνων θείην ἂν ὧν οἶδα: *R.*330E καὶ αὐτός—ἤτοι ὑπὸ τῆς τοῦ γήρως ἀσθενείας ἢ καὶ . . .—ὑποψίας δ' οὖν καὶ δείματος μεστὸς γίγνεται: *Ti.*28B: *Lg.*698E, 811C.

III. Textual difficulties. γοῦν and δ' οὖν are liable to be confused in MSS. In Th.i63.1 and vii82.1 δ' οὖν is read, no doubt rightly, by Poppo and Dobree respectively, for γοῦν: so too by Bekker in Pl.*Lg.*634D and by Elmsley in E.*El.*508. Contrariwise, in Ar.*Av.*1027 Dobree's γοῦν (*sane*, van Leeuwen) for δ' οὖν seems required. I should suggest γοῦν in Pl.*Lg.*653A φρόνησιν δὲ καὶ ἀληθεῖς δόξας βεβαίους εὐτυχὲς ὅτῳ καὶ πρὸς τὸ γῆρας παρεγένετο· τέλεος δ' οὖν ἔστ' ἄνθρωπος ταῦτα . . . κεκτημένος ἀγαθά (des Places, p. 211, renders δ' οὖν 'en tout cas (= quoi qu'il en soit de leur possibilité)'). In *Prm.*130E Proclus's δ' οὖν is certainly more idiomatic than οὖν (*BT*). In X.*Cyr.*viii7.9 Hertlein's δ' οὖν has the merit of accounting for both οὖν and δὲ νῦν, and may perhaps be right, though the sense certainly seems to require οὖν. In Aen.Tact.18.21 δ' οὖν is clearly impossible (and Schoene's δοῦν = δὴ οὖν most unlikely). In *id.*7.1 οὖν (or possibly γοῦν: *q.v.* II) seems to be required. In S.*OT*310 Jebb's σύ νυν is probably right (σὺ νῦν L^{ac}: σὺ δ' οὖν *rec.*) In Is.i10 read, probably, τότε δ' οὖν (for ὅτι γοῦν: see γοῦν, II *ad fin.*). In E.*Or.*530 Hermann's δ' οὖν is perhaps right: but οὖν may possibly stand, as introducing a new point, 'Now, one thing . . .'.

καὶ . . . δὲ οὖν, a stronger form of καὶ . . . δέ, seems only to occur in Pl.*Epin.*977B καὶ τὴν ἄλλην δὲ οὖν φρόνησιν (if the text is sound).

Οὖν δή : δὴ οὖν

These combinations, very common in Herodotus and Plato, are rarely found elsewhere (never in the tragedians, except for οὖν δή in Sophocles.) Klotz observes (ii418) that in Attic they are especially used in questions. This is certainly true of Plato, except that in the *Timaeus*, a dialogue which, by reason of its form, contains few questions, οὖν δή is predominantly used in statements. On the whole, οὖν δή tends to replace δὴ οὖν in Plato's later works. Thus, in the *Timaeus* and *Laws* the proportions of οὖν δή to δὴ οὖν are 14 to 1 and 48 to 4 respectively: and in *Sophist*, *Politicus*, *Philebus*, *Timaeus*, *Critias*, and *Laws* combined, as compared with the earlier dialogues, the proportions are, οὖν δή, 83 to 48: δὴ οὖν 4 to 52 (des Places, p. 85, who refers to H. Kallenberg, *Rh.M.*lxviii(1913)465–76).

On the other hand, in the fairly early *Gorgias*, δὴ οὖν is not found, while οὖν δή occurs 7 times: while in the slightly later *Phaedrus* δὴ οὖν occurs 11 times, as against οὖν δή twice.[1]

It appears impossible to distinguish in meaning between οὖν δή and δὴ οὖν. Kühner (II ii 162) renders 'also offenbar' and 'offenbar also'. But, as both οὖν and δή are used both for connexion and for emphasis, we may perhaps regard the earlier particle in each combination as connective, the second as ancillary. 'Ils ne se distinguent pas dans la pratique', des Places observes. In Hdt.iii 130.2 neither particle is connective: ὁ δὲ ἐνθαῦτα δὴ ὦν ἐκφαίνει: so, too, in places where οὖν δή, δὴ οὖν reinforce other particles (see below).

οὖν δή. S.*Aj.*873 Τί οὖν δή; *Tr.*153 πάθη μὲν οὖν δὴ πόλλ' ἔγωγ' ἐκλαυσάμην: Hdt.i 11.4 οὐκ ὦν δὴ ἔπειθε: 84.4 ὁ ὦν δὴ Ὑροιάδης οὗτος: 115.3 εἰ ὦν δὴ τοῦδε εἵνεκα ἄξιός τευ κακοῦ εἰμι: 174.3 τὸ ὦν δὴ ὀλίγον τοῦτο (after parenthesis): Pl.*Cra.*409E Τί οὖν δή; 440D ἴσως μὲν οὖν δὴ . . . οὕτως ἔχει, ἴσως δὲ καὶ οὔ: *Tht.* 195E ἴθι οὖν δή, σὺ ἀποκρίνου: *R.*359B ἡ μὲν οὖν δὴ φύσις δικαιοσύνης αὕτη τε καὶ τοιαύτη: 360D ταῦτα μὲν οὖν δὴ οὕτω: 360E τίς οὖν δὴ ἡ διάστασις; 459A Πῶς οὖν δὴ ὠφελιμώτατοι ἔσονται; X.*HG*v 3.5 πολλοὶ μὲν οὖν δὴ καὶ ἄλλοι: *Lac.*2.7 ταῦτα οὖν δὴ πάντα (δή *om.* Stob.): Hdt.v 63.1: 96.2: *id. saep.*[2]: Hp. *Genit.*51 (χρή *pro* δή *vulg.*): Pl.*Ti.*21B,24C,26D,27D,30B: *id. saep.*

οὐκοῦν δή: Pl.*R.*459E. In Lys.xxix 4 read, probably, οὔκουν δήπου γ' ὡς (*C.R.*xliv(1930)214).

[1] My statistics are based partly on des Places, partly on unpublished notes of R. W. Chapman. I have not troubled to reconcile slight differences originating in different methods of computation. The two sets of figures agree as near as matters.

[2] The following table (the exact accuracy of which I cannot guarantee) of the examples of ὦν δή, δὴ ὦν in Herodotus, shows that these combinations are, on the whole, rarer in Books VII–IX, which were perhaps written first:—

	ὦν δή	δὴ ὦν		ὦν δή	δὴ ὦν
Book I	8	16	Book VI	5	3
II	6	3	VII	3	1
III	5	12	VIII	—	1
IV	3	3	IX	—	1
V	2	2		—	—
			Total	32	42

δὴ οὖν: Hdt.i18 οὗτος δὴ ὢν ὁ Κανδαύλης: 30 αὐτῶν δὴ ὢν τούτων καὶ τῆς θεωρίης ἐκδημήσας ὁ Σόλων εἵνεκεν: 34,58,59, 69.75,80,82,94: *id. saep.*: Pl.*Euthphr.*4D ταῦτα δὴ οὖν καὶ ἀγανακτεῖ ὅ τε πατήρ: *Cra.*408E Τί δὴ οὖν πρῶτον βούλει; *Tht.* 150C εἰμὶ δὴ οὖν αὐτὸς μὲν οὐ πάνυ τι σοφός: 151D πάλιν δὴ οὖν ἐξ ἀρχῆς ... πειρῶ λέγειν: *R.*369E Τί δὴ οὖν; 497C δῆλος δὴ οὖν εἶ: *Ti.*24D ᾠκεῖτε δὴ οὖν: *id. saep.*: Hp.*Acut.*13.

δὴ ... οὖν: Pl.*Lg.*802E τὸ δὴ μεγαλοπρεπὲς οὖν (here δή seems to go closely with τὸ μεγαλοπρεπές, while οὖν gives the connexion: cf. *Lg.*926A Τί δή τις οὖν ... δρῶν ...;)

δὴ οὖν and οὖν δή reinforcing other particles.[1] Hdt.v124.2 εἴτε δὴ ὢν ... εἴτε (viii 54): Pl.*R.*507A τοῦτον δὲ δὴ οὖν τὸν τόκον ... κομίσασθε: 619B καὶ δὴ οὖν καὶ τότε (οὖν *om.* Proclus): *Lg.*775B οὔτε ... οὔτ' οὖν δή: *Alc.I* 108D ὥσπερ ἐκεῖ ἐγὼ ... καὶ σὺ δὴ οὖν οὕτως ἐνταῦθα τί φῄς; γοῦν δή (only in replies, in Plato: the converse form, γε δὴ οὖν, is not found: R. W. C.): *Sph.*232C Λέγεται γοῦν δή (γοῦν *W*: οὖν *BT*): 232E (δή *W*: *om. BT*): *Plt.*270B,311A: *Lg.*679D.

For γὰρ οὖν δή, see γὰρ οὖν, (4) and (5).

ἀτὰρ οὖν δή: Pl.*Chrm.*154B: *Plt.*269D.

οὖν δή universalizing a relative: Pl.*Lg.*789D ὁπωσοῦν δή.

For οὖν δήπου, see δήπου, *ad fin.*

(For a full list of examples of οὖν δή, δὴ οὖν in Plato, see des Places.)

Μὲν οὖν

We have seen that μέν may be either prospective, adversative (possibly) or affirmative: while οὖν may be either retrospective, logical-progressive, or ancillary and emphatic. Hence the combination of the particles presents a considerable diversity of usage.

(1) Retrospective and transitional οὖν with prospective μέν. μὲν οὖν occurs in the Homeric poems with increasing proportionate

[1] It is hardly worth while to tabulate instances of the collocation of preparatory μέν with connective οὖν δή, δὴ οὖν: μὲν οὖν δή, often in Plato: *Phd.*112E, *Cra.*440D (for which, and for S.*Tr.*153, X.*HG*v3.5, see p. 469): μὲν δὴ οὖν Pl.*Phdr.*252E,256A.

frequency, once in the *Iliad*, five times in the *Odyssey*, and four times in the *Hymns*. In the examples from the *Iliad* and *Odyssey* there is always a backward reference, as in ἐπεὶ οὖν and ὡς οὖν, and usually an echoed word. *I* 550 (543 τὸν δ' . . . ἀπέκτεινεν Μελέαγρος) . . . ὄφρα μὲν οὖν Μελέαγρος ἀρηΐφιλος πολέμιζε, τόφρα δὲ . . .: δ780 βὰν δ' ἰέναι ἐπὶ νῆα θοήν . . . νῆα μὲν οὖν πάμπρωτον . . .: χ448 (437 ἄρχετε νῦν νέκυας φορέειν) . . . πρῶτα μὲν οὖν νέκυας φόρεον: ν122: ο361: ψ142. So, too, *h.Merc.*62 θεὸς δ' ὑπὸ καλὸν ἄειδεν . . . καὶ τὰ μὲν οὖν ἄειδε, τὰ δὲ φρεσὶν ἄλλα μενοίνα: 350. But in the two remaining passages in the *Hymns* μὲν οὖν is purely transitional, 'now': *h.Merc.*577 πᾶσι δ' ὅ γε θνητοῖσι καὶ ἀθανάτοισιν ὁμιλεῖ· παῦρα μὲν οὖν ὀνίνησι, τὸ δ' ἄκριτον ἠπεροπεύει (introducing an explanation of ὁμιλεῖ): *h.Cer.*33 τὴν δ' ἀεκαζομένην ἦγεν . . . ὄφρα μὲν οὖν γαῖάν τε καὶ οὐρανὸν ἀστερόεντα λεῦσσε θεά . . . . It will be noticed in the above examples that μὲν οὖν always comes near the beginning of a sentence, and that, except in two passages which start with καί (ν122: *h.Merc.*62), there is no formal connecting particle. Clearly οὖν, in μὲν οὖν, is well on the way to becoming a connective.

The Pindaric examples (except *N.*6.10: see (2)), and some of the Aeschylean, are purely transitional. Pi.*P.*3.82 ἓν παρ' ἐσλὸν πήματα σύνδυο δαίονται βροτοῖς ἀθάνατοι. τὰ μὲν ὦν οὐ δύνανται νήπιοι κόσμῳ φέρειν, ἀλλ' ἀγαθοί (after describing divine dispensations, it is natural to go on to describe how men bear them: 'Now these ills fools cannot endure'): *O.*1.111: *P.*3.47: *I.*4.7: *Fr.*234(42).3: A.*Pr.*827 'I will describe Io's wanderings up to the present time. ὄχλον μὲν οὖν τὸν πλεῖστον ἐκλείψω λόγων, πρὸς αὐτὸ δ' εἶμι τέρμα σῶν πλανημάτων' ('Now,' 'Well'): *Ch.*700 ('Well, I wish I had brought better tidings': μέν answered by ⟨δέ⟩ in 704): *Th.*615 'Amphiaraus will be involved in the ruin of his evil associates. δοκῶ μὲν οὖν σφε μηδὲ προσβαλεῖν πύλαις . . . ὅμως δ' ἐπ' αὐτῷ φῶτα . . . ἀντιτάξομεν' (after his moralizing, Eteocles turns to the business in hand: 'Well'): *Supp.*134 (μέν answered by δέ in 138).

From the second half of the fifth century, the transitional use of μὲν οὖν is very common. The following verse examples are mostly from Bäumlein: S.*OT* 843 Λῃστὰς ἔφασκες αὐτὸν ἄνδρας ἐννέπειν ὥς νιν κατακτείνειαν. εἰ μὲν οὖν ἔτι λέξει τὸν αὐτὸν ἀριθμόν, οὐκ ἐγὼ 'κτανον . . . εἰ δ' . . . ('Now, if . . .'): *Fr.*420: E.*El.*1270 'You will be acquitted before the Areopagus. δειναὶ μὲν οὖν θεαὶ τῷδ' ἄχει πεπληγμέναι . . . χάσμα δύσονται χθονός, . . . σὲ δ' . . .': 1284 (after directions for the burial of Aegisthus and Clytaemnestra) Πυλάδης μὲν οὖν . . . οἰκάδ' ἐσπορευέτω . . . σὺ δ' . . .: *Ion*1518: *IT*968: *Ph.*438,465,861: *Hec.*1192.

This transitional use is very frequent in prose. E.g. Th.i.138.5 νοσήσας δὲ τελευτᾷ τὸν βίον . . . μνημεῖον μὲν οὖν αὐτοῦ ἐν Μαγνησίᾳ ἐστὶ . . . τὰ δὲ ὀστᾶ φασὶ . . . . Often the μέν clause sums up and rounds off the old topic, while the δέ clause introduces the new one (cf. μὲν δή, p. 258). Hdt.i4 (after describing various ἁρπαγαί) μέχρι μὲν ὦν τούτου ἁρπαγὰς μούνας εἶναι παρ' ἀλλήλων, τὸ δ' ἀπὸ τούτου . . .: Th.i15 τὰ μὲν οὖν ναυτικὰ τῶν Ἑλλήνων τοιαῦτα ἦν . . . ἰσχὺν δὲ περιεποιήσαντο . . .: Ant. i13 ταῦτα μὲν οὖν μέχρι τούτου· περὶ δὲ τῶν γενομένων . . . . Very common in Aristotle: *Pol.*1255b39 περὶ μὲν οὖν δούλου καὶ δεσπότου τοῦτον διωρίσθω τὸν τρόπον. ὅλως δὲ περὶ πάσης κτήσεως . . . . In Pl.*Grg.*465D–E μὲν οὖν comes four times, only the last being answered by δέ: as des Places (p. 92) picturesquely puts it: 'Les trois premiers μὲν οὖν sont de fausses sorties, il entr'ouvre la porte qu'il ouvre pour de bon avec le δέ de 466A2.'

I have grouped together above, as 'transitional', passages ranging from the Homeric *Hymns* to Aristotle. It may appear artificial to talk of 'transitional' μὲν οὖν in speaking of late fifth- and fourth-century literature, by which time οὖν, by itself, has become firmly established as a transitional (and inferential) particle. The transitional force, it might be urged, resides in οὖν alone, which is no more essentially connected with μέν than γάρ is in μὲν γάρ. This objection may be answered by pointing out that μὲν οὖν is already used in transitions, in the Homeric *Hymns*, Pindar, and Aeschylus, at a period when the connective force of οὖν has not yet been developed. (This use of μὲν οὖν may, in fact, have contributed to the development of independent connective οὖν.) Quite possibly (though one cannot be certain) Pindar and Aeschylus felt οὖν as emphasizing μέν, as in (2) below, not as supplying a connexion, whereas Thucydides and Demosthenes cannot have felt it so. Nevertheless, although with different view-points (by 'view-points' I do not mean to imply that the ancient authors theorized about the matter), μὲν οὖν is used both by earlier and by later writers in transitions. And it is for this reason that I group the later and the earlier passages together (while not thinking it appropriate to quote here passages in which οὖν, in μὲν οὖν, has its later, strictly inferential, force). The development of the transitional use of μὲν δή (see pp. 258–9) is closely parallel.

(2) Οὖν emphasizing a prospective μέν. Cf. μὲν δή, p. 258. This usage is not adequately recognized by theorists, and it is rare enough to be a stumbling-block to copyists and editors.[1] It is commoner in Hippocrates and Aristotle than elsewhere: unknown to Aeschylus (except, possibly, *Ch.*931), Euripides, Aristophanes, and the Attic orators (except for one instance in Hyperides: in Lys.xix 60 the second οὖν (*om.* Aldus) is no doubt caused by μὲν οὖν just before).

Xenoph.*Fr.*34 καὶ τὸ μὲν οὖν σαφὲς οὔτις ἀνὴρ γένετ᾽ . . . εἰδὼς ἀμφὶ θεῶν . . . δόκος δ᾽ ἐπὶ πᾶσι τέτυκται: Emp.*Fr.*15 ὄφρα μὲν . . . τόφρα μὲν οὖν εἰσιν . . . πρὶν δὲ . . . οὐδὲν ἄρ᾽ εἰσιν: Melanipp.*Fr.*4 τάχα δὴ τάχα τοὶ μὲν οὖν ἀπωλλύοντο, τοὶ δὲ παράπληκτον χέον ὀμφάν: Pi.*N.*6.10 ἀρούραισιν, αἵτ᾽ ἀμειβόμεναι τόκα μὲν ὦν βίον ἄνδρασιν . . . ἔδοσαν, τόκα δ᾽ αὖτ᾽ ἀναπαυσάμεναι σθένος ἔμαρψαν: A.*Ch.*931 Στένω μὲν οὖν . . . ἐπεὶ δὲ . . . (οὖν, 'it is true', Tucker: but perhaps transitional, 'Well, I lament'): S.*OT*498 ἀλλ᾽ ὁ μὲν οὖν Ζεὺς ὅ τ᾽ Ἀπόλλων ξυνετοί . . . ἀνδρῶν δ᾽ ὅτι μάντις πλέον ἢ 'γὼ φέρεται, κρίσις οὐκ ἔστιν ἀληθής: *Ant.*925 ἀλλ᾽ εἰ μὲν οὖν τάδ᾽ ἐστὶν ἐν θεοῖς καλὰ . . . εἰ δ᾽ οἵδ᾽ ἁμαρτάνουσι . . . (Jebb's note, 'ἀλλ᾽ οὖν, "well then"', is most misleading): Th.iii 101.2 καὶ αὐτοὶ πρῶτοι δόντες ὁμήρους καὶ τοὺς ἄλλους ἔπεισαν δοῦναι . . ., πρῶτον μὲν οὖν τοὺς ὁμόρους . . . ἔπειτα Ἰπνέας: iv 104.5 καὶ ἐβούλετο φθάσαι μάλιστα μὲν οὖν τὴν Ἀμφίπολιν, πρίν τι ἐνδοῦναι, εἰ δὲ μή, τὴν Ἠιόνα προκαταλαβών: Pl.*Phd.*90E προθυμητέον ὑγιῶς ἔχειν, σοὶ μὲν οὖν καὶ τοῖς ἄλλοις καὶ τοῦ ἔπειτα βίου παντὸς ἕνεκα, ἐμοὶ δὲ αὐτοῦ ἕνεκα

[1] Kühner (II ii 157), remarking that 'οὖν weist auf das Vorhergehende hin, und dient zugleich (*sic*) zur Kräftigung des μέν', confuses two idioms which, in post-Homeric Greek, are kept quite distinct, and indiscriminately groups some of the examples which I am about to give with others given under (1).

τοῦ θανάτου: *Ti.*29B ὧδε οὖν ... διοριστέον, ὡς ἄρα τοὺς λόγους, ὧνπέρ εἰσιν ἐξηγηταί, τούτων αὐτῶν καὶ συγγενεῖς ὄντας· τοῦ μὲν οὖν μονίμου ... μονίμους ... τοὺς δὲ τοῦ πρὸς μὲν ἐκεῖνο ἀπεικασθέντος, ὄντος δὲ εἰκόνος εἰκότας ἀνὰ λόγον τε ἐκείνων ὄντας (οὖν *secl.* Wilamowitz): *Plt.*269D ὃν δὲ οὐρανὸν καὶ κόσμον ἐπωνομάκαμεν, πολλῶν μὲν οὖν ... μετείληφεν, ἀτὰρ οὖν δὴ κεκοινώνηκέ γε καὶ σώματος (μὲν οὖν *B*: μέν *cett.*): X.*An.*iv7.2 ἐπεὶ δ' ἀφίκοντο ... Χειρίσοφος μὲν οὖν ... προσέβαλλεν ... ἐπειδὴ δὲ ... (οὖν *om. dett.*): *Ages.*7.7 εἰ δ' αὖ καλὸν καὶ μισοπέρσην εἶναι, ὅτι καὶ ὁ πάλαι ἐξεστράτευσεν ..., ὁρῶσι μὲν οὖν ἅπαντες ταῦτα· ἐπεμελήθη δὲ τίς ἄλλος πώποτε πλὴν Ἀγησίλαος ...; (but οὖν might be resumptive here, with anacoluthon): *Eq.*6 14 (οὖν: *fort.* σύν, Marchant, with very great probability): *HG*v3.7 μάλιστα μὲν οὖν ... ἀτὰρ ... (οὖν *del.* Cobet): Hyp. *Ath.*11 καὶ τῶν ἐράνων εἷς μὲν οὖν, Δικαιοκράτης, ἐνεγέγραπτο, οὗ ἦσαν λοιπαὶ τρεῖς φοραί· οὗτος μὲν .... (οὗ *pro* οὖν *B*).

In two Platonic passages (see des Places, pp. 104–5, 117–8), which are perhaps to be similarly explained, μὲν οὖν introduces an answer; but perhaps οὖν is connective, 'well': cf. the use of οὐκοῦν and τοίνυν in answers (Introd. II.5.i.). *Phlb.*51B Πῶς δὴ ταῦτα ... αὖ λέγομεν οὕτω;—Πάνυ μὲν οὖν οὐκ εὐθὺς δῆλά ἐστιν ἃ λέγω, πειρατέον μὴν δηλοῦν (οὖν *secl.* Badham: see also (4) below): *Sph.*229D Τί δὲ ... λεκτέον;—Οἶμαι μὲν οὖν ... (οὖν *om. W* Stobaeus): cf. X.*HG*vi3.13 (οὖν *om. CF*).

Hippocrates and Aristotle. Hp.*Fract.*4 ἔπειτα ἐπιδεῖν τῷ ὀθονίῳ, τὴν ἀρχὴν βαλλόμενος κατὰ τὸ κατήγημα· ἐρείδων μὲν οὖν, μὴ πιέζων δὲ κάρτα (οὖν *secl.* Withington): *Int.*49 τούτῳ ἢν μὲν οὖν ξυμφέρῃ ... ἢν δὲ μὴ ξυμφέρῃ (μέν *om. H*: οὖν *om. K*): *Fist.*9 μανδραγόρου ῥίζαν μάλιστα μὲν χλωρήν, εἰ δὲ μή, ξηρήν, τὴν μὲν οὖν χλωρὴν ... τὴν δέ γε ξηρὴν ...: *Art.*14 ἄλλοι δ' αὖ τινές εἰσιν οἵτινες ... ἐπιδέουσι μὲν οὖν ... ζώσαντες δὲ ... (οὖν *om. CEKL*): *Mochl.* 2,21: *Foet.Exsect.*5: *Vict.*75,82,89: Arist.*Po.*1458a25 ἢ αἴνιγμα ἔσται ἢ βαρβαρισμός· ἂν μὲν οὖν ἐκ μεταφορῶν, αἴνιγμα, ἐὰν δ' ἐκ γλωττῶν, βαρβαρισμός: *Rh.* 1387a33 καὶ τὸν ἥττω τῷ κρείττονι ἀμφισβητεῖν, μάλιστα μὲν οὖν τοὺς ἐν τῷ αὐτῷ ... εἰ δὲ μὴ ... (οὖν omitted in some MSS.): *Pol.*1252b29 πόλις ... γινομένη μὲν οὖν τοῦ ζῆν ἕνεκεν, οὖσα δὲ τοῦ εὖ ζῆν: 1316a9,1329b3: *EN*1141a11 (οὖν omitted in some MSS.): *SE*169a19.

(3) *Οὖν* emphasizing an adversative or affirmative *μέν*. This use, first found in Aeschylus, is common in verse and prose dialogue, very rare in continuous speech.

(i) In dialogue. Adversative. 'No': 'on the contrary': 'rather'. A.*Ag.*1090 *Πρὸς τὴν Ἀτρειδῶν* (*στέγην σ' ἤγαγεν*) ...—*Μισόθεον μὲν οὖν*: S.*Aj.*1363 *δειλοὺς* ...—*Ἄνδρας μὲν οὖν* ... *ἐνδίκους*: *Ph.*1378 *Ἢ πρὸς τὰ Τροίας πεδία* ...;—*Πρὸς τοὺς μὲν οὖν σε* ... *παύσοντας ἄλγους*: E.*Hel.*1631–2 *εἰ μή μ' ἐάσεις*— —*Οὐ μὲν οὖν σ' ἐάσομεν*.—*Σύγγονον κτανεῖν κακίστην*— —*Εὐσεβεστάτην μὲν οὖν*: *Or.*1521 *Μὴ πέτρος γένῃ δέδοικας* ...;—*Μὴ μὲν οὖν νεκρός*: Ar.*Eq.*911 *Ἀπομυξάμενος* ... *μου πρὸς τὴν κεφαλὴν ἀποψῶ*.—*Ἐμοῦ μὲν οὖν*.—*Ἐμοῦ μὲν οὖν*: *Nu.*71 "*ὅταν* ... *ἅρμ' ἐλαύνῃς* ..." *ἐγὼ δ' ἔφην*, "*Ὅταν μὲν οὖν τὰς αἶγας* ...": *V.*898 *τίμημα κλῳὸς σύκινος*.—*Θάνατος μὲν οὖν κύνειος*: S.*El.*1503: *OT*705: E.*Cyc.*546: *Alc.*821,1113: *Or.* 1511: *IA*893,1537: *Rh.*687: *Hec.*1261: Ar.*Ach.*285: *Eq.*13: *Nu.* 220,1112: *V.*515,953,1377,1421: *Av.*292: *Ra.*556: Pl.*Grg.*466A *κολακεία δοκεῖ σοί εἶναι ἡ ῥητορική*;—*Κολακείας μὲν οὖν ἔγωγε εἶπον μόριον*: *Smp.*201C *σοὶ οὐκ ἂν δυναίμην ἀντιλέγειν* ...—*Οὐ μὲν οὖν τῇ ἀληθείᾳ* ... *δύνασαι ἀντιλέγειν*: *Chrm.*161D *ἢ σὺ οὐδὲν ἡγῇ πράττειν τὸν γραμματιστὴν* ...;—*Ἔγωγε ἡγοῦμαι μὲν οὖν*, *ἔφη* ('On the contrary, I *do* think that he does something'): *Cra.*405A *ἄτοπον* ...—*Εὐάρμοστον μὲν οὖν*: *Tht.*165A *σοὶ λέγω ὅπῃ, ἢ Θεαιτήτῳ*;—*Εἰς τὸ κοινὸν μὲν οὖν*: *Lg.*657A *Θαυμαστὸν λέγεις*.—*Νομοθετικὸν μὲν οὖν*: *Phlb.*25B *Σὺ καὶ ἐμοὶ φράσεις, ὡς οἶμαι*.—*Θεὸς μὲν οὖν*: 34D *οὐδὲν γὰρ ἀπολοῦμεν*.—*Ἀπολοῦμεν μὲν οὖν ταῦτά γε* ('doch'): *Alc.I*129E *Οὐκ ἔχω λέγειν*.—*Ἔχεις μὲν οὖν, ὅτι γε* ...: X.*Mem.*iii 8.4 *Ἆρ' οὖν, ἔφη, πάντα ὅμοια ἀλλήλοις*;—*Ὡς οἷόν τε μὲν οὖν, ἔφη, ἀνομοιότατα ἔνια*: Pl.*Lg.* 673A *οὐκ οἶδ' ὅντινα τρόπον ὠνομάσαμεν μουσικήν*.—*Ὀρθῶς μὲν οὖν* (contradicting the disparaging *οὐκ οἶδ' ὅντινα τρόπον*). *Cri.* 44B: *Grg.*470B: *R.*531C: *Lg.*694E: 832A.

(ii) The second speaker, while agreeing with what the first has said, as far as it goes, shows that he regards it as inadequate by substituting a stronger form of expression. A.*Pers.*1032 *Παπαῖ, παπαῖ*.—*Καὶ πλέον ἢ παπαῖ μὲν οὖν*: S.*OC*31 *Ἦ δεῦρο προσστείχοντα κἀξορμώμενον* (*ὁρᾷς τὸν ἄνδρα*);—*Καὶ δὴ μὲν οὖν παρόντα*: E.*Andr.*837 *Ἀλγεῖς, φόνον ῥάψασα συγγάμῳ σέθεν*;—

Κατὰ μὲν οὖν στένω δαΐας τόλμας: Ar.*Av.*1387 Ἐκ τῶν νεφελῶν γὰρ ἄν τις ἀναβολὰς λάβοι;—Κρέμαται μὲν οὖν ἐντεῦθεν ἡμῶν ἡ τέχνη: *Ra.*612 ὑπερφυᾶ.—Σχέτλια μὲν οὖν καὶ δεινά: *Ec.*377 Ἤδη λέλυται γάρ (ἡ ἐκκλησία);—Νὴ Δί' ὄρθριον μὲν οὖν: *Pl.* 1036 Οὐκ ἀλλὰ κατασέσηπας...—Διὰ δακτυλίου μὲν οὖν ἐμέγ' ἂν διελκύσαις: Pherecr.*Fr.*70.2 Ὑδαρῆ 'νέχεέν σοι;—Παντάπασι μὲν οὖν ὕδωρ: Anaxandr *Fr.*3.3 ἐκάρωσεν ὑμᾶς.—Ἀνακεχαίτικεν μὲν οὖν: Pl.*Phdr.*234D οὐχ ὑπερφυῶς...;—Δαιμονίως μὲν οὖν: *Euthphr.*8C ἤδη τινὸς ἤκουσας ἀμφισβητοῦντος...;—Οὐδὲν μὲν οὖν παύονται ταῦτα ἀμφισβητοῦντες: *Phd.*99D βούλει...;—Ὑπερφυῶς μὲν οὖν, ἔφη, ὡς βούλομαι: *Cra.*391E ἢ σὺ οὐκ οἴει;—Εὖ οἶδα μὲν οὖν ἔγωγε (*R.*556E: X.*Cyr.*v 2.29): *Tht.*181B ὅρα ... εἰ λυσιτελεῖ...—Οὐδὲν μὲν οὖν ἀνεκτὸν ... μὴ οὐ διασκέψασθαι: *R.*444B τοιαῦτ' ἄττα οἶμαι φήσομεν...—Αὐτὰ μὲν οὖν ταῦτα: 498D Εἰς μικρὸν...—Εἰς οὐδὲν μὲν οὖν (608C: *Hp.Ma.* 283C): *Phlb.*42A οὐκ ἔστι ταὐτὸν τοῦτο γιγνόμενον;—Πολὺ μὲν οὖν μᾶλλον: *Euthd.*299D ὁμολογεῖς...;—Ὡμολόγηκα μὲν οὖν ('I *have* admitted it *already*): *La.*192C σχεδὸν γάρ τι οἶδα... ὅτι τῶν πάνυ καλῶν πραγμάτων ἡγῇ σὺ ἀνδρείαν εἶναι.—Εὖ μὲν οὖν ἴσθι ὅτι τῶν καλλίστων (a double correction): X.*Oec.*11.23 εἰ ... μελετᾷς ... δήλωσον.—Οὐδὲν μὲν οὖν ... παύομαι, ἔφη, λέγειν μελετῶν: Pl.*Lg.*640D,655C: *Tht.*181D.

Superlative substituted for positive. Pl.*Phlb.*53B παντάπασιν ἐροῦμεν ὀρθῶς.—Ὀρθότατα μὲν οὖν: *Prt.*309D: *R.*405B: *Prm.* 163C: *id. saep.*

(iii) Assentient in the full sense. This usage is not found before the time of Plato, and is, in all its branches, practically confined to him. Des Places (p. 106) says that in Plato the assentient force is much commoner than the corrective. (But see *Addenda.*) Assentient μὲν οὖν is seen at its purest in (*a*), where a *nonne* question almost always precedes: in (*b*) the second expression is often slightly stronger than the first, and such examples might be classed under (ii): so, even more, might (*c*).

(*a*) With word repeated from the previous speech.[1] Pl. *Euthd.*284B οἱ ῥήτορες ... οὐδὲν πράττουσι;—Πράττουσι μὲν

[1] οὐ μὲν οὖν is not used by Plato, as οὐ μέντοι (p. 402) and (rarely) οὐ μὲν δή (p. 392) are used, in assentient negative answers, echoing a previous οὐ (R. W. C.). But see X.*Hier.*1.21, p. 478 (ii).

οὖν ('Certainly they act'): *Euthphr.*12C οὐ πεφόβηταί τε καὶ δέδοικεν . . . ;—Δέδοικε μὲν οὖν: *Lg.*896C ἀληθέστατα . . . εἰρηκότες ἂν εἶμεν . . . .—Ἀληθέστατα μὲν οὖν: *Chrm.*164B,171A: *Tht.*153B: *R.*353A,456A: *Lg.*665E: *Sph.*237E: *Prm.*161B: *Phlb.*36A: X.*Hier.*10.2. (Pl.*Tht.*196D is corrective rather: ἔοικας οὖν ἐννοεῖν . . . .—Ἐννοῶ μὲν οὖν.)

(*b*) With variation of the previous speaker's words. Alex.*Fr.* 270.5 Διὸς Σωτῆρος;—Οὐκ ἄλλου μὲν οὖν: Pl.*Phdr.*262A Δεῖ ἄρα . . .—Ἀνάγκη μὲν οὖν (I agree with des Places (p. 109): "ἀνάγκη enchérit sur δεῖ"): 230B ἆρ' οὐ τόδε ἦν τὸ δένδρον . . . ;—Τοῦτο μὲν οὖν αὐτό ('The very one'): *R.*443B Οὐκοῦν τούτων πάντων αἴτιον ὅτι . . . ;—Τοῦτο μὲν οὖν, καὶ οὐδὲν ἄλλο: *Lg.*627D Ἀληθέστατα . . . λέγεις.—Καλῶς μὲν οὖν, ὥς γε ἐμοὶ συνδοκεῖν, τό γε τοσοῦτον, τὰ νῦν (I do not think καλῶς can be intended as stronger than ἀληθέστατα, as des Places (p. 110) suggests).

(*c*) With intensive adverbs, πάνυ μὲν οὖν, παντάπασι μὲν οὖν, παντελῶς μὲν οὖν, σφόδρα μὲν οὖν, κομιδῇ μὲν οὖν, etc. These expressions are very common in Plato, particularly as self-contained elliptical answers, but also without ellipse.

Elliptical. Πάνυ μὲν οὖν: Ar.*Pl.*97: Pl.*Prt.*310A: *R.*341A. Παντάπασι μὲν οὖν: Pl.*Tht.*160B,C. Παντελῶς μὲν οὖν: Pl.*R.* 573C: *Prm.*155C. Σφόδρα μὲν οὖν: Pl.*Phlb.*39C,48E. Ὑπερφυῶς μὲν οὖν: Pl.*Tht.*194D,195B: *R.*525B. Πάντων μὲν οὖν μάλιστα: Pl.*Phlb.*11C. Κομιδῇ μὲν οὖν: Ar.*Pl.*833,834,838: Pl.*Tht.*155A: *R.*377B. Πολὺ μὲν οὖν νὴ τοὺς θεούς: Ar. *Pl.*412.

Not elliptical. (Often with echoed word, as in (*a*).) Πάνυ μὲν οὖν: Ar.*Pl.*1195 Πάνυ μὲν οὖν δρᾶν ταῦτα χρή: Pl.*Grg.* 450D Πάνυ μὲν οὖν καλῶς ὑπολαμβάνεις: *Men.*76C χαριοῦμαι οὖν σοι καὶ ἀποκρινοῦμαι.—Πάνυ μὲν οὖν χάρισαι: *La.*181A, 194E: *Chrm.*172A: *Phdr.*238C: *Cra.*411B: *Phlb.*33B. Παντάπασι μὲν οὖν: Pl.*Lg.*801A τιθῶ . . . οὕτως;—Παντάπασι μὲν οὖν τίθει: *R.*341E,409D,545B: *Phdr.*277C. Παντελῶς μὲν οὖν: Pl. *R.*572B: *Prm.*155E. Ὑπερφυῶς μὲν οὖν: Pl.*Phd.*99D. Κομιδῇ μὲν οὖν: Pl.*R.*397C: *Plt.*271C. Πάνυ μὲν οὖν σφόδρα: Pl.*Ap.* 26B: *Cra.*425C.

The frequency of these expressions in the *Plutus* (produced in 388 B.C.) is significant. There is clearly a topical point in the insistence on κομιδῇ μὲν οὖν in 833–8. Epich.*Fr.*171.1 reads Ἆρ' ἐστιν αὔλησίς τι πρᾶγμα;—Πάνυ μὲν οὖν. But Diels, on grounds of form and content, considers the fragment fourth-century work. perhaps from the hand of Dionysius the Tyrant.

Sometimes assent is given to the first or second of two stated alternatives. Pl.*Tht.*202C οὕτως . . . ἢ ἄλλως . . . ;—Οὕτω μὲν οὖν παντάπασιν: *Phlb.*36A: *Hp.Mi.*365E: *Cra.*397D,425C.

Position of μὲν οὖν in answers. Usually μὲν οὖν (whether adversative or affirmative) follows the first (or second) word of the answer. But occasionally it is preceded by:—

(i) An expression of assent. Ar.*Ec.*765 Ἀνόητος;—Οὐ γάρ; ἠλιθιώτατος μὲν οὖν ἁπαξαπάντων: Pl.*Hp.Ma.*288A Εἶεν· πάνυ μὲν οὖν: *Epin.*986A ἆρ' οὐκ ἂν κακὸς . . .;—Πῶς γὰρ οὔκ, ὦ ξένε; κάκιστος μὲν οὖν: *Chrm.*161D ἢ σὺ οὐδὲν ἡγῇ . . . ;—Ἔγωγε, ἡγοῦμαι μὲν οὖν ('Yes, I do, I certainly think so').

(ii) An oath. Ar.*Ra.*1188 Μὰ τὸν Δί' οὐ δῆτ', οὐ μὲν οὖν ἐπαύσατο: *Ec.*786 Ὄντως γὰρ οἴσεις;—Ναὶ μὰ Δία, καὶ δὴ μὲν οὖν τωδὶ ξυνάπτω τὼ τρίποδε: *Pl.*287 πλουσίοις . . . ;—Νὴ τοὺς θεούς, Μίδαις μὲν οὖν: X.*Cyr.*viii 4.25 ἔστι σοι . . . οὐσία ἀξία τῆς παιδός;—Νὴ Δί', ἔφη, πολλαπλασίων μὲν οὖν χρημάτων: *Hier.*1.21 Ἦ οὖν ὁρᾷς τι . . . ;—Οὐ μὰ τὸν Δί', ἔφη, οὐ μὲν οὖν.

(iii) An apostrophe. Pl.*Euthd.*274D ἐκέλευον αὐτὼ . . . ἐπιδείξασθαι . . . εἶπον οὖν ἐγώ· Ὦ Εὐθύδημε καὶ Διονυσόδωρε, πάνυ μὲν οὖν παντὶ τρόπῳ . . . ἐπιδείξασθον.

(iv) A repetition, surprised or contemptuous, of some of the previous speaker's words. Ar.*Th.*206 (ἀπολοίμην ἂν) δοκῶν . . . κλέπτειν . . .—Ἰδού γε κλέπτειν· νὴ Δία βινεῖσθαι μὲν οὖν: 861 πατὴρ δὲ Τυνδάρεως.—Σοί γ', ὤλεθρε, πατὴρ ἐκεῖνός ἐστι; Φρυνώνδας μὲν οὖν: Archipp.*Fr.*35.2 μῶν ἔδακέ τί σε;—Ἔδακε; κατὰ μὲν οὖν ἔφαγε: Pl.*Grg.*466E Ἐγὼ οὔ φημι; φημὶ μὲν οὖν ἔγωγε: *Phdr.*258E Ἐρωτᾷς εἰ δεόμεθα; τίνος μὲν οὖν ἕνεκα κἄν τις ὡς εἰπεῖν ζῴη . . . ; *Euthd.*304E Ποῖον, ἔφη, χαρίεν, ὦ μακάριε; οὐδενὸς μὲν οὖν ἄξιον: *Amat.*132B: X.*Cyr.*viii 3.37.

Usage (3) in continuous speech. The speaker objects to his own words, virtually carrying on a dialogue with himself: 'No.' A.*Ag.* 1396 εἰ δ' ἦν πρεπόντων ὥστ' ἐπισπένδειν νεκρῷ, τῷδ' ἂν δικαίως ἦν, ὑπερδίκως μὲν οὖν: *Ch.*985 δροίτης κατασκήνωμα (προσείπω);

δίκτυον μὲν οὖν ἄρκυν τ' ἂν εἴποις: *Eu.*38 δείσασα γὰρ γραῦς οὐδέν, ἀντίπαις μὲν οὖν: E.*Hipp.*1012 μάταιος ἆρ' ἦν, οὐδαμοῦ μὲν οὖν φρενῶν: *Ph.*551 περιβλέπεσθαι τίμιον; κενὸν μὲν οὖν: *Hipp.*821 κηλὶς ἄφραστος ἐξ ἀλαστόρων τινός· κατακονὰ μὲν οὖν ἀβίοτος βίου: Ar.*Ec.*1102 ἆρ' οὐ κακοδαίμων εἰμί; βαρυδαίμων μὲν οὖν: Hdt.vi 124.1 ἀλλὰ γὰρ ἴσως τι ἐπιμεμφόμενοι Ἀθηναίων τῷ δήμῳ προεδίδοσαν τὴν πατρίδα. οὐ μὲν ὦν ἦσάν σφεων ἄλλοι δοκιμώτεροι ἔν γε Ἀθηναίοισι ἄνδρες οὐδ' οἳ μᾶλλον ἐτετιμέατο (the only instance of corrective μὲν ὦν in Herodotus): Pl. *Lg.*728A οὐδὲ . . . τιμᾷ τότε τὴν αὐτοῦ ψυχήν—παντὸς μὲν οὖν λείπει—τὸ γὰρ αὐτῆς τίμιον . . . ἀποδίδοται σμικροῦ χρυσίου (des Places (p. 113) confirms me in my belief that this is the only Platonic example in continuous speech).

It is characteristic of the dramatic vigour of Demosthenes' style that he, alone of the orators (except the authors of xxv and xlii, if he did not write those speeches), uses corrective μὲν οὖν: xviii 130 ὀψὲ γάρ ποτε—ὀψὲ λέγω; χθὲς μὲν οὖν καὶ πρώην: 140 ἆρ' οὖν οὐδ' ἔλεγεν, ὥσπερ οὐδ' ἔγραφεν, ἡνίκ' ἐργάσασθαί τι δέοι κακόν; οὐ μὲν οὖν ἦν εἰπεῖν ἑτέρῳ: 316 ὑπερμεγέθεις, οὐ μὲν οὖν εἴποι τις ἂν ἡλίκας: xxv 54 δεινῶν γὰρ ὄντων, οὐ μὲν οὖν ἐχόντων ὑπερβολήν: xlii 19 μᾶλλον δὲ λέγε τὸν νόμον αὐτόν. μικρὸν μὲν οὖν, ἱκετεύω, ἐπισχές (' No, stop ').

The few Aristotelian examples (closely similar to each other) represent imaginary dialogue: *Rh.*1399a15 οὐ τοίνυν δεῖ παιδεύεσθαι, φθονεῖσθαι γὰρ οὐ δεῖ. δεῖ μὲν οὖν παιδεύεσθαι, σοφὸν γὰρ εἶναι δεῖ: 1399a23: *MM*1209a11.

Combined with other particles. A.*Pers.*1032 Καὶ πλέον ἢ παπαῖ μὲν οὖν (' Nay, even more . . .'): S.*OC*31 Καὶ δὴ μὲν οὖν ('Nay, actually': Ar.*Ec.*786): Pl.*Phdr.*271B Οὗτοι μὲν οὖν. For γε μὲν ὦν (ὦν strengthening adversative γε μέν) see γε μέν, p. 389.

We have seen that μὲν οὖν is used both in rejecting, and in accepting, the words of a previous speaker, meaning apparently in one place ' no ', in another, ' yes '. How are these strongly contrasted usages to be connected? The authorities either make no attempt to solve the problem, or else, tacitly or openly, whittle down the adversative force of the combination. Thus

Bäumlein talks only of 'Zustimmung' and 'Bestätigung' and renders 'allerdings' in passages like E.*Or*.1521: while des Places (p. 107) follows Navarre in holding that, in apparently adversative passages, 'l'opposition réside uniquement dans la pensée, non dans la particule'. This is not very satisfactory, particularly in view of the fact, which no one seems to have noticed, that the adversative sense is in the field nearly a century before the other. It might rather be reasonable to regard the adversative sense as primary, and the affirmative as secondary, with the intermediate class (ii) (and perhaps also iii.*b* and *c*) acting as a bridge: since to disagree by substituting a stronger form of expression is virtually to agree. (Cf. E.*Alc.* 231 οὐ φίλαν ἀλλὰ φιλτάταν: *Hec.*1121.) Again, where a *nonne* question precedes, μὲν οὖν may be taken as contradicting the negative: 'doch'.[1] All this leaves us with a not very large residue of unequivocally assentient examples. However, with the analogy of μέντοι and μὲν δή before us, it is perhaps safer to conclude that the two opposite meanings of μὲν οὖν derive independently from two opposite meanings of μέν: for which, see that particle, and compare also μέντοι. *

(4) Textual questions. In E.*Or*.169 μὲν οὖν can scarcely stand. Nor can it be retained in Pl.*Phd*.95B (πάνυ οὖν *T*: πάνυ μὲν οὖν *B*). In *Plt*.257B the MSS. read: Εὖ γε . . . καὶ δικαίως, καὶ πάνυ μὲν οὖν μνημονικῶς ἐπέπληξάς μοι τὸ περὶ τοὺς λογισμοὺς ἁμάρτημα. This does not seem to have troubled editors much, and Campbell renders, without comment, 'and most certainly with praiseworthy recollection'—which ignores μὲν οὖν. Could μὲν οὖν be corrective here, καὶ πάνυ μνημονικῶς (καί adverbial) being substituted for δικαίως ('rightly, or, I should say rather, with accurate memory')? There certainly does not seem to be much point in such a correction. *Chrm*.175E ταῦτ' οὖν πάνυ μὲν οὖν οὐκ οἴομαι οὕτως ἔχειν, ἀλλ' ἐμὲ φαῦλον εἶναι ζητητήν: here we should certainly cut out the second οὖν (Winckelmann), probably μέν (which can hardly be answered

[1] I find that I have given two different interpretations and punctuations of Pl.*Chrm*.161D on pp. 475 and 478. I think the second is probably preferable: but I leave the inconsistency deliberately, as an example of the precariousness of classification.

by ἀλλά), and very likely πάνυ as well (Stallbaum). Des Places (p. 118) is inclined to retain οὖν in all three passages, and in *Phlb.*51B (see (2) above), suggesting that πάνυ μὲν οὖν was a 'locution figée', μὲν οὖν adding little to πάνυ. But the frequency of πάνυ μὲν οὖν in Plato may have led a copyist to insert μὲν οὖν after πάνυ automatically, as des Places (p. 104) suggests οὖν was inserted in *Sph.*229D (for which see (2) above).

Περ

In view of the intensive use of περί in Epic (for which cf. the Latin *perquam*, *permagnus*), it seems difficult to question the accepted view that περ is cognate with that word, signifying 'all round', and so 'completely'.[1] As Brugmann puts it (p. 513) 'Die Vorstellung, dass etwas rings umher geschieht und keine Richtung ausgeschlossen ist, ergab den Begriff der Vollständigkeit oder des hohen Grades'. At the same time it is certainly surprising that the use of the particle which best supports this etymology, its intensifying use with adjectives and adverbs, is in fact the most difficult of all to exemplify. The primary use must have been metamorphosed before the time of the earliest extant Greek literature.

Except in combination with καί, οὐδέ (rarely), εἰ, and relative adjectives and adverbs, περ is almost confined to Epic. In its concessive sense (see I.6) it has a rather precarious footing in later Greek. Otherwise, hardly a single instance is to be found. Pl.*Phdr.*235C πλῆρές πως, ὦ δαιμόνιε, τὸ στῆθος ἔχων . . . : the *Aldine's* περ, for πως, can hardly be right, unless Hoogeveen is correct in supposing a quotation from a poet. For Hp.*Genit.*47, οὕτω δή περ, see I.2.

I. Epic (or mainly Epic) use. Exact classification is impossible here, as often in the case of Epic uses.

[1] Boisacq suggests that πέρ : περί : : ὑπέρ : Skr. *upári*.

(1) Intensive. As I have said, examples of this are few. Hom.*T*217 *φέρτερος οὐκ ὀλίγον περ*: *θ*187 *στιβαρώτερον οὐκ ὀλίγον περ* ('far stouter'): *Ω*504 *αὐτόν τ' ἐλέησον, μνησάμενος σοῦ πατρός· ἐγὼ δ' ἐλεεινότερός περ* ('far more to be pitied than he'): *Θ*353 *οὐκέτι νῶϊ ὀλλυμένων Δαναῶν κεκαδησόμεθ' ὑστάτιόν περ* ('at the very last'): *Ξ*295 *οἷον ὅτε πρῶτόν περ ἐμισγέσθην φιλότητι* ('the very first time'): Thgn.1015 *πρίν τ' ἐχθροὺς πτῆξαι καὶ ὑπερβῆναί περ ἀνάγκῃ* (*πρὸς ἀνάγκην* Crusius). With negatives *οὔ περ* = *οὐδαμῶς*: *Ξ*416 *τὸν δ' οὔ περ ἔχει θράσος ὅς κεν ἴδηται*: *θ*212 *τῶν δ' ἄλλων οὔ πέρ τιν' ἀναίνομαι.*

A few examples which some scholars have explained similarly are better taken otherwise. *A*352 *ἐπεί μ' ἔτεκές γε μινυνθάδιόν περ ἐόντα, τιμήν πέρ μοι ὄφελλεν 'Ολύμπιος ἐγγυαλίξαι* (Hartung and Kühner render the first *περ* 'ganz', 'sehr': Leaf, rightly, 'of however short a span'): *Γ*201 *ὃς τράφη ἐν δήμῳ 'Ιθάκης κραναῆς περ ἐούσης* ('durch und durch steinig', Hartung: but the point is, as Leaf says, that Ithaca, though a stony land, bred an Odysseus).

(2) Determinative: closely allied to the intensive use. The particle denotes, not that something is increased in measure, but that the speaker concentrates on it to the exclusion of other things: with, or without, the definite envisagement of some other particular thing thus excluded or contrasted.

Hom *B*236 *οἴκαδέ περ σὺν νηυσὶ νεώμεθα* ('let us have nothing short of return home', Monro: *Π*205): *K*70 *μηδὲ μεγαλίζεο θυμῷ, ἀλλὰ καὶ αὐτοί περ πονεώμεθα* ('let us do something *ourselves*, (not leave everything to others)'): *N*447 *ἐπεὶ σύ περ εὔχεαι οὕτω* ('for *you* boast in this way, (so I will do the same)', Leaf): *Π*31 *τί σευ ἄλλος ὀνήσεται ὀψίγονός περ, αἴ κε μὴ Ἀργείοισιν ἀεικέα λοιγὸν ἀμύνῃς*; (attention momentarily concentrated on posterity): *Φ*308 *σθένος ἀνέρος ἀμφότεροί περ σχῶμεν* (Scamander appeals to Simois for help in what has hitherto been a duel between himself and Achilles): *Ω*130 *ἀγαθὸν δὲ γυναικί περ ἐν φιλότητι μίσγεσθ'*: *υ*7 *αἳ μνηστῆρσιν ἐμισγέσκοντο πάρος περ* (a grim hint that this intercourse will not continue much longer).

In Hp.*Genit.*47 *οὕτω δή περ* seems to be an isolated instance of the survival of this use in post-Homeric Greek.

(3) Limitative. Concentration often carries with it the idea of reservation or limitation (cf. γε): and Homer sometimes uses περ where a later writer would have used γε, to convey that what is said is to be taken within certain definite limits, while the possibility of extension beyond these limits is ignored or excluded.

Hom.*Θ*243 *ἀλλά, Ζεῦ, τόδε πέρ μοι ἐπικρήηνον ἐέλδωρ· αὐτοὺς δή περ ἔασον ὑπεκφυγέειν* ('Even if we fail of our purpose, let us at least save our lives', Leaf): *Λ*789 *ὁ δὲ πείσεται εἰς ἀγαθόν περ*: *N*72 *ἀρίγνωτοι δὲ θεοί περ* (*sc.* 'whatever mistakes one may make about mortals'): δ34 *αἴ κέ ποθι Ζεὺς ἐξοπίσω περ παύσῃ ὀϊζύος* (*in futurum saltem*, since the past has been full of sorrow): ζ325 *νῦν δή πέρ μευ ἄκουσον, ἐπεὶ πάρος οὔ ποτ' ἄκουσας* ('now at any rate'): λ441 *μή ποτε καὶ σὺ γυναικί περ ἤπιος εἶναι* (*sc.* 'whatever you may be to a man': Merry and Riddell's 'even thy wife' is, I think, wrong).

(4) Whereas often in (2) and always in (3) περ implies a contrast between an expressed idea and another, or others, implied, in other passages both contrasted ideas are expressed. περ may then appear either in the first, or in the second, of two coordinated clauses.

(i) In the first clause. Hom.*P*121 *σπεύσομεν, αἴ κε νέκυν περ Ἀχιλλῆϊ προφέρωμεν γυμνόν· ἀτὰρ τά γε τεύχε' ἔχει κορυθαίολος Ἕκτωρ*: *T*200 *ἄλλοτέ περ καὶ μᾶλλον ὀφέλλετε ταῦτα πένεσθαι* ... *νῦν δ'* ...: ε29 *Ἑρμεία· σὺ γὰρ αὖτε τά τ' ἄλλα περ ἄγγελός ἐσσι· νύμφῃ ἐϋπλοκάμῳ εἰπεῖν νημερτέα βουλήν*: ζ282 *βέλτερον, εἰ καὐτή περ ἐποιχομένη πόσιν εὗρεν ἄλλοθεν· ἦ γὰρ τούσδε γ' ἀτιμάζει κατὰ δῆμον*: σ122 *γένοιτό τοι ἔς περ ὀπίσσω ὄλβος· ἀτὰρ μὲν νῦν γε κακοῖς ἔχεαι πολέεσσι*: ο540.

(ii) In the second clause, usually with pronouns. Hom.*Π*523 *ὁ δ' οὐδ' οὗ παιδὸς ἀμύνει. ἀλλὰ σύ πέρ μοι, ἄναξ, τόδε καρτερὸν ἕλκος ἀκέσσαι*: *P*712 *κεῖνον μὲν δὴ νηυσὶν ἐπιπροέηκα* ... *ἡμεῖς δ' αὐτοί περ φραζώμεθα μῆτιν ἀρίστην*: *Σ*151 *Ἀχαιοὶ* ... *φεύγοντες νῆας* ... *ἵκοντο. οὐδέ κε Πάτροκλόν περ ἐϋκνημῖδες Ἀχαιοὶ ἐκ βελέων ἐρύσαντο νέκυν* (their own safe retreat is contrasted with their failure to rescue Patroclus' body): *Υ*119 *Αἰνείας ὅδ' ἔβη* ... *ἀλλ' ἄγεθ', ἡμεῖς πέρ μιν ἀποτρωπῶμεν ὀπίσσω*: δ379 *ἐκ μέν τοι ἐρέω* ... *ἀλλὰ σύ πέρ μοι εἰπέ* (in these last two passages περ almost = αὖ, 'in your turn': cf. δ468): *Α*508: *Ρ*634: *Υ*300.

Further, when subordination, not co-ordination, of clauses is employed, περ may be attached either to the main or to the subordinate clause.

(iii) In the main clause. Hom.*Α*353 ἐπεί μ' ἔτεκές γε μινυνθάδιόν περ ἐόντα, τιμήν πέρ μοι ὄφελλεν Ὀλύμπιος ἐγγυαλίξαι ('*honour*, since he has not granted me long life'): *Λ*796 εἰ δὲ . . ., ἀλλὰ σέ περ προέτω: *Μ*349 εἰ δὲ . . ., ἀλλά περ οἶος ἴτω (*Μ*362): *Π*38.

(iv) In the subordinate clause. Hom.*Ι*514 πόρε καὶ σὺ Διὸς κούρῃσιν ἕπεσθαι τιμήν, ἥ τ' ἄλλων περ ἐπιγνάμπτει νόον ἐσθλῶν: ρ273 ῥεῖ' ἔγνως, ἐπεὶ οὐδὲ τά τ' ἄλλα πέρ ἐσσ' ἀνοήμων: ψ209.

(5) Since the attention is naturally concentrated upon that which is more important or striking than everything else, περ often denotes climax, like καί, οὐδέ. Hom.*Θ*452 σφῶϊν δὲ πρίν περ τρόμος ἔλλαβε φαίδιμα γυῖα, πρὶν πόλεμόν τ' ἰδέειν (*vel antea*: cf.*Ο*588): *Ι*110 ὃν ἀθάνατοί περ ἔτισαν ('the very immortals': cf. *Υ*65 τά τε στυγέουσι θεοί περ: ε73 καὶ ἀθάνατός περ ἐπελθὼν θηήσαιτο ἰδών): *Ρ*239 οὐκέτι νῶϊ ἔλπομαι αὐτώ περ νοστησέμεν ἐκ πολέμοιο (*vel ipsos*: leaving out of account the possibility of rescuing Patroclus' body, which, Menelaus goes on to say, is of less importance than their own skins: Leaf's 'by ourselves at any rate, if we do not get help' is surely wrong): *Ψ*79 ἀλλ' ἐμὲ μὲν κὴρ ἀμφέχανε στυγερή, ἥ περ λάχε γιγνόμενόν περ ('at my very birth'): θ547 ἀνέρι, ὅς τ' ὀλίγον περ ἐπίψαύῃ πραπίδεσσι: τ587 μεμνήσεσθαι ὀΐομαι ἔν περ ὀνειρῷ (τ541).

(6) The sense of climax often carries with it a concessive tone. 'The very gods hate': 'they hate although they are gods'. In this sense περ continues to be found, though rarely, in post-Homeric Greek: in Pindar and Aeschylus, and (with participle) in Sophocles, Euripides, Herodotus, and Plato. (In Is.ix11 the MSS. give: καὶ τοὺς ἄλλους, ὅτῳ ἐπὶ βραχύ περ ᾔδει Ἀστύφιλον χρώμενον. Kühner accepts this, but the text can hardly stand: if it can, περ presumably must go with ἐπὶ βραχύ, not with ὅτῳ: ὅτῳ περ ἔμβραχυ, Cobet.)

Hom.*Δ*421 *ταλασίφρονά περ δέος εἷλεν*: *Π*638 *οὐκ ἂν ἔτι φράδμων περ ἀνὴρ Σαρπηδόνα δῖον ἔγνω*: *Σ*108 *ὅς τ' ἐφέηκε πολύφρονά περ χαλεπῆναι*: *Φ*63 *ἥ τε κρατερόν περ ἐρύκει*: Pi.*P.* 4.237 *ἴυγξεν δ' ἀφωνήτῳ περ ἔμπας ἄχει . . . Αἰήτας*: *N.*3.80 *πέμπω . . . ὀψέ περ*: A.*Ag.*140 *τόσον περ εὔφρων . . . τούτων αἴνει ξύμβολα κρᾶναι*: 1084 *μένει τὸ θεῖον δουλίᾳ περ ἐν φρενί.* *μίνυνθά περ* in Homer is, at any rate usually, concessive, 'though but for a little while'. So, clearly, in *M*356, *Ξ*358, *Ψ*97. *N*573 (etc.) is more doubtful, and the meaning might be 'for quite a little while': *ἤσπαιρε μίνυνθά περ, οὔ τι μάλα δήν.*

The concessive sense is especially common with the participle, *περ* either following the participle, or being inserted elsewhere in the participial clause. Hom.*A*586 *καὶ ἀνάσχεο κηδομένη περ*: *P*459 *μάχετ' ἀχνύμενός περ*: *Ξ*217 *πύκα περ φρονεόντων*: *Ω*593 *εἰν Ἄϊδός περ ἐών*: A.*Th.*1043 *γυνή περ οὖσα*: *Supp.*55 *τὰ δ' ἄελπτά περ ὄντα φανεῖται*: *Ag.*1571 *τάδε μὲν στέργειν, δύστλητά περ ὄνθ'*: E.*Alc.*2 *θῆσσαν τράπεζαν αἰνέσαι θεός περ ὤν*: *Ion* 1324 *οὐ τεκοῦσά περ*: *Andr.*763 *τροπαῖον αὐτοῦ στήσομαι, πρέσβυς περ ὤν*: Hdt.iii 131 *ὑπερεβάλετο τοὺς ἄλλους ἰητρούς, ἀσκευής περ ἐών*: viii 11.1 *ἔργου εἴχοντο, ἐν ὀλίγῳ περ ἀπολαμφθέντες*: 13 *τοῖσι δὲ ταχθεῖσι αὐτῶν περιπλέειν Εὔβοιαν ἡ αὐτή περ ἐοῦσα νὺξ πολλὸν ἦν ἔτι ἀγριωτέρη* ('the night, though one and the same night, was rougher in one place than in another': Kühner can hardly be right (II ii 85) in taking *περ* as strengthening *αὐτή*, 'ebendieselbe Nacht'): Pl.*Epin.*975C *οὐδ' ἡ σύμπασα θηρευτική, πολλή περ καὶ τεχνικὴ γεγονυῖα . . .* (the only Platonic example known to me).

Where a negatived main verb precedes the participial clause, there are two possibilities. Either (i) the participial clause is contrasted with the negation of the idea: Hom.*X*424 *οὐ τόσσον ὀδύρομαι ἀχνύμενός περ* ('though grieved, I do not lament so much'): *κ*174 *οὐ γάρ πω καταδυσόμεθ', ἀχνύμενοί περ, εἰς Ἀΐδαο δόμους*: *I*605: S.*Ph.*1068 *μὴ πρόσλευσσε, γενναῖός περ ὤν.* Or (ii) it is contrasted with the idea which is negatived, as regarded by itself positively: Hom.*A*131 *Μὴ δὴ οὕτως, ἀγαθός περ ἐὼν . . .*, *κλέπτε νόῳ*:[1] *α*315 *Μή με . . . κατέρυκε λιλαιόμενόν περ ὁδοῖο*

[1] But it seems necessary to class T155 (=A 131) with (i): *Μὴ δὴ οὕτως, ἀγαθός περ ἐὼν . . . νήστιας ὄτρυνε προτὶ Ἴλιον υἷας Ἀχαιῶν* ('Though a mighty

('detain me in spite of my eagerness'): ρ13 ἐμὲ δ' οὔ πως ἔστιν ἅπαντας ἀνθρώπους ἀνέχεσθαι, ἔχοντά περ ἄλγεα θυμῷ: 47 μηδέ μοι ἦτορ ἐν στήθεσσιν ὄρινε φυγόντι περ αἰπὺν ὄλεθρον. (I see no reason, in *A*131, ρ13,47, to suppose a causal sense (*satis insolite*, = *quoniam*, Ebeling, II 162b).)

Often the participial clause opens with καί. καὶ ... περ then means 'even though', καί marking the climax and περ the concession. Hom.*B*270 οἱ δὲ καὶ ἀχνύμενοί περ ἐπ' αὐτῷ ἡδὺ γέλασσαν: *E*135 Τυδεΐδης δ' ἐξαῦτις ἰὼν προμάχοισιν ἐμίχθη, καὶ πρίν περ θυμῷ μεμαὼς Τρώεσσι μάχεσθαι ('(he did not return to the battle earlier,) though eager to do so': this interpretation makes Leaf's punctuation unnecessary): *O*30 ἀνήγαγον ... καὶ πολλά περ ἀθλήσαντα: 195 ἀλλὰ ἕκηλος καὶ κρατερός περ ἐὼν μενέτω: υ271 Καὶ χαλεπόν περ ἐόντα δεχώμεθα μῦθον (at opening of sentence): Pi.*Fr*.184(194).4 καὶ πολυκλείταν περ ἐοῖσαν: A.*Fr*. 199.2 καὶ θοῦρός περ ὤν.

καὶ ... περ is also attached, without a participle, to individual words or phrases. Hom.*P*104 ἐπιμνησαίμεθα χάρμης καὶ πρὸς δαίμονά περ: *Ω*750 καὶ ἐν θανάτοιό περ αἴσῃ: δ214 μῦθοι δὲ καὶ ἠῶθέν περ ἔσονται (*sc*. 'though evening is the best time for story-telling'): A.*Ag*.1203 Μῶν καὶ θεός περ ἱμέρῳ πεπληγμένος;

The later form καίπερ, in which the particles are juxtaposed, occurs only once in Homer: η224 καί περ πολλὰ παθόντα: Hes.*Th*.533 (at opening of sentence). καίπερ with participle in post-Homeric Greek is common, though rare in the orators except Demosthenes.* With participle omitted: S.*OT*1141 Λέγεις ἀληθῆ, καίπερ ἐκ μακροῦ χρόνου: 1326 γιγνώσκω σαφῶς, καίπερ σκοτεινός, τήν γε σὴν αὐδὴν ὅμως: *Ph*.647. καίπερ with finite verb, in the following two passages, cannot stand: Pi.*N*.4.36 (καἴπερ, Christ): Pl.*Smp*.219C (καίτοι, Burnet: καί, Schanz).

The corresponding negative form is οὐδὲ ... περ, οὐδέ περ.

man of valour, do not expect impossibilities of the troops'). There is a certain awkwardness in giving different interpretations to a word in dentical lines in different contexts: but I think that Ebeling is right in doing o, though I cannot accept his view of A131 (see below). This is a difficulty one meets with elsewhere in the case of repeated lines in Homer (see Introd., IV). Nor do I agree with Leaf that περ means 'very' in both passages.

As with καὶ . . . περ, καίπερ, Homer almost always separates, while later writers juxtapose, the particles.

οὐδὲ . . . περ (Homer only). Θ201 Ὢ πόποι, ἐννοσίγαι' εὐρυσθενές, οὐδέ νυ σοί περ ὀλλυμένων Δαναῶν ὀλοφύρεται ἐν φρεσὶ θυμός: Λ841 ἀλλ' οὐδ' ὧς περ σεῖο μεθήσω τειρομένοιο: γ236 οὐδὲ θεοί περ: ν294. (But in α59 οὐδέ is connective, 'yet not').

οὐδέ περ. Hom.λ452 ἡ δ' ἐμὴ οὐδέ περ υἷος ἐνιπλησθῆναι ἄκοιτις ὀφθαλμοῖσιν ἔασε (the only instance of juxtaposition in Homer): A.*Supp*.399 οὐδέ περ κρατῶν: *Ch*.504 οὐ τέθνηκας οὐδέ περ θανών: E.*Ph*.1624 τὸ γὰρ ἐμὸν . . . οὐκ ἂν προδοίην, οὐδέ περ πράσσων κακῶς: Ar.*Ach* 222 μὴ γὰρ ἐγχάνῃ ποτὲ μηδέ περ γέροντας ὄντας ἐκφυγὼν Ἀχαρνέας.

II. Ancillary περ. περ is used as an ancillary strengthening particle in various combinations.

(1) ἤπερ (comparative): Epic and Ionic prose only. (ἤπερ in an intrusive gloss in Th.vi40.1: [Pl.] *Alc.II* 149A.) 'Ut sit maius quam alterum quod ipsum magnum est', Ebeling's explanation fits some passages well: Hom.*A*260 ἤδη γάρ ποτ' ἐγὼ καὶ ἀρείοσιν ἠέ περ ὑμῖν ἀνδράσιν ὡμίλησα (where Nestor is trying to be propitiatory): δ819 τοῦ δὴ ἐγὼ καὶ μᾶλλον ὀδύρομαι ἤ περ ἐκείνου: ρ417. But it is quite inappropriate to others, where περ seems rather to stress the extent of the difference expressed by ἤ: Hom.*Π*688 ἀλλ' αἰεί τε Διὸς κρείσσων νόος ἠέ περ ἀνδρῶν: Σ302 τῶν τινὰ βέλτερόν ἐστιν ἐπαυρέμεν ἤ περ Ἀχαιούς.[1]

Democr.*Fr*.181: Hdt.iv50.4 πολλαπλήσιά ἐστι τοῦ θέρους ἤ περ τοῦ χειμῶνος: vii150.1 πρότερον ἤ περ: ix26.7 δίκαιον ἡμέας ἔχειν τὸ ἕτερον κέρας ἤ περ Ἀθηναίους: ix7a2: 28.1: *id. saep.*: Hp.*Haem*.4 οὐδὲν γὰρ χαλεπώτερον ἤ περ . . . περαίνειν ('For it is no more difficult than . . .').

(2) εἴπερ. In Homer, also εἰ . . . περ *separatim*: in *O*372, if εἰ and περ are associated, the interval between them is exceptionally wide. (i) 'If really': common in all styles and periods

[1] For a discussion of different views, see Kühner II ii 302, Anm.1: he seems to be right in saying that περ in this combination tends to lose all its force, as in ὥσπερ, ἐπείπερ.

of Greek:[1] often reinforced by γε, following immediately or at an interval. B.17.53 εἴπερ με νύμφα Φοίνισσα λευκώλενος σοὶ τέκε: A.*Ag*.29 ἐπορθιάζειν, εἴπερ Ἰλίου πόλις ἑάλωκεν, ὡς ὁ φρυκτὸς ἀγγέλλων πρέπει: 1249 Ἀλλ' οὔτι παιὼν τῷδ' ἐπιστατεῖ λόγῳ.—Οὔκ, εἴπερ ἔσται γ'· ἀλλὰ μὴ γένοιτό πως: *Ch*.198 τόνδ' ἀποπτύσαι πλόκον, εἴπερ γ' ἀπ' ἐχθροῦ κρατὸς ἦν τετμημένος: Ar.*Ach*.307 τῶν δ' ἐμῶν σπονδῶν ἀκούσατ', εἰ καλῶς ἐσπεισάμην. —Πῶς δέ γ' ἂν καλῶς λέγοις ἄν, εἴπερ ἐσπείσω γ' ἅπαξ οἷσιν οὔτε βωμὸς οὔτε πίστις οὔθ' ὅρκος μένει; Hom.*B*123: *N*464: E.*Ph*.725: Ar.*Av*.1359: *Nu*.341,930: *Ach*.1228: *Lys*.992: *Ra*. 77,1368: *Eq*.366. Pl.*Prt*.312A εἴπερ γε ἃ διανοοῦμαι χρὴ λέγειν: *Tht*.182C εἴπερ γε δὴ τελέως κινήσεται: Hdt.vi 57.4: vii 143.1: Pl.*Prt*.330B: *Plt*.275E: Isoc.iv 14: D.i 2.

With imperfect, or aorist, of unfulfilled condition. Hom.*Π*618 εἴ σ' ἔβαλόν περ: S.*El*.312 μὴ δόκει μ' ἄν, εἴπερ ἦν πέλας, θυραῖον οἰχνεῖν: 604: Pl.*Ti*.75B μάλιστα γὰρ ἂν . . . ἔσχεν . . . εἴπερ . . . ἠθελησάτην. εἰ μή περ, for εἴπερ μή: Ar.*Nu*.1183 (εἰ μή πέρ γε, a *reductio ad absurdum*): *Lys*.629: Hdt.vi 57.4: Pl. *Alc.I* 124B: X *Oec*.7.17.

(ii) 'Even if': common in Homer. *B*597 στεῦτο γὰρ εὐχόμενος νικησέμεν, εἴ περ ἂν αὐταὶ Μοῦσαι ἀείδοιεν: *Λ*116 ἡ δ' εἴ περ τε τύχῃσι μάλα σχεδόν, οὐ δύναταί σφι χραισμεῖν: *Χ*389 εἰ δὲ θανόντων περ καταλήθοντ' εἰν Ἀΐδαο, αὐτὰρ ἐγὼ καὶ κεῖθι φίλου μεμνήσομ' ἑταίρου: *Γ*25: *K*225: *M*223.245: α167: β246: ν138,143. This use is not to be found outside Homer. Pl.*Euthphr*.4B ἐπεξιέναι, ἐάνπερ ὁ κτείνας συνέστιός σοι καὶ ὁμοτράπεζος ᾖ means that you must prosecute the homicide if, and only if, he shares house and board with you: otherwise he cannot pollute you: see Burnet *ad loc*. and in *C.Q*.viii 233.[2] In Hdt.vi 68.3 εἴ περ πεποίηκας is 'if you really have done', rather than 'even if you have done': in viii 60α ἤν περ καί is 'even if really' (and this may be the correct explanation of Hom.*H*204 εἰ δὲ καὶ Ἕκτορά περ φιλέεις, a much disputed passage).

[1] Jebb's statement (on S.*Tr*.27) that 'the tone of εἴπερ is usually confident', while 'that of εἰ δή is sceptical', perhaps goes rather too far: εἴπερ is clearly sceptical in Ar.*Ra*.634, Pl.*Prt*.319A, *Lg*.902A, and elsewhere: though *often*, no doubt, it is confident. See also δή, I.11, p. 223, n. 1. εἴπερ δή, Arist.*Pol*.1289a24.

[2] Kühner's 'vereinzelt attisch' (II ii 170, 490) is therefore incorrect.

εἴπερ is often used with ellipse, before τις, που, ποτε, etc. S.*Aj*.488 ἐξέφυν πατρός, εἴπερ τινός, σθένοντος (with attraction): Th.iv 55.2 ἐς τὰ πολεμικά, εἴπερ ποτέ, μάλιστα δὴ ὀκνηρότεροι ἐγένοντο: Pl.*Phd*.58E εἴπερ τις πώποτε καὶ ἄλλος: 67B εἴπερ που ἄλλοθι: D.i6 προσέχειν εἴπερ ποτὲ καὶ νῦν.

Sometimes εἴπερ stands quite alone: 'if at all'. Ar.*Nu*.227 Ἔπειτ' ἀπὸ ταρροῦ τοὺς θεοὺς ὑπερφρονεῖς, ἀλλ' οὐκ ἀπὸ τῆς γῆς, εἴπερ; ('if you must'): Pl.*R*.497E (see Stallbaum) Οὐ τὸ μὴ βούλεσθαι . . . ἀλλ', εἴπερ, τὸ μὴ δύνασθαι, διακωλύσει ('if anything'): *Prm*.150B Ἐν μὲν ὅλῳ ἄρα τῷ ἑνὶ οὐκ ἂν εἴη σμικρότης, ἀλλ', εἴπερ, ἐν μέρει: *Euthd*.296B (see E. S. Thompson, *The* Meno *of Plato*, p.262): *Lg*.667A: 900E Καὶ τῶν μὲν προσήκειν ἡμῖν, εἴπερ, ὁπόσα φλαῦρα, θεοῖς δὲ . . .: Arist.*EN*1101a12 οὐκ ἂν γένοιτο πάλιν εὐδαίμων ἐν ὀλίγῳ χρόνῳ, ἀλλ', εἴπερ, ἐν πολλῷ τινι καὶ τελείῳ: *Rh*.1371a17.

This is a curious idiom. There are, as far as I can ascertain, three instances in Plato, and twelve in Aristotle (see Bonitz's Index[1]: I exclude *EN*1180b27, ἀλλ', εἴπερ τινός) of ἀλλ', εἴπερ, by itself, following a negative statement: 'Not . . ., but, if anything, if at all, . . .'. Add *Cael*.268a22 ἀλλ', εἴπερ ἄρα (some MSS. omit ἄρα: cf. εἰ ἄρα, *s.v.* ἄρα III.1). In *GC*321a17 (τὸ δ' ὕδωρ οὐκ ηὔξηται οὐδ' ὁ ἀὴρ . . .· τὸ σῶμα δέ, εἴπερ, ηὔξηται) δέ replaces ἀλλά. There are two further Platonic examples of self-contained εἴπερ not following ἀλλά. Apart from these fourteen Aristotelian and five Platonic instances (three from Plato's later works), there seems to be no example of self-contained εἴπερ other than Ar.*Nu*.227. I have little doubt that Aristophanes is making fun of philosophical jargon here (though no one, reading the line by itself, would suppose he had anything before him but an easy colloquialism): cf. the esoteric meaning of περιφρονεῖν ('meditate on') in the preceding line.[2] Scholars obscure the issue by citing examples of the common elliptical εἴπερ τις, etc., where εἴπερ does not stand alone. In E.*Ion*354 Hermann's Σοὶ ταὐτὸν ἥβης, εἴπερ, εἶχεν ἂν μέτρον lacks all probability, and Mr. E. Harrison has shown (*Cambridge University Reporter*, 1933) that εἶχ' ἂν (with εἴπερ ἦν), is unexceptionable.

[1] But Bonitz has omitted one of the twelve (*Pol*.1269b35), and he may have overlooked other examples.

[2] For examples of similar parody, see *C.Q.*xxi(1927)119–21.

Elliptical *Εἴπερ γε δή*, in answer: Pl.*Prm.*138D.

(3) With relatives and relative conjunctions: *ὅσπερ, ἐπείπερ, ἐπειδήπερ, ὥσπερ, καθάπερ*,[1] etc.: also very common in all styles, *περ* being often followed by *δή* or *καί*. Here, again, Homer often separates *περ* from the relative, while later writers always juxtapose. (Ar.*Ra.*815, where *ἡνίκ' ἂν ὀξύλαλόν περ ἴδῃ* may be the true reading, is epic in colour.) *περ* often has little force: *ὥσπερ*, for example, is in Attic a merely stylistic substitute for the simple *ὡς*.

Hom.*Δ*361 *τὰ γὰρ φρονέεις ἅ τ' ἐγώ περ*: *Λ*126 *τοῦ περ δή*: δ376 *ἥ τις σύ πέρ ἐσσι θεάων* (emphasizing universality of relative): A.*Ag.*607 *οἵανπερ οὖν ἔλειπε*: E.*Alc.*1132 *ἔχεις γὰρ πᾶν ὅσονπερ ἤθελες*: Hdt.vii 168.4 *τῇ περ δὴ καί*: Isoc.iv 66 *τὸν αὐτὸν τρόπον ὅνπερ*: D.ii 5 *ὅπερ καὶ ἀληθὲς ὑπάρχει*: Hdt.v 66.1: viii 82.1: 129.3.

Hom.*Α*211 *ὡς ἔσεταί περ*: *Δ*259 *ὅτε περ*: *Λ*86 *ἦμος . . . περ*: *Χ*250 *ὡς τὸ πάρος περ*: β327 *ἐπεί νύ περ ἵεται*: A.*Ag.*854 *ἐπείπερ ἕσπετο*: Hdt.i 97.1 *ἔνθα περ*: iii 153.2 *ἐπεάν περ*: v 18.2 *ἐπεί περ*: 99.1 *ὅτε περ καί*: Pl.*Prt.*357A *ἐπειδήπερ . . . ἐστὶν ἡ τέχνη*: D.iv 7: viii 22. *ἅπερ*, adverbial: A.*Ch* 381: *Eu.*131, 660: S.*OT* 175. *οἷάπερ*, adverbial: Ar.*Av.*925 (read *οἵαπερ*?)

III. *περ* combined with other particles.

ἅτε περ. Arist.*Pol.*1253a6. *δή περ*: Hom.*Θ* 243: ζ325: Hp. *Genit.*47. *περ δή*: Hom.*Ι* 310: *Ο* 707.

For *καὶ . . . περ, καίπερ, οὐδὲ . . . περ, οὐδέ περ*, see I.6. For *ἀλλά περ, ἀλλὰ . . . περ*, see I.4.iii. For *εἴπερ γε, εἴπερ δή, εἴπερ γε δή*, see II.2. For *ὅσπερ δή*, see II.3.

Που

From *που* meaning 'somewhere' is developed the sense 'I suppose',[2] 'I think', the particle conveying a feeling of un-

[1] *καθάπερ* is common in inscriptions (Meisterhans, p. 257), and gives a formal tone in Ar.*Eq.*8, *Av.*1041, *Ec.*61,75. In Plato's later works it tends to replace *ὥσπερ*.

[2] Brugmann compares *οὐδαμοῦ*, 'by no means', and *ποῦ* in E.*Ion* 528 *Ποῦ δέ μοι πατὴρ σύ*; For further examples of this sense of *ποῦ*, see L. & S.

certainty in the speaker. Hence, further, που is used ironically, with assumed diffidence, by a speaker who is quite sure of his ground. The tone of uncertainty, whether real or assumed, is ill-adapted to the precision of history, or to the assertiveness of oratory. There are few examples in Thucydides (viz. ii 87.2: v 99 (*bis*): vii 68.1: i 107.6 *coni.* Krueger), and (in contrast with the free use of δήπου) very few in the orators: Ant. v 6: Lys. vi 25: Isoc. xv 75: D. xxiii 162 (text doubtful). In D. xviii 51 που is perhaps local, εἶπέ που λέγων, 'somewhere in his speech': cf. xviii 299 πόρρω που, 'somewhere far'. But που (κου), admirably suits the easy, colloquial style of Herodotus and, *par excellence*, the ironical bent of Plato, in whom it is very common.

(1) In direct statements (far commoner than (2) and (3)). Hom. *E* 473 φῆς που ἄτερ λαῶν πόλιν ἕξεμεν (ironical): *M* 272 καὶ δ' αὐτοὶ τόδε που γιγνώσκετε: A. *Ag.* 182 δαιμόνων δέ που χάρις βίαιος: S. *Ant.* 1256 καὶ τῆς ἄγαν γάρ ἐστί που σιγῆς βάρος ('methinks'): *OT* 769 ἀξία δέ που μαθεῖν κἀγώ (the understatement gives dignified confidence to her claim): *Ph.* 1385 Σοί που φίλος γ' ὤν ('I imagine I am your friend, unless I deceive myself': Neoptolemus rather resents Philoctetes' suspicion): *El.* 786 νῦν δ' ἕκηλά που τῶν τῆσδ' ἀπειλῶν οὕνεχ' ἡμερεύσομεν ('Now, if I mistake not, I shall have peace': ironically expressing quiet assurance): *Ant.* 778 κἀκεῖ τὸν Ἅιδην ... αἰτουμένη που τεύξεται τὸ μὴ θανεῖν (savagely ironical): E. *Ion* 251 οἴκοι δὲ τὸν νοῦν ἔσχον ἐνθάδ' οὖσά που (Creusa with difficulty recovers herself): Ar. *Ach.* 97 ἄσκωμ' ἔχεις που περὶ τὸν ὀφθαλμὸν κάτω ('I suppose that's an oar-pad'): *Eq.* 204 Τί δ' ἀγκυλοχήλης ἐστίν;—Αὐτό που λέγει, ὅτι ...: *Ra.* 565 Νὼ δὲ δεισάσα γέ που ἐπὶ τὴν κατήλιφ' εὐθὺς ἀνεπηδήσαμεν (που *V*: πω *RAM*: 'I believe we ran up': she was so frightened at the time that she hardly remembered afterwards exactly what had happened): Hom. θ 541: A. *Pers.* 724, 740: S. *Aj.* 489, 597: *El.* 948: Hdt v 1.3 καὶ εἰπάν κου παρὰ σφίσι αὐτοῖσι ...:[1] vii 157.1 τὸν γὰρ ἐπιόντα ἐπὶ τὴν Ἑλλάδα πάντως κου πυνθάνεαι ('No doubt you know'): Pl. *Ap.* 20E Χαιρεφῶντα γὰρ ἴστε που: *R.* 522B αἵ τε γὰρ τέχναι βάναυσοί

[1] 'I expect they said among themselves ....' Herodotus is fond of divesting himself of the historian's omniscience, and assuming a winning fallibility (cf. i 119.7). This often comes out in his use of κου: cf. i 113.3, 114.2.

που ἅπασαι ἔδοξαν εἶναι (‘We agreed, I believe’. The speaker affects to distrust his own recollection: cf. *Ti.*17C): *Ti.*24B ᾔσθησαί που (‘I expect you have noticed’): Isoc.xv 75 εἶπον δέ που (‘I said, I think’: referring to §51): Pl.*Cri.*53C: *Phd.*62E, 94B: *id. saep.*

In numerical approximations (Herodotus, κου). i 209 ἐὼν τότε ἡλικίην ἐς εἴκοσί κου μάλιστα ἔτεα: ix 102.1 μέχρι κου τῶν ἡμισέων: i 181 μεσοῦντι δέ κου τῆς ἀναβάσιος: vii 223.1 ἐπισχὼν χρόνον ἐς ἀγορῆς κου μάλιστα πληθώρην: iii 3: vii 22: 198.2.

In answers (Plato). *Phd.*71E Πάντως που, ἔφη (‘Absolutely so, I imagine’: *Cra.*416C: *R.*454D): *R.*431E.

(2) In questions. A.*Pr.*249 Μή πού τι προύβης τῶνδε καὶ περαιτέρω; 743 τί που δράσεις . . .; (*Ag.*1646 που perhaps ‘anywhere’): Hom.*I* 40: Pl.*Phd.*103C Ἆρα μή που . . . καὶ σέ τι τούτων ἐτάραξεν . . .;

Especially οὔ τι που, οὔ που in incredulous or reluctant questions: often in Euripides. Pi.*P.*4.87 Οὔ τί που οὗτος Ἀπόλλων (‘Surely this cannot be Apollo?’ The sentence is, in its inception, interrogative): S.*Ph.*1233 οὔ τί που δοῦναι νοεῖς; (‘Surely you don’t mean . . .?’): E.*HF* 966: *Ion* 1113: *Or.*1510: *Hel.*95, 475,541: Ar.*Nu.*1260: *Pax* 1211: *Av.*443: *Lys.*354: *Ra.*522,526 (Xanthias mockingly echoes Dionysus): *Ec.*329,372: Pl.*Tht.*146A: *R.*362D. E.*El.*235 Οὐχ ἕνα νομίζων φθείρεται πόλεως νόμον.—Οὔ που σπανίζων τοῦ καθ’ ἡμέραν βίου; *IT* 930: *Supp.*153: *HF* 1101,1173: *El.*630: *Med.*695: *Hel.*135,575,600,791: *Ph.*1072: *IA* 670 (readings often doubtful, but οὔ που seems everywhere right).

οὔ τί που in a statement, Scol.Anon.11.1 Φίλταθ’ Ἁρμόδι’, οὔ τί που τέθνηκας (‘methinks thou art in nowise dead’).

(3) In subordinate clauses and reported speech. Hom.*K* 105 οὐ . . . Ζεὺς ἐκτελέει, ὅσα πόυ νυν ἐέλπεται: ξ 227 αὐτὰρ ἐμοὶ τὰ φίλ’ ἔσκε τά που θεὸς ἐν φρεσὶ θῆκεν: *Π* 39 ἄλλον λαὸν ὄπασσον Μυρμιδόνων, ἤν πού τι φόως Δαναοῖσι γένωμαι: ω 462 μὴ ἴομεν, μή πού τις ἐπίσπαστον κακὸν εὕρῃ: θ 491 ἀείδεις . . . ὥς τέ που ἢ αὐτὸς παρεὼν . . .: A.*Supp.*400 μὴ καί ποτε εἴπῃ λεώς, εἴ πού τι κάλλοῖον τύχοι, . . .: Hom.*I* 628: *K* 511: *Υ* 453: σ 107: υ 207: S.*Aj.*521,533,546: *OT* 43: Pl.*Smp.*205E ἐὰν μὴ τυγχάνῃ γέ

που . . . ἀγαθὸν ὄν: *Euthphr.*5C εἰδὼς ὅτι καὶ ἄλλος πού τις καὶ ὁ Μέλητος οὗτος . . .: *Tht.*169C τήρει τὸ τοιόνδε, μή που παιδικόν τι λάθωμεν εἶδος τῶν λόγων ποιούμενοι: *Sph.*239D καὶ τἆλλα ὅσα που . . .: *R.*376A ὅτι δέ που δρᾷ ταῦτα, δῆλον: *Lg.*694A,776D: *Sph.*235E: *Cra.*427A: *R.*395A,462C,465A: *Ti.*63B.

With infinitive: Pl.*R.*449D οἰόμενοί σέ που μνησθήσεσθαι ('thinking that you would presumably mention').

With participle: Th.vii68.1 τὸ λεγόμενόν που ἥδιστον εἶναι: Hdt.i113 οὔνομα ἄλλο κού τι καὶ οὐ Κῦρον θεμένη ('I suppose she called him something else, not Cyrus'): iii4 μεμφόμενός κού τι Ἀμάσι.

(4) Position. It is natural that που should be one of the particles which markedly gravitate to an early position, since its function is, not to concern itself with individual words, but to throw doubt, real or assumed, upon the certainty of the import of the whole sentence. Nevertheless there are not lacking cases in which this doubt is thrown as an afterthought, που occurring late, or even last word of all, in clause or sentence.

A.*Ag.*711 μεταμανθάνουσα δ' ὕμνον Πριάμου πόλις γεραιὰ πολύθρηνον μέγα που στένει: Ar.*Ec.*119 οὐκ ἂν φθάνοις τὸ γένειον ἂν περιδουμένη ἄλλαι θ' ὅσαι λαλεῖν μεμελετήκασί που (last word of sentence and of line: cf. A.*Pr.*822: S.*Aj.*469: *El.* 1244: *OT* 43: *OC* 580: E.*Ion* 251: Ar.*Ec.*111): Pl.*Ap.*38B ἴσως δ' ἂν δυναίμην ἐκτεῖσαι ὑμῖν που μνᾶν ἀργυρίου ('and perhaps I could pay you, I suppose, a mina'): *Sph.*244C Τό τε δύο ὀνόματα ὁμολογεῖν εἶναι μηδὲν θέμενον πλὴν ἓν καταγέλαστόν που: *Phd.*70E: *Sph.*267A (last word of sentence): *Plt.*306C (penultimate word): *R.*425E (penultimate word), 464E,543B,544D,605C (last word): *Ti.*26E (last word), 27C (penultimate word), 90C.

(5) Combined with other particles. Except for δήπου, ἦ που (*qq.v.*), where the two particles coalesce closely, these combinations have, for the most part, the air of fortuitous collocations, and are not to be taken too seriously, particularly where a word (or words) intervenes. At the same time, we may recognize in Plato a certain fondness for the juxtaposition of γάρ and γε with που: and there is something characteristic about καί που: while on the other hand, οὖν που is avoided.

ἄρ που: Hom.λ139. ἀτάρ που: Hom.X331.

γάρ που, γάρ που ... γε, καὶ γὰρ ... που. Hom.ξ119 Ζεὺς γάρ που τό γε οἶδε: Pl.*R*.490C μέμνησαι γάρ που: 525D οἶσθα γάρ που: *Phd*.92D ἐρρήθη γάρ που (γάρ που is often used by Plato in such appeals for assent): *Euthphr*.2A οὐ γάρ που καὶ σοί γε δίκη τις οὖσα τυγχάνει (rejecting in advance a possible answer to a question just put: *Cra*.438D): *Phd*.89E: *Cri*.44A: *Euthd*. 280E,297B: Lys.vi25: D.xxiii162 (text doubtful).

γέ που. S.*Aj*.533 Μὴ σοί γέ που δύστηνος ἀντήσας θάνοι ('Aye, lest haply ...'): Eup.*Fr*.314 οἷόν γέ που: Pl.*Plt*.259E Παρεχόμενός γέ που γνῶσιν (γε continuative): *Tht*.200E (γε *BT*: γάρ *W*: γε που almost = γοῦν): *Tht*.147C Ἔπειτά γέ που: *Phdr*. 262C: *Lg*.682C,694A. ἀλλὰ ... γέ που. Pl.*Phd*.117C Μανθάνω ... ἀλλ' εὔχεσθαί γέ που τοῖς θεοῖς ἔξεστι: Ar.*Pax*1047: Pl.*R*.596B: *Men*.75E. δέ γέ που. Pl.*R*.560D,607D: *Phd*.65C,94A. δέ γε ... που. Pl.*Lg*.667D,913A.

δέ που. Pl.*R*.517B θεὸς δέ που οἶδεν εἰ ...: 520D: A.*Pers*. 724,740: *Pr*.822: *Ag*.182: S.*OT*769.

καὶ δή κου. Hdt.ix113.1 σύν τε τοῖσι ἑωυτοῦ υἱοῖσι καὶ δή κού τισι καὶ ἄλλοισι: vi11.1: 128.2: vii12.1.

καὶ δὴ καὶ ... γέ που. Pl.*Lg*.800E. οὐ γὰρ δὴ ... γέ που. Pl.*Lg*.712C.

For δήπου, ἦ που, see pp. 267–8, 285–6.

ἤ που, ἢ ... που. Hom.Z438 ἤ πού τίς σφιν ἔνισπε ... ἤ νυ καὶ αὐτῶν θυμὸς ἐποτρύνει: S.*Aj*.1244 ἀλλ' αἰὲν ἡμᾶς ἢ κακοῖς βαλεῖτέ που, ἢ ... ('No doubt', I think, indignant: not 'somewhere' (Jebb)): Hdt.vii141.4 (oracle) ἀπολεῖς δὲ σὺ τέκνα γυναικῶν ἤ που ... ἢ ...: Pl.*Phd*.82B ἥμερον γένος, ἤ που μελιττῶν ἢ σφηκῶν ἢ μυρμήκων: *Ep*.336B ἤ πού τις δαίμων ἤ τις ἀλιτήριος: Hdt.vii10θ3 (perhaps local): Pl.*R*.496C: *Ti*.83C. ἤ ('than') που. Pl.*Lg*.716C.

θήν που. Hom.N813 ἦ θήν πού τοι θυμὸς ἐέλπεται ἐξαλαπάξειν νηᾶς.

καί που. Hom.ζ190 καί που σοὶ τάδ' ἔδωκε: σ382 καί πού τις δοκέεις μέγας ἔμμεναι: S.*Ph*.293 καί που πάγου χυθέντος ... ξύλον τι θραῦσαι ('and haply'): 308 καί πού τι καὶ βορᾶς μέρος προσέδοσαν οἰκτίραντες ('and perhaps give me'): 1123 (not local, I think): Hdt.v18.5 μαστῶν τε ἅπτοντο ... καί κού τις καὶ φιλέειν ἐπειρᾶτο ('and I expect one of them tried to kiss one'): ix18.1

διετείνοντο τὰ βέλεα ὡς ἀπήσοντες, καί κού τις και ἀπῆκε: Ant. v 6 καί πού τι καὶ ἐξαμαρτεῖν (the first καί must be copulative, and something has dropped out of the text): Th.ii 87.2 καί πού τι καὶ ἡ ἀπειρία ... ἔσφηλεν ('wohl', 'vielleicht', Krüger): in i 107.6 Krüger reads καί τι καί που, for καί τι καὶ τοῦ, with much probability: Pl.*Phdr*.229C καί πού τίς ἐστι βωμὸς αὐτόθι Βορέου.

καὶ . . . γέ που. Pl.*R*.460B Καὶ τοῖς ἀγαθοῖς γέ που: *Euthphr*. 13B,E.

μέν που. Hom.Γ308 Ζεὺς μέν που τό γε οἶδε: Ω488 καὶ μέν που κεῖνοι περιναιέται . . . τείρουσ': Ω46: S.*Aj*.597: Hdt.v 16.2 τὸ μέν κου ἀρχαῖον . . . μετὰ δὲ . . .: vi 98.1 καὶ τοῦτο μέν κου τέρας . . . ἔφηνε ὁ θεός: Pl.*Ap*.34D 'Εμοὶ . . . εἰσὶν μέν πού τινες καὶ οἰκεῖοι (ironical: 'I *have* relations, I imagine'): *R*.422B, 476B,521C,527A.

μέν γέ που. Pl.*Tht*.147A: *R*.478A,559B: *Lg*.747D.

ἀλλὰ μήν που. Pl.*Euthd*.281A. ἀλλὰ μήν που . . . γε. Pl.*Grg*. 477E: *Hp.Ma*.284E: *Hp.Mi*.375C. ἀλλὰ μὴν . . . γέ που. Pl. *Sph*.252D. καὶ μήν που. Pl.*R*.381A,486A. καὶ μὴν . . . γε . . . που. Pl.*Lg*.687D. καὶ μὴν καὶ . . . γε . . . που. Pl.*Lg*.890E. οὐ μὴν ἀλλά που. Pl.*Lg*.722A.

μέντοι . . . γέ που. Pl.*R*.596E. ἀλλ' οὖν . . . γέ που. Pl. *Phd*.102D. τέ που. Pl.*Cra*.395D. γέ τοί που. Pl.*Lg*. 888E.

Τε

Τε is a particle which has attracted considerable attention. Wentzel and Christ have analysed the Homeric use, Schäfer has taken Antiphon, Schmidt the remaining orators, Hoefer Plato, and Hammer Herodotus, Thucydides, and Xenophon. The dissertations of Schmidt and Hammer are models of thoroughness and careful arrangement, while Hoefer's work, though inferior to these, is of considerable value. Only a detailed study of the particle in lyric poets and dramatists is lacking.

While these special studies have shed much light on τε (even though many details remain obscure), the problem of bridging the gulf between the two main branches of its usage (I and II) remains unsolved, and, as often, comparative philology offers little help.[1] It seems fairly certain that τε is related to Sanskrit *ca*, Latin *que*, Indogermanic *q*ᵘ*e*. Indogermanic *q*ᵘ*e* served to connect two parallel nouns or pronouns (perhaps also two parallel verbs): πατὴρ ἀνδρῶν τε θεῶν τε, *noctesque diesque*. Further, it possessed a universalizing sense in Sanskrit *káś ca*. Latin *quisque*. (Brugmann indicates a possible way of connecting the copulative and universalizing meanings when he compares 'wer auch immer'.) A universalizing *q*ᵘ*e* certainly does help us to understand τε. But the uses of *que* in *quisque*, *utcumque* and τε in ὅς τε, ὥς τε are in practice widely different. τε attached to a relative does not universalize the *relative*: ὥς τε λέων does not mean 'in whatever way a lion': nor does it give an indefinite, approximative force to the relation, 'more or less as a lion'. What it does (as we shall see) is to present the *action* described in the relative clause as typical and habitual: 'as a lion always'. Often, in fact, it is palpably impossible to universalize the *relative*: Hom. *A* 86 μὰ Ἀπόλλωνα ᾧ τε σὺ εὐχόμενος θεοπροπίας ἀναφαίνεις: 'to whom, and to no other, you, whenever it may so happen, pray'. This is the Epic τε of habitual action (see II), which bears the same force when it follows relatives as when it follows other particles. Since, then, what happens habitually is on a fair way to happening universally, there is, to that extent, a real logical affinity between universalizing *que* and Epic τε. But in practice the usages of the two particles diverge widely here.

We are driven, then, to abandon philology and fall back on usage. An examination of the uses of τε shows that (I) its commonest significance is combination or addition, and that it denotes, on the whole, a closer connexion than καί. On the other hand (II), as Wentzel and Monro have shown, in certain usages (for the most part Homeric) it appears to express habituation, de-

[1] I follow Brugmann (p. 612) here, so far as philology is concerned. But my statement of the case, and my conclusions, are different. A relation between τε and indefinite τις, asserted by Kvičala, would, if philologically possible, enable us to explain Epic τε, as = 'on some occasion or other': but connective τε is difficult or impossible to explain on this assumption.

noting something which happens constantly or characteristically.[1] Attempts to find a common parentage for (I) and (II) have hitherto failed: and we cannot, perhaps, entirely exclude the possibility that there may be two distinct τε's (not to mention the suffix, for which see Brugmann, p. 297) with different origins. Moreover we are left at the end with a certain residue of intractable phenomena, which no ingenuity has succeeded in relating either to (I) or to (II).

I. Connective and corresponsive. τε, like καί, is used both as a simple connective and as a preparatory particle in corresponsion, τε . . . τε, τε . . . καί. But it hardly, if at all, shares the adverbial function of καί, 'also'. (See II *ad init.*, II.1, and III.) As in the case of καί, it is uncertain which is the primary use. (Kvičala and Brugmann believe that corresponsive τε . . . τε came first.)

(1) Single τε. τε is freely used in verse to connect individual words or phrases, clauses, and sentences.[2] Hom.*A*5 κύνεσσιν οἰωνοῖσί τε πᾶσι: 45 τόξ' ὤμοισιν ἔχων ἀμφηρεφέα τε φαρέτρην: 460 ἔδειραν, μηρούς τ' ἐξέταμον κατά τε κνίσῃ ἐκάλυψαν: Pi.*O.*1.38 ἐκάλεσε . . . ἐς ἔρανον φίλαν τε Σίπυλον: A.*Supp.*274 Βραχὺς τορός θ' ὁ μῦθος: *Pr.*172 σκῆπτρον τιμάς τ' ἀποσυλᾶται: E. *Heracl.*182 εἰπεῖν ἀκοῦσαί τ': *Hel.*696 μέλαθρα λέχεά τ': *Hec.* 560 ἔρρηξε λαγόνας . . . μαστούς τ' ἔδειξε: *Hel.*652 Ἔχεις, ἐγώ τε σέ: *Tr.*1269 (after a particularly strong pause: perhaps read δέ, as certainly in A.*Eu.* 468 (Pearson): but cf. S.*OT* 1001: *OC* 534 (at opening of answer): E.*Hel.*404,785,924: *El.*240: *HF* 854: Ar. *Ec.*458: Hdt.iii 156: see also II.3.ii (τε introducing a question in Homer), and δέ, *ad init.* p. 162): Ar.*Ach.*1062 ὁτιὴ γυνή 'στι τοῦ πολέμου τ' οὐκ αἰτία: E.*Hec.*1072: *HF* 649,1056: *IT* 160–5: *Hel.*1360–4: *Ph.*229–34.

In prose, single connective τε is much rarer. Mainly confined to the historians (more than 400 times in Thucydides, according to Hammer) and Plato (especially in the *Timaeus*), it is seldom

[1] Consequently, to class, as Hartung does, any passage which can conceivably be so taken as connective or responsive, is an artificial proceeding, which often leads to forced explanations and to the supposition of unnatural ellipses.

[2] The units linked by τε (or by καί) are not necessarily *eiusdem generis.* See Jebb on S.*Ant.*383,653, *Ph.*1178.

found in the orators[1] (occasionally in Antiphon, Andocides, and Lysias, and in pseudo-Demosthenes: once each in Isocrates, Aeschines, and Hyperides: never in Demosthenes or Lycurgus: frequent in Isaeus (Schmidt, p. 22) though not proportionately more frequent than in Antiphon and Andocides).

(i) Connecting single words and phrases. This use is much rarer in prose authors generally than (ii) and (iii), though in Plato it is commoner (Hoefer, p. 9). Moreover, the items connected are, for the most part, seldom single words. The tendency in prose is for single τε to couple large units, not small ones: with this exception, that in Plato's latest work (particularly the *Timaeus* and *Critias*) single τε frequently connects single words.

Single words. Hdt.viii 140β3 ἐξαίρετον μεταίχμιόν τε τὴν γῆν ἐκτημένων: Pl.*Phdr.*267A Τεισίαν δὲ Γοργίαν τε ἐάσομεν εὕδειν: *Sph.*227A ὑπὸ γυμναστικῆς ἰατρικῆς τε: *Ti.*17A σὸν τῶνδέ τε ἔργον: 37C νοῦς ἐπιστήμη τε: 40C ἀλλήλοις ἡμῖν τε: 46A ἐντὸς ἐκτός τε: 59D λεπτὸν ὑγρόν τε: 60C ἔθλιψεν συνέωσέν τε: 60E πῦρ μὲν ἀήρ τε: 62C μετὰ τῆς τοῦ κάτω φύσεως ἄνω τε λεγομένης: 88A σμικρᾷ... ἀσθενεῖ τε: *Ti.*39C,64C,66B,66D (*bis*): *Criti.*109C, 110A,113C,115D: *Lg.*643D,679D,733B,969B: *Epin.*974C,981C, 990B: *Ep.*342D.

Phrases. Hdt.vii 190 νέας... λέγουσι διαφθαρῆναι τετρακοσιέων οὐκ ἐλάσσονας, ἄνδρας τε ἀναριθμήτους χρημάτων τε πλῆθος ἄφθονον: ix 80.1 εὕρισκον σκηνὰς κατεσκευασμένας χρυσῷ καὶ ἀργύρῳ, κλίνας τε ἐπιχρύσους καὶ ἐπαργύρους, κρητῆράς τε χρυσέους: 101.2 τῆς αὐτῆς ἡμέρης συνέβαινε γίνεσθαι μηνός τε τοῦ αὐτοῦ: Th.i 12.4 Ἰταλίας δὲ καὶ Σικελίας τὸ πλεῖστον Πελοποννήσιοι (*sc.* ᾤκισαν) τῆς τε ἄλλης Ἑλλάδος ἔστιν ἃ χωρία: 29.1 ἄραντες ἑβδομήκοντα ναυσὶ καὶ πέντε δισχιλίοις τε ὁπλίταις: Pl.*Ti.*58C οὕτω δὴ διὰ ταῦτά τε: X.*Cyn.*1.18 γίγνονται τὰ εἰς τὸν πόλεμον ἀγαθοὶ εἴς τε τὰ ἄλλα: Lys.xxxii 22 πλεῖν ἢ τετρακισχιλίας δραχμὰς ἀνηλωμένας, ἕτερά τε παμπληθῆ: Is.vii 7 εἰσέπραξε τὸ ἡμικλήριον ὧν Μνήσων κατέλιπεν ὅσα τε ἐκ τῆς ἐπιτροπῆς ἀπεστέρησε: Hdt.vii 79: Th.iii 36.6: X.*HG* vi 4.14.

(ii) Connecting clauses. (*a*) Participial. Th.i 76.2 ἀλλ' αἰεὶ καθεστῶτος... ἄξιοί τε ἅμα νομίζοντες εἶναι: X.*Oec.*10.12 καθα-

[1] I quote approximately all the examples below. In prose inscriptions single τε is not found before the Roman period (Meisterhans, p. 249).

ρωτέρα οὖσα πρεπόντως τε μᾶλλον ἠμφιεσμένη: Is.vii 17 ἐκείνῳ οὐκ ἀπιστούντων ἐμέ τε οὐκ ἀγνοούντων: cf. Aeschin.iii 87 Καλλίας... συναγείρας... ὅ τ' ἀδελφὸς αὐτοῦ Ταυροσθένης... διαβιβάσας: Hdt.ii 174: Th.iv 75.1: And.iii 30: Lys.xxxii 1: D.lix 38,62, 115.

(*b*) Infinitival. Hdt.i 112 ἐπιφοιτήσειν γὰρ κατασκόπους... ἀπολέεσθαί τε κάκιστα: Th.i 58.2 πείθει Χαλκιδέας... ἀνοικίσασθαι ἐς Ὄλυνθον μίαν τε πόλιν... ποιήσασθαι: X.*An.*i 9.5 ἔνθα Κῦρος αἰδημονέστατος... τῶν ἡλικιωτῶν ἐδόκει εἶναι, τοῖς τε πρεσβυτέροις... πείθεσθαι: D.lix 67.

(*c*) Finite. Hdt.i 31 τελευτὴ τοῦ βίου ἀρίστη ἐπεγένετο, διέδεξέ τε ἐν τούτοισι ὁ θεός: Th.i 13.1 τυραννίδες ἐν ταῖς πόλεσι καθίσταντο... ναυτικά τε ἐξηρτύετο ἡ Ἑλλάς: Pl.*R.*398A εἴποιμεν δ' ἂν ὅτι... ἀποπέμποιμέν τε...: *Ti.*39B ἵνα... φαίνοι τὸν οὐρανὸν μετάσχοι τε ἀριθμοῦ τὰ ζῷα: *Lg.*859B Καλῶς εἴρηκας, ποιῶμέν τε ὡς λέγεις:[1] X.*An.*i 5.14 ὁ δ' ἐχαλέπαινεν... ἐκέλευσέ τε αὐτὸν...: Lys.i 17 ἀναμιμνῃσκόμενος δὲ ὅτι... ἐψόφει ἡ μέταυλος θύρα... ἔδοξέ τέ μοι...: Isoc.xvii 41 ἐγὼ πλεῖστον εἰσήνεγκα τῶν ξένων, αὐτὸς θ' αἱρεθεὶς... ἐπέγραψα: Is.i 12 ἔσωσεν... ἐπεμελεῖτό τε: Pl.*Phdr.*230B: Ant.i 26: And.i 61,111: ii 15,19: iii 9: Lys.i 6: xiii 1,82: xxiii 3: xxxi 2: Is.vii 10,39: viii 16,18: xi 39: Hyp.*Epit.*42: D.xl 8: xliv 31: xlvi 15: lix 73.

(iii) Connecting sentences, particularly in Thucydides (e.g. i 4: 5.3: 6.5: 13.4: 13.5: 13.6: 14.2). Hdt.i 96,207: ii 37,82,176: iii 156: *id. saep.*: Pl.*Phdr.*248C: *R.*578A: *Ti.*57A (τε αὖ), 68B: *Lg.* 700B,757D,773A: X.*An.*iv 8.13 (*bis*) (but τε in Xenophon seldom connects sentences: and in most of Hammer's examples under this head only a colon precedes)[2]: Ant.ii γ3 (δέ Schäfer), δ7 (δέ Reiske): And.iii 33,40: Is.vii 9 (*bis*): viii 19 (*bis*): x 20: D.xlix 27 (δέ *FQD*).

The conclusion is that after Thucydides the use of τε to connect sentences declines markedly: and that single τε, in general not common in fourth-century prose, is used, where it is used,

[1] Hoefer observes (p. 7) that, except for *Ti.*29D, this type of expression is peculiar to the *Laws* (772E,891B,893A,895A,905D,961C).

[2] I do not mean that sentences must necessarily be separated by full stops: nor that there is a clear-cut line between sentences and finite clauses. But I have taken the punctuation of our printed texts as a rough guide to the strength of the pause, though I have not followed it slavishly.

to connect, neither sentences nor (except in Plato's latest works) individual words, but clauses.

The following peculiarities in the use of single τε may be noted:

(*a*) τε introduces the last item of a series, the previous items being connected by καί or δέ.

(α) Single words. S.*Ph.*581 πρὸς σὲ κἀμὲ τούσδε τε: E.*IA* 1301 ἔνθα ποτὲ Παλλὰς ἔμολε καὶ δολιόφρων Κύπρις Ἥρα θ' Ἑρμᾶς θ' (τε with last two items): Pl.*Ti.*31B σωματοειδὲς δὲ δὴ καὶ ὁρατὸν ἁπτόν τε: 75B σαρκώδη . . . καὶ νευρώδη κρατεράν τε κεφαλήν: *Criti.*112C κήπους καὶ γυμνάσια συσσίτιά τε: *Lg.*792E, 947E: *Criti.*117E,118C. Phrases. E.*Or.*204 ἐν στοναχαῖσί τε καὶ γόοισι δάκρυσί τ' ἐννυχίοις: Hdt.vii 8α1 Κῦρός τε καὶ Καμβύσης πατήρ τε ἐμὸς Δαρεῖος: Pl.*R.*415D: *Ti.*18A,60A.

(β) Clauses. E.*Supp.*831 κατά με πέδον γᾶς ἕλοι, διὰ δὲ θύελλα σπάσαι, πυρός τε φλογμὸς ὁ Διὸς ἐν κάρᾳ πέσοι: Hdt.vii 5.3 ὡς ἡ Εὐρώπη περικαλλὴς χώρη καὶ δένδρεα παντοῖα φέρει τὰ ἥμερα ἀρετήν τε ἄκρη, βασιλέϊ τε μούνῳ θνητῶν ἀξίη ἐκτῆσθαι: Th.i 56.2 ἐκέλευον τὸ ἐς Παλλήνην τεῖχος καθελεῖν καὶ ὁμήρους δοῦναι, τούς τε ἐπιδημιουργοὺς ἐκπέμπειν: Pl.*Ti.*73E μετ' ἐκεῖνο δὲ εἰς ὕδωρ βάπτει, πάλιν δὲ εἰς πῦρ, αὖθίς τε εἰς ὕδωρ (αὖθίς τε *FY*: αὖθις δέ *AP*): *Tht.*157E λείπεται δὲ ἐνυπνίων τε πέρι καὶ νόσων . . . ὅσα τε . . .: Hdt.i 86: Ant.ivα4 (δέ Schäfer): D.lvii 12.

(γ) Sentences. Often in Thucydides τε introduces a clinching or summing up of what precedes: iv 12.3: 14.3: vii 71.4. ἁπλῶς τε: iii 38.7: 45.7. ξυνελών τε: ii 41.1. So, too, Aristotle often sums up an enumerative series by ὅλως τε: e.g. *Metaph.* 981b7,989a26.

(*b*) A word or clause connected by τε is followed by another connected by καί or δέ, with sometimes another τε.

(α) Single words and phrases. Ar.*Av.*701–2 γένετ' οὐρανὸς ὠκεανός τε καὶ γῆ πάντων τε θεῶν μακάρων γένος ἄφθιτον: Pl. *Ti.*92C μέγιστος καὶ ἄριστος κάλλιστός τε καὶ τελεώτατος: *Lg.* 828B ἐξηγηταὶ καὶ ἱερεῖς ἱέρειαί τε καὶ μάντεις: 886A: Lys.ii 39 ποῖαι δ' οὐχ ἱκετεῖαι θεῶν ἐγένοντο ἢ θυσιῶν ἀναμνήσεις, ἔλεός τε παίδων καὶ γυναικῶν πόθος οἶκτός τε πατέρων καὶ μητέρων, λογισμὸς δὲ . . . τῶν . . . κακῶν. Hoefer observes that καὶ . . . τε . . . καί is common in *Timaeus* and *Laws*. (In Pl.*Ti.*80A both τε καί's perhaps couple the units of the pairs, while between the pairs there is asyndeton: *καὶ ὅσοι φθόγγοι ταχεῖς τε καὶ βραδεῖς ὀξεῖς τε καὶ βαρεῖς φαίνονται*: cf. *Epin.*978A: *Lg.*880D,896D: Hdt.iii 157. So, too, in Ar.*Ach.*1016 τε καί seems to mean 'both ... and', *μαγειρικῶς* being analysed into *κομψῶς* and *δειπνητικῶς*.)

(β) Clauses. Pl.*Ti.*41D,78A: Ant.ii β 12 (perhaps).

(*c*) Rarely, τε couples the last two units of an otherwise asyndetic series (cf. δέ, I.A.4: καί, I.1). A.*Pers.*404 *ἐλευθεροῦτε δὲ παῖδας, γυναῖκας, θεῶν τε πατρῴων ἕδη*: *Ag.*1433: S.*Aj.*297 *ἄγων ὁμοῦ ταύρους, κύνας βοτῆρας, εὔερόν τ' ἄγραν*: *OT* 1407 *νύμφας γυναῖκας μητέρας τε*: E.*El.*334 *αἱ χεῖρες ἡ γλῶσσ' ἡ ταλαίπωρός τε φρήν*; *Ba.*694 *νέαι παλαιαὶ παρθένοι τ' ἔτ' ἄζυγες* (*τ' ἔτ' ἄζυγες ex Chr.Pat.*1834, Musgrave: *τε κἄζυγες LP*): *Ph.*1147: *IA* 107 (text doubtful): Pl.*Lg.*775C *εὐπαγὲς ἀπλανὲς ἡσυχαῖόν τε*: *Ti.*76E.*

Or τε following an asyndetic series is followed by a further connective; E.*Tr.*674 *ἄνδρ' ἀρκοῦντά μοι ξυνέσει γένει πλούτῳ τε κἀνδρείᾳ μέγαν* (but more probably the καί links *μέγαν* with *ἀρκοῦντα*): *Hel.*1103 *ἔρωτας ἀπάτας δόλιά τ' ἐξευρήματα ἀσκοῦσα φίλτρα θ' αἱματηρὰ δωμάτων*: Pl.*Ti.*82A *γῆς πυρὸς ὕδατός τε καὶ ἀέρος*. Alternation of copulation and asyndeton is common in the *Persae*: e.g. 959–60 *οἷος ἦν Φαρανδάκης, Σούσας, Πελάγων, [καὶ] Δοτάμας, ἠδ' Ἀγδαβάτας, Ψάμμις, Σουσισκάνης τ'.*

(*d*) The coupling of *πολλά* and a qualitative epithet by τε, instead of the normal καί, in A.*Th.*339 seems unparalleled: *πολλὰ γὰρ ... δυστυχῆ τε πράσσει*. Hence Dobree's *πολλὰ ... χρηστά θ'* in S.*Ph.*584 (for γ'), though often accepted, rests on a fragile foundation.

Two disparate qualitative epithets are coupled by τε in Pi.*P.*12.9 *παρθενίοις ὑπό τ' ἀπλάτοις ὀφίων κεφαλαῖς*. A.*Eu.*559 is harder: *ἐν μέσᾳ δυσπαλεῖ τε δίνᾳ* (Turnebus: *δυσπαλεῖται codd.*): and if *δυσπαλεῖ* is taken as a verb the position of τε is even more difficult. Coupling phrases: S.*Aj.*379 *ἰὼ πάντα δρῶν, ἁπάντων τ' ἀεὶ κακῶν ὄργανον*: E.*Med.*124 *ἐμοὶ γοῦν ἐν μὴ μεγάλοις ὀχυρῶς τ' εἴη καταγηράσκειν* (where Reiske's γ' is probably right). E.*Med.*405 *τοῖς Σισυφείοις τοῖς τ' Ἰάσονος γάμοις*, with its repeated article, can certainly not be defended on these grounds: nor can A.*Supp.*9 *γάμον Αἰγύπτου παίδων ἀσεβῆ τ' ὀνοταζόμεναι* (Paley takes τ' as postponed: ʼξονοταζόμεναι Tucker): nor can Hdt.vii 151 (τε *om. ABCP*).

(*e*) Greek sometimes employs connexion by τε where English prefers an appositional construction. (Cf. δέ, I.A.1: see also καί, I.4.) A.*Supp*.42 Δῖον πόρτιν ... ἶνίν τ' ἀνθονόμον: 62 τᾶς Τηρείας μήτιδος οἰκτρᾶς ἀλόχου κιρκηλάτου τ' ἀηδόνος: *Th*.501 Πρῶτον μὲν Ὄγκα Παλλὰς ἥ τ' ἀγχίπτολις πύλαισι γείτων (see p. 523): *Ag*.10 φέρουσαν ἐκ Τροίας φάτιν ἁλώσιμόν τε βάξιν: 1526 ἐμὸν ἐκ τοῦδ' ἔρνος ἀερθέν, τὴν πολύκλαυτόν τ' Ἰφιγενείαν (πολυκλαύτην, without τε, Porson): 1585 πατέρα Θυέστην τὸν ἐμὸν ... αὑτοῦ τ' ἀδελφόν (τ' is unnecessarily suspected by Elmsley and Verrall): *Ch*.95 ἔσθλ' ἀντιδοῦναι ... δόσιν τε τῶν κακῶν ἐπαξίαν (γε Stanley)*: E.*IA* 1153 τὼ Διὸς ... παῖδ' ἐμώ τε συγγόνω (δέ Matthiae): 1454 Πατέρα τὸν ἁμὸν μὴ στύγει πόσιν τε σόν (γε Elmsley): *Hec*.615 (τε seems to be epexegetic of ὡς ἔχω, 'as best I may, by mustering finery': perhaps γ', Wakefield): *El*.1243: *Ph*.1029 (the μοῦσα *is* an Ἐρινύς). The existence of an appositional use of γε (*q.v.* I.12.i), and the facility with which τ and γ may be interchanged (see e.g. E.*Hel*.426,432,829,1273), often make the reading doubtful.

(*f*) τε is very occasionally employed in anaphora, like καί (I.3) and δέ without μέν (δέ, I.A.2), instead of the more usual μὲν ... δέ or asyndeton. Hom.Θ24 αὐτῇ κεν γαίῃ ἐρύσαιμ' αὐτῇ τε θαλάσσῃ: S.*OC* 1311 σὺν ἑπτὰ τάξεσιν σὺν ἑπτά τε λόγχαις: E.*Tr*.604 οἷος ἰάλεμος, οἷά τε πένθη: S.*Ant*.674 (*coni.* Pearson): E.*HF* 1377 (δέ Hermann). In A.*Pers*.379 θ' is *v.l.* In S.*Aj*.350 read μόνοι ἔτ' ἐμμένοντες (Hermann for μόνοι τ' *codd.*).

(*g*) Occasional other irregularities are to be met with. Lys. xiii 40 πυθομένη δ' ἐκείνη ἀφικνεῖται, μέλαν τε ἱμάτιον ἠμφιεσμένη: the text has been universally suspected, but 'she came, and dressed in black' is natural English idiom, and perhaps not impossible as a colloquialism in Greek, τε almost bearing the force of καὶ ταῦτα: cf. δέ, I.A.3: clearly, τε does not couple the participles. Externally similar, but to be otherwise analysed, is Pi.*P*.6.46 Θρασύβουλος πατρῴαν μάλιστα πρὸς στάθμαν ἔβα, πάτρῳ τ' ἐπερχόμενος ἀγλαΐαν ἅπασαν (where Christ paraphrases ἔβα πρὸς πατρῴαν στάθμαν βαίνων πάτρῳ τ' ἐπερχόμενος).

Pi.*I*.5.19 τὶν δ' ἐν Ἰσθμῷ διπλόα θάλλοισ' ἀρετά, Φυλακίδα, κεῖται, Νεμέᾳ δὲ καὶ ἀμφοῖν Πυθέᾳ τε, παγκρατίου ('both, including Pytheas': see Schroeder *ad loc.*, and Wackernagel, *Ztschr. f. vergl. Sprachf.* xxiii 308, on Hom.*M* 335–6, citing a Vedic parallel, 'we two and Varuna' = 'I and Varuna').

(*h*) Single τε is not used after οὐ (οὔτε, 'and not'), except (occasionally) where a negative clause precedes (οὐ . . . οὔτε, 'not . . . and not': see 4.iii). In Lys.xxv 14 there is an anacoluthon, οὔτε after δικασταί meaning 'neither' (Kühner, II ii 288).

(2) Corresponsive, τε . . . τε. This combination, though rarer in prose than in verse, is yet far commoner in prose than single τε. Excluding εἴτε, ἐάντε, οὔτε, it is rarer (though not, on the whole, absolutely rare) in the orators than in the historians and Plato: the genuine public orations of Demosthenes afford no example.[1]

Verse. (Homer, as Bäumlein and Christ have pointed out, usually employs τε . . . τε to connect words or phrases, seldom to connect clauses.) Hom.*A* 13 λυσόμενός τε θύγατρα φέρων τ' ἀπερείσι' ἄποινα: 544 πατὴρ ἀνδρῶν τε θεῶν τε: Hes.*Op.*669 ἀγαθῶν τε κακῶν τε: A.*Pers.*184 μεγέθει τε τῶν νῦν ἐκπρεπεστάτα πολύ, κάλλει τ' ἀμώμω: 491 πλεῖστοι θάνον δίψῃ τε λιμῷ τ': S.*Aj.*34–5 τά τ' οὖν πάρος τά τ' εἰσέπειτα: Ar.*Ach.* 370–5 τούς τε γὰρ τρόπους τοὺς τῶν ἀγροίκων οἶδα . . . τῶν τ' αὖ γερόντων οἶδα τὰς ψυχάς (an exceptionally wide interval: cf. S.*OC* 765–72).

Rarely with anaphora. S.*El.*1098–9 ὀρθά τ' εἰσηκούσαμεν ὀρθῶς θ' ὁδοιποροῦμεν.

In prose, the units joined are usually clauses, seldom single words or phrases. This applies to Plato as well as to other

[1] But there are some 36 examples in the lawcourt speeches attributed to Demosthenes, including speeches certainly written by him. What is the reason for this difference in usage between Assembly speeches and forensic speeches? Was τε . . . τε felt, perhaps, to be slightly colloquial? In prose inscriptions before the Roman period τε . . . τε is found only with εἰ, ἐάν, οὐ, μή (Meisterhans, p. 249). Spengel (*Rh.M.*xvii(1862)167) notes that there are only two certain examples of τε . . . τε in Ant. I, V, and VI, as against 42 in the *Tetralogies*. Fuhr (*Rh.M.*xxxiii(1878)594–9) observes that τε . . . τε gets rarer during the fourth century.

Schmidt (p. 32) is misleading here: he does not distinguish between τε . . . τε and ἐάν τε . . . ἐάν τε.

prose writers. But, relatively to them, he uses τε to join phrases often, though very rarely to join single words.

Single words. Pl.*Criti.*115B παιδιᾶς τε ὃς ἕνεκα ἡδονῆς τε γέγονε . . . καρπός: 121B παγκαλοί τε μακάριοί τε (there may be some Homeric colour here, as Hoefer suggests).

Phrases. Hdt.vii 8γ3 οὕτω οἵ τε ἡμῖν αἴτιοι ἕξουσι δούλιον ζυγὸν οἵ τε ἀναίτιοι: ix 122.2 ἀνθρώπων τε πολλῶν ἄρχομεν πάσης τε τῆς Ἀσίης: Th.ii 84.3 τοῦ τε ἀνέμου τῶν τε πλοίων: iv 8.8 τήν τε νῆσον πολεμίαν ἔσεσθαι τήν τε ἤπειρον: Pl.*R.*373B οἷον οἵ τε θηρευταὶ πάντες οἵ τε μιμηταί: 520B ὑμῖν τε αὐτοῖς τῇ τε ἄλλῃ πόλει: 578A φόβου γέμειν ἆρ' οὐκ ἀνάγκη τήν τε τοιαύτην πόλιν τόν τε τοιοῦτον ἄνδρα; *Ti.*37E τό τ' ἦν τό τ' ἔσται: *Phdr.*244A ἥ τε γὰρ δὴ ἐν Δελφοῖς προφῆτις αἵ τ' ἐν Δωδώνῃ ἱέρειαι: 245D πάντα τε οὐρανὸν πᾶσάν τε γένεσιν: X.*HG* iv 8.22 εὔχαρίς τε οὐχ ἧττον τοῦ Θίβρωνος, μᾶλλόν τε συντεταγμένος: Hdt.ix 3.2: Th.ii 64.2: iv 108.3: Pl.*Phdr.*276D: *Lg.*951E: *R.* 465C: X *Cyr.*vi 1.29: *An.*iv 5.12.

There are a few examples in the orators, mainly from those of the earliest period. Ant.iiγ3 ὅ τε φόβος ἥ τε ἀδικία: *ib.* ὅ τε κίνδυνος ἥ τε αἰσχύνη: And.iii 2 διά τε τὴν ἀπειρίαν τοῦ ἔργου διά τε τὴν ἐκείνων ἀπιστίαν: 34 φημὶ . . . ἄνδρα στρατηγὸν τῇ πόλει τε εὔνουν εἰδότα τε ὅ τι πράττοι λανθάνοντα δεῖν . . . ἄγειν ἐπὶ τοὺς κινδύνους: Aeschin.ii 145 ὅταν . . . ἔν τε ταῖς ἐκκλησίαις ἁπάσαις πρός τε τὴν βουλὴν διαβάλλῃ τινά.

Clauses. Hdt.i 22 καὶ δύο τε . . . νηοὺς . . . οἰκοδόμησε . . . αὐτός τε ἐκ τῆς νούσου ἀνέστη: Th.i 8.3 οἵ τε ἥσσους ὑπέμενον . . . οἵ τε δυνατώτεροι . . . προσεποιοῦντο: 23.1 τούτου δὲ τοῦ πολέμου μῆκός τε μέγα προὔβη, παθήματά τε ξυνηνέχθη γενέσθαι: Pl.*R.*474C ἅπτεσθαί τε φιλοσοφίας ἡγεμονεύειν τ' ἐν πόλει: 548D πῶς τε γενόμενος ποῖός τέ τις ὤν; X.*Cyr.*i 4.25 οἵ τε ἄλλοι πάντες τὸν Κῦρον διὰ στόματος εἶχον . . . ὅ τε Ἀστυάγης . . . ὑπερεξεπέπληκτο ἐπ' αὐτῷ: Lys.xiii 8 ὑμεῖς τε . . . οὐκ ἠνέσχεσθε ἀκούσαντες . . . Κλεοφῶν τε . . . ἀντεῖπεν: Isoc.iv 137 τήν τε γὰρ Ἀσίαν διωμολόγηται . . . τάς τε πόλεις . . . παρείληφεν: D.xlvii 81 τά τε σκεύη ἐκφορῆσαι τήν τε τιτθὴν συγκόψαι: Th.i 12.3: 26.3(*bis*): 34.3: Pl.*Phdr.*248B: *R.*466C: *Phd.*71B,113D: And.i 24,80,82: Lys.xii 61,64: Isoc.v 72,80,92,104,106,108: Is.i 50: [D.] vii 13: D.xx 16,50: xxiv 8,156: Aeschin.ii 81.

τε . . . τε . . . τε. Sometimes two or more τε's, meaning 'and', follow the first τε. (Xenophon uses triple and quadruple τε more frequently than the other historians: Hammer, p. 94. Multiplication of τε is rare in Plato: Hoefer, p. 12.)

E.*Ba.* 379–81 ὃς τάδ' ἔχει, θιασεύειν τε χόροις μετά τ' αὐλοῦ γελάσαι ἀποπαῦσαί τε μερίμνας: Ar.*Lys.* 40–1: *Ra.* 818–19: Hdt.i 16 οὗτος δὲ Κυαξάρῃ τε . . . ἐπολέμησε καὶ Μήδοισι, Κιμμερίους τε . . . ἐξήλασε, Σμύρνην τε . . . εἷλε, ἐς Κλαζομενάς τε ἐσέβαλε: Th.i 2.3 ἥ τε νῦν Θεσσαλία καλουμένη καὶ Βοιωτία, Πελοποννήσου τε τὰ πολλὰ πλὴν Ἀρκαδίας, τῆς τε ἄλλης ὅσα ἦν κράτιστα: Pl.*Prm.*165A–B πρό τε τῆς ἀρχῆς . . . μετά τε τὴν τελευτὴν . . . ἔν τε τῷ μέσῳ: X.*Cyr.*vi 2.17 ἀλλ' οἵ τε ἵπποι εἰσὶ . . . οἵ τε ἡνίοχοι . . . ἑστᾶσι . . . δρέπανά τε . . . προσήρμοσται: Lys.xix 13 ὑπ' ἐκείνου τε πεπιστευμένους γεγονότας τε ἐπιεικεῖς τῇ πόλει ἔν τε τῷ τότε χρόνῳ ἀρέσκοντας: Isoc.iii 25: v 54: Is. vi 38: vii 34: D.xxi 26: xxvii 16.

The forms εἴτε . . . εἴτε, οὔτε . . . οὔτε are common in all periods and styles, and the second τε is not here normally replaced by καί.[1] (E.*IT* 591 is exceptional: εἶ γάρ, ὡς ἔοικας, οὔτε δυσμενὴς καὶ τὰς Μυκήνας οἶσθα: here there is clearly a change of construction, οὔτε ἄϊδρις, or the like, being expected: Wecklein compares Lucian *DMar.*14.1.) Only deviations from the normal require illustration: these are mainly poetical, and are almost entirely absent from the strict regularity of fourth-century oratorical prose.

(3) εἴτε . . . εἴτε: used both in conditional protases and in indirect questions. The following forms should be distinguished (Kühner, II ii 300):

(*a*) Each conditional protasis has its own apodosis. Th.ii 51.5 εἴτε γὰρ μὴ 'θέλοιεν δεδιότες ἀλλήλοις προσιέναι, ἀπώλλυντο ἐρῆμοι . . .· εἴτε προσίοιεν, διεφθείροντο. Cf. Pl.*Prt.*338B: X. *An.*vi 6.20: Arist.*Pol.*1259b39.

(*b*) The two protases share a common apodosis. Pl.*Ly.*212E Τὸ φιλούμενον ἄρα τῷ φιλοῦντι φίλον ἐστὶν . . . ἐάν τε φιλῇ, ἐάν τε καὶ μισῇ: Th.iv 19.1.

(*c*) The two protases share also a common verb. Hom.*M* 239 τῶν οὔ τι . . . ἀλεγίζω, εἴτ' ἐπὶ δεξί' ἴωσι . . . εἴτ' ἐπ' ἀριστερά:

[1] But Pl.*Lg.*849E ἐάντε . . . καὶ ἂν μή: 863E, 929E. On S.*Fr.*1019.11 (his 1120), see Pearson, *Fragments of Sophocles*. For *Ant.* 328, see pp. 517–18.

Pl.*Men* 92C Πῶς οὖν ἂν . . . εἰδείης περὶ τούτου τοῦ πράγματος, εἴτε τι ἀγαθὸν ἔχει ἐν αὐτῷ εἴτε φλαῦρον; X.*HG* i 6.5.

(*d*) The protases have no verb, and have to borrow one from the apodosis: εἴτε then approximates to ἤ, as 'whether' to 'either'. S.*Ph.*345 λέγοντες, εἴτ' ἀληθές, εἴτ' ἄρ' οὖν μάτην (*sc.* ἔλεγον): *OT* 194,1049: X.*Cyr.*i 1.5.

(*e*) The second protasis has a verb, while the first has to borrow one from the common apodosis. Pl.*Cra.*428C καὶ ἐμοὶ σὺ . . . φαίνῃ . . . χρησμῳδεῖν, εἴτε παρ' Εὐθύφρονος ἐπίπνους γενόμενος (*sc.* χρησμῳδεῖς), εἴτε καὶ ἄλλη τις Μοῦσα πάλαι σε ἐνοῦσα ἐλελήθει. Cf. *Sph.*222B θὲς δὲ ὅπῃ χαίρεις, εἴτε μηδὲν τιθεὶς ἥμερον, εἴτε ἄλλο μὲν ἥμερόν τι, τὸν δὲ ἄνθρωπον ἄγριον, εἴτε ἥμερον μὲν λέγεις . . . .

The negative form οὔτ' εἰ . . . οὔτ' εἰ (e.g. S.*Ant.*905–6) is used also in indirect questions: Hdt.vii 135.3 ἐλευθερίης δὲ οὔκω ἐπειρήθης, οὔτ' εἰ ἔστι γλυκὺ οὔτ' εἰ μή.

Exceptional forms:

(i) εἰ . . . εἴτε. A. *Eu.*468 σὺ δ' εἰ δικαίως εἴτε μὴ (ἔκτεινα) κρῖνον δίκην: S.*OT* 92 Εἰ τῶνδε χρῄζεις πλησιαζόντων κλύειν, ἑτοῖμος εἰπεῖν, εἴτε καὶ στείχειν ἔσω: E.*Alc.*140 εἰ δ' ἔτ' ἐστὶν ἔμψυχος γυνὴ εἴτ' οὖν ὄλωλεν εἰδέναι βουλοίμεθ' ἄν: A.*Ch.*768: S.*OT* 517: E.*Ion* 1121: *IA* 796: Pl.*Lg.*952B εἴ τινα φήμην . . . ηὗρέν τινας ἔχοντας φράζειν, εἴτε καὶ αὐτὸς νενοηκὼς ἄττα ἥκοι: X.*Cyr.*ii 1.7 Ἀλλ' εἰ μὲν ἀνδρῶν προσδεῖ ἡμῖν . . . εἴτε καὶ μή, αὖθις συμβουλευσόμεθα· τὴν δὲ μάχην μοι, ἔφη, λέξον: v 3.57 ὅπως εἴ τί που ἐναντιοῖτο αὐτῷ, ἀπαντῴη . . . , εἴ τέ τί που φεῦγον ὀφθείη . . . διώκοι (ὅπως εἴ τε που *HAG et D*): Hdt.iii 35 (*ABCEP*): ix 54.2: Pl.*R.*503E: *Cra.*424B: *Alc.II* 148A: *Lg.*907D. Essentially similar, Hdt.vii 234.1 εἰπὲ . . . ὁκόσοι τοιοῦτοι τὰ πολέμια, εἴτε καὶ ἅπαντες:[1] cf. ii 53.

(ii) εἴτε . . . εἰ δέ. Here (with a certain degree of anacoluthon) δέ is substituted for τε in order to give an antithetical emphasis

[1] Here ὁκόσοι implies εἰ: 'whether a proportion only, and, if so, what proportion . . .'. So, in X.*An* i 3.11, in a true conditional clause, ἕως means 'if, and as long as'. There does not seem, in principle, to be any reason why τε ('and') should not follow εἰ, without a preceding conditional protasis expressed or implied: εἴ τε, 'and if': in practice the collocation seems to have been avoided.

to the second clause. Pl.*Lg*.952C καὶ ἐάντε μηδὲν χείρων . . . ἐὰν δὲ πολὺ βελτίων . . . : X.*Mem*.ii 1.28 ἀλλ' εἴτε τοὺς θεοὺς ἵλεως εἶναί σοι βούλει, θεραπευτέον τοὺς θεούς, εἴτε . . . εἴτε . . . εἴτε . . . εἴτε . . . εἴτε . . . εἴτε . . . εἰ δὲ καὶ τῷ σώματι βούλει δυνατὸς εἶναι . . . : Pl.*Ap*.33D. In Pl.*Ap*.40C–E the great interval between εἴτε δή and εἰ δ' αὖ makes the anacoluthon imperceptible.

(iii) εἴτε . . . ἤ. E.*Hipp*.142–4 ἦ σύ γ' ἔνθεος, ὦ κούρα, εἴτ' ἐκ Πανὸς εἴθ' Ἑκάτας ἢ σεμνῶν Κορυβάντων φοιτᾷς ἢ ματρὸς ὀρείας; *IT* 272 εἴτ' οὖν ἐπ' ἀκταῖς θάσσετον Διοσκόρω, ἢ Νηρέως ἀγάλμαθ': E.*El*.896: Ar.*Ach*.569: Pl.*Phdr*.277D Ὡς εἴτε Λυσίας ἤ τις ἄλλος πώποτε ἔγραψεν: *R*.375A ὁ μὴ θυμοειδὴς εἴτε ἵππος εἴτε κύων ἢ ἄλλο ὁτιοῦν ζῷον (εἴτε ἄλλο *F* Stobaeus: ἢ ἄλλο *ADM*): *Lg*.739D εἴτε που θεοὶ ἢ παῖδες θεῶν αὐτὴν οἰκοῦσι: 862D εἴτε ἔργοις ἢ λόγοις. Even in the formal language of an inscription (424 B.C.), Meisterhans, p. 256. (But in Pl.*R*.364B–C, which Kühner cites, εἴτε is clearly answered by ἐάν τε, not by ἤ.)

ἢ . . . εἴτε (not, as Kühner says, entirely confined to poetry). S.*Aj*.178 ἤ πού τινος νίκας ἀκάρπωτον χάριν, ἤ ῥα κλυτῶν ἐνάρων ψευσθεῖσ', ἀδώροις εἴτ' ἐλαφηβολίαις; E.*Alc*.115 ἀλλ' οὐδὲ ναυκληρίαν ἔσθ' ὅποι τις αἴας στείλας, ἢ Λυκίαν εἴτε . . .: Pl.*Criti*.115A ὅσα εὐώδη τρέφει που γῆ τὰ νῦν, ῥιζῶν ἢ χλόης ἢ ξύλων ἢ χυλῶν στακτῶν εἴτε ἀνθῶν ἢ καρπῶν.

(iv) εἴτε omitted in the first clause.[1] Pi.*P*.4.76 εὖτ' ἂν . . . μόλῃ

[1] With some hesitation, I retain this traditional heading, and quote the examples in chronological order, refraining from sub-classification. But further analysis seems necessary, though the authorities do not give it us. The passages fall, I think, into two classes: (1) where εἴτε has no verb expressed, and ἤ could be substituted for it, as in (*d*) above, the words preceding εἴτε making grammatical sense independently of the sequel: this includes the passages from Pindar and Sophocles, and the five from Plato: (2) where εἴτε has a verb expressed, and the words preceding εἴτε will not stand if taken independently: this includes the two passages from Aeschylus, which differ, however, pretty widely from one another. In A.*Ag*.1403 εἴτε must clearly be understood before αἰνεῖν, as the thought is definitely disjunctive, 'whether . . . or . . .'. *Ch*.1002 is equally clearly not disjunctive; 'whether she had been a lamprey or a viper' is nonsense, and one understands εἰ, rather than εἴτε, before μύραινα. E.*Tr*.874 occupies a sort of intermediate position: the words preceding εἴτε make sense independently, but εἴτε has a verb expressed.

. . . ξεῖνος αἴτ' ὢν ἀστός: A.*Ag.*1403 σὺ δ' αἰνεῖν εἴτε με ψέγειν θέλεις, ὅμοιον: *Ch.*1002 τί σοι δοκεῖ; μύραινά γ' εἴτ' ἔχιδν' ἔφυ, σήπειν θιγοῦσ' ἂν ἄλλον (γ' εἴτ' Hermann: τ' ἤτ' *M*): S.*Tr.*236 Ποῦ γῆς, πατρῴας εἴτε βαρβάρου; λέγε (the punctuation is doubtful: I follow Jebb): E.*Tr.*874 κτανεῖν ἐμοί νιν ἔδοσαν, εἴτε μὴ κτανὼν θέλοιμ' ἄγεσθαι: Pl.*Sph.*217E ἀπομηκύνειν λόγον συχνὸν κατ' ἐμαυτόν, εἴτε καὶ πρὸς ἕτερον: 224E Καὶ τὸ κτητικῆς ἄρα μεταβλητικόν, ἀγοραστικόν, καπηλικὸν εἴτε αὐτοπωλικόν, ἀμφοτέρως: *Lg.*844D ὃς ἂν ἀγροίκου ὀπώρας γεύσηται, βοτρύων εἴτε καὶ σύκων: *Lg.*814A: *Ti.*56D: *Alc.II* 148C.

For εἴτε καί, see further καί, II.B.7.i: for εἴτε οὖν, see οὖν, II.1, pp. 418–9.*

(4) οὔτε . . . οὔτε (μήτε . . . μήτε), or, where the second clause is positive, οὔτε (μήτε) . . . τε (e.g. Pl.*Prt.*360D Οὐκέτι ἐνταῦθα οὔτ' ἐπινεῦσαι ἠθέλησεν ἐσίγα τε (negative duplicated, as in S.*Ant.* 763, for which, however, see δῆτα, II.1): *Tht.*184A: *Criti.*120C: *et saep.*).

Exceptional forms (see Kühner, II ii 288 ff.).

(i) οὔτε . . . τε . . . οὐ (or τ' οὐ). E.*Hipp.*302 οὔτε γὰρ τότε λόγοις ἐτέγγεθ' ἥδε νῦν τ' οὐ πείθεται: *Tr.*487 κοὔτ' ἐξ ἐκείνων ἐλπὶς ὡς ὀφθήσομαι, αὐτή τ' ἐκείνας οὐκέτ' ὄψομαί ποτε: S.*Ant.* 763. Sometimes also in prose. Th.i 5.2 ὡς οὔτε ὧν πυνθάνονται ἀπαξιούντων τὸ ἔργον, οἷς τε ἐπιμελὲς εἴη εἰδέναι οὐκ ὀνειδιζόντων: 126.6 οὔτε ἐκεῖνος ἔτι κατενόησε τό τε μαντεῖον οὐκ

Here there is no need to supply either εἰ or εἴτε (either would necessitate supplying also κτανεῖν θέλοιμι): simply 'they gave her me to kill, or, if I wished, without killing, to take away', ἄγεσθαι being construed ἀπὸ κοινοῦ after ἔδοσαν and after θέλοιμι.

Hdt.ii 125 is again different: ὅσοι . . . στοῖχοι ἦσαν . . . τοσαῦται καὶ μηχαναὶ ἦσαν, εἴτε καὶ τὴν αὐτὴν μηχανὴν ἐοῦσαν μίαν . . . μετεφόρεον ἐπὶ στοῖχον ἕκαστον. εἴτε thus standing, with verb expressed, as the equivalent of ἤ in an independent clause is, I think, unparalleled: but the colloquial casualness of the language is characteristically Herodotean: 'or whether it was that . . .' ('oder sei es auch dass', Stein, rightly: but he is wrong, I think, in comparing ii 53, grouped under (i)).

The essential point to grasp is that the two Aeschylean passages involve harsh ellipses of εἴτε and of εἰ, of a kind which would scarcely be tolerated in prose: and that they are not really on all fours with the remaining passages.

ἐδήλου: Pl.*Lg*.679B. (Where the negative goes closely with a single word, this construction merges into οὔτε . . . τε.[1])

(ii) τε . . . οὔτε. Extremely rare (Kühner (II ii 292) and Jebb (on S.*OC*367) refuse to allow it at all): E.*Fr*.522 κεῖνοί τ' ἂν οὐδὲν εἶεν οὔθ' ἡμεῖς ἔτι (οὐδ' Trinc.): Pl.*Tht*.159E Οὔκουν ἐγώ τε οὐδὲν ἄλλο ποτὲ γενήσομαι . . . οὔτε ἐκεῖνο . . . . It is to be remarked that in both cases a negative closely follows the τε. Th. i 37.2 can hardly be admitted as an example (see Marchant (for) and Steup (against): I am inclined to believe that Steup is right in taking τε as connective and reading οὔτε μάρτυρα).

(iii) οὐ . . . οὔτε. The addition is an afterthought. Epic, Elegiac, and Lyric. Hom.*Z*451 ἀλλ' οὔ μοι Τρώων τόσσον μέλει ἄλγος ὀπίσσω, οὔτ' αὐτῆς Ἑκάβης οὔτε Πριάμοιο ἄνακτος οὔτε κασιγνήτων: *X*265 (*v.l.* οὐδέ, but οὔτε has preponderating MS. authority: see Leaf): δ566 οὐ νιφετός, οὔτ' ἂρ χειμὼν πολὺς οὔτε ποτ' ὄμβρος: λ483 σεῖο δ', Ἀχιλλεῦ, οὔ τις ἀνὴρ προπάροιθε μακάρτατος οὔτ' ἄρ' ὀπίσσω: Thgn.125 (reading doubtful): 745 μή τιν' ὑπερβασίην κατέχων μήθ' ὅρκον ἀλιτρόν: Pi.*P*.5.54 πόνων δ' οὔ τις ἀπόκλαρός ἐστιν οὔτ' ἔσεται: B.*Fr*.21.1 οὐ βοῶν πάρεστι σώματ' οὔτε χρυσὸς οὔτε . . . .

οὐ . . . οὔτε is also found in the tragedians, and occasionally in comedy and prose. οὔτε is often emended into οὐδέ, but the number of passages is perhaps too large to justify this alteration everywhere.[2] Tyrt.*Fr*.6–7.12 ἀνδρός τοι ἀλωμένου οὐδεμί' ὤρη γίγνεται οὔτ' αἰδὼς οὔτ' ὀπίσω γένεος: S.*Aj*.428 Οὔτοι σ' ἀπείργειν οὔθ' ὅπως ἐῶ λέγειν ἔχω: *El*.1412 Ἀλλ' οὐκ ἐκ σέθεν ᾠκτίρεθ' οὗτος οὔθ' ὁ γεννήσας πατήρ: *OC*496 λείπομαι γὰρ ἐν τῷ μὴ δύνασθαι μήθ' ὁρᾶν, δυοῖν κακοῖν: E.*Med*.1354 σὺ δ' οὐκ ἔμελλες . . . οὔθ' ἡ τύραννος οὔθ' . . .: S.*OC*451: *Tr*.1058: E.*IA* 978,1323: Ar.*Ach*.657

[1] Cf. cases of τε . . . τε correspondence which contain an οὐ going closely with the following word: e.g. E.*IT* 1367,1477: X.*Mem*.i 2.4.

[2] Jebb, on S.*Tr*.1058, wrongly seeks to restrict this use to cases where more than one οὔτε follows the οὐ, in imitation of the 'Homeric usage' (which is itself, however, not entirely so restricted: see λ 483 above). Wilamowitz (on S.*Ach.Conv*.17, *Berliner Klassikertexte* v 2 (1907), p. 65) allows οὐ . . . οὔτε where οὐ is 'erweitert durch einen anderen Zusatz' (μήν, τοι, τις, τι). With Pearson (*Fragments of Sophocles*, vol. i, p. 99), I doubt whether there is much to be said for this canon, though certainly a number of the apparent instances are οὔ τις (τι) . . . οὔτε.

(οὐδ' ... οὐδ' Suidas): X.*An.*iv 8.3 ἐξικνοῦντο γὰρ οὔ, οὔτ' ἔβλαπτον οὐδέν (text uncertain): vi 1.24 σημαίνει μὴ προσδεῖσθαι τῆς ἀρχῆς μήτε εἰ αἱροῖντο ἀποδέχεσθαι (text uncertain): Hdt.iii 155 (οὔτε *RSV*: οὐδέ *cett.*): Ant. v 93: vi 10: Lys.xvi 3: Is.viii 1: D.xix 160 (οὐκ ... οὔτε (οὐδέ Bekker) ... οὐδέ): 19 (οὐδέ Blass). (It is worth noting that four of the Attic prose examples are from Xenophon and Antiphon, writers whose style has a poetical or non-Attic tinge, while a fifth is from Isaeus, who uses single τε freely.)

οὐ ... οὔτ' οὖν. Hom.β 200 ἐπεὶ οὔ τινα δείδιμεν ἔμπης, οὔτ' οὖν Τηλέμαχον ('nor, for that matter, Telemachus'): ι 147 ἔνθ' οὔ τις τὴν νῆσον ἐσέδρακεν ὀφθαλμοῖσιν, οὔτ' οὖν κύματα μακρὰ κυλινδόμενα προτὶ χέρσον (see Merry and Riddell: οὐδ' οὖν Dindorf, La Roche): Pi.*Fr.*207(220) τῶν οὔ τι μεμπτὸν οὔτ' ὦν μεταλλακτόν: S.*Ach.Conv.*17 Diehl Οὐ μὴν ἐπ' ἀκταῖς γ' ἐστὶ κωπήρης στρατός, οὔτ' οὖν ὁπλίτης ἐξετάζεται παρών (where Pearson prefers, but does not print, Wecklein's οὐδ').

The few examples of οὐδὲ ... οὔτε are essentially similar, the δέ in οὐδέ usually marking the connexion, and the οὐ answering the οὔτε. E.*Hel.*747 οὐδ' ἦν ἄρ' ὑγιὲς οὐδὲν ἐμπύρου φλογὸς οὔτε πτερωτῶν φθέγματ' (οὐδέ Kirchhoff): Pl.*Chrm.*171C Οὐ δῆτα. —Οὐδέ γε ἄλλος οὐδεὶς ... οὔτε δὴ ὁ σώφρων: Hp.*Epid.*vii 3 τοιοῦτος παλμὸς ἦν, οἷος οὐδὲ ('not even') ὑπὸ δρόμου οὔτε ὑπὸ δείματος ... ἂν γενηθείη. (In Hom.*h.Cer.*22 Hermann has, for some reason which I cannot fathom, conjectured οὔτε for the second οὐδέ.)

(iv) οὔτε ... οὐ. Here, conversely, the writer intends to express the addition formally, but, for emotional effect, breaks off with an asyndeton. This use is almost entirely confined to serious poetry.[1] A.*Pr.*450 κοὔτε πλινθυφεῖς δόμους προσείλους ᾖσαν, οὐ ξυλουργίαν: Hom.*Hymn.*2.236*: A.*Ch.*291: S.*Ant.*249 (on 257 see Jebb): *OC*972: E.*Med.*1348: *Hipp.*1321 οὔτε ... οὔτε ... οὐ ... οὐ (*Hec.*1235: S.*Ant.*953): *HF*643: *Tr.*934: *IT*354: *Or.*41, 1086: Hdt.viii 98.1 τοὺς οὔτε νιφετός, οὐκ ὄμβρος, οὐ καῦμα, οὐ νὺξ ἔργει (where the Homeric reminiscence is palpable): i 132.1.

Sometimes connexion is resumed after the asyndeton. E.*Or.* 46 μήθ' ἡμᾶς στέγαις, μὴ πυρὶ δέχεσθαι, μήτε προσφωνεῖν τινα:

[1] Hartung (i 199) can find no example in classical prose except the two from Herodotus. Similarly τ' οὐκ ... οὐ, if Hermann's conjecture at E.*IT*373 is right.

Hdt.i 138 ἐς ποταμὸν δὲ οὔτε ἐνουρέουσι οὔτε ἐμπτύουσι, οὐ χεῖρας ἐναπονίζονται οὐδὲ ἄλλον οὐδένα περιορῶσι. In A.*Pr.*479, οὐκ ἦν ἀλέξημ' οὐδέν, οὔτε (οὐδὲ *M*) βρώσιμον, οὐ χριστόν, οὔτε (οὐδὲ codd.) πιστόν may be the right text.

(v) οὔτε for οὔτε . . . οὔτε (Kühner (II ii 291) compares Shakespeare's 'Helen . . . nor yet Saint Philip's daughters were like thee' (1 *Henry VI*, I.ii.143): 'in Faenza ni in Forli gli era rimaso amico'. Cf. also Bunyan's 'Hobgoblin nor foul fiend': Shak. *M.N.D.* II.ii.22).[1] This is confined to poetry, though the corresponding οὐδέ, for οὐ . . . οὐδέ, is not infrequently found in prose. (See οὐδέ, I.2.iii, and cf. Wilamowitz, E.*HF*, p. 272).) Pi.*P.*3.30 κλέπτει τέ νιν οὐ θεὸς οὐ βροτὸς ἔργοις οὔτε βουλαῖς: 6.48 νόῳ δὲ πλοῦτον ἄγει, ἄδικον οὔθ' ὑπέροπλον ἥβαν δρέπων: 10.29 ναυσὶ δ' οὔτε πεζὸς ἰὼν κεν εὕροις . . . ὁδόν: 10.41 νόσοι δ' οὔτε γῆρας οὐλόμενον κέκραται ἱερᾷ γενεᾷ: A.*Ag.*532 Πάρις γὰρ οὔτε συντελὴς πόλις: *Ch.*294 δέχεσθαι δ' οὔτε συλλύειν τινά: S.*Ph.*771 ἐφίεμαι ἑκόντα μήτ' ἄκοντα μηδέ τῳ τέχνῃ κείνοις μεθεῖναι ταῦτα (μηδ' Eustathius: μήτ' *codd.*: μηδέ *A rec.*: μήτε *L rec.*): *Ant.*851 (text doubtful). Where a negative precedes, as in Pi.*O.*14.8, S.*Aj.*1233, *Ant.*267, *OT* 239, it is alternatively possible to regard οὔτε as answering that negative, not as answering an understood οὔτε: see οὐδέ, I.2.iii, and cf. E.*Hel.*747 (iii above).

(vi) οὔτε . . . δέ. (See Kühner, II ii 292: Jebb on S.*Tr.* 1151ff. 'Used', Kühner says, 'when the second clause expresses a contrast to the first'. Mostly, at any rate, so used.) Hom. *H* 433 ἦμος δ' οὔτ' ἄρ πω ἠώς, ἔτι δ' ἀμφιλύκη νύξ: S.*Tr.*143 ὡς δ' ἐγὼ θυμοφθορῶ μήτ' ἐκμάθοις παθοῦσα, νῦν δ' ἄπειρος εἶ: Hom. *Ω* 368: S.*Tr.*1153: *OC* 422: E.*Supp.*225: *HF* 1282: *Or.*293: *Ph.* 347, 892 (δέ *L*: τε *cett.*): Pl.*R.*388E Οὔτε ἄρα ἀνθρώπους ἀξίους λόγου κρατουμένους ὑπὸ γέλωτος ἄν τις ποιῇ, ἀποδεκτέον, πολὺ δὲ ἧττον, ἐὰν θεούς: X.*An.*vi 3.16 ἀλλὰ δὴ ἐκεῖ μὲν οὔτε πλοῖά ἐστιν οἷς ἀποπλευσούμεθα, μένουσι δ' αὐτοῦ οὐδὲ μιᾶς ἡμέρας ἔστι τὰ ἐπιτήδεια: Hdt.i 108.5: Pl.*Lg.*627E: Ant.v 76, 95: Lys.xix 62. In A.*Supp.*987–8 μήτε . . . δέ is impossible, since the negative cannot be carried through: see Paley and Tucker.

For οὔτε . . . οὐδέ, see οὐδέ, I.2.i. For οὔτε οὖν, see οὖν, II.2.

(5) Corresponsive, τε καί, τε . . . καί. This tends very largely to

[1] Other English parallels in Gildersleeve on Pi.*P.*6.48.

replace τε . . . τε. Hom.*A* 17 Ἀτρεΐδαι τε καὶ ἄλλοι ἐϋκνήμιδες Ἀχαιοί: *h.Ven.*113 γλῶσσαν δ' ὑμετέρην τε καὶ ἡμετέρην σάφα οἶδα ('yours as well as ours'): S.*Aj.*647 φύει τ' ἄδηλα καὶ φανέντα κρύπτεται: Pl.*Euthphr.*4D ὠλιγώρει τε καὶ ἠμέλει: Hdt.ix 32.1 Φρυγῶν τε καὶ Μυσῶν καὶ Θρηίκων τε καὶ Παιόνων (closely coupling pairs: cf. ix 31.3–4).

Rarely in anaphora. Hes.*Op.*91 ἄτερ τε κακῶν καὶ ἄτερ χαλεποῖο πόνοιο: D.iii 1 ὅταν τ' εἰς τὰ πράγματ' ἀποβλέψω καὶ ὅταν πρὸς τοὺς λόγους: xxiii 51: Pl.*R.*474E,493B: *Lg.*744C.

Fuhr (*Rh.M.*xxxiii (1878),577ff.) has discussed exhaustively the rarity of juxtaposed τε καί in the orators and in inscriptions. There appear to be not more than a round dozen of examples in the certainly genuine speeches of Demosthenes. In Andocides II (the earliest speech) we find τε καί juxtaposed in almost every other section: while in I it is much rarer, and in III (and also in [IV]) entirely absent. Andocides thus adapted himself gradually to oratorical usage. Fuhr attributes the rarity of τε καί in formal and official language to a desire to avoid the superfluous, since the preparatory τε is not necessary when the connected words are in close proximity. (Contrast the redundance of ballad style, 'a grave both wide and deep'. For particularly redundant τε καί, τε . . . καί, see further below.) The indexes to the several orators now make it possible to supplement Fuhr's statistics. Antiphon never has τε καί, always τε . . . καί: Lysias has τε . . . καί more than three times as often as τε καί: Isocrates has τε καί thirteen times (excluding καλοί τε κἀγαθοί and ἄλλως τε καί), as against hundreds of τε . . . καί's:[1] Dinarchus has τε καί once, Lycurgus four times, as against τε . . . καί three and fourteen times respectively.

Hartung (i 101–2) points out that τε καί (τε . . . καί) is often used by poets, sometimes by prose writers, with a marked redundance, where simple καί would suffice. Hom.ξ 20 τριηκόσιοί τε καὶ ἑξήκοντα: Pi.*O.*1.79 τρεῖς τε καὶ δέκα: S.*Ant.*1278 ἔχων τε καὶ κεκτημένος: Hdt.i 26 μεταξὺ τῆς τε παλαιῆς πόλιος . . . καὶ τοῦ νηοῦ: 31 πολλά τε καὶ ὄλβια: ix 26.1 ὠθισμὸς Τεγεητέων τε καὶ Ἀθηναίων: 29.1: Pl.*R.*453D 479C: 511D: Arist.*Metaph.*

[1] Fuhr (*Rh.M.*xxxiii 334), says that Isocrates rarely juxtaposes τε καί, except in ἄλλως τε καί, unless the first word begins with a vowel, and καὶ . . . καί would entail hiatus, as in v42 ἡμᾶς τε καὶ Λακεδαιμονίους.

997b29,1074a11. In the tragedians,[1] τε καὶ οὐ coupling opposites. S.*OT*1275 πολλάκις τε κοὐχ ἅπαξ: *El.*885 ἐξ ἐμοῦ τε κοὐκ ἄλλης: *OC*935 βίᾳ τε κοὐχ ἑκών: Hdt.viii 88.1 διαφυγεῖν τε καὶ μὴ ἀπολέσθαι.* Schmidt (p. 38) notes the frequency of τε ... καί in the pseudo-Demosthenic speeches supposed to be written by Apollodorus.

(6) Irregular corresponsions.

(i) μὲν ... τε. See μέν, III.2.iii.

(ii) τε ... δέ. δέ is often unnecessarily emended by editors. The explanation of the irregularity probably is that the idea of contrast is added to the original idea of addition: while in those passages in which the particles are separated by a wide interval some degree of anacoluthon is to be assumed.[2]

Hom.*E* 359 κόμισαί τέ με δὸς δέ μοι ἵππους: *H* 418 ἀμφότερον, νέκυάς τ' ἀγέμεν, ἕτεροι δὲ μεθ' ὕλην: S.*El.*1099 Ἄρ' ... ὀρθά τ' εἰσηκούσαμεν ὀρθῶς δ' ὁδοιποροῦμεν ...; (here there is little antithesis, and τε, read by some MSS., is usually adopted): *Tr.* 286 ταῦτα γὰρ πόσις τε σὸς ἐφεῖτ', ἐγὼ δὲ ... τελῶ: Hom.*Ψ* 277: *h.Ven.*110: Pi.*P.*4.81: 11.30: S.*Tr.*333: *Ant.*1096: *Ph.*1313: E.*Alc.*197 (τ' *P*): *Tr.*380: *IT* 995,1415: *Ph.*1606 (text uncertain), 1626 (τε *V*): Hdt.ii 172 ἦν οἱ ἄλλα τε ἀγαθὰ μυρία, ἐν δὲ καὶ ποδανιπτὴρ χρύσεος: Th.i 25.3 Κορίνθιοι δὲ κατά τε τὸ δίκαιον ὑπεδέξαντο τὴν τιμωρίαν, νομίζοντες οὐχ ἧσσον ἑαυτῶν εἶναι τὴν ἀποικίαν ἢ Κερκυραίων, ἅμα δὲ καὶ μίσει τῶν Κερκυραίων: viii 16 3 καθῄρουν αὐτοί τε τὸ τεῖχος ... ξυγκαθῄρουν δὲ αὐτοῖς ...: Pl.*R.*367C ἃ τῶν τε ἀποβαινόντων ἀπ' αὐτῶν ἕνεκα ἄξια κεκτῆσθαι, πολὺ δὲ μᾶλλον αὐτὰ αὑτῶν: X.*HG* vi 5.30 οἱ δὲ Ἀρκάδες τούτων τε οὐδὲν ἐποίουν, καταλείποντες δὲ τὰ ὅπλα εἰς ἁρπαγὴν ... ἐτρέποντο: *An.*v 5.8 ἐπαινέσοντάς τε ... ἔπειτα δὲ καὶ ξυνησθησο-

[1] Also in Plato: see Stallbaum on *Euthd.*283B.

[2] Hartung (i 92–5) adopts a rather over-elaborate classification under five headings, of which Kühner (II ii 244) takes over the first four (omitting the fifth, 'wo die Theile zugleich in ihrem Ebenmaasse und in ihrer Mehrheit oder Vielheit dargelegt werden sollen'): (1) where there is a negative in the first clause: (2) where the second clause opens with ἔπειτα καί, ἅμα καί, etc.: (3) where there is anacoluthon: (4) where there is an idea of contrast, particularly of persons. See also Jebb on S.*Tr.*143, *Ant.*1096: Pearson *C.Q.* xxiv(1930)162. Jebb and Pearson agree that each case must be judged on its own merits.

μένους: Hdt.vi 50.2: ix 19.3: Hp.*Prog.*14: Th.i 11.1: vii 81.3: Pl.*Smp.*186E (τε ... δὲ καί: *Euthphr.*3E: *R.*394C,618A: *Lg.* 782B): *Cra.*406C: *Tht.*203B: X.*HG* iv 5.15: vii 1.24: *Cyr.*iii 3.64: iv 4.3: vi 2.4: *Smp.*8.2: And.i 5,58: Lys.xxv 34: Isoc.iii 33: xv 232: Aeschin.iii 80.

Exceptionally in anaphora. S.*Aj.*835 τὰς ἀεί τε παρθένους ἀεὶ δ' ὁρώσας: Pi.*Fr.*141(155) τί ἔρδων φίλος σοί τε, καρτερόβροντα Κρονίδα, φίλος δὲ Μοίσαις, Εὐθυμίᾳ τε μέλων εἴην, τοῦτ' αἴτημί σε (but perhaps τε is answered by τε here).

τε ... οὐδέ (μηδέ). Hom.φ310 ἀλλὰ ἕκηλος πῖνέ τε, μηδ' ἐρίδαινε: S.*OC* 368 αὐτοῖς ἦν ἔρως Κρέοντί τε θρόνους ἐᾶσθαι μηδὲ χραίνεσθαι πόλιν: E.*IT* 697 ὄνομά τ' ἐμοῦ γένοιτ' ἄν, οὐδ' ἄπαις δόμος πατρῷος οὑμὸς ἐξαλειφθείη ποτ' ἄν: Hom.*h.Ven.*16 (anacoluthon): Pl.*Ti.*33C ὀμμάτων τε γὰρ ἐπεδεῖτο οὐδὲν ... οὐδ' ἀκοῆς.

(iii) ἤ ... τε (very rare). Hom.*B*289 ὥς τε γὰρ ἢ παῖδες νεαροὶ χῆραί τε γυναῖκες (often emended by editors: L. & S. think ἠ should be read): A.*Eu.*524 ἢ πόλις βροτός θ' ὁμοίως.

(iv) τε ... ἤ. S.*Tr.*445 εἴ τι τὠμῷ τ' ἀνδρὶ ... μεμπτός εἰμι ... ἢ τῇδε τῇ γυναικί: Pl.*Ion* 535D ὃς ἂν ... κλάῃ τ' ἐν θυσίαις ... ἢ φοβῆται: *Men.*95B ὁμολογεῖν διδάσκαλοί τε εἶναι ἢ διδακτὸν ἀρετήν (καί *F*): *Tht.*143C περὶ αὑτοῦ τε ὁπότε λέγοι ... ἢ αὖ περὶ τοῦ ἀποκρινομένου: X.*Oec.*20.12 ὑγροτέρα τε οὖσα πρὸς τὸν σπόρον ἢ ἁλμωδεστέρα (γε Stephanus).

(v) τε ... αὐτάρ, τε ... ἀτάρ. Hom.*H*296 ὡς σύ τ' ἐϋφρήνῃς ... αὐτὰρ ἐγὼ ... ἐϋφρανέω: Pl.*Hp.Ma.*295E τά τε γοῦν ἄλλα ... ἀτὰρ οὖν καὶ ....

(vi) τε ... ἔπειτα. Pl.*Lg.*669A δεῖ ταῦτα τρία ἔχειν, ὅ τέ ἐστι πρῶτον γιγνώσκειν, ἔπειτα ὡς ὀρθῶς, ἔπειθ' ὡς εὖ (ὅ τι Boeckh).

For τε ... ἠδέ, τε ... ἰδέ, see ἠδέ, ἰδέ, pp. 287–8. For τε ... καὶ ... δέ, see καὶ ... δέ, p. 203.

(7) τε, τε ... τε, οὔτε ... οὔτε, τε ... καί, are sometimes used (rarely in prose) where the thought implies a more elaborate relationship than that of mere addition.

In Hom.*M.*285 τε is used where we should expect δέ (Heyne): but κῦμα ... ἐρύκεται is perhaps, as Leaf suggests, parenthetical. In E.*Hel.*1485 ἄβροχα πεδία καρποφόρα τε (see Pearson) and *Or.*127, τε stands for *et tamen*: cf. καί, I.8.

τε . . . τε (οὔτε . . . οὔτε), 'just as . . . so . . .'. S.*Tr*.131–2 μένει γὰρ οὔτ' αἰόλα νὺξ βροτοῖσιν οὔτε κῆρες οὔτε πλοῦτος ('*as* night does not abide, *so* neither does woe', Jebb): cf. A.*Ch*. 258–60: Ant.vi 5 ἀνάγκη δὲ τῆς τε δίκης νικᾶσθαι παρὰ τὸ ἀληθές, αὐτοῦ τε τοῦ ἀληθοῦς ('just as a man must submit to an untrue verdict, so he must submit to truth of itself, unexpressed in a verdict'): *ib.* οὔτε . . . οὔτε: Thgn.108–9: Pi.*O*.2.98–100: A. *Ag*.324 (see Verrall): see further Wilamowitz on E.*HF* 101–3. With the emphasized clause coming first: E.*Hel*.770–1 (see Pearson): *Hec*.519–20.

Hom.ζ208 δόσις δ' ὀλίγη τε φίλη τε ('small but welcome').

τε . . . καί, 'just as much as', 'not only . . . but also'. (The emphatic expression may be either the first or the second.) A.*Supp*. 754 εἰ σοί τε καὶ θεοῖσιν ἐχθαιροίατο (= οὐ μόνον σοὶ ἀλλὰ καὶ θεοῖσιν, Tucker): S.*Ant*.1112 ἐγὼ δ' . . . αὐτός τ' ἔδησα καὶ παρὼν ἐκλύσομαι ('as I bound, so will I loose'): 1251–2 ἐμοὶ δ' οὖν ἥ τ' ἄγαν σιγὴ βαρὺ δοκεῖ προσεῖναι χἠ μάτην πολλὴ βοή (where note the reply Καὶ τῆς ἄγαν γάρ ἐστί που σιγῆς βάρος, 'Aye, in silence, too, there is peril'): E.*Heracl*.138.

τε . . . καί, 'when . . . then'. (Cf. καί, I.9: μέν, III.1.i.) See Headlam on A.*Ag*.179 (his 189); S.*Fr*.234.6 εἶτ' ἦμαρ αὔξει μέσσον ὄμφακος τύπον, καὶ κλίνεταί τε κἀποπερκοῦται βότρυς ('and as it declines the grape reddens'): Timocl.*Fr*.21.4 καὶ ταῦτά τε εἴρητο καὶ . . . ἐπόππυσ': S.*Ant*.1186: X.*Eq*.5.10 οὐ φθάνει τε ἐξαγόμενος ὁ ἵππος καὶ . . .: Hdt.ii 93.5 (see Stein): iv 181.3. 199.2: vi 41.1: 134.2: viii 56: Pl.*Phdr*.254B: X.*An*.i 8.1: iv 2.12: 6.2: vii 4.12: *Cyr*.i 4.28: vii 1.26.

τε . . . καί, with a disjunction implied, 'either . . . or . . .', S.*OC* 488 (γ' for τ' *L*). So, too, τε . . . τε: E.*Ion* 853 θέλω . . . θανεῖν τε ζῶν τε φέγγος εἰσορᾶν.

τε . . . καί for μὲν . . . δέ: A.*Eu*.174 κἀμοί τε (γε Casaubon) λυπρός, καί τὸν οὐκ ἐκλύσεται. οὔτε . . . τε (οὔτε . . . οὔτε), for μὲν . . . οὐ . . ., . . . δέ: E.*Alc*.70–1 κοὔθ' ἡ παρ' ἡμῶν σοὶ γενήσεται χάρις, δράσεις θ' ὁμοίως ταῦτ' ἀπεχθήσῃ τ' ἐμοί ('while you will get no thanks, you will have to do it all the same'): Arist.*Rh*. 1369b32 (ὅροι) μήτε ἀσαφεῖς μήτε ἀκριβεῖς ('definitions which, without being exact, are not obscure').

(8) Position of τε. τε, whether copulative or preparatory, is normally placed second in the sentence, clause, or word-group.

But, as in the case of other particles which occupy the second place, there are numerous deviations from this rule.[1] Postponement of τε is common, sometimes even normal, in the following cases:

(i) Article—Substantive (or adjective, or participle)—Particle. A.*Ch.*41 τοῖς κτανοῦσί τε: *Eu.*232 τὸν ἱκέτην τε: S.*Ant.*1090 τὸν νοῦν τ': A.*Pr.*67,830: S.*Ph.*325: Hdt.ii 176 τῇ Ἴσι τε: Hp. *Vict.*27 τὸ πῦρ τε: Th.i 29.4 ὁ κῆρυξ τε: iii 64.3 τὴν τελευταίαν τε: Pl.*Lg.*822E τῶν νόμων τε: X.*Cyr.*ii 3.22 ὁ οὐραγός τε καὶ οἱ τελευταῖοι: vii 1.26 τῷ Ἐνυαλίῳ τε: And.iii 34 τῇ πόλει τε εὔνουν: D.xxi 176 τὴν δίκην τε πᾶσαν. Cf. E.*IA* 203.

Often in Plato, when τε looking forward to καί is thus postponed, a second article has to be supplied after the καί: *Phd.* 82A τῶν λύκων τε καὶ ἱεράκων: *Prt.*313C οἱ περὶ τὴν τοῦ σώματος τροφήν, ὁ ἔμπορός τε καὶ κάπηλος: 355E μεταλάβωμεν δὴ τὰ ὀνόματα πάλιν, τὸ ἡδύ τε καὶ ἀνιαρόν (contrast *Euthphr.*9C τὸ ὅσιόν τε καὶ τὸ ἀνόσιον): *Euthphr.*7C: *Phdr.*254A: *R.*399C. In other cases, again, the article embraces both terms, two things or two actions being regarded as virtually identical, and the position of τε is regular: *Euthd.*303C ἐπὶ τὸ ἐπαινεῖν τε καὶ ἐγκωμιάζειν: *R.*393D ἡ ποίησίς τε καὶ διήγησις: 604D τὸ πεσόν τε καὶ νοσῆσαν: *Phd.*81C ἡ ὁμιλία τε καὶ συνουσία: 82C οἱ φίλαρχοί τε καὶ φιλότιμοι (the two classes are perhaps regarded as identical, whereas the classes in *Cri.*53A are clearly distinct, οἱ χωλοί τε καὶ τυφλοί). Ambiguity sometimes arises from these irregularities: cf. p. 518, n.1.

(ii) Preposition—Substantive (etc.)—Particle: far commoner in Herodotus than the order Preposition—Particle—Substantive (Hammer, p. 31). A.*Pr.*210 ἀμοχθὶ πρὸς βίαν τε: S.*Ph.*1312 μετὰ ζώντων θ' (curiously enough, this is the only place in

[1] It may be well to point out, since Schmidt (p. 18) has gone astray, that there is no postponement of τε in such passages as A.*Pr.*665 ἔξω δόμων τε καὶ πάτρας: Isoc.xv 251 τῶν ἀκμαζόντων τε μᾶλλον ἠγὼ καὶ . . . μὴ φροντιζόντων. In D.xxvii 59, again, πρὸς τὸν χρόνον τε καὶ τὴν ἐκείνου μίσθωσιν, τε is postponed in respect of the article only, not, as Schmidt supposes, of the preposition as well: cf. Pl.*Cri.*52D.

I do not know whether there is anywhere any difference in frequency of postponement between τε preparatory and τε copulative. The authorities draw no such distinction, and my own researches into postponed τε are too slight to form a basis for any conclusion.

Sophocles, according to Ellendt, where τε is postponed after a preposition: and θ', though generally accepted by editors, is attested by *A* alone): Th. i 17 κατὰ πόλεις τε: Pl.*Hp.Mi.*363C περὶ ποιητῶν τε ἄλλων καὶ περὶ 'Ομήρου: X.*HG* iv 2.1 ἐν κινδύνῳ τε: And. iii 12 ἐφ' οἷς τε: Isoc. xii 61 ὑπὲρ αὐτῆς τε (according to Schmidt, p. 19, Isocrates has τε between preposition and substantive (pronoun) only in xii 6 περί τ' ἐμαυτοῦ: but he has the order Preposition—Particle—Article—Substantive in v 2 περί τε τῆς πόλεως ταύτης): D. xxvii 3 μετ' εὐνοίας τε: xxxix 37 ἐξ ἀρχῆς τε: Pl.*Phd.*112E: *R.*563E.

(iii) Preposition—Article—Substantive (etc.)—Particle. A. *Eu.*291 ἐς τὸ πᾶν τε: Ar.*Nu.*1176 ἐπὶ τοῦ προσώπου τε: *Av.* 1427-8 (also exemplifies (i)): Hdt. i 86 κατὰ τὸ χρηστήριόν τε Th. i 141.4 ἀπὸ τῶν ἰδίων τε: iii 81.2 ἐς τὸ "Ηραιόν τε: vii 84.4 ἐς τὰ ἐπὶ θάτερά τε: Pl.*Ti.*85A ἐπὶ τὰς περιόδους τε.: *Cra.*407D: *R.*604D.

(iv) Outside the above limits, postponement of τε is much rarer. Hes.*Th.*272 ἀθάνατοί τε θεοὶ χαμαὶ ἐρχόμενοί τ' ἄνθρωποι: 846: *Sc.*451: A.*Supp.*282 **Κύπριος** χαρακτήρ τ': *Pr.*138 τοῦ περὶ πᾶσάν θ' εἱλισσομένου χθόν' . . . 'Ωκεανοῦ: *Eu.*559 (perhaps: see p. 501): E.*Alc.*819 καὶ κουρὰν βλέπεις μελαμπέπλους στολμούς τε (Murray transposes κουράν and στολμούς, perhaps rightly: τε at the end of a sentence is very harsh: the whole passage is suspect): *HF* 1266 ἔτ' ἐν γάλακτί τ' ὄντι . . . ὄφεις ἐπεισέφρησε: *Tr.*1064 σμύρνης αἰθερίας τε καπνόν: 1069 τέρμονα πρωτόβολόν θ' ἁλίῳ (τε πρωτόβολον *VP*: *trai.* Musgrave): *Hec.*566 οὐ θέλων τε καὶ θέλων (for this postponement of the particle after a negative, much commoner in the case of δέ, cf. Hdt. iv 46.2 μὴ βουλομένους τε: ix 93.4 οὐ πρότερόν τε παύσεσθαι): *Hel.*587: (Barnes): *Tr.* 745: *Ph.*1249: Ar.*Ra.*1009: Scol.Anon.24.3: Hdt. vi. 136.2 ἑλὼν Λῆμνόν τε καὶ τεισάμενος τοὺς Πελασγούς: Pl.*Cra.*403E τέλεος σοφιστής τε: *Lg.*673C "Αρισθ' ὑπέλαβές τε καὶ οὕτω δὴ ποίει: *R.*358E τί ὄν τε καὶ ὅθεν γέγονε δικαιοσύνη: *Ap.*18D ἀνάγκη ἀτεχνῶς ὥσπερ σκιαμαχεῖν ἀπολογούμενόν τε καὶ ἐλέγχειν μηδενὸς ἀποκρινομένου: Lys. xix 23 χαρίσασθαι ἐκείνῳ τε καὶ κομίσασθαι μὴ ἔλαττω (emended by many editors): D. lvii 12 διά τε . . . ἵνα τούτῳ τ' ἐξουσία γένοιθ': Pl.*R.*470C, 474E, 478D: *Lg.*866A, 885D, 890B. (On B.18.52 see Jebb.)

In S.*Ant.*328 ἐὰν δέ τοι ληφθῇ τε καὶ μή (for καὶ ἐάν τε ληφθῇ καὶ μή) the postponement of τε is necessary to avoid the collocation of τε and δέ: cf. A.*Ag.*179: Ar.*Th.*672: Hdt.i 74.3. (See p. liv n. 1.)

In other passages τε (meaning 'both') is placed after a word preceding the two co-ordinated words (or word-groups) and common to both, instead of after the first co-ordinated word (or first word of the first word-group). But it is correctly placed, the word which it follows being supplied in thought in the second word-group: cf. καί in A.*Ag.*324 τῶν ἁλόντων καὶ κρατησάντων: S.*OC*606 τἀμὰ κἀκείνων (see Jebb). Cf. S.*El.*991 (καὶ . . . καί). A.*Ag.*314 νικᾷ δ' ὁ πρῶτος καὶ τελευταῖος δραμών is probably not a case of this usage.

(v) Preposition supplied. A.*Ch.*523 ἔκ τ' ὀνειράτων καὶ νυκτιπλάγκτων δειμάτων: *Eu.*951: S.*Aj.*53 καὶ πρός τε ποίμνας ἐκτρέπω σύμμεικτά τε . . . φρουρήματα: *OC*33: *OT*253: Hdt.i 106.1 ὑπό τε ὕβριος καὶ ὀλιγωρίης: Th.i 18.2: Pl.*R*442C διά τε λυπῶν καὶ ἡδονῶν: *Prt.*316D τοὺς ἀμφί τ' Ὀρφέα καὶ Μουσαῖον: X.*Cyr.*i 4.22: Isoc.iv 159 ἔν τε τοῖς τῆς μουσικῆς ἄθλοις καὶ τῇ παιδεύσει: D.xxi 126 εἴς τε τὴν λῃτουργίαν καὶ τὸ σῶμ' ὑβρίσθην (Isocrates and Demosthenes sometimes, though less frequently, repeat the preposition (Schmidt): e.g. Isoc.xii 5: D.iii 25): Th.i 5.3: iv 35.4: Pl. *Cri.*48C: *Ap.*35B: Ant.i 25: vi 6.

(vi) Article supplied (in general,[1] though not very rare in Plato, much rarer than the above). E.*Ion* 7 τά τ' ὄντα καὶ μέλλοντα (see Owen's note): *Ph.*474: *Hel.*14: Hdt.iii 127.1 εἶχε δὲ νομὸν τόν τε Φρύγιον καὶ Λύδιον καὶ Ἰωνικόν: ix 83.2: Th.i 7 αἵ τε ἐν ταῖς

[1] Probably because the transposition of τε with the article is often misleading, since it implies that the article does *not* apply to both terms: as it sometimes, in fact, does not, e.g. in Pl.*Criti.*116E τῶν τε βασιλέων καὶ ἰδιωτῶν ('*the* kings and (*some*) individuals'). In yet another set of passages the article is applied to a single entity, instead of being distributed over two (cp. p. 516, *med.*): Pl.*Smp.*218D τούς τε πολλοὺς καὶ ἄφρονας (= τοὺς π. τε κ. α.: contrast 189E τοῦ τε ἄρρενος καὶ θήλεος): *R.*430B τήν τε θηριώδη καὶ ἀνδραποδώδη. Laxity in the placing of τε following the article not infrequently results in serious ambiguity, which is not entailed by its displacement after a preposition. Conversely a second article may be added where there is no duality: E.*Heracl.*826 τῇ τε βοσκούσῃ χθονὶ καὶ τῇ τεκούσῃ.

νήσοις καὶ ἐν ταῖς ἠπείροις: Pl.*R*.537A τοῖς τε πόνοις καὶ μαθήμασι: X.*HG*i 1.25 τούς τε ἀπὸ τῶν πόλεων στρατηγοὺς καὶ τριηράρχους: Pl.*Ti*.70B τῶν τε παρακελεύσεων καὶ ἀπειλῶν: Isoc.x 29 παραλιπεῖν τήν τε Σκίρωνος καὶ Κερκύονος καὶ τῶν ἄλλων τῶν τοιούτων παρανομίαν: Pl.*Prt*.357A: *R*.401D,497C,516B,549C: *Euthphr*.15E: *Lg*.697A: *Hp.Ma*.283A: X.*Cyr*.vii 5.41 (τοὺς ἄρχοντας *CE*): Arist.*Pol*.1280a8.

Both article and preposition supplied. (*a*) Hdt.ii 36.1 τάς τε ἐν τῇ κεφαλῇ καὶ τῷ γενείῳ: vii 106.2 οἵ τε ἐκ Θρηίκης καὶ τοῦ Ἑλλησπόντου. (*b*) Pl.*R*.485B περί τε τῶν φιλοτίμων καὶ ἐρωτικῶν: Th.i49.3: X.*HG*.i4.9.

(vii) Word (or words) of another class supplied. A.*Pr*.42 Αἰεί τε δὴ νηλὴς σὺ καὶ (αἰεὶ) θράσους πλέως (where the generally accepted γε δή (see p. 245) is by no means certain): *Eu*.701: S.*OC* 808 χωρὶς τό τ' εἰπεῖν πολλὰ καὶ (τὸ) τὰ καίρια (εἰπεῖν) (Suidas' τὸ καίρια may well be right): E.*Ph*.96 ἅ τ' εἶδον (ἃ) εἰσήκουσά τε: Hdt.i 22.2 ἰδών τε σωρὸν μέγαν σίτου κεχυμένον καὶ (ἰδὼν) τοὺς ἀνθρώπους ἐν εὐπαθείῃσι ἐόντας: iii 71.2 ἐπίστασθαι ὅτι τε ὁ μάγος εἴη ὁ βασιλεύων καὶ (ὅτι) Σμέρδις ὁ Κύρου τετελεύτηκε: v 42.1 Κλεομένης . . . ἦν τε οὐ φρενήρης ἀκρομανής τε (ἦν): Pl.*Cri*.43B ἐν τοσαύτῃ τε ἀγρυπνίᾳ καὶ (τοσαύτῃ) λύπῃ εἶναι: X.*Cyr*.v 2.21 ἅ τε δεῖ φίλια καὶ (ἃ δεῖ) πολέμια ἡμᾶς νομίζειν: D.i5 ἴσασιν ἅ τ' Ἀμφιπολιτῶν ἐποίησε τοὺς παραδόντας αὐτῷ τὴν πόλιν καὶ (ἃ ἐποίησε) Πυδναίων τοὺς ὑποδεξαμένους: Hdt.ii 79.1: vii 197.2: X.*Mem*.iii 5.3: iv 2.40: *Cyr*.ii 1.13.

(viii) Other irregularities (dislocations of order, rather than simple postponements as in (iv)). There remain some passages in which the position of τε cannot be explained on any of the above grounds. Most of them are accounted for by the thought (or the construction) taking a different turn as it develops (anacoluthon would usually be too strong a word). Many of these are the exact counterpart of those grouped under (vii). There, the early position of τε necessitates the repetition, in thought, of the word preceding it. Here, the later position of τε makes repetition unnecessary: but nevertheless repetition, or substitution of synonym, is employed. Contrast Hdt.iii 71.2 (vii) with iii 43.1 (below).

Pi.*O*.6.42 τᾷ μὲν ὁ χρυσοκόμας πραΰμητίν τ' Ἐλείθυιαν παρέστασέν τε Μοίρας: S.*OT* 759 ἀφ' οὗ γὰρ κεῖθεν ἦλθε καὶ κράτη σέ τ' εἶδ' ἔχοντα Λάϊόν τ' ὀλωλότα (the specific mention of Laius' death is perhaps an afterthought): *Tr.*336 ὅπως μαυῃς . . . οὕστινάς τ' ἄγεις ἔσω ὧν τ' οὐδὲν εἰσήκουσας ἐκμάθῃς ἃ δεῖ: *Ant.*204 (μήτε: see Jebb): *Ph.*1412 φάσκειν δ' αὐδὴν τὴν Ἡρακλέους ἀκοῇ τε κλύειν λεύσσειν τ' ὄψιν: E.*Rh.*969 (οὔτε): Hdt.iii 43.1 ἔμαθε ὅτι ἐκκομίσαι τε ἀδύνατον εἴη . . . καὶ ὅτι οὐκ εὖ τελευτήσειν μέλλοι (ὅτι is redundantly repeated, perhaps for the sake of clearness: v 18.5 αὐτίκα οἱ Πέρσαι μαστῶν τε ἅπτοντο . . . καί κού τις καὶ φιλέειν ἐπειρᾶτο ('and one of them tried to *kiss*'): cf. vii 197.2: Th.vi 2.1 ἀρκείτω δὲ ὡς ποιηταῖς τε εἴρηται καὶ ὡς ἕκαστός πῃ γιγνώσκει περὶ αὐτῶν): Pl.*Phd.*117C ἃ δὴ καὶ ἐγὼ εὔχομαί τε καὶ γένοιτο ταύτῃ: *Criti.*121A φθίνει ταῦτά τε αὐτὰ κἀκείνη συναπόλλυται τούτοις (the addition of the second verb is characteristic of Platonic fullness of expression): X.*HG*v 1.29 εἰδότες φρουράν τε πεφασμένην ἐφ' ἑαυτοὺς καὶ γιγνώσκοντες ὅτι . . .: D.xxiv 12 ἔλεγ' ἄλλα τε πολλὰ καὶ διεξῆλθεν πρὸς ὑμᾶς ὡς ἔλαβ' ἡ τριήρης τὸ πλοῖον: Pl.*R.*465E, 550A, 605A. The distorted order in Arist.*Pol.*1339a29 is cured by reading διαγωγήν γε, Coraes (Eucken, p. 15): ἀλλὰ μὴν οὐδὲ διαγωγήν τε παισὶν ἁρμόττει καὶ ταῖς ἡλικίαις ἀποδιδόναι ταῖς τοιαύταις.[1]

II. Epic τε. Having discussed τε as a connective and preparatory particle, meaning 'and' or 'both', it remains to consider certain usages which are, in the main, peculiar to Epic, with which I include early elegiac, lyric, and iambic poetry: though to some extent, and in certain stereotyped forms, they survive in later Greek. Hartung, Kühner, and most other authorities explain τε in such cases as 'responsive', a theory which is at least plausible in a number of instances. But Wentzel's view, that τε expresses habitual action here, appears on the whole preferable, and covers the facts more completely and naturally, though it leaves many passages unexplained. (Indeed, none of the theories of τε hitherto put forward is entirely satisfactory, and all but the most optimistic writers on this particle have felt

[1] Hartung (i 117) maintains that in Ar.*V.*1277 and *Eq.*562 an expression common to both limbs is inserted between them: in the first case ἄνδρα, in the second ἐκ τῶν ἄλλων θεῶν. I believe that both passages are straightforward, and that the expressions belong to the second limbs alone. Hartung extends this treatment, even less convincingly, to other passages which I explain otherwise.

themselves compelled to institute a home for waifs and strays somewhere or other.) Wentzel's remarks have received scant attention from his successors, but they are adopted, in broad outline, by Monro, in his paper to the Oxford Philological Society (*Proceedings* 1881–2, pp. 14–15) and in his *Homeric Grammar*. *Inter alia*, they are supported by the often observed fact that this τε is particularly common in similes and γνῶμαι, where phenomena of general and typical occurence are cited in comparison. Hence the accumulation of τε in such passages as Hom.*E*136–41: *O*271–5,630–6: *Π*157–63: *P*673–8. In the following pages I shall keep the distinction between general and particular statements always in the foreground. The most important of the usages to be discussed are τε with relatives and τε combined with other particles. After considering these, we may turn our attention to other less common idioms.

(1) With relatives. Here the theory that τε is responsive finds some support in the similar employment of καί.[1] But it is to be noted that almost all the examples denote habitual, typical action. The tense is almost always present, or gnomic aorist.

Hom.*A*86 Ἀπόλλωνα . . . ᾧ τε σύ, Κάλχαν, εὐχόμενος Δαναοῖσι θεοπροπίας ἀναφαίνεις: 238 δικασπόλοι, οἵ τε θέμιστας πρὸς Διὸς εἰρύαται: *Γ*61 ὑπ' ἀνέρος, ὅς ῥά τε τέχνῃ νήϊον ἐκτάμνῃσιν: *Δ*483 αἴγειρος ὥς, ἥ ῥά τε . . . πεφύκῃ: *E*340 ἰχώρ, οἷός πέρ τε ῥέει μακάρεσσι θεοῖσιν: *I*5 Βορέης καὶ Ζέφυρος, τώ τε Θρῄκηθεν ἄητον: *X*127 τῷ ὀαριζέμεναι, ἅ τε παρθένος ἠΐθεός τε: *Ψ*845 ὅσσον τίς τ' ἔρριψε καλαύροπα βουκόλος ἀνήρ (ε400

[1] Brugmann (p. 613) adduces a further consideration in support of this view: 'Und zweitens handelt es sich hier immer um postpositive Sätze. Hinter den meisten Relativkonjunktionen, die präpositive Sätze einleiteten, wie ἕως, ὅπως, ὅπῃ, ἦμος, kommt τὲ überhaupt nicht vor. Hiernach ist wohl überall das anknüpfende τὲ anzunehmen'. But this fact can be accounted for partly by the tendency to restrict Epic τε to habitual action, partly by certain conventions of Epic composition. Thus ἦμος (except μ 439) is always found in the first arsis, and is always followed by δέ: and ἦμος δέ τε is thus metrically impossible. Temporal ὅπως is never used of habitual action (see the exx. in Ebeling, ii 69 b *ad fin.*: in Σ 473 ὅππως means 'according as'). I add that non-connective τε does follow prepositive ὅππῃ ('wherever') in M 48.

ὅσσον τε γέγωνε βοήσας): ι254 οἷά τε ληιστῆρες ὑπεὶρ ἅλα: ν300 Παλλάδ' Ἀθηναίην . . . ἥ τέ τοι αἰεὶ . . . παρίσταμαι: ξ221 ἀνδρῶν δυσμενέων ὅ τέ μοι εἴξειε πόδεσσι: 466 καί τι ἔπος προέηκεν ὅ πέρ τ' ἄρρητον ἄμεινον ('of such a kind that': cf. τ161: Ω774): Hes.*Th*.382 ἄστρα τε λαμπετόωντα, τά τ' οὐρανὸς ἐστεφάνωται: Mimn.*Fr*.2.1 ἡμεῖς δ' οἷά τε φύλλα φύει πολυάνθεμος ὥρη ἔαρος: Alcm.*Fr*.94.2 βάλε κηρύλος εἴην, ὅς τ' ἐπὶ κύματος ἄνθος . . . ποτῆται: Hes.*Op*.20,36,92,224,322.

(For ὅσσον τε, οἷός τε, see further (ii) and (iii) below.)

With relative local adverbs, often in geographical or anatomical descriptions. Hom.δ85 Λιβύην, ἵνα τ' ἄρνες ἄφαρ κεραοὶ τελέθουσιν: λ475 Ἄϊδόσδε . . . ἔνθα τε νεκροὶ ἀφραδέες ναίουσι: τ188 ἐν Ἀμνισῷ, ὅθι τε σπέος Εἰλειθυίης: α50: γ321. Hom. Ε305 κατ' ἰσχίον, ἔνθα τε μηρὸς ἰσχίῳ ἐνστρέφεται: Υ478 ἵνα τε ξυνέχουσι τένοντες: Χ325.

In general. Hom.Δ247 σχεδὸν ἐλθέμεν ἔνθα τε νῆες εἰρύατ': Ι441 οὐδ' ἀγορέων, ἵνα τ' ἄνδρες ἀριπρεπέες τελέθουσι: Σ521 ἐν ποταμῷ, ὅθι τ' ἀρδμὸς ἔην πάντεσσι βοτοῖσιν: φ142 ἀρξάμενοι τοῦ χώρου ὅθεν τέ περ οἰνοχοεύει: ξ353: ω507: Mimn.*Fr*.11.5 Αἰήταο πόλιν, τόθι τ' ὠκέος Ἠελίοιο ἀκτῖνες . . . κείαται.

With temporal relatives. Hom.Β471 ὥρῃ ἐν εἰαρινῇ, ὅτε τε γλάγος ἄγγεα δεύει: Κ7 ἢ νιφετόν, ὅτε πέρ τε χιὼν ἐπάλυνεν ἀρούρας: μ22 δυσθανέες, ὅτε τ' ('whereas') ἄλλοι ἅπαξ θνήσκουσ' ἄνθρωποι: Β782: Δ259: Λ87 ἐπεί τ' (562): Hes.*Op*.575 ὅτε τ' ἠέλιος χρόα κάρφει: Thgn.977 ὄφρα τ' ἐλαφρὰ γούνατα: cf. 1015 πρίν τ' ἐχθροὺς πτῆξαι.

ὥς τε, ὡς εἴ τε, in comparisons, often in Homer. Hom.Γ23 ὥς τε λέων ἐχάρη: 381 τὸν δ' ἐξήρπαξ' Ἀφροδίτη ῥεῖα μάλ' ὥς τε θεός ('as a goddess would'): Β780 ἴσαν ὡς εἴ τε πυρὶ χθὼν πᾶσα νέμοιτο: Ι481 καί μ' ἐφίλησ' ὡς εἴ τε πατὴρ ὃν παῖδα φιλήσῃ: ξ254 ῥηϊδίως, ὡς εἴ τε κατὰ ῥόον: Hes.*Op*.112,116: *Sc*.222: Thgn.985,1097: Archil.*Fr*.102.2 ἡ δέ οἱ σάθη ὡς εἴ τ' ὄνου Πριηνέος: Sol.*Fr*.23.20: Ibyc.*Fr*.7.6: Carm.Pop.1.11. Doric, ὧτε: Alcm.*Fr*.1.41,100.

In some passages τε gives a causal colour to the relative, like *quippe*, denoting an inherent, and therefore essentially general, connexion. Hom.Α244 χωόμενος ὅ τ' ἄριστον Ἀχαιῶν οὐδὲν ἔτεισας: 518 Ἦ δὴ λοίγια ἔργ' ὅ τέ μ' ἐχθοδοπῆσαι ἐφήσεις Ἥρῃ: Ρ174 οἷον ἔειπες, ὅς τέ με φῂς Αἴαντα πελώριον οὐχ ὑπομεῖναι: O468: ε357: Thgn.1069 νήπιοι, οἵτε θανόντας κλαίουσ', οὐδ' ἥβης ἄνθος ἀπολλύμενον.

The number of passages in which τε follows a relative in strictly particular statements is very considerably smaller. Hom. E477 ἡμεῖς δ' αὖ μαχόμεσθ', οἵ πέρ τ' ἐπίκουροι ἔνειμεν: N625 Ζηνὸς . . . ξεινίου, ὅς τέ ποτ' ὔμμι διαφθέρσει πόλιν αἰπήν: O130 οὐκ ἀΐεις ἅ τέ φησι θεὰ λευκώλενος Ἥρη . . . ; X115–16 πάντα μάλ' ὅσσα τ' Ἀλέξανδρος . . . ἠγάγετο Τροίηνδ', ἥ τ' ἔπλετο νείκεος ἀρχή: P368 ἠέρι γὰρ κατέχοντο μάχης ἐπί θ' ὅσσον ἄριστοι ἕστασαν (contrast O358 ὅσον τ' ἐπί, habitual action: τε is perhaps stereotyped in this formula): B594 Δώριον, ἔνθα τε Μοῦσαι ἀντόμεναι Θάμυριν . . . παῦσαν ἀοιδῆς: κ417 ἵνα τ' ἔτραφεν ἠδ' ἐγένοντο: Γ189 ἤματι τῷ ὅτε τ' ἦλθον Ἀμαζόνες: M393 αὐτίκ' ἐπεί τ' ἐνόησεν: κ420 ὡς ἐχάρημεν, ὡς εἴ τ' εἰς Ἰθάκην ἀφικοίμεθα: H298: K127 (Bentley), 286: η323: ρ331: Thgn.703 ὅστε καὶ ἐξ Ἀΐδεω . . . ἀνῆλθεν: 1123 πέπονθά τοι οἷά τ' Ὀδυσσεύς, ὅστ' . . . : 1128 ὄφρα τε γῆς ἐπέβη δαιδαλέου τε μυχοῦ: Mimn.*Fr.*12.1 ἐπείτε . . . ἀφικόμεθα: Semon.*Fr.*7.117 ἐξ οὗ τε τοὺς μὲν Ἀΐδης ἐδέξατο.

Survivals of Epic τε following relatives in the fifth and fourth centuries.

ὅς τε is sometimes used in general statements in lyric and tragic poetry. (But even in Pindar this use no longer predominates strongly, while in tragedy it has receded altogether into the background.) Pi.*O.*2.35 οὕτω δὲ Μοῖρ', ἅ τε πατρώϊον τῶνδ' ἔχει τὸν εὔφρονα πότμον: 14.2 Καφισίων ὑδάτων λαχοῖσαι ταί τε ναίετε καλλίπωλον ἕδραν: A.*Eu.*1024 (iamb.) ξὺν προσπόλοισιν αἵτε φρουροῦσιν βρέτας τοὐμὸν δικαίως: E.*Hec.*445 Αὔρα, ποντιὰς αὔρα, ἅτε ποντοπόρους κομίζεις θοὰς ἀκάτους: Pi.*I.*8.40: *P.*4.30: 12.2: *N.*6.9,31: 8.2: 11.1: *Fr.*107(122).3: A.*Supp.*63,559: *Th.*140: *Pers.*42: *Ag.*49,1122: E.*Ion* 882: *IT* 1237: *Or.*321. Ar.*Lys.*1308 (Doric) ᾇ τε πῶλοι, 'like colts'. (In A.*Th.*501 τε is probably copulative (epexegetic), as Tucker takes it: see p. 502.)

More frequently (in tragedy perhaps always) ὅς τε is now no more than, at most, an emphatic relative, 'that very one who', often conveying a generic-causal sense, *quippe qui*: at least, a merely stylistic, and perhaps metrically convenient, substitute for the simple relative. Aeschylus uses ὅς τε far more frequently than the other tragedians, occasionally even in iambics, while in Sophocles and Euripides it is confined to lyrics. (In S.*Ph.*600 Heath's γ' is certainly right.)[1]

Pi.*N.*9.9 ἱππίων ἀέθλων κορυφάν, ἅ τε Φοίβῳ θῆκεν Ἄδραστος: A.*Pers.*297 τίνα δὲ καὶ πενθήσομεν τῶν ἀρχελείων, ὅστε ... τάξιν ἠρήμου θανών: *Ch.*615 φοινίαν κόραν, ἅτ' ἐχθρῶν ὑπαὶ φῶτ' ἀπώλεσεν φίλον: S.*Tr.*824 Ἴδ' οἷον ... προσέμειξεν ἄφαρ τοὔπος τὸ θεοπρόπον ἡμῖν ... ὅ τ' ἔλακεν ...: *El.*151 σὲ δ' ἔγωγε νέμω θεόν, ἅτ' ἐν τάφῳ πετραίῳ, αἰαῖ, δακρύεις: Pi.*P.*2.39: 3.89: *N.*10.47: *I.*2.23: A.*Supp.*49: *Pers.*16: *Pr.*556, 1071 (doubtful): *Th.*753,1060: *Ag.*357: *Eu.*921: S.*OT*694: Hdt.i 74 ὅρκια δὲ ποιέεται ταῦτα τὰ ἔθνεα τά πέρ τε Ἕλληνες, καὶ πρὸς τούτοισι ... (τε hardly seems to look forward to καί, as Stein alternatively suggests. This Herodotean epicism is supported by ὅκως τε (i), ὅσον τε (ii), οἷά τε (iii) below).

In illustrating the following further varieties of τε with the relative in fifth- and fourth-century Greek, it will not be worth while, in view of what has been said above, to classify separately general and particular statements.

(i) With local and temporal adverbs and adverbial phrases. A.*Pers.*762 (iamb.) ἐξ οὗτε τιμὴν Ζεὺς ἄναξ τήνδ' ὤπασεν (*Eu.* 25, iamb.): E.*Ph.*645 καλλιπόταμος ὕδατος ἵνα τε νοτὶς ἐπέρχεται γύας (*Ph.*1751: *IA* 1495): *IA* 573 ἔμολες ... ἦτε ... ἐτράφης: Hdt.ii 108.4 οὗτοι, ὅκως τε ἀπίοι ὁ ποταμός ... πλατυτέροισι ἐχρέωντο τοῖσι πόμασι (τε *secl.* Hude). ἐπείτε is common in Herodotus, and is indistinguishable in sense from ἐπεί: i 34,35, 42.2: *id. saep.*

(ii) ὅσον τε. In phrases like the Homeric ὅσσον τε γέγωνε βοήσας (see (1) *ad init.*, pp. 521–2) τε denotes habitual action. (Hes.*Op.*346 πῆμα κακὸς γείτων, ὅσσον τ' ἀγαθὸς μέγ' ὄνειαρ: 679 ὅσον τ' ἐπιβᾶσα κορώνη ἴχνος ἐποίησεν: Mimn.*Fr.*2.8 ὅσον τ' ἐπὶ γῆν κίδναται ἠέλιος.) From this it is but a short step to phrases in which ὅσον τε, with ellipse of verb, denotes approximation to a definite standard. Hom.ι 322 τὸ μὲν ἄμμες ἐΐσκομεν εἰσορόωντες ὅσσον θ' ἱστὸν νηός: 325 τοῦ μὲν ὅσον τ' ὄργυιαν ἐγὼν ἀπέκοψα: κ 517 βόθρον ὀρύξαι ὅσον τε πυγούσιον. The occurrence of this quasi-adverbial idiom in Herodotus is perhaps

[1] For ὅστε in tragedy, see Ellendt, *s.v.*

an Homeric trait: i 126 ἦν γάρ τις χῶρος . . . ἀκανθώδης ὅσον τε ἐπὶ ὀκτωκαίδεκα σταδίους: ii 96 κοψάμενοι ξύλα ὅσον τε διπήχεα: iii 5 ἐὸν τοῦτο οὐκ ὀλίγον χωρίον ἀλλὰ ὅσον τε ἐπὶ τρεῖς ἡμέρας ὁδοῦ: ii 92,99: iii 30. (The fact that in such cases the sense 'about' is appropriate should be welcome to those who derive τε from indefinite τις.) Adjectival, with verb expressed in relative clause: Hdt.ii 73 τῆς σμύρνης ᾠὸν πλάσσειν ὅσον τε δυνατός ἐστι φέρειν (*quantum fere*, Stein: τε *om. PRSV*: τι Schweighäuser).

(iii) οἷός τε. Hdt.i 93 θώματα δὲ γῆ Λυδίη ἐς συγγραφὴν οὐ μάλα ἔχει, οἷά τε καὶ ἄλλη χώρη (*qualia fere*, Stein: τε *L*: γε Krueger) offers another rare survival of an Homeric use. But οἷός τε, meaning 'able to', is common in post-Homeric Greek, the neuter οἷόν τε being also freely used. In Homer the two senses, 'the sort of man to' and 'able to', are scarcely yet differentiated: τ160 ἤδη γὰρ ἀνὴρ οἷός τε μάλιστα οἴκου κήδεσθαι: φ117 ὅτ' ἐγὼ κατόπισθε λιποίμην οἷός τ' ἤδη πατρὸς ἀέθλια κάλ' ἀνελέσθαι: 173 τοῖον . . . οἷόν τε ῥυτῆρα βιοῦ τ' ἔμεναι καὶ ὀϊστῶν. Monro remarks (on τ160) that οἷος with the infinitive is rare in Homer, and not found at all in the *Iliad*. In later Greek, the sense 'the sort of man to', 'inclined to', is expressed by plain οἷος with the infinitive, οἷός τε being reserved for the meaning 'able to'. οἷά τε, adverbial in a causal sense, like ἅτε: Hdt.ii 175.5 ἀναστενάξαι οἷά τε χρόνου ἐγγεγονότος πολλοῦ: v 11.2: in a comparison, E.*Hyps*.fr.lxiv 20 von Arnim.

(iv) ἅτε, adverbial, with participle, in a causal sense, is unknown to Homer and Hesiod, and, I think, to the tragedians, but is often found in Aristophanes, Herodotus, Plato, and Xenophon. Commoner in the *Problems* than in genuine Aristotle, Bonitz. In the orators[1] the only instance is [D.]xlii 24 ἅτε νέος . . . ὤν. Pi.*P.* 2.84 ἅτ' ἐχθρὸς ἐών: Cratin.*Fr*.295: Ar.*Pax* 623,634: *Av*.75, 285: *Ra*.546,671: *Th*.456: *Lys*.418: *Ec*.37,257: Hdt.i 123 ἄλλως μὲν οὐδαμῶς εἶχε ἅτε τῶν ὁδῶν φυλασσομένων. Pl.*Smp*.179D: Th.iv 130.6: X.*Cyr*.i 3.3: *An*.iv 2.13: 8.27: v 2.1: [X.]*Ath*.1.16: 1.20: 2.14. For further Herodotean examples, see Kühner, II ii 97. For Plato, Xenophon, and Aristotle, see the several indexes. (I have cited all the Aristophanic examples. Cf. Introd. VI. 5.)

[1] My statistics for ἅτε and ἐφ' ᾧ τε in the orators are from Schmidt, with whom the indexes to individual orators agree.

Rarely without participle: Hdt.iii 80 ἄχθεται ἅτε θωπί: i 123: v 66.2: 85.2: Th.v 72.1 (*v.* Steup). Pl.*R*.551E χρήματα μὴ ἐθέλειν εἰσφέρειν, ἅτε φιλοχρημάτους (*sc.* ὄντας): 568B αὐτοὺς εἰς τὴν πολιτείαν οὐ παραδεξόμεθα ἅτε τυραννίδος ὑμνητάς: 619D: *Ly*.212A: Arist.*Mete*.358a35. (In A.*Th*.140 ἅτε = ἤτε.)

Occasionally in tragedy, not infrequently in Pindar and Herodotus, in comparisons, *tamquam*, *velut*. (The adverbial sense of ἅτε does not occur at all in Homer (in *Λ* 779 and *X* 127 ἅτε is not adverbial) or in Hesiod: see Ebeling, ii 316b, and Kühner, II ii 490.) The earliest examples I can find of comparative ἅτε are Alcm. *Fr*.1.62: Ibyc.*Fr*.6.8 (conjectured). Pi.*O*.1.2 ὁ δὲ χρυσὸς αἰθόμενον πῦρ ἅτε διαπρέπει νυκτὶ μεγάνορος ἔξοχα πλούτου: 12.14 ἐνδομάχας ἅτ' ἀλέκτωρ: *P*.2.79: *N*.7.105: *Fr*.225(241): A.*Ch*.381 Τοῦτο διαμπερὲς οὖς ἵκεθ' ἅπερ τε βέλος (τι Schütz): S.*Aj*.168[1] παταγοῦσιν ἅτε πτηνῶν ἀγέλαι (ἅπερ L^{ac}): E.*HF*667 ἴσον ἅτ' ἐν νεφέλαισιν ἄστρων ναύταις ἀριθμὸς πέλει: Hdt.i 200 ἅτε μᾶζαν μαξάμενος: ii 69 ἅτε πολεμίους περιέπουσι ('as enemies'): iii 115: iv 64,146: viii 134.2 (*bis*).

For ἅτε δή, see δή, I.9.v.*b*.

ἅτε περ: Arist.*Pol*.1253a6.

(v) ὥστε. ὥστε in comparisons is pretty common in the tragedians, particularly in the *Trachiniae* and *Bacchae*.[2] It is used both in the iambic portions and in the lyrics. Sometimes ὥστε has a verb to itself: S.*Tr*.112: *Fr*.433: E.*Rh*.972 Βάκχου προφήτης ὥστε Παγγαίου πέτραν ᾤκησε: Far more frequently the verb is understood*: A.*Ag*.628 Ἔκυρσας ὥστε τοξότης ἄκρος σκοποῦ: S.*Tr*.530 κἀπὸ μητρὸς ἄφαρ βέβαχ', ὥστε πόρτις ἐρήμα: *Ant*.586 ὁμοῖον ὥστε . . . ὅταν . . . ('like as when . . .', cf. *Tr*.699): E.*Or*.697 ὁμοῖον ὥστε πῦρ κατασβέσαι λάβρον. (Cf. *Or*.145 σύριγγος ὅπως πνοὰ λεπτοῦ δόνακος . . . φώνει μοι.) In A.*Eu*.628, again, there is hardly a question of understanding a verb from the *context*, and ὥστε stands roughly for οἷά ἐστι, *sc.* τόξα (cf. E. *El*.748[3]). (Sometimes ὥστε follows the word to which it refers,

[1] The only Sophoclean instance of adverbial ἅτε given by Ellendt. Dorville's conjecture at *OT* 478 lacks probability.

[2] Schroeder (*Prolegomena* § 83), following Boeckh, reads ὥτε everywhere in Pindar, though the MSS. often give ὥστε: *O*.10.86: *P*.4.64,10.54: *N*. 6.28: 7.62,71 (for ὡσείτε), 93: *I*.4.18b.

[3] Kayser's νερτέρας βροντῆς is therefore not absolutely necessary.

or is inserted in the middle of the clause: A.*Supp.*751 κόρακες ὥστε: *Ag.*1671 ἀλέκτωρ ὥστε θηλείας πέλας (ὥστε Scaliger: ὥσπερ *codd.*): *Ch.*421 λύκος γὰρ ὥστ' ὠμόφρων: S.*Tr.*537: E.*Hipp.* 1221: *Hec.*205: and for other instances see above.) A.*Pers.*424: *Pr.*452: *Th.*62: *Fr.*57,313: S.*Aj.*300: *El.*444: *Ant.*1033,1084: *Tr.*367,703,768,1071: *OC* 343: *Fr* 210,808: E.*Hipp.*429: *Heracl.* 423: *Hec.*178,337: *HF* 110: *IT* 359: *Hel.*1162: *Ph.*1573,1712, 1722: *Or.*882,1520: *Ba.*543,748,752,778,1188: *IA* 1082: *Rh.*301, 618.

Quite distinct is the Herodotean usage, whereby ὥστε gives a causal force to a participle, either in direct construction or with a genitive absolute: i8 ὥστε δὲ ταῦτα νομίζων: vi 52.3 ὥστε καὶ ὁμοίων καὶ ἴσων ἐόντων: i 73,127: iv 136: v 19.1: 35.3, 42.2: 83.2 (ὥστε δή): 101.2: vi 44.3: 94.1: 136.2: vii 129.1 (ὥστε γε): 129.2: viii 118.2: ix 37.2: 37.3: 70.2: 76.1.

There are two examples in Thucydides, probably due to Herodotean influence: ii 40.4 βεβαιότερος δὲ ὁ δράσας τὴν χάριν ὥστε ὀφειλομένην δι' εὐνοίας ᾧ δέδωκε σῴζειν ('since it is owed to him': this seems to be the correct interpretation of a much disputed passage): vii 24.2 ὥστε γὰρ ταμιείῳ χρωμένων τῶν Ἀθηναίων τοῖς τείχεσι πολλὰ ... χρήματα ... ἐνῆν (ἅτε *B*: ὥσπερ Stahl: here ὥστε seems to go with the participle, 'quippe cum uterentur': see Steup *ad loc.*, and on ii 40.4).

Apart from these two examples, there are no traces of the Herodotean usage in Attic. In A.*Ag.*884 ὥστε σύγγονον βροτοῖσι τὸν πεσόντα λακτίσαι πλέον, it is unnecessary to supply ὄν (on the analogy of Th.ii 35.1 ὡς καλόν, where again see Steup), since we can perfectly well read ὥς τε, 'and saying that'. Nor can an ellipse of ἐστι be supported by A.*Th.*13, where Paley's defence of the generally accepted ὥστε (for ὥστι, ὥστις) is inadequate. (*C.R.*xlvii(1933)163–4.)[1]

ὥς τε, consecutive, with indicative, is not found in Homer: with infinitive, only in *I* 42 and ρ21: Hes.*Op.*44 ὥς τέ σε κεὶς ἐνιαυτὸν ἔχειν. Originally, no doubt, the consecutive relation is expressed by the infinitive alone, and ὡς means 'as' (ὥς τε

[1] The explanation of ὥστε with participle in And.iv 20, Is.ix 16, and other passages is of course different: here a consecutive clause dependent on a participle is assimilated into the participial construction: see Kühner, II ii 96, 514 *Anm.*3.

νέεσθαι, 'wie um zurückzukehren'). But later the consecutive sense is felt to reside, not in the infinitive, but in the ὥστε (Kühner, II ii 500: Monro, on ρ21): and in later Greek ὥστε is the normal substitute for ὡς in the consecutive sense.

ὡσείτε: Pi.*P*.1.44 (false reading for ὥτε in *N*.7.71). But in S. *Ant*.653 ἀλλὰ πτύσας ὡσεί τε δυσμενῆ μέθες, Jebb is probably right in taking τε as copulative: 'Nay, with loathing, and as if she were thine enemy'.

(vi) ἐφ' ᾧ τε, 'on condition that', is used with the future indicative and with the infinitive. Hdt.iii 83 ἐπὶ τούτῳ δὲ ὑπεξίσταμαι τῆς ἀρχῆς, ἐπ' ᾧ τε ὑπ' οὐδενὸς ὑμέων ἄρξομαι: Th.i 103.1 ξυνέβησαν . . . ἐφ' ᾧτε ἐξίασιν (only here in Thucydides, in *ABEFM* alone): Pl.*Ap*.29C ἀφίεμέν σε, ἐπὶ τούτῳ μέντοι, ἐφ' ᾧτε μηκετί . . . διατρίβειν (the only Platonic instance known to me): X.*HG*ii 3.11 αἱρεθέντες δὲ ἐφ' ᾧτε συγγράψαι νόμους. Like ἅτε, ἐφ' ᾧτε is very rare in the orators: it is found once in Isocrates (xvii 19), twice in Aeschines (iii 114, 183), once in genuine Demosthenes (xli 4). Contrast its frequency in [D.]lvi(3,5,20,42,49): add [D.]xxvi 13. It is very rare in verse: but cf. Ar.*Th*.1162: *Pl*.1000: 1141: Cratin.*Fr*.279. Prose: Hdt.i 22.4: vi 65.1: vii 153.3: 154.3: 158.5: viii 4.2: X.*HG*ii 4.38: vii 4.10: *An*.vi 6.22. In an inscription of 329 B.C. (Meisterhans, p. 253).

(I take no account of ἔστε, since it seems uncertain whether the τε in ἔστε has anything to do with the particle.)

(2) τε following other particles. Since ideas which are presented antithetically or disjunctively may simultaneously be presented as simply added to one another, the combinations μέν τε, δέ τε, ἤ τε present no difficulty to those who derive all meanings of τε from the root idea of 'addition'. Equally easily explained on this hypothesis are γάρ τε, ἀλλά τε, and even the redundant καί τε (as 'and also'). But the great majority of passages in which τε is coupled with another particle contain general propositions, or describe habitual action. And there are strong reasons for believing that here too, as in the case of relatives, τε generalizes the action, its association with particular particles being almost as loose and fortuitous as that, for example, of μέν with γάρ.

(i) *μέν τε, δέ τε.* Hom.*A*403 *ὃν Βριάρεων καλέουσι θεοί, ἄνδρες δέ τε πάντες Αἰγαίωνα*: *B*90 *αἱ μέν τ' ἔνθα ἅλις πεποτήαται αἱ δέ τε ἔνθα*: 210 *σμαραγεῖ δέ τε πόντος*: *E*138 *ὅν ῥά τε ποιμὴν . . . χραύσῃ μέν τ' αὐλῆς ὑπεράλμενον οὐδὲ δαμάσσῃ*: *N*493 *γάνυται δ' ἄρα τε φρένα ποιμήν*: Hes.*Op.*233 *ἄκρη μέν τε φέρει βαλάνους, μέσση δὲ μελίσσας*: Xenoph.*Fr.*13.3 *ἵπποι μέν θ' ἵπποισι, βόες δέ τε βουσὶν ὁμοίας, καί κε θεῶν ἰδέας ἔγραφον*: Hom.*η*124: *μ*93: Hes.*Th.*596: *Op.*218,311,631: Thgn.148, 359: Emp.*Fr.*35.7,11,16: Sapph.*Fr.*117: Cleobul.4: Philox. *Fr.*e4.

δέ τε in apodosi: Hes.*Th.*784 *καί ῥ' ὅς τις ψεύδηται . . ., Ζεὺς δέ τε Ἶριν ἔπεμψε.*

(ii) *οὐδέ τε.* Hom.*β*182 *ὄρνιθες δέ τε πολλοὶ ὑπ' αὐγὰς ἠελίοιο φοιτῶσ', οὐδέ τε πάντες ἐναίσιμοι*: *λ*123 *οἳ οὐ ἴσασι θάλασσαν ἀνέρες, οὐδέ θ' ἅλεσσι μεμιγμένον εἶδαρ ἔδουσιν*: *Ξ*18 *οὐδ' ἄρα τε προκυλίνδεται*: Emp.*Fr.*27a *οὐ στάσις οὐδέ τε δῆρις ἀναίσιμος ἐν μελέεσσιν.*

(iii) *γάρ τε.* Hom.*A*63 *καὶ γάρ τ' ὄναρ ἐκ Διός ἐστιν*: *I*406 *ληϊστοὶ μὲν γὰρ τε βόες*: 410 *μήτηρ γάρ τέ μέ φησι* ('says habitually': cf. *A*521): Hes.*Op.*761 *φήμη γάρ τε κακὴ πέλεται*: Hom. *B*481: *γ*147: *δ*397: Hes.*Op.*30,214: Thgn.281: Phoc.*Fr.*7.2.

(iv) *ἤ τε.* Disjunctive: Hom.*I*276 *ἣ θέμις ἐστίν, ἄναξ, ἤ τ' ἀνδρῶν ἤ τε γυναικῶν*: *Λ*410 *ὃς δέ κ' ἀριστεύῃσι μάχῃ ἔνι, τὸν δὲ μάλα χρεὼ ἑστάμεναι κρατερῶς, ἤ τ' ἔβλητ' ἤ τ' ἔβαλ' ἄλλον.* Monro (*HG.*[2] § 340) remarks that 'considering the general difficulty of deciding between *εἰ* and *ἤ* in the text of Homer, we cannot regard the form *ἤ τε* as resting on good evidence'.

Comparative: Hom.*π*216 *ἀδινώτερον ἤ τ' οἰωνοί.* In *Δ*277 Monro (§ 332) thinks Bekker's *ἠέ τε*, for *ἠΰτε*, may be right.

(v) *καί τε.* Hom.*K*224 *σύν τε δύ' ἐρχομένω, καί τε πρὸ ὃ τοῦ ἐνόησεν*: *ξ*465 *οἶνος . . . ὅς τ' ἐφέηκε πολύφρονά περ μάλ' ἀεῖσαι καί θ' ἁπαλὸν γελάσαι, καί τ' ὀρχήσασθαι ἀνῆκε*: *τ*537 *χῆνές μοι κατὰ οἶκον . . ., καί τέ σφιν ἰαίνομαι εἰσορόωσα*: Emp.*Fr.* 23.8 . . . *καὶ ὑδατοθρέμμονας ἰχθῦς καί τε θεοὺς δολιχαίωνας*: Hom.*A*521: *h.Merc.*559: *h.Ven.*30: *h.Ath.*4: Hes.*Op.*515–16: *Th.*420: Thgn.138,662.

καί τε, 'also', 'even': Hom.*I*159 *τοὔνεκα καί τε βροτοῖσι θεῶν ἔχθιστος ἁπάντων*: *ρ*485 *εἰ δή πού τις ἐπουράνιος θεός ἐστι. καί τε θεοὶ ξείνοισιν ἐοικότες ἀλλοδαποῖσι . . . ἐπιστρωφῶσι* πόληας: Hes.*Op.*360 ὃς δέ κεν αὐτὸς ἕληται . . . καί τε σμικρὸν ἐόν, τό γ' ἐπάχνωσεν φίλον ἦτορ.

Exceptionally, καί τε . . . καί τε, corresponsive: Emp.*Fr.* 129.6 ῥεῖα . . . λεύσσεσκεν ἕκαστον καί τε δέκ' ἀνθρώπων καί τ' εἴκοσιν αἰώνεσσιν ('in ten, yea twenty, lifetimes').

(vi) ἀλλά τε. Hom.*B*754 οὐδ' ὅ γε Πηνειῷ συμμίσγεται ἀργυροδίνῃ, ἀλλά τέ μιν καθύπερθεν ἐπιρρέει: μ44,64,67: Hes.*Th.* 797. *In apodosi* (following εἴ περ in protasis: 'even if . . . still'): Hom.*A*82 εἴ περ γάρ τε χόλον γε καὶ αὐτῆμαρ καταπέψῃ, ἀλλά τε καὶ μετόπισθεν ἔχει κότον: *K*226: *T*165: *Φ*577: *X*192.

(vii) ἀτάρ τε. Hom.*Δ*484 λείη, ἀτάρ τέ οἱ ὄζοι ἐπ' ἀκροτάτῃ πεφύασι.

(viii) εἰ πέρ τε, 'even if'. (For πέρ τε after relatives, see (1) above.) Hom.*K*225 μοῦνος δ' εἴ πέρ τε νοήσῃ, ἀλλά τέ οἱ βράσσων τε νόος, λεπτὴ δέ τε μῆτις: *Λ*116 ἡ δ' εἴ πέρ τε τύχῃσι μάλα σχεδόν, οὐ δύναταί σφι χραισμεῖν.

(ix) οὔτε . . . τε. Here the redundancy is intolerable, if τε is taken as responsive. Hom.*E*89 τὸν δ' οὔτ' ἄρ τε γέφυραι ἐεργμέναι ἰσχανόωσιν, οὔτ' ἄρα ἕρκεα ἴσχει.

(x) μέν τε (with affirmative μέν: for τε following prospective μέν, see (i) above). Hom.*Δ*341 σφῶϊν μέν τ' ἐπέοικε μετὰ πρώτοισιν ἐόντας ἑστάμεν: *O*203 στρεπταὶ μέν τε φρένες ἐσθλῶν: ε447 αἰδοῖος μέν τ' ἐστὶ . . . ὅς τις ἵκηται ἀλώμενος.

(xi) νύ τε. Hom.α60 οὔ νύ τ' Ὀδυσσεὺς . . . χαρίζετο . . . ; 347 οὐ νύ τ' ἀοιδοὶ αἴτιοι.

(xii) καὶ δέ τε. Hom.*Y*28 καὶ δέ τέ μιν καὶ πρόσθεν ὑποτρομέεσκον ὁρῶντες (the only example of καὶ δέ τε in Homer, Leaf: καὶ δέ τι Aristarchus, with some MSS., but I agree with Leaf that 'the pronoun is insufferably weak'.)

There remains a strong minority of passages in Epic where τε is associated with other particles in particular statements. But the number should probably be materially reduced. As Monro points out, in his paper to the Oxford Philological Society and in his *Homeric Grammar*: (*a*) τε is often omitted in some MSS.: (*b*) in some places τε is clearly inserted, to avoid a supposed hiatus, by a scribe ignorant of the digamma: (*c*) in others emendation is probably needed.

(*a*) Hom.*X*166 θεοὶ δέ τε πάντες ὁρῶντο (δέ, δ' ἐς *al.*): υ252 ἐν δέ τε οἶνον κρητῆρσιν κερόωντο (ἐν δ' ἄρα *al.*: but cf. κ317 ἐν δέ τε φάρμακον ἧκε): *Π*96.

(*b*) *Z*367 οὐ γάρ τ' οἶδα, most MSS. (κ190 οὐ γάρ τ' ἴδμεν): *Λ*406 οὐδέ τ' ἔδησαν (οὐδέ F' ἔδησαν, Leaf: cf. *B*165, 181 : *Λ*437).

(*c*) In particular, δ' ἔτι, οὐδ' ἔτι are often read by editors for δέ τε, οὐδέ τε : a ready expedient, which has sometimes, perhaps, been abused.[1] In *Ω*337 ὡς ἄγαγ', ὡς μήτ' ἄρ τις ἴδῃ μήτ' ἄρ τε νοήσῃ Bentley conjectures μή τίς Fε ἴδῃ μήτ' ἄρ Fε νοήσῃ. In *Ω*17 read probably τὸν δ' ἐάεσκεν (see Leaf).

There still remain, however, some awkward passages, which are not easily emended. Hom.*E*118 δός δέ τέ μ' ἄνδρα ἑλεῖν : *K*466 δέελον δ' ἐπὶ σῆμά τ' ἔθηκε (see Leaf): *Π*836 σὲ δέ τ' ἐνθάδε γῦπες ἔδονται : *Φ*456 νῶϊ δέ τ' ἄψορροι κίομεν : Hes.*Th.* 688 ἐκ δέ τε πᾶσαν φαῖνε βίην (δέ γε *D*): 423 οὐδέ τ' ἀπηύρα : Hom.δ497 : ο428 : ρ25,270. Hom.*Λ*64 ὅτε μέν τε μετὰ πρώτοισι φάνεσκεν, ἄλλοτε δ' ἐν πυμάτοισι : *Π*28 τοὺς μέν τ' ἰητροὶ πολυφάρμακοι ἀμφιπένονται : ε331 ἄλλοτε μέν τε Νότος Βορέῃ προβάλεσκε φέρεσθαι, ἄλλοτε δ' αὖτ' Εὖρος : *N*47 Αἴαντε, σφὼ μέν τε σαώσετε λαὸν Ἀχαιῶν : Hes.*Sc.*359. Hom.*Υ*156 Ἀτρεΐδη, σοὶ γάρ τε μάλιστά γε λαὸς Ἀχαιῶν πείσονται μύθοισι (but this is half-general, 'will listen, as they always do'): *Ω*602 καὶ γάρ τ' ἠΰκομος Νιόβη ἐμνήσατο σίτου (here, perhaps, a historic precedent is taken as equivalent to a general proposition) : *M*245. Hom. *Γ*235 οὕς κεν ἐῢ γνοίην καί τ' οὔνομα μυθησαίμην : τ342 πολλὰς γὰρ δὴ νύκτας . . . ἄεσα καί τ' ἀνέμεινα . . . Ἠῶ. καί τε, as Christ points out, is especially common in the Hymn to Aphrodite, where it is used in particular, as well as in general, statements: e.g. 30,51. In *h.Merc.*133 καί τε means 'although': καί τε μάλ'

[1] In the first edition of his *Homeric Grammar* (§ 332) Monro allowed, as 'isolated Epic uses', (1) τ' ἄρα after interrogatives, (2) ἤ τε, (3) ἤ τε (comparative), and (4) οὐδέ τε, μηδέ τε: this last with the rider that, except in Λ 437 (Φ 596) and Φ 248, 'there is generally some marked parallelism between the words of the two clauses' (e.g. B 179 (μηδέ τ' *vulg.*), μ 198): while 'in most, if not all, instances' the emendation οὐδ' ἔτ', μηδ' ἔτ' is 'at least possible'. In the second edition (*ib.*) only (1) and (2) remain: in (3) τε is rightly regarded as akin to τε in similes, and therefore as possessing a generalizing force: while in (4) Monro everywhere unequivocally reads οὐδ' ἔτ', μηδ' ἔτ'. (It must be admitted, however, that in Ψ 730 (οὐδέ F', Brandreth) and Ω 52 ἔτι is not very suitable.)

ἱμείροντι. Hom.*P* 42 *οὐδ' ἔτ' ἀδήριτος ἤ τ' ἀλκῆς ἤ τε φόβοιο* (some MSS.: see Leaf): *T* 148 *δῶρα μὲν αἴ κ' ἐθέλῃσθα παρασχέμεν, ὡς ἐπιεικές, ἤ τ' ἐχέμεν παρὰ σοί* (some MSS. *εἴ τ'*, perhaps rightly: Monro *HG*² §340). Hom.*α* 188 *ξεῖνοι δ' . . . εὐχόμεθ' εἶναι . . . εἴ πέρ τε γέροντ' εἴρηαι*: 204 *οὔ τοι . . . ἔσσεται, οὐδ' εἴ περ τε . . . .*

(xiii) *ἦ τε.* This combination presents peculiar difficulties on any theory of *τε*. There is no trace here of any generalizing force: in fact the examples are all, I believe, particular. In some passages *τε* might conceivably be copulative: but this explanation is nowhere a very natural one (it will not fit Hes. *Sc.* 79, if *τε* is right there): moreover Christ observes that *τε* in Homer never, or scarcely ever, couples sentences. For the most part scholars are content to regard this *τε* as, at most, emphatic: at least, formal and superfluous.[1]

Hom.*Γ* 56 *ἀλλὰ μάλα Τρῶες δειδήμονες· ἦ τέ κεν ἤδη λάϊνον ἕσσο χιτῶνα* ('otherwise'): *E* 201 *ἀλλ' ἐγὼ οὐ πιθόμην (ἦ τ' ἂν πολὺ κέρδιον ἦεν)*: *Λ* 362 *ἔφυγες θάνατον, κύον· ἦ τέ τοι ἄγχι ἦλθε κακόν*: *ν* 211 *οἵ μ' εἰς ἄλλην γαῖαν ἀπήγαγον· ἦ τέ μ' ἔφαντο ἄξειν εἰς Ἰθάκην*: Hes.*Sc.* 79 *Ἥρως ὦ Ἰόλαε . . . ἦ τε μέγ' ἀθανάτους . . . ἤλιτεν Ἀμφιτρύων* (*τε* Peppmüller, *τι* (*τοι* *IM*) *codd.*): Hom.*Γ* 366: *Λ* 763: *Σ* 13: *ω* 28.

Apodotic.[2] Hom.*K* 450 *εἰ μὲν γάρ κέ σε νῦν ἀπολύσομεν . . . ἦ τε καὶ ὕστερον εἶσθα*: *E* 350: *X* 49: *α* 288: *μ* 138.

The use of *τε* after other particles is virtually confined to epic and elegiac poetry. The few apparent examples in drama and prose are palpably corrupt, or highly doubtful.

γάρ τε. Pi.*Fr.* 131 (143). 1 *κεῖνοι γάρ τ' ἄνοσοι καὶ ἀγήραοι πόνων τ' ἄπειροι*: in E.*Ion* 1099 (lyr.) Verrall conjectures *γάρ ⟨τ'⟩*.

δέ τε. B. 13. 129 (see Jebb): *Fr.* 4. 1: A.*Ch.* 490 (iamb.: certainly to be emended): S.*OT* 18 (read *οἵδε τ'*, or *οἱ δ' ἔτ'*): E.*IA* 1580 (iamb.: in a passage which cannot be taken seriously): *Fr.* 732 (iamb.: *δέ γ'* Matthiae): Ar.*Av.* 641 (*δέ γε* is certain):

[1] Christ and Kühner call it 'accessory': Bäumlein, roundly, 'räthselhaft'.

[2] Hartung (i 70) makes this the basic sense of *ἦ τε*: but his argument is highly artificial.

Hp.*Fract.*26 μᾶλλον δέ τε δεῖ (other MSS. τι, no doubt rightly): *Vict.*5 φοιτεόντων δ' ἐκείνων ὧδε, τῶν δέ τε κεῖσε (so some MSS., perhaps rightly: all things are possible in the *de Victu*).

μέν τε. E.*Med.*1094 (lyr.: τ' kept by Verrall alone).

καί τε. Hp.*Vict.*5 καί θ' ἃ μὲν πρήσσουσιν οὐκ οἴδασιν, ἃ δὲ οὐ πρήσσουσι δοκέουσιν εἰδέναι· καί θ' ἃ μὲν ὁρέουσιν οὐ γινώσκουσιν (Mack omits θ' in each case: 'Correction inutile', Littré observes, 'c'est la locution καί τε'. Perhaps: as I have said, the author of this treatise is capable of anything).

(3) Other uses of τε in Homer.

(i) With indefinite τις. In almost every case the sentence is a general one. (Exceptional, *Ξ*90 σίγα, μή τίς τ' ἄλλος Ἀχαιῶν τοῦτον ἀκούσῃ μῦθον (τ486).) Those who accept the theory of a generalizing τε are therefore not driven (with Kühner, II ii 240) to seek always in such cases to combine the particle with another word in the sentence. *B*292 καὶ γάρ τίς θ' ἕνα μῆνα μένων ἀπὸ ἧς ἀλόχοιο ἀσχαλάᾳ: *I*632 καὶ μέν τίς τε ... ποινὴν ... ἐδέξατο: υ45 καὶ μέν τίς τε χερείονι πείθεθ' ἑταίρῳ: *Γ*12: *M*150: *Π*263: ε120: τ265: ψ118.

(Where τε follows another particle, μέν or γάρ, it is perhaps preferable to regard τε as adhering to that particle, rather than to the indefinite pronoun. Where it follows ὡς, it should certainly be regarded as adhering to ὡς: one cannot differentiate between *Γ*23 ὥς τε λέων and *P*133 ὥς τίς τε λέων).

(ii) With interrogatives. Here τε is, I believe, invariably followed by ἄρα, and the question, lively or surprised in tone, usually forms the opening words of a speech. (Sometimes the vocative of the person addressed precedes the interrogative.) *Γ*226 Τίς τ' ἄρ' ὅδ' ἄλλος ...; *Σ*188 Πῶς τ' ἄρ' ἴω μετὰ μῶλον; *Λ*656: *N*307: α346: γ22: ν417. This appears to be the normal connective τε.[1] (If so, we must admit an exception here to the rule by which τε in Homer couples words or phrases, not sentences.) Like δέ and καί, it adds a note of liveliness to the interrogation. Nor is there any difficulty in assigning a connective sense to τε in *A*8 and *B*761, in which passages it is used

[1] Monro, however (*H.G.*[2] § 332), holds that the ancient grammarians who merged the particles in one (ταρ) were probably right in so doing, τε having lost its own force in the process of amalgamation.

transitionally in continuous speech. (τε, which, in general, may connect after a strong pause (I.1), is found in Attic at the opening of a speech: S.*OT* 1001, though the connexion with the preceding words is there very close: Ar.*Ec.*458, at the opening of a question: cf. E.*Ph.*1515 (τίς τ' ἄρ' *B*): and in S.*Ph.*441 the τε of *LA* is perhaps possible, though probably δέ (*rec.*) is right.

(iii) With ἄλλος. The association of τε with ἄλλος is curious. ε 29 Ἑρμεία, σὺ γὰρ αὖτε τά τ' ἄλλα περ ἄγγελός ἐσσι, νύμφῃ ἐϋπλοκάμῳ εἰπεῖν: ρ 273 'Ρεῖ' ἔγνως, ἐπεὶ οὐδὲ τά τ' ἄλλα πέρ ἐσσ' ἀνοήμων: Ψ 483 Αἶαν..., ἄλλα τε πάντα δεύεαι Ἀργείων. A generalizing force is appropriate in all three passages.[1] (In Ξ 90 τε should be referred to τις rather than to ἄλλος: *v. supr.*, (i).)

Kühner points to two strange survivals (as he thinks) of this use of τε: Meisterhans, *Gr. d. att. Inschr.*[2] 208,2 (267–5 B.C.) ἐπεὶ τά τε ἄλλα πράττουσιν καλῶς, ἀναθεῖναι αὐτοῖς καὶ στήλην: Lycurg.100 τά τε ἄλλ' ὢν ἀγαθὸς ποιητὴς καὶ τοῦτον τὸν μῦθον προείλετο ποιῆσαι (ἦν Blass: the text can hardly stand).

(iv) With ὅδε. The two passages in which τε is associated with ὅδε are a godsend to the supporters of τε's deictic origin, an embarrassment to others: ν 238 εἰ δὴ τήνδε τε γαῖαν ἀνείρεαι (one good MS. γε): ο 484 οὕτω τήνδε τε γαῖαν ἐγὼν ἴδον ὀφθαλμοῖσι (γε Bothe). Obviously there is no generalizing force in τε here.

(v) Apodotic (?). Apodotic ἀλλά τε, ἦ τε have been considered above (2.vi and xiii). τε is also used apodotically in the following passages. *A* 218 ὅς κε θεοῖς ἐπιπείθηται, μάλα τ' ἔκλυον αὐτοῦ: *Δ* 161 εἴ περ γάρ τε..., ἔκ τε καὶ ὀψὲ τελεῖ, σύν τε μεγάλῳ ἀπέτεισαν: *M* 48 ὅππῃ τ' ἰθύσῃ, τῇ τ' εἴκουσι στίχες ἀνδρῶν: 304 εἴ περ γὰρ..., οὔ ῥά τ' ἀπείρητος μέμονε σταθμοῖο δίεσθαι. Here, again, all the statements are universal: and it is natural to regard τε as having a generalizing force, rather than as marking the correspondence between protasis and apodosis. (The latter view, however, receives some support as regards μ 138 (ἦ τε) from the fact that the parallel passage λ 111 has καί κεν ἔτ'.)

In examining the Epic use of τε (1) with relatives, (2) with other particles, and (3) with certain other words, and *in apodosi*, we have seen that most of our examples are in universal state-

[1] In the first two Kühner interprets 'also': in the third (where, for other interpretations, see Leaf) he regards τε as 'rein formelhaft'.

ments, and thus that there is reason to attribute to Epic τε a generalizing force. It might be expected that the particle would bear this generalizing force in other cases, apart from any association with this or that word. This, however, is not so: instances of generalizing τε, outside the above limits, are extremely rare: but cf. *Π* 688 ἀλλ' αἰεί τε Διὸς κρείσσων νόος ἠέ περ ἀνδρῶν (*P* 176): *T* 221 αἶψά τε φυλόπιδος πέλεται κόρος ἀνθρώποισιν: α 392 αἶψά τέ οἱ δῶ ἀφνειὸν πέλεται καὶ τιμηέστερος αὐτός (though τε here might, just conceivably, look forward to καί). *Ψ* 310 is a curious case of non-connective τε in a particular statement: ἀλλά τοι ἵπποι βάρδιστοι θείειν· τῷ τ' οἴω λοίγι' ἔσεσθαι (κ', γ' *al.*).

What is the explanation of this apparently arbitrary restriction of the generalizing use? Why does a particle which has a generalizing force cling to other particles and to relatives? And why has Greek no particle whose function it is, without such restriction, to express this generalizing sense? (To a certain extent, τοι, which has some contacts with τε, fills the bill: cf. *O* 203 στρεπταὶ μέν τε φρένες ἐσθλῶν: *N* 115 ἀκεσταί τοι φρένες ἐσθλῶν: but the essential force of τοι is different.) These are insoluble problems: these, and the problem of the relationship between τε copulative or preparatory and Epic τε.

III. Supposed sense 'also'. In a few passages in drama and prose it has sometimes been suggested that τε, usually in combination with other particles, may mean 'also'.

καὶ . . . τε appears sometimes in the text of Thucydides to mean 'and also'. The occurrence of several examples of the same oddity in a single author causes some weight prima facie: but in fact there are only three cases of καὶ . . . τε in Thucydides in which the primary MSS agree and there is no independent reason to suspect corruption: i 9 3 ἅ . . . παραλαβὼν καὶ ναυτικῷ τε ἅμα ἰσχύσας: vi 44.3 καὶ πρός τε τοὺς Ῥηγίνους λόγους ἐποιήσαντο: vii 78.3 καὶ ἐπειδή τε ἐγένοντο ἐπὶ τῇ διαβάσει . . . ηὗρον ἐπ' αὐτῷ παρατεταγμένους . . . καὶ τρεψάμενοι αὐτοὺς . . . ἐχώρουν ἐς τὸ πρόσθεν. In i 43.3 τε and δέ are variants: in i 145 τε is in *ABEF* only and is therefore not the archetype's reading: in viii 68.2 *M* omits τε and the context is in any case seriously corrupt: and in viii 76.5 corruption in the context is almost certain. Also, the phenomenon is not confined to Thucydides: it appears in Is.xi 41, which is demonstrably corrupt for other reasons, and in Is.iii 80. (Hdt.vii 175.2, of course, is not an example.)[1]*

(2) *τε γάρ.* Aristotle, in several passages, appears to use *τε γάρ*, without following *τε* or *καί*, for *γάρ* or *καὶ γάρ*: *namque, etenim.* Eucken (pp. 17–21) denies this use: but Bonitz (Index, *s.v.* *τε*, and *Ztschr. f. d. öst. Gymn.* 1867, pp. 672–82), while admitting that Eucken's criticism disposes of most of the apparent examples, maintains that the supposed use is to be recognized in certain passages: *APo.*75b41: *deAn.*405a4: *PA* 661b29: *Pol.*1318b,33 1333a2. The MSS. of Thucydides show a *τε γάρ* of this kind at v 26.2 and vi 17.6: similarly Ant.iv α2. In S.*Tr.*1019–20 the MSS. read *σὺ δὲ σύλλαβε. σοί τε γὰρ ὄμμα ἔμπλεον ἢ δι' ἐμοῦ σῴζειν*: Campbell heroically keeps all this, 'the Epic use of *τε*': but the Epic use is *γάρ τε*, not *τε γάρ*: less courageous editors emend. Anacoluthon explains E.*Ph.*1313 (if *τε γάρ* is sound: but see Pearson), and D.xix 159. In Lys ii 17 *τε* seems to be answered by *δέ*. In Pl.*R.*522B the speech is interrupted. In Hdt.i 3.1 read *οὐδέ*, Schaefer.

(3) A.*Ch.*557 *ὡς ἂν δόλῳ κτείναντες ἄνδρα τίμιον δόλῳ τε καὶ ληφθῶσιν ἐν ταὐτῷ βρόχῳ* (almost universally emended: see Tucker): S.*Aj.*1312 *τῆς σῆς ὑπὲρ γυναικός, ἢ τοῦ σοῦ θ' ὁμαίμονος λέγω*; (emended by editors generally, though Campbell thinks it 'barely possible that *ἢ* . . . *τε* may = *ἢ καί*'): *El.*1416 *Ὤμοι μάλ' αὖθις.—Εἰ γὰρ Αἰγίσθῳ θ' ὁμοῦ* (*γ'* Hermann: Jebb thinks the MS. reading, with *τε* meaning 'also', 'very awkward, though not impossible'): Hp.*Prorrh.*ii 1 *ἕτερος δὲ τρόπος προρρήσιος . . . ἄλλο τε δὲ σχῆμα προρρήσεων τόδε λέγεται* (*τε* *HK*: *om. vulg.*): *Prog.*20 *οἵ τε γὰρ εὐηθέστατοι τῶν πυρετῶν . . . οἵ τε δὲ κακοηθέστατοι* (*δέ* omitted in some MSS.). In Hdt.viii 101.4, if *τε* is sound, as it well may be, it picks up an anticipatory *γάρ* (cf. pp. 70–72). It cannot mean 'also': nor can it be purely formal, as Stein takes it.)

The passages cited in the last three paragraphs afford little evidence for the sense 'also'. Although three of the most plausible examples are from one writer, Sophocles, the abnormalities seem too strong, and too diverse, to be attributed to the experimentalizing of an individual author.

[1] See Hartung, i 113: Hammer, p. 56: Schmidt, p. 22: K. W. Krüger, Classen-Steup and Marchant on the Thucydides passages. For further discussion, see references in Classen-Steup.

Τοι

That *τοι* is to be identified with the (ethic) dative of *σύ* is etymologically plausible and entirely consonant with the usage of the particle.[1] Its primary function is to bring home to the comprehension of the person addressed a truth of which he is ignorant, or temporarily oblivious: to establish, in fact, a close rapport between the mind of the speaker and the mind of another person. As a natural corollary, *τοι* implies, strictly speaking, an audience, and preferably (owing to the intimacy of appeal which it suggests) an audience of one: though in certain combinations (*γάρ τοι*, *οὔ τοι*, *ἐπεί τοι*) its original force tends to atrophy, and it often does little more than add emphasis. In English, 'you know', 'I tell you', 'mark my words', 'See!', 'Hark!', cover some of the ground: though often gesture, or tone of voice, furnishes the true equivalent.

τοι, I have said, strictly speaking implies an audience. We must consider to what extent this limitation holds good.

Epic. Homer, who has *τοι* over seventy times, always uses it in speeches, except for *ὅς δή τοι* twice (K316: *υ*289): *h.Merc.*138 *ἐπεί τοι* (*τοι A*: *om. cett.*: *ἐπειδή M*). Hesiod has *τοι* thrice in narrative in the *Theogony* (94 (*γάρ τοι*), 126 (*δέ τοι*), 448) and twice in the *Shield* in speeches (110,353). But the great majority of the Hesiodic instances are in the *Works and Days*, where the poet is talking to the 'great fool Perses'. Hesiod has *ἦ τοι* in narrative several times.

Philosophical Epic. Parm.*Fr.*19 *οὕτω τοι κατὰ δόξαν ἔφυ τάδε*: Emp.*Fr.*17.14 *ἀλλ' ἄγε μύθων κλῦθι· μάθη γάρ τοι φρένας αὔξει.* Both poets address themselves to an individual (Empedocles to Pausanias: see *Fr.*1), and use the 2nd pers. sing. freely.

Lyric and Elegiac. Pindar uses *τοι* in addressing a victorious

[1] So, doubtfully, Bäumlein: confidently, Nägelsbach and Brugmann (pp. 460, 607, 612). (In many places it is hard to say whether *τοι* is a particle or a pronoun.) This derivation is not invalidated by the use of the particle in addressing a number of people: especially since, as Nägelsbach points out, the use of *ἄγε*, *φέρε*, *ἰδέ* is similarly extended. For other derivations, see Hartung (who is unhappy in his treatment of *τοι*) and Kühner.

athlete, Hiero, and Zeus (not to mention the island of Delos (*I.*1.6) and his own θυμός (*O.*2.90)), and in addressing his audience. In lyric and elegiac fragments we sometimes find τοι used in addressing an audience: Simon.*Fr.*4.28 πάντα τοι καλά, τοῖσιν αἰσχρὰ μὴ μέμεικται (in a scolium): Tim.*Fr.*6d 40 ἔνθα τοί τ[ις Πέρσης] πέδιος ἀνήρ: in other elegiac passages a context is lacking: Tyrt. *Fr.*6.11 (where μαχώμεθα and ὦ νέοι follow): Sol.*Fr.*1.63,65,74.

In the lyrics of tragedy, where τοι is far less common than in iambics, there is a marked divergence between Aeschylus and his successors. The Aeschylean chorus often uses τοι in the air, as it were, without any obvious personal reference: *Supp.*88,688, 1047: *Th.*332: *Ag.*362,1001,1014: *Eu.*840. Sophocles seems to furnish no example of this use: *El.*495 and 498 are addressed to Electra, who is still on the stage: in other passages there is a lyric dialogue between chorus and actor (*Ph.*837,854,855,1140: *OC*517), in others, apostrophe (*OT* 1193: *OC* 1578). This consideration tells against the acceptance of Dindorf's τοι in *Ph.*686 (nor is τοι in itself appropriate: read, surely, δ' αὖ, with Wecklein and Wunder). In Euripides, there is lyric dialogue in *El.*195, and apostrophe in *Alc.*570: *Heracl.*906: *El.*1169: *Supp.*379,1006: *Hel.*1358: *Ph.*183. In *Alc.*93 (see Murray), *Ion* 205 the passage is divided between individual choreutae. Only *Andr.*774 (οὔτοι) and *HF* 678 remain: in these passages the chorus seem to be addressing the audience or each other. *Or.*1498 ἤτοι in the monody of the Phrygian.

(Aristophanic characters sometimes use τοι in asides or soliloquies: *Lys.*919 Ἦ τοι γυνὴ φιλεῖ με ('You know, she's fond of me'): *Th.*904 ἀφασία τίς τοί μ' ἔχει: *Ec.*321 ἡ πανταχοῦ τοι νυκτός ἐστιν ἐν καλῷ; so, too, Euripides in *HF* 1105 (cf. 1094, ἰδού), and perhaps in *Fr.*300 οἴμοι· τί δ' οἴμοι; θνητά τοι πεπόνθαμεν. But on the whole there is a homeliness and *naïveté* in this use of τοι that makes it unsuited to serious drama.)

Prose. In historical narrative, τοι occurs in Hdt.ii 120 (δέ τοι) and iii 33 (νύν τοι), and the possibly less vivid ἤτοι in ii 120. (It is perhaps relevant that Herodotus' history was designed for reading aloud, and that he is fond of rhetorical questions.) In prose treatises, τοι is exceptionally found in X.*Lac.*10.3 εἰκότως δέ τοι καὶ σπουδάζεται οὗτος ὁ ἀγών: Critias*Fr.*32 ἄρχομαι δέ τοι ἀπὸ γενετῆς ἀνθρώπου· πῶς ἂν . . .; Anaximenes, *Rh.Al.*30

([Arist.]1437a38) (reading uncertain). Aristotle has only οὔτοι, μήτοι, ἤτοι, ἦ γάρ τοι (otherwise never γάρ τοι). In set speeches included in a history τοι is sometimes used: only three times (excluding ἤτοι) by Thucydides (ii 41.4: iii 40.4: vii 77.2: in iii 104.4 τοι, in a quotation from an Homeric hymn, is probably dative singular): more often by Xenophon [1] (*HG*ii 3.32: 4.13: v 1.16: *An.*iii 1.37: *Cyr.*i 5.13: *id. saep.*). Of the Attic orators, Antiphon uses τοι (excluding ἐπεί τοι, γάρ τοι) more frequently than all his successors put together (i 27 (δέ τοι): iv γ 5 (δέ τοι): v 48,72,91,94 (οὔτοι), 95 (δέ τοι), 96). The only other examples in the orators [2] are: And.i 3: Lys.*Fr.*59 (γέ τοι): Is.xi 4 (εἰ δέ τοι): D.iii 20 (οὔτοι: iv 18): xxxiv 32 (δέ τοι: so *S*): xl 32 (τἄν: μέντἄν *al.*): Aeschin.iii 130. In Hyp.*Eux.*11 τοι has considerable probability. (D.lii 8 and Aeschin.i 83 (μέντοι *al.*) are quotations, the former from conversation. I exclude ἤτοι, ἐπεί τοι and γάρ τοι, in all of which, perhaps, the vividness of τοι is somewhat weakened. Schmidt (p. 40) remarks that τοι hardly survives in the orators after Antiphon except in the combination καὶ γάρ τοι.) In prose dialogue τοι occurs constantly.

The conclusion which emerges from this survey is that τοι is exceedingly common in dialogue, prose and verse: is less frequently employed in addressing an audience: and outside these limits is scarcely found at all. We must now consider the various usages: and we shall find that τοι is far commoner in direct statements than in questions, wishes, commands, or subordinate clauses.

I. In direct statements.

(1) In general. Hom.*E* 801 Ἦ ὀλίγον οἷ παῖδα ἐοικότα γείνατο Τυδεύς. Τυδεύς τοι μικρὸς μὲν ἔην δέμας, ἀλλὰ μαχητής: ι 259 Ὦ ξεῖνοι, τίνες ἐστέ; . . .—Ἡμεῖς τοι Τροίηθεν ἀποπλαγχθέντες Ἀχαιοὶ . . . ἤλθομεν: A.*Supp.*370 ἐγὼ δ' ἂν οὐ κραίνοιμ' ὑπόσχεσιν πάρος, ἀστοῖς δὲ πᾶσι τῶνδε κοινώσας πέρι.—Σύ τοι πόλις, σὺ δὲ τὸ δάμιον: *Eu.*791 δύσοιστα πολίταις ἔπαθον· ἰὼ μεγάλα τοι κόραι δυστυχεῖς Νυκτὸς ἀτιμοπενθεῖς: E.*Heracl.*589 μέμνησθε τὴν

[1] In Xenophon τοι is much commoner in *Memorabilia*, *Oeconomicus*, *Symposium*, and *Cyropaedia* than in *Anabasis* and *Hellenica*.

[2] The indexes to all the orators, supplemented by Schmidt's examination of all the orators, confirm me.

σώτειραν ὡς θάψαι χρεών. κάλλιστά τοι δίκαιον: *Tr.*448 ἢ κακὸς κακῶς ταφήσῃ... Δαναϊδῶν ἀρχηγέτα. κἀμέ τοι νεκρὸν φάραγγες ... θηρσὶ δώσουσιν δάσασθαι ('mark my words'): *Rh.*432 (after giving an excuse for his tardy arrival) τοιάδε τοί μ' ἀπεῖργε συμφορὰ πέδον Τροίας ἱκέσθαι ('Such, you must know...'): *IA* 4 Σπεύσεις;—Σπεύδω. μάλα τοι γῆρας τοὐμὸν ἄυπνον ('be sure'): Ar.*Pax* 511 ἀλλὰ πᾶς ἀνὴρ προθυμοῦ.—Οἵ τοι γεωργοὶ τοὔργον ἐξέλκουσι κἄλλος οὐδείς ('You know, the farmers are doing all the work'): *Lys.*86 Ἡδὶ δὲ ποδαπή 'σθ' ἡ νεᾶνις ἡτέρα;—Πρέσβειρά τοι ναὶ τὼ σιὼ Βοιωτία ἵκει ποθ' ὑμέ ('She's from Boeotia, you know'): Hom.ο272: Thgn.1123: A.*Supp.*390,407: *Pers.*287, 1076: *Pr.*1040: *Th.*715: *Ag.*348,877: S.*Aj.*776 (Hermann): *El.* 984: E.*Cyc.*450: *Alc.*256: *Andr.*212: *El.*415,1008: *Or.*585: Ar.*Eq.*683: *Av.*600: *Th.*1104: *Ec.*35,1150: Pl.*Grg.*499B οὐ ταῦτα ἀνάγκη, ὦ Καλλίκλεις;—Πάλαι τοί σου ἀκροῶμαι, ὦ Σώκρατες, καθομολογῶν: *Prt.*316B προσῆμεν πρὸς τὸν Πρωταγόραν, καὶ ἐγὼ εἶπον· Ὦ Πρωταγόρα, πρὸς σέ τοι ἤλθομεν ('we've come to see *you*, you know'): *La.*195A Οὔκουν φησί γε Νικίας.—Οὐ μέντοι μὰ Δία· ταῦτά τοι καὶ ληρεῖ: *Phd.*63A ὁ Σωκράτης ἡσθῆναί τέ μοι ἔδοξε τῇ τοῦ Κέβητος πραγματείᾳ, καὶ ἐπιβλέψας εἰς ἡμᾶς, Ἀεί τοι, ἔφη, ὁ Κέβης λόγους τινὰς ἀνερευνᾷ: *Chrm.* 155B: *Phd.*66B: *Tht.*184D: *Plt.*264D: *Min.*315D: *Lg.*857B: *Hp.Ma.*304A: *Hp.Mi.*369D: *Alc.I* 114B: X.*Mem.*i2.46: 6.11: iii5.1: *Oec.*3.1: *An.*vi5.24: 6.34: *Cyr.*v2.23: vii3.10: viii7.17.

A precise classification of the various nuances of τοι in statements is impossible. But some sort of rough grouping may be of service.

(2) Boasting. Hom.*Δ*405 ἡμεῖς τοι πατέρων μέγ' ἀμείνονες εὐχόμεθ' εἶναι: E.*Or.*1167 Ἀγαμέμνονός τοι παῖς πέφυκα ('Look you, I am Agamemnon's son'): A.*Supp.*536.

(3) Threatening. A.*Supp.*952 Ἀλλ' ἄρσενάς τοι τῆσδε γῆς οἰκήτορας εὑρήσετε: *Eu.*729 Σύ τοι τάχ'... ἐμεῖ τὸν ἰόν: E.*Ba.* 516 ἀτάρ τοι τῶνδ' ἄποιν' ὑβρισμάτων μέτεισι Διόνυσός σε: A.*Pr.* 1021: E.*Cyc.*698.

(4) Hortatory, deprecatory, persuasive, soothing, or remonstrating. Hom.*B* 298 αἰσχρόν τοι δηρόν τε μένειν κενεόν τε νέεσθαι: A.*Ch.*923 (Orestes is weakening here): *Eu.*727 Σύ τοι... οἴνῳ παρηπάτησας ἀρχαίας θεάς (whining: whereas Σύ

τοι in Apollo's retort (729, *v.supr.* (3)) has a sharper, threatening tone): S.*Aj.*1353 *Παῦσαι· κρατεῖς τοι τῶν φίλων νικώμενος*: *Tr.* 321 *Εἴπ', ὦ τάλαιν', ἀλλ' ἡμὶν ἐκ σαυτῆς· ἐπεὶ καὶ ξυμφορά τοι μὴ εἰδέναι σέ γ' ἥτις εἶ* (a caress): *Ph.*480 *ἴθ'· ἡμέρας τοι μόχθος οὐχ ὅλης μιᾶς*: 801 *ἔμπρησον, ὦ γενναῖε· κἀγώ τοί ποτε τὸν τοῦ Διὸς παῖδ' . . . τοῦτ' ἐπηξίωσα δρᾶν*: E.*Heracl.*733 *Ἔπειγε . . .—Σύ τοι βραδύνεις* (a gentle remonstrance: 'It's you that are lagging, you know'): *Med.*344 *οἴκτιρε δ' αὐτούς· καὶ σύ τοι παίδων πατὴρ πέφυκας*: 1015 *Θάρσει· κάτει τοι καὶ σὺ πρὸς τέκνων ἔτι* ('be sure'): *Ba.*1118 *Ἐγώ τοι, μῆτερ, εἰμί, παῖς σέθεν*: Ar.*Ach.* 752 *Διαπεινᾶμες ἀεὶ ποττὸ πῦρ.—Ἀλλ' ἡδύ τοι νὴ τὸν Δί', ἢν αὐλὸς παρῇ* (consolatory: 'Well, that's very nice, you know'): *Nu.*861 *εἶτα τῷ πατρὶ πιθόμενος ἐξάμαρτε· κἀγώ τοί ποτε, οἶδ', ἐξέτει σοι τραυλίσαντι πιθόμενος . . .*: *Lys.*84 *Ὡς δὴ καλὸν τὸ χρῆμα τιτθίων ἔχεις.—Αἴπερ ἱερεῖόν τοί μ' ὑποψαλάσσετε* (impatient): Hom. *E* 873: A.*Ch.*1056: S.*El.*624: *Tr.*1255: E.*Alc.*38: *Supp.*379: Ar.*Pax* 1096: *Av.*1642: *Ra.*1039: *Ec.*972: Pl.*R.*499E *Ὦ μακάριε . . . μὴ πάνυ οὕτω τῶν πολλῶν κατηγόρει. ἀλλοίαν τοι δόξαν ἕξουσιν, ἐὰν αὐτοῖς μὴ φιλονικῶν ἀλλὰ παραμυθούμενος . . . ἐνδεικνύῃ . . . .*

(5) In response to a command. A.*Pers.*944 *Ἵετ' αἰανῆ πάνδυρτον δύσθροον αὐδὰν . . .—Ἥσω τοι τὰν πάνδυρτον*: 1065 *Διαίνου δ' ὄσσε.—Τέγγομαί τοι*: E.*Ion* 205 *ἄθρησον . . .—Πάντᾳ τοι βλέφαρον διώκω*: 760 *Εἴφ' . . .—Εἰρήσεταί τοι*: *Rh.*571 *Ὅρα κατ' ὄρφνην μὴ φύλαξιν ἐντύχῃς.—Φυλάξομαί τοι*: Ar.*Av.*1437 *πτεροῦ.—Νῦν τοι λέγων πτερῶ σε.*

(6) Revealing the speaker's emotional or intellectual state (present or past). A.*Eu.*968 *Τάδε τοι χώρᾳ τἠμῇ προφρόνως ἐπικραινομένων γάνυμαι*: S.*OT* 746 *ὀκνῶ τοι πρὸς σ' ἀποσκοποῦσ', ἄναξ*: *El.*871 *Ὑφ' ἡδονῆς τοι, φιλτάτη, διώκομαι*: 928 *θαῦμά τοί μ' ὑπέρχεται*: E.*Hipp.*342 *Ἔκ τοι πέπληγμαι*: 433 *ἐμοί τοι συμφορὰ μὲν ἀρτίως ἡ σὴ παρέσχε δεινὸν ἐξαίφνης φόβον*: *Andr.* 56 *Δέσποιν'—ἐγώ τοι τοὔνομ' οὐ φεύγω τόδε καλεῖν σε*: *Or.*682 *Ὀρέστ', ἐγώ τοι σὸν καταιδοῦμαι κάρα*: 1047 *Ἔκ τοί με τήξεις*: *Rh.*663 *Σύ τοί με πείθεις*: *El.*767 *Ὦ φίλτατ', ἔκ τοι δείματος δυσγνωσίαν εἶχον προσώπου*: S.*OT* 1193: *Ant.*278: *OC* 517: E.*Med.*1116: *Ph.*1327: *Or.*544: *IA* 1613: *Rh.*568: Ar.*Eq.*1355: *V.*784: *Pl.*29,377: Pl.*Euthphr.*5C *Καὶ ἐγώ τοι . . . μαθητὴς ἐπιθυμῶ γενέσθαι σός*: *Chrm.*172E *Νὴ τὸν κύνα, ἔφην, καὶ ἐμοί τοι δοκεῖ*

οὕτω: *Grg.*454B Καὶ ἐγώ τοι ὑπώπτευον ταύτην σε λέγειν τὴν πειθώ: *Tht.*177B Οἶδά τοι: *R.*499A.

(7) Conveying a criticism, favourable or unfavourable, of the previous speaker's words. A.*Pers.*245 Δεινά τοι λέγεις: S.*Tr.* 1131 τέρας τοι ... ἐθέσπισας: Ar.*Pax*934 Εὖ τοι λέγεις: *Pl.*198 Εὖ τοι λέγειν ἔμοιγε φαίνεσθον: Pl.*Lg.*837D Πάντῃ τοι καλῶς, ὦ ξένε, . . . εἴρηκας.

(8) With the second person singular pronoun (usually accusative), conveying a summons to attention, often peremptory in tone. S.*Aj.*1228 σέ τοι, τὸν ἐκ τῆς αἰχμαλωτίδος λέγω: *El.*1445 σέ τοι, σὲ κρίνω, ναὶ σέ: *OC*1578 σέ τοι κικλήσκω, τὸν αἰένυπνον (in urgent prayer: cf. A.*Ch.*456: Ar.*Th.*1145 δῆμός τοί σε καλεῖ γυναικῶν): E.*Ion*219 Σέ τοι, τὸν παρὰ ναὸν αὐδῶ: Ar.*Av.*274 Οὗτος ὦ σέ τοι: 406 ἰὼ ἔποψ, σέ τοι καλῶ: E.*IA*855: Ar.*Pl.* 1099. A.*Ag.*1047 Σοί τοι λέγουσα παύεται σαφῆ λόγον.

(9) Directing a person's eye or ear to a sight or sound: 'See!' 'Hark!' A.*Th.*369 Ὅ τοι κατόπτης ... πευθώ τιν' ἡμῖν ... νέαν φέρει: *Ag.*1444 ἡ δέ τοι ... κεῖται φιλήτωρ τῷδ' ('and lo! there lies...'): *Ch.*332 Κλῦθί νυν, ὦ πάτερ ... δίπαις τοί σ' ἐπιτύμβιος θρῆνος ἀναστενάζει: S.*Ph.*855 οὖρός τοι, τέκνον, οὖρος: *Indag.* 112 Diehl Ἔα μάλα· παλινστραφῆ τοι ναὶ μὰ Δία τὰ βήματα εἰς τοὔμπαλιν δέδορκεν: Carm.Pop.1.11 νεῦμαί τοι, νεῦμαι ἐνιαύσιος, ὥστε χελιδών: Pl.*Ly.*211C πάρεστι δέ τοι αὐτός—οὐχ ὁρᾷς;—Κτήσιππος.

The following are really similar, though the appeal is to the mind, not to the senses. A.*Ch.*542 κρίνω δέ τοί νιν ὥστε συγκόλλως ἔχειν ('And lo! I interpret it'): 1065 ὅδε τοι μελάθροις τοῖς βασιλείοις τρίτος αὖ χειμὼν . . . ἐτελέσθη: Pi.*N.*6.11: 7.77: 10.22.

(10) With a proverb or general reflection, far commoner in serious poetry than in comedy or prose.[1] τοι is used here to point the applicability of a universal truth to the special matter in hand: it forces the general truth upon the consciousness of the individual addressed: 'Don't forget, please'. Very frequent in

[1] Undue prominence has sometimes been attributed to this use, as though τοι invariably or predominantly accompanied gnomic utterance. Thus Jebb on S.*Ph.* 81 'τοι would be bluntly sententious'. See also Verrall and Tucker on A.*Th.*715, and, in correction, Headlam, *On editing Aeschylus*, p.124: 'That τοι always indicates a proverbial sentiment is another notion of schoolboys'.

gnomic writing: *e.g.* Hes.*Op*.287,302,713,719,730: in Theognis, every few lines: *e.g.* 153 *τίκτει τοι κόρος ὕβριν*: cf. Phoc.*Fr*.5,8, 11: frequent, too, in Pindar, and in the sententious fragments of Euripides. The rarity of *τοι* in so markedly gnomic a writer as Democritus is surprising: but cf. *Fr*.229 *φειδώ τοι καὶ λιμὸς χρηστή*. The tense is usually present or gnomic aorist, rarely future (A.*Supp*.732): but *ἐστί* is often omitted.

Hom.*I* 158 *Ἀΐδης τοι ἀμείλιχος*: *M* 412 *πλεόνων δέ τοι ἔργον ἄμεινον*: *θ* 329 *κιχάνει τοι βραδὺς ὠκύν*: Alcm.*Fr*.109 *πεῖρά τοι μαθήσιος ἀρχά*: Emp.*Fr*.17.14 *μαθὴ γάρ τοι φρένας αὔξει*: Pi.*O*. 4.18 *διάπειρά τοι βροτῶν ἔλεγχος*: *P*.2.72 *καλός τοι πίθων παρὰ παισίν*: A.*Pr*.39 *Τὸ συγγενές τοι δεινόν*: *Supp*.385 *μένει τοι Ζηνὸς ἱκταίου κότος*: S.*El*.945 *Ὅρα, πόνου τοι χωρὶς οὐδὲν εὐτυχεῖ*: E.*Andr*.181 *Ἐπίφθονόν τοι χρῆμα θηλείας φρενός*: *Or*.229 *φίλον τοι τῷ νοσοῦντι δέμνιον*: Ar.*Lys*.16 *χαλεπή τοι γυναικῶν ἔξοδος*: *Th*.1130 *σκαιοῖσι γάρ τοι καινὰ προσφέρων σοφὰ μάτην ἀναλίσκοις ἄν* (in Euripides' mouth): Hom.*N* 115: *Φ* 184: *Ψ* 315: *θ* 351: *τ* 43,592: Sol.*Fr*.14.1: Simon.*Fr*.75: Pi.*P*.2.94: 5.122: *N*.8.17: A.*Pr*.277,698: S.*Aj*.580,1350: *El*.415,916: *Ant*.243, 580,1028: E.*El*.343,422: *HF* 101: *IT* 650,1064: *Or*.397,486: Pl.*Smp*.219A *ἥ τοι τῆς διανοίας ὄψις ἄρχεται ὀξὺ βλέπειν ὅταν ἡ τῶν ὀμμάτων τῆς ἀκμῆς λήγειν ἐπιχειρῇ*; X.*Cyr*.viii 7.15 *ἑαυτοῦ τοι κήδεται ὁ προνοῶν ἀδελφοῦ*: Pl.*R*.595C: X.*Cyr*.viii 7.14: 7.16 (viii 7.6–28 contains the behests of the dying Cyrus to his sons). Somewhat analogous, perhaps, is *τοι* in Thgn.193, marking a typical instance: *αὐτός* (or *ἀστός*, Diehl) *τοι ταύτην εἰδὼς κακόπατριν ἐοῦσαν εἰς οἴκους ἄγεται χρήμασι πειθόμενος*.

(11) In negative statements, *οὔ τοι, οὔτοι*. (It is a matter of indifference which we write: the practice of editors varies.) Common in tragedy and (in oaths) Aristophanes. Perhaps here, as far more noticeably in the case of *γάρ τοι, ἐπεί τοι*, the particle loses some of its peculiar flavour, and does little more than add force to the negation.

Hom.*B* 361 *οὔ τοι ἀπόβλητον ἔπος ἔσσεται*: *π* 187 *Οὔ τίς τοι θεός εἰμι*: A.*Eu*.64 *Οὔτοι προδώσω*: S.*El*.773 *Μάτην . . . ἥκομεν.—Οὔτοι μάτην γε*: *Aj*.915 *πᾷ κεῖται . . . Αἴας;—Οὔτοι θεατός*: *Ant*.523 *Οὔτοι συνέχθειν, ἀλλὰ συμφιλεῖν ἔφυν*: E.*Med*.469 *οὔτοι θράσος τόδ' ἐστὶν οὐδ' εὐτολμία*: Ar.*Ec*.522 *Οὔτοι παρὰ τοῦ μοιχοῦ γε φήσεις* (*ἥκειν με*) (elsewhere, Aristophanes has *οὔτοι* in oaths only, rarely preceded by μὰ . . . (*V.*299: *Th.*34), usually followed by it, the verb being usually in the future: *Nu.* 814 Οὔτοι μὰ τὴν Ὁμίχλην ἔτ' ἐνταυθοῖ μενεῖς: *Eq.*235,409 435, 698: *Ra.*42: *Th.*533: *Pl.*364: *id. saep.*: cf. E.*Med.*1060 μὰ τοὺς . . . ἀλάστορας, οὔτοι ποτ' ἔσται τοὖθ': Ar. *V.*1122 is a strong asseveration verging on an oath): Hom.*Γ*65: *Z* 335: *N* 151,811: α 203: ι 27: Archil.*Fr.*3.1: Xenoph.*Fr.*16.1: Pi.*N.*5.16: S.*OT* 629: *OC* 176: E.*IT* 116: *El.*195: *Andr.*774: Hdt.vii 141.2 Ὦναξ, χρῆσον ἡμῖν ἄμεινόν τι περὶ τῆς πατρίδος . . .· ἤ οὔ τοι ἄπιμεν ἐκ τοῦ ἀδύτου: Pl.*Prt.*360E Οὔτοι . . . ἄλλου ἕνεκα ἐρωτῶ πάντα ταῦτα: X.*An.*vii 6.11 (reinforcing a preceding negative) ἀπετραπόμην . . . οἴκαδε ὡρμημένος, οὐ μὰ τὸν Δία οὔτοι πυνθανόμενος . . .: Arist.*Metaph.*1035a30 ταῦτα δ' οὐ φθείρεται, ἢ ὅλως ἢ οὔτοι οὕτω γε (reading uncertain): Pl.*R.*345A,423D: *Alc.II* 143D: X.*Mem.*i 4.10: iii 12.5: *Cyr.*viii 7.19: Ant.v 94: D.iii 20: iv 18.

Οὔτοι, by itself, in an answer ('No'): Pl.*Alc.I* 114E ἄλλῳ γε λέγοντι μὴ πιστεύσῃς.—Οὔτοι, ἀλλὰ ἀποκριτέον.

οὔτοι . . . μή: S.*Aj.*560 οὔτοι σ' Ἀχαιῶν, οἶδα, μή τις ὑβρίσῃ. κοὔτοι: S.*Ant.*678: *Tr.*491. ἀλλ' οὔτοι: S.*El.*137: X *Cyr.*vi 3.20. γὰρ οὔτοι: A.*Supp.*884. οὔτοι . . . οὐδέ: X.*Cyr.*iii 1.39 (the MSS. vary).

(12) In potential clauses, with ἄν (not very common in prose). τοι often immediately precedes ἄν, and coalesces with it by crasis, τἄν: cf. μεντἄν. A.*Pr.*397 ἄσμενος δέ τἂν . . . κάμψειεν γόνυ: *Eu.*700 τοιόνδε τοι ταρβοῦντες ἐνδίκως σέβας ἔρυμα . . . ἔχοιτ' ἄν: S.*Aj.*962 ἴσως τοι, κεἰ . . ., θανόντ' ἂν οἰμώξειαν: *El.*582 εἰ γὰρ κτενοῦμεν ἄλλον ἀντ' ἄλλου, σύ τοι πρώτη θάνοις ἄν: *OT* 1469 χερσί τἂν θιγὼν δοκοῖμ' ἔχειν σφας: E.*Hipp.*1043 ἔκτεινά τοί σ' ἄν: A.*Ag.*870: E.*Alc.*197: *Hipp.*1413: *IA* 965. οὔ τἄν: A.*Eu.* 888: S.*Ant.*747: E.*Med.*867. Pl.*Grg.*452B Θαυμάζοιμί τἄν: *Ap.*29A δεινόν τἂν εἴη: *Alc.I* 104E οὐ γάρ τοι εἴη ἂν θαυμαστόν: *R.*545C (γέ τοι ἄν): X.*Cyr.*iv 2.46: vi 3.20 οὔτοι ἄν.

τοι nearly always precedes ἄν, very rarely follows it, the particle gravitating to an early position. But A.*Pers.*706 ἀνθρώπεια δ' ἄν τοι πήματ' ἂν τύχοι βροτοῖς. (In Hom.*O* 69 τοι is probably dative singular: ἐκ τοῦ δ' ἄν τοι ἔπειτα παλίωξιν . . . τεύχοιμι.)

For ἦ τἄν, see VI.8 below.

II. So much for *τοι* in statements. In other independent clauses (questions, commands, and wishes) the particle is much less common.

(1) Questions (a rigid line cannot be drawn between questions and statements). Ar.*Ec.*321 *ἦ πανταχοῦ τοι νυκτός ἐστιν ἐν καλῷ*; Pl.*Phlb.*48B *Τό τοι νυνδὴ ῥηθὲν ὄνομα φθόνου πότερα λύπην τινὰ ψυχῆς θήσεις, ἢ πῶς*; *Tht.*168E *Τί δέ; οὐ πολλῶν τοι Θεαίτητος . . . ἄμεινον ἂν ἐπακολουθήσειε λόγῳ . . .*; *Sph.*238E *τὸ μὴ ὂν γὰρ φημί. συνίῃς τοι.—Ναί* (virtually a question): X. *Mem.*iii 4.10: *Oec.*8.8: D.lii 8. (In Hom.*N* 219 (*ποῦ τοι ἀπειλαὶ οἴχονται . . .*;), 770,772, Hdt.vii 48 *τοι* is, or may be, dative.)

(2) Commands. Anacr.*Fr.*88.3 *ἴσθι τοι, καλῶς μὲν ἄν τοι τὸν χαλινὸν ἐμβάλοιμι* (S.*El.*298: *Ant.*473): A.*Th.*179 *φιλοθύτων δέ τοι πόλεος ὀργίων μνήστορες ἐστέ μοι*: E.*El.*659 *πάλιν τοι μῦθον ἐς καμπὴν ἄγε*: Ar.*Av.*1229 *φράσον δέ τοί μοι*: *Lys.*94 *Μύσιδδέ τοι ὅ τι λῇς ποθ' ἁμέ* (Bentley, for *μυσιδδέτω*): Pl.*Grg.*461E *ἀλλὰ ἀντίθες τοι* (Crates Com.*Fr.*15.1).

Negative commands. Thgn.155 *μήποτέ τοι πενίην . . . πρόφερε* (*μοι* Stob.): A.*Pr.*436 *Μή τοι χλιδῇ δοκεῖτε . . . σιγᾶν με*: S. *Ant.*544 *Μήτοι, κασιγνήτη, μ' ἀτιμάσῃς*: *OC* 1439 *Μή τοί μ' ὀδύρου*: Ar.*Ach.*655 *ἀλλ' ὑμεῖς τοι μή ποτ' ἀφῆσθε*: A.*Pr.*625: S.*OC* 1407: E.*Med.*178 (reading doubtful): *Heracl.*691: Pl.*R.* 438A *Μήτοι τις . . . ἀσκέπτους ἡμᾶς ὄντας θορυβήσῃ.* With ellipse of verb: X.*Cyr.*ii 3.24 *διπλῆν ὑμῖν δίκαιον καὶ τὴν εὐωχίαν παρέχειν. Μὰ Δία, ἔφη ὁ ταξίαρχος, μήτοι γ' ἐν μιᾷ ἡμέρᾳ* (*μήτοι CE*: *μήτι cett.*). *μὴ γάρ τοι*: Pl.*Grg.*505D: *Min.*319A (*τι AF*: *τοι vulg.*)

(3) Prayers and wishes. A.*Supp.*688 *καρποτελῆ δέ τοι Ζεὺς ἐπικραινέτω*: *Ag.*974 *Ζεῦ . . . τὰς ἐμὰς εὐχὰς τέλει· μέλοι δέ τοι σοὶ τῶνπερ ἂν μέλλῃς τελεῖν.* (But in Hom.*ρ* 513 *τοι* is perhaps dative.)

III. In subordinate clauses.

(1) Causal, *ἐπεί τοι*. Hom.*N* 382 *ἐπεὶ οὔ τοι* (*β* 372: *υ* 264: Hes.*Sc.*110): *h.Merc.*138 *αὐτὰρ ἐπεί τοι πάντα κατὰ χρέος ἤνυσε δαίμων* (temporal: *δή M*): Pi *I.*2.45 *ἐπεί τοι οὐκ ἐλινύσοντας αὐτοὺς ἐργασάμαν*: S.*El.*323 *Πέποιθ', ἐπεί τἂν οὐ μακρὰν ἔζων ἐγώ*: E.*Andr.*540 *σοὶ δ' οὐδὲν ἔχω φίλτρον, ἐπεί τοι μέγ' ἀναλώσας ψυχῆς μόριον Τροίαν εἷλον*: Ar.*Pax* 628 *ἐπεί τοι τὴν κορώνεών γέ*

μου ἐξέκοψαν: S.*OC*433: E.*Cyc.*198: Pl.*R.*595C ἐπεὶ πολλά τοι . . .: Hdt.vii 103.3: Hp.*Fract.*16 (ἐπεί τοί γε): *Art.*48: *Acut.*2: X.*Smp.*3.4: Ant.vi 14: Lys.vi 39: viii 18: D.iv 2.

Frequently (in Euripides and Plato almost invariably[1]) ἐπεί τοι is followed immediately by καί. E.*Med.*677 Μάλιστ', ἐπεί τοι καὶ σοφῆς δεῖται φρενός: *Heracl.*507,744: *Andr.*89: *Supp.* 879: Ar.*Ach.*933: *Ra.*509: Hdt.iii 36: Pl.*Chrm.*154E,162B: *Tht.*142B: *R.*567E: *Hp.Ma.*288C. ἐπεί τοί γε καί: Ant.vi 9.

ὅτι τοι: Pl.*R.*343A τίτθη σοι ἔστιν;—Τί δέ; ἦν δ' ἐγώ· . . .;—"Ὅτι τοί σε, ἔφη, κορυζῶντα περιορᾷ: X.*Oec.*1.7.

(2) In conditional protasis, εἴ τοι, εἰ δέ τοι. Tyrt.*Fr* 6.11 εἰ δ' οὕτως ἀνδρός τοι ἀλωμένου οὐδεμί' ὤρη γίγνεται . . ., θυμῷ γῆς πέρι τῆσδε μαχώμεθα: S.*OT* 549 Εἴ τοι νομίζεις . . ., οὐκ ὀρθῶς φρονεῖς (countered by Εἴ τοι νομίζεις in 551: the tone is defiant): *Ant.*516 Οὐ μαρτυρήσει ταῦθ' ὁ κατθανὼν νέκυς.—Εἴ τοί σφε τιμᾷς ἐξ ἴσου τῷ δυσσεβεῖ (for the contradictory sense, 'doch', cf. οὔτοι, S.*El.*773, *OT* 629): E.*El.*77 Εἴ τοι δοκεῖ σοι, στεῖχε: Pi.*N* 4.79: A.*Supp.*387: *Ag.*1659: S.*Ant.*327: E.*Hipp.*507: *Hec.*747: Ar.*Lys.*167: *Av.*1630: Hdt.iii 145 ἀλλ' εἴ τοι σύ σφεας καταρρώδηκας, ἐμοὶ δός: ii 120.3: v 39 2: Hp.*Morb.*ii 14,27: X.*An.* ii 1.19: *Cyr.*iii 3.54: Is.xi 4.

(3) In relative clause. Hom.β88 φίλη μήτηρ, ἥ τοι περὶ κέρδεα οἶδεν: Orpheus *Fr.*21.5 τῇ τοι γάννυα πιαίνεις τῇ σῇ: Thgn.221 ὅστις τοι δοκέει . . ., κεῖνός γ' ἄφρων ἐστί: Pi.*O.*6.29 πρὸς Πιτάναν . . . ἐλθεῖν . . . ἅ τοι . . . λέγεται . . .: Ar.*Th.*899 Ὁπόσα τοι βούλει λέγε: Pi.*Fr.*50(61).2, reading doubtful: Pl.*R.*330B Οὔ τοι ἕνεκα ἠρόμην, ἦν δ' ἐγώ, (ἔστιν) ὅτι . . . .

(4) In final clause. S.*El.*1469 χαλᾶτε . . ., ὅπως τὸ συγγενές τοι κἀπ' ἐμοῦ θρήνων τύχῃ: *Tr.*190 ἀπῇξ', ὅπως τοι . . . πρὸς σοῦ τι κερδάναιμι: Hp.*Morb.*ii 33 μόλιβδον ποιησάμενος ὥς τοι καθίκῃ πρὸς τὸ ἕλκος: 61 ὅκως τοι εὔροον ἔῃ.

(5) In indirect speech. A.*Eu.*765 ὁρκωμοτήσας . . . μήτοι τιν' ἄνδρα . . . ἐποίσειν . . . δόρυ: Pl.*Lg.*859E ἴδωμεν δέ ὡς, εἰ . . ., τῶν πάντων τοι καὶ τὰ παθήματα ἡμῖν ἐστιν: *Tht.*190B (see IV.2 below).

(6) μή τοι . . . γε, with infinitive (in S.*Aj.*472 with participle), 'at any rate not', is equivalent to οὔκουν . . . γε in a direct con-

[1] Kugler (p. 7) says that καί is invariably added in Plato: and I find no case where καί is absent, except *R.*595C (above), where ἐπεί and τοι are not juxtaposed.

struction. It appears to be confined to Sophocles, Plato, and Aristotle. τοι has lost all, or nearly all, its vividness here. Cf. ἀλλ' οὔτοι . . . γε (VI.1).

S.*Aj.*472 πεῖρα . . . ἀφ' ἧς γέροντι δηλώσω πατρὶ μή τοι φύσιν γ' ἄσπλαγχνος ἐκ κείνου γεγώς: *El.*518 ὅς σ' ἐπεῖχ' ἀεὶ μή τοι θυραίαν γ' οὖσαν αἰσχύνειν φίλους: Pl.*Phlb.*67A ἀπήλλακτο . . . μή τοι τἀγαθόν γε αὐτὸ . . . εἶναι: *Epin.*983C δεῖ δὲ . . . μή τοι ληροῦντά γε . . . φαίνεσθαι: *R.*352C ἢ αὐτοὺς ἐποίει μήτοι καὶ ἀλλήλους γε καὶ ἐφ' οὓς ἦσαν ἅμα ἀδικεῖν: 388B–C δεησόμεθα μήτοι θεούς γε ποιεῖν ὀδυρομένους . . . εἰ δ' οὖν θεούς, μήτοι τόν γε μέγιστον τῶν θεῶν . . .: Arist.*Pol.*1308b15 εἰ δὲ μή, μή τοί γ' ἀθρόας δόντας ἀφαιρεῖσθαι πάλιν ἀθρόας: 1315a10 ἐὰν δὲ ἄρα τινὰ δέῃ ποιῆσαι μέγαν, μή τοι τό γε ἦθος θρασύν.

In final clause: Pl.*Tht.*168E ἵνα μή τοι τοῦτό γε ἔχῃ ἐγκαλεῖν (so *B*).

IV. Position. τοι, being designed to arrest the attention, is usually placed early in the sentence. But:

(1) It fairly often comes early in the apodosis of a conditional sentence. Hom.*X*488 ἤν περ γὰρ πόλεμόν γε φύγῃ . . ., αἰεί τοι τούτῳ γε πόνος καὶ κήδε' ὀπίσσω ἔσσοντ': Pi.*P.*3.65 εἰ δὲ σώφρων ἄντρον ἔναι' ἔτι Χίρων . . ., ἰατῆρά τοι κέν νιν πίθον . . . παρασχεῖν: A.*Ch.*548 εἰ γὰρ . . ., δεῖ τοί νιν . . . θανεῖν βιαίως: Pi.*P.* 1.87: A.*Th.*404: S.*Aj.*456: *OT*518 (οὔτοι: 852: *OC*1351: E. *Heracl.*438: *Tr.*409: *El.*363: *Rh.*60: *Supp.*182): S.*Tr.*279: *Ph.* 854: E.*Hipp.*1043: Ar.*Ach.*788: Pl.*Epin.*983E εἰ δ' οὖν δεῖ νικᾶν . . ., δυοῖν τοι θάτερα θετέον αὐτά: Hdt.i 89,115 (perhaps dative): iii 69 (οὔτοι): Th.iii 40.4: Pl.*R.*365E: *Lg.*859E. For ἀλλ' οὔτοι apodotic (Arist.*Pol.*1282a11) see VI.1, below.

Much less frequently after a temporal or relative protasis. E.*IT*111 ὅταν δὲ . . . μόλῃ, τολμητέον τοι: *Ba.*515 ὅ τι γὰρ μὴ χρεών, οὔτοι χρεὼν παθεῖν: And.i 3 ὁπόσοι μὲν γὰρ . . ., εἰκότως τοι καὶ ὑμεῖς τοιαῦτα περὶ αὐτῶν γιγνώσκετε. After causal protasis (ἐπεί), Pl.*Sph.*261C.

(2) In general, τοι occasionally occupies a late position in the sentence or clause, the arousing of attention being deferred till the crucial moment. Hes.*Op.*319 αἰδὼς . . ., αἰδώς τοι πρὸς ἀνολβίῃ . . ., αἰδώς (cf. 579): A.*Fr.*70 Ζεύς ἐστιν αἰθήρ, Ζεὺς δὲ γῆ, Ζεὺς δ' οὐρανός, Ζεύς τοι τὰ πάντα: 175 ἀλλ' Ἀντικλείας

ἆσσον ἦλθε Σίσυφος, τῆς σῆς λέγω τοι μητρός: *Eu*.755 Ὦ Παλλάς, ὦ σώσασα τοὺς ἐμοὺς δόμους, γαίας πατρῴας ἐστερημένον σύ τοι κατῴκισάς με: Ar.*V*.1192 λέγειν . . . ὡς ἐμάχετο . . . ἤδη γέρων ὢν καὶ πολιός, ἔχων δέ τοι πλευρὰν βαθυτάτην: Hdt. i41 πρὸς δὲ τούτῳ καὶ σέ τοι χρεόν ἐστι ἰέναι: Hp.*Art*.47 ἀλλ' ἐσιδέειν γε ἀπρεπὴς ταύτῃ τοι γινομένη ἡ κατάτασις (τοι *om*. *C*: perhaps dative): Pl.*Prt*.346D οὐ τοῦτο λέγει, ὥσπερ ἂν εἰ ἔλεγε πάντα τοι λευκά: *Tht*.190B Ἀναμιμνῄσκου δὴ εἰ πώποτ' εἶπες πρὸς σεαυτὸν ὅτι παντὸς μᾶλλον τό τοι καλὸν αἰσχρόν ἐστιν: X.*Cyr*. vii 5.53 καὶ νῦν δὴ νενικήκαμέν τε . . . καὶ . . . καὶ . . . καὶ μὰ τὸν Μίθρην ἐγώ τοι ἐχθὲς . . . ('and, by Mithras, yesterday, I tell you . . .'): Anaximenes, *Rh.Al*.30([Arist.]1437a38) ἐκ μὲν οὖν τοῦ παρόντος χρόνου οὕτω τοι διαβολαὶ . . . γενήσονται (τοιαῦται γενήσονται, for γενήσονται, V^b, omitting οὕτω τοι).

(3) Like other particles, τοι is often placed between article and substantive (etc.), or preposition and substantive. Thgn.655 σύν τοι, Κύρνε, παθόντι: Pi.*O*.2.90 ἐπί τοι Ἀκράγαντι: S.*Ph*.637 ἤ τοι καίριος σπουδή: 894 τό τοι σύνηθες: E.*Hec*.606 ἔν τοι μυρίῳ στρατεύματι: *El*.767 ἔκ τοι δείματος: Ar.*Ec*.972 διά τοι σέ: A. *Th*.438: *Fr*.22: S.*OC*880,1187: *Fr*.855.1: E.*Hipp*.610: *Fr*. 222: Ar.*Ra*.1046: *Pax*511: Pl.*Phd*.108D περὶ γάρ τοι γῆς (60C): *Sph*.261C τό τοι μέγιστον: X.*Smp*.8.18 διά γέ τοι τὰ τοιαῦτα ἔργα: Pl.*Tht*.190B: *Smp*.219A.

Between a preposition and a verb compounded with it. E. *Hipp*.934 ἔκ τοι πέπληγμαι (*HF*1105): *Or*. 1047 Ἔκ τοί με τήξεις: Ar.*V*.784 Ἀνά τοί με πείθεις.

The order in X.*Mem*.i2.46 is strange: Μάλα τοι . . . καὶ ἡμεῖς τηλικοῦτοι ὄντες δεινοὶ τὰ τοιαῦτα ἦμεν.

V. Repetition of τοι. Hom.K477 Οὗτός τοι, Διόμηδες, ἀνήρ, οὗτοι δέ τοι ἵπποι (perhaps datives: so, certainly, Τ409 ἀλλά τοι ἐγγύθεν ἦμαρ ὀλέθριον· οὐδέ τοι ἡμεῖς αἴτιοι): S.*Aj*.359 σέ τοι, σέ τοι μόνον δέδορκα: *Ph*.1095 Σύ τοι, σύ τοι κατηξίωσας.

VI. τοι combined with other particles. (For καίτοι, μέντοι, τοιγάρτοι, τοίνυν *v.s.vv.*) τοι stands second of the two particles (except in τοι ἄρα, τοι δή). On the whole, there is not much cohesion between τοι and the other particle: τοι brings the point home to the person addressed, while the other particle retains its normal force: γέ τοι is the only combination which bears a meaning appreciably different from that of its component parts: but γάρ τοι also is, in certain authors, distinctive, for reasons given below. Certain collocations are, for no apparent reason, avoided: τέ τοι, quite needlessly conjectured by Buttmann at S.*Ph.*823 (for τέ τοι in Ar *Ec.*473 γέ τοι should no doubt be read, with Suidas): οὖν τοι. If δέ τοι is allowed, why not τέ τοι, if τοιγάρτοι, why not οὖν τοι?

(1) ἀλλά τοι, ἀλλὰ . . . τοι.

ἀλλά τοι. Hom.ν341 ἀλλά τοι οὐκ ἐθέλησα Ποσειδάωνι μάχεσθαι: Pi.*P.*3.19 οὐκ ἔμεινε . . . ἀλλά τοι ἤρατο τῶν ἀπεόντων: S.*Tr.*1239 ἀλλά τοι θεῶν ἀρὰ μενεῖ σ' ἀπιστήσαντα: E.*Hel.*744 ἀλλά τοι τὰ μάντεων ἐσεῖδον ὡς φαῦλ' ἐστί: Hom.σ230: Thgn. 656: Pl.*Grg.*461C Ὦ κάλλιστε Πῶλε, ἀλλά τοι ἐξεπίτηδες κτώμεθα ἑταίρους . . . ἵνα . . . ('But, you know, my dear Polus'): *Prt.*335B: *R.*474A,497A: *Sph.*231C: *Tht.*171C: X.*Oec.*12.2: 12.5: *Mem.*i2.36: ii2.7: iii6.10: *Cyr.*i6.9: viii8.13.

ἀλλὰ . . . τοι. Hom.Φ110 ἀλλ' ἔπι τοι καὶ ἐμοὶ θάνατος: Pi.*I.* 4.37 ἀλλ' Ὅμηρός τοι τετίμακεν: S.*El.*298 ἀλλ' ἴσθι τοι τείσουσά γ' ἀξίαν δίκην: *Ph.*1255 Ἀλλὰ κἀμέ τοι ταὐτὸν τόδ' ὄψῃ δρῶντα: Epich.*Fr.*170a1 ἀλλ' ἀεί τοι θεοὶ παρῆσαν: Ar.*Ra.*1046 ἀλλ' ἐπί τοι σοὶ . . . 'πικαθῆτο: A.*Supp.*952: *Pers.*795: *Ag.*1304: S.*Aj.*743: *Ant.*834: E.*Cyc.*698: *Ph.*1659: *IA*312: *Fr.*133: Ar.*Pax*334: *Av.*356: *Lys.*56: *Ec.*604: Pl.*Smp.* 207C Ἀλλὰ διὰ ταῦτά τοι . . . παρὰ σὲ ἥκω: X.*Oec.*4.21: *Cyr.*iv4.3.

ἀλλ' οὔτοι . . . γε: Pl.*Grg.*450D Ἀλλ' οὔτοι τούτων γε οὐδεμίαν οἶμαί σε βούλεσθαι ῥητορικὴν καλεῖν: Arist.*Pol.*1282a11 εἰ γὰρ καὶ . . ., ἀλλ' οὔτοι τῶν εἰδότων γε μᾶλλον (so one MS.).

ἀλλ' οὖν . . . τοι: E.*IA*983 ἀλλ' οὖν ἔχει τοι σχῆμα . . δυστυχοῦντας ὠφελεῖν.

(For ἀλλ' οὐδέ τοι, see (5).)

(2) αὐτάρ τοι, ἀτάρ τοι. Hom.O45 αὐτάρ τοι καὶ κείνῳ ἐγὼ παραμυθησαίμην: X181 ἀτὰρ οὔ τοι: E.*Ba.*516 ἀτάρ τοι τῶνδ' ἄποιν' ὑβρισμάτων μέτεισι Διόνυσός σε.

(3) γάρ τοι. In writers who use τοι freely, each particle retains its proper force. Hom.*E*265 τῆς γάρ τοι γενεῆς . . .: ρ572 εἵματα γάρ τοι λύγρ' ἔχω: K250: Pi.*P.*3.85: A.*Ag.*1040: S.*Tr.*1228: *Fr.*846: E.*Heracl.*435,533,716: *Supp.*312,564: *El.* 606: *Hel.*93: Ar.*Eq.*180: *Nu.*365: *V.*588,603,787: *Av.*1225:

*Th.*81,171: *Lys.*46: *Ra.*73: Pl.*Grg.*484C *φιλοσοφία γάρ τοί ἐστιν . . . χαρίεν*: *Prt.*310C *ὁ γάρ τοι παῖς με ὁ Σάτυρος ἀπέδρα*: Hdt.vii 172.2: Pl.*Grg.*455B,458B,E: *Prt.*314E,340E,349E: X. *Oec.*7.2: 7.18: 13.5: 20.25: *HG* iii 3.2: v 1.17. Xenophon, like Euripides and Aristophanes, but unlike Plato,[1] sometimes uses *γάρ τοι* in assentient answers (see *γάρ*, VIII.3).

But in writers who only use *τοι* in the combinations *ἐπεί τοι* and *γάρ τοι* the particle has clearly lost its vividness and is now merely ancillary. Thus in Isocrates we only find *τοι* in *καὶ γάρ τοι*, which occurs eight times: in Lysias (excluding, as spurious, *Fr.*59, *γέτοι*), only in *καὶ γάρ τοι* (seven times) and *ἐπεί τοι* (twice). Gorgias *Fr.*8. Aristotle only uses *γάρ τοι* in *ἦ γάρ τοι* (*Pol.*1281a12: *Ph.*254a18: *GA*734a16).

(For *καὶ γάρ τοι* see pp. 113–14.) *ἀλλὰ . . . γάρ τοι*: S.*Ph.* 81 (so *A*).

(4) *γέ τοι.* In this combination *τοι* retains its vividness, since *γέ τοι* is only found in writers who use *τοι* freely. At the same time, the *τοι* usually strengthens, and coheres with, the (limitative) *γε*, so that *γέ τοι* is practically a livelier form of the much commoner *γοῦν*, 'at any rate'.

(i) Giving a reason, valid so far as it goes, for accepting a proposition: a colloquial idiom, common in Aristophanes and Plato. S.*Aj.*534 *Μὴ σοί . . . ἀντήσας θάνοι.—Πρέπον γέ τἂν ἦν δαίμονος τοὐμοῦ τόδε* ('Certainly that would have consorted well with my genius'): *Tr.*234 *δίδαξον, εἰ ζῶνθ' Ἡρακλῆ προσδέξομαι.—Ἔγωγέ τοι σφ' ἔλειπον ἰσχύοντά τε καὶ ζῶντα* ('He was alive when I left him, anyhow'): 1212 *τἄλλα γ' ἔργασαι.—Φορᾶς γέ τοι φθόνησις οὐ γενήσεται* (partial consent): *Ph.*823 (*γε τοι* gives a partial confirmation of the belief that Philoctetes will soon fall asleep: *γάρ* in the line before purports, less cautiously, to give full confirmation: *δέ τοι F*): Ar.*V.*934 *οὐ καὶ σοὶ δοκεῖ, ὦλεκτρυόν; νὴ τὸν Δί' ἐπιμύει γέ τοι*: 1416 *ἔρχεται καλούμενός σε· τόν γέ τοι κλητῆρ' ἔχει*: *Av.*307 *ἆρ' ἀπειλοῦσίν γε νῷν; οἴμοι, κεχήνασίν γέ τοι καὶ βλέπουσιν ἐς σὲ κἀμέ*: E.*Cyc.* 224: *Ph.*730: Ar.*Ach.*947: *Eq.*787: *Nu.*878: *V.*912,1146: *Pax*820,821: *Th.*775: *Ec.*76: *Pl.*147,424,1041: Diph.*Fr.*73.6: Pl.*R.*545C *Κατὰ λόγον γέ τοι ἄν, ἔφη, οὕτω γίγνοιτο*: *Men.*89B

[1] In fact the only place in Plato where *γάρ τοι* introduces an answer of any kind is *La.*200C (Hoefer, p. 19).

Εἰκός γέ τοι (*Alc.I* 126D): *Cra.*416D *Δεῖ γέ τοι* (X.*Mem.*iv 2.18): *La* 20:D: *Cra.*393B: *Chrm.*159B: *Alc.I* 118C,138A,147E: *Hp.Mi.* 367B: *Mx.*236B: X.*Smp.*8.18. Perhaps class here [Lys.]*Fr.*59.

(ii) Restrictive *γέ τοι* in general. Ar.*Nu.*327 *Νῦν γέ τοι ἤδη καθορᾷς αὐτάς* ('You see them *now* at any rate, if you didn't before'): *Av.*1614 *Νὴ τὸν Ποσειδῶ ταῦτά γέ τοι καλῶς λέγεις*: *Eq.*1054: X.*Mem.*iv 2.33: 4.21. In relative clause: Pl.*Lg.*901A *τόν γε θεὸν οὐ ῥητέον ἔχειν ἦθος τοιοῦτον, ὅ γέ τοι αὐτὸς μισεῖ* (*quos quidem ipse mores oderit*: *τοι* not in all MSS.). *In apodosi*: S.*OC* 1324 *κεἰ μὴ σός, . . . , σός γέ τοι καλούμενος*: X.*An.* ii 5.19 *εἰ δ' ἐν πᾶσι τούτοις ἡττῴμεθα, ἀλλὰ τό γέ τοι πῦρ κρεῖττον τοῦ καρποῦ ἐστιν*: *Hier.*1.14 *εἰ ἐν τοῖς θεάμασι μειονεκτεῖτε, διά γέ τοι τῆς ἀκοῆς πλεονεκτεῖτε.*

(iii) Less often, *γε* is emphatic or exclamatory, and *τοι* stands more apart. A.*Ag.*1001 *μάλα γέ τοι τὸ μεγάλας ὑγιείας ἀκόρεστον τέρμα* (*γάρ τοι Fl*: *γέ τοί δή Fa*): S.*Ant.*1064 *Ἀλλ' εὖ γέ τοι κάτισθι* (though this and *Tr.*1107 might be classed under (ii)): Ar.*Pax* 509 *Χωρεῖ γέ τοι τὸ πρᾶγμα πολλῷ μᾶλλον*: Pl.*Grg.*447B *Ἐπ' αὐτό γέ τοι τοῦτο πάρεσμεν* ('That's just what we've *come* for, you know': clearly not to be classed under (i): cf. *Euthd.*274A *Ἐπ' αὐτό γε τοῦτο πάρεσμεν*).

In Ar.*Th.*887 *γε* goes closely with the preceding *καί*: *Κακῶς τ' ἄρ' ἐξόλοιο κἀξολεῖ γέ τοι.* In X.*Hier.*6.6 *δέ τοι* should possibly be read. (If *γέ τοι* is retained, we should class under (iii): '*Fear*, you know . . .'. But Xenophon is adding a new point: 'How perpetually terrified the tyrant is! And fear, besides being unpleasant in itself, ruins everything else'. In such a case asyndeton seems to me unnatural (Introd. II.4), and I hardly think *γε* can be quasi-connective here (cf. *γε*, III.2).)

(iv) *γέ τοι δή*, in sense (i) or (ii) above. S.*OT* 1171 *Ἦ δοῦλος, ἢ κείνου τις ἐγγενὴς γεγώς;— . . . Κείνου γέ τοι δὴ παῖς ἐκλῄζεθ'*: Ar.*Nu.*372 *Νὴ τὸν Ἀπόλλω τοῦτό γέ τοι δὴ τῷ νῦν λόγῳ εὖ προσέφυσας* (*δὴ τῷ νῦν* Porson: *τῷ νυνί codd.*): Pl.*Cri.*44A *Φασί γέ τοι δή*: *R.*476E,504A: *Phdr.*264B. Ar.*Ra.*1047 is curious: *ὥστε γε καὐτόν σε κατ' οὖν ἔβαλεν.—Νὴ τὸν Δία τοῦτό γέ τοι δή* ('She *did that*, by Jove!'. The ellipse of *ἐποίησε* is rather difficult. Merry's 'That's one for *you*' would need *σοί* for *τοι*, an emendation which has crossed my mind).

γέ τοί που: *Pl.Lg.*888E.

(5) δέ τοι. (This collocation is a good deal commoner in Xenophon than in Plato.) Hom.*I* 654 ἀμφὶ δέ τοι τῇ ἐμῇ κλισίῃ . . . Ἕκτορα . . . σχήσεσθαι ὀΐω: Pi.*O*.8.59 τὸ διδάξασθαι δέ τοι εἰδότι ῥᾴτερον: A.*Pers*.506 πῖπτον δ' ἐπ' ἀλλήλοισιν· ηὐτύχει δέ τοι ὅστις τάχιστα πνεῦμ' ἀπέρρηξεν βίου: Hom.π470: Pi.*O*. 9.21: *P*.2.94: A.*Supp*.393: *Pr*.1021: *Th*.179: S.*Aj*.1157: *Tr*. 327: E.*Andr*.636: *Hel*.253,747: Ar.*Ec*.1150: Pl.*Cra*.423D (δέ τι *BT*): *Ly*.211C: X.*Oec*.7.41: *Ap*.7: *HG* ii 3.32: *An*.ii 1.19: iii 1.37: *Cyr*.iii 3.54: *Lac*.10.3.

καὶ . . . δέ τοι, Xenophon only (Xenophon favours καὶ . . . δέ). X.*Cyr*.viii 3.44: *HG* v 1.16: *Oec*.8.8.

οὐδέ τοί. Hom.*N*252 ἠέ τευ ἀγγελίης μετ' ἔμ' ἤλυθες; οὐδέ τοι αὐτὸς ἧσθαι ἐνὶ κλισίῃσι λιλαίομαι: ρ17 Ὦ φίλος, οὐδέ τοι αὐτὸς ἐρύκεσθαι μενεαίνω. ἀλλ' οὐδέ τοί: S.*Ph*.1252: E.*Supp*. 1068: Pl.*R*.395A. καὶ γὰρ οὐδέ τοι: E.*IA* 1385.

(6) δή τοι, τοι δή.

(i) δή τοι occasionally after relatives in Epic. Hom.*K*316 ὃς δή τοι εἶδος μὲν ἔην κακός: *X*12: *Ω*731: υ289: Hes.*Op*.385: *Th*.1015.

There are a few examples of δή τοι in prose: Th.ii 41.4 μετὰ μεγάλων δὲ σημείων καὶ οὐ δή τοι ἀμάρτυρόν γε τὴν δύναμιν παρασχόμενοι: Pl.*Prt*.311E τί τοιοῦτον (ὄνομα) περὶ Πρωταγόρου ἀκούομεν;—Σοφιστὴν δή τοι ὀνομάζουσί γε, ὦ Σώκρατες, τὸν ἄνδρα εἶναι ('Well, you know, they *call* him a sophist': the particles express Hippocrates' embarrassment): *Mx*.245C οὕτω δή τοι τό γε τῆς πόλεως γενναῖον καὶ ἐλεύθερον βέβαιόν τε καὶ ὑγιές ἐστιν. ὡς δή τοι, introducing a sentence, is a Platonic idiom (for ὡς δή, see p. 229): *Phdr*.242C ὡς δή τοι, ὦ ἑταῖρε, μαντικόν γέ τι καὶ ἡ ψυχή: *Ti*.26B ὡς δή τοι, τὸ λεγόμενον, τὰ παίδων μαθήματα θαυμαστὸν ἔχει τι μνημεῖον: *R*.366C. (δή τοι has been conjectured, for δ' ἄν τοι, in A.*Pers*.706. But the combination, as Wilamowitz observes, is not found in Aeschylus (nor in any other dramatist).)

γὰρ δή τοι: Hom.*O*201.

(ii) τοι δή (positive) is generally accepted in S.*Ph*.245 Ἐξ Ἰλίου τοι δὴ τανῦν γε ναυστολῶ (δῆτα νῦν *codd*.). οὔτοι δή (Plato only): *Cri*.43D ἢ τὸ πλοῖον ἀφῖκται . . .;—Οὔτοι δὴ ἀφῖκται, ἀλλὰ δοκεῖν μέν μοι ἥξει τήμερον. Elsewhere always followed by γε, οὔτοι δὴ . . . γε being the negative form of γέ τοι δή, as οὔκουν . . . γε of γοῦν (οὖν, II.5). *Euthphr.*2A οὐ γάρ που καὶ σοί γε δίκη τις οὖσα τυγχάνει . . . .—Οὔτοι δὴ Ἀθηναῖοί γε . . . δίκην αὐτὴν καλοῦσιν ἀλλὰ γραφήν ('Well, the *Athenians* don't call it a δίκη'): *Cra.*438D Οὔτοι δὴ δίκαιόν γε: *Alc.I* 124D: *Lg.*656C.

(7) ἤτοι.

ἤτοι . . . ἤ (often ἤτοι . . . γε . . . ἤ) is common in Plato and Aristotle. It is difficult to say what degree of vividness τοι retains here. On the one hand, Thucydides confines ἤτοι, like simple τοι, to speeches: ii 40.2: vi 34.2: 38.2: 40.1: this suggests that he felt τοι as vivid in the combination. On the other, the frequency of ἤτοι in the matter-of-fact style of Aristotle suggests that for him τοι did nothing more than emphasize the disjunction. In the orators the only examples are: And.ii 2: Isoc.xv 33: D.xiv 40: xxii 32: xxv 51: lviii 7: Aeschin.iii 40: Din.i 50: never in Antiphon (who has simple τοι relatively often), Isaeus, Lycurgus, or Hyperides. (In Lys.*Fr.*284, Baiter and Sauppe, *Oratores Attici*, ἤτοι is not, I think, part of Tzetzes' quotation from Lysias.)

A.*Ag.*849 ἤτοι κέαντες ἢ τεμόντες: 662: *Ch.*497: S.*Tr.*150: *Ant.*1182: E.*Med.*1296: *Ion* 431: *Hel.*1175: *Or.*1498: *Rh.*817: Hdt.i 11,137: ii 120,173: iii 83: Pl.*Phd.*68C,76A,103A,104B: *id. saep.*: X.*Mem.*iii 12.2: iv 6.13: *Cyr.*iv 5.22: Arist.*Metaph.*1039 a27: *id. saep.* (For ἢ γάρ τοι in Aristotle see (3) above.)

ἤτοι meaning 'or' is very rare. Pi.*N.*6.5 ἢ μέγαν νόον ἤτοι φύσιν (cf. *Fr.*123(138) *Antiatt.* in Bekk.*Anecdot.*i 99.2 ἤτοι οὐκ ἄρχον ἀλλ' ὑποτασσόμενον· Πίνδαρος Θρήνοις: but perhaps = ἤ τοι here): Pl.*R.*344E Ἔοικας, ἦν δ' ἐγώ (*sc.* τουτὶ ἄλλως ἔχειν οἴεσθαι)—ἤτοι ἡμῶν γε οὐδὲν κήδεσθαι: 400C οἶμαι τὰς ἀγωγὰς τοῦ ποδὸς αὐτὸν οὐχ ἧττον ψέγειν τε καὶ ἐπαινεῖν ἢ τοὺς ῥυθμοὺς αὐτούς—ἤτοι συναμφότερόν τι: 433A τοῦτό ἐστιν, ὡς ἐμοὶ δοκεῖ, ἤτοι τούτου τι εἶδος ἡ δικαιοσύνη: Arist.*EE* 1225b4.

ἤτοι . . . ἤτοι: Arist.*Fr.*144,1502b27 ἤτοι ὅτι . . . ἤτοι ὅτι.

(8) ἦτοι = ἦ τοι (variously written ἦ τοι, ἤτοι, ἦτοι, the last accentuation being the correct one: see Schroeder on Pi.*O.*2.3, Wackernagel *Gr. Akzent*: ἤτοι L. & S., 9th ed.). Strictly, τοι serves to bring home a truth of which the certainty is expressed by ἦ: 'Verily, I tell you'. But perhaps τοι here has lost some of its vividness (it is significant that it occurs not infrequently in

narrative, where τοι is, generally speaking, rare), and is on its way to becoming a mere ancillary.

Hom.*A*68 ἤτοι ὅ γ' ὣς εἰπὼν κατ' ἄρ' ἕζετο: 211 ἀλλ' ἤτοι ἔπεσιν μὲν ὀνείδισον: *Δ*22 ἤτοι Ἀθηναίη ἀκέων ἦν: *H*451 τοῦ δ' ἤτοι κλέος ἔσται: *Λ*24 τοῦ δ' ἤτοι δέκα οἶμοι ἔσαν: γ419 κρήηνατ' ἐέλδωρ, ὄφρ' ἤτοι πρώτιστα θεῶν ἱλάσσομ' Ἀθήνην: ε24 οὐ γὰρ δὴ τοῦτον μὲν ἐβούλευσας νόον αὐτή, ὡς ἤτοι κεινοὺς 'Οδυσεὺς ἀποτίσεται ἐλθών; μ61 Πλαγκτὰς δ' ἤτοι τάς γε θεοὶ μάκαρες καλέουσι: ο6 εὗρε δὲ Τηλέμαχον καὶ Νέστορος ἀγλαὸν υἱὸν . . . ἤτοι Νεστορίδην μαλακῷ δεδμημένον ὕπνῳ· Τηλέμαχον δ' οὐχ ὕπνος ἔχε γλυκύς: ω154 ἵκοντο προτὶ ἄστυ περικλυτόν, ἤτοι 'Οδυσσεὺς ὕστερος, αὐτὰρ Τηλέμαχος πρόσθ' ἡγεμόνευε: Pi.*O*.2.3 ἤτοι Πίσα μὲν Διός· 'Ολυμπιάδα δὲ . . . . Hom.δ238: ο488: Hes.*Op*.166,333: *Sc*.413: Pi.*O*.2.30: 12.13: 13.84: *P*.12.13: *N*.5.43. (Except in *O*.12.13, where a vocative precedes, ἤτοι in Pindar always opens a sentence.)

Kühner (II ii 146) observes that ἤτοι is commonest in Epic, not uncommon in Pindar, but rare in tragedy, and only found there in combination with ἄν or ἄρα. (S.*El*.498 appears to be an exception: but possibly ἤτοι may be disjunctive, 'or else'.) ἤ τἄν: A.*Th*.552 ἤ τἂν πανώλεις παγκάκως τ' ὀλοίατο: S.*OC* 1366: Ar.*Ra*.34. ἤ τἄρα: E.*Alc*.642 ἤ τἄρα πάντων διαπρέπεις ἀψυχίᾳ: 732: *Heracl*.651: *Hipp*.480,1028.

(Pi.*P*.12.29 is exceedingly difficult: ἐκ δὲ τελευτάσει νιν ἤτοι σάμερον δαίμων. If ἤτοι goes closely with σάμερον, 'verily to-day' (Christ takes the words as a hesitating question, 'Will it be to-day?'), its position is unparalleled. Schroeder takes ἤτοι as answered by the following ἀλλά, in the sense μὲν . . . δέ: but his parallels do not justify his interpretation. Perhaps ἤτοι means 'either', and there is an anacoluthon (Hartung's ellipse of ἤ ὕστερον is impossible).

ἤτοι (= ἦ τοι) μέν, Epic only. (For an elaborate analysis, see Mutzbauer, ii 20–35.)

(i) With indicative. Hom.*Λ*442 Ἆ δείλ', ἦ μάλα δή σε κιχάνεται αἰπὺς ὄλεθρος. ἤτοι μέν ρ' ἔμ' ἔπαυσας: *T*23 νῦν δ' ἤτοι μὲν ἐγὼ θωρήξομαι: *Υ*435 ἀλλ' ἤτοι μὲν ταῦτα θεῶν ἐν γούνασι κεῖται: Hes.*Th*.116 ἤτοι μὲν πρώτιστα Χάος γένετ': 1004 αὐτὰρ Νηρῆος κοῦραι, ἁλίοιο γέροντος, ἤτοι μὲν Φῶκον Ψαμάθη τέκε: Hom.*E*809: τ124,560.

(ii) (Rarely) with imperative or optative. Hom.Π451 ἀλλ' εἴ τοι φίλος ἐστὶ . . ., ἤτοι μέν μιν ἔασον: κ271 Εὐρύλοχ', ἤτοι μὲν σὺ μέν' αὐτοῦ: Ρ509: μ385. *In apodosi*: Hom.Δ18 εἰ δ' . . ., ἤτοι μὲν οἰκέοιτο πόλις Πριάμοιο ἄνακτος.

(9) τοι ἄρα, ἄρα τοι. E.*HF*623 καλλίονές τἄρ' εἴσοδοι τῶν ἐξόδων πάρεισιν ὑμῖν ('So your going in is happier than your coming out, eh?'): *Ion* 337 ἀλλ' αἰδούμεθα.—Οὔ τἄρα πράξεις οὐδέν: Ar.*Ra*.253 Δεινά τἄρα πεισόμεσθα: *Eq*.366 Νὴ τὸν Ποσειδῶ κἀμέ τἄρα . . .: A.*Ag*.1252 (Hartung): *Cho*.112,221: 224 (Bamberger): *Fr*.363: S.*El*.404: *Tr*.322: *OC*1442: *Ph*.1253: E.*Med*. 703: *Hel*.85: *Or*.1335: *Hipp*.441: *Ph*.712: *IA* 1189[1]: Ar.*V*.299, 1262: *Av*.895,1017: *Lys*.20,435: *Ra*.656: Hdt.viii 57.2 εἶπε· Οὔ τοι ἄρα, ἢν . . ., οὐδὲ περὶ μιῆς ἔτι πατρίδος ναυμαχήσεις. *In apodosi*: Philol.*Fr*.2 ἐπεὶ τοίνυν φαίνεται . . ., δῆλόν τἄρα ὅτι . . .

ἤτἄρα . . . ἤ' . . .: E.*Fr*.645.5.

For ἦ τἄρα, see (8) above.

ἄρ τοι: Hes.*Op*.372 πίστιες ἄρ τοι ὁμῶς καὶ ἀπιστίαι ὤλεσαν ἄνδρας.

(10) νύ τοι. Hom.Χ11 ἦ νύ τοι οὔ τι μέλει Τρώων πόνος: Hes.*Op*.424. (In Hom.Τ421 read probably τό.) νύν τοι: Hdt. iii 33 οὔ νύν τοι ἀεικὲς οὐδὲν ἦν . . . .

(11) οὔτοι μὲν οὖν: Pl.*Phdr*.271B.

Καίτοι

This compound is not found in Homer or in Hesiod: (in Hom. Ν267 Καί τοι ἐμοί . . ., καί goes closely with ἐμοί ('Know that for me too . . .'): in ζ32 τοι is dative singular): Sappho 68.7 is perhaps the earliest example. The primary force is, no doubt, 'and, I would have you know'. But the purely connective sense is, throughout classical Greek, far less common than the secondary, adversative sense, which is the only meaning borne by the particle in so early a writer as Aeschylus (in whom καίτοι is only found

[1] Here I am convinced that οὔ τἄρα συνετούς (Wecklein) is the true reading, with no question-mark at the end of the sentence: E.*Supp*.496 is closely similar.

three times, in *Pr.*: *Eu.*848 is corrupt). The connective sense, though *prima facie* the earlier, makes its appearance, in fact, later than the adversative: while with καὶ μήν the contrary is the case. The evolution of an adversative sense from a connective is not a difficult process: and we have seen that simple καί is occasionally used (see καί, I.8) where an adversative force is implied by the context: see also καὶ μήν, (8). There is usually a certain combative tone in καίτοι. For this reason it is not common in unimpassioned, cold-blooded exposition. It is significant that out of 24 Thucydidean examples all except i 10.2 are from speeches (viii 72.1 reported speech).

(1) Adversative. (I will take this, as the commoner use, first.)

(i) In general. καίτοι introduces an objection (often couched in interrogative form) of the speaker's own, which tends to invalidate, or cast doubt upon, what he has just said, or to make it appear surprising: or is, in general, opposed to it in tendency: 'yet', 'and yet'. For the very rare use of καίτοι in answers (where καὶ μήν usually takes its place) see (v).

A.*Pr.*439 δάπτομαι κέαρ, ὁρῶν ἐμαυτὸν ὧδε προυσελούμενον. καίτοι θεοῖσι . . . γέρα τίς ἄλλος ἢ 'γὼ παντελῶς διώρισεν; S.*El.* 520 οὐδὲν ἐντρέπῃ ἐμοῦ γε· καίτοι πολλὰ πρὸς πολλούς με δὴ ἐξεῖπας ὡς θρασεῖα: *Ant.*948 Ἔτλα καὶ Δανάας οὐράνιον φῶς ἀλλάξαι δέμας . . .,· καίτοι καὶ γενεᾷ τίμιος . . . καὶ . . .: E.*Alc.* 648 οὐδ' ἐτόλμησας θανεῖν τοῦ σοῦ πρὸ παιδὸς . . . . καίτοι καλόν γ' ἂν τόνδ' ἀγῶν' ἠγωνίσω: *Or.*1668 οὐ ψευδόμαντις ἦσθ' ἄρ', ἀλλ' ἐτήτυμος· καίτοι μ' ἐσῄει δεῖμα, μή τινος κλύων ἀλαστόρων δόξαιμι σὴν κλύειν ὄπα: Ar.*Nu.*876 πῶς ἂν μάθοι ποθ' οὗτος . . .; καίτοι γε ταλάντου τοῦτ' ἔμαθεν Ὑπέρβολος: Pi.*I.*4.52: A.*Pr.*642: S.*Aj.*158,441,552: *El.*338: *OT* 393,1455: *Ant.*904: *OC*270,775,919: E.*Alc.*290: *El.*1080: *Ion* 352: *IT* 720: Ar.*Ach.* 357,611; *Eq.*885,977: *Nu.*921,1045: *V.*980,1301: *Av.*264: *Lys.* 509,905,1030: *Ec.*20: Pl.*R.*350E . . . ἐπειδήπερ οὐκ ἐᾷς λέγειν. καίτοι τί ἄλλο βούλει; *La.*195E (an objection put in the form of a dilemma): *Euthd.*289D Ἱκανόν μοι δοκεῖς . . . τεκμήριον λέγειν, ὅτι οὐχ αὕτη ἐστὶν ἡ τῶν λογοποιῶν τέχνη . . . . καίτοι ἐγὼ ᾤμην ἐνταῦθά που φανήσεσθαι τὴν ἐπιστήμην ἣν δὴ πάλαι ζητοῦμεν: *Phdr.*272B Ἀδύνατόν που . . . ἄλλως (ἀποδέχεσθαι λεγομένης λόγων τέχνης)· καίτοι οὐ σμικρόν γε φαίνεται ἔργον: *Ion* 539E ἢ οὕτως ἐπιλήσμων εἶ; καίτοι οὐκ ἂν πρέποι γε ἐπιλήσμονα εἶναι ῥαψῳδὸν ἄνδρα (*deprecantis*): Isoc.iv 11 καίτοι τινὲς ἐπιτιμῶσι (introducing an adverse criticism: cf. iv 138): Hdt.ii 148: iii 80, 152: Th.i 10.2: 37.5: vii 77.2: Pl.*Ap*.17A,24A,D,41D: *La*.199C: *Phdr*.228A: *Ly*.214E: *Euthd*.299B: *Men*.99E: *R*.362D,596E: X.*Oec*.14.4: Ant.v 53: Isoc.vi 11: viii 86: D.xv 5: xviii 108,171: xlv 23.

(ii) Used by a speaker in pulling himself up abruptly: the sharper 'but' is sometimes perhaps a better translation here than the quieter 'yet': though, strictly, 'but' is ἀλλά, ἀλλὰ γάρ, ἀτάρ, rather than καίτοι. A.*Pr*.101 καίτοι τί φημι; S.*Aj*.855 ὦ θάνατε θάνατε, νῦν μ' ἐπίσκεψαι μολών· καίτοι σὲ μὲν κἀκεῖ προσαυδήσω ξυνών: *OC* 1132 καίτοι τί φωνῶ; E.*Med*.1049 χαιρέτω βουλεύματα. καίτοι τί πάσχω; (*Ion* 1385): *HF* 501 ἐγὼ δὲ σέ, ὦ Ζεῦ, . . . αὐδῶ . . . ἀμύνειν . . . . καίτοι κέκλησαι πολλάκις· μάτην πονῶ: *Ph*.695 Χώρει σὺ καὶ κόμιζε . . . Κρέοντ' . . . . καίτοι ποδῶν σῶν μόχθον ἐκλύει παρών: Ar.*Ach*.466 'Απέρχομαι. καίτοι τί δράσω; *Lys*.926 ἐκδύομαι. καίτοι, τὸ δεῖνα, προσκεφάλαιον οὐκ ἔχεις: *Ra*.1304 ἐνεγκάτω τις τὸ λύριον. καίτοι τί δεῖ λύρας ἐπὶ τούτων; *Ec*.299: Pl.*Cra*.401E δίκαιον 'Ρέαν καὶ Κρόνον ἐπισκέψασθαι. καίτοι τό γε τοῦ Κρόνου ὄνομα ἤδη διήλθομεν: *Tht*.164C Τί οὖν δῆτ' ἂν εἴη ἐπιστήμη; πάλιν ἐξ ἀρχῆς, ὡς ἔοικεν, λεκτέον. καίτοι τί ποτε μέλλομεν, ὦ Θεαίτητε, δρᾶν; *Lg*. 708E ἔοικα . . . ἐρεῖν τι καὶ φαῦλον . . . . καίτοι τί ποτε δυσχεραίνω; *Hp.Mi*.368D καίτοι τό γε μνημονικὸν ἐπελαθόμην σου . . . τέχνημα ('But I've forgotten your *memoria technica*').

This use is hardly to be found in the orators. And.iv 10 ἀναμνῆσαι βούλομαι. καίτοι ἀπορῶ γε . . . πόθεν ἄρξομαι, quoted by Schmidt (p. 48), is not really a true example: the speaker does not go back on his own words here.

(iii) Not infrequently (particularly in Plato, whose characteristic fullness of style this idiom suits) the objection introduced by καίτοι is countered, palliated, or modified by a following adversative clause. E.*Hipp*.1297 ἄκουε, Θησεῦ, σῶν κακῶν κατάστασιν· καίτοι προκόψω γ' οὐδέν, ἀλγυνῶ δέ σε. ἀλλ' ἐς τόδ' ἦλθον . . . : *Hel*.950 'I will not weep. καίτοι λέγουσιν ὡς πρὸς ἀνδρὸς εὐγενοῦς ἐν ξυμφοραῖσι δάκρυ' ἀπ' ὀφθαλμῶν βαλεῖν. ἀλλ' οὐχὶ τοῦτο τὸ καλόν, εἰ καλὸν τόδε, αἱρήσομαι 'γώ': Ar.*Ra*.43

Οὔ τοι . . . δύναμαι μὴ γελᾶν· καίτοι δάκνω γ' ἐμαυτόν· ἀλλ' ὅμως γελῶ: E.*Andr.*220: Pl.*Euthphr.*3C *καταγελῶσιν ὡς μαινομένου· καίτοι οὐδὲν ὅτι οὐκ ἀληθὲς εἴρηκα ὧν προεῖπον, ἀλλ' ὅμως φθονοῦσιν ἡμῖν*: *Prm.*128B *σὺ δ' οὖν τὴν ἀλήθειαν τοῦ γράμματος οὐ πανταχοῦ ᾔσθησαι. καίτοι . . . εὖ μεταθεῖς τε καὶ ἰχνεύεις τὰ λεχθέντα· ἀλλὰ πρῶτον μέν σε τοῦτο λανθάνει*: *La.*183C (*καίτοι . . . δέ*), 186C, 194A: *Ap.*40B: *Men.*80B: *Grg.*499C: *Smp.* 177E: *Phd.*68E(*bis*): *Prm.*136E: *Lg.*707E (*καίτοι . . . δὲ δή*): D. xviii 219: xxi 62.

(iv) A variant of the above is the forecasting of the following adversative by *μέν*. In such cases '*καίτοι* covers the *μέν* clause only: so that *δέ*, while formally balancing *μέν*, really goes behind *μέν* to answer *καίτοι*' (R.W.C.). Pl.*R.*532D *ἀποδέχομαι οὕτω. καίτοι παντάπασί γέ μοι δοκεῖ χαλεπὰ μὲν ἀποδέχεσθαι εἶναι, ἄλλον δ' αὖ τρόπον χαλεπὰ μὴ ἀποδέχεσθαι*: *Criti.*107A *τοῦτο παραιτοῦμαι. . . . καίτοι σχεδὸν μὲν οἶδα παραίτησιν . . . ἀγροικοτέραν μέλλων παραιτεῖσθαι, ῥητέον δὲ ὅμως*: *Lg.*809C. Cf. *R.* 595B, where the *μέν* clause introduces a fresh sentence.

(v) *καίτοι*, though it belongs properly to continuous discourse, is occasionally used at the opening of a speech, where its place is normally taken by *καὶ μήν*. S.*Ph.*1257 *Καίτοι σ' ἐάσω* (here Odysseus' change of intention ignores Neoptolemus' words, to which he hardly listens: see Jebb): Pl.*Phdr.*241D *ἀλλ' ἤδη σοι τέλος ἐχέτω ὁ λόγος.—Καίτοι ᾤμην γε μεσοῦν αὐτόν.* In Ar.*Ec.*47 Cobet's *καίτοι*, for *καί μοι*, must be right: but it is by no means certain that a speech opens at *καίτοι*.

(vi) *καίτοι* in parenthesis. *καίτοι* being the characteristic means of expressing an objection or reservation in continuous discourse, it is not surprising that it should be used in parentheses. Ar.*Lys.*1035 *'Αλλ' ἀποψήσω σ' ἐγώ, καίτοι πάνυ πονηρὸς εἶ, καὶ φιλήσω*: Pl.*R.*414D *Λέγω δή—καίτοι οὐκ οἶδα ὁποίᾳ τόλμῃ . . . χρώμενος ἐρῶ—καὶ ἐπιχειρήσω . . .*: *Plt.*284C: *Lg.*723D, 728E. The parenthetical nature of the *καίτοι* clause is particularly obvious when it is sandwiched in between antithetically balanced clauses: Pl.*Phdr.*264E *μὲν . . . καίτοι . . . δέ* (*R.*339A): *Cra.*423D *πρῶτον μὲν . . . καίτοι . . . ἔπειτα.* In *Alc.I*108E the *καίτοι* clause is less definitely isolated. (Punctuation in these cases is not always an easy matter: but to put a comma at the beginning of the *καίτοι* clause and a colon at the end of it, as the Oxford text does in the last two passages, gives the misleading impression that the particle introduces a subordinate clause.)

Isoc.v 14 καίτοι . . . εἰπεῖν is hardly a regular parenthesis: there is anacoluthon here and in x 42. In the following the verb is exceptionally omitted: Hp.*Art.*14 οὔτε γὰρ μόνιμα οὐδένα χρόνον, οὐδ' εἰ κατακέοιτό τις—καίτοι ἐγγυτάτω ἂν οὕτως—: D.xx 117 συγχωρῶ καὶ ὑμᾶς ταὐτὸ τοῦτο ποιῆσαι, καίτοι τοῦτό γ' αἰσχρὸν ὁμοίως (so H. Wolf: text doubtful).

(vii) At the same time, the use of καίτοι in parentheses shows a tendency on its part to develop from an adversative particle introducing a main clause into a concessive particle introducing a subordinate clause (an opposite evolution to that of *quamquam*). And this explains the concessive use of καίτοι with the participle, very rare and dubious in classical, but common in later, authors (e.g. Philostr.*Imag.*ii 9.1: 29.1).

Simon.*Fr.*4.5 οὐ δέ μοι ἐμμελέως τὸ Πιττάκειον νέμεται, καίτοι σοφοῦ παρὰ φωτὸς εἰρημένον: Ar.*Ec.*159 ἀνὴρ ὢν τὼ θεὼ κατώμοσας, καίτοι τά γ' ἄλλ' εἰποῦσα δεξιώτατα (εἶπας σύ, Blaydes): Lys.xxxi 34 καίτοι πολλά γε παραλιπών: Pl.*R.*511D καίτοι νοητῶν ὄντων μετὰ ἀρχῆς: [Pl.]*Ax.*364B καίτοι γε . . . διαχλευάζων: Arist. *HA* 541a10 καίτοι κύστιν ἔχουσα: *Mete.*369a20 καίτοι πεφυκότος ἄνω τοῦ θερμοῦ φέρεσθαι παντός: [Arist.]*Mu.*397a28,398b26,399a3: *Pr.*929a16: Further, in Hdt.viii 53.1 καίτοι περ ἀποκρήμνου ἐόντος τοῦ χώρου is the reading of *ABCP* (καίπερ *DRSV*).

Bolling maintains (*AJP.*1902, 319–21 and again *Language* 1935, 261) that καίτοι with the participle is wholly post-classical: he explains Simon.*Fr.*4.5 as a parenthesis, emends Pl.*R.*511D and Lys. xxxi 34, and suggests that in Ar.*Ec.*159 Praxagora's 'syntax reveals her sex', like the νὴ τὼ θεώ to which she takes exception.

(2) Continuative. The purely continuative use of καίτοι (as distinct from the syllogistic, or argumentative, use examined below) is rare, and hardly to be found at all in verse. In S.*Tr.* 719 Jebb's 'howbeit' gives the right idea: Deianeira regards her intended suicide as in some manner compensating her unintentional homicide. In E.*Andr.*662 καίτοι φερ' is almost equivalent to ἀτάρ, and marks something of a new departure.

Hp. *VM* 3 'Animals live on grass, and so on. καίτοι τὴν ἀρχὴν ἔγωγε ἀξιῶ καὶ τὸν ἄνθρωπον τοιαύτῃ τροφῇ κεχρῆσθαι' ('And indeed'): *Cord.* 8 ἔστι δὲ ὄργανα τοῖσιν ἡ φύσις ἁρπάζει τὸν ἠέρα. καίτοι δοκέω τὸ ποίημα χειρώνακτος ἀγαθοῦ: Pl. *R.* 440D ὥσπερ κύων . . . ;—Πάνυ μὲν οὖν, ἔφη, ἔοικε τούτῳ ᾧ λέγεις· καίτοι γ' ἐν τῇ ἡμετέρᾳ πόλει τοὺς ἐπικούρους ὥσπερ κύνας ἐθέμεθα ('And in fact'): 583B Ταῦτα . . . δύ' ἐφεξῆς ἂν εἴη καὶ δὶς νενικηκὼς ὁ δίκαιος τὸν ἄδικον· τὸ δὲ τρίτον . . ., ἄθρει ὅτι . . . . καίτοι τοῦτ' ἂν εἴη μέγιστόν τε καὶ κυριώτατον τῶν πτωμάτων ('And this, in fact, would seem to be the decisive round') : *Ion* 533C καίτοι ὅρα τοῦτο τί ἔστιν ('Now consider what the meaning of this is': the only place, apparently, where Plato uses καίτοι with the imperative: Hoefer, p. 30): *Cra.* 418D Νῦν δέ γε τετραγῳδημένον οὐδ' ἂν κατανοήσαις ὅτι βούλεται ἡ "ἡμέρα". καίτοι τινὲς οἴονται, ὡς δὴ ἡ ἡμέρα ἥμερα ποιεῖ, διὰ ταῦτα ὠνομάσθαι αὐτὴν οὕτως ('And in fact some people actually suppose . . .') : X. *An.* i 4.8 'I could catch the deserters if I chose: but I do not choose. καίτοι ἔχω γε αὐτῶν καὶ τέκνα καὶ γυναῖκας . . . ἀλλ' οὐδὲ τούτων στερήσονται' (a new point: 'Again'): Theopomp. Hist. *Fr.* 205 Χάρητός τε νωθροῦ τε ὄντος καὶ βραδέος, καίτοι γε καὶ πρὸς τρυφὴν ἤδη ζῶντος ('and besides': exceptionally, after a weak stop): Ant. v 43 (a new argument, from τὸ εἰκός, reinforces the evidence of witnesses): Lys. vi 13 ('In fact his line will be, not to defend himself, but to accuse others'): D. iii 23 'The old orators were outspoken, the new have ruined their country by their servility. καίτοι σκέψασθε . . . ἅ τις ἂν κεφάλαι' εἰπεῖν ἔχοι τῶν τ' ἐπὶ τῶν προγόνων ἔργων καὶ τῶν ἐφ' ὑμῶν': viii 55 'People complain of expenditure. But money spent on national security is not wasted. καίτοι ἔγωγ' ἀγανακτῶ καὶ αὐτὸ τοῦτο . . . εἰ τὰ μὲν χρήματα λυπεῖ τινας ὑμῶν εἰ διαρπασθήσεται . . . τὴν δ' Ἑλλάδα πᾶσαν Φίλιππος ἁρπάζων οὐ λυπεῖ': Aeschin. ii 148 'My relations on my mother's side are all free men. καίτοι, ὦ Δημόσθενες, ἡ μὲν ἐμὴ μήτηρ ἔφυγε μετὰ τοῦ αὐτῆς ἀνδρὸς εἰς Κόρινθον καὶ μετέσχε τῶν πολιτικῶν κακῶν, σὺ δὲ . . .' ('And further'): Hp. *Art.* 35: *Fract.* 27.

καίτοι καί. D. xix 337 οὐχ ἕξει τί λέγῃ, ἀλλὰ τὴν ἄλλως ἐνταῦθ' ἐπαρεῖ τὴν φωνὴν καὶ πεφωνασκηκὼς ἔσται. καίτοι καὶ περὶ τῆς φωνῆς ἴσως εἰπεῖν ἀνάγκη ('And in fact I must say something about that voice of his': but perhaps rather καίτοι introduces a diversion here, like ἀλλὰ γάρ or ἀτάρ: cf. I.ii above): iv 12 καίτοι καὶ τοῦτο· εἴ τι πάθοι . . . ('Then again there is *this* consideration'): xviii 122 καίτοι καὶ τοῦτ', ὦ ἄνδρες Ἀθηναῖοι.

In many other passages (including some cited by Kühner, II ii 152) where καίτοι at first sight appears to be purely continuative, a closer examination reveals an adversative or argumentative force. In Pl.*Phlb.*26C καίτοι is adversative, looking forward to the δέ clause, πολλὰ . . . γένη being virtually a μέν clause, subordinate in thought. *Grg.*519B: 'The old politicians corrupted the city, the politicians of to-day will unjustly get the blame. Yet, on reflection, *no* politician *can* be unjustly treated.' In Hdt.viii 68α1, which Kühner cites, καί τοι (dative singular) is probably the correct reading.

(3) Logical. καίτοι often marks the transition from premise to premise, almost invariably from minor to major, only very rarely vice versa. It is, however, but seldom so used in formal syllogisms, ἀλλὰ μήν, δέ γε, etc., being used instead: far more frequently in rhetorical syllogisms or enthymemes. 'The argumentative, not to say quarrelsome, colouring of the group of passages is unmistakable. The common type is a negative or destructive argument of a loose kind. You state your opponent's position or develop its implications; then you place it in its most unattractive light by means of a sentence opening with καίτοι θαυμαστὸν ἂν εἴη or the like (Isocrates' favourite formula is καίτοι πῶς οὐκ ἄτοπον . . .;), and leave the rest to the imagination'. 'καίτοι occurs in 125 places in Isocrates. In 68 of these it introduces a rhetorical question, either persuasive in tone, appealing to the reader's good sense, or confuting the adversary with a triumphant *reductio ad absurdum.*' 'καίτοι is constantly found (in Isocrates) with terms of obligation (χρή, προσήκει, δίκαιον, αἰσχρόν), terms of reason and unreason (εἰκός, εὔλογον, ἄλογον, ἄτοπον, καταγέλαστον, οἱ εὖ φρονοῦντες), and terms of demonstration (ἐπιδεῖξαι, φανερόν).' 'In Lysias only 27 examples out of 106 are questions, and in Lysias the adversative value is more pronounced.' (R.W.C.)

(i) Occasionally in a complete syllogism, with conclusion expressed. Hdt.ii 142 'The priests give the period as 341 generations. καίτοι 341 generations = 11,340 years. οὕτως ἐν μυρίοισί τε ἔτεσι καὶ χιλίοισι καὶ πρὸς τριηκοσίοισί τε καὶ τεσσεράκοντα ἔλεγον . . .': Pl.*Tht.*148B Καὶ μὴν . . . ὅ γε ἐρωτᾷς περὶ ἐπιστήμης οὐκ ἂν δυναίμην ἀποκρίνασθαι ὥσπερ . . . . καίτοι σύ γέ μοι δοκεῖς τοιοῦτόν τι ζητεῖν· ὥστε πάλιν αὖ φαίνεται ψευδὴς ὁ Θεόδωρος: X.*Mem.*i 1.5 πολλοῖς τῶν συνόντων προηγόρευε . . . . καίτοι τίς οὐκ ἂν ὁμολογήσειεν αὐτὸν βούλεσθαι μήτ' ἠλίθιον μήτ' ἀλαζόνα φαίνεσθαι τοῖς συνοῦσιν; ἐδόκει δ' ἂν ἀμφότερα ταῦτα, εἰ προαγορεύων . . . καὶ ψευδόμενος ἐφαίνετο. δῆλον οὖν ὅτι οὐκ ἂν προέλεγεν, εἰ μὴ ἐπίστευεν ἀληθεύσειν: S.*OT*855 (conclusion introduced by ὥστε): Hdt.vii 10γ2 (ὦν): Pl.*Prt.* 339D (ὥστε): *Chrm.*164C (οὐκοῦν): Lys.vi 14 (οὔκουν): [D.]vii 10 (δή).

In the following, the conclusion precedes the premises. Ar. *Pl.*586: Pl.*R.*522D Παγγέλοιον . . . στρατηγὸν Ἀγαμέμνονα . . . ἀποφαίνει. Agamemnon couldn't even count. καίτοι ποῖόν τιν' αὐτὸν οἴει στρατηγὸν εἶναι; (here, for αὐτόν, we should expect τὸν τοιοῦτον): *R.*376B (in this logical structure, composed of two syllogisms, the first major premise is introduced by καίτοι, the second by ἀλλὰ μέντοι, and the conclusion of the whole argument ('the dog is a philosopher') is placed at the beginning. The conclusion of the first syllogism, which is also the minor premise of the second ('the dog is a lover of learning'), is understood): Hdt.iii 81. In X.*Mem.*i 6.11 the conclusion both precedes the premises and is repeated after them (δῆλον δὴ ὅτι . . .).

(ii) Far more frequently the conclusion of the syllogism is left to the imagination. Usually the minor premise precedes, the major follows, often in the form of a rhetorical question.

E.*Heracl.*973 Οὐκ ἔστι τοῦτον ὅστις ἂν κατακτάνοι.—Ἔγωγε· καίτοι φημὶ κἄμ' εἶναί τινα: *HF*1320 'The gods sin, but get on very well all the same. καίτοι τί φήσεις, εἰ σὺ μὲν θνητὸς γεγὼς φέρεις ὑπέρφευ τὰς τύχας, θεοὶ δὲ μή;' Ar.*Nu.*1052 Ποῦ ψυχρὰ . . . εἶδες Ἡράκλεια λουτρά; καίτοι τίς ἀνδρειότερος ἦν; (*sc.* 'therefore hot baths aren't effeminate'): 1428 σκέψαι δὲ τοὺς ἀλεκτρυόνας καὶ τἄλλα . . . ὡς τοὺς πατέρας ἀμύνεται· καίτοι τί διαφέρουσιν ἡμῶν ἐκεῖνοι . . .; (*sc.* 'therefore why shouldn't *we* beat *our* fathers'): *V.*915 Κοὐ μετέδωκ' αἰτοῦντί μοι. καίτοι τίς ὑμᾶς εὖ ποιεῖν δυνήσεται, ἢν μή τι κἀμοί τις προβάλλῃ τῷ κυνί; E.*Rh.* 757: Ar.*Nu.*371,1074,1082: *Pl.*498,531: Pl.*Phdr.*231C 'The lover will always desert the old love for the new. *καίτοι πῶς εἰκός ἐστι τοιοῦτον πρᾶγμα προέσθαι τοιαύτην ἔχοντι συμφορὰν . . .;*' (*sc.* 'therefore don't trust the lover'): *Phd.*65B 'Are eye and ear infallible? *καίτοι εἰ αὗται τῶν . . . αἰσθήσεων μὴ ἀκριβεῖς εἰσιν . . . σχολῇ αἵ γε ἄλλαι*' (*a fortiori*): *R.*433C *Δοκεῖ μοι . . . τὸ ὑπόλοιπον . . . τοῦτο εἶναι . . . . καίτοι ἔφαμεν δικαιοσύνην ἔσεσθαι τὸ ὑπολειφθὲν ἐκείνων*: X.*HG*iv 1.35 'If you join us, you will be independent. *καίτοι ἐλεύθερον εἶναι ἐγὼ μὲν οἶμαι ἀντάξιον εἶναι τῶν πάντων χρημάτων*': Hp.*deArte*5: Pl.*Cri.* 44C: *Phd.*73A: *Grg.*452E: *R.*360C: *Hp.Mi.*372C: *Lg.*656B: 801C: X.*HG*iii 5.14: iv 1.36: 8.5 (*a fortiori*): 8.14: *Mem.*i 7.2: iii 14.6: *Cyr.*iii 3.19: v 4.25: *Ages.*6.4: Ant.vi 47,48: Isoc.iv 25, 31,37: D.ix 16: xviii 137,215,264: xix 146: Lycurg.37.

(iii) If the relationship of the *καίτοι* sentence to the preceding sentence is regarded in isolation, apart from the role played by both in a syllogistic structure, it is usually adversative in tone. S.*Aj.*1071 *οὐ γὰρ ἔσθ' ὅπου λόγων ἀκοῦσαι ζῶν ποτ' ἠθέλησ' ἐμῶν. καίτοι κακοῦ πρὸς ἀνδρὸς ἄνδρα δημότην μηδὲν δικαιοῦν τῶν ἐφεστώτων κλύειν* (the *καίτοι* clause, considered by itself, revolts against such indiscipline: regarded as a major premise, 'and that is how a bad man behaves', it leads on to the implied conclusion, 'therefore Ajax was a bad man'): E.*Tr.*671 (an *a fortiori* argument). In tragedy, the syllogistic force of *καίτοι* is still, perhaps, in its infancy. Pl.*Phd.*77A '*Ἱκανῶς* (*sc. ἀποδεδεῖχθαι Κέβητι δοκεῖ*) . . .· *καίτοι καρτερώτατος ἀνθρώπων ἐστὶν πρὸς τὸ ἀπιστεῖν τοῖς λόγοις* (Cebes' normal scepticism is contrasted with his openness to conviction on the present occasion: at the same time, the fact that he is convinced is an indication, *a fortiori*, that anybody else must be convinced): *Grg.*482B (*deprecantis*, recoiling from the contemplation of discord in the soul): *Prt.*317C *ὥστε . . . μηδὲν δεινὸν πάσχειν διὰ τὸ ὁμολογεῖν σοφιστὴς εἶναι. καίτοι πολλά γε ἔτη ἤδη εἰμὶ ἐν τῇ τέχνῃ* (his immunity from harm is contrasted with the frequency of his opportunities for suffering harm: at the same time, the conclusion is implied, 'Therefore, if one admits one is a sophist, there is no danger').

Far less frequently, the relationship of the *καίτοι* sentence to the preceding sentence, regarded in isolation, is positive in tone. Pl.*Tht.*187C *ἐὰν γὰρ οὕτω δρῶμεν, δυοῖν θάτερα, ἢ εὑρήσομεν ἐφ'* ὃ ἐρχόμεθα, ἢ ἧττον οἰησόμεθα εἰδέναι ὃ μηδαμῇ ἴσμεν· καίτοι οὐκ ἂν εἴη μεμπτὸς μισθὸς ὁ τοιοῦτος ('and that is a reward worth having': an adversative force would be inappropriate here). Cf. Pl.*R*.433C, *Hp.Mi*.372C, *Phd*.73A, and other passages cited under (ii) above.

The syllogistic use may perhaps be regarded as descended both from the adversative and from the simple connective use. (The same may be said of other syllogistic particles, δέ γε, ἀλλὰ μήν, καὶ μήν.)

(4) καίτοι combined with other particles.

(i) καίτοι γε, καίτοι . . . γε. An emphatic word following καίτοι is often stressed by γε. The juxtaposition καίτοι γε is much rarer.[1]

καίτοι γε: Hippon.*Fr*.31: E.*IT* 720: *Fr*.953.10 (spurious): Ar. *Ach*.611: *Nu*.876: (doubtful at *Lys*.1035): Hdt.vii 9β1 (γε *om. ABC*): Hp.*Prorrh*.ii 2: *Acut*.9.14: Pl.*R*.332A,440D: *La*.194A (καίτοι ἀήθης γ' *T*: καίτοι γ' ἀήθης *W*): *Min*.318E (γε *A*: τε *F*): [Pl.]*Ax*.364B,369A: X.*Mem*.i 2.3: iv 2.7: *Cyr*.iii 1.38 (γ' ἔφη *om. CEDF*): Arist.*Mete*.370a5: *Metaph*.1008b23 (*v.l.* καίτοι . . . γε), 1061a20, 1092b7 (γε *om.* Bekker): *Po*.1454a21: [Arist.]*Mu*.396a33: *Col*.798b22: Theopomp.Hist.*Fr*.205: And.i 72: Lys.i 42: viii 11: xi 7: xxvi 16: D xxiv 113 (καίτοι . . . γε Cobet): vii 12 καίτοι γε πλείους γε (γε *post* καίτοι *add. SL*[1]: *om. vulg.*: obviously one γε must go): lviii 36 (καίτοι τάς γε *A*: καίτοι γε τάς *SQFD*): Lycurg.90.

(ii) καίτοι περ. See I.vii above.

(iii) In A.*Eu*.849 neither καίτοι μέν (*M*) nor καίτοι γε μήν (*Fl, Fa*) is possible.

καίτοι in crasis: Ar.*Lys*.509 καἰτοὐκ: *V*.599 καἰτοὐστίν.

[1] References to authorities in Klotz, ii. 655. Kühner holds that in καίτοι γε, γε stresses καίτοι, in καίτοι . . . γε, the word it follows. But the particles, even when separated, cohere in thought: see γε, V.1.

Τοιγάρ, τοιγαροῦν, τοιγάρτοι

The first syllable of *τοιγάρ, τοιγαροῦν, τοιγάρτοι* is quite distinct from the particle *τοι*, and is allied to the stem *tŏ-*, of which the Homeric *τῶ*, or rather perhaps *τώ*, 'therefore' (later *τῷ*), seems to be the instrumental case.[1] *τῷ τοι* is found in A.*Pr.*239, and is read by some MSS. in Pl.*R.*409B (*τοιγάρτοι al.*), *Tht.*179D (*τοῦτο T*), and *Sph.*230B (*καὶ γάρ τοι T*): cf. [Arist.]*Plant.*825a37: Philostr.*Imag.*ii 14.2. *τῷ* alone, S.*OT* 510. *τό*, meaning 'therefore', S.*Ph.*142.

Τοιγάρ

τοιγάρ, formed by a combination of this *τοι* and *γάρ* as suffix, is found in Homer, drama (almost always in iambics, usually first word in the line: very rarely in comedy[2]), and very occasionally in Ionic, though never in Attic, prose. There are no examples in Pindar, and I have noted none in Hesiod or in early Elegiac or Lyric: later Lyric, Arist.*Fr.*625. *τοιγάρ* bears a strong logical force, 'therefore', 'in consequence', even 'that is why', never sinking to the rank of a mere progressive particle, 'well', 'now', 'further'. As a natural consequence, it invariably opens a sentence.

(i) In Homer, as Bäumlein points out, *τοιγάρ* is only used by a person preparing to speak or act at another's request: *A*76 *Ὦ Ἀχιλεῦ, κέλεαί με, Διῒ φίλε, μυθήσασθαι . . . · τοιγὰρ ἐγὼν ἐρέω*: *δ*612 *Αἵματός εἰς ἀγαθοῖο, φίλον τέκος, οἷ' ἀγορεύεις· τοιγὰρ ἐγώ τοι ταῦτα μεταστήσω* (Menelaus to Telemachus, after the latter has declined the gift of horses): *K*413: *η*28: *θ*402: *id. saep.* . . . (Otherwise, *Batr.*152.)

(ii) In subsequent writers, *τοιγάρ* is used both (*a*) thus and (*b*) in other ways. (*a*) S.*Tr.*1249 *Πράσσειν ἄνωγας . . . τάδε;—Ἔγωγε.—Τοιγὰρ ποήσω*: Ar.*Lys.*901 *Μὰ Δί' οὐκ ἔγωγ'* (*sc. βαδιοῦμαι*

[1] Brugmann, pp. 269, 471, 615–16. That *τοι* in *καίτοι, μέντοι* is (as Brugmann suggests) this *τοι*, not the particle, seems to me, on grounds of usage, quite impossible.

[2] Thrice only, in the *Lysistrata*: 516, 901, 902: in the last, Myrrhine mockingly catches up Cinesias' pompous *Τοιγάρ, ἢν δοκῇ*.

πάλιν), ἢν μὴ διαλλάχθητέ γ' ...—Τοιγάρ, ἢν δοκῇ, ποιήσομεν καὶ ταῦτα: 902: S.*El*.29. (*b*): A.*Ch*.894 Φιλεῖς τὸν ἄνδρα; τοιγὰρ ἐν ταὐτῷ τάφῳ κείσει: *Eu*.901 μεθίσταμαι κότου.—Τοιγὰρ κατὰ χθόν' οὖσ' ἐπικτήσει φίλους: S.*Aj*.666 ἐχθρῶν ἄδωρα δῶρα κοὐκ ὀνήσιμα. τοιγὰρ τὸ λοιπὸν εἰσόμεσθα μὲν θεοῖς εἴκειν: E.*Cyc*.124 Βρομίου δὲ πῶμ' ἔχουσιν ...;—Ἥκιστα· τοιγὰρ ἄχορον οἰκοῦσι χθόνα ('in consequence'): *Med*.622 αὐθαδίᾳ φίλους ἀπωθῇ· τοιγὰρ ἀλγυνῇ πλέον: *Supp*.577 Πράσσειν σὺ πόλλ' εἴωθας ἥ τε σὴ πόλις.—Τοιγὰρ πονοῦσα πολλὰ πόλλ' εὐδαιμονεῖ: Ar.*Lys*.516 Γυ.[a] Ἀλλ' οὐκ ἂν ἐγώ ποτ' ἐσίγων.—Πρ. Κἂν ᾤμωζές γ', εἰ μὴ 'σίγας.—Λυ. Τοιγὰρ ἔγωγ' ἔνδον ἐσίγων: Arist.*Fr*.625 (*Hymn to Virtue*) 1583b22 τοιγὰρ ἀοίδιμος ἔργοις: A.*Th*.1038: *Pers*. 607,759,813: *Eu*.603: *Supp*.309 (but there is a good deal to be said for Tucker's Τῇ γάρ): 656(lyr.): S.*Aj*.1389: *El*.1165: *Ant*. 931(anap.),994: *OC*868,1370,1380: *Fr*.210(doubtful): E.*Alc*.588 (lyr.),662,859: *Med*.458,509: *Heracl*.331: *Hipp*.687: *HF*1241: *Ion*274: *Tr*.73: *El*.482(lyr.): *Hel*.1626: *Ba*.32,964,1303.

Prose. Hdt.viii 114.2 εἶπε· Τοιγάρ σφι Μαρδόνιος ὅδε δίκας δώσει (the only Herodotean example, Hoffmann, p. 50[1]: τοιγάρτοι, *s.v.*). The only other (apparent) prose example known to me is Hp.*Cord*.10: here τῇ γάρ (= ταύτῃ γάρ) has been conjectured: 'Il n'y a rien à changer', remarks Littré, but he translates 'là, en effet', and τοιγάρ gives a quite unsuitable sense.

Τοιγαροῦν, τοιγάρτοι

These combinations virtually replace τοιγάρ in comedy and prose, and are also common in tragedy. The ancillary use of οὖν is paralleled in ἀλλ' οὖν, γὰρ οὖν, etc.: that of τοι in καίτοι, and also (though there the particle has more independence) in γάρ τοι, ἐπεί τοι. Attempts to differentiate in meaning between τοιγαροῦν and τοιγάρτοι are unconvincing and the two must be regarded as synonymous. Both particles are strongly emphatic, and sometimes even convey the effect that the logical connexion is regarded as more important than the ideas connected. Hence they approximate in force to διὰ ταῦτα καί, δι' ὃ δὴ καί.

Both particles, as a natural consequence of their strength, are

[1] In iii 3.3 *CPRSV* read τοιγάρ: τοιγάρ τοι *cett.*

placed first in the sentence:[1] except that in Hippocrates τοιγαροῦν is invariably placed second: *Int.*41 αὕτη τοιγαροῦν ἡ νοῦσος . . .: *Vict* 35,89: *Int.*47: *Genit.*50. Cf. [Pl.]*Ax.*365E: [Arist.]*Plant.*824a34,826a30. (Hoogeveen observes that τοιγαροῦν is sometimes placed second in Lucian.)

τοιγάρτοι first occurs in Aeschylus, τοιγαροῦν in Sophocles: Euripides, I think, has neither: Aristophanes both (once each), Herodotus both (once each). Schmidt observes (p. 44) that τοιγαροῦν gradually tends to replace τοιγάρτοι, and that certain writers show an individual preference for the one or the other. Thus Andocides, Lysias, and probably Aeschines (i 114 is doubtful) use only τοιγάρτοι: whereas Aristotle, Lycurgus, and Demosthenes in the genuine speeches (except for viii 66 and xxiii 203, in both of which the MSS. vary between τοιγάρτοι and καὶ γάρ τοι) use only τοιγαροῦν. τοιγαροῦν alone, I think, is found in Xenophon (who uses it very frequently, at least eighteen times) and Hippocrates. Isocrates, on the other hand, uses both: so does Plato, but he has τοιγαροῦν in late dialogues only (*Sophist* and *Laws*) and in the doubtful *Alcibiades II* (Hoefer, p. 40). In general τοιγαροῦν is about twice as common as τοιγάρτοι.

τοιγάρτοι. A.*Supp.*654 τοιγάρτοι καθαροῖσι βωμοῖς θεοὺς ἀρέσονται: Ar.*Ach* 643 τοιγάρτοι . . . ἥξουσιν ἰδεῖν ἐπιθυμοῦντες τὸν ποιητὴν τὸν ἄριστον: Emp.*Fr.*145: Hdt.iii 3 (see p. 566, n. 1): Th.vi 38.3: Pl.*Grg.*471C,494D: *Smp.*179D: *Euthd.*276E: *La.*183A: *Phd.*82D: *Tht.*174B: *R.*454C,568B: *Hp.Ma.*290A: And.i 108,119: iv 12,22: Lys.xxvi 20: xxxi 24: Isoc.vii 52: xv 126: Aeschin.i 92,140: ii 140: iii 132: [D.]vii 43: x 4,48: D. xxiii 203 (καὶ γάρ τοι *F*, according to Schmidt): Din.ii 26.

τοιγαροῦν. S.*El.*1257 Ξύμφημι κἀγώ. τοιγαροῦν σῴζου τόδε: Ephipp.*Fr.*2 οἱ μεθύοντες ἀεὶ τὰς μάχας πάσας μάχονται.—Τοιγαροῦν φεύγουσ' ἀεί ('That's why they always run away'): S.*OT* 1519: *Ph.*341: *Aj.*490: *Fr.*574.9 (Pearson): Ar.*V.*1098: Eup.*Fr.*116.1: Antiph.*Fr.*165.2,194.13: Aristophon,*Fr.*14.1: Pl.Com.*Fr.*186.5: Gorg.*Fr.*6: Pl.*Sph.*234E,239C,246B: *Lg.*695D,

[1] Hdt.iv 149 appears at first sight to be an exception, with τοιγαρῶν picking up an anticipatory γάρ (see γάρ, IV. 3 and 4): ὁ δὲ παῖς οὐ γὰρ ἔφη οἱ συμπλεύσεσθαι, τοιγαρῶν ἔφη αὐτὸν καταλείψειν. But I believe that τοιγαρῶν does not pick up γάρ, but is the first word of the reported speech: Τοιγαρῶν σε καταλείψω (Introd. II.5.iii).

790B: *Alc.II*138C,148C: X.*An.*i.9.9: 9.15: *id. saep.*: Anaximenes *Rh.Al.*15,35([Arist.]1432a7,1440b26): Arist.*Pol.*1271b3: Theopomp.Hist.*Fr.*217: Isoc.iv 136,152: vii 48: xi 6,17: xv 138: D.iv 36: xviii 40,134: [D]x 30: xiii 20,32: lx 16: Lycurg.72,88,105, 109,114,133: Hyp.*Eux.*36.

Τοίνυν

Kühner (II ii 327) and Brugmann (p. 616) regard **τοι** in **τοίνυν** as identical with τοι in τοιγάρ: but Wackernagel (*Indog.Forsch.*i (1891) p. 377) holds that the *particle* **τοι** coalesced with **νυν** to form **τοίνυν**. There can be little doubt that Wackernagel is right, and that the connective force resides in the **νυν**. Wackernagel's derivation accounts for the fact that τοίνυν is never, in classical Greek (though occasionally in later writers), placed at the opening of a sentence, like τοιγάρ, τοιγαροῦν, and τοιγάρτοι, and that its logical force is for the most part not very strong, rather weaker, on the whole, than that of οὖν, which comes nearest to it in meaning. 'Then', 'well then', 'well now', rather than 'therefore', are usually the best equivalents, and in II.2 (a usage, first clearly present in Aristophanes, in which **τοίνυν** has some affinities with **καὶ μήν**), 'further', 'again'.

τοίνυν is absent from Homer and Hesiod: it is rare in Lyric: much commoner in comedy than in tragedy:[1] commoner in Attic, than in Ionic, prose: and commonest in those parts of Attic prose which approach most closely to the idiom of ordinary speech. This last point is well brought out by Rosenberg, who gives statistics for the distribution of τοίνυν in the Attic orators: Antiphon, rare (commonest in V): Andocides, much commoner: Lysias, about once in every 6 sections (almost absent from pseudo-Lysias): Isocrates, rarer than in Lysias: Isaeus, same frequency as Lysias: Lycurgus, about once in every 9–10 sections: Hyperides, rare (he prefers οὖν):

[1] Seven examples in Sophocles, 3 or 4 in Aeschylus (*Th.*994 is doubtful): I have only noticed 5 in Euripides (excluding *Hel.*838, *coni.* Canter), but there may be more: Todd cites 80 from Aristophanes.

Demosthenes, much commoner in forensic speeches (about once in every 2–3 sections) than in political: Aeschines, once in every 13–15 sections: Dinarchus, rare: sophistic declamation (Gorgias, etc.) very rare. For further statistics see Kalinka, who points out that Thucydides uses *τοίνυν* in Athenian speeches only (iii 45.4: v 87,89,105.1: viii 53.3). Out of seventeen Herodotean examples which I have noted, only four (i 57: ii 142.4: vii 5.1: 139.2) are from the narrative.

τοίνυν is, then, essentially an Attic, and a colloquial, particle. Being conversational and lively, it is absent from the *Timaeus*, and in Plato, speaking generally, is much commoner in dialogue than in continuous speech: in about half the Platonic instances it goes with imperative or hortative subjunctive (des Places). All the 80 Aristophanic examples occur near the opening of an answer.

I. Logical.

(1) In general.

(i) In continuous speech. This use is entirely absent from drama. and is rare in Plato. Pi.*O*.6.27 *κεῖναι γὰρ ἐξ ἀλλᾶν ὁδὸν ἁγεμονεῦσαι ταύταν ἐπίστανται . . . · χρὴ τοίνυν πύλας ὕμνων ἀναπιτνάμεν αὐταῖς*: *P*.5.43: Hdt.i 57 *εἰ τούτοισι τεκμαιρόμενον δεῖ λέγειν, ἦσαν οἱ Πελασγοὶ βάρβαρον γλῶσσαν ἱέντες. εἰ τοίνυν ἦν καὶ πᾶν τοιοῦτο τὸ Πελασγικόν, τὸ Ἀττικὸν ἔθνος ἐὸν Πελασγικὸν ἅμα τῇ μεταβολῇ τῇ ἐς Ἕλληνας καὶ τὴν γλῶσσαν μετέμαθε* (in narrative): 209 *οὐκ ὦν ἔστι μηχανὴ . . . τὸ μὴ οὐ κεῖνον ἐπιβουλεύειν ἐμοί. σὺ τοίνυν τὴν ταχίστην πορεύεο ὀπίσω ἐς Πέρσας*: D.i 1 *ὅτε τοίνυν τοῦθ' οὕτως ἔχει . . .*: iv 7 'Philip owes his success to his vigour. *ἂν τοίνυν . . . καὶ ὑμεῖς ἐπὶ τῆς τοιαύτης ἐθελήσητε γενέσθαι γνώμης νῦν . . ., καὶ τὰ ὑμέτερ' αὐτῶν κομιεῖσθ' . . . κἀκεῖνον τιμωρήσεσθε*': Hdt.vii 162.1: ix 42.3: Pl.*Smp*.178D: *Lg*.793A,829B,888B: D.ii 29.

(ii) In dialogue, introducing an answer. *τοίνυν* represents the answer as springing from the actual words, or general attitude, of the previous speaker.[1] The logical force is often not very

[1] This includes passages in which the previous speaker has merely expressed his assent to what has been said (e.g. Pl.*Men*.76A *ἐπίπεδον καλεῖς τι . . .;* —*Ἔγωγε καλῶ.* —*Ἤδη τοίνυν ἂν μάθοις μου ἐκ τούτων σχῆμα ὃ λέγω*: Ar.*Ec*.160): though in such cases we can, if we like, say that *τοίνυν* looks back to the principal speaker's previous remark.

strong, and 'well' or 'well then' are frequently the best renderings.

A.*Ch*.911 *Ἡ Μοῖρα τούτων, ὦ τέκνον, παραιτία.—Καὶ τόνδε τοίνυν Μοῖρ' ἐπόρσυνεν μόρον* ('well', rather than 'then', gives the force: *τοίνυν* merely denotes that Orestes' retort springs out of Clytaemnestra's excuse): S.*Aj*.127 'We are but shadows'.—*Τοιαῦτα τοίνυν εἰσορῶν ὑπέρκοπον μηδέν ποτ' εἴπῃς αὐτὸς ἐς θεοὺς ἔπος*: *El*.1050 *Χρ. Πάλαι δέδοκται ταῦτα . . . .—Ηλ. Ἄπειμι τοίνυν· οὔτε γὰρ σὺ τἄμ' ἔπη τολμᾷς ἐπαινεῖν οὔτ' ἐγὼ τοὺς σοὺς τρόπους* (the particle refers to Chrysothemis' general attitude, as well as to the particular words she has just spoken: cf. *OT* 444): *Tr*.71 *Λυδῇ γυναικί φασί νιν λάτριν πονεῖν.—Πᾶν τοίνυν, εἰ καὶ τοῦτ' ἔτλη, κλύοι τις ἄν*: E.*Hipp*.1405 *Τρεῖς ὄντας ἡμᾶς ὤλεσ', ᾔσθημαι, Κύπρις.—Πατέρα γε καὶ σὲ καὶ τρίτην ξυνάορον.—Ὤιμωξα τοίνυν καὶ πατρὸς δυσπραξίας*: *IA* 1539 *θαυμαστά σοι . . . σημῆναι θέλω.—Μὴ μέλλε τοίνυν, ἀλλὰ φράζ'*: Ar.*Ach*.818 *Ὤνθρωπε ποδαπός;—Χοιροπώλας Μεγαρικός.—Τὰ χοιρίδια τοίνυν ἐγὼ φανῶ ταδὶ πολέμια καὶ σέ*: *Eq*.1259 'What's your name?'—'Agoracritus'.—*Ἀγορακρίτῳ τοίνυν ἐμαυτὸν ἐπιτρέπω* ('Very well, then, I put myself into Agoracritus' hands'): *Nu*.356 *διὰ τοῦτ' ἐγένοντο γυναῖκες.—Χαίρετε τοίνυν, ὦ δέσποιναι* ('Well, good morning, ladies'): 1406 'I used to be an ignorant fellow, with no mind for anything but horses. But now I can prove to you that it's right to punish one's father'.—*Ἵππευε τοίνυν* ('Then you'd better stick to your horses'): *Ec*.339 *δέδοικα μή τι δρᾷ νεώτερον.—Νὴ τὸν Ποσειδῶ ταὐτὰ τοίνυν ἄντικρυς ἐμοὶ πέπονθας*: *Ach*.904,911: *Eq*.30,299: *Nu*. 392,435: *V*.164,367,385: *Pax* 1219: Hdt.i 112 *ὡς δὲ οὐκ ἔπειθε ἄρα τὸν ἄνδρα, δεύτερα λέγει ἡ γυνὴ τάδε· Ἐπεὶ τοίνυν οὐ δύναμαί σε πείθειν . . .* (cf. iii 134 *Ὦ γύναι, ἐπεὶ τοίνυν τοι δοκέει . . .*: v 40.1: ix 42.2: 46.2): Pl.*Chrm*.156A *ἄνευ δὲ τῆς ἐπῳδῆς οὐδὲν ὄφελος εἴη τοῦ φύλλου.—Καὶ ὅς, Ἀπογράψομαι τοίνυν, ἔφη, παρὰ σοῦ τὴν ἐπῳδήν*: 162B *ἢ τινος ἠλιθίου ἤκουσας τουτὶ λέγοντος . . .;—Ἥκιστα . . . .—Παντὸς τοίνυν μᾶλλον . . . αἴνιγμα αὐτὸ προύβαλεν* (the only other alternative): *Euthphr*. 15E *εἰπὲ οὖν . . . καὶ μὴ ἀποκρύψῃ ὅτι αὐτὸ ἡγῇ.—Εἰς αὖθις τοίνυν . . .· νῦν γὰρ σπεύδω* ('Some other time, then'): *R*. 398C *οὐ πᾶς ἂν εὕροι . . .; καὶ ὁ Γλαύκων ἐπιγελάσας, Ἐγὼ τοίνυν, ἔφη, . . . κινδυνεύω ἐκτὸς τῶν πάντων εἶναι· οὔκουν ἱκανῶς γε ἔχω . . . συμβαλέσθαι . . . : 430D Πῶς οὖν ἂν τὴν δικαιοσύνην εὕροιμεν, ἵνα μηκέτι πραγματευώμεθα περὶ σωφροσύνης;—Ἐγὼ μὲν τοίνυν, ἔφη, οὔτε οἶδα οὔτ' ἂν βουλοίμην αὐτὸ πρότερον φανῆναι, εἴπερ μηκέτι ἐπισκεψόμεθα σωφροσύνην: *Ion* 542B πολὺ γὰρ κάλλιον τὸ θεῖον νομίζεσθαι.—Τοῦτο τοίνυν τὸ κάλλιον ὑπάρχει σοι παρ' ἡμῖν, ὦ Ἴων, θεῖον εἶναι: X.*An.*ii 3.5 οἱ δ' ἔλεγον ὅτι περὶ σπονδῶν ἥκοιεν ἄνδρες οἵτινες ἱκανοὶ ἔσονται . . . ἀπαγγεῖλαι . . . . ὁ δὲ ἀπεκρίνατο· Ἀπαγγέλλετε τοίνυν αὐτῷ ('Well, then, tell him . . .'): Pl.*R.*358A,450D: X.*An.*vii 2.13: 5.3: 5.10: *Cyr.*vi 1.38.

In reported speech: X.*Cyr.*vi 3.17 εἰπόντος δὲ Κύρου ὅτι τούτων μὲν τοίνυν εἴη ἅλις . . . .

Certain varieties of logical τοίνυν deserve special notice:—

(2) In conclusions of formal syllogisms (rare, οὖν, οὐκοῦν, and ἄρα being normally used instead). Pl.*Chrm.*159D Φαίνεται . . . κατά γε τὸ σῶμα οὐ τὸ ἡσύχιον . . . κάλλιστον ὄν. ἦ γάρ;—Πάνυ γε.—Ἡ δέ γε σωφροσύνη καλόν τι ἦν;—Ναί.—Οὐ τοίνυν κατά γε τὸ σῶμα ἡ ἡσυχιότης ἂν . . . σωφρονέστερον εἴη, ἐπειδὴ καλὸν ἡ σωφροσύνη: *Sph.*238B,255B.

(3) Responding to an invitation to speak: the answerer either announces his intention of speaking, or plunges at once *in medias res.* Frequent in Plato, with whom the answerer often repeats a word from the preceding speech. Ar.*Nu.*429 Λέγε νῦν ἡμῖν ὅ τί σοι δρῶμεν . . .—Ὦ δέσποιναι δέομαι τοίνυν ὑμῶν . . . ('Well, ladies, what I want of you is . . .'): 961 τὴν σαυτοῦ φύσιν εἰπέ.—Λέξω τοίνυν . . . : *V.*1181 (λέγε λόγους) οἵους λέγομεν μάλιστα τοὺς κατ' οἰκίαν.—Ἐγῷδα τοίνυν τῶν γε πάνυ κατ' οἰκίαν ἐκεῖνον . . . (cf. 1205) : Pl.*Euthphr.*5D Λέγε δή, τί φῂς εἶναι τὸ ὅσιον . . .—Λέγω τοίνυν . . . : 12E Πειρῶ . . . διδάξαι . . . —Τοῦτο τοίνυν ἔμοιγε δοκεῖ: *Phd.*60D εἰπὲ τί χρὴ λέγειν.—Λέγε τοίνυν . . . τἀληθῆ: 89C καὶ ἐμὲ . . . παρακάλει . . .—Παρακαλῶ τοίνυν: 108E τὴν μέντοι ἰδέαν τῆς γῆς οἵαν πέπεισμαι εἶναι . . . οὐδέν με κωλύει λέγειν.—Ἀλλὰ . . . καὶ ταῦτα ἀρκεῖ.—Πέπεισμαι τοίνυν (picked up by πρῶτον μὲν τοίνυν . . . τοῦτο πέπεισμαι 109A): *Grg.*494D ἀποκρίνου μόνον.—Φημὶ τοίνυν . . . : *Prt.*318A ὅτι οὖν ἀποβήσεται, ἐάν σοι συνῇ, ἡδέως ἄν φησι πυθέσθαι . . .—Ὦ νεανίσκε, ἔσται τοίνυν σοι, ἐὰν ἐμοὶ συνῇς . . . ('Well, my

lad ...'): *Lg.*891D ἀλλ' ὅπῃ, πειρῶ φράζειν.—Ἔοικεν τοίνυν ἀηθεστέρων ἀπτέον εἶναι λόγων: X.*Mem.*i4.3 Λέξον ἡμῖν, ἔφη, τὰ ὀνόματα αὐτῶν.—Ἐπὶ μὲν τοίνυν ἐπῶν ποιήσει Ὅμηρον ἔγωγε μάλιστα τεθαύμακα: Pl.*La.*192B: *Smp.*173E,185E: *Chrm.*158E: *Prt.*342A,353C: *Grg.*463A: *R.*458C: *id. saep.*: X.*Cyr.*iii1.15: vi3.19: viii4.11: 4.13. Cf. E.*Ion*936,987 (Ἄκουε τοίνυν: Ar.*Pl.* 649: Pl.*Phd.*96A).

(The invitation to speak may be conveyed indirectly, as in Pl. *Prt.*318A above (cf. *R.*470A ἡδέως ἂν ἀκούσαιμι), instead of by a blunt imperative. The mere asking of a question might, in fact, be taken as implying an invitation to answer it: but I do not think that this use of τοίνυν is actually extended so as to include answers to straightforward direct questions. For example, in Pl.*Men.*77B εἰπὲ τί ἐστιν ἀρετή is answered by Δοκεῖ τοίνυν μοι ... ἀρετὴ εἶναι ...: but I doubt if τοίνυν would have been possible after a direct question (τί ἐστιν ἀρετή;) without the expression or clear implication of a command or invitation. Again, in S.*OT*1167 ('Well, he was ...') I believe that τοίνυν is conditioned by the command ('Speak!') implied in the threat of 1166: and that the particle would be unsuitable if 1167 formed a direct answer to the question in 1164. But I should not be surprised if a passage or two were found to the contrary. Certainly, inceptive-responsive καὶ μήν, which is used in much the same way as τοίνυν here, sometimes introduces the answer to a question, as in Pl.*Tht.*158C: see καὶ μήν, (5).)

(4) A rejoinder introduced by τοίνυν sometimes conveys a comment on, or criticism of, the previous speaker's words. S.*OT* 1067 Καὶ μὴν φρονοῦσά γ' εὖ τὰ λῷστά σοι λέγω.—Τὰ λῷστα τοίνυν ταῦτά μ' ἀλγύνει πάλαι ('Well, I am getting tired of your "thinking for the best"'): Ar.*Av.*511 'That's what the bird on the sceptre means'—Τουτὶ τοίνυν οὐκ ᾔδη 'γώ ('Well now, I never knew *that* before': cf. *Pax*615): *Nu.*1236 κἂν προσκαταθείην γ' ὥστ' ὀμόσαι τριώβολον.—Ἀπόλοιο τοίνυν ἕνεκ' ἀναιδείας ἔτι ('Well now, damnation take you for your shamelessness'): *Lys.*34 ἢ μηκέτ' εἶναι μήτε Πελοποννησίους— —Βέλτιστα τοίνυν μηκέτ' εἶναι νὴ Δία ('Well, that's the *best* that could happen'): Pl.*R.*358A Οὐ τοίνυν δοκεῖ, ἔφη, τοῖς πολλοῖς ('Well, that isn't what *most* people think'): *Sph.*242B Φοβοῦμαι

. . . *μὴ . . . μανικὸς εἶναι δόξω.—Ὡς τοίνυν ἔμοιγε μηδαμῇ δόξων μηδὲν πλημμελεῖν . . . θαρρῶν ἴθι τούτου γε ἕνεκα* (' Well, don't think that *I* shall criticize you ') : *Lg*.688D *ταῦτ' οὖν . . . πειράσομαι . . . δηλοῦν . . . .—Λόγῳ μὲν τοίνυν σε . . . ἐπαινεῖν ἐπαχθέστερον, ἔργῳ δὲ σφόδρα ἐπαινεσόμεθα.*

Especially *καλῶς τοίνυν*, etc., with or without ellipse of verb, conveying approval. Ar.*V*.856 *Οὗτος σὺ ποῖ θεῖς;—Ἐπὶ καδίσκους.—Μηδαμῶς. ἐγὼ γὰρ εἶχον τούσδε τοὺς ἀρυστίχους.—Κάλλιστα τοίνυν· πάντα γὰρ πάρεστι νῷν ὅσων δεόμεθα* (' Excellent, then '): *Pl*.1092 *Θάρρει, μὴ φοβοῦ. οὐ γὰρ βιάσεται.—Πάνυ καλῶς τοίνυν λέγεις*: 1190 *Παντ' ἀγαθὰ τοίνυν λέγεις*: Pl.*Chrm*.162E *πάνυ συγχωρῶ . . .—Καλῶς γε σὺ τοίνυν, ἦν δ' ἐγώ, ποιῶν*: *Cra*.433A . . . *εἰ μέμνησαι . . . .—Ἀλλὰ μέμνημαι.—Καλῶς τοίνυν* (' Very good, then ' : *Lg*.653C) : *Lg*.813A *Ἀληθῆ καὶ ταῦτα διείρηκας.—Ἀληθέστατα τοίνυν* (*τοίνυν* is certainly very curious here, and one would expect *μὲν οὖν*).

The use of *τοίνυν* in Ar.*V*.1141 is also curious : *ἔγνως γὰρ ἄν· νῦν δ' οὐχὶ γιγνώσκεις.—Ἐγώ; μὰ τὸν Δί' οὐ τοίνυν* (' Well, now, I don't ' : *οὔτοι νῦν γ'* Starkie : *οὐ ταυνῦν γ'* A. Palmer).

(5) *τοίνυν* at the opening of an account or narration announced in advance by the speaker or writer (' Well ') is particularly common in the minor works of Xenophon. Pl.*Phdr*.253D *ἀρετὴ δὲ τίς τοῦ ἀγαθοῦ ἢ κακοῦ κακία, οὐ διείπομεν, νῦν δὲ λεκτέον. ὁ μὲν τοίνυν αὐτοῖν* . . . : X.*Lac*.4.3 *ἐξηγήσομαι· αἱροῦνται τοίνυν* . . . : 9.3 *καὶ τοῦτο καλὸν μὴ παραλιπεῖν· ἐκεῖνος τοίνυν* . . . : Ar.*Pl*. 567 : Pl.*Lg*.739B,767B,810B,815B : X.*HG* vii 2.2 : *Lac*.5.1 : 11.2 : *Eq.Mag*.1.9 : 1.17 : 2.1 : 5.4 : *Eq*.3.1 : 4.3 : 5.1 : 7.1 : 9.2 : 10.6 : 12.1 : Isoc.v 99 : viii 75.

(6) Xenophon's occasional use of *τοίνυν* at the opening of a set speech may be compared with his similar use of *ἀλλά* (*q.v.* II.8). *An*.v 1.2 *ἐκ δὲ τούτου ξυνελθόντες ἐβουλεύοντο . . . ἀνέστη δὲ πρῶτος Λέων Θούριος καὶ ἔλεξεν ὧδε. Ἐγὼ μὲν τοίνυν, ἔφη, ὦ ἄνδρες, ἀπείρηκα* . . . : *Cyr*.vi 2.14 *ἐπεὶ δὲ συνῆλθον, ἔλεξε τοιάδε. Ἄνδρες σύμμαχοι, ἐγὼ τοίνυν ὑμᾶς συνεκάλεσα.* As these are the opening speeches of a debate, *τοίνυν* seems, as Kühner puts it, to represent the speech as arising out of the present situation : ' Well, gentlemen '.

Similarly, as Rosenberg remarks, *τοίνυν* is used at the opening of *δευτερολογίαι*: Lys.xviii: Is.xii: [D.]xxvi.

(7) *τοίνυν*, usually in association with *οὗτος*, is sometimes used by Plato to round off a long argument: 'Well, that is the conclusion to which we come'. *R.*397B *Ταῦτα τοίνυν, ἦν δ' ἐγώ, ἔλεγον τὰ δύο εἴδη τῆς λέξεως* (the topic propounded at 392D): 603A *Τοῦτο τοίνυν διομολογήσασθαι βουλόμενος ἔλεγον ὅτι* ... ('Well, that is what I meant': in the formal argument which precedes, the steps are made by *οὐκοῦν* and *ἄρα*): 438D: *Phd.* 83E: *Sph.*236C: *Lg.*822D.

II. Transitional. This use merges imperceptibly into the logical, and no sharp line can be drawn between I and II. In continuous speech transitional *τοίνυν* is particularly common in Lysias, Isaeus, and Demosthenes (Schepe, p. 13).

(1) Marking a fresh step in the march of thought (or action).

(i) Dialogue. A.*Pr.*760 'You would like Zeus to fall?'—'Certainly'.—*Ὡς τοίνυν ὄντων τῶνδέ σοι μαθεῖν πάρα* ('Well, he *will* fall'): *Supp.*459 'I have girdles'.—'Naturally'.—*Ἐκ τῶνδε τοίνυν, ἴσθι, μηχανὴ καλή*: Ar.*Nu.*255 'You would like to talk to the Clouds?'—'Very much.'—*Κάθιζε τοίνυν ἐπὶ τὸν ἱερὸν σκίμποδα.—Ἰδοὺ κάθημαι.—Τουτονὶ τοίνυν λαβὲ τὸν στέφανον* ('Now take this crown': the first *τοίνυν* is logical, 'then', the second introduces the next stage in the hocus-pocus: an instructive juxtaposition of two shades of meaning): Pl.*Phd.* 59B *πάντες οἱ παρόντες . . . οὕτω διεκείμεθα . . . εἷς δὲ ἡμῶν καὶ διαφερόντως, Ἀπολλόδωρος—οἶσθα γάρ που τὸν ἄνδρα . . . .—Πῶς γὰρ οὔ;—Ἐκεῖνός τε τοίνυν παντάπασιν οὕτως εἶχεν, καὶ αὐτὸς . . . καὶ οἱ ἄλλοι* ('Well, *he* was in that state . . .'): *R.*394D, 572D (*bis*): *Lg.*693E.

(ii) Continuous speech. E.*El.*1030 *τούτων ἕκατι παῖδ' ἐμὴν διώλεσεν. ἐπὶ τοῖσδε τοίνυν καίπερ ἠδικημένη οὐκ ἠγριώμην* ('Well': a good example of what a bad rendering of *τοίνυν* 'therefore' sometimes is): Hdt.vii 5.1 *ἡ βασιληίη ἀνέχωρησε ἐς . . . Ξέρξην. ὁ τοίνυν Ξέρξης* . . .: Pl.*Lg.*888B 'There are always atheists. *τόδε τοίνυν σοι, παραγεγονὼς αὐτῶν πολλοῖσι, φράζοιμ' ἄν*' ('Well, I've met many of them, and this is what

I would say to you'): Hdt.vii 9β2: 50.2: 50.3: 50.4: 139.2: X.*Cyr*.i 1.2.

In oratory, resuming the thread of a speech after the recitation of evidence, laws, or other documents. And.i 15 *δευτέρα τοίνυν μήνυσις ἐγένετο*: Lys.xvi 14,15,18: Is.ii 6: D.l 14: *et saep.*

(2) Introducing a fresh item in a series: a new example or a new argument. *τοίνυν* is, on the whole, rather more static here ('further', 'again'), rather more dynamic ('well', 'now') in (1): but the point cannot be pressed.

(i) Dialogue. Ar.*V*.578,698: *Pl*.563 (in all three passages adding a new point, after an interpellation by another speaker): Pl.*R*.514B *ἰδὲ* . . . .—*'Ορῶ, ἔφη.—"Ορα τοίνυν παρὰ τοῦτο τὸ τειχίον* ('And now see . . .'): *Hp.Ma*.288C "*Εἶεν*", *φήσει δή· "τί δὲ λύρα καλή; οὐ καλόν;" φῶμεν, ὦ 'Ιππία;—Ναί.—'Ερεῖ τοίνυν μετὰ τοῦτ' ἐκεῖνος . . . "τί δὲ χύτρα καλή;"* *Tht*.147E *Τὸν ἀριθμὸν πάντα δίχα διελάβομεν· τὸν μὲν δυνάμενον . . . ἰσόπλευρον προσείπομεν.—Καὶ εὖ γε.—Τὸν τοίνυν μεταξὺ τούτου . . . προμήκη ἀριθμὸν ἐκαλέσαμεν*: *R*.564E *ἐν μὲν γάρ που τὸ τοιοῦτον γένος ἐν αὐτῇ ἐμφύεται . . . 'Άλλο τοίνυν τοιόνδε ἀεὶ ἀποκρίνεται ἐκ τοῦ πλήθους.*

(ii) Continuous speech. Hp.*Art*.57 *οὐδ' ὑγιαίνοντες δύνανται κατὰ τὴν ἰγνύην ἐκτανύειν τὸ ἄρθρον . . .· οὐ τοίνυν οὐδὲ ξυγκάμπτειν δύνανται* ('Nor, again'): Hdt.ii 142 *ἐν μυρίοισί τε ἔτεσι καὶ χιλίοισι καὶ πρὸς τριηκοσίοισί τε καὶ τεσσεράκοντα ἔλεγον θεὸν ἀνθρωποειδέα οὐδένα γενέσθαι . . . . ἐν τοίνυν τούτῳ τῷ χρόνῳ τετράκις ἔλεγον ἐξ ἠθέων τὸν ἥλιον ἀνατεῖλαι*: Pl. *Phdr*.231E *εἰ τοίνυν τὸν νόμον καθεστηκότα δέδοικας* ('If, again . . .': opening a new paragraph): *Prt*.319D 'The conduct of Athenian politics implies the view that political wisdom cannot be taught. *μὴ τοίνυν ὅτι τὸ κοινὸν τῆς πόλεως οὕτως ἔχει, ἀλλ' ἰδίᾳ* . . .': *R*.362B *πρῶτον μὲν ἄρχειν ἐν τῇ πόλει . . . ἔπειτα γαμεῖν ὁπόθεν ἂν βούληται . . .· εἰς ἀγῶνας τοίνυν ἰόντα* . . .: X.*Mem*.i 4.13 (after describing the physical benefits conferred by Providence) *οὐ τοίνυν μόνον ἤρκεσε τῷ θεῷ τοῦ σώματος ἐπιμεληθῆναι, ἀλλὰ . . . καὶ τὴν ψυχὴν κρατίστην τῷ ἀνθρώπῳ ἐνέφυσε*: Is viii 15 *ἡμεῖς τοίνυν καὶ ἄλλα τεκμήρια πρὸς τούτοις ἔχομεν εἰπεῖν*: Hyp.*Epit*.19 'The battle was a glorious one. *ἄξιον τοίνυν συλλογίσασθαι καὶ τί ἂν συμβῆναι νομίζοιμεν μὴ κατὰ τρόπον τούτων ἀγωνισαμένων'*: X.*Vect.*4.49: Lys.i 45: iii 37: xiii 33: Isoc.iv 38,41,47: Lycurg.122.

ἔτι τοίνυν. Hp.*VM*19: Pl.*Cri.*52C: *Phd.*109A: *Tht.*178A: *Smp.*188B: *R.*491C: *Lg.*633B: *id. saep.*: X.*An.*v 1.8: *Cyr.*i 1.2: Aen.Tact.10.25: Lys.iii 35: Isoc.v 66: vi 29: Is.i 16,22,27.

τοίνυν ... ἔτι. Pl.*Plt.*281C *Πρὸς τοίνυν ταύταις ἔτι ...*: *Lg.* 681D *Τρίτον τοίνυν εἴπωμεν ἔτι πολιτείας σχῆμα γιγνόμενον.*

(3) Marking the transition from the enunciation of a general proposition to the consideration of a particular instance of it. Pl.*Cra.*399B 'Various transformations occur in words'.—*Ἀληθῆ λέγεις.—Τούτων τοίνυν ἓν καὶ τὸ τῶν ἀνθρώπων ὄνομα πέπονθεν* (cf. 410A): X.*Ages.*1.10 *πῶς ἄν τις σαφέστερον ἐπιδείξειεν ὡς ἐστρατήγησεν ἢ εἰ αὐτὰ διηγήσαιτο ἃ ἔπραξεν; ἐν τοίνυν τῇ Ἀσίᾳ ἥδε πρώτη πρᾶξις ἐγένετο* (group perhaps under I.5): *Ages.*7.5.

Not infrequently, in such cases, *τοίνυν* introduces what is virtually a minor premise, the preceding general proposition being the major premise, while the conclusion is left to the imagination. Isoc.iii 15 '"Equal rewards for all" is a bad political principle. *αἱ μὲν τοίνυν ὀλιγαρχίαι καὶ δημοκρατίαι τὰς ἰσότητας τοῖς μετέχουσι τῶν πολιτειῶν ζητοῦσι ... αἱ δὲ μοναρχίαι πλεῖστον μὲν νέμουσι τῷ βελτίστῳ ...*' (here the major premise is repeated in a different form in §16 *καίτοι τίς οὐκ ἂν δέξαιτο ... τοιαύτης πολιτείας μετέχειν, ἐν ᾗ ...*): iv 103 'Political hegemony is to be judged by its effects on the ruled. *ἐπὶ τοίνυν τῆς ἡμετέρας ἡγεμονίας ...*': X.*Mem.*i 2.29: D.xix 52,119. In Pl.*R.*368E the minor premise precedes, and *τοίνυν* introduces the major, the conclusion being introduced by *οὖν*.

(4) In other cases, the general proposition is implied from a particular instance of its application. *τοίνυν* is then almost invariably associated with *οὗτος, τοιοῦτος, οὕτως*, which emphasize the second, crucial, application. This use is closely similar to that of *μέντοι* noticed on pp. 408–9. Pl.*Chrm.*156D 'Doctors often have to treat the whole body in order to cure a particular part'. (This implies the general proposition that the health of the part depends on the health of the whole.)—'Yes.'—*Τοιοῦτον*

τοίνυν ἐστὶν . . . καὶ τὸ ταύτης τῆς ἐπῳδῆς ('Well, it is just the same with this charm'): *Euthphr*.12C: *Plt*.294E.

In other cases, again, a general proposition is formulated, or implied, and followed, first by a preliminary instance of its application, and then by the crucial instance introduced by τοίνυν. Pl. *Smp*.205D 'We call the species (sexual passion) by the name of the genus (love)'. A parallel instance, that of ποίησις, is given. 'Οὕτω τοίνυν καὶ περὶ τὸν ἔρωτα' ('Well, it is the same in the case of love'): *Grg*.482A 'Men universally accept what is said by those they love. You do so yourself, Callicles, ὥστε . . . ἴσως εἴποις ἂν . . . ὅτι εἰ μή τις παύσει τὰ σὰ παιδικὰ τούτων τῶν λόγων, οὐδὲ σὺ παύσῃ ποτὲ ταῦτα λέγων. νόμιζε τοίνυν καὶ παρ' ἐμοῦ χρῆναι ἕτερα τοιαῦτα ἀκούειν': *Ly*.217E.

(5) τοίνυν, like καὶ μήν, marks a fresh beginning after a strong stop. It rarely follows a light stop: but cf. Pl.*Ap*.33E πάρεισιν αὐτῶν πολλοὶ . . ., πρῶτον μὲν Κρίτων οὑτοσὶ . . . ἔπειτα Λυσανίας . . ., ἔτι δ' Ἀντιφῶν . . . , ἄλλοι τοίνυν οὗτοι: X.*An*.vii 6.19 συνεπόμνυμι μηδὲ ἃ οἱ ἄλλοι στρατηγοὶ ἔλαβον εἰληφέναι, μὴ τοίνυν μηδὲ ὅσα τῶν λοχαγῶν ἔνιοι.

(6) Apodotic. The occasional apodotic use of τοίνυν, analogous to the commoner apodotic οὖν, springs from the substitution of paratactic for hypotactic expression in the course of a long sentence whose construction is beginning to get out of hand. We can speak, without exaggeration, of anacoluthon here. And.iii 30 Συρακούσιοι δ' ὅτε ἦλθον ἡμῶν δεόμενοι . . ., ἡμεῖς τοίνυν εἰλόμεθα: D.xviii 249 καὶ μετὰ ταῦτα συστάντων . . ., ἐν τοίνυν τούτοις πᾶσι . . .: xlvii 64 ἐκτίνοντος δέ μου τῷ Θεοφήμῳ . . . ἐπειδὴ ἐξέτινον . . ., λαβὼν τοίνυν παρ' ἐμοῦ . . . .

Cf. the following Platonic passages, where a second speaker's answer intervenes: *Plt*.275D ἦν γὰρ ἔφαμεν αὐτεπιτακτικὴν μὲν εἶναι τέχνην . . .—μέμνησαι γάρ;—Ναί.—Ταύτης τοίνυν πῃ διημαρτάνομεν: *R*.562B: *Tht*.207B.

III. τοίνυν combined with other particles.

(1) καὶ τοίνυν, καὶ . . . τοίνυν ('and further'), in Plato almost confined to the later works: as Rosenberg remarks, not found in the orators.

(i) *καὶ τοίνυν*. Pl.*Sph.*234A *καὶ γὰρ ζῴων αὐτὸν εἶπες ποιητήν.—Φημί, καὶ πρός γε θαλάττης καὶ γῆς . . .· καὶ τοίνυν καὶ ταχὺ ποιήσας αὐτῶν ἕκαστα πάνυ σμικροῦ νομίσματος ἀποδίδοται*: *Plt.*280C *τὴν μὲν διετέμομεν . . . .—Μανθάνω.—Καὶ μὴν τὴν . . . .—Πάνυ μὲν οὖν.—Καὶ τοίνυν τὴν . . .*: X.*Cyr.*i 3.16 *ὁ διδάσκαλός με . . . καθίστη δικάζειν. καὶ τοίνυν, φάναι, ἐπὶ μιᾷ ποτε δίκῃ πληγὰς ἔλαβον*: Pl.*Sph.*245D: *Plt.*299B: *Lg.*678E,782D,842A: X.*HG* vi 1.6: *Cyr.* i 1.5: 6.20: ii 2.25: iii 3.41: iv 2.35: v 1.4: *Hier.*1.38.

(ii) *καὶ . . . τοίνυν*. Ar.*Pax* 543 *Ἴθι νῦν ἄθρει οἷον πρὸς ἀλλήλας λαλοῦσιν αἱ πόλεις διαλλαγεῖσαι . . . .—Καὶ τῶνδε τοίνυν τῶν θεωμένων σκόπει τὰ πρόσωφ', ἵνα γνῷς τὰς τέχνας* ('Yes, and look at the faces of the *audience*'): *Pl.*989: Pl.*Chrm.*165D *Εἰ τοίνυν με, ἔφην, ἔροιο σύ . . . εἴποιμ' ἂν ὅτι . . . .—Ἀποδέχομαι.—Καὶ εἰ τοίνυν με ἔροιο . . .*: X.*HG* vi 1.10 *καὶ μὴν Βοιωτοί γε καὶ οἱ ἄλλοι πάντες ὅσοι Λακεδαιμονίοις πολεμοῦντες ὑπάρχουσί μοι σύμμαχοι· καὶ ἀκολουθεῖν τοίνυν ἀξιοῦσιν ἐμοί, ἂν μόνον ἀπὸ Λακεδαιμονίων ἐλευθερῶ αὐτούς*: Pl.*Tht.*194A: *R.*489B: X.*Cyr.* i 1.2: ii 2.24: Arist.*Pol.*1287a17. (In Pl.*R.*424C it is more natural to take *τοίνυν* as the connective and *καί* closely with *ἐμέ*, 'me too': *ὥς φησί τε Δάμων καὶ ἐγὼ πείθομαι.—Καὶ ἐμὲ τοίνυν . . . θὲς τῶν πεπεισμένων*: cf.*Grg.*516B: *R.*450A,509B: *Phlb.*15C,64B.)

Occasionally in the middle of a sentence, after a weak stop. X.*HG* vii 4.3 *ἐκλεξάμενος . . ., καὶ συνθέμενος τοίνυν . . .*: *Oec.*5.2 *πρῶτον μὲν γὰρ ἀφ' ὧν ζῶσιν οἱ ἄνθρωποι, ταῦτα ἡ γῆ φέρει ἐργαζομένοις, καὶ ἀφ' ὧν τοίνυν ἡδυπαθοῦσι, προσεπιφέρει*: *Eq. Mag.*7.3: 7.6: Diph.*Fr.*55.1 (probably).

(2) *δὴ τοίνυν* (except for Ar.*Fr.*535 *φέρε δὴ τοίνυν*, Plato only,[1] almost entirely in his later work). Pl.*Phlb.*33A *Ἄγε δὴ τοίνυν*: *Lg.*707E *Λέγε δὴ τοίνυν τὸ τούτοις ἑξῆς*: 712C *Φέρε δὴ τοίνυν*: 817E *Ἔτι δὴ τοίνυν* (*Phlb.*51E): *R.*588D: *Lg.*803B,895C.

The reverse order, *τοίνυν δή*, is doubtful. In Pl.*Grg.*459A the MSS. vary between *Ἔλεγές τοι νυνδή*, *Ἔλεγες τοίνυν δή*, and *Ἔλεγες τοίνυν νῦν δή* (*F*): the asyndeton of the first is surely impossible in this passage of formal reasoning: I believe *F*'s reading to be correct (or *τοίνυν νυνδή*), and should be inclined to read *Τὰ τοίνυν* ⟨*νυν*⟩*δὴ λεχθέντα* in *Lg.*718D (*C.R.*xlvii(1933)216).

[1] I exclude the juxtaposition *καὶ δὴ τοίνυν*: Ar.*Av.*550: Gorg.*Fr.*11a.7,11.

(3) Other combinations. These have, on the whole, very little significance. μὲν τοίνυν occurs often in Plato (e.g. *R.*536D: *Grg.*473D: *Men.*71D: *Phlb.*41A: *Lg.*643A. Des Places observes that Plato prefers μὲν οὖν in continuous speech, μὲν τοίνυν in dialogue, which accords with his general use of οὖν and τοίνυν). But the special considerations which made it worth while to investigate transitional μὲν οὖν are not present here, and I cannot agree with des Places that μὲν τοίνυν 'mérite une étude spéciale'. Nor is there any significance in the following: Pl. *Lg.*666C Εἰς μέν γε τὸ προάγειν τοίνυν αὐτούς: 816B πολλὰ μὲν δὴ τοίνυν ἄλλα . . . τούτων δὲ ἓν καὶ τὸ . . . . In Ar.*Av.*481 it is not quite clear whether δὲ . . . τοίνυν means 'and further', like καὶ . . . τοίνυν: or whether the meaning is 'And that the gods, then, . . .': Ὡς δ' οὐχὶ θεοὶ τοίνυν ἦρχον τῶν ἀνθρώπων τὸ παλαιὸν . . . πόλλ' ἐστὶ τεκμήρια τούτων. In Pl.*Epin.*979E μηδέ seems to go closely with σφώ: ἀλλ' ὅμως μὴ ἀποκάμῃς λέγων ὃ φῄς.—Ναί, μηδὲ σφὼ τοίνυν ἀκούοντε. Ar.*Pl.*1157 is more deserving of notice: τί οὖν Ἑρμῆν παλιγκάπηλον ἡμᾶς δεῖ τρέφειν;—Ἀλλὰ δόλιον τοίνυν ('Well, as Hermes the god of guile, then'). In Pl.*Phdr.*243D γε goes closely with τοῦτον: Τοῦτόν γε τοίνυν ἔγωγε αἰσχυνόμενος . . . (cf. Ar.*Ec.*105). In *Tht.*210B, *B* reads Ἐὰν οὖν τοίνυν (Ἐὰν τοίνυν *cett.*): clearly impossible.

IV. Position. τοίνυν is not often placed later than second word in the sentence, though Plato allows himself considerable licence in this respect. Most of the exceptions (as in the case of other particles) are clearly traceable to a desire to avoid separating words which form a logical unity. Other postponements are caused by the combining of τοίνυν with other particles (see III *passim*).

S.*OC*404 Τούτου χάριν τοίνυν: Ar.*Th.*157 Ὅταν σατύρους τοίνυν ποιῇς: *Pl.*863 Νὴ Δία καλῶς τοίνυν ποιῶν ἀπόλλυται (after oath: cf. *Ec.*339: Pl.*Tht.*207E): *Pax* 1023 is corrupt: Alex.*Fr.* 143.1 ἥξω φέρουσα συμβολὰς τοίνυν ἅμα: Pl.*Euthphr.*12C (after article and another word: 5 other examples in Kugler): *Ap.*26B (after preposition and another word: 9 other examples in Kugler: contrast *Lg.*800C Ἐν τοίνυν τοῖς . . .): *Plt.*303E (after preposition, article, and another word: *Sph.*226C: *R.*459D: *Lg.*907D): *Phd.* 59B (after a word and τε: 4 other examples in Kugler): *Prt.*

318A Ὦ νεανίσκε, ἔσται τοίνυν σοι: *Tht.*145E Τοῦτ' αὐτὸ τοίνυν (*Plt.*292C): *Phlb.*20C Μίκρ' ἄττα τοίνυν: *Lg.*821C Ταῦτ' ἔστι τοίνυν: 867C Πάλιν ἐπανελθόντες τοίνυν: *Sph.*225A Οὐκ ἀπὸ τρόπου τοίνυν: *Plt.*294E Καὶ τὸν νομοθέτην τοίνυν (*R.*509B): *R.*523C Ὡς ἐγγύθεν τοίνυν ὁρωμένους λέγοντός μου διανοοῦ: D.xliv 52 τὸ μετὰ ταῦτα τοίνυν: Pl.*Chrm.*162E: *R.*509C: *Phlb.*65B: *Lg.* 664B,812B,900D.

The order in Pl.*Lg.*715E is remarkable: "Ἄνδρες" τοίνυν φῶμεν πρὸς αὐτούς: cf.772E.

Where τοίνυν follows μέν, the particles are usually juxtaposed. But Plato separates them in *Ly.*214C, *La.*198C, *R.*535A, *Hp.Mi.* 365C, *Lg.*666C (μέν γε . . . τοίνυν): des Places, p. 314. For examples in the Apollodorus speeches attributed to Demosthenes, see Introd. *ad fin.*

ADDENDA AND CORRIGENDA

p. 27. (3). Neil (on Ar.*Eq*.780), citing *Lys*.427, is another supporter of the view that ἀλλ' ἤ originated in ἄλλο ἤ. In *Ra*.442–3 he places the question-mark (rightly, I am sure) after στρώμασιν: the question is equivalent to a negative statement.

p. 46. (3). ἆρα expecting a positive answer. Pearson (on E.*Hel*.256) compares D.lv 15. *Hel*.256 is differentiated by the strength of the expression τέρας from the other examples of this use, in which the question is couched in terms of a studious moderation which commands the assent of all. 'Am I a miracle?', expecting the answer 'yes', would be equally unnatural in English. 257–9 are *versus suspecti*. Perhaps 256, as well as they, is also an interpolation, inserted to lead up to τέρας in 260, and 256 is a statement, not a question (cf. p. 48, n. 1).

p. 62. III. 2. Add S.*OT*220 ('I was a stranger to the affair (and have remained a stranger to it), for . . .': for other interpretations of γάρ here, see Jebb *ad loc.*, and Pearson in *C.Q.*xi 62): E.*IT*1015 (supply, with Paley, after εἰσιδεῖν, 'and I will make the attempt': but many editors suppose a lacuna before 1015): *Hel*.497 (Pearson finds difficulty in γάρ here, and has proposed a transposition of lines: I find no difficulty whatever, if the lines are sympathetically read. Reluctant at first to credit the accumulated coincidences, Menelaus ends up with a bewildered 'I don't know what to make of it!' This admission of utter perplexity leads him naturally to consider anew the possibility that the coincidences may be credible after all).

p. 65. (6). In E.*Hel*.257–60, if the text is sound, both γάρ-sentences explain 256 (so Paley: the second γάρ is not, as Pearson says, 'impossible': but the text is doubtful). In A.*Supp*.202–3 μέμνησο δ' εἴκειν· χρεῖος εἶ ξένη φυγάς. θρασυστομεῖν γὰρ οὐ πρέπει τοὺς ἥσσονας there are, logically speaking, two γάρ clauses, though the first is introduced asyndetically; both give the reason, but in slightly different forms, for μέμνησο εἴκειν.

p. 69. Second paragraph. In Tragedy, a vocative followed by a γάρ clause is most often used immediately on the arrival of the person addressed. So in S.*OC*891: there, as in E.*Rh*.608, there cannot be any forward reference.

p. 71. (v). In E.*IA*804 England regards γάρ as 'proleptic' and as resumed by οὖν in 810. But this produces an awkward asyndeton at 804, the interval between γάρ and οὖν is wide, and there is little trace of anticipatory γάρ in drama. The sequence of thought is, I think: 'Call Agamemnon. For the circumstances of each individual are different, and I should like to tell him of mine.'

p. 92. (i). In A.*Pr*.152 the wish may refer to 143 φρουρὰν ἄζηλον ὀχήσω; the Scholiast, however, points out that τὰ πρὶν πελώρια in 151 refers to the Titans, and Prof. Thomson in his edition takes Prometheus' wish to mean 'Would I were in Hades, like the Titans'. If this is right, the passage should be classified under (iii) below: but we should perhaps expect ἐμέ rather than με.

p. 149. 2. i. In Hom.*A*299 ἐπεί μ' ἀφέλεσθέ γε δόντες Leaf takes γε as prepositive. This is possible, but ἐπεί . . . γε (p. 142) is an alternative explanation. Dr. Sheppard takes exception to the position of γε in S.*OT*65 (ὥστ' οὐχ ὕπνῳ γ' εὕδοντά μ' ἐξεγείρετε). But ὕπνῳ εὕδοντα is a unified phrase (cf. *Aj*.812) into which γε is inserted.

p. 152. (2) (i). In general, for τοί (καίτοι, μέντοι) γε, with references to earlier authorities, see Neil, *Knights*, p. 194.

p. 155. 4. i. Dobree's δέ γε in E.*Ion*1316 is, I think, improbable.

p. 158. In E.*Med*.608 W. M. Edwards rightly suggests that καί is adverbial: 'I am a curse, if it comes to that, to your house too'.

p. 162. Note 3. δέ in A.*Ch*.986 does not couple single words. If it is kept (τ' Hermann), put a colon after οὖν, with Tucker.

p. 166. (2). Dr. Sheppard, in his note on *OT*379, opposes Jebb's view that δέ means 'nay' here, and holds that both here and in *OC*1443 δέ connects with the speaker's previous words. That method of connexion is sometimes employed (Introd.II.7), but I do not think it is to be assumed here. In S.*Tr*.729 and *OC*395 Sheppard says that δέ could be rendered 'Yes, but'. That is true, but δέ is stronger in those passages than it usually is.

p. 173. 2. iii. In Hom.*N*260 ἔρχομαι . . . ἔγχος . . . οἰσόμενος . . .. δούρατα δ' αἴ κ' ἐθέλησθα, καὶ ἓν καὶ εἴκοσι δήεις ἑσταότ' ἐν κλισίῃ there is nothing unnatural in the use of δέ. ('I am going to get a spear'.—'And you will find plenty'. Leaf suggests that δ' is for δή, or that γ' (*C*) should be read.)

p. 182. Top. Ebeling cites Hom.*Θ*20: but we may either put the colon after κρεμάσαντες (Leaf) or read τ' with *C* (Monro and Allen).

p. 187. A. 5. Pl.*Smp*.199A is different: οὐκ ᾔδη ἄρα τὸν τρόπον τοῦ ἐπαίνου, οὐ δ' εἰδὼς ὑμῖν ὡμολόγησα . . . ('I did not know . . . and it was in this ignorance that I agreed . . .', δέ having no adversative force, and οὐ going closely with εἰδώς: but we should perhaps read οὐδ' with Stallbaum, 'Nor did I in knowledge of it agree . . .').

p. 190. οὐδέ is not connective in Pl.*R*498D μὴ διάβαλλε . . . ἐμὲ καὶ Θρασύμαχον ἄρτι φίλους γεγονότας, οὐδὲ πρὸ τοῦ ἐχθροὺς ὄντας ('not before either') or in D.xviii43 πάντ' ἐκεῖνος ἦν αὐτοῖς· οὐδὲ φωνὴν ἤκουον εἴ τις ἄλλο τι βούλοιτο λέγειν ('not even'). In Th.i10.4 I think the sense is 'without even having covered-in ships', and that ἐφέλκεσθαι is right in i42.3 (so that the negative answers καὶ οὐκ ἄξιον κτλ.).

p. 191. 1. i. This use of οὐδέ is implied in Headlam's (to my mind very improbable) emendation of A.*Ag*.168, οὖλός τις: with the MSS. οὐδ' ὅστις (and Ahrens's generally accepted οὐδὲ λέξεται) each οὐδέ exercises its force independently, 'not even he who was great shall even be spoken of': this is distinct from the duplication of οὐδέ illustrated on p. 197 (ii). (Or perhaps the first οὐδέ means 'nor'.) οὐδέ in A.*Eu*.665 might be explained as a balancing adversative: πέλας μάρτυς πάρεστι παῖς 'Ολυμπίου Διός, οὐδ' ἐν σκότοισι νηδύος τεθραμμένη.

p. 194. II. 1. But there are certain passages in which οὐδέ seems to add a negative idea to a *positive* one: A.*Supp*.958 καὶ δώματ' ἐστὶ πολλὰ μὲν τὰ δήμια, δεδωμάτωμαι δ' οὐδ' ἐγὼ σμικρᾷ χερί: *Ag*.1523: S.*OT*325 (p. 195). Add Pl.*Phd*.108A ('For, had it been simple, it would also have needed no guide': οὐδέν Stob.): D.xx94 ('For, had he done so, you, on your side, would not have been persuaded . . .': οὐδὲ ὑμεῖς almost = ὑμεῖς αὖ οὐ: οὐ γάρ, for οὐδὲ γάρ, *AF*). In these two passages (which might also have been cited for γάρ = 'for otherwise') the preceding negatives have nothing to do with the case.

p. 197. III. I have not seen the possibility of this sense of οὐδέ discussed anywhere. I find that Wecklein renders οὐδέ 'gar nicht' in E.*El*.981, comparing A.*Eu*.228, S.*Ant*.731: but in fact all three passages should be otherwise explained.

p. 198. Hdt.viii25.2. Here οὐδέ seems to contrast what is untrue with what *is* true: cf. καί IIc.7, pp. 321–2. Cf. Pl.*Phdr*.232B τοὺς δὲ μὴ ἐρῶντας οὐδ' αἰτιᾶσθαι διὰ τὴν συνουσίαν ἐπιχειροῦσιν ('They *don't* attempt to blame the non-lover, whereas they *do* blame the lover'). It is possible, however, that οὐδέ goes with ἐπιχειροῦσιν, in spite of the order (cf. V, p. 199): 'they do not even *attempt* to blame'.

p. 253. (v). If Reiske's δὴ σῇ for τῇ σῇ is right in E.*Andr*.334, δή has the force of καὶ δή.

p. 255. (2). In E.*Ph*.337 σὲ δ', ὦ τέκνον, καὶ γάμοισι δὴ κλύω ζυγέντα, καί is deleted by Hermann on metrical grounds but kept by Wilamowitz (*Griechische Verskunst*, p. 572).

p. 276. (3). In A.*Supp*.207–10 Hermann's transposition makes ἴδοιτο δῆτα follow immediately after ἴδοι (cf. 216): Tucker argues, perhaps rightly, that the echo is not absolutely necessary: but in 359, which he cites, there is an echo, of ἄνατον.

p. 280. *Ἦ.* As ἦ is not common in Aristophanes, and as I have already cited the great majority of the instances in him, I am tempted to add the remainder from Todd's Index, particularly since his examples are not classified. (1) ἦ *simplex*. (i) Affirmative. *Ach*.543: *Eq*.1290: *V*.478: *Pax*568,910: *Lys*.256: *Ec*.145: *Fr*.333. (ii) Interrogative. *Nu*.483: *Av*.292: *Fr*.346 (*add*. Bergk): 362. (2) ἦ που. *Ra*.803,814: *Fr*.79. I will also take the opportunity to add here: ἀλλ' ἦ: *Fr*.125,607: ἦ μήν: *Fr*.198.3.

p. 288. (θην). In Pi.*Fr*.192(203).1 Schroeder reads ἄνδρες θήν τινες ἀκκιζόμενοι [Σκύθαι] νεκρὸν ἵππον στυγέοισι λόγῳ κείμενον ἐν φάει (ἄνδρεθάν τινὲς *vel* ἄνδρες τινὲς *codd*.).

p. 290. (1). In A.*Pers*.683 τίνα πόλις πονεῖ πόνον; στένει, κέκοπται, καὶ χαράσσεται πέδον it is possible that πέδον is not the subject of all three verbs. Two explanations have been offered for A.*Ag*.899: (1) that καί links two distinct series of comparisons: (2) that φανεῖσαν παρ' ἐλπίδα applies to μονογενὲς τέκνον as well as to γῆν. (2) is preferable, but there is something to be said for Blomfield's γαῖαν.

p. 291. (4). Where καί is used in anaphora, there is always a fairly marked contrast between the two ideas, whereas δέ in anaphora regularly conveys the emphasis of accumulation. Hence ἐκεῖνος . . . κἀκεῖνος at Ar.*Ra*.788–90 cannot both refer to Sophocles.

p. 299. (6). Pearson on E.*Ph*.497 draws attention to Wyse's valuable note on Is.v25. Wyse combats the view that εἰ καί is never equivalent to καὶ εἰ. εἰ καί, he says, is often used to 'emphasize the general validity of the apodosis by selecting an extreme case', meaning, not 'although (as a matter of fact)', but 'even if'. In support of this thesis, he quotes a number of passages from the orators in which the meaning is 'even if'. In many of them, however, there can be no 'extreme case', as only two possibilities are envisaged: and Wyse has, I think, obscured the true line of division, which I have given at the opening of (6). On the other hand, I entirely agree with him that εἰ καί is very often used for καὶ εἰ. Wyse points out that Isocrates avoided καὶ εἰ on grounds of euphony: there is only one case in his works, and that in a doubtful speech (xxiii), whereas εἰ καί is commoner in Isocrates than in all the other orators put together. Demosthenes 'does not like καὶ εἰ (a feeling shared by Aeschines), but is not so pedantical as to deny himself the use of it'. He often avoids it by using κἂν εἰ (Wyse's examples of which should be added to mine on p. 302). 'The absence of καὶ εἰ in Isaeus, Lycurgus, and Dinarchus is probably an accident.'

p. 306. First line. In *R*.571C the sense required is 'And which desires do you *mean*?'. Perhaps we should read τίνας δὲ καὶ λέγεις . . .;

p. 308. 9. ii. See van Leeuwen on Ar.*Nu*.624. I add from his list the following doubtful examples: Ar.*Nu*.409: *Pax*890 (κᾆτ' ἀγαγεῖν Herwerden): *Av*.1455.

p. 320. (4). In Hom.γ196 ὡς ἀγαθὸν καὶ παῖδα καταφθιμένοιο λιπέσθαι ἀνδρός the meaning may be 'a son as well as wealth' (Bothe).

p. 320. (5). Pearson regards E.*Heracl*.660, 745, and 884 as similar to Pl.*R*.573D τοῦτο σὺ καὶ ἐμοὶ ἐρεῖς ('epitatic').

p. 323. II *ad fin.* I believe that the much disputed passage Arist. *Po*.1447b22 belongs here: τὸν μὲν ("Ομηρον) ποιητὴν δίκαιον καλεῖν, τὸν δὲ ('Εμπεδοκλέα) φυσιολόγον μᾶλλον ἢ ποιητήν· ὁμοίως δὲ κἂν εἴ τις ἅπαντα τὰ μέτρα μιγνύων ποιοῖτο τὴν μίμησιν, καθάπερ Χαιρήμων . . ., καὶ ποιητὴν προσαγορευτέον. (Empedocles is *not* to be called a poet in virtue of his consistent metre: Chaeremon *is* to be called a poet in spite of his inconsistent metre: καί stresses προσαγορευτέον.) In Pl.*Cra*.436E καί may be similarly explained: 'Consistency (συμφωνεῖν) in nomenclature does not prove that the names are correct. οὐ μέντοι ἀλλὰ θαυμάζοιμ' ἂν εἰ καὶ τὰ ὀνόματα συμφωνεῖ αὐτὰ αὑτοῖς' ('But I should be surprised if the names actually are [as supposed above (436C)] consistent': καί goes closely with συμφωνεῖ).

p. 324. (1). Since καί . . . καί couple disparate ideas, A.*Ag*.677 καὶ ζῶντα καὶ βλέποντα can hardly be right. In E.*Hel*.1422 ἔστιν τι κἀκεῖ κἀνθάδ' ὧν ἐγὼ λέγω, whatever that very obscure line may mean, the thought implies a more elaborate relationship than merely 'both . . . and'. Cf. p. 514 (7).

p. 338. Wilamowitz on A.*Th*.538 (*Interpretationen*, pp. 110–11) goes astray through assuming that οὐ μήν must be adversative.

p. 348. (2). On A.*Th*.1062 σύ γε μὴν πολλῶν πενθητήρων τεύξῃ Tucker translates 'Thou indeed', but a concessive sense of γε μήν is not warranted, and the adversative sense is appropriate there.

p. 350. (5). In Thgn.1129 Stobaeus' οὔτε γε μήν is clearly wrong. Hp.*Acut*.11 δέ γε μήν in one MS. only.

p. 353. (2). In Pl.*La*.199E καὶ μήν can alternatively be regarded as adversative. In general, syllogistic μήν, ἀλλὰ μήν, and καὶ μήν can often be so regarded. Cf. my remarks on καίτοι, p. 563 (iii).

p. 353. (3). 'Logically speaking . . . left unexpressed.' This analysis may appear inconsistent with my procedure (p. 343) in connecting the corresponding use of ἀλλὰ μήν (3) with use (2) of that combination (assentient), not with (6), transition to second premise. But progressive ἀλλὰ μήν (4), of which the syllogistic use is a variety, is very rare in verse. It would therefore be artificial to derive (3), which is already found in tragedy, from (4), and thus to connect it with (6). On the other hand, progressive καὶ μήν (1) is very common in tragedy, and it is therefore natural to derive (3) from (1): though it is true that 'assentient' καὶ μήν (4) also may have helped to produce 'substantiating' καὶ μήν (3).

This is a good example of the difficulty of classifying the usages of particles. It also, I think, illustrates the need for flexibility of method. A treatment which takes into account the actual evolution of usages is to be preferred to a more symmetrical treatment founded on abstractions.

p. 356. (6), cf. p. 331. καὶ μήν, introducing a character upon the stage, is used in the following ways:

(1) As the first words of an actor, often.

(2) As the first words of a short anapaestic system, forming a division between scenes: S.*Ant.*526,1257: E.*Hipp.*1342: *Andr.* 1166.

(3) As the first words of an iambic distich, spoken by the coryphaeus, at the end of a choral ode: S.*El.*1422: E.*Hipp.*1151.

(4) As the first words of a short anapaestic system at the end of a choral ode: E.*Andr.*494: *Supp.*980: *Tr.*230: *Or.*348. Cf. Ar.*Lys.*1072, at the opening of a pair of anapaestic tetrameters followed by a pair of iambics (the only instance I can find in Aristophanes of this καὶ μήν outside iambics).

p. 365. Second paragraph. In Lys.viii5 μέν after οἵτινες can hardly stand: its presence is perhaps accounted for by the μέν after λάθρᾳ. If sound, the first μέν may look forward to the second.

p. 367. First paragraph. Verrall's 'therefore' is really a *non sequitur*. That an affirmative answer is a necessary preliminary to subsequent discussion does not indicate that subsequent discussion is desired, or its possibility assumed, by the questioner. 'Lend me five pounds.'—'Are you *of age*? (If not, I will not consider the proposition.)' Cf. E.*Hel.*1226, quoted in the text.

p. 367. Second paragraph. The use of μέν in questions looks conversational, and all the Euripidean examples are in dialogue. E.*Supp.*1143 πάτερ, σὺ μὲν σῶν κλύεις τέκνων γόους; is an exception, if μέν is sound: it gives irregular but possible metrical corresponsion.

p. 372. See further Jebb on S.*Aj.*372 (χερσὶ μέν *codd.*: χερὶ μέν Hermann) and *Ph.*279. At E.*Hec.*120 all MSS. except *LP* have ἦν δ' ὁ τὸ μὲν σὸν σπεύδων ἀγαθόν. Murray accepts this, but the position between article and adjective seems impossible.

p. 379. (*b*). In *OT* 302 matters are complicated by the picking up of the main (μέν) clause after the conditional clause by an apodotic δέ (see p. 181), and we seem to have a blend of φρονεῖς μέν, εἰ καὶ μὴ βλέπεις and εἰ καὶ μὴ βλέπεις, φρονεῖς δέ. (εἰ καὶ μὴ βλέπεις is, of course, the 'δέ' clause (see note 1), and the δέ after φρονεῖς does not answer μέν, as in the preceding paragraph.) But I would rather leave all this coil alone, for I am more convinced than ever that Jebb is, in essence, right: though I am now inclined to believe that the logical antithesis to the μέν clause starts with the relative clause in 303: 'You know the state of the *patient* (the city): now for the *treatment*'.

p. 384. IV. 1. Pl.*Lg.* 655A differs from the other examples cited under (1) in that the second μέν introduces a dependent (consecutive) clause, not an independent one. But it rightly belongs to (1), not to (2), because the second μέν clause arrives to amplify a μέν clause that is already structurally complete.

p. 429. (5). For ὦν in tmesis and Lithuanian *ai*, see W. Prellwitz in *Glotta* xix (1930) 106–11, and cf. adverbial ὦν in Semon.*Fr.* 7.45.

p. 437. (*a*). The MSS. give οὐκοῦν with second person imperative in E.*Or.* 1238 and *IA* 528. This is certainly impossible in fifth-century Greek (I do not know if there are any fourth-century examples), and both passages are rightly altered by editors.

p. 480. The more I consider μὲν οὖν, the less evidence I find for a genuinely affirmative usage of the combination. Out of some 38 passages that Dr. Chapman has collected in which an emphatic word is repeated from a previous speaker, almost all are in answer to a *nonne*-question, so that μὲν οὖν can be taken as corrective (p. 480). Again, in answers to disjunctive questions (p. 478) μὲν οὖν may be taken as rejecting one alternative, not as accepting the other. There remain two passages in which a word is repeated in an answer to a *statement*: *Lg.* 896C (quoted under iii.*a*): *Plt.* 282D (not quoted) Οὐκοῦν χρή.—Χρὴ μὲν οὖν (but οὐκοῦν χρή should perhaps be taken as a *nonne*-question: see p. 437). iii.*b* and *c* may, as I have observed on p. 480, be regarded as half-corrective, though no doubt in *c* the corrective force has almost vanished.

p. 486, καίπερ. Statistics of the relative frequency of καίπερ in the orators are given by Bolling in his review of the First Edition of this book in *Language*, 1935, p. 261.

p. 501. (c). In A.*Pr.* 502 χαλκόν, σιδηρόν, ἄργυρον χρυσόν τε the MSS. have δέ, which is clearly wrong (τε Robortelli). Despite the close connexion of gold and silver, I think this passage should be classed here.

p. 502. (e). In A.*Th*.1078 ἡμεῖς δ' ἅμα τῷδ' ὥσπερ τε πόλις καὶ τὸ δίκαιον ξυνεπαινεῖ Tucker renders 'Aye, as . . .', but it is better to regard τε as displaced.

p. 508, εἴτε. If Matthiae's οὔτε . . . οὔτε is right for the εἴτε . . . εἴτε of *LP* in E.*Ba*.206–7 οὐ γὰρ διῄρηχ' ὁ θεός, οὔτε τὸν νέον εἰ χρὴ χορεύειν οὔτε τὸν γεραίτερον, this is a strange conversion of εἴτε . . . εἴτε into οὔτε . . . εἰ . . . οὔτε after a preceding negative.

p. 510. (iv). In Hom.*h.Cer*.236 the interval between οὔτε and οὐ is particularly short: οὔτ' οὖν σῖτον ἔδων, οὐ θησάμενος γάλα μητρός: which is in favour of Wilamowitz's conjecture in A.*Ag*.496: ὡς οὔτ' ἄναυδος οὗτος, οὐ δαίων φλόγα.

p. 513. E.*IT* 591–2 (p. 505) appears to be the only example of οὔτε . . . καί.

p. 516. (i). In contrast to the Platonic examples quoted in the text, at *Phdr*.242B the article is superfluously repeated: τὸ δαιμόνιόν τε καὶ τὸ (τό *BT* Proclus: *om. al.*) εἰωθὸς σημεῖόν μοι γίγνεται. But perhaps δαιμόνιον is a substantive here: see Stallbaum.

p. 526. (v). 'Far more frequently the verb is understood.' This is, in fact, the case with all the passages cited on p. 527 from A.*Supp*. 751 to E.*Rh*.618. *HF* 120 appears similar, but 119–23 are corrupt: that Wilamowitz's ⟨ἔκαμε⟩ provides ὥστε with a finite verb tells against his emendation. A.*Fr*.39 ὥστε διπλόοι λύκοι νεβρὸν φέρουσιν is a badly mutilated fragment, but ὥστε φέρουσιν looks sound: in S.*Fr*.756 μολυβδὶς ὥστε δίκτυον κατέσπασεν the subject is probably not μολυβδίς but some word corresponding to Plutarch's κακία. E.*Ba*.1066–7 is much disputed, and Scaliger's ἑλκεδρόμον may well be right.

p. 536, on καὶ . . . τε. καὶ . . . τε has twice been restored by editors in fifth-century inscriptions: but in one case (*S.E.G*.x 11.32) the starting-point was an excessively corrupt copy of a lost stone, and in the other (*S.E.G*.x 67.16) Professor Meritt, who originally read τε[, now reads τ[(*Athenian Tribute Lists* II D 21). Even if the restorations were correct, neither case would have anything in common with the alleged Thucydidean use of καὶ . . . τε.

BIBLIOGRAPHY[1]

I. *Works dealing, in whole or in part, with the particles generally.*

Bäumlein, W. Untersuchungen über griechische Partikeln. Stuttgart, 1861. (Rev. *N. Jahrb.* lxxxv (1862) 467–87.)

Devarius, M. De Graecae linguae particulis, edidit R. Klotz. Lipsiae, 1835–42.

Hartung, J. A. Lehre von den Partikeln der griechischen Sprache. Erlangen, 1832–3.

Hoogeveen, H. Doctrina particularum linguae Graecae. Lugd. Bat., 1769. Idem, in epitomen redegit C. G. Schütz. Glasguae, 1813.

Klotz, see Devarius.

Paley, F. A. A short treatise on the Greek particles. London, 1881.

Schraut, J. Die griechischen Partikeln im Zusammenhange mit den ältesten Stämmen der Sprache. Progr. I, II, Neuss. 1847–8. (Rev. *N. Jahrb.* lvi (1849) 412–18.)

Brugmann, K. Griechische Grammatik, 4te Auflage, bearbeitet von A. Thumb. München, 1913.

Kühner, R. Ausführliche Grammatik der griechischen Sprache, 3te Auflage in neuer Bearbeitung besorgt von B. Gerth., vol. 2, Hannover und Leipzig, 1898.

Meisterhans, K. Grammatik der attischen Inschriften[3]. Berlin, 1900.

Monro, D. B. Grammar of the Homeric Dialect, 2nd ed. Oxford, 1891.

Schoemann, G. F. Die Lehre von den Redetheilen nach den Alten dargestellt und beurtheilt. Berlin, 1862.

Viger, F. De praecipuis Graecae dictionis idiotismis liber cum animadversionibus H. Hoogevenii, J. C. Zeunii et G. Hermanni, ed. 4. Lipsiae, 1834.

[1] In compiling this Bibliography, Bursian's *Jahresbericht* has been of the greatest service, supplemented by E. Hübner's *Grundriss zu Vorlesungen über die griechische Syntax* (Berlin, 1883) for the Dark Ages which lie behind 1873. My list is, I hope, fairly complete. It can be made more complete by reference to Ebeling and Ellendt (under the various particles), and also to Hübner, who includes some works that I omit, and (particularly on the etymological side) to Brugmann. I have occasionally referred to reviews of the works cited. A few of the items in the Bibliography are inaccessible to me. Of the rest, there are some (especially of the older general treatises) that I have merely skimmed or not read at all.

II. *Special Works.*

Abbott, T. K. On δή after relatives in Plato. *Hermath.* vii (1890) 44–5.

Arnim, H. von. Sprachliche Forschungen zur Chronologie der Platonischen Dialoge. *Sitz. d. Wien. Ak. d. Wiss.* clxix. 3 (1912).

Βαλασσίδης, X. περὶ τοῦ ‘ οὐ μὴν ἀλλά ’, ‘ οὐ μέντοι ἀλλά ’, ‘ οὐ γὰρ ἀλλά ’. Ἀθηναῖον, Ἔτος Η', Τόμος 8, 221–7.

Bekker, I. Homerische Blätter, Band I (xviii τί ἤ, ἐπεὶ ἤ : xxvi δέ und γάρ nach dem zweiten Wort). Bonn, 1863.

Birkler, W. Die oratorischen Transitions- und Argumentations-Phrasen τί δέ; τί δέ δή; τί οὖν; τί δαί; τί δῆτα; Progr. Ehingen u. Tübingen, 1867–8.

Bodin, L. et Mazon, P. Extraits d'Aristophane et de Ménandre, pp. 336–61 (index of particles). Paris.

Bolling, G. M. καίτοι with the participle. *Am. J. Phil.* xxiii (1902) 319–21.

Bonitz, H. Über den Gebrauch von τε γάρ bei Aristoteles. *Ztschr. f. d. öst. Gymn.* xviii (1867), 672–82.

Breitenbach, L. Über die Part. οὔκουν und οὐκοῦν. *Ztschr. f. Alt.* viii (1841) 105–12.

Brinkmann, A. Lückenbüsser (μέντοι γε, καίτοι γε). *Rh. Mus.* lxviii (1913) 320.

Broschmann, M. De γάρ part. usu Herodoteo. Diss. Lipsiae, 1882.

Brugmann, K. Über ἄρα, ἄρ, ῥα und litauisch *ir*. *Sitz. d. Gesell. d. Wiss. zu Leipzig*, 1883, i–ii, 37–70.

Buchwald, O. De interrogativarum ἦ et οὔκουν part. apud Graecos poetas tragicos usu. Breslau, 1865.

Bury, J. B. μὲν . . . τε. Appendix A (pp. 153–61) to *Isthmian Odes* of Pindar. London, 1892.

Buttmann, P. De vi et usu part. δέ in apodosi positae. Excursus xii to edition of Demosthenes, *Midias*, ed. 5. Berlin, 1864.

Bywater, I. Apodotic δέ (Contrib. to Text. Crit. of *Nicomachean Ethics*, p. 34). Oxford, 1892.

Campbell, L. Plato's *Republic*, vol. ii, 199–213. Oxford, 1894.

— Introduction to *Sophist* and *Politicus* of Plato (p. xxxvi). Oxford, 1867.

Capelle, C. γάρ (rev. of Pfudel and Sernatinger). *Philol.* xxxvi (1877) 700–10.

Chapman, R. W. ἀλλὰ . . . μέν. *C.R.* xxv (1911) 204–5.

Christ, W. Der Gebrauch der griechischen Part. τε mit besonderer

Bezugnahme auf Homer. *Sitz. d. Münch. Ak. d. Wiss.* 1880, 25–76. (Rev. *Phil. Anz.* xi 7–10.)

Cohn, L. μέντοι. *Herm.* xvii (1882) 645–7.

Collitz, H. The etymology of ἄρα and μάψ. *Trans. Am. Phil. Ass.* xxvi (1895) xxxix.

Dittenberger, W. Sprachliche Kriterien f. d. Chronologie der platonischen Dialoge. *Herm.* xvi (1881) 323–45.

Doederlein, L. Homerica part. γάρ nusquam refertur ad insequentem sententiam. Erlangae, 1858.

Eberhard, E. Die Part. καί im homerischen Verse (καί in arsis and thesis). *Ztschr. f. öst. Gymn.* xl (1889) 581–99.

Eucken, R. De Aristotelis dicendi ratione. Pars I. Observationes de part. usu. Diss. Gottingae, 1866. (Rev. *Ztschr. f. öst. Gymn.* xvii (1866) 804–12.)

Fairclough, H. R. A study of ἆρα in Plato. *Proc. Am. Phil. Ass.* xxxvii (1906) xlvi.

Fraenkel, H. Griechische Wörter: (4) περ. *Glotta* xiv (1925) pp. 6–13.

Franke, F. De usu part. οὐδέ et οὔτε (= De part. negantibus linguae Graecae commentatio II). Rintelii, 1833.

Frederking, A. Sprachliche Kriterien f. d. Chronologie der platonischen Dialoge. *Jahrb. f. klass. Phil.* cxxv (1882) 534–41.

Fritsch, E. A. *Nam, enim, etenim,* ἄρα, γάρ. Progr. Wetzlar, 1859.

Fritzsche, F. De part. οὐδέ usu Sophocleo. Diss. Rostochii, 1897.

Frohberger, H. Miscellen (δέ without preceding μέν). *Philol.* xv (1860) 342.

Fuhr, K. Excurse zu den attischen Rednern (τε . . . καί: τε . . . τε: οὐ μέντοι: οὐ μήν). *Rh. Mus.* xxxiii (1878) 334, 578–99.

Funkhaenel, K. H. ὁ δέ, etc., without preceding μέν. *Ztschr. f. Alt.* v (1847) 1075–9.

Gebauer, G. De hypotacticis et paratacticis argumenti ex contrario formis quae reperiuntur apud oratores Atticos. Zwiccaviae, 1877.

Green, E. L. περ in Thucydides, Xenophon, and the Attic orators. *Proc. Am. Phil. Ass.* xxxii (1901) cxxxv–vi.

Grosse, E. Quaest. gramm. de part. Graec. specimen. I. De part. copulativis τε et καί apud Pindarum. Aschersleben, 1858.

Haacke, A. Quaestionum homericarum capita duo. I. De part. ἄρα. Diss. Nordhusae, 1857.

Hammer, B. De τε part. usu Herodoteo, Thucydideo, Xenophonteo. Diss. Lipsiae, 1904.

Hand, F. De part. Graecis dissertatio secunda. De part. τε cum aliis vocabulis coniuncta. Diss. Ienae, 1824.

Hartung, J. A. Commentatio de part. δή et ἤδη. Erlangae, 1828.

Havet, L. Notes critiques sur Eschyle. Enquête sur τε et δέ dans les tragédies d'Eschyle étrangères à l'Orestie. *Rev. de Phil.* xlvii (1923) 108–40.

Heinze, H. Griechisches τε . . . καί. *Wissenschaftliche Monatsblätter* vi (1878) x 150–1.

Heller, H. De part. ἤδη et δή. *Philol.* viii (1853) 254–308.

Heller, J. C. De part. ἄρα. *Philol.* xiii (1858) 68–121.

Herbst, L. Thukydides (notes on particles, *passim*). *Philol.* xxiv (1867) 610–730.

Hermann, E. Griechische Forschungen I. Die Nebensätze in den griechischen Dialektinschriften. Leipzig, 1912.

Hiller, E. Die Part. ῥα. *Herm.* xxi (1886) 563–9.

Hoefer, H. De part. Platonicis capita selecta. Diss. Bonnae, 1882.

Hoffmann, V. De part. nonnullarum apud Herodotum usu. Diss. Halis Saxonum, 1880.

— Über den Gebrauch der Part. ὦν bei Herodot. Progr. Schneidemühl, 1884.

Horn, W. Quaestiones ad Xenophontis elocutionem pertinentes (pp. 32, 64, καὶ . . . δέ). Diss. Halis Saxonum, 1926.

Hude, K. Über γάρ in appositiven Ausdrücken. *Herm.* xxxvi (1901) 313–15: xxxix (1904) 476–7.

Jahn, C. F. Grammaticorum Graecorum de coniunctionibus doctrina. Greifswald, 1847.

Jones, W. H. S. καὶ οὐ, ἀλλ' οὐ, οὐδέ. *C.R.* xxiv (1910) 51.

Jurk, J. Ramenta Hippocratea. Diss. Berolini, 1900.

Kalinka, E. De usu coniunctionum quarundam apud scriptores Atticos antiquissimos. Wien, 1890. (Rev. *Berl. Phil. Woch.* vii (1887) 770–1.)

Kallenberg, H. δὴ οὖν, οὖν δή. *Rh. Mus.* lxviii (1913) 475–6.

— οὐδέ statt καὶ (ἀλλὰ) οὐ bei Herodot. *Ztschr. f. d. Gymn.* li (1897) 193–222.

Kayser, W. C. On μέν, μάν, and μήν in Homer. *Philol.* xviii (1862) 672–4.

Keelhoff, J. εἰ δ' οὖν peut-il être synonyme de εἰ δὲ μή? *Rev. de l'instruction publique en Belgique*, xxxv. 3. 161–76.

Kratz, H. Über καὶ γάρ. *Ztschr. f. d. Gymn.* xx (1866), 599 ff.

Krueger, G. T. A. De formulae ἀλλ' ἤ et affinium part. natura et usu commentatio. Brunsvigiae, 1834.

Kühlewein, H. Observationes de usu part. in libris qui vulgo Hippocratis nomine circumferuntur. Diss. Gottingae, 1870.

Kugler, F. De part. τοι eiusque compositorum apud Platonem usu. Diss. Basileae, 1886.

Kvíčala, J. *Ztschr. f. öst. Gymn.* xv (1864) 313–34 (δέ), 393–422 (τε).

Lahmeyer, L. De apodotico part. δέ in carminibus Homericis usu. Diss. Lipsiae, 1879.

Lammert, R. De pronominibus relativis Homericis: Cap. III. De pron. rel. cum τε part. coniunctis. Diss. Lipsiae, 1874.

Linke, R. De part. δέ significatione affirmativa apud Sophoclem. Diss. Halis Saxonum, 1873.

Ljungdahl, S. De transeundi generibus quibus utitur Isocrates. Upsaliae, 1871.

Ludwig, T. De enuntiatorum interrogativorum apud Aristophanem usu. Diss. Regimontii Prussorum, 1882.

Lutoslawski, W. The origin and growth of Plato's Logic: chapter iii, 'The Style of Plato'. London, 1897.

Marold, C. Über die gotischen Konjunktionen, welche οὖν und γάρ vertreten. Progr. Königsberg, 1881.

Matthiae, K. Beitrag zur Lehre von den griechischen Part. (γε, ἄρα, μέν, δέ). Progr. Quedlinburg, 1845.

Menrad, J. Homerica. (1) τε im Nachsatz? (2) δέ mit Ellipse des Verbums? *Blätter f. bayr. Gymnasialschulwesen* xlix, 232–5.

Misener, G. The meaning of γάρ. Diss. Baltimore, 1904.

— The εἰ γάρ wishes. *C. Phil.* iii (1908) 137–44.

Monro, D. B. τε in Homer. *Trans. Oxf. Phil. Soc.* 1882–3, 14–15.

Mosblech, P. W. Einiges über die Part. τε. *Ztschr. f. Alt.* v (1838) 948–50.

Mueller, F. Quaestiones grammaticae de γάρ particulisque adversativis enuntiata eorumque membra coniungentibus. Diss. Gottingae, 1910.

Mutzbauer, C. Der homerische Gebrauch der Part. μέν, I, II. Progr. Köln, 1884–6.

Naber, S. A. On μέν, μάν, and μήν in Homer. *Mnem.* iv (1855) 195–8.

Nägelsbach, C. F. Commentatio de part. γε usu Homerico. Nürnberg, 1830.

Nägelsbach, C. F. Anmerkungen zur Ilias (Exkurse I μήν, μάν, μέν: II τοι, ἤτοι: III ἄρα: IV γε bei pronominibus: V ἤπερ: XI δέ im Nachsatze). Nürnberg, 1834. (Rev. *Ztschr. f. Alt.* 1836, 1875–7.)

Näke, A. F. De ἠδέ et ἰδέ part. apud Homerum (Opusc. i. 218 ff.). Bonn, 1842.

Navarre, O. Études sur les part. grecques. *Rev. des ét. anc.* vi (1904) 320–8 (δῆθεν): vii (1905) 125–30 (τοίνυν): x (1908) 293–335 (οὖν).

Neil, R. A. The particle γε (App. I to Ar., *Knights*). Cambridge, 1901.

Oeltze, O. De part. μέν et δέ apud Thucydidem usu. Diss. Halis Saxonum, 1887.

Peile, T. W. Edition of *Agamemnon* (1839), pp. 378–94; note on τε.

Pfudel, E. Beiträge zur Syntax der Causalsätze bei Homer. Progr. Liegnitz, 1871.

Places, É. des. Études sur quelques part. de liaison chez Platon. Paris, 1929.

Platt, A. ἀλλὰ . . . μέν. *C.R.* xxv (1911) 13–14.

Radermacher, L. Drei Deutungen. III δέ? *Rh. Mus.* lvii (1902) 480.

— Bemerkungen zur Sprathe des Sophokles (*repetition of* ἀλλά). *Wien. Stud.* xlvi (1928) 130–2.

Ramsay, W. M. καί meaning 'or'. *C.R.* xii (1898) 337–41.

Rassow, J. De collocatione particularum τε, καί, οὔτε, οὐδέ in fabulis euripideis: Analecta Euripidea, Pars II, Progr. Griefswald, 1889.

Rhode, A. M. T. Über den Gebrauch der Part. ἄρα bei Homer. Prog. Moers, 1867.

Riddell, J. Digest of Platonic idioms (App. B to edition of *Apology*). Oxford, 1867.

Ritter, C. Untersuchungen über Plato. Die Echtheit und Chronologie der platonischen Schriften. Stuttgart, 1888.

— Review of Platonic literature. Bursian's *Jahresbericht*, 1921, 1–227.

Rosenberg, E. Die Part. τοίνυν in der attischen Dekas. *Jahrb. f. klass. Phil.* 1874, 109–21.

Rosenthal, W. De Antiphontis in part. usu proprietate. Diss. Berolini, 1894.

Rost, V. C. F. Über Ableitung, Bedeutung und Gebrauch der Part. οὖν. Gothae, 1859.

Saeve, H. Quaestiones de dicendi usu Thucydidis. I. De vi et usu part. γάρ. Upsaliae, 1864.

Sagawe, K. δέ im Nachsatz bei Herodot (Auszug). Breslau, 1893.

Schäfer, H. De nonnullarum part. apud Antiphontem usu. Diss. Gottingae, 1877.

Schepe, K. De transitionis formulis quibus oratores attici praeter Isocratem, Aeschinem, Demosthenemque utuntur. Progr. Bückeburg, 1878.

Schmidt, C. De usu part. τε earumque quae cum τοι compositae sunt apud oratores Atticos. Diss. Rostochii, 1891.

Schneider, E. Quaestionum Hippocratearum specimen (pp. 6–27, τε). Diss. Bonnae, 1885.

Schonack, W. Curae Hippocrateae (pp. 65–105). Diss. Berolini, 1908.

Schraut, J. De particulis γε et ἄρα. Rastatt, 1849.

— Über die Bedeutung der Part. γάρ in den scheinbar vorgeschobenen Sätzen. Progr. Rastatt, 1857.

Seiler, J. Wie 'gewinnen wir Homer die Art ab'? *Ztschr. f. d. Gymnasialwesen* lxii (1908), 161–81 (on Homeric particles).

Sernatinger, B. De part. γάρ, Partes I et II. Progr. Rastatt, 1874–5. (Rev. *Philol.* xxxvi (1877) 700–10: Bursian's *Jb.* 1878, 272.)

Shorey, P. On δέ γε in retort. *C. Phil.* xiv (1919) 165–74, 291.

— On the *Erotikos* of Lysias (καὶ μὲν δή). *C. Phil.* xxviii (1933) 131–2.

— Statistics of style in the Seventh Platonic Epistle (δ' οὖν). *C. Phil.* xxi (1926) 258.

Spengel, L. τε in Antiphon. *Rh. Mus.* xvii (1862) 166–9.

Spitzner, F. Homeri *Ilias*. Excurs. viii μέν, τε, τοι, ῥα: xxiii εἰ καί, καὶ εἰ. Gothae et Erfordiae, 1832.

Ssobolewski, S. οὐδέ and καὶ οὐ. *Russ. Phil. Rundschau* II. i. 48 (in Russian).

Stahl, J. M. Über eine besondere Bedeutung von γάρ. *Rh. Mus.* lvii (1902) 1–7.

Stürmer, F. Über die Part. δή bei Homer. *Berl. Phil. Woch.* xxxii 1844–5.

Thiemann, C. Über den Gebrauch der Part. δή und ihre Bedeutung bei Homer. *Ztschr. f. d. Gymn.* xxxv (1881) 530–4.

Thiersch, F. De analogiae Graecae capitibus minus cognitis, I–III (ἦ, μήν, δή, τοι). *Abh. d. Münch. Ak. d. Wiss.* vi (1852) 415–54: vii (1855) 309–25.

Thomas, F. W. ἤδη and δή in Homer. *J. Phil.* xxiii (1894) no. 45, 81–115.

Tournier, E. Sur la signification de quelques part. grecques. *Rev. de Phil.* vii (1833) 33–44, 133–9.

Usener, H. Grammatische Bemerkungen. VII δὴ ἄν. *Neue Jahrb. f. Phil. und Paed.* xlviii (1878) i. 66–7.

Uthoff, H. Quaestiones Hippocrateae. Diss. Marburgi, 1884.

Vahlen, E. Appositional γάρ (Aristotle *Poetics*, ed. 3 (1885) 99–102).

Wackernagel, J. Beiträge zur Lehre vom griechischen Akzent (20 ff. ἦ τοι: ἤτοι). Basel, 1893.

— Über ein Gesetz der indogermanischen Wortstellung (position of enclitics). *Indog. Forsch.* i (1891) 333–436.

— Sprachliche Untersuchungen zu Homer, pp. 169 (δαῦτε), 177–82 (μάν, μέν, μήν), 182–3 (οὖν), 191–5 (ἐπειδή, ἐπειδάν). *Glotta* vii (1916).

— δήπου, δήπουθεν. *Ztschr. f. vergl. Sprachf.* xxxiii (1893) 23.

Waehdel, H. Über Gebrauch der Part. οὖν bei Aristophanes. Stralsund, 1869.

Weber, H. γάρ. *Phil. Rundsch.* iv 1078.

Wehr, J. Quaestiones Aristophaneae. Pars I, De part. nonnullarum usu. Diss. Gottingae, 1869.

Wentzel, E. Über den Gebrauch der Part. τε bei Homer. Progr. Glogau, 1847.

Wetzell, C. Beiträge zu dem Gebrauche einiger Part. bei Antiphon. Frankfurt a. M., 1879.

Wilson, J. Cook. On the use of ἀλλ' ἤ in Aristotle. *C.Q.* iii (1909) 121–4.

Zycha, F. Der Gebrauch von ἐπεί, ἐπείπερ, ἐπειδή, ἐπειδήπερ. *Wien. Stud.* vii (1885) 82–115.

III. *Lexicographical.*

Liddell and Scott. Greek-English Lexicon, ed. 9. Oxford, 1925–40.

Boisacq, E. Dictionnaire étymologique de la langue grecque. Paris, 1916.

Herwerden, H. van. Lexicon Graecum suppletorium et dialecticum. Lugduni Batavorum, 1902.

Lexicon Homericum, ed. H. Ebeling. Lipsiae, 1879–80.

Lexicon Pindaricum. J. Rumpel. Lipsiae, 1882.

Lexicon Aeschyleum. W. Dindorf. Lipsiae, 1886.

Lexicon Sophocleum. F. Ellendt. Regimontii Prussorum, 1835.

Index Aristophaneus. O. J. Todd. Cambridge, Mass., 1932.

Lexicon Herodoteum. J. Schweighaeuser. Oxonii, 1840.

Index Thucydideus. M. H. N. von Essen. Berolini, 1887.

Lexicon Platonicum. F. Ast. Lipsiae, 1835–6.

Lexicon Xenophonteum. F. G. Sturz. Lipsiae, 1801–4.

Index Aristotelicus. H. Bonitz. Berolini, 1870.

Index Antiphonteus. F. L. van Cleef. Cornell, 1895.

Index Lysiacus. D. H. Holmes. Bonnae, 1895.

Index Andocideus, Lycurgeus, Dinarcheus. L. L. Forman. Oxonii, 1897.

Index Isocrateus. S. Preuss. Lipsiae, 1904.

Index Demosthenicus. S. Preuss. Lipsiae, 1892.

Index Aeschineus. S. Preuss. Lipsiae, 1896.

Index to Hypereides (in Blass's Teubner text, Leipzig, 1894). H. Reinhold.

The following indexes, while not aiming at completeness, contain much valuable information about the particles:

A. C. Pearson, vol. iii of *The Fragments of Sophocles*, index to the tragedies and fragments. Cambridge, 1917.

K. W. Krueger, Wörterverzeichniss zu den Anmerkungen, in his edition of Thucydides. Berlin, 1860.

C. Rehdantz, Index to Demosthenes, *Philippics*. Leipzig, 1866.

INDEX OF COMBINATIONS

Notes.

1. A combination whose function is to co-ordinate two or more sentences or members of a sentence is written thus: μέν/δέ; one which constitutes an inseparable group of words, thus: ἀλλ' ἆρα; one which is always split by another word or words, thus: ἀλλὰ . . . γὰρ οὖν; one which is sometimes split and sometimes not, thus: ἀλλὰ (. . .) ἄρα.
2. A combination traditionally written as a single word (e.g. δήπου, καίτοι) is treated as such.
3. Where a combination is found in the same sense both in Attic and in other dialects only the Attic form is included.
4. Where a combination involves either οὐ or μή only the form with οὐ is included.
5. Elided words are treated as if unelided.
6. Some of the combinations involve words which are not particles; they are included for the reader's convenience.

INDEX OF REFERENCES